SCHOOL AND SOCIETY

WITH WHICH ARE COMBINED THE EDUCATIONAL REVIEW, ESTABLISHED IN 1891, THE TEACHERS MAGAZINE, ESTABLISHED IN 1878, AND THE SCHOOL JOURNAL, ESTABLISHED IN 1874.

EDITED BY J. McKEEN CATTELL

Volume 39 | SATURDAY, JANUARY 6, 1934 | Number 993

WHAT HAS THE FUTURE FOR BOOKS AND LIBRARIES?[1]

By H. M. LYDENBERG

ASSISTANT DIRECTOR OF THE NEW YORK PUBLIC LIBRARY

JULY, 1893, just forty years ago, and the American Library Association in its sixteenth session in this city of Chicago, the meeting then as now part of an international congress of librarians. A year much like the four we have just lived through—financial crises in this country, Italy, India and Australia, staggering and rocking industrial and economic life; failures and receiverships for banks and railroads so common as to excite little more than passing comment; unemployment a vital and pressing problem.

Librarians were talking about the new building for the Chicago Public Library, one cornerstone just laid in May, the other to be laid in November; about the final settlement of the litigation over the John Crerar will; about the bequest for the Rosenberg library in Galveston, about the Arizona museum and Arizona territorial library recently established, about the purchase of the Copinger collection of Bibles for the General Theological Seminary library in New York City. It was still an era of printed catalogues for such libraries as could afford them. The Rudolph indexer, some thought, was fated ultimately to take the place of printed catalogues and card catalogues. The Cutter expansive classification and the Dewey decimal system had gradually worn down their other competitors and were now settling into the final rounds of their duel.

And here I should pause for some one to rise to remind me that when Dr. Dewey opened the sixteenth conference of the A. L. A. forty years ago he announced he "would make no formal report and would defer any extended remarks." His worthy precedent has not been followed consistently since then, but I shall do my best this evening to keep close to his commendable example.

It is not unfitting, however, that on such an occasion as this we should recall the earlier meeting in this city, that we should note how it, just forty years from us, stood then just forty years from the first general meeting of librarians in this country in New York City in 1853. It certainly is not unfitting that on such an occasion we should glance at the ground behind us, should study carefully the path before us that indicates in general but indefinite fashion some of the pleasant meadows we may hope to traverse soon and warns of those bogs and swamps, those perilous passes and difficult crevasses, that cause some stout hearts to greet the future with apprehension.

[1] From the address of the president of the American Library Association, Chicago, October 18, 1933.

I

As librarians our life is an integral part of the surrounding world. As librarians our life is completely separated from the surrounding world. Phrase it as you will: Each is true, neither is true—alone. When the storm broke four years ago this very month I am sure we all realized we were certain to be affected in some degree, but I doubt if many had any idea the flood would ravage our shores with the biting fierceness these years have shown, few thought the whirl and swirl of the market place would sweep into our reading rooms to fill them with unaccustomed readers and to drag from them some we had come to count as intimate partners of our daily life. It all gave us one more opportunity for fruitful study of the closeness of connection between our work and that of our neighbors and fellow citizens. But whether we are detached observers swung high aloft in the crow's nest or are part of the crew laboring at the pumps and sweeps, none can deny or doubt that the economic and industrial upheaval has had a lasting effect on our present and our future fortune.

What kind of an effect has it had?

Well, for one thing, it has shown us just what kind of part the library plays in this world. Some of us have had the instructive experience of standing before those in control of the public purse and presenting our appeal for funds for the library, an experience as chastening as instructive. We show by diagrams and tables, by word of mouth and written and printed support, how the use of the library has grown, how responsive it has been to these increased demands, how sympathetically and helpfully it has worked with its public, how it has sought to anticipate those needs. We build up what seems to us a convincing case, its accuracy and strength demonstrated beyond cavil or doubt.

Yes, and we have seen that eloquent and moving plea met with devastating thunder and conviction. "The library is a luxury, and in times like these luxuries must go first and must be cut deepest. Do you realize that so and so many thousand dollars of last year's taxes are unpaid? Do you really want us to spend more money for books when so and so many families lack money to pay their water bills? Do you know how many empty coal bins are being filled by gifts from kindly neighbors? Do you really want us to take public money to buy more books for your readers while such distress but a few hundred yards from here calls to high heaven for help? You'll be asking us to supply picture puzzles next!"

When we hear honest, public-spirited men, your friends and neighbors and mine, saying such things, what can we reply?

We insist that the library is no luxury, that it is an essential part of the life of every citizen and every community that rate the mind above the body. "Man shall not live by bread alone" is as true to-day as when the Teacher quoted it nineteen hundred years ago.

Ah, yes, my friends, it is easy to say such things here before a friendly and understanding audience. No matter whether it is easy or difficult to say them before a hostile audience, it is the duty of each of us who cares for more than the next fleeting moment to ask why it is that honest, intelligent men speak and feel this way about libraries. We certainly have failed to convince them that our work is as essential, as fundamental, as necessary, as worth while as we so fondly and honestly believe it to be.

Would it be necessary if we had shown them as youths what books could do? If we had proven to them then that books can be free from the stigma of text-books and the hateful memories of instruments thrust upon them by school teachers? What have we done to show the youngster how to read? Given him story hours, I admit.

Yes, and provided carefully graded lists for this age and that. But if men with a semblance of education answer our pleas with such replies, tell me how to rate our efforts to demonstrate that books are vital and essential?

May our future efforts at demonstration be more potent and more successful than those we look back on in the immediate past.

II

What are the achievements the association can set to its credit this year just passing? What are the problems facing us?

For one thing I rank high the efforts to keep the profession young. It is difficult to speak too strongly of the work of the committee on pensions and annuities. I am sure I voice the feeling of every member of the association and of every well-wisher of library work in this country when I congratulate the association on the results of this work and thank the committee for its happy solution of the problem.

Closely akin to this in spirit has been the way the new members, the younger folk, have been recognized the past few years. Every one of us wants to give this new blood a chance to strengthen and enliven our fellowship, to give these new brooms a chance to demonstrate that they can sweep effectively — whenever and wherever their elders have failed.

We all rejoice that the first payment—one half of the total expected—has been made by the Carnegie Corporation on account of the million increase in endowment secured as the result of the constant, persistent, unceasing labors of the special membership committee. But the income of this half million, say $20,000, will not set us free from thought and care. The year for the association began with a deficit, and our activities have been hampered by the necessity of first making good on that deficit and second adjusting ourselves to decreased income.

A salary cut of 14 per cent. applied to the headquarters' staff is the demonstration of our earnest determination to live within our income. The spirit with which this was met by the devoted band in the secretary's office redounds emphatically to their credit. Let me remind you also that the headquarters' staff ranks among the first to join the annuity plan announced early this year. We all hope that in the not too distant future we may be able to change the arrangement from the present "employee pay-all" plan to a joint sharing of contributions by employer and employee.

Something like three fifths of our income, 60 per cent. of our annual receipts, comes from membership dues, conference registration, sales of publications, the whole making a factor closely controlled by you, me, each of us. One new member brought in by each one now enrolled will double our income. Responsibility for the future progress of the work rests squarely on our own shoulders.

I want to call attention to the part we have played in the movement for adult education. Steady, constant thought and effort prove that we unquestionably see an advance here as compared with our position a year ago. We have been more concerned with studies, experimentation, investigation, thought, than with promulgation or propaganda. The next major step may perhaps be an examination of the library implications of the numerous adult education experiments now under way.

For library extension the year has been marked rather by emphasis on fundamentals, on foundation work, than by startling expansion. Revision of public library standards by a special committee, beginning of the study of the public administration aspects of public library service, a notable meeting at the University of North Carolina, continuation of the regional field work in the Southeast, a demonstration from the Knoxville library covering ten counties in the Tennessee valley area, the survey of "Libraries in Canada," and the grants to Canadian college libraries by the Carnegie Corporation parallel to those great helps made in this country a year or so ago, these stand out as some of the things to remember in this field. The most serious setback came in state library extension work, which suffered distressingly at the hands of state legislatures.

It is a satisfaction to recall that the Library of Congress has found itself able to take over the task of supplying D. C. numbers on its printed cards. Another advance not spectacular, but none the less beneficial, has been the establishment of a scheme of cooperative cataloguing destined undoubtedly to decrease administrative costs for each of us and to increase the help we can give scholarship and research when they turn to us.

There is less satisfaction in recalling that we still have vacant the post of assistant at headquarters charged with the supervision of our work in the field of adult education, that the statistical service and the school library department and the college library advisory service are all likewise deferred.

III

So much for the immediate past. What about to-morrow, next year, the next decade?

Let me mention a few of the problems that face us. What part are we librarians to play in control of this new leisure voluntarily sought or involuntarily thrust upon this new world? What are we to say to the next generation of librarians? What are we to do about new phases of book production? What do we know about the cost of storage of books, the cost of supplying books to readers? How are we to justify the cost of our work to the community that supports us? What are we doing to adapt our administrative problems to the new conditions that face us? How shall the work of libraries (adult education, reference, circulation) be revamped to meet the needs of the new social order and to fit the new philosophy of education with its renewal of emphasis on independent study?

How soon shall we be able to tell the new generation of librarians just what qualification we feel the library schools should set before them as preliminary to their decision about joining our ranks? Have we in the past emphasized too much the material rewards when we set before us the task of recruiting for librarianship? Much of the success that crowns the next generation will depend on the way we of to-day insure the ease of access of those fitted for our work, and help to other careers those who there will be happier and more successful.

Mass production has swept into the world of books. The output of typewriter, machine compositor, high-speed presses has increased prodigiously; the reading public is larger, though perhaps not proportionately increased; the space for shelving and the capacity for digesting, absorbing, using this Gargantuan mass lag far behind. The same specialization that besets us in our industrial or professional life demands observance in the book life. Are economic and book world alike condemned to this welter of uncertainty until they develop and apply proper controls? If so, it certainly behooves us as librarians to ponder our responsibility and our fate.

I sometimes wonder if we to-day are witnessing a change in book-making as far-reaching and as portentous as that in Mainz when Johann Gutenberg produced a book mechanically, without the slightest use of the pen, as some of his followers described it. Certainly the mechanical production of books has far surpassed in speed and quantity any forecasts the previous generation would have dreamed of voicing in its most daring moods. And now when the camera, the offset process, the rubber blanket, the film slide, the phonograph record—to say nothing about radio broadcasting, television, sound pictures—are so emphatically at our elbow, what can we as librarians do but ask earnestly where we may find the man with vision extensive enough and accurate enough to picture exactly whither we go and what we are to encounter? We certainly shall be unfaithful to our trust, unappreciative of our opportunities if we fail to realize that a change is imminent, indeed is on us.

Our scientific friends have come to feel recently that storage of books in our modern cities is dangerous, the polluted air of urban environment doing irreparable damage to paper and leather there subjected to its ravages, while the purer air of the country, less beridden with noxious gases, offered a more welcoming haven to paper and binding. Does this look towards the removal of the bulk of our books to storage warehouses far out in the country, with daily shipments to the reading rooms located in the midst of busy city life and strife?

For the study of these storage conditions we ought certainly to pause long enough here to pay tribute to the Carnegie Corporation, which made possible the long and thorough examination of methods of caring for books carried on for several years by the Bureau of Standards at Washington for the National Research Council. To the Corporation, the Council, the Bureau should go our thanks as librarians, and (within the family circle) let me ask if you feel it to the credit of this association of librarians that such an investigation should have been made on behalf of another organization than our own? Never a word of appreciation or approval from the American Library Association!

Now and then we hear a protest against the size and growth and vastness of our modern museums, hospitals, other typical institutions, suggesting that better results would follow if these huge plants were broken up into smaller ones, highly specialized, located at strategically convenient points. To be sure, the voice of the market place is by no means unanimous, but the mere raising of the question is significant. I sometimes wonder if our library schools and centers of research and investigation might find it profitable to devote the time and effort of a competent student to determine when the weight of the library administrative machinery requires more energy than can be profitably devoted to such a purpose.

I can not solve these problems. But I do not fear to set them before you for consideration, thought and pondering. Every one of us will say without qualification that we want to simplify our life, to lessen the complications that beset us on every side, to define the fundamentals and to relegate the less important to the sidelines. No difficulty in stating the premises. But application of the general principles is not so simple when it comes to applying them to surrounding conditions.

IV

And now, friends, what is the substance of the whole matter? Which of these questions must be faced and answered today? Which in time will answer themselves?

This is neither the time nor place to decide whether an era is past and we are entering on a new world, or whether there has been no essential change beyond a shrinking in paper values. A change certainly has come, a new vision has been seen. But interpret and explain it as you will, never do you find a prophet who dreams of a world without books, without contact with those records of what has been said and done and thought in the past, those inspirations and stimulations for new visions in the future. It is a new world, with a new emphasis on the machine. But it is also an old world with the simple moral and spiritual values still the motivating forces behind the processes of reconstruction. It is certainly a better world in which to do library work. No need for us to seek a rating for our achievements, as compared with the physician struggling with physical ills, the lawyer righting social wrongs, the clergyman calling to right living—we know how we help the community, we live daily with the inspiration of tendering satisfaction to the reader's desire. We see over and over again what books can do for the material, physical, intellectual life of their readers. But, an integral and vital part of all that, far transcending any single element in its meaning and its result, is the conviction and assurance that the message of the book, the mission of those who spread that message abroad, is a lasting and penetrating part of the spiritual life of the community.

I do not mean to preach. I do mean to remind us one and all of the privilege granted us by this opportunity of working with books. With no desire to lessen the importance of study of the technique of the use and care of books, I do want to urge the duty, privilege, responsibility, the lasting reward connected with this interpretation of the message, the value, the power, the essence of this world of books, this realm granted to us librarians for cultivation. We have little to do with the seed as it is sown. We have much to do with the fate of the plant as it struggles through the soil and rises toward harvest. The fruit itself and the service it renders others are affected in large measure by the spirit and the skill of the librarian who cares for it. Appreciation of that duty and that reward is safely left in your hands.

Many of our questions undoubtedly will long remain unanswered. But there never has been nor ever will be any question that books and those that deal with books will constantly bear a larger part in this new world opening around us.

EDUCATIONAL EVENTS

THE SITUATION ON STUDENTS IN GERMAN UNIVERSITIES

AN Associated Press dispatch from Berlin, printed in *The Christian Science Monitor,* reports that owing to the fact that recent college graduates are finding professional positions with difficulty, the number of students admitted to German universities next year will be sharply limited, with one woman scholar for every ten men students.

A decree issued on December 28 by Dr. Wilhelm Frick, Minister of the Interior, will fix matriculations at 15,000, the restriction being motivated "by the constantly growing difficulties graduates encounter in finding the professions overcrowded when they leave school."

"Persistent and effective measures will be taken," the order said, "to guide the surplus of would-be students into practical callings." It pointed out that the numbers of "jobless persons with doctors' degrees" has of late grown alarmingly.

Matriculations of both sexes have doubled in recent years compared with pre-war figures; the number of women scholars alone has increased eightfold or ninefold. Last year 24,700 persons started their college work, of whom 4,400, or about 17 per cent., were women.

Dr. Frick's decree maintained that this hardship was only apparent because "it is obviously far better to restrict admissions than to leave young men and women stranded later with only the slenderest chance to obtain adequate employment." It will go into effect at the beginning of the spring term. In this connection a scheme which was announced five months ago for the elimination of mediocre students from institutions of higher learning was recalled.

Aims of the new education are the ejection of mediocre characters from academic careers and the strengthening of the will of highly gifted students.

Another recent measure required Jewish students to obtain special permits to gain entrance to classes in German universities. Also playing a part in the National Socialist reorganization of the educational system is the doctrine of Hedwig Foerster, head of the woman's department in the Prussian Ministry of Education, that "learning is not for the German girl," and that there should be "less learning and more body building."

Herr Bernhard Rust, Prussian Commissioner for Culture and Education, announced last summer that all male university students must spend a year at compulsory labor.

UNDER-NOURISHED CHILDREN IN NEW YORK CITY

THE much-discussed question of whether school children are actually under-nourished as a result of the depression has been answered in the affirmative for a group of more than five hundred children, typical of a relatively poor neighborhood in New York City. These children were especially examined by physicians in a study conducted by the Milbank Memorial Fund, in collaboration with the U. S. Public Health Service and Dr. Shirley W. Wynne, commissioner of health of New York City.

In families with a weekly income of less than $4.00 per person it was found that 41 per cent. of the children were suffering from malnutrition, according to Clyde V. Kiser, Ph.D., and Regine K. Stix, M.D., of the Milbank Fund staff, who wrote the report in the current *Quarterly Bulletin* of the fund. This rate, they say, is much higher than that found in families with weekly incomes of $6.00 or more per person and is above that ordinarily found in the general population.

The effectiveness of "home relief" is shown, according to the survey, by a larger proportion of well-nourished children in families receiving it than in poverty-stricken families without this particular form of relief.

The Milbank findings are based upon medical examinations of 514 school children from families included in an extensive economic and health survey in New York City. The New York study is a part of a nation-wide survey of the health of the wage-earning population conducted by the Milbank Fund and the U. S. Public Health Service.

The nutritional phase of the survey in New York and elsewhere was undertaken partly in order to check the various reports of increased malnutrition that have recently appeared. The examinations of children were made in accordance with specifications of the Federal Public Health Service and were conducted by carefully selected physicians from the New York City Health Department, assisted by physicians and nurses from the Milbank Fund's staff and technicians from the Public Health Service. "The physician's estimate of nutrition," says the report, "made immediately after completion of the physical examinations, was based on an appraisal of the child's general physical condition, with special emphasis on amount of subcutaneous fat present, texture of skin and hair, quality of muscle tone." The economic condition of the families from which the children were selected was not known to the examining staff, which graded the children upon clinical evidence. Moreover, the information as to family economic condition was obtained by a still different set of investigators.

The results of the study are summarized by Dr. Kiser and Dr. Stix as follows:

Without attempting to discuss their implications at this time, the indications afforded by the examinations of 514 New York school children in a poor area in 1933 as related to family income and relief may be summarized briefly:

1. Within this group of children there is a direct association between nutrition and income. Forty per cent. of children from the lowest income groups were rated "poor" or "very poor," while only 25 per cent. of the children from the higher income groups were so rated.

2. A lowering of nutritional status appears to be associated with drop in family income in as short a time as a year.

3. In the lowest income group, children from families receiving aid from the Home Relief Bureau had somewhat higher nutrition ratings than those from families receiving other types of relief or having comparable incomes from sources other than relief. This is of especial interest in view of the fact that, although the per capita weekly income of families receiving home relief was lower than that in either of the other categories, the cash income given had to be spent for food.

4. The proportion of children suffering from

malnutrition in the group examined appears to be considerably larger than the proportion of malnourished children we should expect to find in a non-depression era. While we have no records for other groups of children which are directly comparable with our data, the difference in the prevalence of malnutrition among children of low income families as compared with that among children from the highest income families, in which there has been relatively little change in income since 1929, is definitely shown for the group included in this study.

The Milbank Memorial Fund expends the larger part of its income in the field of public health, and is now engaged in a number of projects for the improvement of public health procedures. John A. Kingsbury is secretary of the fund, Edgar Sydenstricker is director of public health activities, and the board of directors of the fund is composed of Albert G. Milbank, *president;* Edward W. Sheldon, Thomas Cochran, Frank L. Polk, Linsly R. Williams, M.D., Roland S. Morris and Cornelius N. Bliss.

RESEARCH TO PROMOTE PROGRESS IN EDUCATION

THAT research workers in education, representing 124 colleges and universities throughout the United States, completed more than 3,000 studies in one year, is brought out in the sixth annual survey of educational research conducted by the Office of Education.

The Bibliography of Research Studies in Education, 1931–1932, prepared by the library division, lists 3,121 titles of masters' and doctors' theses reporting investigations in 24 different fields of education. The bibliography is published as Bulletin 1933, No. 6, and can be obtained from the Superintendent of Documents, Washington, D. C.

"What invention is to industry research is to education," said United States Commissioner of Education George F. Zook, in announcing publication of the list of the latest investigations in education. "Progress in education is being built on the foundation of facts revealed by research studies of school problems. The abundance of educational research reported to the Office of Education reveals that educators are diligently promoting progress in education."

The majority of studies are master of arts theses, numbering more than 2,000. Reported doctors' dissertations number 357. Others are classified as "faculty research" studies.

The field of special problems of the curriculum, dealing with reading, writing, science and other school subjects, is the most popular one for research. Vocational training, including such related problems as agricultural education and home economics, is next in order. School health and physical education attracted the attention of research workers as never before, with 166 theses written in these fields during 1931–32.

Many of these studies are available through inter-library loan or for consultation at the library of the Office of Education, which has 768 unpublished works on file. "Use of the thesis loan collection is growing rapidly," according to Ruth A. Gray, author of the Research Bibliography.

The Federal Office of Education publishes the series of Bibliography of Research Studies to stimulate research in education and to prevent duplication of effort in educational studies being made throughout the United States.

PLATFORM OF THE NEW YORK STATE CONGRESS OF PARENTS AND TEACHERS

A PLATFORM was adopted at the recent annual meeting of the New York State Congress of Parents and Teachers which is in part as follows:

Because the home is the most important influence in the life of the child, we believe in the need for understanding parents, who accept full responsibility to provide for each child such favorable conditions as are necessary for the normal development of his mind, character and emotions from birth through adolescence.

We stand for the ideals of the home as expressed in the Children's Charter and we urge these rights for every child.

That parents may appreciate and assume the responsibility of the home, we recognize the need of a wider interest in parent education.

In order that the home may meet its responsibility for parent understanding of and cooperation with the school, we recommend the study of the objectives, the curriculum, the administration and the financing of the public schools in New York State.

We believe that the schools of New York State should provide an education for each child broad enough to suit his educational needs and interests which develop to the full his abilities and possibilities from kindergarten through high school. We reaffirm our conviction that the State of New York should continue to grant full state aid to education as provided in the state aid law, the purpose of which is destroyed by arbitrary limitation.

Because "Children are the Nation's greatest asset," we believe that every community should carefully safeguard these assets by providing for its children modern efficient health services, every possible safety precaution, educational facilities to meet the needs of every child, year round recreational facilities under trained supervision, adequate program of prevention and protection for delinquent and dependent children and the enactment and enforcement of laws safeguarding education and the welfare of our children.

ADMISSION OF UNEMPLOYED STUDENTS TO THE UNIVERSITY OF MINNESOTA

A GROUP of students that may number as many as 800 at the University of Minnesota will be enabled to remain in college during the winter quarter as a result of steps now under way.

Taking advantage of a great number of small economies throughout the institution during the fall quarter, the university has been employing 300 students at various types of work since college opened in October. These men and women receive $50 for the quarter's work. Ways are now being sought of continuing the arrangement for these students, and it is expected to go on.

It is now expected that the Federal Relief Administration will assign an additional 500 students to the University of Minnesota at the opening of the winter quarter and finance them under its plan for sending 1,000 young people to colleges in Minnesota. These men and women will be divided among the various colleges proportionately to their enrolment, and this will give slightly more than half of them to the university.

Inasmuch as only unemployed persons can be named in this group, students already holding university jobs will not be eligible. The federal relief students will receive slightly higher pay than the others, but will have a monthly earning limit of $25.

The second project, which is now being put into effect in many states of the union, has come about as a direct result of the project for educating the unemployed which Governor Floyd B. Olson promulgated with the assistance of President L. D. Coffman and other educators in the state of Minnesota. It is expected to provide education for thousands this winter who otherwise would have had to remain out of college.

Young people whose parents are on the relief rolls will be given first choice. The students will be selected by Dr. Harold F. Benjamin, professor of education in the university, who is in charge of the state project for education of the unemployed.

CALIFORNIA STATE COUNCIL OF EDUCATIONAL PLANNING AND COORDINATION

THE school code enacted by the 1933 California Legislature provides for a State Council of Educational Planning and Coordination, consisting of the superintendent of public instruction and the president of the University of California as *ex-officio* members, and seven other members, each to serve for a one-year term, appointed jointly by the State Board of Education and the Board of Regents of the University of California upon the joint nomination of the two *ex-officio* members. Five of these seven must be lay persons. The nominations of the superintendent of public instruction and the president of the University of California were approved by their respective boards on November 24 and November 28.

The membership of the council is as follows:

Charles Albert Adams, attorney at law, San Francisco.

Allen T. Archer, member of the State Board of Education.

Miss Annie Florence Brown, president of the Oakland Forum.

Mrs. William B. Hayes, president of the California Congress of Parents and Teachers, Burlingame.

H. Gurney Newlin, attorney at law, Los Angeles.

Chester H. Rowell, member of the Board of Regents, University of California, and editor of the *San Francisco Chronicle*.

Will C. Wood, vice-president of the Bank of America, Oakland.

Vierling Kersey, superintendent of public instruction.

Robert Gordon Sproul, president of the University of California.

The code provides: "The function of the State Council of Educational Planning and Coordination is to study problems affecting the relationships between the schools of the public school system and the University of California, and to make recommendations thereon jointly to the State Board of Education and the regents of the University of California through the superintendent of public instruction and the president of the University of California."

COMMITTEE ON PENAL SCHOOLS IN NEW YORK STATE

FORMATION of a commission for the study of the educational problems in penal institutions for the aid of youth was announced by Governor Lehman on December 26 and is reported in *The New York Times.* For more than a year the Department of Correction has been at work on a program of education for inmates of state institutions. Gratifying progress has been made at the Elmira Reformatory, upon which institution efforts have been centered. It is expected that new ideas will be incorporated in the curricula with those that have proved to be wise and practical.

Governor Lehman reported that "the project has already excited the interest of correctional departments and educators from other states and several states have sent representatives to Elmira to observe the work."

To extend the cooperation which the project already has received from experts in the field of education, the following committee has been named:

Dr. Herbert B. Bruner, professor of education, Teachers College, Columbia University.

Dr. Edmund de S. Brunner, professor of education, Teachers College, Columbia University.

Edward R. Cass, general secretary, American Prison Association.

Dr. William E. Grady, associate superintendent of schools, New York City.

Miss Julia K. Jaffray, secretary of the National Committee on Prisons and Prison Labor.

Dr. Franklin J. Keller, director of the national occupational conference.

Dr. Daniel J. Kelly, superintendent of schools, Binghamton.

Sam A. Lewisohn, formerly chairman of the commission to investigate prison administration and construction.

Dr. J. Cayce Morrison, assistant commissioner for elementary education, New York State Education Department.

Dr. Goodwin Watson, associate professor of education, Teachers College, Columbia University.

Dr. Jesse F. Williams, professor of physical education, Teachers College, Columbia University.

Dr. N. L. Engelhardt, professor of education, Teachers College, Columbia University.

Dr. Lewis A. Wilson, assistant commissioner for vocation and extension education, New York State Education Department.

EDUCATIONAL NOTES AND NEWS

DR. EDWARD L. THORNDIKE, professor of psychology and director of the division of psychology in the Institute of Educational Research, Teachers College, Columbia University, was elected president of the American Association for the Advancement of Science at the recent Boston meeting. Dr. Guy Thomas Buswell, professor of educational psychology at the University of Chicago, was elected chairman of the Section of Education, and Dr. John E. Anderson, professor of psychology and director of the Institute of Child Welfare at the University of Minnesota, was elected chairman of the Section of Psychology.

DR. S. A. MITCHELL, professor of astronomy at the University of Virginia and director of the McCormick Observatory, was elected president of the American Association of University Professors at the meeting held in Philadelphia last week.

PORTER H. ADAMS, who became vice-president of Norwich University last June, has been appointed president to succeed Colonel Charles A. Plumley, who has been nominated for election to Congress. Colonel Plumley has been president of the university since 1920. His resignation becomes effective in July. Mr. Adams has been actively interested in aviation since 1915, and is now chairman of the executive committee of the National Aeronautic Association and president of the Boston Municipal Air Board. He is a commander in the United States Naval Reserve Corps.

LORD EUSTACE PERCY, formerly president of the British Board of Education, has been invited by the Governors of Armstrong College, Newcastle, to become president of the college in succession to the late Viscount Grey of Fallodon.

DR. EDWIN A. LEE, professor of education and director of vocational education at the School of Education of the University of California, has been elected superintendent of the San Francisco schools. He succeeds Superintendent Joseph Marr Gwinn, who becomes technical adviser to the school administrators.

ASSOCIATE SUPERINTENDENT JOHN E. WADE was recently reelected a member of the Board of Superintendents of New York City for a six-year term. Mr. Wade, who was first elected to the board in 1927, is chairman of the building and sites committee and has been temporarily assigned as supervisor of the teaching personnel.

PROFESSOR J. L. MCBRIEN, professor of rural education and director of community activities at Central State Teachers College, Edmond, Oklahoma, has been appointed supervisor in the Division of Secondary Education in the Nebraska State Department of Public Instruction. Mr. McBrien was president of the Nebraska State Teachers Association in 1891 and was from 1905 to 1909 state superintendent of public instruction in Nebraska.

CLARENCE S. MARSH, known in the field of adult education for his work at the University of Buffalo Evening Session, of which he has been the dean since its founding in 1923, has accepted the appointment of educational director for the Civilian Conservation Corps. With headquarters in the U. S. Office of Education, in Washington, Dean Marsh will have general charge of the whole educational program, working under the supervision of Dr. George F. Zook, commissioner of education. In scope the new educational plan will affect the 300,000 men who are enlisted in the corps, and will include a staff of nine regional directors and 1,466 educational advisers in the various forest work camps.

THE Downtown Brooklyn Association's Gold Medal, awarded annually to the citizen who has performed "the most distinguished service for Brooklyn," will be presented to Frederic B. Pratt, president of the board of trustees of Pratt Institute, at the annual meeting of the association on January 24.

DR. J. MCKEEN CATTELL, editor of *Science* and of SCHOOL AND SOCIETY, was given a dinner at the University Club, Boston, at the time of the meeting of the American Association for the Advancement of Science. Dr. Karl T. Compton, president of the Massachusetts Institute of Technology, presided, and Dr. John Dewey, emeritus professor of philosophy, Columbia University, made the principal address.

DR. SAMUEL B. HECKMAN, professor of educational psychology and director of the Educational Clinic of the College of the City of New York, was the guest of honor at the semi-annual luncheon of the Education Club of the college on January 4.

A DINNER in honor of Colonel Timothy F. Donovan, division supervisor of the Bureau of Attendance of the New York City Board of Education, was tendered to him on December 21 by the men and women over whom he has had supervision in the department. Colonel Donovan retired on January 1 after many years of service.

CHANDLER RATHFON POST, professor of Greek and of fine arts at Harvard University, has been appointed to the William Dorr Boardman chair of fine arts, formerly occupied by the late Arthur Kingsley Porter. Professor Post graduated from Harvard College in 1904 and has been a member of the Harvard teaching staff since that time. He has resigned as an associate of Eliot House, where his place will be taken by Dr. Walter B. Cannon, George Higginson professor of physiology at the Harvard Medical School.

THE New York State educational associations meeting in Syracuse during Christmas week elected presidents as follows: Associated Academic Principals of New York State, Hugh C. Williams, of Canton; New York State Association of Elementary School Principals, Rollin W. Thompson, of Utica; New York State Vocational Association, Donald M. Kidd, of Syracuse; New York State Association of Science Teachers, Irving H. Buckmaster, of Lockport.

PROFESSOR JOHN A. WALZ, of Harvard University, was elected president of the American Association of Teachers of German, meeting in St. Louis on December 27. Professor A. R. Hohlfeld, of the University of Wisconsin, is the retiring president.

DR. LENT D. UPSON, professorial lecturer in political science in the University of Michigan and director of the Bureau of Governmental Research in Detroit, will conduct, under the auspices of the Census Bureau, a federal survey of tax delinquency in 309 cities in the United States with a population of over 30,000 each.

THE Social Science Research Council has appointed President L. D. Coffman, of the University of Minnesota, chairman of a Commission of Inquiry on Public Service Personnel. Other members of the committee are Louis Brownlow, of Chicago, representing the public administration clearing house; Ralph Budd, president of the Chicago, Burlington and Quincy Railroad; Dr. A. L. Day, director of the Geophysical Laboratory of the Carnegie Institution, and Dr. C. E. Merriam, professor of political science in the University of Chicago. Dr. Luther Halsey Gulick, Eaton professor of municipal science and administration at Columbia University, will be the full-time secretary.

PROFESSOR FREDERICK E. BOLTON, of the University of Washington, spent the month of October in Alaska visiting schools for the Northwest Association of Secondary and Higher Schools. He inspected the Alaska College of Agriculture and the School of Mines at Fairbanks, which is the college farthest north in the world. He visited nearly all the public high schools and made a special survey at the request of the school board of the schools of Juneau.

DR. J. ANTON DE HAAS, William Ziegler professor of international relationships at the Harvard Graduate School of Business Administration, lectured on the problems of European Jews at an open forum of the Boston Young Men's Hebrew Association held on December 10.

THE annual Christmas week lectures for young people on the James Mapes Dodge Lecture Foundation were given in the hall of the Franklin Institute, Philadelphia, on December 27 and 28. Charles Bittinger, artist-physicist of Washington, D. C., spoke on "Adventures in Color."

CLIFTON D. GRAY, president of Bates College, was the principal guest and speaker at the meeting of the Boston Bates Club held at the University Club in Boston on December 8. He spoke on "Ideas Made in Germany." On the same day he spoke at the Huntington School in Boston and at the Medford High School, and on Sunday, December 10, he preached at both the morning and evening services in the First Baptist Church in Winchester, Mass.

DR. JONATHAN RIGDON, president emeritus of the Central Normal College at Danville, Indiana, died on December 30 at the age of seventy-five years. Dr. Rigdon was professor of philosophy at Central Normal College from 1888 to 1901. During the last three years he served also as president. He became professor of ethics and philosophy at Clark University in 1902. In 1908 he founded Winona College at Winona Lake, Indiana, and served as its president until 1916. Two years later he was again elected president of Central Normal College, serving for eleven years.

DR. THOMAS W. ATKINSON, formerly president of Louisiana State University, died on December 25 at the age of sixty-eight years. He was elected president in 1929, serving until 1931, when he retired and was succeeded by Dr. James Monroe Smith. Dr. Atkinson joined the faculty of the university in 1891 and was dean of the school of engineering from 1907 to 1927, when he became acting president.

RICHARD ADDISON SEARING, known for his work in the establishment of free medical clinics for school children and for forty years secretary of the New York State Teachers Association, died on December 20 at the age of seventy-one years. Mr. Searing at his death was treasurer of the association. Between 1890 and 1930, the period in which he was secretary, it grew from a few hundred members to more than 40,000. The growth has been attributed largely to his efforts. Mr. Searing was principal of the City Normal School, Rochester, New York, from 1898 to 1904 and superintendent of schools at North Tonawanda, New York, from 1904 to 1920.

DR. ARCHER BUTLER HULBERT, professor of American history at Colorado College, died on December 24 at the age of sixty years.

CHARLES PHILLIPS, professor of English literature at the University of Notre Dame, died on December 29 at the age of fifty-three years.

DR. CHARLES EDWIN CLEMENS, professor of music at Western Reserve University and also in the Flora Stone Mather College, died on December 27. He was seventy-five years old.

FRANK A. WELD, editor of *School Executives Magazine,* died on December 26 at the age of seventy-five years. Before engaging in editorial work, Dr. Weld served as president of the State Teachers College at Moorhead, Minnesota, from 1899 to 1919, when he resigned. Before that, he was a high-school principal at Farmington and at Zumbrota, Minnesota. He was also superintendent of schools at Fergus Falls and Stillwater, Minnesota.

THE death at the age of seventy-eight years is announced of Samuel Bower Sinclair, of Toronto. Mr. Sinclair had been principal at Ridgetown public school, vice-principal of the Ottawa Normal School, dean of Teachers' School, MacDonald College, Quebec, and lecturer on rural school consolidation for the Ontario Department of Education.

ANATOLY VASILIEVICH LUNACHARSKY, Soviet ambassador to Spain and formerly People's Commissar for Public Instruction of the Soviet Union, died on December 26.

AT the Philadelphia meeting of the American Association of University Professors three institutions were dropped from the eligible list. These were Rollins College, of Winter Park, Fla.; Brenau College, of Gainesville, Ga., and the U. S. Naval Academy. It is reported that in the last case the action refusing to recognize a new degree of bachelor of science soon to be given at the academy was taken "in view of unsatisfactory tenure conditions and the lowering of qualifications for instruction in general subjects." The dispute began last year with disapproval of the dismissal of thirteen civilian instructors.

STUDENTS of Bennington College, Vermont, have scattered for two months to continue their education in various parts of the United States, Mexico, the West Indies and Europe. On their return on February 23 they will bring with them reports, essays, paintings, sculpture or other products of their work during the recess. The experiment of a long "working vacation," instead of the usual two-week winter holiday, was first tried last year, and is said to have convinced both students and faculty of its value. The summer vacation is somewhat shortened, so that no recitation time is lost.

DISCUSSION

1934 AS A CENTENNIAL YEAR IN THE HISTORY OF EDUCATION

IN continuation of previously published lists[1] of centennial dates in the history of education, the following group of significant 1934 dates is presented. Additional details regarding events and persons mentioned may be found in the standard encyclopedias and histories of education.

B. C. 267

Andronicus brought as a slave to Rome, later to become teacher of Greek and Latin languages.

B. C. 167

Founding of the first library in Rome, with books brought from Greece by the conqueror Paulus Emilius.

Crates, Greek grammarian and head of the library at Pergamum, establishes first grammatical school at Rome.

A. D. 534

Codification of Roman law in the Justinian Code.

A. D. 1034

Birth of Anselm of Canterbury, leader in influential church conference in latter part of eleventh century, especially concerned with the nature of knowledge.

A. D. 1434

Founding of Regia Universita Degli Studi di Catania, Italy.

[1] See SCHOOL AND SOCIETY, January 7, 1933, for list for 1933 and for references to similar lists from 1926 to 1932.

A. D. 1534

Founding of the "society of Jesus" or the "Jesuit Order," influential Catholic teaching order which organized hundreds of schools and colleges and concerning whose educational practises, Bacon said: "As for the pedagogical part, the shortest rule would be, Consult the schools of the Jesuits, for nothing better has been put in practise."

A. D. 1734

Birth of Rolland, who in 1768 as president of the Parliament of Paris outlined a comprehensive system of public education for France.

Founding of the University of Göttingen, Germany.

A. D. 1834

Death of Malthus, who in his famous "Essay on Population" urged the necessity of a widespread system of public instruction for England.

Founding of the University of Brussels, Belgium.

Founding of the Cantonal University at Bern, Switzerland.

Abolition of the rate-bill in Pennsylvania.

Publication in New York of Victor Cousin's report to the French government on education in Prussia.

Establishment of the first public evening school in the United States at Louisville, Kentucky.

Beginning of a permanent school fund in Massachusetts.

First free school law in Pennsylvania, creating 987 school districts in the state.

Enactment by the legislature of New York of the first law in the United States providing for the professional education of teachers for the common schools.

Founding of the University of Delaware.

Founding of the Hartford Seminary Foundation, Connecticut.

Founding of Franklin College, Indiana.

Founding of Tulane University, Louisiana.

Founding of Wheaton College, Massachusetts.

Founding of Wake Forest College, North Carolina.

Birth of Charles W. Eliot, distinguished president of Harvard University.

Walter Crosby Eells
Stanford University

THE TEACHER'S PART IN COMMUNITY LIFE

It was at a school executives' conference that I met Taylor. "Oh, yes," he said, "I remember you. Seven years ago you applied to me when I was superintendent at Tobia. You were the best candidate for the position, but the man who was leaving belonged to the ——— Church and taught in their Sunday school. So we had to elect some one to take his place as Sunday-school teacher and you were of another denomination, so we elected a young fellow from State College. He was a fine Sunday-school teacher, but couldn't teach his subject-matter in the public schools at all." Small-town superintendents are all too familiar with the pleas of local social organizations to elect a teacher who can do this or that or the other thing in the social life of the community.

Placement bureaus can tell us that a candidate's ability to play in a band or an orchestra, to sing in the choir, or to play on the independent basketball team may often be the decisive factor in the selection of teachers. Some years ago I was notified by a placement bureau to apply for a position as teacher of science and mathematics, coach of basketball and player on an independent basketball team. A note was added to the effect that special consideration would be given to men qualified to take charge of the Boy Scouts and direct a church choir. I wonder what that teacher did in his spare time!

The development of a truly professional teaching corps certainly demands that some definite understandings should be established concerning the part that teachers should play in the non-school social life of a small town.

In the first place, how much does a small town have the right to expect of its teachers in social leadership? People are apt to regard teachers as especially talented in many lines. Teachers dislike to refuse any reasonable request that they take part in community work, with the result that often teachers carry a heavy part of the burden of social activities in the community. In general we might say that a community should expect no more of its teachers than it does of other people of the same educational attainment and of the same abilities. Others should not be allowed to make the teacher bear the burden of their shirking.

However, communities do have the right to expect teachers, as well as others, to use special talents for community benefit. The teacher who is a good singer but refuses reasonable requests that she appear in public or the teacher who can teach Sunday-school but refuses to do so are not being fair to the community of which they are a part. The teacher has no right to shirk her share of community work.

Teachers must avoid over-emphasis of non-school activities. Too often the willing teacher is too heavily burdened with social affairs to do justice to her teaching. It must be remembered by all involved that the teacher is employed to teach and that nothing should be allowed to interfere with her work. A few years ago one of my teachers, who was a good dramatic reader, appeared on three programs on three successive school nights. As a result of the combination of late hours and midnight lunches she was not a very fit teacher by the end of the week.

School boards should not consider a teacher's work in community affairs as a decisive factor in the selection or retention of teachers. It is infinitely more important that the best possible chemistry teacher be secured than that the base-ball team gets a teacher who can play first base. A few years ago the board of a neighboring school was forced by community pressure to reelect a teacher who had proved a failure, because he was a star center on the independent basketball team. No trust of the people could be more foully abused than was the duty of a school board in this case to hire teachers on the strength of their records as teachers. If all other things are equal, however, preference should be shown to those who have ability to aid in community affairs.

Teachers must guard against appearing to force themselves into positions of honor in social organizations. Often others are coyly waiting for the position which a teacher accepts unhesitatingly. It is easy to give offense in this way.

It is also inadvisable for a teacher to take an active part in the inception of a long-term project. Any work of a community nature undertaken by a teacher should be of such a nature that it can be, without great loss, discontinued at the end of a school term. For example, it would appear unwise to organize a troop of Boy Scouts or Girl Scouts unless others permanently residing in the community will carry on the work. Yet I have recently seen a schoolman start a Scout troop in April though he had not been reelected to his position for the next year.

Finally, school people should not accept community responsibility to such an extent as to allow community interest to atrophy. The P. T. A. which depends on the teachers to furnish its programs, the Sunday school which must close for lack of teachers when the public school teachers leave town, and the basketball team which must have a good forward in the seventh and eighth grade teaching position have all ceased to be community organizations in the truest sense and have become parasites upon the school.

In conclusion, a community has the right to expect teachers to be as active in community affairs as are others of the same ability. Teachers have the right to the same freedom in participation in social affairs as others enjoy. The school has the right to expect that there will be no interference from community organizations in its selection and retention of teachers and that community affairs will be held secondary to school work by its teachers.

W. B. McPHERSON,
Superintendent of Schools
WILLIAMS, MINN.

QUOTATIONS

PROBLEMS OF HIGHER EDUCATION IN AMERICA

IN earlier reports, particularly those for the years 1925 and 1931, fundamental questions relating to the organization and development of universities in the United States were presented in some detail. Each year continues to make it plain, however, that the confusion in the public mind, and even in what may be called the educational mind, between college and university still persists and is obviously most perplexing to European visitors and observers. It is this confusion which makes American educational statistics of higher education, whether official or unofficial, as these are printed and widely circulated, wholly meaningless for comparison with statistics in other countries, owing to the lack of any clearly thought-out and sound method of classifying institutions of higher education according to their real character rather than according to their self-assumed names. Nothing is easier than for a college in this country to call itself a university, even though it has not the first characteristic of university organization, method or ideal. All it need have is ambition to be something which it is not and can not be. Moreover, the Government of the United States, through the Office of Education in the Department of the Interior, persists in classifying universities and colleges as either public or private. There is, and can be, no private university or private college in the United States, unless, perchance, some state or the District of Columbia be sufficiently loose in its legislation to permit an individual or a corporation to seize upon either name and use it for private profit. Every genuine college and university in the United States is a public institution and is grounded upon the law of the state in which it exists. The only real distinction between these institutions grows out of their differing methods of financial support and control. They are either tax-supported or non-tax-supported colleges and universities. In either case they are public institutions. The mere notion that any one could establish and maintain a private university would not occur to a person with any sense of humor.

It must be repeated over and over again that the ground for all this confusion arises in failure to distinguish between the threefold division of the period following upon the elementary school which exists in America, and the twofold division of that period which exists on the continent of Europe. In America this period is divided between secondary school, college and university, while in Continental Europe it is divided between *lycée* or Gymnasium and university. The American college, it must again be repeated for the hundredth time, covers the field which on the Continent of Europe is occupied by the upper years of the *lycée* or Gymnasium and the first year of the university. All this confusion is made still more confounded by the fact that our colleges derived their origin from England, where the term university was used in still another sense and was, in the case of both Oxford and Cambridge, an organization composed of largely independent and self-governing colleges, rather than something built upon those colleges as the American university is supposed to be built upon the American college. Out of all this arises the fact that while there are but 11 universities in England, 4 in Scotland and 1 in Wales, 5 in Belgium and 8 in Holland, 17 in France and 23 in Germany, 3 in Austria, 4 in Hungary, 25 in Italy and 11 in Spain, there are no fewer than 263 universities, colleges and technological institutions in the United States approved by the Association of American Universities. Of these 36 are institutions having a more or less complete university organization equipped with schools for graduate study and with some, at least, of the usual professional or technological schools. This leaves 227 colleges and technological institutions which are approved by the Association of American Universities. On the other hand, various books of reference give the public a quite different impression. The World Almanac lists 579 universities and colleges in the United States, the Directory of the United States Bureau of Education lists 567 and the Statesman's Year Book for 1933 is able to find no fewer than 1,078 universities, colleges and professional schools.

It so happens that every genuine university in the United States has a college incorporated in its educational system, and in the vast majority of cases the college looms larger before the public than does the university. It is the undergraduates of the college who carry on intercollegiate sport and who in a hundred different ways interest the public and attract its attention. The older body of more advanced students is very little in the public eye and is composed of mature and well-disciplined men and women who have fixed their minds on a definite intellectual goal and are doing their best to reach it with credit and with honor.

What may be called the interpenetration of the American college and the American university has very greatly influenced both institutions. While logically, no doubt, it would have been better to separate each type of institution, as is done on the Continent of Europe, historical conditions and sentimental relationships have made this quite impossible in the United States, since, with the exception of the Johns Hopkins University and Clark University, every existing American university is the outgrowth of an earlier and older college, and for both of these an organization for undergraduate work was quickly provided. It is important to dwell from time to time upon these fundamental facts and distinctions, since there can be no clear thinking relative to higher education in the United States and its problems unless they are known and observed.

The task of the American college is, or should be, reasonably definite and well understood. It is to take the youth at about the age when in ancient Rome he put on the *toga virilis* and offer him for three or four years opportunity for carefully directed and supervised study in some part or in many parts of the field of liberal arts and sciences. The purpose of this carefully supervised and directed training is to give him the benefit of his rich human inheritance, so far as that may be practicable, and thereby better to prepare him for such specific task as may await him in the years of mature life. Deprived of this rich inheritance, the youth must of necessity be correspondingly impoverished and put under the necessity of making most strenuous efforts in later years to make good the loss which he has had to suffer. The old days when the substance of this inheritance could be transmitted through a few carefully chosen and prescribed subjects of study have gone forever. They have gone, not because those studies were not excellent in their time and adequate to the needs of that time, but rather because times have changed and the human inheritance has taken on a more many-sided and richer form than it once was known to have. Nature and its study have offered new and splendid vistas to both knowledge and imagination. The creative arts have unfolded themselves in striking fashion for a century past as educational instrumentalities of highest value. The structure and underlying principles of the social and political order, first examined and interpreted in classic fashion by Aristotle, have now taken on many new forms and guises, each with its own appeal and its own capacity for usefulness. It is for reasons such as these that the task of the college faculty has become more difficult than ever before, since it must, within a very limited time and for youths from all sorts and conditions of home, family and school background and environment, offer that opportunity to understand and to grasp the rich human inheritance which it is the first business of the college to transmit.

The university student has a quite different outlook and a quite different method of approach to his field of intellectual interest. He has already come into possession, adequately or inadequately, of the essential elements of his intellectual and spiritual inheritance, and, so taught and disciplined, he is now to approach some particular part of the field of organized knowledge with a view to making himself familiar with it, to understand its method and its interrelations, and to prepare himself to use all this knowledge either in the field of pure scholarship, or in that of one of the learned professions, or in what it is the fashion to call the business of everyday life. The true and profitable university student will first have been a college student. Whether the college student shall also become later a university student is a matter for his own choice, often largely determined by the personal and economic circumstances which surround and confront him. It is important not to confuse the two, which is so easily done, since both college and university are, in the United States, so uniformly parts of one and the same corporate educational system.—*From the annual report of President Nicholas Murray Butler, of Columbia University.*

EDUCATIONAL RESEARCH AND STATISTICS

PREDICTING SUCCESS IN ALGEBRA

KNOWLEDGE of the probable success in algebra would be most desirable to educators (for purpose of counseling and guidance in mathematics), particularly if such knowledge might be available before the eighth year. Until recently the published evidence relating to success in algebra favored mental ability as the most significant single influence on success. The study reported in this article was devoted in part to an investigation to answer the following two problems: (1) What are the comparative predictive values of certain measures available before instruction is begun in algebra? (2) What is the best combination of these measures in predicting algebraic success?

TABLE I

CORRELATIONS OF SUCCESS IN ALGEBRA WITH VARIOUS MEASURES USED IN PREDICTING THAT SUCCESS

Measure	Correlation
South Pasadena Prognostic Test	.400 ± .036
8A Mechanics Test	.375 ± .035
8A Reasoning Test	.439 ± .041
Teacher Estimate	.634 ± .027
I.Q.	.337 ± .030
South Pasadena Prognostic Test and Teacher Estimate (multiple correlation)	.688
8A Mechanics Test and Teacher Estimate	.636
8A Reasoning Test and Teacher Estimate	.634
Teacher Estimate and I.Q.	.635
(All other combinations of 2 measures yielded a multiple R or less than .600)	
South Pasadena Prognostic, 8A Mechanics Test and Teacher Estimate	.670
8A Mechanics, 8A Reasoning Test and Teacher Estimate	.636
8A Reasoning Test, Teacher Estimate and I.Q.	.640
South Pasadena Prognostic Test, 8A Reasoning Test, and Teacher Estimate	.704
South Pasadena Prognostic Test, I.Q. and Teacher Estimate	.694
8A Mechanics Test, I.Q. and Teacher Estimate	.636
(All other combinations of 3 measures yield a multiple R of less than .600)	
South Pasadena Prognostic Test, 8A Mechanics Test, 8A Reasoning Test and Teacher Estimate	.690
South Pasadena Prognostic Test, 8A Mechanics Test, I.Q. and Teacher Estimate	.641
8A Reasoning Test, 8A Mechanics Test, I.Q. and Teacher Estimate	.698
South Pasadena Prognostic Test, 8A Mechanics Test, 8A Reasoning Test, Teacher Estimate and I.Q.	.691

In this article success in algebra is measured by the mark received the second semester of algebra.

All pupils who completed the exploratory course in mathematics in the eighth year at the South Pasadena Junior High School, South Pasadena, California, and who subsequently completed a year's course in algebra at the same school during the years 1930–1933 are included in this investigation. Two hundred forty pupils were involved. The scores on the South Pasadena Prognostic Test in Algebra, the 8A Mechanics Test, the 8A Reasoning Test, the Teachers' Estimate of Mathematical Ability, and I.Q. as determined by the Terman Group Test were the measures used. The scores on these measuring devices were determined prior to regular algebraic instruction. Marks in second semester algebra were taken from the records at the South Pasadena Junior High School.

The two problems under consideration may be solved by the method of correlations. A comparison of the predictive values of the measures may be made by the relative values of the coefficient correlation. The Pearson "r" method for zero order and multiple correlations was used throughout. The correlations in the zero order were made between the raw scores on the tests and the actual marks received in algebra.

The correlations of second semester algebra marks, with the various measures used in prediction, appear in Table I.

The best combination of the measures above in predicting algebraic success is the combination of the South Pasadena Prognostic Test, 8A Reasoning Test and the Teacher Estimate of Mathematical Ability.

G. H. AYERS

JUNIOR HIGH SCHOOL
SOUTH PASADENA, CALIF.

NEW BOOKS IN EDUCATION

FERRISS, EMERY N. and others. *The Smaller Secondary Schools.* Pp. viii + 236. U. S. Government Printing Office.

KNAPP-FISHER, H. C. *The Modern World.* Pp. 447. Dutton. $2.50.

SPAULDING, FRANCIS T. and others. *The Reorganization of Secondary Education.* Pp. xii + 423. U. S. Government Printing Office.

SWIFT, FLETCHER H. *European Policies of Financing Public Educational Institutions.* Vol. I, *France.* Pp. xvi + 179. University of California Press.

EDUCATIONAL REVIEW

Edited by Nicholas Murray Butler, 1891–1919, Frank Pierrepont Graves, 1920–1924, and William McAndrew, 1924–

MONTHLY REVIEW OF EDUCATIONAL BOOKS

By WILLIAM McANDREW

GOVERNMENT FOR STATUS QUO

AMAZINGLY familiar with American civic affairs, political-scientist Brogan,[1] of the London School of Economics, writes his brilliant "study in the American political system and how it works." It is, says Professor Harold Laski, the most illuminating treatise on our government since Bryce's "American Commonwealth" appeared fifty years ago.

Our Constitution was a clear effort to protect a certain view of property from invasion by the multitude. This fact has been unrecognized or ignored while the opportunities of a new continent have favored the humble man. He has not thought it necessary as his brother in Europe to ask questions about the fundamental policies of state. England's security rests on foundations absent from America: a neutral civil service, supremacy of legislature over judiciary, clear and measurable power of the executive, local government largely free from the taint of business corruption, party organization representing the economic needs of the whole country, a method of discovering, not by a lottery, leadership in the national sphere.

Mr. Brogan puts emphasis on those aspects of our system which in origin and development are most American. He uses our history with consummate understanding. He fears you may think him willingly making an unworthy picture of the United States. If you write on politics this must be so, as politics is the least noble of our aspects. It is unfortunate, he says, that such a course calls for much attention to the pork barrel and none to the Panama Canal, a whole section on the spoils system and nothing for the Bureau of Standards.

Starting with the Constitution and its makers' doubts regarding it, the book moves rapidly with abundant incident, authority, and comment through parties, sectionalism, the president, congress, spoils, pensions, the machine, city corruption, Tammany, rural political crookedness, conventions, candidates, campaigns and prospects of reform. Hamilton lives again in these pages; Jefferson expounds; Marshall decides; Jackson upsets. Approaching our day, Mr. Brogan puts the cold light of disillusioned scrutiny on Lincoln, Grant, the Roosevelts, Wilson, Taft, Harding, Coolidge, Hoover and those who managed them or couldn't.

Almost from the start the Constitution got into the hands of a priesthood, the lawyers, who from time to time have told the multitude the judgment of the ancestors on situations which the ancestors never dreamed of. The wealthier classes have used the Constitution as a means of gaining power and personal prosperity. It has never been a tool for action, for its makers feared to give power to government. But with comparative ease it has been adapted to the needs of the rich and made an obstacle to satisfying the wants of the commonality.

THE TONE BUSINESS GIVES

American parties have had their life drained out of them and are now mere shells: collections of professional politicians trading on the unthinking loyalties of the mass of the voters. The Republicans have all the faults bred by too long success. The fidelity with which this party served the dominant lords of business by tariff, farm policy and foreign relations leaves it unable to meet the altered demands of the new society. The Democratic party is no better. Its incoherence paralyzes it. The victory of 1932 is meaningless in relation to party fortunes. In the name of the immortal principles of Jefferson, millions support policies that he could not reconcile with his creed. Lincoln was scarcely buried before his party was using his name to carry measures which he would have fought to the end. "Times have been that when the brains were out the man would die" was not written of American parties. No observer from another land can see any reason in the system, any method in the madness.

[1] D. W. Brogan, "Government of the People." Harper and Brothers, New York. 415 pp. $4.00.

With vigor like this our author, singularly specific, discusses the sweep of Mr. Franklin Roosevelt. But you can't teach the old guard new tricks. The Republican leaders are not now looking for a master statesman but for another Harding.

The chapter on municipal politics and the machine as a kindly instrument for giving service with a smile is pungent. The bosses continue to give picnics, balls, coal and dinners to the poor; they save them from the law. They grow rich and powerful; they continue to draw pay for protecting speakeasies, brothels and crime, but this tribute is paltry as compared with the payments to the machine by respectable business. In a society whose tone is set by business there is no reason to be surprised at the relation between business and the bosses. At every stage of our history business has been found asking for favors or worse. Business is the buyer of wares offered for sale by the state machine and its agent the state government. No change of form to commission government or city manager will better things if the community is willing for business to bribe its way into success. Harding's was a business administration. He put more thieves and liars into his cabinet than any president since Grant.

The machine will lose its hold, observes Mr. Brogan, as soon as public opinion really reprobates the control of cities, counties, states and the nation by business in its own interest or in its own defense. That time has not yet come.

But there is, to-day at any rate, he says, more chance for purity in politics than there was at any time since the great war. To-day faith in the values of business, in its powers of self-adjustment, is waning. The intrusion of business into politics is now getting its challenge more and more. More rigorous taxation with less accommodation for the rich, less buying of privilege and immunity, possibly the acceptance of inefficiency in the management of utilities when publicly owned in order to remove corruption, are written in the prospectus.

This book is easier reading than Bryce's masterpiece. It will not be so pleasing to the complacent. The learned lord accepted as half-justified practises which Brogan shows to be seeded with revolution. This is a book written for the layman, but the schoolmaster, wallowing in texts devoted to solacing the generation with belief that we have the best government in the world, will find this inspiringly different.

UNDERSTANDABLE ECONOMICS

Economics Professor Haney,[2] New York University, has the talent of getting into the head of the average man a coherent understanding of the difference between the basic theories of economics and the practical difficulties of their operation. Wealth, competition, supply, demand, standard of value, good money, gold, credit, inflation, exchange, production, consumption, distribution, wages, capitalism, business cycles, speculation, tariffs, price fixing, government interference with business, socialism and such topics are treated in short, crisp paragraphs. In the light of present conditions you are set to thinking what the troubles are and how they may be mitigated.

Economics has been hidden in cloistered recesses. The public is coming into them where heretofore have been mostly the theorists. The trials of 1929 and following years provoked the book. Straight thinking upon our problems is a crying need. Economics has been urged as a necessary study among the offerings of public education now accepting the claim that schools are bound to contribute to civic welfare. But economics is in a pitiable state. A hundred fifty "economists" sign a petition to inflate the currency. Fifteen hundred of their brethren regard this as a pitiful spectacle. So-called "leading economists" who are young men without experience or mature thought will advocate anything from greenbacks to national isolation. The public gets to regard one economist as good as another. It will accept a slogan without analyzing the principles behind, if there are any. Various institutions that might function well have been tampered with. Many people have lost morale. The stock-minded have often lost their heads. The notion that the way to make money is to spend it has intoxicated too many. Government has been conceived as a magic power apart from ourselves.

These observations are enough to show you that the author is no faith healer. He finds

[2] Lewis H. Haney, "Economics in a Nutshell." The Macmillan Company, New York. 213 pp. $2.00.

the readiness of accountants, statisticians and engineers to pose as economists shows them to be afflicted with the business-leader complex. The simon-pure economist is devoted to the general welfare, not to the making of profits. He must be trained by years of study of history and social benefits.

Economics is the social science which deals with human wants and their satisfaction by production. It is, truly, a science. It does deal with results and causes. It does discover laws in its field. The greatest good of the greatest number has not been supplanted by any better aim of government. The trouble with our politics has been its emphasis on the party's own interest instead of on the general good. The Hoover administration did not stand for broad individualism or the common interest of all of us as consumers but rather for the benefit of certain groups of producers. The Roosevelt philosophy professes the common welfare of the people and emphasizes the interests of farmers too much.

Government should step into business when the managers of that business are running counter to the general welfare. But government operation is rigid, formalized, slow to make needed improvements, lacking in the tests of competition, prone to costly mistakes affecting great multitudes. Business fraud accompanies private operation; graft comes with government control.

These samples should assure you that this is no pussy-footing book. It is concise; it is positive; it discloses both strength and weakness of current proposals. It is concerned with the economic condition of to-day. It is refreshingly understandable.

LEONARD AYRES AND RECOVERY

AFTER 18 years of service in the public-school ranks, a leader in pulling education out of guesses and unproved assertion, Leonard Ayres, fourteen years ago, became vice-president of the Cleveland Trust Company. Economic adviser to the United States government, he writes books that are, as was his work in education, demonstrations of the use of facts and reason in the cure of defects in administration. His latest publication[3] is devoted to solution of the present national problems. It is written with such directness and clarity as to become a favorite with teachers who wish to offset the common criticism that schools are neglecting the pressing issues of to-day and to-morrow. For there never was a time in our history, says this economist, when it was so important as now to clarify discussion and reconcile the teachings based on theory with the judgments derived from observation and experience. Measures and policies are now changing from week to week. We should consider measures for getting out of this depression. We should give support to those most promising.

After an estimate of the situation, Dr. Ayres takes up the courses of early and later depressions that invariably follow wars. He uses the researches of Cornellians Warren and Pearson, charting the national prosperity and hard times since 1750. He takes up debts and prices, the crisis in banking, what government can do, agricultural relief, the industrial recovery act, inflation, orthodox *versus* managed recovery and foreign trade.

If we could put the unemployed producers of durable goods back to work the depression would be over. These are the people who furnish things made of metals, lumber, cement, glass and other enduring materials. Automobiles, ships, locomotives and cars belong in this group. The demand for these goods is elastic because there is almost no limit to the amount we can use if we can get them and also because we can postpone the purchase of them. But consumption goods—food, clothing, tobacco, gasoline, domestic fuel, articles of rubber, paper, leather and textiles—are consumed in almost unchanging amounts. About twenty-six million workers produce these two kinds of goods. About twenty-three million provide services. The employment of these service workers depends heavily on the amount of production of those who provide goods of both kinds. About half the unemployed were producing durable goods. Their unemployment drags into idleness almost as many persons providing ser-

[3] Leonard P. Ayres, "The Economics of Recovery." The Macmillan Company, New York. 189 pp. $1.75.

vice. The main steps of the NRA are to spread work by reducing hours, to increase purchases by raising wages of the most poorly paid workers, to spend three billion three hundred million dollars on public works. The first two projects will fail because they do not increase the demand for durable goods. The NRA is not aiming at the right target. The public works program is to expend less than four billions on durable goods. In 1929 the country produced 40 billion dollars worth of these commodities. For building construction alone we spent eight billions. The solution, concludes Dr. Ayres, is to be found in the expansion of private enterprise, the flow of long-term credit, a market for originating and distributing bonds, for equipment trusts, for real estate mortgages, diminishing the flood of federal borrowing, permitting the flow of private borrowing.

From these extracts you may see that here is a book that is positive, plain-speaking and clear, however it may coincide or conflict with your beliefs.

ELECTRICITY AND SECRECY

To the science teacher who wishes to offset the now common criticism that the instruction practises in public schools remain isolated from current public benefit the little book[4] which Morris Cooke edits will be a boon. It consists of papers read at a convention of the Institute of Public Engineering by engineers, professors of economics, researchers, public officials, managers of power plants, accountants and statisticians.

One of the major problems of the nations, says Engineer Cooke in his comments on these essays, is getting the products of agriculture and industry distributed at the least possible expense. It is up to the engineers to get the facts of electricity costs into such shape that the man on the sidewalk will see the soundness of them. Mr. Cooke believes there is little in this collection of papers that can not be grasped by the ordinary reader without specialized engineering training.

Electricity in domestic life has only just begun. In the United States during the past three years the average annual use in homes has varied from 550 to 600 k.w.h. Throughout Ontario the comparable figure is 1,800 k.w.h., in Winnipeg, 4,000 k.w.h. One circuit in Seattle has an annual use per customer of over 9,000 k.w.h.

If distribution cost-finding methods are developed for electricity they will doubtless be largely applicable to gas and water. In the paper of Engineer Ross, of the Seattle Board of Public Works, you scent something suspicious in the woodpile when he shows that a layman may know the cost of generating plants and of transmission lines, but when he seeks figures on the cost of distribution the vast majority of power systems will give out no usable figures. The information has repeatedly been compiled, but analysis of it is forbidden.

Requests for total figures have the promise that the answers will be confidential. Even the Federal Government can't give out these costs. Since state regulation is a partnership with public-utility corporations, how can a state make a "fair valuation" when it can not know costs? Every state should demand these figures, insists Superintendent Ross.

It seems to me this is a book that physics teachers, teachers of civics and economics will find rich in topics for highly profitable class discussion.

THE NEW DEAL REVIEWED

AT the moment of issuing the national survey by Observers Beard and Smith[5] little bitter and dogmatic opposition has created any formidable danger to the drastic program of legislation and administrative orders that began last March. Earlier American ideals have been upset. Hysteria has not been absent. Conservative business interests were stunned. They were apparently unable to cope with a crisis which their operations had created. There was no rallying point, except a President with a program. What brought the crisis of March 4, 1933, what marked its early days, the problems of governmental economy and efficiency, of industry and transportation, of agriculture, of finance and of

[4] Twenty-eight authors, "What Electricity Costs." The New Republic, New York. 267 pp. $1.00.

[5] Charles A. Beard, George H. E. Smith, "The Future Comes." The Macmillan Company, New York. 178 pp. $1.75.

relief and public works are the subjects of this book.

The startling events that have occurred since the present administration took hold are covered concretely and in an orderly fashion. Getting most of our information from the newspapers we are not sure to realize how inexorably the New Deal grows out of the Old Deal. It is easy to imagine that President Roosevelt is making history. Reading Beard and Smith you are reminded that he also has to be made by it. Wilson's "New Freedom" was based on the old tradition. The answer of history has shown the futility of the Wilson ideas. Momentous decisions will be made in the coming months to settle a present difficulty. They may beyond all present measurement make a fateful future. The purpose and provisions of the various acts of the administration are briefly told in this volume. The views of the critics are presented. We have seen great economic interests moving at electric speed while ideas and ideals of the ox-cart days have persisted. At the best we are at only the beginning of a transition.

WORLD AFFAIRS SUMMARIZED

RESEARCH DIRECTOR BUELL[6] opens the series of booklets projected by the Foreign Policy Association and the World Peace Foundation. There are to be ten of these essays issued yearly with the intent of helping the citizen to understand contemporary international problems and to promote cooperation. Mr. Buell's style of treating topics in short interpretative paragraphs makes his essay admirably fitted for use in classes. He presents the demands of Germany and Japan, South American wars, disarmament, Fascism, Hitlerism, militarism, depression, the Roosevelt program, isolation and international planning.

Members of either of the publishing organizations will get the booklets free. To others yearly subscription at $2.00 will bring the publications in paper covers; $4.00, in cloth bindings.

HISTORY FOR CHILDREN

PROFESSOR KNOWLTON'S project for teaching children history by selecting phases which best come within their understanding proceeds under the title "The Westward March" through "Beginnings in the Past" and "Western Europe."[7]

From primitive man, his tools, inventions and customs, through the myths and cultures of Egypt, Mesopotamia, Palestine, Phoenicia, Greece and Rome, the generously pictured stories proceed through the fall of Rome, the northern invasions, the Moors, the new European nations, England, the castle and cathedral builders, chivalry, religions and discoverers. The design of giving the young American a contact with the cultural stream on which he is riding is well carried out with abundance of adventure and awakening of valuable curiosity. The story is to be carried on by two more books, "When We Were Colonies" and "Since We Became a Nation." The books are written by those whose experience with children has developed skill of animated story-telling.

SUCCESSES AND FAILURES OF THE NATIONS

HARR WAGNER'S idea of a stream of history on which to float our young Americans takes the form of a beautifully printed and illustrated text,[8] the work of three teachers devoted to the newer conceptions of social science. Teach achievements, they say, so as to awaken imitation, a powerful impulse of youth. Teach failures so as to result in resolutions of avoidance. We have here the triumphs and mistakes of the old nations, including India, China and the advanced civilization of the Incas, Aztecs and Mayas. There are chapters on beliefs, languages, records, sciences, arts and governments. "Things to do" follow each chapter. "Other books you may want to read" are listed in large numbers. The authors have mastered an easy story-telling style in a vocabulary adapted to the ages of school children. "Things to think about" are related problems requiring more than memory to solve.

6 Raymond Leslie Buell, ''The World Adrift.'' Foreign Policy Association, New York, or World Peace Foundation, Boston. 38 pp. Cloth, 50 cents; paper, 25 cents.

7 Armand J. Gerson, 242 pp., 57 cents; Mary A. Wheeler, 346 pp., 92 cents. American Book Company, New York.

8 Homer Ferris Aker, B. Lloyd Nelson, Vanza Nielsen Aker, ''Yesterday the Foundation of Today.'' Harr Wagner Publishing Company, San Francisco. 467 pp. $1.40.

DELICIOUS AMERICAN HISTORY

Speaking of history and poetry, Rosemary Benet and her husband, Vincent John Brown's Body Benet, with the aid of brilliant Charles Child, picture-maker, offer a hundred and fourteen delicious pages of verse and prints.[9] You and your children, domestic and official, will devour these choice things over and over. They are not like anything we had in school. They are fresh, tuneful, quaint and with the tang of a different humor. "Columbus discovered our country by thinking it couldn't be there." "The Americans did the Indians and frequently remarked to them it was for their own good." You will renew acquaintance with De Soto, Pocahontas, Stuyvesant, Captain Kidd, Washington, Paul Jones, Johnny Appleseed, Dolly Madison and many old friends.

> Jefferson said "the many";
> Hamilton said "the few."
> Like opposite sides of the penny
> Were these exalted two.
>
> Aaron Burr was bold and bad
> Or else a deeply injured lad.

Our men who were odd or incompetent have their oddities and failures whimsically paraded here. Our Washingtons, Lincolns, Clevelands, Walter Reeds and others are biographed in thrilling Epic verse.

> We've had quite a lot of presidents
> They come from near and far,
> A few have tried to avoid the job
> A couple merely annoyed the job
> But no one ever enjoyed the job
> With the gusto of T. R.

The book is "a marching panorama of our past and present drama and we shan't know all the answers till we're history ourselves." That's the way it closes. Its opening gives you the conviction you are going to enjoy this volume. It starts with the dedication of Father and Mother Benet (Professor Mawson's "Book of Names" says you pronounce it Ben-ay without accenting either syllable) "to Stephanie, Thomas, and Rachel, our other works in collaboration."

[9] Rosemary and Stephen Vincent Benet, "A Book of Americans." Farrar and Rinehart, New York. 114 pp. $2.00.

A DOCTOR COMMENTS ON MORALS

To my thinking Dr. Cabot's is a great book.[10] You come through it with a feeling of exaltation, as if having stood on a height with a superb view, or having heard a great piece of music, or as if you had been on a long walk with a master of life and mind. Practitioner and teacher of medicine, author of a shelf of books on the healing art, often reprinted, this untiring New Englander fills two chairs in Harvard, as professor of clinical medicine and as professor of social ethics.

One must presume he has studied many texts. They have not smothered him. His every-day, matter-of-fact presentation of great themes marks him as a philosopher on his own.

Why make another book on ethics? he asks. Because we face new events, new ideas, that will support, destroy or modify current beliefs about right and wrong. So, then, we go with him through materials gathered directly from life rather than from books: desires, agreements, needs, growth, honesty, self-deceit, recklessness, unsolved problems, art, autocracy, confession, conscience, war, habit, happiness, law, laziness, mental hygiene, rewards, punishments, praise, reformers, worry and the sporting spirit. These are not treated as you are used to hear them.

The devil of idleness is the great preventer. If he has you he lets you think you like mental comfort. But this is a sort of waking sleep, a portion of death.

Growth is insured by desire. Ministers, exploiters, reformers, teachers, work from the outside to spur your desire for growth. The great triumph is to create your own desire.

Take a look at self-deceit on the map of the mind and note the space it occupies. It covers an area as huge as all the sins of man.

The solidarity of nations is that of people trying to get out of a burning theater.

Until very recently in academic circles it has been hardly respectable to go along without refuting some eminent scholar.

As to freedom, why shouldn't you do as you please? The answer is because you prefer conscious, intelligent life to mental suicide or chronic somnolence.

[10] Richard C. Cabot, M.D., "The Meaning of Right and Wrong." The Macmillan Company, New York. 463 pp. $3.50.

You can not live without some semblance of a consistent purpose.

You can't say that every one finds his place. No one ever finds it except approximately.

If you grow you are getting what you want. To know this is to enjoy it and yourself.

Joy recharges your batteries. It flashes the green light on the road ahead.

When you deceive others you may never be found out. When you deceive yourself you are always and instantly caught for you destroy a portion of your own substance and have just so much less self left.

Poetry is adequate words for the expression of beauty.

Public-school teachers are efficient in teaching the three R's because they are learning nothing new about them. But the hope of the country is in the inefficient children because they are growing. We are efficient only so long as we stick to what we have mastered. This is to stop growing.

Such are the terse conclusions sprinkled through this Religio Medici, keen, original and stimulating.

SEVENTEEN EDUCATIONAL MOULDERS CRITICIZED

Norman Woelfel, psychologist, research specialist, educational measurer, an explorer for an American philosophy of education, selects seventeen prominent leaders among teachers and analyzes their later published output.[11] Then he essays the always dangerous task of classifying living men. Six he groups as educators stressing American historical tradition; six are for the ultimacy of science; five are stressing the implications of modern experimental naturalism. It is not for me to tell you whom he puts into each chosen group. The entertainment of guessing is too enjoyable to be taken from you. Nor shall I say who the seventeen moulders are. One each is in the universities of New York, Minnesota, Iowa and Stanford; two are in Ohio State University; three in the University of Chicago and eight in Columbia. All are professors of education and its philosophy. There is not a president or superintendent, principal or public-school teacher in the assortment, for Dr. Woelfel says he selected the seventeen men because he is influenced by the fact that these particular ones have most affected his professional thinking. He has read their writings. By their works ye shall know them. He has considered the influence of this age upon them. Present conditions he has summarized in pungent pages. His summaries of what each of the seventeen stand for, his criticisms of each moulder are keen-cutting, never malicious. He works like a gentleman surgeon. You will find yourself believing he sees sometimes things that are not there. It is regrettable that the documentation of passages on which he bases his conclusions are separated from the appraisals and put into an appendix. I feel that many readers, when, like me, they read a characterization that controverts an opinion they have formed of the man in question, would like to see the authority then and there. Otherwise we seem to be getting the beliefs of a speaker from some one who heard the address. To one of his galaxy Dr. Woelfel gives the enthusiastic admiration of hero worship. To all the others, praise for something, gentle cynicism to other doctrines. But the analyses are so well done that I would be willing to wager something of considerable value that, of the fourteen of the selected eminences I have known pretty well for years, a dozen of them would recognize their own portraits if their names were removed. And reading these appraisals will do the seventeen good. Wasn't it Disraeli who said those who will not read criticism will rarely merit to be criticized? Dr. Woelfel is a welcome relief in giving us something different from the usual educational biography—all praise. He exhibits the skepticism which Lowell insisted is part of the make-up of a good critic.

He does not leave the problem with this summary or comment involving the views of seventeen prominent educators. He offers a closing discussion in which a philosophy of American education, teaching aims and terse conclusions are given in such summary form that no justice could be done to it by any quotation short of what would violate the coypright laws.

[11] Norman Woelfel, "Moulders of the American Mind." Columbia University Press, New York. 304 pp. $3.00.

MOVIES, MORALS AND EMOTIONS

THIRTEEN attractively bound volumes of studies of motion pictures and youth are now listed in the series sponsored by the Payne Fund for Educational Research. The Dysinger-Ruckmick study[12] is the work of professors of psychology at the University of Iowa. After a historical survey of experimental investigations of emotions, the authors describe the methods of the present study, in laboratory and theater. It is clear, they conclude, that the influence of the picture is a matter of individual mental lives. You must know your child; you must know the particular picture. The average greatest emotional intensity was found in children under twelve, but the most extreme stimulation was discovered near the age of 16.

Bound with the study are 285 pages of Professor Peters' discussion of moral effects.[13] A short history of morals opens the essay. Then comes a highly interesting discussion of measuring morals and the development of rating. There are chapters on aggressiveness of girls in love, kissing in the movies, divergence from social democracy, how parents behave on the screen, morality and success of a film. Eighty-five pages of cases selected from motion pictures show the divergences from moral standards chosen for these measurements.

ENJOYING THE CINEMA

So much of the educational literature regarding the moving-picture houses has seemed to be based on a notion that this form of entertainment is going to be suppressed that Edgar Dale's[14] sensible acceptance of the movies as a source of commendable entertainment, involving beauty, art and genius, is a pleasant change. In the educational series of the Payne Fund he has written a manual of motion-picture criticism for the use of high-school students. He argues that appreciation of the cinema is as proper a part of public instruction as is appreciation of music, literature, the graphic arts and nature. He gives a history of the movies, a visit to a studio, talks on how the stories are obtained, acting, photography, settings, sound, music, directors, what are the pictures for? what next? He has over a score of beautiful full-page pictures from different motion-picture plays. He has built upon the universal fascination of the screen a sober, solid, entertaining and edifying offering of culture and refinement that will bring him the thanks of millions of teachers, parents and youth.

[12] Wendall S. Dysinger, Christian A. Ruckmick, "Emotional Responses of Children to the Motion-Picture Situation." The Macmillan Company, New York. 285 pp. $2.00.

[13] Charles C. Peters, "Motion Pictures and Standards of Morality" (with preceding).

[14] Edgar Dale, "How to Appreciate Motion Pictures." The Macmillan Company, New York. 243 pp. $1.20.

OUR HESITATING HIGH SCHOOLS

THOMAS BRIGGS is so gentle and impersonal in his reproof that this new book of his,[15] instead of exploding bombs in the medieval high-school structure we still have with us, is concerned to show what American education was intended to be and asks how you can get the most needed returns. There must be a new course of studies that will function in a democracy. Historian James Sullivan, when he was principal of the Brooklyn Boys' High School, a typical American one, used to say that a sixteenth century youth would feel comfortably at home in our secondary schools. Dr. Briggs pays his respects to the National Survey of Secondary Education and concludes that the program of what the schools should do is yet to be made. A new curriculum appropriate to the needs of a new civilization is no armchair job. It requires prodigious effort. It is well worth it. An attempt to construct such a plan, if given proper explanation and publicity, will undoubtedly, he says, meet with a large degree of popular approval. Only a revolutionary remaking is of real importance. Continual tinkering with a curriculum that has come down from the past and that springs from aims no longer pertinent will still further undermine public confidence, which is already dangerously weakened. Dr. Briggs' stirring book is concerned mostly with what high-school education should and may be.

Nowhere has rigidity and inertia been more apparent than in high-school courses of study. The first ones were copied as exactly as possible from England, where the schoolmaster had prevented their adaptation to the many changes in

[15] Thomas H. Briggs, "Secondary Education." The Macmillan Company, New York. 577 pp. $2.50.

life subsequent to the Renaissance. Education was behind the times in its own old country and more so in Colonial America. Franklin, Noah Webster, Benjamin Rush and a score of eminent statesmen riddled its pretensions, but a persistent snobbery in propaganda that this education made one a gentleman was kept alive by professors. They built up a traditional resistance to change. Dr. Briggs' discriminative historical sketch of American education makes this startlingly evident. He reproduces Dean William Russell's chart, where, side by side, the doings of the school are contrasted with those of the world surrounding them.

It is obvious, says our author, that in this age with newspaper, platform, pulpit and legislative chamber ringing with the demands of a changing social and civic order the studies that were adopted to fit a society that was can not now suffice. The curriculum must be changed.

Tell How We are Bamboozled

Who is to do it? The author's answer is that a central body of most competent men and women should be working continuously, having adequate resources and an appreciation of responsibility. There are at least, says the doctor, forty-five basic questions to be answered, the conclusions to be the guiding principles of the new courses. The civic ideals of our society must be formulated. It is obvious that the success of the democracy depends on an understanding by every citizen and on his devotion to its principles. The teaching of the mechanics of government, which is now about all that civics study does, will not insure understanding or devotion. It is too much a study of a perfect government. It ignores the woful defects we are suffering. The records of libraries, the output of publishers, show there is a great demand for books on politics, economics and sociology now. But the high schools are not concerned with civic and economic affairs. They are under the spell of the old love. They carefully avoid the teaching that would result in an improvement of politics and economics. Politics is not taught as practised—a game, a graft. The sooner the youth is taught how we are bamboozled by politicians the sooner will he become an intelligent and active citizen.

High schools have amazingly increased in membership. The lures that have drawn children to them are of doubtful value. False hopes have been woven into a questionable salesmanship, an educational evangelism. The uninformed public and unformed pupils have assumed, not found, that the education offered by the high schools is appropriate. Half our youth do not enter high school; half of those who do are not willing to finish the course. We must examine the high-school philosophy to see why. A 70 per cent. achievement is satisfactory in school; nowhere else. Fourteen per cent. of those who have begun Latin continue it beyond the second year. In modern languages the record is similar. The use outside of high school of subjects taught in it is ridiculously infrequent. Evaluated by the amount of contributions to the communities which support it, the high school is bankrupt.

These are sober reflections selected here and there from the pages.

The main thesis of the book is that the founders of our democracy provided education so as to insure the continuance of the nation and to promote the general welfare. For this, lavish expenditures of public funds are made. It is hard to understand how careless Americans have been in seeing to it that the teaching they pay for is devoted to the ends for which it was made a public cost.

These sad strictures of an experienced practitioner and observer have no reprimands attached. No one knows better than Author Briggs that the host of American teachers does constitute an army under orders. The orders are the contents of the curriculum and the authorized text-books. Accordingly, having by his historical summary and his array of facts established the need of the educational revolution, Dr. Briggs, in reasonable argument and earnest persuasion, shows what a high-school curriculum and supplementing text-books ought to be. This he does by his chapters on issues, functions, customs, interests, attitudes and adolescence, concluding with a noble chapter, "A Vision of Secondary Education."

HYGIENE WITH INTEREST

Dr. Etheredge[16] does know how to put life

[16] Maude Lee Etheredge, M.D., "Health Facts for Students." W. B. Saunders Company, Philadelphia. 342 pp. $2.00.

into an old subject. The devil of contumacy makes me, and maybe you, balk at duty. The reading of any book on hygiene is somehow associated in my mind with duty. This volume is pushed upon me with the command to review it. Miracle! The first chapter is so gently persuasive, so quietly logical, so distinctly interesting, that it leads one to think a woman can write a better hygiene than a man. Now that I have read through, I'm sure of it.

Your health, observes Lady Etheredge, depends much on your outlook on life. This is your own. You needn't take a long journey to reach the house with the golden windows. Get the right angle and your own are full of glorious luster.

For college you do need a new adjustment. You never were so close to so many kinds of people before. The strong personality usually becomes stronger from these contacts; the weaker one slumps. For this reason, know about mental and social hygiene. It is a ladder for reaching your highest level.

So, here we go through chapters on the nervous system, the relation of booze to it, the upset of the system at puberty, conflicts, complexes, fears valuable and destructive, worry, failures, play, fatigue, rest, sleep, foods, indigestion, constipation, overeating, teeth, the reproductive organs, the respiratory system, the circulation, bones, muscles, the glands, skin, hair, beauty, the sense organs, clothing, first aid, community health.

The descriptions of the body are only detailed far enough to make proper care more intelligent. But the usual absurd omission of the sex organs is quietly ignored. Their nature and care are covered. Painful menstruation in college girls is usually because of mental or physical strain. The hygiene of this condition is presented as it is for the diseases that afflict the college student from measles to cancer. There is a chapter on venereal ailments.

This is a business-like book. President Ray Lyman Wilbur, who is, himself, a doctor of medicine, says Dr. Etheredge is an expert adviser, wise in the experience of answering questions that pour upon her in her position as medical consultant to the students of the University of Illinois.

You will offer to add that she knows how to write.

CAN YOU PRONOUNCE?

I WONDER whether President Ruthven, of the University of Michigan, knows that his name is properly pronounced *Rivn.* Roosevelt is *Rozyvelt.* Saare is *Sayry* but Saarbrucken is *Zarbruken.* Louisiana is *Looeezeana,* Louisville is both *Looisvill* and *Looyvill.* If you mean the capital of Senegal you must say *Sanlooee,* but for the metropolis of *Missoory* or *Mizoory* you may say *Saint Looy* or *Saint Looiss.* All this and the pronunciation of 9,240 more proper names you may learn from Dr. Mawson's volume.[17] He sent letters to men and women in all parts of the world, asking how they pronounce their own names and those of the places in which they live. Foreign legations, learned societies and others, able to furnish first-hand information, gave the facts sought. Every entry, says the compiler, is backed by authority. You should know Dr. Mawson by now from his editions of the Roget Thesaurus. A decidedly valuable feature of the book is the author's spicy discussion of pronunciation, of the twists that get fixed in the names of men and places, the bad breaks of lecturers and broadcasters, the English and American form of foreign places, essential sounds of vowels and consonants in foreign words, accents. France accents every syllable, Bohemian or Czech, Estonian, Finnish, Hungarian or Magyar, Lettish, Slovak, always the first; Armenian, Burmese, Persian, generally the last syllable. Forty-four languages are listed as to accents.

The book will be found full of surprises. *Hindenboork* is the proper sound. Saint John is the place, but *Sinjen,* the man, if he is a Briton. *Illinoi* or *Illinoiz; Iowah* or *Ioway* always accented on the first; *Ipsylanty.* Reading is *Redding* in both England and America. *Portsmuth, Lowss Angeless* (hard g) *Lowss Anjeless* or *Lowss Angeleez,* always with a long *o; Baytoven, Moosoleenee.* Percy Mackaye is *Maki,* accented on the last, Belloc is *Belluk,* on the first; Beauchamp is *Beecham;* Methwold, *Mu-al;* Taliaferro, *Toliver.* Consult the book

[17] C. O. Sylvester Mawson, ''International Book of Names.'' Thomas Y. Crowell, New York. 308 pp. $2.00.

before you make a speech. If you want some entertainment at a dinner of intelligentsia get some names from the book, put them on place cards and give a prize to the best pronouncer.

WHY TEACHERS OF FOREIGN LANGUAGE?

Helen Eddy[18] visited 264 high-school classes in foreign language, ascertained what schools have the reputation for superior work, examined 207 of their courses of study and wrote monograph 24 of the Koos survey under the auspices of the United States Office of Education. She finds this school subject in a state of transition. The survey reports that the first objective now aimed at by teachers of language in America is a knowledge of other countries. The second purpose is that of gaining a knowledge of relations between the foreign tongue and English words and grammar. The continual charge of the followers of Snedden, Counts, Frasier and the Great Unsatisfied, that the rule of *status quo* in high schools is unbroken, shows no sign of worrying any of the contributors to this survey. The list of objectives proposed by the study is based on the testimony of selected teachers, on scores attained in standardized tests and on enrolment figures showing that only 57 per cent. of pupils who begin a study of foreign language hang on for two years.

It reminds me of a remark made by a member of the New York State Legislature to a committee of teachers: "You good people want us to support the teaching of your specialty on the basis that you teachers believe it ought to be taught. It's the same as having the chauffeur decide what car to use and where it ought to go."

If there is anything indicated in this present crisis of education, is it not that there should be a sound answer to the question, Why should there be a school tax? On the answer should be based all the studies selected and all the "objectives" of them. Until this is done the defenses of high-school education are alarmingly vulnerable.

In the same mail with this report comes a circular from Teachers Woelfel, Grossman, Counts, Hook, Hullfish, Kilpatrick, Newlon, Overstreet, Rugg and Spear, proposing an organization to get education remade on the basis of reconstructing the social order. State teachers associations are resolving in their general sessions that the school must select its activities in accordance with this aim. The resolvers then walk into the special section meetings and proceed as though we should start with subjects and build from their peculiar objectives the main aim of education in general.

Little correlation, observes Miss Eddy, is found between language study and the rest of the course. There is opportunity for linking it with social studies. The local course is generally a reflection of the text-book used. The College Entrance Examination Board requires translation; therefore, we must teach it. There is a tendency to load the pupils with programs impossible of achievement.

For Latin, the report finds a persisting influence derived from the Classical Investigation of 1924, whose conclusions Commissioner Butterfield condensed into "Latin should be taught because we teach it." Miss Eddy finds 69 per cent. of those who begin Latin continuing it as long as one or two years. Five per cent. of those taking it to get into college continue it after they get there. Its chief evil is an excessive amount of grammar in the first year; and, thereafter, of reading. As a result there is neither mastery of Latin nor a realization of its values. J. Caesar's war book is being cut to five months of study. The most potent influence on courses of study is the College Entrance Examination Board. Many schools establish an alibi for responsibility by printing: "The teaching of Latin has for its direct aim the satisfaction of college requirements."

Why should George Counts ask his now famous question, "Can the schools make a new social order?" when their courses are laid out for them by gentlemen and scholars in higher institutions of learning that accept the dictum of the young president of the University of Chicago on the colleges' immunity from teaching citizenship?[19]

Miss Eddy has done a thorough piece of work.

[18] Helen M. Eddy, "Instruction in Foreign Languages." U. S. Superintendent of Documents, Washington, D. C. 61 pp. 10 cents.

[19] School and Soceity, February 11, 1933.

She has made a panorama of a devoted company of hard-working upholders of a special brand of scholarship. Their loyalty to themselves and their subject is more than ever in the public eye.

It is surprising how sedulously the committees in charge of telling us what the aims of foreign language should be avoid saying that enjoyment is an important objective. A stack of new texts delights the eye. You do not get very far into any without discovering that the compilers are determined that you shall have a good time.

German

The authors of "A Second German Book"[20] scatter, even among the exercises for straightening grammar, a wealth of fascinating pictures of German town-and-country life, sports, quaint old engravings and modern pretty girls. Reading ability and human interest are the confessed aims of the authors. Ease and enjoyment are not synonymous. Easy reading keeps the pupil in the baby class. Curiosity will urge towards enough work to understand the stories. Adhering to this principle, Messrs. Betz and Holzwarth, long experienced in teaching huge classes of adolescents, have hit the bull's-eye beautifully.

Spanish

Pittaro and Green[21] accept the recommendations of the Modern Foreign Language Study and make reading ability and cultural information their guiding stars. Interesting and easy reading selections lure to the higher and brighter field, with a fine array of thought-provoking creative projects. The *lecturas culturales* are twenty in number, concerned with the geography, industry, art, literature and eminent leaders of Spain. Silent reading is pushed. It must have plenty of material at a given level unobstructed by too many grammatical hurdles. The exercises in matching synonyms and antonyms, derivatives, Spanish-English cognates, are used to secure high comprehensibility. Frequent dictation is employed to develop reading without translation. All through the book is the recognition of a common stupidity of language teaching, the habit of clogging progress by a load of grammatical aids in which the implements get more attention than the product. The grammar is here in abundance but stored neatly in the tool-rack to be used when wanted. The pictures are alluring.

Latin

Professors Carr and Hadzsits[22] write their beginning Latin book in that spirit. Beginning with picturae, sellae, tabulae, mensae, et ceterae, pictured, written and spoken, they arrive, by dialogues, anecdotes, poems, songs, music and games, to extracts adapted from the classic authors.

A committee of Latin teachers in Baltimore,[23] after eight years of experimenting with seventh-grade pupils in the junior high school, have pooled their experience in a bright text of pictures, talk, reading and general facts of language abounding in easy stories and furnishing varied information on Roman life and letters.

The Chicago University Latin booklets[24] are illustrated with special drawings. The books are based on the dictum, "you learn to read by reading." They use, early and often, words that occur most frequently in Latin literature. The primer uses a combination of pictures and short sentences in accordance with the universal practise in teaching the mother tongue. Forty chapters bring the beginner to reading lessons a page in length. Topics for composition, lessons in dictation, assorted vocabularies follow. "Cornelia" is the story of the adventures of a little American girl. "Carolus et Maria" tells in Latin the doings of every-day Charles and Mary and their friends.

[20] Frederick Betz, Charles Holzwarth, "A Second German Book." American Book Company. 492 pp. $1.60.

[21] John M. Pittaro, Alexander Green, "Progressive Spanish." D. C. Heath and Company, Boston. 554 pp. $1.72.

[22] Wilbert Lester Carr, George Depue Hadzsits, "The Living Language." D. C. Heath and Company, Boston. 404 pp. $1.36.

[23] Mary T. Brennan, chairman, "Exploring Latin." American Book Company, New York. 190 pp. 80 cents.

[24] Mima Maxey, Marjorie J. Fay, "New Latin Primer," 138 pp., 90 cents; Mima Maxey, "Cornelia," 78 pp., 70 cents; Marjorie J. Fay, "Carolus et Maria," 98 pp., 70 cents. University of Chicago Press.

MAKING HISTORY HUM

Reviewers hailed "Arundel" and "Lively Lady," the first a historical novel of Arnold's expedition against Quebec, the other a gallant sea adventure in the War of 1812, as better stories and better histories than any American work in this line. Vigor, simplicity, humor, stirring adventure, courage, tragedy, comedy and genius they found abundant. You will agree with them when you read this author's latest story of Burgoyne's expedition.[25]

In it there is small nourishment of the cherished romantic fallacy that courage and ability bring greater recognition than mediocrity and bluster, that virtue always triumphs and that cowards surely get fit punishment. Peter Merrill, shipbuilder, sea captain, soldier scout, of Arundel, Maine, tells of the genius, daring, skill and devotion of Benedict Arnold and the indignities put upon him by Old Woman Gates and the nincompoops in Congress, how in spite of jealousies and slanders he saved the nation from disseverment by Burgoyne and Howe, and preserved the Union.

You will love roaring Cap Hubb and old Doc Means. Doc "scratched" all the recruits with vaccine. In ten days young Nathaniel said he was sick. "You ain't sick," said Doc, "you're scairt."

The others insisted that Doc should give him a puke as all the real doctors do.

"No reason, no reason at all!" shouts Doc. "Every doctor sets up a smallpox hospital and pukes everybody. Why is that? So's his patients'll think they're sick. How's a doctor going to make a living if his patients don't think they're sick? The trouble with a puke is it makes you feel sicker'n you are. What I say is if you don't feel sick you ain't sick."

When the whole troop began to feel the workings of the inoculation they howled for food. But Doc gave them only a cup of warm milk now and then, with maybe a pinch of Digby's sympathetic powder.

"When a dog's sick," he said, "he crawls under the barn, don't he? He don't fill himself with all sorts of gurry guaranteed to rip his insides to pieces. He lays there and sleeps and don't eat nothing. If you was sick that's the kind of medicine I'd give you, too—let you sleep and give you nothing to eat."

"If doctors ain't no good," protested Cap Hubb, "what you want to carry that doctor book around with you for?"

"So's to see what the best doctors recommend and then do different," said Doc promptly.

All through the campaign this bonesetter and bullet-prober kept his men aware that "there ain't nothing ails you unless you think there is."

He made decoctions of the common white mullein for fluxes of the belly, for cramps and convulsions, for toothache and piles, for obstructions of the bladder, for inflammation of the throat, for wounds in the flesh, for various aches and pains.

"Does it cure all these things?" asked Peter Merrill.

"I guess mebbe," said Doc placidly, "if you think it will. There ain't nothing that does you much good unless you think it does."

Captured by the Indians, his skill brings Doc the honor of initiation into the Midewiwin, the grand order of Medicine Men recognized by all the tribes.

"I don't know about this," said Doc. "It might make you a regular doctor and then you'd have the ethics. That's ticklish business. If one doctor sees another purging a patient to death he can't say nothing; ethics says you mustn't. No, I don't want to be a regular doctor, for ethics makes you do all the fool things the others do."

If you can bear to be shaken in your cherished myths, this book will do it for you. "Wolfe should have been court-martialed for putting his troops where he did. Montcalm should have been court-martialed for abandoning an impregnable fortress to fight in an open field."

"People believe anything bad about a big man —anything that shows he hasn't behaved himself with a woman, or money, or rum. There ain't one man in a thousand who won't talk himself black in the face about things he knows nothing of. Nine times out of ten the worst in the lot are folks who think they're educated."

From the sprightly talk of the actors in these

[25] Kenneth Roberts, "Rabble in Arms." Doubleday Doran and Company, Garden City, New York. 870 pp. $2.50.

stirring scenes you get the atmosphere of those terrible times: militiamen enlisting for bounties and running back home, political incapables supplanting real commanders, jealous plotters against Washington, Schuyler and Arnold, a whiffling Congress knowing nothing of war, or men mussing into everything.

This book, in your school library, will be soon worn out. It will put much vitality into your teaching of history.

BOY AND GIRL STORY

A LIVELY story of children whom you would like to spend a summer with is published by the Viking Press.[26] It has adventures of work and play, unemployment, dramatics, school, woods, streams, quaint folks and a jolly American boy with a boy's instinct for building. It is a hearty book for youngsters of the junior and senior high-school age.

WOBBLY COMMERCIAL EDUCATION

ONE of the jolliest books that has come to this reviewery in a long time is that in which Professor Nichols,[27] of the Harvard Graduate School, plies hammer and tongs upon high-school commercial education tradition. What makes you think, he asks, that your commercial course, framed in the armchair, used as a dump for children failing in academic subjects, losing its boys, and now almost entirely a girls' course, does anything but waste time? Isn't it rather a confidence game to encourage so many youngsters to look forward to office work without your taking stock of the blind alleys in it? The verdict that "they are not college material" has kept many boys and girls out of the academic classes. It is time in the interest of the economy of human hopes and successes that you should decide whether or not your business pupils are "commercial material."

Most of your commercial students are girls. They are trained for one thing, but according to research they are employed for something quite different. A changing economic order and a static form of school education for business have combined to eliminate the boys from your commercial classes. They elect the college preparatory course and as soon as they graduate from it seek commercial employment. Worse yet, employers prefer them over the boys that have taken the commercial studies.

There will be about fourteen million people receiving vocational education by 1935. Half of them will be commercial students. As early as 1928 there were a million pupils definitely preparing for business. The increase of the number is appalling. The grip of tradition on academic teaching is deadly, but it is more persistent in the commercial courses.

For many years the high-school managers treasured the solacing belief that the dropping out of students was due to economic conditions at home. Many still cling to this fallacy. Indisputable proof is available, showing that only 15 per cent. of withdrawals are due to this cause. The lure of wage-earning, with its promise of better clothes, more freedom, more "good times," is the greatest force taking young people out of school.

You should test your students in those qualities on which business success depends. Those who have them should be given a new course made especially for the business of to-day. A commission of business men, of heads of schools maintained by large business concerns for training their own workers, of the most advanced educators, could map out a course for the new deal and watch its operation. For the other children you can give a general business course such as you now use as a retreat from academic difficulties.

Professor Nichols' book is mostly constructive after he has distinctly diagnosed the failures of the present scheme. He has been a keen student of vocational education for twenty-five years. Always he has been an apostle of the truth that better business must follow better teaching. His advocacy of changes and reforms have been backed, as in this volume, by facts and figures.

His present book, in these days of educational criticism from without, is indispensable to the high-school principal and to the commercial teacher, for it shows where the defenses are weakest and how the whole line can be made invulnerable.

26 Lincoln Fay Robinson, "Jack's House." The Viking Press, New York. 258 pp. $2.00.

27 Frederick C. Nichols, "Commercial Education in the High School." D. Appleton-Century Company, New York. 513 pp. $3.00.

SCHOOL AND SOCIETY

WITH WHICH ARE COMBINED THE EDUCATIONAL REVIEW, ESTABLISHED IN 1891, THE TEACHERS MAGAZINE, ESTABLISHED IN 1878, AND THE SCHOOL JOURNAL, ESTABLISHED IN 1874.

EDITED BY J. McKEEN CATTELL

Volume 39 SATURDAY, JANUARY 13, 1934 Number 994

MEASUREMENT IN EDUCATIONAL EXPERIMENTATION WITH SPECIAL REFERENCE TO THE PROGRESSIVE EDUCATION ASSOCIATION PROJECT[1]

By Dean MAX McCONN

LEHIGH UNIVERSITY

I

THE title of this paper has been carefully composed so as to look and sound decorously drab and unexciting. This has been done in accordance with that code of etiquette which proscribes any semblance of human interest in the titles of addresses at educational meetings. As a matter of fact, however, the real topic which my title so punctiliously drapes is a distinctly controversial one.

The nature of the controversy may be indicated by reference to the four groups sponsoring this "Second Educational Conference," as listed on the first page of our program. You have all scanned that list. It includes (1) the American Council on Education Committees on Personnel Methods and on Educational Testing, (2) the Cooperative Test Service, (3) the Educational Records Bureau and (4) the Progressive Education Association's Commission on the Relation of School and College. It will be noted at once that the first three of those groups are concerned, not solely, of course, nor ultimately, but directly and immediately, with testing and measurement and records; whereas the fourth group, the Commission of the Progressive Education Association, has much wider objectives, among which testing and measurement and records may be regarded as playing only a very minor and incidental rôle.

It might be expected that some difference of attitude and emphasis and point of view would develop among partners thus assorted, and it is a fact that such difference has actually developed to a point which I fear fully justifies the word controversy. As a controversy it has so far been kept for the most part under cover, in the form of doubts and reservations and smouldering suspicions, freely and fervently expressed by the members of each party among themselves, but not as yet flung openly in each other's teeth.

But this stage could not last much longer, and in any case it is not a happy or healthy situation. Accordingly, it is the purpose of this paper to drag this controversy forth into the light of day, to air it somewhat thoroughly, and quite possibly to give occasion for a still more thorough airing at the discussion session this afternoon.

[1] Presented at the third annual meeting of institutional members of the Educational Records Bureau, Hotel St. Regis, New York City, November 3, 1933.

II

The dragging-forth process I hope to accomplish by stating in turn, as well as I can, the two opposing points of view; and, here at the beginning, I shall endeavor to present each side with some of that exaggeration and heat and bias in which the proponents of each are inclined to indulge in their private "bull sessions" together. Because, in this case, as in many others, the exaggeration and heat and bias are essential parts of the controversy. Perhaps, in fact, it may turn out that those aspects of the matter represent the major part of the difference.

First, then, let me try to set forth the doubts and questionings of those devotees of tests and measurement who are just now looking somewhat askance at the project of the Progressive Education Association. They are inclined to say that the progressives don't really know what they want to do or how they want to do it, that they have not been able to agree on any common curriculum or common subject-matter, and that, since they appear to be unwilling to have their results measured by any standardized and comparable tests, neither they nor anybody else will know, when they get through, what, if anything, they have accomplished or demonstrated. One lively correspondent of mine has expressed it thus—that their whole project seems likely to degenerate into "a disjointed series of spasms on the part of individual schools and bolshevistic individual teachers, without any common or understandable measuring rod being applied to any two of the institutions or classes."

Perhaps that may serve for that side. Now for the retort of the more radical progressives.

They are wont to declare—these more radical progressives—that the existing tests are no good. Or, in milder mood, they may assert merely that they are "inadequate"—which, however, means, I take it, much the same thing. More specifically, they claim that the existing tests measure only mere information, mere facts.

You will all recall that Miss Daisy Ashford, in "The Young Visiters," described certain persons as being "very mere." That is the way some of the progressives apparently regard information and facts; they practically never refer to them without calling them "mere." But this is a digression. To continue:

The members of this group assert that they are very little interested in information, facts, whether "mere" or otherwise—that what they are concerned with in their students is such things as growth and power, attitudes, understandings, appreciations and the like, and that the existing tests do not measure any of these things, and therefore are of no substantial use.

And then, by way of counter-offensive, carrying the war into the enemy's country, they are likely to claim that any existing test or group of tests, if it is known that it is to be used, will inevitably become a goal of instruction, will be prepared for, "crammed" for, so that the pupils may make a good showing, and will thus come to dominate the curriculum and the subject-matter of individual courses and the methods of teaching, and consequently will check free experimentation and kill spontaneity and stifle and devitalize the whole business. If we are to have tests, they say, why not go on as we were, with the College Board examinations? Why should we go to great trouble to set up a so-called experiment if we are merely to exchange our old shackles for new ones which may be equally galling?

This, you will see, comes close to being the exact opposite of the position taken by the more conservative testers. And so we have the setting for a very pretty quarrel, or, to speak soberly, a somewhat ugly quarrel, which, if it develops, may do substantial damage to both causes, that of educational testing and measurement and that of progressive education.

III

So let us examine these two opposing positions, which I have deliberately stated above with some exaggeration and bias, as I proposed at the beginning to do—but certainly with no more of these attributes than I, and most of you, have actually seen and heard exhibited in conversations among the extremists on both sides; let us examine the two positions, as calmly as we can, to see if we may be able to strip away the exaggeration and bias and find what remains on each side that is valid and significant. If we should be successful in doing only that, we should make a substantial contribution to both causes.

But, as a matter of fact, I propose also to suggest in my conclusion what seems to me a possible synthesis, a method of procedure in testing in educational experimentation which may solve the apparent dilemma—may satisfy those who are chiefly interested for the present in educational measurement, and yet may be acceptable to the most freedom-loving and experimental progressives.

This, of course, is a large order, and my proposed synthesis may draw only brickbats in the discussion this afternoon. But even so my temerity may stimulate some more successful conciliator and synthesizer to follow either this afternoon or later.

Since I have several times used the somewhat ugly word "bias," it may be only proper at this point for me to take time out for a couple of minutes to give you what the astronomers would call my own "personal equation," my own bias and prejudice. Looking at myself as objectively as I can, I should say that in this matter I am that despicable and unhappy creature, a middle-of-the-road man, who can, of course, expect sympathy and support from neither side. I am like Mr. Snell of the Rainbow Inn in "Silas Marner," inclined to cry, "You're both right and both wrong; the truth lies atween you." More specifically: I am deeply interested in educational tests; of the technical side of these instruments I know substantially nothing; but as a personnel officer, a counselor of college students, I make daily use of test results, and I am thoroughly convinced that with the help of these results I am able to do my work with much better success than I was able to attain before such aids became available. On the other hand, I subscribe with equal conviction to the progressive doctrines of interest and individualization; indeed I agree with the progressives even in regard to the "mereness" of information; I too have little use for facts in education, except as they may contribute to worth-while understandings and attitudes and appreciations; and I deplore as strongly as any one any domination and standardization of curriculum or methods by any testing or measurement program. In short, it is—of course—exactly my own prejudice and bias that lead me to attempt, in my own thinking, to synthesize the two movements and conserve the values I seem to see in both.

With that out of the way, let us turn now to the position of those measurement people who are distrustful of the progressive program.

When those people say that the progressives do not know what they want to do or how they want to do it, I disagree with them entirely. What those people should say in this connection is that *they* don't understand what the progressives want to do or how. The progressives themselves have, as a matter of fact, attained a quite remarkable unanimity on these points.

The proof of this assertion, for me, lies in the proceedings at the conference held in Atlantic City last March by that commission of the Progressive Education Association which is one of the sponsoring groups for these meetings. The purpose of that conference was the final selection, by the commission and its directing committee, of the twenty-odd secondary schools to participate in the current project for progressive experimentation at the secondary level; and the selection was to be based, in the main, on the plans for experimentation to be presented there by the representatives of nearly fifty schools. Please note that these plans were entirely devised and formulated by the faculties of the different schools, working separately and independently; the commission having laid down no specifications and in fact having offered no suggestions. Yet the many plans presented exhibited the most remarkable homogeneity, not only of purpose and general direction and general pattern, but in concrete proposals for the organization of curricula, subject-matter content, subject-matter grouping and teaching methods. Before I was privileged to attend that conference I too sometimes wondered whether we progressives represented anything more than a congeries of assorted bolsheviks; but since that conference I am convinced that it is the progressives who do know what they want to do and why and how. In these days it is rather the conservatives who have no answers to such questions; else why, in the face of revolutionary change, should they continue to do only what has always been done in the past?

But when the measurement people go on to say that if the progressives will not have their results measured by standardized and comparable tests, neither they nor anybody else will know, when they get through, what, if anything, they have accomplished and shown, then my sympathy and conviction swerve sharply to their side. On this point they seem to me indisputably right. The Progressive Education Association's commission constantly refer to their project as an experiment. It is as an experiment that it has been accepted by more than 250 colleges. It is as an experiment that it has been supported financially through the Carnegie Foundation and the Carnegie Corporation, and as an experiment that it has attracted the interest of the general educational public. And the word "experiment," drawn from the vocabulary of the exact sciences, unquestionably implies a procedure that shall be watched and checked and measured with all possible precision and shall yield results expressed as far as possible in exact, quantitative, comparable terms.

It seems to me perfectly clear, therefore, that if this progressive project is to retain, during its progress, the support of the colleges and of the foundations and the interest of the educational public, it must call to its aid every available kind of measurement. And that it must do this also if its final report, when the project is concluded in 1944, is to have any wide effect on secondary education in this country or on the attitude of the colleges towards progressive schools or progressive procedures in schools. Neither the schools in general nor the colleges will take much stock in generalized claims of achievement or personal qualitative appraisals; but they can be convinced, even against their prejudices, by comparable measurements.

IV

But it is time now to listen again to the caveats of the more radical progressives against what they usually style "the existing tests."

I have quoted them as declaring that all the existing tests are "inadequate." Well, if by that they mean, as I think they do, that no existing test or group of tests can measure the attainment of the more general, long-term goals of the educative process—such goals as the progressives suggest, without precise definition, when they use such words as "power" and "understandings" and "attitudes" and "appreciations"—then I agree absolutely, and I have yet to encounter the most rabid tester who does not also agree. So we may concede that much.

But the same people go on to make their charge more specific by saying that the existing tests test only for information, facts. With that assertion I am not prepared to concur quite so fully. Let us agree that it is partly true, perhaps even largely true. But certainly the measurement people are consciously attacking this deficiency with both vigor and ingenuity. You will listen at one o'clock this afternoon to Dr. Lindquist, of the University of Iowa, on "The Technique of Constructing Tests in Relation to Various Uses of Test Results." I presume, and hope, that he will mention, at least in passing, that for several years now the Iowa Achievement Tests have been constructed with the deliberate purpose to defeat rote learning and mechanical drill procedures. As I have written elsewhere[2] of these tests: "The questions used regularly demand, not mere facts—names, dates, definitions, formulae, laws—but the interpretation of facts by the recognition of relationships, sequences, causes, results, implications, contradictions, and the like." Of course I mention these Iowa tests as one example only of what all the testers are now striving to do. How well they have thus far succeeded in this effort I am not competent to judge; but in view of their truly remarkable achievements in general during the brief quarter century they have been at work, I have a good deal of faith that they will advance, slowly, perhaps, but surely, into this difficult terrain.

But of course the radical progressive objectors do not believe that, as yet, the testers have made any worth-while progress in this respect. So far, they say, all the tests are information tests, pure and simple. So be it! I do not myself think they are quite right when they say that—I think they are a little behind the times—but for the sake of argument let us grant that it is so. What then? It does not seem to me to follow that even mere information tests are of no value to progressives. It seems to me that admittedly factual tests can be of the greatest utility in the *indirect* measurement of the kinds of achievement to which the progressives aspire.

Let me pause to point out that the minute we leave the exact sciences, physics and chemistry, we leave behind for the most part the possibility of direct testing and measurement. In geology and astronomy, in biology, and still more in psychology and sociology, our scientists can seldom measure directly the total phenomenon or result or development in which they are interested. Usually they must content themselves with measuring some aspect or incident or symptom, for which they have been able to devise a technique of measurement, and then draw inferences as to the meaning of their results with respect to the total process with which they are really concerned. In medicine, for example, what the physician really wants to measure is the progress of a disease or a cure. He can almost never do that directly, any more than we can measure directly growth in power or improvement of social attitudes. But the physician does not therefore repudiate all measurement. On the contrary, he assiduously and systematically measures everything he can measure, temperature, pulse, blood count, urinal content, etc., and from his exact and comparable data relating to these mere incidents and symptoms draws, by inference, important indications for diagnosis and therapy. In the field of education, where all the uncertainties of biology, psychology and sociology are intermingled and concentrated, we can hardly complain if we must usually proceed by a similar indirection.

[2] "Educational Guidance Is Now Possible," in *The Educational Record,* Vol. 14, No. 4, October, 1933.

The application of all this to the use of information tests in progressive education will be obvious. Granted that as progressives we are not interested in information for its own sake, any more than the physician is interested in pulse or temperature as such, we may still be deeply and constantly interested in the results of factual tests for their indications of progress or lack of progress towards our own legitimate goals.

Choosing to be tedious rather than to risk vagueness, I propose to try to drive this point home—because it seems to me really important. It is the faith of progressives that if we faithfully employ in the teaching process and in curriculum building and in guidance the principles of interest and individualization we shall attain an effectiveness in learning that can not possibly be achieved when these principles are ignored, as they commonly are in current schooling; that a student working in a particular field because of a genuine self-felt interest will master the material in that field with extraordinary thoroughness and precision and retain it with equally remarkable completeness and accuracy. True, we are not much interested in the mere volume of information thus acquired and held in memory. We are interested rather because we believe that facts and ideas mastered in this way penetrate to the active intellectual life, as compelled rote learning never does, reach the emotions, develop what we call understandings and attitudes and appreciations and eventuate in conduct and code. But incidental to the total process is the peculiarly effective mastery of factual material in the student's chosen field. And there is the one point in the whole process where we can at present test and obtain comparable quantitative data. We can not do much perhaps in the measurement of interest at the beginning of the process, or anything at all as yet in the measurement of emotional reactions and understandings and appreciations at the end. But we do have in the standardized objective achievement test a sort of stethoscope which can be applied in the middle. And so it seems to me we ought to be eager and systematic in the use of that available instrument.

If in particular cases we find a fine mastery of materials in the students' chosen fields, we may be reasonably sure that we have been successful in our use of the principles of interest and individualization and are making progress towards our higher goals. And if in other cases the achievement tests uncover ineffective learning even of facts—I do not mean in all the usual fields, but in the chosen fields—then it seems to me we may well question whether we have been successful in our attempted use of progressive principles and whether we are on our way to progressive goals or any goals at all.

I confidently expect, moreover, that if we will make free use of achievement tests —granting that they are mere information tests—in the schools now working under the commission of the Progressive Education Association, and in other progressive experimentation in school and college, we shall, by this device alone, demonstrate the overwhelming superiority of progressive procedures. It seems to me obvious in advance that students working eagerly and ardently in fields in which real interest has been aroused will acquire, even incidentally, a mastery of factual material in those fields surpassing anything that routine procedure can produce. I venture to assert that this has already been demonstrated at those colleges—Swarthmore, Lehigh and others—which have adopted the progressive device of the major field and the comprehensive examination therein, and I am confident of the same outcome at the secondary level.

In passing, let me call attention to the

splendid strategic value of thus beating the enemy on their own ground.

V

But we have still to examine the most serious objection which the radical progressives raise against the existing tests and—if I understand them correctly—against any conceivable tests, namely, that any testing program inevitably becomes itself the goal of instruction and hence dominates, standardizes, stifles and devitalizes the whole of the teaching process subjected to it.

On this point we must, I think, admit that the objectors have history on their side. Such has certainly been the outcome of many notable testing programs in the past. We all know what the Regents' Examinations have done to the high schools of the state of New York and what the College Board examinations in their old original form did to the whole group of Eastern preparatory schools.

It should be noted, in parenthesis, that the present situation with respect to the College Board examinations, since the board has developed its Comprehensive Examinations and Scholastic Aptitude Test, is very different from what it used to be. In fact, in view of its newly proposed "placement examination" program, I am tempted to say that we have here the first recorded case in natural history in which the leopard has changed his spots. But to continue:

The Pennsylvania Study, in giving new-type comprehensive examinations only three times in the colleges of Pennsylvania, uncovered pretty clear evidence of attempts to "coach" for those examinations. And all of us, working in either school or college, have watched general departmental examinations operate in the same way, becoming goals and standardizers for all the teachers and students in the department. It is not necessary to multiply examples.

But it may be worth while to inquire whether these unhappy results are inherent in the nature of the tests and examinations themselves—whether they have not followed rather from the use we have hitherto made of tests and examinations.

Up to the immediate present we have been accustomed to use examinations exclusively on crucial occasions, to be followed by immediate and drastic results for the examinee, based upon one spasmodic deliverance on his part under conditions of special stress and strain. We have used them to determine whether a man shall receive the degree of doctor of philosophy or the license to practise medicine or law; whether a college student shall be graduated; whether a high-school boy may be admitted to the college of his choice; and at all levels whether students shall be promoted or left behind and be awarded praise or blame.

So long as we use examinations and tests, of any type whatsoever, in that fashion, I agree with the radical progressives that the examination program will inevitably become the actual goal of instruction for students and teachers alike, and will tend to defeat all worth-while educational purposes.

But there is another possible way of using examinations and tests, which has been tried in part in a very few schools for a very few years, and which seems to me to conserve and enhance their measurement values and to avoid their dangers. And this brings me to that attempt at a constructive proposal of which I warned you at the beginning—a possible synthesis, a method of procedure in testing in educational experimentation which may solve the apparent dilemma. This suggestion is offered, I trust, with due modesty, certainly with some trepidation. It may serve at least as something to shoot at in the discussion group this afternoon. It is simply this:

That in the schools working under the current project of the Progressive Education Association and in other progressive experimentation we should abandon once for all what I will call the end-examination: the examination or test of any kind given at the end of the student's course, or at the end of the year or semester, or at other regular or stated intervals, to determine either in whole or in substantial degree graduation or failure to graduate, promotion or demotion, honors, prizes, demerits, exclusion, or the like. But that we should by no means abandon examination and testing.

That we should rather multiply examinations and tests, of many kinds, using them frequently, but always informally, casually and skeptically; record the results, of course; correlate and study these results; study particularly the pattern of results in each student's cumulative record, in conjunction with personal impressions, teachers' grades or better teachers' estimates, and all available facts in regard to the student's background and achievements; and base the necessary administrative decisions with respect to graduation, promotion, classification and guidance on the total picture of the student's abilities, aptitudes, character and potentialities—to which total picture a considerable number of comparable test results would seem to me to contribute a vitally necessary part.

I have said that in my opinion this kind of examining and testing would escape the dangers which have historically accompanied examination procedures. The fact is that we humans, old and young, enjoy tests—provided we are not going to be hung if we do badly. Please recall the vogue of the "Ask Me Another" books; the publishers found it worth while to issue three successive volumes. And every crossword puzzle is a test. So is every game of bridge or chess or billiards or tennis or golf —a competitive test of some kind of ability or achievement, and a test yielding comparable results. If all human games and sports partake of the nature of tests, why can not we make of our necessary academic testing another school sport? We can do this if we dissever it from the extraneous and illogical rewards and punishments which we have hitherto attached to it. The trouble is we educators have professionalized this sport of being tested. What we need to do is to give it the amateur status and keep it strictly amateur.

To be concrete: It seems to me that if I were in charge of a school engaged in an educational experiment I should spring tests frequently throughout the year, using practically every kind that the Educational Records Bureau could find for me—psychological tests, aptitude tests, vocational interest tests, personality rating scales and quite a lot of achievement tests. I think I should even give some of the College Board examinations, which are probably the finest examinations of the subjective type which have ever been concocted or administered, and which have done harm only because of the purpose for which they have been used. And of course I should have all the results recorded on each student's cumulative record. But I should not base any decision on any one result or any two or three results, but only on the total picture or diagram for the individual student, to which any one examination or test would contribute only a single stroke or dot. And because it would be known that that was the case, I believe the fear and strain of examinations and all thought of "coaching" for them or modifying procedures on their account would die out and they would take their place as an important amateur sport.

Let me add, in conclusion, that if some such solution as this should enable the schools working in the current project of the Progressive Education Association to make full and free use of measurement and testing without injury to the freedom of experimentation, the student records sent up to the colleges would in my opinion—and I speak as the chairman of a committee on admissions—prove so convincing and helpful that they would quickly supersede all other methods of admission.

Obviously, also, such a solution would find us furnished at the end of the experiment with an ample body of definite and comparable data, to be used in a report which, we may hope, will prove the case for progressive education up to the hilt, and may lead to far-reaching changes in educational practise throughout the nation.

HIGHER EDUCATION AND SOCIAL CHANGE[1]

By Dr. ERNEST H. WILKINS
PRESIDENT OF OBERLIN COLLEGE

Oberlin College is one hundred years old to-day.

On our first 3rd of December, Oberlin was still mainly forest; the smoke of burning trees and bushes rose from the edges of the little clearing; the log cabins of a dozen settlers were strung out along what is now South Main Street. At a point southwest of what is now the crossing of Main and College Streets there stood the one and only building of the Collegiate Institute—a three-story frame building known simply as "the boarding hall," containing offices, the common dining-room, and the chapel, and serving as dwelling place for students and for the founder, Shipherd, and his family.

The college did not come into complete being on that 3rd of December. The three departments which we now know were still in the future, though the college proper and the seminary were soon to emerge from dream into reality. The two departments which opened on that far-off Tuesday morning were the Preparatory Department, taught by John F. Scovill, and an Infant School, taught by Eliza Branch.

How one would like to reverse the years and look in upon the first classes, witness the first teaching, hear the very first words spoken! One wonders what those first words were. In all probability, they were words of prayer.

In the evocation of those early days, the passionate piety of our founders is surer than all else. The burning bushes at the clearing's edge were but the symbol of a divine enthusiasm. For one purpose, double and yet single, had they gathered here—colonists, teachers, students—"to glorify God, and do good to men, to the utmost extent of their ability."[2]

Have we kept the faith, through the hundred years? Could the founders suddenly stand among us, in their homespun, brought unadvised from their distant decades to confront our scenes, our ways, our words, their first shocked answer would be: "No, you have not kept the faith." But could there be conveyed to them some sense of the swift evolution of the intervening generations, could they know the high mental and spiritual strivings of their successors, could they follow Oberlin's efforts in the many-phased struggle for human liberation, could they trace the long rays of the star they kindled, they would answer, in bewilderment but in benediction: "Yes, you have kept a changing yet enduring faith."

Grateful and resolute in the memory of our past, let us, on this Centennial Day, look forward.

Oberlin's past is a hundred years long.

[1] An address delivered on December 3, 1933, the one hundredth anniversary of the opening of Oberlin College.

[2] Quoted from Shipherd's letter of August 6, 1832, to his parents.

How long is Oberlin's future to be? Another hundred years? Two hundred? A thousand? Ten thousand? Longer still?

We can not tell. The forces which will, in their own time, give answer proceed in part from the surrounding social order; and in part from the inner spirit of Oberlin.

All educational institutions exist, in the last analysis, in response to the desires and the needs of society. Society, like every other evolving organism, will change; its desires and its needs will therefore change; the institutions which exist in response to those desires and those needs must therefore change—or else wither and die. Society, to be sure, has always tolerated a considerable lag in the response of its institutions; but if the lag becomes too great, social support ceases, society moves on and the institution falls away.

What is the course of society to be in the next hundred, the next thousand years?

It will not be a straight and unbroken course. The difficulties of the physical and the social terrain are too great for that. Rather will it be a course of advances and retreats, of false starts and of new explorations, of obstacles surmounted at great cost, of rough and hard-hewn trails made wide and smooth at last.

The course of society will be more self-directed than it has been. Primitive as we are, we are just beginning to learn that the social world is no less modifiable than the material world; that if it be left unmodified it limits, thwarts and imperils us; and that it may presumably be so modified as greatly to enhance the significance and the value of human life. The very concept of social *laissez-faire* has in it an element of childish helplessness. We are just beginning to outgrow that helplessness. As the generations pass, society will learn—slowly, painfully, yet ever more surely—to direct its own course.

That course will be toward a greater fulness of life for all men: toward the giving of life that shall be worth the name to the children of that present sad majority for whom life is but existence; toward the achievement, for every man and for every group, of the full range of possible physical, mental and spiritual resource; toward the smoothing of all barriers save those which shut out ugliness from beauty, falsehood from truth and hate from love. I have small hope that great gains are to be made easily or soon. It may even be that the conflict of contending forces will for a time—for a long time, perhaps—drive us back rather than advance us on our course. There is menace not only in reaction but in the impatience and the unwisdom of the very forces which seek Utopia. But I have faith that there is in man enough of the all-pervading creative spirit to enable him to win through, eventually, to a life far better than the life we know.

Toward a society in the throes of such evolution, the response of any institution of higher education—if it is significantly to survive—must be twofold. On the one hand, it must in large measure accept such social changes as may be in fact accomplished, and must consent to share in any great experimentation which may hold promise of ultimate social good. On the other hand, its primary attitude toward social change should be active rather than passive: it should do its best to equip its students to play a wise and efficient part in the directing of social change.

To this end American higher education should become—will indeed inevitably become—more socio-centric: should focus its strength more and more upon the problems of social behavior and social organization. I foresee, therefore, for the social sciences and the sciences most closely allied to them, an importance much greater, in fact and in recognition, than that which they now possess. This is not to maintain that the social sciences have as yet deserved such importance. I predict their centrality, not on the basis of their past performance, but on the basis of our future need. Yet those do ill, even now, who depreciate them because they are different in nature from the sciences which are relatively more exact. The social sciences deal with an extremely complex and elusive material; they are still young; they have sometimes claimed too much; they have fallen into divisions which are traditional rather than organic; but they carry the seeds of an abundant harvest. They must themselves evolve; their own evolution must be directed; and in their evolution lies our main hope—on the side of intelligence—for the building of a scheme of things which shall by sure design be nearer to the heart's desire.

To say that the social sciences are to become more central is not to deny the value of other studies. In the society which the social sciences will help to build, the values of many other studies will indeed be enhanced by the very fact that there will be more chance for the perception and the utilization of those values, more chance for the development of all that which serves in any way to increase the energy and to exalt the quality of human life.

In a changing society any educational institution must itself face the prospect of change, both in content and in form. It must face that prospect whether it will or no; it should face that prospect intelligently, courageously and gladly.

The independent four-year college certainly faces the prospect of formal change. Fifty years ago it stood unrivaled in the field of higher education, and seemed, as a form, to be well-nigh eternal. To-day the four-year college is overshadowed by the university, and in its reduced prestige is challenged by the swiftly growing junior college. It no longer derives its form from a single unifying educational ideal. It no longer corresponds, in its upper and lower limits, to points of development which are of major physical or educational significance. The problems of adult education are beginning to impinge upon those of college education. The four-year college has been in the past the chief educational pride of the American people. It has rendered, and is still rendering, excellent service; and the stronger four-year colleges may continue for many years to render such service. Yet the time is close at hand, here and elsewhere, for major decisions as to the future of the four-year college. It may be that some new principle of unity will justify its continuance; it may be that it should soon give way to some other educational form or forms.

In Oberlin, change lies inevitably ahead, with more or less immediacy, not only for the college but for the school of theology and the conservatory as well. Fortunately, we have in Oberlin two great sources of strength which, while they should not and can not serve to prevent change, may serve to mitigate the impact of change, to make change rather a growth than a rending. The first is the fact that Oberlin, as a complete institution, is greater than any one or than all of its three departments, possesses a powerful inclusive vitality which may, if need be, reabsorb and recreate any one of its departments. They share in a common life which, however forms may change, should carry forward, in one great enterprise, the values which they severally represent.

The second source of strength is the fact that each of the three departments does represent a fundamental human value. It is no matter of mere coincidence that in their characteristic emphases they correspond—college, seminary and conservatory—to the three elements of the Platonic triad—the true, the good and the beautiful.

Of the specific changes which lie ahead, even those which are within the range of prophecy are still too immature to justify discussion at this time. There may be mentioned, however, four conditions of progressive change which should operate here—as, indeed, in any educational institution which deliberately seeks growth.

In the first place, change must be challenged. Change is essential to progress, but change does not in itself constitute progress. Change in itself is neither good nor bad. Resistance to change is in itself neither good nor bad. Progress results when change, challenged and perhaps modified by resistance, finally overcomes that resistance. Challenge plays an indispensable part in the phenomenon of progress; challenge is therefore to be expected and to be desired when changes are proposed for Oberlin.

In the second place, such change as we may experience here should be directed change, rather than change forced upon us as a belated counsel of despair. We should do willingly and with careful thought that which, if we delay, we may have to do with ill grace and ill success. We aspire to qualify our students to help in the planning of society: the least we can do is to plan our own future.

In the third place, change and the planning of change should be in the direction of enabling us, through our students, to render ever better service to society. Our very confidence in the excellence of the thing we have been doing tends to make us satisfied with perpetuation, tends to obscure the implications of our ultimate social aim. Yet the disturbing consciousness of that aim must in the end prevail.

In the fourth place, change should involve only the least possible hardship for any person who has cast in his permanent lot with the lot of the college. The college seeks to create in its students a sense of social-mindedness in all human relations. It should evince that social-mindedness in dealing with the members of its own staff. Yet the application of this principle should not seriously delay the advent of approved change. What is essential is not that the old should quickly go, but that the new should come. If time enough be given for the coexistence of the old and the new, the new will ultimately come the better into its own.

If Oberlin is significantly to survive it must, then, be plastic, susceptible of change, free to evolve.

Yet there is that in the spirit of Oberlin which should never change. Oberlin's past has been illumined with high intelligence, has been inspired with an invincible good-will toward men, has been blessed with a reverent consciousness of the creative spirit which moves through all life. Oberlin, if it is significantly to survive, must continually be so illumined, so inspired and so blessed.

High intelligence is indispensable. The successive waves of social problems can not possibly be surmounted by good-will alone, not even by passionate good-will. Passionate good-will, indeed, if it be not bridled with intelligence, is likely to do more harm than good. The problems which increasingly press upon us are difficult in the extreme, intricate in the extreme. Certainly it is the part of an institution of higher education to face them in accordance with its own specific genius. The intelligence of our students is not their plaything, nor is it ours; it is not their property, nor is it ours. Their intelligence is an instrument which they and we together hold in trust for society, an instrument which they and we together are in honor bound to refine and to strengthen, to the best of our joint ability, in order that it may be used for the benefit of mankind.

But the possession of high intelligence highly trained does not guarantee its rightful use—does not even guarantee that it will be used at all. The more powerful an instrument is, the greater are its potentialities for injury as well as for creation. I do indeed believe that intelligence itself is on the side of the good, and carries within itself a certain motive power; and that it is only the as-yet-inevitable imperfection of our intelligence which leaves in it so large a tendency to inertia, so large an element of menace. But until that imperfection shall have put on perfection, good-will toward men will be an indispensable guide for the truly progressive use of high intelligence. And good-will toward men, beyond and above its directive function, is, in itself, an inexhaustible joy.

Good-will toward men merges into that supporting consciousness of the more-than-human which has been for so many generations the greatest source of human strength in time of trouble, the greatest motive force for the achievement of a kingdom worthy to be called the Kingdom of God. Concepts of the creative spirit which moves through all life have changed, will change. It is not the *creed* of our fathers to which we sing allegiance. And I believe that as the centuries pass, as the initial excitements of discovery gradually yield to permanent clarity of understanding, as the impeded thrust of human and social evolution gains freedom, reveals more and more its tremendous dynamic urge, the faith of our fathers, though transformed perhaps beyond their recognition, will yet find a fulfilment nobler than the noblest of their dreams.

Oberlin's past is a hundred years long. How long is Oberlin's future to be? A hundred years? A thousand years? Ten thousand? Longer still?

We can not tell. This much at least is sure: the longer our future is to be, the more important it is that the impulses we send rippling down the distant years be impulses of vital thought and of vital love.

EDUCATIONAL EVENTS

THE NEW UNIVERSITY IN TURKEY

THE correspondent of the London *Times* writes that the Swiss Professor Malche, who made a report to the Ministry of Education last year about the reform of Constantinople University, was invited by the Turkish Government to return to Turkey this summer to supervise the work of reorganization which he had proposed. The work had hardly begun, however, when it was realized that something more than reorganization was called for, and on August 1 the government dismissed all the staff, suppressed the old foundation, and set out to form an entirely new university.

The problem of finding new professors now confronted the government. They determined to engage as few as possible of the former staff, as it was regarded as responsible for the decline of the old university (Dar-ül-funun). Accordingly successors were sought abroad. At Zürich Dr. Philip Schwarz, who until recently was professor of pathological anatomy at the University of Frankfurt, had set up an organization to find employment for others who, like himself, were prevented for political or religious reasons from following their professions in Germany. Through him thirty-five professors were engaged, most of whom are wholly or partly Jewish, and he himself accepted the chair of pathological anatomy.

Among those appointed to chairs are: Dr. Rudolf Nissen, late surgeon at the hospital of La Charité in Berlin, surgery; Dr. Wilhelm Lepman, of Berlin, gynecology; Dr. Hugo Braun, of Frankfurt, bacteriology; Dr. Julius Hirsch, of Berlin, hygiene; Dr. Hans Winterstein, of Breslau, experimental physiology; Dr. Joseph Egersheimer, of Frankfurt, ophthalmology; Dr. Siegfried Obandof, of Munich, experimental pathology; Dr. Vernon Lipsicz, of Frankfurt, biological chemistry, and Dr. Karl Lervental, of Berlin, histology. Dr. Sauerbruch, the eminent surgeon, is taking a keen interest in the new Medical School and is expected to make periodical visits to the university to act as adviser.

Others equally distinguished in other branches have also been engaged.

The new university, Istanbul Universitesi, has now been opened, and the professors have entered upon their duties under five-year contracts. At the end of three years they will be expected to lecture in Turkish. Meanwhile they are lecturing through interpreters, of whom there is unfortunately a great dearth, for, though it is easy to find Turks with a knowledge of German, there are few who have also an adequate knowledge of the subjects in which they are required to interpret.

The ban on Jews in Germany, according to the correspondent, has proved to be a blessing to Turkey, as it has enabled the government to secure at moderate cost the services of men at the top of their profession, who must have an incalculable influence on the culture of the new Turkey and not least on the health of the Turkish nation.

SUPPORT FOR THE NATIONAL HIGH-SCHOOL STANDARDS STUDY

REGIONAL associations of United States colleges and high schools have voted their support of a proposed plan to study high-school standards and accrediting procedures. The Federal Office of Education reports that this action practically assures the launching of such a nation-wide study early in 1934.

The regional associations which have thus approved the survey represent 4,600 of America's largest and most influential high schools in forty-seven states, the District of Columbia, Alaska and the Canal Zone. They are: The North Central Association of Colleges and Secondary Schools, New England Association of Colleges and Secondary Schools, Southern Association of Secondary Schools and Colleges, Middle States Association of Colleges and Secondary Schools and the Northwest Association of Secondary and Higher Schools. The four associations first mentioned have already appropriated $4,500 toward planning the study and getting it under way.

Proposal to make this study was made at a recent meeting of the Committee for Cooperative Study of Secondary School Standards and Accrediting Procedures, held in Washington, D. C. At that time it was suggested that new standards or guiding principles for high schools and preparatory schools throughout the United States should be developed through such an investigation, extending over a three-year period. These standards are expected to be "more comprehensive, more valid, more stimulating to the continued improvement, more flexible in operation and more adaptable to scientific administration than any applied at the present time."

What is a good high school? How can a good high school be made a better one? How may the effectiveness of a high school be evaluated? How can high schools be stimulated to better progress? Answers to these and similar questions are expected to result from the study which will be under the direction of the several regional accrediting associations, with headquarters in Washington.

Regional accrediting associations at the present time appropriately may perform certain functions, such as, passing on the adequacy of the educational environment surrounding the pupil, judging of the effectiveness with which that environment is used, and stimulating the school personnel to introduce progressive and continuous improvements in the environment and its utilization. The proposed study, it is expected, will result in a more scientific approach to these three important functions, demanded by parents and pupils.

G. E. Carrothers, high-school visitor, University of Michigan, is chairman of the general committee. E. D. Grizzell, chairman of the Accrediting Commission of the Middle States Association of Colleges and Secondary Schools, is chairman of the executive committee for the study. Carl A. Jessen, specialist in secondary education in the U. S. Office of Education, is secretary of both the executive and general committees.

STATE FUNDS FOR PAROCHIAL SCHOOLS

FINANCIAL relief for parochial schools has been asked in an open letter to Governor Lehman and the State Legislature printed in the current issue of *The Tablet,* the official publication of the Roman Catholic Diocese of Brooklyn, and quoted in *The New York Times.*

Contending that "religious public schools" of the state are suffering "untold" hardships, the letter says that in former years the supporters of Lutheran, Catholic and "other religious public schools" were willing to bear "this heavy burden, but to-day the economic situation makes it too heavy to carry."

The letter continues:

The Catholic population of the state is one quarter of the whole. The number of religious public schools maintained by Catholics total 994, the number of pupils 531,323, and the number of teachers is about 13,283. An investment of many millions of dollars is represented.

Assuredly if state schools, which draw upon the compulsory taxes and assessments and which are made the recipients of state appropriations, are in difficulty, how much harder must it be for religious public schools which receive none of this assistance. What makes the burden more onerous is that those who maintain the religious schools also pay their share of the taxes for the non-religious public schools. In other words, they are suffering the unjust burden of double taxation.

The Catholic citizens of this state, and we believe the other religious public-school bodies, would welcome relief. The national emergency particularly demands it. Some of us have a program of relief which we will gladly recommend, but we first ask you, Governor Lehman, and the fair-minded Legislature, to look into the question. We believe the justice due such a large part of our citizenry demands a new deal in education.

MILITARY TRAINING AT THE OHIO STATE UNIVERSITY

LONG agitation against compulsory military drill at Ohio State University reached a crisis on January 5 when five students were expelled. The dismissals were made in the face of widespread protest from ministers and church organizations. Five others indicated their refusal to take the work which means their ultimate dismissal.

As reported in *The Christian Science Monitor* and elsewhere, the move, directed by Dr. George W. Rightmire, president of the university, and his committee, established a precedent with their order to the 10 men, "either take the prescribed courses or leave the institution." The committee is composed of Dr. Louis Morrill, vice-president of the university; Mr. Joseph A. Park, dean of men, and Colonel Grosvenor Townsend, head of the Reserve Officers' Training Corps unit.

In presenting the ultimatum, although not a written communication, Dr. Rightmire is reported to have said the students had "no alternative."

The committee heard the pleas of thirty-one conscientious objectors and recommended to the president that fifteen be exempted. In a letter addressed to the other sixteen students the committee members said they were "unable to find that their reasons grew out of conscientious objections." Dr. Morrill was quoted as saying, "The sincerity of these students was questioned." The fifteen students who were excused after a study of their cases must take courses in political science and physical education.

Support for the expelled men was crystallized at a meeting of fifty students and members of the ministry from both Cleveland and Columbus, as well as a Cleveland attorney. The meeting was held to determine what steps might be taken to prevent the university dismissing the students. No action was taken.

The land upon which the school is located was acquired through a land grant from Congress and the compulsory military training is a clause specified in the grant. All male students, physically able, are required to take two years of training, amounting to three quarters a year, or one hour a day, five days a week.

The students concerned are members of the University Young Men's Christian Association, which is understood to be unofficially backing their pacifist stand.

THE INDEPENDENT STUDY PLAN OF THE UNIVERSITY OF CALIFORNIA

IN pursuance of the plan outlined in the issue of SCHOOL AND SOCIETY for December 9 for independent study at the University of California in fields not covered by regular courses but of university grade, regulations have been drawn up "to encourage students to become interested in subjects for the sake of the subjects themselves, and to regard the examination as a mere detail, necessary but not terrifying, in the routine of obtaining formal university credit."

The new regulations, interpreted in the light of the action of the Academic Senate, give the deans of the several colleges and schools of the university authority to approve or reject any application for such examination, and charge them with the administration of such examinations as they may approve.

The new rules are:

The deans are authorized to approve an examination in the subject-matter of any course announced in the current announcement of courses.

Subjects not included in the provisions of the preceding paragraph must be reported to the Committee on Courses for special action.

The subject-matter in which the student seeks to be examined must be of a kind that may properly be tested by examination. In certain laboratory, field and practise courses an examination may not be a satisfactory test.

Credit in a foreign language which is in the mother tongue of the applicant is not available, except in advanced courses.

Credit is not available for subjects for which the university has no competent examiners.

To be eligible an applicant must be registered and in good standing.

The examination may be the regular final examination of a course or it may be a special examination, as shall be determined by the examining officer.

No fee will be charged for these examinations.

Results of the examination shall be reported as A, B, C, or "not passed."

"It is not intended that the new procedure shall cancel or modify any of the existing rules relative to curricula, prescribed courses, majors, residence or study list limits, save as arrangements may be made individually with the dean concerned," said Thomas B. Steel, recorder of the faculties. "The student's preparation for examination may be made during the regular sessions, during vacation periods, or while he is on leave of absence; in the latter case credit may be obtained on passing the examination subsequent to his return and registration," he explained.

FELLOWSHIPS AND SCHOLARSHIPS OF THE AMERICAN LIBRARY ASSOCIATION

THE American Library Association, under the provisions of a grant from the Carnegie Corporation of New York, is again offering a limited number of fellowship and scholarship grants for the study of librarianship to residents of the United States and Canada.

The purpose of the grants is to encourage and aid those who are capable of making specific contributions to the library profession, by enabling them to pursue a year of study or research in library problems. Candidates should be graduates of approved colleges or universities. They should also have had at least one year of work in a library school and satisfactory experience in library work. The work of candidates who are given awards must be carried on in connection with an educational institution recognized as appropriate for the supervision of their studies, but not necessarily be in residence. It is intended that students shall give full time to their work, the results of which will be expected to constitute a definite contribution to library science and be made available to the profession.

The stipend for a fellowship will be $1,500 or more, and will vary according to the requirements and qualifications of the recipient. Scholarships varying in amount from $750–$1,000 may be awarded to persons with more limited training and experience. Present employment conditions and the need for restraint in recruiting incline the committee to devote the larger part of these funds to fellowships rather than to scholarships. Grants will be conditional upon the acceptance of the applicant by the institution chosen to supervise the work.

Applicants should address Harrison W. Craver, chairman of the American Library Association Committee on Fellowships and Scholarships, Engineering Societies Library, 29 West 39th Street, New York, N. Y., before February 1, 1934.

THE "TEACHERS' TREK" AT THE UNIVERSITY OF DENVER

UNDER the direction of Gilbert S. Willey, professor of education and principal of the Training School of the University of Denver, who acted as chairman of the Trek Committee, the sixth annual "Teachers' Trek" took place on December 29. At the general meeting, held in Mayo Hall, there was a panel discussion on the general subject, "Education of Teachers for To-day." Under the leadership of well-known teachers of the state, this theme was treated under these four questions:

1. What courses in college have been of greatest value to you as a teacher, administrator or supervisor; as a citizen and as a leader of culture in your community?
2. What additional educational experiences in college have been of greatest value to you in these same three phases?
3. In what ways did your college experiences

notably fail to prepare you for these same three phases?

4. What suggestions have you for the improvement of the offerings at the University of Denver?

As a means of summarizing the discussion for each person present, this question was asked: "If you were to begin your college course again, in the light of your present knowledge, what courses and experiences would you consider of greatest importance for your (1) preparation for educational work, (2) preparation for citizenship and community responsibilities, and (3) the enrichment and enjoyment of your own personal life?"

Sectional meetings on varied subjects followed the panel discussion. The topics discussed ranged from the problems of the primary teacher to the trials of the public-school administrator in these days of lowered income.

Several hundred attended the Trek. The University of Denver began these holiday conferences five years ago with the hope of being a help to those of her alumni who had chosen the teaching profession. That the meetings have been of value is indicated by the larger numbers who attend each year and by the eager participation in discussions. Dr. R. J. Walters, dean of the College of Liberal Arts and professor of education, served as chairman of the general meeting.

IN HONOR OF SAMUEL B. HECKMAN

A DINNER in honor of Professor Samuel B. Heckman, of the School of Education of City College of the College of the City of New York, will be given by colleagues and friends at the Hotel Roosevelt on Saturday evening, January 20. The occasion will celebrate the twentieth anniversary of the founding of the educational clinic of the college, the first of its kind in the country. Since its inception, Dr. Heckman has been its only director.

Born in Union, Ohio, in 1870, Dr. Heckman received a Ph.D. degree from Earlham College in 1893 and followed this up with post-graduate work at Harvard and the University of Pennsylvania. Between 1895 and 1897 he served as professor of English literature and modern languages at Juniata College, later taking a post at the Cheltenham Military Academy, where he remained until 1900, when he became Assistant Commissioner of Education at Porto Rico.

After two years as professor of psychology in Temple University, Dr. Heckman joined the department of education of the College of the City of New York in 1908 and in 1913 organized the Educational Clinic.

Controlled and subsidized by the college, the clinic treats children between the ages of four and eighteen who are recommended to it by accredited social agencies or public schools. The children are given complete medical, psychological and neurological examinations, which serve as the basis for recommendations to the agencies. At present the clinic is helping, through investigation and advice, in the reorganization of the administration and objectives of teaching in several Bronx schools.

In the twenty years of its existence the clinic has studied almost 18,000 children individually. The number of children examined yearly is increasing rapidly, the present number being twice that of five years ago. Last year 2,812 children were examined. Forty elementary schools, three high schools and seventeen social agencies sought help.

The staff of the clinic is composed of a group of highly specialized experts, each of whom is studying for a doctorate in psychology. Mrs. Elise Muster, assistant director, was formerly State Director of Education in Wyoming.

Speakers at the dinner in his honor will include Dr. Leta Hollingworth, Teachers College, Columbia University; Mrs. Lucille Neumberg, director of the Vocational Guidance Department of the Jewish Social Service Association; Professor Egbert M. Turner, School of Education; Mr. Eugene Gartland, principal of P. S. 42, Bronx, and Mrs. Muster, assistant director of the clinic. Dean Paul Klapper will be toastmaster.

A portrait of Professor Heckman is being painted by Joseph Margolies and will be presented at the dinner.

THE RESIGNATION OF PRESIDENT BOARDMAN OF THE UNIVERSITY OF MAINE

DR. HAROLD S. BOARDMAN, since 1926 president of the University of Maine, has submitted his resignation to the Board of Trustees.

Dr. Boardman's letter of resignation follows:

It has been my privilege to be associated with the University of Maine first as a student and afterwards as a member of the staff for over forty years. I am proud to be an alumnus and proud that my *alma mater* has given me the opportunity to serve her in the various grades of instructor, professor of civil engineering, dean of the College of Technology and finally, for the past nine years, as president.

During this long period it is only natural that my roots have become firmly imbedded in the soil of the institution as well as in that of my native state. I have seen the institution grow from a small college into a state university that is known and respected in educational and professional circles throughout our land. To have had a part in this development during the major part of my life's work will always remain a cherished memory.

The term of a state university president rarely exceeds ten years, in fact the average for the country is only five. When I accepted the presidency I realized that my connection with my institution was drawing near a close. It is, therefore, only after much thought that I have decided that the time has come when I should soon sever my official relations. Conditions of the past few years have had their effect upon my vitality and I feel that a change in the presidency will not only be beneficial to the institution but to myself as well.

The past few years have been most difficult in the financial world with the result that higher education has been passing in review and is receiving the most careful scrutiny not only by those not directly connected with institutions of learning, but also by educators themselves. It is possible that the near future may witness radical changes. I am, therefore, tendering my resignation to take effect at the end of the academic year. I am placing it in your hands at this time as I realize that time is an important factor in the selection of my successor.

It is with sincere regret that I sever my connection with all those with whom I have worked and who have given me their loyal and whole-hearted support. The friendships which I have formed have been priceless and I shall be leaving the university with feelings of warm affection. If in the future I can be of service to the board or to my successor you will find me ready.

Harmon C. Allen, president of the board of trustees, in his letter accepting Dr. Boardman's resignation, wrote:

It is with deep regret that we learn of your determination to resign as president of the University of Maine. Your long and faithful service to your *alma mater* as assistant professor, professor, dean, and lastly president of the college has endeared you in the hearts of all who have come in contact with you. For nearly forty years you have given to your college the best that was in you and now that you are about to give up your work here, we feel that the college has met a very distinct loss.

Therefore, in accepting your resignation we, the board of trustees, do so reluctantly, feeling that the college has suffered a loss that will be felt throughout the state.

EDUCATIONAL NOTES AND NEWS

DR. HAROLD G. CAMPBELL, deputy superintendent, was elected superintendent of the New York City schools on January 10, by unanimous vote of the Board of Education. He will take up the work on the retirement for age on January 31 of Dr. William J. O'Shea.

W. E. PHIPPS, superintendent of schools of North Little Rock, has been appointed State Superintendent of Public Instruction of Arkansas.

J. F. WADDELL, of Evansville, Wis., has been appointed assistant state superintendent of public instruction, to succeed O. H. Plenzke. Mr. Waddell is a graduate of the Wisconsin State Normal School at Whitewater, and the University of Wisconsin, and for the past five years has served as state supervisor of high schools.

THE new library building at the University of Utah, now being erected at a cost of $550,000 as part of the state building program financed by the Public Works Administration, will be named the George Thomas Library, in honor of the president of the university.

THE Inglis lectureship for 1934 at the Harvard School of Education was delivered on January 12 by Professor Isaac Leon Kandel, of Teachers College, Columbia University. Professor Kandel spoke on "The Dilemma of Democracy." The Inglis lectureship in secondary education was established by the Harvard Graduate School of Education in honor of the late Professor Alexander Inglis, a member of the faculty of the school, who at the time of his death in 1924 had become a leading scholar and writer in the field of secondary education.

FOR the first time in one hundred and twenty-one years the Connecticut State Medical Society on January 5 exercised its charter right to confer the honorary degree of doctor of medicine. The recipent was Dr. Russell H. Chittenden, professor emeritus of physiological chemistry and emeritus director of the Sheffield Scientific School of Yale University. The ceremony was a feature of the one hundred and fiftieth anniversary of the founding of the New Haven Medical Association. In conferring the degree, Dr. Ralph A. McDonnell, president of the state society, said: "This honor, now held by no living man, is about to be conferred upon you in recognition of your valuable contributions to our knowledge of the human body and because of the inspiration derived from your instruction by many who later achieved marked success in the practise of medicine."

DR. STEPHEN P. DUGGAN, director of the Institute of International Education and formerly professor of government in the College of the City of New York, has been nominated as president of the alumni of the college.

DR. WILLIAM E. PRAEGER, since 1905 head of the department of biology at Kalamazoo College, Michigan, has recently celebrated his seventieth birthday anniversary. Next June he will terminate twenty-nine years of active service at the college, primarily in the teaching of botany.

GEORGE E. HARTMANN, formerly on the faculty of the State College at Montgomery, West Virginia, has been appointed dean of the recently organized Beckley College, sponsored by the business men of Beckley, West Virginia.

DR. FRANCIS A. CAVENAGH, professor of education in University College, Swansea, England, has been appointed professor of education at the University of Reading, as from September 30.

DR. MELCHIOR PALYI, formerly chief economist for the Deutsche Bank and professor in the Berlin Handelhochschule, has been appointed for the current year visiting professor of economics at the University of Chicago. He plans to give courses on "Monetary Theory," "European Banking Systems and Problems" and, during the summer, a course on "Business Cycles." Dr. Palyi's appointment was made possible by gifts to the university and he will divide his time between the university and several groups in Chicago interested in banking and monetary policy.

DR. BRUNO BIRNBAUM, formerly member of the faculty of the University of Berlin and chief judge of the Industrial Court of Appeals in Germany, has accepted the chair of political economy at Yeshiva College, New York City. A dinner in his honor will be held on January 28 in the Waldorf-Astoria. Dr. Rudolph Kayser, now in exile in Holland, who is the son-in-law of Professor Albert Einstein, has also been invited to be a member of the faculty.

DR. ARVILLE O. DEWEESE, director of student health service, Ohio State College, Kent, was elected president of the American Association of School Physicians at the annual meeting in Indianapolis.

DR. J. HAROLD WILLIAMS, professor of education at the University of California at Los Angeles, has been elected president of the Southern California Society for Mental Hygiene.

LORD IRWIN, the newly elected chancellor of the University of Oxford, has consented to act as president of the Oxford Society.

DR. CARGILL SPRIETSMA has become director of the Maison Française of Columbia University for 1934. He succeeds Professor Louis Cons, who has been director for the past two years.

MISS MARGARET TRACY, assistant professor in the Yale University School of Nursing and assistant superintendent of nursing at the New Haven Hospital, has been appointed director of the Training School for Nurses in the University of California, and to serve also as superintendent of nurses at the University of California Hospital, San Francisco.

The Personnel Journal notes that Dr. Dorothy Stratton has become dean of women at Purdue University; Miss Helen Moreland has taken up her work as dean of women at Albany State Teachers College, and Miss Lois Bennink has been appointed to a similar post in the State Teachers College in Santa Barbara, California.

DR. L. A. PITTENGER, president of Ball State Teachers College, Muncie, Indiana, has been appointed chairman of a committee to make a survey of the Indiana State Teachers College at

Terre Haute. The work will be done by Harry E. Elder, registrar of the Terre Haute College, and W. E. Wagoner, secretary-registrar of the Muncie institution. The committee will report to Governor Paul V. McNutt.

J. LEE FAIRBANKS, professor of art, has been made chairman of the museum committee at Oregon State College, which will take over the supervision of the large historic and prehistoric collections assembled by the late Dr. John B. Horner, professor of history. Dr. Horner's death came at the age of seventy-seven years, just prior to the opening of the fall term, after he had served as a member of the college faculty for forty-two years.

PROFESSOR ALVIN H. HANSEM, of the University of Minnesota, has been appointed, under the Social Science Research Council, full-time secretary of the Commission of Inquiry on National Policy in International Economic Relations.

THREE members of the Oregon State College faculty have recently become associated with the federal service. Wallace L. Kadderly, for eighteen years a member of the staff and program director of the state-owned radio station, KOAC, since its establishment at the college in 1926, on November 15 became director of the Western Farm and Home Hour, a radio broadcast sponsored by the U. S. Department of Agriculture over the National Broadcasting Company daily from San Francisco. Dr. E. N. Bressman, professor of farm crops, a recognized authority on hops culture and disease control, was named scientific adviser to Secretary of Agriculture Wallace and took over his work in Washington early in December. H. P. Barss, professor of botany and plant pathology at the college for twenty-two years, has resigned, effective on April 1, to become principal botanist and assistant to the chief of experiment stations in the U. S. Department of Agriculture.

As a part of the celebration of the fiftieth anniversary of the founding of Goucher College a history of the institution is being written by Mrs. Anna Heubeck Knipp, a member of the first class to be graduated and now senior member and secretary of the Board of Trustees, and Dr. Thaddeus P. Thomas, professor of economics and sociology and senior member of the faculty.

DR. ROBERT M. HUTCHINS, president of the University of Chicago, was the chief speaker at a recent meeting of the Social Science Research Council in New York City.

DR. EUGENE A. BISHOP, professor of education at the University of Washington since 1929, died on December 31.

THE REV. C. B. SCHRANTZ, since 1905 president emeritus of St. Charles College, Catonsville, Maryland, died on January 4 at the age of eighty-eight years.

GEORGE WASHINGTON CRAM, secretary for appointments at Harvard University, died on January 1. He was sixty-seven years old and had been connected with the administration of the university for forty years as recorder and secretary to the Faculty of Arts and Sciences.

DR. WILLIAM HANNIBAL JOHNSON, chief editorial writer of *The Columbus Evening Dispatch* since 1920 and before that for twenty-five years professor of Latin at Denison University, Granville, Ohio, died on January 4. His age was seventy-three years.

DR. JACOB WITTMER HARTMANN, professor and chairman of the department of Germanic languages at Long Island University, died on January 4. He was fifty-two years old.

MRS. SARAH IRWIN MATTINGLY, who was president of the Washington College for Women at Washington from 1896 to 1899, died on January 6 at the age of eighty-two years.

The School Board Journal reports the death of L. A. Mahoney, superintendent of schools of Moline, Ill., from 1915 to 1931, on December 2. He was fifty-eight years old. Mr. Mahoney resigned from active work in 1931, to serve in an advisory capacity as assistant superintendent, but retired in June, 1933, because of failing health.

The Technology Review reports that this autumn friends and alumni of Victoria University College, New Zealand, undertook to commemorate in a series of portraits to be hung in the college library the work of their four foundation professors, of whom the late Dr. Richard C. Maclaurin, who later became president of the Massachusetts Institute of Technology, was one. Apprised recently of the plan, the corporation voted to present to Victoria College a copy of Frank W. Benson's oil portrait of Dr. Maclaurin, which now hangs in the president's office. The copy will be made by Leslie P. Thompson and will be sent to New Zealand, where it will hang as a memorial to the earlier achievements of Dr. Maclaurin.

TEN students and graduates of The City College, of New York City, were elected members of the Gamma Iota Chapter of Kappa Delta Pi at a recent meeting at Columbia University. In addition the following were elected to honorary membership: Professor Egbert M. Turner and Dr. Harold Abelson, of City College; Professor Joseph G. Cohen, of Brooklyn College, and Dr. Elias Lieberman, of Thomas Jefferson High School, Brooklyn.

THE California State Board of Education has approved the appointment of the following persons establishing a State Council of Educational Planning and Coordination: Robert Gordon Sproul, president of the University of California; Chester H. Rowell, member of Board of Regents, University of California and editor of *The San Francisco Chronicle;* Allen T. Archer, member of the State Board of Education; Annie Florence Brown, president of the Oakland Forum; Charles Albert Adams, attorney at law, San Francisco; Will C. Wood, vice-president of the Bank of America, Oakland; H. Gurney Newlin, attorney at law, Los Angeles; Mrs. William J. Hayes, president of the California Congress of Parents and Teachers, Burlingame, and Vierling Kersey, Superintendent of Public Instruction. These names are the joint nominations of the superintendent of public instruction and the president of the University of California. They have been approved by the Board of Regents. The program of activities will be prepared by President Sproul and Superintendent Kersey. The council is set up for the purpose of studying various problems in the field of higher education and making recommendations to the Board of Regents of the State University and to the State Board of Education.

THE New School for Social Research, New York City, will issue an international journal of political and social science under the joint editorship of the members of the graduate faculty.

THE school of education, University of Southern California, announces the publication of a series of monographs to include research studies which are outstanding in current interest. "The primary purpose of inaugurating this new project is to make the results of worthy educational investigations available to the teaching profession and to the general public," according to Dr. Lester B. Rogers, dean of the school of education. Dr. Willard S. Ford is chairman of the publications committee, which includes also Dr. A. S. Raubenheimer and Dr. William G. Campbell. The University of Southern California plans to publish approximately eight numbers of the series during the current academic year, the first two to be ready for distribution within the next month.

THE English-Speaking Union, London, points out in the London *Times* that interchange appointments between secondary school teachers in British and American schools can be arranged by a joint committee composed of representatives of the English-Speaking Union, the British Federation of University Women, the Incorporated Association of Headmistresses and the Association of Assistant Mistresses, working in conjunction with committees in the United States. These appointments, which are for one year, are only open to teachers who at the time of their application are holding a position in a school in Great Britain. Any subject in the usual school curriculum may be offered, but English, history and mathematics are the most suitable for interchange appointments. Whether a teacher is paid during her year's exchange by her own educational authorities or by the American school to which she is appointed, full pension rights are preserved.

A DECREE of the Prussian minister of public instruction concerning instruction in heredity and in ethnology in the schools went into effect on October 1. Until the final revision of the curriculum has been completed, it is decreed that, in the graduating classes of all schools, the following subjects must be incorporated in the curriculum: science of heredity, ethnology, eugenics, family history and demographic science. The essential basis for such instruction will be biology, for which, according to the decree, an adequate time (from two to three hours a week), if necessary at the expense of mathematics and foreign languages, must be found. Since biologic thinking is to constitute the basis of instruction in all branches, likewise other subjects, such as German, history and geography, must be brought into the service of such instruction. In all final examinations, every pupil must be tested as to his knowledge of the new subjects, and no person may be exempted from such tests. The minister will appoint commissioners to supervise the results of the examinations.

DISCUSSION

SCHOOLMASTERS AND SCHOOL WRECKERS

IN the midst of the hysteria for "economy" at the expense of the schools, now being exploited by alliances of large taxpayers throughout the country, and the struggle against the school-wrecking policies of boards of education by a teaching staff which has always been "ruggedly individualistic" and unwilling to organize as an economic unit, one may well pause and ask a question. Why is it that these taxpayers and board members, most of whom have been in the public schools at some time in their lives, have not been so impressed with the value of the public-school system that they would fight to preserve rather than to cripple it? In other words, how is it that no great public sentiment has been built up around this most valuable of all public institutions, the school?

Numerous answers have been offered. One of the most plausible and best-supported mentions the fact that, since most of the members of "taxpayers' alliances" send their children to private schools, the fate of public schools is of no importance to them. This is very probable as far as it goes. It does not, however, explain the apathy with which closed schools and slashed schedules are looked upon by the general public.

I believe that the present plight of education can be laid at the very doorstep of educators themselves. I believe that the teachings of our schools, the attitude of our teachers and the whole atmosphere of the public-school system has been favorable to the development of school-wreckers and others who acquiesce in school-wrecking.

School teachers (and in this category may be included both secondary and college instructors) are, on problems of economics and politics, the most uniformly illiterate class known. The great preponderance of votes for Hoover in the straw vote taken in 1932 in educational institutions shows the strong tendency of educators to cling to the *status quo,* to try nothing which is new and different.

The weight of the schools has always been on the side of conservatism. Teaching things as they are, and the necessary rightness of these things, is a shibboleth of American education. After eleven years of school and seven of college, I found myself completely ignorant of the defects of our economic system, the corruptness of our politics, the vicious way in which our government is dominated by economic interests. In economics classes I was taught that the profit system was the best adapted to American conditions; that money must be based on gold or some other accepted physical standard; that business operated for profit was more efficient than non-profit institutions. In psychology classes I was told nothing of the prevalent false ideas, such as that the profit motive is necessary to a successful economic system, or that wars are a natural expression of an inherited impulse. One course in American government proved to be so thoroughly desiccated that I never ventured near that department again. In short, I found my academic education to be "academic" in the worst connotation of that word, devoid of life and civic value.

The attempts of teachers to be "impartial" in their presentation of material are also characteristic of the current system. Impartiality, to these educators, means refusing to criticize any existing institution. Some of this is due, undoubtedly, to reactionary superiors, school boards and regents. More is due to the reactionary character of educators themselves, perpetuating itself from generation to generation.

The stereotyped thinking of these educators, and of the students they send forth, must inevitably react to the detriment of the educational system. Men who accept the principles of the capitalistic system as right and inevitable must, as a result of that training, reach the conclusion that the liberal, academic type of education should be curtailed. Nothing is further from the ideals of capitalism.

Most teachers do not realize that public free education was grafted more or less by force upon the capitalistic system, and that it is inevitable in times of depression that this "unprofitable" enterprise be reduced to a minimum. As a matter of fact it is exactly during a depression that education is most needed and is of the greatest public value. The use of a period of enforced idleness to train men for a period of social need is so obviously the correct policy that one can not understand opposition to it. And yet it is clear that education is supported by taxes, taxes come in considerable share from the capitalist class and in times of depression this class will inevitably insist on reductions in the expenditures for education—notwithstanding the pressing social need for more rather than less educational effort.

These conditions—the conservatism and lack of decisiveness in educational policies—result immediately from the types of personality found in our teaching staffs. These individuals enter the academic monastery because they fear the competitive conflict of business. They hope to get away from the scramble for profits into a life of service and security. Having once obtained a position they abjure change and all suggestion of change. And in thus grasping eagerly after security, they make their own positions more insecure!

The advantages of a system managed for use rather than for profit would be great to the educators of America. Much that hampers our educational and research work could be scrapped if this change were made. It is very strange that schoolmen, rather than eagerly accepting the idea of a non-profit system, have been apathetic or positively antagonistic toward it.

The social benefits of an educational program planned without consideration of financial gain or any other goal than that of service to society would be incalculable. The educators of America have an opportunity to help build such a system if they escape from their lethargy. If they become educated and alert on questions of public policy, they can mold the opinions of an entire generation, and pilot the course of America along a safer channel than the history of the last thirty years shows us to be heading for. The possibilities in store for us if education remains a dead weight upon the forces making for progress are somewhat too unpleasant to contemplate.

ROSS STAGNER
UNIVERSITY OF WISCONSIN

CHALLENGE GATE

ONE morning, on my daily matinal jaunt into the country before school, I chanced to see a new gate leading into a hill-crest farm. The boards of the gate were as yet unpainted and bore the words "Challenge Gate," to which was appended the name of a local lumber concern. How those words had come there I was at a loss to ascertain. Suffice it to say that they arrested my attention, and I stopped my car to take in the entire ensemble. As I was vainly trying to apply some rhyme or reason to these words, a school bus rattled by, packed to the guards with rural Young America.

Suddenly the thought came to me that the name of the gate was intrinsically bound up with that school bus. Where do we go from here? Do we go N. R. A.? Or is the pendulum of public school education to swing back to those three stalwart bulwarks of an older type of education, R. R. R.? Educators can not but acknowledge that once more education is faced with a crisis totally aside from financial. Education, too, is confronted with a new, unpainted gate, emblazoned "Challenge Gate." And while educators ponder the approach to this new gate and the *modus operandi* after "crashing" the gate, part of Young America confidently waits beside rural mail-boxes for the yellow buses that are to take them into a world filled with riches other than those delivered up of Mother Earth.

As I drove back to school, slowly, savoring to the full the picture of these boys and girls from the farms, eager, hopeful, healthy, level-headed, typical robust youngsters, an integral part of America's core and fiber, I pondered over this new challenge thrown to us as educators. The challenge involves the assimilation of the rural element of Young America with the Young

America of the street, of the laborer, of the white-collar man, of the foreigner into the huge melting pot of education. The resultant mass, molten in form, is poured into the various molds, hardened and put out on the world market as salable. This has been our recent process taken in its entirety. Through growing numbers the process has had to become almost completely mechanical in its workings. But the recent economic chaos into which we have been tossed has taught us that, after being inspected by the so-called giants of industry, these molds have been found wanting.

The plight of Young America, graduated from the best foundries America affords, refined and super-refined, is pitiful. Youth had felt so safe, its time so carefully scheduled, its life so painstakingly supervised, its 'isms so specialistically tested, that, confronted by jobs (if any) requiring a slightly different mold, Youth has become fatalistic. Youth perforce has lost the very characteristic which makes of it an essential contribution to professions and business of all sorts.

So what? The answer to this question lies behind "Challenge Gate." How to find that answer lies within the inner citadel of each and every one of us—those intangible depths of every alive human being, where thoughts are engendered and where the courage to answer the challenge is born.

First and foremost we, as educators, must take inventory of curricula and then ask ourselves quite honestly—Can the curricula now existent stand the test of more leisure time? Are we planning our curricula so as to give opportunity for the development of self-sufficiency? Bridge, sports, amusements pall now. When the average person receives less actual money than he is now accustomed to (even though the number of such average persons be increased) and when he has many more hours per week unaccounted for, unscheduled, what then is to be his test? This, and this alone—has he enough self-sufficiency to derive pleasure as well as profit from this added leisure time?

Academicism *per se* is not to be advocated for the majority. But surely we will have to approach our "Challenge Gate" in a more academic manner, or at least in a manner commensurate with the lasting cultural effects of academicism. No academician is superficial. But I think that many of my readers will agree with me when I say that the results of modern public school education tend to lead to a superficial approach to life and life's problems. This tendency can not be blamed entirely upon the modern generation. Nor can the guilt be laid at the door of education and educators.

Our present curricula are the results of a vicious four-point circle—college requirements, the necessary high-school requirements to meet college exigencies, economic conditions causing fewer pupils to leave high school at an early age to seek a livelihood and, lastly, a desire on the part of educators to consider each human part of the system as a separate entity worthy of individual attention. This last in the face of the fact that curtailments in school budgets are forcing a heavier teaching load as well as foisting upon individual teachers jobs for which they are in no wise trained!

"Utopially" speaking, education should be far enough removed from economic conditions to study them without becoming sufficiently involved to impair its daily workings. Then to mold raw material into the various shapes required by a changing economic system could be successfully and efficiently accomplished. But it would seem that we are inextricably bound up with nearly every phase of economic progress. So that our "Challenge Gate" is but a new entrance to the same road along which all business, all professions, all modern life must travel. Not to be a part of this life while preparation is in progress would, of course, be ideal. Since this is impossible, we must enter "Challenge Gate" along with the others, with the realization that whatever withdrawing there is on our part must be done unobtrusively. We must keep one eye upon the progress of our fellow challengers in their different fields, and the other eye focused upon the necessity of creating a curricular content that will develop a deeper, more self-sufficient education in our pupils.

Unless we ourselves feel the urgent need for an inner citadel, a reservoir of thought, ideals and those intangible somethings which can be called upon to make leisure moments profitable and pleasurable, there is, obviously, no need to attempt an entrance through "Challenge Gate."

Once completely convinced of this need, however, "Challenge Gate" should hold no terrors for educators; for they have ever been of the stuff that brooks no lasting toleration of obstacles in the path of their ideals!

As I once more turned and looked through the challenge gate that led to the hill-crest farm, I somehow felt a renewed faith. There may have been a new gate leading to that farm perched high up on the hill, but the trees were flaunting the same gorgeous challenge to winter that they have flaunted throughout all changing civilization! The hill was part of the good, rich earth that has yielded man's harvest for eons. And the sun shone down in the same old way that has been its unchanging custom for many thousands of October mornings! This challenge gate looked in upon a scene as old as the hill itself, offering but a new approach. Fundamentally our educational "Challenge Gate" leads us into familiar haunts requiring but a slight adjustment, necessitated by a new curve in the road!

Helen R. Stilwell

Oakwood High School
Oakwood, Dayton, Ohio

QUOTATIONS

ECONOMY CUTS ABROAD

The International Federation of Teachers' Associations has been collecting information concerning the cuts in teachers' salaries and the unemployment among teachers which have resulted from the general economic crisis. The replies to questions sent out to the teachers' associations in various countries are summarized in bulletins recently issued. Most of the information given has passed through the medium of teachers' newspapers in a dozen different languages, and has been much condensed, and translated into French. The situation, moreover, has changed in some respects even since the Federation's October-November bulletin was prepared, but the summaries which the bulletins give may be taken as a conspectus of general tendencies.

In Germany a cut of 6 per cent. in the salaries and pensions of teachers and Government employees was made in December, 1930; and in June, 1931, there was a further reduction of from 4 per cent. to 8 per cent., against which the two largest teachers' federations organized a campaign of protest. In September of the same year a number of young teachers were displaced on account of the rigorous cutting down of educational budgets. In October three teachers' training colleges in Prussia were closed, and there were no new admissions to the ten remaining colleges. These were reduced to six in December, 1931, when the age of retirement was lowered to 62 and salaries were reduced by another 9 per cent. This, as the *Allgemeine Deutsche Lehrerzeitung* pointed out, made a total reduction of 40 per cent. in some cases. The *Bremische Lehrerzeitung* of February 27, 1932, reported that in Oldenburg the teachers had received no pay for several months. In Prussia in June, 1932, there was a new reduction of 5 per cent. for unmarried and 2½ per cent. for married teachers. The *Preussische Lehrerzeitung* in November, 1932, stated that there were in Prussian schools more than 140 classes of over 60, and some classes numbered as many as 90. The *Rheinische Lehrerzeitung* is quoted to the effect that there was at the time a method of payment in vogue in various German States by which each month's salary was paid so late that the authority gained one month in twelve. Not much is said about the changes that have since taken place, except that the *Allgemeine Deutsche Lehrerzeitung* quotes an order of the Minister of the Interior of August 5, 1933.

> Since the National-Socialist Government has taken upon itself the exclusive administration of the State, it is the Government which defends the interests of its employees. In consequence demands and representations of Government employees and of their organizations, addressed to the authorities, and in particular to the Ministers, relative to salaries, re-classification and service, are not only superfluous but inadmissible, and will in future not be accepted. All representations which criticize superiors, and therefore the administration, which alone is responsible, are forbidden. Personal demands must pass through the administration.

In France, in protest against cuts of from

2 per cent. to 8 per cent., imposed early this year on salaries of officials over 12,000 francs a year, there was a "half-hour strike" of Government employees and teachers. Under the Herriot and Boncour Administrations, it is pointed out, French Government employees' salaries were almost untouched, but there was a long quarrel with the Daladier Administration. The present Administration has, it is stated, not made its financial intentions known.

Italy saw a reduction of 12 per cent. in employees' salaries in 1930. In Spain matters have been complicated by the creation of what is practically a new educational system. There are one-class schools with more than 100 pupils, but it is hoped that in two years no class will be larger than 60. In Denmark, in the beginning of 1932, 44 per cent. of teachers were out of work, and since then school building and admission to training colleges have been slowed down. In Sweden the number of training college students has been reduced and colleges have been closed, as a result of the fall in the birthrate. There have been heavy salary reductions in Austria (up to 25 per cent. for unmarried women teachers in some parts). The beginning of the school year in Bulgaria was attended by a large reduction in the numbers of teachers. Hungarian teachers (according to *Tanitok Lapja*) have been in a bad way, not having been paid even their greatly reduced salaries with any regularity for some time past. Those who are paid in kind are better off, but a great many schools are closed for lack of funds to pay for heating and cleaning. The course of affairs in Russia appears to have been characteristically up-and-down. Ninety thousand new teachers were recruited in 1931 and a series of six-month training courses were set up for them. In 1933 the establishments of Government employees were reduced by from 10 to 50 per cent.

Last month the Latvian Government had before it a scheme by which the salaries of teachers in Riga would be reduced by 35 to 45 per cent., but after what is described as *une lutte acharnée* on the part of the teachers and other municipal employees the project was defeated in the Latvian Parliament. There are, it is stated, about 16,000 more children this year than last year in the primary schools, and 320 new teachers' posts have been created, which the Government are seeking to fill at 300f. a month. It is stated that at the time the bulletin was issued there were still 170 teachers needed, but that the Government had not the money to pay them.

The organization of education in Switzerland is complicated; each canton is autonomous so far as education is concerned and makes its own laws. The conditions in the towns are quite different from those of mountain districts. All federal subventions, including those for primary education, are to be reduced, it is pointed out, by 20 per cent. for six years. The federal Government planned a reduction of 7 per cent. in all employees' salaries, and a referendum taken this May, with contrary results, has only had the effect of slightly modifying the Government's plans for 1934 and 1935.

The Dutch Government proposed in 1931 a cut of 2½ per cent. in all employees' salaries, against which the teachers' organizations started a campaign. A further proposal of a cut of 8 per cent. for married and 15 per cent. for unmarried teachers was followed by a street demonstration by teachers at Amsterdam. In January of this year cuts were made averaging 4 or 5 per cent. Two hundred and thirty-five State schools were closed in July, and a further temporary reduction of 5 per cent. was made in salaries. The Queen's speech at the opening of the States General foreshadowed further large reductions of expenditure. In Finland a cut of 10 per cent. is projected for 1934 in the salaries of unmarried employees, and of the married if their pay is not the main resource of the family. The reports have much to say about the *opiniâtreté inlassable* of the National Union of Teachers, thanks to whose efforts the cuts in teachers' salaries in England are of a temporary and conditional character. In no other country has there been anything in the way of organized resistance which approaches the "monster petition."

The most interesting of the efforts at settlement are reported from Norway, where both Government and teachers appear to regard economy as a regrettable national necessity. In view of the great amount of unemployment among teachers in Norway the chief teachers' association proposes that man and wife should not, as a rule, be allowed to hold teaching posts, and that the retiring age for women should be 55 and for men 60. Teachers who can live without their pay are advised by the association to resign, so that work and food may be more equitably divided. One branch of the association suggests the closing of all training colleges until the present teaching staff have found work, and that teachers who had been longest out of work should have the first claim. As a result of friendly negotiations between employees and the Government, employees in general accepted a voluntary cut of from 2 per cent. to 5 per cent., and in May similar negotiations took place between the Government and the teachers' association. As a result of these a proposal was made that a 4 per cent. reduction should be made, on the basis of the cost of living—if this rose there would be no further reduction, and if it fell the reduction might be increased. Almost all teachers accepted this arrangement, and those who refused have continued to receive their full salaries.—*The London Times Educational Supplement.*

REPORTS

THE PROFESSIONAL LIBRARY IN THE SCHOOL SYSTEM

THE PUBLIC LIBRARY NOT A SUBSTITUTE

EVERY school system should have a library of professional reading materials. In a large system, ideally, each building should have such a library. Even though there is a good public library, it is not a substitute for the teachers' library. The public library is organized on an entirely different basis. It caters to the demands of the general public and probably has few of the special books and magazines needed by the teacher. Even if it contains the professional books and magazines, they are not immediately at hand and constantly accessible.

The superintendent in the small community or the building principal in the larger one should constantly refer teachers to certain books or magazines, and those should be right at hand so as to be used that day, if desirable, and not at "some time" when the book or magazine happens to be at the public library. The special teachers' library is exactly as necessary to success as text-books and collateral books for the pupils. The professional library is not something for the teachers' personal benefit, but a part of the equipment which is of immediate benefit to the public.

BUILDING THE PROFESSIONAL LIBRARY

In the average community, especially in depression days, a professional library can not be assembled in a day. A beginning should be made at once, and by careful planning a very useful library can be assembled in time. The following suggestions may be found helpful.

(1) At one of the teachers' meetings, have for the central theme "A Teachers' Library for This School." The superintendent should be prepared to discuss it in a concrete way. It would be well to talk over the matter informally beforehand with some of the teachers, especially the principals and librarians.

(2) Have each of the teachers agree to subscribe for at least one educational magazine and to place it in the library immediately after being read by the owner. In this way from ten to twenty-five magazines would be made available to all. The magazines should be accessioned and loaned the same as other library materials. This will insure their preservation. All magazines or books loaned by the teachers should belong to the respective individuals unless and until donated to the school. At the close of a year or a period of service the respective teachers would have the choice of taking their materials or donating them to the school. Most teachers would donate the magazines because of the difficulty of transporting.

(3) Many teachers will be glad to loan a few books on the same basis as the magazine materials. They may be willing to loan some special books for a particular purpose and for a limited time. Other books might be loaned for the year or during the term of service of the teacher. These books should be marked in such a way as to indicate the private ownership. They could be catalogued in some special way so that a record would be preserved. The card index file should list all books so as to make them of the largest possible use. As the books will be handled only by the teachers, it is be-

lieved that the wear will not depreciate the books greatly. They should be covered so as to preserve them as well as possible. Each book would probably be used only a few times in a year, but each of those times might be very important.

(4) The district should set aside a small amount of the annual library fund for professional materials. A superintendent will usually have no difficulty in convincing the board that this is a most important part of the school equipment.

(5) Many articles of great importance on education appear every month in the popular magazines. By informing the patrons through the local paper, the school paper, through messages communicated in the school assembly, occasional circular letters, announcements in the parent teachers' meetings and casual personal interviews they will be glad to donate those magazines to the school. These articles may be detached, placed in convenient paper binders and regularly catalogued.

(6) All the materials sent gratis by the U. S. Office of Education should be secured and preserved. A great wealth of materials in the form of leaflets, pamphlets and bulletins are distributed annually. If possible all the publications of that office should be subscribed for and secured as issued. For example, the U. S. Office of Education is now issuing the bulletins prepared by the Survey of Secondary Education. There are 28 most valuable bulletins and the total cost is only $3.80. Likewise, the various publications of the National Education Association should be accumulated. The Children's Bureau publishes a large number of pamphlets each year, which may be secured free of charge.

(7) The librarian should card index the outstanding titles in the magazines. Each of the teachers should render assistance in this by indicating the titles of special interest. If magazines or books are withdrawn permanently by the owner the card could be marked "withdrawn." The reference should be left in the card index file, as it might be of assistance even if the material had to be secured from another library.

(8) Magazines that belong to the school and that are received continuously should be bound each year.

In these ways a valuable up-to-date professional library can be assembled. Of course, it will be limited in size and scope and will not be a substitute for a great university library. Under proper guidance of a live superintendent such a library, however, would prove a great stimulus to many who would otherwise do absolutely no professional reading. Many teachers would consult it constantly of their own accord, others when preparing something for a teachers' meeting or for a parent-teachers' association. I frequently receive S.O.S. calls from former graduates teaching in a small community who have been scheduled for a talk at a parent-teachers' meeting and who have no available materials.

Dr. Carter Alexander, of Teachers College, Columbia University, has suggested that many teachers are starved for professional vitamins and that they should find them in the best educational magazines. In his article[1] he indicates

> "some earmarks by which magazines rich in professional vitamins may be identified. These magazines all have one distinctive quality—they are thought-provoking. When this quality is further studied, it seems to be due to the emphasis on worth-while or important matters and to the treatment of these in well-written and authoritative articles. Emphasis on important matters appears in such things as the selection of fundamental problems of educational theory, methods or policies. . . . These magazines treat current educational needs, problems, accomplishments or failures, rather than those of a generation or so ago. They constantly emphasize new ideas, new relationships, new applications of old data and new interpretations of old views or data. They do not neglect the past, but they use it to suggest what we ought to do or not to do in education now and in the future. . . .
>
> The educational magazines rich in professional vitamins are authoritative and well written. They enjoy their eminence not by the size of their subscription lists, but because of the inherent worth of their contents. Their articles are interesting, challenging, not pedantic, trite or platitudinous. They are intelligently and scientifically critical and are not merely promoting a cult or commercial interest. Where possible their articles are based on

[1] Carter Alexander, "Selecting Magazines for Teachers Starved for Professional Vitamins," *School Executives Magazine*, April, 1933, pp. 268, 269.

evidence and the results of sound research, rather than on mere opinion or the limited personal experience of the writers.

The articles in these magazines are orderly presentations, more or less complete in themselves, of problems that can be adequately treated in the available space. These periodicals do not attempt to cover in an article something that requires a book for satisfactory treatment. . . . Their articles are clear and definite presentations without undue wordiness, just enough to state the case clearly, convince the reader and incite him to any advisable action. One of the best actions to which a good teacher can be incited is the reading of suitable professional books.

Naturally, most of the articles in the good professional magazines are by authors of accepted standing. But these periodicals do not take any old manuscript from an author in this class. The editors know only too well that even such authors sometimes turn out very inferior work, hastily revamp their old expression and preach an old sermon. These magazines maintain their standards for all and will take work from unknown beginners as readily as from the old established leaders if it measures up to their specifications.''

A Minimum Magazine List

The following magazines are indispensable in every small school system and in large cities should be in duplicate in each school building. The list is far from exhaustive and constitutes merely a "minimum essentials" list. Large numbers of most excellent periodicals are omitted from the lists. Some of them largely duplicate those listed, while others are technical and used mainly by specialists and research workers. The list given here is intended to represent the minimum essentials in a good working professional library in a small school system. Probably only a few of those given in the list for specialized groups could be secured in the average community.

Alexander lists seven magazines, which he believes contain such professional vitamins as indicated above. They are starred in the accompanying list. I believe that those not starred are equally as important.

(a) For Superintendents and Principals

The American School Board Journal. The Bruce Publishing Company, Milwaukee. Monthly. $3.00 per year. A periodical of school administration. Concrete studies in school administration. News items regarding school projects, school laws, board actions. Illustrated.

The Nation's Schools. The Nation's Schools Publishing Company, Chicago. Monthly. $2.00 per year. Devoted to the application of research to the building, equipment and administration of schools. Concrete, scientific, well illustrated. Especially good on modern buildings and equipment.

The School Executives Magazine. The School Executives Magazine Company, Lincoln, Nebraska. Monthly. $3.00 per year. Brief, challenging articles interpreting education; current procedures in school organization and administration. News and notes. Especially for superintendents and principals.

School Life. Official Organ of the United States Office of Education. Monthly, except July and August. 50 cents per year. Provides a national perspective of education. Notes important educational movements in foreign countries. Excellent notices of publications of the U. S. Office of Education and of much other educational literature.

**Journal of Educational Research.* Public School Publishing Company. Monthly, except July and August. $3.30 per year. Established to support educational research in all phases.

**Progressive Education.* The Progressive Education Association, 716 Jackson Place, Washington, D. C. Monthly, 8 numbers. $3.00 per year. Designed to interpret critically all ideas that are intended to make for progress in education from the nursery school through college. Many of the articles relate to public school education. Notes from the field and news from the association.

(b) For All Teachers

*School and Society. The Science Press. New York. Weekly. $5.00 per year. Indispensable for all teachers. Best current educational interpreter. One or more interpretative articles each week, usually some great address; educational news, home and foreign; one brief research study.

The Journal of the National Education Association. Washington, D. C. Monthly, except July, August, September, $2.00 per year, which includes membership in the National Education Association. Contains in each issue a leading article on a focal education topic, notices of meetings and activities of the National Education Association, feature articles on selected topics, notes and announcements. Every teacher should be a member of the N. E. A. and also read the journal.

Education. The Palmer Company, Boston. Monthly, except July and August. $4.00 per year. Devoted to the science, art, philosophy and literature of education. Each month most of the number on a selected phase of education, including administration, secondary education, high-school subjects, elementary school problems, special education, etc.

Journal of Education. New England Publishing Company, Boston. Bi-monthly, September to June. $3.00 per year. Established by Dr. Albert E. Winship, 1875. Important news items. Stimulating, brief articles on current topics in educational philosophy, organization, methods.

Washington Education Journal. Monthly, except June, July, August, September. $2.00 per year. Every teacher should read his state education journal. In other states, of course, the respective state journals should be substituted.

**Educational Method.* Published by the Bureau of Publications of Teachers College for the Department of Supervisors and Directors of Instruction of the National Education Association. Monthly except June, July, August. $3.00 per year. A journal of progressive public schools. Scientific, readable and should be of interest to all grade and high-school teachers. Articles on principles of method and methods in the various subjects.

(c) For High School and Junior High School Teachers

**The School Review.* The University of Chicago Press. Monthly, except July and August. $2.50 per year. A journal of secondary education. The oldest magazine devoted to the general problems of the secondary school. Reports of many actual experiments in high-school work.

**The Clearing House.* 32 Washington Square, New York. Monthly, 9 months. $3.00 per year. A challenging journal for liberal people. All editors are connected with New York University. Associate editors from various positions in secondary education, which is the special field cultivated.

The High School Teacher. Published by the High School Teacher Company, Blanchester, Ohio. Devoted to the interests of workers in junior and senior high school fields. $2.00 per year.

(d) For Elementary and Primary Teachers

**Elementary School Journal.* Published by the School of Education, University of Chicago. Monthly, except July and August. $2.50 per year. General problems of organization and methods in elementary schools. Many of the articles describe and interpret practises in the laboratory schools of the University of Chicago. Other contributors from the field.

American Childhood. Milton Bradley Company, Springfield, Massachusetts. Monthly, except July, August. $2.00 per year. Includes nursery and kindergarten as well as grades.

Grade Teachers' Magazine. Educational Publishing Company, 425 4th Avenue, New York City. Monthly, except July, August. $2.00 per year. Includes nursery and kindergarten as well as grades.

The Instructor. Owen Publishing Company, Bansville, N. Y. Monthly, except July, August. $2.00 per year. Includes upper grades as well as primary.

Childhood Education. Published with the cooperation of the Association for Nursery Education, 1201 16th Street, N. W., Washington, D. C. $2.50 per year. Covers nursery, kindergarten and primary education. The most important one in the kindergarten field.

(e) For Various Specialized Groups

School Arts Magazine. The Davis Press, Worcester, Mass. Monthly, except July and August. $3.00 per year. An illustrated publication for those interested in fine and industrial arts.

The English Journal. University of Chicago Press. Monthly, September to June. $3.00 per year. The official organ of the National Council of Teachers of English.

The Historical Outlook. McKinley Publishing Company, Philadelphia. Monthly, except June, July, August, September. A journal for readers of history and the social studies. Published with the endorsement of the American Historical Association. $2.00 per year.

Journal of Home Economics. American Home Economics Association, Baltimore, Md. Monthly. $2.50 per year. Scientific, current theory and practises.

The Mathematics Teacher. 525 W. 120th Street, New York City. Monthly, except June, July, August, September. $2.00 per year. Devoted to the interests of mathematics in elementary and secondary schools.

Mind and Body. Published by the Mind and Body Publishing Co., New Ulm, Minn. Monthly. $2.00 per year. A journal of physical education. Theory and practise of physical education in elementary and high schools.

School Music. Keokuk, Iowa. Bi-monthly. $2.00 per year. A magazine for music teachers, elementary and secondary.

Music Supervisors' Journal. Music Supervisors' Conference, 64 E. Jackson Boulevard, Chicago. Five numbers per year. $1.00 per year. Ideals, methods, practises.

School Science and Mathematics. Published by the Central Association of Science and Mathematics Teachers, Menasha, Wisconsin. $2.50 per year. Monthly, October to June, inclusive.

Recreation. (Formerly *The Playground*) 315 4th Ave., New York City. Monthly. $2.00 per year. In the interests of the National Recreation Association, formerly the Playground Association of America.

The American Shorthand Teacher. The Gregg Publishing Company, New York City. Monthly, except July and August. $1.00 per year. A magazine for teachers of shorthand and other commercial subjects.

FREDERICK E. BOLTON
UNIVERSITY OF WASHINGTON

EDUCATIONAL RESEARCH AND STATISTICS

THE DISTRIBUTION OF MEMBERSHIPS IN THE EXTRA-CURRICULAR ACTIVITIES OF THE LIBERAL ARTS COLLEGE

EXTRA-CURRICULAR activities are rather generally accepted as a significant part of the total educational program of the liberal arts college. A very common administrative problem in connection with these activities has to do with the regulation of their distribution in the student body. Social fraternities and sororities covet very much the honors and privileges that go with the non-academic enterprises of the campus. These groups usually succeed in securing a monopoly of the campus extra-curricular activities and come to regard them as of greater importance than studies and class work. As a consequence scholarship and intellectual advancement become secondary considerations and the institution falls short of accomplishing its real educational purposes. When properly regulated the out-of-class activities can be made to contribute materially to the widening of the intellectual atmosphere of the college. But when not so regulated they constitute a serious encumbrance to the educational development of its students.

In this study data are submitted bearing on the extra-curricular situation in Transylvania College which show a condition regarded as typical of a great many other liberal arts institutions. It is believed that the serious consideration of such data is a first step in the solution of the problem presented. Table I displays the distribution of students in the two groups, social fraternities and sororities, on the one hand, and, on the other, the group of students not identified with these social organizations. The table gives the numbers of each class of students by semesters for the five years from 1926–27 to 1930–31, inclusive. It is apparent from the table that the fraternity group year after year is not greatly different in size from the non-fraternity group; on the average the former group is about 10 per cent. smaller than the latter.

TABLE I

NUMBERS OF REGULAR STUDENTS CLASSIFIED ACCORDING TO MEMBERSHIP OR NON-MEMBERSHIP IN SOCIAL FRATERNITIES, BY SEMESTERS FOR THE FIVE YEARS FROM 1926–27 TO 1930–31, INCLUSIVE

Group — Year / Semester	1926–27 I	1926–27 II	1927–28 I	1927–28 II	1928–29 I	1928–29 II	1929–30 I	1929–30 II	1930–31 I	1930–31 II	Five-year totals
Fraternity	138	131	116	113	138	127	164	158	144	128	1,357
Non-fraternity	131	136	143	158	152	170	139	133	174	180	1,516

Table II displays the distribution of extra-curricular memberships in the two groups for the corresponding five years. These memberships were determined by consultation of the student annual or year book for each of the years considered. Exclusive of their extra-curricular memberships in social fraternities, the fraternity group is seen to have on the average considerably more than two thirds of the total.

An effort was made to classify the extra-curricular activities into five groups—cultural, ethical, athletic, political and social, respectively. Table III displays the totals in each group for the five-year period considered. The cultural activities group includes memberships

TABLE II

DISTRIBUTION OF EXTRA-CURRICULAR MEMBERSHIPS (EXCLUSIVE OF FRATERNITY MEMBERSHIPS) BY FRATERNITY AND NON-FRATERNITY GROUPS BY YEARS FOR THE FIVE YEARS FROM 1926–27 TO 1930–31, INCLUSIVE

Group	1926–27	1927–28	1928–29	1929–30	1930–31	Five-year totals
Fraternity	216	217	185	202	218	1,038
Non-fraternity	84	138	100	68	78	468

in literary, forensic, dramatic, musical and professional organizations, both active and honorary; the ethical group includes memberships on the honor council, and officers and committee chairmen of the Y. M. C. A. and Y. W. C. A.; the athletic group includes memberships on the various athletic squads, football, basketball and baseball, as well as honorary athletic organizations; the political group includes the officers of the freshman, sophomore, junior and senior classes, special student body recognitions, memberships in the various general honorary junior and senior societies, the "pep" organization of the campus, and the staff of the college annual; the social activities group includes the five-year totals of social fraternity and sorority annual memberships.

TABLE III

DISTRIBUTION OF THE MEMBERSHIPS IN THE CLASSIFIED GROUPS OF EXTRA-CURRICULAR ACTIVITIES BETWEEN FRATERNITY AND NON-FRATERNITY STUDENTS, GIVEN IN FIVE-YEAR TOTALS FOR THE INTERVAL 1927–28 TO 1930–31

Group	Cultural	Ethical	Athletic	Political	Social	Totals
Fraternity (1)	424	101	258	255	736	1,774
Non-fraternity (2)	265	53	88	62	0	468
Ratio (1)/(2)	1.6	1.9	2.9	4.1	∞	3.8

The table also displays the relative degrees of concentration of these different types of activities memberships by giving the ratios of fraternity memberships to non-fraternity memberships. It is apparent from this table that the fraternity group has a decided monopoly on every type of activity, and that this monopoly is least evident in the cultural and ethical activities and most pronounced in the social and political activities.

Table IV displays the distribution of the students of highest scholarship records, *i.e.*, those with B-average grades or better, between the fraternity group and the non-fraternity group. It is seen from this table that for each of the ten semesters the majority of the students of superior scholarship records were not members of social fraternities or sororities. This fact, coupled with the opposite character of the distribution of extra-curricular memberships, is fraught with significance.

TABLE IV

DISTRIBUTION OF STUDENTS OF SCHOLARSHIP RECORDS OF B-AVERAGE GRADE OR BETTER BETWEEN FRATERNITY AND NON-FRATERNITY GROUPS, BY SEMESTERS FOR THE FIVE-YEAR PERIOD, 1927–28 TO 1930–31

Group / Year	1926–27		1927–28		1928–29		1929–30		1930–31		Five-year totals
Semester	I	II	I	II	I	II	I	II	I	II	
Fraternity	30	33	20	30	39	33	35	41	27	22	310
Non-fraternity	46	52	63	67	55	66	49	49	50	59	556

Needless to say, there should be a unity of intellectual purpose in the student body. That unity of purpose is, of course, not present in a college where almost one half of the student body place campus activities and honors above achievements in scholarship. The remedy for the situation does not necessarily require either the abolishment of extra-curricular activities or the elimination of social fraternities. It does, however, call for such regulation of the out-of-class activities through a functioning point system as will prevent them from interfering with the success of the educational program of the institution.

CHARLES A. MANEY

LEXINGTON, KENTUCKY

SCHOOL AND SOCIETY

WITH WHICH ARE COMBINED THE EDUCATIONAL REVIEW, ESTABLISHED IN 1891, THE TEACHERS MAGAZINE, ESTABLISHED IN 1878, AND THE SCHOOL JOURNAL, ESTABLISHED IN 1874.

EDITED BY J. McKEEN CATTELL

Volume 39 SATURDAY, JANUARY 20, 1934 Number 995

LEARNING AND LEISURE[1]

By Dr. W. B. BIZZELL

PRESIDENT OF THE UNIVERSITY OF OKLAHOMA

A LITTLE more than three months ago I presented diplomas in this hall to nearly a thousand students. Many of those who graduated at that time entered college in September, 1929—about the time of the great stock market crash. As I faced that great group of graduating seniors on that June morning, I found myself thinking of the changes that have come over the world in the four years that these students had been in college. An era of unprecedented prosperity had closed with registration days in 1929. The four years that followed were characterized by indescribable distress. The carefree years of the nineteen-twenties had been followed by years of anxiety and suffering. Those who were graduating on that eventful day in their lives were to go into a vastly different world from whence they came when they entered college.

Many of you who are entering college for the first time to-day, no doubt, are looking forward to your graduation in 1937. You are probably selecting your courses with a view to your needs when college days are over. What kind of a social order will confront you as you go forth from college? What opportunities will you have in the vocation or profession for which you are now beginning to make preparation? There is implied in the selection of your courses of study a prophecy of the future. Upon the accuracy of your insight will depend your future happiness, as well as your success. Events are reshaping human affairs with such rapidity that it is difficult to predict world conditions a few years hence. It is reasonable to assume, in the light of what is happening to-day, that the world into which you will go after your graduation will be vastly different from what it is to-day. This dynamic situation makes it exceedingly difficult to select a course of study in preparation for the needs and requirements of the years that are ahead.

THE PASSING OF INDIVIDUALISM

Thoughts and habits are changing so rapidly to-day that it is impossible to appraise their consequences. The fact that these changes are being accelerated by ballyhoo and noisy demonstration doesn't lessen their significance. We see things happening to-day that we have never seen before. An irresponsible individualism is being superseded rapidly by regulated and cooperative capitalism. It is profoundly significant that an individualistic society can surrender a long and cherished conception of life and can accept almost over

[1] Convocational address delivered by President W. B. Bizzell at the opening of the forty-second annual session of the University of Oklahoma on Tuesday, September 19, 1933.

night a radically different philosophy, involving mass action and group consciousness.

The growing conflict between individualism and collectivism was discussed by Dr. Charles W. Eliot in his Barbour-Page Foundation lectures at the University of Virginia in 1909. According to this great intellectual American, "individualism values highly not only the rights of the single person, but also the initiative of the individual left free by society. Collectivism values highly social rights, objects to an individual initiative which does mischief when left free, holds that the interest of the many should override the interest of the individual, whenever the two interests conflict, and should control social action, and yet does not propose to extinguish the individual, but only to restrict him for the common good, including his own." After pointing out the strong natural hold that individualism had on American democracy, Dr. Eliot contended that individualism was slowly losing ground in its conflict with collectivism and prophesied that ultimately it would be overcome by its protagonist. That prophecy has been fulfilled in our day.

The conflict between individualism and collectivism in education has been going on for a long time. In the past, education was directed to the needs of the individual child. Montaigne developed his theory of education around the interest of a single gifted child whose intellectual life was guided by one capable tutor. He never thought in terms of mass education. While Rousseau approached the problem somewhat differently, he had very much the same idea. Thomas Jefferson founded the University of Virginia upon the ideal of free choice of subjects and the personal wishes of the student. Ezra Cornell, the founder of the great university that bears his name, expressed the wish that the institution should be a place where any one might pursue any subject that appealed to him.

The spirit of collectivism has made many inroads in recent times upon this individualistic conception. The fact that the collective interest of society often promotes individual welfare has made it easy to move in this direction. Compulsory education, restriction on the choice of subjects and state adoption of text-books are examples of the tendency toward collective action in education. The collective interest of society was responsible for the establishment of state-supported institutions of higher learning; and their courses of study, while apparently designed to meet individual needs, have been primarily determined by social objectives. In recent times, we have seen all kinds of arbitrary standards set up for admission to state-supported institutions and very definite legal requirements for the practise of the professions. The latest steps in collective action are restrictions on enrolment and limitation of numbers in various professional courses. There is much to indicate that this tendency will be carried much further in the immediate future. It is fortunate, of course, that many of the restrictions upon individualism have been brought about through the cooperation between collective and individualistic influences. Bertrand Russell, in his recent book, "Education and the Modern World," says: "A sense of citizenship, of social cooperation, is therefore more necessary than it used to be; but it remains important that this should be secured without too great a diminution of individual judgment and individual initiative." It is certainly questionable how much further collectivism in education can go without infringing seriously upon the rights, as well as the needs of the individual. There is a need for the searching of hearts in the future consideration of all these tendencies in American life.

Collectivism in business, as reflected in the several industrial codes recently promulgated by the National Recovery Administration and accepted by industrial enterprises, raises the question of restriction on individualism in education. Will state-supported educational institutions, for example, be utilized to promulgate popular theories of political practises? We have seen this brought about in a most ruthless manner in Germany recently. Acceptance of a particular conception of governmental policy has been made the basis of employment rather than intellectual attainments, character and personality. A similar attitude has prevailed in Italy for some years. Of course, we do not expect to see this happen in America, but these examples illustrate the extreme to which collective action may go under the domination of a Hitler or a Mussolini.

The Obligations of Education to the Social Order

Whatever view we may hold with reference to the limitations of collectivism on education, there can be no question that our educational institutions have an obligation to the social order. Our schools are functional agencies of society. As such, they must adjust their objectives and conform their programs to the changing world that they are designed to serve. There is a popular belief that our educational institutions have not always fulfilled their obligations to society, but any one who is familiar with the changing objectives of education in America during the last hundred years must be convinced that our schools have made a serious effort to adjust their curricula to the changing social order that they are designed to serve.

The changes that are taking place to-day impose new obligations, as well as new opportunities, upon our schools. The National Recovery program is bringing about important changes in the lives of our people. The industrial codes that are being formulated in conformity with this program are limiting the hours of labor to 35 or 40, out of a total of 168 hours for the week. This releases the energies of thousands of people to be utilized in other than bread-winning employment. Is this free time to become a social asset or a social liability? The misuse of unhired time is as serious a problem as the unwise use of wealth. Sociologists and others have recognized this fact for years, but it has taken an unprecedented crime wave and a state of demoralization never experienced before in our history to drive the fact home to all of us.

Throughout our history, we have glorified work. The willingness to work and the ability to do good work have been recognized as supreme virtues. John Ruskin expressed the thought in one connection as follows: "Every man should do good work for his bread and every man should have good bread for his work." The pioneer spirit in America gave validity to this accepted code. In our early history, men had to work hard to live and the lazy idler was regarded as a social drone. It was a necessity during pioneer days that a man who did not work should not eat. In those days survival and security depended upon every one working hard, spending sparingly and saving rigorously. The virtues of work, thrift and sobriety have endured as supreme virtues.

These virtues have not been discarded, but their position in the hierarchy of virtues has changed. Machinery and industrial organization have been for a generation constantly increasing the efficiency of man power. The results have produced consequences of great significance. It is claimed that automatic machines and organization methods make it possible to-day to dispense with one third of all the 48,832,589 workers listed as gainfully employed in 1930 and to produce sufficient goods to maintain the present standard of living and only require the average employee to work thirty-six hours per week.

This situation has not only produced a reappraisal of the social virtues, but it has changed our estimates of social values. In the past, we have measured success by the possession of worldly goods. Prestige and power have always gone to those who possessed large wealth. Idleness and wasteful display have been the evidence of economic surplus. It is now a possibility that a new conception of social values may appear. Is it too much to expect in the future that prestige may come to those who use their leisure for the enrichment of personal and social life? The time may be at hand when the making of a great life may be recognized as at least as important as the making of a great fortune. There is wisdom in the words of an eminent sociologist who has said recently: "We must face and welcome a world in which leisure is more important than money making and where both earning and spending will be judged by the quality of life they produce, rather than by the wealth, the power, the excitement or the display."

Education for Leisure

The proper use of leisure time is not a new problem to us. Shorter working hours have come to thousands in recent years. When industry, business and transportation accepted the eight-hour day, the proper use of leisure time became a popular topic for discussion. Dr. L. P. Jacks predicted in a lecture at Glasgow University that the hours needed for mass production and mechanized labor would fall so low as "to leave the leisure hours the major quantity" for all classes of workers. This prophecy has probably been fulfilled much earlier than he realized at the time. Dr. Jacks has said more recently, "I name education for leisure as an outstanding need of the present age." Quite recently Mr. H. G. Wells, in his monumental book entitled "The Work, Wealth and Happiness of Mankind," surveys the history of the increase and possibilities of leisure time. "One inevitable consequence of continuing human progress," he says, "is a steady increase of human leisure and human resources." Mr. C. E. M. Joad has written a little book entitled "Diogenes or the Future of Leisure," in which he surveys the place of leisure time in modern civilization. But the industrial codes that have been promulgated in recent weeks by the Federal Government bring the problem of leisure time squarely before us as one requiring serious consideration. The *New York Times,* in a recent editorial, has said that "a code looking to the better education of the people in a sensible use of their leisure time may, as one has suggested, come in time to be known as a second Magna Charta of liberty." That education for leisure is as necessary as training for work is recognized by all those who have given serious consideration to the problem.

In fact, there is an intimate interrelation between work and leisure. The use made of free time has an important influence upon the quality of employed time. The reverse is not equally true, but the proper attitude towards one's vocation should give direction to one's avocational and recreational activities. Dr. Jacks believes that if an individual makes all the proper adjustments in life, he should make work and play essentially interchangeable. The wise employer will, therefore, be concerned about what his employees do during their unhired time. No argument is necessary to sustain the contention that a man who spends his free time in exhausting frivolity can not render a high quality of service during his working hours.

It is equally true that a student's use of his free time largely determines his accomplishments in college. It is not an exaggeration to say that a student's grades are, in general, the result of the use he makes of his week-ends and holidays rather than by his regularity in attending classes. Learning is a serious business. The acquisition and the assimilation of knowledge involve much more than reading text-books and listening to a professor's exposition of his subject. No man or woman can acquire an education by attending classes fifteen or sixteen hours a week. Learning involves much more than this. It involves a state of mind, as well as conformity to a schedule of instruction. Dissipation of any kind is the antidote to learning. The Greek word for school (σκολή) means leisure, the Latin word for college (*collegium*) means bringing together or assembling, while study (*studium*) means effort. A school, then, is a place of leisurely meditation where a group of earnest young people are assembled for sustained effort in the acquisition of knowledge. Perhaps, this definition sounds far-fetched to you. A more accurate definition, according to the general impression of many people, might be stated as follows: A school is a place where a group of young people are assembled and required to attend lectures, in which few of them are interested, for five days, during which they plan for their week-end parties or automobile trips to neighboring cities. But this is not the classical conception of what an educational institution should be. The poet Wordsworth, in one of his sonnets, described quite accurately what the trouble is with our educational institutions. He says:

> The world is too much with us; late and soon,
> Getting and spending, we lay waste our powers.

The world *is* too much with us these days. It is difficult to keep from dissipating our powers of mind and heart in profitless and wasteful activities. My point is that both in industry and education the use we make of our free time determines to a large extent our success in scheduled hours of work.

Avocational and Recreational Education

The development of the whole man—body, mind, heart and soul—has long been accepted as a comprehensive task of education. We now need to realize that education must take into account the entire time at the disposal of man in the fulfillment of this task. Our educational system, up to the present, has done little more than prepare man to utilize approximately a third of his time. Many of the evils in our society are due to the fact that we have ignored the other two thirds of the twenty-four hours at our disposal. The late Arnold Bennett wrote a remarkable book some years ago entitled, "How to Live on Twenty-four Hours a Day." He tells us we have only this much time extended over an uncertain number of days, months and years in which "to spin health, pleasure, money, content, respect and the evolution of an immortal soul." The thought running through this book is that man needs to live well for every second, minute and hour of each full day, and not merely for a fractional part of this time.

Professor Walter B. Pitkin, of Columbia University, tells us in his recent book entitled "Life Begins at Forty" that

> everybody comes into the world with a certain chance of acquiring a working capital of a round half million. Half million what? Half million hours, of course. They will be on hand, ready for investment, as fast as the new-born promoter crawls from his cradle and toddles forth to meet the dawn. They will be paid in full if he is skillful enough and lucky enough to stick around until he turns the mossy corner of three score years and ten.
>
> He can not give away his minutes. He can not borrow minutes from a friend. He can not steal minutes. Money is a mere medium of exchange. Time is neither a medium nor is it exchangeable. It is the inmost stuff of life itself.

This may sound quite quixotic, but there is wisdom in these thoughts. Our inalienable and universal heritage is time—a sufficient amount of it to produce a great life. We can not dispose of it. We must consume it. But the methods of consumption determine whether we are to be ignorant or scholarly, wise or foolish, successes or failures, libertines or gentlemen.

Youth needs guidance in the use of this priceless inheritance. Avocational and recreational education comes into the picture to supply this need. The industrial revolution produced the vocational objective in education more than a half century ago. The economic revolution of to-day brings us squarely to the need for avocational and recreational education. Educational institutions will not abandon the older aims, but new conditions will subordinate them in point of emphasis. We have already found that training for a single vocation is unwise. Demand for skilled workers is shifting rapidly. The times call for versatile workers. This means many adjustments in educational policy.

We need to recall the magnificent contributions that men have made in leisure pursuits to science, art, literature and public welfare. Leonardo da Vinci was an artist, but his varied structural designs have caused him to be called the father of engineering and aeronautics. Chaucer was a collector of customs, but his poetry has made him immortal. Benjamin Franklin was a printer; but his title to fame rests on his literary accomplishments, his scientific discoveries and his statesmanship. Mendel was an abbot of a monastery, but his place in the sun is due to his contributions to genetics. Leeuwenhoek, the great Dutch scientist and the author of "Arcana Naturae," was a merchant. Fabre was a teacher of the classics in France, but observations made by him in his back-yard gave him world-wide recognition as an entomologist. Priestley, the discoverer of oxygen, was a preacher with an impediment in his speech. His interest in scientific research probably caused him to inflict many a poor sermon upon his parishioners; but, if it had not been for this avocational interest, Priestley would never have been heard of beyond the confines of his local parish. These are only a few of the names of men who have enriched the world in one field or another by having some abiding interest outside the work they performed for their daily bread. Much of the world's best work through all the ages has been done by men outside the hours of their regular employment.

The idle time now being consumed by irresponsible people who are depressed, desperate or delinquent must be conserved for constructive leisure. If this free time, which is the priceless possession of thousands to-day, could be utilized properly, the sum total of human happiness would be greatly enlarged. The problem, of course, is a partnership one, in which both society and the individual must share. Countless thousands of people to-day, who are unemployed, desire to work and to earn not only subsistence for themselves, but a surplus that might be used in profitable ways. This is society's responsibility, and the fact that after all these centuries man has not been able through organized effort to prevent these cycles of wide-spread unemployment is a severe indictment of his insight and ingenuity. On the other hand, the individual, as a partner in the social group, has not always been wise in the use of his full time when conditions enabled him to acquire a surplus of this world's goods. Insurance against periodic unemployment, shorter working hours and a wage scale sufficiently high to create a surplus are society's responsibilities to the individual at this time. With this security the home, the school and the church should face seriously the task of training men and women to utilize every hour of the twenty-four at their disposal in the interest of public welfare and individual happiness.

This means that avocational and recreational education must be assigned a place in the curriculum equal in dignity with courses in vocational and professional education in every college and university in the land. This, of course, means a rather thorough reorganization of existing programs of study. But the time has come when courses must be adapted to the needs of students rather than made to conform to the interest and predilections of faculty groups.

Both character and knowledge are required to render acceptable service in positions of public trust. Deficiency in these qualities accounts for scandals and inefficiency that are constantly occurring in public life. The mismanagement of our city governments, the shortsightedness of school board officials, and numerous other services of this character are due to these causes. If our public school system is to hold its place in popular esteem and justify the theory on which it is sustained, it is absolutely necessary for it to train men and women to serve the public with competency, devotion and honesty. I admit this is not a very original thought, but it never needed emphasis more than it does to-day.

I am making a distinction between avocational and recreational education. The two concepts are usually thought of as different aspects of one thing, but to my way of thinking they are quite different. Avocational education, to me, means training for useful public service that is no part of regular employment and for which the individual receives little, if any, remuneration. Recreational education is training one to enjoy his free time largely for his own benefit. Avocational education has a social objective, while recreational education is concerned with the individual's needs and requirements.

Recently a prominent American citizen said in a mild criticism of the NRA that every man had an inalienable right to work eight hours per day. I recall that in the late years of the nineteenth century men were saying that a man's time was his own and that he had a right to work as many hours per day as he desired. There is both truth and error in these generalizations. I freely admit that if a man can not or will not profitably utilize his free time for wholesome ends, it is better for him to be employed than to be idle. This conclusion, though logical, need not follow. Men can be taught and directed to utilize their unemployed time in just as profitable ways as they can be taught to utilize their employed time efficiently and well. The tragedy in American life is that so few mature men can get satisfaction out of leisure hours. Professor Walter B. Pitkin, in the book previously quoted, brings out this fact. There are many forms of recreation that give satisfaction to those who participate in them. Travel, reading, conversation (now nearly a lost art), walking, swimming, golfing and numerous other activities are profitable ways of utilizing leisure time. A man does not have to be a professional athlete to enjoy a wholesome game. I have been playing golf for many years. I do not recall having ever won a foursome, but I have found great enjoyment in the game and some of the friendships I value most in life have been made on the golf course.

It has long been my belief that every college student should be taught at least two games that he could play with enjoyment after his graduation. But this type of education is not more important than education for travel, reading, music and art appreciation, and many others too numerous to mention that contribute to enjoyment and contentment. It is fortunate, indeed, that at a time when the energies of thousands are being released from arduous toil there should be so many profitable and interesting ways to utilize leisure time. The radio, picture shows, museums, art galleries, dramatic productions, playgrounds, national parks, inexpensive means of travel and a thousand other agencies for profitable enjoyment are available to all.

CONCLUSION

A new synthesis of values needs to be made—something similar to what Plato called harmony and Aristotle happiness. The *summum bonum* is to be found in a new appraisal of work, play, love and worship. This new appraisal is your chief task as you begin this new college year. The earnestness and fidelity with which you pursue the work at hand and the ways by which you utilize your leisure time will indicate to what extent you are really preparing to live the good and useful life in the world into which you will go in a few fleeting years.

Much more is involved than the making of high grades or avoiding contact with the faculty committee on conduct. You are expected to live a life characterized by high purpose. The thing that gives supreme value to college life is that it is the one place in society where all the powers of mind and heart have an opportunity for exercise and development. The fact that you have a wide range of choices of conduct does not mean that you are to choose the easy or the sordid way.

You are expected to learn to live here as well as to learn to know. Learning to live well is as important as to learn the subject-matter of books. But one is not contradictory of the other. They are supplementary rather than contradictory. The life of thought should reenforce the life of action. Time is at your disposal. It is your priceless heritage, and this college environment is your supreme opportunity to consume it day after day in the making of a good and useful life.

EFFECTIVE LEARNINGS OF CULTURES BY LESS ABLE PERSONS

By Dr. DAVID SNEDDEN
PROFESSOR OF EDUCATION, TEACHERS COLLEGE, COLUMBIA UNIVERSITY

I. THESES

THE central thesis herein argued is that present widely operative, or even still formative, plans for extended scopes and enriched contents of American educations are deplorably unrealistic and ineffectual as respects cultural educations for the less able two thirds of American youth at age levels 12 to 20.

It is assumed that all effective educational plannings are and must be the products of expert educators and hardly at all of laymen. Laymen have already given noble foundations and scaffoldings—financial, legislative, civic, and as supporting popular faiths. But only educational specialists can provide plans for more improved adaptations to class needs, for more functional contents and for effective methods.

The now operative as well as contemplated plans of American educators for democratized cultural educations for learners of less than high abilities are here held to be deplorably unrealistic and ineffectual for several reasons: First, because nearly all present plans for cultural educations of learners of secondary and collegiate school ages are still based excessively on traditions of class adaptations, subject-matter contents, and prevailing pedagogical methods derived from times and social conditions when only the aristocratic, the well-born and well-bred were deemed able to profit from secondary school and liberal college, cultural educations; second, because such plannings are based on no reliable analyses of the distinctive qualities and values which derive from really functional cultural educations of at least three species (distinctive, that is, from qualities and values of vocational, health conserving, religious, civistic and other kinds of non-cultural educations) which can and should be made the objectives of school educations; third, because such plannings have been based upon no adequate study of the prodigiously rich resources for, and profitable possible objectives of, two upper divisions of cultural educations for less able minds as made possible by modern advances in cultural contents and technological means; and, finally, because such plannings are based upon no adequate recognition of the many and diversified avenues along which in our times and under our conditions of democratized culture and leisure really functional cultural educations are practicable.

II. What Learnings Are of Most Worth?

There can be no really effective applied science of education until extensive agreements have been reached among the abler of our educational policy-makers as to classes, optimum measures and optimum adaptations of learnings. And, amidst present confusions of philosophies of educational purposes, methods and adaptations, no writer proposing improvements in education can hope to be intelligible or helpful to others unless he first gives clear expression to the theories or hypotheses of educational values which are basic to his proposals. Hence the following formulations of some salient articles of the writer's educational creeds:

All human beings are learners from the cradle to the grave. Their learnings constitute one great class of their growths. Such learnings play relatively far more important rôles in the safe and effective survivals and satisfactory living of human beings than they do in the cases of birds, mammals and insects, notwithstanding that all these are creatures which in some degree acquire new learnings throughout their lifetimes.

All the learnings acquired by human beings have functions—that is, they have uses, they give satisfactions. But these functions are as various as the felt impulses and the purposed activities of persons, whether babies trying out bodily motions, young adults seeking to solve important problems or old peasants eager for some current gossip. Perhaps the great majority of the learnings, like large proportions of the other activities, of either children or adults are playful, casual, impulsive, amusing. All such learnings, which give color or flavor or health or immediate satisfactions to life, may have very little of the values which we attach to purposed growths, to planned constructions, to deliberate cultivations.

But human beings, and above all the kinds of human beings whom we like to think of as civilized, introduce much planning into at least large proportions of their learnings and in less measure into some other growths. Parents plan for some, but not all, the learnings of their children. Foresighted and self-controlled young adults make extensive plans for acquisition of vocational or cultural or health conserving or etiquette learnings. Even old adults, relaxing from focused pursuits of economic security or social prestige or avocational skills, often lay out plans for new cultural learnings through travel, or reading, or for new civic learnings through study of, and sharing in, political action.

Planned learnings are, obviously, always designed to serve valued ends or purposes

—valued, that is, by the learner himself if he does the planning, or valued by his guardians and well-wishers if they are the planners on his behalf. Schools have always been intended to be agencies for finding and offering planned learnings. Teachers, tutors, preachers, advertisers, legend tellers, seers, prophets and numberless other kinds of social persuaders or propagandists have always sought in large measure to insure planned learnings in others. In a broad sense, all eager experimenters, readers of newspapers, seekers after gossip, patrons of libraries and interested travelers are in pursuit of more or less self-planned learnings.

On such foundations, all commonplace enough to the unconfused understanding of mature thinkers, must be erected the postulates, theories and experimental programs which can be assembled as philosophies of educational values. In past centuries leaders in education or other large affairs only occasionally became excited over problems of educational values, because the slow processes of custom-growth and tradition-transmission usually gave fairly stable, even if only faith-based, values and valuations. But the intellectual riches of our times, the greatly increased demands we now tend to make upon purposed controls of learnings, our progressive democratizations of opportunities, and, perhaps above all, our progressive large-scale quests after higher economies and efficiencies in all the collective affairs of men have brought sweeping changes. In hundreds of sections of the civilized world, and amongst scores of unlike types of large-scale collective work, leaders are seeking, demanding and researching after more reliable and more scientific foundations of educational values—that is, standards and criteria of the values of all those kinds and degrees of learnings which can be self- or alter-controlled to the ends of higher human well-being.

III. Criticisms of Present Cultural Educations for the Less Able Analyzed

In the first section of this paper four criticisms of present practises and proposed plans of cultural educations in schools and colleges were briefly stated. Let it be recalled that this paper is not concerned with cultural educations of the naturally most gifted or the environmentally most favored. It is concerned with practises and plans for cultural educations of the intellectually less able-minded two thirds of our youth, and especially of those being reared in culturally inferior environments.

First, the cultural educations in literature, history, natural science, drama, etc., now available to these relatively disadvantaged classes in secondary schools and liberal colleges are excessively antiquated, aristocratic, "high brow." Formerly only selected minorities attended such schools. Now, these schools are being rapidly democratized, or rather, in rapidly increasing proportions the less able and less well-environed sections of our populations are demanding appropriate advanced cultural educations throughout the ages from 12 to 18, whilst also steadily mounting proportions are seeking opportunities at collegiate age levels from 17 to 20.

Present high-school curricula, and especially the dominant conceptions of educational values underlying them, have not been materially changed as planned accommodations for these newcomers. A wealth of current criticisms of educational experts is to that effect.

Because of such prevalent agreement that present conditions are bad, it is the second of the criticisms stated at the outset that is most serious. Though our abler and more articulate educators unite in condemning present upper-level school offerings for the multitude of less able minds now claiming further educational advantages, they are in utter disagreement as to what other offerings should be made instead. Worse than that even, they agree on no clearly defined formulations as to what are valid classifications of the values or valuable outcomes which should control provision of any school opportunities for controlled learnings between ages 12 and 20. Their theories of educational values are excessively subjective and aspirational and, in consequence, their formulations of such theories are too vague, generalized and romantic to admit of effective application to the construction of courses and curricula—that is, of working plans and programs for school-directed educations.

The theories of these critics, for example, rarely give any realistic recognition to such unlike functionings of the activities of men as those for economic production (vocational competencies), for political cooperations (civism), for conservation of physical well-being (hygiene, medical service, body building) and for culture.

Nowhere do such theories take into account the several easily distinguishable types of utilization culture which are everywhere in evidence among adults—namely common or all-purpose cultures, euthenic or material utilization cultures and advanced intellectual and esthetic, or spiritual, cultures.

The third criticism is that current plannings take no adequate account of the prodigious riches of the means—literatures, histories, current journals, music, moving pictures, natural sciences, social sciences, geographies, plastic arts, crafts, etc.,—now abundantly available for the cultural educations of the less able at age levels 12 to 20. Instead, they cling obstinately to traditionally formalized and often excessively desiccated, studies of mathematics, foreign language, classical English literature and abstract expressions of natural science.

Finally, such plannings are as yet nowhere based upon sociologically sound findings as to who, for our day, are men and women of optimum cultures. The time has long gone by—in reality there never was such a time except for certain self-approving castes or "intellectuals" or "esthetes" —when to be "cultured" (meaning of superior or optimum cultural attainments) must connote in all persons similar attainments (beyond minimum essential manners and common knowledge). The "cultures" optimum for men and women in democratic societies without leisured classes — but where all persons have some leisure—must be greatly diversified—for some perhaps much music and little natural science, for some entrancing craft avocations but no foreign language, for some much reading but little travel.

IV. CONSTRUCTIVE PROPOSALS

Assume: That presently all the children of all the people will be in full-time attendance on local, non-vocational schools to 18 years of age; that no educations for consciously vocational objectives will be permitted until after 18 years of age and then only in central, not local, schools; that all youth from 12 to 15 will attend junior high schools irrespective of grade reached or intelligence quotient; that all youth 15 to 18 will attend senior high schools irrespective of grade reached; and finally, that in junior and senior high schools time allotments to cultural educations will average 50 per cent. of all school time, to civic and moral educations 20 per cent., and to physical welfare educations 10 per cent.—but with very considerable flexibilities according to varying needs—or in some degree preferences—of learners.

The problem then is: What kinds, what scopes, to what ends and by what means can really functional cultural educations be provided for, let us say, the two thirds of lowest powers of receptivity at ages 12 to 18 in such junior and senior high schools?

First, let us group all practicable objectives of cultural—as distinguished from health and vigor fostering, socializing and vocational preparation—objectives of school educations into three classes: the "common" or "all-purpose" cultural objectives; the "euthenic" or material utilizing cultural objectives; and the "spiritual" or intellectual and "esthetic advanced," cultural objectives.

Second, recognize that whereas large proportions of needed "all purpose" or common cultural objectives—in history, geography, arithmetic, English language, etc., —will have been presented or covered in grades before the seventh, nevertheless for dull or slow or apathetic pupils these should be given yearly review, revival or refreshed applications even into upper grades.

Third, focus objectives of "euthenic" cultures in accordance with probable future wholesome living standards of these persons—in areas of sumptuary utilizations of foods, shelter, dress, decorations, sense-satisfying recreations, diversions, etc., and of thrift, saving, insurance, etc.

Fourth, in areas of "spiritual" cultural objectives make much of varied appreciational approaches to riches of current literatures, current natural sciences, recent plastic arts, present and prospective personality cultures, popularized histories and social sciences, and other means now so abundantly used by American adults sharing in our splendidly democratized cultural resources. Recognize that these cultures are now accessible to, and in some degree used by, nearly all adults, even of inferior native powers; but that schools will seek to assure more elevated, more really culturing, more growth-conserving uses. Accept democratic inevitability of: Tabloids, wood-pulp magazines and hack-produced fiction; popularized science, biography and history; commercialized recreational resorts, moving pictures, radio, window-shopping, auto travel, etc., etc., and proceed to invent and use school courses to refine, upgrade and otherwise elevate cultures in such areas.

EDUCATIONAL EVENTS

THE AMERICAN UNIVERSITY UNION

OFFICERS of the American University Union in London and Paris have recently submitted to the Institute of International Education, which finances and controls them through a special committee of its board of trustees, their reports for the academic year 1932–1933.

The following comments are made in the *Bulletin* of the institute on the basis of those reports: Dr. Horatio S. Krans, director of the Paris office, notes with satisfaction that the problem of admission of American students to French medical faculties has been settled by the Ministry of Public Instruction in accordance with recommendations made by the union. The new regulation provides that no applications for admission to medical faculties will be considered unless such applications have been previously submitted for evaluation to the Association of American Medical Colleges. From both the French and American points of view such action was recognized as a method of eliminating undesirables from French medical faculties, and, hence, from a profession already overcrowded in both France and America.

The Paris office has collaborated with the Institute of Intellectual Cooperation in the preparation of conferences of the directors of pedagogic centers and directors of higher education. The union recruited the American delegation of some thirty students to attend a Franco-American Student Conference at Lyon. A students' broadcasting competition was also arranged. Six vacancies as postes d'assistants d'Anglais in French lycées were filled by recommendation of the union. A series of causeries d'orientation were also arranged. The Paris office has become with the years more widely known both in this country and in France because professors and students turn to it in increasing numbers for all sorts of information and advice; and because collaboration with other organizations, French and American, has become closer and more constant. Visitors during the academic year averaged 36 for each working day.

The director of the London office reports that there have been a larger number of American scholars in England in the past year than in the ten years prior, although these men were neither unemployed nor fugitives from chaos. The fact that some were absent from America in order to ease the strain on the budget of their college may account in part at least for the increase.

Visitors at the London office represented in the main five geographical areas—New England, New York to Maryland, North Carolina, the Chicago region and California. The majority of American scholars in England for research represented either English literature or history or economics. During the past year, while English held its first place, economics outnumbered history.

In accordance with its policy of facilitating personal contact between American and British scholars, the union arranged again last year a series of "week-end lectures." During the past two years thirty such lectures have been arranged; the American professor generally spending a week-end as a guest of one of the newer universities, delivering one lecture and engaging in informal discussions with his colleagues. A lecture fee and traveling expenses are furnished by the union with funds supplied by the Carnegie Endowment. The following men were "week-end lecturers" during the past year: Professor Edward H. Warren, of Harvard; Professor T. M. Parrott, of Princeton; Dean T. L. Hood, of Trinity College, Hartford, Connecticut; Professor H. J. Cadbury, of Bryn Mawr; Professor Jerome D. Greene, of Harvard and University College, Aberystwyth; Professor Harvey Walker, of the Ohio State University; Professor E. F. Gay, of Harvard University; Professor Howard M. Jones, of Michigan University, and Professor Arnold Post, of Haverford College.

RELIGIOUS EDUCATION AT THE UNIVERSITY OF DENVER

FOUR years ago the University of Denver established a Commission on Religious Education, composed of seven members of the faculty, seven students and three members of the Board of Trustees, and charged it "to study the entire campus situation, with a view to discovering and encouraging those activities, experiences and influences which are contributing to the religious and moral development of students; locating and defining further needs in this field; developing and evaluating methods whereby these needs can be met most adequately." Protestants, Catholics and Jews are included in the commission's membership. An executive officer, a member of the faculty with the title of director of religious activities, is responsible for carrying out the commission's policies. There follows a brief report of the program of religious education which has been developed under the guidance of the commission.

Closely related to teaching is the personal counsel of members of the faculty. An advisory system, still in process of development, provides for each student in the university a faculty adviser, whose functions are conceived as broader than educational guidance alone, including counsel for the student in whatever problems he may encounter. Supplementing this are the advisory services of the dean of women, the adviser of men, the director of religious activities and the secretaries of the Christian associations.

Religious interests are regularly included in the public meetings of the university. An important feature of the college year is the annual series of addresses on religion, extending through one week, and delivered by a speaker of proved ability. The speakers of the last three years and their topics follow:

1931—Dr. Albert W. Palmer, "Building Your Own Philosophy of Life."

1932—Dr. Henry N. Wieman, "The Nature and Functions of Religion."

1933—Dr. Bruce Curry, "Religion as a Resource for Modern Life."

At least half the student body have regularly attended these addresses. In addition, one of the weekly university assemblies in each month is planned as an occasion for worship. A voluntary attendance of from four hundred to six hundred students out of a student body of a thousand is indicative of the student response.

Further, the university seeks to cooperate as fully as possible with the churches of Denver, with which most of the students have contacts through their families. The university relationship at most extends through but four years, while the church relationship may be life-long. It is therefore believed to be important that the student should take an active part in the life of some church while he is in college, and that his church, on the other hand, should be prepared to aid him in the readjustments of religious thought and practise which are normally a part of the maturing experience of the college student. An interchurch committee of representative students is the agency through which this part of the religious education program is carried out.

VOCATIONAL EDUCATION AND UNEMPLOYMENT

ECONOMIC retrenchment and unemployment are assigned by Secretary of the Interior Harold L. Ickes, in his annual report, for the falling off in the enrolment in vocational education classes last year over the year before. It is the first time in the history of the vocational education program in this country that the enrolment in vocational schools has not increased from one year to another. It is pointed out, however, that most of the decrease has occurred in trade and industrial schools, which by their very nature are affected by unemployment, and that enrolment in schools of agricultural and home economics, which have not been so directly affected by the unemployment situation, increased during 1933.

The reduction in total enrolment is one inevitable consequence of reduction in federal, state and local revenues available for vocational education. In support of this declaration it is pointed out that $3,276,000 less money was invested in vocational schools in 1933 than in 1932. As a result opportunities offered for vocational education were correspondingly reduced, and funds were not available for promoting vocational education in new areas, however urgent the need in such areas for widening the range of vocational training to embrace new occupations.

No surprise is expressed by Secretary Ickes over the decreased enrolment shown in his report in evening and part-time trade and industrial schools. He takes pains to point out, however, that enrolment in all-day, full-time trade and industrial schools increased. "It is obvious," he says, "that the enrolment in evening and part-time industrial schools, which are established primarily to serve employed workers who desire additional training and instruction along the lines of their daily employment, must drop off in a period of unemployment such as has prevailed during 1933. Moreover, it is inevitable that some unemployed workers, who under normal conditions enroll for vocational training during part of their working day, should take advantage of full-time day school classes to prepare themselves for future employment, thus swelling the enrolment in these schools."

As in previous years enrolment in vocational schools during 1933 was made up of employed adult workers in evening classes who desired training along the lines of their daily employment; of young workers who had dropped out of full-time day school and had enrolled in a vocational course for part-time instruction, and of boys and girls taking vocational courses as regular full-time pupils in day schools.

Of the 1,149,495 boys and girls and adults of all ages who enrolled in vocational schools last year, 265,978 were farm boys and girls and adult farmers enrolled in courses in vocational agriculture; 537,512 were boys and girls and adult workers in trade and industrial courses, and 346,005 were girls and women in courses in home economics.

PLANS OF THE JOINT COMMISSION ON THE EMERGENCY IN EDUCATION

THE Joint Commission on the Emergency in Education, appointed by the National Education Association and the Department of Superintendence, plan to ask the Federal Government to appropriate money for the aid of schools in the present educational crisis. Following close upon the announcements that more than 2,000 rural schools had shut their doors, and that the schools of some large cities will be forced to close by March 1, a nation-wide campaign for emergency relief to public education was initiated in Washington at a conference of educators at which both the Joint Commission on the Emergency in Education and the Legislative

Commission of the National Education Association were represented.

Relief will be sought either through congressional or administrative action at the earliest possible moment. Participating in the effort to prevent the complete collapse of the American public schools, are forty-eight state education associations with a total membership of 600,000 teachers and school officers.

Reports placed before the recent Washington Conference showed a gradual decline in educational opportunity throughout the entire nation, and included accounts of pitiful sacrifices of teachers and parents to provide their children with even a meager portion of their American birthright of education. Teachers were found copying texts in long hand in order that there might be a sufficient supply of books for the pupils to study. Many teachers have taught months without any kind of pay. A total of more than $40,000,000 is now owed to teachers by school districts which will be able to provide only a few more weeks of school this year for their children unless substantial assistance comes from the Federal Government.

One out of every four cities has already shortened its school term this year. The terms in practically every great American city are to-day one or two months shorter than they were seventy to one hundred years ago. The nation is literally stepping back into the educational opportunities of the early nineteenth century.

One out of every four teachers is now being paid a rate less than that established for factory hands under the Blanket Code of the Federal Administration. Children are being herded into schoolrooms under conditions in which individual instruction is impossible. The recent ban on child labor has freed many additional children who expect a chance to continue their schooling, and in many states are required by law to do so. Twenty-five thousand teachers have been dropped from the schools, while a million more pupils have come into them.

The action taken by the Washington Conference follows the endorsement of the fundamental principle of federal relief to schools as an integral part of the recovery program, by leaders of such civic groups as the National Congress of Parents and Teachers and the American Federation of Labor. With the assistance of all organized groups interested in the welfare of children, it is hoped to secure action by the congress before the schools of the nation are closed and educational efficiency is wrecked.

THE CIVIL WORKS ADMINISTRATION AND NURSERY SCHOOLS IN NEW YORK

CHILDREN between the ages of two and four years whose parents are needy will receive specialized training, under the Civil Works Service program, that has been made available in the past only to small numbers of fortunately placed children. Nursery school projects are being approved for cities throughout New York State and the drafting and training of unemployed teachers to conduct the schools will continue while the locations are being selected, according to an announcement made by Mrs. Charles H. Sabin, chairman of the advisory committee for women's projects for the State Civil Works Administration.

Not only teachers, but carpenters, doctors, nurses, nutritionists and garment workers will find employment in establishing and conducting the nursery schools. Twenty children will make up each group and will be attended during the day while their parents are working or seeking employment.

In New York City the program will be started with twenty-five units, with the possibility of extending the number and size of the units later on. Up-state forty-six schools are planned tentatively for the following districts: Buffalo, Ithaca, Niagara Falls, Oneonta, Poughkeepsie, Rochester, Syracuse and Tompkins and Dutchess Counties.

Salaries of the personnel will be met out of federal relief funds through the Civil Works Service Bureau. The cost of housing the schools and such items as rent, heat and light, however, will be met by private welfare, religious and educational institutions or by public departments interested in furthering the project.

The schools, it is stipulated, will be open to children of every race and creed, regardless of the organization sponsoring any individual school.

The program is under the supervision of the State Department of Education and is sponsored on a national scale by the U. S. Office of Education.

Dr. Ruth Andrus, chief of the bureau of child development and parent education in the State Department of Education, will have direct charge in New York City and will supervise the schools throughout the state. Garth Akridge will be director of the schools in New York City.

Explaining the operation of the project, Miss Inez Ross, director of the Civil Works Service Bureau for New York State, said that children whose homes were found unsuitable for healthy growth would spend the entire day in the schools. Uniforms will be provided for each child, and the children will be fed at regular intervals and receive cod liver oil. They will be put to sleep for a period during the afternoons. The routine corresponds to systems worked out in Teachers College and other institutions.

Each school will be staffed at all times by a supervisor, a teacher, a nurse, a nutritionist, a parent educator, a cook, a cleaning woman and laundress and part of the time by a pediatrician.

THE SCHOOLS OF KANSAS

Mr. Roy Buckingham, editorial correspondent, writes to *The New York Times* that curtailed incomes resulting in tax delinquencies have worked the heaviest hardship on Kansas rural schools. A thousand fewer rural schools are open now than a year ago and before spring two or three hundred others will have to close because of inadequate funds. There are 6,893 district schools in operation now. This time last year 7,243 schools were open.

The present apparent jeopardy of the rural school program in Kansas is ascribed to the cash basis law, the limitation of school levies and the income slump. One of the first acts of the Landon administration was to establish every unit of government on a cash basis. At the time deflation was the general practise in the United States. Lavish spending was barred. Budget slashes were demanded.

The Legislature made drastic cuts in salaries. The order of the day was to make outgo meet income, so the cash basis law prevented the usual budgetary extensions and amortizations.

Some temporary relief through the CWA is in sight and schools which have been closed because of drained treasuries will employ teachers. In towns where educational facilities have been curtailed courses will be restored with teachers on the CWA basis. Several towns are taking advantage of the CWA to improve their school health programs.

According to Mr. Buckingham, so much emphasis has been placed on city institutions that the rural school has struggled along like a poor relation. Its teachers have been paid less, its standards have been lower and the advantages of school politics have not been turned its way. Lately, however, the closer integration of rural and urban communities has made the people conscious of the rural school and the realization that country boys and girls are entitled to every advantage is taking hold.

The school of fewer than seven pupils is said to be doomed. Hundreds of the schools which failed to open this year are in this group. But because there are a thousand fewer schools in operation does not mean that pupils are denied educational privileges. Probably the rural school enrolment for the year will be near the average. The explanation is consolidated districts.

The friends of better schools, however, regard the emergency as a plain indication of the need for a better rural school system which takes into consideration the thousands of miles of all-weather highways, better school buildings and facilities and better qualified teaching staffs. This will be brought about by redistricting, which will provide fewer but larger school districts with superior facilities.

THE SUPERINTENDENT-ELECT OF THE NEW YORK CITY SCHOOLS

Dr. Harold G. Campbell has been elected Superintendent of Schools for a term of six years by vote of the Board of Education. Dr. Campbell will succeed Dr. William J. O'Shea, the retiring superintendent, on February 1. One vote was given to Dr. William E. Grady, associate superintendent, who has been identified with progessive education activities. The vote later was made unanimous.

The new commissioner is a Republican, a Presbyterian and is regarded as a conservative in education.

Descended from Scotch Presbyterian stock,

Dr. Campbell was born January 13, 1884, in Fraserburgh, Scotland, the son of a shoemaker. He was brought to the United States when he was four years old and received his elementary education at Public School 34, in Brooklyn. He was graduated from the Boys High School, Brooklyn, in 1901 and from the Brooklyn Training School for Teachers in the following year.

His career in the New York public school system began in 1903 with his appointment as a teacher at Public School 25, in Brooklyn, and he remained an elementary school instructor until 1910, when he was appointed teacher of history at the Eastern District High School in Brooklyn. Seven years later he was promoted to administrative assistant of the school, holding that office until his appointment in 1920 as principal of the Flushing High School in Flushing, Queens.

Dr. Campbell was elected associate superintendent of schools in 1924. *The New York Times* remarks that "although his stand on various educational matters has not always escaped condemnation, his critics have generally admitted him to be a vigorous, suave and tactful administrator, tremendously likable, with a huge capacity for labor or politics."

Dr. Campbell's present position carries a salary of $12,000. The Superintendent of Schools receives $20,000 since the reduction from $25,000.

EDUCATIONAL NOTES AND NEWS

Dr. William J. O'Shea, who will retire on January 31 as superintendent of schools of New York City, was the guest of honor on January 18 at a dinner given by the New York Academy of Public Education at the College of the City of New York. The Academy Medal was presented to Dr. O'Shea "for distinguished service in the field of education" by Dr. William O'Flaherty. Dr. Harold G. Campbell, newly elected superintendent of schools, and Dr. George J. Ryan, president of the Board of Education, were among the speakers. President Frederick B. Robinson, of the College of the City of New York, presided.

Dr. John H. Finley, president of the College of the City of New York from 1903 to 1913 and now associate editor of *The New York Times,* was guest of honor at a dinner given on January 13 by the class of 1911 of City College in the Fifth Avenue Hotel. Part of the baccalaureate address delivered by Dr. Finley in 1911 was read by Stephen K. Rapp, presiding officer. An etching of Dr. Finley was presented to him by William Auerbach Levy, a member of the class. Dr. Finley, in his response, recalled incidents connected with his administration of the college.

Dr. John Dewey, professor emeritus of philosophy at Columbia University, delivered the Terry Lectures at Yale University on January 17, 18 and 19. He spoke on "Religions *versus* the Religious," "Emancipation of Faith" and "Community Life and the Religious Attitude." The Dwight H. Terry Lectureship was made available in 1923 for lectures on "religion in the light of science and philosophy." Former lecturers on the foundation include Robert A. Millikan, Arthur H. Compton, William Ernest Hocking, Herbert S. Jennings, Henry N. Russell and J. Arthur Thomson.

President Ernest H. Wilkins, of Oberlin College, has recently accepted membership on the Advisory Council of the Anglo-American Institute of the First Moscow University of the U. S. S. R.

Dr. Livingston Farrand, president of Cornell University, returned from a trip to the West Indies on January 5.

Dr. George D. Strayer, of Teachers College, Columbia University, has been asked to conduct a survey of the public school system for the Board of Education of Yonkers, New York. The object of the survey is to effect economy and bring about improvements in the school system.

Leave of absence from Columbia University of Dr. Rexford G. Tugwell, assistant secretary of agriculture, has been extended. It is reported that the position of under secretary of agriculture will be created for Dr. Tugwell if the Congress approves of an appropriation of $10,000 for his salary.

Abbé Ernest Dimnet, of France, will be

visiting professor at the University of California and at Stanford University in the fall of 1934, lecturing on the Brontës.

AT the Boston meetings Professor Arthur H. Compton, of the University of Chicago, was elected president of the American Physical Society and Professor R. W. Wood, of the Johns Hopkins University, was elected vice-president; Professor A. B. Coble, of the University of Illinois, was elected president of the American Mathematical Society.

PROFESSOR GEORGE H. PARKER, director of the zoological laboratory of Harvard University, has been elected president of Sigma Xi. Dr. Edward Ellery, professor of chemistry and dean of the faculty of Union College, continues as secretary.

AT a meeting held in Washington, on December 28, Professor Elizabeth Hazelton Haight, chairman of the department of Latin at Vassar College, was elected president of the American Philological Association and chairman of the advisory council of the American School of Classical Studies in Rome.

THE decoration of Companion of Honor has been conferred in the British New Year's List of Honors on Thomas Ethelbert Page, editor-in-chief of the Loeb Classical Library. The completion of the great Oxford English dictionary is recognized in the title of Commander of the British Empire, awarded to Dr. Charles Talbut Onions, joint editor of the dictionary since 1913 and chief author of the supplementary volume issued this year.

MARGARET T. CORWIN, executive secretary of the Yale University Graduate School, has been appointed dean of the New Jersey College for Women. She succeeds the late Mrs. Mabel Smith Douglass, who was drowned in Lake Placid in September.

DR. HERMON L. SLOBIN, head of the department of mathematics at the University of New Hampshire, has been appointed acting director of the summer school for 1934.

PROFESSOR LEWIS FREEMAN MOTT will retire at the end of this term as chairman of the English department of City College, New York, after fifty years' service, thirty-six of which were spent as chairman of the department. He is the senior member of the faculty.

MARVIN T. HERRICK, associate professor of English at the University of Pittsburgh, has been appointed acting associate professor in the department of English of Princeton University. Professor Herrick will replace temporarily Associate Professor Robert R. Cawley, who has received leave of absence for the second academic term.

DR. JOHN S. ROBERTS, district superintendent and executive assistant to the retiring superintendent, Dr. William J. O'Shea, and Stephen Fielding Bayne, district superintendent, have been elected for six-year terms associate superintendents of the New York City schools. They succeed Charles W. Lyon, retired, and Dr. Eugene A. Colligan, who resigned to become president of Hunter College. The election of a successor to Dr. Harold G. Campbell as deputy superintendent was deferred.

R. H. LATHAM has been elected superintendent of schools at Asheville, North Carolina, to succeed W. L. Brooker.

WILLIAM P. KELLY, head master of Rutgers Preparatory School since 1911, has resigned because of poor health. Mr. Kelly will withdraw from active management of the school at the close of the first semester, on February 1, but will be on leave of absence until the end of the academic year, in June. For the present Professor William A. Cook, assistant head master, will be acting head master.

THE Harvard Corporation has granted to Edward H. Chamberlin, assistant professor of economics, leave of absence for the second half of the academic year, in order that he may serve with the Committee on Government Statistics and Information Services in Washington. This bureau was set up by the Social Science Research Council and the American Statistical Association, and acts in a general advisory capacity to various government bureaus and departments.

LEAVE of absence for the balance of the present college year has been granted to William I. Nichols, director of the Harvard University News Office. During this period, Mr. Nichols will assist Mayor Richard M. Russell in the preparation of a development survey of Cambridge and other matters.

DR. HARRY F. WARD, executive secretary of the Methodist Federation for Social Service and professor of social ethics at the Union Theological Seminary, recently gave the first of the fireside lectures, sponsored by the Foundation for the Advancement of the Social Sciences of the University of Denver. His subject was "The New Deal and the Five-Year Plan: A Comparison." Dr. Ward has lately returned from a two-year sojourn in Russia, during which he made a study of the social and economic experiment of that country.

SIR DONALD MACALISTER, principal of the University of Glasgow from 1907 until his retirement in 1929 when he was made chancellor, died on January 14 at the age of seventy-nine years. Sir Donald was a distinguished physician and prominent member of congresses of the universities of the empire.

THE University of Michigan is the recipient of a portrait of the late Alice Freeman Palmer, of the class of 1876. The portrait is an oil likeness and comes to the university from the estate of Professor George H. Palmer, of Harvard University, who died last spring. Dr. Alice Freeman Palmer became the first dean of women at the University of Chicago and later was president of Wellesley College.

A GIFT to Amherst College of the mathematical library owned by the late Dr. George E. Olds, president of Amherst from 1923 to 1926, has been presented by Mrs. George E. Olds. Consisting of the many mathematical and scientific papers and books, the library will be housed in a room of Walker Hall, formerly the quarters of Dr. Olds, and will be under the care of Professor Thomas C. Esty, vice-president of Amherst. Professor Esty holds the Walker professorship of mathematics formerly held by Dr. Olds. This room will be equipped and furnished by the class of 1895, of which Dr. Olds was an honorary member.

THE Progressive Education Association will hold a Regional Conference at Temple University, Broad and Montgomery Avenues, Philadelphia, on February 9 and 10. The theme of the conference will be "Developing Social Responsibility through the Schools." The speakers will include Dr. Eduard C. Lindeman, New York School of Social Work, Dr. Lois H. Meek, Dr. Jean Betzner, Dr. Thomas Briggs, Dr. John Childs, all of Teachers College, Columbia University; Dr. Forrest E. Long and Dr. Robert K. Spear, of New York University; Dr. Vivian Thayer, director Ethical Culture Schools; Dr. Harold E. B. Speight, Swarthmore College; Dr. Armand J. Gerson, associate superintendent, Philip A. Boyer, director of educational research and William H. Welsh, director of school extension, all of the Philadelphia Public Schools.

ON January 10, a conference of the Supervising Principals of Bucks, Montgomery, Chester and Delaware Counties (southeastern Pennsylvania) was organized at the University of Pennsylvania. This is a voluntary organization the purpose of which is to facilitate an exchange of experiences in order that each supervising principal may attack his problems with an enriched background. Through it an attempt is also to be made to give more concerted cooperation in the solution of the pressing educational problems of the state. Of the seventy-five supervising principals invited to attend, forty-five were present. The problems presented, the experiences related and the ensuing discussion indicated the values of the conference. The conference was called by Dr. James C. Miller, Dr. LeRoy A. King and Dr. Theodore L. Reller, of the Division of Educational Administration of the School of Education, University of Pennsylvania. While they will continue to assist in the work in every way possible, it is an independent, voluntary conference of supervising principals.

FOR the third time Yale has received the Medal of the Alumni Association of the Graduates in Architecture of the Ecole des Beaux Arts in Paris. Dean Everett V. Meeks and several other members of the faculty of the School of the Fine Arts are members of this organization. The medal was presented by Frank C. Farley, president of the American group of the society, and received for the university by President James Rowland Angell, who delivered it to Dean Meeks, who made a brief address of acceptance.

THE University of Arkansas has recently been

granted by the Federal Public Works Administration a loan of $1,665,000, including a grant of 30 per cent. of the cost of labor and materials. Out of this fund $1,165,000 will be used to erect a library building and a chemistry building at the main university at Fayetteville and the remaining $500,000 will be used to construct a building for the Medical School at Little Rock. Plans and specifications for all three of the buildings are ready and it is expected that construction will begin within the next two months.

CONSTRUCTION of a new arts building on the campus at Ball State Teachers College, Muncie, Indiana, was assured when official announcement of the federal grant of $95,000, about one third of the estimated cost of the building, was received. No further action can be taken until rules and regulations governing the grant have been sent to local officials from the Civil Works Administration. Art, music, English and allied departments will be housed in the new structure. Between 80 and 100 men will be employed for about a year on the construction of the new building. The tunnel which will furnish heat and power is now being constructed. A number of other CWA projects, employing about 100 men, are being carried out on the campus. In each project the college has furnished the materials and supervision, and the CWA the labor.

WASHINGTON COLLEGE, Chestertown, Maryland, has received a gift of $1,500 for the establishment of a memorial reading room and library of current literature and magazines in Reid Hall, the women's dormitory of the college. The gift has come from Mrs. Frank Madison Dick, of Cambridge, Maryland, librarian general of the Daughters of the American Revolution, and is in memory of Elihu Cullen Dick.

ABOUT three and three fourths acres of land has been presented to the board of regents of the University of Colorado, to be used as an athletic field for students and members of the faculty. The property, which adjoins the campus of the medical school and Colorado General Hospital, Denver, will be named in honor of the donor, Dr. Horace G. Wetherill, Monterey, Calif., who was professor of gynecology in the medical school for many years.

THE University of Montreal, which has been in financial difficulties for several years, is the recipient of a gift of $100,000 from P. V. Rougier, a Paris manufacturer. The sum is to be devoted chiefly to the medical laboratories of the university.

THE Association for the Aid of Crippled Children, New York City, will receive more than $10,000,000 from the estate of Milo Merrick Belding. Mr. Belding, who died on October 13, 1931, was former president of Belding Brothers and Co., silk manufacturers. The gift consists of a trust fund whose present value is $7,223,452, and the residuary amounting to $3,107,731. Mrs. Annie K. Belding will receive the income from these funds during her life, the institution to receive them upon her death, to constitute the Milo M. Belding Fund. The trust fund provides that in case a hospital association is organized at Belding, Mich., a town named for the testator's family, and sufficient land is obtained for the hospital, then the hospital is to receive $200,000 of the fund.

DISCUSSION

THE ADVENTURES OF ALICE THROUGH THE LOOKING CLASS

THE GRADUATE FORMULA

WHEN Alice awoke she looked about her uncertainly, for everything seemed blurred and unfamiliar. "I wonder where I am now," she said, half aloud.

"A very foolish question indeed," said a squeaky little voice behind her. She turned around quickly and beheld a little formula, dressed like a gnome and holding an adding machine under one arm.

"Who are you?" asked Alice, somewhat surprised at his sudden and also his peculiar appearance.

"I am Formula," he pouted.

"Oh, how do you do," said Alice, remembering her manners almost too late; for the little fellow was on the point of bursting into tears at not being derived at once. "May I ask which Formula you are?" she continued, as politely as possible. "I'm sure I have heard the name before."

"Graduate Formula," he answered, somewhat mollified, though he continued to dab at his eyes with a huge red pocket handkerchief.

"But I thought a graduate . . ." began Alice.

"You thought nothing of the sort," he snorted, suddenly getting very angry. "If you don't know any better than that, you must come to my school and see for yourself." He seized her hand and pulled her along at a rapid rate.

"I never saw a Formula that went like this," panted poor Alice to herself. And then, all of a sudden, they were in the midst of an open grove surrounded by pillars.

"The graduate school," her new guide announced.

"But where is the graduate?" asked Alice, as soon as she had got her breath.

"And where is the post?" her guide was saying to himself. "The post, the post." He seemed somewhat bewildered. "It was right here this morning," and he looked hopelessly into a little hole in the ground.

"That must have been the *Morning Post*," said Alice, trying to help him, "and there won't be another edition until evening."

"Then we'll have to wait," he replied. "Meanwhile—meanwhile . . ." and his voice fell away hopelessly into a little quaver, while he absent-mindedly dug his toe into the post-hole.

"Meanwhile," said Alice, "what is the difference between a graduate and a post-graduate?"

"I don't like conundrums," the Formula answered, "and, besides, there isn't any."

After a long silence, Alice began again: "Do you work very long hours?"

"I don't really work very well," said the Formula, "but I am employed quite regularly," he added with a touch of pride. "And that is something, these days."

"It is nice to be employed, even if you don't work," agreed Alice. "Who employs you?"

"The Literary College and the Education School, and I think there are some others," he said, pensively. "You see, I am really quite simple; I don't remember exactly. It is something like this: To be a Graduate you have to have so many points."

"Good points, or bad points?" Alice asked.

"It doesn't make any difference so long as they are honor points," answered the Formula. "The exchange is different in different places, however; they have the double standard. Take the Education School. There, the points aren't so good, so you have to have 25 per cent. more."

"More than what?" asked Alice.

"Hours, of course," answered the Formula.

"I didn't think anybody *had* hours," said Alice. "I thought they spent them."

"They do," replied the Formula, "and the more you spend, the more you have."

"How nice!" exclaimed Alice excitedly, clapping her hands. "Could I have some like that to take home?"

"That's all they are good for," replied the Formula, "but you have to spend them to earn them. Come along with me, and I'll show you how it's done."

He led her behind some of the pillars, where a man with whiskers was mumbling queer words to some people who were looking at him—at least some of them were, and writing in little note-books, though some in the back rows were sound asleep. "The Looking Class," whispered the Formula. "They are spending their hours looking at him. That's what they are there for."

"Are they getting any points?" asked Alice, for the man with the whiskers seemed to be making one at the moment.

"Some will," said the Formula. "It all depends on the alphabet. For you see the alphabet really is important. If you get an A, you get three points; if you get a B, you get two points, and so on. That is why they call it the Literary College: you have to make your letters."

"Do they make them here?" Alice asked.

"Oh, no," said the Formula. "They only get their hours here. Come this way and I'll show you how they make their letters."

They walked along through the grove until they came to an office. Inside, a young man with a large letter on his sweater was saying that if he didn't get his B, he couldn't play on the team. The other man, who looked like a Reader, and who sat behind a desk, yelled back at him, "*Your* B! How long since it was yours!"

"I deserve it," said the Sweater. "On the examination, you asked for ten advantages of a cultural education, and I gave them."

"They were not the reasons given in the book," said the Reader.

"Well," countered the Sweater, "You asked for the seven cardinal sins of education, and I gave the seven that were in the book. I know, because I copied them out of it."

"You should display more originality and think up your own answers," said the Reader.

"It's a racket," shouted the Sweater.

"Certainly," said the Reader. "The sooner you dumb, muscle-bound athletes learn that college is no place for you, the better."

"I'm not muscle-bound," snarled the Sweater.

"I think the letter on his sweater is all he'll get, don't you?" whispered Alice.

"It looks bad," said the Formula. "Come, and I'll show you another way."

They wandered on through the grove until they came to another office, where a charming Co-ed was working for her letters and points.

"But I don't see why I should get a C," said the Co-ed, almost in tears. "We have been *such* good friends."

"Did my Reader give you a C?" asked the Instructor. "Well, I'll fix that. Let's see your paper. Well, well, it is pretty bad. There doesn't seem to be any punctuation in it, except the periods."

"Well, those are points, aren't they? And I've got to have my points."

"You have them, my dear," replied the Instructor.

"I think she'll be a Graduate," whispered Alice.

"Yes, I can't stop her," replied the Formula.

By this time it was evening, and the *Post* had arrived. "It says," said the Formula, hastily scanning the headlines, "that the standards of the Literary College are higher than they ever have been, and that the scholarship of the Co-eds is consistently higher than that of the men students."

"That doesn't mean the standards, does it?" Alice asked.

"Oh, no," replied her guide.

"I think a literary education must be wonderful," Alice sighed. "I should so like to be a Graduate."

W. T.

SPECIAL CORRESPONDENCE

SCHOOLS IN SMYRNA, AFTER TEN YEARS OF THE TURKISH REPUBLIC

October 29, 1933, marks the tenth anniversary of the proclamation of the Turkish Republic. Now, after a decade under the leadership of the new Turkish Republic régime of Mustafa Kemal Pasha, is an appropriate time to evaluate the educational progress. This article will deal with the Smyrna or Aegean area of Turkey, the fertile western quarter of the country. Smyrna, the chief export city of Anatolia, is the political and commercial center of the area and very naturally the educational center.

When the Republic was first proclaimed ten years ago, the immediate problem was the rehabilitation of the damage caused by the retreating armies. Not only had part of Smyrna been burned, but also much of the fertile back country on which her prosperity depended had been devastated. Nevertheless, the department of education began at once a well-considered plan of school advance.

The first necessity was an adequate supply of teachers trained in modern methods. Two normal schools were soon enlarged and modernized, one for men and one for women. The poverty caused by years of war made it difficult to get enough students able to finance themselves, so the educational department undertook the student expenses, handling them much as do West Point and Annapolis. These normal schools have been enlarged so that they have supplied sufficient teachers to man the rapidly increasing number of schools.

The second problem was that of raising educational standards, especially in primary education. This was approached from three angles. The National Government brought in certain foreign experts. Dr. John Dewey came and made a comprehensive survey for the whole country. The Smyrna department of education engaged Professor Adolphe Ferriere, of the J.

J. Rousseau Institute of Geneva, and later Professor Pierre Bovet, also of Geneva. These men studied the actual situation and gave much practical advice for improving the quality of work, following Professor Ferriere's principle of "l'école active."

The next approach was compulsory summer school work for all teachers trained under the old régime of the Sultanate. These summer schools were guided by Hikmet Bey, head of the Boys' Normal School, and Mutafa Rahmi Bey, a graduate of the J. J. Rousseau Institute and a professor at the International College. These courses made available to old-time teachers the modern methods demanded by the department.

Finally, Hikmet Bey and Rahmi Bey edited an educational magazine, *Fikirler,* which is the Turkish representative in the international progressive education movement. This was sent to all teachers in the Aegean area. A comprehensive series of pamphlets on teaching methods have also been produced under Rahmi Bey's direction and sent out. Fuat Bey, formerly director of education for the Aegean area, stood solidly behind these new advances, and much of the improvement is due to his vision. The classes in primary education to-day are unified, all courses being built into a common classroom experience, with a single work-book for all class work.

When the devastated areas were rebuilt and the quality of teaching greatly improved, the time came for material expansion. The Smyrna governor, Kazim Pasha, aided by Nailly Bey, superintendent of schools, outlined a plan to cover every village in the area and adequately to staff the urban centers.

This program of mass production got the hearty support of the general population, and in 1928 a great program of building was put into effect. This was greater than the statistics quoted below would indicate, for as new buildings went up many old type buildings were abandoned.

The following figures speak for themselves: Night schools have taught 56,600 adults to read and write during the past five years.

PRIMARY SCHOOL STATISTICS, PROVINCE OF SMYRNA

	1923	1933
School buildings	191	466
Teachers	530	800
Students	15,100	33,798

In Turkey as a whole primary students have increased from 313,000 in 1923 to 538,000 in 1933.

Further, secondary schools and lycées have been built in all important centers to handle the graduates of the primary schools. Commercial, industrial and agricultural schools have been developed. More educational progress has been made in the ten years of the Republic in Smyrna than in the preceding hundred years under the Sultans.

All this has been done at a time when war losses and economic depression make expansion of any enterprise difficult. Further, it has been done when school budgets are under attack, even in America.

This movement is an answer to those who ask if the Turkish revolution is engineered wholly from the top. The Smyrna educational progress had of course the active sympathy and support of the officials in Ankara, but it is actually the result of local Smyrna leadership and the popular demand for schools. It is another illustration that the Turkish revolution is rooted in the popular desire for the benefits of modern life.

Smyrna, ten years after, has a record of educational progress, both quantitative and qualitative, which is probably more striking than that of any other area during the same period.

LEE VROOMAN

INTERNATIONAL COLLEGE
SMYRNA, TURKEY

QUOTATIONS

PROFESSOR THORNDIKE'S NEW HONOR

FOR the first time in many years the Association for the Advancement of Science has chosen as its president a man who is widely known as a teacher and a teacher of teachers—Professor Edward L. Thorndike. He has had an important part in developing Teachers College in Columbia University. But first and last he is a scientist, and his psychological studies have resulted in the establishment of a truth that is a major contribution to human advancement. He has demonstrated the continuing ability of the mind to learn even into old age. The chief reason why adults seldom learn a new language or a new trade, he contends, is not the lack of ability but the lack of opportunity or desire. Faculties are kept, provided the interest and application continue. This is not a mere generalization based upon a few experiences or observations, such as Cicero made in his "De Senectute," but a conclusion reached after innumerable experiments made with the greatest scientific precision. Moreover, this continuing ability was found to exist not only in those of high intellectual pursuits but also in those in ordinary walks of life—a Promethean gift to mankind that enables it to extend its empire over the realm of the mind without fixed bounds.

He also discovered certain laws of learning, beginning with his researches in the field of animal intelligence, and devised methods of measuring mental altitudes. So has he been and will be helpful to many in finding what the destinies of their aptitudes are—their prescriptions at birth, especially. He also offers the comforting philosophy that the work of education is "to make desirable activities pleasurable and to inhibit their opposites by discomfort." There is, however, another law which is not so pleasing—that improvement in any single mental function rarely brings about equal improvement in any other function. Each has to depend largely upon itself for its development and highest exercise.

All who come near Dr. Thorndike, it is said, are made the subjects of his researches. Their I.Q.'s are consciously or unconsciously registered. But they must all be improved by the hopeful spirit which his own doctrines of adult improvement evoke. William James' view, that outside their own business the ideas gained by men before they are 25 are practically the only ideas they will have in their lives, that "they can not get anything new," left the average man without hope of intellectual advance. The philosophy of Thorndike writes over the entrance even into middle life ("nel mezzo del cammin di nostra vita") "recover hope all ye who enter here." It is encouraging to all and especially to those beyond the days of youth that one with such a gospel should lead on at the head of the scientists.—*The New York Times.*

MESSAGE OF SUPERINTENDENT-ELECT CAMPBELL

May I take this opportunity to extend a word of thanks to the many teachers and other members of the educational staff from whom I received congratulatory messages? These expressions of confidence have made me very happy, particularly because I am aware that whatever measure of success I may have in the office to which I have been elected will depend upon the wholehearted cooperation of the teaching and supervisory staff.

It shall be my aim, with the help of all the teachers and other educational employees, to seek, as Dr. O'Shea has sought, to make the New York city school system the very best school system in the world and to offer every child as an individual the fullest opportunity for development and growth.

It is my view that the schools are a social as well as an educational agency, and it should be our purpose in harmony with the purpose of the government itself to make possible for every child "a more abundant life."

The problems before us are numerous, and we are confident that in their solution we shall continue to have the helpful cooperation of the State Legislature, the State Department of Education and of the Board of Estimate.

I note that the Mayor has already spoken of the desirability for cooperation. It will give me the greatest of pleasure to cooperate with the Mayor and with all others interested in the welfare of the children of the city of New York. The records will show, and the State Commissioner of Education will confirm the fact, that he has always had the fullest possible cooperation from me.

Without attempting to list our problems in the order of their importance, it may be said that most pressing among them are the resumption of the building program, the necessity for increased state aid to education, the extension of opportunities for vocational education and the provision of more special courses and special classes to meet the varying needs and abilities of the children.

The enormous growth of registration in our

secondary schools has brought about a problem of first magnitude, and special provision must be made both for those who wish to take the traditional school courses and for those who seek special training.

It has been and will continue to be our aim to individualize instruction to make the schools an agency for broader service, caring for the health and the well-being of each child in addition to his educational needs, and assisting him in the solution of all his personal problems, whether social, economic or educational.—*Dr. Harold G. Campbell, superintendent-elect of the New York City Schools, in the New York Sun.*

THE NATIONAL EDUCATION ASSOCIATION

THE SIXTY-FOURTH CONVENTION OF THE DEPARTMENT OF SUPERINTENDENCE

THE sixty-fourth Annual Convention of the Department of Superintendence will meet at Cleveland, Ohio, from February 24 to March 1.

The tentative program of the general sessions follows:

SATURDAY, FEBRUARY 24

Registration all day. Exhibits open at 12:00 noon

SUNDAY, FEBRUARY 25, 4:00 P. M.

Vesper Service

Presiding, Paul C. Stetson, superintendent of schools, Indianapolis, and president, Department of Superintendence.

Invocation, Reverend Harold C. Phillips, First Baptist Church, Cleveland.

Welcome to Cleveland, Charles H. Lake, superintendent of schools, Cleveland.

Religion and Democracy, William Lowe Bryan, president, Indiana University.

MONDAY, FEBRUARY 26, 9:30 A.M.

Education for the New America

Presiding, Paul C. Stetson, president, Department of Superintendence.

Invocation, Reverend L. C. Wright, Epworth-Euclid Church, Cleveland.

The Contribution of Colleges of Education, William F. Russell, dean, Teachers College, Columbia University.

The New Leisure Challenges the Schools, John H. Finley, *New York Times.*

The Contribution of the Public Schools, Harold G. Campbell, superintendent-elect of schools, New York.

MONDAY, FEBRUARY 26, 2:00 P.M.

General Subject Committees

I. The Administration of Teacher Training.
II. A Comprehensive Program of Public Education.
III. Financing Public Education.
IV. Education for the New America.
V. Public Education and Public Welfare.
VI. A National Outlook on Education.
VII. Interpreting the Schools to the Public.

MONDAY, FEBRUARY 26, 6:30 P.M.

Dinner Meeting

Presiding, Paul C. Stetson, president, Department of Superintendence.

Music and Entertainment.

Economy, Wise and Otherwise, in Municipal Government, Charles E. Merriam, University of Chicago.

TUESDAY, FEBRUARY 27, 9:30 A.M.

Some National Problems in Education

Presiding, Paul C. Stetson, president, Department of Superintendence.

Invocation, Reverend John R. Hagan, superintendent of Cleveland Catholic Schools.

Planned Teacher Production, Arthur B. Moehlman, School of Education, University of Michigan.

Interpreting the Schools to the Public, Merle Sidener, president, Sidener, VanRiper and Keeling, Advertising, Indianapolis.

The Case for the Public Schools, Wm. J. Shroder, president, Board of Education, Cincinnati.

Presentation of the Yearbook—Critical Problems in School Administration, Ben G Graham, superintendent of schools, Pittsburgh.

Report, Committee on Resolutions.

TUESDAY, FEBRUARY 27, 2:00 P.M.

General Subject Committees

I. The Administration of Teacher Training.
II. A Comprehensive Program of Public Education.
III. Financing Public Education.
IV. Education for the New America.
V. Public Education and Public Welfare.
VI. A National Outlook on Education.
VII. Interpreting the Schools to the Public.

TUESDAY, FEBRUARY 27, 8:30 P.M.

Presiding, Frank Cody, superintendent of schools, Detroit.

Progress and Problems in Negro Education, Robert R. Moton, president, Tuskegee Normal and Industrial Institute.

Education at the Crossroads, Payson Smith, state commissioner of education, Massachusetts.

WEDNESDAY, FEBRUARY 28, 9:30 A.M.

Public Education and National Welfare

Presiding, David E. Weglein, superintendent of schools, Baltimore, and second vice-president, Department of Superintendence.

Invocation, Rabbi Barnett R. Brickner, Euclid Avenue Temple, Cleveland.

Public Education and National Welfare, George F. Zook, United States commissioner of education, Washington, D. C.

Public Education and the Nation's Business, Edward A. Filene, merchant, Boston.

Our National Dividends from Public Education, E. C. Hartwell, superintendent of schools, Buffalo.

WEDNESDAY, FEBRUARY 28, 2:00 P.M.

A Comprehensive Program of Public Education

Presiding, Carroll R. Reed, superintendent of schools, Minneapolis.

The Elementary Schools, Frank G. Pickell, superintendent of schools, Montclair, New Jersey.

The Relationship between Secondary Education and Present Economic Trends, Howell Cheney, manufacturer, South Manchester, Connecticut.

The Secondary Schools, Thomas W. Gosling, superintendent of schools, Akron, Ohio.

Higher Education, James B. Edmonson, dean, School of Education, University of Michigan.

WEDNESDAY, FEBRUARY 28, 8:30 P.M.

Financing Public Education

Presiding, Jessie Gray, president, National Education Association.

The Cleveland Symphony Orchestra.

Financing Public Education—A Report of General Subject Committee III, Frank W. Ballou, *chairman,* and superintendent of schools, Washington, D. C.

THURSDAY, MARCH 1, 9:30 A.M.

Reports of General Subject Committees

Presiding, Paul C. Stetson, president, Department of Superintendence.

Invocation, Reverend Dan F. Bradley, Pilgrim Congregational Church, Cleveland.

Reports of Committee Chairmen:

The Administration of Teacher Training, Edward D. Roberts, superintendent of schools, Cincinnati.

A Comprehensive Program of Public Education, J. Stevens Kadesch, superintendent of schools, Medford, Massachusetts.

Education for the New America, Willard E. Givens, superintendent of schools, Oakland, Calif.

Public Education and Public Welfare, Leslie A. Butler, superintendent of schools, Grand Rapids, Michigan.

A National Outlook on Education, John K. Norton, Teachers College, Columbia University.

Interpreting the Schools to the Public, Frank A. Jensen, superintendent of schools, Rockford, Illinois.

REPORTS

PROGRAM PROPOSED BY THE FEDERAL ADVISORY COMMITTEE ON EMERGENCY AID IN EDUCATION

(1) THE emergency problem of keeping elementary and secondary schools open on as nearly normal a basis as possible during the school year 1933–34 should be met by a federal appropriation of $50,000,000 to be allocated according to emergency needs in the several states. This sum may be provided in one of two ways: (a) By a special provision in the relief act, or less preferably (b) by a separate federal appropriation. In either case such appropriation shall be administered preferably by a board of which the U. S. Commissioner of Education shall be chairman and executive officer.

(2) In view of the fact that the inability of many communities adequately to maintain schools is certain to continue during the fiscal year 1934–35 a federal emergency appropriation or allocation of not less than $100,000,000 should be made available beginning July 1, 1934; this appropriation or allocation to be distributed in an objective manner, determined by a board of which the U. S. Commissioner of Education shall be chairman and executive officer, and based upon reasonable evidence of needs and resources.

(3) That the instability of educational support even in the abler states and communities, due to the shrinkage of local ability to support schools during the depression, constitutes an aspect of the present emergency of such proportion as to endanger the effectiveness of the schools throughout the nation. The fundamental relief which is necessary in order that public educational institutions may be adequately supported can be secured only through the adoption of measures for the federal emergency aid to education during 1934–35. The situation is so critical in education that the people are justified in using federal funds to insure the normal operation of schools. Accordingly, it is recommended that a substantial sum be distributed from the federal treasury to the various states to assist them in meeting this phase of the emergency.

It is the sense of this conference that the method of distribution should provide first, that a flat sum objectively determined be distributed to all states; second, that a supplemental sum objectively determined but weighted to meet the needs of the poorer states be included in the distribution, and third, that the method of distribution be stated in the statutes, provided that a contingent fund not to exceed ten per cent. of the amount so provided for 1934–35 be reserved for distribution to states and local units to meet exceptional and unforeseen needs under the direction of a board of which the U. S. Commissioner of Education shall be chairman.

(4) Local funds should be released for school maintenance by:

(a) Refinancing school district indebtedness or such municipal or county indebtedness as may have been incurred in behalf of the schools.

(b) Providing federal loans to school districts or to municipal or county corporations, where (in the case of the latter) the loan is to be used for educational purposes; *provided* that in both instances the loan shall rest on the security of delinquent taxes, frozen assets in closed banks, or other acceptable securities.

(5) Out of any new appropriations made for public works not less than 10 per cent. should be allocated for buildings for schools, colleges and other educational enterprises. Such grants shall be available provided that an approved survey has been made, and that the survey shows the need for the buildings. In cases where such surveys have not already been made these surveys shall be made under the direction of the Office of Education through a decentralized regional organization. The cost of these surveys shall be charged to the public works appropriation for school plants. We recommend that the grants for such projects be made on a 100 per cent. basis. In administering this fund major attention should be given to the needs of the rural schools.

(6) A federal appropriation or allocation of $30,000,000 should be provided to assist students to attend institutions of higher education for the period ending July 1, 1935, by (a) special provision in existing acts, or (b) by a separate federal appropriation.

This fund should be administered by the U. S. Office of Education.

EDUCATIONAL RESEARCH AND STATISTICS

DIFFERENTIAL PREDICTION OF SCHOLASTIC SUCCESS

FOR some time now general scholastic ability and ability in different subjects on the secondary level have been predicted through general ability tests, prognostic tests and tests of interests and various achievements. The efficiency of these measurements for purposes of guidance is determined by noting the relationship between these test results and later success as measured by high-school or college marks or achievement test scores in different subjects. This relationship is pictured best, probably, by the correlation coefficient. Knowing the predictive correlation coefficient for a certain test or combination of tests, the limits of the prediction for an individual student's success can be obtained. This probability is shown by the measurements known as the Standard Error or the Probable Error. We are able by these measures to say, within limits, for instance, for a certain group of students by using the American Council Test and a placement test with entering college students, what the average mark of a given pupil is likely to be. The predicted mark may be a B or 2 ± .3. The ± .3 is the Probable Error and indicates in the group concerned, or similarly situated groups, the chances of a measure falling within .3, .6, .9 or within any other number of points of the predicted mark. The worth of the advice to the students and the regulations made by the institution will be limited by the possibilities expressed by these Probable Errors. This kind of prediction is very important, because through it the limits of possibility for general scholastic success or success in any particular subject may be ascertained.

There has been a growing need during the last few years for a measurement which will predict the chance of success in one college subject or curriculum as against another. This need has been growing during the last decade because of the great number of students who are asking for training in our colleges and universities. Since students are entering colleges in such large numbers an important question is: In what subject or curriculum will the student do best? The satisfaction of this need is consistent with our educational philosophy of to-day which recognizes our responsibility for creating the opportunity for all students to develop to the limits of their ability.

To answer this need for more accurate guidance data in educational measurements the method of differential prediction was developed. New formulas for measuring the accuracy of this new kind of prediction were developed[1] and at the same time an application of the method was made to show how it would operate on the college level. The method of differential prediction, like direct prediction which has been described very briefly, uses tests of various sorts. However, since the object is to differentiate, as, for instance, between success in engineering against that of social studies the search is not toward general tests, such as general intelligence tests, but tests of aptitudes, interests, etc. Investigation of the use of such a general instrument as the American Council on Education shows, however, that its parts do have some differentiating power.[2] The total score on this test is used as a factor in this study because it was available.

Some tests will be found to be of greater value than others for purposes of differential prediction. The more independent the tests the more valuable they will probably be. In the original study,[3] using this method on the college level, the Cowdery Vocational Interest Blank, which is the forerunner of the Strong Interest Blank, was found to be of value. This study investigates the value of the different interest scores made on the Strong Interest Blank[4] and the scores on the different parts of the Iowa High School Content Examination[5] for the differential prediction of success in college subject groups. The Strong Vocational Interest Blank is now used by college personnel departments for purposes of vocational guidance, and the Iowa High School Content Examination is being used by high schools in aiding to determine the achievement of their high-school students and by colleges for purposes of guidance in college. Any values found for purposes of differential prediction are therefore of particular practical importance.

The data were obtained from the records of 100 junior college boys who had filled out the Strong Questionnaires and taken the Iowa Test at the time of entrance to junior college and who had finished one year's work. The marks made by the boys in each of four colleges subject fields were averaged. These average marks are used as our criterion marks. The total score on the American Council on Education Psychological Examination was also available for each student.

From a preliminary analysis of the data and from a consideration of Strong's recommendations[6] regarding the most independent of the

[1] David Segel, "Differential Prediction of Ability as Represented by College Subject Groups." *Jour. Educ. Research*, xxv: 1 and 2 (January and February, 1932).

[2] David Segel and J. R. Gerberich, "The Value of the American Council Psychological Examination for the Differential Prediction of Achievement." To be published in the *Journal of Applied Psychology*."

[3] D. Segel, *ibid.*

[4] Published by the Stanford University Press, Stanford University, California.

[5] Published by the Bureau of Educational Research and Service, Extension Division, State University of Iowa, Iowa City, Iowa.

[6] Manual of Directions for the Vocational Interest Blank, Stanford University Press.

interest scores, the vocational scores used were reduced to six. These were engineering, medicine, law, life insurance, personnel management and purchasing agent. The factors which were used in the investigation were as follows:

1. Score on the American Council on Education Psychological Examination (1931 Edition).
2. Score on English Literature (Iowa H. S. Content Examination).
3. Score on Mathematics (Iowa H. S. Content Examination).
4. Score on Science (Iowa H. S. Content Examination).
5. Score on History and Social Science (Iowa H. S. Content Examination).
6. Engineering Interest Score (Strong Blank).
7. Medicine Interest Score (Strong Blank).
8. Law Interest Score (Strong Blank).
9. Life Insurance Interest Score (Strong Blank).
10. Personnel Management Interest Score (Strong Blank).
11. Purchasing Agent.

The intercorrelation coefficients between these factors are given in Table I. The zero order correlation coefficients between the factors and differences between marks in certain college subject groups are given in Table II. The differential correlation coefficients for this table and for the study were all obtained by the use of the formula

$$r_{(a-b)x} = \frac{r_{ax}\,\sigma_a - r_{bx}\,\sigma_b}{\sqrt{\sigma_a^2 + \sigma_{b-2}^2\, r_{ab}\,\sigma_a\,\sigma_b}} \quad [7]$$

since the direct correlations had been calculated for a study of direct prediction. The coefficients using this formula come out in favor of the first subject over the second. In English-Languages the +.23 means that better scores on the American Council Test are indicative of a prediction of better English marks than Language marks. Similarly, the +.36 means that the better scores on the English Literature part of the Iowa test are indicative of prediction of better English marks than Language marks. If the coefficient has a minus sign such as the −.16 of the Strong interest score in Life Insurance, it means that the prediction is for better marks in languages than in English. The meaning of these signs for subject pairs is uniform throughout this study.

This table (II) bears close examination. The results with the American Council Test gives a differential meaning to its scores in favor of English (English-Languages, +.23; English-Mathematics and Science, +.14) and History (Languages-History, −.30; Mathematics and

[7] J. Murray Lee and David Segel, "The Utilization of Data for Simple or Direct Prediction in the Development of Differential Prediction Regression Equations," *Jour. Educ. Psychol.*, xxiv: 7, pp. 550–54, October, 1933.

TABLE I

INTERCORRELATIONS BETWEEN THE SCORES ON THE AMERICAN COUNCIL TEST, THE STRONG VOCATIONAL INTEREST SCORES, AND THE SCORES ON THE PARTS OF THE IOWA HIGH-SCHOOL CONTENT EXAMINATION (100 CASES)

	1 American Council	2 Iowa English Literature	3 Iowa Mathematics	4 Iowa Science	5 Iowa History and Social Science	6 Strong Engineering	7 Strong Medicine	8 Strong Law	9 Strong Life Insurance	10 Strong Personnel Management	11 Strong Purchasing Agent
2	+.62										
3	+.57	+.42									
4	+.64	+.53	+.64								
5	+.59	+.70	+.39	+.48							
6	+.10	−.10	+.49	+.36	−.16						
7	−.02	−.11	+.28	+.29	−.05	+.62					
8	.00	+.09	−.03	−.01	+.09	−.06	+.35				
9	−.12	−.04	−.27	−.29	+.08	−.46	−.31	+.20			
10	−.08	+.10	−.15	−.17	+.04	−.32	−.46	−.18	+.06		
11	−.32	−.43	+.04	−.26	−.26	+.16	−.18	−.21	+.08	+.10	

TABLE II

ZERO ORDER CORRELATION COEFFICIENTS BETWEEN THE SCORES ON VARIOUS PREDICTION FACTORS AND DIFFERENCES BETWEEN MARKS IN CERTAIN COLLEGE SUBJECT GROUPS (DIFFERENTIAL PREDICTION CORRELATION COEFFICIENTS)

Differences in marks between	1 American Council	2 Iowa English Literature	3 Iowa Mathematics	4 Iowa Science	5 Iowa History and Social Science	6 Strong Engineering	7 Strong Medicine	8 Strong Law	9 Strong Life Insurance	10 Strong Personnel Management	11 Strong Purchasing Agent
English-Languages (62 cases)	+.23	+.36	+.12	+.14	+.21	−0.1	−0.7	+.04	−.16	−.07	−.08
Languages-Mathematics and Science (68 cases)	−.09	−.27	−.37	−.26	−.09	−.23	−.07	+.22	+.23	−.06	−.12
Language-History (41 cases)	−.30	−.36	+.02	+.07	−.26	+.38	+.12	+.10	+.06	−.34	+.03
English-Mathematics and Science (66 cases)	+.14	+.09	−.25	−.12	+.12	−.24	−.14	+.26	+.07	−.13	−.20
English-History (42 cases)	−.07	.00	+.14	+.21	−.05	+.37	+.05	+.14	−.10	−.05	−.41
Mathematics and Science-History (44 cases)	−.21	−.09	+.39	+.33	−.17	+.61	+.18	−.12	−.17	−.28	+.15

Science-History) as opposed to Languages and Mathematics and Science but does not show a differential as between English and History (English-History −.07).

The English Literature test results give a differential in favor of English over Languages (+.36); Mathematics and Science over Languages (−.27); and History over Languages (−.36). Iowa Mathematics gives a differential prediction particularly well as between mathematics and science marks as opposed to Languages, English and History (−.37, −.25, +.39). Similarly, each of these tests may be analyzed to discover its particular value in predicting differential success. The Probable Errors for these coefficients are substantial, so that the smaller coefficients can not be considered too seriously. We have in the main considered coefficients of .20 and above as indicating a relationship.

Although many of these coefficients may be of sufficient size to be taken into account in theoretical discussions, each of them (with one possible exception) may be considered to have little value as an individual correlation coefficient to be used for purposes of guidance. However, an inspection of the intercorrelations given in Table I revealed the fact that many of the intercorrelations were low. Therefore, it seemed possible that combinations of the proper factors might result in giving relationships of value to guidance.

An examination of Table II indicates that the first criterion: English-Languages had very few correlation coefficients of any magnitude. This difference criterion was omitted from our further consideration. The other criteria seemed to have possibilities in this connection. The multiple correlation coefficients indicating the efficiency of predicting these five criteria were obtained using those factors in each case which had a significant relationship with the criterion. These results (given in Table III) show that these factors when combined do have important relationships to the criteria. It is to be remembered that these criteria consist of teachers' marks which in turn have been based on various marks and ratings, mostly subjective, made by the teacher on a scale of five points.

To discover more effectively the relation of the factors of academic achievement when the unreliability of marks would not be present we attacked the problem from another approach. As stated before, the Strong questionnaire was filled out and the Iowa test given at about the

TABLE III

MULTIPLE CORRELATION COEFFICIENTS FOR THE PREDICTION OF DIFFERENCES IN COLLEGE MARKS USING VARIOUS FACTORS

Criterion (differences in marks)	Factors	Multiple correlation coefficient
Languages-Mathematics and Science	1. Iowa English Literature 2. Iowa Mathematics 3. Iowa Science 6. Strong Engineering 8. Strong Law 9. Strong Life Insurance	.49
Languages-History	1. American Council 2. Iowa English Literature 5. Iowa History and Social Science 6. Strong Engineering 10. Strong Personnel Management	.58
English-Mathematics and Science	3. Iowa Mathematics 6 Strong Engineering 8. Strong Law 10. Strong Purchasing Agent	.40
English-History	4. Iowa Science 6. Strong Engineering 11. Strong Purchasing Agent	.48
Mathematics and Science-History	1. American Council 3. Iowa Mathematics 4. Iowa Science 6. Strong Engineering 10. Strong Purchasing Agent	.72

same time at the beginning of the college year. The different parts of the Iowa test correspond fairly well with the college subject groups which are chosen. The main difference being that the Iowa test has one part on science and one part on mathematics, whereas in other groups mathematics and science were considered as one group.

The relationship between measures taken at the same time can not be considered strictly as a predicting relationship. In this case it can be considered such only in so far as the relative relationship between achievements such as are measured by the parts of the Iowa test remain constant over a period of time. It is assumed here that the change over a one-year period would not be great. The only measures which can be used as factors for discovering the differences in achievement as represented by the parts of the Iowa test are the interest scores on the Strong blank. The American Council test was not considered of value in this case because of its uniform relationship with the various parts of the Iowa test.

In considering the relationship between interest scores and achievement scores we can not assume that the interest is the cause of the achievement or the achievement the cause of the interest. It is possible that there is mutual reaction between them, *i.e.,* that sometimes interest stimulates certain activities and at other times activities may stimulate interest, or it is possible that interest and achievement are but outward manifestations of an underlying mental activity. As a practical working instrument for guidance it is not necessary to know the nature of this relationship.

The difference between the English Literature and History and Social Science and between the Mathematics and Science parts of the Iowa test did not show any appreciable correlation with the Strong interest scores and were omitted from further consideration.

The zero order correlation coefficients, showing the relationships between the Strong interest scores and the difference between the scores on the parts of the Iowa test, are given in Table IV. The interest scores in law had little or no relationship with the Iowa scores and have therefore been omitted from this table. These differential correlation coefficients show that there is considerable differential power in these interest tests.

TABLE IV

ZERO ORDER CORRELATION COEFFICIENTS BETWEEN THE SCORES ON INTEREST AND THE PARTS OF THE IOWA HIGH-SCHOOL CONTENT EXAMINATION (DIFFERENTIAL PREDICTION CORRELATION COEFFICIENTS)

Criterion (Differences between Test Scores)	6 Strong Engineering	7 Strong Medicine	9 Strong Life Insurance	10 Strong Personnel Management	11 Strong Purchasing Agent
Iowa English Literature-Mathematics	−.55	−.36	+.22	+.23	−.44
Iowa English Literaature-Science	−.46	−.41	+.25	+.28	−.20
Iowa Mathematics-History and Social Science	+.57	+.29	−.31	−.17	+.28
Iowa Science-History and Social Science	+.53	+.34	−.37	−.21	....

The differential relationships given here show that these interest tests have more power to differentiate between these achievements than they do to show the achievements themselves. Using the relationship as a predictive one this means that these interest scores will predict differences between achievement in subjects better than they will predict absolute achievement in single subjects. Statistically, the reason for the difference of the results in differentiating ability and the direct relation with ability lies in the nature of correlations of these interest scores with the achievement as measured by the parts of the Iowa tests. As will be noted, some of these are positive and some negative. In finding the differential correlation coefficient the negative and a positive direct relationship coefficient are brought together and the effect is an additive one.

The multiple correlation coefficients resulting when the effect of all these factors are brought together in each case is given in Table V. These results show that there is a fairly high relationship existing between some of the Strong interest scores and achievement as measured by the parts of the Iowa test. These relationships are high enough to be considered as factors in the guidance of the student.

TABLE V

MULTIPLE CORRELATION COEFFICIENTS SHOWING THE RELATIONSHIP BETWEEN DIFFERENCES IN ACHIEVEMENT BETWEEN THE PARTS OF THE IOWA HIGH-SCHOOL CONTENT EXAMINATION AND THE SCORES ON THE STRONG VOCATIONAL INTEREST BLANK

Criterion (Differences between Test Scores)	Factors	Multiple Correlation Coefficient
Iowa English Literature-Mathematics	(6) Strong Engineering (7) Strong Medicine (9) Strong Life Insurance (10) Strong Personnel Management (11) Strong Purchasing Agent	.68
Iowa English Literature-Science	(As above)	.54
Iowa mathematics-History and Social Science	(As above)	.61
Iowa Science-History and Social Science	(As above, except No. 11)	.87

In this study we have shown the relationship existing between vocational interest scores and differences between marks in college subject groups and differences between achievement test results. These relationships have been found substantial. The study also shows that these differential relationships may be stronger than direct relationships. The use of this method gives added value to the results of tests which are now often given by high schools and colleges. The method is much more accurate than any now existing in giving information upon which a decision may be made regarding the relative possibilities of success in different scholastic subjects, curriculas or occupations.

DAVID SEGEL

U. S. OFFICE OF EDUCATION

SCHOOL AND SOCIETY

WITH WHICH ARE COMBINED THE EDUCATIONAL REVIEW, ESTABLISHED IN 1891, THE TEACHERS MAGAZINE, ESTABLISHED IN 1878, AND THE SCHOOL JOURNAL, ESTABLISHED IN 1874.

EDITED BY J. McKEEN CATTELL

Volume 39 | Saturday, January 27, 1934 | Number 996

HOW CAN THE COLLEGE PHYSICAL EDUCATION ASSOCIATION BEST SERVE EDUCATION?[1]

By President WILLIAM MATHER LEWIS

LAFAYETTE COLLEGE

DEPARTMENTS of physical education in colleges and universities have passed beyond the experimental or haphazard stage and are now, in many of the best institutions, well organized and scientifically conducted. The problem now is to get the proper coordination between the work in physical education and that in other departments. Such coordination must be based upon several conditions.

First, the purpose and policy of each college and university must be clearly defined and all members of the staff thoroughly acquainted with these aims. There is in most of our institutions the weakness of water-tight compartment departmental systems. The average student in chemistry is too often treated as if he were to be a professional chemist; the student in Latin as if he were to be a teacher of that subject; the student in the physical education department as if he were to be a professional athlete or a coach. In properly exalting his own department, the professor is apt unconsciously to overlook others and to neglect the essential problem of giving each student the best all-around cultural equipment that can be provided for him. It is an unusual institution which successfully emphasizes the unity of human knowledge. Much of departmental over-emphasis does not come from any narrowness among professors but from the lack of institutional policy. We know perfectly well what an automobile factory or a tin-plate mill or a cement works is supposed to produce but are somewhat put to it to describe just what we expect to turn out at this college or that university. The higher institutions of learning in England, France and Germany have found much less difficulty in defining their purpose in the world than have ours. First then let us challenge the institutions with which we are connected to give their excuse for living; to state how they answer the needs of the present social order.

Having the definition, the faculty of an institution should be persuaded to interpret it into action—first, by enthusiastic presentation of each individual branch of instruction, and, second, by a helpful attitude toward all other subjects in the curriculum. It seems clear that an effective way of improving the present deplorable situation in regard to the use of English by college students is to have every class in the institution to some degree a class in English; insisting on correctly spoken and written

[1] Address at the thirty-seventh annual meeting of the College Physical Education Association, Chicago, December 28, 1933.

expression, whether the class be one especially devoted to English or physics, civil engineering or what not. In like manner each class should have its interest in physical education—with requirements for proper posture in sitting and standing, together with proper ventilation, lighting and humidity of classrooms and laboratories. I can hear many remark when they read this suggestion—"Does this man think the dear old university is a kindergarten?" One has only to look at the stoop-shouldered, anemic, run-down graduates of our colleges to get the answer to this question. One has only to give casual attention to vital statistics to realize that the breakdowns coming with increasing frequency among our most highly educated class; that the emotional instability; that the mental disorders of this driven age are due to lack of balance between the mental and the physical. The speeded-up engine is shaking the frail machine to pieces. Much of this is due to the neglect of a sound physical education program by administrations and faculties; to an attitude that this is a matter not worthy of academic rating. Such a position demonstrates ignorance of the fact that much of the listlessness and lack of response among students may be traced to physical causes, such as faulty nutrition, lack of sleep and proper exercise. The fatigue element in classes meeting late in the day is not enough appreciated and dealt with. Many instructors teaching in institutions having evening classes mistake for attention the docility due to fatigue. Such situations are remedied where there is proper cooperation between departments.

Other departments have their contribution to make to the department of physical education. The department of chemistry should study the proper chlorination of swimming pools, should advise concerning the chemistry of foods and render other expert service; the biology department should make a distinct contribution in the fields of physiology and personal and social hygiene. The departments of psychology and physical education have much in common. Researches on specific items in the psychology of athletics have been initiated in the last few years. There is not much factual data at hand, but the work is progressing. Work may be done to find if there are any special aptitudes for athletics in general, or for special kinds of athletics analogous to a special talent for music or drawing. Through psychology may be determined the significant elements in staleness, esprit de corps, motivation. The two departments can together contribute much to student welfare in devising and applying proper tests of emotional stability. Along these and many other lines departmental cooperation will produce highly desirable results.

The public which supports our institutions, seeing the fine physical specimens upon the football teams and other athletic organizations, has the comfortable feeling that the men on the campus are young Adonises—just as over the lapse of centuries we feel that every Greek youth was a person of physical and mental perfection. Wilenski, in "The Meaning of Modern Sculpture," says, "There is a conspiracy to persuade us that the Athenians produced final perfection in sculpture and had clear heads and true tastes, because they lived in a city which was beautifully disposed, and clean and clear. But the propagandists know that Athens and its inhabitants were filthy, because the city was always short of water; that the streets were miserably unpaved lanes; that the majority of houses were mean; that there was no sanitation and that the 'sane and wholesome pagans' splodging through mud in unlighted streets at night thought themselves lucky if they did not receive a shower bath of household garbage on their heads." That frank description gives us something of a shock, and so likewise does any true statement relative to the gap between the best physical specimens in our colleges, the average and the subnormal. When the situation is made clear, when the academic implications of physical fitness are fully understood, faculties will be more willing to move over a little and give the department of physical education a seat in their councils.

And this brings us to the consideration of departmental organization. Naturally, but unfortunately, work in physical education and athletics grew up in most of our institutions as a thing apart. Many times this was due, not to the desire of those promoting the physical interests to have it so but because of hostility or lack of interest on the part of those having the curriculum in hand. That point has, however, been passed, and to-day we realize that there should be the same departmental organization in the physical as in all other departments. The work in physical education, athletics and health should be under one competent head with full professorial rank and with fine professional training, and associated with him should be various specialists, in so far as possible appointed upon a full-time basis, as in other departments.

It is not for me here to make detailed suggestions as to the essential work in these various branches of the physical education department. Certain random observations may not, however, be amiss. The college physician must have the authority and the facilities to make the catalogue statement that each student receives regular physical examinations a reality rather than a generality, and must make those examinations thorough and searching rather than hurried and superficial. Nothing is more essential in the proper coordination of physical education with the general work of the college than this. Vital facts never known before the boy entered college are constantly being discovered where searching examinations are given entering freshmen. Incipient tuberculosis, cancer, conditions of eyes and other abnormalities are located which indicate the necessity of withdrawal from college for immediate drastic action or continuing treatment and the proper assignment of work in the institutions. There are, for instance, an increasing number of students who have been crippled by infantile paralysis entering our colleges each year. The success of President Roosevelt in overcoming this handicap suggests the contribution which our colleges with their swimming pools and other modern equipment can give to society in making over these young people during their four years of college life. Careful examination for all those going into athletics of any kind, cultivation of the "infirmary habit," teaching students not to spread disease, but to report to the college physician as soon as they become indisposed; all these things are extremely important to the individual student and to the welfare of the college community. Ignorance and carelessness in regard to the individual's responsibility for health conditions in his community are still wide-spread even among well-educated people. We constantly have instances of students with colds, grippe, scarlet fever and other infectious and contagious ailments who spread illness through a whole fraternity house or dormitory. Effective physical education should eliminate this error and prepare students to be health leaders when they leave college.

We have all watched with interest and gratification the growth of intramural sports programs in many colleges. A note of warning, however, seems to be necessary if they are to be fully successful. With the growth of physical contact games such as campus football, junior varsity and 150 pound intercollegiate football, soccer, basketball and even touch football, the matter of injuries has assumed increasing importance. There have not always been the proper facilities in equipment; in first aid and in trainers that is essential. In other words, the organization of teams has outstripped the facilities to safeguard the players. No matter how informal the games, it becomes increasingly evident that before participation there must be reasonable conditioning processes and careful physical examinations. Failing in this the intramural policy defeats its own purpose.

Of intercollegiate athletics, particularly football, little need be said here because the matter is being so thoroughly covered in other meetings this week. However, one who from a college administrative post has followed this activity over a period of years observes many indications that this sport is being put on a better basis as time goes on. The coaches are more and more realizing their place in the general scheme of education. The ethics of sport are receiving more consideration on the gridiron; the slave-driving methods of preparation, which turn a game into a dreary grind, are less and less evident. More college coaches are constantly showing their ability in developing football players from the rank and file of the student body and not merely organizing and teaching new plays to star prep school players who are brought to them. Time was when we very frequently found better teachers of football among the secondary school coaches than among the college group. The former made players; the latter simply lined them up. This situation is being changed. On many teams we now find not a few men who never played before entering college, and they often play with a dash and fire lacking in those who played on preparatory school teams for years before entering college. Some day an expert on athletics will make a study of football playing efficiency, showing where the average player reaches his peak. In this connection my guess is that it will be shown that the average player does not keep developing in proficiency over a period of four years on a secondary school team, a year on a freshman team, and three years on the varsity—but that he often reaches his peak early in his college experience. Here the fatigue element as well as the routine may be found to be important factors.

Again it is to be noted that the best coaches are giving more and more intelligent attention to the welfare of the players on the field. It is rare to-day to see any high-grade, experienced coach push a player to the point of exhaustion, even if the winning of an important game depends upon it. This is a matter to be emphasized, because the athlete who works to the point of exhaustion in any sport pays the price immediately, or as the years go on.

In regard to the matter of subsidizing, which also is showing many evidences of improvement, Major John L. Griffith, president of the National Collegiate Athletic Association, was quoted recently as saying in "a statement of principles" to be put before the association, "in the interest of equal competition and with the idea of conserving ethical standards in athletics, that the colleges that are ethical in the administration of their athletics should schedule games only with institutions which observe the same high standards." This appears to be an intelligent stand in the matter. As a matter of fact, this policy is to some degree already in existence. It is not difficult in going over the schedules of all the colleges each fall to ascertain which have a high standing with sister institutions and those whose policy is questioned. When we find an institution whose schedule is made up of the highest rating institutions in its own part of the country—natural competitors, in other words—we may assume that consideration is given to maintaining or improving ethical standards. When such schedules are not the rule doubt naturally arises. We may here paraphrase a Scripture statement and say, "By their schedules ye shall know them."

In serving the general educational scheme of the institution the department of physical education should give due consideration to strengthening the moral as well as the physical fiber of the students. This may be done by sound teaching as to the results of temperate and intemperate living, in eating, drinking, habits of work and recreation and other activities. One great omission during the period of national prohibition was that of education in temperance. For many years preceding that period sharp attention had been paid to teaching youth the results of alcohol on the human system and the results of intemperance in the social order. When the 18th Amendment came into effect the educational and ethical elements connected with the use of alcoholic drinks were forgotten, and the entire question became a political football. It is the task of those connected with education, particularly physical education, now to stress effectively the educational side of the question. Let no one think that we solved the problem when we repealed the 18th Amendment. We merely changed the emphasis. In New York last week I saw more men and women on the streets and in the hotel lobbies under the influence of liquor in one evening than I had seen in a month during the last few years. This may be a passing phase; an inevitable step in the process of readjustment. Let us hope that it is and let us do our part through the agency provided us in education to build up that temperate attitude, that resistance and self-control without which no one can be truly successful in life.

Finally, this organization can serve education effectively by preparing college students properly and profitably to use their leisure time. With the regulations of the N. R. A. and the more permanent trends in the conduct of industry and business, it becomes evident that the great task before us is not so much to prepare people to work as it is for that use of leisure which will make for the abundant life. A great leader in national thought recently said, "Leisure should not be just time to play. It should be opportunity to realize hopes and ideals; the possibility of attaining real citizenship and true achievement." Usually when we speak of the duty of teachers of physical education in providing means for the proper use of leisure time, we have in mind training the student in the technique of carry-over sports, such as golf, tennis and swimming. Such a program is good, but it is not broad enough. There is much food for thought in that sentence, "Leisure should not be just time to play." From the opposite conception comes our attitude relative to "killing time," the "tired business man" and the rest. Out of leisure time properly spent have come the greatest achievements of civilization. As Henry Ford recently said, "To be out of hire is not necessarily to be out of employment." Some men who have been out of a job during the past three or four years have spent their enforced leisure time in hopeless inactivity; others have improved their minds; have devised means of useful employment; and in numerous instances have done creative work of a much higher and more remunerative type than could have been expected. Thus the great opportunity is not merely to teach people how to fill their leisure time with play. It is to build up in students that abounding physical and mental energy which shall give them the vigor to do creative, constructive things in their leisure time. Thus equipped, they will not be under the necessity of contributing, as do the unfit, altogether too much to hired entertainers or to find their only relaxation in play. The coming generation must be more resourceful, more alert, more fit than any which has preceded it. It must go out from the college halls with a spirit of high adventure and the strength to realize its dreams, if the new day for which we all so greatly yearn is to become a reality.

How can this organization best serve education? The answer is, I believe, first to inspire in its members a great desire to aid in defining the real purpose of the institutions with which they are connected; second, to stimulate a lofty desire to place physical education on a par with any activity in the college; third, to emphasize true sportsmanship, particularly in intercollegiate athletic relationships; fourth, to appreciate that the department should make a distinct contribution to the broad cultural equipment of every student in the institution; fifth, to aid in developing a sane program of individual living, in which self-control, physical fitness and normal reactions have a large part; in short, to furnish on the physical side every incentive and opportunity for an abundant life. In the great enterprise of furnishing sound, valuable recruits for the armies of progress, I am sure the departments of physical education in our colleges are to have an ever-increasing part.

ENRICHING THE LIFE EXPERIENCE OF EXCEPTIONAL CHILDREN*

By Professor PAUL A. WITTY
NORTHWESTERN UNIVERSITY

FOR education, our largest social enterprise, we have spent several billion dollars yearly. Recently, there has been a check upon all expenditures and a public demand for scrutiny of every phase of education has resulted. Some of our newer educational enterprises and innovations have been sharply criticized. Indeed, special education has been assailed as wasteful and inefficient. We have been accused of providing palaces for the subnormal and of indulging in extravagant excesses for the superior child. Let us examine briefly the facts concerning such polemics.

Examination of the nature and amount of special education reveals a paucity of provision for all deviates and an expenditure of public funds by no means in accord with the magnitude of the problem, nor in terms of the social benefits which can be obtained through special education.

For example, a conservative estimate shows that there are 300,000 crippled children in the United States. Special education appears essential for about one third of this number. Less than 15,000, however, are being provided for through the public schools. There are at least 50,000 children who need special education because of defective vision; 5,000 (10 per cent.) only are cared for in our 350 special classes; 348 of these classes are located in cities. The deaf are infrequently provided for in 64 residential and 114 public schools for the deaf.[1]

Two to 6 per cent. of the general population are decidedly restricted in potentiality for mental development. Nevertheless, only 15 states have enacted special laws to promote identification and care for this large group. A study for one state showed that less than 6 per cent. of the estimated number of feebleminded are being given any kind of special educational provision at public expense.

Scarcely a beginning has been made in

* Address given before the Division upon Special Education, National Education Association, Stevens Hotel, Chicago, July 3, 1933.

[1] *Cf.* in this connection: White House Conference Report on Child Health and Protection. ''Special Education: The Handicapped and the Gifted,'' Section III. The Century Company, New York, 1931.

efforts to essay special educational opportunities for the gifted. The term "gifted" has been used by L. S. Hollingworth to apply to those of I.Q. 130 plus; by H. Rugg to those above I.Q. 125; and by L. M. Terman to those of I.Q. 140 and above. The first classification refers to about 1 per cent. of public-school children; the second, to 3 per cent.; and the third to children estimated by one writer to be found once in every six hundred cases. "Gifted" has been interpreted more broadly by the Committee on Special Classes in the White House Conference Report, "Special Education: The Handicapped and the Gifted." Six per cent. of the school population, approximately 1,500,000 children, require, the workers think, special education to realize their potentialities.

Certainly our greatest natural resource appears to reside in these mentally gifted children. Nevertheless, only forty cities reported a total of 150 classes. Again, the glaring inadequacy of our provision for atypical children looms large. The story is similarly distressing for the remaining types of deviates.

The expenditures for all types are negligible in terms of our total educational budget; the uncompromising fact is that we have failed utterly to provide educational opportunity for these groups of children.[2] Of the special types, there is only one for whom one may question expenditure. This is for the delinquent group: it seems socially inappropriate and questionable to place the stigma of "social undesirability" upon children whom we wish to rehabilitate.

Available facts seem to point to the conclusion that *any child whose behavior is unsatisfactory should have thorough physical, mental, pedagogical and behavior examinations.* Particular needs, then, should be met by prudent expenditure of public funds. The school has four ways of proceeding: through child study departments; through adult and parental education; through mental hygiene instruction for teachers; and through modification in goals and in methods of instruction. In none of these has scientific progress been conspicuous; in each, progress is sufficient to make us hopeful. The public school is the great social enterprise and laboratory in which the potential delinquent may be identified and through which he can be rehabilitated.[3]

Through appropriate education, delinquency may be lessened without recourse to the devastating stigma of the special class. It seems essential, however, that special classes be formed for the other types of children.

The first need in dealing with all atypical children is early identification. Criteria for identification of the several types have been carefully set up by the White House Commission upon Special Education; and through these, and by prudent use of mental tests we can identify early and reliably those children for whom special education seems imperative.

There is one group, the needs of which are exceedingly important, at a time when leadership is so conspicuously needed. This is our group of gifted children. Educational workers and psychologists have sharply criticized our school leaders for their failure to recognize superior children and for their dilatoriness in providing educational reform.

2 Of course, number provided for is only a partial measure of adequacy. The inadequacy of provision is clearly revealed also in the type of work provided and in the money spent. For detailed data, see White House Conference Report on "The Handicapped and the Gifted"; and Witty and Beaman, "Practices in Special Classes," *Educational Trends,* Vol. I, No. 1, January, 1932.

3 *Cf.* in this connection: White House Conference Report on "The Delinquent Child," The Century Company, New York, 1932; and "Crime Prevention through Education," *Research Bulletin of the National Education Association,* Vol. x, No. 4.

How can we best provide for variation in the physical and in the social maturity of the gifted? Some have urged that acceleration be adopted as a general school practise in dealing with the gifted.

After recognizing and considering the difficulties in obtaining valid indexes for selecting gifted children, and after thinking carefully regarding the difficulties in modifying curricula, Freeman defends acceleration as a general educational policy.

> Acceleration actually provides enrichment. The work of the advanced grades is intellectually superior because the method which is pursued and the content are superior to those of the lower grades. From the point of view of the intellectual adjustment, then acceleration accomplishes both the saving of time and the enrichment of the instruction. The difficulties with this mode of adjustment are not of an intellectual nature but of a social nature. These difficulties may be met by proper forms of organization and they are being progressively diminished by the very increase in the frequency of acceleration itself.[4]

This recommendation favoring widespread use of pedagogical acceleration is now made after careful consideration has been given to the claims for the value of homogeneous grouping. The failure of homogeneous grouping thus far to justify the claims made for it arises in part from the lack of agreement over the validity (and consequent selection) of devices to provide homogeneity. The apparent failure of many classes actually established is to be attributed no doubt in large measure to the neglect or to the inability of educators: to provide workable methods for the segregated, to modify curricula and to define and practise enrichment.

Let me hasten to add that acceleration is an expediency measure, not a solution to the problem. Failure to give opportunity to the one million and one half very promising children in America is a neglect that the country can now ill afford to make. Let us take steps to enable teachers accurately to identify the gifted and to actuate the administrative officers to provide the necessary adjustments in the form of acceleration and enrichment.

For the majority of gifted children acceleration seems to be advisable. But indispensable also is enrichment, since from the ranks of the gifted we hope our future leaders will emerge. And the development of leadership undoubtedly implies provision of particularized materials as well as the development of special methods of education.

Of great social value should be experiments dealing with the results of special class instruction for gifted children. In more than a decade of experimentation, we have developed astonishingly few enrichment programs, but some (notably the Los Angeles and Cleveland efforts) are promising. The following are some points wherein enrichment may mean the merging of life experience with worth-while school endeavor for atypical children.

(1) The Language Arts

(*a*) *Reading:* Through free choice of reading from carefully graded, extensive book-lists, children may be led to develop the permanent habit of reading as a leisure activity. However, important is it that the gifted child's reading be directed, since he appears to neglect, when allowed spontaneous free choice, several areas of experience which are associated with wholesome growth.

L. M. Terman's study shows a continuous increase in amount of reading as the gifted child matures. The height of the "reading craze," heralded as inevitable for the average child at age 13, seems not to have been reached at age 17½ by gifted children. My most recent study of 50 gifted children who have been followed

[4] F. N. Freeman, "The Treatment of the Gifted Child in the Light of Scientific Evidence," *Elementary School Journal,* Vol. xxiv, pp. 652–661, May, 1924.

since 1924 reveals a progressive and appreciable yearly increase in the amount of reading which these unsegregated gifted children do. The girls are found consistently to read more and better books than do the boys.

It is not without significance that among the gifted children little interest is exhibited in the books dealing with the fine arts, music and drama. And for the boys poetry also attracts little or no interest. Small wonder, then, that newspapers and "middle-grade" magazines absorb practically the whole of the portion of leisure time set aside for reading by the average adult. Certainly the reading for gifted children as well as that of adults can not be considered other than a serious reflection upon the effectiveness of the school in instilling and developing permanent interests in reading as a leisure activity. Although the spontaneous reading of the gifted is relatively high in quality and in amount, it appears by no means to be that which we desire for maximum growth and development of these promising children. Several important fields of human endeavor are neglected, and the liberalizing effect of reading in the arts is conspicuously absent. Herein, we find an opportunity for guidance that may prove as fruitful as it is expedient.

The guidance should include the following practises: Analysis of each child's interests, discovery or a development of a predominant interest, direction of book choice in accord with mental maturity, and an association of reading with other spontaneous activities and extra-curricular interests. Book lists, assembled according to maturation levels in ability and interest, will prove a help in intelligent guidance, but no substitute can be made for intensive case study of every gifted child; this should be followed by suggestions for extensive reading. In the field of social science an unusual opportunity is offered in the guidance of these children. For the boys especially a guidance toward reading about music, art and other phases of the esthetic seems essential.

(*b*) *Creative work in writing:* Noteworthy is it that eleven of the fourteen promising youthful writers chosen by Terman for intensive study were girls. Three boys only were selected, and in no case did the writing of a boy reach in quality that of the most inferior writing of the eleven girls. All seven of the most talented, most promising were girls. Surely, the gifted boys have similar inchoate ability which should be fostered by creative free writing. Herein, especially, do we need to readjust our teaching procedures and to provide an opportunity for expression that will afford outlets for real interests and engender a development of superior written expression, which, in terms of the superior mental background of gifted children, should reach unusual heights.

(2) THE FINE ARTS

It is of much import that musical ability, painting, drawing and other specialized abilities are not exhibited in marked degree by the fifty gifted children whom I have studied. Two boys only give promise of attaining high rank in the arts. These have produced meritorious though quantitatively unmeasured evidences of unusual superiority in music.

Several writers have reported very low coefficients of correlation between musical ability (Seashore Test results) and intelligence. Nevertheless, the measures of innate musical ability are not unassailable from the views of validity. I believe, with Terman, that "without the support of a high intelligence a special talent is not likely to mature into achievements of very unusual merit." Early identification and early and continuous stimulation of special talents are essential in nurturing to rare attainment those special abilities which characterize many gifted children in their youth. But special abilities do not spring full grown in the mature genius. Attention must be directed toward providing gradual development through study of maturation levels in artistic ability. The psychological aspect of this development is relatively untouched, but exploratory efforts are surely demanded.

(3) Curriculum Flexibility

The curricula for the gifted should contain many electives. A pupil's load should be selected in terms of his interests and abilities, but it is essential that challenging and mentally provocative tasks be introduced in a way such as to elicit full use of the superior ability. Several studies show clearly that the gifted child can save 50 per cent. (or more) of the time ordinarily allotted to subject-matter acquisition. It is the English and social studies fields that offer many possibilities for enrichment during the time saved from school routine. These fields offer opportunity for developing worth-while projects, for creative writing and for original work or research. In addition, special interests and abilities should have opportunity for expression and development.

(4) Leadership

Our contemporary leadership in every line of human activity appears impotent to meet current social-economic issues and needs. But the leadership which we have and deplore is a product of our own making. Indifference to the character of political leaders has characterized many worth-while citizens; the present dilatoriness in effecting reform shows a failure of our people to demand and to follow mentally superior and socially minded public leaders.

There must be given to children an educative experience which will create leadership, but it is equally important in addition that children learn to respect, to demand and to follow the highest type of leaders.

Knowledge of significant social, political and ethical events and issues is important if intelligent choice of leaders is to follow. A new generation must be led to participate in and to evaluate vital problems and controversies; a permanent child-adult interest in social-economic events and issues will develop from early and continuous participation in the activities associated therewith in the public schools. Obviously, social-minded and informed teachers are needed, but the root of our social-economic failure may be traced largely, I think, to the methods and the materials with which children have been educated for citizenship. Fixed, outmoded social codes have been transmitted by rigid, stereotyped procedures which preclude active participation in vital present-day social and economic problems and issues.

Elasticity in school demand and freedom to develop individuality are essential in the new school, if maximum growth is to take place. Uniformity and excessive conformity are foes to growth. Outmoded codes must be abandoned, and we should aim, through cooperative reconstruction of experience, to develop more adequate values. In this process of creation, cooperative endeavor is a most important determiner of growth. Mechanical drill and compulsory "learning" of subjects having little or no present meaning should be replaced by the whole-hearted purposive activities that have a vital grip in the present interests of children. Vital living *now* is emphasized; this procedure stressing universal cooperative activity appears to be the most propitious background for the development and emergence of true leaders.[5]

(5) Activity Programs and Recreation

In natural play groups, children educate each other; often, they develop their

[5] See J. L. Childs, "Education and the Philosophy of Experimentalism," New York, The Century Company, 1931.

own regulative standards and checks. Indeed, the group which utilizes spontaneous interests and activities exercises perhaps the most powerful influence in the development of desirable individualities, each of whom has a high respect for the personality of the others.

The utilization of play activities appears appropriate in creating interest and desire in education. Furthermore, the development of play curricula can effect a rather complete merging of school and life. Nevertheless, play activities vary in their educational value. Many spontaneous interests of children are actually harmful; others are of doubtful utility in a worth-while educational program.

Characteristic play activities should be discerned for children of the several school ages, and these should be utilized and evaluated as a starting point in an educational program which stresses maturation levels. Dorothy Van Alstyne has assembled typical play activities for children of ages 2 to 5. Lehman and Witty have listed and described the play performances and play interests of boys and girls of school ages.[6] Witty and Beaman have studied the play of subnormal children and have suggested modifications in the special class curricula in terms of the results.[7] These studies present data which may be utilized effectively as points of departure in developing activity programs. Miss Beaman's curriculum for the special class is a pioneer effort to adapt interesting experiences and activities to the maturity levels of special class children.

In the special class for the mentally sub-average, there is abundant opportunity for capitalizing the values to be derived from prudent use of play activities. The lag of teaching behind theory is illustrated by the fact that, in a survey recently completed by Miss Beaman and the writer, it has shown that the majority of 588 special classes offer simply the traditional subject curriculum supplemented by handwork, and by the fact that activity curricula are seldom initiated.

In the survey, one hundred teachers of special class children cooperated in describing the play activities and play curricula in their schools. Play was interpreted by the teachers usually to mean games, and these were seldom graded in terms of known facts of abilities of children at various stages of development. Revision of play curricula might well provide:

(1) A well-balanced program requiring play activity not predominantly of the game type.

(2) An integrated program of play activities providing progressively for growth in social experience. The haphazard introduction of highly organized games which now characterizes the programs should be abandoned.

(3) The recognition of interests, however immature, of special class children through provision for an increased amount of "free-play" under stimulating conditions.

(4) The realization that play activities serve as a salutary motivating and educative influence in the social and academic education of special class children.

Our study revealed also the inadequacy and inappropriateness of the selection and classification of mentally sub-average children. The range in I.Q. of the classes was 20–116; the mean was 63.

The special classes are dealing apparently with many children who are below as well as with many who are above the

[6] I am directing my attention to selected phases only of special education for the sub-average since other papers on this program consider in detail curriculum, method and objectives.

[7] See Lehman and Witty, "The Psychology of Play Activities," Barnes and Company, 1927; or Dorothy Van Alstyne, "Play Behavior and Choice of Play Materials of Pre-School Children," University of Chicago Press, 1932. In addition, see Witty and Beaman, "The Play of Mental Deviates," *Mental Hygiene,* forthcoming issue, and especially F. N. Beaman, "An Experimental Curriculum for Special Classes," Master's Thesis (unpublished) Northwestern University, 1932.

educable limits of the special class. If the two extremes of low and high mental age are to be dealt with in the public-school special classes, more adequate provision in the form of pre-primary rooms should be made for those of immature mentality, and remedial measures and psychiatric service must be provided for those of the problem type. On the whole, however, when the newness of special education is kept in mind, one observes that great strides have been made to place the selection, admission and classification of mentally retarded pupils upon a scientific basis.

Nevertheless, we have barely made a start in special education. Teachers, administrators and the public should be led through our efforts to realize the significance and the expediency of the following objective from the Children's Charter: "For every child who is blind, deaf, crippled, or otherwise physically handicapped, and for the child who is mentally handicapped, such measures as will early discover and diagnose his handicap, provide care and treatment, and so train him that he may become an asset to society rather than a liability. Expenses of these services should be borne publicly where they can not be privately met."

EDUCATIONAL EVENTS

THE OXFORD SOCIETY

THE report of the Oxford Society for the year 1932–33, according to a summary in the London *Times,* shows that the society is now well established, the membership is over 6,000, the first annual general meeting has been held, at which a formal constitution was adopted and officers elected, and a permanent office organization has been set up in Oxford and is in touch with branches all over the world. Not only have all running expenses been met, but a sum of over £8,000 has been invested to form the nucleus of an endowment fund.

The general aim of the society is to unite all Oxford men and women for service to the university and to each other. The formulation of practical methods of service will early engage the attention of the executive committee. The issue of an authoritative publication, which shall supply both authentic news and intelligent discussion of it, is a question of urgent importance, according to the report. For the time being the annual report of the university (now expanded to include semi-official and unofficial, as well as strictly official, news) is being circulated to all members. Another function which experience shows that the society can perform is that of an information bureau. An increasing number of letters is received from members requesting information on a wide variety of subjects.

While the work of the appointments committee has developed satisfactorily in recent years, the staff employed by the university can not make all the contacts which might be made in the field of employment. The report points out that membership of the Oxford Society presents an excellent opportunity for voluntary service in this respect. Oxford men actually engaged in vocations can report new opportunities of employment to the secretary, who will place the information at the disposal of the appointments committee. The report urges that members of the society can serve better in this matter of employment by acting through the society and the appointments committee than by attempting to obtain posts for Oxford men on their own account.

About 230 groups or branches of the society have been established in all parts of the world. Each local committee in an industrial area is asked to appoint (as has already been done in some centers) a few of its members to act as a special employment panel, which would conduct propaganda for the employment of university men and make a survey of available posts, reporting results to the central office. The establishment of local branches overseas has been welcomed. In places where the English community is small, and often widely scattered, the opportunities of social meetings which the society affords are highly appreciated. The central office endeavors to inform each local secretary of any member proceeding as a stranger to his district, so that he may be welcomed on arrival and introduced to people who may be willing to give him such help as he requires.

An arrangement has been made with the appointments committee, whereby the secretary of the society is informed of the name and address of any member of the society obtaining an appointment through the committee; thus the local secretary of the branch in the district to which he is going can immediately be notified of his advent and asked to extend a welcome to him. Again, the distinguished visitor from Oxford can be received among friends in almost any part of the world, and Oxford graduates, perhaps long severed from direct contact with the university, have the opportunity of meeting him and hearing news of Oxford.

The report concludes by saying that almost the last public work done for Oxford by the late Lord Grey of Fallodon was to launch the Oxford Society. His interest in its progress was real and personal.

PER CAPITA COSTS IN CITY SCHOOLS

The extent which schools have cut costs to meet losses in income due to the depression is revealed in the annual study of "Per Capita Costs in City Schools, 1932–1933," just released by the Federal Office of Education.

Reports from 299 typical cities scattered throughout the nation show reductions in per-pupil cost running as high as 41 per cent. in a single year. Per-pupil costs dropped between 15 and 30 per cent. in one third of the cities in a single year's time. The average decrease for all cities for the year is 22 per cent. The average total cost of educating a child for the year 1933 in 299 cities was $87.65. This compares with $113.03 for 1932.

Statistics separately organized for four groups of cities ranging from small cities to cities of over 100,000 population show the shift from 1932 to 1933.

In Group 1 cities, 100,000 population and up, average per-pupil cost dropped from $118.61 to $91.69. Cities which have a per-pupil cost close to this average are: Somerville, Massachusetts, $92.81; Indianapolis, Indiana, $90.60; Grand Rapids, Michigan, $90.18; St. Paul, Minnesota, $89.46; Des Moines, Iowa, $89.04; Minneapolis, Minnesota, $89.02.

In Group 2 cities, 30,000 to 100,000 population, the drop was from $95.55 to $80.82. Cities which have a per-pupil cost close to this average are: San Bernardino, California, $83.32; Cedar Rapids, Iowa, $82.72; Chester, Pennsylvania, $82.47; Lansing, Michigan, $81.31; Saginaw, Michigan, $81.31.

In Group 3 cities, 10,000 to 30,000 population, the drop was from $79.06 to $68.02. Cities which have a per-pupil cost close to this average are: Fremont, Nebraska, $69.05; Logansport, Indiana, $68.47; Hastings, Nebraska, $67.81; Stevens Point, Wisconsin, $67.36; Oskaloosa, Iowa, $67.00.

In Group 4 cities, 2,500 to 10,000 population, the drop was from $84.90 to $73.23. Cities which have a per-pupil cost close to this average are: Jerome, Arizona, $74.12; Rockville, Connecticut, $73.78; Columbus, Indiana, $73.57; La Grande, Oregon, $73.16; Chehalis, Washington, $70.63.

How wide-spread the movement to reduce costs has been is shown by the fact that 96 per cent. of the cities show a decrease in per-pupil cost between 1932 and 1933.

Largest decreases for cities in the various groups are: *Group 1,* San Antonio, Tex., 36.1; Akron, Ohio, 33.4; New Bedford, Mass., 30.9; El Paso, Tex., 29.7; Grand Rapids, Mich., 27.8. *Group 2,* Kokomo, Ind., 34.9; Kenosha, Wis., 34.3; Kalamazoo, Mich., 33.7; Jackson, Mich., 31.6; Shreveport, La., 31.0. *Group 3,* Great Falls, Mont., 41.7; Selma, Ala., 34.3; Sedalia, Mo., 33.0; Findlay, Ohio, 32.2; Iron Mountain, Mich., 30.5. *Group 4,* Jerome, Ariz., 36.7; Helena, Ark., 36.6; Andalusia, Ala., 34.4; Bisbee, Ariz., 32.8; Downers Grove, Ill., 31.2.

The averages for all four groups are lower than for all years going back to 1924 when statistics for a selected group of cities were first collected.

The study of per-pupil cost does not indicate in detail what factors are operating to bring about such extensive decreases.

Other studies indicate that the current expense for operating American schools, both city and rural, in 1933–34 is approximately $368,000,000 less than in 1930.

THE APPOINTMENTS BUREAU OF COLUMBIA UNIVERSITY

Columbia University, through its Appointments Office, placed more than 5,400 students in full or part-time jobs last year, according to a report made by W. Emerson Gentzler, secretary of appointments. Needy students were helped further through the distribution of more than $533,000 in scholarships and loans.

Mr. Gentzler pointed out that improvement in the number of opportunities for recent graduates had been shown in the chemical industry and its branches, with the result that frequent calls for men with special training in that field had been made.

Part-time jobs during the academic year involving men students are only twenty-seven fewer than the peak year of 1929–30, and the total number for winter and summer of the past year shows an increase of 487 placements over those for the preceding year. This increase is considerably greater than has before been achieved from any one year to another, and in volume of employment makes the record a better one than in any previous year except for the peak year 1929–30.

The number of full-time commercial positions and teaching positions has decreased considerably during the past two years, however. One might safely infer that the number of teaching appointments may be still further diminished during the next few years.

Over 2,000 temporary and service placements were made within the university itself, in the dining halls, libraries, the bookstore, department of buildings and grounds, and other departments. As many as 300 students were sometimes employed on a single Saturday at football games, with wages and commissions to the student workers amounting to more than $5,000 for the season. Seventy-nine students earned approximately $8,000 through the operation of student laundry, newspaper, magazine, blotter and other agencies.

According to Mr. Gentzler, the college employment office is faced with new problems due to the diminished number of student employment opportunities in and around New York. He points out that the problem is that of evaluating the relative needs of students, in order to give help first of all where it is most needed. Because of the limited number of jobs, it is not a matter, therefore, of putting the first man in the first job for which his qualifications, his hours and his individual needs fit him. Consideration must be given in addition to his situation in relation to that of all other needy students.

THE CONDITION OF SCHOOL BUILDINGS IN THE EARTHQUAKE ZONE IN CALIFORNIA

THE following facts are taken from an article by Chapin Hall, editorial correspondent of *The New York Times:*

The California Grand Jury, after months of investigation by an expert committee, has announced that all public-school buildings which failed to comply with the earthquake resistance building code adopted by the state after the Long Beach earthquake of last March should immediately be abandoned. This order affects more than 30 per cent. of the schools, housing approximately 250,000 pupils.

Recently in Long Beach, where scarcely a school building remained intact, the voters turned down a proposed reconstruction bond issue and that city is now operating with hastily erected, one-story frame bungalows until such time as a permanent building program can be financed.

In Los Angeles inspection showed that 146 masonry school buildings were so badly damaged that rehabilitation or complete reconstruction will be necessary, while 710 of other types required extensive repairs to restore the safety factor which existed prior to the quake—this out of a total number of 2,600 school structures. The Board of Education has placed an order for 1,700 floored tent schoolhouses, dividing the school day so that one tent will do double duty, and vacating hundreds of perfectly equipped structures.

A permanent building program is now in process of formulation providing for one-story buildings of the Mission type, a feature which in itself means the acquiring of very extensive real estate holdings, as practically all of the present buildings are of two or more stories. Another feature of the plan contemplates operation of the temporary schools on a twelve-month basis, which would help take up the slack.

A bond election is to be called as soon as practicable, probably for an initial sum of $30,000,000, and the Reconstruction Finance Corporation will be invited to buy the issue.

Mr. Hall points out that should the election result negatively, "the fifth city of the United States will present the curious spectacle of educating a quarter of a million or more of its children under canvas—a spectacle to which it is committed in any event during a reconstruction period of at least three years."

THE CATHEDRAL OF LEARNING OF THE UNIVERSITY OF PITTSBURGH

APPROVAL of a $300,000 grant for labor for the completion of the Cathedral of Learning of the University of Pittsburgh has been awarded by County Administrator James Lyall Stuart, of the Civil Works Administration, in an effort to finish the building by February 15.

Under the proposal, presented by Chancellor John Bowman, of the university, at least 1,000 men would be put to work immediately at a labor cost of $300,000, with the university furnishing more than $250,000 worth of materials.

If the plan is approved the lower floors of the massive stone and brick building would be closed in, and partitions would be built in the lower floors. It is expected that these operations can be completed by February 15, when the Civil Works Administration program is tentatively scheduled to terminate.

The work that was left to be completed when the depression cut off donations included the placing of outside stone-work on the first two floors, completion of the top, which will make the building 45 to 50 feet higher than at present, the installation of a heating plant and the finishing of the interior.

Whether Congressman Henry Ellenbogen will continue his efforts to secure a federal loan to put the actual finishing touches on the building and to erect a $1,000,000 dormitory for students could not be learned. He proposed several weeks ago to ask the Federal Public Works Administration for outright grants of 30 per cent. of the funds necessary to complete the plant, the remainder to be advanced to the university as a loan.

All laborers, skilled workmen and engineers who would work on the Civil Works Administration project would be selected from the rolls of the Federal State Employment Bureau, giving work to stone masons, bricklayers, plumbers, steam-fitters, iron-workers, painters, engineers and laborers.

NEW BUILDING FOR TEACHER-TRAINING AT INDIANA STATE TEACHERS COLLEGE

THE Public Works Administration at Washington, D. C., has granted the allotment of $98,000 for the construction of a teacher-training building at Indiana State Teachers College.

For the last several years a new training and demonstration school has been planned. The project was first blocked by the lack of a suitable site upon which to build. Citizens of Terre Haute rallied to the cause and after considerable discussion, the Heminway Park site was purchased from the City Park Board.

On account of economic conditions during the last two years funds which were rapidly becoming available under the Improvement Fund tax were cut off by act of the General Assembly and it seemed that all plans must wait for a considerable time at least. Several weeks ago, the project was revived when Governor McNutt gave his approval to the application for the Federal allotment and personally interceded at Washington for its grant. Building operations will probably be started within the next few weeks.

The building will be 210 by 138 feet. The type of structure is English Gothic and when completed and landscaped, it is expected to be one of the most attractive buildings in the city.

Controller C. C. Connelly has announced that the college has available at present $281,000 for this project. In the original request for the allotment, a grant of $115,000 was asked, but an allotment only of $98,000 was given. There will thus become available at once $379,000, which will be spent in the erection of the building.

The old training school has been outgrown for the last several years and the new building has been urgently needed. Its completion, it is said, will not only be a great aid to the college in its teacher-training work, but an adequate training school will also do much to elevate the rating of the college among other teacher-training institutions of the state and of the Middle West.

PROPOSED INVESTIGATION OF THE NEW YORK CITY SCHOOLS

MAYOR FIORELLO H. LA GUARDIA, of New York City, would have authority to appoint three members on a committee to make a searching investigation of the school system under a resolution presented to the Board of Education on December 31 by Commissioner Louis S. Posner.

It was, in amended form, a proposal that Mr. Posner has been pressing for about two months and which has encountered the bitter opposition of President George J. Ryan. Efforts to induce Mr. Posner to modify the resolution are said to have spurred him to make it more drastic. The chief objection of board members is to having outsiders on the committee.

Commissioner Walter J. Carlin forced a postponement of action on the measure by exercising his privilege of objection to immediate consideration.

Although primarily designed to determine the effects of financial retrenchment and eliminate waste, the resolution would allow a broad study of all aspects of school work with a view to fundamental reforms. Mr. Posner has explained that the survey would differ from that of the State Education Department into "pedagogical efficiency" in that it would make a concrete attack on financial problems and an examination of objectives.

The resolution follows:

The Board of Education of this city has conformed to the general necessity for stringent economy in the expenditure of public funds and has yielded to budget reductions to such extent as it believed would not adversely affect the educational standards of the public school system of the city or the welfare of its pupils.

Our schools have been operating under reduced budget for nearly two years and survey should now be made to determine to what extent, if any, their efficiency has been impaired and whether further economies should be effected or an increased budget required.

In addition such study should include, among other matters, detailed data and recommendations concerning the physical condition and maintenance of school properties, matters of administration, curriculum and school methods and such changes and readjustments as may be advisable in the light of changed economic and social conditions.

It is, therefore,

Resolved, That a committee be forthwith appointed to make a study, report and recommendations with all due speed to this board concerning the matters set forth in this preamble; further

Resolved, That such committee shall consist of seven, one of whom shall be a member of the Board of Education to be appointed by its president, three of whom shall be unconnected with the Department of Education, to be appointed by the Mayor of the City of New York, the remaining three to be designated by the superintendent of schools from among the employees of the department. The superintendent of schools shall be *ex officio* a member of the committee. The committee is authorized to designate advisory and other assistants, and, with the approval of the superintendent of schools, secretarial and other assistants from among the school personnel; and the auditor and all other officials and employees of the department are directed to furnish such assistance, data and records, and access thereto, as may be required by the committee in the course of its investigations and studies.

THE AMERICAN ASSOCIATION OF TEACHERS COLLEGES

THE Eighteenth Annual Meeting of the American Association of Teachers Colleges will be held at the Carter Hotel, Cleveland, on February 23 and 24, 1934.

The preliminary program is as follows:

Friday morning, February 23.

I. The abilities, aptitudes and capacities that a teacher should have in the fields of psychology, mental hygiene and emotional adjustments.

Daniel A. Prescott, Rutgers University.

Carleton Washburne, superintendent of schools, Winnetka, Illinois.

Maud E. Watson, director Child Guidance Division, Children's Fund of Michigan.

Friday afternoon, February 23.

II. The personal and social traits necessary in a successful teacher and how they can be achieved.

Ned H. Dearborn, director of the Institute of Education, New York University.

Caroline B. Zachry, Mental Hygiene Institute, State Teachers College, Upper Montclair, New Jersey.

George A. Selke, president, State Teachers College, St. Cloud, Minnesota.

Friday evening, February 23.

III. The education of teachers for a changing social order.

Professor John Dewey.

George F. Zook, U. S. commissioner of education.

Third speaker still to be selected.

Saturday morning, February 24.

IV. Training school facilities and techniques.

Willard Beatty, superintendent of schools, Bronxville, New York.

Earle U. Rugg, State Teachers College, Greeley, Colorado.

Charles C. Ward, principal, State Normal School, Plattsburg, New York.

Saturday afternoon, February 24.

V. Differences in the education of teachers in the teachers colleges and in the liberal arts colleges.

W. E. Peik, University of Minnesota.

Albert Lindsay Rowland, president, State Teachers College, Shippensburg, Pennsylvania.

After each session the discussion will be opened by a member of the association not yet selected, followed by general discussion from the floor.

EDUCATIONAL NOTES AND NEWS

RALPH N. TIREY, superintendent of schools at Bloomington, Indiana, has been elected president of the Indiana State Teachers College at the meeting of the Teachers College Board. At the same time, George C. Cole resigned as state superintendent of public instruction and was appointed vice-president and business manager of the college.

A DINNER in honor of Dr. Frank Cody's fifteenth anniversary as superintendent of the Detroit Public Schools was given by the administrative division of the Detroit Teachers Association on January 12.

GOVERNOR MOORE, of New Jersey, announces that Professor Albert Einstein has accepted an invitation to a state-wide reception in his honor in March at the Atlantic City Convention Hall. The event is being sponsored by New Jersey Jews, seven hundred of whom dined with the governor at the Jewish Community Center in Jersey City on January 21 to further plans. Governor Moore served as honorary chairman and named a reception committee of educators, industrialists and public officials.

A BANQUET in honor of three members of the faculty of mathematics at the University of Wisconsin was recently given by friends, associates and students. These were Professor Charles S. Slichter, dean of the Graduate School; Dr. E. B. Skinner, professor of mathematics, and Dr. E. B. Van Vleck, emeritus professor of mathematics. The three men have a combined service record in the university of a hundred and sixteen years. Among representatives of the departments of mathematics of other universities who were present were Professor George D. Birkhoff, of Harvard University, who formerly taught at Wisconsin; Professors G. A. Bliss and E. P. Lane, of the University of Chicago, and Professor T. F. Holgate, of Northwestern University. In addition, Professor Warren Weaver, who left Wisconsin two years ago to join the Rockefeller Foundation in New York, returned for the occasion. President Glenn Frank; Dr. E. A. Birge, president emeritus of the university; George C. Sellery, dean of the College of Letters and Science; Professor Birkhoff and Dr. Weaver were speakers at the banquet. The guests of honor also spoke, and Professor Mark Ingraham, of the department of mathematics, acted as toastmaster.

DEAN CRAVEN LAYCOCK, Dartmouth College, '96, who is retiring in June after thirty-five years of service at the college, was the guest of honor at the annual dinner of the Dartmouth Alumni Association on January 18. Speakers included Dr. Ernest M. Hopkins, president of Dartmouth, Dr. Harry Woodburn Chase, chancellor of New York University, Dartmouth, '04, and Dr. E. Gordon Bill, dean of the faculty.

PROFESSOR GILBERT A. BLISS has been awarded the Martin A. Ryerson Distinguished Service Professorship for his "brilliant and fruitful service to the University of Chicago." Of the nine distinguished service professorships two are now held by members of the department of mathematics, the Eliakim Hastings Moore Distinguished Service Professorship having been awarded to Professor Leonard Eugene Dickson several years ago.

The Jusserand Medal, awarded only three times since the first presentation in 1925, "for a published work of distinction on any phase involving the history of the intellectual relations between the United States and any foreign country," was received by Howard Mumford Jones, professor of English in the University of Michigan, at the recent meeting of the American Historical Association. The award was made in recognition of the publication of Professor Jones's book, on "America and French Culture, 1750–1848." The fund establishing the medal was given by Jules Jusserand, war-time ambassador to the United States, and is administered by the association.

Dr. Bert A. Nash, associate professor of educational psychology and director of the Educational Clinic at the University of Kansas, was recently elected president of the Kansas Mental Hygiene Society.

The Eastern Association of College Deans and Advisers of Men elected the following officers at the fifth annual meeting held in Atlantic City, New Jersey: *President,* Director Theodore A. Distler, New York University; *Vice-president,* Dr. Robert A. Brotemarkle, University of Pennsylvania; *Secretary-treasurer,* Dean Edward H. Heyd, Rutgers University; *Executive Committee,* in addition to the three officers listed above, Dean W. E. Tilberg, Gettysburg College; Dean Samuel T. Arnold, Brown University; Dr. Maurice S. Sheehy, The Catholic University of America; Dean Arthur A. Hauck, Lafayette College; Dean Norman Alexander, University of New Hampshire, and Dean R. H. Rivenburg, Bucknell University.

Dr. William Emory Smyser, who has been dean of the College at Ohio Wesleyan University, Delaware, for the last seventeen years, has tendered his resignation effective at the close of the present semester on January 29, 1934. He retains his professorship in English and will continue to give his full time to his classes.

Dr. Donald G. Tewksbury, who was granted leave of absence for 1933–1934 to assume the acting deanship of St. Stephen's College for the year, has been promoted from assistant professor to associate professor of education at Teachers College, Columbia University.

The department of economics and sociology at Mount Holyoke College announces the appointment of Professor Edwin D. Harvey, of Dartmouth College, to fill the vacancy made by the release of Professor Conrad Taeuber, who recently became assistant analyst in the Bureau of Statistical Research at Washington, undertaking special work for the Federal Emergency Relief Administration.

Dr. Henry J. Gerling, superintendent of schools at St. Louis for the past four years, was reelected by the Board of Education on January 9 for a second term of four years. Dr. Gerling has been connected with the St. Louis school system continuously for the past thirty-three years as teacher, principal of elementary school, assistant superintendent and superintendent.

Dr. Silas O. Rorem has retired as superintendent of schools in Port Chester, N. Y. Lorenzo H. Knapp, principal of the Port Chester High School, has been named acting superintendent.

Leon J. Cook, superintendent of schools of the first supervisory district of Ontario County, New York, retired on November 27 after a service of thirty-eight years as teacher, principal and superintendent of schools in the State of New York.

H. E. Kentopp, formerly superintendent of schools at Central City, Nebr., has accepted an elementary school principalship in East Orange, N. J., where he will work under the supervision of Superintendent Clifford J. Scott.

Appointment of Redfield Proctor, formerly governor of Vermont, to the executive committee of the Massachusetts Institute of Technology, is announced. Mr. Proctor will serve during the absence of Professor Elihu Thomson, now recovering from an illness. Mr. Proctor is president of the Technology Alumni Association.

Professor James D. McGill, of the University of Rochester, has been elected president of the Rochester, N. Y., Board of Education.

Howard W. Beers, instructor in the department of rural social organization at Cornell University, has received an appointment with the Federal Emergency Relief Administration. He will be assistant to Dr. Ellis L. Kirkpatrick, who heads the research work on the cost of living in rural areas in various states. Dr. Kirkpatrick is now on leave from the University of Wisconsin.

PROFESSORS M. C. DEL MANZO, Donald P. Cottrell, F. B. O'Rear and Clarence Linton, of Teachers College, Columbia University, have recently completed a brief investigation of the scope and character of the work of the Graduate School for Jewish Social Work in New York City. This study was undertaken at the request of the Board of Trustees of the school in order to clarify future policies.

PROFESSOR ELIJAH W. BAGSTER-COLLINS has leave of absence from Teachers College, Columbia University, for service with the Emergency Committee in Aid of Displaced German Scholars.

PROFESSOR JOSEPHINE FOSTER, of the Institute of Child Welfare of the University of Minnesota, has been elected a member of the executive board of the National Association for Nursery Education.

GEORGE WHARTON EDWARDS, of Greenwich, Conn., will go this month to Mexico City with the Commissioner of Education and Publicity of Mexico, Senor E. E. Noro, to paint and study Mexican types and scenes for a forthcoming volume of impressions under the patronage of the Mexican Department of Education.

PROFESSORS W. E. SIKES, G. L. Maxwell, R. W. McWilliams and G. Eleanor Kimble, of the University of Denver, are members of the newly organized Crime Prevention Committee of the city of Denver. Working in cooperation with Sergeant Young of the Denver Police Department, the committee, headed by Granville B. Johnson, is making a thorough study of the delinquent areas of Denver with the purpose of correcting present conditions.

DR. N. L. ENGELHARDT, professor of education at Teachers College, Columbia University, has been appointed chairman of Governor Herbert H. Lehman's Commission for the Study of the Educational Problems of Penal Institutions for Youth.

DR. PAUL DENGLER, director of the Austro-American Institute of Education, Vienna, spoke at the University of Minnesota on January 17, discussing "The Crisis of Education in Europe."

NORMAN THOMAS on January 9 spoke to the members of Iowa State College on "The Choice Before Us" and on "The New Deal or Socialization." He also took part in a radio forum together with Dean Friley and Professor Starrak, of the college. Mr. Thomas was a guest of the college chapter of the League for Industrial Democracy.

THE Foundation for the Advancement of the Social Sciences announces that Dr. George Norlin, president of the University of Colorado, was the speaker at the second of the 1934 series of fortnightly luncheon lectures held on January 20 at Denver. Dr. Norlin was in residence in Berlin, Germany, as Roosevelt Lecturer during the academic year 1932–33. His subject will be "Significant Trends in Central Europe and What They Suggest for American Policy."

A PICTURE of the late Dr. Arnold L. Jacoby, director of the Psychopathic Clinic in connection with the Recorder's Court in the City of Detroit and the chief of the neuro-psychiatric service in Harper Hospital, was presented by a group of his friends to the Arnold L. Jacoby School on the occasion of its formal dedication. Superintendent Frank Cody presided. The presentation speech was made by Dr. Grover C. Penberthy, surgeon-in-chief of the Children's Hospital. A pupil of the school gave a brief speech of acceptance. Formal acceptance of the picture was made by Mrs. Laura F. Osborn, president of the Board of Education. Professor Charles Scott Berry, of the University of Ohio, delivered the principal address. The Arnold L. Jacoby School is the first school for intellectually limited boys to be erected in the City of Detroit.

DR. W. CHARLES WALLACE, president of Westminster College, New Wilmington, Pennsylvania, from 1916 until his resignation in 1931, died on January 18 at the age of fifty-eight years.

DR. LINCOLN HULLEY, president of Stetson University, Deland, Florida, since 1904, died suddenly on January 20, at the age of sixty-eight years. Dr. Hulley had been president of the Florida Bankers Association for one term and a member of the State Senate for two terms.

He was a trustee of Bucknell University and Crozer Theological Seminary.

THE REV. DR. WILLIAM FLETCHER MCMURRY, Methodist Episcopal Bishop of Kentucky, Western Virginia and the Baltimore District, formerly president of Central College, Fayette, Missouri, and president of the board of finance of the Methodist Episcopal Church, South, died on January 17, at the age of sixty-nine years.

DR. ULRICH BONNELL PHILLIPS, professor of American history at Yale University, a student of the economic, social and political history of the South, died on January 21. He was fifty-six years old.

MARY A. HALL, retired professor of chemistry in the College for Women in Constantinople, died on January 1. She was seventy-three years old.

MISS LUELLA A. PALMER, for the last twelve years director of kindergartens in the public schools of New York City, died on January 13, at the age of sixty-seven years.

A NEW magazine, *Social Research*, the editorial board of which will include members of the faculty of the University in Exile of the New School for Social Research, 66 West Twelfth Street, will appear on February 1. It will be published quarterly in English. The first issue will be entirely the product of German professors driven from their country by the Nazi Government. The contributors and their subjects are: Emil Lederer, economist, formerly of the University of Berlin, "Social Control Versus Economic Law." Eduard Heimann, economist, formerly of the University of Hamburg, "Sociological Preconceptions of Economic Theory." Karl Brandt, agricultural economist, formerly of the University of Kiel, "Toward a Panic-Proof Industrial Structure." Arthur Feiler, "The Pressure for Monetary Depreciation." Gerhard Colm, formerly head of the economics department of the University of Kiel, "Why the Papen Plan for Economic Recovery Failed." Frieda Wunderlich, economist and sociologist, formerly of the Berlin Training College, "New Aspects of Unemployment in Germany." Hans Speier, formerly on the faculty of Berlin University, "The Salaried Employee in Modern Society."

THE National Council of Geography Teachers held their twentieth annual meeting at Northwestern University on December 28, 29 and 30. A half day session was devoted to each of the following topics: "Geography in the High School," "Research Studies," "Field and Laboratory Work," "Effective Use of Tools and Methods" and "Content Units in Geography." At the banquet held on the evening of December 29, Professor H. C. Morrison, of the University of Chicago, gave the annual address. A feature of this evening meeting was the presentation of the Distinguished Service Award to Professor R. H. Whitbeck, of the University of Wisconsin. The presentation was made by Professor L. O. Packard. This Distinguished Service Award was established a year ago and Professor William M. Davis, of Harvard University was the first recipient. At the end of this year Professor Whitbeck will have completed twenty-five years of service at the University of Wisconsin. For the coming year Miss Edith P. Parker, of the University of Chicago, has been elected as president of the council.

THE fifth meeting of the Institute for Education by Radio will be held at the Ohio State University, Columbus, Ohio, from April 30 to May 2. This fifth meeting marks a milestone in radio broadcasting and the papers and discussions at the meeting will be an appraisal of what has happened in the last five years. Interesting and informed speakers have already been secured and the complete program will be announced shortly. This year a special session will be devoted to broadcasting by educational stations. The Association of College and University Broadcasting Stations will have charge of this part of the program. It has already secured speakers from university stations in the country. Other sessions of the institute will be devoted to the use of radio in schools, methods of presenting educational programs, administration of educational programs, relation between educational broadcasting and newspapers, and the Canadian Radio Broadcasting Commission will be represented by a speaker who will report on the progress made in national broadcasting in Canada. Sample recordings of programs will be played at the institute and criticized. An award will be given to the program which is most interesting to listeners and which is best from the standpoint of presentation. Members of the institute will help rate these programs. The round table discussion groups will be held again this year with the topics: commercial stations; college and university stations; school broadcasting, and research in radio education.

DISCUSSION

READING FOR YOUNG PEOPLE: THE WASHINGTON PLAN

OVER a term of years superintendents of schools, teachers, members of library commissions and librarians, many of whom have studied at first hand the library service given by the Washington Public Library to the elementary and junior high schools of the District of Columbia, have urged that this service be described in print. In the last two years such requests have been even more insistent because of the wide-spread threat to children's reading in the general reduction of school budgets.

I therefore requested two members of my staff, because of their long experience with, and study of, school problems to prepare a paper showing the type of work being done in Washington and the economy of the plan. This was done in the hope that the Washington plan might prove suggestive for other communities.

In a recent radio address Governor Ritchie of Maryland called attention to the incidence of governmental expenditures:

> It is curious how indifferent or ignorant people have been in regard to government appropriations. It seems almost as if they thought government funds came like meteors from the sky. . . . The truth is, of course, that the government, whether national, state, or local, can spend nothing it does not collect, and everything it does collect comes from the people.
>
> There is no royal road to lower taxes. It does no good to reduce one kind of taxation and increase another kind or add a new kind. The only way to really lower taxes is to spend less money.

One way to spend less money might well be to eliminate the costly library in the elementary school. In their article, "The Taxpayer and Reading for Young People: Would a Library in Every School Justify the Cost?" published in the *Library Journal* for January 1, 1934, Charlotte H. Clark, supervisor, work with schools, and Louise P. Latimer, director, work with children, of the Washington Public Library, give tables of the comparative costs of the library in the elementary school and book service to school children from a public library reservoir supplying the classroom. Basing their figures on the cost of establishing 175 school libraries in Washington and the expense of their annual support, in comparison with the actual cost of equipping and supporting the central agency in the public library, they find that the school libraries' establishment cost in Washington would be 11 times that of the public library method, while supporting costs annually would be 15½ times as much for individual libraries as for a central distributing agency.

That the school-library movement is being urged on every elementary and junior high school in the country is indicated by "The National Elementary Principal" for June, 1933, the yearbook of the Department of Elementary School Principals of the National Education Association. While some schools and school systems have developed a satisfactory method, a large per cent. of the schools are either giving a poor book service or, if giving efficient service, doing so at a tremendous cost. The fact that the cost of library service in schools as so often administered adds a considerable cost to the school budget prevents the inadequately funded or the prudent school from attempting what is regarded as the *sine qua non* of education, an adequate book supply. In the light of the distressing facts on school budgets and especially on teachers' salaries presented in *Harper's Magazine* for November, 1933, by Avis D. Carlson in "Deflating the School," the wisdom of establishing and supporting a general reading library for every building may well be challenged.

There is no denying that supplementary reading for the school curriculum and cultural reading for school children is unquestionably necessary to a sound education. The real problem is to find a satisfactory and economical way to supply it.

After weighing the costs; the validity of the school library program as put forward by its advocates; the teacher-librarian problem; and the book collection frequently built up by the methods in popular use, through gifts and supplementary curriculum texts; after considering the school library from the teacher's point of view; and reviewing the community center plan frequently linked to the library in the school, the writers are able to come to definite conclusions in their summary of the comparative merits of the two systems:

> The school library movement is dangerous to the taxpayer because of its terrific cost; it is dangerous to the schools, because, in order to meet the costs of the school library, officials' and teachers' salaries, already low in many places, may be cut or not raised; because the schools may not be able to afford an adequate number of teachers; because necessary school building programs may be curtailed; and because school energies may be diverted to a collateral activity.
>
> It is dangerous to the child because in times of enforced economy provision for children's reading may be abandoned altogether; because, even in normal times, makeshift libraries will almost surely be established throughout the country; because the public library may be hampered in its legitimate work; because the child may fail to form the public library habit; and most of all because cultural reading is likely to be sacrificed to school problems with the tragic result that the child may grow up without acquiring a love of reading.

A careful reading of the entire article in the *Library Journal* by school officials and educators generally is invited.

GEORGE F. BOWERMAN,
Librarian

THE PUBLIC LIBRARY
WASHINGTON, D. C.

A PROGRAM OF ACTION FOR THE DEPARTMENT OF SUPERINTENDENCE

CLOSING of many public schools and restriction of activities of many others are inevitable consequences of the relationship between our school system and our economic system.

Further collapse of local school districts can not be prevented, in most cases, by local measures. It can not be prevented by appeals based on wishful thinking or based on a conception of economic conditions such as prevailed when local communities were self-contained and self-supporting.

We can't restore prosperity to our schools by mere propaganda any more than we can restore prosperity to business, to labor and to agriculture by propaganda alone.

The Department of Superintendence, therefore, should give its attention immediately to the adoption of an economic program compatible with America's resources, and along these lines:

(1) *Abolition of child labor,* with full educational opportunities for children and youth.

(2) *Work for every adult who is able to work.* This will mean support of such an employment program as the government has already initiated and which must go much further to achieve its goal.

(3) *High standard of living for all workers.* America has abundant resources—enough to provide adequate food, decent housing, sufficient clothing, wholesome recreation, for all. This means the more equitable distribution of wealth, such as has been suggested by Secretaries Ickes, Wallace and Tugwell.

(4) *Insurance for those unable to work*—and this should include every aged person.

(5) *A just and unified system of taxation.* The very essence of this would be to place the tax burden on those who can most easily bear it.

This program would involve permanent federal support of public education. It need not imply federal control of education, any more than present state-support systems involve state control of curriculum and teaching personnel in local communities.

With such an economic program must be an appropriate educational program, to include:

(1) *Physical and health education,* with medical and dental treatment provided at state expense.

(2) *Preparation for wholesome family life.* Many homes are such that the school must definitely supplement them in preparing boys and girls to participate in family life and to become intelligent and worthy parents.

(3) *Vocational preparation.* Such provision, of course, is futile if young people can not get jobs. Hence the need for an economic program which assures work to every able adult.

(4) *Preparation for civic life.* This involves realistic examination of current conditions in politics and economics. It would be attacked by politicians and by business interests who think that the school, like the church, should keep out of politics.

(5) *Recreational life.* In our new age of leisure the schools should emphasize the very things now being abandoned as wasteful.

(6) *Creation of a humane civilization.* Our children should be given a vision of the kind of America we might have under a democratic co-operative economy.

What steps should the department take to win acceptance for these economic and educational ideals? The department should do these things:

I. Create at once its connection with the national office of the department a full-time bureau with a personnel of trained newspaper writers. In this respect the department would follow the example of President Roosevelt, as described by Paul Mallon in the *New York Times Magazine* of Sunday, November 19, 1933:

> Mr. Roosevelt knows his publicity as no President ever has. . . . The country may not know it, but good publicity is a prime requirement for good statesmanship. . . .
>
> Mr. Roosevelt is building up quietly and indirectly a contact with the men and women of the country that transcends anything heretofore known in politics. Through the newspapers, radio, the camera and other avenues he and all the members of his private and official family are reaching out through the country to shake hands daily with millions. . . . Start with the secretariat. . . .
>
> Mr. Roosevelt chose to surround himself with three very good newspaper reporters. . . .
>
> These three men think and act in terms of publicity. It is their life.
>
> With their cooperation Mr. Roosevelt has established a personal relationship with working news men closer than any previous President has had. Indeed, a substantial number of Washington correspondents have been absorbed into the official New Deal fold; they have been given publicity jobs in various government departments or official positions outside the realm of publicity. These men were all top-notchers in the corps. They are friendly with most of the experienced Washington news gatherers. . . .
>
> Their employment in the New Deal is a legitimate efficiency move. They have far more ability and experience than the average politicians who ordinarily get such jobs. . . .

II. Persuade local school superintendents to follow Mr. Roosevelt's example in publicity. On the staff of every superintendent of schools, there should be a competent teacher with newspaper training.

This specialized worker, knowing news and what makes news, and being familiar, too, with education and its relationship to the economic conditions of the community and the economic program of the nation, would devote full or part time in helping to reveal the local schools as they are and *as they might be*.

. . . He would help to open the schools to free and uncensored inspection by press and citizens.

III. Train young men and women for public-school publicity work. Ask schools of journalism to include in their curricula a course in education.

IV. Introduce courses in education and economics into the public schools. Create a textbook embodying the points of the economic-educational program for use in all junior and senior high schools. Use a simplified edition in elementary schools and for distribution to parents.

V. Require a course in public relations of every person training for school administration. Techniques of news writing and of cooperating with the press should be well known to every superintendent.

VI. Convert state teachers associations and other groups to the economic-educational program. Make allies of farm groups, labor groups, parent groups, church groups. Get these to join the campaign for the economic-educational program. Supply them as well as individual superintendents with information, suggestions and plans for national and local publicity and action in persuading school boards, state legislatures and Congress to make the program effective.

Pursuit of this program would greatly strengthen the state and national educational associations, make them purposeful, active, militant.

Only such a concrete, tangible program based

upon a plan which in itself reflects American axioms of cooperation and welfare can produce the militancy which is essential if school executives and teachers are to help the American people achieve better schools in a more humane economy.

CLYDE R. MILLER

TEACHERS COLLEGE
COLUMBIA UNIVERSITY

SPECIAL CORRESPONDENCE

THE NEW EDUCATION IN THE REPUBLIC OF ARMENIA

THE republic of Armenia is of recent origin. It was organized after the world war, and on May 28, 1918, Armenia was declared independent. It continued its independent existence until November 29, 1920, when the Communists seized the control of the government. Since then Armenia is an autonomous republic, federated with U. S. S. R. (Russia), under the administration of an Armenian Soviet party. This new republic has a territory of 11,000 square miles, rich in copper mines and marbles. A little more than one million Armenians live within its boundaries. About one and a quarter million Armenians dwell in the adjacent and neighboring countries—450,000 in Georgia; 350,000 in Aizerbaidjan; and 450,000 in Transcaucasia and Southern Russia.

The new régime launched itself with great enthusiasm on a program of unified public education, secular, compulsory, supported and supervised by the state. At the head of this new educational organization stands the Commissariat of Education (Lousavoroutiun Commissariat).

Since 1920 the Commissariat of Education has been organizing, improving and perfecting the system of public education in the republic. In August, 1923, the compulsory education act was passed. The proper age for entrance into the public schools was made four years. Preschool education begins at this age. At eight years the pupil should enter the public school, which he can leave at twelve.

One of the most important problems with which the Commissariat of Education had to contend was the elimination of illiteracy. It is understood that prior to the organization of the new republic the Armenians under the rule of the Tsarist régime of Russia had only private and parochial schools. Even though the élite of the nation were well educated, the masses of people did not have access to free public schools. Hence the illiteracy of a great majority of people—almost 70 per cent. of the rural population—was a fact to be faced by the Commissariat of Education of the new republic. The new régime, therefore, turned its attention to the problem of lowering the rate of illiteracy. Schools for adults were opened, where young men of eighteen years of age and up could receive free education. Besides these schools, cottage reading rooms, clubs and other similar agencies have been able to combat successfully the evils of illiteracy. "It is a very small thing to teach a man how to read and write; it is necessary to make him half literate and then fully literate. For this reason great attention is paid to this problem and a network of institutions are spreading more and more widely in Armenia."[1]

The educational ideals of the new régime are greatly colored by their social and economic ideas. Education must be real, education must be for life, education must be universal and especially it must be the privilege of the lower classes—workers and peasants. These are the ideals of education reiterated in almost all the issues of the official educational magazine, *The Popular Illumination*. Education for life means that the school must represent life as it is, and not as it ought to be. The real life and not the ideal life, the material life and not the unmaterial or spiritual life is considered as the problem of the schools. Here one clearly sees the realistic and materialistic philosophy of Leninism.

If the school must be related to real life, it must take into consideration the actual environment of the child and must be closely related to the life of the community in which he lives. The students must actually take part in the social, economic and industrial activities of the community. Hence much stress is laid upon industrial, agricultural and polytechnic subjects. In addition to these, humanistic studies, such as history and literature, are organized on a different basis and with a different purpose.

[1] *The Popular Illumination* (Joghovertagen Lousavoroutiun), No. 11, 1927, p. 7.

To cultivate the spirit of collectivism and social cooperative production is the chief aim of these subjects. In order to bring the school in closer contact with the community, a new subject-matter called *Kavarakidoutiun* (the science dealing with the problems of the interior provinces) has been added.

In connection with the development of the spirit of collectivism, the students are given opportunity to become accustomed to useful production. The dignity of labor is exalted in every conceivable way. The pupils must learn to engage in productive labor suited to their particular capacities. In short, the philosophy of education is permeated through and through with one idea, namely, that the collective self is of more importance than the individual self.

In the realm of methods the old methods of education have been discarded and new ones have been adopted. As the purpose of education is to be entirely practical and real, the methods of teaching must be practical and real. "Complex" is a term to describe a method somewhat similar to our project method. There are three steps in the application of this method.[2]

In the first step, the teacher, through a didactic method, presents to the pupils certain aspects of a problem. The pupils select the problem. The teacher already has in his mind a detailed plan for the solution of the problem, but he is not supposed to tell it directly to his pupils. He must lead the students to select a plan almost similar to his own for the solution of the "Complex."

The second step consists of finding out the actual knowledge of the pupil in the various aspects of the "Complex"; also his attitude toward it, and his experiences toward it. The pupil must be led by the teacher to express himself in every possible means of expression in order that he may gain habits of self-expression in an objective way.

The third step consists of gathering new data and working on them by means of new observations and experiments. Excursions, researches and the collection of concrete data are the activities characterizing the third step. Diagrams, statistical tables and synthesis are the final phases of the solution of the "Complex."

[2] *The Popular Illumination,* No. 4, 1926, pp. 32–35.

It is believed that through this method the pupil will find an opportunity for self-activity and self-expression. It is contended, also, that according to the "Complex" method of teaching there will be no opportunity for the isolation of the various subject-matters, and the gulf which separates one subject-matter from the other is bridged over. Throughout all this one can see the traces of the modified concept of Herbart in regard to correlation and apperception, as well as the motor expression theory of Froebel.

In different classes the pupils take up different "Complexes." In one[3] class the "Complex of Community" is studied. In another the "Economic Status of the Local Community" furnishes the material. In still another group the "Interrelations of City and Country Life" are solved by this method.

Another plan which is in use, after having been tried in an experimental school in Erivan, is the Dalton plan, to meet the problem of the individual differences of the school children. The Dalton plan is well known in the United States; hence it will be superfluous to elaborate on this method.

Our own project method also is much talked of and discussed in educational circles. It is asserted, however, that the project method needs to be modified to encourage the spirit of collectivism. Therefore, the projects are expected to be solved by groups of cooperating students rather than by one individual student.

Laboratory and experimental methods are emphasized also. The real motive in the selection of these methods is to make education practical, to have it related to life, and to lead to actual participation in the activities of life.

To realize the aims of the new republic the following educational institutions are organized, with a unified program of studies, under the supervision of the Commissariat of Education.

(1) *The Community Center Schools in Rural Districts:* These represent an effort to offer preschool training to the children of neglected rural districts. During the summer months the government organizes these out-of-doors schools, which are established in the center of the village. Very small children with their mothers, usually illiterate, are gathered in these centers, and the following program is carried out:

[3] *The Popular Illumination,* No. 4, 1928, p. 345.

(a) Children are offered an opportunity to learn proper hygienic habits. The use of soap and towels, and bathing and swimming are taught.

(b) Children are organized in groups to train for self-service, self-help and also for mutual helpfulness and ideals of collectivism and cooperation.

(c) They are offered opportunities to observe the life of the village in all its phases. They gain knowledge in the use of agricultural tools and machinery. They obtain rudimentary notions about the interrelations of rural activities and the economic phases of city life, as well as about community holidays, etc., by means of excursions, story-telling and discussions.

(d) An effort is made to free the child from superstitious fears and to inculcate in him a sane knowledge of the working of natural phenomena. They work in their own truck gardens, struggle against the pests and insects, etc.

(e) Medical inspection is afforded the young children of the village.

(f) Various athletic games are encouraged, with the purpose of developing the spirit of collectivism and cooperation.

This is entirely a new type of institution. It has grown out of the particular needs of peasant life in the remotest corners of the republic. "The community center school is becoming a center of cultural pursuits (in the villages) which on account of its close contact with the home, especially with the mother, is proving to be a revolutionizing factor in favor of the improvement of rural life."[4]

The motto is: "Lead the child through the village community center to the kindergarten."

(2) *Kindergartens:* In 1920–1921 there were very few kindergartens. The Froebelian and Montessori ideals and methods were prevalent. The modified form of Froebelianism was more in line with the educational conceptions of the leaders of the republic than the old type of Froebelianism. But a new modification is introduced in the kindergarten ideals and methods. According to the new plan, the child must be brought in actual contact with the real activities of the community in which he is living. He must participate as far as possible in some of these activities in his own way. His childish interests must be linked with the real interests of the community. It is expected that in this way the kindergarten in rural districts will become a revolutionizing factor in the improvement of rural community life.

(3) *Four Year Schools:* This institution functions as the elementary school in the Republic of Armenia. Students enter this school at the age of eight and normally finish the course at twelve. But the age limit varies a great deal at the present time, owing to the newness of the public-school organization and the weakness of compulsory education enforcement.

(4) *Seven Year Schools:* These schools correspond to our institutions of secondary education. They are established usually in the cities, and more of them are gradually expected to be established in rural districts.

(5) *Nine Year Schools:* These schools represent the extension of secondary education. They combine the four years of elementary schools, three years of purely secondary education and two years of gymnasium or higher education, corresponding to the training given in our junior college. There are at present very few nine year schools established.

(6) *Technical Schools:* The Republic of Armenia is a small country of the size of Belgium. A considerable part of the country is uninhabitable on account of marshes and unirrigated and unreclaimed lands. This accounts for the need of industrial and technical training. The present government emphasizes this phase of the educational program. The country needs reconstruction and the need of technically prepared workers is of paramount importance. In November, 1921, the first industrial and technical school was established in Erivan. In 1922 another was established in Leninakan. All industrial occupations which are found in Armenia are taught in these schools. Carpentering, masonry, metal-working, electrical engineering, stenography, accounting and typewriting are taught. Shoemaking and dressmaking schools were established in Erivan in 1922; a school of bookbinding was established in Leninakan in 1923, and a central trade school in Erivan in June of 1923.

(7) *Agricultural Schools:* Agriculture is the chief occupation of the present population of

[4] *The Popular Illumination,* No. 11, 1927, p. 51.

Armenia. This explains the great emphasis upon agricultural education.[5] The purpose of these schools is not to prepare highly advanced specialists, but simply to train better qualified farmers. It is expected that the graduate of these schools will be familiar with the use of new and improved farming machinery, and the modern ideas in regard to the selection of better seeds and stock, etc. The immediate purpose is to prepare farmers to improve both the quality and the quantity of their products.

There are agricultural schools of seven years established in suitable locations. The state university also has a strong department in agricultural science.

(8) *Art Schools:* The Armenian people, in general, have shown great love for the cultivation of art. Especially have they shown marked talent in architecture, music and poetry. The leaders in present-day education are emphasizing art education. Three types of art schools are established.

(a) *Conservatory of Music:* This was established in 1921, on December 22. The purpose of this institution is to prepare: Musical technicians of mediocre talent, to fill various places in the musical institutions; musical artists of high-class talent and genius. "The Conservatory of Music is not an institution isolated from life."[6] Frequently musical programs are given for the benefit of the common people.

(b) *Studio of Classical Dancing:* The purpose of this institution is to study the origin and development of the Armenian folk dances, to restore the art of folk dancing and, if necessary, to improve and modify it.

(c) *Professional School of General Arts:* This was founded in 1921, with the purpose of preparing qualified specialists in artistic productions, as well as training teachers of painting and drawing for public schools. It has departments of painting and sculpturing. There are also attached to this institution training schools of artistic embroidery and jewelry.

(9) *Workers' Universities:* These institutions[7] were organized in 1923 in Erivan and Leninakan. The purpose of these institutions with pretentious name is to prepare in three or four years' time workers and peasants of high intelligence for admission to the state university, where they are expected to take special courses in *Hasarakidoutiun,* the subject of general culture in history, the humanities and institutional life of the country. These specialists are expected to take a leading part in the political reorganization of the republic. In these workers' universities, technical industrial training is also given, together with the general cultural studies.

(10) *The State University:* To crown the public educational system of the Republic of Armenia, the state university was organized on January 21, 1921, in Erivan, capital of Armenia.

The university has the following departments (faculties): Agriculture, Technology, Medicine, Humanities. The latter is subdivided into History and Literature, Law, and Pedagogy.

The state university is an institution of high scholastic standing. The members of the faculty are a select group, thoroughly trained. The majority of them are educated in the universities of Germany, Switzerland and Russia. The department of pedagogy especially is very strong. It has a pedagogical museum, representing the pedagogical and scientific activities of the Armenian schools.

K. A. SARAFIAN

LA VERNE AND CLAREMONT
COLLEGES, CALIF.

[5] *The Popular Illumination,* No. 3, 1927, p. 6.

[6] "Khorhertayin Hayasdan," p. 303.

[7] *The Popular Illumination,* "The Requirements for Admission," No. 2, 1926, pp. 70–74.

QUOTATIONS

REQUIREMENTS FOR ADMISSION TO COLLEGE[1]

THE financial depression did not react unfavorably upon college attendance until some time after its beginning. There is reason to believe that even in the event of prompt financial recovery the downward tendency in enrolment will continue for a time.

Decreased pressure for admission will doubtless lead to some general relaxation in entrance

[1] Dr. Adam Leroy Jones, director of admissions, in his annual report to the president of Columbia University.

requirements in undergraduate and professional schools as well as in graduate schools. Qualitative standards will probably be lowered in many institutions and we may expect, also, that there will be a tendency to throw overboard certain prescribed entrance subjects which might keep out a greater or smaller number of applicants.

Excellent and inspiring reasons can doubtless be found for removing this kind of obstacle to admission. It will be argued that if a person can become educated without knowing algebra or French—and perhaps he can—elementary mathematics and foreign languages should not be required for admission. If he can be educated without knowing any given subject, why ask him to know any specified subject when he enters college?

There is evident in many parts of the country a tendency of exactly this sort. Specific subject-matter requirements are being given up. Entrance requirements are being stated in vague terms and college curricula are being adjusted to the needs of a body of students who may have had little or no preparation in common and no instruction in any subject beyond the barest rudiments. Indeed, the tendency is one which in effect practically eliminates secondary school training as a prerequisite for college work.

The first years in college would presuppose no specific information. On this plan there may be little or nothing in the first two years of the college course which a student could not get in a first-rate high school and at the end of the college course he may have progressed no further if as far in intellectual achievement than the graduate of a European secondary school. For admission to a college under these conditions preparation, in the older sense, is no longer necessary. A modicum of intelligence and a mastery of the three R's are all that are presupposed.

This surely would mean in most colleges the debasement of the baccalaureate degree. In exceptional cases with exceptional faculties and leadership it may be possible to achieve values which will offset the loss due to lack of preparation for advanced work, but in other institutions the loss will not be compensated for. Indeed, from the standpoint of preparation for more advanced intellectual endeavor, the high-standing graduate of many a metropolitan high school is better prepared than the graduate of certain colleges. He knows something and he has learned to use his mind.

No doubt there have been in some institutions a literalism and formalism in curriculum and in instruction which have called for sharp correction. Many state universities have been compelled by law to receive any graduate of an approved high school whatever he may have studied or not studied. Other institutions have often framed their requirements to meet those of the state universities. Schools have brought constant pressure against requirements for specified subjects. Colleges have yielded to pressure all along the line.

Changes have been made even in some of the strongest colleges, but the doctrine that preparation is unnecessary for college work has not made much progress in such institutions. In Columbia College, in particular, there has been no tendency to eliminate subjects which have been required for admission for the past twenty years and more and which supply the foundation upon which the college course is based.

Columbia University is tightening its requirements for the admission of graduate students. Once admitted, the weak graduate student is difficult to eliminate.

A common practise in graduate schools is to admit a student on the presentation of a bachelor's degree from an approved college. Sometimes there is a requirement that a certain amount of undergraduate work must have been completed in the field in which the applicant desires to specialize, but aside from this it seems to be widely assumed that a mere bachelor's degree from a respectable college is evidence of fitness for graduate study.

A recent study of graduate students at another university shows that, while many weak students are eliminated from other schools of the institution, weak graduate students often seem to linger on indefinitely. It seems probable that such a state of affairs would be found in most institutions.

This study shows clearly also a fact that any sensible person might have known—namely, that graduation from an approved college is not in itself a guarantee of ability to do graduate work. Doubtless no one ever really supposed that it was, but in admitting students to graduate schools it was so much less trouble to act as if it were that the achievement and promise of the individual applicant were taken for granted if he had a degree from an approved college.

The better selection of graduate students is a subject which has recently received increasing attention in the graduate schools. It is unfortunate that decreases in enrolment because of business conditions will probably stand in the way of any general adoption of more effective methods of selection. In so far as such methods have been put into effect in Columbia University, the results have been found to be very satisfactory.

SOCIETIES AND MEETINGS

THE SOUTHERN INTERCOLLEGIATE MATHEMATICS ASSOCIATION

A NEW organization, known as the Southern Intercollegiate Mathematics Association, was organized at Centenary College, Shreveport, Louisiana, on October 21, 1933. This association embraces the colleges and universities in the states of Mississippi, Louisiana, Texas and Arkansas. Its chief object is to promote and support contests in mathematics and to encourage mutual and intellectual fellowship among its members.

As is well known, competition in mathematics is not new. In earlier times individual mathematicians often engaged in such contests. Moreover, intercollegiate contests in general are not new. It may also be pointed out that intercollegiate contests of all kinds will inevitably contain certain elements in common because, presumably, the objectives to be attained are either the same or similar. Nevertheless, what is perhaps new in education is the organization of this association.

Membership in the association is restricted to universities and senior colleges in these states. The four states have been arbitrarily divided into four regions in such manner as to make the number of members in each region approximately the same. The officers of the association have been so chosen as to make it thoroughly representative.

The contests have been divided into regional contests and final contests. The regional contests consist of preliminary examinations, and the final contests of final examinations. The preliminary examinations are held at the individual institutions at the same time and are the same for all institutions.

The regional winners are eligible for the final contests, which are held at the same time and place as the annual meeting of the association. It was decided that, in both the preliminary and final examinations, the "grade" shall be the average grade obtained by a given institution in all the examinations. Thus, the winner will be the institution and not the individual.

The contests are restricted to undergraduate students. The constitution of the association defines, among other things, the eligibility of the students, the types of contests, prizes and the methods of grading and making out examinations. The association obligates each member to recognize the students taking part in these contests by awarding to each of them a "letter" or an equivalent insignia.

Intellectual competition does not seem to have met with universal approval. It has been said that "it seems predicated upon the conviction that popularity means success." It would, indeed, be very unfortunate if popularity were mistaken for success or for scholarship. Such criticism, however, really betrays a lack of sympathetic understanding of intellectual contests. Any one who examines the possibilities of such contests as are contemplated by the Southern Intercollegiate Mathematics Association with a sympathetic attitude will see that, if properly conducted, such contests will, among other things: (1) give more importance and greater dignity to scholastic attainments; (2) divert some of the interest, enthusiasm and energy from athletics (especially football) to the intellectual domain; (3) help spread the conviction that our enduring pleasures and interests are in the last analysis intellectual; (4) benefit the schools participating in these contests by bringing them into closer intellectual cooperation; and (5) benefit the mathematics departments themselves in various ways.

Our attitudes toward what we do, what we observe, what we are—in short, our attitudes toward life and its concomitants—are the most important of all things; and the attitude we take toward such an association, and that with which we carry on its work will determine its success and just what it may be expected to achieve.

I. Maizlish
Centenary College of Louisiana

EDUCATIONAL RESEARCH AND STATISTICS

STATUS OF THE JUNIOR COLLEGE IN THE UNITED STATES, 1933–34

Continued increase in the number of junior colleges, coupled with an apparent (but not real) slight decrease in enrolment in them over the corresponding figures reported in School and Society[1] a year ago, is shown by reports received from this group of institutions of higher education in the United States up to November 20, 1933.

Detailed information regarding each of these institutions may be found in the "Directory of the Junior College, 1934," compiled by Dr. Doak S. Campbell, of Peabody College, secretary of the American Association of Junior Colleges, and published in the issue of the *Junior College Journal* for January, 1934. A synopsis of some of the more significant facts and summaries will be of general interest.

The total number of junior colleges (including some institutions which are prevailingly high school, academy or seminary in character, but all of which are doing some junior college work) is reported as 519—an increase of 22 or 4.4 per cent. over the number reported in 1933. The total enrolment for 1932–33 was reported as 105,457, an apparent decrease of less than one half of one per cent. over that of the previous year. That this loss is apparent rather than real is shown by two considerations. The 1934 Directory gives the list of institutions in existence during the year 1933–34, but reports enrolment data for the preceding completed year, 1932–33. Therefore the current Directory does not contain the name of Crane Junior College, unfortunately abolished this year by the astonishing action of the Chicago Board of Education. During 1932–33 the enrolment at Crane was close to 4,000. Had this figure been added to the reported enrolment of 105,457, it would have made a gain for the year of 3.3 per cent. instead of a loss of 0.5 per cent. as the published figures actually show. A second consideration showing the inadequacy of the published data is that in the current directory no enrolment data are given for fifty institutions, while last year there were only twenty-eight for which no enrolments were available. There is no question that the actual enrolment in these twenty-two additional "no-report" institutions, independent of the Crane College situation, would more than remove the apparent small loss in enrolment in the published figures.

[1] W. C. Eells, "Status of the Junior College in the United States, 1932–33," School and Society, xxxvii, 198–200, February 11, 1933.

The number of junior colleges and enrolment in them, as shown by successive issues of the Directory for the past seven years, has been as follows:

Year	Number	Enrolment
1928	408	50,529
1929	405	54,438
1930	429	67,627
1931	436	74,088
1932	473	99,476
1933	497	106,016
1934	519	105,457

Public and Private Institutions

Of the entire group of 522 institutions, 214 (41 per cent.) are public institutions and 305 (59 per cent.) are private. Corresponding figures last year were 192 public institutions and 305 private ones. The public institutions not only are increasing more rapidly in number, but they have much the larger proportion of the enrolment. Sixty-eight per cent. of the enrolment (last year 66 per cent.), or 72,100, is found in the public junior colleges, as compared with 33,357 in the private junior colleges.

Distribution by States

The number and enrolment in each type of junior college for each state are shown in Table 1.

California leads in total number of junior colleges, with 54; Texas is next with 43; followed by Iowa with 37, Missouri with 24, Okla-

TABLE 1

Number and Enrolment in Public and Private Junior Colleges in the United States

State	Total		Public		Private	
	No.	Enrolment	No.	Enrolment	No.	Enrolment
Alabama	8	483	1	...	7	483
Arizona	2	891	2	891	0	...
Arkansas	12	2,057	6	1,642	6	415
California	54	34,814	35	33,515	19	1,299
Colorado	5	522	2	250	3	272
Connecticut	5	321	0	...	5	321
Delaware	2	276	1	51	1	225
Dist. Columbia	9	433	0	...	9	433
Florida	7	643	1	201	6	442
Georgia	17	2,029	10	1,234	7	795
Idaho	7	1,537	3	986	4	551
Illinois	18	3,403	5	1,878	13	1,525
Indiana	7	520	2	...	5	520
Iowa	37	2,676	27	1,904	10	772
Kansas	17	3,704	10	3,330	7	374
Kentucky	18	2,739	1	192	17	2,547
Louisiana	9	649	2	548	7	101
Maine	3	153	0	...	3	153
Maryland	5	561	1	13	4	548
Massachusetts	9	674	1	44	8	630
Michigan	11	3,718	8	3,522	3	196
Minnesota	10	2,412	7	2,222	3	190
Mississippi	20	3,240	11	2,522	9	718
Missouri	24	4,762	8	2,427	16	2,335
Montana	2	379	1	379	1	...
Nebraska	7	746	2	131	5	615
Nevada	0	...	0	...	0	...
New Hampshire	2	190	1	...	1	190
New Jersey	4	235	0	...	4	235
New Mexico	1	209	1	209	0	...
New York	10	954	0	...	10	954
North Carolina	21	3,206	3	319	18	2,887
North Dakota	2	421	2	421	0	...
Ohio	12	3,563	1	1,215	11	2,348
Oklahoma	23	2,795	20	2,643	3	152
Oregon	2	...	0	...	2	...
Pennsylvania	7	995	0	...	7	995
Rhode Island	1	25	0	...	1	25
South Carolina	4	306	1	20	3	286
South Dakota	6	352	3	233	3	119
Tennessee	14	1,762	2	174	12	1,588
Texas	43	8,528	20	4,949	23	3,579
Utah	6	1,522	3	675	3	847
Vermont	1	101	0	...	1	101
Virginia	11	1,492	0	...	11	1,492
Washington	6	739	4	502	2	237
West Virginia	7	887	1	290	6	597
Wisconsin	6	906	1	689	5	217
Wyoming	0	...	0	...	0	...
Philippines	4	1,865	3	1,817	1	48
Canal Zone	1	62	1	62	0	...
Total	519	105,457	214	72,100	305	33,357

homa with 23, North Carolina with 21 and Mississippi with 20. Nevada and Wyoming are the only states in which none are found. One is reported this year for the first time in the Canal Zone.

Public junior colleges are found in 37 states, as compared with 31 states last year. California stands first with 35, followed by Iowa with 27 and by Texas and Oklahoma with 20 each. Private junior colleges are found in all but five states, the largest number being in Texas, California, North Carolina, Kentucky and Missouri in the order named.

California leads in total enrolment with 34,814, almost one third of the total enrolment in the country. Texas is second with 8,528, followed by Missouri with 4,767.

Increased enrolments are found in the public junior colleges in 20 states, decreased enrolments in 12, and no change in 3 states, the net increase being 3.3 per cent. The most notable increase in enrolment in public junior colleges occurred in California with an increase of 4,767 regular students (22 per cent.), but a decrease of 1,545 in special students, making a net gain of 3,222 or 11 per cent. for the year. A strong factor in this steady growth in California, even in times of severe economic stress, is the complete absence of tuition charges of any kind. Decreased attendance has resulted in some states in which substantial tuition charges have been imposed in the public junior colleges.

Increased enrolments are found in private junior colleges in 18 states, decreased enrolments in 24 states, and no change in one state, the net decrease being 7.9 per cent. Private junior colleges, with relative high tuition charges, have suffered severely in many cases, even though they have made substantial reductions in tuition.

Type of Institution

The junior college is prevailingly a coeducational institution and is becoming more so, 372 being reported of this type this year, as compared with 345 last year. Two institutions for men and two for women are reported in the public group, all the others being coeducational. Of the private group 47 are for men and 96 are for women. Corresponding numbers last year were 43 for men and 105 for women.

Fifty-eight per cent. of the private group are reported as under denominational auspices, the Methodists leading with 45, followed by Baptists, 33; Catholic, 27; Lutherans, 19; Presbyterians, 15; and sixteen other groups with one to six each, 38.

A considerable variety of types of administrative organization are found, which are summarized in Table 2. The percentage distribution for the same six types last year, based upon 463 cases, is added for comparison. The most notable changes seem to be in the decrease in the number and proportion of the six-year type (from 32 to 23) and of the four-year type (from 29 to 19), and the corresponding increase in the two-year type, which now includes practically 90 per cent. of the junior colleges in the country.

TABLE 2

DISTRIBUTION OF JUNIOR COLLEGES IN THE UNITED STATES ACCORDING TO TYPE OF ADMINISTRATIVE ORGANIZATION

Type	Number 1934	Percentage 1934	Percentage 1933
6-year	23	4.9	6.9
5-year	2	0.4	0.4
4-year	19	4.0	6.3
3-year	2	0.4	0.4
2-year	422	89.5	85.1
1-year	4	0.8	0.9

SIZE OF COLLEGES

The size of the 469 junior colleges for which enrolments are reported are summarized in the following tabulation:

0– 49	82	700– 799	8
50– 99	124	800– 899	4
100–199	120	900– 999	1
200–299	66	1,000–1,999	9
300–399	26	2,000–2,999	3
400–499	17	3,000–3,999	2
500–599	4	4,000–4,999	0
600–699	2	5,000–5,999	1

While the junior college is still a comparatively small institution, much too small in many cases for the highest efficiency, yet it is growing steadily. It is significant that there are 77 which have enrolments exceeding 300, as compared with 75 last year, and 15, even not including Crane, which exceed 1,000 as compared with 14 last year (including Crane.) The largest institution in the country is now Los Angeles Junior College, with a reported enrolment last year of 5,009.

ENROLMENT BY CLASSES

Enrolment by classes, as far as this distinction was observed, may be summarized as follows. A percentage distribution for last year is added for comparison.

Class	Number 1932–33	Percentage 1932–33	Percentage 1931–32
Freshmen	53,558	55.9	57.1
Sophomores	29,330	30.6	28.3
Specials	12,964	13.5	14.6
Total	**95,852**	**100.0**	**100.0**

The proportion of sophomore students has made a distinct increase over the previous year. If the special students are eliminated from consideration, 33 out of each 100 regular students were sophomores in 1931–32; 35 in 1932–33.

NUMBER OF INSTRUCTORS

The Directory reports 3,639 full-time instructors and 2,464 on a part-time basis in 394 junior colleges, an average of 15.5 per institution, as compared with 15.7 last year. If it be assumed that two part-time instructors are equivalent to one working full time, the equivalent of 4,871 full-time instructors, an average of 12.4 per institution, is found in these 394 reporting junior colleges. California is credited with 1,310 instructors, Texas with 472, and Missouri with 300.

CHANGES IN ADMINISTRATORS

A comparison of the 1933 and 1934 directories reveals a change in the administrative head on the part of 74 junior colleges, or 16 per cent. of the entire group. Last year a similar change of 12 per cent. was reported. In the public junior colleges the change was 18 per cent., in the private ones, 15 per cent.

WALTER CROSBY EELLS
STANFORD UNIVERSITY

NEW BOOKS IN EDUCATION

MEYER, ADOLPH E. *Modern European Educators.* Pp. xiv + 241. Illustrated. Prentice-Hall. $2.50.

PALM, FRANKLIN C. *Europe Since Napoleon.* Pp. ix + 890. Illustrated. Ginn. $4.00.

SCHOOL AND SOCIETY

WITH WHICH ARE COMBINED THE EDUCATIONAL REVIEW, ESTABLISHED IN 1891, THE TEACHERS MAGAZINE, ESTABLISHED IN 1878, AND THE SCHOOL JOURNAL, ESTABLISHED IN 1874.

EDITED BY J. McKEEN CATTELL

Volume 39 SATURDAY, FEBRUARY 3, 1934 Number 997

CITIZENSHIP TRAINING AT THE COLLEGE LEVEL

By Professor E. J. ASHBAUGH

DEAN, SCHOOL OF EDUCATION, MIAMI UNIVERSITY, OXFORD, OHIO

PAST AND PRESENT STATUS

HIGHER education has never accepted citizenship as a major objective. The colleges of liberal arts have stated their objective—to teach young people to be at home in the world; to develop culture; to liberalize the mind. The professional schools have each considered a specific vocational objective—the preparation needed for the practise of law, medicine, engineering, teaching, etc. None of these comprehend citizenship. Of course both types of schools hope that their graduates will be good citizens. Both point with pride to alumni who have been and who are good citizens. But the most higher education has done is to hope that this good citizenship was a resultant of its training.

"To be at home in the world" does not guarantee good citizenship. It does not even imply it. It implies rather a sufficient knowledge selected from the whole realm of knowledge to enable the possessor to converse intelligently with others who are at home and to meet life's situations in a manner comfortable to the individual. The college seeks to attain this for its students by requiring a given number of hours of work in each of four or five general fields, and a major of not more than X hours in one. Since each of these fields, however, includes rather distinct subject-matter departments, it assumes that four years, 120 semester hours of passing grade, variously distributed among, perhaps, an ancient language, a pure science, history, mostly ancient or medieval, and English, perhaps mostly speech, will achieve this goal. If it conceives this to prepare for the acceptance of the duties and obligations of citizenship, it must be on the basis of a faith in faculty psychology and formal discipline that almost staggers the imagination.

Fundamentally, the college staff believes its function is the production of scholars. Sound scholarship is its pride and highest joy. There is more rejoicing over one alumnus who goes on and makes good in a graduate school than over ninety and nine who go out and attempt to live on the basis of undergraduate work.

Since this is true, college courses are almost without exception organized in terms of the logical development of the subject and the prospective succeeding courses at both undergraduate and graduate levels. In other words, there is an effort to organize the materials into a logical sequence which leads directly from the most elementary principles to the farthest development on the frontiers of knowledge. Course 1, or 10, or 100 or whatever the first course may be numbered must be taken before course 2, 20 or 200. In fact, it forms a prerequisite for the succeeding course. In like manner the second course forms a prerequisite for the third, the assumption continually being that the primary purpose for taking one course is preparation for taking the next one. The mastery of this segment of the world's total knowledge, the ability to master and represent the work studied, the ability to utilize this knowledge in a further study of the field, become dominating and domineering objectives in the whole college course.

The college campus is a cloistered spot and, while each individual faculty member will admit that this is a world of economic, political and social problems, a frontal attack on the problem of preparing young people to solve these problems is considered out of place. It smacks of trade and vocations, of the "making a living" motive instead of the transcendental concept of "making a life."

Of course some practise in meeting miniature samples of economic, political and social problems is permitted. Some students may be permitted to work for their board and room and even manage boarding houses and the business side of dances and student publications. They may indulge in the game of politics in student elections and in social affairs, such as fraternities, sororities and individual dates. All these, however, are strictly extra-curricular, tolerated or at best encouraged to thereby prevent difficulties of one sort or another and not a part of the college program of training for citizenship in a democratic society.

In his introduction to an interesting book published some years ago, Chancellor Capen, of the University of Buffalo, who has had wide experience in the field of higher education, says:

> Conservatives are always partly right as well as partly wrong,—that is what makes them so hard to deal with. One of the purposes of education is to preserve and to pass on to the next generation the accumulated achievements of the race. But academic conservatism does not stop there. It closes its eyes to new conditions calling for new materials and new adjustments. The college, more than any other part of the educational system, is the stronghold of conservatism.

Of course, new departments have been created year after year in our colleges. A comparison of the typical college catalog of a century ago, even a half century ago, with one of to-day reveals many additions. Most of these represent divisions of fields that were formerly thought of as a single unit. The tremendous increase in knowledge has doubtless justified these divisions, and our emphasis in the training of college teachers on research and specialization has accelerated the movement. This emphasis, however, perhaps as much as traditional conservatism, has emphasized subject-matter fields and knowledge for its own sake to the exclusion of preparation for the most vital things which young people encounter when they leave the institution. Thirty-seven undergraduate courses in botany, 33 in economics, 24 in physics and 28 in school administration are but random samples from the catalog of one large state university. That there is sufficient material for this number of courses in each of the respective fields is not questioned. That each may be serving a worthwhile purpose may also be accepted. But that they have been conceived from the standpoint of the preparation of young people for modern citizenship could hardly be claimed.

A Ray of Hope

However, the picture is not altogether black. From time to time there have been individuals who have had a vision of a college education which would prepare directly for the duties and responsibilities of present-day life. For the most part they have been individual voices "crying in the wilderness." Occasionally there have been individuals entrusted with some administrative responsibility and who consequently have endeavored to get such ideas into a working program. An outstanding example of such an attempt occurred a few years ago at the University of Toledo, where the program of required courses for the freshman year included: Principles of Human Behavior, College Life, English Language, Modern American and English Literature, Problems of Modern Social Life, Modern History, Economics, and Modern Problems of State and City Governments. The aims of these various courses were set forth in the following manner:

Principles of Human Behavior. Aim: To help you [addressed to student, you note] to discover how and why you and other people behave as you do so that you may more intelligently influence the behavior of others as well as more effectively control your own conduct.

College Life. Aim: To discuss with you some of the most important problems of college life, the solution of which will enable you to get the most out of your college life.

English Language. Aim: To help you to improve your ability to express most effectively, in writing, thoughts which you feel are worth communicating to others. There is a great demand for men and women able to say what they want to say in the most forceful and telling way.

Modern American and English Literature. Aim: To give you a chance to read, discuss and appreciate the best of our modern literature. A study of the literature which is influencing the lives of men and women of to-day.

Problems of Modern Social Life. Aim: To help you to understand the complex society in which you find yourself, a rapid survey is made of the more primitive forms of social life and of the evolution of the most important of our own social institutions. When people live together in groups there always result problems. A study is made of these problems and of the efforts which are being made toward their solution.

Modern History. Special attention is given to the study of the social, industrial, commercial and civic aspects of the history of modern Europe and America.

Economics. A study of the most important topics in economics from the point of view of the individual, the family and the community.

Modern Problems of State and City Governments. Our people in their endeavors to develop democratic governments in their states and cities are confronted with all sorts of problems which they are attempting to solve in a variety of ways. It is the purpose of this course to study these problems and what is being done in Europe and America toward their solution.

The sophomore year likewise was set up with the same specific idea in view of giving the student a training for present-day life. The courses were set up as follows:

Physics of Every Day Life, or Chemistry of Every Day Life. Aim: As indicated by their titles, these courses aim to help you to discover the laws and principles of either physics or chemistry, a knowledge of which will enable you to understand many important phases of your complex physical environment.

Preventive Measures. Aim: We are to-day preventing rather than curing diseases. We study how the body works, and what we must do to make it work with ease, and not dis-ease. Most of our physical troubles can be prevented if we know what to do in time. This course teaches us what to do and why we do it.

Foreign Life Studies. Each foreign language department will offer a course devoted to a study of the important phases of the life of the people whose language and literature the department teaches. While students will be allowed to choose which of these courses they desire to take, the course is not required of students who continue the study of a foreign language, which may be done in either the Freshman or Sophomore year.

Modern Logic. Aim: We all admire the logical thinker. Most of us, however, tend not only to make serious mistakes in our thinking, but also be misled by fallacies in the thoughts of others. It is the aim of this course to help you to discover and incorporate in your own thinking the principles underlying efficient thinking, as well as to acquaint you with the mistakes and errors most commonly made.

The president and the board of trustees were in complete agreement that the fundamental purpose should be to develop socially efficient American citizens.

As might be expected, however, the program aroused immediate antagonism. A letter from a member of the faculty to the president is illustrative: "The unwisdom in the selection and distribution of courses is manifest in demanding Sociology, Economics, and Political Science in the first year or at least by the close of the second year. These subjects do not offer the strict intellectual discipline which other studies afford." Little need be said regarding the final results of this attempt to provide college training aimed directly at the preparation of citizens. Suffice it to say that the conservative faculty insisted upon the prerogative of their traditional departmental organization, and almost before the experiment started it ceased to exist.

The junior college movement has, in some instances, conceived of its function in these same terms: First, a recognition that all students, whether or not they graduate from college, go into the world of affairs with the responsibility of citizenship and hence should have had a preparation which would enable them to be more intelligent about present-day problems and second, that a larger proportion of the students who enter college neither complete the four-year course nor indeed expect to do so when they enter. To the extent that the junior college program has been conceived, independent of its integral relationship with senior college and university programs, emphasis has been placed upon present-day living and citizenship preparation. The pressure of the minority, however, who are definitely bound for college graduation, has seriously tended to formalize the junior college program in terms of the traditional college pattern.

Another effort, while not directed principally toward the ideal of effective citizenship, has been the organization of orientation or generalized courses in many of our colleges. The fundamental objective was the giving of students a broad over-view of the whole field of science or the whole field of history, for example, rather than an intensive study of a comparatively small area. These courses have not met the favor of the subject-matter specialists. They have been severely criticized as lacking in sound scholarship. In the science field particularly, though to some extent in others, it is regularly claimed that no one knows enough about the larger field to teach the course properly. Teachers of one science profess an amazing ignorance of all the other fields of science. One is led to suspect, however, that the real basis of the opposition lies in departmental jealousies and ambitions for large enrolments within these restricted preserves.

The School of Education at Miami University is engaged at present in an interesting experiment in this direction. Perhaps it has not progressed far enough yet to be called an experiment, but a committee representing the School of Education and the College of Liberal Arts, which furnishes the subject-matter service in the training of prospective teachers, is attacking the problem from this standpoint: What preparation can the university give prospective students for effective participation in our changing social order? What are the major problems about which effective citizens must be intelligent? By what means can we introduce college students to these major problems in such a manner as to secure the fundamental knowledge necessary for intelligent action and the attitude which shall determine desirable action.

In facing the problem of preparation for citizenship in this manner we are momentarily, at least, attempting to forget the high barriers of departmentalization, thinking, not in terms of history, government, sociology, economics, etc., but in terms of major problems of modern life and then asking what these departmentalized fields can contribute to the adequate understanding of the problems, to their solution and to the desirable next step in our social progress.

I think we understand some of the difficulties involved in a program of this kind: (1) We must reach some sort of general agreement regarding the major problems about which prospective teachers should be intelligent. (2) We must devise ways and means of organizing the worthwhile knowledge from the various subject-matter fields around these problems in such a way that a course or courses may be developed, sound in scholarship, rich in content and challenging to genuine intellectual endeavor. (3) We must find a way to permit such a course or courses to be offered and evaluated on the basis of its own merits without too much of a handicap from departmental jealousies and natural conservatism. (4) We must recognize that in addition to knowledge genuine training for citizenship involves also the development of ideals and attitudes which cause an individual to wish to utilize the knowledge he possesses and to put forth his best judgment regarding live problems into definite action. Furthermore, to whatever extent is possible there should be provision for the utilization of this knowledge and the strengthening of these ideals and attitudes by actual practise in the field of citizenship on the level of the student himself.

These are the problems upon which the committee is definitely at work. This is the line of approach to civic training on the college level which seems to me to be most hopeful. In my judgment we dare not continue indefinitely to focus our attention solely upon the acquisition of subject-matter largely selected and organized from the standpoint of subject-matter itself, particularly within the single field, but must face live problems, utilize all the resources of the university in helping students to understand these problems and to develop socially desirable attitudes and ideals. We must accept the responsibility for citizenship as a major objective in higher education.

EDUCATIONAL EVENTS

SUMMER COURSES AT THE UNIVERSITY OF MOSCOW

A NEW venture in international education sponsored in Soviet Russia by the People's Commissaria of Education and Voks (the Society for Cultural Relations with Foreign Countries), and in the United States by the Institute of International Education, Inc. For the first time since the revolution of 1917, the University of Moscow is offering for foreigners summer courses of interest to school teachers, social workers and students of the social sciences. The unique feature of the plan is that these courses are taught in English by a faculty of Soviet professors, and are especially designed to meet the summer needs of English and American students and educators.

The program offered, which includes courses in education, economics, psychology, sociology, criminology, art and literature and advanced Russian, is coordinated and executed by the Anglo-American Institute of the First Moscow University. The institute, which was recently organized, has a two-fold purpose. The first is to provide foreign visitors to the Soviet Union with the academic facilities and programs necessary for serious research and study. The second is to publish material on Soviet educational, social and cultural movements for the information and use of educators and students in all English-speaking countries. These two functions are inter-related, since it is planned to publish the results of research and study of the students. It is hoped that the program to be offered during the summer of 1934 will no doubt serve as a means of furthering cultural contacts between American, English and Russian students and teachers.

The plan offered by the institute involves four weeks of resident study at the University of Moscow and two weeks of supervised travel field work through the Soviet Union. University credit is certified by the University of Moscow. The summer session begins in Moscow on July 15. Rates for attendance, including travel and full maintenance, have been materially reduced for students, teachers and social workers only. Further information can be obtained from the Institute of International Education, at 2 West 45 Street, New York City.

AN EXHIBIT OF INDUSTRIAL CHEMISTRY AT THE NEWARK MUSEUM

The Newark, N. J., Museum has in preparation an exhibit for the layman which will be known as "Chemistry Changes Our World: an Exhibit of the New Discoveries for Industry and the Home." It will open about the middle of March. This is in furtherance of the museum's policy of presenting exhibits related to the industries of its community, but because of the scope and timeliness of the exhibit of industrial chemistry, it is expected to attract national interest.

Already over a hundred national firms have accepted invitation to cooperate. Among the first to offer cooperation were: E. I. du Pont de Nemours and Company, Incorporated, Celanese Corporation, the Bakelite Corporation, the Beetleware Corporation, E. R. Squibb and Sons, the Celluloid Corporation, Westinghouse Electric Company, Public Service Electric and Gas Company, Texas Gulf Sulphur Company and others. Among those who have offered to act in an advisory capacity to the exhibit are Dr. E. C. Worden, of the Worden Laboratories; Professor William T. Read, of Rutgers University; Dr. John H. Schmidt, chairman of the North Jersey Section of the American Chemical Society, and Donald Deskey, decorator, of New York City.

Special educational features of interest to the general public are being scheduled for the duration of the exhibit. A series of speakers prominent in the field of industrial and research chemistry are being invited to talk in explanation of various aspects of the exhibit. A series of educational moving pictures dealing with chemistry is also being arranged. A living room, designed by Donald Deskey, the New York decorator, and furnished entirely with synthetic materials, is expected to be one of the most popular features.

Previous industrial exhibits held by the Newark Museum include an aviation exhibit, held in 1932, which had an attendance of 85,000; a leather exhibit, held in 1920, which had an attendance of 75,000, and exhibits of pottery, floor coverings and textiles. The "Chemistry Changes Our World" exhibit will remain at the Newark Museum, opposite Washington Park, Newark, N. J., for two months at least.

THE GEOGRAPHIC PLAYERS, INC.

Dr. Roy Chapman Andrews, with a group of geographers, explorers and other scientific men, has organized in New York City a new theater, "The Geographic Players, Inc." It is planned, according to *The New York Times,* to present programs combining motion pictures, lantern slides, lectures and native music and dancing.

> To establish a legitimate theater with stage and screen where the world's geographers, explorers and scientists may present their experiences and records in a popular way.
>
> To foster through the spoken word and pictures appreciation for reality and natural beauty, which has been developed by scientific researchers who work with camera, microscope and telescope, whether under sea, on the earth or in the air.
>
> And to present this knowledge of the truth of life and the customs of the different peoples who live in the world, so that it may become of educational and inspirational value to the public.

The Geographic Players will present all their programs for the time being at the Waldorf-Astoria Hotel. Carveth Wells, the explorer, will be master of ceremonies.

The first program on China was given on Sunday, January 21. It was directed by Princess der Ling, first lady-in-waiting to the late Empress Dowager of China.

Other participants who spoke were Dr. Andrews, who showed motion pictures and lectured on his explorations in China; Lucille Douglass, archeologist, presenting painted slides of Far Eastern gardens, and Chester Su and Miss Han, who gave a program of Chinese music.

The people and life of Mexico will be the subject of the second program by the players, on Sunday night, February 4. Russell Hastings Millward, the explorer, is director of the program. He will also show motion pictures and lecture on the Mexican jungle and its products, present-day life and customs of the Mexican people and native dances and music.

Major James C. Sawders, explorer, will illustrate his lecture on the ancient civilization of the Mayas and Aztecs in Mexico with lantern slides. Motion pictures of Popocatepetl and the Floating and Borda Gardens of Mexico, to be shown by Julia Barrett Rublee, artist, and a series of songs and dances by native Mexicans, directed by Mrs. Mary Richards Bauer, well-known musical director, will be other features of this program.

The Italian program on Sunday night, February 18, will be supervised by Professor G. A. Borgese, Italian author and visiting professor at Smith College. He will speak on Italian literature. Maestro Sturani, of the Metropolitan Opera Company, will be heard in a program of Italian songs, and motion pictures will be presented of the most interesting places in Italy, featuring a travelogue of famous Italian gardens and villas.

Among members of the advisory board are: Dr. Mary E. Woolley, president of Mount Holyoke College; Dr. Wallace W. Atwood, president of Clark University; Dr. Charles B. Davenport, Dr. Ferdinand W. Haasis and Dr. Morris Steggerda, of the Carnegie Institution; Professor Mark A. May, of Yale University; Dr. L. A. Wolfanger, of Columbia University; Dr. Erwin Raisz, of Harvard University, and Dr. Elmer D. Merrill, director of the New York Botanical Garden.

THE FINANCIAL CONDITION OF THE ALABAMA SCHOOLS

Reports received by the Alabama State Department of Education showed, according to *The Christian Science Monitor,* that all public schools, for white and Negro, would be closed in February in 29 counties and 13 cities. Detailed reports from the 67 counties and the larger cities had not been received, and the opinion was expressed that local authorities were waiting for all hope to be exhausted before reporting definitely that the schools must be closed.

Montgomery County and City schools, all operating under one system, have been closed to 20,000 children and 500 teachers. Mayor W. A. Gunter is said to have expressed the hope that "something can be done" to reopen for the second semester, but no definite announcement has been made as to how the city and county hopes to raise the money.

"The board of education will act on the matter of resuming operation of the schools when it has been assured that the money will be provided with which to operate them," according to L. C. Cardinal, president of the board. W. R. Harrison, superintendent of schools is reported to have said that the anticipated revenue for the rest of the school year would not be sufficient.

Lieutenant-Governor Hugh D. Merrill, of Anniston, and Mr. A. M. Tunstall, Greensboro, Speaker of the House of Representatives, have suggested to Governor B. M. Miller that he call a special session of the Legislature to consider the problem. Governor Miller already had written Mr. Tunstall outlining his views on the question. Although, according to the *Monitor,* he expressed a willingness to discuss the matter further, the Governor set forth "certain principles which I believe are fundamental and which I must insist upon" if an extraordinary session is called. He opposes further reductions in the salaries of officers and employees of the state, but the carrying out of economies through consolidation of departments and other measures. He is "unalterably opposed" to the state's borrowing money "in violation of the constitution," and believes that "we should provide the revenue now and should not borrow and trust to getting the money in the future." He believes that the budget law, passed last year and providing that the state must operate within its income, should not be weakened.

REGROUPING OF DEPARTMENTS AT HARVARD UNIVERSITY

The regrouping of several departments in Harvard University, designed to make possible more effective administration and instruction, has been announced by President James Bryant Conant. One of the changes involves the consolidation of the three departments of botany, zoology and general physiology into a single, coordinated department of biology within the Division of Biology.

A second change substitutes for the former Division of Philosophy a Division of Philosophy and Psychology, with two departments, a department of philosophy and a department of psychology.

In accordance with this vote, Professor Oakes Ames, chairman of the division, has appointed the following committee to consider the general details of the reorganization: Professors Alfred C. Redfield, *chairman,* Henry B. Bigelow, William H. Weston, Jr., Ralph H. Wetmore, Jeffries Wyman, Morgan Upton and Edward S. Castle.

Commenting on the change, Professor Ames expressed his hope that the change will cause the teaching and study at Harvard "to become broader in scope, and break down the artificial barries which have often hampered those engaged in biological research."

In the new Division of Philosophy and Psychology, Professor Ralph Barton Perry will serve as chairman of the division, and also as chairman of the department of philosophy, and Professor Edwin G. Boring will become chairman of the department of psychology. The change, Professor Perry stated, "gives administrative form to a difference in the teaching and research methods of psychology and philosophy which has developed in recent years. The tendency of psychology has been increasingly to follow the scientific and experimental method. A separation between philosophy and psychology already exists in almost every university. But Harvard has for some years occupied a peculiar position with respect to this question, owing largely to the fact that many of its distinguished psychologists, such as James, Münsterberg and McDougall, were at the same time philosophers."

APPOINTMENTS OF THE OREGON STATE BOARD OF HIGHER EDUCATION

APPOINTMENT of acting presidents for the University of Oregon and Oregon State College has recently been approved by the Oregon State Board of Higher Education on recommendation of Chancellor W. J. Kerr, who has been head of the Oregon state system of higher education, comprising six institutions, for nearly two years.

George W. Peavy, dean of the school of forestry at the state college for twenty-four years, became acting president of Oregon State College, and Dr. C. V. Boyer, dean of the College of Arts and Letters since the reorganization of the state system of higher education in 1932, was chosen as acting president of the University of Oregon. Both executives will be directly responsible to Chancellor Kerr in their capacity as acting presidents and both will continue as deans of their respective schools.

Although the state board of higher education on March 18, 1932, approved the continuance of the administrative identity of the college and the university as well as the ultimate appointment of a president for each, for reasons of economy the appointment of these executives had been delayed. In the meantime, the administrative work of the institutions has been performed by the chancellor, the inter-campus deans and directors, and the executive secretaries.

With an increasing need arising for more local administration, which would also relieve Chancellor Kerr of much detail and permit him to devote more attention to major policies, the board accepted the chancellor's recommendation that acting presidents now be placed in charge.

Dean Peavy has built up one of the leading schools of forestry in the country since he was called to Oregon State College in 1910 after he had spent several years in the federal forest service in different parts of the West. He received both his bachelor's and master's degrees from the University of Michigan. He has had wide experience as an educator, both in the public schools where he was principal of one of the largest high schools in Michigan for seven years, and in institutions of higher learning.

Dr. Boyer joined the faculty of the University of Oregon in 1926, going to Eugene as head of the department of English after serving on the staff of the University of Illinois. He later became dean of the college of arts and letters of the state system of higher education in 1932. After receiving his bachelor's degree from Princeton in 1902, Dr. Boyer studied law at the University of Pittsburgh and later attended the University of Oxford and the American Academies in Rome and Athans. He received his master's degree in 1909 and his Ph.D. degree in 1911, both from Princeton University.

THE NATIONAL SOCIETY OF COLLEGE TEACHERS OF EDUCATION

THE National Society of College Teachers of Education will meet under the presidency of Stuart G. Noble, of Tulane University, at Cleveland, from February 24 to 28, during the meeting of the Department of Superintendence.

The tentative program follows:

SATURDAY, FEBRUARY 24, 1934

2:15 P. M.

Joint Meeting with the American Association of Teachers Colleges

"The Differences in the Training of Teachers in Liberal Arts Colleges and in Teachers Colleges," W. E. Peik, University of Minnesota.

MONDAY, FEBRUARY 26

Luncheon, 12:15 P. M. *to 1:45* P. M., *Hotel Cleveland*

Speaker, Edgar W. Knight, University of North Carolina.

MONDAY, FEBRUARY 26

Open Meeting, 2:15 P. M.

Presiding, Paul W. Terry, University of Alabama.

THEME: A Better Integration of Academic and Professional Studies in Teacher-Training Institutions.

"Training Teachers in a Knowledge of the New Social Order," Harold O. Rugg, Teachers College, Columbia University.

"Activities of the Committee on Education of the American Political Science Association," Earl Crecraft, *chairman,* the University of Akron.

"A Liberal Arts View of the Professional Training of Teachers and Administrators," Kenneth P. Williams, Indiana University, *chairman* of committee Q of the American Association of University Professors.

"Cooperation of Teachers of the Liberal Arts with Teachers of Education," Ralph W. Tyler, the Ohio State University.

Discussion led by: Ernest Horn, University of Iowa; Edgar W. Knight, University of North Carolina; Edward H. Reisner, Teachers College, Columbia University.

Business Meeting.

TUESDAY, FEBRUARY 27

Round Table Conferences, 9:15 A. M.

SECTION I. For Teachers of History, Principles and Philosophy of Education.

Newton Edwards, *chairman,*
University of Chicago

"A Functional Concept of the History of Education," Thomas Woody, University of Pennsylvania.

"The Philosophy of Education in a Changing Social Order," H. G. Hullfish, the Ohio State University.

"Comparative Education as a Subject of Professional Study," I. L. Kandel, Columbia University.

"Education of Teachers of the History of Education," Edgar B. Wesley, University of Minnesota.

SECTION II. For Teachers of Educational Psychology and Educational Sociology.

E. H. Cameron, *chairman,*
University of Illinois

"Intellectual Growth of Children," F. N. Freeman, University of Chicago.

——————————, David Snedden, Columbia University.

"The Foundations of Educational Psychology," C. R. Griffith, University of Illinois.

"Visual Aids in Educational Psychology," W. C. Trow, University of Michigan.

SECTION III. For Teachers of School Administration, Elementary Education and Secondary Education.

Ralph E. Wager, *chairman,*
Emory University

"Improvement in the Academic Preparation of Teachers," John E. Stout, Northwestern University.

"Criticisms and Recent Developments in the Teaching of Elementary Education," Edwin H. Reeder, University of Vermont.

"An Evaluation of Current Criticism of the Teaching of Secondary Education," Forrest E. Long, New York University.

"An Evaluation of Current Criticism of the Teaching of School Administration," Fred Engelhardt, University of Minnesota.

"Critical Issues in Public School Control," John R. McClure, University of Alabama.

Discussion.

TUESDAY, FEBRUARY 27

2:00 P. M.

Joint Session with American Educational Research Association
Presiding, Clifford Woody,
University of Michigan

WEDNESDAY, FEBRUARY 28

General Meeting, 2:00 P. M.

Presiding, George L. Jackson,
University of Michigan

"The Significance of the Experience of Foreign Countries in the Preparation of Teachers," I. L. Kandel, Teachers College, Columbia University.

Report of the National Committee on Courses for the Training of Teachers, Thomas Alexander, *chairman,* Teachers College, Columbia University; Frank E. Baker, State

Teachers College, Milwaukee; Frank P. Bachman, George Peabody College for Teachers; J. B. Edmonson, University of Michigan; Forest C. Ensign, University of Iowa; W. G. Gifford, State Teachers College, Harrisonburg, Virginia; Charles H. Judd, University of Chicago; W. W. Kemp, University of California; Alonzo Myers, New York University; Raleigh Schorling, University of Michigan; Willis L. Uhl, University of Washington.

Discussion of the various aspects of the report led by members of the committee.

Business Meeting.

EDUCATIONAL NOTES AND NEWS

IN order that the editor of SCHOOL AND SOCIETY may be able to meet other engagements, and with a view to possible future developments, the journal will be edited for a period of six months, beginning on February 10, 1934, by Professors R. D. Lindquist and W. H. Cowley, of the Ohio State University. Editorial communications should be addressed to the Editors of SCHOOL AND SOCIETY, Education Building, Ohio State University, Columbus, Ohio.

DR. KIRTLEY F. MATHER, professor of geology at Harvard University, has been appointed director of the Harvard Summer School for 1934. He succeeds Assistant Professor N. Henry Black, who directed the school in 1932 and 1933. The school was founded in 1871, and Dr. Mather is the tenth director. In addition to acting as director of the school, he plans to give one course in geology.

THE resignation, to take effect in June, has been announced of Dr. Richard Eddy Sykes, as president of St. Lawrence University; Owen D. Young, president of the university corporation, has also resigned. Dr. Sykes will become president emeritus and Mr. Young, who will remain a member of the board of trustees, has been elected honorary president of the corporation. He will be succeeded by Millard Jencks, a member of the publishing firm of Ginn and Company.

DR. C. E. RARICK has been appointed acting president of Fort Hays Kansas State College for the remainder of this year. Mrs. W. A. Lewis, widow of the late president, has been appointed acting librarian.

JOHN E. WADE has been elected deputy superintendent of schools by the Board of Education of New York City. Mr. Wade will succeed Dr. Harold G. Campbell, who recently was elected Superintendent of Schools. Both took up their new work on February 1. Mr. Wade has been connected with the public school system for thirty-five years and has been associate superintendent since 1927. He was educated in the city schools, the College of the City of New York and Columbia University. He served several schools as principal and then was made district superintendent.

DR. ALBERT Z. MANN has been appointed dean of Springfield College, succeeding Dr. F. N. Seerley. Professor Lawrence K. Hall has been appointed director of the new Division of Social Science and Dr. Hartley W. Cross director of the Division of Arts and Science. Dr. Mann has been acting dean since last October.

SIX professors who have served Colgate University for many years will retire or resign this year. Dr. Alfred Edward Alton, professor of Biblical literature, who has served for twenty-four years, is resigning because of an injury. Those who will retire because they have reached the age limit of seventy years are Dr. Robert Webber Moore, professor of German language and literature, who has served for forty-four years; William Franklin Langworthy, professor of botany, forty-four years; Frank Lucius Shepardson, professor of Greek, once treasurer of the university, thirty-eight years; Dr. Freeman Harlow Allen, professor of history and politics, twenty-six years, and William Henry Hoerrner, professor of music, twenty-four years.

OWEN D. YOUNG was reelected president of the Academy of Political Science at the annual corporation meeting held on January 22 at Columbia University. Other officers elected were: Dr. Albert Shaw, Jackson E. Reynolds and Dean Roswell C. McCrea, of the Columbia University Business School, *vice-presidents;* Professor Parker T. Moon, of Columbia University, *secre-*

tary and *editor* of *The Political Science Quarterly* and *The Proceedings;* George A. Plimpton, of Ginn and Company, *treasurer,* and Miss Ethel Warner, *director* and *assistant treasurer.* The following directors were reelected for three years: Dr. W. Randolph Burgess, Alanson B. Houghton, Dean McCrea, Ogden L. Mills, Professor Edwin R. A. Seligman, of Columbia University, and Dr. Shaw.

DR. WILLIAM J. O'SHEA, retiring superintendent of schools of New York City, was the guest of honor on January 27 at a testimonial dinner given by the Emile Pedagogical Society at the Waldorf-Astoria. The dinner, attended by about 300 teachers and guests, marked the forty-sixth anniversary of the founding of the society. Among the speakers were: Max Schonberg, president of the society; Dr. James J. Reynolds, a district superintendent of schools, who was toastmaster; Dr. George J. Ryan, president of the Board of Education; Dr. William E. Grady, associate superintendent; Dr. Harold G. Campbell, who succeeded Dr. O'Shea; Dr. John P. Conroy, retired district superintendent, and others.

DR. WILLIAM MATHER LEWIS, president of Lafayette College, was elected president of the Association of American Colleges at its twenty-third annual meeting at St. Louis. Other officers elected are: David A. Robertson, president of Goucher College, *vice-president;* LeRoy E. Kimball, comptroller of New York University, *treasurer;* Sister Antonia, president of the College of St. Catherine; Dean C. S. Boucher, of the University of Chicago; J. R. McCain, president of Agnes Scott College, and Dr. E. D. Soper, retiring president, *members of the executive committee.*

DR. JOSEPH MARR GWINN, retiring superintendent of the San Francisco schools, was honored recently at a banquet in San Francisco attended by more than five hundred school people. The dinner was held under the auspices of the Principals Association of San Francisco; George Learned, principal of Portola Junior High School and president of the association, presided. There were numerous speakers. Dr. Gwinn and Mrs. Gwinn were presented with tokens of esteem, also with a parchment testimonial.

A TESTIMONIAL dinner in honor of Dr. Henry J. Gerling, who was recently re-elected for a second term of four years superintendent of schools of St. Louis, Missouri, was given on January 18. It was attended by over thirteen hundred principals, teachers and others. The speakers included Mayor Bernard F. Dickmann; Chas. M. Hay, city counselor; Wm. L. Igoe, president, board of police commissioners; Stephen M. Wagner, member, board of election commissioners; William R. Gentry, lawyer, and various members of the Board of Education.

A DINNER in honor of Dr. G. S. Hopkins, on his retirement as active professor in the New York State Veterinary College, was given at Willard Straight Hall, Cornell University, on January 12. Dr. Hopkins is an original member of the faculty of the college. The dinner was sponsored by the alumni and was attended by over two hundred friends and colleagues. Dr. W. A. Hagan was toastmaster. The speakers were: President Farrand, who represented the university; Professor S. H. Gage, the original faculty; Dr. D. H. Udall, the present faculty; Dr. L. E. Moore, the alumni, and Dr. Hopkins, who responded.

A PORTRAIT of the late Dr. William Hand Browne, professor of English at the Johns Hopkins University, painted by Willem Wirtz, has been presented to the university by Miss Lucy Hand Browne.

THE latest issue of *The Bulletin of Bibliography,* a bi-monthly magazine, is dedicated to Dr. William W. Bishop, university librarian and head of the department of library science at the University of Michigan, as a tribute to his progressive librarianship. A full-page picture of Dr. Bishop is used as a frontispiece. He is now on leave of absence to attend the meeting to establish the policy of operation for the recently completed League of Nations Library, at Geneva. The library, the gift of John D. Rockefeller, Jr., has been erected at a cost of $2,000,000. Dr. Bishop acted on the building committee and is the only librarian on the advisory committee.

PROFESSOR HERBERT E. SLAUGHT, emeritus professor of mathematics of the University of Chicago, was at the Boston meeting elected honorary president for life of the Mathematical Association of America.

The ceremonies connected with the celebration of the semi-centennial of Temple University, Philadelphia, will take place from February 11 to 18. Those on whom honorary degrees will be conferred include United States Senator Royal S. Copeland, of New York; Dr. Glenn Frank, president of the University of Wisconsin; Dr. Albert L. Midgley, secretary of the Dental Educational Council of America, and Dr. George E. de Schweinitz, emeritus professor of ophthalmology at the University of Pennsylvania.

Dr. Harlan H. Horner, New York state assistant commissioner for higher education, recently received the degree of doctor of laws from Alfred University. Dr. Horner delivered the Founders' Day address at ceremonies commemorating the ninety-eighth year of the university.

Superintendent J. G. Moore, of Fargo, has been elected president of the North Dakota Education Association. Mr. Moore has served as superintendent of the Fargo school system since 1921.

Dr. Filmer S. C. Northrop, who is a member of the faculty of Yale University, has been elected vice-president of the Eastern Division of the American Philosophical Association. He will serve as visiting professor of philosophy at the University of Virginia during the leave of absence of Professor Scott Buchanan.

Dr. Herbert E. Bolton, professor of history and chairman of the department of history at the University of California, and Charles Tucker Brooke, professor of English at Yale University, will join the faculty of the University of Wisconsin for the summer session.

Dr. Harry M. Little, of Texas, has recently gone to Pittsburgh, Pennsylvania, to be psychologist at the Pittsburgh Child Guidance Center, which was recently established under a grant by the Buhl Foundation.

The Senate confirmed on January 27 the nomination of Walter M. W. Splawn, formerly president of the University of Texas, as a member of the Interstate Commerce Commission.

Professor Joseph L. Klamon, of the Washington University School of Business and Public Administration, has been granted leave of absence until March to accept an appointment as principal agricultural economist in the Agricultural Adjustment Administration. Professor Klamon is now in Washington, where he expects to work in the Dairy Division and in the Commodities Division of the Department of Agriculture.

Dr. Guy Stanton Ford, dean of the Graduate School at the University of Minnesota, has been appointed a member of the Commission of Inquiry on National Policy in International Economic Relations. The commission is a creation of the Social Science Research Council, of which Dean Ford is chairman of the committee on program and plans. The establishment of the commission was made possible by an appropriation from the Spelman Fund.

Dr. Scott M. Buchanan, professor of philosophy at the University of Virginia, has been granted leave of absence to carry on nine months' intensive work in the history and philosophy of medicine. He will work at the Institute for History of Medicine at the Johns Hopkins University. For the past six months he has been acting as philosophical adviser to the Josiah Macy, Jr., Foundation of New York in its attempt to formulate and solve some of the professional problems of medicine. Two reports of medical commissions, one on medical education, and one on the costs and efficiency of medical care, are the focal points of the study to be undertaken.

Albert K. Eaton, instructor in economics at Harvard University, has resigned to engage in research for the Deputy Minister of Finance of the Canadian Government. The position falls under the provisions of civil service and therefore is permanent.

Officers of McGill University have asked the government to make inquiries into the reported arrest of Dr. Kiang Kang-hu, chairman of the department of Chinese at the university, who, according to dispatches published in a Chinese-language newspaper of Toronto, has been arrested by police of the Nationalist government at Nanking on suspicion of aiding the rebel cause in China.

The Carnegie Foundation for International Peace has suspended all work in Germany, leaving vacant professorial chairs in that country, on account of charges that the School of International Politics in Berlin has become an organ of propaganda. Dr. Earle B. Babcock, European administrative director of the endowment, is reported to have stated that Dr. Hajo Hilborn, permanent professor at the Hochschule, had left Germany. The second chair which the endowment maintains is filled annually by four visiting professors.

DR. PAUL R. MORT, director of the School of Education of Teachers College, Columbia University, has been appointed chairman of a committee on the emergency in education of the Progressive Education Association. Other members of the committee, which will study the financial problems of education, include Dr. Robert M. Hutchins, president of the University of Chicago; Dr. Fletcher H. Swift, professor of education at the University of California; Dr. Alfred D. Simpson, assistant commissioner of finance of the New York State Department of Education; Dr. Sidney B. Hall, state superintendent of public instruction in Virginia; Dr. Homer W. Anderson, superintendent of schools in Omaha, and Dr. Charles A. Lee, state superintendent of schools in Missouri.

DR. ABBOTT LAWRENCE LOWELL, of Harvard University, will be the commencement speaker at Middlebury College, Vermont, next June.

DR. FRANK AYDELOTTE, president of Swarthmore College and American secretary of the Rhodes Scholarship Trustees, will be the speaker at the annual dinner of the alumni of the Massachusetts Institute of Technology, on Saturday evening, February 17.

DR. JOHN GREEN HARRISON, dean of the Mercer University School of Christianity, died suddenly on January 28 at the age of sixty-five years. Dr. Harrison was ordained a Baptist minister in 1896 and was pastor of the Tattnall Square Baptist Church in Macon, 1899–1905. He was professor of philosophy and education at Mercer University, 1907–15.

DR. ARTHUR GRANVILLE BEACH, professor of English literature at Marietta College since 1913, died on January 27. He was sixty-three years old.

ON February 9 and 10, the Department of Speech and Dramatic Arts at the University of Denver will again be hosts for the third annual Rocky Mountain Speech Conference, which is held for the teachers, students and speakers of the elementary and junior and senior high schools, of the colleges and of the churches of Colorado and the neighboring states. There are thirty sessions, ranging in subject-matter from debates for high-school and college students, voice and diction, and recent trends in speech training, to verse speaking, the telling of heroic and romantic tales and play production for school assemblies, little theaters and churches. This is the first time that the conference has definitely considered the religious drama and pageantry. This session will consider such subjects as what drama and pageantry are, when and how to use them for adults and for children, and how to present them from the point of view of costuming, lighting, make-up and music.

THE new dormitory recently given to Connecticut College by Mrs. Edward S. Harkness is to be called Mary Harkness House. The plans are now being completed by Shreve, Lamb and Harmon, the architects of Windham House, the dormitory finished in the fall. It is hoped that the new building will be ready for occupancy next autumn.

DISCUSSION

SHALL THE COLLEGES BE CLOSED?

HAS America gone mad in the matter of higher education? In our academic centers of higher learning are now registered four times as many men and eight times as many women proportionate to our population as are found similarly enrolled in England, France and Germany. The ancient's vision of cattle on a thousand hills fades before the panorama of youth in a thousand halls of higher learning. The metaphor is more than a mere figure of speech. By including five hundred junior colleges, the number of these institutions rises to fourteen hundred. The majority of these comprises those typically American institutions, the liberal arts colleges or the colleges of letters and sciences.

From all sides we hear of the difficult straits

in which many of these institutions find themselves. If the youth of the country were clamoring for admission to these colleges, our problem would be an easy one: namely, to equip these schools to care for their needs. In many cases, however, the tables are turned and the colleges are clamoring for students. Recruiting agencies have been set up and high-powered methods are being used. The problem has become one of adjusting the number and the quality of the colleges to meet the student demand.

What will the outcome be? The question must be answered individually for each college. The answers will vary with such factors as financial stability, quality of leadership, location and specialized function. A generalized answer for all liberal arts colleges must comprise a variety of suggestions. The following alternatives present themselves to each institution:

(1) *It may continue as a strong independent liberal arts college per se.* This alternative is open to those colleges which are firmly established in the performance of a function for which there is an obvious demand.

(2) *It may continue as a strong church college.* This alternative is open to those colleges which enjoy separatist support. They will continue in a worth-while function as long as they have a constituency which requires the service of such a college. The curtailing of immigration has an important bearing upon their problem. For another half century at least these colleges are likely to be meeting a genuine need.

(3) *It may become a municipal university.* This development can, of course, proceed only in large centers of population. The municipal university is one of the most recent developments in American higher education. Any private college located in a growing population center without a competitor may be enjoying a false sense of security. If the municipality feels the need of a university of its own, the private college may well examine carefully the function it is performing and perhaps conclude that its obligation and its privilege lies in becoming the nucleus of the new institution.

(4) *It may become a junior college.* This alternative may present an attractive field to many small colleges at present. It does not imply that these colleges reluctantly take the first step toward disintegration. It implies that they become thoroughly conversant with the functions of this new institution and with energy assume those functions. It does not imply that these colleges drop their two upper years and become a truncated two-year school. It implies that they actively participate in the reorganization of the American educational system which will eventually place them at the top of the secondary educational structure as one of the great four-year upper secondary schools, performing two years earlier in the lives of their students the great cultural function which they were originally designed to perform.

(5) *It may merge with some stronger college.* This alternative is open to those colleges which are located near some larger and stronger institution. To perpetuate its traditions by such a merger will prove very difficult, but it affords a graceful and convenient way of terminating the career of an institution that has outlived its usefulness.

(6) *It may close its doors and dissolve its organization.* How many small colleges have already taken this step and how many more are on the verge of doing so is a question that should be answered in the interest of a clearer evaluation of this phase of higher education in the United States.

Which of the above alternatives shall a college in difficult straits accept? At present no machinery exists that can render disinterested aid in helping such a college to arrive at a decision. In the absence of such machinery the writer proposes the following: (1) A commission appointed by the regional accrediting association; (2) a commission appointed by the denominational board of education; (3) a commission appointed by the Association of American Colleges.[1]

The commission of the Association of American Colleges will be the dominant agency and will serve all colleges throughout the country that request its services. It will call into consultation the commission of the particular accrediting association of the region in which the college is located. If the college is a church college, the denominational commission will also be consulted. The deliberations of these com-

[1] The appointment of these commissions is dependent upon the readiness of the organizations involved to cooperate.

bined commissions will be based on pertinent objective data previously gathered by an investigator appointed by the Association of American Colleges. The commission will render an advisory opinion, leaving, perforce, to the controlling body of the college freedom of judgment to act in conformity with its advice or to follow a contrary opinion. No attempt is here made to set up in detail a workable plan. The import of the above proposal is to emphasize the necessity of making some provision for salvaging, to the best advantage of all concerned, the assets of a rapidly disintegrating portion of America's higher educational system.

Irwin J. Lubbers
Carroll College
Waukesha, Wisconsin

PATENTS ON SOCIAL INVENTIONS

I am indebted to A. T. Deinboll, engineer, of Oslo, Norway, for sending a translation of a short article in the Norwegian encyclopedia "Kringla Heimsens," on organizational inventions, in which the idea is expressed that patents or protection by law might conceivably be granted for this type of invention. Mr. Deinboll was moved to send the translation through having read the article, "Will There be an Age of Social Invention?" in the *Scientific Monthly* for October, 1932, in which article, however, the idea of patenting social inventions is not expressed.

The conception of patenting this type of invention is not so far-fetched, after all. Familiar as we are with multitudes of mechanical inventions protected by patents, and knowing that for the last three years patents have been issued for the invention of new varieties of plants, we should admit the possibility of extending legal encouragement to the socially inventive. If a new variety of carnation can be exhibited by its patentee, as in New York City this winter, why not hold out a reward for plans to improve social conditions?

Difficulties enough would no doubt be encountered in reducing the idea to practise, but even to have it proposed is a gain. Just to conceive a better status for social inventiveness is something, when the person of creative turn of mind interested in organizational change is too frequently subjected to a barrage of decayed vegetables and antiquated eggs, or risks jail for radicalism.

The translation, as given, of the article in the Norwegian encyclopedia is quoted:

> *Organisation Inventions.* By organisational inventions (as contrasted with technical inventions) the right of the inventor is not recognized. And this in spite of the fact that it is primarily through organisation inventions that we may hope to reach a solution of the social problems, such as the problem of unemployment. It is conceivable however, that in the future a practically serviceable way of protecting by law also this type of inventions will be found. (Lit.: Sylwan: The Cultural Value of Inventions. Rossman: The Psychology of the Inventor.)

Arland D. Weeks

SPECIAL CORRESPONDENCE

THE CHICAGO PLAN ADAPTED TO A STATE COLLEGE

Fort Hays Kansas State College has revised its curriculum, the new feature of which included an adaptation of the Chicago Plan. This plan had a number of features which appeared to be good, such as, generalized instead of specialized courses, integrated instruction instead of scattered courses, and emphasis on achievement rather than on serving time.

In reconstructing our curriculum with reference to the Chicago Plan, we strove to reach the following goals: (1) An integrated general education in the lower division which should serve the double function of finishing off those who should not go farther and also prove an adequate preparation for the upper division; (2) a more extensive and a better organized major in the upper division; (3) a fair recognition of individual differences; (4) an objective measure of achievement as a requirement for graduation from both divisions, and (5) provision for experimentation on problems of college instruction. Provision was made for an integrated education by condensing the existing nine groups of courses (English, Foreign Language, Mathematics, Physical Science, Biological Science, Social Science, Philosophy and Biblical

Literature, Psychology and Vocational and Applied Arts) into four, namely: Biological Sciences, Humanities, Physical Science and Social Science. There is to be a general introductory or survey course which is a prerequisite for the departmental courses in each group. The survey courses are to be taken by all entering students unless exempted by freshman tests, which show that a student has sufficient general knowledge of a group to justify his taking the more specialized departmental courses. Even if a student is exempted from all the survey courses he must after all take from eight to ten sequential hours in departmental courses in each of four subjects distributed over three groups. In the upper division, he must have a major of at least forty semester hours related to one subject. These need not be all in the major department but must be advised by the major professor.

Provision is made for individual differences in the following ways: (1) A student may be exempted from survey courses if freshman tests show him to be qualified; (2) a student may secure advanced standing by passing a special examination in the course; (3) the load is adjusted to the student's abilities from a minimum of ten hours to a maximum of twenty hours, the average being fifteen hours; (4) a student may enter the upper division after one year in college if examinations show him to be qualified.

Provision is made for experimentation by keeping a permanent curriculum committee of twelve faculty members whose duty it is to revise the curriculum and to make recommendations once a year or oftener but never to make a final report. This committee not only encourages experimentation, but its members conduct experiments in problems of college instruction. This year an extensive experiment is being conducted in the possible advantages of ability groupings.

Not all these provisions will go into effect at once. This year two survey courses, one in the Humanities and one in English, are in operation. Next year there will be one in the Biological Sciences, and in the following year, we hope that the reorganization will be completed, except for minor improvements.

HOMER B. REED
FORT HAYS KANSAS STATE COLLEGE

QUOTATIONS

STUDENTS IN THE UNIVERSITIES OF INDIA

THE decision of the German Government to make drastic reductions in the number of students in the universities, technical colleges and other establishments which prepare candidates for professional life is certain to attract great attention in India, where the problem of middle-class unemployment is most acute. We saw last week that Sir George Anderson, Educational Commissioner with the Government of India, has called attention to the "grave complications" arising from the excessive number of undergraduates, and has pointed to the possibility that the machinery of the universities, which has already shown ominous signs of strain, may collapse altogether.

Sir P. S. Sivaswamy Aiyer made unqualified admissions on the subject at the annual convocation of Lucknow University last month. He may have had in mind the claim of the Uriyas for a university for their proposed new province when he said that far more important than an addition to the number of universities was an improvement in their quality and efficiency. He ranged himself with Sir George Anderson and other well-qualified observers in the opinion that many of the students resorting to the Indian universities lacked capacity to profit by so doing, and that it was desirable in their own interests that, instead of becoming undergraduates, many should turn to some technical or vocational course better suited to their aptitudes. He gave some illustrations of "woful ignorance" on the part of candidates at Delhi for the Indian Civil Service. Several candidates were unable to name even the provinces of India or their capitals. Sir Sivaswamy added that many of the students had not acquired even the habit of consulting a dictionary. The narrow range of their intellectual interests could be judged from the poor quality of the books and the journals they read.

Except that unemployment is intensified, the picture drawn in 1917 by the then Director of Public Instruction in Assam for the Calcutta University Commission is still true to-day. He wrote of the constant conflict in educational policy between the government and the people —the one desiring to improve the standard of education, the other crying on behalf of the hungry who were not fed, for the relaxation of standards and the wider spread of education, good or bad. The privileged classes did not take to commerce or industry; the unprivileged followed their lead. It was only by matriculating, wrote the D.P.I., and by taking part in the after-life which had been reserved for those who had matriculated, that the lower castes could raise themselves to consideration. Only so could they raise a representation strong enough to fight for their social and political interests.

The census superintendent for Assam, who tried in 1931 to get figures of the educated unemployed, states that matriculation has assumed much the same importance in the social sphere as a public school education has done in England. The ambition to "make a gentleman" of their son is not confined to the parents of the lower classes of any one country, and in Assam this takes the form of matriculation followed by a job which does not involve manual labor.—*The Educational Supplement of the London Times.*

REPORTS

THE AIM OF HARVARD UNIVERSITY[1]

ON November 21, 1932, President A. Lawrence Lowell tendered his resignation to this board, in June he presided for the last time over the commencement exercises, and on September 1 he turned over to his successor the direction of the university. With profound sorrow the Harvard community realized that this was to be the last year of Mr. Lowell's wise leadership. It is unnecessary for me to enumerate the many accomplishments of his administration. Almost twenty thousand men have graduated from Harvard College during the presidency of Mr. Lowell, and these alumni can testify to the marvelous change he wrought in the attitude of the undergraduates toward scholarship. This he accomplished by the modification of the elective system, the introduction of the tutorial system, the establishment of the freshman dormitories and finally by the inauguration of the house plan. The whole university has felt the dominating personality of the president and rejoiced in the free and vigorous intellectual atmosphere which his firm stand insured even in times of great stress. An eventful and significant epoch in Harvard history has closed. We who inherit the fruits of his labors unite in wishing President Lowell a long life and much happiness in the well-earned rest of his retirement.

Since this is my first annual report as president of the university, it may not be inappropriate if I discuss certain general problems in regard to our future. According to the account written nearly three hundred years ago, Harvard was founded "to advance learning and perpetuate it to posterity." We can all agree that these few admirable words still describe our aims, although the methods of advancing learning and the modes of perpetuating it have changed greatly in the course of three centuries. Our Puritan ancestors thought of education and theology as inseparably connected. It is hard for us to recapture their point of view; to-day, learning has become secular. Indeed, the universities are now the residuary legatees of many of the spiritual values which were guarded by the church three centuries ago. Our responsibilities are correspondingly increased and our ideals must be clearly defined. If future generations are to have that high regard for the achievements of the human mind which is essential to civilization, there must be a true reverence for learning in the community. It is not sufficient to train investigators and scholars, no matter how brilliant they may be; a large body of influential citizens must have a passionate interest in the growth of human knowledge. It is our ambition to inspire the undergraduates

[1] From the annual report of President James Bryant Conant of Harvard University to the Board of Overseers.

in Harvard College with an enthusiasm for creative scholarship and a respect for the accumulated intellectual treasures of the past. This is one way in which we to-day perpetuate learning to posterity.

Learning must be advanced as well as perpetuated. Indeed, in the last analysis it is only by advancing learning that it is possible to perpetuate it. When knowledge ceases to expand and develop, it becomes devitalized, degraded, and a matter of little importance to the present or future. The community loses interest, and the youth of the country responds to other challenges. Able young men enlist in an enterprise only if they are persuaded that they, too, may contribute by creative work. A zest for intellectual adventure should be the characteristic of every university. In the future, as in the past, our teachers must be scholars who are extending the frontiers of knowledge in every direction. I hope there will never be a separation of our faculty into those who teach and those who carry on creative work. No line should be drawn between teaching and research. Our strength in the past has lain in the fact that the spirit of scholarship has pervaded our teaching and our scholars have seen the importance of perpetuating the ideals of scholarship as well as advancing knowledge in their own specialty.

A university is a group of men—a community of scholars and students—and here lies the real problem in regard to the future of all institutions of higher learning. Harvard's success will depend almost entirely on our ability to procure men of the highest caliber for our student body and for our faculty. We have been fortunate in the past, largely due to the wisdom of my predecessors but partly in virtue of the historical accident of our early development. For a long period, also, Cambridge was located more nearly in the center of the population of the United States than it is at present. The problem of the immediate future is to devise ways and means to insure that we shall continue to obtain men of the greatest promise.

Harvard must endeavor to draw to its staff the most able investigators and teachers of the world. We have to-day a faculty of which we may be justly proud, but we can not ignore the fact that it is increasingly difficult to attract from other universities and research institutes the outstanding men whom we desire. I need not stress the necessity of our having at Harvard great scholars and investigators. Our ultimate contribution to society will depend on their scholarly output and their stimulating teaching. What they accomplish and those whom they inspire will be the measure of our success. If we have in each department of the university the most distinguished faculty which it is possible to obtain, we need have little worry about the future. If we fail in this regard, there are no educational panaceas which will restore Harvard to its position of leadership.

Together with other institutions of higher learning, we are the trustees in whose hands lies the fate of the future of human knowledge. We have at Harvard unusual advantages for scholarly work: libraries, museums, laboratories and special institutes. In some fields we can provide opportunities for investigation which are unequalled in this country. It is clearly our first duty to see that our permanent staff is composed of those who can use these facilities most effectively and wisely. We must provide every opportunity for the ambitious, brilliant young scholar to come to Harvard and demonstrate his worth. In order to obtain such men for our faculty, the academic life in Cambridge must be made more attractive in a number of ways. Sufficient time should be allowed for writing and investigation; a satisfactory balance must be struck between teaching and research. The governing boards might well give serious consideration to the problem presented by the transformation of the living conditions in Cambridge which has occurred in the last twenty-five years. Suitable houses for our faculty have become increasingly scarce and expensive. It is no longer as pleasant or easy to live in Cambridge as in many other university communities. This fact is a serious handicap to our development.

In the future even more than in the past, we should attract to our student body the most promising young men throughout the whole nation. To accomplish its mission Harvard must be a truly national university. The young men who enter the college and our professional schools are to-day drawn from no single locality and no single class. Student aid and student employment have enabled many with small means to complete their Harvard course. It is very difficult, however, for a student without any financial resources to continue his education in a privately endowed institution. It is particularly difficult if he comes from a distance. Yet we should be able to say that any man with remarkable talents may obtain his education at Harvard, whether he be rich or penniless, whether he come from Boston or San Francisco. This is an ideal toward which we must work; to-day our fellowship and scholarship funds are woefully inadequate. In my opinion we should have a large number of fellowships paying as much as twelve hundred dollars. The universities in this country should be the apex of a pyramid based on our highly developed school system. A path to the top should be open to all of exceptional talent. The privately endowed institutions must keep the way clear for the gifted youth with limited means.

EDUCATIONAL RESEARCH AND STATISTICS

THE RÔLE OF EYE MOVEMENTS IN DIAGNOSTIC AND REMEDIAL READING

THE marked educational handicap due to reading deficiencies among students has received an increasing amount of attention from both educators and research workers during recent years. It has been convincingly demonstrated that carefully planned and executed remedial treatment, based upon accurate diagnosis, relieves to some degree the reading disabilities due to specific causes.[1] If the subject is adequately motivated, he will, in most cases, show definite improvement.

Abundant data are at hand showing that inefficient reading is accompanied by characteristic oculomotor behavior. There are many and long fixation pauses, and irregular sequences of fixations along the line of print. At times these movements approximate an aimless roaming to and fro. This condition, of course, is the opposite of eye-movement patterns in the efficient reading of most material. On the basis of this apparent relation between disorganized eye movements, and reading disability some writers have concluded that the eye movements are important causal factors producing the deficiency, *i.e.,* peripheral motor habits are determinants of central perceptual processes. In the light of this conclusion, it is further assumed that training the eye movements will improve reading proficiency. Gray,[2] Robinson,[3] Pressey[4] and others have attempted to develop effective eye movements as a method of improving reading.

Another group of investigators claim that faulty eye movements do not cause reading deficiency. In none of his cases did Gates[5] find that inefficient eye movements were the basis of reading disability. Careful consideration of the problem led Tinker[6] to conclude that, in practically all cases, faulty eye movements are merely symptoms rather than causes of poor reading.

The efficiency of reading clinics rests on adequate methods of diagnosis and treatment. A critical examination of the rôle of eye movements in clinical programs should yield a clearer understanding of the importance of emphasis upon training eye movements as a technique for improving reading.

To the uncritical reader there seems to be some evidence that training eye movements improves reading. Both Gray (*op. cit.*) and Robinson (*op. cit.*) found that after training, fixations were fewer and more regular, and reading was more efficient. Examination of their procedures, however, discloses other training besides "pacing" the eye movements. There were usually included: (1) Emphasis on motivation for increased efficiency; (2) exercises

[1] M. A. Tinker, "Diagnostic and Remedial Reading," *El. Sch. Jour.*, 33: 293–306; 346–357, 1932.

[2] W. S. Gray, "Remedial Cases in Reading," Suppl. Ed. Monog., No. 22, 1922.

[3] F. P. Robinson, "The Rôle of Eye Movements in Reading with an Evaluation of Techniques for Their Improvement," Univ. Iowa Stud. No. 39, 1933.

[4] L. C. Pressey, "A Manual of Reading Exercises for Freshmen," Columbus, 1928.

[5] A. I. Gates, "The Psychology of Reading and Spelling with Special Reference to Disability," Teachers College Contr. to Ed., No. 129, 1922.

[6] M. A. Tinker, "Use and Limitations of Eye Movements in Reading," *Psychol. Rev.*, 40: 381–387, 1933.

to widen span of recognition; (3) emphasis on increasing speed of reading; and generally (4) emphasis on improving comprehension. Is the improvement in reading due largely to "pacing" the eye movements or to these other forms of instruction? When the latter program or its equivalent is employed, improvement in reading proficiency and also in regularity of eye movements is achieved just as readily as when "pacing" eye movements is included in the instruction. Furthermore, in several very successful methods of remedial reading, as in Monroe's[7] and Gates'[8] techniques, no attempt is made to train eye movements. In clinical practise there is no unequivocal evidence that eye-movement training as such produces improvement in reading. There is no sound basis in work of this kind, therefore, for concluding that faulty eye movements cause reading disability, or that training eye movements improves reading proficiency.

The inaccuracy of the return sweep from the end of one line to the beginning of the next may be mitigated by specific practise. This is quite different from "pacing" the eye movements within a line of print.

There are ample data which indicate that variations in eye movements are controlled mainly by changes in processes of perception and apprehension. Some of these will be cited: (1) A change in reading attitude or mental set produced either by changes in reading material or instructions to the reader produces changes in perception and apprehension which yield characteristic variations in oculomotor patterns.[9] (2) Whenever a complex relationship difficult to understand, as in certain mathematical formulae, occurs in context,[10] apprehension becomes slower and less certain. This is immediately reflected in an increased number of fixations and regressions, which are grouped around the formula. (3) In reading a foreign language, (Judd and Buswell, *op. cit.*), oculomotor sequences are fairly regular as long as apprehension of successive words proceeds in an orderly manner. If the apprehension is difficult, the eye movements become irregular, and if little or no comprehension is present (*i.e.,* there is mental confusion) the progress of the fixations approximates a random wandering back and forth over the passage. (4) In any reading situation where apprehension and perception shifts from large (word wholes) to smaller units (letters or syllables) the number of fixations are increased correspondingly. These examples, and others which might be cited, all indicate that central processes of perception and apprehension are to a large degree determinants of eye movements in reading.

The remarkable ability of eye-movement patterns to adapt themselves to each new reading situation emphasizes the rôle exercised by the central processes of perception and apprehension in determining oculomotor performance. New eye-movement habits are easily established, and they are just as easily modified. This modification occurs without any conscious sign of interference from previous eye-movement habits. The motor behavior of the eyes is, therefore, very flexible. Any modification in the perceptual and apprehensive process in reading is immediately reflected in the character of the eye movements.

The facts warrant the following conclusions: (1) There is no evidence that training eye movements as such develops effective motor habits which improve reading ability. (2) On the contrary, there are data from many sources which indicate that the nature of oculomotor performance in reading is largely determined by central processes of perception and apprehension. In other words, eye-movement patterns do not cause, but merely reflect efficient or poor reading performance.

The implications of these conclusions for diagnostic and remedial reading are clear. The measurement of eye movements, which requires elaborate apparatus and is costly if done accurately, may be dispensed with in the reading clinic. In the remedial treatment the training or "pacing" of eye movements may be omitted without lessening the effectiveness of the instruction.

MILES A. TINKER

UNIVERSITY OF MINNESOTA

7 M. Monroe, "Children Who Can Not Read," Chicago, 1932.

8 A. E. Gates, "The Improvement of Reading," New York, 1927.

9 C. H. Judd and G. T. Buswell, "Silent Reading," Suppl. Ed. Monog., No. 23, 1922.

10 M. A. Tinker, "A Photographic Study of Eye Movements in Reading Formulae," Genet. Psychol. Monog., 3: 65–182, 1928.

EDUCATIONAL REVIEW

Edited by Nicholas Murray Butler, 1891–1919, Frank Pierrepont Graves, 1920–1924, and William McAndrew, 1924–

MONTHLY SURVEY OF EDUCATIONAL BOOKS

By WILLIAM McANDREW

SUCCESS IN CIVIC FAILURE

RECORDER RUSSELL'S[1] much study is no weariness to your flesh. Out of every seeming abortive effort of America to reform he squeezes elixir. There is a law of conservation in moral energy no less than in physical. No good deed is ever lost. This quality in Russell's books: "Uprising of the Many," "Songs of Democracy," "These Shifting Scenes," "Wendell Phillips," and this last view of the waves of revolt from 1880, make them rich additions to high-school and college libraries. Added to this quality there is practical force, a moving stride that gives his books the quality of staying in your hand until they are read to the last word.

Your boys and girls ought to know Millholland, and Inez his queenly daughter, Edmond Kelly, Percy Grant, Father McGlyn, Weaver, DuBois, Mailly, Henry VanDyke, Dakota Townly, Edwin Ladd, Erskine Childers, Eamon de Valera. They are the sort that public schools must produce if education's original aim is not lost. Russell shares his acquaintance of them and admiration generously with you. There is little of civic life in our time that he has not, as a newspaper editor, or a crusader, been in.

The real source of our grievous distress, he says, has been production for profit rather than for general welfare. Free Trade is dead everywhere and will so be until we learn from panic and disaster to discard this insane obstacle to providing man with his needs.

All through the years of civic incompetency and corruption the truest element of the strength of the political machine has been the chronic indifference of the average citizen. The schools, says Editor Russell, failed in the education of the citizen to his responsibilities. No doubt they made bond-salesmen, electricians, lawyers; but they did not make citizens. The American does not know the history of his own bunking by the bosses. Schools don't teach it. Their graduates are ready to be caught in the same old traps.

After the story of each of the several betterment movements in which he has worked, Dr. Russell gives you an autopsy. A tart cynicism flavors each. You might set him down in the group of many men over fifty who have soured on improving the state of man. Russell wouldn't stay there. The shafts of his sarcasm have pierced no sincere person—including shooter Russell himself. He is quite unpoisoned. By brushing the dust off declarations of principles which were formulated by the reviled a few years back, he shows these demands now fulfilled and accepted as desirable.

Often he stops in his story of some apparently forlorn hope and disproves the Nordic fallacy that every effort is futile which fails. Whatever the virulence of ridicule, any organization working to establish a world without war, without poverty, without spoilation of the worker, with an opportunity for all to live and know what life really means, is no failure even if it appears to accomplish nothing.

Russell talks with his old friend, Steffens and shows him plenty of improvement where Steffens holds there is none.

No revolt ever totally fails. We don't get all we want but we get something. We move slowly. But when we get rid of the social system that has cursed mankind we shall speed up. All this can be done without shedding one drop of blood or locking anybody up. Can be and will be.

This quality in Russell's writing, together with the virile snap in it, makes him especially valuable for high-school libraries at this time.

EDUCATION, REFORM AND PUBLIC INDIFFERENCE

THE third printing of Dr. Counts' survey of the American world[2] comes to SCHOOL AND SOCIETY as evidence that this critic is being listened to. The conservative view of the Ameri-

[1] Charles Edward Russell, ''Bare Hands and Stone Walls.'' Charles Scribner's Sons, New York. 441 pp. $3.00.

[2] George S. Counts, ''The American Road to Culture.'' The John Day Company, New York. 194 pp. $2.50.

can school's influence upon the political health of the country, he says, hangs on although our leading educational thinkers take the position that the school should serve as a leavening and creative force in the social order. But the people as a whole lack the revolutionary spirit of their ancestors. America believes that the state should control the schools for the purpose of making good citizens. But the type of good citizen is merely one who reveres the names of the founding fathers who left the American form of government almost divinely ordered. There is little responsibility left for keeping it clean or making it better.

Dr. Counts reviews American faith in education, governmental responsibility, local initiative, worship of the individual go-getter, inclination toward education for its money value, democratic traditions, mechanical efficiency, low regard for intellectual achievement, weakness of educational philosophy, which are some of the large topics critically examined. The material of this book is fundamental for educational success. The treatment is deeply in earnest; the conclusions, inevitably disconcerting; the effect, stimulating.

AS A FRENCH OBSERVER SEES US

A journey through modern American history in company of Mr. Faÿ[3] means enjoying entertaining company. This historian and biographer is one of the French authors best known in America because of his "Washington," his "Franklin," and his service in universities here. Part I, "In Search of America," pictures the discoverers and inventors. Part II considers our financial pirates of steel, of the golden calf, wreckers, gravediggers and the three wooden kings—Harding, Hoover and Coolidge, each of whom lost America. Part III is America finding herself again, led by Franklin Roosevelt.

America to most Europeans, says the author, is a big factory where everybody is following rules set by Messrs. Edison, Ford, Hoover and Owen Young. Nobody seems to remember that America is a nation which has already gone through several stages and kinds of civilization. Her real greatness has been to forge ahead and to develop from generation to generation constantly new forms of life and culture.

[3] Bernard Faÿ, ''Roosevelt and His America.'' Little, Brown and Company, Boston. 345 pp. $2.75.

With every new president America adopts a new aspect as an amiable woman changes her hat and expression to please each new lover; always activity reigns supreme. Work is America's discipline; success, her goal. Everything has been sacrificed in order to exalt production of things. The machine multiplies the effectiveness of every movement. Politicians, priests, professors, women, children, conform to the rule. Every one acts; every one hurries. It is the apotheosis of work. And it is a catastrophe. The American is attracted toward crisis. The Englishman is fascinated by passivity. The American wants a violent reaction and enjoys an explosion.

American scholars and their students are instinctively realizers. They make tools, machines and appliances. They do not so much fill their minds with knowledge as their country with things.

American politics does not represent a battle of ideas as in numerous European countries where parties use set programs, nor has America any acute class-conflict; for every citizen believes himself capable of arriving by his own efforts at the top of the social scale if he works hard enough and has luck. American politics is guided by those who have the sinews of war, the financiers. No ambitious young man can be elected unless his expenses are supplied by wealthy backers.

Mr. Faÿ's observation of American family life is that the executive power is in the hands of the mother. The legislative power lies in the children. The father has hardly any power other than that of going away, which is easy, the country is so large.

In the United States the schools, colleges and universities are invaded by millions of young persons who have little interest in ideas, in the arts or sciences, little desire for excessive refinement and little inclination for intellectual labor. They are eager to taste the joy of life. They go to college for immediate happiness and to win success in sport, the reputation of being a good fellow, which will win them a good position in life.

The American is proud. It irritates him not to be able to understand. The prestige of professors is not high.

The nomad farmer has reached the last frontier. He is defeated. He must either adopt the old custom of Europe or invent new methods.

These are some of the appraisals I have gathered here and there from the volume.

For the present chief executive this Frenchman has an enthusiastic esteem. Franklin Roosevelt is a genius in understanding and guiding the people's mind. The President is determined that captains of industry shall put the general interests of the country before profits and returns on investments.

Professional men seem likely to pay a higher price for the recovery program than any one else will. They can not organize and fight as the workmen do nor follow the combinations of the business men. They have no lobby at Washington, no possibility of codes. They will work harder and earn less than other groups. The middle class will pay for the war between capital and socialism. They have not enough capital to defend capital. They have enough to be injured.

WELLING'S VISION OF SOCIAL STUDIES

MR. WELLING'S[4] fifteen-page booklet is making a stir. Joy Morgan says a study of it should be required in every high school. New York State Commissioner of Education Graves congratulates it as a very worthwhile contribution to civics teaching and stimulative to greater emphasis on the practical and functional duty of instruction. Cayce Morrison believes it presents the most challenging and vital issue before the public schools at the present time.

It asks why the schools, founded as they were to enlighten public opinion so as to give force to good government, are so notoriously avoiding references to the quality of government that surrounds them. Every study of American affairs in books written by other than teachers portrays politics in rural communities, villages, towns, cities, states and nation, as no rule by the people for the people, but as a cleverly manipulated business for the benefit of spoilsmen. To know the theoretical purpose of road commissioners, park departments, water works and other public services, says Attorney Welling, is a good start. The community-civics texts portray the whole governmental machinery in its perfection and do it superbly. They allow the young citizen to go into the civic world with the childlike belief that government is rendering these services splendidly. Why should he bother with any idea of his responsibility? The appalling fact is that these services are in every state in the hands of manipulators more concerned with their own profit than with the general welfare. Our public service, whatever statistics you study, is more inefficient and corrupt than that of any of the enlightened nations of the world—and our schools are the most expensive. They were set up on the promise that they would make politics their main study. They avoid it.

If the management of a medical college, confronted with an outbreak of typhoid in the town, should make it a point to avoid all teaching about typhoid, its prevention and cure, they would be following the example of the public schools.

New York civics teachers avoid presenting the history and methods of Tammany. Chicago, Philadelphia, every American city, sees its youngsters going through high school untaught as to the actual way in which its own political machine debauches government. Lyman Beecher Stowe, invited to address a New York high school assembly, said he would talk on the Seabury findings. The principal would not permit it. Which is more effective for good government, asks Author Welling, saluting the flag or showing what must be done to get good government?

There are warm paragraphs on the merit system, proportional representation, grand jury, law enforcement, current events study, newspaper reading, practical politics and books that high-school boys and girls should study.

Active for a long lifetime in the cultural and civic life of New York this persistent apostle of a school system making an effort to live up to the promises its founders made when they saddled its cost of education on the whole community, regardless of whether taxpayers have children in public schools or not, clings to the belief that teaching political responsibility can be done by the public schools and is the most patriotic, interesting and enjoyable pursuit an educator can find.

It is certain, he says, that when the intelli-

[4] Richard Welling, "Civics as it Should be Taught." National Self Government Committee, 80 Broadway, New York. 15 pp. 10¢, 25 copies, $2.00.

gence and loyalty of our army of teachers is turned to this duty they will give us a Republic such as our founders visioned.

PROJECT FOR ALL HIGH SCHOOLS AND COLLEGES

To be taken in small doses and along with Mr. Welling's booklet of which I just spoke, both to be thoroughly chewed by the teeth of discussion, is Professor Dewey's[5] case study of city politics. It is a digest and interpretation of typical American government. A committee of educators and civic workers under Dr. Dewey's chairmanship prepared it. I call it a typical situation because Lincoln Steffens, Charles Edward Russell and Judge Seabury, experienced investigators, have averred that your state, county, city or town has the same sort of trickery and corruption in its government. The world generally considers it an American disease.

This booklet is civics teaching based upon how government actually works, who works it, what they make out of it, recommendations for cure.

Every high-school class in automobilistics goes as thoroughly as possible into care and repair of the machine. Every medical school spends most of its time on diseases. English language study devotes attention to the correction of errors. All the surveys of civics teaching and social studies affirm that it misses the main points: investigation of actual trouble, emphasis on responsibility of those trained in the public schools, duty of making government a general welfare proposition, not a scheme for individual profit.

The much advertised question of the Tammany boss was, "What are you going to do about it?"

Ask your children the same, day after day. Try the Hamilcar-Hannibal morning set-up.

You have acclaimed John Dewey, *primus inter primos,* your leader. For the land's sake, follow him.

AMERICA'S QUEST FOR FREEDOM AND HAPPINESS

ADAMS' epic,[6] fourteenth printing, new edition, has the sweep of the great river which "just keeps rollin' along." The author likes to revert to it as a type of the progress of the nation. Here is history elevated to the heroic but with such a sure touch of the seasoned artist that the color, the movement, the sentiment everywhere is germane to the event. Allen Nevins, professor of history at Cornell and Columbia universities, has called this the best single volume on American history in existence. It is a splendid picture of the procession from Columbus to Henry Ford. It is, says its author, the working out of a desire to discover how the ordinary American became what he is to-day in outlook character and opinion. The dream of a bigger and better nation than any yet appearing on earth has been that of riches and happiness for all citizens of every rank. That dream has been present from the birth of the nation. It is the greatest contribution we have made to the thought and welfare of the world. The frontier now vanished, was a safety valve from over-tension. A new prosperity may bring a greater danger to the dream than any encountered in the past. We have merely glimpsed the vast temptations of a new frontier of the exploitations of applied science. The struggle will be a severe one for the ordinary man to hold fast to those rights of life, liberty, and happiness which were vouched to us on parchments and in the vision of statesmen.

The epic theme, the great ideal, the American dream, is present in the thought of historical-painter Adams in his treatment of each epoch. The settlement of our country was different from earlier migrations in history. It was not led by warrior lords with followers dependent on them. It was one in which the common man was hoping for greater freedom and happiness for himself and his children. But none of the leading men of the English colonists who came over to settle expected or wished to see any democratizing of social or political life. Most of them feared and detested democracy. John Winthrop cursed it as the meanest and worst of all forms of government. The American dream owes more to wilderness and the necessity of individual will and cooperative help than it does to its early leaders.

Historian Adams finds no need of preserving the myths of Revolutionary days in order to

[5] John Dewey, "New York and the Seabury Investigation." City Affairs Committee of New York, 112 E. 19th St. 49 pp. Paper 25¢, $15.00 per hundred.

[6] James Truslow Adams, "The Epic of America." Little, Brown and Company, Boston. 446 pp. $2.50.

make the real glory clear. The frenzy over the Boston "Massacre" was made by the tricks of propaganda. There is no recorded instance of a British soldier offering any affront to a Boston girl. Local orators ranted over "our beauteous virgins exposed to all the insolence of unbridled passion."

Mr. Adams shows no fear of the burning of his books on bonfires of the super-patriots of to-day. He rejects the mistake of thinking of America of 1776 as a nation of patriots pressing their services to aid the war for freedom. It was hard to get men into the army and to keep them there.

In no American history is there a better interpretation of what the concentration of wealth has done to the dream. For the most part the gatherers of riches have been as ruthless as any pirate who ever trod a bloody quarterdeck. The owners of great fortunes have, at their death, been held up by newspapers and clergymen as models for youth.

In the chapter, "The Age of the Dinosaurs," the epic comes to tragedy. The Hamiltonian system has run amuck. The simple problems of 1787 have become so overwhelmingly complex that it is a question whether we can solve them by intelligence or whether we shall become the victims of uncontrolled forces.

Old and young, teacher and pupil, Americans all, have a boon in this remarkable book.

FOR A UNITED EUROPE

NATIONALISM has no future. The European states are incapable of carrying on their present isolation. Europe can only become a whole when it feels itself a whole. The entire history of Europe teaches this can not be brought by force. The importance of the French spirit in bringing this union is the theme of the brilliant Cohen-Portheim study.[7]

The legacy of the ancient world, Latin France, the Gothic period, the culture of the grand Epoch, the age of gallantry, Voltaire, Rousseau, the Revolution, Napoleonic Era, and each succeeding epoch, furnish chapters on the literature, art, drama, music, science, and civilization of the French nation.

The idea that Paris is France and the rest of the country is nothing gets firmly fixed during the last hundred years in the minds of all nations. It is a complete illusion. As its importance grew, Paris cut itself off more and more from the life of the country. But there are thirty-seven millions of Frenchmen outside of Paris. They are the real France, with the real traditions. Paris is only France in intellectual and artistic matters. In every other respect it is not France but its exact antithesis. Paris matters more to the rest of the world than to France itself.

In the commonly assumed decadence of nations France is one of the soundest states in Europe. Far from showing any symptoms of either mental or physical degeneration it has all the vitality characteristic of the Latin races as a whole through the generations. The foreigner's idea of Paris, based on the things he is looking for and which are provided solely to meet his demand, his thoughts of naughtiness, finds no echo in the Frenchman's mind. Those things he views with pious horror combined with a desire to explore the modern Babylon for himself.

Cohen-Portheim's presentation of the origin of the arts of the different epochs is refreshingly simple and clear. Balzac was the first to depict in art the driving force of modern life, money. The heroes of earlier literature were far too exalted for money to direct their actions. Flaubert is strong where Balzac is weak, in style. Zola is the Balzac of the second empire. Taine is a writer to whom psycho-analysis can be traced back. Without Taine modern intellectual life would be unthinkable.

France has her unemployed generals, her fire-eating clergy, and her small minded folk who say that because war and hatred have always existed they always will exist; but their influence is on the decline. France is free of any victory-complex. The French nation is thoroughly sound, the least hysterical, the least extreme of any people in present-day Europe. It is in such a healthy condition that it has the leisure, the peace of mind and the inclination to create. From time immemorial it has had respect for the opinion of its intellectuals such as no other nation has shown. It is still the country where a Voltaire, a Rousseau, a Zola could make history and where Rolland, Duhamel, and Barbusse are making it to-day.

[7] Paul Cohen-Portheim, "The Spirit of France." E. P. Dutton and Company, New York. 214 pp. $3.00.

These are not encomiums by a Frenchman. Cohen-Portheim was born in Berlin of an Austrian mother, spent his boyhood in her native land, and thereafter painted in France and England. Alan Harris' translation of this book preserves the fascinating verve of the original.

A JOURNALISTIC ABBOT'S PROGRESS

WILLIS ABBOT, class of '84, was for us freshmen at Ann Arbor a boast and a model. He ran the college paper. He wrote without a dictionary. The text-book of the first year English classes: "Abbott's "How to Write Clearly" was attributed to him. For wasn't he, born in the shadow of Yale, of a family of writers? John S. C. Abbott of Bowdoin, author of a library of histories including the famous Life of Napoleon Bonaparte was his grandfather. Jacob Abbott of the famed Rollo books was his grand uncle; Lyman Abbott, a cousin. When the popular "blue jacket" histories of exploits of the American navies appeared, we of that time bidding for a momentary importance used to say "I was in college with him."

In his latest book[8] Abbot tells how one of the t's was dropped from the family name. He begins the story with his experience as a cub on the New Orleans *Times-Democrat.* He takes you a companionate trip through newspaperdom in New York, Chicago, Kansas City and Boston. He knew Jefferson Davis, every President since Cleveland. Bryan confided in him. Hearst employed him. He held high post on the *Sun* in its bright days. The affairs he describes are fascinating in themselves. The author's interpretation and comment make them glow. No one has given so illuminating an account of Bryan's "Cross-of-Gold" electrification of the Chicago convention. Roosevelt the First, Champ Clark, Woodrow Wilson, Jim Creelman, Calvin Coolidge, William Randolph Hearst, Mussolini, Robert La Follette, John Altgeld, Herbert Hoover, politicians, statesmen, martyrs, cranks, journalists, come to you portrayed not as the author learned of them second hand but as he saw and heard them.

Abbot adds a significant feature to his accounts; a habit of seeing the gains in other than wealth and material possessions that have come to the country. In Abbot's boyhood Johann Most, saloon-keeper, was the hero of American socialists, a name anathema to most of the country. As the author writes his pages, a Congregational minister, Princeton graduate, Norman Thomas, is the leader of the party and invited as speaker by college lecture associations.

We take for granted phenomena in politics more amazing, more incredible than incidents and results of armed revolutions in other parts of the world.

As a journalist on a Hearst newspaper Dr. Abbot can tell you how much his employer had to do with bringing on the silly Spanish War. The story is something not to be missed.

Collier's Weekly sent investigator Abbot to the chief industrial communities to study the economic results of prohibition. He was instructed to give Old John Barleycorn a square deal. The mission turned the researcher into an advocate. There is only one side to the story, he writes. Prohibition enhanced the efficiency and improved the condition of labor. Banks and insurance companies got the money that used to go over the bars. People were better clad. Children came to school better fed. Every sort of legitimate business reported increased trade and ascribed it to the closing of the saloons. These things, says the recorder, he saw with his own eyes. They were true then; they are true now.

One of the most interesting features of Dr. Abbot's moving narrative is his account of the cure that allied him to Christian Science, the experience of the *Monitor* newspaper of that church and of the journalism that works by the motto: "Injure no one; bless all mankind."

This book is so interestingly wholesome that the school and college library will be much enriched by it.

WORKABLE SELF-TRAINING

PROFESSOR PITKIN[9] returns to his thesis that however much you are doing, you can do more. How?

By the art of which most people know too little, the art of making the most of your energies. His latest book is a working technique of this.

He shuns guesses and wishes. He gathers and coordinates facts well established. He

[8] Willis J. Abbot, "Watching the World Go By." Little, Brown and Company, Boston. 358 pp. $3.00.

[9] Walter B. Pitkin, "More Power to You." Simon and Schuster, New York. 298 pp. $1.75.

shows that schools can double the efficiency of the population and reduce to the vanishing point unhappiness caused by lost motion.

The source of human energy, its creation and use, diet, exercise, temperature, working posture, rhythms, getting warmed up to work, duration, attention, interest, boredom, fatigue, sleep, rules of the workshop, are some of the chapters outlining a program for the worker and based on the findings of the experimenters in human laboratories.

Essential for all the rules is your need of trying them until you fit your own case, for you are all different. Some are logy from too much sleep. Some are poor workers from too little. Naps in the day time buck up Carl Seashore. They ruin Walter Pitkin's day.

Wallace Irwin can't do good work after noon. Franklin Adams does his best by artificial light. Frank Stockton chose the noisiest place he could find for his literary workshop. Thomas Carlyle padded his to keep out the little sound from a quiet Chelsea street.

When your work hour begins, jump in at your hardest. Easy beginning makes a bad ending. The well-known "time o' dread" disappears like mist in the sun if you energize at the start. Failure to observe this is playing hob with children who are in the charge of certain favorite educators. Starting with the correct belief that men do well only what they are interested in doing, these pedagogues distort the thought into an absurdity.

A line of penetrating studies of workers has brought out the amazing waste of their energy due to wrong relations of supervision. Except where home affairs are in a mess the worker's attitude toward his immediate superior is the most influential factor. The boss who tries to get the most out of his gang by a stiff pace and by bawling out the slow workers ends with an output far below the cheerful supervisor who explains patiently what the work is, why rest periods should be used and the easiest way to work. Charles Frohman was the greatest praiser in the theatrical field and developed the best actors. The age-long resentment of teachers against tyrannical school boards in a large American city has kept instruction at a level much below the average of metropolitan schools.

A more lavish waste of human energy would be hard to find in the chronicles of mankind than our tragic American education. It has been an enthusiastic, grandiose, expensive mistraining of a generation of incompetent, disillusioned, confused, rebellious adults.

Only now and then does Psychologist Pitkin break out into these indignations. The general tenor of his book is cheery, confident, exact and not too hardly workable. School people need it, as who does not? It is rich in material for discussion by high-school and college classes where, if anywhere, the appetite for learning how to live is active.

THE FINE ART OF GROWING OLD

PROFESSOR FERRIS,[10] now past seventy-one, writes the best of the many de-senectute books I have read. He tells his own experiences as the unwelcome signs of a change kept intruding upon him. How a sense of humor can be cultivated after you pass your seventieth birthday, how extraverting is acquired and how good it is for you, the need of some high-class reading every day and of some of your best writing, the cultivation of a more refined enjoyment of food, the advantage of paying more attention to dress and to athletic events, and many other matters of import and interest are covered by this agreeable essayist with charm and cheer.

You do well to get out of your regular job before you are seventy and let the public have the services of some younger and fresher man in that position. But you have in your lifetime accumulated a lot of private things you want to do, you really do not retire until you turn your face to the wall and pass out.

AS SCHOLARS SEE THIS REVOLUTION

MR. LINDEMAN'S essay[11] is an interpretation of a ten-year inquiry by a group of scholars concerned with the chronic conflicts in American life following the world war.

The great scientific revolution by which there will be scientific thinking about human relations and social issues is yet to come. It will ensue, says the author, when men collectively and cooperatively organize knowledge to achieve and make secure the social values. The book covers experimental living, interpretation of American life, research, the use of facts, class conflicts,

[10] Elmer E. Ferris, "Who Says Old?" Sears Publishing Company, New York. 205 pp.

[11] Eduard C. Lindeman, "Social Education." The New Republic, New York. 233 pp. $1.00.

business and ideals, racial disturbances, international relations, inter-sectarianism, community, conference and education.

The fact that the social sciences are so extensively taught in the public schools, elementary, high and collegiate, gives evidence of a deep-seated longing for social goals. Indeed, the "American dream" of a society governed with the consent of the governed constitutes one of the boldest of social aims. The entire American tradition has pointed in this direction. But the ease with which power groups may influence and direct public opinion increases with our size and the attendant lessening of the individual's influence. The daily press, with few exceptions, has become primarily a business enterprise. It thus tends toward that political and economic opinion which resists change and protects the status quo. Those who view public issues in the light of reason have largely concluded that false convictions and prejudices have become the primary movers in our affairs.

The cry for less government in business is futile. Business could not run without government protection. Business could not be free of government restraint without putting all government in jeopardy. The kind of industry, corporationalism, civilization, that has emerged implies increasing social controls all along the line.

Now that the perfervid period of economic expansion is over and we begin to see that we have created a civilization of things and machines for which our managerial skill is inadequate, planning in the interest of a more valid control will hopefully ensue.

The three concluding chapters, although not specifically intended for educational administrators, are applicable to them at almost every point. Discussion, conference, selection of means most likely to reach the larger aims, rejection of the traditional less vital methods, are of immediate necessity.

EDWIN BROWN'S HAPPY HIT

To my mind Edwin Brown's new book[12] of classroom cases and problems lacks only one thing, an index, to make it as perfect a manual as I have seen. One of the author's maxims slipped in well along in the book is, "only thoughtfully acquired information is usable." Apparently Professor Brown has come to believe only used information is thoughtful, for his book is one continuous requirement of making you use and think. It has infinite variety, running from Irvin Cobb to Glenn Frank, a defense of Benedict Arnold, a business man's roast of education set against the enduring Ratio Studiorum, everything in such order that the dictum of the early artists, "unity in diversity" seems here fulfilled. And the questions, batteries of them! "What is the difference between Dr. Bagley's proposal and Dr. Coffin's?" "Here are definitions of education by thirteen eminent leaders. Which one do you think best? Why?" "Now clear your mind by writing a paragraph on your meaning of education and don't copy it from any author."

This Brown man has abundant enthusiasm for teaching. He sees it as a profession of exalted devotion, immense importance and great powers of giving satisfaction to the practitioner, but he does not slop over nor preach about it. He repeats enheartening passages by masters whom you can not discount; he puts questions up to you which you can not answer without acknowledging that education is essentially in the front rank of all the activities forever respected. Then, after an exaltation produced by the masterful content of a page, you will be answering the persistent questioning so as to be saying that no inspirational crooning over the nobility of teaching gets you anywhere unless you know your stuff, where you intend to take your youngsters, and what is the road for getting there.

After a spirited trek through educational aims during which you, rather than the guide, tell what you see, Conductor Brown gets you through the whole realm of teaching, discipline, testing, planning, organizing, promoting, keeping up attendance, vivifying incentives, using the curriculum without formalizing everything, developing your own self, getting your own fun and sloughing off the traditional notion that your supervisor is a pest.

These matters are not presented as didacticum. They are a series of occurrences in town, in school, in teachers' meetings, where live persons say and do what they are saying and doing all through American educationdom.

It is a course in the training of intending

[12] Edwin J. Brown, "Everyday Problems in Classroom Management." Houghton Mifflin Company, Boston. 306 pp. $1.80.

teachers. Dr. Brown has developed it in his own classroom where he keeps young men and women very lively on the toes of their mind. It has authorities and their works listed at the close of each chapter. It has other features of a good working text but beyond that it is a remarkably interesting composition and will carry even a lone reader profitably to the end.

A STURDY EDUCATION

FIVE large units are chosen by Butterweck and Seegers[13] as basis for their view of the educational field. These are the school to-day, how it came to be, its unrealized ideals, the scientific method, guiding the learner, school organization, the teacher. Each unit begins with a preview followed by the discussion, the problems, the questions, the collateral readings. The arrangement throughout shows high-grade workmanship, the result of much experience in teaching the subject with skill in combining thoroughness with interest.

The seventy-four pages devoted to unrealized ideals are sure to make the oldtimer wince. Much of what the school does it does because of unexamined tradition. Many subjects must be thrown out. The authors have no awe for the present curriculum, elementary, high, or collegiate. The college still dictates the subjects to be taught below it. For a time the academies revolted and set out to be people's schools but in turn came under the collegiate yoke. It was not until 1919 that the high schools adopted the seven cardinal objectives and omitted college preparation from the list of main duties. But the masters have taught the college requirements so long that they can not vision a school other than one conditioned by the teaching of these subjects. Result: generations wedded to the status quo.

The authors realize that they must deal with the two educational camps: those who wish to teach the earth as flat; those who will teach it round. Accordingly, with much cleverness they show how methods must be improved (a) "if traditional subjects are retained," (b) "if traditional subjects are largely discarded."

When I read their presentation of the school's political-civic duty I am sure that these two genial professors must have written with tongue in cheek when they outlined improvements for schools in which traditional subjects are retained. There is full treatment of the main ills and absurdities of American government and society, with forthright declaration that public education has sidestepped its main civic duty. They propose revolution in aims and methods. They show that change is inevitable. They want you to wake up and make it, now.

[13] Joseph S. Butterweck, J. Conrad Seegers, "An Orientation Course in Education." Houghton Mifflin Company, Boston. 399 pp. $2.00.

EDUCATION ON A SCIENTIFIC PLAN

IT seems to me that psychologists Powers and Uhl[14] would see some truth in Bill Hurley's declaration: "A schoolmaster always knows he's right—and sometimes he is." Their book is rich with accumulation of experimental evidence that many of the commonest things we teachers are doing are contrary to principles of mental hygiene.

The lady so intent on keeping her personal indignation out of punishing her pupils that, to be more nearly just, she always postponed penalty for a week got herself intensely disliked because they had forgotten their offenses and ascribed the punishment to her desire of inflicting it.

Timing instruction to a theory that children develop at different ages an instinct for building, then for collecting, for fighting, for religion, and so on, is to count as a fact what investigation shows to have very little foundation.

Giving "failing" grades as a spur is contrary to the findings of research. Psychologically there is much to be said for giving no failing marks.

The effect of leaving tasks undone, problems unsolved, the accuracy of results undetermined, break down interest, ambition and ability. Completion, decision, should be developed into habit. Hundreds of chances occur daily in the classroom that can be made to strengthen these powers. Goals attainable should be set up. Every one works with more power when the goal is in sight.

Very few teachers know the possibilities of games in the subjects taught. The spirit of play, rivalry, social influence, enjoyment of competition, group approbation and many other social forces furnish a hearty drive.

[14] Francis F. Powers, Willis L. Uhl, "Psychological Principles of Education." D. Appleton-Century Company, New York. 570 pp. $2.50.

The two authors have composed a text for teacher-training schools, for college, for teachers in service. Nothing more firmly based upon so wide an application of the findings of the psychological laboratory has been published. It abounds in definite cases, documented in bottom-of-the-page references and full bibliographies. It is gloriously indexed. Its "Education as Conduct," "Mental Functions," lead into a remarkable exposition of motivation pregnant with corrective application to teaching.

The teacher proposed is one who provides the content of learning (this is the old type), but the Powers-Uhl teacher also motivates activity and directs progress.

A well-advertised proposal coming into doubt is that a teacher should be credited with the difference of ability of a child when finishing the grade as compared with that child when entering it. Doctors Powers and Uhl damage this easy claim. They deal in a similar way with certain assumptions on the ratings of teachers. Their presentation of teaching procedures, curricula, learning, subjects, conduct, production of abnormalities, character education, keeps within the logical bounds of the accredited facts of psychology. You come through with a level head, a sadder, maybe, but a wiser man and converted to their main thesis that education is conduct. This is a great book.

THE PROBLEMS OF GIRLS

A SKILLED and sympathetic observer[15] writes a study of the normal girl and her change to womanhood. Miss Chadwick, an experienced practitioner, treats of the adolescent girl among primitive races, in fairy tales, in the past, in the present, her conflicts at home and in school, and how she is helped and hindered.

The girl has her eyes looking toward the future rather than on the past. She has a vision of what might be. She has enthusiasm to attempt things the realization of which is not certain. She has the spirit of adventure. You who have her in charge are a misfortune to yourselves and to her if you have lost her eager inquiry and have joined the mutterers of "Safety First." The attitude of looking backwards rather than to the future is the main cause in the parent or teacher of the great gap separating them from an understanding of the girl and from sympathy with her.

The girl's best idea of being grown up is that of being an independent person who has some individual contribution to make, not to be like all the rest as a coral insect. Often her rebellion against the usages of school is due to her dread of the boredom of being like all the other amiable, docile, good little girls. She assumes a daring exterior which may be a covering for her sense of inferiority. If you take as little notice as possible of her lack of discipline and her effort to lead a rebellion you may be taking the best solution of the problem. It is impossible to keep up a war when you have no one to fight. If someone can gain her confidence and without criticism or preaching let her see why the best way is to accept discipline much good may come. But, don't forget this, that the cultivated faculty for following directions, the mass-production method of school, may extend beyond school into after life and stifle it.

Curiously enough, schools calling themselves progressive advertise free time for the children and so supervise it that it is as much directed as the other activities.

"Do you ever have a half holiday?" one of the boarding-school girls is asked.

"Yes, indeed, practically every afternoon. We do all our work in the morning."

"But what do you do in the afternoon? Is all arranged?"

"Yes."

"When do you have any free time to do as you like?"

"But all our afternoons are free; don't you understand?"

"Not quite. I mean time to do anything one likes, when one likes, or nothing at all."

This girl, insists our author, is speaking of the liberty the adolescent needs. She does require some time in the day to be all her own with the absence of criticism concerning her use of it.

Here, then, is a champion of the girl in her peculiar time of life. Here is a wise friend who knows that even the best meaning mothers, fathers and teachers do the girl much harm by not understanding her. Miss Chadwick dispels much of this bewilderment.

DISCONTENTED BOYS

DR. ARMSTRONG[16] is psychologist in the Children's Court, New York City. Her book is a

[15] Mary Chadwick, "Adolescent Girlhood." The John Day Company, New York. 303 pp. $3.50.

[16] Clairette P. Armstrong, "Six Hundred Runaway Boys." The Gorham Press, Richard G. Badger, Boston. 208 pp.

study of why boys desert their homes. By tabulating the case studies she has made, Dr. Armstrong shows the distribution of the probable causes of runaways, together with much valuable suggestion for parents and teachers.

A PRACTICAL SUCCESS-BOOK

DIRECTOR BENNETT'S manual[17] for college students and for teachers in secondary and higher institutions is in the front rank of books dealing with problems of self-discovery and self-direction. The author, experienced as a guidance counsellor in public school and junior college, makes his book on the basis of the questions and problems he finds most young people eager to consider.

After the world war humanity went crazy chasing pleasure. It laughed scornfully at serious thought and conscientious effort. This spirit swept into colleges and universities to the dismay of earnest teachers.

The depression has awakened the nation to hard and stern realities. The rah-rah spirit has waned. A quest for truth, beauty and meaning in life is emerging.

In tune with this new spirit the book asks you what college is for, how you can satisfactorily live your time in it, what are the proved best ways of studying, distributing time, note-taking, remembering, using the library, and so forth. The ways of success, the pitfalls on the path are talked of here with eminent skill. The author has taken a great road and charted it thoroughly. His style is free from a manner of preaching that often repels. He knows what the healthy youngster really wants. The means that successful men and women have used are made clear.

The dear old myth that the best success in after life is made by him whose name is engrossed more distinctly in the table in Nat Drake's beer hall than on the dean's roll of honor is upset by the statistics, Mr. Bennett quietly records.

There are some significant figures showing the increase of school success achieved by students who have been given lessons on the management of mind.

There are illuminating pages on the nature of adolescence.

The hints on mind-mastery are detailed with notable clearness accompanied by reasons why this or that technic is the best yet found. Inventories for self-diagnosis come in frequently at the close of an exposition of a particular technic and are in line with the general personal direction of the book.

This is far and away in advance of the common success books which use so much space discussing why you should make the most of your powers that they have few pages left for telling you how. The Bennett book assumes you are for the best you can do. It goes immediately into ways and means.

STOP PLAYING WITH ADULT EDUCATION

THE influences which have brought the wide support to adult education, says Dr. Kotinsky,[18] in her forward-looking book, have grown out of social changes. Unless the adult schools in an intelligent way adjust themselves to the changing scene they are useless. If it continues its present mechanical interpretation of the American scene as existent, this education will contribute nothing to getting a better social order. To what extent is adult education purely a schoolish affair? To what extent is it a factor in remaking life outside of school? How does it measure up to the conception of the original founders of American public education who called upon it to make a conscious reconstruction of institutions to human ends by the human beings participating in them?

Dr. Kotinsky's answers to these questions are forthright. She does know the field. The chapter on the adult mind of America is brilliantly lucid. So are "The conscious movement," "Worthy leisure and labor," "Current conceptions of adulthood, and the different sorts of maturity." The obvious conclusion of the whole discussion is that your adult classes must not go along imitating the methods used in teaching children. It is useless to transpose the infant's tune a scale or two higher so as to be fit for a man.

Let me speak a minute. Without study or preparation I found myself ordered to be superintendent of adult education in the American Metropolis. I was given charge of good-natured teachers who had no more special

[17] M. E. Bennett, College and Life.'' McGraw-Hill Book Company, New York. 456 pp. $2.75.

[18] Ruth Kotinsky, ''Adult Education and the Social Scene.'' D. Appleton-Century Company. 208 pp. $2.00.

preparation than I had. The texts they used were babyish; the methods they employed were infantile; the aim seemed to be to turn an adult Italian into a large American baby. These teachers were busy most of their working time with their day schools under the most urging supervision to be found in any public-school system. The only modification of their night teaching was such as could be secured by infrequent professional conferences and from the use of new text-books. In Chicago the situation was similar. In Newark, in Boston, I know, and in other places I guess, the same conditions existed. Praise to the full everything the teacher-training institutions are doing to make the teacher more than the book, the fact remains that we all seek the easiest path. That path in education is the text-book.

"Along came Ruth," said a popular stage play. Well, do come along, milady, and write a series for use by adult classes and cap it with a stiff manual for teachers. Of all the essays I have been obliged to read regarding adult education yours is the most adequate. You have the big objective. I saw this before I read William Kilpatrick's enthusiastic praise of your book. This is no stopping place for you.

TEACHING ADULTS TO READ

WHAT the researchers have discovered about learning to read has been long enough seeping from the elementary schools into the classes for adults. Two gentlewomen of Springfield, Massachusetts[19] continue producing books based upon newer experiments. With interesting information about the United States as content the authors have organized their experience so as to equip the new American with habits of efficient eye-span, grasp of the paragraph, and accuracy and speed of comprehension. To cherish citizenship, to read newspapers, magazines and library books and to do this reading silently are aims so evident all through the book as to shame the babyfied instruction that still persists in many classes where the teacher almost wholly disregards in night instruction what she has been required to make constant in the daytime.

19 Josephine Dwight Mason, Gertrude E. O'Brien, ''A Practical Reader for Adults,'' Book III. D. C. Heath & Company, Boston. 229 pp. $1.12.

PICTURED HISTORY OF THE ATLANTIC

OUR school librarian tells me it is unwise to put all the new lures on the reading table at one time. Display a novelty every now and then. A beautiful one is the Viking Press's pictorial history of the mastery of the sea.[20] This is a feast of color and story from the dark days of ignorance to the time of aeroplane and zeppelin. The authors delved in libraries in New York, Paris, and Oslo in search of designs to use in connection with each historical epoch.

AMERICAN BIOGRAPHIES BY THE POETS

THE longer I know Burton Stevenson, Master Librarian of Chillicothe, Ohio, the more puzzled I am to figure how he turns out such an enormous amount of first-class work. When I met him twenty-three years ago he had just published "The Spell of Holland" which, in my prejudiced opinion, is the most charming travel book of the century. He then had to his credit fifteen volumes of history, stories, juveniles, mysteries, and accurate researches. It was he who organized and directed the library service for the American Army in Europe and afterwards built the American Library in Paris. I never saw him hurried, I never saw him working, but when I last met him, two years ago, he had done twenty-five more books including histories, anthologies, books for boys and girls, and that prodigious Home Book of Verse. If he can imagine the struggles most of us must make in trying to keep the pile of undone work down to unalarming height will he please write a book on how to get worthwhile things done. Stevenson's latest[21] is a reproduction of two hundred and thirty-seven poems grouped in this way: Washington, Lincoln, presidents between, from Garfield to Wilson, great statesmen and public men, soldiers, sailors, the Civil War, writers, adventurers and miscellany. Historical comments introduce the different sections and each of the poems. It is an inspiring American history and biography of obvious importance to school libraries as a jewel mine for history study, pageants and anniversaries.

20 Ingri and Edgar Parin d'Aularre, ''The Conquest of the Atlantic.'' The Viking Press, New York. 55 pp. 10 x 12 inches. $2.50.

21 Burton Stevenson, ''Great Americans as Seen by the Poets.'' J. P. Lippincott Company, Philadelphia. 494 pp. $3.00.

SCHOOL AND SOCIETY

WITH WHICH ARE COMBINED THE EDUCATIONAL REVIEW, ESTABLISHED IN 1891, THE TEACHERS MAGAZINE, ESTABLISHED IN 1878, AND THE SCHOOL JOURNAL, ESTABLISHED IN 1874.

EDITED BY J. McKEEN CATTELL, R. D. LINDQUIST AND W. H. COWLEY

EDITORIAL COMMUNICATIONS SHOULD BE ADDRESSED TO THE EDUCATION BUILDING, THE OHIO STATE UNIVERSITY, COLUMBUS, OHIO

Volume 39 | Saturday, February 10, 1934 | Number 998

WILLIAM JAMES' PHILOSOPHY OF HIGHER EDUCATION

By Dr. MAURICE BAUM

KENT STATE COLLEGE, KENT, OHIO

The Function and Methods of College Instruction

William James wrote no treatise on higher education,[1] but in various addresses at commencements and reunions he expressed convictions which constitute a genuine philosophy of higher education. These addresses, "The True Harvard" (1903), "Stanford's Ideal Destiny" (1906), and "The Social Value of the College Bred" (1908) have been available and familiar to students of James' philosophy since the appearance in 1911 of the posthumous volume, "Memories and Studies." A short paper, "The Ph.D. Octopus" (1903), which was also reprinted in this volume, is the only additional writing of James on higher education that has heretofore been accessible to all.

To base one's final estimate of James' philosophy of education on this material alone, however, would be to overlook certain earlier and later writings which in some instances confirm and in other instances elaborate the opinions and conclusions expressed in the better-known addresses. Moreover, to neglect these writings would be to sacrifice entirely James' incisive treatment of certain perennially important educational problems.

The first of these earlier writings, "The Teaching of Philosophy in our Colleges,"[2] was published in 1876, twenty-seven years before the appearance of "The Ph.D. Octopus," the essay which inaugurated his later discussions of higher education. Stanley Hall's letter to the *Nation*, expressing dissatisfaction with the current state of affairs regarding the teaching of philosophy in American colleges, afforded James an opportunity to present his own views on the purpose and function of higher education. Although these convictions were thus first expressed in relation to the teaching of philosophy, even at this early date James applied them to the whole field of college instruction.

James believed and argued that higher institutions of learning in addition to their professional subjects should offer courses which aimed "to give young men a wider openness of mind and a more flexible way of thinking[3] than special technical training

[1] James' philosophy of secondary education is contained in his "Talks to Teachers on Psychology; and to Students on Some of Life's Ideals," published in 1899.

[2] *Nation*, Vol. 23, pp. 178–179. The following four quotations are from this selection.

[3] Nine years before the publication of this

can generate.'' The development of mental perspective, of the ability to gain some insight into the general relationships between things, so that old narrow habits of judging and one-sided bigoted conclusions would be abandoned, he felt should be the true goal of our American colleges.

He likewise declared that real liberalism in education is more a matter of attitude and method than of subject-matter. With true prophetic vision, he foresaw that the time would come (as it inevitably did come) when the question would be raised whether Greek should be an obligatory study. And his answer to the problem of the place of the classics in the curricula of American colleges was based directly on the assumption previously made regarding the aim of higher institutions of learning. In so far as Greek or any other study provides a means of enlarging the mental perspective of the student and affords an opportunity of teaching him to appreciate attitudes and values other than his own, it constitutes a valuable element in the curriculum.

''As philologic training,'' he wrote, ''Greek is but a language among others. Its value to the universal college student literally consists in its being a 'humanity'—in its bringing him into contact with a different human life from that which he sees, but one whose eminent worth he must nevertheless acutely feel. Its function is what we have called philosophical as distinguished from technical. Teach all sciences in a liberal and philosophic manner, and Greek ceases to be indispensable. Teach Greek in a dry, grammatic fashion, and it becomes no better than Gothic.'' Against one possible interpretation of Stanley Hall's recommendation, namely, that the application of philosophical systems to history, politics and law be taught separately from the ordinary historical, political and legal courses, he protested, ''All branches must be taught from the first in a philosophic manner, must be saturated with the liberal spirit, for any good to be effected.''

The college was not an agency, he concluded, to provide definite answers or given solutions for all possible problems, but an institution primarily to stimulate personal insight and vision, as well as practical foresight. Hence the value of individual variations and individual experimentation! ''What doctrines students take from their teachers,'' he declared, ''are of little consequence, provided they catch from them the living, philosophic attitude of mind, the independent, personal look at all the data of life, and the eagerness to harmonize them.''

When it is realized that James himself was a teacher of natural science at this time, having begun his teaching career only three years earlier as an instructor in anatomy and physiology, and that therefore he had no professional interest in the aims and methods of philosophical instruction, or in the development of the kind of attitude which he identified with the educated mind, it becomes apparent that his philosophy of higher education was not a later and accidental by-product of circumstances. Indeed, more than thirty years of subsequent teaching in a variety of fields only confirmed these deep-seated convictions of his early career.

As he grew older and observed the vast expansion and greater degree of organiza-

article, James had defined education in similar terms. In a letter to Thomas Ward, written from Berlin in 1867, he referred to his late discovery of the ''importance and nature of *education* (*i.e.*, getting orderly habits of thought, and by intense exercise in a variety of different subjects, getting the mind supple and delicate and firm).'' *Cf.* ''Letters,'' Vol. 1, p. 119. James repeated this conviction twenty years later in a letter to Mrs. James written from Chautauqua. ''Altogether, what with the teachers . . . and others whom I've met,'' he wrote, ''I'm put in conceit of college training. It certainly gives glibness and flexibility, if it doesn't give earnestness and depth.'' *Cf. ibid.*, Vol. II, p. 41.

tion in American higher institutions of learning, he became more and more critical and dissatisfied with the educational theories and practises involved. His letters[4] and later addresses[5] all tell the same story—a definite distrust of the regimentation of students and the standardization of methods and ideals so prevalent at American colleges and universities.

The introduction of this topic, however, makes necessary an explanation of James' emphasis upon individualism in his philosophy of higher education—an emphasis prominent in his very first educational article, "The Teaching of Philosophy in our Colleges."

No doubt there was much in the heritage, the early home-training, formal education and personal experiences of his youth to foster such an attitude and emphasis. Henry James, Sr., was himself the very incarnation of triumphant individualism, which he had come by honestly enough. His own father, the first William James, after emigrating from Ireland at the age of eighteen with more courage than money in his possession, had forged ahead in orthodox fashion by dint of his own efforts, and had become a self-made business man of considerable eminence in his local community. His friendly and sympathetic nature, however, had not prevented him from inflicting so rigorous a Presbyterianism upon the members of his family that two of his sons had become estranged from him in later years on account of theological differences.

One of these sons was Henry James, the father of William James, who, ironically enough, at the early age of twenty-six deserted the Princeton Theological Seminary, after two years of work, for the free air of personal experimentation and faith. The later years of his life saw him express "with abounding scorn and irony" the full measure of that antipathy to all ecclesiasticism, which he had first conceived under the stimulus of the Princeton orthodoxy. Thus the individualism of Henry James revealed itself not in the realm of business but in the realms of ethical and religious speculation and conduct, wherein he consistently played the rôle of iconoclast.

Upon at least two of his children, Henry James, Jr., and William James, he bestowed his own unique gifts of individuality of character and expression. He taught them to live their own lives at their own risk, and to despise, more than anything else, moral hypocrisy and sham. It is not surprising, therefore, to read that William James, in the words of his son, "above all . . . was encouraged early to trust his own impulse and pursue his own bent."[6]

That James did so is evident from the record of his formal education, which was largely a matter of patches and shreds, a fact which James himself deplored.[7] For after much irregular schooling abroad between the years 1855–1858, consisting mainly of instruction in the private schools of London and Paris and a brief attendance at the Collège de Boulogne, where he passed his sixteenth birthday, and at the Academy of Geneva, he decided to test his artistic ability in the studio of William Hunt at Newport. The trial ended in his conviction that he was not born to be an artist, and he then turned voluntarily to his other major interest, science. He entered the Lawrence Scientific School in 1861, and during his three years' attendance there he decided, again for himself, on a professional career. Choosing medicine because it embodied the advantages of

[4] *Cf.* "Letters," Vol. II, pp. 227, 228, 229, 243–244, 280.

[5] See especially, "The Ph.D. Octopus" and "Stanford's Ideal Destiny" in "Memories and Studies."

[6] "Letters," Vol. I, p. 22.

[7] *Ibid.*, Vol. I, p. 20.

both business and pure natural science,[8] he entered the Harvard Medical School in 1863. But he did not hesitate to interrupt his studies in 1865 to join Agassiz' expedition to the Amazon. On his return from Brazil in 1866, he resumed his medical studies, and after another interlude of eighteen months' duration abroad, due to poor health, a desire to perfect his knowledge of German and to study physiology in the new German laboratories, he took his medical degree in 1869. Protracted ill health, however, compelled him to go into retirement during the next four years. He emerged in 1872 to accept an appointment to teach anatomy and physiology at Harvard College, thereafter progressing by degrees from one department to another until he finally taught philosophy only.

If James' individualism was thus a product of a definite heritage, home-training and formal education, it was likewise partly the product of a certain cosmopolitanism generated in him at an early age by multiple and vivid contacts with a constantly changing panorama of persons and things. "Clearly, there was profit for him also," declares his son, "in the restlessness which governed his father's movements and which threw the boy into quickening collision with places, people and ideas at a rate at which such contacts are not vouchsafed to many school-boys. From so far back as his nineteenth year (there is no evidence to go by before that) William was blessed with an effortless and confirmed cosmopolitanism of consciousness. . . . Probably his active and inquiring intelligence could not have been permanently cribbed and confined by any schooling, no matter how narrow and rigorous. But, as nothing was to be more remarkable about him in his maturity than the easy assurance with which he passed from one field of inquiry to another, ignoring conventional bounds and precincts, never losing his freshness of tone, shedding new light and encouragement everywhere, so it is impossible not to believe that the influences and circumstances which combined in his youth fostered and corroborated his native mobility and detachment of mind."[9]

That this attainment of a cosmopolitan standpoint so early in life should have affected his whole outlook is not surprising. In many fields of reflection, however, it produced exceedingly important and novel results. This was especially true in the field of education, where it led James to an exalted appreciation of individual differences and to an almost fanatical opposition to all educational organizations and ideals which seemed to threaten the survival of individual spontaneity and variation.

At all events, the irregular formal education and youthful travels of William James conferred upon him one benefit which a more standardized preparation seldom begets, namely, an insight into other ways of thinking and an appreciation of values alien to his own.

THE MEANING OF A LIBERAL EDUCATION

In 1891, or twelve years before the delivery of the first of his well-known addresses on higher education, James published a long defence of the projected three-year A.B. degree at Harvard. This defence entitled, "The Proposed Shortening of the College Course,"[10] contains many of the fundamental ideas which he later elaborated to form his mature philosophy of higher education. It is important, however, for more than its genetic significance as the first concrete expression of some of James' ideals of education; it contains in

[8] At this time, James openly acknowledged his preference for pure natural science, but practical considerations made the choice of such a career unwise. *Cf.* his statements regarding this problem, "Letters," Vol. I, pp. 44–46.

[9] "Letters," Vol. I, pp. 21–22.

[10] *Harvard Monthly*, Vol. 11, pp. 127–137.

addition an analysis and solution of one great problem in American educational theory which he never discussed again elsewhere. In the light of recent developments in the field of college and university reorganization, this analysis and solution have proved to be prophetic utterances of uncommon solidity and depth.

James declared in his paper in 1891 that American colleges and universities must discriminate between two different but equally worthy types of students—the type who seeks only a liberal and modest acquaintance with certain fields of knowledge and the type who is preparing, and is mentally equipped, to do advanced professional work—and must adjust their curricula and graduation requirements accordingly. He insisted, however, that in both cases college life must not constitute merely a poetic interlude in one's journey through a hard, practical world; it should, on the contrary, help to shape men's ideas and ideals, to discipline their emotions and correct their ignorance, to fashion them into beings of superior insight and courage equipped to face and to deal effectively with things as they are in this world.

In point of style and logical rigor of argument, in breadth of view and factual insight, this defence of the proposed shortening of the college course constitutes one of the most memorable writings in James' discussions of educational theory and practise.

Individualism in Art and Education

Twelve years later, when he was asked to speak at the dedication of the New Germanic Art Museum at Harvard, he utilized the opportunity to contribute certain additional elements to his philosophy of higher education, elements which form the basis of his later addresses, "Stanford's Ideal Destiny" and "The Social Value of the College Bred." What makes his "Remarks on the Dedication of the Germanic Museum" especially noteworthy is his direct application of certain philosophic distinctions and principles, familiar to all readers of his popular philosophic books and essays, to the field of education.

In his logical and metaphysical writings, James had drawn a vivid contrast between the men of fact and the men of principle, the lovers of experience in its crude particularity and the worshippers of experience pruned and shaped into an object of esthetic perfection and delight. Too long, he declared as early as 1879,[11] had the ideals of the latter dominated modern philosophy, with the result that a sterile intellectual tradition had settled, like a suffocating blanket, over men's moral and spiritual aspirations. Therefore he had fought for the recognition of opaque fact in the realm of logic and of pungent uncertainty in the realm of metaphysics.[12] Fact spelt reality as it actually came to us in the form of brute, unintelligible shocks and surprises; and real uncertainties suggested dramatic and inspiring moral and religious possibilities.

Now he was to appeal for the recognition of a similar situation in the field of higher education. Let human differences and variations constitute the ultimates in educational theory and practise, just as facts and uncertainties constitute the ultimates in logic and metaphysics. A pluralistic world of values demanded a pluralistic system of education. Just as there was no one absolute and final truth in logic and metaphysics, so there could be none in education; and all pedagogical arrangements and devices which aimed to produce such an artificial simplicity must be heartily condemned. German art and education, he felt, illustrated graphically the unique and valuable results which might follow from

[11] *Cf.* "The Sentiment of Rationality," reprinted in "Collected Essays and Reviews."

[12] *Cf.* "Absolutism and Empiricism," published in 1884 and reprinted in "Essays in Radical Empiricism."

taking this standpoint seriously. It was only the unwarranted prejudice and opposition of the classicists and rationalists in both art and education that had led to the denial, and the attempted concealment, of the values which flow from the recognition and reward of individual differences. Harvard, too, he believed, had prospered because she had earned a reputation for devotion to this ideal of individualism in education; an explicit acknowledgment of its value was all that was needed to accelerate the eventual triumph of this ideal in all American higher institutions of learning.

A survey of all James' writings on higher education thus reveals that here, as elsewhere, his concern was primarily with the individual, with the discovery and enhancement of his point of view. Educational needs and demands must be determined accordingly; only thus could society itself profit most through the attainments and the achievements of its more gifted members. As early as 1876 and as late as 1908, adopting this aim and ideal as his standpoint, James attacked all that stood for mere professionalization and systematization in this field.

The attainment of personal vision rather than the acquisition of information, or better, the formation of a mental perspective upon the basis of sound knowledge, seemed to him, both at the beginning and at the end of his career, the only desirable goal of higher education. The materials and methods of such an education, therefore, must be as flexible as individual variations warranted. For closed systems and fixed curricula, James had only a profound distrust. These would but nullify, if not obliterate, the one great reality toward which all educational theory and practise should be orientated—the preservation and enrichment of the individual's experience.

PERSONALITY AND THE ATHLETIC GIRL

By Dr. EDWIN G. FLEMMING
NEW YORK, N. Y.

IN general discussions it has often been said that the emphasis upon athletics by the modern girl is spoiling her. It is argued that athletics do something to the personality of their participants that detracts from the desirable and delightful qualities of femininity.

Since it is generally supposed that the athletic men are "he-men," crude, coarse, rough, hardy and other things that are supposed to be associated with masculinity, and since up to a few years ago athletics were almost the exclusive occupation of men, it seems logical that participation in athletics by any one would tend to develop the supposedly typical mannish characteristics. Observers who have contended that athletics were spoiling the young girl athletes could always point to examples to prove their point. Single examples and illustrations may test a rule, but they never can establish a law.

The purpose of this study is to determine what, if any, traits or characteristics of personality may be associated with athletic ability or participation, or rather with that type of girl known as athletic to a greater extent than with the average girl; then to examine such traits, if there be such, in order to estimate their worth from a social point of view.

The subjects were 84 girls of the Horace Mann High School for Girls, Teachers College, Columbia University, comprising the junior and senior classes.[1] At the Horace

[1] It is necessary that I acknowledge my indebtedness to Dr. Cecile White Flemming, director of the division of pupil adjustment of the Horace

Mann High School athletic activities open to the girls are indicated in the school manual as follows:

> A wide and varied program of sports is offered; the most popular are field hockey, basketball, swimming and tennis.
>
> Field hockey is the major fall sport and is played by the four upper classes in the high school, culminating in an interclass tournament for first and second teams and the selection of one squad of the most advanced players who have several friendly games with other schools on Saturday mornings.
>
> Basketball and swimming fill the winter season. Besides regular basketball team practises for each class, there are elective periods for individual coaching and a schedule of interclass games.
>
> Class games with Lincoln School and a few outside games by a selected squad are also played. The final championship game is the big event of the season. . . .
>
> In swimming there are splash parties and other events all through the year, with the interclass meets in the spring.
>
> Tennis is played by all classes in a doubles and singles tournament. Instruction in strokes and playing strategy is given in regular class periods.
>
> Other sports such as badminton, archery, baseball, golf, and horseback riding are offered as electives throughout the year.

It is obvious that general participation in such a program of activities would not necessarily make the girls athletic. So in order to determine who the athletic girls were, as well as to get data upon the other traits studied, the teachers were given lists of forty-six traits, including "athletic," and asked to check for each girl each item that could be attributed to the particular girl. The traits were:

Intelligent	Cultured	Beautiful or pretty	Competent
Sense of humor	Helpful	Amusing	Idealistic
Interesting in conversation	Modest	Frank	Neat
Considerate of others	Dependable	Understanding	Industrious
Talented in some field of art	Unselfish	Generous	Tolerant
"Good sport"	Good judgment	Sociable	Entertaining
	Witty	Loyal	Natural, unaffected
	Individuality	Sympathetic	Fair
		Good natured	Well informed
		Athletic	Adaptable
		Courteous	Pleasant voice
		Sincere	Wide interests
		Attractive personal appearance	Not easily excited
		Honest, truthful	Smiling countenance
		Clever	Tactful
		Lively	Original

At least three teachers checked a list for each girl, while in a few cases six teachers gave ratings for a particular girl. The average number of lists checked per girl was 3.6. Since each check list was the reaction of a different person to an individual we might consider the traits checked on each list as representing a distinct personality. In that case there was a total of 303 personalities analyzed.

In addition, each girl indicated on a scale of ten the intensity of pleasant feeling that she subjectively associated with every other girl of her class. This gave me a measure of what may be termed the pleasingness of the personality of each girl. There was an average of over 35 ratings for each girl on this factor of personality.

The teachers also on a scale of ten indicated the amount of personality that each girl possessed. For this measure there were not fewer than three ratings for each girl. The average rating was taken as the measure of personality.

For a measure of leadership we took into consideration the positions of leadership or responsibility actually held by the girls during the ninth, tenth and eleventh grades in the Horace Mann School for Girls. The senior year was not included because only about half of the subjects had completed the last year. Also due to the fact that a

Mann School, who gathered the data which made this study possible, and to express appreciation for the cooperation of the teachers and girls in the school who participated in this inquiry.

number of girls had not been in attendance at the school for all three years there were only 71 subjects considered for the study of relationships to leadership. Various positions received various points of credit according to a schedule determined by the school authorities for the purpose of allocating credits to the girls for extra-class activities, and which are made a routine part of the school record.

The method of determining the degree of association between athletic and the other traits and characteristics was by means of the coefficient of contingency described by H. E. Garrett in "Statistics in Psychology and Education," pp. 195–201. A two-by-two-fold table was used. In interpreting results it is necessary to bear in mind that for a two-by-two-fold table the highest possible coefficient is .707, whereas theoretically perfect association should yield a coefficient of 1.00. It is probable, then, that the actual association is somewhat more definite than is indicated by the coefficients of contingency found.

The coefficient of contingency, C, between athletic and personality is .19. Between athletic and the pleasingness of the personality as indicated by the girls the coefficient of contingency is .18. And between athletic and leadership the coefficient is .20. It then appears that there is a positive tendency for athletic to be associated with personality, pleasingness of personality and leadership among girls of the high-school age. While no necessary causal relationship is indicated by these coefficients, it seems reasonable that among girls, as among boys, athletic prowess would make them stand out and be sufficient reason for the admiration of their contemporaries and sympathetic elders. In that sense athletic ability would be a contributing cause of personality, pleasingness to others and would tend to provide opportunities to hold positions of leadership. In addition to such probable causal relation, athletic ability may be and probably is the concomitant of general good health and well-being, maintains and fosters energy and buoyancy of spirit, which in turn are linked up with personality, pleasingness and leadership.

Obviously, there can be no attempt from this study to indicate anything about the personality, or the personality traits and leadership of athletic boys. The results are confined merely to girls.

TABLE 1

SHOWING THE COEFFICIENTS OF CONTINGENCY BETWEEN ATHLETIC AND VARIOUS OTHER TRAITS AND CHARACTERISTICS

"Good sport"	.24
Fair	.23
Lively	.21
Pleasant voice	.21
Wide interests	.18
Beautiful or pretty	.17
Interesting in conversation	.15
Honest, truthful	.15
Helpful	.15
Amusing	.14
Attractive personal appearance	.14
Adaptable	.14
Intelligent	.12
Unselfish	.12
Individuality	.12
Competent	.12
Tactful	.11
Sense of humor	.10
Generous	.10
Witty	.10
Tolerant	.10
Natural, unaffected	.10
Good natured	.09
Sociable	.08
Sympathetic	.08
Sincere	.08
Modest	.08
Dependable	.08
Idealistic	.08
Courteous	.07
Entertaining	.07
Loyal	.06
Good judgment	.06
Neat	.06
Well informed	.06
Considerate of others	.04
Understanding	.04
Industrious	.04
Smiling countenance	.04
Talented in some field of art	.02
Frank	.01
Cultured	.00
Clever	–.02
Original	–.02
Not easily excited	–.08

The coefficients of contingency between athletic and each of the traits and characteristics on the check list presented to the teachers are indicated in Table 1. The most noteworthy information revealed by the table is that none of the coefficients is particularly high. We would be warranted, then, in concluding that the athletic type of girl is not especially distinguished from the average girl of her group by the possession or lack of possession of any of these 45 traits. It is possible that there are other traits that may be more positively associated with athletic ability and participation by girls.

However, coefficients of .15 or more are probably of some significance, though slight, and indicate a tendency for those traits to be associated more often with the athletic girl than with the average run. Thus arbitrarily taking .15 as the limit of association of some significance there are nine traits that appear to be positively related to athletic. They are "good sport," fair, lively, pleasant voice, wide interests, beautiful or pretty, interesting in conversation, honest or truthful, and helpful.

As for the probable causal relation between athletic and these nine traits we probably have a circular effect, the possession of the trait tending to push the individual into athletics and athletic participation tending to develop the trait. This is almost certainly true with "good sport," lively and wide interests. With the exception of pleasant voice and beautiful or pretty good sense would seem to suggest that participation in athletics would have a causal relationship to the other seven traits, even though the possession of the trait might also have some effect upon athletic participation.

In conclusion, then, we would be inclined to say from the results of this study that the athletic type of girl is not strikingly different from the non-athletic type, except in her interest in athletics. If there is any difference it is that the athletic type of girl is rather more of a "good sport," fairer, livelier, has a more pleasant voice, has wider interests, is more beautiful or pretty, is more interesting in conversation, is more honest or truthful and more helpful than the average. These traits being desirable and of the kind that schools and society would foster, athletic programs in our schools would tend to improve the personalities of our girls rather than to detract from them. The athletic type of girl also tends slightly to have more personality, to be more pleasing to other girls than the average, and to be found in more numerous or more significant positions of leadership.

EDUCATIONAL EVENTS

INTER-AMERICAN CONFERENCE ON EDUCATION

CHILE will be the first Latin-American country to hold an Inter-American Conference on Education. This conference will be held in Santiago from September 12 to 17, under the joint auspices of the Minister of Education and the National Cooperating Committee for Chile of the Inter-American Federation for Education. Among the members of the Chilean committee are representatives from the ministries of foreign relations and education, leading universities, the national directors for primary and secondary education and for industrial and commercial education, the president of the National Teachers Association and an outstanding Pan-American woman educator, Mrs. Amanda Labarca. The chairman of the committee is Dr. Agustin Edwards, a distinguished publicist and educator. Dr. Raul Ramiraz, professor of English at the University of Chile, is secretary of the Chilean committee.

The first conference of the federation was held from July 1 to 3, 1929, at Atlanta, in connection with the annual meeting of the National Education Association. Ten countries were represented at this preliminary organization conference. Nineteen of the twenty-one Pan-American countries are now members of the federation. Ministers of education in these countries serve as an advisory council of the federation. There is also an organization committee with representatives, one each from Brazil, Mexico, Uruguay, Guatemala, the Dominican Republic and the United States. National cooperating committees in all countries function either through the ministers of public education or leading educational associations. Dr. Glen Levin Swiggett, of Washington, is chairman of the organization committee of the federation.

Pan-American accord and understanding through better education is the main purpose in the program of this federation. To achieve this purpose, says Dr. Swiggett, it will be necessary that these conferences stress elementary vocational and character training, and seek to have national programs of public education in all Pan-American countries based upon thorough and adequate courses of study that will increase the earning power, social sense and civic understanding of their peoples.

FEDERAL AID FOR SCHOOLS AND COLLEGE STUDENTS

On February 2, Harry L. Hopkins, Federal Relief Administrator, announced the availability of an indefinite grant to be used for relief of schools in communities up to five thousand population. The grant is being made to keep the schools from closing and to give relief to unpaid and unemployed teachers.

The funds will be administered by the Federal Emergency Relief Administration in cooperation with the United States Office of Education, and will be used for elementary and secondary schools where unavailing efforts have been made to keep the schools open. Only certified teachers will be recipients of assistance, and none of the funds can be used for administration, maintenance, equipment, or supplies. None of the money can be used, furthermore, to pay back wages or to redeem warrants. As yet no definite statement has been made concerning the amount of money appropriated for this teacher-relief program.

In a second announcement on the same day Mr. Hopkins gave out plans for federal assistance to students who have been unable for financial reasons to continue their college work. The plan calls for financing part-time employment for 100,000 needy students and for a budget of from five to seven million dollars.

Mr. Hopkins has authorized state emergency relief administrators to provide part-time jobs at colleges for students up to 10 per cent. of each college's enrolment as of October 15, 1933. Students will apply to their college authorities for assistance, and they in turn will submit requests for allotments to the state relief administrations. About three quarters of the students to be helped will be those who dropped out at the end of the first quarter or semester for financial reasons and about one quarter will be new students who would otherwise be unable to enter.

From $10 to $20 a month will be paid students for work of the kind customarily done in the institution by students working their way through college including clerical, library, research, work on building and grounds, and in dormitories and dining halls, but not regular class instruction. These jobs will be in addition to those now provided by the various institutions. Where the institutions are not under public control, jobs may not include construction and repair but such jobs may be provided on nearby property.

Men and women will be given jobs in proportion to the enrolment of each. To obtain work, students must possess character and ability "to give assurance that they will do high grade work in college," the rules state. The rate of pay is to be such as is commonly paid by the institution for the type of service rendered but not less than 30 cents an hour. A 30-hour week and an 8-hour day are set as maximums. The average allotment will be $15 a month per student employed.

College and university presidents will be responsible for the program in their institutions and they must waive all fees for registration, tuition, laboratories and other purposes for the students receiving federal aid.

A CITIZENS' CONFERENCE ON THE CRISIS IN EDUCATION

Because of the financial emergency in education throughout the country, Ohio State University is organizing this year two series of meetings at the time of its educational conference:

First, a national conference for citizens, and, second, a somewhat different conference than heretofore for school people.

The first of these two series of meetings, which will be called the Citizens' Conference on the Crisis in Education, goes into session on Thursday, April 5, the keynote being "Education—A Crisis in American Democracy." Four large meetings will be held, one on Thursday and three on Friday. Among those who have already accepted invitations to speak are the following: Mrs. Franklin D. Roosevelt; Newton D. Baker; President Glenn Frank, of the University of Wisconsin; President Robert M. Hutchins, of the University of Chicago; Governor Paul McNutt, of Indiana, and Superintendent William J. Bogan, of the Chicago Public Schools. Among those who will act as chairmen of these meetings are Governor George White; Federal Judge Walter C. Lindley, of Illinois; Commissioner George F. Zook, of the U. S. Office of Education, and Frank P. Graves, commissioner of education of New York State. Other prominent speakers will be announced later.

The United Press, the Associated Press and other national press associations have agreed to give considerable advance publicity throughout the United States and they are sending special representatives to cover the meetings for their large chains of newspapers. The United Press is now in the process of planning a series of feature articles, one to be published each day for two weeks before the conference convenes. These articles will describe the school situation in various parts of the country, and each will call attention to the Citizens' Conference. Furthermore, the National Broadcasting Company will probably put several of the addresses on a national radio hook-up.

On Saturday morning, April 7, the four citizens' meetings will be followed by a series of eight or nine discussion groups, each of which will be led by a nationally known educator—to be announced soon. These discussion leaders will seek to interpret the addresses made at the citizens' conference into programs of action.

The function of the speakers at the general sessions will be to arouse public opinion to the importance of the crisis in education. The function of the discussion leaders will be to inform the public about programs that need to be followed. The discussion groups planned are the following: The Elementary Curriculum; The High School Curriculum; The Administration of Large City School Systems; The Administration of Small City School Systems; The Administration of County School Systems; Crime and Delinquency; Education for Leisure Time; The Training of Teachers; Legislation and Finance.

The Ohio State Educational Conference proper will be held between the Citizens' Conference, which ends on Friday night, April 6, and the discussion groups, which begin on Saturday morning at 10:30. They will meet from 8:30 until 10:15 on Saturday morning, and the keynote will be the same as that of the Citizens' Conference: "Education—A Crisis in American Democracy." All the thirty-nine sections of the conference will hold meetings, concentrating their attention upon the conditions in their fields of interest and the steps that need immediately to be taken.

EDUCATIONAL PROGRAM OF THE NATIONAL CONFERENCE OF JEWS AND CHRISTIANS

Plans for an intensive educational campaign to eliminate causes of friction between members of different religious faiths were, according to *The New York Times,* announced on February 4 by the National Conference of Jews and Christians.

Newton D. Baker, a Protestant, is one of the three co-chairmen of the conference. The other co-chairmen are Professor Carlton J. H. Hayes, head of the department of history at Columbia University, a Catholic, and Roger W. Straus, a Jew.

The campaign, an outgrowth of the recent "pilgrimage of understanding" made by a Catholic priest, a rabbi and a Protestant clergyman to thirty-seven cities throughout the country, will be nation-wide in scope.

At the start four principal aims will be emphasized. These are:

To suggest to high schools, both public and private, that they invite a Catholic priest, a Protestant minister and a rabbi to appear together before assemblies and speak on "The American Tradition of Religious Freedom" during the week of George Washington's Birthday.

To encourage church and synagogue youth organizations to discuss civic relationships of Protestants, Catholics and Jews.

To extend college and city "seminars" and round-table programs.

To form a women's committee of 1,000 state leaders, which Mrs. Dorothy Canfield Fisher will head, and which will parallel the existing men's advisory council of 1,000 national community leaders.

"It is the judgment of the conference," Professor Hayes has observed, "that the pilgrimage revealed a general demand for a constructive educational program for the achievement of genuine understanding between the three great religious and cultural groups in this country, and as a result of an executive meeting held in New York a few days ago it was decided that certain definite procedures be adopted at once."

He explained that the conference plans to make available to schools material designed to clear up in the minds of the young misunderstandings which create friction and to approach church young people's groups with a special view to stimulate frank discussions of Protestant-Catholic-Jewish relationships. The conference will promote periodic community meetings and form local or regional "teams," composed of a minister, a priest and a rabbi, who will be prepared to appear together to speak on such subjects as "Citizenship" and "American Human Relations."

THE CHILD LABOR AMENDMENT

BOTH Dr. A. Lawrence Lowell, president emeritus of Harvard University, and President Nicholas Murray Butler, of Columbia University, have voiced opposition to the Child Labor Amendment. Dr. Lowell gave out a statement on February 1, and Dr. Butler expressed his protest in a nation-wide radio hook-up on February 2.

Dr. Butler called the amendment "social revolution of the most extreme sort." He urged that state legislatures be informed of the "overwhelming objections" to it. "There is no movement," he declared, "in any part of this country, nor could there be, to defend child labor or to protect those who would use the labor of children to their own profit and advantage." He further said:

> The people have themselves found ways and means to get rid of child labor without undermining their form of government, as it can only be gotten rid of, through the force of public opinion and by the action of local authorities, and without putting our federal government in a position toward the family, the school and the church which even the most advanced communists might well admire.
>
> "Child labor is abolished," said President Roosevelt in his message to Congress on January 3. Since we have the assurance of the president that child labor no longer exists and since no one desires to reestablish it in any wise, the proposed amendment can have no effect whatever upon the problem of unemployment or of child welfare.

The National Child Labor Committee has not as yet replied to Dr. Butler, but Mrs. Gertrude F. Zimand, research director of the committee, has given an interview to the newspapers in reply to Dr. Lowell, in which she declared it absurd to believe that the Federal Government would enter the home and dictate the actual conduct of children, as Dr. Lowell fears. She expressed the opinion that attacks upon the amendment on this score are merely smoke screens to conceal some other basis of opposition. *The Christian Science Monitor* reports her interview with the press as follows:

> The progress of the child labor amendment has reached a crisis, and from this point on until the thirty-sixth state ratifies it, the struggle between its supporters and its opponents promises to be intense.
>
> Recent acceleration of the speed of ratification has brought forward all the forces of opposition, in which the committee beholds one newcomer, the press.
>
> Since the newspapers in their NRA code were denied the right to hire boys of 14 to sell their papers, they have shifted their stand on the child labor amendment, bitterly attacking it and closing their columns to the supporters of the amendment.
>
> With the exception of the press, the opposition lines up just about the same, with the Manufacturing Association, the Roman Catholic Church and farm groups, marshaling all their forces to stop the ratification of the amendment, which has been indorsed by about 10 states in the last year—as many as in the preceding eight years. At present 20 states have ratified, leaving 16 to act favorably before it becomes part of the Constitution.
>
> The committee regards New York State and Massachusetts as strategic points. If the amendment passes these states, with their large Roman Catholic composition and their reputed liberalism,

tremendous impetus will be given to its ultimate passage.

The opposition, it was revealed, is trying a new offensive, which consists of effecting passage of resolutions in the states, declaring the amendment dead, because of the long period it has been before the legislatures.

THE PROPOSED HIGH SCHOOL OF ART FOR NEW YORK CITY

IN an address on January 31, before the Women's City Club of New York, Harold G. Campbell, newly appointed superintendent of New York City schools, announced that Mayor La Guardia has asked the Board of Education to establish a "high school of art." Mr. Campbell's announcement came as a surprise to some but not to those who have been familiar with Mayor La Guardia's educational theories.

The mayor, before he took office, revealed to a few friends, according to the *New York Herald-Tribune,* that he hoped to set up a separate high school for music and art. He said that time he saw no reason why the city should waste money on giving art and music lessons once a week to all students, a method which he regarded as wasting the time of those not interested and of no real value to those showing promise.

Instead, he held, classes should be set up in a separate high school, with the students drafted from the regular high schools and the teachers similarly recruited. After the separate high school had been set up, the development of that institution into a conservatory, under municipal control, would be the next step, under the mayor's plan. It was understood that if the expenditure of any great amount of money would be entailed, the project would be delayed until the city was in a better financial position.

Dr. Campbell in his address also defended the so-called fads and frills of education. He said that under the new administration he expected no difficulty with budget-cutters seeking to go back to the three R's.

He said he quarreled with the budget-cutters not because he did not recognize the need for economy, but because they wanted to cut where society could not afford to cut. Eliminating health education, he declared, as some propose, would wreck the next generation. In teaching drawing, for example, the schools no longer attempt to make artists of all students, but seek to insure that all the graduates will have at least some appreciation of art. "What is the use of having these programs for use of the new leisure time," he asked, "if you haven't a population that knows how to use these opportunities?"

CONFERENCE ON "OVERWORKED" TEXT-BOOKS

AT a recent conference on better hygiene in handling books used in common in schools, held at the call of United States Commissioner of Education, George F. Zook, it was reported that one unhappy result of reduced expenditures for educational purposes is that thousands of children are using text-books which have become not only unsightly but also unsanitary. Need of immediate attention to this problem was suggested to Commissioner Zook.

Among those who took part in the conference were: Mrs. F. J. Flagg, president, Professional Women's Club, Newtonville, Mass.; Mrs. Fred L. Pigeon and Mrs. Carl W. Illig, Jr., General Federation of Women's Clubs; W. Elwood Baker, general secretary, National Congress of Parents and Teachers; Miss Anne Whitney, director education service, American Child Health Association; Dr. E. Blanche Sterling, U. S. Public Health Service; Ernest Bryan, National Education Association, and members of the staff of the Federal Office of Education.

It was pointed out that the useful life of an elementary school text-book was approximately three years. Due to lack of funds, this usage is being extended considerably. Often these overworked books have pages missing and not a few are out of date.

The conference urged that the relatively small outlay for text-books and other materials handled by children should not be reduced and that facilities for cleanliness of school children should be ample.

While it was reported that studies undertaken to date fail to furnish positive proof of transmission of disease through common use of text-books, the conference asked that school administrators put forth more efforts to prevent children with infectious diseases from attending school and to insure safer handling of books by children.

The Federal Office of Education was requested to prepare a circular on the supply and handling of text-books for the information and guidance of school administrators and civic groups interested in the schools.

SURVEY FOR THE DEAF AND HARD-OF-HEARING

To determine the types of occupations for which young people who are deaf or hard-of-hearing can be successfully trained, and to discover employment possibilities for them under Civil Works and Public Works Administrations, is the aim of a survey launched by the Office of Education through a grant from the Civil Works Administration.

According to a recent estimate, there are about 300,000 children in our schools whose hearing is so seriously impaired that they need special educational attention. One of the major functions of the school program organized for them is to guide them into vocations in which they can be gainfully employed, despite their handicap.

An extensive survey is being carried on under the immediate direction of Elise H. Martens, specialist in the education of exceptional children in the Office of Education, and Herbert E. Day. Mr. Day was co-author of a survey made in 1925 of American schools for the deaf. He was called to the Federal Office of Education for the special purpose of assisting in this project.

In thirty different states and the District of Columbia, executives of schools for the deaf, and others interested, have volunteered their services in acting as coordinating agents between the Office of Education and the field. To these will be due much of the success of the survey, since they are responsible for organizing and directing the work carried on by the field workers in the selected areas assigned to them.

Three hundred and seventy field workers are assigned to the various states for a period of six weeks. These come from the ranks of the unemployed who are registered with the Civil Works Administration. Social workers, nurses, teachers and other trained persons are eligible for employment on the project. More than $65,000 will be paid out in salaries.

The field workers will be responsible for making contacts with deaf and hard-of-hearing adults within their respective territories. They will also interview the employers of these persons. They will secure the information needed for an analysis of the occupational history and problems of the deaf and hard-of-hearing, which will be transmitted through them to the Office of Education.

It is expected that the survey will yield much information which will be of value. Obstacles in the way to gainful employment of the deaf will be disclosed, and means will be sought to remove them. The findings will have a direct bearing upon the educational program provided for them in the schools.

An advisory committee for the project has been chosen, representing national organizations. The members of this committee are:

Elbert A. Gruver, superintendent, Pennsylvania Institution for the Deaf.

Howard McManaway, president, American Association to Promote the Teaching of Speech to the Deaf.

Percival Hall, president of Gallaudet College, and chairman of the Executive Committee of the Conference of Executives of American Schools for the Deaf.

Betty Wright, executive secretary, American Federation of Organizations for the Hard-of-Hearing.

Norman McManaway, associate superintendent, Volta Bureau.

John A. Kratz, chief, Rehabilitation Division, Vocational Educational Division of the Office of Education.

EDUCATIONAL NOTES AND NEWS

Dr. William M. Jardine will assume the presidency of the Municipal University of Wichita, Kansas, on March 1. He served as Secretary of Agriculture in the cabinet of President Coolidge and as American Minister to Egypt under President Hoover.

Lloyd K. Neidlinger, former Dartmouth football player and Princeton hockey coach, will become dean of Dartmouth College at the end of the present academic year, succeeding Craven Laycock, who is retiring.

Dean John W. Withers, of the School of Education of New York University, was elected on January 29 chairman of the Save the Children Fund of America. He succeeds Dr. A. T. McCormick, director of public health in Kentucky. Colonel Theodore Roosevelt was named chairman of a committee of sponsors and the Rev. Dr. S. Parkes Cadman, vice-chairman.

DR. HENRY B. VAN HOESEN, chairman of the department of bibliography at Brown University, has been elected president of the American Library Institute, succeeding Dr. Theodore W. Koch, librarian of Northwestern University.

HENRY A. MORSE, who has been a life member of the corporation since 1924, has been announced as acting treasurer of the Massachusetts Institute of Technology. Dr. Vannevar Bush, vice-president of the institute, has been appointed assistant treasurer.

WILLIAM F. SCHMIDT, president of the St. Paul-Luther College, has announced his resignation, effective on July 1.

DR. BRADLEY M. PATTEN, associate professor of histology and embryology at Western Reserve University, has resigned to assume the assistant directorate for medical sciences of the Rockefeller Foundation, New York.

PROFESSOR ROBERT M. SCOON was appointed chairman of the department of philosophy at Princeton University on January 31, succeeding Professor Robert B. C. Johnson, who is now on leave of absence.

PROFESSOR V. S. FINCH, chairman of the department of geography at the University of Wisconsin, received the honorary degree of doctor of science at the celebration of the one hundredth anniversary of the founding of Kalamazoo College.

CLARENCE P. HOUSTON, director of physical education and Braker professor of law at Tufts College, has recently been reelected president of the University Club of Boston.

ALFRED ROSENBERG, chief of the Nazi private ministry of foreign affairs and chief editor of Chancellor Hitler's two newspapers, has just been appointed Comptroller of Intellectual Activities in the third reich. In that capacity, he will dictate the philosophy which is to be expounded in the schools, on the lecture platforms, by printed matter and over the radio.

DR. HARLOW SHAPLEY, director of the Harvard College Observatory, delivered the third annual James Arthur lecture on "Time and Its Mysteries" on February 6 at New York University.

THE twenty-fourth anniversary of the founding of the National Council of the Boy Scouts of America will be observed from February 8 to 14. President Roosevelt will address Boy Scouts over the radio at noon on February 10.

JAMES GEDDES, JR., professor of romance languages; Marshall Livingston Perrin, professor of Germanic languages and Sanskrit, and Joseph Richard Taylor, professor of Greek and drama, three of the oldest professors in the college of liberal arts of Boston University, were honor guests at a reception and dinner given on February 3 by three hundred alumni of the university.

NORA ARCHIBALD SMITH, pioneer kindergarten teacher and sister of the late Kate Douglas Wiggin, died in Portland, Maine, on February 1. She was seventy-five years of age. In 1880, Miss Smith and her sister founded the Silver Street Kindergarten in San Francisco, the first free kindergarten west of the Rocky Mountains.

DR. JULIUS SACHS, emeritus professor of secondary education at Teachers College, Columbia University, and active professor in the subject from 1902 until his retirement in 1917, died in New York on February 2. He was eighty-four years old. Dr. Sachs established the Sachs School for Boys in 1872 and the Sachs School for Girls in 1891.

CHARLES RAMSDELL LINGLEY, professor of history at Dartmouth College, died in Hanover, N. H., on January 30, at the age of fifty-six years.

DR. MANUEL AUGUSTO MONTES DE OCA, until recently professor of constitutional law at the Argentine National School, died in Buenos Ayres on January 27. Dr. de Oca had served as foreign minister of the Argentine, president of the fifth Pan-American Conference, special envoy to Brazil and special ambassador to Great Britain at the coronation of Edward the Seventh. He was sixty-six years of age.

ALBERT MORTON LYTHGOE, founder and curator emeritus of the department of Egyptian art of the Metropolitan Museum of Art, died in Boston on January 29, in his sixty-sixth year. Before joining the staff of the Metropolitan Museum in New York he had organized the Egyptian department of the Boston Museum of Fine Arts. Among his many excavations in Egypt was included his assistance to Lord Carnarvon in 1922–23 at the tomb of Tut-ankh-Amun.

FLORA STONE MATHER COLLEGE of Western Reserve University has been named ultimate beneficiary of the estate of Andrew Squire, dean of the Cleveland bar, who died on January 5. Mrs. Eleanor Seymour Squire, the widow, will have the use of the estate, estimated at $1,270,000, during her lifetime, after which it will be held in trust for the college. This trust endowment is to be built up ultimately to a permanent principal amount of $3,000,000. Mr. Squire's will provides for the immediate transfer to the college of Vallee-vue, his country estate.

THE Reynolds Memorial Training School for Nurses at Moundsville, West Virginia, will receive $10,000 from the estate of Miss Emma Thorne, who died in New York on January 17.

BEQUESTS for educational purposes totaling $200,000 have been made by the late Evans Searle Pillsbury, of San Francisco. Bowdoin College is to receive $50,000.

THE University of Pennsylvania is to receive the residue of the $150,000 personal estate of the late Baroness Fontana, formerly Margaret Dulles. The money must be used for the establishment of a cancer hospital, to be known as the Crothers Dulles Hospital. If the University of Pennsylvania trustees do not accept the fund it is to go to the University Hospital, and if rejected by that institution, to the Jefferson Medical College, for similar purposes.

SEVEN fellowships, awarded to women who give promise of distinction in science, literature and the arts, have been announced by Dr. Kathryn McHale, general director of the American Association of University Women. Five were granted to residents of the United States for study in this country or abroad. One fellowship is awarded annually to a Latin-American woman, and an international fellowship is given to enable the holder to carry on research in some country other than her own. A total of 208 fellowships have been distributed since 1889.

PRESIDENT ROOSEVELT, it is reported, will soon issue an executive order against the proposed economy cuts in agricultural education. The economy provisions would have cut $1,732,750 from the regular annual appropriations to land-grant colleges, and a total of $6,516,766 from all the educational services combined.

New Moon, a magazine in raised type for the sightless, is now on the press at the Braille Institute of America in Los Angeles. The periodical will carry a digest of world news, the latest political events in the nation and foreign countries, bits of humor, household hints and an occasional short story. The magazine, which is to be issued monthly, is named in honor of Dr. William Moon, the Englishman who perfected a type for the blind in 1847.

THE surplus of doctors of philosophy in Czechoslovakia is so great, it is reported by the *New York Herald-Tribune,* that nearly one hundred of them have been given jobs in the sales department of a large shoe manufacturing concern.

THE Board of Education of the Methodist Episcopal Church met in Chicago on February 2 to review the work of its 90 educational institutions and of 24,000 Sunday church schools. Enrolments in Methodist educational institutions in the autumn of 1933 were 58,305, as compared with 60,220 enrolled in 1932. The world total of enrolment in Methodist Sunday schools is 4,360,691.

TWENTY thousand Montgomery County, Alabama, children returned to school on January 30, after a ten-day vacation during which the school board and city and county officials sought means of raising money to run the system for the remainder of the year. A majority of the county's five hundred teachers agreed to the proposal offered by the board of education. The teachers are to receive part payment in cash and the remainder in interest-bearing warrants, maturing not later than January, 1935.

SIXTY-TWO unemployed teachers from the Metropolitan area and Connecticut, who have been selected to fill positions in the Federal

Emergency Nursery Schools, are being given a short intensive training period in Teachers College of Columbia University. The nursery school and kindergarten department, of which Dr. Patty S. Hill is director, is offering these courses with the cooperation of the Child Development Institute of the college.

THE U. S. Office of Education announced on February 3 the results of its studies of the financial reports of 299 typical cities scattered over the country. Some of the facts brought out are the following: Per-pupil costs range from $72.23 in small towns to $91.69 in large cities. The average reduction in 1933 in per-pupil cost was 2 per cent., but in some cities it ran as high as 41 per cent. The average cost of educating a child for the year 1933 in these 299 typical cities was $87.50, as compared with $113.03 for 1932. Especially large decreases were made in San Antonio, Texas; El Paso, Texas; Akron, Ohio; Kenosha, Wisconsin; Selma, Alabama; Helena, Arkansas; Sedalia, Missouri; Bisbee, Arizona, and New Bedford, Massachusetts. In submitting these statistics to the public, Commissioner George F. Zook, observed that "it is evident from this survey that schools have undertaken heroic measures to adapt themselves to the exigencies of the depression. Some of the reduction has come from true economy, in which approximately equivalent service is provided at a lower cost. On the other hand, the reductions represent in part a lowering of the standards of education in American cities."

THE Carnegie Corporation late in January began to distribute to American colleges sets of equipment designed to provide all that is necessary for a complete basic education in music. The sets consist of 824 records, a phonograph, 251 scores and 129 books. The equipment also includes a cabinet to contain the 136 albums into which the records fit, another cabinet for the scores and a bookcase for the books, the 129 volumes of which represent 106 titles. The records and scores range in subject-matter from Gregorian chants to Gershwin's "Rhapsody in Blue" with many samples of the work of Bach, Beethoven, Brahms and Wagner. The books range from Leopold Auer's "Violin Playing as I Teach It" to Grove's "Dictionary of Music and Musicians," and include other reference works, biographies, histories of music, treatises on special forms and works on theory. The sets cost $2,500 each.

A STANDING committee of five members representing the various fields of knowledge was appointed by the Council of the American Philosophical Society to make recommendations to the council in regard to appropriations for the advancement of knowledge through investigation. This committee is now organized and prepared to consider applications. The applicant's name with the names of the sponsors of the enterprise submitted and the amount of funds requested must be forwarded with the application to the Secretaries of the American Philosophical Society, 104 South Fifth Street, Philadelphia.

THE Presbyterian board of Christian education in a statement issued in Philadelphia on February 4, asserts that the Presbyterian college financial situation is much brighter now than it has been for a number of years. The statement, dealing with the financial condition of 35 of the 45 colleges operated with the cooperation of the Presbyterian Church in the United States, points out that 19 institutions showed an operating surplus last year as against nine showing such surplus the preceding year. The board also announced that total enrolment at Presbyterian colleges, junior colleges and academies increased in 1933 for the first time in several years. Twenty-three of the forty-nine schools reporting showed gains. The largest increases were reported by MacAlester College in St. Paul, Pikeville Junior College at Pikeville, Ky.; University of Tulsa at Tulsa, Okla., and Buena Vista College at Storm Lake, Iowa. The enrolment of 125 at Pikeville is 36.8 per cent. higher than a year ago. In 1931 the institution more than doubled its enrolment and in 1932 it reported a 25 per cent. increase.

THE expenditure of $1,000,000, granted by the Carnegie Corporation for the purchase of books of interest and use to undergraduates in 85 American universities and colleges, is centralized through the order department of the University of Michigan Library, of which Dr. W. W. Bishop is librarian. The system has been operating since 1931. Each institution has from

$5,000 to $25,000 to be expended in from two to five years, and each school makes its own selection.

The Reich Minister of the Interior has issued a summary of leading principles to be followed in the running of German schools. It emphasizes the resolve that the school and the Hitler Youth Organization shall work in the closest cooperation with parents and that the whole upbringing of German youth shall be in the spirit of National-Socialism. Special attention is paid to the health of children and limits set to the hours they devote to organized activities. Pupils who are members of the S.A. or Hitler Youth may wear their uniforms in school and the previous orders that teachers and pupils should always exchange the German greeting are repeated. "Non-Aryan" children are left free to choose whether they give the salute or not. At the beginning and end of all holidays the children will assemble to honor the flag and sing one stanza of the Deutschland Lied and the Horst Wessel Lied.

The Republic of Turkey, according to the *News Bulletin* of the International Institute of Education, for the past several years has been increasingly looking to the United States for advice and leadership in her educational and economic regeneration. The most recent indication of the former is the resolution of the Turkish Ministry of Education to send larger numbers of government students to the United States for graduate study rather than to Europe, as has been the practise for the past hundred years. There are at the present time over 450 Turkish government students doing graduate work in foreign countries. An even greater number are doing so independently of any government assistance. Although there are 64 Turkish students in this country, only 5 receive government assistance. In accordance with the new policy of the Ministry of Education, the first group of 17 government students will arrive in the United States this fall. Selected by competitive examination, 10 of these men are experienced teachers, graduates of Turkish normal schools, who have shown great ability in their chosen profession. They will devote their time to the study of rural education and educational extension work, to become leaders of rural communities in Turkey upon their return. One of the greatest desires of the Turkish Government is to educate and enlighten the adult peasants, mentally, socially and economically. These students will be important factors in this campaign. The remaining 7 men are recent graduates of Turkish lycées. They will be trained as high-school teachers in mathematics, physics, chemistry and science. Turkish educational authorities are said to be of the opinion that not only are educational advantages in the United States superior to those of other countries, but that here they can obtain a better conception of the true meaning of the word "democracy."

DISCUSSION

CURRENT HISTORY

While we emphasize social studies in schools and colleges, are we not failing to develop an intelligent knowledge of current history? Many of our college students read newspapers, if at all, very superficially. In order to test the familiarity of his students with important names that recur in our news dispatches, the writer recently asked 155 students a series of 24 questions. These students appear to be of the mental range of undergraduate college students in general. None of them has recently taken a course in contemporary historical problems, but all are sophomores or upper classmen. The questions, with brief discussions of the responses, are here given.

(1) *What is Mussolini's office?* Fifty-four, or about one third of the students, replied that he is premier or prime minister of Italy. Ninety called him a dictator. Evidently his position is generally familiar, although one called him president, one chancellor, and one made him "dictator of Germany." Four students gave no answer.

(2) *Who is chancellor of Germany?* Hitler was named by 126, Von Hindenburg by 10,

Bruening by two. Sixteen did not answer. One said Mussolini.

(3) *What is the U. S. S. R.?* This question was left unanswered by 55 students. Most of the remainder gave various formulae that indicated a general knowledge that these letters symbolize soviet Russia. The largest number, 45, agreed on "United States of Soviet Russia." Only two named the true answer: "Union of Socialist Soviet Republics." There were several scattering guesses, such as "United States Scientific Research" and "United States Ships and Railroads."

(4) *Who is prime minister of Great Britain?* MacDonald was named by 123, but 24 students gave no answer, while a few others named Baldwin, Lloyd George or Borden. One loyal Pennsylvanian named Andrew Mellon.

(5) *Who is the chief justice of the Supreme Court?* This question was correctly answered by 59 students, but a larger number, 69, gave no answer. William Howard Taft was resurrected by nine, Justice Holmes was recalled and promoted by sixteen, and two students named Brandeis.

(6) *Who is the Vice-president of the United States?* Are vice-presidents without honor in their own country? Not altogether, for the correct answer was given by 104, but 32 gave no answer, while from one to seven in each case mentioned Hughes, La Guardia, Curtis and Dawes.

(7) *Who is Cordell Hull?* The majority seem to know nothing about our Secretary of State, blanks being left by 85 persons. The question was correctly answered by 41, but others gave him the portfolios of the Treasury, the Interior, Agriculture, War, and the Navy. One says he is connected with Hull House, of which institution two others make him the owner. One says he is Secretary of State of Soviet Russia.

(8) *What is the Kuomintang?* This question stumped 137 students, while others attempted scattering guesses. Perhaps six had a vague idea of the meaning of the term, the best answer, as representing the policy of the party, being "China for Chinese."

(9) *What is the Manchoukuo government?* This is called by 21 the government of Manchuria. Five call it the province taken from China by Japan. About 20 others connect it with China or Japan as a government or an organization. A few answers are altogether erroneous, such as: "government of India" or "government in or under Russia." The question was left unanswered by 93.

(10) *Who was Clemenceau?* Eighty papers show a more or less clear idea of the place of Clemenceau in French history. Twenty-one others erroneously call him a president of France. A scattering few assign him to Germany, Russia and the new Cuban government. The question is left unanswered by 39.

(11) *Who is Mustapha Kemal?* His position was quite correctly indicated by 17 students, but 101 left the space blank. The remaining papers assigned him to a marvelous variety of duties and nations. Six call him the Sultan. One student was wisely content to call him "another famous fellow."

(12) *Who is Mahatma Gandhi?* The Mahatma seems to be a generally familiar figure, though some can describe him only as "the man with the sheet and goat," or "the man from India who resists England and wears few clothes." There are only twelve blanks, while 85 call him an Indian leader. He is thought by 18 to be a ruler or dictator. Several call him a religious leader, a reformer or a radical.

(13) *Who is the President of Germany?* Von Hindenburg is named by 79, but 34 name Hitler, and 35 give no answer. Three assert that Germany has no president at present, while one says: "Hindenburg was—Hitler is now." One student says the president is "Heidelburg."

(14) *Who is Pilsudski?* This was a poser for 104, while scattered others assign him to Russia. Forty students seem to know something about him, calling him dictator, premier, president, statesman or marshal of Poland.

(15) *Who is Venizelos?* There are 133 blanks. Only four students show any real knowledge of Venizelos, and only one of these correctly names him as a former premier of Greece. The others assign him to various countries, the shrewdest guess being that he was the founder of Venezuela.

(16) *Where is Guatemala?* This question was correctly answered by 60 students, while 19 others placed it in South America, and 48

confessed ignorance by writing nothing. The remaining students scattered Guatemala all over the world map, from the West Indies to New Zealand.

(17) *What is Fascism?* There were 48 blanks after this question. It was called the party in control in Italy by 28, and an Italian form of government by 25. No one described it as a movement or as the principles of the Fascisti. One student created an eponymous hero, saying that the word "comes from Fascisti, the founder of the party."

(18) *What is the N. R. A.* Here there are no blanks, although a wide variety of interpretations of the initials is to be seen. All seem to know the general significance of the term. By 99 it is interpreted as the National Recovery Act, while 27 say it is the National Recovery Administration.

(19) *In what country is Prague?* There is a wide distribution here. Czecho-Slovakia is named by 28, but 27 say Germany, 14 name Austria, and smaller numbers mention nearly all the countries of Europe and some on other continents. The question was left unanswered by 32.

(20) *Who is Stalin?* The answer that is nearest to a correct statement of his office is "Chairman Central Committee, U. S. S. R." That he is a Russian leader, statesman, premier or government head is indicated by 68. Four persons evidently confound his name with that of Lenin.

(21) *Who is Dollfuss?* There are 113 blanks. Seventeen papers indicate some knowledge of him although only five give him the correct title of chancellor of Austria. One student confounds him with Dreyfus.

(22) *Who is Daladier?* Although a few days before these questions were presented the newspapers were full of the news of the fall of the Daladier government in France, only 18 students identified him as premier, and only four mentioned his recent defeat. There are 113 blanks. Nine call him President of France.

(23) *What country is governed by a Shah?* This was correctly answered by 34, but 74 attempted no answer. Various countries other than Persia were mentioned by from one to seven persons each.

(24) *Who is La Guardia?* La Guardia's election as mayor of New York a few days before was recognized by 39 students, and 24 others named him as mayor, which at that time, of course, he was not. These two groups, however, may indicate the number who recognize his relationship to New York City. There are 70 blanks and a few scattered designations such as "president of Cuba" or "new French premier." Eight students call him governor of New York.

Doubtless there are hundreds of American colleges whose undergraduates would show a similarly sketchy knowledge of the important men and movements of our day. If this is true, is it not clear that a distinct educational emphasis should be placed upon the vitalization of contemporary history in our schools?

E. LEIGH MUDGE
STATE TEACHERS COLLEGE
EDINBORO, PENNSYLVANIA

THE PRONUNCIATION OF "LIMINAL"

IN the galley proofs of the forthcoming "Dictionary of Psychology and Cognate Sciences" Professor H. C. Warren, the general editor, says that "liminal" should be pronounced "lĭm-." As the pronunciation recommended was strange to me, I queried it, only to have a rule of pronunciation quoted to me that "the long vowel in the noun is, in accordance with Latin etymology, shortened in the adjectival form."

The rule, if it is a rule, finds ready illustration (*e.g.,* stamen-staminal; semen-seminal; nomen-nominal; crime-criminal), but instances to the contrary—*i.e.,* where the vowel in the noun remains long in the adjective—occur also with great frequency (*e.g.,* cerumen-ceruminal; lumen-luminal; lay-laical; labium-labial; and the adjectival form of words ending in "tion," *viz.,* notion-notional; sensation-sensational, etc.).

It must, furthermore, be pointed out that Latin etymology offers no sanction for the rule mentioned above. The long "ī" in "līmen" and "vīta," for example, *remains long* in the adjectives "līminālis" and "vītālis." But as Jespersen says, "in Latin words it is not the classical quantity that is decisive, but the English school-pronunciation, which followed its own rules."[1] The rule followed in this case is the so-called "three-syllable rule" that "when a stressed syl-

[1] O. Jespersen, "A Modern English Grammar," pt. 1, 131, 1909.

lable is followed by two (or more) weak ones, there is a strong tendency to shorten it."[2]

Rules, since they are known by their exceptions, and examples, since they are merely specific instances of usage, offer an insecure basis upon which to determine the correct pronunciation of any given term. The final arbiter in questions of this kind is authoritative usage. "Limen" and "liminal" are psychophysical terms. The psychologists, and in particular the psychophysicists, have, therefore, a right to be heard.

In order to discover the pronunciation actually used by competent men, I sent postal reply-cards to 64 psychologists: to the past presidents of the American Psychological Association, to the psychophysicists of this country[3] and to the heads of our foremost departments. I asked them to designate upon the reply cards, which carried the alternative pronunciations diacritically marked, the pronunciation that they used. Without having recourse to a "follow-up," I received 61 replies. Two of this number, however, count as blanks: one because my correspondent said he used both pronunciations indiscriminately, and the other because he did not know which, if either, was correct. Of the 59 positive replies,[4] 32 indicated the usage of "lim-," and 27 of "li-."

An analysis of the replies reveals striking differences among the three groups circularized. As there is considerable overlapping among the groups—many past presidents, for example, are heads of departments and some are psychophysicists—a dichotomy was made for every group.

About two thirds of the presidents (18 to 8) shortened the vowel in the adjectival form; whereas the majority of those not having held this office (19 to 14) used the long vowel.

The results of the poll of the presidents stand strikingly in opposition to those obtained from the psychophysicists, for the great majority of the latter (21 to 6) use "li-." The non-psychophysicists use the alternative pronunciation, "lim-," in even greater proportion, (26 to 6). The division here is so marked that pronunciation may be taken as a rough indicator of interest in psychophysics. Indeed, one of my correspondents, a past president, a psychophysicist and a head of a department, predicted this result. He wrote, " 'li-' is usual in psychophysics, 'lim-' more usual in psychical research and in the psychopathology of 1910 *et ante*."

The replies of heads of departments and "not-heads" were about equally divided between the alternatives, being respectively 16 to 13 and 16 to 14 in favor of "lim-." Not significant differences in either case.

In order to discover whether pronunciation was geographically conditioned, a regional classification was made of the replies. The proportion of "li-" to "lim-" is 8 to 6 in New England, 8 to 9 in the East, 2 to 4 in the South, 8 to 7 in the Mid-West, and 1 to 6 in the Far West. With the exception of the Far West, which shows a decided preference for "lim-," the returns are about equally divided. These results are not, however, fair indicators of geographical influence, for pronunciation in every case was doubtlessly established long before the correspondents attained their present positions. Since we are dealing with a technical term, one not learned in childhood but only in professional study, a better indicator would be the place of study. Geographical classifications were accordingly made for the first degree, and—since the term may not have been met sufficiently often in undergraduate study to condition pronunciation—for the doctorates. The results show slight deviations in both classifications but nothing to indicate sectional preference.

Since the past presidents, the majority of whom received their professional training before the turn of the century, show a bias in favor of "lim-," it may well be that this pronunciation is the older, and that "li-," the pronunciation of the psychophysicists, has only gradually come into usage with the advance of psychophysics in this country. In order to test this conjecture, the replies were classified upon the basis of date of the doctorates. Of those

[2] *Op. cit.*, 122. *Cf.* also the section on quantity in Romance—Latin and French—words (pp. 130–145, esp. 139 *f.*), which exhibits many examples of the pattern "liminal" as well as exceptions "in some modern (chiefly learned) words."

[3] I counted as psychophysicists all those who had published articles on that subject or were at present teaching courses in it.

[4] One of the correspondents, a past president, wrote that he used "lim-" but preferred "li-." Since we are interested in usage, his reply was tallied as "lim-."

receiving their professional training before 1900, the numbers using "li-" and "lim-" are respectively 3 and 12; between 1900–1910, 5 and 12; between 1911–1920, 11 and 8; and since 1921, 8 and 1. Though this analysis gives added warrant to our conjecture, it shows that there is no unanimity at any period and further that pronunciation is listing decidedly in the direction of "li-."

In view of these results a lexicographer is certainly not justified in being dogmatic. If he records usage he can do no less than to give both pronunciations of "liminal." If he wishes to standardize usage he can not, without flaunting the present trend, declare for "lim-" and against "li-."

KARL M. DALLENBACH

CORNELL UNIVERSITY

SPECIAL CORRESPONDENCE

SOME FACTS RELATED TO STUDENT LIFE AS FOUND IN A SURVEY AT THE UNIVERSITY OF COLORADO, MARCH, 1933

THE student body of any institution of higher learning may be divided into two groups—those who must work all or part of their way while in college and those who are wholly supported by some one else. Both groups must make adjustments upon entering college which are for the majority outside of the realm of previous experience. Those who are not employed must learn how to use their time constructively, while those who work carry a double responsibility and if they succeed must learn to do both passingly well.

A man or woman who is employed while in college is in many instances doing his first independent work. Said a freshman to me in discussing his program—"I am working eight hours a day more than I ever worked while in high school." He was washing dishes three hours a day for his meals and found it necessary to study five hours a day to keep up his work. This was his daily work program in addition to his classroom and laboratory schedule.

In a survey made in March, 1933, at the University of Colorado, it was found that students who are employed work a median of twenty hours per week. This in our student community is the equivalent of earning one's board, since it is the custom to serve twenty meals per week at boarding houses, and a student is expected to work one hour for each meal.

It was found that 42.3 per cent. of all men in the university are employed while in school—13.3 per cent. must earn their entire way, while 29 per cent. earn only a portion of their expenses. Thirty cents per hour or its equivalent is the rate paid student help for all kinds of unskilled labor. This nets the average student worker approximately $200 per year or its equivalent, which for many is the largest item of their expense. The women of the university fare somewhat better than the men in that 18.5 per cent. are employed part-time, while only 2.5 per cent. must earn their entire expenses. The proportionate number of men to women covered by the survey was approximately two to one.

Closely related to the problem of working while in college is the fact that a goodly portion of the students have been previously employed; 63.6 per cent. of the men and 37 per cent. of the women have held positions, carrying a salary or wages, prior to coming to the university. The blank filled in by the students called for names and addresses of former employers, as well as rate of pay and duration of employment. The information secured regarding work experience is found to be very valuable in learning of the background of each student and for reference in case of consideration for future employment.

The fact that an education is considered a good investment is borne out when we learn that 40.7 per cent. of the men have borrowed money to pursue their schooling. The median amount borrowed per man was $279. Again, the women students appear to be in better financial circumstances, for only 16.5 per cent. find it necessary to borrow money, and the median amount borrowed was $200.

Eighty per cent. of the men students and 30 per cent. of the women students report that they had savings to their credit upon entering the university. The median amounts saved were $300 per student for the men, and $150 for the women.

When one considers the individual effort and expenditure entailed in securing an education he is convinced that planning an education becomes a serious problem and should be given more thought and study.

The survey also called for a report of the students' outside activities while attending the university. In this field of endeavor the women have a slight advantage over the men, in that 84.4 per cent. participate in activities, while 80 per cent. of the men take part. However, the men make up for the smaller percentage in that they spend more time in activities each week. The median number of hours per week spent by the men is 6.6 hours, while the women give but 4.6 hours per week. The variety of activities affords a most liberal education and supplements the more formal class and course work by giving the great majority of students the opportunity to develop their many interests and thereby gain valuable experience.

The survey further reveals that men members of social fraternities participate in activities to a greater extent than non-fraternity members. The proportion is 91 per cent. to 74 per cent. Also, the fraternity men spend more time in outside affairs, the hours spent being 7 per week for fraternity men and 5 per week for non-fraternity men.

Of the sorority women 95.4 per cent. take part in activities, while 81 per cent. of the non-sorority women participate. In the matter of employment the difference in the two above-named groups of women is still greater. Only 5.4 per cent. of the sorority women are employed, while 28.6 per cent. of the non-sorority women find it necessary to have employment.

For the men the percentage of those employed is nearly equal, 42.5 of the fraternity men and 44.4 per cent. of the non-fraternity men being the proportionate number employed.

In making a special study of the undergraduates who hold scholarships it was found that in the case of the men a greater percentage holding scholarships were employed while attending school than was shown by the whole group—56 per cent of scholarship men as compared to a total of 42.3 per cent. was the proportion. Also, it was found that more scholarship students were employed before entering the university or during summers fewer borrowed money and fewer had savings accounts.

In the case of the women students the facts were somewhat different. Proportionately twice as many holding scholarships were employed part-time while in college than was shown by the whole student body; fewer holding scholarships were employed before coming to the university; more scholarship people found it necessary to borrow, but more had savings accounts.

The facts of this survey emphasize the need for careful planning by those who intend to enter college and pursue an education, and also produces evidence to prove that the administration of student affairs, including activities, finances and employment, is second to none in importance to all problems connected with student life. The question may well be asked—do we as college administrators give the time and study to these problems commensurate to their importance in the plans of each individual student involved? The facts revealed should cause us to rethink our responsibility in this regard.

FRED E. ADEN
UNIVERSITY OF COLORADO

QUOTATIONS

EDUCATION IN JAPAN

JAPANESE army leaders have served notice on civilian educational authorities that the entire educational system must be drastically reformed in accordance with definitely outlined conceptions. They have made it clear that unless the reforms they ask are promptly applied, they intend to take charge of the educational system themselves, with the support of Nationalist civilian groups.

What are the reforms which the army demands? The public utterances and writings of army leaders provide the answer to this question. Briefly, the army and its Nationalist supporters insist that the nation's entire attention should be concentrated upon expanding and consolidating the Eastern Asiatic Empire which they regard as Japan's "manifest destiny."

For more than two decades, they declare, international-minded Japanese have diverted the nation from its destined path. Often uncertain themselves what they desired, such leaders are declared to have associated themselves and their country with such international undertakings as the League of Nations to the detriment of the only program which will give Japan the position to which it is entitled: namely, an unassailably dominant control of Eastern Asia.

The expansion and consolidation of this Eastern Asiatic Empire, they declare, is probably the work of several generations. The children of Japan should therefore be trained to carry on this task, and the present educational system is not properly devised to that end.

Japan's modern educational system has always been something more than mere "schooling"; it has included a program of "Japanization" more intensive than any "Americanization" or other program of the sort which has been applied anywhere else in the world. Every tourist to Japan has been impressed by the fact that he encounters crowds of school children everywhere, visiting temples, shrines and beauty spots in all parts of the country. Led by their teachers, boys and girls trudge for miles to stand for a few moments before some shrine commemorating a national hero or a temple dedicated to some Japanese deity.

Every school child in Japan, which means almost every child, takes at least six "cultural trips" each year to national shrines and temples. They are given extraordinarily cheap rates on the government railways and their itinerary usually is restricted to the district in which they live. The average expenditure for these trips is therefore only about 80 cents per family per year. But if any families are too poor to afford even this amount, their children are taken along at the government's expense.

The cumulative effect of these constant visits is naturally very great. In the six years of compulsory primary school education, every child makes 36 such trips, under auspices designed to impress upon him a love of country such as few, if any, other governments, foster so carefully.

The writer visited this winter the Grand Shrine of Ise, the principal Shinto shrine of Japan, where the sacred mirror, one of the three sacred treasures, is kept. To the Grand Shrine every Japanese aspires to make at least one pilgrimage during his lifetime. There was no special festival at the shrine during the writer's visit, but nevertheless he encountered a constant procession of school children. Some of them were very young and others were older, but all of them marched earnestly behind their teachers and all bowed reverently before these impressively simple shrines, in their perfect natural settings of mountains, trees and waterfalls, and made their offerings to the sun goddess, who is considered the ancestress of Japan's Imperial family.

In other countries one might expect a great amount of chattering and laughter among so many young children on such an outing, but these Japanese children had been prepared for a great occasion, and they visited the shrines in a spirit of reverence which had been inculcated by months of previous instruction. And on this same day, at lesser shrines, other groups of children were bowing in the same reverent spirit.

This effectual method of instilling patriotism, moral and religious concepts and love of country has been used for generations, but has been intensified since the expansion program was revived in 1931. The army insists that the emphasis of these trips, as of the school curriculum, must be laid in future upon those things which will develop in the children's imagination the conception of Japan as a supreme Asiatic power, and of the sacrifices which may be necessary to attain that end. They insist that all tendencies toward pacifism and "softness" must be rigorously eradicated, and the natural "fighting qualities" of the Japanese people emphasized.

There has been considerable resistance to the army's proposed domination of the educational system, not because any groups object to the expansion policy, but because army leaders are not believed capable of directing a balanced educational program. Army leaders are regarded as men with "one-track minds" who want to use the educational system for a single purpose, whereas more thoughtful Japanese realize it should serve several.

The training of army officers, even as compared to that of naval officers, has been decidedly limited. Until recently they studied only the German and Russian languages in addition to their own, and one close observer remarked that most of them read only *old* German and Russian textbooks and philosophical works, which means that they were nurtured in the pre-war Prussian and Tsarist concepts. Public utterances of the higher officers to-day clearly reveal these influences.

Army officers seldom have left Japan except to visit the adjacent Asiatic mainland, whereas naval officers travel constantly and see much of other countries. Naval officers have studied English and French, and their reading in these languages has made their outlook different from that of army officers.

The army, however, initiated the revival of the expansion policy which has aroused so much popular enthusiasm, and the army is pressing for domestic reforms which appeal to the popular imagination. Popular support is therefore assured for the army's insistence upon educational reforms, and the educational system is already being reshaped to mold the conviction of the oncoming generation that an Eastern Asiatic Empire is Japan's "manifest destiny," the attainment of which is the primary purpose of all national effort.—*Demaree Bess, Staff Correspondent of The Christian Science Monitor.*

REPORTS

"THE SEARCH FOR VALUES"[1]

MORE than 500 college and university presidents, deans and professors, representing nearly 300 institutions of higher education in the United States and Canada, attended the sessions of the twentieth annual meeting of the Association of American Colleges, which was held on January 18 and 19, 1934, at the Hotel Jefferson in St. Louis, Missouri. The central theme of the meeting was "The Search for Values," and the various papers and reports presented bore upon phases of the present seeking on the part of the college world for higher spiritual and social values.

Four sessions were held—three on January 18 and one on January 19. At the first session the reports of officers and chairmen of permanent commissions and special committees were presented. Two formal papers and one committee report were presented at the second meeting. Three addresses were delivered at the annual dinner. The meeting closed with a business session and the presentation of papers on the general theme by representatives of four accrediting agencies, Phi Beta Kappa and the American Association of University Women.

The president of the association, President Edmund D. Soper, of Ohio Wesleyan University, presided over the gathering. The meeting was opened with an address of welcome by Chancellor George R. Throop, of Washington University, on behalf of the colleges and universities of the trans-Mississippi region.

[1] Twentieth annual meeting of the Association of American Colleges, held in St. Louis, Missouri, January 18–19, 1934.

In his annual report as executive secretary of the association, Dr. Robert L. Kelly reviewed the work of the association during the past year, referring to the appearance of the Brethren and Friends Colleges Surveys, Architectural Planning of the American College and More and Better Wills; the authorization of a supplementary volume on comprehensive examinations within the field of the social sciences and a monograph on College Instruction in Art; progress in the College Music Study; the distribution of college alumni, alumni clubs and other groups, in leading cities, as a possible aid to college financing; the regional conference under the joint auspices of the association and the Council of Church Boards of Education at Dallas; participation in the regional conferences on the emergency in education in Detroit and Hartford, and considerable other field work, including some state college conferences; and the publication of some successful current methods of financing colleges.

While describing historically the relation of the colleges to national recovery, he cited particularly the efforts and achievements, in behalf of the colleges, of the joint committee representing the American Council on Education, the Association of American Colleges, the National Catholic Welfare Association and the National Education Association. It was as a result of the work of this committee that the ruling was secured from the NRA that "schools, colleges, universities, churches, hospitals, and charitable institutions supported by public subscriptions, not operated for profit, except so far as they may be engaged in the operation of trade or industry, need not come under the provisions of the National Recovery Act."

On the authority of the executive committee, Dr. Kelly presented for the consideration of the association the following question raised by our present situation:

> Shall new legislation be attempted to overcome the present disposition of certain federal authorities to discriminate, in certain areas of operation, against privately controlled, publicly supported, non-profit making institutions of higher learning?

Subsequently, at the afternoon session on January 18, the following resolution was adopted and embodied in a telegram which was sent to the President of the United States:

> Since many young men and women qualified to enroll in our colleges and universities have not been able to do so through lack of funds, and since it is evident that many students now enrolled will have to drop out at the end of this semester, thereby increasing the number of unemployed;
>
> We therefore petition the United States Government through the CWA, CWS, or other appropriate funds, to provide financial aid for college and university students in tax supported and endowed colleges and universities (chartered not for profit) through the agency of the institutions themselves;
>
> We further petition the United States Government through the RFC or some other agency
>
> (1) To lend money directly to the colleges and universities on secured student notes given in payment for tuition and other regular fees;
>
> (2) To lend money directly to the colleges and universities for the purpose of refinancing existing obligations at a low rate of interest, similar to the plan under which such loans are granted to tax supported institutions, and
>
> (3) To lend money to colleges and universities, at a low rate of interest, to carry through to completion building projects which had been projected and announced at least three years ago.

Arrangements were also made for the appointment of a representative of the association, a college president, to be sent to Washington to promote the adoption of the relief program embodied in this telegram, by securing administrative and legislative action.

In discussing recent developments in "the campaign for perseverance" and the interest aroused among trust companies, insurance companies and members of the bar in support of the colleges and other cultural agencies, Dr. Kelly emphasized the fact that "there is a deeper meaning in all of this than the possible securing of funds."

> More important, however, is the keeping of the currents of benevolence sensitively fluid. If our total educational program drifts or is driven into some form of state socialism, a calamity of the first order will be the result. It is the glory of American education that it is not everywhere and always answerable to the state, and subject to its dictation.
>
> By insisting that church-related and independent institutions are publicly supported and are rendering a service to the public, even though privately controlled, we are in that very act rendering an important public service.

He also reminded his audience that "at the moment when higher education in the United States, like all other phases of education, is passing through its greatest crisis, the college of liberal arts and sciences stands out conspicuously in the confidence and esteem of the people," that "the people of the United States believe in their colleges, with all their faults," and that "the colleges which actually are able to deliver the finer things of life, are balance wheels in our disturbed social machinery."

Reverting to the general theme of the meeting, he said:

> The day of objective minimum standards is passing, and the day of general maximum principles and ideals is dawning. Indeed, standardization is giving way to accreditment through the evaluation, by highly competent men, of individual and institutional achievement in the light of definitely outlined objectives.

The treasurer of the association, Comptroller LeRoy E. Kimball, of New York University, in his annual report announced that the association had closed the year with a balance.

The report of the Commission on College Athletics, read by President Daniel L. Marsh, of Boston University, in the absence of the chairman of the commission, President Thomas S. Gates, of the University of Pennsylvania, traced the tremendous growth of college athletics during the era of prosperity and indicated that the depression had caused a deflation in the importance of intercollegiate athletics, adding that "the extension of intramural sports in the last three years has been remarkable."

In 1930 there were the first symptoms of a collapse of this condition of inflation. There was a drop of 6 per cent. in attendance and 9 per cent. in receipts. In 1931 there was a drop of 10 per cent. in attendance and a still sharper decline in receipts, and in 1932 the receipts fell off to the extent of about 27 per cent. Preliminary reports for 1933 show a substantial increase in attendance, but it is doubtful if there was a corresponding increase in receipts, as many institutions lowered admission prices sharply.

The Carnegie Foundation report No. 23, on athletics, was cited as "a great relief to the harassed president of many a college." Responses to a questionnaire submitted to college presidents by the commission clearly indicated that there is a growing resistance to the commercialization of athletics and that those institutions which persist in it must look to a loss of prestige in the college world. The report ended with the observation that:

The last three years have shown an increasing realization among the leaders in the college world of their responsibility for the physical welfare of the student and that physical education in its varied forms, extending from the individual care of the under-developed lad up to giving his more favored classmate the honor of representing his college in intercollegiate contests, forms a vital part of a well-rounded program in our institutions of learning.

Auditor T. L. Hungate, of Teachers College, Columbia University, in his report as chairman of the Commission on the Cost of College Education, referred to new techniques now available for the study of educational costs in individual institutions. The two great areas of economy open to colleges, he said, are in the field of institutional coordination of effort on a state-wide basis and in institutional internal administration. The immediate problem is to balance the budget and retain teaching standards, reducing expenditures without lowering standards.

In the report of the Commission on Educational Surveys, the chairman of that commission, President David A. Robertson, of Goucher College, mentioned the analysis being made by Dr. Walter C. Eells of all surveys in the field of higher education, commended for study the surveys of the University of Chicago and of the colleges affiliated with the Methodist Episcopal Church and the report of the American Association of University Professors on college and university teaching, and urged the establishment of a standard terminology which would contribute greatly to the value of educational surveys, especially for comparative purposes.

A brief report for the Commission on Permanent and Trust Funds, prepared by the chairman of that commission, F. L. Jackson, of Davidson College, was read by the executive secretary.

As chairman of the Committee Sponsoring the College Music Study, which the association is conducting under a subvention from the Carnegie Corporation, President Ernest H. Wilkins, of Oberlin College, presented a progress report in which he summarized the procedures employed by the director of the study, Mr. Randall Thompson, on his visits to thirty colleges and universities and in the preparation of the report which it is anticipated will be ready for publication this spring.

President E. E. Rall, of North Central College, presented a report of the achievements of the National Committee on Standard Forms for Institutions of Higher Education. As he indicated, the work of this committee has been along three lines: (1) the study of practises in accounting and reporting as they existed; (2) the formulation of recommended forms, reports, principles and procedures; and (3) the effort to secure acceptance of forms and procedures proposed. The committee has published seven bulletins thus far and has several others in process. President Rall reported that nine national organizations and 164 institutions, as well as the U. S. Office of Education and a number of state departments of education, have adopted or plan to adopt, in principle or in detail, the forms and procedures recommended by the committee.

The report of the Committee on Classification of Institutions of Higher Education was read by Dean Howard D. Roelofs, of the University of Cincinnati. During the past three years this committee has prepared a classification of institutions of higher education for the use of administrators, professors and others desiring to compare enrolment statistics, finances, material equipment, library volumes and other data.

The report included an interpretative summary of attendance trends in higher education, prepared by the chairman of the committee, President Raymond Walters, of the University of Cincinnati:

> Liberal training maintains its hold. Young men and women in practically undiminished numbers are continuing to take liberal arts courses in the universities almost equally in the privately-controlled institutions having tuition fees as in the institutions under public control where tuition is free, with varying incidental fees. In the independent colleges of arts and sciences, which are very largely privately-controlled with tuition fees, about 95 per cent. of last year's enrolment is reported this year.
>
> There is a definite attendance trend away from certain types of professional and vocational training. Preparation for teaching is the most pronounced instance of this; there are decreases of around 13 per cent. in university graduate schools which prepare largely for teaching in schools and colleges, and decreases likewise in university schools and departments of education and in separate teachers colleges. Engineering and architecture reflect recent industrial conditions in their decreased enrolments. There are similar enrolment drops in journalism, music and pharmacy.
>
> There are small attendance increases and decreases in other professional and vocational fields. As to schools of law, medicine and divinity, there are indications of limitation in numbers admitted; the totals this year in each are slightly higher than last. The university schools of business administration report totals less than 4 per cent. under those of 1932. The decreases in agriculture, forestry and dentistry are about this same percentage.

Believing that in view of certain recent dismissals of college presidents and professors reestablishment of the association's Commission on Academic Freedom and Academic Tenure may be of service to its membership, the association, on recommendation of the executive committee, voted to reestablish that commission. The following were elected members of the commission: President J. L. McConaughy, of Wesleyan University, *chairman;* Chancellor S. P. Capen, of the University of Buffalo, President Meta Glass, of Sweet Briar College, President R. A. Kent, of the University of Louisville, and President Edmund D. Soper, of Ohio Wesleyan University.

Under the general theme, "The Search for Values," President Homer P. Rainey, of Bucknell University, read a stimulating paper on "The Search for Values through Expression" and Dr. William S. Learned, of the Carnegie Foundation for the Advancement of Teaching, presented a searching critique on "Testing for Values in Education."

President Rainey called attention to the need for a new emphasis in education if the colleges are to lead the American people in their search for spiritual values. "In the dark days of the depression the colleges have stood for the supremacy of spiritual values," but "we have tried to reduce too much education to pure reason."

> We are just now coming to realize that the training of the emotions and the imagination is not a mere by-product of education, but is one of its central tasks. . . . We have sought to train students to think, which is all very good, if we had not at the same time neglected to teach them to act.

The solution, he believed, is to be found in a vital college program organized around the principle of action and expression.

> This principle is that all learning or education is a process of experience-getting, and a recognition of the further fact that no experience becomes vital until the learner has made an effort to give a successful expression of the experience which he has received. . . .
>
> Because of the significant place which all the sciences hold in contemporary life, and because of the objectivity of the scientific method of investigation the scientists on college faculties have exerted an influence on college curricula and methods of instruction out of proportion to their value in life. . . .
>
> The scientific point of view has, in recent years, virtually robbed the arts college of its fine arts program. It has insisted that such subjects as music, painting, and sculpture have no place in the curricula of the arts college. . . . Literature has been the only one of the arts to survive this attack, and it has survived at the cost of surrendering almost completely to a scientific method of study.

The speaker summarized his conception of the liberal college in the following terms:

The college will really function when it reaches the level of creative productivity in all the great areas of human experience. This means that the college must find ways of leading its students through the great areas of human experience in such a way that they shall be able, insofar as possible, to re-create the experiences of mankind for themselves. It is in this process of re-creation of experiences that the principle of expression becomes operative and is of such tremendous value. It is in the field of the various arts that this opportunity for the re-creation of experience finds its fullest expression. The arts constitute the successful expression of all the experiences of man. Hence, if one wishes to re-create any experience of man he finds his medium in one or more of the various forms of art.

He advanced the following six objectives of a program for the arts:

(1) It will give the arts a significant and vital place in the program of the college—a place which they rightly deserve, and which the contemporary needs of society demand.

(2) By providing for and encouraging creative activities in the arts it will loose them from their shackles and will provide an important stimulus for a real period of creative productivity in American art.

(3) It will offer wide opportunities for the entire student population of the colleges to participate in art activities.

(4) It will greatly enrich the cultural life of the campus by presenting to the campus opportunities to hear, see, and appreciate all forms of good art.

(5) The campus will become a cultural center for the immediate community and the surrounding territory.

(6) The college will discover art interests and abilities which it will encourage and develop and will select students for a continuation of their work into advanced study and eventually into a career.

The task of education, according to Dr. Learned, is to increase the student's store of important thoroughly mastered knowledge, and to make this knowledge useful to him by requiring him to think out its meanings.

The unit- and credit-earning procedure of our schools and colleges makes it difficult for the student to learn the supreme importance of reflection; of reading and re-reading until he understands; of putting together the values of many courses into a thoroughly organized knowledge of a subject; or of working out a clear picture of the world about him and of his own place in it.

The result is that the student has little respect for accurate, coherent knowledge or the power to get and retain it. The Pennsylvania tests appear to show that more than one-third of the college seniors in that state can easily be matched by the seniors in good high schools so far as their general thinking in the field of liberal education is concerned. This simply means that many colleges are essentially high schools in this respect.

It is the duty of the college to find out first what its students are, what they know and can do. On the basis of this information they can then be guided into profitable study, and required to attain reasonable standards. Well constructed achievement tests are of great importance in bringing this about.

In his presidential address, delivered at the annual dinner, President Edmund D. Soper, of Ohio Wesleyan University, discussed "The Search for Values through Character Development."

If centuries of education in Europe and Asia, not to speak of America, have taught us anything at all they surely have made it clear that unless moral values are made a part of the aim in education it is futile. . . . Character is an ultimate in our educational program and is to be sought as an end and not as a means to a more significant end beyond itself. . . . The final solution of the problem of character development is a belief in Christianity.

Dr. John A. Lapp, chairman of the Chicago Regional Labor Board, made a strong plea for a new conception in the teaching of the social sciences in colleges in his address on "The Search for Values through Social Work." "When we think in terms of the social values connected with the protection of the integrity of human beings," he said, "we have four major values, namely, the protection of the physical integrity of human beings; secondly, the protection of the economic integrity; third, the protection of the political integrity; and, fourth, the protection of the moral and spiritual integrity."

The greatest trouble in this country, according to Dr. Lapp, is that we do not get our knowledge out where it can be used effectively.

> We have been making progress in storing up things, in the social sciences, but we have not been making progress, and I say it with a great deal of deep regret, in getting the knowledge of politics and economics and sociology out among even the leaders of business and of professional life and of other parts of our society. If we had been successful in that, we would not now be in the condition we are in in this country. . . .
>
> We need a renaissance of social science, research and social science teaching, that will reach more widely than we have ever reached before, in order that our people may plan effectively, to the end that we may protect human beings in their essential integrities. And out of this present disaster may come the leadership which may take us in that direction, but let us understand as college presidents, college professors, college deans, that we must buttress that plan against the possibility that with the revival of prosperity we may go back to the gay and thoughtless life that we passed through in that period from 1921 to 1929, when we thought that there was nothing but economic prosperity continually unfolding in larger and larger amounts, only to discover that we had built a house of cards.

Principal Walter T. Brown, of Victoria University, was presented as the representative of the one Canadian member college of the association. He spoke briefly but very comprehensively on the problems of higher education common to Canada and to the United States.

At the final session, President Henry M. Wriston, of Lawrence College, on behalf of the North Central Association of Colleges and Secondary Schools, of which he is this year president, and President William Mather Lewis, of Lafayette College, on behalf of the Middle States Association of Colleges and Secondary Schools, of which he was last year president, told what their respective organizations are doing in the search for values. President James R. McCain, of Agnes Scott College, described what the Southern Association of Colleges and Secondary Schools is doing in this connection; Dr. Adam Leroy Jones, of Columbia University, what the Association of American Universities is doing; President David A. Robertson, of Goucher College, what Phi Beta Kappa is doing, and Director Kathryn McHale, of the American Association of University Women, what that organization is doing.

The following officers of the association were elected for the ensuing year: President William Mather Lewis, of Lafayette College, *president;* President David A. Robertson, of Goucher College, *vice-president;* Comptroller LeRoy E. Kimball, of New York University, *treasurer,* and as additional members of the executive committee: Sister Antonia, of the College of St. Catherine, Dean C. S. Boucher, of the University of Chicago, President James R. McCain, of Agnes Scott College, and President Edmund D. Soper, of Ohio Wesleyan University.

Archie M. Palmer,
Associate Secretary, Association of American Colleges

EDUCATIONAL RESEARCH AND STATISTICS

THE STATE ORGANIZATION AND ADMINISTRATION OF TEACHER PREPARATION

There is a scarcity of literature dealing with the state organization and administration of teacher preparation. This may be due to the comparatively recent creation of divisions of teacher preparation in state departments of education, the small number of divisions of teacher preparation which are functioning as such, or the fact that few students have availed themselves of the opportunity to do research work in this field.

The educational organization varies in the several states. Consequently, the form and composition of the state departments of education vary accordingly. The state school laws of Alabama and Maryland define the term "state department of education" as an office consisting of the state superintendent, or commissioner of education, and his assistant staff. The school laws of Connecticut and New Hampshire contain no specific references to a state department of education, but specify that the state board of education shall have control and supervision of the educational interests of the state, appoint subordinate officers and prescribe their duties. The school laws of California specify that the state department of education shall be administered through:

(1) The state board of education, which shall be the governing and policy determining body of the department.

(2) The state director of education, in whom all executive and administrative functions of the department are vested and who is the executive officer of the state board of education.

The term "state department of education" as used in this study designates an office composed of the state superintendent, or commissioner of education, and his assistant staff.

A division or bureau of teacher preparation in the state department of education is found in the following states: Alabama, California, Connecticut, Indiana, Louisiana, Maine, Massachusetts, Missouri, New Jersey, New York, North Carolina, Ohio, Pennsylvania, Virginia, West Virginia and Wisconsin. The office of state director of teacher preparation is found in those states in which there are a large number of students enrolled in teacher preparation courses. Over half of the students enrolled in teacher preparation courses are found in those states in which there is a division or bureau of teacher preparation in the state department of education. It would appear that the magnitude of the work of teacher preparation has caused the chief executive officer of the state school system to delegate the responsibility to a professional state officer or officers.

The state control of education necessitates a "planning" department, or state department of education. The most important duty of the state department of education is to lead the educational forces of the state. If the department of education has the confidence of the public, the public will regard it as a cooperating friend, a body of organized experts working for the children of the state, leading, not driving.

If the state is interested in providing competent teachers for the children in the schools, it follows that it should have supervision of normal schools, teachers colleges and all other teacher preparation agencies. Certification standards, curricula, entrance requirements and graduation standards are all problems of a state nature which demand the constant and careful attention and study of the professional officers of a state department of education.

Control of Teacher Preparation by State Departments of Education

	Yes	No	No state board
State boards operating through a state department of education in the administration of the state normal schools and teachers colleges	18	25	5
State boards operating through a state department of education in the supervision of the state normal schools and teachers colleges	19	24	5
Regulations of the state department of education subject to the approval of the state board of education	32	11	5
State board of control for the state normal schools and teachers colleges separate from the state board of education	24	24	
Local boards of control for each state normal school and teachers college	15	33	
Local boards elected	1	14	
Local boards appointed	14	1	
State councils, composed of state normal school principals and teachers college presidents	17	31	
Teacher certification procedure, based upon examinations only	18	30	

State officers who approve selection of teachers college presidents	Total states
Chief state school executive officer	6
State board of normal school trustees	7
State superintendent and director of teacher preparation	1
State board of higher education	1
State board of control	2
State board of education	11
Board of administration	1
Governor	1
State board of regents	4
Local teachers' college boards	4
Commissioner nominates, state board approves	3
None	7
Total	48

Mark E. Stine
State Teachers College
Millersville, Pa.

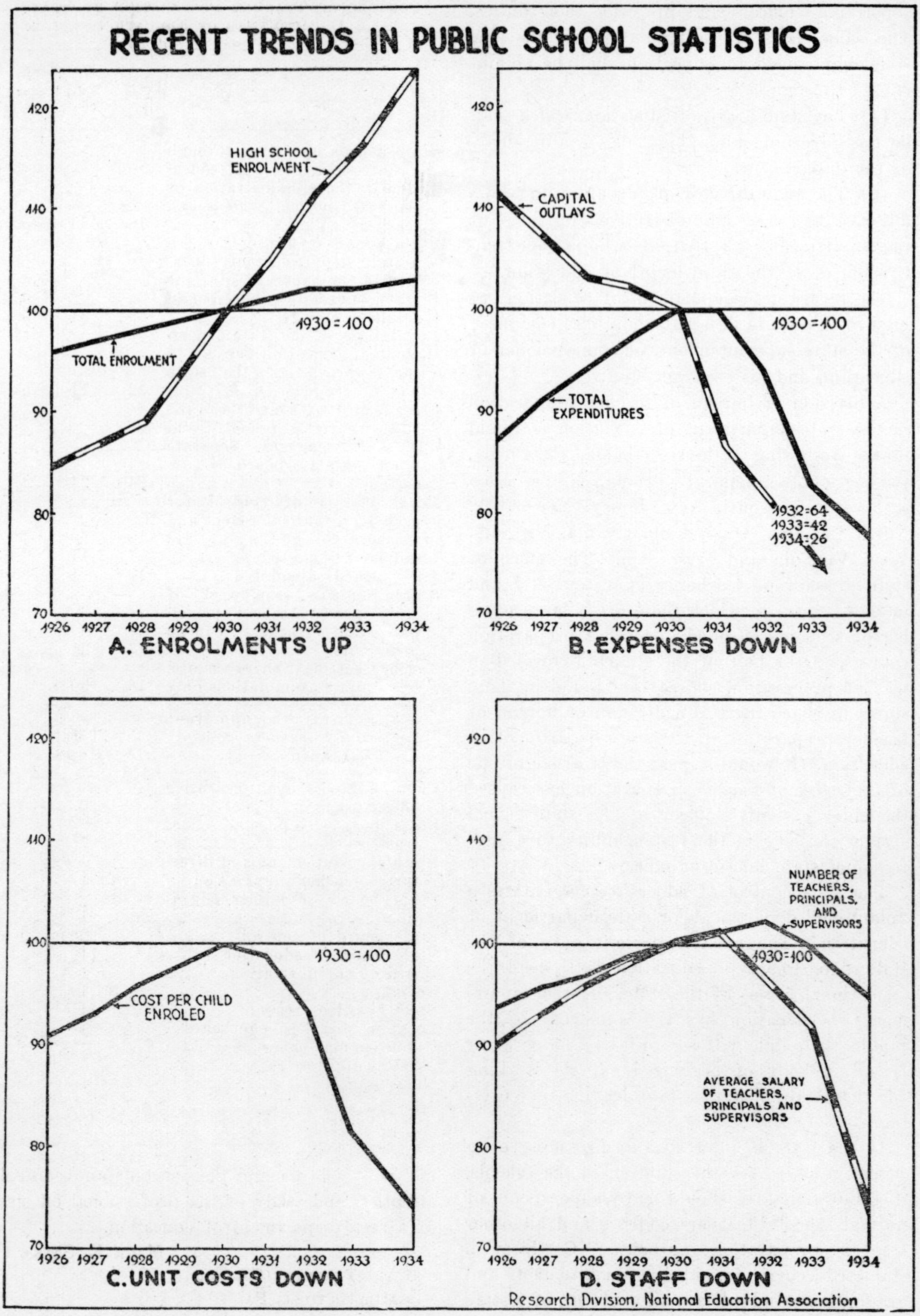
RECENT TRENDS IN PUBLIC SCHOOL STATISTICS
HIGH SCHOOL ENROLMENT
TOTAL ENROLMENT
1930=100
A. ENROLMENTS UP
CAPITAL OUTLAYS
TOTAL EXPENDITURES
1930=100
1932=64
1933=42
1934=26
B. EXPENSES DOWN
COST PER CHILD ENROLED
1930=100
C. UNIT COSTS DOWN
NUMBER OF TEACHERS, PRINCIPALS, AND SUPERVISORS
1930=100
AVERAGE SALARY OF TEACHERS, PRINCIPALS AND SUPERVISORS
D. STAFF DOWN
Research Division, National Education Association

SCHOOL AND SOCIETY

WITH WHICH ARE COMBINED THE EDUCATIONAL REVIEW, ESTABLISHED IN 1891, THE TEACHERS MAGAZINE, ESTABLISHED IN 1878, AND THE SCHOOL JOURNAL, ESTABLISHED IN 1874.

EDITED BY J. McKEEN CATTELL, R. D. LINDQUIST AND W. H. COWLEY

EDITORIAL COMMUNICATIONS SHOULD BE ADDRESSED TO THE EDUCATION BUILDING, THE OHIO STATE UNIVERSITY, COLUMBUS, OHIO

Volume 39 — SATURDAY, FEBRUARY 17, 1934 — Number 999

YOUTH AND THE CRISIS IN AMERICAN LIFE,[1] WITH PARTICULAR REFERENCE TO COLLEGE JOURNALISM

By JOY ELMER MORGAN

EDITOR, JOURNAL OF THE NATIONAL EDUCATION ASSOCIATION

I APPRECIATE the privilege of meeting personally this pioneer organization of student leaders. It is from such groups as this that we shall recruit the civic and intellectual leadership of to-morrow which must guide this country in its continued growth. I have profound respect for the student mind, for the mind of youth unspoiled by the thousand and one illusions and disillusionments that too often accumulate with the years. One of the most inspiring facts of American history is the youthfulness of the men who founded this nation. Alexander Hamilton at 23 was writing documents on our federal financial policy which would do credit to the great scholars of all time. He put his mind to the task of dealing with intercolonial financial problems, just as the young people of our day must tackle the task of international financial problems. The human mind matures much earlier than is generally supposed and the development which takes place later is the accumulation of experience rather than an increase in sheer brain excellence.

In speaking of youth and the crisis in American life, I have in mind the facts of the present situation as the raw materials with which college journalism should be constantly dealing. The major problem of college journalism is not the organization of staff or the technology of printing, finance or circulation. It is the content, the ideas and the spirit which are to parade through the pages of the college periodical and to leave their impress upon the habit of mind, the outlook, the interests and the attitudes of the generation of youth who are served by the college periodical. And so most of what I have to say this morning will concern itself with the points in the present crisis which are of immediate importance to young people everywhere who wish to face realistically the actualities of to-day's life.

There is an old paradox that every strength is a weakness and that every weakness is a strength. As I have watched the years and the decades go by I have been increasingly impressed by the truth of that paradox as applied both to the individual and the collective life. And so I believe that the new hope which President Roosevelt has inspired during 1933 rests upon

[1] Address before the ninth annual convention of the National Student Federation of America, Washington, D. C., December 29, 1933.

sound foundations, even though I also believe that the gravest of our difficulties are still ahead. If it be true that the hardest part of the trail is still ahead, let that fact be a challenge to youth to gird its loins, conserve its strength and push forward, thankful to live in this great day and to have its part in the eternal struggle for life, liberty and the pursuit of happiness.

May I begin with a confession of faith? I believe:

(1) That people come first, that they are more important than property.

(2) That it is possible to build from the best elements of to-day's civilization a new order which shall bring untold benefits to the whole of humanity.

(3) That the entire people in their collective experience and wisdom are wiser than any group or class.

(4) That freedom of thought and of teaching are fundamental to the growth and improvement of mankind.

(5) That representative democracy is the best form of government.

(6) That public opinion and ballots are more powerful than bullets.

(7) That teaching is more effective than fighting.

(8) That, excepting only the home and the church, the free common school has done more to lift mankind than any other agency.

(9) That the spirit of a people is more significant than their material resources; and

(10) That in the present worldwide struggle between humanity and special privilege, humanity will win.

I come now to the crisis in American life. I have already told you that I believe the most difficult part of the path lies ahead. I want to speak first of the spirit which in my judgment should characterize the student, particularly during this crisis. He can not be a student and ally himself with any party or class. This does not mean that he will not take active part in the rough and tumble of current policy, but it does mean that in his collection, examination, analysis and synthesis of facts, he must achieve a reasonable detachment from partisanship, prejudice, wishful thinking and the limitations which intense preoccupation with the immediate present imposes upon us. The inescapable logic of events is stronger than the wills of individual men, and the real student of affairs is more interested in getting at the roots of the logic of events than he is in praise or blame or the success of any group or party, even of his own group.

The real student is careful in the use of labels. He knows that labels can be counterfeited, that they can be shifted from one bottle to another and that the important thing is not the label but the content behind it. And so the realistic student is not fooled by the catchwords, the shibboleths and the slogans that are invented for a purpose and that usually hide rather than reveal the real current of thought. Such words as capitalism, fascism, communism, have a thousand meanings to a thousand different people, and their use means little unless at the same time one sets forth the exact facts which he has in mind. In the end we have to deal with conditions as they are and to adapt our labels to the conditions and not to our prejudices or wishes.

I do not propose now to catalog the current social problems of the world with which I assume you are all more or less familiar. They fall in three main groups: *First,* the task of bringing about internal harmony in the affairs of our own country. *Second,* the task of establishing mutually helpful working relations between our people and the other peoples of the world. *Third,* the task of developing a system of money and banking which will stabilize the standards of value generation after generation, and make money the servant rather than the master of mankind.

I believe the problems of our own country come first, because we can not do much for the rest of the world if we are not able to put our own house in order; and I believe the problems which concern youth are more important than any of the other problems which face the nation. I am not unaware of the tragedies in the lives of millions of people who to-day are in the sunset years. I am not unfamiliar with the problems which face those who in middle life must maintain their families in the face of uncertainty and unemployment. I know those problems are pressing, but I believe the problems of youth are crucial. In all nature there is a point at which growth takes place, at which new beginnings are made. For human society that point is the place where young people become a part of the active community and contribute their fresh courage and their new outlook.

America to-day has largely closed the doors to youth. Take one profession after another—teaching, medicine, law, engineering, architecture, journalism—or take the best opportunities in business and industry —they are closed to youth. Talk with your friends who are in their fifties and sixties and you will find that they are supporting not only their children but their grandchildren because their children are unable to find a place in life. Go into your communities and states and make a survey of the population between 16 and 25 and you will find hundreds of thousands—a total for the nation of more than three million—young people for whom there are neither jobs nor schools. Appoint a committee in your college and make a study of the graduates who have gone out during the past five years to find what they are doing and you will encounter a most discouraging and disheartening lack of opportunity. The gates are closed. For most of these youth there is not even a toehold by which they may climb the path of life. They are referred to casually as the "lost generation." There can not, there dare not, be a lost generation in America. A lost generation means a lost nation. It means the destruction of what our forefathers have worked centuries to build up.

And so I regard the problem of unoccupied youth as the major problem of our time, as an inescapable insistent problem that will not down and that will continue to get worse until we gather the facts, face the situation and recognize frankly the character of the present stage in our national existence. We are at the end of an epoch; this is not an ordinary depression or a mere aftermath of war; it is not the product of broken faith and violated trust, however great the mismanagement of our financial and industrial leadership may be. The present stage of our society is the product of a deeper evolution of which the war and the financial collapse are mere incidents; the present crisis is a breakdown not primarily of men but of the system itself; and what we face in the United States is the reconstruction of the system out of the ruins amidst which we now live.

I do not believe that we shall achieve that reconstruction by denying youth its chance. I believe that youth is the major factor in that reconstruction, that it has more at stake than we of older years; and further that if we who are older wish any real security of life in the years ahead, we shall find that security not in stocks and bonds—the world is already 300 billion dollars in debt—but in seeing that youth has its chance. Out of that chance which we give youth to-day will come our own security and happiness to-morrow.

Our problems are not insoluble. We have a rich and varied continent, a veritable Garden of Eden in which to live. We have a diverse and mighty people. We are the victims of no devastating act of God. Obviously the trouble is not in our environment; it is in ourselves, in our purposes, our planning, our outlook on life, and because our difficulty is in ourselves I believe that the way out is in education. The school, from kindergarten through college, is the real instrument of recovery, and only by making the school better, by making it more truly representative of the common need and aspiration of the people can we work our way into a better day.

You have already heard from our distinguished United States Commissioner of Education, who discussed the crisis in education. There is no problem which concerns you more than this crisis in education. It is more than the financial crisis. The schools to-day are under the stress of four great pressures.

First, the imperative demand for a lengthened period of schooling. Responsible public commissions in two of our leading states, California and New York, have suggested that possibly the period of free and universal schooling should be extended two years beyond the present high school, making a total of 14 years of formal school opportunity for our population.

Second, the schools face the necessity for a higher quality of education if they are to maintain their self-respect and keep pace with the life around them.

Third, the schools face a sudden and terrific reduction in their financial resources, which makes it doubly difficult to bring about the internal improvements in education demanded by these times.

Fourth, there is a very real and far-reaching effort on the part of our giant industry and business directly and indirectly to dominate education so as to destroy its freedom to deal with the great social and economic problems which require intelligent study for their solution.

Of these problems the immediate task of school finance may seem most pressing, but it is only apparently so. It will do us little good to keep the schools open if we can not maintain their freedom, vitality and excellence.

These four great pressures on American education are natural enough. They grow out of the general conditions of our common life. The machine has replaced workers; child labor is not needed; there is nothing else for youth to do, and the obvious thing is to continue in school. The school of the past does not meet the needs of this vastly extended demand for education on the higher levels, and so the curriculum must be revised to take account of the new strain on character, the increased leisure, the more varied vocational situation and the urgent demand for an informed citizenship. The economic system has collapsed. The national income is less than half of what it was a few years ago. Taxes which then seemed easy to-day seem burdensome or impossible, and the pressure of great corporations to escape the burden is the logical consequence of that state of affairs. Our political, financial and industrial policies are in a state of flux. There is an intense struggle between special privilege and the common good and we need not be surprised if this struggle makes itself felt in the administration of every phase of education.

The important thing is for youth to stand by the schools, to understand them, to seek to make them better, to refuse to be fooled by the foolish propaganda which would limit or tear down the very institution which has made us what we are. Wherever you go, whatever occupation you follow, you as a member of the great brotherhood of educated people have an obligation to stand for intelligence as a way of life and to do your part for the great institutions which seek to make intelligent living the common habit of mankind.

And now a word about college journalism. The college periodical, rightly edited, may easily become the major intellectual and spiritual opportunity of the college life. It can bring about right attitudes and an eager and informed college spirit. It can deal so constructively with the problems of college life and with the great currents of life outside the college that students will look forward to each issue with anticipation.

Whether the college periodical is to take this larger place or is to be merely a weakly portion of ballyhoo and triviality, will depend upon the purposes, the ideals and the working technique of the journalistic staff. No one should be chosen for editorial responsibility who is not willing to recognize the character of that responsibility, who does not know how to learn and to organize his learning for others. We get our ideas from our own experiences, from our observation of life about us, from conversation with our associates, from the reading of books. No one can be a great editor who is not a reader and a thinker, who is not able to deal with an idea as an idea, to separate it from the verbal trappings in which it is clothed, and to make it his very own.

I make bold therefore to suggest to you two short lists of books which I believe every editor would wish to read. The first list gives a general background of philosophy and outlook. It includes the following:

(1) "A History of the Freedom of Thought," by J. B. Bury.

(2) "The Work, Wealth and Happiness of Mankind," by H. G. Wells.

(3) "The New Exploration," by Benton Mackaye.

(4) "Constructive Citizenship," by L. P. Jacks.

(5) "Other People's Money," by Louis D. Brandeis.

(6) "Recent Social Trends in the United States," text-book edition.

(7) "A Sociological Philosophy of Education," by Ross L. Finney.

The second list deals more specifically with the immediate problems of to-day's life. It may be out of date almost before I give it, because new and better books may be produced during the months ahead, but it is a good starting point. It includes the following:

(1) "Looking Forward," by Franklin D. Roosevelt.

(2) "The Roosevelt Revolution," by Ernest K. Lindley.

(3) "The Industrial Discipline," by Rexford G. Tugwell.

(4) "Concentration of Control in American Industry," by H. W. Laidler.

(5) "The Modern Corporation and Private Property," by Berle and Means.

(6) "A Planned Society," by George Soule.

(7) "The Coming Struggle for Power," by John Strachey.

(8) "The Social Economic Goals of America," which can be secured from the National Education Association, Washington, D. C., in pamphlet form or in the *Journal* of that organization for January, 1934.

Both of these lists have two weaknesses—they are too narrow and too short. The editor must deal with life as a whole. In an age of intense specialism, when things are broken up into such small parts that they tend to lose their meaning, it is the task of the editor to be not a specialist but a generalist who acquires some knowledge of many things so that he can point out their significance and interrelationships.

There is a by-product of college journalism which I shall note in passing. It is a wonderful training ground for professional journalism. I would like to think of it as a training ground for a new type of *community journalism*. There are unusual opportunities to-day for community journalism of a sort more dynamic and creative than anything which has so far developed. National and international news is much better handled to-day than local news. I have been traveling across the United States for more than a decade and have lived for a short time in all its leading cities and in many of its middle-size cities. Looking back over that experience, I can not recall a single city where local affairs are reported and treated in such a fashion as to enable the citizen to know enough about them to take his part intelligently in the common life of the community.

I make this observation not as a criticism of present journalistic efforts, but merely as a suggestion for those who are looking for new opportunities upon which to build a life of service. I can conceive of a community paper which would be quite willing to leave national and international affairs to others and to dedicate itself to a comprehensive and vigorous interpretation of the community life, to an intelligent and dramatic presentation of the sort of information that is found in that great study of "Recent Social Trends," which would handle this information not from the point of view of commercial interests but from the point of view of the people themselves, giving them the straightforward facts, much as Consumers Research is now doing in its own field. Under such a newspaper policy, problems which intimately concern the lives of the people would be constantly played up—the planning of the city itself, housing, schools, churches, all the local budgets of the community, conditions of life in the community, with suggestions for their improvement.

I doubt that such a newspaper can be a commercial enterprise in the old sense of that term. I doubt that it can be maintained by advertising. But I believe that it might be maintained on the basis of subscriptions or by an association of people interested in the common welfare rather than in profits. On a national scale we have such a newspaper to-day in the *American Observer.* If you are not familiar with this paper, which is widely used as a text in high schools and colleges, you can obtain samples of it by writing to the publishers, Civic Education Service, 744 Jackson Place, Washington, D. C.

May I not close this discussion by suggesting very tentatively a few points that might be included in a program for the youth of 1934?

First, take hold of your life with courage and faith in your power to dream, to do and to be.

Second, like Benjamin Franklin, put yourself under a daily discipline that will bring out the best in you.

Third, ask yourself what kind of a life you want and push resolutely toward that life.

Fourth, ask yourself what kind of a country you want and seek to do your part to build such a country.

Fifth, make yourself a student of one or more of the great national problems.

Sixth, throw yourself into the thick of the fight.

Seventh, avoid the softening influence of luxury and extravagance.

Eighth, associate yourself with some great cause and grow with it.

Ninth, keep yourself from alliances which will interfere with your reasonable freedom of thought and action.

Tenth, and finally, be patient and reasonable. Many things which seem difficult or impossible to-day will seem easy and natural to-morrow. The conditions of life in America at this moment which to many of us seem harsh would be a veritable heaven to some of our less fortunate human brethren in other parts of the globe.

AN ARCHITECT'S CRITICISM OF THE USE OF COLLEGIATE GOTHIC IN THE DESIGN OF GIRLS' COLLEGE DORMITORIES

By I. HOWLAND JONES

FELLOW OF THE AMERICAN INSTITUTE OF ARCHITECTS

It is rather surprising to realize the number of Collegiate Gothic dormitories, both for boys and girls, that have been built in our colleges in recent years, when one considers how entirely unsuited this type of architecture is for this special sort of building. It is unsuitable enough for most college buildings, but it is especially so for dormitories and more especially so for girls' dormitories.

A large proportion of our college girls come from modest American homes and most of them go back to them when their college life is over, and one wonders why these few years should be spent in an atmosphere which is so entirely different from that of the rest of their lives. Surely a girl's surroundings at this period of her life play an important part in her education, and if she is surrounded by common, familiar homelike things in good taste, will she not be better prepared to go back to her home and fit contentedly and naturally into it than she will if she has lived for four years in the unnatural atmosphere of buildings of the Gothic period.

I can best explain, perhaps, what I mean by this atmosphere by describing parts of some of the buildings I have seen this fall during a little tour of some of the colleges in the eastern part of the country.

I visited one recently, where I entered under an elaborately carved stone porte-cochère which would have been a fit approach to the palace of a millionaire, and after passing through a heavily moulded oak door, which may have weighed a ton, I entered a dark panelled oak hall, with an immense stone fireplace, a richly carved staircase and stained glass windows which shut out every ray of sunlight from an already gloomy room.

The living room of another dormitory was about as unsuited to the informal, intimate life of a group of college girls as one could imagine. The room was high, with a flat, heavily beamed ceiling, and extended across the width of the building so that it had three windows along each of its two opposite sides. These windows were monumental in scale and were filled with Gothic tracery, with "antique" leaded glass with coats of arms in color, so that there was no possibility of getting the faintest glimpse of the blue sky nor of the trees and lawns of the beautiful campus outside.

The floor of the room was of wood, but to give the proper medieval atmosphere as one approached the room from either end, the two vestibule floors were paved with rough split-faced slate slabs laid in irregular shapes with wide joints, and the jambs of the two entrance doors were of stone carved with Gothic mouldings—a well-designed and well-proportioned room, but entirely unsuited to its purpose.

The living room of another dormitory was a beautifully designed little chapel with a pointed roof and heavy oak trusses. The walls were unusually low, with flat-topped tracery windows with stained glass. This room had a tiled floor with rugs and a stone fireplace and chimney which extended up to the roof at the end of the room opposite the entrance. The walls were rough gray plaster and the furniture was heavy dark oak, with refectory tables and big brass candle-sticks and all the other proper fittings of the period. There was not a single light feminine touch possible anywhere in the room, and I could not picture it filled in the evening with a lot of gay and pretty college girls.

It would have been a most picturesque setting for a costume party if the girls were dressed in the clothes of Queen Elizabeth's time, but for daily use as a modern living room for young girls it was, I thought, in extremely bad taste, because it was totally unsuited to its use.

I visited another college, where I saw a group of girls' dormitories that had been completed two or three years ago. The buildings outside are beautifully designed and, in their setting under a growth of old trees, they are as fine an architectural composition as one can imagine, and when time has mellowed them and they have settled into their surroundings they will be even finer. They are of brick and limestone, with steep roofs of heavy, graduated green slate. In the upper stories there are small Gothic windows, with stone mullions and trim, and in the lower story many of the larger windows of the more important rooms are filled with quite elaborate Gothic tracery, and all the windows are fitted with hinged bronze casement sash with leaded glass in small panes. They are a fine example of the best Collegiate Gothic work. I did wonder where all the money came from to pay for them and whether it had been spent wisely, because the cost had evidently not been considered when they were designed.

I wondered, too, if the buildings inside were really going to meet the requirements for which they were designed, especially in regard to the girls' own rooms. They were built to be a home for modern young American girls for four years or more. Many hours of the girls' time would necessarily be spent in their rooms, and they should, of course, be comfortable, homelike and well lighted.

I found them thoroughly in keeping with the type of building. They have rough gray plaster walls, the floors are concrete, painted with a glossy drab concrete paint, and there is one stingy little rug beside each bed. The doors are of oak, stained dark brown with painted metal door frames and trim. The picture mould is metal and set in the plaster so that it shows as an ugly crack around the room. The stone mullion and trim of the window, which are a part of the exterior design, also appear inside the room with the bronze metal casement sash with their small panes of leaded glass. They are placed so high above the floor that a girl would with difficulty be able to look out when sitting down, and they are not large enough really to light the whole room adequately.

There is, of course, no possibility of hangings of any sort at the windows. The furniture is of oak and was evidently designed to be in keeping with the general design of the building. There is nothing domestic or feminine or homelike about these rooms and no possible chance for a girl to add anything to soften the stern, cold, cheerless place. She might hang a few pictures from the unsightly crack in the wall and put a scarf on the bureau, but that is all. The whole conception of the building, it seemed to me, both outside and in, is entirely out of keeping in every way with our modern standards of life—an affectation.

Now, after presuming to criticize some of the best work of some of the foremost architects of the country, and my very good friends, because it is Collegiate Gothic, I want to suggest a type of building that seems to me to answer all the requirements of the problem in a simple, natural, modern and economical way. The type I have in mind is the eighteenth century English or American building, similar to the old buildings at Harvard or Brown or Williams or any of the older colleges in this country and some of the buildings of the same period in the English schools and colleges. And we have some admirable examples in some of our new college groups.

In the first place, they are economical to build, are perfectly suited to our modern fireproof construction and may be built of either brick or stone. We may feel that they are only suited to be a part of a formal group of buildings on a level campus, but it is easily possible to design a most picturesque group on sloping or uneven ground, with partially enclosed quadrangles at different levels, and there is no reason why it is not possible to make just as charming and informal a group as is possible with Gothic buildings. The old buildings of the Temple in London are an admirable example.

To describe a group of dormitories of this type that I visited recently: The buildings are placed around three sides of a small quadrangle, opening to the south, which is made more attractive by two huge elms which overhang the buildings. These are of red brick, with white painted trim around the windows, and the porches and cornices of the buildings are of wood, painted white. The roofs with their dormer windows are of gray-green slate. The only cut stone is comprised in some little keystones over the first-story windows, and I was reminded of the tons of expensive cut stonework which had been lavished on the other buildings, and necessarily so, in order to conform to the type.

The paths in the quadrangle are paved with red brick, with green moss in the joints, and where they branch to the several entrances there is a paved circle, with a little fountain in the center—as quiet and homelike a little place as one could imagine, nothing striking or theatrical about it, but just good, plain American college architecture.

The central building is entered from a brick-paved terrace, slightly raised above the campus, under a simple Georgian porch, and there are chairs and a table on the terrace and a white balustrade along the edge.

The entrance hall is a long, comfortable-looking, sunny room, with windows going to the floor along one side, and there are alcoves where the girls may receive their callers with a little privacy. The furniture has a simple domestic look about it, and there is a piano and a nice big comfortable fireplace with chairs grouped around it.

At one end of the hall are double doors, which open into the living room, and at the other end two single ones, which lead into the dining room. The woodwork of the hall is painted ivory-white and the walls are painted a soft dull yellow tone. The windows have shades of about the same color, which give a warm light, and the hangings are of bright-colored, flowered cretonne.

The living room has its longest dimension at right angles to the axis of the hall, and opposite the entrance is a fireplace with a simple mantel up to the ceiling, with a beautiful old gilt-framed mirror hanging in the big panel. The walls are papered with an old-fashioned wall-paper, and there are hangings of a soft rose color at the windows, with cream-colored net curtains beneath. There is a low-panelled wood dado up to the window-sill level, and a simple wood cornice. The furniture, too, is simple, well-designed American furniture, in both maple and mahogany, and there is enough of it arranged in groups to give a most livable and homelike look to the room.

The dining room is much the same size and shape as the living room and has a most attractive glazed landscape paper on the walls above a low-panelled dado. The hangings at the windows are of soft grayish-white monk's cloth, and the furniture is all of early American design in maple, with little spindle-backed chairs with wood seats, varying slightly in design at the several tables.

The floors of all these rooms are of cork tile, which has been kept carefully waxed until they have taken on a delightful soft tawny tone and are most pleasant to walk on.

The impression one has of the whole place is that of a big comfortable American country house, as simple and livable as possible, very much the sort of home the girls are accustomed to, only probably much larger and more carefully designed, and the sort of thing they would be glad to remember if the opportunity came later to plan homes of their own.

The girls' own rooms on the second and third floors have been very carefully thought out in all their details. The closet has been planned in every case so that it comes next the corridor wall, and its door is at right angles with the corridor and in a little entrance alcove, leaving the walls of the room unbroken and available for furniture. The ceiling of this alcove is dropped to the height of the doors, which leaves the ceiling of the room a simple rectangle.

There are both double and single rooms, the double rooms coming at the corners of the building. These have two windows on adjacent sides, and the single rooms have one window each. They are, of course, common double-hung windows, with twelve panes of glass, with screens outside and shades and curtains inside, with none of the complications in this respect that always come up with hinged casement windows, and the windows are big enough really to light the whole room.

There is in each room a low plain cream-white painted dado up to the level of the window-sills, and above that the walls are painted a light cheerful color, varying in the different rooms, up to the white picture mould, which forms a narrow trim against the ceiling. All the wood finish, including the sash and the door, is, of course, painted white, and there are small, thin, old-fashioned brass door-knobs, with a flat oval keyhole escutcheon beneath. The windows all have some little bright-colored curtains, and the furniture is simple maple and Colonial in design and in nice scale with the rooms.

The few rooms on the north side of the building are papered above the dado with pretty, sunny, flowered papers, which are glazed so that they can be easily cleaned. The floors of all the rooms and corridors are of cork tile that has been waxed for several years until they are in beautiful condition, and they are quiet and warm and homelike. Altogether, there is an air about these upper floors of bedrooms that is as dainty and feminine as can be, and you are impressed with the feeling that they are just the sort of place for a lot of nice college girls to live in.

I visited this group of buildings this fall a short time after I had seen the other ones, and I was more than ever convinced that Collegiate Gothic is not suited for the use to which we are putting it. In the first place, considering these buildings externally, they do not fit into our American surroundings but always have a look of belonging somewhere else and wishing they could be taken home. It is always rather a shock to come upon a building of such a pronounced type that it looks as if it had been picked up bodily in some other part of the world and brought over here and transplanted into our surroundings. This, I think, is true of any type of building if its character and all its details are merely a copy of some old type we are familiar with, whether it be an Italian palace or a French château or a Chinese tea-house or a Spanish church. There is an interesting thought, though, in this statement. The Spanish churches and houses in California seem to be quite at home there. Is it because of the character of the landscape or because we naturally associate Spain with that part of the country on account of the early settlers? I think it is because these buildings are suited to the country and the climate, and for this reason they seem to belong there.

On the other hand, the Gothic buildings were developed to fit the conditions of a civilization entirely different from ours, and the small windows and deep reveals and leaded glass and stone floors and all the other Gothic accessories seem to me to be distressingly out of place in a modern college in this country.

Is it not worth considering that a girl's surroundings during her college life must make a very lasting impression and really are an important part of her education and that, if they are not an affectation but are in good taste and are of a simple domestic character, they may have an influence on her which she will be glad to carry away and which some day may be of value to her when she has a home of her own?

In any case, I am sure she will have a more affectionate remembrance of her college associations if her surroundings have been suited to her life there and have been natural and homelike and beautiful.

ANDREWS, JONES, BISCOE AND
WHITMORE, ARCHITECTS
BOSTON, MASSACHUSETTS

EDUCATIONAL EVENTS

REFORMS IN GERMAN INSTITUTIONS OF HIGHER LEARNING

THE regular Berlin correspondent of the American Medical Association reports that the reorganization of German institutions of higher learning is now being carried out. New regulations concerning habilitation at Prussian institutions have been established. Henceforth the demonstration of scientific performances or qualifications before the faculty in question will not suffice to secure permission to lecture at a Prussian institution of higher learning. An applicant must have served several months in a field station or a work camp and must have completed a course of training in an academy for the training of instructors in higher institutions of learning, which academy is to be newly created. When these two courses have been completed satisfactorily, a candidate for habilitation in a university or other higher institution will present his credentials to the faculty of the school in question, which will act on his application in the same way as heretofore. In the reorganization of the universities and other institutions, special importance is placed in the training of the oncoming generation of academic instructors. In the new regulations, it is emphasized that the decision whether an applicant has the necessary qualifications to become an instructor in a given institution was heretofore left to the faculty of that institution, and in some cases entirely to the single representative of a department, since, with the growth of the faculties, the faculty as a whole could not always form a judgment concerning the applicants. The result was, one reads further, that the selection of candidates was controlled more and more by departmental points of view and that the more general considerations were necessarily forced into the background. Thus capable scholars in a given field were selected, and the general qualifications were left to chance. If the universities are to undergo a real reorganization, a fundamental change in the method of selecting new instructors must be made. The new decree of the Prussian minister of public instruction, it is pointed out, has in two ways taken account of this need; for in the work camp the candidate has an opportunity to reveal his true character, in surroundings that are not academic. The testimonial issued by the work service will have great weight in determining a candidate's suitability for habilitation. The Dozentenakademie (for the training of instructors) will receive acceptable candidates from the Arbeitsdienst (work service) and will provide regular courses for candidates seeking admission to the various departments of the university. In this academy, candidates will participate in a strictly organized community life and will study courses of a general scientific character. Here, again, the candidate will have to prove his worth in fields outside his specialty. As a result of close collaboration with his fellows in the academy, a candidate is expected to develop the general impulses requisite for his scientific work in his specialty. The examination of the candidate in his specialty, which follows in due course, is, according to the new regulations, only the final step in the habilitation procedure. It is emphasized that no one will be selected as instructor solely on the basis of his capacity in his scientific specialty.

The *dozenten* of Prussia (instructors in universities and higher institutions of learning) have been organized into a society. Several different posts have been created in keeping with the duties to be performed. There is a scientific bureau, which will deal with all questions bearing on the scientific training of the oncoming generation of instructors, questions pertaining to reforms in the curriculum, and the question of the rights and privileges of Germans who have emigrated to foreign countries. There is also a bureau for work service, which is closely connected with the corresponding bureau of the German student body. Further bureaus have been created to aid in the solution of the technical problems at the various universities and higher institutions. At the several universities, a corresponding organization will be effected before the opening of the fall semester. The local directors were recently admitted to a field station. Assistants and instructors who have no fixed appointment must become members of the dozentenschaft, or society of instructors; but instructors holding definite posts, and assistants in research institutes and in municipal hospitals attached to a university, may join or not, as they see fit.

The University of Giessen in Hesse has adopted somewhat different regulations. In Hesse the rector of a university may grant the venia legendi to a privatdozent if the ministerial department having jurisdiction has given its consent; at first for a period of seven years, subject to cancellation. If, before the end of the seventh year, a privatdozent, or instructor, has not been appointed to a professorship, he automatically severs his connection with the instructional staff. This provision applies also to those instructors who have been previously appointed. Any one who is called by the government to occupy a chair is appointed as professor. The federal governor may appoint a privatdozent as a professor after at least five years of teaching activity. A privatdozent may, through the mediation of a colleague, appeal to the dean of the faculty and request that he be appointed as professor.

HOBART COLLEGE STUDIES A NEW TYPE CALENDAR

THE proposed new college calendar at Hobart College and William Smith College, coordinate institutions, has been favorably accepted by a seven-to-one affirmative student vote. Tabulation of the student opinion has shown that 93 per cent. of the William Smith undergraduates and 86 per cent. of the Hobart students favor the plan.

The Hobart plan, which is new to the educational institutions of the East, provides for two unbroken semesters of approximately seventeen weeks each. The first semester, which will start on the Tuesday following Labor Day, will conclude about December 22, being followed by a vacation of three or four weeks. The second semester, which will start in January, will run, without interruption, until late in May. Commencement will be held some time between May 20 and May 29. The plan makes no attempt to upset the established school year, but aims to increase the efficiency of teaching during the year. It is based upon approved scientific tests in learning and aims to eliminate the detrimental influence of the present interrupted semesters.

The present system, the three-term system and the Hobart plan have been carefully studied by the college officials, and the conclusion has been reached that the two unbroken periods of the Hobart plan offer the greatest opportunity to increase teaching efficiency. Dr. Forrest L. Dimmick, professor of experimental psychology and research associate at Hobart and William Smith Colleges, maintained that "psychological work on memory has shown that the attitude of the learner and unification of the material are both important for retention. For both of these, the continuous period of study made possible under the Hobart plan is highly advantageous. Within limits the longer the period over which learning is spread, the more efficiently the work is accomplished. A semester of seventeen weeks falls well within the limits of this rule, so that, for example, three hours a week for seventeen weeks will prove much more effective than five hours a week for ten weeks."

Dr. Murray Bartlett, president of the institutions, has stated that there are many factors which must be taken into consideration by the administration of the two colleges before definite action can be taken. Students who voted against the plan will be asked to state their reasons for so voting in order that these reasons may be tabulated and studied. The administration will attempt to determine the effect of the adoption of the plan upon the schools by sending a questionnaire to all Hobart and William Smith alumni in the teaching field. Every conceivable test of the plan will be applied before a final decision by the corporation is reached. Dr. Milton Haight Turk, dean of Hobart College, is the sponsor and originator of the plan.

CITIZENS LIBRARY PLAN FOR SOUTH CAROLINA

A PROGRAM for public library development in South Carolina was recently adopted by a citizens' conference on the needs of the state, meeting at Clemson College. The conference was a direct outgrowth of the meeting of southern leaders held at Chapel Hill in April, 1933, under the auspices of the American Library Association and the Southeastern Library Association.

More than 1,000,000 people are without any type of library service in South Carolina. Barely 25 per cent. of the rural people have even the opportunity of borrowing books from libraries. Only three counties—Charleston, Greenville and Richland, have fully developed county-wide library systems. Besides, Dillon and Laurens counties make small appropriations to provide such service. While there are still hundreds who, unfortunately, can not read, yet there are thousands who can read and who are eager for books and magazines. This is evidenced by the fact that the three counties with developed library service have a combined circulation of over 1,000,000 books a year—more than the combined circulation of all the other 43 counties of the state. The citizens' program, as adopted, makes the following declaration:

Good libraries are increasingly necessary in these swiftly changing times. The rapid development of adult education; the opportunities for the fruitful employment of the new leisure; the need for quick and wide dissemination of information and ideas; the necessity for wholesome recreation; the desire for vocational knowledge and guidance—all these make imperative demands for the more speedy development of our library facilities. In a genuine democracy access to books is not limited to any one class. Libraries are now being considered as essential for adults as schoolhouses are for children.

Ultimately South Carolina should have: (1) Library service, supported from public funds, organized on a county or regional basis, within easy reach of every person in the state. (2) A state library extension agency to provide trained leadership, professional advice and counsel, book-lending service, and financial aid for new and struggling libraries.

The immediate and urgent need, however, is for sufficient financial support for the South Carolina Library Board, established by act of the legislature in 1929 as the state agency for the development of a more adequate library service. Handicapped by lack of funds, this board has been unable to perform the duties expected of it. With proper support it could begin a book-lending service, stimulate the increase of county libraries through financial assistance and actual demonstrations, help secure trained personnel and aid in improving the efficiency of existing libraries.

For the continuance of its work the conference authorizes the appointment of a standing committee to secure support for the State Library Board and to organize committees in the several counties to aid in the development of an adequate program of library service.

To the accomplishment of its aims this Conference on the Library Needs of South Carolina invites and urges the active assistance of all concerned with the spread of enlightenment and the increase of those opportunities that should characterize a truly democratic society.

Members of the committee are: *Chairman,* Mrs. Hagood Bostick, librarian Columbia Public Library and secretary of the State Library Board; J. P. Coates, S. M. Derrick, McDavid Horton, W. P. Jacobs, Mrs. T. S. Leitner, Miss Claudia Phelps, Fant Thornley, Marion Wright, Miss Mary E. Frayser, Miss Parmelee Cheves, Dr. R. C. Grier and D. B. Anderson.

MASSACHUSETTS AND THE CHILD LABOR AMENDMENT

FOLLOWING the opposition expressed last week by Dr. A. Lawrence Lowell to the child labor amendment, Dr. Manley O. Hudson, Bemis professor of international law at Harvard and a member of the Hague Permanent Court of Arbitration, appeared before the committee of the Massachusetts Legislature which is considering the amendment and advocated its passage. According to the *Boston Herald,* he said:

The real thing behind much of the present opposition to the child labor amendment is a hangover from the opposition to the 18th amendment, but I refuse to allow that experience to warp my thinking about our national problems and to poison my attitude toward the Federal Government. The great vice of the 18th amendment was that it embodied in the constitution a legislated policy on a very controversial subject, with the result that no road was left open for the exercise of legislative judgment on that subject. The child labor amendment does nothing of the kind. It merely confers power on Congress, without attempting to dictate for all time how that power is to be used. I refuse, therefore, to be stampeded in my approach to the child labor amendment.

Now some very wild things are being said as to what Congress might do if it were given this new power.

I must deal with one of these arguments, for it shows how extreme, how fantastic, how bankrupt is some of the opposition to this amendment. I have read statements in the newspapers which attribute this argument to Mr. A. Lawrence Lowell, but knowing and admiring Mr. Lowell I shall refuse to believe that he made any such argument until I hear it from his own lips. The point has been made that if this amendment were adopted Congress might under its new power conscript children under 18 for military training and military service. Any one who knows our constitution knows that Congress needs no new power for conscripting such children. It now has that power. The constitution gives Congress a general power "to raise and support armies."

It has had that power since 1789, and the power has never been exercised as to children under 18. To contend that under the guise of labor legislation, Congress would take such a course is to show a complete lack of confidence in our Federal Government.

The problem is indeed a federal one. For years I have heard it said that Massachusetts can not do certain things because other states will not keep the pace. Massachusetts workers should not be competing with the children workers of other states. We have already seen what can be done along this line under the NRA. I want to make that gain permanent. Fairness to the workers of Massachusetts demands it.

Alexander Lincoln, one of the leaders of the opposition, presented a summation of the opponents' case. He also read letters from Cardinal O'Connell, head of the Boston archdiocese, and Bishop William Lawrence, retired head of the Episcopal church in Massachusetts, voicing emphatic opposition to the proposed amendment.

The Rev. George O. Lillegard placed the Boston Lutheran Pastors' Association on record in opposition to the amendment. He declared that apparently those chiefly backing the measure are "educators itching for power" and Communists seeking to overthrow the government. The latter, he said, seek to regulate the religious beliefs of youth and to wipe out parochial schools, some of which are conducted by his church.

Others speaking in opposition were John W. Regan, head master of the Dorchester high school for boys; Eben W. Burnstead, of the Massachusetts Civic Alliance; Mrs. John V. Ballard, state regent of the Catholic Daughters of America; Mrs. Cornelius G. Flynn, president of the League of Catholic Women.

Dean Albers, of the Boston University Law School, asserted that the adoption of the amendment would mean "Russianization of the American child." He said that every encroachment on American liberty is dangerous, and that power, once given, is always used to the utmost.

TWO UNIVERSITIES SUBMIT PUBLIC REPORTS

THE Columbia University Commission of Economic Reconstruction on February 5 made public its survey of national economic problems. Two days later the faculty of the division of public administration of New York University published a report of its study, the management of New York City demonstrating how the city might save from fifty to seventy-five million dollars annually. Both reports have received considerable news and editorial comment in New York newspapers and illustrate the significance of public service undertakings by university faculties.

The Columbia study has been under way for over a year, with a group of economists and sociologists cooperating. Eleven individuals signed the report, including Professor Robert M. MacIver, chairman of the commission, James W. Angell, Joseph W. Barker, John M. Clark, Arthur D. Gayer, Alvin H. Hansen, Alvin Johnson, Wesley C. Mitchell, Harlow S. Person, George Soule and Josef Schumpeter. Three members of the commission, which was appointed by President Butler, withdrew from the discussions to join the Roosevelt administration. These were Professors James H. Rogers, A. A. Berle, Jr., and Leo Wolman.

The commission made twelve recommendations and reached nine conclusions. The recommendations included the suggestion that special care be taken to make sure that the national recovery act shall not be made a means for the competitive limitation of output by organized industries; the return of the United States to an international gold standard only after a number of reforms in the working of the standard have been effected; monetary stabilization without delay; measures to maintain an equilibrium in the cost-price structure; a permanent public works program; the establishment of a system of unemployment and consumers' reserves; the further regulation of large-scale corporations; the regulation of all organizations which are concerned with the supply of capital and credit; reciprocal tariff agreements and the reconstruction of a world monetary system; and finally the establishment of a National Social-Economic Council, of a purely advisory nature, for continuous study of economic and social planning.

The New York University report has attempted to accomplish much the same thing for the government of New York City as the Columbia report has attempted for the national government. The report has been submitted directly to Mayor La Guardia by President Harry Woodburn Chase, and in general recommends a new system of government under the leadership of a mayor nominated by petition and elected by preferential vote in a city-wide election on a non-partisan ballot. Under him all administrative functions would be placed. He would be supported by a cabinet of twelve department heads of his own appointment.

The report proposes that all county offices be abolished and that a single council of twenty-five members replace the several legislative units that now exist. The report also proposes widespread changes in the judicial and financial organization of the city. It recommends that both the Board of Education and the Board of Higher Education be retained, the former, however, to be called the Department of Education.

HIRAM COLLEGE REVISES ITS ACADEMIC DAY

PRESIDENT KENNETH I. BROWN, of Hiram College, has announced the establishment of a new plan of organization which will make it possible for students to give the major part of their attention to a single course or subject during an entire day. The curriculum will be divided, under the new plan which goes into effect next fall, into courses of two types: old-type courses, which will meet for an hour each day, and courses which will meet from nine-thirty daily until four-thirty. The latter are to be known as "intensive courses." Each student will carry one old-type course, in such subjects as language and creative writing, and one "intensive course."

"Orthodox college teaching and learning," Dr. Brown has remarked in his announcement, "require that the student and faculty member dissect his attention and effort into five equal parts, each to be assigned to a different and frequently unrelated course. At eight o'clock on a certain morning of the week Student Jones may go to a class in British literature. At nine, when the bell rings, he will shift his mental gear and turn his thought to the mysteries of chemistry. By the time his interest in atomic weights has been warmed, the bell reminds him that his presence is required in the group studying the sociological backgrounds of the family. So the days and weeks pass with so much scattering of attention that the learning process is retarded or, more correctly, never allowed to become established with any degree of vigor."

The Hiram plan calls for the completion of a year's academic work in each "intensive course" of nine weeks. During this period the student's time is at the command of the instructor for lectures, discussion groups, research problems, off-campus visitation or study. The plan has been in operation in Hiram summer sessions since 1931.

EDUCATIONAL NOTES AND NEWS

DR. ROBERT REDFIELD, anthropologist, has been appointed dean of the division of social sciences of the University of Chicago. He succeeds Dr. Beardsley Ruml, who has resigned to become treasurer of R. H. Macy and Company. Dr. Redfield has also been promoted from associate professor of sociology to the rank of professor. Both appointments are effective on March 1. Dr. Redfield is thirty-six years of age and has taken all his studies, from elementary school through his graduate work, at the University of Chicago. He received the Ph.B. degree in 1920 and the degree of J.D. from the Law School in 1921.

DR. THOMAS W. GOSLING, superintendent of schools at Akron, Ohio, has resigned to become director of the Junior Red Cross, according to an announcement made on February 7 at the headquarters of the American Red Cross.

PROFESSOR MYRON W. WATKINS, head of the economics department of University College,

New York University, has recently joined the staff of the Consumers' Advisory Board of the NRA as a special consultant on trade regulation.

Dr. William L. Bragg, professor of physics at Manchester University and winner of the Nobel Prize in 1915 for his research in the structure of solids, arrived in the United States on February 5. He will serve as visiting professor at the chemical laboratory of Cornell University for the next four months.

The Federal Emergency Relief Administration on February 7 revoked its original requirement that colleges taking advantage of the relief program for its students must waive tuition fees. Mr. Harry L. Hopkins, Federal Relief Administrator, announced that jobs for students must be allocated on the basis of colleges' enrolment of full-time students on October 15, that the pay will be from $10 to $20 per calendar month, and that from the money he earns a student may be required by the college to pay his tuition fees.

Dr. Ray Lyman Wilbur, president of Leland Stanford University, was the guest speaker at the observance of Public Health day of the Chicago Woman's Club on February 13.

Signor Pietro Parini, minister plenipotentiary in the Italian Department of Foreign Affairs, visited Wellesley College on February 6 as the guest of the Italian Department, whose famous Plimpton collection of rare Italian books and manuscripts he examined. Signor Parini's special function in his government is the supervision of the education of Italians outside of Italy.

Dr. Stanley King, president of Amherst College, delivered the principal address at the ninth annual conference of the Secondary Education Board held at the Hotchkiss School, Lakeville, Conn., on February 16 and 17.

Dr. Frank L. McVey, president of the University of Kentucky, on February 8 made the principal address before the staff and alumni of Louisiana State University. Dr. McVey remained at Baton Rouge for the meeting of the Southeastern Athletic Conference, of which he is president.

Dr. William F. Albright, director of the American School of Oriental Research in Jerusalem, and Dr. Nelson Glueck, professor of Biblical History at the Hebrew Union College in Cincinnati, were guests of honor at a dinner given in New York on February 14. The dinner was under the auspices of the American Friends of the Hebrew University, Jerusalem, of whose Institute of Oriental Studies Dr. Albright is an honorary member. Dr. Glueck, who last year was director of the Jerusalem School of Oriental Research, left for Palestine on February 15 to continue an archeological survey.

Dr. Eugene A. Colligan, president of Hunter College, was guest of honor at the annual Associate Alumnae breakfast, held on February 17, to celebrate the sixty-fourth anniversary of the founding of the college. Dr. Harold G. Campbell, Superintendent of Schools of New York City, and Professor Walter Pitkin, of Columbia University, were the speakers.

Dr. Leonard Dupee White, professor of political science at the University of Chicago, has been nominated by President Roosevelt as a Republican member of the Civil Service Commission to succeed Thomas E. Campbell.

Dr. Arthur C. Howland, a member of the University of Pennsylvania faculty for thirty years, has been elected Henry Charles Lea professor of history. He succeeds Dr. Edward Potts Cheyney, who has retired after fifty years of teaching to become Henry Charles Lea emeritus professor of history and curator of the Henry Charles Lea Library of Medieval History.

Wayne L. Morse, dean of the school of law of the University of Oregon, has recently been elected to membership in the American Council of the Institute of Pacific Relations.

Donald H. Wallace, instructor in the Department of Economics at Harvard University, has been awarded the David A. Wells Prize in economics for his thesis on an original investigation in economics.

Professor Lewis Freeman Mott, chairman of the Department of English at the College of the City of New York since 1897, has announced that he will retire at the close of the present college term.

Dr. Lucy L. W. Wilson, principal of the South Philadelphia High School for Girls, received the Philadelphia Award for 1933 on February 8. Dr. Wilson, whose teaching career began in 1892, established the first evening high school for women in Philadelphia, and in 1918 opened the war emergency high school for technical instruction for more than five hundred war workers. The award, founded thirteen years ago by Edward Bok, includes a medal, a scroll and a check for $10,000. Dr. Wilson is the first woman to receive the award.

MRS. FREDERICK E. STOCKWELL, sister of President Henry Noble MacCracken, has been appointed field secretary of the Summer Institute of Euthenics of Vassar College.

PROFESSOR RALPH FLETCHER, statistician in the School of Business and Public Administration at Washington University, has been appointed state supervisor of a federal survey of employment and payrolls in Missouri.

DR. CHESTER K. WENTWORTH, associate professor of geology at Washington University, has been appointed geologic engineer for the Board of Water Supply of the City of Honolulu.

PROFESSOR JOSEPH M. KLAMON, of the Washington University School of Business and Public Administration, has been appointed principal agricultural economist in the A. A. A.

WALTER BIDDLE SAUL, a member of the Philadelphia Board of Education, has been named chairman of a committee to investigate the admission standards of the Philadelphia Normal School. Special emphasis will be laid on the non-scholastic requirements for the prospective teachers.

FREDERICK M. DAVENPORT, formerly Representative in Congress from New York, has been appointed visiting professor at Connecticut Wesleyan University for the second semester.

DR. HAROLD G. CAMPBELL, Superintendent of Schools of New York City, has been presented with the Italian silver medal of merit for distinguished accomplishment in education. Italian Consul General Antonio Grossardi made the award on February 9 aboard the Italian liner *Roma*.

DELAND STOWE, Pulitzer prize winner in 1930 for the best example of foreign correspondence and Paris representative of the *New York Herald-Tribune,* delivered the Block Foundation Lecture at Yale University on February 12.

ARCHIBALD T. DAVISON, professor of choral music, organist and choirmaster at Harvard University, has been honored with the degree of doctor of music by the University of Oxford. He is the first American to receive this honor.

PROFESSOR MARSHALL E. DIMOCK, of the University of Chicago, is making an investigation of Canal Zone railroads for Secretary of War Dern.

HARRIS C. ARNOLD, deputy attorney general of Pennsylvania, announced on February 7 that school districts which dismiss teachers and then reemploy them at lower salaries are violating the School Code. In a formal opinion submitted to the Department of Public Instruction Mr. Arnold declared that a schedule of minimum salaries and minimum increases has been established by the code and must be respected.

DR. THOMAS A. JOHNSTON, president of the Kemper Military School, died on February 5 in Boonville, Mo., at the age of eighty-five years.

DR. ST. JOHN WILLIAM HEBEL, professor of English at Cornell University, died in Ithaca on February 7 at the age of forty-two years.

DR. CARLOS HUNTINGTON STONE died in Suffern, N. Y., on February 2 in his seventy-seventh year. He had served from 1887 until 1916 as head master of the Stone School, later known as the Storm King School.

DR. DALE S. YOUNG, director of research in the Tennessee Department of Education and formerly a member of the state department of education in Alabama, was killed in an automobile accident in Gadsden, Ala., on February 1.

DR. HUNTINGTON RICHARDS, physician and instructor of Latin at St. Paul's School since 1892, died on February 4 in Boston in his eighty-fourth year.

DR. WILLIAM M. DAVIS, professor of physiographical geology at the California Institute of Technology, died on February 5. Dr. Davis, who was eighty-three years old, served on the faculty of Harvard University from 1879 to 1912, when he became professor emeritus of geology.

JAMES W. ROBERTS, former teacher of English in the Chicago public schools, died in Chicago on February 3 at the age of seventy-eight years.

Before going to Chicago in 1893, Mr. Roberts was superintendent of schools in Tacoma, Wash.

Dr. Nicholas Murray Butler, president of Columbia University, announced on February 8 the receipt by the institution of gifts totaling $21,684.16. The largest individual donation, amounting to $4,500, has been made by the General Education Board for research in the processes of motor development in children. This research will be conducted by the Normal Child Development Clinic.

A Greater Cleveland chapter of the National Teachers Federation, affiliated with the American Federation of Labor, has been organized. Application for a charter was made on February 10. Three hundred and fourteen teachers, representing fourteen schools, constitute the initial membership of the union. Two hundred more teachers have signified their intention of joining the group. As soon as the charter is granted, the group will elect delegates to the Cleveland Federation of Labor. Mr. George Davis, teacher of English and dramatics at East Technical High School, has been chosen as president. The local tax situation and the present school financing in other cities are among the first concerns of the union, according to Mr. Davis. The majority of those who have joined the new organization are members of the Cleveland Teachers Federation.

All married women teachers in the Everett, Mass., schools will receive notices that their contracts will not continue after a thirty-day period, as the result of a 6-to-2 vote of the school committee. The action, ending a controversy of three years, will affect twenty teachers. In supporting the measure, Committeeman Charles E. Hill stated that of the twenty women, eleven had not even a normal school education.

Lewis E. Lawes, warden at Sing Sing penitentiary, has invited twelve professors from the New York University School of Commerce, Accountants and Finance to deliver a series of lectures on "Modern Business" to two hundred interested inmates, according to an announcement made on February 7 by John T. Madden, dean of the School of Commerce, Accountants and Finance. The first lecture was delivered on February 8 by Dr. Alfred M. Neilson, professor of economic geography. This program of lectures has been conceived by Warden Lawes as part of a plan to rehabilitate and keep up the morale of those prisoners who have sufficient ability to comprehend college work. Many of those who are expected to attend the lectures have been part way or completely through college. The whole educational program is under the supervision of Harry L. Masson, who has been selected by civil service examination.

Surrounded by a student guard of fifty undergraduates in brown shirts and swastika banners, Chancellor Adolf Hitler on February 7 announced to a large assembly of professors and students congregated in the Berlin Philharmonic Hall the creation of the "reichsshaft," a new student organization. The reichsschaft, created by law, will be the only German undergraduate organization. It puts students under Nazi party control, following the pattern for trade unions, church societies and other groups. The new organization will be under the direction of the Minister of the Interior, who will appoint a student president.

A new unit has been established at Rutgers University to be known as University College. The work formerly carried on by the extension division will be transferred to the new college, which will grant degrees. According to President Clothier, this step will give adequate status to those branches of the university's work which provide educational opportunities to persons of more advanced years and to those who are not free to become full-time resident students. Administrative direction of University College will be vested in Professor Norman C. Miller, director of the university extension since the division was established in 1926.

To maintain and strengthen the bond which exists between Drexel Institute and its alumni, special courses for the alumni have been established. The courses, which are for graduates only and are given without charge, consist of classes in current economics and public speaking. Sixty graduates, men and women, have enrolled for the work, which is to extend over a period of twenty weeks.

A preliminary statement in connection with the importance of revising the various types of credentials in the field of adult education has been authorized by the California State Department of Education. The rapid growth together with changing conceptions of the aims and purposes of adult education seem to make it imperative that present practises and provisions governing the issuance of credentials be revised. A special committee of the State Board of Education, consisting of Superintendent R. E. Gelway, chairman, Miss Alice H. Dougherty and Miss Alice Rose Power, has been designated to cooperate with the State Department of Education and the state superintendent in preparing suggestions for consideration by the board.

THE American Association for Adult Education, 60 East 42nd Street, New York City, has undertaken a study of the place of science in the field of adult education. The study will be in charge of Benjamin C. Gruenberg, associate in science. It is especially desired to get information as to successful practises and as to existing needs that are not being met. Scientific men and educators who are interested are invited to send their suggestions and inquiries to the above address.

DISCUSSION

A MATHEMATICAL SOLUTION DEVELOPED DURING MORE THAN THREE MILLENNIUMS

IT took the mathematicians more than three thousand years to solve the general quadratic equation in its modern form as now taught to our high-school students. During the last five or six years various solutions of special numerical quadratic equations which appear on Babylonian tablets of about 2000 B. C. have been deciphered by O. Neugebauer, Copenhagen, Denmark; F. Thureau-Dangin, Paris, France, and others. The former of these named concluded that the Babylonians then knew that some of the quadratic equations considered by them have two roots, while the latter expressed the view that they were interested in only one root of such an equation. A noted German mathematical historian, J. Tropfke, recently traced the history of the quadratic equation during a period of thirty-five hundred years and supported the view that the ancient Babylonians were interested in only one of the roots of the quadratic equations considered by them.[1]

The most striking fact in the history of the development of the solution of the quadratic equation is that the Babylonians solved certain numerical quadratic equations by a method which is similar to our modern method of solving these equations. As they did not use negative or complex numbers, they obviously could not solve quadratic equations having either two negative roots or two complex roots. In fact, no instance is known in which a quadratic equation of the form $x^2 + px + q = 0$, where p and q represent positive numbers, was solved before 1685, when such a solution appeared in the noted "Algebra" by John Wallis. A little earlier (1657), J. Hudde first used the same letter to represent both positive and negative numbers, and thus made it possible to reduce every quadratic equation to the same normal form, as is now commonly done in our text-books on elementary algebra used in the schools.

In Volume 2 of Euclid's "Elements," propositions 4, 5 and 6, the classical treatment of the quadratic equation is presented in a geometric form. This geometric treatment relates only to the outward appearance, but it represents the main contribution made by the ancient Greeks towards the solution of the general quadratic equation. Only a few years ago it was commonly assumed that the solution of the quadratic equation as far as known by the ancient Greeks was discovered by geometry, but the recent discoveries relating to Babylonian mathematics make it clear that this assumption should be abandoned. The algebraic nature of the ancient Babylonian mathematics seems now to be well established, and it removes some of the historical support for the emphasis on geometry in the early mathematical courses in the schools. It should, however, be noted that the geometric solutions of certain quadratic equations by the ancient Greeks apply also to irrational roots, but such roots were not then considered in the *numerical* solutions, since the number system of the ancient Greeks did not embrace the irrational numbers.

The point of greatest interest in this connection is that the ancient Greeks, as well as their

[1] *Jahresbericht der Deutschen Mathematiker-Vereinigung*, Vol. 43, page 106, 1933.

predecessors, never found explicitly the two roots of the quadratic equations which they treated, even in the cases when these equations have two positive rational roots. It may be somewhat surprising that, notwithstanding this fact, some mathematical historians believe that the ancients knew that two such roots actually exist in certain cases. The difficulty along this line can be partly explained by the fact that the quadratic equations which they considered often arose from the consideration of the following two symmetric equations:

$$x + y = a$$
$$xy = b$$

It seems, therefore, immaterial whether we find the value of x or the value of y in the quadratic equation resulting from the elimination of one of these unknowns. From this point of view the consideration of the second root of a quadratic equation appears somewhat trivial, since the original equations are not affected by the interchange of x and y. Somewhat similar remarks apply to the algebraic equations of higher degrees.

The fact that certain quadratic equations have two distinct roots was explicitly recognized by the Hindus and the Arabs, and H. Cardan made a slight beginning in the use of complex roots in his noted "Ars Magna" (1545). From this time onward the development of the solution of the quadratic equation proceeded more rapidly and it took only a little over a century longer until all the possible cases were considered under a single normal form as noted above. Clear light on the subject was, however, not possible until negative and complex numbers were fully explained at about the beginning of the nineteenth century. Hence the history of the development of our modern solution which is now commonly taught to the high-school students extends over almost four thousand years. A knowledge of this long period of development should impress the student. There are probably not many intellectual achievements whose successive steps upwards can be traced so clearly throughout such a long period of time and which are now supposed to be a part of the intellectual equipment of all educated people.

G. A. MILLER

UNIVERSITY OF ILLINOIS

BASIC ENGLISH

AN article by Mr. G. M. Moment, printed in the issue of SCHOOL AND SOCIETY for October 21, 1933, is said "but for the quotations" to be "written in Basic" English.

I have compared this article with the list of Basic words and usages contained in "The Basic Words"[1] and am unable to trace the following words (or uses) employed by Mr. Moment in his article:

(1) Tower
(2) Résumé
(3) Outdo*
(4) Orient
(5) Continent
(6) Moreover*
(7) Gotten*
(8) The Blacks*
(9) Diplomacy
(10) Pictorial*
(11) Length*
(12) Scientific*
(13) Troublesome*
(14) Dictionary
(15) Information
(16) Mankind*

Those words marked with an asterisk are compounds of words contained in the Basic vocabulary, but the compounds themselves are not listed in "The Basic Words." In any case does a foreigner's knowledge of "out" and "do" enable him to guess the meaning of "outdo"? Or does knowledge of "more" and "over" help him to translate "moreover"? Basic uses the suffixes *-er, -ed, -est, -ing* only; hence *Pict-orial, Scien-tific, trouble-some* will not be understood. In Basic English "kind" means *bien, bienveillant;* "sort" is used for the other sense. (We might, of course, emend the passage to "the de-Babelization of mansort.")

A critique of the Basic English prepared by M. West and E. Swenson, with the help of F. L. Russel and K. M. Fawkes, is shortly to be issued by the Department of Educational Research of the Ontario College of Education. I would earnestly ask those interested in the system to suspend judgment until they have investigated it, and its implications, thoroughly.

MICHAEL WEST

[1] C. K. Ogden, Kegan Paul & Co., 1932.

SPECIAL CORRESPONDENCE

WORK CAMPS FOR THE YOUTH OF GERMANY

NEARLY three hundred thousand young men between the ages of eighteen and twenty-five are working in the forestry camps of the United States. As part of President Roosevelt's "New Deal" these young unemployed men are lodged, clothed and fed by the government and receive thirty dollars a month for their work. The camps in the United States find precedents in German, Bulgarian, Welsh, Dutch and Swiss camps which contain over 325,000 young people.

The system of camps in Germany offers the best analogy to those in the United States from the standpoint of numbers of youth cared for and type of work performed. The German camps came into existence in 1923 as an attempt of several sport and Christian organizations to care for unemployed youths and to break down the political, social and religious barriers which seriously divided them. The war and its aftermath left many of the youth of Germany weak physically and depressed spiritually. It was felt that they could best be cared for by placing them in camps. The wholesome food and outdoor work was to rebuild them physically. A program of recreation and education was to raise their morale and intelligence and help them understand the problems of Germany.

These camps developed as a venture of private organizations and individuals until 1931, when there were about thirty such camps scattered over Germany. In July of that year the German government decided to establish camps of this kind for the thousands of young unemployed. By a series of Reich emergency decrees a system of camps was set up which by the fall of 1932 contained nearly 275,000 young people between the ages of eighteen and twenty-five.

The camps were voluntary, and the participants received eight to ten cents a day besides their room, board and work clothes. Most of the camps contained unemployed peasants, workers and students. The youth constructed roads and trails, drained marsh, meadow and forest land and did flood control work on a small scale. The type of work done was restricted by law to: (1) Projects which promoted the general welfare; (2) projects which could not be done by regular laborers; (3) projects that did not take work from employed workers.

The youth worked six to seven hours a day beginning early in the morning. The late afternoons and evenings were thus left free. During this leisure time much was done to raise the educational level of the recruits. The law which set up the German camps restricted the participants to young people between the ages of eighteen and twenty-five, but allowed the recruiting agencies to include one person over the age of twenty-five for every twenty-five youth in a camp. This provision was designed to allow unemployed intellectuals to take part so that they might assist in the recreational and educational programs.

Discussion groups were organized. Books were made available to the men. Professors and lecturers came to the camps to speak on such subjects as the unemployment problem, the fundamentals of citizenship, the economic crisis and the trend of population toward the cities. In every case an attempt was made to show the young German his place in society. Communists and National Socialists, Junkers and common laborers lived and worked together and thus came better to understand their mutual problems. Under the Nazis these camps have been continued, though their purpose and programs have been considerably modified.

The camps were originally organized, first, to care for the unemployed; secondly, to do valuable work for poor areas; thirdly, to bring the different classes together and thus break down the strata of German society. Besides the voluntary exchange of ideas among the different classes of youth in the camps, discussion groups were arranged which provided for the presentation of the ideas of the different classes on problems of mutual interest. The educational phase of the camps was considered to be of significant importance.

To-day their first purpose is to convert and confirm the youth of Germany to National Socialism, thus obliterating class and political distinctions; secondly, to care for the unemployed and develop them physically; thirdly, to do valuable work for the poor areas. Before the advent of Hitler the camps were voluntary, but to-day the tendency is to make them compulsory.

The symbol of the *arbeitdienst* is a shovel and three heads of grain, with the historic words of Frederick the Great, "Where one head of grain grows there must be two." Before the Hitler régime young women took part in the same camps as the men. Usually they worked in the kitchen, waited on table and mended the clothes of the workers. In a few cases they did the lighter manual work with the men. At present the women are in separate camps, where they raise vegetables and other food products used in the camps of the men. The camps for the women, like those for the men, are overwhelmingly National Socialist and hotbeds of ardent supporters of Hitler.

Where last year some 3,000 students from the colleges and universities took part in the camps, there are about 17,000 this year. Nine thousand of them have just finished high school. The others come from the colleges and universities. No Jews are allowed to take part in the camps. The German Studentenshaft were only morally bound to do service in the camps during the summer, but now they are required by law to go to camps before and during their college or university course for a minimum of forty weeks. Up to the present time, however, the limited number of camps has not permitted participation by all students. This participation of students in the camps is in line with Hitler's desire to break down class differences and create one great unified group of Germans. The number of students has increased from 75,000 before the war to 150,000 since the war. There are enough trained experts to-day to take all professional jobs for the next ten years. Since Germany feels that there are already too many students they hope that some of them may be reorientated in the direction of agriculture or industry.

To facilitate the interchange of ideas among the different classes in the camps, discussion groups are organized during the leisure time. Prior to the advent of Hitler the camps were non-military and neutral politically. To-day they are a means for converting and confirming German youth to the Nazi party. *Wehrsports* and marching make them a potential army of organized youth. Nazi emblems and flags, while banned before Hitler became chancellor, are very much in evidence this season. Where before discussions were generally on subjects of a non-political nature, to-day they are just the opposite. In many camps this important educational phase of the project has been lost. Many of the more intelligent German youth deplore this loss of the "basic ideals of the work camps." Originally an explanation of the German state and the basic principles on which the nation rests led to a consideration of the governments of other states. But to-day they seldom get beyond the swastic horizon.

The subject of the majority of the discussions, as one would imagine, is National Socialism and its various aspects. They discuss "Fascism," "The Structure of the German State" and "The Aspects of Citizenship in New Germany." They strive to teach love of country and an appreciation of its grandeur. They are trying to break down the idea of the state as the protector and the individual as a benefactor of this protection. A true citizen of Germany must be an active, participating, militant National Socialist. The fervor with which this statement is repeated by ardent young Nazis leaves no doubt that young recruits must, at least outwardly, be National Socialists or take the consequences. Any one who can not be converted may find a berth in a concentration camp where more persuasive methods are used.

The leaders of the camps are either old army officers who are National Socialists or members of the Steel Helmets. They are first sent into training camps for a period of six weeks where they are taught to administer the camps and carry out the programs of political education and recreation. They receive about 60 marks per month, besides their board, room and uniforms.

The younger Nazis are not satisfied with these leaders and talk of another revolution in which these older men will be replaced by younger and more ardent National Socialists. They predict the change will take place before March.

The youth usually enroll for a period of 40 weeks. This can be extended if they are unable to find employment by the end of the period. Of course the government hopes eventually to place all the young people in regular jobs, and now that the *"Traegers der Arbeit"* are the

Federal Unemployment Bureaus the camps are more directly controlled by the government. The recruits are registered in the bureaus and their records filed. If requests for workers come to the bureaus which can be filled by any of the young workers, they are placed in this manner. While they are in the camps an attempt is made to determine their interests and abilities. A definite attempt is made to interest college and university students of mediocre ability in non-academic pursuits. One reason the government officials insist that students spend several weeks in the work camps is to see if some of the students can not be directed into non-professional fields of endeavor. At the same time, if peasants and workers show exceptional ability, they are given an opportunity to enter schools of higher learning.

If, in the course of a service period, an unemployed decides he would like to become an agricultural settler on the land reclaimed by the workers he is eligible for governmental assistance. He is given preference over the unemployed who have not served in the camps and is eligible to receive a loan from the government to purchase land and farm equipment. In a like manner some of the large estates which are already much in arrears on taxes will be divided and settled by young National Socialists.

While it would be unfortunate if the men in the Civilian Conservation Corps Camps were propagandized for any political party, there is an opportunity to carry out an informal educational program which would not interfere with the work of the men but would greatly benefit them individually. Under the direction of Dr. Clarence S. Marsh, dean of Buffalo University, and the U. S. Bureau of Education, an educational program is being worked out for the Conservation Corps Camps which promises to meet the needs of the young men. According to present plans, no formal program will be applied to all the camps. The program for each camp will vary according to the ability of the men and the facilities in the vicinity of the camp. Discussion groups and field trips will be used rather than the formal lectures and the reading of text-books which characterize much of our education. The Civilian Conservation Corps Camps offer a great opportunity to the adult education movement in America, and it would seem that the camp commanders are now willing to cooperate with the commissioner of education in carrying out a program on a national scale.

KENNETH HOLLAND
INTERNATIONAL STUDENT SERVICE,
NEW YORK, N. Y.

REPORTS

THE WORK OF THE NEW YORK STATE EMERGENCY COLLEGES

MR. THURSTON CHILD, in the *New York Herald-Tribune* of February 4, summarizes the recent report of Lewis A. Wilson, assistant commissioner of education for New York State, on the twelve emergency colleges that have been established during the past year in that state. These institutions have been set up to offer educational facilities to high-school graduates who have been financially unable to continue their education and who, at the same time, have been unable to find employment. As the winter of 1932–33 passed it became evident to many thoughtful educators and relief administrators of this state that a large number of recently graduated high-school students were unable to go on to college for financial reasons. At the same time it was discovered that there were available many highly trained and experienced college instructors who were temporarily without teaching positions. It therefore was decided to bring these two groups together, and steps were taken to establish a series of emergency collegiate centers. Part of the relief funds allocated to education were set aside to pay the salaries of the instructors who were to teach at the centers and their salaries were to be uniform—$15 per instructor a week.

The response to this plan was immediate and enthusiastic. By the end of March centers were established at Albany Buffalo, Garden City, Rochester, Syracuse and White Plains. Registration at the different centers varied. At White Plains 100 students were enrolled, while at Buffalo more than 500 young people applied for admission. At the other centers the registration averaged 200.

In order to make certain that a high standard of work would be maintained, the State Department of Education asked for the cooperation of the heads of state or city colleges already established in the localities where it was decided to open the centers. The State Colleges for Teachers at Albany and Buffalo sponsored the centers located in those cities, while the centers at White Plains and Garden City were opened by the president of the College of the City of New York.

The presidents of these sponsoring institutions selected the faculties for the centers, outlined the curricula to be pursued, set up the entrance requirements for the students who applied for admission, and in many cases turned over the facilities of their institutions to the centers. After the machinery had been set in motion, the direction of the center was turned over to a dean or registrar.

The courses offered at the centers were the usual freshman survey courses corresponding to the courses offered to the freshmen of the sponsoring institutions. This was to make easier the transfer of credits when the student finished his work at the center and was ready to enter a standard college. But a surprisingly large number of students registered who had already had one year of college work, and it was decided to offer courses in English and American literature, government, sociology, public speaking and economics to meet the special needs of these young people.

In an effort to make the student life at the centers similar to the student life at the sponsoring colleges, the centers developed interesting and varied extra-curricula activities. Two centers organized active dramatic and musical groups; other centers issued weekly newspapers, mimeographed for economy's sake, but as full of news and jokes as many regular college papers. Several of the centers organized independently or in cooperation with the sponsoring colleges athletic teams, tennis, base ball, etc.

The work of these six original centers was so successful that the state decided early last fall to continue them. This decision was amply justified by the advance registration. In almost all cases the registration figures showed a decided increase over last spring. At White Plains thirty more students applied for admission, while at Garden City the number of registrants jumped from 256 to 457.

Due to this increased registration and due also to the difficulties of providing inexpensive means of transportation in the upstate sections it was decided to open additional centers. Branches of the Emergency Junior College at Albany were opened at Troy and Schenectady, while centers were also opened at Auburn, Cortland, Little Falls and Newark.

In most cases the activities of the old centers were enlarged. The work was made to conform to the standard requirements of the first year of a junior college. A 75 per cent. regents' average was set as the minimum entrance requirement. New courses were added. The faculties were increased. At Buffalo eight instructors volunteered their services.

SOCIETIES AND MEETINGS

MEETING OF THE DEPARTMENT OF SUPERVISORS AND DIRECTORS OF INSTRUCTION OF THE N. E. A.

THE Department of Supervisors and Directors of Instruction of the National Education Association will hold its fourteenth annual meeting in Cleveland on February 27 and 28. The program is as follows:

TUESDAY, FEBRUARY 27

9:30 A. M., Ballroom, Public Auditorium

Presiding, Mildred English, president.

Topic: "The Use of Scientific Methods in a Program of Supervision."

"The Scientific Method and Creative Supervision," Bess Goodykoontz, Assistant Commissioner of Education, U. S. Office of Education.

"The Scientific Method and Cooperative Supervision," Elizabeth Hall, assistant superintendent of schools, Minneapolis, Minnesota.

"The Use of Objective Measures in Evaluating Instruction," W. A. Brownell, Duke University.

"Presentation of the Seventh Yearbook," Paul T. Rankin, supervising director of instruction, Detroit, Michigan.

"Evaluation and Appraisal of the Yearbook," Clifford Woody, University of Michigan.

Tuesday, February 27

12:15 p. m., Lake Room, Hotel Statler

Presiding, Leonard Power, first vice-president.

Discussion: "Supervision and the Needs of Childhood," Worth McClure, superintendent of schools, Seattle, Washington.

Wednesday, February 28

9:30 a. m., Ballroom, Public Auditorium

Presiding, Mildred English, president.

Topic: "The Redirection of the Educational Program to Meet the Needs of the Present Crisis."

"The Type of Instruction Demanded by the Present Educational and Social Crisis," Ernest W. Butterfield, commissioner of education, Connecticut.

"The Challenge of the Present Crisis for a New Type of Supervision," Laura Zirbes, Ohio State University.

"Self-Supervision by Teachers, a Practical Way to Help Meet the Need," William T. Melchior, Syracuse University.

"Wise and Unwise Economies in a Program of Supervision," E. E. Oberholtzer, superintendent of schools, Houston, Texas.

Immediately following the program on Wednesday, February 28, the annual business meeting of the department will be held. The annual meeting of the board of directors will be held on Monday, February 26, at 7:30 a. m., in the Tavern Room of the Hotel Statler. The executive committee will meet at the same place immediately after the meeting of the board of directors. The membership committee will meet on Tuesday, February 27, at 7:30 a. m., in the Tavern Room of the Hotel Statler. Miss Maybelle G. Bush is chairman of the committee.

THE CONFERENCE ON CHILD DEVELOPMENT, CARE AND TRAINING

The Conference on Child Development, Care and Training, under the auspices of the Mooseheart Laboratory for Child Research, will be held at the New Willard Hotel, Washington, D. C., on February 22 and 23. Senator James J. Davis will serve as honorary chairman and Martin L. Reymert, director of the Mooseheart Laboratory, as chairman. The program follows:

Thursday, February 22

2:00 p. m.

Address of Welcome, Senator James J. Davis.

"The Mooseheart Laboratory," Martin L. Reymert.

"Future Lines of Clinical Research on Children," Edgar A. Doll, director, The Training School, Vineland, N. J.

"Psychiatry and the Modern Child," Paul L. Schroeder, director, Institute of Juvenile Research, Chicago, Ill.

"The Importance of the Mooseheart Laboratory to a Nation-wide Parent Education Program," Louise Stanley, chief, Bureau of Home Economics, U. S. Department of Agriculture.

Friday, February 23

10:00 a. m.

General meeting of the Advisory Council and Governing Officials of the Loyal Order of Moose (Board of Governors of Mooseheart and the Supreme Council of the Loyal Order of Moose).

2:00 p. m.

"Research in the Field of the Psychological Development of the Child," Charles H. Judd, dean, Graduate School of Education, University of Chicago.

"The Modern Child and Curriculum Construction," Ernest Horn, College of Education, University of Iowa.

"Physical Growth of the Child," T. Wingate Todd, Department of Anatomy, Western Reserve University.

"Research on the Young Child, a Retrospect and a Forecast," John E. Anderson, director, Institute of Child Welfare, University of Minnesota.

"The Modern Child in Relation to Vocational Education," C. A. Prosser, director, William Hood Dunwoody Institute, Minneapolis, Minn.

7:00 p. m.

"The Growing Child as a Problem in Pediatrics," H. F. Helmholz, M.D., head, Section of Pediatrics, Mayo Clinic.

"The Growing Child as a Problem in Physiology," A. J. Carlson, Department of Physiology, University of Chicago.

"The Growing Child in the Family and the Play Group," E. W. Burgess, Department of Sociology, University of Chicago.

EDUCATIONAL RESEARCH AND STATISTICS

THE CONSTRUCTION AND RESULTS OF A TWELVE-HOUR TEST IN ENGLISH COMPOSITION

I. BACKGROUND

IN accordance with the general plan of the Board of Examinations of the University of Chicago, the seventh qualifying examination in English composition was given in May of this year to 680 New Plan students.[1] The examination differed radically from any of the preceding ones. It was given, at the request of the English department, in four periods of three hours each, one period on each of four successive Mondays; the total testing time was thus twelve hours, spread over four weeks. Originally the plan was to have relatively "free" writing ("write a theme on ...." type of writing) in these periods, the hope being that the student would within this time period supply sufficient evidence upon which a sound estimate of his writing ability could be based. It was also hoped that the size of the sample would facilitate reliable judging of the quality of the papers. As evidence from the past experimentation seemed to constitute proof that reliable reading of free themes was virtually unattainable without extensive training of the readers, the original plan was abandoned. The views of the instructors of English were varied on this decision; some of them felt that free writing should be given this final trial. However, the committee in charge decided against it.

With the aid of members of the staff and in cooperation with the examiner, an examination committee of English instructors constructed the examination. Although the task of preparing a qualifying test in English must always be laborious, the particular arduousness of the task on this occasion and the time required for it can be appreciated only in the light of the state of flux which the English course was in at that time. The examination was, nevertheless, as much as anything could be at that time, the product of the combined efforts of the instructors of English composition. A greater amount of time and energy was spent by the instructors on this examination than had been spent on any previous one.

II. DESCRIPTION OF THE EXAMINATION

The aim of the first three-hour session was to test the students' ability to put a research paper into proper form. The point to be proved, the outline to be followed and sufficient notes (with informal references to sources) for construction of the paper were given. The student was instructed to write and document the paper and to make a formal bibliography. The material proved to be too difficult in content for the average student to master and work into form in the three hours allowed. In particular, putting the formal bibliography into proper form and making the proper footnote entries were more time-consuming than had been estimated. The general type of exercise was felt by the group concerned to be a valuable one, but the material was slightly too difficult.

The second three-hour session was designed to test the ability to organize into an effective essay a given body of ideas upon a subject. The subject of the paper was given, together with a collection of ideas on the subject in the form of sentences arranged in chance order. The student was required to outline the paper and then to write it. Again, many of the students felt pressed for time.

The third three-hour session, devoted to the short exercise type of test, consisted of four parts. Part A, a sentence exercise, gave two paragraphs of short, choppy sentences. The student was required to rewrite the paragraphs, showing proper subordination and coordination. In Part B, the student had to make certain specified construction changes in given sentences, together with any other necessary changes, the purpose being to test the students' power over sentence structure. Part C gave two paragraphs adequately organized and written, and required that they be rewritten according to a second general type of organization.

[1] See John M. Stalnaker, "Attempts to Measure the Ability to Write with Clarity and Accuracy," SCHOOL AND SOCIETY, 37: 69–72, 1933, and John M. Stalnaker, "Tests of Acceptable and Reliable Habits of Writing," *The English Journal*, December, 1933, for a description of the English composition courses offered and the general examination problem at the University of Chicago.

In exercise D, the student was to fill in with the appropriate word or phrase certain blanks left in a descriptive paragraph, the purpose being to test accuracy and fullness of vocabulary rather than literary feeling.

The fourth three-hour session of the examination was entirely objective. The sections were labeled: Organization, Paragraph Unity, Reading, Sentence Structure, Grammar, Punctuation, Diction, Vocabulary and Bibliography and Research Paper Form. Each label is an obvious indication of what the section tested.

III. Scoring the Examination

The instructors read the papers for this examination without the students' names appearing on them. Rather than have each instructor read all of a small batch of examinations, the examination committee assigned certain instructors to read all the examinations for certain exercises. By having the instructors work in small groups, it was hoped that agreement on standards would be reached more quickly and that greater reliability of reading would be achieved. The results obtained justified the procedure.

IV. The Reliability of Reading

Various checks on the consistency or reliability with which the themes were read had been made on most of the past examinations with the result that no examination was found to have been read with high reliability. In fact, reliabilities as low as .30 were found, and none as high as .75 or .80. These low reliabilities indicate that the mark a student receives is more dependent on the mood of the reader than on the quality of the student's writing. An educational system that stresses examinations is rendered pointless without reliable measuring instruments.

The readers, being aware of the previous studies of reliability, determined to make this reading reliable. They agreed very thoroughly on the standards to be used, and then checked over many papers to insure that their standards were not shifting. The amount of effort which the instructors put into the reading of these papers was incalculable. It was hoped that the initial training, together with the fact that the

TABLE I

Point Scoring of the Examination Units

Unit	Theoretical score range	Weight	Total possible score	Percentage
First session				
Footnotes	0–50	3	150	25
Bibliography	0–50	1	50	8
Essay	0– 5	80	400	67
Total			600	100
Second session				
Outline	0–20	1	20	20
Essay	0– 4	20	80	80
Total			100	100
Third session				
Sentence exercise	0–10	10	100	32
Construction shifts	0–27	4	108	34
Paragraph construction	0– 8	10	80	25
Description	0–27	1	27	9
Total			315	100
Fourth session				
Organization	0–94	1	94	17
Paragraph unity	0–20	2	40	7
Reading	0–10	4	40	7
Sentence structure	0–45	2	90	16
Grammar	0–21	3	63	11
Punctuation	0–35	1	35	6
Diction	0–43	1	43	8
Vocabulary	0–60	1	60	11
True-false	0–51	2	102	18
Total			567	101

Note: To obtain the total score, a procedure equivalent to adding standard scores was used. See John M. Stalnaker and M. W. Richardson, "The Combination of Test Scores," *Journal of General Psychology*, 8: 460–463, 1933.

writing on this examination was more rigidly restricted than that on any previous examination, would result in reliable reading of the papers. The results, however, far exceeded the expectations.

In order to secure a measure of the consistency of reading, 90 papers were reread. Every effort was made to have this check made independently of the first reading, and in general the readers were unaware of the fact that they were rereading a set of papers. No names or marks were made on any of the papers. The instructors cooperated excellently and were as interested as the Board of Examinations in maintaining an experimental attitude toward the reliability study.

All reliabilities were high, ranging from .98 to .73, with an average reliability of .88. Table II gives the results for the various sections.

TABLE II

READER RELIABILITY, DETERMINED BY HAVING A GROUP OF 90 PAPERS INDEPENDENTLY REREAD

Examination section	Obtained reliability
Session I	
Essay	.80
Footnotes	.91
Bibliography	.95
Session II	
Essay	.89
Outline	.73
Session III	
Sentence exercise	.82
Construction shifts	.98
Paragraph organization	.91
Description	.97
Average	.88

These high reliabilities show that it is possible, with careful reading of papers on highly restricted writing, to obtain agreement in grading.

V. ASSIGNMENT OF LETTER GRADES

The letter grades, A, B, C, D and F, were assigned by arbitrarily dividing the distribution of total scores into five parts, in conformity with the general grade distribution of all other examinations.

TABLE III

THE DISTRIBUTION OF GRADES

Grade	Number	Percentage	Score range
A	72	11	20.6–
B	113	17	18.9–20.5
C	288	42	15.4–18.8
D	103	15	13.6–15.3
F*	104	15	0.0–13.5
Total	680	100	

* F is the only failing grade.

VI. CORRELATIONAL STUDIES

There is a certain amount of value and considerable interest in a study of the relationships which obtain for the various parts of this examination. As the final score on the total examination was made up of 18 unit scores, the number of possible simple relationships (zero-order correlations) among the parts would number 153. If the intelligence test scores and the initial placement test scores were also considered, there would be 190 different correlations possible. Only a few of these possible correlations have been computed. In addition, the scores on certain related sections of the test have been combined into a single score and the relationships between the scores so obtained have been computed. Most of the computations were made on a sample of 150 cases selected at random from 680 available cases.

As each of the four examination periods constituted a unit, the relationships among them were found:

TABLE IV

THE RELATIONSHIPS BETWEEN THE SESSIONS

Session	Correlation
I and II	.24
I " III	.48
I " IV	.61
II " III	.38
II " IV	.42
III " IV	.63
Total and I	.76
" " II	.64
" " III	.80
" " IV	.85

The first and second sessions were devoted to writing, while the third session consisted of exercises and the fourth of objective material. The first session was graded for (1) essay, (2) footnotes, (3) bibliography; the second session for (1) essay and (2) outline. Thus the essay scores constituted only a part of the total score for each session. In determining the correlation between the two essay scores, the total population of 680 cases was used. The correlation was .25. A simple conclusive explanation of this low correlation between the two essay scores, in spite of the high reliability of the grading, can not be given. Several explanations are possible, two of which are obvious. It may be that both tests measured the same ability, but the student varied markedly in his performance from day to day. Possibly the two tests, although both required writing, in reality measured very different abilities.

The objective section of past English examinations has proved to be a rather stable measure. In this examination, the total score correlated more highly with the objective section than with any other section, although the objective section contributed no more to the final score than did any other section. A study of the correlation of the essays with the objective score was therefore indicated. Essay I and the objective total gave a correlation of .58; essay II and the total objective, .25; essays I plus II and the objective, .66.

Other correlations between the individual units are given in Table V. (The Roman numerals refer to the session of the examination.)

Much might be written about these correlations. Consider the correlation of .25 between the outline grade of session II and the grade on the objective organization test (IV). If both tests measure the ability to organize (assuming that such an ability exists), they should show a much higher relationship, say .85. If they measure different abilities, what are those abilities? Naming them is trivial, but it is important to know whether or not they are part of the complex which makes up writing ability. Were some valid external criterion available, one could easily determine the answers to these questions. At present, there is no answer.

All the correlations are low. Each unit of the test appears to be measuring some ability which is different from the ability measured by the other units. When the various units of the test are perfected, an application of the newly developed factor analysis technique may result in the discovery of the different abilities which go together to make up the complex ability of writing.

The total test score and the intelligence test score gave a correlation of .57. The initial placement test scores correlated with the present test .63.

TABLE V

CORRELATION BETWEEN TEST UNITS

Units	Correlations
Outline II—Organization IV	.25
Sentence structure IV — Construction shifts III	.49
Sentence structure IV—Sentence exercise IV	.40
Paragraph unity IV—Paragraph construction III	.03
Paragraph construction III—Sentence exercise IV	.35
Sentence exercise III—Construction shifts III	.27
Paragraph construction III—Construction shifts III	.18
Construction shifts III—Grammar IV	.37
Construction shifts III—Vocabulary IV	.35
Sentence structure IV—Grammar IV	.47
Sentence structure IV—Punctuation IV	.39
Grammar IV—Punctuation IV	.41
Footnotes I—Bibliography I	.30
Footnotes I—Research paper form IV	.43
Description III—Vocabulary IV	.44
Reading IV—Vocabulary IV	.48
Diction IV—Vocabulary IV	.38

Although the correlations are not high enough to justify the conclusion that any two of the unit tests measure the same ability, certain of them should, from their nature, measure the same general type of ability. On the basis of this descriptive nature of the unit parts, various combinations were made.[2]

(1) *Essay:* Essay I and essay II. (The Roman numerals refer to the test session or day.)

(2) *Organization:* Outline II and organization IV.

(3) *Paragraph writing:* Sentence exercise III, paragraph construction III and paragraph unity IV.

(4) *Mechanics:* Construction shifts III, sentence structure IV, grammar IV and punctuation IV.

[2] Certain arbitrary weights were given to these unit scores in combining them into the larger groups for correlation work. No discussion is given to the weights used, as it can be demonstrated that the correlation coefficients between the groups are not sensitive, in the ranges here concerned, to minor variations in the weighting of the units which make up the groups.

(5) *Documentation:* Footnotes I, Bibliography I and Bibliography and Research Paper Form IV.
(6) *Word sense:* Description III, Reading IV, Diction IV and Vocabulary IV.

The correlations obtained among these total groups are (the group number is indicated in parentheses):

Essay (1) and unit vocabulary of IV	.47
Essay (1) and organization (2)	.51
Essay (1) and paragraph writing (3)	.44
Essay (1) and mechanics (4)	.56
Essay (1) and documentation (5)	.36
Essay (1) and word sense (6)	.52
Outline (2) and paragraph writing (3)	.35
Outline (2) and mechanics (4)	.52
Outline (2) and documentation (5)	.29
Outline (2) and word sense (6)	.41
Paragraph writing (3) and mechanics (4)	.39
Paragraph writing (3) and documentation (5)	.25
Paragraph writing (3) and word sense (6)	.51
Mechanics (4) and documentation (5)	.31
Mechanics (4) and word sense (6)	.47
Documentation (5) and word sense (6)	.20

It is particularly interesting to note that the highest correlations, although they are not high, are found between the "mechanics" group and the "word sense" group, with the other combinations. Certainly a sound measure of the student's knowledge of the mechanics of writing and of his ability to use words is necessary for a complete picture of the ability to write.

The correlation between the essay grade (1) and the total objective grade (all of session IV) is .66. Correlations from previous examinations have been .59, .65, .55, .61 and .36.

VII. Additional Studies of Validity

A. Pre-examination reports from instructors

The instructors in English submitted, just before the examination was given, the names of the 10 per cent. of their students whom they judged to be the best and the 10 per cent. of their students whom they judged to be the worst. As they knew that their lists were to be checked against lists of high and low ranking students on the examination, what they tried to do was to predict the results of the examination. One hundred and eight names were ranked: 50 high and 58 low.

The students rated high by their instructors had an average percentile rank on the intelligence test of .70, as compared with the average intelligence percentile of .24 for the group rated by the instructors as low. In other words, the high group was on the average bright and the low group on the average dull.

The following table shows the performance on the examination of the listed students. It is to be noted that of the 49 students rated high by the instructors, 43 per cent. were found to be among the highest 10 per cent. (68 students) on the examination. Of the 53 rated low, 19 (36 per cent.) were actually among the lowest 10 per cent. (68 students) on the examination.

TABLE VI

Records of Students Rated by their Instructors

	Instructors' Rating	
	Highest 10 per cent.	Lowest 10 per cent.
Total number	50	58
Number completing examinations	49	53
Number not completing examinations	......	3
Number not taking examinations	1	2
Number in upper 10 per cent. on total examination	21	......
Number in lower 10 per cent. on total examination	......	19

The percentile ranks of the scores which these students obtained on the examination are shown in the following table. It is interesting to note that of the 53 rated as low, 7 or 13 per cent., score over the average of all students taking the examination, and 26 (50 per cent.) are in the upper three quarters. On the other hand, of the 49 high-rated students, 3 (6 per cent.) are in the lower half of the group taking the examination, and 16 (33 per cent.) are in the lower three quarters. The percentile ranks of the average scores for the two groups show, nevertheless, how widely separated they are on the average, in spite of a certain amount of overlapping of the two groups.

TABLE VII

Percentile ranks on total examination	Students rated by instructors as	
	High	Low
90–99	22	......
80–89	7	......
70–79	7	......
60–69	5	3
50–59	5	4
40–49	2	4
30–39	1	12
20–29	......	7
10–19	......	8
0– 9	......	15
Total	49	53
Percentile rank of average score for group	84	20

TABLE VIII

	Rated by the examination	
	High	Low
Total number	68	68
Had no English course	3	4
Had taken English 101 and/ or 103*	22	17
Had taken English 102*	43	47
English 102 students rated high or low by instructor	21 (49%)	19 (40%)
English 102 students not rated high or low by instructor	22†	28
Average intelligence percentile	70	19

* The English Department, previous to the school year 1931–32, offered two courses in English composition which, under the old plan, were *required:* English 101, usually taken upon entrance, and English 103, usually taken during the sophomore year or later. These two courses are no longer offered. English 102 is a new course in composition, and in a sense it takes the place of both English 101 and English 103.

† The two highest scores on the examination were obtained by English 102 students who were not rated in the upper group by the instructors. The highest scoring student was rated as a B student by his instructor. The second highest student was a colored student whose instructor made this comment: "A first-rate student; he worked slowly but well. 85 percentile."

We can consider also the highest and lowest 10 per cent. on the examination. Table VIII indicates the extent of the preparation of these students and their ratings.

The names of those students who fell in the highest 10 per cent. or the lowest 10 per cent. on the examination, but whose names had not appeared on the rating lists were sent to the instructors with a request for a letter rating. The two groups were arranged in one alphabetical list, so that there was no way of determining which were the highest and which the lowest. The instructors did not know how the names on the list had been selected. There were 22 from the highest 10 per cent. and 28 from the lowest. A tabulation of the ratings follows:

TABLE IX

THE INSTRUCTORS' RATINGS OF THE STUDENTS WHO SCORED IN THE UPPER OR LOWER 10 PER CENT. ON THE EXAMINATION, BUT WHO HAD NOT BEEN INITIALLY RATED BY THE INSTRUCTOR AS HIGH OR LOW

Instructor rating[3]	Highest group on examination	Lowest group on examination
A		
A –	3	1
B	5	
B –	3	1
C	5	3
C –	1	1
D +	1	
D	2	9
D –		5
F		10
Total	20*	29*

[3] The possible grades are A, B, C and D for passing, and F for failing.

* No ratings for two in high group; no rating for 1 in low group, but 2 ratings for 2.

Since, of the highest 68 students on the examination, only 43 were English 102 students, and of the 68 lowest students, only 47 were English 102 students, a more valid comparison would be between the 49 high students and the 53 low students as rated by the instructors and the 49 highest and the 53 lowest English 102 students on the examination. When this comparison is made, 23 (46 per cent.) of the 49 highest English 102 students on the examination are found to have been rated by the instructors as in the highest 10 per cent. of their class and 20 (38 per cent.) of the 53 lowest English 102 students on the examination are found to have been rated by the instructors as in the lowest 10 per cent. of their classes.

While these comparisons do not show any remarkable degree of consistency between predicted high and low, and high and low as obtained on the examination, there is some satisfaction to be found in the fact that no student ranked as high fell into the lowest 10 per cent. on the examination, and no student ranked as low fell into the upper 10 per cent. on the examination. No doubt, the satisfaction of this fact is lessened by noting that in the post-examination ratings of the special group, two top-scoring students were rated D, and one low-scoring student, A –.

B. Preparation of the Students

Most of the students who took this examination were English 102 students, but a few (128) were English 103 students (who in general had also had English 101), 28 had had only English 101, 3 had advanced standing, and 30 had had no English training at a university. There is a large spread of scores in each of the groups, and the amount of overlapping of scores is great. The rank order of the groups is shown in Table X.

The groups which have had the most training and have received the best grades are on the average superior. The students graded poor are poor on the examination. The degree of overlapping of the distribution of the scores for these groups, it must be remembered, is great.

VIII. Conclusions

The interpretation of the results of a controlled experiment is usually an easy task. The examination which has here been considered has been loosely called an experiment In the sense that we were trying new types of material, it was. But the set-up was by no means that of a controlled experiment. Hence, the conclusions to be drawn must be as unsatisfactory as was the experimental set-up.

In general, one may say that this examination

TABLE X

	Average Score
1. Advanced standing students (3 only)	18.3
2. English 102 students, graded Satisfactory	17.6
3. English 103 students, graded Satisfactory	17.1
4. English 103 students, no grade report	17.0
5. English 101 students, graded Satisfactory	15.7
6. Students with no English courses	15.7
7. English 103 students, graded Unsatisfactory	14.2
8. English 102 students, graded Unsatisfactory	13.8
Total	16.8

was from almost all points of view the most satisfactory qualifying examination in English which we have given. The assignment of letter grades on the basis of the total examination was generally in conformity with those which would have been given by the instructors. The conclusions from the validity studies are indefinite and unsatisfactory, largely because of the lack of a sound criterion.

While the total examination was successful, the various units did not agree with related units in any striking fashion. Thus, it is not possible to feel certain just what any given unit of the test measured. However, when all the units were put together, the resulting score seemed to be the most adequate measure of the ability to write we have yet developed.

The unusually high degree of consistency in the reading of the papers which was achieved constitutes a definite and sizable step forward. Some of the new types of exercises in restricted writing which were developed and tried out look very promising.

While an examination of this size and elaborateness will not be given again very soon, the experience gained from it has been valuable. The next examination, patterned largely after the successful units of this examination, will be a six-hour one, given during a single day.

John M. Stalnaker
University of Chicago

[4] Students under the new plan are graded by the instructors as satisfactory, unsatisfactory, or registered, but no grade report.

SCHOOL AND SOCIETY

WITH WHICH ARE COMBINED THE EDUCATIONAL REVIEW, ESTABLISHED IN 1891, THE TEACHERS MAGAZINE, ESTABLISHED IN 1878, AND THE SCHOOL JOURNAL, ESTABLISHED IN 1874.

EDITED BY J. McKEEN CATTELL, R. D. LINDQUIST AND W. H. COWLEY

EDITORIAL COMMUNICATIONS SHOULD BE ADDRESSED TO THE EDUCATION BUILDING, THE OHIO STATE UNIVERSITY, COLUMBUS, OHIO

Volume 39 | Saturday, February 24, 1934 | Number 1000

FEDERAL AID FOR PUBLIC SCHOOLS

By Professor ALFRED P. JAMES

UNIVERSITY OF PITTSBURGH

The distribution of wealth and of income vitally affects education. What might be termed maldistribution is certainly of serious import for the so-called public schools. Anything which at the same time might remedy maldistribution and specifically aid public school education would be doubly a service. Some analysis of matters seems to show such a possibility.

In more remote times the distribution of wealth and of income may have been greatly influenced by warfare, plunder and violence. But to the historical student it appears that in more recent times distribution has been affected and in many ways determined by governmental arrangement and policy.

Five principal factors, all of them subject to the legalized arrangements of governmentally organized society, have influenced the present distribution of wealth and of income in the United States. One of these is the ownership and inheritance of property. Another is the control and exploitation of natural resources. A third factor is commerce in its broadest sense as exchange of goods and services. Finance in the sense of both currency and banking is a fourth factor, while taxation is the fifth.

If governmental arrangement and policy in regard to such factors as these have in large degree been responsible for the present maldistribution of wealth and of income a corollary is that, at least in a political democracy, it can be used for the correction of this maldistribution. One may certainly hope that what has been the result of arrangement and policy may be improved by rearrangement and a better policy.

A magazine article is insufficient for a summary discussion of even one of the five principal factors mentioned. It is possible to consider merely a feature of one of them. It happens that the factor of taxation presents such a feature.

Charles Austin Beard and Mary Beard, in the first volume of their "Rise of American Civilization" (pp. 318–319), claim that "the shifting of taxes" is "one of the grand devices of politics for the transfer of wealth from one class to another." Undoubtedly taxation is, above all other factors in the distribution of wealth and of income, a specifically governmental matter. The incidence of taxation is a problem both difficult and significant. It should be in the hands of experts. But even the inexpert can see that some "shifting of taxes" may with the present maldistribution be a matter of great importance to education.

The regions of the United States which at present are having trouble in adequate provision for public schools are the rural states and rural sections of other states. It is of course notorious that some urban centers, such as Chicago, have experienced difficulty, but one has a strong suspicion that mismanagement both of taxation and expenditure has been responsible. Rural regions, on the other hand, appear to suffer from an actual inadequacy of wealth and of income as a basis for revenue from taxation.

Any one familiar with rural taxation knows that the bulk of local taxes is for three main kinds of expenditures. The first of these is for the maintenance of local government. Any relaxation of this burden must come from consolidation of governmental subdivisions. Important movements in this direction are in the air, but only a beginning has been made. It is a common saying that our governmental subdivisions are a relic of the horse-and-buggy age, while we are living in the automobile age. It might be added that we are rapidly entering the flying age. Granted good paved roads, a county seat of a county fifty miles square to-day would be more accessible than the county seat of a county twenty miles square fifty years ago.

The second great outlay of local revenues is for roads. For a long time this burden has been met in part by actual work upon the roads, in lieu of money payment in taxes. More recently aid for hard-surfaced road construction has been secured from larger governmental units, not only from the state but also from the Federal Government. A definite tendency in the direction of the enlargement of such aid is clearly apparent.

The third great outlay of local revenues is for education. It is at present in many local communities the heaviest of local expenditures. Partly owing to the maldistribution of wealth and of income, the local economic base does not seem to furnish the possibility of sufficient revenues from taxation to maintain adequate free compulsory education. Already state aid has in many places been brought to the support of education in distressed communities. But many rural states now begin to experience state-wide inability to finance an adequate public school system. To many it seems that this situation is in part due to large regional maldistribution of wealth and of income caused by factors much subject to the influence of governmental arrangement and policy. And one of these very factors is taxation itself, both state and federal, but particularly the latter.

With better governmental arrangement and policy, especially in matters of commerce and finance, there can be little doubt that the United States as a whole has sufficient real wealth which can be organized in such a way as to produce sufficient public income and taxes to support adequate educational facilities. Since the federal government so largely controls the factors in the distribution of wealth and of income, is it not time for it to assume some responsibility for the establishment and maintenance of adequate public school education throughout the country? To the student of governmental and economic facts it seems that somewhat too meekly educators have accepted the idea that public school education is a local or at best a state concern. And in the light of the history of the United States such an idea is hardly justified.

Central government aid for education is not without very old and somewhat continuous precedent. If it be assumed that the central government in colonial times was, so far as America alone was concerned, located at the colonial capital, there is nearly a century and a half of sporadic colonial precedent. Even during the disturbed conditions of the American Revolution the idea did not disappear. Reflections of the idea appear in some of the early state constitutions. The idea of national governmental aid for public schools found notable expression in the Survey Ordinance of 1785, a national instrument which set aside one section of land in each township of the Northwest for the support of public schools. Later with the acquisition of the Far West, two sections of land in each township of that region were thus set aside.

Recently the present commissioner of education of the United States has done some research in the early national history of constitutional and political opinion in regard to the matter of federal aid for public schools. Research in a later period of our history proves even more valuable. Extended study of the quarter of a century from the Civil War furnishes abundant argument for federal aid to public schools as well as a story of intrinsic interest on its own account.

In matters of education the period of the Civil War is best known for the Morrell Act, providing land grants for the establishment of agricultural and mechanical colleges. This Act of July 2, 1862, and its results are so widely and well known that mere mention of them here is sufficient.

But the Civil War brought up the question of the education of the Negroes of the South, and, motivated by this problem, a strong agitation for federal aid for public school education was carried on for more than twenty years. A study of this movement reveals many of the facets of the whole matter of federal aid to local education.

Warfare between the states may have begun about the division or preservation of the Union, but it rapidly became involved with the status of slaves and Negroes. As refugees, early in the war, Negro slaves flocked to the Union armies in many places, thereby producing serious complications of many kinds.

The Emancipation Proclamation, announced in September, 1862, and promulgated on the first of January, 1863, was immediately followed by activity for the care of the proposed freedmen. A "Bureau of Emancipation" in the federal government was demanded by various Emancipation Leagues. Congressman Eliot of Massachusetts in the latter part of January, 1863, introduced a bill to this effect. When it failed to pass, he introduced in December, 1863, another similar bill, which likewise failed to pass. Two years indeed went by without important action.

But in the summer of 1864, a convention of freedmen's associations in Indianapolis, Indiana, in a petition to the government had asked for the establishment of a bureau of freedmen's affairs in the Federal Government. In the second session of the thirty-eighth Congress the time for successful action had arrived. In February, 1865, Congressman Eliot, from a committee set up for that purpose, reported a bill for the establishment of a freedmen's bureau. President Lincoln, February 9, 1865, laid before Congress a memorial from the officers of private freedmen's societies asking the establishment of the proposed bureau. A statement of this memorial might well be the slogan of those to-day seeking federal aid for education. "It is the magnitude, not the nature of the work that appalls us and drives us to the government for aid and support," said the memorialists of 1865. On March 3, 1865, the bill establishing the Bureau of Refugees, Freedmen and Abandoned Lands passed Congress and was signed by President Lincoln.

This bureau, under the direction of General Oliver Otis Howard, as commissioner, while set up originally for one year only, was by later enactment continued for about five years. Among its varied activities was promotion and supervision of the education of the freedmen. Not only private contributions, but also federal funds were used for this purpose. In Congress impassioned speeches were made in support of such educational work. Congressman Ignatius Donnelly of Minnesota pleaded ardently for federal aid, rejecting the idea that the matter should be left entirely to the individual states.

In the thirty-ninth Congress another important step was taken in the establishment of a national Bureau of Education. In the long debate on the bill for this purpose, the whole theory of federal responsibility for education was explored. Both the constitutionality and the expediency of it were fully discussed by very able men. On February 26, 1867, four days before the bill was finally enacted, Congressman Howe used prophetic language in his statement, "The struggle to educate the nation is just commencing, and commencing with this bill."

Contemporary with the passage of the legislation for the establishment of the national Bureau of Education was the establishment in the House of Representatives of the Committee on Education and Labor and in the Senate of the Committee on Education, later changed to the Committee on Education and Labor to correspond with the name of the similar committee of the House of Representatives.

In his final report in 1869 on the work of the Freedmen's Bureau, General Howard recommended that the general Government take the matter of the education of the freedmen in hand. "The law of self-preservation," he said, "will justify the national legislature in establishing through the Bureau of Education, or some other agency, a general system of free schools." Probably as a result of this recommendation, President Grant, in his first annual message to Congress, in 1869, remarked, "I would respectfully call your attention to the recommendation of the Secretary of the Interior for uniting the duties of supervising the educating of freedmen with the other duties developing upon the Commissioner of Education."

Following upon these recommendations, a number of bills to carry out such ideas were introduced in the second session of the forty-first Congress. Congressman Prosser of Tennessee in a speech on one of the bills on January 25, 1870, pointed out that the United States had previously appropriated 78,576,802 acres of land for education in a portion of the states and territories. He suggested that one half of the expense of the schools desired be met by the federal government and proposed for immediate expenses an appropriation of $2,200,000. Having in mind particularly education in the South, he proposed that Congress "come forward with aid and encouragement for the organization and maintenance for some years of schools." He was of the opinion that they should be "maintained for the space of at least two scholastic generations." To such proposals there was of course violent and determined opposition. In the debate party politics and regional interests are very apparent. A very detailed and careful study would be necessary to determine all the factors and ramifications. The general impression derived from reading the discussion is that philanthropic interest in freedmen and education was greatly supplemented by Republican Party hope to educate the freedmen for service in that party. But, though a bill to discontinue the Freedmen's Bureau and turn its funds over to the Commissioner of Education passed the House of Representatives, April 5, 1870, nothing resulted from other bills for federal aid for education.

In the third session of the forty-first Congress a bill was introduced by Congressman Arnell of Tennessee to set apart and devote to the common schools of the South all money arising from the sale of public lands for five years. For three months spasmodic debate occurred on this and other educational bills, but with no enactment of such legislation. President Grant, however, in his third annual message of December 4, 1871, championed Congressman Arnell's proposal in his statement, "Educational interest may well be served by the grant of the proceeds of the sale of public lands to settlers." Bills to carry out this presidential approval were promptly introduced in the second session of the forty-second Congress. In the extended debate which followed, Congressman Perce of Mississippi asserted that "the application of the proceeds of the public lands to educational purposes is not a new or startling measure," while like others at an even earlier time, Congressman Walls took the position that "if the State Governments are unwilling to provide equal facilities for all, then let the national Government take the matter in hand." To-day the matter is more one of inability than unwillingness, but the essential idea is much the same. A bill to provide an educational fund from the proceeds of the sale of public lands passed the House of Representatives on February 8, 1872, by a vote of 117 to 98, with 24 not voting. It failed to pass the Senate, but President Grant in his fourth annual message, December 2, 1872, recommended it as "a measure of such great importance to our real progress and so unanimously approved by the leading friends of education" that he commended it to the favorable attention of Congress. No immediate legislative result followed.

Again in the first session of the forty-third Congress, which met in December, 1873, educational bills were promptly introduced and ardently advocated, but with no resulting legislation.

In his seventh annual message, December 7, 1875, President Grant asserted that "the education of the masses becomes the first necessity for the preservation of our institutions." He recommended a constitutional amendment requiring states to furnish free schools. A flood of educational bills and debate followed in the first session of the forty-fourth Congress in the winter following, but again with no enactment of legislation. President Grant seems to have at last become weary of useless educational recommendations, for he dropped all mention of education from his eighth annual message of December 5, 1876. But congressional advocates of federal aid to education presented bills as usual. The defeat of such a bill in the House of Representatives March 3, 1877, by the overwhelming vote of 141 to 9 may indicate the waning of hopes and interest as well as weariness and pressure of business on the last day of the session.

President Rutherford B. Hayes, however, may be said to have revived and continued the agitation for federal aid to public schools. From the general tenor of his life it may be assumed that his interest in the matter was something more than mere party politics. In his inaugural address he said, "Universal suffrage should rest upon universal education. To this end," he added, "liberal and permanent provision should be made for the support of free schools by the State governments, and, if need be, supplemented by legitimate aid from national authority." Bills to apply the proceeds from the sales of federal lands to education were, therefore, promptly introduced in the first or special session of the forty-fifth Congress but without results in legislation. Undeterred, President Hayes in his first annual message of December 3, 1877, made the somewhat too strong statement, "The wisdom of legislation upon the part of Congress, in aid of the States for the education of the whole people in those branches of study which are taught in the common schools of the country is no longer a question." He promised his assent to any such measures.

No such measures, however, came forth from Congress. Again, in his second annual message, December 2, 1878, President Hayes urged educational legislation, using the argument of preparation for citizenship in his emphasis upon education, "as the resource for the advancement of the people in the requisite knowledge and appreciation of their rights and responsibilities as citizens." A bill was accordingly introduced in the first session of the forty-sixth Congress to apply the proceeds of the sales of public lands to popular education, but it failed to pass either house and therefore did not become law.

In his third annual message, December 1, 1879, President Hayes repeated his educational recommendations. "No more fundamental responsibility," he said, "rests upon Congress than that of devising appropriate measures of financial aid to education, supplemental to local action in the States and Territories and in the District of Columbia." Such aid he believed to be in accordance with precedents since 1787 and he advocated "measures in accordance with this traditional policy." In his fourth annual message, December 6, 1880, Hayes again recommended federal aid for public schools, in a plea which would fit to-day. "The means," he said, "at the command of the local and State authorities are in many cases inadequate to furnish free instruction to all who need it." "Whatever Government can fairly do to promote free popular education," he proclaimed, "ought to be done." He again urged the establishment of an educational fund from the net proceeds of the sales of the public lands. But in spite of all recommendations of President Hayes no legislation of the kind was passed during the four years of his term. In his second Congress, the forty-sixth, an educational bill did pass the Senate, but that was all that was done.

In his inaugural address in 1881, President Garfield took up the cudgels. He emphasized the dangers of illiteracy among voters, especially in the South with its recently enfranchised Negroes. Responsibility for education as a remedy he made national. The whole spirit of his inaugural address suggests that the assassination of President Garfield was a loss to national education.

With somewhat more reservation President Arthur adopted the program of his three predecessors. Any federal fund for such purposes he suggested might be "wisely distributed in the different states according to the ratio of illiteracy." In accordance with his recommendation, bills were introduced for federal aid to schools in the first session of the forty-seventh Congress. Long debates and masses of historical, legal and statistical data were the only result. In his second annual message, December 4, 1882, President Arthur again suggested federal aid as a supplement to other resources for the provision of public schools. After serious and lengthy debate the effort to pass such legislation was defeated in the Senate, February 24, 1883, by a vote of 82 to 80. But President Arthur returned to the subject in his third annual message of December 4, 1883. "I again submit," said he, "for the consideration of Congress whether some Federal aid should not be extended to public elementary education wherever adequate provision therefor has not already been made." In the first session of the forty-eighth Congress more bills were introduced making Federal appropriations for the purpose. Senator Blair, of New Hampshire, chairman of the Committee on Education and Labor, in promoting such measures, pronounced them "the logical consequence and true conclusion of the war," meaning of course the Civil War twenty years earlier. An educational bill passed the Senate, April 7, 1884, by a vote of 33 to 11, but since no action was taken in the House of Representatives, nothing in the way of legislation resulted.

For some reason not clearly apparent, President Cleveland in neither his first term, 1885–1889, nor his second term, 1893–1897, showed much interest in education. Nevertheless, such bills were introduced in the first session of the forty-ninth Congress and one of them passed the Senate, March 5, 1886, by a vote of 36 to 11, but again there was no action by the House of Representatives. In the second session of the same Congress only one bill for federal aid to schools was presented and no attention was paid to it. On the whole, the Democratic Party President and House of Representatives seemed to have been indifferent to educational moves of the Republican Party Senate.

Following the victory of the Republican Party in 1888 and the election of Benjamin Harrison as President, a new crop of bills for federal aid to public schools were introduced, most of which were buried in the Committee on Education and Labor and not one of which reached final enactment. In his first annual message of December 3, 1889, President Harrison took up the now twenty-five-year-old agitation. As his statement is the last of this particular series, it might be considered in detail. It will suffice here, however, to quote only three sentences: "National aid to education has heretofore taken the form of land grants, and in that form the constitutional power of Congress to promote the education of the people is not seriously questioned. I do not think it can be successfully questioned when the form is changed to that of a direct grant of money from the public treasury. Such aid should be as it always has been, suggested by some exceptional circumstances." In spite of this statement by this great lawyer, only one bill was introduced in the first session of the fifty-first Congress about federal aid for public schools, and it never came out of the committee to which it had been referred. Questions such as the tariff and currency now absorbed attention. The end of an era had also come with the restoration of complete Democratic Party and white control in the "solid South."

Largely owing to the maldistribution of wealth and of income, "exceptional conditions" again face the United States, and education is again in many places in need of federal aid. The quarter of a century after the Civil War has furnished us with much precedent for the demand, much factual data on the historical policy toward education of the Federal Government and an unusually complete array of the arguments and reasons for such federal aid. Incidentally federal aid to public schools in distressed areas of the country would help in the redistribution of wealth and of income, a thing greatly to be desired.

IN THE LIBERAL ARTS COLLEGE—THE REFERENCE LIBRARIAN, A PROFESSOR?

By PAUL ALLEN

REFERENCE LIBRARIAN, DARTMOUTH COLLEGE

Is the reference librarian to be the professor of the future? If one holds with a speaker at the Chicago convention of the American Library Association, the answer is in the affirmative. Those who too sharply criticize the speaker's assertion might consider the implications inherent in curricular changes instituted by the University of

Chicago. With the passing of a comprehensive examination the sole requirement for credits which are elsewhere earned only through the course system, the Chicago undergraduate may conceivably complete much of his college course without resort even to the syllabi and reading lists that are furnished when he registers. If one considers the speaker's idea improbable, would he agree with the opinion that the reference librarian will become merely a skilled technician on the card catalog? Between these alternatives lies the whole future of reference librarianship in the liberal arts college. The more conservative of those connected with education probably believe that neither professors nor librarians make any pretense that the one is able to do the other's work. And while this is probably true, many of those who so believe would also agree that a closer cooperation between professor and reference librarian is needed to increase the value of the work done by each.

Briefly, a proposal to effect this cooperation is that the number of reference librarians in a college library shall be increased and that they shall function in a manner similar to that of the consultants at the Library of Congress, or the research librarians at the University of Pennsylvania and Cornell. In libraries that have large reference staffs or in institutions where there are departmental libraries or many special collections in separate rooms, the system already obtains to a greater or lesser degree. Undoubtedly the proposed plan could be introduced most effectively in libraries which are intended to house all the book collections, without departmentalization, and where, hitherto, the reference department has functioned chiefly as an information bureau or has established itself as the means of answer to almost any question.

For many liberal arts colleges, a beginning might be made with a staff of five members, each responsible in a single field—English literature, economics, political science, history and sociology. In time there would be appointed members responsible in foreign literatures, the natural sciences, the exact sciences, and, as required, in other fields. In so far as this arrangement is based primarily on the book classification and secondarily on the usual academic organization of departments, it would be but little affected by changes in the latter. Such a staff would be in attendance during the hours that the library is open, and each member would have to be prepared, while doing his turn at the public desk of the department, to "double in brass." Let this not be considered undesirable, but rather think of the possibilities for keeping a staff alert, through the necessity of being able to furnish information on such varied subjects as death customs among the Aztecs, the Lancaster mutiny, the composer of the "Chocolate Soldier," pictures of the caps and gowns of foreign universities, the history of Fascism and a description of the course in contemporary civilizations at Columbia University.

Primarily, the members of such a department would be specialists in a particular field. In order to attract the right type of individual for this work, they should be members of the faculty, perhaps as "tutor" or, with longer service, as assistant professor or professor of their subject. Indeed, they might have been prepared to teach and at first might have one section of a course. However, if this work should grow, and as Mr. Borden pointed out in an article on "Creating Services," the tendency is for services offered in a library to have ever-increasing demands made upon them, shortly the entire time would have to be devoted to the library, and possibly an assistant would be required for an especially popular department. Though not active teachers, faculty status would make each member of the reference staff more familiar than he otherwise could be with the point of view of his respective department. Through close cooperation with his teaching colleagues, each would have a familiarity with the material offered by the department with which he was connected. Each reference librarian might help in the preparation of bibliographies and syllabi for his department's courses, particularly those instituted subsequent to his appointment. As a result of this familiarity with the department and its work, the reference librarian would be able to answer much more satisfactorily the questions of the students after lectures that present points in which they become interested or which they fail to understand. Such familiarity would eliminate the confusion that is often caused when the idea is garbled on the way from the classroom to the library, with the result that little or no assistance can be given. A trivial though indicative example of this sort of thing which sometimes requires reference librarians to be mind-readers, though not always successfully, was furnishing the student with "Democracy" by Scott Nearing, when the actual inquiry was for "Nearing Democracy" by Scott. And finally, in the departmental relationship, an important duty of such a reference librarian, would be as liaison agent between the library and the academic department—handling the department's requests and book-orders—keeping the members advised regarding accessions in their own and related fields.

In colleges, to-day, the method of instruction, even where the "tutorial" system has been adopted, is based largely on lectures or recitation groups, with the expectation that the student will accomplish a great deal of reading on which reports will be made; generally a "term" paper and sometimes several additional papers are required during the semester. The preceding statement applies to but a single course: ordinarily the student's schedule has five such courses! The proposed cooperation would be especially valuable for this system, and particularly so in the case of "majors," for the reference librarian would recognize immediately those majoring in his department and, through consultation with his colleagues and attendance at department and faculty meetings, would know the type of work expected of each student and the manner in which it should be performed. The reference librarian would be responsible for giving instruction to the students in the use of the bibliographical material in his field. For even though this is sometimes attempted under the present system, the experience has been that it is not satisfactory, when not obligatory, or when informally attempted with each student, who brings a problem in a field different from that of the previous inquirer. Usually the best that can be done is to indicate the most promising sources of the material, with a brief explanation of their use, while the less obvious sources, though no more difficult to use, and possibly of greater specific value, must be ignored because somebody is waiting for information on Mendel's law, or the ineffectiveness of "Journey's End" and "All Quiet on the Western Front" as incentives to peace. Again, as a member of the department, such a reference librarian well might have the authority to set the limit of the work which the student should perform in connection with his problem. Under the present system it is rather presumptuous for him to indicate that he considers certain material of little value—rather, he must present as much as possible to the student, who will make his choice from it or ask his instructor's advice. And, even if it were not presumptous, it would be almost impossible for the reference librarian to do such a thing, because his duties seldom allow him to thoroughly familiarize himself with the material of more than one or two fields of knowledge, and at best he has a rather superficial acquaintance with a rather wide range of things. And it is rare, by comparison, that a student presents a question dealing with a subject in which the reference librarian is interested and in whose literature he is well versed.

Under the proposed system the reference librarian would be responsible for a good background in his particular field, and need it be said, the extent of the library's collections in it. In such cases the reference librarian's advice might help to prevent the assignment of outside work in a phase of the field in which the library's resources were inadequate. Or, with faculty rank, the reference librarian might have the authority to set the student at work. For example: In the usual circumstances, the student talks enthusiastically with his professor in October about the paper he will do for that term. Then, on the day before Christmas vacation begins, the same student comes to the library and withdraws the few books on his subject that are still to be found in the library. These books are taken home for the vacation with the expectation that even if he does not return with the paper written, at least the reading for it will be accomplished. Alas, he returns in January with nothing read, and the first few days are lost in matching accounts of holiday experiences. And then mad work is begun on the paper and on several "book-reports" that must be handed in for other courses. And finally, the paper is turned in, if the student is fortunate, at the last class of the semester; if not, possibly by late afternoon of the day of the final examination in the course. Under the proposed system, the reference librarian would receive the names of the students and their selected topics, and possibly the instructor's suggested outline, immediately after a choice had been made. He would be advised of any important changes or developments at future conferences between the student and the instructor. Then, if the student has not reported within reasonable time to the reference librarian, and a definite bibliography prepared, the reference librarian would have authority to send for him, and have the work begun. In this connection there are two benefits which probably would result immediately. First would be the decrease in lost and damaged books, if one holds with the theory that many disappearances and mutilations result because the student is pressed for time. Second, would be the partial elimination of the turning in of cribbed or plagiarized work, which is discovered in almost every case to be a result of the dilatory nature of the collegian, and the sudden realization that a dead-line is upon him—which perhaps is encouraged somewhat by "theme bureaus" and similar rackets.

It may be objected that this is too paternalistic an attitude, but I believe that it is a reasonable and desirable function of the reference department, if it is adequately staffed to do it and has been given the necessary sanctions. Under the present system of college instruction there is often no opportunity for the instructor to have the necessary freedom to direct his student in the "outside" work. The classes are too large, and again, many students have a complex about bothering the instructor. As a consequence, a topic is selected, possibly in consultation with the instructor—many times from a list of subjects that is furnished the class, and the instructor hears no more of it until he finds the paper on his desk for grading. A closer relationship between the reference librarian and a department would enable the reference librarian to handle some of the details, recognized as desirable, but impossible to do in connection with this work. With comparatively long office hours, he would be available almost always to the students, so that they would not feel that they were intruding on private time. If the reference librarian of a particular field were not available when a student called, his colleagues on duty might take a few notes for him, and arrange a definite appointment. When the student again called, there might be a brief bibliography prepared for him; at least the literature available in the library on the particular subject of the paper would have been surveyed, so that the first meeting would be productive. On the other hand, the reference librarians on duty should still be able to dispose of those questions to which an answer must be furnished immediately. However, with the previously mentioned authority to call a student for consultation, it is probable that much of the student work requiring an answer instantly would disappear.

It may be objected also that much of this is properly the work of the teacher, but it is also true that much of it is routine work, from which the teacher should be and must be freed if he is to carry on his teaching successfully. Besides teaching, preparation and necessary outside activities, there is little time to direct individually the work of twenty-five, fifty or one hundred students in the preparation of a bibliography for their papers, even once a semester, let alone the several times that is required in some cases. Obviously, if the work is going to be done, it might logically be done in the library, and if not by the instructor, possibly by the reference librarian. But if the reference department is going to be considered solely as an information desk, it will not be staffed to undertake a program which involves so much additional work, nor will the staff have been given authority to lend effectiveness to the little that it can do.

To digress, it has often been said that one may lead a horse to water but one can not make him drink. In considering the problem of the college student, one sometimes wonders if he has even been led to the water (of knowledge) and if he has, has any inducement or effort been made to make him take a swallow? For usually, if one can succeed with that, the drinking comes easily. It is sometimes said that the solution of state universities for the problem of large admissions that are forced upon them is to let every student work out his own salvation—"flunking out" the hindmost at the end of the first semester. This may be so. Probably the state has done its share in providing the facilities for an education. However, a different attitude should apply in a private institution. For it would seem that an institution dependent on private funds and the good will of a private clientele has a responsibility to those whom it admits to do all in its power to inspire them to learn. It is not an adequate answer to say that a private institution has provided facilities and that it is up to the admitted individual to make the best of them, because as a result of his admission, two others had to be denied the privilege. Such an argument is specious if one accepts that, of the three applicants, the best was selected, and the two rejected were lacking in qualities the college considered desirable. On the contrary, all three applications were made because it was expected that the private institution would give them something that could not be got elsewhere. Those who sought only facilities would have found them at less expense, and sometimes superior in quality, at their state university.

In many cases, one is convinced that the failure of students to do more than the necessary minimum in the liberal arts college, even though they come with fine secondary school records, is due largely to the impersonal educative system to which they are subjected. Note the difference between those prepared in good secondary schools, where classes are small, and those who enter from the average high school. (We can not consider here the volte-face that often occurs before the class is graduated, but it is commonly accepted that in September of the freshman year, the advantage is all to the student from the good private school.) If we are going to continue to have the lectures and group recitations in college, and expect the student to work with few restrictions, save his presence at class, then he should be furnished some additional assistance which will help him in those matters to which his instructors can not give attention, or which he is unwilling to bring to the attention of the instructor. If we do not do this I believe that the liberal arts college has failed in its responsibility to education, and we may say that, instead of leading a student to an oasis, he is being directed to a mirage, towards which we ourselves would not move.

And finally, besides rendering valuable service to the department and to students, the value of such a reference librarian to the library would be inestimable. The collections in his particular field might be built up under his direction, in which he would have a more objective point of view, ordinarily toward the complete library resources, than those who are teachers of the subject. His services would be valuable also in aiding with the classification and cataloging so that these would better serve both patrons in general and the faculty of a particular department.

In partial support of the whole matter, may we point to the departmental librarian, from whom patrons receive, and rightfully expect, much more expert service and advice, ordinarily, than in the same given field they might obtain from the reference librarian. But are there not great potentialities in a system such as is proposed, where the reference librarian could confine his efforts to a single field, and have at his disposal in one building, unhampered by departmental collections, the entire library resources of a college?

It is not intended that the suggested program should usurp in the slightest degree any prerogative which properly belongs to the teacher. Rather it is an attempt to point out certain things which it seems desirable for a liberal arts college to undertake in greater degree than it has done in the past, and to suggest that they be centered upon the reference department and the reference librarian as the place and person for the most convenient and effective performance of these duties. The advantages of such a closer cooperation between the reference library and the academic department seems to provide a way and to promise great benefits. And lastly, the whole proposal is made, not with a fixed plan in mind, but rather for the express purpose of inviting critical suggestions from which a more specific and definitely valuable program might be evolved.

EDUCATIONAL EVENTS

THE EDUCATIONAL SITUATION IN CHINA

NEWS from the United States, that school appropriations have been curtailed because of a temporary financial depression, is greeted in China to-day almost with incredulity, according to Dorothy Gould, special correspondent of *The Christian Science Monitor*. In China it is regarded as axiomatic that "the hope of our nation is in its youth" and, more now than ever before, interest is focused on education and child welfare work.

Statistics revealing that there are 3,000,000 illiterate children in Hopei, the province in which Peiping and Tientsin are located, while only 700,000 children there go to school, seem discouraging at first glance. But when one considers that Hopei now is virtually a buffer state between Japan and China, over which bombing airplanes have been flying daily, it seems remarkable not so much that children lack primary schooling there, as that any one should care enough to compile such statistics.

All over China a similar census is being taken. Nanking, the capital city, confesses that it has 56,317 children of school age, only 20,000 of whom are being educated. The Ministry of Education there reports that only seven of every 10,000 Chinese citizens obtain the equivalent of a high-school diploma.

The most important thing that these figures disclose is that, for the first time in its 4,000 cultured years, China is taking keen interest in all its children. An entirely new conception of primary education is being inaugurated. Instead of preparing a few favored youths to be mandarins, the government now is devoting its chief attention and most of its educational funds to giving elementary learning to as many children as possible.

This new type of schooling aims to provide complete courses for its pupils, instead of merely introducing them to a higher education which few of them can afford to complete at present. A primary school graduate, according to the new program, will be fitted for duties as a citizen and will have acquired a vocation. Every approved primary school in China must now offer vocational courses.

Compared with China's traditional ideas of education, such changes are revolutionary. Only one generation ago, under the stern rule of Confucian teachers, little boys sat from dawn until dusk in sweltering rooms in summer and freezing rooms in winter, droning out loud the "Four Books" and the "Five Classics," which they were too young to understand. When slightly older, they composed essays based on these classics and wrote poems. They were released for the day only when it became too dark to read any more.

This, until a few years ago, formed the sum total of Chinese teaching. A great improvement was made when the Nationalist Government introduced a new type of text-book to take the place of dull lists of names and archaic philosophy. The new readers had simple illustrated stories about boys, animals and household affairs, but were marred by undue emphasis on international politics, a subject almost as unsuitable for young minds as the Confucian Analects. Especially unfortunate was the anti-foreign propaganda which blighted the pages of these otherwise attractive primers.

A revised edition of these Nationalist primers has now been issued. The ideals of Dr. Sun Yatsen and the Kuomintang Party are not slighted, but instead of picturing fat foreign men smoking cigars and grinding poor China under their feet, the new text-books have page after page of foreigners realistically portrayed in their native homes. Stories of Chinese heroes are interlarded with illustrated biographies of George Washington, Thomas Edison and other worthy foreigners.

THE AMERICAN PEOPLES COLLEGE IN EUROPE

One-month Pocono study tours will be made possible this summer for the first time by the American Peoples College in Europe. The short trip, designed for those who wish to make a short vacation count for the most possible, will include five days at the informal college center in Oetz-in-Tyrol, one of the most picturesque spots in the Austrian Alps, where lectures may be heard by outstanding European leaders on current European conditions, and where the life of a typical little Tyrolean village may be enjoyed. The study tour will include Paris, London, Milan, Venice, Innsbruck and Brussels.

Besides the regular nine-and-a-half-week and three-month study tours in psychology, economics, physical education, youth and youth movements, adult education and general cultural and social developments abroad, given under the auspices of the American Peoples College, two new travel-study courses were given last year, one in drama and one in European gardens and horticulture. Both proved so successful that they will be repeated this year.

The drama courses, under the direction of Lucile Hoerr Charles, varying in length from nine weeks to a year, not only give an opportunity for American amateurs to study the theater at first hand in the dramatic centers of Europe and come into personal contact with European actors, producers and playwrights, but also make it possible for those so inclined to tour up and down the Tyrolean valley near the college, presenting American plays in the picturesque village inns and schoolhouses. The courses this year will, of course, include attendance at the Passion Play at Oberammergau.

"European Gardens and Horticulture" is a study tour designed for amateur as well as professional gardeners and landscape architects.

During the time spent in the Tyrol there will be lectures and discussions on recent studies in the fields of plant culture, gardening and garden arrangement, as developed in the various European countries, and private and public gardens and horticultural schools will be visited in Paris, Geneva, Vienna, Prague, Dresden, Berlin, Helsinki, Copenhagen and London, with an opportunity given to spend some time in Italy.

The American Peoples College was founded five years ago as a non-profit-making institution in an effort to make a combination of European study and travel possible for young Americans of limited means and thus bring about a better international understanding. Through the cooperation of foreign governments and foreign educational organizations the college has been able to reduce the cost of living and travel in Europe to a minimum for those taking their Pocono study tours.

Soren A. Mathiasen is the educational director, and the advisory committee includes Professor John Dewey, William H. Kilpatrick and Goodwin Watson, of Columbia University; Professor Harry A. Overstreet, of the College of the City of New York; Dr. J. B. Nash, of New York University; Dean Alvin Johnson, of the New School for Social Research, and Dr. Nat T. Frame, of the University of West Virginia. Full particulars about this year's program may be obtained from Mr. Webster Bowers, American Peoples College in Europe, 545 Fifth Avenue, New York City.

THE FEDERAL RELIEF AGENCIES AND EDUCATION

COMMISSIONER GEORGE F. ZOOK has summarized in a press release from the Office of Education the names and functions of the emergency agencies of the Federal Government which are sponsoring or cooperating with educational undertakings.

Through its codes the NRA (National Recovery Administration) has banished child labor, thus increasing school enrolment, has affected all supplies bought for schools, has set up training standards and wage rates for apprentices and learners, and has sharply increased the extent of the problem confronting schools in helping Americans to make advantageous use of their leisure time.

The PWA (Public Works Administration) has allotted more than $50,000,000 of its $3,300,000,000 in grants and loans for the construction and repair of school buildings.

The plans of the FHC (Federal Housing Corporation) for slum clearance and large-scale housing include consideration of nursery schools, playgrounds and other educational projects.

The CWA (Civil Works Administration) has engaged thousands of unemployed persons to paint and repair schools, improve school grounds and playgrounds which had been neglected due to lack of funds. CWA workers are making an occupational survey of the deaf and hard of hearing to provide schools with data for the guidance of handicapped persons.

The FERA (Federal Emergency Relief Administration) is employing 40,000 unemployed teachers on six kinds of projects: (1) to teach in rural schools, which otherwise would have to close due to lack of funds; (2) to teach adults to read and write; (3) to provide general adult education; (4) to teach persons in need of vocational education; (5) to teach persons suffering from physical handicaps; (6) to organize and teach nursery schools. Members of the Office of Education staff have been assigned to help the states carry out these undertakings.

The Office of Education is developing an educational program in cooperation with the War Department for the ECW (Emergency Conservation Work, also called Civilian Conservation Corps). Educational advisers are being selected for 1,468 camps.

The AAA (Agricultural Adjustment Administration) is enlisting the aid of vocational education in the development of the farm product control program.

The TVA (Tennessee Valley Authority) is combining work and study for its workers in the big hydroelectric projects in order that when those employed return to their communities they will be trained to carry on other activities.

The FSHC (Federal Subsistence Homesteads Corporation) has planned to have schools serve the educational, social and recreational needs of the community.

The Federal Office of Education is advising and cooperating with nearly all the emergency agencies on the educational aspects of their tasks. Commissioner Zook has called more than twenty conferences of prominent educators in various fields of school work to help solve the problems arising in connection with recovery program activities. Members of the Office of Education staff are helping to direct emergency educational projects and are also acting as liaison workers, reporting to school officials throughout the United States the implications for education in recovery program developments. Hundreds of questions from school administrators about the recovery program as it applies to education are received and answered daily by the Office of Education. Through circulars and publications the Federal Office of Education is keeping more than 7,000 county and city superintendents in constant touch with new activities in Washington.

FELLOWSHIPS AT HARVARD COLLEGE

FIVE new Harvard College prize fellowships have been created and will be awarded for the first time in July, 1934, to students entering the freshman class the following September, according to an announcement made by President James Bryant Conant on February 15. The new fellowships are unique in that they are large enough to provide for full college expenses, with maximum stipends of $1,000 in the freshman year and of $1,200 thereafter. They are conceived, it is stated, with the express purpose of bringing together at Harvard College outstanding students from every section of the United States. At the outset, they will be reserved for young men now living and attending school in six Middle Western states—Ohio, Illinois, Indiana, Michigan, Wisconsin and Minnesota. If this initial experiment proves successful, President Conant states, it is hoped to establish additional fellowships for students from other sections of the country.

It is provided that the fellowships will be open not only to students who enter Harvard College by taking the examinations of the College Entrance Examination Board, but also to those who enter under the Harvard "upper-seventh plan." This plan, inaugurated in 1924, permits the entrance without examination of students who stand in the highest seventh of their graduating classes and have the unqualified recommendation of their high-school principals. An endeavor to meet the needs of those who have attended public high schools in rural communities, towns or small cities, and whose courses are not specially designed to meet the requirements of the College Entrance Examination Board, gave rise to this system of admissions.

Stipends for the fellowships have been set to cover all essential college expenses, making it possible for recipients to devote their undivided attention to college work, however limited their financial resources. For students in the upper classes, the maximum is increased to $1,200, in order to provide a somewhat larger allowance for books and for board and rooms in the Harvard houses. Provision is made for the fellowships to be adjusted downward, so that students with some resources of their own would receive less than the maximum stipend.

At the present time, the committee on scholarships awards approximately 540 scholarships to students, representing a total amount of $168,000. The ultimate objective, according to President Conant, will be to have full-term fellowships sufficient to provide for 10 or 15 per cent. of each class.

REPORT OF THE NATIONAL SURVEY OF SECONDARY EDUCATION

THE failure of research bureaus in city school systems to conduct more frequent investigations which promise to modify and improve educational practises is declared "highly unfortunate" in a monograph on "Research in Secondary Schools," recently issued by the Government Printing Office. This criticism, however, is offset by the facts that the research movement in education is relatively new, that each bureau of research has had to work out its own problems and that bureaus must at first render services to administration. It is shown that the major portion of the time of research bureaus is confined to the compilation of facts and statistics. "If bureaus of research in city systems are to lead the way to a sounder educational program, they will find it necessary to place emphasis on fundamental problems of educational practise rather than on the mere compilation and publication of facts and statistics," the report stresses.

Prepared by William H. Zeigel, Jr., specialist in school administration of the National Survey of Secondary Education, the monograph discloses that from the establishment of the first bureaus in 1912, the number has grown rapidly until there are at present 150 bureaus of research in city school systems, and about 95 others divided among state departments of education, state educational associations, state universities and colleges, teachers colleges and secondary schools. About half of the bureaus have been established since 1925, and a fourth since 1928.

The scope of the investigation concerning research in secondary schools involves a study of the personnel of educational research bureaus, the undertakings of research departments in city school systems and in individual secondary schools, the research undertakings carried on by individual secondary school staff members not officially connected with research bureaus or departments, and the nature of research conducted in secondary education within schools and school systems. It was found that few bureaus of research have been organized in secondary schools and that nearly all research in secondary education carried on in school systems is conducted by bureaus of research in city school systems.

An examination of the functions of bureaus of research revealed 24 different specific activities, most of them administrative or supervisory. The functions performed involve such activities as: To administer achievement and mental tests, to classify pupils, to train teachers for special testing, to prepare and publish reports, to disseminate educational information, to guide and supervise research studies carried on by teachers, to answer questionnaires for the school systems and to give educational guidance.

In listing the types of studies most frequently made, Dr. Zeigel states that "the greatest proportions of bureaus are authorized to conduct investigations concerning pupil failures and promotions, but the greatest proportions of bureaus reported the completion of studies involving standardized examination and achievement tests."

In 1929–30 a total of 1,116 studies was reported in progress in 53 bureaus of research. Of this number, 653, or approximately half, relate primarily to the field of secondary education. In the field of secondary education, curriculum studies, standardized examinations and achievement tests constitute nearly 31 per cent. of the total number of studies reported to be in progress. About 40 per cent. of the total number of studies relating primarily to secondary education deal with some form of test administration or test construction. Slightly more than 50 per cent. of the total number of reports from studies in 1929–30 were mimeographed.

THE ESTABLISHMENT OF A CHILDREN'S FILM BOARD

The establishment of children's departments in the offices of all motion picture producers was urged by Dr. W. W. Charters, of the Ohio State University, before the quadrennial convention of the International Council of Religious Education in Chicago, at which educational leaders of 41 Protestant churches were assembled, as reported by *The Christian Science Monitor*.

In learning how to control movies for the public good, a lesson might be taken, Dr. Charters said, from the publishers of school text-books and children's literature, who, although in business for profit, give the most careful attention to the desires of parents and teachers. Commissions of educators examine text-book manuscripts to make sure that they contain nothing "bad for the child," and the publishers are scrupulous in revising the books to meet recommendations. But there are as yet no standards set by the public for the children's motion pictures. As a result, young people are getting an unbalanced diet, with three fourths of the pictures shown in 1931 built around themes of crime, sex and romantic love.

Dr. Charters thought that, if pictures more suited to children were brought out, producers might find a larger undeveloped market for their product in schools, churches and other places where children congregate, since parents and educators would undoubtedly be eager to show pictures which they believed valuable in the education of children.

Such pictures would be of the utmost educational value. "Good pictures with religious ideals," Dr. Charters said, "could do more than any other character-building material could do in the same amount of time. It has been shown by actual tests that a single exposure to great ideals in movies will have a permanent effect on children, actually changing their attitude on a given subject. Certainly if bad movies can debase taste, good ones can raise it."

More vigorous public control not only of motion pictures but of the channels of the air, that the radio as well as the movies may be used to serve social purposes, appears necessary in Dr. Charters' opinion, and the public will no doubt find suitable "techniques of control" in the next 25 years.

That something other than legislative control must be looked for to bring about better use of the nation's radio channels was suggested by Joy Elmer Morgan, editor of the *Journal of the National Education Association.* His recent experiences in Washington had convinced him, he said, that neither of the political parties could be expected to do much to control radio, since both were deeply in debt to the two leading broadcasting companies for radio services during the last presidential campaign.

On the other hand, he thought that the public itself is demanding more educational service from the radio. A recent broadcast on "How Can a Man Educate Himself?" brought letters from all parts of the United States. An expansion of the educational facilities of the country may be expected, as the people come to see that with technological improvements fewer people are needed in bread-and-butter occupations, and more can spend their time in services for the benefit of humanity, whether in the field of education, religion or recreation.

CONFERENCE OF NATIONAL ORGANIZATIONS FOR PHYSICALLY HANDICAPPED CHILDREN

New York University, in cooperation with the National Council on the Physically Handicapped and the National Committee for Mental Hygiene, will conduct a national conference on the education and rehabilitation of handicapped children on March 9 and 10 at the university. Eighteen national organizations, concerned with the problems of nearly ten million handicapped children, will participate in the conference, which will have as its chief purpose the coordination of efforts of the many agencies interested in unfortunate children.

The School of Education of the university will act as conference host, with Professor Harvey W. Zorbaugh, director of special education, as chairman of the committee on arrangements. The forthcoming convocation was believed by Professor Zorbaugh to be the first occasion when so many national organizations would join in a discussion of their common problems.

Seventy recognized experts in the many phases of physical, mental, vocational and social handicaps of children will participate in the formal speaking program, and other specialists will take part in group discussion in the individual section-conferences of each member organization. Professor Zorbaugh expected 2,500 persons to attend the conference.

National organizations which will be represented include: The International Society for Crippled Children, the National Rehabilitation Association, the American Occupational Therapy Association, the National Society for the Prevention of Blindness, the American Foundation for the Blind, the American Federation of Organizations for the Hard of Hearing, the National Education Association, the Department of Lip Reading, the National Association of the Deaf, the National Tuberculosis Association, the American Heart Association, the American Orthopsychiatric Association, the American Society for the Study of Disorders of Speech, the Child Study Association of America, the American Association for the Study of Mental Deficiency, the National Conference of Juvenile Agencies and the American Association of Visiting Teachers.

On the basis of recent surveys, Professor Zorbaugh states that one of the greatest problems confronting social agencies at the present time is that of malnutrition. Approximately six million children are suffering from malnutrition, he said, while three million others are suffering from serious specialized handicaps and an additional 625,000 are suffering from diseases of the heart.

"The present nation-wide tendency to cut the budgets of public schools and community welfare funds bears down most heavily on physically and mentally handicapped children," Professor Zorbaugh asserts. "Throughout the country boards of education have been curtailing special services for handicapped children as a means of balancing budgets and meeting deficits.

"It is natural, in a time of social stress and crisis, to think less in terms of the individual and to turn our attention to fundamental problems of social organization and broad social programs. As a result of this shift of public attention, the individual, unless he is economically dependent, is left to shift for himself. For the handicapped child, in need of special educational and social services, this tendency is fraught with tragedy, which will be felt long after we have forgotten the present economic depression.

"The organizations participating in the conference believe that it will result in more cooperative planning among the many agencies throughout the country which are interested in the problems of the handicapped, a cooperation which is as urgently needed in this field as in other fields of endeavor."

EDUCATIONAL NOTES AND NEWS

AMOS W. W. WOODCOCK, formerly federal prohibition administrator, was elected president of St. John's College, Annapolis, Md., on February 17 to succeed Dr. Douglas Huntly Gordon.

OWEN D. YOUNG was elected a member of the Board of Regents of the University of the State of New York on February 13.

PRESIDENT ROOSEVELT has designated six college and university presidents and one dean as members of the board of visitors to the United States Naval Academy for 1934. The board includes Dr. R. B. von KleinSmid, president of the University of Southern California; Dr. K. C. M. Sills, president of Bowdoin College; Dr. M. L. Brittain, president of the Georgia School of Technology; Dr. Charles R. Richards, president of Lehigh University; Dean H. E. Clifford, of the School of Engineering at Harvard University; Rear Admiral Ralph Earle, retired, president of Worcester Polytechnic Institute, and the Reverend W. Coleman Nevils, S.J., president of Georgetown University.

DR. BESSIE CARTER RANDOLPH was inaugurated as president of Hollins College on February 21.

DR. S. PARKES CADMAN was elected to the board of trustees of the Berkeley Institute, Brooklyn, N. Y., at the annual meeting of the board on February 17. Dr. Cadman will serve for three years.

PROFESSOR SIMEON E. LELAND, of the University of Chicago, was appointed recently by Secretary of the Treasury Morgenthau to work out a program for federal aid to municipalities.

DR. GLENN FRANK, president of the University of Wisconsin, received the honorary degree of doctor of laws from Temple University on February 15 on the occasion of its fiftieth anniversary celebration. Dr. Frank delivered the founder's day oration.

DR. EDWARD ELLERY, acting president of Union College at Schenectady, N. Y., announced on February 17 the chairmen of the four divisions of study into which the departments of the college have recently been integrated, as follows: Dr. Harrison G. Coffin, professor of Greek, chairman of the division of languages and literature; Dr. Earl E. Cummins, professor of economics, chairman of the division of social studies; Dean Charles F. F. Garis, professor of mathematics, chairman of the division of mathematics and science. Dean Ernst J. Berg, professor of electrical engineering, has been chairman of the division of engineering since 1932.

THE New York Economic Council has announced the formation of an educational advisory committee to serve in the interests of public school officials. Members of the committee include Dr. Henry Holmes, dean of the Harvard Graduate School of Education; Dr. William S. Learned, of the Carnegie Foundation for the Advancement of Teaching; Dr. Charles R. Mann, director of the American Council on Education; Dr. Albert B. Meredith, head of the department of school administration at New York University, and Dr. Frank E. Spaulding, professor of education in the Graduate School of Yale University.

ABEL DECAUX, professor of organ at the Eastman School of Music in Rochester, New York, and formerly professor of organ at the Schola Cantorum in Paris, has recently been awarded the cross of the French Legion of Honor for his services as composer and teacher of music.

DR. ANNIE J. CANNON, professor of astronomy at Harvard University, has utilized the prize of $1,000 awarded her last year by the Association to Aid Scientific Work by Women to found an award which will honor other women for distinguished contribution to astronomy. The American Astronomical Society will administer this endowment, and the first award of the Annie J. Cannon Prize in Astronomy will be made next December. Women of all countries will be eligible to the award, which will be made triennially.

JAMES M. SPINNING, deputy superintendent of schools of Rochester, N. Y., has been elected by the Board of Education to succeed Superintendent Herbert S. Weet, who has resigned after twenty-two years of service.

THE REVEREND FREDERICK R. MARTINEZ, C. M., professor of Spanish and sociology at De Paul University, has been appointed assistant dean of the College of Liberal Arts and Sciences of the university.

MRS. ANNIE NATHAN MEYER, founder and trustee of Barnard College, was the guest of honor at a reception held at the college on February 19, her sixty-seventh birthday.

DR. WILLIAM H. HOLMES, superintendent of schools in Mount Vernon, N. Y., received a memorial book from the high-school students of the city at their Washington's Birthday exercises. The event celebrated his twentieth year as head of the Mount Vernon school system.

JOSE CLEMENTE OROZCO, visiting professor of art at Dartmouth College since 1932, was guest of honor on February 16 at a banquet held to celebrate the completion of his frescoes, "Epic of Civilization on the American Continent," which cover more than three thousand square feet of wall space in the Baker Memorial Library of the college.

A PORTRAIT of Professor Vida D. Scudder, poet and professor emeritus of English literature at Wellesley College, was unveiled on February 10 in the art museum of the college at the meeting of the Wellesley College Alumnae Council.

HARRY BRYANT CENTER, head of the department of journalism at Boston University since its founding twenty years ago, was the guest of honor at a dinner given on February 16 by one hundred alumni and undergraduates.

HERBERT A. BORK, comptroller at the University of Wisconsin since 1927, has resigned his position to become business manager for the Oregon State Board of Higher Education.

PROFESSOR CALVERT MAGRUDER, vice-dean of the Harvard Law School, has been appointed vice-chairman of the New England Regional Labor Board.

DR. CHEVALIER JACKSON, originator of the bronchoscope, has recently joined the faculty of the Woman's Medical College of Pennsylvania as professor of bronchoscopy and chief of the new bronchoscopic clinic at the college hospital.

DR. N. L. SIMS, professor of sociology at Oberlin College; F. C. McFarlane, principal of Dunbar High School, Dayton, Ohio, and R. H. Garner, state director of the Young Men's Christian Associations in Ohio colleges, have been elected to membership on the board of counselors of the Ohio International Institute. These elections, increasing the board membership to twenty-five, were held at the fourth annual meeting of the institute at Wilberforce University on February 12.

DR. HAROLD J. NOBLE, associate professor of history at the University of Oregon, has been elected a member of the American Council of the Institute of Pacific Relations.

DR. SERGE ELISSEEFF, formerly of the University of Paris and recently appointed professor of Far Eastern Languages at Harvard University, has been made director of the Harvard-Yenching Institute. He will assume his new duties in September.

PROFESSOR HOYT H. HUDSON, chairman of the department of English at Princeton University, has accepted an invitation to become a visiting scholar at the Huntington Library and Art Gallery at San Marino, California.

PROFESSOR ARCHIBALD A. HILL, professor of English at the University of Virginia, has been granted a fellowship by the General Education Board to study methods of linguistic research at Brown University, under the direction of Professor Hans Kurath.

THE REVEREND CHARLES W. BALDWIN, one of the original committee responsible for the founding of Goucher College and the oldest living graduate of Yale University, will be the principal speaker at the fiftieth anniversary celebration of Goucher College to be held on March 8.

DR. JOHN LIVINGSTON LOWES, Francis Lee Higginson professor of English literature at Harvard University, delivered an address on "The Modern Language Association and Humane Scholarship" before the Harvard Modern Language Conference on February 19.

THE board of trustees of Vassar College announced the following promotions on February 15: H. Marjorie Crawford, assistant professor of chemistry, to associate professor; Marie H. Lelavandier, assistant professor of French, to associate professor; Louise Fargo Brown, associate professor of history, to professor, and Ruth M. MacKaye, instructor in zoology, to assistant professor.

THE following appointments at Yale University have been announced by President Angell. Cornelius B. Osgood has been named curator of anthropology in the Peabody Museum of Natural History; Hugh M. Wilson, assistant professor of radiology, and Jean Boorsch, assistant professor of French.

NEW YORK UNIVERSITY has added thirty-two members to its instructional staff, according to an announcement issued on February 8. The list of appointments includes twenty-one instructors, nine assistants, one lecturer and one faculty lecturer.

FOUR members of the faculty of Wellesley College have been granted leaves of absence: William A. Campbell, associate professor of art; Alice M. Ottley, associate professor of botany; Edith Smaill, assistant professor of speech, and Helen Sard Hughes, professor of English literature and chairman of the department.

WESLEY J. MCCARTY, professor of accounting at Boston University for the past sixteen years, died on February 11, at the age of sixty years.

HENRI B. GALLIETT, professor of French at Wilmington College, died on February 13 at the age of sixty-eight years.

DR. FRANK PUTERBAUGH BACHMAN, director of surveys and field studies at George Peabody College and a former director of the General Education Board of the Rockefeller Foundation, died on February 17. Dr. Bachman was sixty-eight years of age.

DR. JOSEPH A. MOSHER, associate professor of public speaking at the College of the City of New York since 1907, died on February 6. He was fifty-two years of age.

DR. ERNESTO QUESADA, who in 1916 became the first occupant of the Chair of Latin-American History and Economics at Harvard University, died on February 8, at the age of seventy-six years.

DR. WALLACE NELSON STEARNS, authority in the field of Biblical literature and education, died on February 4. He was sixty-seven years old.

MRS. IRENE WHALEN, formerly superintendent of girls at Mount Holyoke College and at Rosemary Hall, died on February 8.

THE University of Minnesota's medical research and graduate student fund, established by a $1,500,000 donation from Dr. William J. Mayo and Dr. Charles Mayo in 1915, has recently been augmented by an additional gift of $500,000 from the original donors.

DAVID E. ROSS, president of the board of trustees at Purdue University, has presented a tract of 122 acres to the university. This land and an adjoining tract of 340 acres, donated to the university several years ago, will be used as a site for an airport.

WALTER STALB, bursar of the College of the City of New York, announced on February 13 that the members of the faculty of the college had contributed over $10,000 to a fund providing for employment for needy students in the period from January, 1933, to January, 1934. More than five hundred students have been assisted by this fund.

THE Helen Kenyon Hall of Physical Education at Vassar College, named in honor of Helen Kenyon, chairman of the board of trustees, was dedicated on February 23. Dr. William Darrach, a trustee and dean emeritus of the College of Physicians and Surgeons at Columbia University, delivered the dedicatory address.

THE Board of Education of New York City moved, on February 14, to eliminate multiple job holding in the public schools of the city. The resolution putting the plan in effect stated that no person in the system should hold both day and night school positions unless specifically certified by the Board of Superintendents and approved by the Board of Education. Dr. Harold G. Campbell, superintendent of schools, declared that the plan would not disrupt the existing organization but that in new appointments no teacher would be assigned more than one position.

AN expansion program, calling for the expenditure of $1,000,000 at Susquehanna University, has been announced by Dr. Morris Smith, president of the institution. Four new buildings, including a gymnasium to replace the one recently destroyed by fire, will be erected. Work on the gymnasium will begin immediately.

THIRTY-SIX thousand Michigan school boys and girls, organized into safety patrols and auxiliaries to protect children at street crossings, have reduced the state's accident rate by 25 per cent., according to the 1933 report of H. O. Rounds, director of the safety and traffic division of the Automobile Club of Michigan. Mr. Round reports that 85 per cent. of the schools are cooperating in the movement.

DISCUSSION

SUBSISTENCE HOMESTEADING AND PROGRESSIVE EDUCATION: THE SIGNIFICANCE OF DENMARK'S EXPERIENCE

FOR some years, I have been impressed by a general lack, among American students of education, of knowledge of, or at least of interest in what seems to me to be one of the most important and inspiring chapters in the whole history of education. This chapter, moreover, deals with an institution whose purpose and results are quite closely related to the philosophy of those who call themselves Progressive educators and who occupy such a large part of the educational stage to-day. This institution is the Danish folk high school.

This impression concerning American educators was confirmed by what I observed at and learned about the National Conference on Subsistence Homesteading, which was held in Dayton, Ohio, on December 8, 9 and 10. (I may say, in passing, that I regard it as one of the most interesting and valuable conferences which I have ever attended.) Those who arranged the program recognized that subsistence homesteading has very important educational bearings, and that these are in close alignment with the objectives of Progressive education. Hence they very properly provided for one session devoted to a discussion of "Educational Organization," in which Progressive educators had the leading places. At this session, many interesting and important things were said, but the Danish folk high school, the example *par excellence* of an educational institution in our part of the world, which has a record of successful accomplishment in remaking life for the masses, was not so much as mentioned.

Surely few topics could be more pertinent to a discussion of educational questions by Progressive educators at a conference on subsistence homesteading. Progressive educators believe that the school can and must be made an effective instrument for the progressive improvement of the social order, rather than merely a means for the initiation of the younger generation into life as it now is. Many Progressive educators, like other enthusiastic missionaries of a new gospel, have not been distinguished for the accuracy of their historical knowledge, or their fairness in appraising the merits and defects of older philosophies and institutions. When all this has been said, however, there remains a very large measure of truth in their assertion that the school heretofore has been an instrument for the preservation of the *status quo,* through the inculcation of the knowledges, skills and attitudes which are currently accepted. Broadly speaking, the school has followed and has been influenced by, very much more than it has initiated or helped to bring about, important social changes. There is all the more reason, therefore, for an interest in an institution which was originated for the definite purpose of social and national regeneration and which has had such an extraordinary success.

Denmark possesses relatively few natural advantages for the attainment of a comfortable standard of living or a high level of popular culture. There is neither water power nor mineral deposits. The majority of the population are necessarily engaged in agricultural pursuits, but under rather unfavorable conditions. The land is low and flat; the soil is sandy and not of high natural fertility. Until recently, much was a heath, overgrown with heather and unfit for agricultural purposes. The climate is never extremely cold, but the winds are damp and chilly. Live stock has to be stabled for much of the year, while the dampness frequently interferes with the harvest. There is fog for an average of ninety-four days per year, while Copenhagen has only about fifty days of sunshine annually.

Political events and social conditions in the nineteenth century, combined with these natural disadvantages, led to the economic, intellectual and spiritual degradation of the country. While communism in the ownership of land and serfdom had been abolished in the 1780's, the mass of the peasantry lived not much above the level of the medieval serf. Much of the land was held in great estates, which were parceled out to tenant farmers, who worked without ambition, hope or initiative. The government was conservative; so far as it was concerned, the peasant was the forgotten man. The Napoleonic wars brought the bombardment of Copenhagen, the destruction of the fleet and the loss of Norway. The embargo on foodstuffs growing out of this struggle ruined the country, which in 1813 was officially declared bankrupt. Between 1823 and 1825, nearly half the large estates were sold. About the middle of the century the United States, Russia and Argentina, utilizing virgin soils and large-scale production methods, began to compete for the grain markets of the world. Against this competition the small-scale farming of Denmark could not hold its own. Things were made worse when Germany, which had been its best customer, set up a protective tariff against Danish agricultural products. In 1864, Schleswig and Holstein, the richest of all the provinces, were taken by Prussia.

It is not strange that under such circumstances the spirit of the people was crushed and that they became the victims of apathy bordering on despair. But it is remarkable that in a period of fifty years, this country was transformed into one of the most prosperous, progressive, cultured and contented countries in the world. Its prosperity and its culture are unique in that they are the possession not of a small favored class but of the whole people.

But there are other reasons why Danish experience should be of interest to those concerned with Progressive education and subsistence homesteading. Homesteading implies the development of the cooperative spirit to a high degree, and of community life in the best sense of that term; Progressive education stresses the importance of training children for cooperative community living. Denmark furnishes the outstanding example of successful cooperation. Indeed it is the success of the cooperative organizations for manufacturing, buying, selling, stock breeding, banking, etc., that account in large measure for the economic rehabilitation of the country. The rural population of Denmark has developed to a high degree the art of community living; the school and the church are integral parts of the community; the pastor and teacher are members of the community in the fullest sense of the word.

Homesteading seeks to provide a comfortable standard of living on relatively small incomes; the Danish people, many thousands of whom live on farms of from one and one half to twelve acres, offers an object lesson of first-rate importance. Homesteading means the utilization to the fullest possible extent of scientific discoveries and inventions. One of the distinguishing characteristics of Danish life is the extent to which even the smallest farmers utilize the latest discoveries of science.

Nor is it on the material side alone that the experience of Denmark is relevant. The leaders in the homesteading movement believe that a real community life close to the soil can result in popular culture of a high order and can produce the durable satisfactions that result when one's daily work is made intelligent and touched with imagination.

The dull, drab life of the factory worker of the great city has a good deal in common with the dull apathetic existence of the peasant in the older Denmark. The new way of life which homesteading envisages is exemplified in Denmark, which has proved that rural life on small farms can be both profitable and attractive.

Visitors to Denmark are amazed at the ability of the masses of the people to get their satisfactions from their work, whose scientific bases and whose cultural significance they appreciate, as well as from good books, periodicals, lectures, music and art. Surely here is exemplified on a large scale the art of living the good life, in sharp contrast to the life of the masses of our cities, and similar to what the leaders of the subsistence homesteading movement seek to promote.

At certain sessions of the Dayton conference, speakers recognized the importance of studying Danish experience. But the speakers at the educational session were apparently innocent of any appreciation of it, and particularly of the folk high school, which, in the opinion of those knowing most about the subject, has had a leading part in making possible the changes which I have touched on so briefly. It is almost if not quite unique as an example of an educational institution that was definitely established for the purpose of remaking social life and that has had a very large measure of success.

The apparently wide-spread ignorance of this institution on the part of American educators is all the more remarkable in view of the fact that it has been the subject of study by sociologists, statesmen and educators from many different countries, and that there is a considerable number of easily accessible books in the English language dealing with it. These books, however, do not seem to have gotten into the main stream of the professional reading of our educators. There are some who would be unkind enough to say that this is to be explained by the fact that the professional study of education in this country has not yet passed the adolescent stage; that we are like the youth who is so much interested in his own ideas, plans and hopes that he is not interested in the experiences of other people, no matter how relevant they may be to his own aspirations. It is to be hoped that as the professional study of education becomes more mature there will be a much greater interest in the experiences of other peoples. Surely educators, no less than economists, political scientists and sociologists must rise above provincialism in their study and their thinking.

R. H. ECKELBERRY

THE OHIO STATE UNIVERSITY

A DISCOURAGING ANALOGY

IT hasn't been so long ago that the teachers of Latin were contending that those pupils who took much work with them in high school were an unusually gifted group. Many data were advanced, demonstrating that Latin majors did better in their college work than other high-school graduates, that they were superior with respect to intelligence, that they made better grades in all their other subjects and that a greater proportion of them appeared in "Who's Who." All this was true, only the teachers of Latin were not satisfied with so prosaic an exposition and felt it necessary to add that the reason for all this superiority was the fact that the boys and girls had taken that particular subject—*post hoc ergo propter hoc.*

It was men professionally interested in the field of education who first called attention to the logical error implicit in the above explanation. The point was rather laboriously made and reiterated that the reason for the success of the young people who had majored in Latin in high school was not that this subject had contributed much in the way of transfer values, but that its reputation plus college requirements had served to discourage inferior students. In other words, Latin acted as a hurdle or sieve rather than as superior training. Certain authorities have since taken the obvious next step and wondered if this select group might have been even more successful had none taken Latin.

The above is rather ancient history for all but a few of the members of the American Classical Association, but we educators are making exactly the same mistake in our attempts to defend teacher-training institutions. Quite a number of reports have recently been made of the comparative teaching success of graduates of liberal arts and teachers colleges. In these studies the careers of a large number of instructors trained in the two types of schools are traced in order to see which group received the better salaries, taught in the larger schools, attended the greater number of professional meetings, took more graduate work and enjoyed the greater tenure of office.

Such studies are of questionable value in the first place because there is almost no mention made regarding which of the two groups had the more beneficial effect upon the pupils taught.

This factor would seem to be of prime importance, yet any pertinent generalizations must be inferred from data whose implications have never been established. But passing over this matter, the criticism which places us in much the same position as the teachers of Latin is as follows: Even if we do establish the fact that teachers college graduates are better instructors than liberal arts college graduates, no one knows whether this is so because the teachers colleges tend to select students with a greater initial interest in the profession of education or because professional training really functions as such. There is already considerable evidence that teachers college students constitute a select group on a number of bases.

Of course one can claim that no matter what the reason, if teachers college graduates are the better teachers, that in itself is sufficient justification for the insistence upon separate institutions for teacher training. That type of argument, however, carries with it some dangerous insinuations regarding our entire professional curriculum. It would be interesting were some large institution to find itself able to accommodate but half of the applications for its teacher-training curriculum, forcing the other half to matriculate in the liberal arts college. Ten years later the success of the two groups would make a rather fruitful field for study. At least the factor of initial interest in teaching would be removed, and until that is done, any judgments regarding the value of professional training are apt to be somewhat premature.

Stephen M. Corey
Teachers College
University of Nebraska

GAMBLING

I have just been reading Mrs. Franklin Roosevelt's admirable book, "It's Up to the Women," and can say of it that I have rarely seen so much practical wisdom packed in a small space. There is, however, a passage on gambling, which seems to me to need clarifying. On page 224 we read:

> The spirit of gambling seems to be in all people. We may regret it, we may legislate against it, but in one way or another, the gambling spirit seems to spring up again—on the race course, in the stock market, in the lotteries which are so popular in European countries or in card games in the drawing-room and crap games in the street. Therefore, it seems impossible to say to people—you shall not gamble.

If we ask ourselves what it really is, which "seems to be in all people," we find that it is essentially the love of adventure or hazard. Or perhaps we may say, that hope which "springs eternal in the human breast," on the wings of which we daily face an uncertain future. This spirit has been the very fountain of progress, most characteristic of the highest types of humanity. We play our game with the universe, hoping to win enough to justify the effort.

But most unfortunately, this universal feeling has in large measure got linked up with the desire to acquire other people's property without earning it. This is a vice, from any social or pragmatic standpoint. It is, in its various forms, one of the leading causes of the miseries of the world. It should be taboo, just as robbery and murder are held taboo; and with suitable education and the pressure of public opinion it could undoubtedly be outlawed. Even its mildest manifestations are objectionable, because the matter is one of principle.

Such an analysis of the gambling spirit gives us, I believe, the key to reasonable methods of control. Recognize the good spirit, which is really universal, give it ample opportunities for expression and exclude the vice which has, quite needlessly, become associated with it.

T. D. A. Cockerell
University of Colorado

SPECIAL CORRESPONDENCE

THE DIFFICULTIES FACING THE HIGHER EDUCATION IN BULGARIA

Of all the Balkan countries, Bulgaria is said to have made the greatest educational progress in the shortest length of time. Though the country is poor, and especially because of the defeat in the world war and because of her predominantly agricultural structure, it is eager for progress.[1]

[1] See: W. F. Russell, "Schools of Bulgaria" (Teachers College, Columbia University, 1924);

To-day Bulgaria has five institutions of higher learning: The University of Sofia with seven faculties (arts, physical sciences, law, medicine, agriculture, theology and veterinary surgery), and some 3,400 students (of which about 25 per cent. are women); the Polytechnical School with 2,100 students, the Commercial Academy of Varna, the Academy of Arts and Music of Sofia, and a Military Academy in Sofia. There is also a high school for agriculture in Plovdiv. In addition to the state university there is in Sofia a "Free University," known also under the name of "The Balkan Institute of the Near East," a private enterprise, but recognized by the state. It has courses supplementing those of the state university in the following departments—diplomatic and consular service, administration and finance, and commerce and economics. In 1928–29, it had 1,836 students (1,738 men and 98 women).

At the present time Bulgaria is confronted with serious difficulties because of the growing number of graduates from these higher institutions of learning who are out of positions and with little, if any at all, likelihood of getting positions of their choice. In spite of the fact that some 70 per cent. of the Bulgarians live in villages, Bulgaria is unable to solve the problem of her intelligentsia.

Though the Kingdom of Bulgaria started her national career with a lack of university trained men, the situation began to change very soon after the end of the world war. In the second year after the establishment of peace, there were not enough schools, and it became obvious during the third post-war year that too many young people overflooded the educational organizations. It was a regular attack of the young Bulgarians on the Bulgarian educational facilities. All of them wanted to learn certain professions, and especially those which would eventually lead to a political career. It seems that in Bulgaria every school teacher thinks that he will reach the goal of his ambitions if he can succeed in getting elected into the national parliament.

During this period the state did its best to satisfy the demands of the students. Numerous secondary schools were opened in smaller cities and larger villages, which were preparing its registrants for further secondary and higher institutions. The Chamber of Commerce and Industry built up, with the state help, the High Commercial Academy in Varna; the cooperative movement succeeded in having the Higher Cooperative School founded in Sofia; then the "Popular University" for civic and political sciences made its appearance. The university was enlarged by the addition of the four new faculties, medical, veterinary, economics and theological.

But no sooner were these schools started than they were overcrowded with new students. Others went abroad. Most of them came from the villages; but, instead of studying the subjects which could be used in connection with agriculture, they have shown an excessive tendency to specialize in law, music, arts, philosophy, etc. A Bulgarian authority estimates that Bulgaria has some 10,000 of such students at home and abroad, *viz.*, seven or eight times more than in the pre-war days.[2] Furthermore, their ranks are being increased every day. Up to four or five years ago, these students could find positions in industrial, judicial, administrative and educational institutions. But to-day there are hardly any positions available at all. Some 5,000 Bulgarian graduates are vainly seeking employment.

The situation seems to be really hopeless and is aptly expressed by the popular saying in Bulgaria: "It is just too bad to possess a university graduation certificate; but is terrible not to have it." The abolition of some pedagogical

R. H. Markham, ''Meet Bulgaria'' (published by the author, Sofia, Bulgaria, 1931), Chapter X, ''Getting Wise,'' pp. 184–206; Veliko Yordanov, ''L'Instruction Publique en Bulgaria'' (La Bulgaria D'Aujourd'hui,'' No. 13, Sofia, Imprimerie de la Cour, 1926); ''The Near East Year Book 1931–1932'' (The Near East, London, 1931), pp. 241–246; D. P. Stephen Taylor, Ed., ''Handbook of Central and East Europe, 1932–33'' (Zurich, Central European Times Publishing Co., 1932), p. 148; C. Luther Fry, ''Bulgaria,'' in ''The Near East and American Philanthropy,'' by F. A. Ross, C. L. Fry and E. Sibley (New York, Columbia University Press, 1929), pp. 102–106. For the introduction of American methods, see the pamphlet: ''Near East Foundation'' (New York, 151–5A., New York), pp. 21–23.

[2] Chr. Gandev, ''Bulharská Akademická Mládež po Válce,'' in ''Slovanský Přehled,'' Vol. xxv: pp. 277–281, December, 1933.

and professional institutes has not improved the situation; the same applies to the doing away with the Higher Cooperative School. Those who do not find schools to enter simply take the trains for abroad, where they have an opportunity to graduate.

Behind it all is really the desire of the Bulgarian peasant to offer better education to at least one member of his family. Many are spending their last penny to send their son into a secondary school or into the Sofia or a foreign university. Such a son is not only the pride of the family but also an invested capital, which should (so the family thinks) bring eventual returns on the original investment. From another point of view, this represents a flight from the land, from the hard work on the farm, the desire to avoid private responsibility, which results in the ambition of each graduate to find a position in state or private service, known to us as the "white-collar job."

The situation is complicated by the inroads of women graduates into the available positions. There are very few professions in Bulgaria in which women are not represented. There are even women graduates in forestry and theology. But their main ambition is to study for the teaching professions. To them can be added thousands of Bulgarians who emigrated into Bulgaria from the territories lost to the neighboring countries.

The social life of these students is naturally very interesting to the foreign observer. Most of them do not attend the university lectures before noon, and many of them spend most of their available time by working in restaurants, newspaper offices, orchestras, just as is done in America. Their spare time is much more social than in America. They love to debate—a famed Slavic trait. Being by inclination and experience very democratic, they spend much of their time in social gatherings of from five to fifteen persons. Then, as a unit, the members prepare for examinations, arrange picnics, attend theaters, administer a common savings, etc, Others form public "corporations," composed of the students coming from certain districts or cities, which have their own rules, discipline and honorary courts. Their task is not only social, but also the arrangement of lectures in the outlying communities, the creation of public interest in the needs of the students and the discussion of local and regional questions.

Possibly the strongest philosophical influence on the Bulgarian student comes from the Russian sources. The Russian literature is best known to him. For example, the moral ideals of Tolstoy have found a strong expression in the famed "Tolstoyism," an idealistic movement with its principles of vegetarianism, abstinence, peace and simple natural life. Some thirty vegetarian and non-alcoholic dining halls are kept up by the secondary and university students. Other moral movements are much favored by the Bulgarian: the Red Cross, Y. M. C. A., Christian associations, etc. In contrast to the American conditions, sport is very little favored by the young Bulgarians, who think it a loss of time. But they are attracted by politics, and many work in various academic sections of the Bulgarian political parties. In this respect the most successful are the legal students.

But it can not be denied that the situation is dangerous. The hopelessness of the situation is driving many students (as well as others) into the fold of communism. Ideologically and by all his inclinations the Bulgarian is not a communist. But the communist demagogue is able to appeal to the university graduates because of their drastic condition. It will be worth while to watch for future developments in Bulgaria. Just as the German youth was driven into the folds of Fascism, the Bulgarian student might be driven into another similar movement—unless something can be done to get him a job and save his self-respect.

JOSEPH S. ROUCEK

PENNSYLVANIA STATE COLLEGE

FREDERICK W. STAEBNER—A TRIBUTE

FREDERICK W. STAEBNER, scientist and teacher of science, died at his home in Willimantic, Conn., on January 14, at the age of 78 years.

Rarely does one find a teacher with such a combination of talents as Mr. Staebner possessed. His early interest in nature took him over the open fields and rocky knolls of Morningside Heights in his native city of New York. Very naturally scientific interests directed the trends of his life work. He was well versed in his general subject. He was also a successful collector and gathered an unusually valuable collection of minerals. From the Ward Laboratories in Rochester, where some of his early work was done, he went in 1882 to the Westfield, Mass., State Normal School to take charge of the biological and mineralogical work there. In 1897 he became professor of science in the Willimantic, Conn., State Normal School, which later became a State Teachers College, from which position he retired in 1932. He was a markedly successful teacher, who, because of striking personal qualities and attainments and sound educational principles, made an unusual impression upon his students. His methods were inspired or reinforced by a remarkable normal school principal, Joseph G. Scott, of the Westfield, Mass., State Normal School, whom he loyally and joyfully assisted in that pioneer and famous institution, one of the earliest normal schools to adopt and exemplify the objective principles of Pestalozzi and also of Louis Agassiz, under whom Mr. Scott studied on Penikese Island.

Mr. Staebner brought varied talent to his work, which made him a better teacher and brought him enviable favor and popularity and, best of all, success in teaching. He was a delineator and artist of marked ability and a natural actor, which gave him a unique place in school and community dramatics. He loved nothing better than to direct dramatic work, and he was successful in it. Withal he was skilful with his pen, well read in general literature and an impressive literary critic. In his personal bearing he was neither assuming nor presuming. He was a quiet, modest, faithful workman with no penchant for head-lines.

A rare teacher has passed.

Mr. Staebner is survived by a noble wife and a family of six sons and one daughter, well-educated, able, useful.

Frank Webster Smith

Winter Haven, Fla.

QUOTATIONS

ECONOMIC TRENDS AND THE WEIGHT OF CHILDREN

The continuance of the economic depression has given rise to many predictions as to its dire consequences to human health. Without doubt a prolonged period of unemployment and hardships incident to failing incomes is likely to affect seriously the standard of living in any country in which such situations arise. Economic collapse may naturally be expected to affect the food distribution of the population almost as readily as the failure of corps or the blockades of warring nations. The menace usually seems most threatening to the child population, for this represents groups of persons who, on the one hand, are least able to make adjustments on the spur of the occasion and, on the other, have peculiar needs represented by the demands of growth.

Malnutrition among children, always an interesting problem, has been emphasized recently through the publicity associated with the Child Health Recovery Conference called at Washington early in October by the Secretary of Labor. This conference was said to be called for the purpose of considering an emergency in child health due to the depression. Specifically, it was alleged that from six to seven million children in the United States are suffering from malnutrition due more or less directly to the economic crisis through which the country has been struggling for the past four years. The meeting disclosed certain fundamental differences of opinion. During the discussion of the recommendations of the executive committee of the conference, which called for an extensive program of physical examinations on a nation-wide scale for the discovery of malnutrition, it became evident that many of those in attendance, including physicians with long experience in public health work, were by no means convinced that any increase in malnutrition has been demonstrated. The statistics presented in support of the claim that millions of children are underweight as a result of the depression were challenged. The opinion was advanced that a preventive program consisting merely of providing funds for supplying bread and milk in adequate amounts was all that would be necessary to guard against the possible development of undernourishment among children.

In the light of this conflict of opinions, special interest attaches to the study by Palmer[1] of growth in children in relation to the economic depression. This study was carried out in Hagerstown, Md., chosen because approximately twenty million of our people live in communities of similar character. In the composition of its population, employment, charitable agencies and other community characteristics, including financial, it is reasonably representative of others of like size. Palmer[2] had already made studies of variability of weight among elementary school children in Hagerstown from 1921 to 1927. These studies were available to serve as a control for the current observations. Palmer concluded that the average weight of children in the two periods presents no consistent or statistically significant differences and that the variability of body weight, measured by the standard deviation, is not consistently different for the two periods as far as boys are concerned, but that the weight for girls is slightly more variable in 1933 than from 1921 to 1927. He found four fewer boys and forty-one more girls who were 12 per cent. or more underweight in 1933 than would have been expected if the same proportions had been found underweight as in the earlier study. A further classification disclosed that among families of the unemployed, those of the partially employed and those of the regularly employed, the same differences existed as are commonly found between children of different socio-economic classes. Palmer concluded that there has been no obliteration or widening of the class differences during the period of the depression. A still further classification into groups receiving aid from charity and those not receiving aid shows that children in the former class are from 2½ to 9 pounds lighter than in the latter, and Palmer infers that children who are most in need of supplementary aid are probably receiving it.

It is acknowledged that weight alone is not a satisfactory criterion of nutrition, except in a general way, but may be used to a limited extent as a convenient general index. Comparative studies such as those of Palmer are more significant than the statistics derived from the routine weighing of thousands of children, often without supervision, by nurses and teachers. The situation in Hagerstown, as described by Palmer, is probably fairly representative. It does not justify hysteria about the increase of malnutrition as a result of the depression. That thousands of children are under-weight may be conceded; unfortunately, that has always been so. That well considered measures ought to be taken for the correction of such a condition may also be conceded, as may the possibility pointed out by *The Journal*[3] that the results of the economic catastrophies of the past four years may not be manifest at once. At the same time, care should be taken that measures advocated are sound and may reasonably be expected to accomplish the end sought.

The program advanced by the executive committee of the Child Health Recovery Conference leaves much to be desired, especially with respect to the proposal to examine, in what must be a hurried and superficial manner, millions of children. Fortunately the program was adopted as a recommendation only, and the state medical societies are to have a voice in its further development in the respective states. Emphasis on adequate food relief seems most sensible and immediately effective, utilizing the knowledge of health and nutritional conditions in the various communities, already possessed by physicians, by public health and relief officials and by social service organizations.—*Journal of the American Medical Association.*

REPORTS

ADMISSION REQUIREMENTS IN TEACHERS' COLLEGES

THE professional training of teachers as a state function may be said to have begun with the establishment of the normal school at Lexington, Massachusetts, in the year 1839. The academic requirements for this early institution were as follows:

[1] C. E. Palmer, "Growth and the Economic Depression," *Pub. Health Rep.*, 48: 1277, October 20, 1933.

[2] C. E. Palmer, "Variations of Growth in Weight of Elementary School Children, 1921–1928," *Pub. Health Rep.*, 48: 993, August 18, 1933.

[3] "Depression Death Rates," editorial, *Jour. Am. Med. Assoc.*, 99: 13, October 15, 1932.

Candidates "must undergo an examination and prove themselves to be well versed in Orthography, Reading, Writing, English, Grammar, Geography, and Arithmetic."

Since the establishment of the first state normal school, teacher-training institutions have steadily increased in number until in the year 1927–28 there were 137 teachers' colleges of four-year rank in the United States. Since that date the number has not changed significantly.

In the decade from 1890 to 1900 much interest was displayed in the articulation of secondary schools with colleges. Until 1890 the standards set for beginning teachers were so low and the salaries so small that teachers could not afford to invest much money in professional training, and it was not until 1894 that any definite announcement was made that candidates for entrance to normal schools must be graduated from a secondary school or have equivalent training.

To-day, teacher-training is unquestionably vocationalized and its aims differ materially from those of the cultural college. The number of candidates presenting themselves for entrance has increased to such an extent that opportunity now exists for the careful selection of those who enter a teacher-training institution with the view of preparing for the teaching profession. It should be pointed out, however, that such selection rarely, if ever, exists.

From the interest displayed in the decade, 1890 to 1900, with regard to the articulation of secondary schools and colleges, various regional associations have developed which to-day determine to a great extent the rules and regulations governing admission to college.

However, like its ancestor of the early nineteenth century (the first state normal school in America), the teachers' colleges of to-day have an academic subject requirement, in this case to be completed in high school, before the prospective teacher is admitted to professional training. Due to the fact that "The Articulation of the Units of American Education" was the general topic of the Department of Superintendence, Seventh Yearbook, 1929, and that especial emphasis was given to methods of admission and matriculation requirements in colleges and universities in that study with little or no emphasis given to the teachers' college, the writers deemed it advisable to consider the articulation problem from the view-point of the teacher-training institution.

The data used in this study were gathered from the latest catalogues available from teachers' colleges of four-year rank, as listed in the Educational Directory and represent 114 institutions in 34 different states. Each institution considered possesses the degree-granting privilege. The subjects chosen to be studied were those commonly offered by our high schools, *viz.*, English, foreign language, mathematics, science and social science.

Since the various regional associations mentioned previously very large influence the subject offering, the writers have used the regional association as a basis of comparison. For the purposes of this study the grouping is as follows: I (New England Association); II (Middle States and Maryland); III (North Central Association); IV (Southern Association); V (Northwest and Western).[1] When the division was completed it was found that the groups were represented by the following number of institutions: Group I, six institutions; II, eleven; III, sixty-three; IV, twenty-seven, and V, seven.

English Requirements

When a careful study of the catalogues was made it was found for the teachers' college as well as for its sister institution, the liberal arts college,[2] that English is the one outstanding subject requirement that must be fulfilled in the high school before the candidate may be admitted to teacher training. One hundred and eleven institutions (97 per cent.) set a definite amount of English as being prescribed. Only one institution does not state that it requires English, this institution is in the North Central Association (Group III).

Although practically all the institutions require English, there is considerable disagreement as to what the unit amount of credit shall be. Three units is the most common require-

[1] This group included California and Nevada which are not members of any regional association or group.

[2] Edwin J. Brown and William Martin Proctor, "Methods of Admission and Matriculation Requirements in Three Hundred Thirty-one Colleges and Universities," in Department of Superintendence, Seventh Yearbook, 1929.

ment being found in 98 (76 per cent.) of the institutions. Four units are required in 19 (17 per cent.) of the teachers' colleges.

FOREIGN LANGUAGE REQUIREMENTS

The survey indicates that foreign language is infrequently required as an entrance subject to the four-year teachers' colleges of the United States. The number of institutions requiring language work of the accepted student for his graduation is, of course, outside the field of this study. Of the total institutions studied (114) only 12 (11 per cent.) have any definite language requirement for entrance. One hundred and two (89 per cent.) by making no mention of a language requirement for admission indicate the absence of such a requirement.

In Group I, no one of the six institutions considered has a language requirement. In Group II, nine (82 per cent.) of the institutions require no language for entrance, while two (18 per cent.) do have definite requirements. In Group III, 53 (86 per cent.) require no foreign language, nine (14 per cent.) do require language. In Group IV, twenty-six (96 per cent.) of the twenty-seven institutions fail to mention a requirement, one only (4 per cent.) states that it has such a requirement. No teacher-training institution in Group V has a language requirement for entrance.

MATHEMATICS REQUIREMENTS

In the field of mathematics most of the teachers' colleges hold to a prescribed amount of work for entrance. Seventy-six (67 per cent.) have a definite requirement, while thirty-eight (33 per cent.) have no requirement. Approximately 94 per cent. of the so-called liberal arts colleges require mathematics for entrance.

While the requirement of some mathematics for entrance to a teachers' college is quite general, the amount required differs much in the various regional associations. One unit each of algebra and geometry is required in twenty-five colleges. This is 22 per cent. of the total. Two units of "any mathematics" is acceptable in 19 per cent. of the institutions. Two units of algebra and one unit of geometry is the mathematics requirement in eight colleges. This is about 7 per cent. of the total. Thirty-eight institutions (33 per cent.) report in their catalogues no specific requirement.

SCIENCE REQUIREMENTS

It was found that science is a requirement which must be fulfilled in the majority of cases by the candidates seeking entrance to teachers' colleges. Fifty-three (46 per cent.) institutions apparently have no definite requirement for science. Sixty-one (54 per cent.) state they have a definite requirement for admittance. These figures agree perfectly with requirements for the liberal arts college in science.

In the New England Association no institution states that it requires science for entrance. In the Middle States and Maryland the opposite is true for here eleven institutions (100 per cent.) require science for entrance. In the North Central Association over one half of the institutions, thirty-four (54 per cent.), require definite amounts of science. Twenty-nine (46 per cent.) indicate no requirement in science for admittance. The majority lean toward the "no science" requirement in the Southern Association. Eighteen (67 per cent.) make no mention of a science requirement, while nine (37 per cent.) state a definite requirement for admission. All the seven institutions studied in the fifth grouping, arbitrarily called the Northwest and Western Association, indicate they have a science requirement.

There exists in the science requirements, as in many of the other subjects, a very wide range of unit credit as well as a none too uniform selection of subjects. Thirty-seven (32 per cent.) require one unit for entrance. They will accept, according to their catalogues, any laboratory science. Nine teachers' colleges of the 114 studied require two units of a laboratory science in secondary school before admitting the candidate to college standing. This is about 8 per cent. Nine institutions specify "general science or biology," one unit.

SOCIAL SCIENCE REQUIREMENTS

The study shows that there is quite definitely a social science requirement for entrance to teachers' colleges. Of the 114 institutions in the study, 97 (85 per cent.) require social science for entrance. There are only 17 (15 per cent.) that fail to mention a social science requirement. The unit requirement here is higher than for its sister institution, the liberal arts college, McKown and Brown agreeing in their studies of 1913 and 1928 that social science was not required for entrance at either date in more than 75 per cent. of the liberal arts institutions.

In Group I, five of the six (83 per cent.) have a social science requirement for entrance; only one institution (17 per cent.) fails to mention a requirement. All the eleven institutions in Group II have a definite requirement. In Group III, 49 (79 per cent.) of the 63 institutions require social science. Only 14 (21 per cent.) do not require social science for entrance to college. In a like manner the catalogues show that in Group IV, the majority of the institutions require social science. Twenty-five of the total 27 institutions (93 per cent.) have this requirement, only 2 or 7 per cent. admit without social science. In Group V, all (seven) the institutions studied require social science for entrance.

Although 97 (85 per cent.) of the total 114 institutions require social science for entrance, there is considerable variation in the amounts prescribed. Fifty-eight institutions require one unit for entrance. This is 51 per cent. of the total studied. Twenty-six (23 per cent.) require 2 units. Ten or 9 per cent. require 4 units. Two institutions (2 per cent.) require the candidate to present 1½ units. One institution requires 3 units. One requires ½ unit, and one requires from 1 to 3 units.

The study found very little if any agreement as to what the social science subjects or subjects submitted should be. There are sixteen different combinations of subjects in social science accredited toward admission to teachers' colleges.

Edwin J. Brown
Victor T. Trusler
Kansas State Teachers College,
Emporia

EDUCATIONAL RESEARCH AND STATISTICS

NEW HAMPSHIRE AS A NEW FRONTIER

Our several years residence and study of conditions in New Hampshire have led us to posit the statement that this state is becoming a new frontier, as the old frontier has moved westward, pushed by the discontented and more ambitious groups from the East. Taking a cue from Professor Clough's "Wyoming and the Westward Movement,"[1] we made an investigation of the birthplaces of a group of students (357), their parents and their grandparents. The findings of the two groups are given below.

[1] *American Journal of Sociology*, xxxv: 808–15.

Since the University of New Hampshire and the University of Wyoming enroll approximately 87 per cent. in-state students, a comparison of the two sets of data reveals some pertinent facts. Our group is much more deeply rooted to the soil of its native state. In fact it has received practically no new blood from the states outside New England. Only 5 students, 29 parents and 26 grandparents were born beyond the Appalachians. On the other hand, the Wyoming group, its parents and grandparents drew heavily from other states. More than half the students, nearly three fourths of the parents and over one third of

Natal Statistics of Two Groups of Students, Their Parents and Their Grandparents in Percentages

Birthplace	New Hampshire			Wyoming		
	Students	Parents	Grand-parents	Students	Parents	Grand-parents
Native state	58.8	34.6	18.1	47.4	06.3	00.1
Other states	39.0	39.6	23.9	51.0	71.5	37.8
Foreign countries	02.2	23.5	34.1	01.6	21.1	45.0
Unknown	00.0	02.3	23.9	00.0	01.1	17.1
New England states (including N. H.)	90.8	64.5	36.8			
Other states (excluding New England)	07.0	09.7	05.2			

the grandparents were born in other states. In so far as our samples are representative of the two states, this comparison proves that, "While the major population groups of an Atlantic Coast state will be the native stock, and the first to third generation foreign born, the Rocky Mountain states in particular will show a large third group, native-born Americans who have migrated westward and are not native to the state of their residence."[2]

Comparing our findings with two census reports which were tabulated to show the percentages of native-born whites claiming New Hampshire as their birthplace, we found practically the same tendencies for the state. For the decades ending 1900 and 1910 approximately 75 per cent. of native-born persons in New Hampshire gave that state as their birthplace, 95 per cent. New England, and 98 per cent. New England and the Middle Atlantic states.

The New Hampshire and the Wyoming groups drew from foreign countries in about the same proportions, but in our study these drawings were not representative of the foreign elements in the state. Our data showed a preponderance of Teutonic blood, but the 1930 census report gave a predominance of Mediterranean with some Slavic. Of the foreign-born 45.6 per cent. were French Canadians and 5.0 per cent. Poles, while the English-speaking Canadians numbered only 16.1 per cent., the Irish 7.0 per cent. and the English 4.7 per cent. For the past 40 years the native whites of native parentage have been slowly decreasing. These population changes are not without significance.

New Hampshire has kept her population relatively free from the effects of interstate migration, but she has failed to reflect the progressive spirit and thrift that caused the earlier inhabitants to gather stones from the rock-ribbed fields and build mile after mile of walls and to construct farmhouses that would dwarf many a Southern planter's residence. Tumbling fences, falling timbers and deserted farmsteads testify to the change that has taken place, and dirty-faced children, littered yards and sleek cattle bespeak that New Hampshire has been recruited by a foreign element that has not developed an appreciation for the culture of the older stock.

[2] *Ibid.*, p. 808.

No doubt many of the older stock crossed the Appalachians seeking a place where opportunities were thought to be greater, and no doubt the foreign element came to the state for the same purpose. Although the farm lands are not highly productive, the forests are exhausted and the mineral wealth is nil, the land-hungry peasant finds his opportunities in cheap land and cheaper rents. In the manufacturing establishments he finds work for himself and family. With the decaying farm life and the slow movement of manufacturing toward the South, the native finds his opportunities slipping away, but the ignorant and economically oppressed immigrant sees his increasing.

The old so-called cultural centers have dwindled in population and importance, and the manufacturing cities are losing in population and in business. The heavy influx of French Canadians and the scattered Greeks and Poles are making heavy inroads upon Protestantism. Coming from the humbler walks of life, these people have little real appreciation for higher education. In fact, very few French Canadians even enter college. Thus New Hampshire, one of the original colonies, ninth to enter the union, and formerly a leader in intellectual and literary excellence, has passed through the cycle and is entering a new frontier stage. Who knows but that Wyoming, representing the last frontier stage, may also become another last frontier as the New Hampshire movement pushes out again from a state that has so little natural wealth to offer?

H. G. Duncan
Winnie Leach Duncan
University of Colorado

NEW BOOKS IN EDUCATION

Briggs, Thomas H. *Seconday Education.* New York: Macmillan Company, 1934. 577 pp. $2.50.

Johnsen, Julia E. *Federal Aid to Education.* New York: H. W. Wilson Company, 1934. $.90.

McKown, Harry C. *Home Room Guidance.* New York: McGraw-Hill Book Company, 1934. 447 pp. $3.00.

Mooney, James D. *The New Capitalism.* New York: Macmillan Company, 1934. 229 pp. $3.50.

Otto, Henry J. *Elementary School Organization and Administration.* New York: D. Appleton-Century Company, 1934. 652 pp. $3.00.

Smith, Milton. *Guide to Play Selection.* New York: D. Appleton-Century Company, 1934. 174 pp. $1.25.

SCHOOL AND SOCIETY

WITH WHICH ARE COMBINED THE EDUCATIONAL REVIEW, ESTABLISHED IN 1891, THE TEACHERS MAGAZINE, ESTABLISHED IN 1878, AND THE SCHOOL JOURNAL, ESTABLISHED IN 1874.

EDITED BY J. McKEEN CATTELL, R. D. LINDQUIST AND W. H. COWLEY

EDITORIAL COMMUNICATIONS SHOULD BE ADDRESSED TO THE EDUCATION BUILDING, THE OHIO STATE UNIVERSITY, COLUMBUS, OHIO

Volume 39 SATURDAY, MARCH 3, 1934 Number 1001

SINCERITY IN THE PRESENT SITUATION[1]

By THOMAS H. BRIGGS

TEACHERS COLLEGE, COLUMBIA UNIVERSITY

WHEN I received my assignment to participate in a discussion of sincerity in the present situation I immediately recalled a conversation between two young women. "Let's discuss each other with perfect truth and sincerity," said one. "No," replied the other; "I think we'd better remain friends." In Gilbert's satiric comedy, "few care to stay above a day or two" in the palace where by magic every one must tell the truth, and entire sincerity proves dangerous. When the artist declares the queen too fat, King Phanor replies,

> Bear in mind . . .
> You have a palate, and a set of teeth,
> And several delicate contrivances
> That aid digestion. Tell her she's too fat,
> And she may take offense; and, if she does,
> She'll throw that apparatus out of work.

But there is little danger in declaring before educators the faults of education. In professional meetings it is one of the popular indoor sports. It never fails to get amused attention—and it seldom gets anything else. We are entertained by it, but we do not feel a compulsion to go out and act so differently that the criticisms can not be justly repeated. Something ought to be done, we say; but let George do it. And George is busy holding his job, knowing that something ought to be done, but keeping the secrets of the lodge from a complacent public. The unforgivable sin is of so informing the public that it makes the administrator uncomfortable. Then the critic is not loyal to the profession; perhaps, it is insinuated, he does not believe in the great democratic institution of education; perhaps he is under the influence of the United States Chamber of Commerce. At any rate, it is demanded that he present a complete and detailed program for improvement—or else keep quiet.

The fact that he has previously presented constructive phases which the profession has neglected matters little. He is called upon to do what is impossible for any one man, to construct instanter the whole program complete in all its details. Perhaps even the hired secretary of the professional association fires a pop-gun or two at him, thus safeguarding his job and advertising that loyalty to employers is greater than loyalty to the cause of education. Yes; we may be as sincere as we please before the National Council. It's all good fun here in the lodge room. Something indeed ought

[1] Address before the meeting of the National Council of Education, at Cleveland, Ohio, February 24, 1934.

to be done about it, but the very bodies that ought to be active, the great professional organizations that have the influence and the power, possessed by no individual, to set the machinery in motion and to keep it steadily moving, organizations like the very one under whose auspices we are meeting, are too busy with other things. They meet, it is true, only once a year; and after adjournment there is another program for the new officers to prepare, other speakers who must be invited to tell what's wrong with the world and to assert that it can be saved only by an undefined and undirected mystery called education.

Lest I seem to be merely destructive in what I have just said, let me recall that repeatedly I have attempted constructively to outline what should be done to prepare a comprehensive program for the difficult and tedious preparation for the new education, an education that will reflect life as it has become to-day and as it will upbuild the democratic society in which we believe. I am ready to present the outline again and yet again, to argue for its soundness and its promise of success, and cooperatively to contribute all that is within my power to its development. But, unfortunately, what is said critically always sounds louder and is remembered longer than what is suggested constructively. This is not peculiar to educators; it is true with men in all walks of life. I am perfectly safe in prophesying that the "news" of the meetings this week at Cleveland will be the assertions of short-comings, the "fights," the denunciations discovered or invented by perfectly human reporters for perfectly human readers, while the accounts of school successes and the constructive proposals for betterment, especially if they require time and money, will be found, if at all, at the bottom of the last column on an inside page.

But I still have faith that some day the leaders of education—meaning you, ladies and gentlemen—will manifest that you are really leaders and use the organized power that you have to demand and to direct the long, slow-moving rebuilding of the educational structure, beginning with the foundations and working upward, in accord with a logical and consistent plan, to the loftiest minaret. You are too wise and too experienced really to expect miracles. We are never going to wake up some bright morning and find the job all done, the portals of the palace that we have not painstakingly built wide open and inviting us to enter into a paradise of possibilities. First must come a vision and planning and courage and unremitting labor and patience—and then more labor. Since it is vastly more important and ambitious we shall have to plan for and provide for this palace more carefully and more skilfully than men with other responsibilities have planned for physical buildings; a myriad of expert workers of all needed types must be assigned to full-time labor on the project. It can not be done by voluntary part-time service.

One reason why we dally and make less progress than we should is that so few of us become concerned about the same problem at the same time. Once, years ago, I was a trustee of a church in which one of my educational colleagues was a deacon and in which three others were communicants. We formed a small group somewhat separated socially and culturally from the rest of the membership. I have no doubt now, as I had none then, that had we at any time united our forces we could have helped that church greatly. But when I became excited about the finances I found my diaconic colleague lethargic because I had not put my shoulder to the wheel when he was periodically active to stimulate the spiritual welfare of the congregation, and our other colleagues never got their temperatures up at the same moment that we were at the steaming point. So in these meetings. We hear speaker A rail at deficiency x, B exhorts us over failure to remedy y, and C berates us because we have not met the emergency at z. Our emotions as well as our judgments are divided, and we fail to enroll actively in any camp. I wonder why my friend Dr. Morrison does not join me to force the making of a comprehensive long-term program of secondary education, and he, in turn, is disappointed that I should take the time to present my proposals after he has so clearly told us what should be remedied. Perhaps some day we shall all unite at the same time on the same problem and continue at it until there are solution and wide-spread remedial action.

Pledged to sincerity, I must reiterate that I trace all our educational ills, or almost all of them, to a failure in fundamental conceptions. How can we agree on the sort of education that we should have unless first we have agreed on the sort of society that we want? How can organization or details of administration or proposals for new units of subject-matter or novel methods of teaching be evaluated except in terms of the product that we need for the promotion and betterment of the society in which we live? And where shall we find that agreement? It can not be found ready made. Out of all the thoughtlessness and heterogeneity of opinion it must be teased out, interpreted, organized, supplemented to a whole consistent with the democratic ideal, and then popularized so that the vast majority of the public shall understand and approve it. There is, I firmly believe, far more agreement—much of it passive, no doubt—than is ordinarily suspected. If the public were made conscious of the social alternatives toward which our practises are divergently tending, there is little question in my mind but that the great majority would declare itself on the side of the democratic tradition. And on that tradition could then be built a consistent comprehensive program that would have the support of that majority which cares enough to promote or to demand modifications.

So long as education is a popular fetish, it is insecure. So long as the public looks on the schools as pleasant places where children are somehow mysteriously benefited, there should be no surprise that in periods of economic stringency appropriations are disastrously reduced. Education then suffers along with other luxuries. It rested on a fetish rather than on an informed faith because its foundation was not understood by any significant fraction of the profession. I have elsewhere and repeatedly argued at length that the only justification of education furnished free by the public is that it is the only possible means that society has of preserving itself and of promoting its own interests. Only as this principle is understood and as it forms the foundation on which the whole program is developed can free public education be justified. And only as the program is thus justified are we in a position to argue that education is a necessity, the starvation of which will inevitably result in social suicide.

Because teachers, and even administrative leaders, have not understood this, have not assimilated the principle so that it is directive in all planning and in all activities, we have come to the woeful condition that is pinching every one of us. That would not concern me so much, since every man has unsuspected powers of sacrifice and endurance, if I did not so clearly see that our failure in the past and our unconcern to think fundamentally and constructively about the future, are imperiling the social and the political ideals that are expressions—imperfect, it is true, but expressions none the less—of the ideals toward which we have painfully struggled through centuries of history. The race is not between catastrophe and a mystery called education. Catastrophe for us can be prevented only by an education that grows out of the democratic ideals and is purposefully planned to perpetuate them and to achieve what they imply for mankind.

Sincerity forces me reluctantly to declare that a not inconsiderable part of the money, the genius and the effort expended on secondary and college education is wasted. It is worse than wasted, indeed, for students are fed what gives sustenance neither to them nor to the supporting society, thereby preventing the acquisition of nourishing food. It is common knowledge, repeatedly emphasized by individual observation and by data scientifically collected for large groups, that our schools above the elementary level neither generally provide curricula suitable to the needs of their heterogeneous students nor teach what they do offer in such ways that they insure to any considerable number permanent mastery, interests and subsequent use. No credits are so frozen as many that are given by high schools and colleges. The facts are a professional scandal. We all know them; but realizing our individual impotence, we cover them up from the public and fail to demand the only remedy that promises success—a continuing central committee of the best minds in the profession and in related fields to define pragmatically our objectives and then to direct the construction by experts, likewise continuously employed, to develop at least in outline the detailed program. We can never expect teachers, however competent they may be for instruction, to create courses of study in their spare time. The job is too difficult and too complex. It can never be done with any degree of satisfaction by any group of experts even with unlimited time and resources until fundamental principles are agreed on and widely popularized.

Curriculum construction is an unending task anyway. Civilization is not static, and education must not only reflect conditions as they are but prepare as well as possible for those that may be. The Nestor of this program has recently declared in a published letter that he knows of only two radical changes that have recently come in society. With all deference to his observation, which I have found usually to be as exact as his judgments are wise, I am amazed that he detects so few of the scores passing on the screen of the current panorama. (Sincerity compels me to make this statement.) Recently attempting to list the significant changes that have occurred in my part of the world, and I think they may be found in as remote places as Chicago too, I gave up after using some thirty printed pages for the enumeration. My list is far from complete; and though we may disagree somewhat as to the magnitude of each, I am bold to assert that every one of them is significant for the new curriculum. Education can not justify itself if it continues to teach the language of Caesar and Chaucer to the neglect of effective speech of this day, the literature that has chiefly historical interest while blinding itself to what this generation actually reads not only for enjoyment but also for a large determination of its ideals, the science of Aristotle and Roger Bacon, or even of the first decade of this century, when weekly discoveries are made in the laboratories of Compton, Millikan and scores of other geniuses, the morals and manners of Victorian England or of the America of "Little Women" closing its eyes to what the modern generations do with general, though not always pedagogic, approval.

Why the lag of education in a changing world? Again the answer is the same. We have no sincere agreement on fundamental principles; one of which would assuredly be that education should reflect life as it is and direct it toward such a course as is consistent with ideals to which we are consciously and intelligently devoted. And individually impotent in the press and swirl of other duties, we have set up no competent central body to observe, interpret and construct a program for us. Far better that educators, those to whom the responsibility has been entrusted by society believing them expert and reliable, should initiate and promote such machinery than that the public lose faith and starve their efforts or that it force upon them inadequately considered and dangerous innovations.

The plain fact, a statement of which is again impelled by the magic of the Palace of Truth, is that not all who have been licensed to teach or to administer schools are either competent for responsibility or, worse still, sincerely interested in education. A false sense of loyalty has led us into a campaign to protect in this time of economic depression all "teachers," whereas a greater loyalty to education and to society would have seized the opportunity to rid our ranks of the mistakes of licensing agencies. The responsible agent of a board of education directed a superintendent because of the necessities of economy to discharge a certain number of teachers, suggesting that he had an unusual opportunity to strengthen the corps by selecting those who had not proved valuable or promising, and pledging full support of the board. In consequence he got rid of every such teacher—who died or moved from the city. Why have so many who have slipped into the educational system by mistake of one kind or another been protected, while younger men and women of greater promise have been discharged or debarred? The answer is all too easy. Of course the problem is complex and there is a reasonable argument of social justice for the individual and a fear of loss of morale; but the larger loyalty to society as a whole points clearly to the courageous seizing of the opportunity to clean house, to eject the incompetent from the schools. Society may need to care for them by dole until they find some field in which they can earn a living. But it is rank injustice to demand that helpless children should pay for what they are not given. And, in simple truth, there is misfeasance in office if an administrator does not live up to the trust that society pays him to accept.

Another expression of sincerity and I am through, though the temptations to prolong the opportunity are strong. It is not every day that one is commanded to say without restraint exactly what he thinks. Is it not about time that we demand exact definitions of terms that are used so frequently in educational writing and speaking as to have become clichés? Some years ago a witty writer ridiculed the language of "pedaguese" so that for a time there was a tendency to talk simply about education. But of late the inventors of Lagado have been busy again. I have no objection to the invention of a new term to express an idea for which the English language contains no generally understood symbol. I even have no objection to the use of a picturesque novel phrase to give color or emphasis to an idea, new or old. As a matter of fact the new educational argot is usually introduced by some one who has an idea that he wishes to convey as effectively as possible. But the idea is not conveyed at all if it is expressed in phrases that are imperfectly or inaccurately understood. But, unless I am mistaken we love picturesque phrases, whether we understand them or not; and after they are introduced numerous imitators use them frequently with little or no conception of exact meaning.

There is one remedy that sincerity provides, and I suggest that you use it at these meetings whenever you hear a speaker utter a phrase of which you are suspicious: immediately demand that he give you a satisfying definition. If every speaker who impresses us by using "the new social order," the "emerging" or "dynamic" this or that, "the climate of opinion," "the frame of reference," "inclusive thinking," "shared decisions," "the life situation," "the integrated personality," "adversive compensation," and the like were challenged to express himself in simple English so that even we can know precisely what he means, the meetings would be more profitable. And perhaps the next ones would be shorter.

EDUCATIONAL EVENTS

THE REORGANIZATION OF JAPANESE EDUCATIONAL IDEOLOGY

An educational revolution as remarkable as the one that occurred when medieval Japan adopted over night modern educational methods is now taking place in that country, according to Willard Price, special correspondent for the *New York Herald-Tribune*. This revolution consists of an effort to hold all that has been gained and at the same time step back to the ways of the past. Strong nationalism, which has swept back into vogue throughout the world, is nowhere more evident than in Japan.

His Excellency, Ichiro Hatoyama, minister of education for the empire, is more powerful than the education official of any other country, and the success of his administration is evidenced by the fact that no nation is higher in literacy today than Japan. Her school attendance surpasses that of the United States, 99.5 per cent. of her children of school age being in school. Mr. Hatoyama stated in an interview with Mr. Price, that "the progress of Japanese education is owed very much to the educational methods of the West. But as a result of over sixty years' experience, we are now able to develop a method peculiar to this country." The beginning of state education was strongly influenced by mission precedents. Also, investigators were sent abroad to study Western systems. And in 1872, a system was promulgated that savored of many lands, particularly France.

Japan did not, however, adopt the French "duplicate school system," which provides an elementary school system and a secondary school system side by side. Instead was established the "simple school system," now existing in America, which is in the nature of an educational ladder reaching from the elementary school to the middle school (which corresponds to the Western secondary school), and then to the university.

At that time we owed a great deal to America, particularly in connection with methods of elementary and normal education.

The Japanese educational system spans seventeen years instead of sixteen—six years of elementary school, five years of middle school, three years of high school, three of university. Moreover, the number of school days in the year are half as many again as in America. Summer vacations are only a month or six weeks long. This crowding is made necessary by the fact that Japanese children are expected to learn not only Japanese subjects, but American, English, French, German, Russian and Chinese. They are trained to be world-citizens.

English is taught in all middle schools. Sometimes the teachers are Americans or Englishmen, but in the vast majority of cases they are Japanese. The result of this proponderance of Japanese teachers of English is that an extraordinary brand of English has grown up. Students taught by Americans have difficulty in passing the university entrance examinations, their pronunciation being at variance with accepted Japanese English. But the chief value of English to the Japanese lies not in the ability to speak it, but in the ability to read it. This they can do—and the whole range of English literature is open to them.

Japanese education regards the cinema very seriously. Every middle school and high school has its motion picture study club. Foreign pictures are not disregarded. Grave consideration is given to the comparative art of Greta Garbo and Marlene Dietrich; and a study group recently announced as the subject for its next discussion, "Mickey Mouse—Analysis of Motivations and Reactions."

But the chief attention is paid to Japanese subjects. The authorities supply for class use a constant flow of new pictures on the history of Japan, Japanese prowess in war, the taming of Manchukuo, respect for the Emperor—as well as more technical pictures on geography, physics, chemistry, natural history and even mathematics.

The reason for special stress upon the cinema is the belief of educators that Japanese students are peculiarly eye-minded. Therefore the board of education itself produces a large volume of films, not leaving this task to commercial concerns. Also it is insisted that the films be used, not as supplementary or extracurricular material, but as an integral part of classroom work.

The most distinctive characteristic of education in Japan is, according to Mr. Hatoyama, "that we are fostering national morality through Japanese history illustrating the national character of Japan. This is the basis of our national education."

RELATIVE UNIVERSITY STANDINGS IN "AMERICAN MEN OF SCIENCE"

HARVARD UNIVERSITY and the University of Chicago lead all American institutions in the number of members of their science faculties who are recognized as outstanding and in the number of their alumni who have achieved distinction in science, according to Professor Stephen S. Visher, of Indiana University. In an article in a recent issue of the *University of Chicago Magazine,* Dr. Visher arrives at this conclusion by an analysis of the last three editions of "American Men of Science," edited by J. McKeen Cattell and Jaques Cattell. These volumes mark with stars the names of those who are acknowledged as research leaders by vote of their colleagues throughout the country.

Fifty-eight members of the faculty of Harvard University are among the 851 added to the starred list in the editions of "American Men of Science" for 1921, 1927 and 1933. Chicago is second with 41, and other leading universities are represented as follows: The University of California, 31; Columbia University, 29; Yale University, 28; the University of Michigan, 27; the Johns Hopkins University, 26; Cornell University and the University of Minnesota, each 23; Princeton University, 22; the University of Illinois and the University of Pennsylvania, each 21; Leland Stanford University, 20; the University of Wisconsin, 15; Washington University, 14; the Ohio State University and the Massachusetts Institute of Technology, 12 each; the California Institute of Technology, 9; the University of Iowa, 7, and Northwestern University, 6.

Scientific men starred in the first two editions of the volume, 1903 and 1910, are not included in the tabulations because a large proportion of them have died or are inactive. Of the 250 scientific men awarded stars for the first time in the 1933 edition, 43 won the doctorate as graduate students at Harvard University, 29 took the doctorate at the University of Chicago, 22 at Columbia University, 15 at the Johns Hopkins University, 13 at Princeton University, 12 at Yale University, 11 at Cornell University, 10 at the University of Illinois and 8 at the University of Wisconsin. In a comparison of leading institutions regarding the undergraduate training of future scientific men, Dr. Visher points out that of those most recently starred, 19 received the bachelor's degree at Harvard University, 14 at the University of Chicago, 9 at Cornell University and 8 at the University of Michigan.

Dr. Visher summarizes the comparative strength of university science departments, as revealed by the recently starred men who received the doctorate some ten or twenty years ago as follows:

Anatomy and astronomy: Chicago leads in the number of the recipients of the doctorate who were starred in 1927 and 1933.

Botany: Chicago stands first for 1927 and 1933 combined, with 9; Harvard and Columbia each have 6, and Johns Hopkins has 5.

Chemistry: For 1927 and 1933 combined, Harvard has 8; Columbia and Chicago each have 7.

Geology: For 1921, 1927 and 1933 combined, Yale leads with 16; Chicago has 14 and Harvard 8.

Mathematics: Chicago and Harvard each have 14 and Princeton has 6, in 1921, 1927 and 1933 combined.

Pathology: Johns Hopkins stands first, Columbia, second, and Chicago, third.

Physiology: Harvard takes the leadership in the 1933 group from Chicago, which led in 1927 and 1921. Johns Hopkins is third.

Physics: Chicago has 10 in a combination of the 1927 and 1933 groups; Harvard has 6 and Princeton has 6.

Psychology: The totals for 1921, 1927 and 1933 are: Columbia, 9; Chicago, 7, and Harvard 6.

Zoology: Harvard leads, Columbia is second, and Chicago, third.

Commenting on these data the magazine *Time*, in its February 26 issue, makes the following observations:

Harvard and the University of California have faculties of nearly 2,000; Columbia of more than 2,000. Small college men felt that Surveyor Visher should have taken faculty size into consideration as well as number of star-winners. If his ranking were recast on that basis, these ten universities would lead:

Number of Star-winners (since 1921) Per 100 Faculty Members (in 1933)

Chicago	7.07	Yale	3.57
Princeton	7.03	Stanford	3.48
Calif. Inst. Tech.	4.97	Michigan	3.47
Johns Hopkins	4.31	Harvard	3.28
Minnesota	3.97	Cornell	2.67

DEFEAT OF THE BILL TO AID PAROCHIAL SCHOOLS IN OHIO

STATE aid for parochial schools was defeated in the Ohio Legislature on February 15. The proposal to appropriate $2,000,000 of the public funds for the benefit of religious schools failed, owing in large measure to a strong sentiment for the separation of church and state.

While it is believed no effort will be made to revive the amendment at present, it is anticipated that a new attempt will be made in behalf of the parochial schools later, during the further consideration of the needs of the public schools. The innovation of a state appropriation for parochial schools was lost in the lower house because it lacked the required constitutional majority of 68 votes. The vote was 56 for and 49 against.

The project came up in connection with legislation for the financial assistance of the public schools. This plan calls for an annual statewide subsidy for all public schools. The yearly expenditure, estimated at $23,000,000, would be parceled out to all school districts on a per pupil basis. The bill was amended to provide for an additional $2,000,000 from the state treasury for the aid of parochial schools during 1934, and as amended came to a vote in the House early in February. It failed because there were three votes short of a majority.

Upon reconsideration, demand was made that a separate vote be had on the parochial school amendment. Separation of the amendment from the bill required the concurrence of at least 10 members. This was easily acquired, but the rider was voted upon and lost while the bill itself carried by a vote of 82 to 15.

When the parochial school proposal was first introduced, during the special session in the fall of 1933, it lost by a vote of 52 for and 41 against, 68 votes being required for passage. Some 35 members were absent during the balloting. Debate was extended at that time, arguments favoring and opposing the measure being given a full hearing. The proposition then entailed appropriating $1,500,000 for last year and $2,500,000 for this year.

Sponsors of the church schools urged that they embraced 170,000 pupils, that if they were forced to close and transfer their children to the public schools, the cost to the public-school system would be multiplied by many millions. It was also argued that the supporters of the parochial schools were taxed for maintenance of the public-school system, and in the emergency should be given a share of the tax money. The aid sought, it was also said, was but temporary.

Advocates of maintaining the traditional separation of church and state held, on the other hand, that the parochial schools were started as private enterprises, charged a tuition fee and were maintained to further the doctrines of the churches sponsoring them.

THE ADULT EDUCATION PROGRAM OF NEW YORK UNIVERSITY

THE New York University Extension Division series of lectures on "Local Problems in Modern Society," a new experiment in adult education, opened on February 23 with an address on "Geography and Culture," by Dr. Ellsworth Huntington, research associate in geography at Yale University.

Designed to present an integrated study of the chief social problems of the present day, the experimental series of twelve lectures was arranged by Paul A. McGhee, executive secretary of the extension division. The other speakers in the group and their subjects are as follows:

"The Unity of Social Science," by Dr. John Dewey, professor emeritus of philosophy at Columbia University.

"Race and Civilization," by Dr. Franz Boas, professor of anthropology, Columbia University.

"Technology and Production," by Walter N. Polakov, consulting engineer to the Tennessee Valley Authority.

"Money and the Price System," by Frank A. Vanderlip, formerly Assistant Secretary of the Treasury.

"Trends and Problems in Income Distribution," by Dr. Carl A. Taeusch, professor of business ethics in the Harvard Graduate School of Business Administration.

"Economics and Politics of Population," by Dr. Henry P. Fairchild, professor of sociology at New York University and president of the Population Association of America.

"The State, Culture and Minorities," by Dr. Horace M. Kallen, lecturer on philosophy at the New School for Social Research.

"Education and the Problems of Social Control," by Dr. George S. Counts, professor of education at Teachers College, Columbia University.

"Psychology and Psychopathology of Personality in the Machine Age," by Harry A. Overstreet, professor of philosophy at the College of the City of New York.

"Esthetic Experience in the Machine Age," by Dr. Joseph Wood Krutch, associate editor of *The Nation*.

"Philosophy and Social Action," by Dr. Sidney Hook, professor of philosophy at New York University.

Paul McGhee, executive secretary of the university, made the following statement in his announcement of the course:

Until now "adult education" has been a vague phrase. There has been no serious effort to integrate these studies into a meaningful pattern; often there has been no explicit philosophy of what the educational process for adults in a changing social world should be.

In the numerous schools and private institutions which are conducting programs in adult education one finds a vast number of single courses, representing every special field from astronomy to domestic science. All represent isolated interests of individuals, and are entered upon much as if the subject matter was suspended in a social vacuum. This may often satisfy individual needs, but adult education must offer more than this for students to-day. The concept of a social problem now involves more than bread lines and old age pensions.

The experiment to be conducted here is based upon the premise that a serious educational course for adults to-day must be built up around the questions: What are the chief patterns of individual experience which are made possible and accessible in a changing social order? What constitutes a social problem, and how is individual life related to it? What phases of personal experience are involved in the widest conceptions of a social problem? What are the chief social problems in this widest sense? How can they be most widely settled in the light of existing materials and conflicting social ideals?

Our plan to find the answers to these questions is to get adult classes to enter into a sustained mental experiment, working under instructors drawn from various universities and walks of life, using the results of research and the methods of analysis and imaginative social reconstruction.

The present course will be an introductory summary to a complete course of two years' duration which will open next fall. It will be open to all who are interested in the problems. The proposed course is planned to link up the processes of adult education with the actual experiences of the student in his ordinary and social and practical activities.

SPECIAL INSTRUCTION COURSES FOR FARMERS

Farmers who desire instruction in the reorganization of their business to meet changing present-day conditions are provided for in the evening classes in vocational agriculture organized in the principal rural high schools throughout the country, George F. Zook, U. S. Commissioner of Education, announced on February 15. In explanation of his statement, Dr. Zook observed that special emphasis is being laid in these vocational agricultural courses upon instruction in farm reorganization. He called attention to the fact that the Office of Education has cooperated with the Agricultural Adjustment Administration in preparing and distributing three pamphlets designed to aid vocational agriculture teachers in helping evening school farmers to utilize land withdrawn from production under the cotton, wheat and corn-hog acreage reduction programs.

As a further evidence of the effort of the Office of Education to help farmers adjust themselves to agricultural changes, Dr. Zook pointed to a recent publication, "Reorganizing the Individual Farm Business," which contains definite suggestions to agricultural teachers for setting up courses in this subject in their evening classes. An effort is made in presenting the farm organization course to help farmers decide whether it is advisable for them to change their types of farming and, if so, what crops they should grow, what and how much live stock to produce, how much of each crop to produce, what kind and amount of equipment to have and how to set up budget estimates.

No attempt is made to urge a farmer to follow a particular plan. Rather, the instructor assists him in marshaling all the facts in the case and encourages him to make his own decision. Particular stress is laid in the farm reorganization courses on financing and marketing farm crops and the use of crop outlook and similar information issued from time to time by the U. S. Department of Agriculture, state agricultural colleges and experiment stations and other organizations. Increasing numbers of farmers, Dr. Zook said, are turning to the evening vocational agriculture classes for assistance in adjusting themselves to new conditions.

THE STATUS OF INTRAMURAL AND INTERSCHOLASTIC ATHLETICS

INTERSCHOLASTIC athletics among outstanding high schools in the United States are usually confined to only a few sports, most of which have no carry-over value in later life, a fact which was revealed in the National Survey of Secondary Education, as reported in a new Federal Office of Education monograph, entitled "Intramural and Interscholastic Athletics," prepared by P. Roy Brammell, specialist in school administration of the survey. The report shows that about two thirds of the pupils who practise for intercholastic contests actually participate in them, and in certain sports those practising constitute a small number compared with the pupils engaging in intramural activities in the same sports. There is a tendency in high schools throughout the United States to make intramural athletics and physical education correlate fully. The close relationship of interscholastic athletics to health work, physical education and intramural athletics is usually recognized.

There is no indication that the movement of intramural athletics, which came into full swing about 1925, is losing momentum. Of the 327 secondary schools included in Dr. Brammell's study, 231 reported a program of intramural athletics. As the enrolment increases, the percentage of schools having intramural programs also increases. In many instances, larger schools foster games which have a carry-over value. Football is more prominent as an intramural sport among the four-year high schools than among any other type of school. Comparatively large amounts of in-school and out-of-school time are given to practise and contests.

Nine goals which seem to be recognized as desirable of attainment in conducting intramural athletics are proposed in the report. Among these is the suggestion that full financial support of the programs should be assumed more generally by boards of education; that no physical education credit should be given for participation in intramural sports, as such, unless they are administered definitely as a part of the regular program of physical education; that there should be careful avoidance of eligibility rules which would defeat the objective of "participation by all," and that there should be more active use of the sports program in launching health habits.

That part of the report which treats of interscholastic athletics calls attention to the fact that almost without exception the 327 selected schools report that they engage in interscholastic contests especially for boys. On the other hand, increasing numbers of schools are abandoning such contests for girls. In contrast to 65 sports reported by 231 secondary schools in the list of intramural games, only 26 sports are listed by approximately 500 schools in interscholastic contests.

The interscholastic contests in athletics are limited primarily to five sports—basketball, football, track and field, baseball and tennis. Golf and swimming are fostered by a smaller number of schools. In many secondary schools the lists of sports in which interscholastic contests are held is made up altogether of sports recognized as having no carry-over value whatever. In the small high schools, interscholastic athletics are limited to a small number of sports.

Athletic coaches, the study discloses, are usually members of the faculty and teach regular classroom subjects. Two hundred and twenty-three of the 327 schools included in the study reported that regular coaches are employed to coach the teams in interscholastic sports. The success of the coach in 47 schools is gauged by his ability to develop winning teams. Twenty per cent. of the four-year high schools reported this as the criterion of his success, and 24 per cent. of the schools having enrolments of 300 or fewer pupils also rate him on this basis.

In securing coaches, it appears that more attention is given to the applicant's records as a player than to his training in physical education, or in how to coach the sport which he is employed to direct. It is pointed out, however, that in some parts of the country, steps are being taken to place more emphasis on his training in physical education. The Department of Education in Ohio has recently set up regulations requiring a special professional certificate of full-time or part-time teachers of physical education, health or athletics.

EDUCATIONAL NOTES AND NEWS

DR. DIXON RYAN FOX, professor of history at Columbia University and president of the New York State Historical Association, has been elected president of Union College at Schenectady, N. Y. His inauguration will take place in June. As president, Dr. Fox will also become chancellor of the graduate departments, located at Albany. These include the Albany Medical College, the Albany Law School, the Albany College of Pharmacy and the Dudley Observatory. The election of the new president followed the action of the trustees in granting the request of Dr. Edward Ellery that he be relieved of his duties as acting president in order to resume his teaching of chemistry.

DR. MATTHEW LYLE SPENCER, formerly dean of the School of Journalism at the University of Washington and president of the university from 1927 to 1933, has accepted the deanship of the new Syracuse University School of Journalism, which will open on April 1. Dr. Burges Johnson, professor of English, will serve as associate dean of the school.

DR. HENRY H. APPLE, president of Franklin and Marshall College, received the Hungarian Cross of Merit on February 27. John Pelenyi, minister from Hungary, made the award. Franklin and Marshall College is the only educational institution in the United States which has a department for the study of Hungarian language, literature and history.

DR. JESSE H. HOLMES, of Swarthmore College, has been endorsed as Socialist candidate for Governor of Pennsylvania.

A SPECIAL convocation for the awarding of honorary degrees was held at the Ohio State University on March 2, in connection with the centennial program of the College of Medicine of the university. The honorary degree of doctor of science was awarded to Dr. Henry S. Houghton, associate dean of biological sciences at the University of Chicago; Dr. Torald H. Sollmann, dean of the College of Medicine at Western Reserve University, and Dr. William S. McCann, director of the medical school and physician-in-chief of the Strong Memorial Hospital in Rochester, New York.

PRESIDENT FREDERICK B. ROBINSON, of the College of the City of New York, announced on February 19 the promotion of three members of the faculty to heads of departments and the retirement of the head of the department of physics. Professor Frederick G. Reynolds has been named head of the department of mathematics; Professor Harry C. Krowl, acting head of the department of English, and Professor Charles A. Corcoran, acting head of the department of physics, succeeding Professor William Fox, who is retiring.

SUSAN J. GINN, director of vocational guidance in the Boston public schools, has been elected president of the National Vocational Guidance Association.

DR. O. M. W. SPRAGUE, Edmund Cogswell Converse professor of banking and finance at the Harvard Graduate School of Business Administration, who was for three years economic adviser to the Bank of England, and more recently held a similar position in Washington, has been appointed a member of the advisory board of the Massachusetts Investors Trust.

DR. W. F. GEPHART, formerly dean of the School of Commerce and Finance at Washington University, has recently been elected to the Board of Directors of the United States Chamber of Commerce, with the specific function of finance director. He is also chairman of the Foreign Trade Bureau of that organization.

DR. BEN M. CHERRINGTON, director of the Foundation for the Advancement of the Social Sciences at the University of Denver, has recently been appointed a member of the Colorado State Relief Committee by Governor Johnson.

DR. R. C. MOORE, head of the department of geology at the University of Kansas, has been assigned as director of a geological survey of mountain structure in the Rocky Mountains. The research, under the auspices of the Geological Society of America, will begin next summer and will involve the expenditure of $40,000.

WILLIAM WOODWARD and Sylvester W. Labrot, members of the board of visitors and governors of St. John's College, on February 17 announced their intention to resign, following the election of Amos W. W. Woodcock as president of the institution.

ADOLF A. BERLE, associate professor of law at Columbia University and chamberlain of the City of New York, has obtained a leave of absence for the winter session of the academic year 1934–35. Leave of absence for the remainder of the current year has also been granted to Joseph D. McGoldrick, deputy controller, another Columbia professor active in the La Guardia administration.

PROFESSOR RUSSELL FORBES, director of the Division of Research in Public Administration at New York University, has been granted a leave of absence to accept the appointment of commissioner of purchase for the City of New York.

DR. JAMES ROWLAND ANGELL, president of Yale University, will be the speaker at the sixty-sixth Charter Day exercises of the University of California to be held in Berkeley on March 23.

WALTER LIPPMANN, a graduate of Harvard University in the class of 1910 and a member of the board of overseers, has been selected as the Godkin lecturer at the university for the current academic year.

GOVERNOR LANDON, of Kansas, delivered the Founders' Day address at Marietta College on February 15.

THE Rockford College for Women will celebrate its eighty-seventh anniversary on March 4. Dr. Walter R. Agard, professor of Greek at the University of Wisconsin, will deliver the annual Charter Day address.

DR. ARTHUR FISKE WARREN, head master of the Collegiate School in New York City from 1911 until his retirement in 1929, died on February 17 at the age of fifty-nine years.

DR. FRANK WEBSTER KEATING, superintendent of the Rosewood State Training School for thirty-seven years, died in Baltimore on February 18.

HARLAN HOGE BALLARD, librarian of the Berkshire Athenaeum in Pittsfield, Mass., for forty-six years, died on February 18 in his eighty-first year.

WILLIAM K. KLINGAMAN, state supervisor of high schools in Maryland since 1927, was killed by a train in Baltimore on February 19. Mr. Klingaman was forty-two years old.

DR. JENNY B. MERRILL, one of the founders of the kindergarten system in New York City and its director from 1893 until 1911, died on February 19. Dr. Merrill was eighty years of age.

PROFESSOR JARED F. SCUDDER, Latin instructor at the Albany Academy for nearly fifty years, died on February 20 at the age of seventy years.

MISS HARRIET M. JOHNSON, co-director of the Bureau of Educational Experiment in New York City, died on February 21 in her sixty-eighth year.

NORTON HALL, the new student union building of the University of Buffalo, was opened and dedicated on February 26. The new union, which is the gift of the late Chancellor Charles P. Norton, has been designed in the Georgian style of architecture and cost approximately $250,000.

PROFESSOR HARRY STEENBOCK, of the University of Wisconsin, and his sister, Mrs. Robert Bruce Brinsmade, have given the sum of $7,250 to the university for the establishment of a fellowship in home economics. The fellowship will be named in honor of their mother, Christine Margaretha Steenbock, and will be awarded annually.

WABASH COLLEGE will ultimately receive $80,-

000 from the estate of the late William B. Austin, Chicago mortgage banker. Mr. Austin's will created four trusts whose incomes will be paid to various agencies during the lifetime of his daughter, Mrs. Virginia Hill. At Mrs. Hill's death, these trusts will be terminated, and the principal will be given outright to the college.

THE tenth annual Junior High School Conference under the auspices of the School of Education of New York University will be held on April 13 and 14, instead of on April 6 and 7, as previously announced.

THE eighth annual meeting of the National Association of Collegiate Deans and Registrars of Negro Schools will be held at Florida A. and M. College, Tallahassee, Florida, from March 7 to 10. The guest speakers will be Fred McCuistion, executive agent of the Association of Colleges and Secondary Schools in the Southern States, and Dr. W. W. Alexander, president of Dillard University.

THE much discussed merger between the University of Chicago and Northwestern University has been abandoned, according to a joint announcement made by Presidents Robert Maynard Hutchins and Walter Dill Scott. In place of a merger plans for close cooperation will be evolved. These, it is announced, will very likely include the specialization of both universities in particular fields so that students may be directed to one or the other university. The formal announcement was as follows: "The committees of the boards of trustees . . . which were appointed by the respective boards to study the possibility of closer cooperation, including merger, met separately and at the conclusion of their meetings authorized the following announcement: The committees recommend to their respective boards, (1) that the proposal of a merger of the two universities be laid aside and the committees discharged; (2) that the presidents of the two universities continue to consider the possibility of such closer cooperation as will produce the best results for higher education."

PENNSYLVANIA STATE COLLEGE observed on February 16 the seventy-fifth anniversary of the day on which its first students, 69 in number, entered the institution. The college now has an enrolment of 4,500.

INDIANA public school teachers are now required by a new state law to teach temperance and the effects of alcohol to their pupils. The Indiana Anti-Saloon League is also sending speakers throughout the state to foster this educational program and to cooperate with the state board of education in administering the law.

Two buildings at the University of Denver were sold on February 20 for $145,000 of delinquent special improvement taxes by the Denver manager of revenue, who observed that other buildings would be sold if overdue taxes were not paid. The university had claimed tax exemption, but the revenue authorities insisted that special improvement taxes are not actually taxes but benefit assessments.

WITH the recent action of the governing body of DePauw University, all Methodist-controlled schools have now abolished military training as part of their educational activities. The decision to request the government to withdraw the unit was arrived at by a vote of 33 to 2, by the Board of Trustees. The action was in accordance with views of the Methodist Church on military training as expressed in resolutions emanating from the 1928 and 1932 General Conferences. When Dr. G. Bromley Oxnam became president of the university in 1928, one of his first acts was to declare the courses in military training optional instead of compulsory.

A NEW plan for the election of alumni representatives to the board of trustees of Princeton University was recently approved. The alumni henceforth will be represented on the board by four trustees at large and four regional trustees, instead of by eight regional trustees as at present. One trustee at large and one regional trustee will be elected each year, the former by the entire alumni body and the latter by the alumni resident in the region which the trustee would represent.

THE Board of Trustees of Franklin College have voted that the college should go out of the banking business, so far as its students were concerned. A good many institutions in the past three or four years particularly, and some of them over a longer period, have taken notes from students for payment of tuition. A study of this item at Franklin College brought out the following facts. (1) All such notes were signed in good faith by the students, but (2) unforeseen items coming up after the college days were over caused the postponement sometimes of interest as well as principal, until a feeling of discomfort at returning to the campus was created, and the practise proved to have a dividing, not a unifying effect. (3) A mounting number of notes held by the college were not collectable. (4) Some students did not desire to pay, feeling that if they had "worked" the situation correctly, they might have received a scholarship instead of having the obligation of a note. According to the new policy, the college is on a cash basis.

The trustees of Syracuse University have announced that the university balanced its budget last year, as a result of various economies. The only reductions in salaries were the voluntary contributions, ranging from ten to fifteen per cent., made by members of the faculties during six months of the last fiscal year. While the salaries this fall have been paid at the same reduced rate, announcement has been made that there will be no additional reduction. At the same time checks were mailed to the faculty refunding 25 per cent. of last year's voluntary contributions, with the statement "we hope to make another refund of some proportion later in the year."

An enrolment of 7,933 students from every state in the union and 38 foreign countries and United States possessions is announced for the present academic year by Harvard University. Massachusetts leads the list with 3,122 students. New York comes next with 1,267, followed by Pennsylvania, 372, and New Jersey, 347. Ohio leads in the Middle West with 265 students, California in the West with 200 and Texas in the South with 72. Students attending the university from places outside the United States include 42 from Canada, 22 from Hawaii, 18 from China, 11 each from England and Japan and 10 each from France and Germany. Other countries represented include Brazil, Bulgaria, Chile, Denmark, Greece, Switzerland, Syria and Turkey.

Under Wesleyan University's revision of "generalization" requirements, effective with the next freshman class, a student need not continue with either Latin or mathematics. Only one instead of two laboratory sciences is required, and a half-year course in art or music may be counted in any of the three generalization divisions. The student may also satisfy modern language requirements by taking two more years in the language presented for admission. Only the social sciences, physical education and freshman English requirements are unchanged.

A bill now before the House of Commons would regulate the flow of juveniles into industry by empowering the government at discretion to raise the school-leaving age—now 14 years—by one term at a time up to a maximum of 15 years. The bill would also enable education authorities to grant employment certificates to applicants in cases where suitable posts were obtained. Such certificates would lay down conditions as to the hours of work. They would also provide for the attendance of the young person at courses of instruction. One of the provisions included would empower the government Minister of Labor to make regulations for the granting of certificates up to such limits as to correspond with those of the opportunities likely to be available for employment.

The *Journal* of the American Medical Association reports that although its construction was provided for by the decree of May 22, 1925, the Sanatorium des étudiants, Paris, has only recently been opened to patients. There have been many delays owing to lack of funds. The sanatorium is situated at St. Hilaire du Touvet, in the department of Isère, at an altitude of 1,150 meters, well protected on the north by mountains. A beautiful view of Mont Blanc is afforded. There are 180 beds, with a separate pavilion of thirty beds for the admission, later, of women students. Only students of French universities belonging to the Association nationale are ordinarily admitted. But the directing council has the authority to admit, by way of exception, students who are not affiliated with this association; pupils from higher institutions of learning not of university rank, and even university professors. The maintenance charge is placed at 40 francs ($2.40, current exchange) per day, the government assuming any deficit that occurs. Unless there are medical reasons requiring isolation, each room accommodates two or three boarding patients. Everything is provided for the comfort of the patient. To a partial extent, students are able to continue their studies, the sanatorium being provided with study halls, a fine library and lecture courses held by professors from the University of Grenoble near by. All examinations on work done are given at Grenoble.

DISCUSSION

AN EXPERIMENT IN THE HONORS TREATMENT OF STUDENTS IN ELECTRICAL ENGINEERING[1]

PRACTISING engineers express the view that graduates of engineering schools are usually well-equipped to handle a segregated part of a typical engineering problem, but that they are too frequently unable to meet new situations adequately.

That the system of independently-taught subjects and the associated system of independent examinations in each subject commonly employed in engineering schools may foster a situation such as outlined is a conclusion which is reached by reasoning *a priori*. Ordinarily students deal only with problems which are fragments of larger problems, the wholes of which they never see. The fragments are handed to them, carved out and isolated. Certain specific questions are asked. The examinations usually are set and rated by the same man or group of men who provide the instruction. The examinations usually are relatively brief, are likely to emphasize details and too frequently are of a nature conducive to the mere employment of the memory to recall classroom examples; they usually relate only to things which have been "covered." The students guide the scope of their study accordingly. This scheme of things is in fact of such long standing that if students are asked questions the answers to which they have not previously been told, or to which complete, undebatable (preferably numerical) answers can not readily be found, they are likely to consider the conditions unjust. Even professors may gloss over an uncommonly poor set of answers to a question on the ground that the question really was not wholly fair because the point had not been emphasized particularly in class.

The experience with the Honors Group Plan conducted by the Department of Electrical Engineering of the Massachusetts Institute of Technology during the past eight years is significant of what can be done towards placing engineering education on a more sound basis. The students in these groups have been selected at the end of the sophomore year largely on the basis of the excellence of their academic records and the opinions of their instructors regarding their qualifications for profiting from a situation granting greater freedom of work and demanding more exercise of responsibility and judgment. During the junior and senior years they have been given freedom from the requirement of class attendance and from routine problem and laboratory work. They have been encouraged to do more extensive reading and studying independently and to carry on their problem and laboratory work in an investigative spirit, subject to the advice and guidance of members of staff. With the exception of the comprehensive examinations mentioned later, they have been subject to most of the usual examinations and quizzes. Judged by the records earned on this basis, the honors-group students have stood very high indeed. These results demonstrate that the conditions of work provided by the plan, which have granted greater freedom from routine and greater opportunity for independent study and reflection, at least have not prevented the students from meeting the usual tests most creditably, and probably with greater credit than otherwise would have been the case. Furthermore, the quality of the laboratory work has been particularly improved. Most important of all, the students have been influenced to recognize to a larger degree than is common their own responsibility in connection with the problem of education.

However, for the past three years, following a previous three-year period of preliminary experiment, a comprehensive examination has replaced the usual quizzes and final examina-

[1] Presented at the meeting of Section Q—Education, American Association for the Advancement of Science, Boston, December 29, 1933.

tions of the second term of each senior year. These comprehensive examinations have been set by committees consisting of members of staff and outside examiners invited from industry and other engineering schools. Each examination has consisted of a written part, extending over a two-weeks' period, followed by a day of oral examination about a week after the end of the written examination. The examination problems have been largely of a project nature, each in itself more or less comprehensive, involving the interrelationships of the material of several subjects, and of a nature which have made a demand upon originality, resourcefulness and judgment. The intention has been to outline a situation rather than to request a single numerical answer, an important part of the work being to formulate the problem. Sufficient time has been allowed so that the answers given could be the results of careful analysis and mature reflection. The results of these examinations have been substantially less creditable than the results of the usual examination in separate subjects.

This circumstance is rather strong evidence that high records earned in accordance with the usual system of isolated instruction and isolated examinations are somewhat of a delusion as indication of the competence of students to deal with more life-like situations. While the usual type of examination is not in itself without value, its exclusive use appears to interfere seriously with the ideal functioning of the Honors Group Plan in that it tends to discourage rather than encourage the exercise of vision and initiative on the part of the students in the pursuit of their education. Consequently certain modifications have been made in the plan this year.

(1) In some junior- and senior-year subjects there is a weekly seminar conducted for honors-group students. Various members of the staff are invited to participate. Problems of a more comprehensive nature than is common in the usual classroom procedure are attacked. The results of laboratory investigation are reported and discussed. A particular effort is made to illustrate the interrelationships and analogies between subjects of the curriculum. In connection with each seminar, a syllabus of subject-matter, a list of reading references and a set of comprehensive practise problems are given to each student as an aid in planning and testing his mode of study.

(2) All the usual term examinations of the junior and senior years will be waived. A comprehensive examination will be introduced at the end of the junior year. This examination and the comprehensive examination at the end of the senior year will be characterized by problems of the nature outlined for the previous senior-year comprehensive examinations, though they will include also certain quotas of questions dealing more particularly with the details of individual subjects, the producing of accurate results under pressure of limited time, and the testing of the memory, to the extent that such aspects of the usual examinations seem valuable. Each of these examinations will relate not only to the work of the particular year, but also to previously studied foundation and collateral material.

If the results of the trial this year with the students of the junior class prove to be as favorable as expected, it is hoped that the new examination plan can be continued year by year for juniors, in association with the senior comprehensive examination already permanently established; and that the seminar method of instruction can be extended.

RICHARD H. FRAZIER

MASSACHUSETTS INSTITUTE
OF TECHNOLOGY

MATCHING "ONES"

"ONE should not always insist on one's rights." I suppose that a grammatical stickler would say at once that such a sentence is perfectly correct, but that if I should write, "One should not always insist on *his* rights," then I should be committing an egregious blunder. Perhaps so. Yet if I should express the same idea thus, "No one (or nobody) should always insist on *his* rights," he would have to admit the grammatical correctness of the statement. I have to confess that I can not see the logic of his position.

Why all this pother about "one" and "one's?" "One" is an inoffensive word, and at least the intelligentsia usually know what it means. I take it that the purpose of writing is to convey ideas, and that the high aim of every writer is to convey them in language that does not grate on the ear. It irks me to read: "If one does not wish to get into trouble, then *one* should mind *one's* own business." The repetition of "one" here grates on my ear. I much prefer myself to write: "If one does not wish to get into trouble, then *he* should mind *his* own business," and I defy anybody with a grain of common sense to say that he does not know exactly what the sentence means.

Some very good people, in their effort to be grammatically correct, certainly seem to lean backwards. Let us match a few "ones" together and see how far back we can lean. Suppose one matches one's only silver dollar against another one's only silver dollar and loses the match. Then we might express it in this way: "Once one's one one is won by someone else's one one, then one no longer has one's one one."

Now I submit that this is perfectly correct English, the sort that the grammatical stickler insists on, but I surmise that even he would admit that it is a bit stilted. But perhaps not, provided it were his one one that won.

HORACE J. FENTON

SPECIAL CORRESPONDENCE

POLICIES AND PROCEDURES OF THE COLLEGE ENTRANCE EXAMINATION BOARD

SINCE its foundation in 1900 the College Entrance Examination Board has served as the agent for the effective cooperation between the schools of this country and the colleges of the eastern seaboard. This cooperation has been implemented by the board's definitions of requirements, framed and revised from time to time by commissions of high competence representing both schools and colleges. The history of the board may be regarded as a series of treaties between colleges *inter se* and between colleges and schools. By means of these treaties the confusion of many separately administered examination policies has given way to an orderly plan for the transfer of secondary-school students to higher institutions on reaching recognized levels of accomplishment.

The board's present high position in the educational world is the direct result of its efficacy as a form of institutional control, while its chief weakness lies in its somewhat inadequate descriptions of individuals seeking admission to college. The board's examinations have been directed at institutions rather than individuals.

Many people working in the field of mental measurement have long been keenly and painfully conscious of the unreliability of their measuring devices. People, with this background of experience, tend to appraise board examinations from a novel point of view. They think of the candidate's grade, not as an exact point, but as one particular grade drawn by chance from a hat which contains all that candidate's grades obtained from an infinite series of examinations set and read to measure exactly the same trait. They think of a plus or minus value which would include about two thirds of the grades above and below the average of such an infinite series of measurement—the probable error of estimate of an individual's mark.

The discovered unreliabilities of examinations have led to the effort to eliminate some of the elements of unreliability by objectivity of scoring. The desire to rate an individual more fairly has led to the objective test movement and has given that movement many of its reform characteristics. The objective testers have plunged in with the individual rather than the institutional point of view. Questions of the content of the curriculum, or the effect of such examinations on the curriculum, have simply not been raised, or, if raised, have been regarded as heretical.

One can not now ignore the important relationships between examinations and the content of a course of study as the objective test movement has done. The movement is founded on a sound principle of a minimum of error in assigning a grade to an individual, but has erred by regarding good devices for measuring as a prescription of what should be measured. Therefore, beginning without any notions of definitions of requirements, the new testers have really written requirements which are in fact whatever their tests may happen to measure.

The College Entrance Examination Board is aware of the dilemma between the institutional and individual aspects of examinations and proposes to resolve it, if possible, experimentally. At the November, 1933, meeting of the board, several resolutions were adopted looking toward an eventual solution, among them the two following:

That the existing definitions of requirements be liberally interpreted as indicating in a general way the nature and extent of preparation considered necessary, and not interpreted as prescribing any definite form of instruction, method of preparation, or teaching technique.

That all statements concerning the technique of examining or "descriptions of examinations" in the existing definitions of requirements be rescinded, and the committees of examiners instructed to prepare examinations designed to describe individual candidates with the smallest possible error of measurement.

The essential machinery for launching this new attack on the problem was set up by making a central committee of revision responsible for all examination policies, and by directing the permanent staff of the board to analyze former examinations subject by subject in order to discover methods of increasing their validity and reliability. It is possible to investigate these questions in such a way that the results will throw light on the examinations and thus lead to their improvement.

The board also voted to re-scale marks in all subjects before reporting them to the colleges. In the past, marks have fluctuated widely from year to year, and in the face of such eccentric results it seemed more conservative to assume that the populations were comparatively stable and that the examinations varied in difficulty than to assume that the examinations were constant and that the selection of pupils and the quality of preparation varied.

The board also directed the modern language examiners to work away from the two-, three- and four-unit concepts and develop placement examinations in the modern foreign languages. The appointment of two new commissions was also authorized, one to consider the possibility of introducing comprehensive examinations in history, the other the possibility of a comprehensive examination in science, each examination to be set as representative of the goal of a three-year or four-year course of study. Another commission, recently appointed, is now studying the problem of examining in mathematics.

Carl C. Brigham

Princeton University

QUOTATIONS

PLANNING IN EDUCATION

An attempt is now being made in Nazi Germany to fit supply to demand by cutting down production in a field where the application of this method will be regarded as a startling innovation even by the most enthusiastic advocates of economic planning. Moved by the plight of the "breadless army of graduates" who are unable to earn a living in a country overstocked with doctors and lawyers, the Ministry of the Interior has given orders for drastic reductions of the number of students in the universities, technical colleges, and other establishments which are the gateways to the various professions. Out of nearly 40,000 candidates who have passed their matriculation examination only 15,000 are to be admitted in the coming year, and of these, by a characteristic Nazi touch, not more than one tenth are to be women. Further reductions are to be made if necessary in future years, and at the same time the supply of candidates for admission is to be curtailed by reducing the number of secondary school pupils allowed to complete their course. The qualifications for proceeding to a higher education are to be intellectual and physical fitness, character, and, of course, "national reliability." No one, it may be assumed, who is not a professed Hitlerite need expect any more consideration under the Nazi educational system than an anti-Communist would get in Russia.

The official statement announcing these restrictions points out that all the professions are hopelessly overcrowded, and that the number of university students has risen from 62,900 in 1911 to 123,000 in 1931, 19,700 of whom were women. The intention of the Government is to stem this influx and to divert the would-be professional men and officials into occupations where there is more room for them, and where efforts will be made to find them suitable posts. This interesting experiment, which will have to be judged by its results, is part of a revolt against the exaggerated importance which the educational system in Germany, as indeed in most other countries, has attached to intellectual qualifications and to the acquisition of book learning. The new authorities are determined to secure that more attention is paid to the development of character, and that manual work is recognized as no less dignified than intellectual. According to present plans, in a few years' time every university student will have spent some weeks in a labor camp as an essential part of his education. But the tendency is to be less concerned with universities and secondary schools than with the primary schools, in which the great majority of the people receive their training and which therefore have the first claim on the attention of the state. It is a pity that what is healthy in the Nazi doctrine should be marred by the cruel racial intolerance which is as obvious in its educational as in its other manifestations.—*Educational Supplement of The London Times.*

REPORTS

THE FACULTY AND ADMINISTRATION AT THE UNIVERSITY OF MICHIGAN

FITTING the university budget to a reduced income, giving to the teaching staff a greater voice in the management and planning of educational policies, taking the first step toward dormitories for men students, expansion of adult education, the establishment of a graduate center in Detroit and the inauguration of professional school scholarships marked the year 1932–33 at the University of Michigan, according to President Alexander G. Ruthven, in his annual report.

Large colleges and universities in America today, with their enormously varied programs of instruction and research, have long outgrown the management suited to small institutions, in which the president can be responsible for all details of planning and administration, Dr. Ruthven stated. This has been vaguely recognized, but as such institutions have grown, it has been the common practise to manage college affairs with "a rigid, vertical line of executives appointed by a board of trustees," which "inevitably means in a large school stereotyped instruction and the submergence of individuality."

Dr. Ruthven believes that a business can properly place all executive duties on directors, because in a corporation only the management, and not the employees in general, is responsible to the stockholders; in a school, however, the trustees, administrators and teaching staff are all responsible to the student and society.

Members of faculties are supposedly educational experts. They may, then, be safely trusted not only to discuss policies and administrative procedure, but actually to take part in administration and to exercise executive authority in the educational field. If the educator is as interested as he should be in the progress of his profession, he will profit by opportunities to test his opinions and experiment in educational procedures. Common sense would dictate that this conclusion does not mean that every staff member can be a law unto himself or that an institution can operate with every person trying to be a dean. It does mean, however, that, within properly circumscribed spheres, every member of the staff would have administrative responsibilities and that the facilities would assist in executive activities.

At the University of Michigan, it is believed that proper participation in administration is accorded the faculty by placing each school or college under the direction of a dean, assisted by an executive committee selected by the regents from a panel nominated by the faculties, and by placing other activities under directors assisted by advisory committees selected by the president from panels nominated by the university council. It is further believed that, as far as possible, each staff member should be given administrative responsibilities and that every effort should be made to give executive officials time for instruction and research. The curse of modern university administration has been the attempt to set up two groups of staff members —the administrative and the instructional. Much of the discussion has been academic and the distinctions often imaginary, but a tendency toward a double staff has been discernible. It is believed that the best interests of education will be served if our universities are operated by closely knit organizations of educators rather than by dual staffs of instructors and executives.

EDUCATIONAL RESEARCH AND STATISTICS

A TECHNIQUE FOR INVESTIGATING READING COMPREHENSION

THE solution of the problem of the accurate measurement of reading comprehension has long resisted the best efforts of educational investigators. A large number of investigations have been carried on in the field. As a rule these studies have emphasized the effect of a single factor on reading comprehension, such as: (1) The effect of pupil vocabulary, (2) the effect of sentence length, (3) the effect of sentence pattern, (4) the effect of mental set, (5) the effect of changes in punctuation and (6) the effect of paraphrasing. In each case some one factor was singled out for study which could be measured by objective tests. In general, it appears that these studies are open to criticism on at least two grounds. In the first place, the results of these studies have been based upon scores made on various verbal objective tests, upon certain types of which a recent study by Rhynesburger[1] has cast some suspicion. This investigator found that the true-false test did not measure adequately the pupil's comprehension of a controlled test item. She showed that any particular child might answer a true-false test item correctly and then show in a picture test that his word answer was merely words the meaning of which were not understood. An investigation by the writer[2] corroborated these findings and seemed to indicate that absolute confidence can not be placed in the results of any written test. Even picture tests do not give accurate results when they are checked by oral interviews. In the second place, most of these studies have been extensive statistical investigations in which the individual difficulties have been covered up in the group results.

In order to avoid both difficulties mentioned above, the writer set out to devise a technique which would not be open to criticism on these grounds. The technique devised was the individual oral interview. The Iowa Oral Language Recording Machine was used to record everything said either by the pupil or by the investigator. This machine was devised by Betts,[3] who says that it may be expected to be about 99 per cent. accurate in the recording of oral speech.

This apparatus is a radio microphone connected to a dictaphone. The dictaphone was set up in a room separate from the room in which the interviewing was done. The microphone was placed upon a desk or table in front of the subject being tested but was concealed from the child so that he would not know that his words were being recorded. In this way a pupil was not subjected to microphone nervousness and was natural in his responses. No third person was in the room while the interviewing was being done.

During the interview the investigator may probe as deeply as he can into the pupil's understanding of what he has read and everything said will be recorded. To some extent the interview can be made concrete. The pupil can be given concrete materials and asked to show, not tell in words, just what he means. By his remarks to the pupil the investigator can record just what the pupil did.

After the records of the interview have been made, they are carefully transcribed by typists who have had dictaphone experience. After this transcription has been completed it may be checked by using the records again. This produces an accurate record of everything that has been said by the pupil and by the investigator. With these data in hand to be studied at will it seems that the investigator can really begin to study and analyze individual reading comprehension difficulties. It is probable that the individual interview technique will aid greatly not only in the diagnosis of individual reading comprehension difficulties but will enrich our understanding of the total reading process.

JOSEPH C. DEWEY

LINDENWOOD COLLEGE

[1] Amelia H. Rhynesburger, "A Study of Reading Comprehension in Silent Reading," University of Iowa, M.A. thesis, 1930.

[2] Joseph C. Dewey, "A Case Study of Reading Comprehension in American History," Ph.D. thesis, University of Iowa, 1931.

[3] E. A. Betts, "An Experimental Appraisal of Certain Techniques for the Study of Oral Composition," University of Iowa, Ph.D. thesis, 1931.

EDUCATIONAL REVIEW

Edited by Nicholas Murray Butler, 1891–1919, Frank Pierrepont Graves, 1920–1924, and William McAndrew, 1924–

MONTHLY SURVEY OF EDUCATIONAL BOOKS

By WILLIAM McANDREW

WHERE ARE WE?

For the live teacher smarting under common criticism that the public school neglects teaching the defects of government and the duty of repairing them Peter Odegard's[1] detailed diagnosis is indispensable. The author is professor of political science in Ohio State University. He has vision of what we could be, but his main task here is showing what we are as to social behavior, as to family, church, school, press, political parties, popular will, propaganda, arts, movies, radio and censorship. The array of facts is assembled with the completeness a physician might use in preparing for a consultation over a very sick patient.

With vital instances Dr. Odegard composes a vivid concept of the limping nation. The plain intent of setting up a wide-spread educational service was to prevent the civic infirmity now evident. But, notes our author, the usage of putting unmarried women and girls in charge of so essential a public service would have been resisted by the public-minded had America been less generously supplied with opportunities of getting rich from her natural resources. We used the schools as a vast public charity. Instead of a purifier of politics the public school became a means of giving jobs to those with political pull. Most school boards are not looking for teachers who can lead but for those who will convey to the rising generation the humdrum habits of the existing order. Whoever questions the political system as existing is a radical and not likely to be retained as a teacher any longer than the next school-board meeting. With a few outstanding exceptions teachers have become the most tight-lipped timorous creatures of any profession in the country. Teachers are dismissed not because of incompetence but for teaching doctrines unpleasant in the ears of those in control. So far as Professor Odegard can find, there is no case where a professor or student has been disciplined or dismissed because he is too subservient to the interests which exploit the masses of the people.

This is a very warm book, pulling the wool from over the eyes. It is full of specific anecdotes pointing to the current evils of economic and political life. Nobody need lie down because the Founding Fathers left us nothing to do.

A NOVEL OF THIS CRISIS

Mills, harassed employers, soap-box orators, a bright young chap with honest intentions lured by hope of riches and the love of a beautiful girl of a higher social grade, a sterling school mistress, hunger marchers, the hollowness and moral inadequacy of commercial civilization, its prevention of the basically noble from acquiring full vigor, are painted by Phyllis Bently's sure touch.[2] She writes a gripping novel of man's mechanical victory and his moral failure. His face is toward the future. The time is pregnant with human desire. On this industrial battlefield the fate of mankind is surely being prepared. Two forces delay its progress—fear and the lust for power. Tasker's skill and courage, Crosland's public-mindedness, Walter's noble enthusiasm, Elaine's inspiring beauty—these had the power that could remake a world.

SLOW SOCIAL STUDIES

In his sampling of the offerings of social science teaching[3] Mr. Kimmel, American Historical Association, shows evidence of trying hard to find things to praise. He selects schools reputed to be the best in this line of teaching. He pays extended attention to their advances, but the now numerous writers who are deploring the failure of civic teaching to produce the right kind of voter will not fail to find in this survey corroboration of their criticism.

[1] Peter Odegard, "The American Public Mind." Columbia University Press, New York. 308 pp. $2.50.

[2] Phyllis Bently, "A Modern Tragedy." The Macmillan Company, New York. 435 pp. $2.50.

[3] William G. Kimmel, "Instruction in the Social Studies." Superintendent of Documents, Washington, D. C. 105 pp. 10 cents.

Conventional content, stereotyped by long use, predominates, says Surveyor Kimmel. In civics teaching, stipulated qualifications for public officers seem more important than the way these agents are performing their duties or than the grave problems that need settling. Controversial issues are avoided wherever possible presumably with a view to safety yet no advance, no reform, no progress in civic affairs is ever started and secured except through controversy. The crux of healthy civics teaching is how to train citizens to keep their ear to the ground and to analyze the floods of misinformation and propaganda submerging the voter on all sides. All this matter is controversial. Why, of all places, should the high school, the selected agency for preparing the citizen to grapple with real problems, sidestep the most important ones? It is necessary, suggests the author, to eradicate much of the smug complacency which is implied in the current courses. The pressure toward civic conformity in the schools is relentless. Fear of criticism obliterates desirable goals of civic instruction.

Little or no attention, notes Mr. Kimmel, is directed to local conditions. How long must civics lag behind geography, which long ago saw the advantage of starting from immediate surroundings? Local politics, expenditures, local labor conditions, improvements, needs, receive little or no attention. Economics is a study of the activities of people working together to secure from their surroundings whatever they do secure. This is the accepted definition. But the courses examined seem to belong to an earlier conception of the subject.

Sociology is listed as an offering in high schools, but social forces are not particularized. Social conflict is strictly avoided. Human relations in face-to-face situations, crises and maladjustments receive practically no consideration. Specific study of the local community is included in only one course. Really to be effective, remarks the surveyor, the study should bring pupils to see their community in a different light. We need teaching that is not afraid of the revelation of unpleasant facts.

In the courses called Problems of Democracy small cities and towns do better than the larger ones. New York omits Tammany Hall. Perhaps it is not a problem but a settled fact.

What do you think of this? "There seems to be a tendency in certain school systems to offer the courses in problems of democracy to the less capable pupils," as manual-training, commercial studies and "art" used to be used as a dump for the low I.Q's. Lord help us! Taking wages as producers of citizenship and giving it mostly to the morons!

"Current Events" is one of the best kinds of approach to the knowledge of civic needs that is available to the high school. Mr. Kimmel finds that interpretation of facts, recognition of trends that are a threat to civic wholeness, receive very little attention.

In his last pages, after an extended effort to be as encouraging to educators as we want every one to feel toward them, Dr. Kimmel concludes that, considering the available courses in the light of contemporary needs, they seem to sink immeasurably in significance. The need of prophylactic social studies is of tremendous importance. The crisis is a challenge to the educational army. Behind a system of dykes which are broken and leaking, we are star-gazing instead of training workers in methods of embankment.

INDIGNATION AS A SCHOOL ACTIVITY

How a small group of protesting citizens tackled the graft, corruption, and waste of boss-rule in Cincinnati and set up an efficient and economical government improving all the municipal services; how they are saving big money for the population, is told in a first-class story by Attorney Taft,[4] one of the campaigners in the fight. He describes Cincinnati in the good old days of machine rule. Her politicians robbed her in the typical American style. He recounts the successive victories for good government and the new charter provisions devised for preventing the old pilfering. As a school book this is much more valuable than the history of any war—Peloponnesian or World. The author has a deft brush for portraits, abundant humor and courage—the traits of the happy warrior. His various comments on municipal politics in general are especially valuable just now.

The *Yale Daily News*, he says, advises collegians not to go into politics because it is too dirty; but the real reason is that it seems hope-

[4] Charles P. Taft, "City Management: the Cincinnati Experiment." Farrar and Rinehart, New York. 275 pp. $2.50.

less. The citizen, if he has a spurt of patriotism, goes back to his business and lets government slump once more.

The machine makes politics its business 365 days in the year. Professors act on the assumption that the doings of the machine are no part of the science of government which should be taught, but the boss's technique is effective science of prostituting government.

"I oppose," says Author Taft, "to all this pessimism the faith proven worthy by ten years' experience in a typical city. A citizen's organization can establish good government and maintain it permanently on a business basis without patronage, without yielding to either national political party or injuring either."

One urge by Mr. Taft strikes me as novel and tremendously important: Every school should cultivate indignation in its students. A good helper for it is a study of Frank Kent's two books: "The Great Game of Politics" and "Political Behavior." May I say for the fearless Taft that his book may well be added? In Harry Overstreet's "We Move in New Directions" there is a similar demand: "The schools should teach loathing."

In this account of citizens' effort to purify their government we teachers, so often called the bulwarks of democracy, do not appear. A Cincinnati clergyman who did sturdy work in the campaign remarks that he never found any teachers among the volunteers or workers. For getting the 250,000 signatures necessary to get an amendment to the State Constitution so as to improve county government the campaigners got no cooperation from the school folks. Mr. Jefferson, General Washington and the statesmen who made education a public charge "for good government and the happiness of mankind" would grieve.

This book is a needed supplementary reader for high school and college.

NEW NOTE IN CIVICS

PRINCIPAL SPINDT and Professor Ryan[5] begin their civics for junior and senior high schools with a thoroughly modern note: Have pupils read present periodical literature. Allow free discussions of politics in class. Avoid the question-and-answer type of recitation. When students make reports of matters studied get class discussion of the propositions.

These authors show some of the good old Jefferson influence: "The school should teach what is going on now and should imbue each boy with the intent to make his part of the world go on right."

These teachers have produced a book which is interesting. Their history of our government is continuously related to present situations. Their treatment of the constitution is so narrative as to secure a more interested attention than is usual. Their projects and questions are provocative. The authors go farther into the forbidden fields of public utilities, local misgovernment, initiative, referendum and recall than the average high-school text-book. If this kind of courage grows, the first thing you know you will have civics texts centered on the present defects of government and practical exercises in tackling some of the civic ills in one's own town.

CURE FOR BLUES

PRESUMING a desire to achieve, Mr. Roberts[6] finds failure to be due to lack of method and training. He reduces these to ten principles. He recognizes luck as a factor, grossly overestimated, of no use to your scheme of life because you can't count on it, plan for it or reduce it to habit. But faith, investigation, purpose, planning, economy, learning, enthusiasm, application, sincerity, growth, can be habituated. They are paths to success.

With abundant striking anecdotes and crisp remarks of well-known men of this present time Mr. Roberts conducts you cheerfully through mental attitude, investigation, direction, planning, adequate knowledge, mental capacity, economy of time and effort, application, the will to win and putting yourself across.

This is the sort of book to give to a teacher obsessed with the inevitability of the normalcy curve and the intelligence quotient fatalism. These are devices that are said to show human achievements as they are. No scientific study has ever shown that there has to be such failures as these curves and quotients show. On the contrary, no one has been found who lacks capacities still unfilled. The attitude stimulated

[5] Herman A. Spindt, Frederick Lynne Ryan, "The Foundations of American Government." D. C. Heath and Company, Boston. 500 pp. $1.80.

[6] J. C. Roberts, "Personal Achievement." McGraw-Hill Book Company, New York. 306 pp. $2.50.

by this book is the conviction, while there's life there's the possibility of moving ahead.

WELCOME TO LEISURE

ABOUT ten years ago there was a drama on the boards: "Meet the Missus." In that part of it where the adventurer tells the business man of the joy of doing as one wishes, free of the trammels of wealth and the Joneses, the audience was strangely quiet and intense. A good writer can get a similar grip on readers if the joy of freedom is the theme. Gove Hambidge[7] is such a one. He knows the rich overtones of life, the enjoyments that poverty can not destroy, the satisfactions that steal away the sharpness of hardship and induce tranquillity.

Hambidge threw away the security of an editor's desk, took his wife and children into the country, cut his working time to five hours a day and the family needs to what he could earn on the premises. His little book is full of warmth and sparkle, work, building, mending, sports, food, clothes, friends, civic duties.

Machine perfection, he notes, will flood people with leisure. You needn't fear that Americans will squander it in idleness and vice. That is not the American habit or trend. It is more than likely that many intelligent people will see the duty of devoting themselves to public affairs with the same gusto they have put into earning their living. There will no longer be the excuse, "I haven't time." There is going to be more spare time than people ever saw. The energy is here. There is no question of the need. It is, he says, up to education to see that those it trains are turned in this direction.

NEW LIGHT ON LAUGHTER

IT is safe to say that Dr. Walsh's book[8] is not only the best but the only one of its kind—like the genial author, himself, medical sociologist and psychologist, master of many modern ideas which he has brought to life from forgotten lore. Every one in my neighborhood calls him Father Walsh and, when he is on the platform, hears him with delight. His present volume is a scientific presentation of the hygienic need of laughter. Man's body is built as though intended for a horizontal position with the internal organs hanging from the spine. Man has gotten himself upright and needs some influence to give those organs an influence to counteract their compact. So, come humor and laughter, which no other animal has.

The influence of the laugh on lungs, heart, liver, pancreas, spleen, stomach, intestines and ductless glands is given seven convincing and entertaining chapters. Laughter causing other physiologic action, laughter and surgery, laughter and the mind, have chapters, also. This book will awaken in the minds of teacher readers a train of novel thought.

As principal of a high school I succeeded a disciplinarian whose desk contained hundreds of cards: "———— ———— is reported to the principal for the following *offence*: ————." On these, many of the girl offenders were reported for "laughing." But laughter is so common an activity of people as to suggest it as one of nature's curative agencies. Dr. Walsh so regards it. When William Lewis was head of the William Penn School in Philadelphia he took me to visit a class in laughter. It was a delight. We used to have joke contests in the Washington Irving High School, New York. Ida Benfey Judd and a committee of New York intelligentsia are campaigning for a Mark Twain Memorial traveling professorship of humor. Let's dedicate, also, a monument to Father Walsh while he is alive—and laughing.

THE BEAUTY OF THE LIFE OF MAN

How much of the present ferment in American literature and the arts is mere reaction, disillusion? How much is it the fragmentary assertion of something new? What are the prospects of culture in America? Europe is skeptical of us. Americans are eager to know. The go-getter ideal has collapsed. Its result is dissatisfaction. Economist Orton,[9] in modest mood, fearful of claiming too much, exposes in a masterly and fascinating essay evidences that the cultural capacities of the American people and materials for realization are rich and full of promise. Here is a book on a topic that every teacher I ever knew professes an interest in and feels obligated to know more of. In covering it Mr. Orton paints the beginnings and

[7] Gove Hambidge, "Time to Live." McGraw-Hill Book Company, New York. 144 pp. $1.50.

[8] James J. Walsh, M.D., "Laughter and Health." D. Appleton-Century Company, New York. 197 pp. $1.50.

[9] William Aylot Orton, "America in Search of Culture." Little Brown and Company, Boston. $3.00.

growth of American refinement. He does it with a freshness of view and a fascination of interest. He touches the builders of New England houses, the artistry of Thomas Jefferson, the poetry of Poe, the deterioration of our once worshipped liberty, the intoxication brought by science, the push forward out of confusion. In the procession of events march Louis Mumford, Frank Wright, the rejected Rivera of Radio City, Bertrand Russell, Walter Lippmann, flag-worship in the schools, poets, politicians, critics, the movies, maudlin morality, Will Hays, radio ballyhoo and the public-school teacher.

American education is bedeviled by the business-man idea. To keep down costs the need of a cultural wage for a teacher is disregarded. The value of travel and study is belittled. Salary and prestige are necessary to attract the best talent into teaching.

The land is full of scholars who are called masters of arts and doctors of philosophy. They have wandered through the academic groves and emerged as naked and homeless as when they went in.

For the student who collects credits term by term like beads on a string culture is impossible. He never has time to enjoy the experience of studying.

By the end of the nineteenth century esthetic appreciation had become the Cinderella of education. It had slipped out of the position it held in the Renaissance. A public that is content with the present offerings of the press, the cinema and the radio is incapable of a noble social life. The extension of interest in the arts among the American people is notable. The backwardness of men's colleges in this respect is a curious illustration of academic inertia.

Mr. Orton holds interest to the last page; he cauterizes with mordant criticism; he warms with substantiated praise; he sparkles; he glows. His pictures are abundant, on special paper, and magnificent in subject, execution and illustration of the text. It is a gripping book.

EDUCATIONAL POLICIES OF THE WORLD

SCHOOLED in both the French and German educational systems of his native Alsace, directing education in Odessa for the first three years of the Soviet revolution, participating in the higher seminar of the education department of King's College, London, Nicholas Hans, bringing out a book on comparative education, was given much acclaim by the King's College professor of education, Dr. J. Dover Wilson. The book made a distinct impression on English readers. Revised and enlarged[10] it begins with an examination of democracy and education. Massachusetts was the first example of democracy in education as shown by her law of 1647 when she declared: "The universal education of youth is essential to the well-being of the State. It may fix a standard which shall determine the kind of education and the minimum amount. Opportunity must be provided at public expense for youths who wish to be fitted for the University." The people fell away from this intelligent attitude. Compulsory education slumped until 1852 when Massachusetts again led the way until in 1918 Mississippi followed the other American commonwealths and enacted a compulsory law. Dr. Hans traces this movement through the countries of the world. He discusses the state and the church and the family, the ups and downs of centralization and dispersion of authority, the class policy, the care of exceptional children, vocational education, the training of teachers, curriculum regulations, universities, adult schooling, finances, education and politics, nationalistic interpretation of history, the campaign for internationalism. The author's array of facts, his analysis of the doctrines of the great educational reformers of all nations, his summary of educational philosophies, make this a masterly presentation of the history of educational advance.

EDUCATION IN THE DEPENDENCIES

Two new Kandel-lights on education in the world have come from the International Institute of Teachers College, New York.[11] The '31 yearbook covers education in colonial dependencies in Asia and Africa: fourteen accounts by persons associated with the service. Education in this field, remarks Dr. Kandel, in a summary of the volume, is at the crossroads. The attempt to transplant the educational sys-

[10] Nicholas A. Hans, "Principles of Educational Policy." P. S. King and Son, London. 276 pp. 8s 6d.

[11] I. L. Kandel, editor. Educational Yearbook, 1931. Teachers College Press, Columbia University, New York. 721 pp. $4.00. Also, 1932. 497 pp. $3.50.

tem of one people to another has failed. Our experience of twenty-five years with the Philippines and Porto Rico shows the futility of transplanting to a different environment what at the time of its approval for those dependencies was regarded as the most advanced experiment in democratic schooling.

RELIGIOUS EDUCATION AND POLITICS

THE yearbook for 1932 is devoted to discussions by appraisers of religious education in Australia, Belgium, Canada, China, Czechoslovakia, England, France, Germany, Holland, India, Italy, Japan, Latin America, Mexico, Norway, Scotland, Sweden, South Africa and the United States. For the last-named there is presented a Protestant view, a Roman Catholic and a Jewish. As usual, Dr. Kandel gives a comprehensive summary. Generally there are emerging troublesome questions known only to modern times: What rights have the religious minorities? Has the State the right to exclude teaching other than that germane to its purpose in maintaining schools? France, fifty years ago, decided that the influence of the church must not be political in the schools. England has endeavored to satisfy its religious groups. Italy's easier solution has not escaped trouble. The Orient is troubled by the problem. Religious education is becoming a political question, and disconcerting.

A SCHOOLMASTER'S TIP-TOP NOVEL

FAR up on the heights of New York City a college professor of education is speaking: "The public schools are owned and controlled by the interests that own the government. The schools teach mass worship of big business, conformity to present anti-social institutions, the doctrine of individualism, which excuses the few for trampling the many. Our task as educators is to help Americans study their surroundings and to develop the spirit of cooperative action to the end that our graduates will refuse a life beset with meager wages, by curtailed freedom of speech and action, by inequalities and oppression."

"But," excitedly asks a bespectacled young man, "mightn't we be fired from our jobs?"

These two ideas weave in and out of a thrilling novel by Schoolmaster Shields,[12] a handsome young supervising principal of Winston-Salem. This is no amateurish attempt. He knows how to tell a rattling good story with live people in it: Rotarians, lovely schoolmarms, cattish ones, too, the "business-man" superintendent who has forgotten his responsibility for getting good teaching done, the gossips who charge immoral conduct against the progressive woman, and, mussing through it all, the lumbering members of the school board. There's no drag in the story. Its pictures of the life the school worker leads are vivid and authentic.

ARE SCHOOL BOARDS FIT FOR THEIR TASK?

A THREE-MAN school board leads to such intimacy with the superintendent that if he is a good fellow he loses the healthy check of criticism by his board. A larger committee saves the schools this damage. Mr. Dudley[13] in his study of local control of public schools takes up many practical matters like that. He finds ample wealth for supporting the kind of education the people need, he queries the local unit system's suitability for giving equal opportunity, evidence of adequacy of lay boards, whether their professional leadership is filling the need.

This is a broad-minded but careful penetration of the large question of school control and support, matters which in this time of revolution have assumed greater importance than ever.

WHERE DEPRESSION HITS THE TEACHER

PROFESSOR EELLS' study of educational wages and costs[14] grows more pertinent as the stringency continues. Teachers' salaries have never been high. They lagged in the rise of 1915 to 1930. America has been paying for instruction for more than 300 years and has no logical basis for adjusting wages to maintenance of educational efficiency. The Eells study abounds in matter that teachers' associations and school defenders will do well to understand when appeals are made to dispensers of public funds. He handles the cost-of-living index figure with lucidity. He expounds the changes

[12] James M. Shields, ''Just Plain Larnin'.'' Coward-McCann, New York. 344 pp. $2.00.

[13] L. Leland Dudley, ''The School and the Community.'' Harvard University Press, Cambridge. 179 pp. $2.50.

[14] Walter Crosby Eells, ''Teachers' Salaries, and Cost of Living.'' Stanford University Press, California. 94 pp. $1.00.

in the cost of board and lodging, diagrams the lag in salary adjustments. School salary is like the electric cable under the elevator, the last to go up, the first to come down. The investigations in this book, the models of argument, are applicable to every district in the country.

TEACHING TEACHERS BY FILMS

A SERIES of talking films for teachers' training classes in education throws upon the screen and delivers the words of Boyd Bode, Arthur Gates, William Kilpatrick, Guy Buswell, Hughes Mearns and others, thirteen in all. A syllabus[15] is available reproducing the lessons of the speakers and describing the films. The themes are: philosophy of education, methods, measurements and guidance.

HOW DO WE REVISE CURRICULUMS?

SOME systems have been, through a special organization, maintaining a yearly revision of their courses of study for the past ten years. Some are complacently holding on to the course sanctified by the schoolmasters of our fathers. Of 800 private schools interviewed 90 are paying some attention to making changes. This and much other interesting information is derivable from Mr. Lide's monograph[16] in the series of a National Survey of Secondary Education. The compiler gives a summary of many procedures. He pays particular attention to some revisions done by a method which he considers superior.

If one were able to exclude from his mind the concepts of education which he has absorbed by working in high schools, one of the striking aspects of all these revisions would be the assumption that subjects are the basic necessity. The high-school structure has always been a patchwork in the old importation from monarchical Europe. It was brought here before the Revolution. Even the national association of school superintendents, by resolutions, reject its objectives and "Again remind ourselves that our American systems of education were established to preserve and improve our political institutions. We pledge ourselves that not culture, nor scholarship, nor college, shall turn us from the needs of our civic life and a determination to improve it."

A study of the pamphlets reviewed by Allen Oscar Hansen in his "Liberalism and Education in the Eighteenth Century" show statesmen, after the adoption of the Constitution, making curriculums based on the need of a citizenry capable of handling the political and economic responsibilities of cooperative government. These men were not schoolmasters, but they pushed a new plan of taxing for education those who have no children in school. They justified this taxation without representation on the ground that the schools were preponderatingly to be devoted to political and economic education. There is little in Mr. Lide's findings to show that the high schools are revising on this basis. He finds forty-nine which say they are revising "from the ground up." From what ground? If it is from the revolutionary ground promised by those who got schooling made a public charge you will not find it in the monograph. You find no revision starting with the historical and financial sanction for taxing a community instead of parents for a political, economic education centered on citizenship needs not on a "child-centered school." Until revisionists set down these objectives first and then select from all known subjects and activities such daily exercises as have the highest civic voltage, giving what time is left to the present enjoyable high-school pursuits your curriculum revision will continue a patchwork on the educational machine of the gentlemen of Queen Anne's court.

A DELICIOUS PLAY BOOK

MAUDE LYNCH, M.A., master of the art of games that develop observation, skill, individuality and good nature, joins with a charming illustrator, Margaret Freeman, in the production of a delightful manual[17] for worthwhile occupations of younger children. Here is building, cut-ups, scrap-book making, pencil plays, parties, home museums, and games. Mrs. Lynch says she would like a letter from such children as enjoyed the book if they will be sure to tell their ages. Here's mine:

[15] Thirteen Speakers, "Modern Trends in Education." Erpi Picture Consultants, 250 W. 57th Street, New York. 300 pp. Cloth, $1.50, paper, $1.00.

[16] Edwin S. Lide, "Procedures in Curriculum Making." Superintendent of Documents, Washington, D. C. 99 pp. 10 cents.

[17] Maude Dutton Lynch, "I'm Busy. A book of play activities." Houghton Mifflin Company, Boston. 162 pp. $1.50.

Dear Madam,

You are a dear. It's all right for me to say this, for I am seventy and over.

ANOTHER HIGH SCHOOL ECONOMY

How school costs may be reduced and the public served by correspondence courses is outlined by rural specialist Gaumnitz[18] of the Office of Education. Australia and Canada are working the plan successfully. Costs, courses, cases and check-ups are gone into extensively by this timely bulletin.

BENEFIT-SERVICE IN SCHOOL

AN enheartening contrast to the general selfish basis of high-school extra curriculars is visioned in a pamphlet by two gentlewomen[19] of the faculty of the Horace Mann School, New York. These children, as the writers remark, will soon be of adult American society. What good to it will they be? What influence is distinctly able to increase that good? Why not have school do this? For several years, the pamphlet says, the haphazard, unorganized aims of extra-curricular activities have been a feature lacking integration with the accepted purpose of school as a social benefactor.

The progress the Horace Mann School has made in correcting this anomaly constitutes the main theme of the description of the spirit and organization of the Mann activities as far as they have been developed. I note the responsibilities taken by pupil government for almost all the doings of the school other than teaching the curriculum subjects.

I rejoice in these student-faculty committees, their elections, their girl hostesses, their avoidance of retaining good pupil officers to the exclusion of others who need the practise. The whole extended outline of organization is a workable model. But the thing that warms the heart is the prevalence of "otherness" in the spirit of the activities. Services in the nearby public nursery is done for others. Study of unemployment, assisting in relief, penny-boxes for self-denying contributions to social service, making garments and toys for the welfare agencies, helping in the library of the Hudson guild are regular Horace Mann stunts in the practise of what the highbrows call by the high-sounding name of altruism. For these youngsters it is a "project." Every chapter of the school league has one. It isn't what you know about your country, remarked old Benjamin Franklin to the graduate, 150 years ago, it's what you do for it.

If curricular requirements teach citizenship and there is no practise of it, any amateur psychologist knows how scanty the results. If a school can give rooms and teacher-sponsors for the present multitude of enjoyment clubs, it can turn many of them into the direction of bettering the social order. Take Fairhaven, Massachusetts, for instance. Superintendent Prior told me the high-school pupils voted to take 50 per cent. of the money received from all admission tickets to shows, games, etc., and to devote it to town service. Every room in every school in Fairhaven maintains a public benefit club. Nothing more striking than the slowness of teachers to direct the growing social sense of pupils into worth-while action is justification for the doubts expressed by such critics as Counts, Snedden and Robins on whether the American teacher really cares to better the social order. But I can tell you that the mere enjoyment of dramatic clubs, orchestras, athletic contests and such things is doubled when you harness them to community service outside the school. In our town an amateur dramatic society gave shows, dividing the profits among the participants. It soon fizzled out. A schoolman revived it by devoting all its earnings to the town library. This community spirit kept a delightful choral society together and gave la-crosse, cricket and ball matches a big spirit. School children are entitled to the joy of direct town service. If they fail to get it their teachers are not awake to what civic service is.

A SANE SEX BOOK

I HAVE seen no book that gives a boy the necessary knowledge of sex dangers so simply and inoffensively as a handsome little volume by Dr. Rice,[20] professor of pathology, Indiana University Medical School. He comes to the

18 Walter H. Gaumnitz, "High School Instruction by Mail." Superintendent of Documents, Washington, D. C. 69 pp. 10 cents.

19 Helen M. Atkinson, Cecile White Flemming, "Education for Constructive Social Influence through Student Organizations." Teachers College Press, Columbia University, New York. 31 pp. 50 cents.

20 Thurman B. Rice, M.D., "In Training." American Medical Association, 535 N. Dearborn Street, Chicago. 48 pp. 25 cents; per hundred, $16.00; more than a hundred, 14 cents each.

theme through a natural discussion of the universal desire of making a success of life. He is effective in putting the facts of sleep, cleanliness, vigor and self-knowledge in a way to attract boys. The old false exaggerations which cause prolonged anguish to many a frightened lad are frankly met and answered in the light of scientific truth, as are given the real facts of sex. The tone of the book is singularly wholesome. It will transmit to the young reader the healthy spirit in which it is written.

NEWER OBSERVATIONS IN ADOLESCENT CHANGES

CINCINNATI UNIVERSITY's head of its department of child care and training, Dr. Arlitt,[21] writes fourteen chapters embodying the new aspects of adolescent behavior heretofore but dimly apprehended. The book is for students in college and training schools as well as for teachers at work. Four of Dr. Arlitt's chapters are on the intelligence and learning ability at this period and the proper mental hygiene. It is an understanding review simply and effectively told.

HANDBOOK OF LEADERSHIP

A SOLID little book is Counsellor Stock's[22] discussion of training for leadership. A careful study of the interests of the older young people, he says, brings disappointment because they seem indifferent about so many important matters. Look into the abundant extra-curricular activities to which teachers are giving so much attention—dances, games, dramatics, sundry very paltry interests compared with the serious needs of present social, political and economic problems. In view of the worth-while things that young people can be brought to do with real enthusiasm, the high schools offer an amazing array of barren trivialities. Make an outline of the present interests of youth in detail, says our author, then make another one of needs. Note the difference. You can set down fifty worth-while activities, beginning with the nature of life and ending with marriage. Get your youngsters to check ten matters on your list which interest them. One of the tasks undertaken by a typical high-school faculty is to "give them what they ask for" and nothing more. This, he says, is utter folly. Mr. Stock is for teachers listing for each boy and girl the particular qualities for leadership that each has and for developing these talents.

He is chiefly concerned with moral and religious education. He writes on a definite and practical program with a high ideal. He is interesting to every teacher who is still alive.

FACE-TO-FACE LEADERS

LEADERS, says a late monograph[23] issued by Indiana University School of Education, can be pretty well considered as of two kinds—men of thought, men of action. The Smith-Krueger study is of the leader face to face with his group. These are the dynamic infusers like Billy Sunday and Aimee Semple; the prophet; a leader without an office; the boys' gang leader; the professional leader; clergyman, teacher, and others. This monograph is remarkably valuable for high-school and college officers. Educational institutions have long professed training in leadership. Here is a treatise analyzing it. What is its genius? Where are leaders found in larger numbers? What are the types? What are the traits of followers? What are the techniques of leadership? How can it be taught? These and related questions are handled in this modest but important review.

TELLING THE PUBLIC

NEWSMAN FARLEY'S volume[24] in the High-School Survey series is a meaty review of the best ways education is being interpreted to those who are paying for it. There are discussions on the ways of getting cooperation of newspapers, putting students up to a realization of their obligation to the community, reaching the homes, getting the public to school, humanizing reports, and so on. As usual in this series the practises are real. They are accounts of methods now in use.

21 Ada Hart Arlitt, "Adolescent Psychology." American Book Company, New York. 246 pp. $1.80.

22 Harry Thomas Stock, "Young People and Their Leaders." The Pilgrim Press, Boston. 167 pp. 75 cents.

23 Henry Lester Smith, Levi McKinley Krueger, "Brief Summary of Literature on Leadership." Bureau of Research, School of Education, Indiana University, Bloomington. 80 pp. 50 cents.

24 Belmont Farley, "Interpreting the Secondary School to the Public." Superintendent of Documents, Washington, D. C. 113 pp. 10 cents.

SHOULD A PROFESSOR STUDY PEDAGOGY?

"THE majority of the faculty are skeptical in admitting that there is any value to the college teacher if he takes courses in education." This is the reply of the only faculty committee whose answers are printed in connection with the questions sent by the Association of College Professors[25] to its chapters. I am old enough to remember similar skepticism toward organized preparation for their profession voiced by country doctors, pharmacists, lawyers, shipbuilders and architects. I recall the loud protests of teachers and board members against insertion in Mr. Maxwell's requirements for intending teachers in the city schools, a provision that they pass examinations in pedagogy. Isn't it interesting that studying the art of teaching is required for every school field except for the highest where teaching is commonly said to be at its worst? If researchers were set loose appraising the learning of boys under professors who have studied the teaching art and of boys under those who haven't, there could be something more definite to wrangle over. So long as a professor need not study his profession nor be subjected to supervision nor have his work tested, his heel is Achillesian, isn't it?

Nevertheless, this volume is full of active sap. What is the purpose of teaching? How good is it in college? Is it drawing high talent into professorial chairs? Does good pay pay? How about research? Are there practical ways to measure a professor? Is he responsible in any degree for college policy? The discussion of these matters and other themes in the report is full of interest—and caution. The professors, God bless 'em, are as reluctant to have the yardstick applied to their work as were the clergymen to consider John Tyndal's prayer-test. And maybe they are right.

SHOTS INTO THE FLANK

IN connection with the study just reviewed one may remember the warm report of the University Professors Committee Q.[26] This was the work of a three-year-old committee which was impressed by the thought of many professors that the preparation of high-school teachers had an excessive amount of professional training. Committee Q's investigation on its own account brought it to the belief that the public high schools are controlled to a large extent by people who are definitely committed to heavy professional requirements and that inquiries should challenge the right of continuance of such control. Committee Q thought attention should be paid to the manner used by the Cooper-Koos national surveyors in selecting the people to answer the inquiries on professional training of high-school workers.

Committee Q sent a question blank to 136 larger private schools asking opinions on professional training of teachers. Thirty-seven did not desire it, twenty-five were slightly influenced by it, ten distinctly desired it. The "born teacher" tradition had its warm advocates. "Know the subject and know boys" was a favorite maxim. The ex-cathedra decisions included: "The best teachers have had none," "Success depends on personality," "In thirty years I have *proved* the uselessness of it." The upholders of professional training were fully as positive. All the evidence, both ways, was personal opinion. No one knew of any scientific proofs, control cases and statistical tests, bearing on the question.

The committee sent question blanks to 1,800 teachers, enclosing stamps, and promising to protect anonymity. Why do teachers have to be babied so? Q got back 425 replies, of which 391 were used. The answers reproduced are about as rich criticism on the teachers of teachers as Mr. Mencken could phrase. Of those who approve professional training the majority favor practise teaching, methods and educational psychology. Committee Q finds these teachers in agreement with Artemas Ward: "This is 2 mutch."

Committee Q was appointed with the belief that a well-defined movement had been started to impose upon university teachers professional requirements comparable to those exacted of high school teachers. Committee Q believes that its findings effectively destroy any arguments for the movement. We have not met the enemy, but we have defeated him.

The two reports are milestones on the road of

[25] William B. Munro and eight professors, "Report of the Committee on College and University Teaching." American Association of University Professors, 744 Jackson Place, Washington. 122 pp. 50 cents.

[26] Kenneth P. Williams, Chairman, and seven professors, "Report on Required Courses in Education." American Association of University Professors, 744 Jackson Place, Washington, D. C. 63 pp. $1.00.

educational history much more worth preserving than the tracts printed when proposals to set up normal schools were gaining strength. They create a superb project for the foundations to finance. They indicate an opportunity for some heroic professorial Walter Reed to volunteer for inoculation with the virus of pedagogical science. Me? I never took one of these courses, nor wrote a book on high school, but I had what I call my mind injured by my collegiate experts in their subjects who knew nothing of teaching and cared less. No one supervised them. Nobody dared tell them they were botches in a great art which does have measurements of efficiency and principles of success.

ALERT APPRAISALS OF NEEDED CHANGES

No counsel to let the storm blow over is volume V of the annual Proceedings of the Institute for Administrative Officers of Higher Education.[27] The Institute's prospectus promises critical discussions of current tendencies. This yearbook bristles with sharp comment on educational policies in the present revolutionary time. You are, in the first few pages, told that changes in civic training are inevitable. The economic situation will secure new functions of political organization. A world steeped in tradition, insists Charles Merriam, in a stirring address, has a prime social need, reorganization. This is the essence of necessary civic education. The Merriam essay ought to be reprinted in the Journal of the National Education Association in order that educators everywhere may have easy access to it. Its analysis of the present public mind is convincing. Government has always been tinged with doctrine that it is in some way divine, something handed down from above, not to be changed. In this democracy there are those who teach the Constitution as a sacred book, instead of the experiment its makers considered it, subject to further experimentation as time goes on.

Homer Ferguson as president of the United States Chamber of Commerce will have you believe that the worst government, the weakest, is the best. A New York state legislative report proclaims: "No person who is not eager to combat social change should be entrusted with the task of fitting young or old for the responsibilities of citizenship."

Professor Merriam compares the spirit of civic education with that of agriculture, commerce and science. The first discourages change; the others urge inventiveness and experiment. The times emphatically call for the abandonment of the blind worship of the past and for a utilization of experience and the spirit of science in molding the present and the future.

In this volume Arthur Klein shows the need of a thorough reappraisal of university activities from the standpoint of the country's distress. Homer Rainey sees the social program of the college as largely passive. It has taken no responsibility for the formulation of a civic program. It has taught an idealism wholly out of harmony with political and economic usefulness. It has almost incapacitated its students for active economic and political leadership. Contemporary society requires economic intelligence and ability for political planning.

Charles Judd's recommendations touch upon the tenacity of the academic mind in holding to traditions of scholarship to the neglect of familiarity with civic and economic problems. George Zook summarizes findings adverse to the bugaboo raised regarding large classes. He treats college entrance requirements in a healthy critical mood. All grades of education, he remarks, have enjoyed peculiar popularity. It has been difficult to appreciate the sudden reversal of opinion on the part of a good proportion of the mass of the people. Nelson Metcalfe talks on readjustment of athletics to the end that every student will take part in vigorous games, play them well, and with enjoyment.

Simeon Leland showers cold hard sense in his discussion of taxation. Those seeking government aid for education miss too often the connection of education to government. If education gets money by public taxation or, what is, in a degree, the same thing, if its property pays no taxes, its duties to the peoples government are as important as is the management of police, street sweeping and highway construction. Educational finance and garbage finance are of the same sort. The traditional separation of education from government has led educators to assume that their work is not a part of the political system. This aloofness leaves educa-

[27] William S. Gray, Editor, Seventeen authors, "Needed Readjustments in Higher Education." University of Chicago Press. 283 pp. $2.00.

tional forces with little appreciation of the problems of government. It has created an attitude of the educational craft that they are entitled to financial support free from requirements of government. Taxation for the support of higher education, like that for the common schools, is taxation to maintain the State. Higher education is being dispensed to confer an alleged prestige or to improve the recipients' culture, or their economic status, or their enhanced value as citizens. The problems of today require more than a common school training. They must have a constant raising of the educational level and the push of research into civic economic problems farther than the fringes. Developing the citizen intelligent in the economic and political field is an inescapable duty of higher education.

CONDUCTING A UNIVERSITY

THREE years' work scrutinizing every essential detail of nearly fifty large projects are summarized in a round dozen volumes.[28] According to the laws of this university, the president is to exercise such supervision over all educational departments as will promote their efficiency. He is the official medium between faculties and trustees, the same agent for students. He is responsible for the discipline of the university. Messrs. Reeves, Kelly, Russell and Works, who write the volume on administration, go farther and say that in the eyes of the public he is the personification of the university. He provides the vision to inspire its major developments.

There is no denying that these functions of a president are the commonly accepted ones in the United States and that no small amount of carefully reasoned arguments in print show their respectable writers' conclusions that this monarchical form of university government built up by captains of industry is a large obstacle to the service higher education ought to be rendering. Volume III of the survey repeats the words of the first president that the greatest university danger is possible lack of harmony in the faculty.

[28] Floyd W. Reeves, director and ten writers, "Trends in University Growth, University Organization and Administration, Faculty, Instructional Problems, Admission and Retention of Students, Alumni, Libraries, Extension Service, The Plant, Student Problems, Class Size and Costs, Oriental Institute." University of Chicago Press. 12 vols. $22.50.

"Direct public service has played a small part in the selection of professors. It arises as a by-product."

The emphasis on research, note the surveyors, must not be interpreted as a neglect of instruction. The two have at times been in sharp conflict. This university's recent reorganization is aimed to give instruction more emphasis. Tables show the teaching loads and what percentage of instruction and other work the staffs do. Volume IV is devoted to policies and methods of instruction and the ways of improving it.

In Volume V the never unvexed question of what students to admit and whom to retain is given extended attention. A chapter especially germane to the public schools covers the kind of men and women who are taking courses in education. The median age of these at the time of receiving their bachelor's degree in education is 25; at receipt of master's degree 34 years. Twenty-seven per cent. of the masters entered into teaching in higher education; 40 per cent. entered public schools as administrators and supervisors; 26 per cent., as public school teachers; 7 per cent. went into other service.

Those getting doctor's degrees in education have a median age of 42 years. Eighty-five per cent. enter teaching in institutions above high school grade, 11 per cent. become educational administrators in public school systems.

The volume on student problems touches on the old query, What rank do honor students attain in after life? Scholarship holders from this university are 20 per cent. more frequently listed in "Who's Who" than are those who obtained no scholarship awards. This volume discusses student loans, effect of living environment on college success, the reading done by students, evaluation of chapel services, and so forth.

The monograph on class size cites the conclusions reached in Volume III of this survey that the size of class is not responsible for any differences of importance in the teacher's burdens but of great weight as affecting costs. The disputed question of instructional efficiency in small or large classes is untouched.

Professor Breasted closes the series with a fascinating account of the explorations of the Oriental Institute and enlivens it with a profusion of pictures, many in color.

SCHOOL AND SOCIETY

WITH WHICH ARE COMBINED THE EDUCATIONAL REVIEW, ESTABLISHED IN 1891, THE TEACHERS MAGAZINE, ESTABLISHED IN 1878, AND THE SCHOOL JOURNAL, ESTABLISHED IN 1874.

EDITED BY J. McKEEN CATTELL, R. D. LINDQUIST AND W. H. COWLEY

EDITORIAL COMMUNICATIONS SHOULD BE ADDRESSED TO THE EDUCATION BUILDING, THE OHIO STATE UNIVERSITY, COLUMBUS, OHIO

Volume 39 — SATURDAY, MARCH 10, 1934 — Number 1002

FEDERAL AID—BOON OR BANE[1]

By Dr. WILLIAM F. RUSSELL

DEAN OF TEACHERS COLLEGE, COLUMBIA UNIVERSITY

THE public schools are dear to the hearts of the American people. We love them because they belong to us. No national government forces them upon us. No minister of education prescribes their operation. We take educational order from no higher power. The public schools are our own. We created them. We, the people, determine who shall learn, who shall teach, what shall be taught and by what methods, what the school shall be like, where it shall be located—and we reach down in our own pockets and pay the bill. American schools are folk-made, and they are folk-controlled and folk-directed as well. This system is America's pride and joy. In it we all take great delight.

When we look overseas, we find no envy for the highly centralized school system of France, where most of the funds are supplied by the nation as a whole and most of the control rests in Paris. Nor do we find much to imitate when we look upon Australia, with its huge states each in complete control of its schools. There all the money comes from the state as a whole; the locality makes no contribution. All powers reside at the capital. The parents have nothing to say.

We can go from country to country in the world to-day and note the way in which certain of the strongest governments are using their highly centralized school systems to entrench themselves for years to come. Citizens in disagreement are being coerced; the recalcitrant are banished; rebels are stood before firing squads. But these measures are not necessary with the citizens of to-morrow. The young are being enticed, their minds are being seduced, helpless in the powerful grasp of propaganda through nation-wide compulsory education completely under national control. The minds of the oncoming generation are being poured into a mould.

Thus the American has only to examine education in Russia, Japan or Nazi Germany to come to appreciate the precious treasure that he has in the American public schools. They are locally controlled. They are sensitive to the will of our people. By their place in our plan of government, they are at the focus of a myriad of conflicting interests. They are almost perfectly protected from nation-wide partisan or transitory desires. There is a remote chance that some Hitler in some future time might be elected to high office in the United States; but he would have a difficult time, indeed, to win control of our schools and colleges.

That is, he could not have dominated the schools in the past; but a new day is at hand. Our government is changing. The

[1] Address given before the Department of Superintendence, Cleveland, Ohio, February 27, 1934.

depression is modifying the balance of power between the localities, the states and the Federal Government; and there is a good possibility that measures now pending, if adopted, may alter fundamentally the American method of school administration, and make our schools more like those in Europe or Asia that I have cited.

It is unnecessary for me at this time, for this audience, to give in detail the argument which justifies federal participation in the financing of education. We know that this is no new idea. It was advocated in the days of the Confederation. It was implied in the Ordinance of 1785. It was suggested several times in the Constitutional Convention and was in mind when the general welfare clause was drawn. It was advocated both by Alexander Hamilton and Thomas Jefferson. Constitutional amendments to provide it were recommended to Congress by Madison and Monroe. Step by step, in the distribution of the national surplus, in the first Morrill Act and in the succession of acts down to the present day, the Federal Government has played an increasing part in supporting education in the states. We also understand the gradual obsolescence of the taxing system which has tried to support education upon the proceeds of a tax upon the property of a limited taxing area. There was once a time when wealth, as measured by land and buildings, and educational burden, as measured by children in the district school, were roughly proportional from area to area and from state to state; but the growth of transportation and communication, the development of technology, the flight from country to city and the concentration of capital—all manifestations of the machine and power ages—have disturbed this balance. Financial resources and educational burdens within the borders of the states have been found to vary so widely from community to community that state equalization of financial support has been found necessary.

Following a similar line of reasoning, experts in school finance have come to believe that federal aid is necessary. From the study of the efforts made by the state to assist localities to provide minimum educational programs, they have come to learn what was hidden from the layman—that, just as a remote district in many a state is unable to support even a minimum educational offering and in consequence state aid is needed, so an entire state, like Arkansas or South Carolina or South Dakota, may be similarly disqualified from being able to support *as a state* the kind of educational program that the American people deem to be the minimum. Even if there had been no depression, it would have been necessary for the national government to take a share in the financial support of education in order to maintain a minimum standard throughout the United States. 1929 was a boom year in the stock market. 1929 was the culmination of an era of great prosperity; 1929 marked a high point in the general use of automobiles and radios; but, even in that golden age, American children in many states in no small numbers went to hovels for schools, remained there for short terms and were taught by the kind of ignorant teacher that starvation wages would employ. Federal aid would have had to come, depression or no depression!

But the economic conditions of the last four years have hastened a development which otherwise might have been long delayed. Decreases in incomes, shrinking property values, collapse of basic industries, the desperate state of agriculture and manufacturing, the failure of the banks—all these factors in whole or in part removed the ability to pay from a substantial part of the population. Taxes could be levied on real estate, but they could not be collected. The result is the lamentable situation of the moment. Schools are closed. Children are on the street. Teachers are paid in script or not at all. Essential services have been discontinued and institutions abandoned. This distress tugs at our heart strings. This social stupidity stirs us to action. One thing comes to mind. Let us strive to reform state laws and institute new modes of taxation; but the truth is that every time the Federal Government devises a new tax or increases an old one, it is all the more difficult for the states to correct their present systems. In fact, some tax experts are now advocating that all tax collections be made by Washington, because the Federal Government, by taxing incomes and imports and by its large sales taxes on automobiles, alcohol and tobacco, has removed from the states the only taxes which could be collected. Thus the real difficulty in the present educational situation has not been caused by the depression. It has merely intensified a difficulty that has been growing for many years. The Federal Government has absorbed the sources of revenues, and it must share these with the states and localities. Many of us, realizing this situation, have devoted our best efforts to this problem for many years; and we have worked harder than ever since the time of the last meeting of this department. Federal aid to education in some form some time is bound to come.

Now the question which I would discuss to-night is this: Shall we do America a service in bringing the Federal Government to the support of the schools? Are we in danger of destroying the American heritage? At the moment our schools are controlled by us. They are safe from the sinister influence of the small politician. Shall we sell our control of the mind of the American child?

It is said that he who pays the piper calls the tune. Like many an old adage, this is a half truth. Of course, it would have been possible for the laird of the castle to have made such an arrangement with the piper. He could have said that he would make no payment unless the piper played the particular tune he desired. He could specifically have retained discretionary authority, and himself have called the tune. But there are other ways of paying pipers. The laird might find one night on his estate a band of pipers, cold, wet and starving, because they had been paid in scrip. They might even have been forced to sell or pawn their pipes. There is nothing to stop the laird from saying that all who might wish to play at his feast would be fed, clothed, sheltered and provided with new pipes. Or the laird could offer ten shillings to each piper who would play, regardless of what tune he chose. Or he could apply to the pipers' union and agree to pay the wage scale fixed by the code for 36 hours of piping a week, and then hang out a blue eagle. Or he could offer a fixed sum to all musicians, pipers included. It is not necessary that he who pays the piper calls the tune. Whether he calls it or not depends upon the particular arrangement made between the two contracting parties.

I suppose that there are no schools in the world, even in the United States, so free from domination by central authority as the schools of England, Scotland and Wales. There the control rests in education committees, subcommittees of governmental bodies elected locally. The schools of a borough or an urban district are quite free of domination by the central authorities, and even within a particular school system the details of the curriculum, the choice of text-books, the nature of the instruction and the spirit of the school itself are often within the prerogative of the individual school, even of the individual teacher himself. Central authorities will bring influence to bear upon the local committees by hints, by the publication of comparisons and statistics, by research and by advice. One of the most important reorganizations of education in England was stimulated by a small brochure entitled

"Some Suggestions for the Consideration of Teachers." In spite of this local autonomy, more than half of the bill for public education in Great Britain is paid by the central government, by Parliament in Westminster. Why is it that this system did not transfer control? Because the man who pays the piper does not choose to call the tune. Because the pipers would refuse to play if some one else called the tune. He pays half the salary of the piper; he pays half the cost of keeping the audience in health so that it can hear the tune when played. He takes a definite share in certain other expenses. Parliament does not say that it will grant the president of the Board of Education £88,000,000 to use as he sees fit. It does not appropriate the equivalent of $427,000,000 to be used as the Board of Education, the central authority, may deem wise. The whole program is put down in black and white *in detail,* and administration thenceforth is automatic. This is what is meant by a government of *laws,* not a government of *men.*

This is the plan which I hope that we shall follow in the United States in the long run. But there are certain powerful influences and certain colorful personalities in education and public life in the United States to-day who, for reasons which to themselves are adequate, are forcing us away from the English example and pushing us toward a form of federal participation in education which is likely to weaken local control and strengthen discretionary authority at Washington. These influences and personalities fall into three groups.

There are those who have been accustomed to rescue the perishing. Most of the argument for federal aid is based upon distress, and this has its particular appeal to members of welfare organizations, clubs for social service and charity and aid societies, who, individually and corporately, know how to extend the helping hand. Definite methods have been developed by years of experience in charity organizations; and it is only natural that those who have learned how best to relieve the distressed, help the indigent, cure the sick and care for the unemployed should assume that the same methods can be applied to the relief of a distressed school system. The method is to grant an adequate sum of money to an efficient and kindly individual who will study the individual cases which present themselves to him, dole out aid and adjust and readjust his program according to particular needs as they emerge. It is only natural that the members of this group would prefer to meet the emergency in education by granting a large sum of money to an individual or a board in Washington to hand out according to best judgment upon evidence of acute distress. We readily appreciate the public spirit and logic of this point of view; but we who are connected with schools, above all others, should see the danger that is certain to follow. You can put authority over poor people at Washington; you can grant power to deal with the unemployed; you can give funds to relieve human misery caused by a flood, an earthquake or a depression; but, if you put schools in this class, no matter how great their need for aid may be, discretionary authority and power inevitably will grow at Washington.

The second group, composed in the main of lawyers and professors of political science, from its study of local and state government has become impatient of the delay and inefficiencies of legislatures, boards of aldermen and commissions. They know that there is stupidity and occasional corruption in our state and city governments, and it is only natural for them to infer that this applies equally well to school boards. The argument for centralization of power under the New Deal appeals greatly to them. They like its experimental attitude. In all future relations of the Federal Government to education, they say, let us apply these general principles. Place the control of funds in an individual or a board at Washington. Only in that way will the money go where it is needed. Only with authority in Washington can misuse and misappropriation of funds be avoided. This plan of administration appears to have worked very well in the last year in helping to solve the problems of the farmer, in developing the NRA and in constructing public works. It would be successful and welcome in the building of school buildings, in transporting pupils and in the purchase of supplies and equipment. We do not greatly object to centralized control of cotton and wheat, roads and canals, or codes which regulate business; but we must not forget that the American people can not afford to lose their immediate control of the interna—what is taught and how—in their public schools. No person, no board should be given the power to force local authorities to conform to any set pattern. The administrative techniques of the New Deal, excellent though they may be, must not be applied to our schools.

It is a little more difficult to define the third group. Many members of our own profession belong to it. It is composed of those who are just one step behind the procession in the study of school finance. In the early days, in devising plans for the state distribution of school funds, it was thought satisfactory to distribute a sum of money in proportion to the number of children of school age, to the number enrolled or to the number in average daily attendance. Students of school finance found these plans to be inadequate, and schemes were devised to distribute funds according to effort and need. It was thought that the distressed districts should receive more aid than would be provided by such a measure as the number of the pupils; and in some states equalization funds were set up for distribution to the poorer districts according to the judgment of the state superintendent or the state board of education. To stimulate effort grants were made with provisos attached. A state would offer a certain sum toward the erection of a certain type of building, the equipping of a laboratory or the provision of a special teacher. Sometimes communities were offered aid, provided that they raised a proportionate sum themselves. The members of this third group have reached this stage in their thinking. They want federal aid to be set up on some such basis as this. They hope to see a federal board created which will study the effort and need of the states and the localities, and in its discretion be empowered to make grants upon as objective a basis as possible. You and I readily appreciate that this point of view seems sensible, but we must remember one thing. It was the power to distribute state funds which brought discretionary authority to state departments of education. It was the fact that localities had to match funds by the states, that there was a certain *quid pro quo,* which worked for the appointment of inspectors and the centralization of educational control. If similar programs are advocated and adopted for the distribution of federal funds to the states, I fear that inevitably power and authority will grow in Washington.

During the last six months, a number of us, as representatives of various educational, labor and social organizations, have been meeting together in Washington, in the effort to draft a plan for federal aid during the emergency upon which we could all agree. We canvassed the field. We called for advice from all the experts that we could find. We considered the problem not only from the point of view of the schools, but we looked at it in the light of the relation of schools to other governmental and social agencies. We have come to an agreement upon a program; one that is printed in the current number of the *Journal of the National Education Associa-*

tion. But our agreement was only the result of a long and bitter struggle. Most of us agreed that emergency aid in almost any form was needed for the balance of this school year, merely to keep the schools in operation. Whatever way this aid would be given, whether by a separate Act of Congress, or by the interpretation of an existing act under the discretionary authority of a special board or agency, or even of a single official, we agreed that this would be all right for the emergency during the balance of this year. We recommended a grant of $50,000,000 at once, and this has been taken care of through the interpretation of a statute and the administration of Mr. Hopkins. We also recommended a grant of $100,000,000 for the next school year, to be distributed upon as objective a basis as possible by a board in Washington.

But the big question was what to recommend for the balance of the period of the emergency. The three groups just mentioned each advanced its point of view. Those who approached it from the point of view of charity suggested discretionary authority to be conferred upon an individual in Washington. Those who were suspicious of local government wished discretionary authority and experimentation at Washington. Those who were one step behind the school finance procession wished a national board of education at Washington which would devise a plan for distribution designed to stimulate effort and compensate for need. The representatives of the National Education Association, the Department of Superintendence and the Progressive Education Association stood together. They recommended the appropriation of a large sum of money, possibly $400,000,000, to be distributed to the states and localities on an objective basis, to be administered in an automatic way, preferably by some auditor or accountant or bookkeeper. This is in accord with the modern theory of the distribution of school funds. In fact, the latest idea is somewhat amusing, because the experts in school finance, upon the basis of new premises, have come to an old conclusion. We know how ancient housewives' remedies sometimes anticipate later scientific studies in medicine. We know that the Chinese did not catch cholera or typhoid because they boiled their water and ate no raw food. The boiling of the water and the cooking of the food were not based upon modern scientific medicine. I suppose it came as the result of the workings of the law of natural selection. Similarly, French and Russian housewives fed their children from the soup pot, and thus provided a diet rich in all the requisite vitamins. It is modern research, by its studies, that has revealed the worth of these old customs.

So it has been in the field of school finance. In the early days it was deemed satisfactory to distribute money in proportion to the number of children of school age, to the number enrolled or to the number in average daily attendance. This was later shown to be absurd, and schemes were devised to distribute funds in proportion to effort and need. This in turn has more recently been succeeded by another series of formulae designed to give equality amongst the various localities. The first step was to secure a measure of the cost of the standard minimum educational program which should be offered to every child. It was then necessary to determine the rate of local taxation which would raise this sum in the richest district. Then each district in the state would be compelled to tax itself at the same rate upon an equalized assessment; and the central authority would automatically provide the balance. This is distribution of school funds according to what is termed the *principle of equality.* According to this plan, one district within a state gets nothing. All the others get something, much or little according as they have heavy or light educational burdens, and in proportion as they are poor or rich.

But there is another principle of aid from central to local authorities which is finding favor. This is termed the *principle of efficiency.* The idea is that a free people can not rest content with a bare minimum educational program. Education must be moving onward and upward. Certainly every child must have a certain minimum offering, but unless there is opportunity here and there for something better, for a new development, for a readjustment or advance, educationally we should be in the doldrums. There is a good deal to be said for encouraging "that extra something." Central authorities can well afford to shore up the entire educational structure. One of the greatest fallacies commonly believed in this depression is that distress is confined to the schools which have been closed. Our people should realize that there is just as much distress where home economics has been eliminated, where physical education instructors have been discharged, where equipment has not been purchased, where supervisors have been eliminated, where the curriculum has gone back to the 3 R's. If we are to have an alive and alert system, we must go beyond a dead and uniform minimum. It is to provide and encourage development all along the line that the *principle of efficiency* was advanced. Under this formula something is given to every locality, large or small. Aid is given to help the poor and the weak, but it is also provided to foster variation everywhere. If you are interested in following this argument, I suggest that you read Dr. Mort's discussion in the recently published New Jersey report.

Now the amusing thing about this modern theory of school finance is this: When you grant state aid upon the combination of these two principles, that of equality and that of efficiency, it comes out very close to the old school population basis. In fact, if the principle of equality and the principle of efficiency were to be applied to the nation as a whole, we should be safe in recommending to Congress that by far the best way to meet the immediate emergency in education would be to grant to each state a sum of $11 per pupil in average daily attendance for the school year 1932–33, with a slight additional amount for the less densely settled states. No board of strategy would be needed. No discretionary authority would be retained. Minimum programs would be cared for. Schools could be reopened at once. The whole financial structure would be propped up. Local control would be preserved. It would be the best way to meet the emergency.

I now find myself in a somewhat embarrassing position. When our committee finally came to an agreement in Washington on the particular program which we should advocate, we all said that we would stand firmly behind the six point program: (1) $50,000,000 for immediate aid for the balance of this year to keep schools open, to be administered on any basis by a board or individual in Washington; (2) $100,000,000 for next year for the same purpose, to be administered by a board in Washington upon some objective basis; (3) a substantial sum (we thought of $300,000,000 or $400,000,000) upon the principles of *equality* and *efficiency;* (4) loans to the localities secured by frozen assets in banks and taxes anticipated; (5) grants for school buildings, and (6) $30,000,000 for college students.

I want to stand squarely behind this program. I want to urge your cooperation, but I must make plain that this means *the whole program.* The Federal Emergency Relief Administration has looked with favor on No. 1 and No. 6, and has now practically incorporated these suggestions in its own program. It probably will look with favor on Item No. 2. Items No.

4 and No. 5 are in line with certain other governmental policies. What we should fear is the passing-over of Item no. 3. There are many men and women close to the administration in Washington who can not see the force or wisdom of a general grant to all the states to be administered upon an objective basis in an automatic way. The relief-minded (the first group which I discussed) wish to give the money to the Relief Administration. The political scientists of the New Deal distrust state and local government and want to give out federal money according to the dictates of a federal board or official. The advocates of distribution of state funds upon the basis of effort and need want to duplicate at Washington the older experience of the less advanced states.

These are powerful forces to combat. Right now, hearings are being held before Congress in Washington, upon the measures submitted to fulfil this six-point program. There the relief-minded will say their say, and if their point of view prevails, control will grow at Washington. The political scientists of the New Deal will advocate all items except the third, and power will grow at Washington. The older order of state financial experts will advocate effort and need, and centralization of school administration will develop in the nation just as it did in the states.

I shall agree with anybody upon any plan of national aid to education *for the next six months.* But for any time beyond that, it is my public duty, it is your public duty, it is the duty of the Department of Superintendence, to express not only our hopes but our fears. We have a plan for federal aid to education, expressed in the third point of the six-point program, which gives aid to all the states upon an automatic, objective basis. It has been carefully developed. It has been adequately studied. It has been tested. It will bring immediate relief in the emergency. It will leave the power in the states and localities where it should remain. It will enable the Federal Government to help pay the bill. Federal aid in any other form will tend to transfer the power away from the people. It will become repugnant to us. Mistakes made now may take years to correct; and federal aid of the wrong kind and the growth of the beginnings of educational despotism, however slight, will retard the development of American education for generations to come.

Let us stand whole-heartedly behind the whole program. Let us put special emphasis upon the third, the advanced, step. Only if this is included, only if this becomes the basis for future action, will federal aid, so desperately needed at the moment, become a boon and not a bane.

THE CLEVELAND MEETING[1]

By WILLIAM DOW BOUTWELL

EDITOR-IN-CHIEF, U. S. OFFICE OF EDUCATION

THERE is a possibility that this may be the next to the last report of an annual meeting of the Department of Superintendence as an organization bearing the name it has borne (with slight variation) for 64 years and organized in as close relation to the National Education Association as it has been organized since 1922.

Resolution No. 1, adopted by the Department of Superintendence, announces this probability. Because the chairman of the resolutions committee, E. E. Oberholtzer, of Houston, Texas, was elected president of the department, it may be regarded as a certainty that Resolution No. 1 is not a mere pious New Year's gesture.

[1] A review of the annual convention of the Department of Superintendence, National Education Association, at Cleveland, Ohio, February 24 to March 1.

This resolution reads:

We recommend that the president of this department appoint a committee whose duty it shall be to study, investigate and recommend such changes in the name, the objective, the functions and the structure of this organization as will enable it to provide more effective and aggressive leadership. We also recommend that this committee report its findings to the executive committee and this department at the February, 1935, meeting of the Department of Superintendence. We make these recommendations because we feel that the prestige, and consequently the influence of the Department of Superintendence, is hampered, for the reason that its full national significance is not realized outside our profession, and because we feel that with the rapid changes now taking place, a longer planned program for the Department of Superintendence is necessary if it is to keep abreast of modern educational thought.

Two days after the close of the Cleveland meeting I had the pleasure of a conversation with Superintendent Oberholtzer in Washington. He informed me that he regarded Resolution 1 and point 9 under Resolution 4 as the most important business before the school superintendents during the coming year (see text at the close of this report). Point 9 calls for a continuation, amplification in duties and personnel and change of name of the Joint Commission on the Emergency in Education. It proposes appraisal of education and long-term planning for changes in school programs, "to enable our schools to meet as effectively as possible the challenge presented to them by the changing social, industrial and economic order."

The spirit of change abroad in the land is obviously affecting the internal as well as the external affairs of education. A number of groups are reported to be studying the problem of the reorganization of the professional education organizations. The school superintendents have shown increasing irritation with the "side shows" that have become attached to their annual meeting. They have urged other groups to stay away from their February meeting. This year they cut down sharply on listings of programs of their little brother and sister departments of the N.E.A. and other camp follower groups. At Cleveland the irritation of the superintendents was not diminished by three developments, premeditated or accidental: First, that pre-convention meetings, addressed by Professors John Dewey, H. C. Morrison, Thomas H. Briggs and others, gave a color to the meeting in the public mind quite contrary to the majority opinion of the rank and file of superintendents; second, that the Progressive Education Association moved onto the scene before the superintendents had packed their grips, poked fun at the resolutions the superintendents had adopted, and by voicing "advanced" ideas ran off with the headlines; and third, the adoption by allied groups of resolutions at variance to those of the superintendents, thus adding to the general confusion. In short, the superintendents called the meeting, paid the bills and filled the hotels, but when it was all over they were not sure whether it was their convention or that of a couple of dozen other educational organizations. You can hardly blame them for being irritated.

Outwardly, the Cleveland convention was distinctly pink, and will probably be so reported in many periodicals. Closer observation disclosed the superintendents, in meeting after four years under the tightening screw of depression, to be cool-headed, quietly determined to undertake some important changes, but distinctly averse to joining the Columbia torch-bearers at the barricades.

In organization the most conspicuous aspect of the 1934 convention was the topic group approach introduced by President Paul Stetson. Dissatisfied with the usual parade of the usual speakers, President Stetson began last spring the planning of a working convention in contrast to a listening convention. One of the chief reasons the convention went to Cleveland was that this lake city is probably the only one whose hotels could handle 77 committees all meeting simultaneously.

Before going to Cleveland, each member of the Department of Superintendence was assigned to take part in one of the 77 topic groups. Subjects assigned range from "Public Relations Techniques" to "In the Light of the Present Social, Economic and Civic Changes, to What Extent Should the Scope and Variety of the Educational Offerings of the Public Schools Be Expanded and Reorganized to Emphasize the Need of an Understanding and a Solution of the Social, Economic and Civic Problems of the Community, State and Nation?" Fitting together, a "Bird's Eye View of Education in 1934" in 77 pieces was the objective. The topic groups reported to 7 general subject committees. These in turn welded the reports into documents submitted to the convention.

On one afternoon I personally visited 10 topic groups in session. At Topic Group A, Committee VI, Harold Rugg, *chairman,* subject, "Our Social-Economic Situation and the New Education," some 200 gathered. On a dais sat a panel with Rugg as the keystone, Goodwin Watson on the right wing (imagine that!), Superintendent J. W. Studebaker of Des Moines on the *left,* and Professor Henry Harap, Dr. Lois Meek, the lone woman, and eight or nine others on both flanks. Spirited discussion, in which the audience was included, produced agreement that we were moving or must move toward a socialized, cooperative society. The question at issue, and undecided, was, How shall we get from here to there, with the gradualists (if you believe in slow and steady evolution you are a gradualist) or with the anti-gradualists, Watson carrying the banner, in organizing local groups into a party which would in an election take over the government, which would take over nearly everything?

More typical of the topic group meetings were small gatherings of ten, twenty or thirty persons engaged in earnest discussion.

This innovation in convention procedure revealed, as might be expected, both good and bad points. Good points: (1) passive listening was replaced with active participation; (2) every one had a chance somewhere to let off steam and present his opinion; (3) a testing ground was provided for the finding and development of new leadership, which never has a chance to show itself under the speaker battery system; (4) the products of committee activities, while spotty in quality, contain much promising and fresh material, notably that of Subject Committee II, "A Comprehensive Program of Public Education," Superintendent J. Stevens Kadesch, Medford, Mass., in charge; (5) it is a practical application of democracy and the activity program which superintendents often advocate; (6) it served to inaugurate useful inquiries which will continue (one committee respectfully asked permission to continue into next year); (7) it prompted more preparation than is usually in evidence; and (8) finally, it enables a convention to cover far more ground than would otherwise be possible.

On the red side of the ledger must be placed: (1) the lack of interest on the part of some superintendents in the subject to which they were assigned; (2) the lack by some groups of sufficient knowledge to approach their subjects intelligently; (3) the fact that the reports read in part like an overlong set of resolutions without the whereases, and (4) the complicated machinery of handling so many committees.

I made it a point to ask various convention-goers their opinion of the innovation. Most replies were favorable. Some expressed belief that it will improve with age. President Oberholtzer says he heard more commendation for the topic group working convention than condemnation.

Outstanding problems confronting education as reflected in the reports and speeches seem to be these:

(1) What shall we teach?

(2) What shall we do about the teacher-training problems?

(3) How can democratically-decentralized education be reconciled with centralization implicit in the parade toward cooperation?

(4) Expanding the service of education.

(5) Federal aid, which last year was an argument, but this year is a policy.

(1) What Shall We Teach?

"The divergence of the opinion expressed by members of various topic groups," says Superintendent Kadesch's Committee II report, "disclosed a lack of unanimity in the acceptance of our present educational organization and educational procedures, and indicated that there is imperative need of constructing an educational program suitable to the new changing social order. Yet hasty change of an educational system that has given us effective service in the past is not wise and does not necessarily indicate progress until we know whither we are bound."

The superintendents are bucking. They have definitely concluded not to pass on to children ideas which would help make possible a return to the pre-Rooseveltian United States. They have decided, as Edward Filene suggested in his wise and far-sighted address, to turn the present curriculum in for a new model. But they haven't decided what make.

"Our disillusionment was quite thorough," said Harold G. Campbell, new superintendent of schools for New York City. "The gods of business and finance had a queer code of ethics and very little knowledge of economic laws or social problems. They were not fair in their dealings even with one another and were motivated almost wholly by a desire for personal gain. Left to themselves, they were found to be nearly helpless. What should be of deepest concern to us is the fact that most of these men who failed so miserably were the products of our system of education. They, and those who worshipped them and found them to be false gods, were once in our schools, public or private. Either we failed to teach them the proper way of life or, having taught them, they deliberately ignored the lesson. The likelihood is that we did not give them a real understanding of social, economic, political or moral principles. There is no excuse for us now. The public school of to-day takes the child at a much earlier age and has him in its care until he has grown to manhood. . . . We have called upon the people for vast sums of money to make possible this new educational program, and if we are to survive as the social agency we now conceive ourselves to be, we can not fail in the task that is before us."

What the "new model" might look like Superintendent Campbell suggested: "We must, of course, proceed with the individualization of the educative process, but in dealing with each of our students as an individual we must make clear that he is one of a group and that successful living depends upon cooperative effort by the individual in the group."

Making it specific, Rabbi Abba Hillel Silver said, "Our children should be trained to think less in terms of their careers and their personal success and material advancement and more in terms of a helpful and joyous co-worker in the common social task. The model for emulation set before the growing child should not be the poor boy who by dint of work and thrift became rich, but the boy who by dint of the cultivation of his character and the exercise of his talents became a valuable member of the community, a builder of the better social order."

That studies and plans for the educational chassis, new style, are under way was reported by Committee VI, John Norton, *chairman:* "A preliminary survey just completed by the Joint Commission on the Emergency in Education lists 150 groups which have recently completed or are now conducting important investigations which are pertinent to education recovery and reconstruction." The department's resolution for national appraisal and planning of what we teach was recommended by the commission. It is a logical outcome of the determination for a new curriculum deal.

Will it be a 16-cylinder indoctrination which some leaders tried to sell a couple of years ago? Apparently not. Indoctrination is out, if the convention is any indicator.

Edward Filene, although not a professional educator, put it better than any one else, saying, "Orthodoxy in teaching is the death of education. Teaching children what to think can not possibly fit them for life in these changing times."

(2) The Teacher Training Problem

This question figured importantly in the convention for at least three reasons; first, because it is close to President Stetson's heart, second, unemployment of 200,000 teachers paints graphic evidence of education's conspicuous failure in this area, and third, lack of trained teachers and oversupply has been criticized by President Roosevelt. Committee I, which had this problem in charge, declared that "Teacher training programs must be coordinated. . . . In the various states such coordination is the direct responsibility of state departments of education, which should make use of all professional agencies in the state as well as of regional and national professional and accrediting agencies. The United States Office of Education may help in an advisory capacity." Professor Arthur B. Moehlman, in an address before the general session, shed considerable light on this question and rendered particular service by pointing out the falsity of two assumptions; first, "that if we go on producing more and better trained teachers they will by some miracle quickly replace the inadequately trained now in service, and second, that we can arbitrarily cut off the lower 25 per cent. in service and substitute for them the better trained newcomers."

(3) Reconciling Democracy and Centralization

This problem is closely tied into the question of "What to teach" and federal aid. The best statement of the problem and suggested solution was provided, perhaps by Committee II: "There is no good reason why the state should not determine by law certain standards having to do with external matters, school sites, buildings, budget practise, licensing, etc. . . . The internal affairs of the school system, having to do with the organization of schools, the curricula and courses of study and with methods of teaching, should be left to the local administrative and supervisory officers."

That declaration squares with democracy, all right, but it remains to be seen how the superintendents' new model curriculum (see "What to teach"), when and if it arrives, can be installed with any promptitude in 127,000 educational "garages."

(4) Expanding Education's Service

Any institution which stands still goes backward. Tested against this rule education, currently on view at Cleveland, is one of the healthiest of American institutions. It is amazing that education with an acute shortage fund is actually making greater advances into new territory than in any period since the rise of the high school. And it is laying plans for further extensions. Adult education, long a hope, is now, with the stimulus of the Federal Emergency Program, a satisfying reality for hundreds of thousands of American men and women.

"The key to our situation," said U. S. Commissioner of Education George F. Zook, "is quite consciously to adopt the policy of making the schools of the future for men and women as well as for boys and girls. . . . Many a parent would do well to take to himself some of the words of advice as to wasted opportunities which he so freely imparts to his youthful offspring.''

Pre-schools have sprung from isolated demonstration centers to become treasured additions to school service in hundreds of communities. Dean Clarence S. Marsh, educational director of the Civilian Conservation Corps, told the convention of the inauguration of instruction for 300,000 boys in the camps. How important this is he revealed by reporting that in one typical corps area of every 100 boys 2 had no schooling, 50 had attended elementary school but only 23 graduated, 44 attended high school but only 15 graduated, and 4 had attended college.

Here are some other bright ideas of things for schools to do as soon as they have money, or perhaps even if they have no money:

''A satisfactory educational program for elementary school children can not be confined to the school alone. The school is an integral part of the community. It is the one organization within the community where race and creed prejudices can be eliminated in community planning. The school then is in the most strategic position to lead in planning a 24-hour day program for children of elementary school age.''—*General Subject Committee II.*

''Even though juvenile delinquency is on the decrease we must admit there is more than a modern progressive society can afford. . . . The schools should organize more flexible curricula to meet the varying types of ability and aptitudes; employ better trained attendance officers with background for social work; employ an adequate visiting teacher force, definitely trained for social work; promote closer cooperation on the part of the home, the school, juvenile courts and other agencies; develop more extensive use of the schools as social centers for both children and adults; expand recreational activities for children for which the school assumes responsibility, etc.''—*Committee V.*

''The teacher's work is not concerned wholly with classroom instruction. It is his task to see that what he teaches is reinforced in community life and that the forces of the community, both individual and organized, are led into a sympathy and a practise that will make school and life a unity.''—*Committee V.*

(5) Federal Aid

This was on every one's lips. While the convention met, a House of Representatives committee was holding hearings on bills designed to carry into effect the 6-point federal aid program recommended by the advisory committee to the Office of Education. What many considered the most important meeting of the convention was that of the Joint Commission on the Emergency in Education, at which Dr. Paul Mort, having emulated his revered namesake in a dash to Washington, reported on his reception by the House Education Committee. Other recent arrivals from the capital also reported.

There was more to this meeting, however, than reports from the Washington front. The report of work accomplished, recommendations for educational reconstruction (which found their way into the resolutions) and the businesslike atmosphere revealed the National Education Association as a hard-hitting, social organization, driving straight and unwavering toward carefully chosen goals.

Dean William F. Russell's address on ''Federal Aid, Boon or Bane'' reflected the extensive thinking and research that he, Paul Mort and others have been giving to this subject. It also reflected the strenuous discussions of this problem in the recent Washington conferences. Dean Russell pointed to the English example and the attacks on the problems of aid without control which have been made in the states, as offering a method and guarantee that federal aid to education can be provided without sacrificing local school autonomy.

Many events combined to make the Cleveland meeting colorful and memorable. Not the least was a blizzard and zero weather. On Tuesday night was held the first convention banquet in recent years. Tables were laid in the big hall for 2,200 people. After a variety of entertainment President Stetson rose to undying fame as a toastmaster who successfully managed a banquet at which neither of the two chosen speakers of the evening appeared. Dr. Merriam was ordered to remain in Chicago by his doctor; Rabbi Silver, on 24 hours notice, delivered an excellent address. Then President Stetson announced that Governor McNutt's train was delayed. Finally he had to dismiss the session. Governor McNutt arrived at 11:30 and left at 3 A. M. to preside at a hearing for a man scheduled to be electrocuted, so he was unable to deliver his address.

The exhibit by the book and school equipment companies was large once again, indicating the return of prosperity or hope. Especially interesting was the U. S. S. R. exhibit and the vast improvement in sound motion pictures.

It was the first meeting since the repeal of prohibition. Drug stores filled with gleaming bottles of all manner of liquors and well-patronized bars did not cause a ripple; yet this was the same convention which four years ago had hissed a superintendent who had the temerity to suggest the withdrawal of the resolution advocating prohibition.

A number of men who have recently ascended to superintendencies of our large cities addressed the convention; Harold G. Campbell of New York, Ben Graham of Pittsburgh, Charles H. Lake of Cleveland and Edwin A. Lee of San Francisco. Most missed person was William McAndrew.

Other groups which met at Cleveland included the American Educational Research Association, which heard reports of unusual interest, the Departments of Elementary School Principals, Rural Education, Secondary School Principals, Supervisors and Directors of Instruction, Vocational Education, Adult Education, Art Education, Classroom Teachers, Supervisors and Teachers of Home Economics, Visual Instruction, the National Association of High School Inspectors and Supervisors, the National Council of Childhood Education, the National Council of Education, the National Council of State Superintendents and Commissioners of Education, the National Society for the Study of Education, the National Society of College Teachers of Education, the American Association of Teachers Colleges, the American College Personnel Association, the National Association of Secretaries of State Teachers Associations, the National Council for the Social Studies, the National Vocational Guidance Association, the Society for Curriculum Study, and others.

Dr. David E. Weglein, superintendent of schools at Baltimore, was nominated to the presidency of the department but withdrew.

Officers elected were in addition to E. E. Oberholtzer, president: A. J. Stoddard, Providence, R. I., to be second vice president, George C. Bush, South Pasadena, Calif., to be a member of the executive committee taking the place of Charles B. Glenn, Birmingham, Ala., whose term expires, and Ben G. Graham, Pittsburgh, Pa., to the executive committee in place of Herbert S. Weet, who has recently retired from the superintendency at Rochester, N. Y.

Resolutions adopted are as follows:

REPORT OF THE RESOLUTION COMMITTEE
SUBMITTED FEBRUARY 28, 1934

I. A longer planned program for the Department of Superintendence:

We recommend that the president of this department appoint a committee whose duty it shall be to study, investigate and recommend such changes in the name, the objective, the functions and the structure of this organization as will enable it to provide more effective and aggressive leadership. We also recommend that this committee report its findings to the executive committee and this department at the February, 1935, meeting of the Department of Superintendence. We make these recommendations because we feel that the prestige and consequently the influence of the Department of Superintendence is hampered for the reason that its full national significance is not realized outside our profession, and because we feel that, with the rapid changes now taking place, a longer planned program for the Department of Superintendence is necessary if it is to keep abreast of modern educational thought.

II. Functional relations:

(1) We recommend that the control of the public schools be more strictly defined in accordance with the following principles:

(a) Members of boards of education should be chosen solely because of their fitness to hold this important office. Their qualifications should be adequate to scholastic training, successful experience in vocational pursuits, social vision, acceptable personality and fine character.

(b) The superintendent of schools should be the professional executive in charge of the educational program. His service should be evaluated on the basis of executive leadership and administration; on his background of training and preparation; on his ability to inspire confidence and support of all citizens interested in the welfare of youth as well as his ability to secure significant educational results.

(2) In harmony with an obvious trend in the history of American education toward professionalization of all the services rendered by school systems, we recommend that the relationships between boards of education and superintendents be more strictly defined in accordance with the following suggestions:

(a) The functions of the board of education should be clearly legislative and judicial, and this authority should be applied to such policies of control as will effect improvement of the schools.

(b) The functions of the superintendent and the board of education should be more clearly defined by state law. Good practise should recognize the fact, demonstrated by the experience of American schools, that lay control of administrative details is both disastrous and undesirable.

(c) Personal relationship between the board of education and superintendent should be one of mutual respect, confidence and loyalty, instilled by sincere devotion and service in support of a worthy educational program.

III. An adequate educational program:

We believe that America must maintain its place among the nations as a progressive leader, and that there must be guaranteed to every child, according to his abilities, an opportunity to acquire an education which will enable him to make his greatest contribution to society with satisfaction to himself.

We therefore recommend an adequate educational program for every community, irrespective of social or economic status. We also recommend that this program be interpreted accurately, intelligibly and effectively to the citizens of each school community by means of effective and continuous publicity concerning the social purposes and work of the school. This program should be constructed on such principles as the following:

(1) An opportunity for every child to acquire educational training from early childhood to the age at which employment is socially desirable, and for continued education in adulthood as social conditions necessitate.

(2) In every classroom a competent teacher, one capable of interpreting and guiding the learning situations, who shall be maintained at an economic level sufficient to secure a high quality of socially motivated and broadly trained professional service.

(3) In every system a school board that is independent of political and class control, responsive to the will of the people, with freedom to develop efficiently, economically and impartially all policies in support of an adequate school program.

(4) Adequate revenues derived from a stable, varied and flexible tax system sufficient to support the school program without restricting adequate opportunities for all children.

(5) State support of the schools, supplemented by non-control federal aid sufficient to permit every district to maintain an acceptable minimum program of education, yet safeguarding local initiative and autonomy in every local district which can function effectively in the conduct of the schools.

IV. Socio-economic conditions:

(1) We express our profound appreciation of the stability, the saneness, the optimism and the patriotism displayed by the great body of American teachers throughout the present crisis. We urge all teachers, executives and others in positions of leadership to join in the closest cooperative effort for the maintenance of high professional ideals and service. The time has come for more effective organization in order to bring to the attention of the citizens of this country the imperative necessity of providing for the education of

the rising generation. Educational privileges have been so curtailed in recent months that the next generation will not receive its due share of this nation's resources. This department, therefore, declares itself committed to a reorganization of its working relations to all other educational forces of the nation to the end that the natural heritage of youth, a useful education, shall not perish.

(2) We recommend that educational leaders join with all other leaders who desire to cooperate in setting up a program of relief for and correction of maladjustments in the socio-economic world. We commend our former president's research committee on social trends for its suggestion that a national council on social economic planning be created and we respectfully urge the President of the United States to establish such a council. We commend President Franklin D. Roosevelt, Secretary Harold Ickes, Relief Administrator Harry L. Hopkins and the U. S. Commissioner of Education, Dr. Geo. F. Zook, for their splendid support in aiding unemployed teachers and for the encouraging public utterances with respect to the significance of education in building this nation. We express further our appreciation for the recent effort made by them and the Federal Government to assist the states and localities in the maintenance of their schools.

(3) We recommend that a thorough-going analysis of the school and its processes, together with proper interpretation to the public, be made to each community in America. We regret that certain organized forces and agencies have arisen which seek to restore economic prosperity by destroying the birthright of the children, through curtailment, restriction and destruction of the activities, effectiveness and usefulness of the school.

(4) We believe that the schools should keep step with the changes that are occurring in the country and throughout the world. We point to the fact that the schools in America have never produced war, have never taught intolerance nor can they be charged with the responsibility for the depression. We believe that if the leaders of America had not forgotten the lessons of education, this country and much of the entire world would not be experiencing its present distress.

(5) We commend our President and the National Congress for the abolition of child labor and the safeguarding of child health.

(6) We believe there is grave danger to-day that the social, political and industrial changes will move forward at such a speed that they may outstrip the schools. To this end we urge that more attention be given to study of the social, political and economic conditions which affect the life and welfare of our people and we recommend that a more vigorous and systematic education be given regarding the harmful effects of alcohol and narcotics upon the human body.

(7) We point out that the curriculums of many schools are deficient in courses which deal with social and economic problems. Far too many traditional subjects have been retained in school programs because communities have insisted upon having the young people educated in the same way that the older generation was trained years ago. Many new subjects have been injected into the school curriculum as a result of pressure exerted on legislatures by groups of well-meaning reformers having no broad view of the purposes or methods of education. The time has come when the curriculum, like all other aspects of modern life, must be revised. Curriculum revision is an obligation of the schools no less important than teaching. The public must be prepared to support curriculum revision as fully as it supports other aspects of school work.

(8) We recommend that the department through a proper commission take steps in the interest of economy and greater effectiveness toward initiating a study to ascertain the most desirable organization for our public school system. Such a study should relate to objectives, materials, the length of the program of general education, and to the ascertaining of what secondary education should include. We believe that the junior high school, junior college and vocational education have been developed sufficiently to prove their value and that these should become generally an integral part of public education.

(9) We commend the splendid work of the Joint Commission on the Emergency in Education and we recommend:

(a) That this committee be continued for the purpose of completing whatever projects it may now have under way and for meeting such additional emergency demands as may later arise.

(b) That the scope of the work of this commission be broadened to include an appraisal of the present educational program and to include long-term planning for such changes in programs as may be required to enable our schools to meet as effectively as possible the challenge presented to them by the changing social, industrial and economic order.

(c) That such additions to the personnel of the commission be made as may be deemed necessary to enable it to meet this larger responsibility as judiciously and intelligently as possible and that the name of the commission be so changed as to describe more adequately the enlarged scope of its work.

(d) That the executive committee of the Department of Superintendence be requested to take such steps as may be necessary to put into effect the foregoing resolutions.

(10) Federal emergency aid for education:

Inexorable forces generated by the depression have forced various groups to appeal for federal relief. Finance, business, industry, agriculture and welfare have found it necessary to request financial credit and assistance which the Federal Government alone is capable of commanding in this time of crisis. The progressive deterioration of public schools during the past three years has reached the point where education must now appeal for temporary federal aid in order that schools may continue to operate and that children may not be denied the educational opportunities essential to the present stability and future development of this nation.

It is the judgment of the educational executives of the nation that the present emergency in education calls for further, substantial and prompt action on the part of the 73rd Congress. We appeal for emergency aid for education in sufficient amount to permit the states and localities to provide adequately for public education throughout the nation, this aid to be granted in a manner which does not involve federal control over state or local educational policies. Such assistance is indispensable to economic recovery and the perpetuation of democratic government.

We call upon our representatives in Congress and the Federal Administration to enact at this session of Congress the legislation which is essential to these ends.

The Department of Superintendence of the National Education Association calls upon organization of teachers and of laymen—national, state and local—to bring to the attention of Congress and the President of the United States an accurate picture of the present plight of education, and to urge the enactment of appropriate legislation providing for emergency funds without federal control.

We endorse the general program of legislation proposed by the National Committee for Federal Emergency Aid for Education and pledge our full support in securing its enactment.

FURTHER EXPRESSIONS OF APPRECIATION

We desire to express our appreciation of the planned program which has been rendered at these meetings as a result of the vision and planning of President Paul C. Stetson; we commend the initiative and energetic action of President Paul C. Stetson of the Department of Superintendence and President Jessie Gray, president of the National Education Association, for their leadership in our profession during these trying times.

We desire also to express our thanks to Cleveland Radio Stations for the use of its broadcasting facilities, to the National Broadcasting Company and the Columbia Network for their effective cooperation, and to the local and national press for the intelligent and sympathetic publicity given to the proceedings of the convention.

To Superintendent Charles H. Lake, his staff and his local committees, to the Board of Education and to the people of Cleveland, we express our deep appreciation of their cordial welcome and their gracious hospitality which has found expression not only in the many individual courtesies but also in the splendid accommodations during these meetings.

(*Signed*)

E. E. OBERHOLTZER, *Chairman*, superintendent of schools, Houston, Texas.

GEORGE T. CANTRICK, superintendent of schools, Monroe, Mich.

GEORGE C. DIETRICH, superintendent of schools, Piqua, Ohio.

GEORGE W. HUG, superintendent of schools, Salem, Ore.

FRANK M. LEAVITT, assistant superintendent of schools, Pittsburgh, Pa.

LAWRENCE W. MAYBERRY, superintendent of schools, Wichita, Kans.

CECIL K. REIFF, superintendent of schools, Oklahoma City, Okla.

GEORGE H. SANBERG, superintendent of schools, Rochester, Minn.

ANNA LOIS SHINN, superintendent of schools, River Forest, Ill.

G. ARTHUR STETSON, superintendent of schools, Titusville, Pa.

FRANK M. UNDERWOOD, assistant superintendent of schools, St. Louis, Mo.

EDUCATIONAL EVENTS

THE CHARLES WILLIAM ELIOT CENTENARY

THE centenary of the birth of Dr. Charles William Eliot, president of Harvard University from 1869 to 1909, will be observed on March 20 by a program at Cambridge sponsored by the Charles William Eliot Memorial Association.

The program includes the unveiling, in the courtyard of Eliot House, a unit of the Harvard House Plan, of a bronze bust of President Eliot, a gift from the association to the house. The presentation address will be made by Professor Bliss Perry and Professor R. B. Merriman, master of Eliot House, will respond. The bust will be unveiled by Charles William Eliot, 3d, four-year-old great-grandson of President Eliot. Admission to the ceremony will be by ticket and will be limited to members of the association, invited guests and representatives of the press.

In the evening there will be in Sanders Theater a memorial meeting, at which Charles Francis Adams will preside. The program will consist of an invocation by Bishop Lawrence, an address by the governor of Massachusetts, a reading by Charles William Eliot, 2d, from the writings of President Eliot, or from writings relating to him, and an address by President W. A. Neilson, of Smith College. From 10:30 to 11:00 there will be a nation-wide broadcast of brief addresses by President James Bryant Conant, of Harvard University, former President A. Laurence Lowell and Chief Justice Charles Evans Hughes. The evening meeting will be open to the public but with precedence for members of the association and invited guests.

Other features of the memorial celebration will be a meeting for Cambridge school pupils in the auditorium of the Rindge Technical School, which will be addressed by John W. Wood, headmaster of the school; a meeting at the Harvard Law School, at which there will be an address by Dean Roscoe Pound, and a meeting at the Harvard Medical School, to be addressed by Dr. W. B. Cannon.

As part of the anniversary celebration, *The Harvard Teachers Record* devoted the entire issue of February 17 to commemorating the work of President Eliot, including Dr. Eliot's essay on "Education for Efficiency"; a bibliographical and critical sketch of President Eliot's influence on education, by Paul H. Hanus, professor emeritus of the history and art of teaching at Harvard University, and tributes by Edwin H. Hall, president of the Memorial Association, Dr. John H. Finley, of the *New York Times* Sir John Adams, professor emeritus of the University of London, and President Nicholas Murray Butler, of Columbia University.

THE NATIONAL CONFERENCE ON THE EDUCATION OF NEGROES

The National Conference on Fundamental Problems in the Education of Negroes will be held in Washington, D. C., some time between April 15 and May 15, under the sponsorship of the Federal Office of Education. Exact dates for the meeting will be announced later. Dr. Ambrose Caliver, senior specialist in the education of Negroes, will act as director of the conference and as chairman of the planning committee. This committee, appointed last November by Commissioner Zook, is composed of twenty-eight representatives of various agencies in the educational, economic, social and religious life among the Negroes.

The preliminary work of the conference is to be performed by several committees of eighteen to twenty members each, whose function will be to study the financial support of education and certain fundamental and special problems which are involved in the education of the Negro. These groups, designated as functional committees, will emphasize the relationship of education to the channels or agencies through which life functions, namely, the home, vocation, citizenship, leisure, health and character.

The chairmen of the committees are as follows: Mrs. Mary McLeod Bethune, chairman of the committee on home life; Mr. T. Arnold Hill, vocations; Dean V. E. Daniel, citizenship; Mr. E. T. Attwell, leisure; Mr. F. O. Nichols, health; Mr. Fred McCuistion, finance, and Dr. Willis J. King, ethics and morals. Each committee will study the principles, problems and methods involved in making education contribute to the specific life-function considered at the various educational levels.

The second step of the conference will be its division into five sections called administrative groups. All delegates concerned with or interested in any one of the designated educational levels, namely, the elementary, the secondary, the collegiate, the rural and the adult, will meet with that particular group. These groups will consider ways in which the various educational levels may contribute to the development of the knowledge, skills, appreciations, and ideals needed in each of the activities considered by the functional committees.

The third division of the conference separates

the delegates into two groups—those interested in public education of the Negro and those interested in his private education. These are called organization groups and will consider special problems and functions of each kind of education and suggest ways and means of effecting greater cooperation between the different institutions in each division.

Delegates to the conference are to be representative of every organization or agency having any control of or interest in the education of Negroes, including state superintendents, state directors of education, city and county supervisors, members of boards of education, officers of church boards and foundations, representatives of national, state and local teachers' associations, representatives of white accrediting associations and universities, classroom teachers, and school and college administrators.

A SURVEY OF UNEMPLOYED ALUMNI

THOUSANDS of college graduates, many with high-grade professional training, are among the ranks of the unemployed, as disclosed in a recent survey conducted by the American College Personnel Association. Under the direction of Dr. Esther Lloyd-Jones, assistant professor of education at Teachers College, Columbia University, and Clyde R. Miller, director of the Bureau of Educational Service, the study embraced fifty-four colleges and universities located in every section of the United States. The confidential records of these fifty-four institutions revealed that at the present time 21,974 men and women holding degrees from these colleges are without positions.

"The figures revealed by this survey do not pretend to completeness," Mr. Miller reports. "They include only those individuals who have notified the appointment bureaus of their colleges that they are without work. Scores of colleges are not included in the association, and the appointment bureaus of the member colleges have no information concerning the status of large numbers of their alumni who have not communicated with them. It is safe to say that at the present time hundreds of thousands of college graduates are unemployed. Many of them are technically trained men and women of proven ability and splendid achievement."

Many professions are represented, the teaching profession leading with 12,420 unemployed. Engineers are next in rank, listing 2,845 unemployed graduates, the larger number being electrical, mechanical and civil engineers. Business graduates also suffer greatly, the survey showed, as 2,436 business executives are unemployed.

Over 100 different occupations are listed, together with the number of unemployed graduates in each field. Some of the most frequent groups include architects, agriculturalists, bankers, chemists, educational administrators, dietitians, journalists, librarians, social workers, salesmen, laboratory technicians, religious educators, advertising men, draftsmen, artists and biologists.

Of the colleges and universities which listed unemployed alumni, the Ohio State University has the greatest number, with 2,097. The University of Chicago has 1,798; the University of Illinois, 1,445; Teachers College, Columbia University, 1,255; Princeton University, 450; the Carnegie Institute of Technology, 844; New York University, 575; the University of Minnesota, 528; Temple University, 687; the College of the City of New York, 550.

"This survey was undertaken to help the Federal Government in its reemployment program," Mr. Miller said. "It makes available through the U. S. Office of Education and other federal offices which have received copies of the findings the names and records of thousands of men and women competent to fill positions of importance. The study makes it possible for the government in employing an individual to have confidential information concerning his professional training and the quality of his work since he left college or a graduate school. Thus the American College Personnel Association, through this survey, makes it a relatively simple matter for the government in filling these positions to decide, on the basis of merit alone, who will receive any position."

THE BUILDING SHORTAGE AT AMERICAN EDUCATIONAL INSTITUTIONS

A SURVEY just completed on building conditions in American colleges and universities indicates that a large percentage of the higher educational institutions are suffering from marked inadequacy in housing for students and academic activities. In a group of 221 representative schools 65 per cent. are in definite need of new construction or rehabilitation of existing structures, according to this survey, which is based on statements from leading educators in thirty-five states and the District of Columbia.

Only 11 per cent. of the 221 colleges and universities reported adequate buildings throughout. The remaining 24 per cent. did not disclose information sufficiently specific for an accurate index.

The report shows that the most urgent need is for student housing, mainly dormitories. Second in importance are library structures, which are needed only slightly less.

Next among the needs listed in the order named are fine arts buildings, gymnasiums, class and schoolroom buildings, chapels, laboratories and administration buildings. A wide variety of other structures, including engineering buildings, medical buildings, infirmaries, auditoria, faculty housing and other types, are among the less common needs.

The survey covers a selected cross-section of the institutions of higher education in the United States and closely follows, geographically, the comparative number of schools in different sections of the country. Needed construction for which estimates were made amounts to about $93,000,000.

Allowing for a reasonable approximation of costs where a specific project is named but no estimate is given, the aggregate needs of schools that reported amount to about $135,000,000. If this is a truly representative cross-section of the country as a whole, the total needs of the nation are close to $900,000,000 and call for upwards of 2,200 projects and structures or additions or improvements to existing structures.

Among the reasons given for this building shortage, the difficulty of raising funds, the shutting off of subscriptions, the low cash value of securities and other reactions from the general deflation appear to have created serious hardships. Overcrowding is mentioned frequently and the need for additional construction is variously described as "grave," "urgent," "crying" and even as "desperate."

A number of institutions reported that work already planned and approved or actually under construction has been held up on account of present conditions.

THE SCHOOL OF PUBLIC AFFAIRS AT THE AMERICAN UNIVERSITY

THE American University announced on March 2 the establishment of a School of Public Affairs to serve as a laboratory for the study of government through direct contact between students in round-table discussions with government officials. The new school will offer a course lasting only one semester. It is hoped that the session will be attended by university and college students from all parts of the country.

If sufficient enrolments are received to warrant opening the school this summer, according to the announcement, it will be an "Institute for the Study of Emergency Agencies of the Government." It stated further:

Plans for the new school include the extending of invitations to colleges and universities to send to Washington a limited number of their best graduate and undergraduate students in the field of the social sciences for a one-semester intensive training in the field of government.

The university hopes that it will be possible to hold the first session of the school during the summer of 1934, in which event it will be conducted as an institute for the study of the emergency agencies of the government.

Students enrolling in this school will carry on their studies in an entirely different manner from that of the ordinary college classroom.

Courses will be featured by round table discussions, and invitations will be extended to senators, members of the House of Representatives, leading administrative officials and outstanding leaders in the field of business who are in Washington at the present time serving on the government's various advisory boards to participate in them.

Students particularly interested in a special phase of governmental work will be provided with every possible opportunity to make a first-hand study of their field of interest.

Although actual contact with the work of the Federal Government will be given primary emphasis in the new school, the organization of the courses will be under the direction of some of the outstanding social scientists of the nation.

In addition to the permanent faculty of the School of Public Affairs, an outstanding man in the field of the social and political sciences will be invited to serve for a stated period as a "visiting dean of the school."

As soon as his period of service has ended, another leader of the same type will be invited to become associated with this phase of the university's work, and this procedure will be followed indefinitely, so that over a period of time the new school will have the cooperation and guidance of a large group of the most eminent men in the field.

The university will also invite distinguished teachers in the field of the social and political sciences to come to Washington for one semester or for one academic year to observe the progress in operation, and to give at least one lecture per week.

EDUCATIONAL NOTES AND NEWS

EDISON ELLSWORTH OBERHOLTZER, superintendent of schools at Houston, Texas, was elected president of the Department of Superintendence of the National Education Association at the recent Cleveland meeting. Paul C. Stetson, superintendent of schools at Indianapolis, Mr. Oberholtzer's predecessor as head of the department, becomes first vice-president.

THE REVEREND HENRY IRVIN STAHR, executive secretary of the Board of Christian Education of the Reformed Church in the United States, has been appointed president of Hood College to succeed Dr. Joseph Henry Apple.

WILLARD W. BEATTY, superintendent of schools at Bronxville, N. Y., has been reelected president of the Progressive Education Association. Other officers elected are: Elsie R. Clapp, of Louisville, Ky., *vice-president;* Clyde R. Miller, director of the Bureau of Educational Service, Teachers College, Columbia University, *treasurer,* and Dr. John Dewey, of Columbia University, *honorary president.*

RUFUS D. SMITH, dean of the Washington Square College of New York University, has been appointed provost of the university, an administrative office recently established by the council of the university. Dean Smith, working under Chancellor Harry Woodburn Chase, will direct the instructional budgets of the several schools and divisions of the university and will deal with educational problems and interrelationships growing out of such budgets.

DR. JOSEPH M. M. GRAY, formerly pastor of the Central Methodist Church at Detroit, was inaugurated as chancellor of the American University on March 3.

LEON HENDERSON, of the Russell Sage Foundation, has been appointed chief of the research and planning division of the National Recovery Administration, to succeed Colonel Robert H. Montgomery. Mr. Henderson formerly taught industrial management at the University of Pennsylvania and served as professor of industrial economics at the Carnegie Institute of Technology.

THE Board of Trustees of the University of Illinois will hold its regular monthly meeting in Chicago on March 13, at which time the selection of a president of the university will be considered. Ballots containing the names of Dr. Charles M. Thompson, dean of the College of Commerce; Dr. Albert J. Harno, dean of the College of Law; Judge Sveinbjorn Johnson, legal counselor of the university, and Arthur Cutts Willard, acting dean of the College of Engineering, have been distributed to members of the university senate. The senate members will mark their first, second, third and fourth choices, it is understood, and members of the faculty committee will be given the sealed, unsigned ballots, from which they will choose a president.

DR. L. L. HENDREN, dean of administration at the University of Georgia, has been elected president of the Association of Georgia Colleges. Other officers are: Dr. John B. Clark, dean of Mercer University, *vice-president,* and Dr. W. D. Hooper, secretary of the University of Georgia faculty, *secretary-treasurer.*

ROY W. CLOUD, secretary of the California Teachers Association, has been elected president of the National Educational Press Association.

PROFESSOR THOMAS C. HOLY, of the Bureau of Educational Research at the Ohio State University, has been elected president of the American Educational Research Association.

PRESIDENT H. W. DODDS, of Princeton University, was on March 3 awarded the honorary degree of doctor of laws by the American University.

FRANCIS FERGUSSON, executive secretary of the New School for Social Research from 1932 to 1934, has been appointed to the English department of Bennington College at Bennington, Vt.

Peter Manniche, founder and principal of the International People's College at Elsinore, Denmark, who is now traveling in the United States, will visit the University of Wisconsin on March 19.

Dr. Mordecai W. Johnson, president of Howard University, has been appointed by President Roosevelt to serve on an advisory council to assist the Virgin Islands in formulating a plan for the social and economic advancement of their population. Secretary of the Interior Harold L. Ickes and Secretary of Agriculture Henry A. Wallace are also members of the council.

Dr. Adam Leroy Jones, director of admissions at Columbia University since 1909, died on March 2 at the age of sixty years.

Dr. Henry Churchill King, president of Oberlin College from 1903 until his retirement in 1927, died on February 27 at the age of seventy-five years.

Dr. Chalmers Martin, formerly president of the Pennsylvania State College for Women and professor of Old Testament history and literature at Wooster College from 1903 until his retirement in 1929, died on February 28. Dr. Martin was seventy-four years of age.

Dr. Ross Lee Finney, professor of educational sociology at the University of Minnesota, died on February 24. He was fifty-eight years old.

Frank S. Gilkey, principal emeritus of the high school at Medford, Mass., and for thirty-seven years head of the classical department, died on February 28, in his sixtieth year.

Dr. David Misrach, founder of the Talmud Tora School, the first Jewish school in Cincinnati, died on March 1 at the age of seventy-four years.

Dr. Thomas Clachar Brown, formerly professor of geology at Columbia University, Middlebury College and Bryn Mawr College, died on February 28. He was fifty-one years old.

The annual Schoolmen's Week, under the auspices of the University of Pennsylvania, will be held in Philadelphia from March 14 to 17. The conference will be conducted in joint meetings with the Southeastern Convention District of the Pennsylvania State Education Association. Dr. William J. Cooper, formerly U. S. Commissioner of Education, and Dr. A. T. Allen, state superintendent of public instruction in North Carolina, will be the principal speakers.

Perrin C. Galpin, secretary of the Commission for Relief in Belgium Educational Foundation, Inc., has announced the awarding of advanced fellowships for study in Belgium. Awards for a full academic year, beginning in October, have been granted to Dr. C. Hawley Cartwright, of Indianapolis; Dr. Florence Edler, research associate of the Medieval Academy of America; Dr. Milton S. Plesset, National Research Council fellow at the Institute for Theoretical Physics at Copenhagen; Dr. Jerome S. Smiser, instructor in geology at Princeton University, and Dr. E. Clark Stillman, of Ann Arbor, Michigan. Fellowships for more limited periods were awarded to the following: Paul D. Evans, professor of history at the University of Vermont; Edward G. Misner, professor of farm management at Cornell University, and Charles B. Read, assistant geologist in the U. S. Geological Survey.

Syracuse University recently announced the establishment of a school of education to absorb the present teachers college of the university and to take charge of all teacher training in the institution. The faculty of the school will consist of thirty-five or forty members, including approximately twelve from the college of liberal arts, ten from the present teachers college and the balance from the other colleges and schools in which prospective teachers are enrolled. The appointees will hold membership both on the faculties of their respective colleges and on the faculty of the school of education.

The American Council on Education has appointed the following as members of an exploratory committee on the relation of emotion to the educational process: Dr. Daniel A. Prescott, professor of education at Rutgers University, *chairman;* Dr. Frederick H. Lund, professor of psychology at Temple University; Dr. John H. MacCracken, associate director of the American Council on Education; Dr. James

Stuart Plant, director of the Essex County Juvenile Clinic at Newark, N. J.; Dr. Edward Sapir, professor of anthropology at Yale University; Dr. Vivian T. Thayer, educational director of the Ethical Culture School, New York City; and Dr. M. Ernest Townsend, principal of the New Jersey State Normal School at Newark. The work of the committee will be financed by a grant of $5,000 a year for two years from the Josiah Macy Junior Foundation.

THE Arizona State Board of Health, in conjunction with the Civil Works Administration, will make a survey of all children in the elementary schools to determine the amount of malnutrition present, the prevalence of tuberculosis and the number of crippled children in the state. In addition, information will be gathered to assist in a program to eliminate trachoma and other diseases endangering the health of children attending the public schools.

THE Pacific North West Association for Adult Education, which draws its membership from Idaho, Montana, Oregon and Washington, will meet in annual convention on April 3, 4 and 5 in Spokane, Washington. Dean Rhoda M. White, of Spokane, is president of the association.

THE fifth annual history conference for teachers of history in the high schools, academies and colleges of Western Pennsylvania will be held at the University of Pittsburgh on March 17, under the auspices of the department of history and the extension division of the university. The guest speaker will be Dr. Carl Wittke, professor and head of the department of history at the Ohio State University.

BY a vote of nearly four to one at a special election held on February 20, the taxpayers of St. Louis, Mo., authorized the continuance of the present school tax rate of 85 cents on $100 for the next four years. The citizens' school tax committee has made a determined effort to acquaint the voters with the necessity for continuing the present rate. Because of a constitutional limitation of 60 cents on $100, any increase must be submitted to the voters every four years. The 85 cents tax rate has been in effect since 1921.

COLONEL DANIEL W. MACCORMACK, commissioner of immigration and naturalization, in a recent address before the National Council of Naturalization and Citizenship and the New York Committee on Naturalization, urged the adoption of uniform educational standards for aliens desiring to become American citizens. Emphasizing his point that educational standards for citizenship constitute one of the most difficult problems in connection with naturalization, Colonel MacCormack also declared that the prior educational advantages of the aliens, their ages, their opportunities for study and their capacity for further learning must be considered in setting up these standards.

THE P. K. Yonge Laboratory School at the University of Florida was formally dedicated and presented to the university on February 17. Governor David Sholtz, of Florida, and President John J. Tigert, of the University of Florida, were the principal speakers at the dedication ceremonies. Dr. Walter P. Percival, director of Protestant education for the province of Quebec, and Dr. Boyd H. Bode, of the Ohio State University, delivered addresses at the educational conference held in connection with the dedication.

THE University of Wisconsin has received $300,000 in trust for the establishment of a cancer research center to extend the studies carried on by Professor Michael F. Guyer of the university. The money has been left for this purpose by the will of Miss Jennie Bowman.

CONSTRUCTION of the Sullivan Memorial Library of Temple University, made possible through a legacy of $278,196 left to the university by the late Thomas D. Sullivan and a Public Works Administration loan of $550,000, will soon begin. It is reported that the project will provide work for nearly two hundred men for nine months.

DR. CHARLES G. MAPHIS, dean of the University of Virginia, was one of five persons to receive a parchment of distinction from the New York Southern Society on March 2. The society annually honors those persons who have contributed unusual achievements in the perpetuation of the history and traditions of the South. Dr. Maphis' work in the founding and directing of the Institute of Public Affairs at the University of Virginia was recognized in the award.

A SALA ITALIANA has been established at Yale

University and will form another center for the foreign language groups, which already include El Centro Español, Les Thelemites and Der Deutsche Verein. The inauguration of the sala, located in Saybrook College and done in the style of the Italian Renaissance, took place on March 1. Commendatore Antonio Grossardi, Italian consul general at New York City, presented to the university a collection of three hundred books, the gift of the Italian Government.

THREE hundred and fifty Italian students, representing twenty-six universities, will arrive for a good-will tour of the United States early in September, according to plans being formulated by Italian-American groups. Mario Ferraris, spokesman for the group of Fascist educational institutions, arrived in this country on February 28 to hold preliminary conferences with consulates and with various university officials. Through Mr. Ferraris, the Italian students will extend invitations to American students to visit Italy in 1935.

THE *Christian Science Monitor* reports that the teachers in Hungary believe that the unemployment in their profession could be met by cutting into sections the over-large classes which at present exist in the schools. Anxious to find some way of dealing with the problem of unemployment in the educational world, Mr. Balint Homan, Minister of Public Instruction, recently put forward the proposal that teachers who are regularly employed in schools might provide work for those not so employed by refraining from giving lessons to private persons outside school hours. But the teachers did not see the force of the argument. Teaching, they pointed out in meetings held all over the country, is so poorly paid nowadays that even those regularly employed in it find it next to impossible to live on their salaries.

FIGURES showing that numbers of London school children are suffering from malnutrition were given at a recent conference of the London Teachers Association. Miss A. E. Phillips, in her presidential address, stated that more than ten out of every one thousand school children in the poorer districts were malnourished, while in the London secondary schools alone, 7.5 per cent. of the boys and 12.2 per cent. of the girls were found, from the point of view of nutrition, to be below normal.

THE primary schools of Turkey, although financed from the treasuries of the different provinces, are under the general supervision of the central government. Lee Vrooman, dean of the International College at Smyrna, reports that the government has recently issued an order giving teachers' salaries precedence over all other items in the provincial budgets.

DISCUSSION

MORE ACTUAL TEACHING NEEDED

FROM the beginning the purpose of the school has been to make available to the greatest number of children the best possible instruction. This has by no means been accomplished, and strong leadership is still needed in the realization of the ideal. There are two aspects to the problem, which can be designated as over-teaching and under-teaching. In connection with the first it is sheer ignorance of the true character of efficient instruction that is responsible. Habits of routine, excessive red-tape, debilitating verbalism, meaningless manipulations, irrelevant interpolations, tiresome repetitions and offensive mannerisms are some of the forces that interfere with effective pupil learning. Even teachers of extensive training and protracted experience have faulty conceptions of the elements of successful instruction. They manage daily to remove from the classroom and laboratory natural learning situations of supreme importance. They joke or scold while the golden opportunity slips out of sight, and they laugh off pertinent pupil comment as insignificant or out-of-order. Frequently they frown down juvenile questionings as mischievous. They drill and drive toward the mastery of the so-called minimum essentials as the major intellectual crises of young lives are passed off lightly. There are probably 50,000 American instructors who because of their too much talking and moving about in pedagogical busy-work really do not teach. On the basis of a term of ten months of twenty days each this would mean a possible annual loss of 55,000,000 learning hours. A replacement group of 50,000 skilful directors of pupil learning would strengthen our class-rooms inestimably. Progressive education requires that this substitution be gradually brought about.

The problem of under-teaching is even more serious and the educational loss more appalling. In visiting many schools one is impressed by the absence of actual instruction. Every one seems to be waiting for school to begin. A prolonged warming-up process seems to be unavoidable before genuine teaching gets under way. This means that learning situations and study projects are difficult for some teachers to get established and that for them vigorous mental activity is not easily motivated. These teachers have no ability to generate an interest in those educational pursuits for which the school was supposedly organized. Instructors are found in their home-rooms *waiting* for the bell to notify the army of children that they may go to the scene of greater instructional exposure. In other schools one sees pupils calmly *waiting* for the clock to register exactly nine, allowing no reading, no questions, no discussion and no evidence of eagerness to learn on the part of any child. One sees frequently these stately teachers standing before their docile subjects *waiting* for the hands of time to point to noon precisely, murdering precious moments by insisting on absolute silence and suicidal submissiveness. This absence of the learning process is also conspicuous as the school day draws to a close. There they are—*waiting* for the instrument of dismissal to indicate four, *waiting* with funereal and vacuous inanity, perfectly protected from any possibility of cerebration or inspiration. Inaction is as undesirable as over-activity and probably much more expensive, as there are undoubtedly more than 50,000 instructors who seem either never to get started or to stop before any real teaching is inaugurated. Physical dignity and intellectual austerity are no worthy substitute for genuine instruction; they are the sheerest camouflage that fails to conceal the shameful impotence of the incompetent.

There is another phase to under-teaching. Educational leaders are too far removed from the classroom and too frequently away from their "seats" of professional work. There are so many organizations demanding attendance on their meetings, activity in connection with committee assignments, correspondence concerning the spread of propaganda and thought relative to political movements both in and out of the organization. At an annual winter meeting there will be 10,000 of the best teachers and administrators at the sessions of a prominent professional association. They will miss on the average easily five days each from their posts of service. On the basis of a modest six-hour day this will mean a loss of 300,000 hours of expert educational labor in behalf of the many young teachers and tender children who need their supervision. Perhaps the commendable, experimental program of 1934 with its novel feature of every member participating will be the first to bring tangible and compensating returns from the huge February investment. Programs of other years have brought benefits to a small circle of active participants, but hardly equivalent to the heavy outlay of time and money involved.

There are at least 25,000 skilled educators not doing any teaching whatsoever; owing to their superior abilities they have been relieved of classroom duties. They receive more pay and in many instances do less work of a directly fruitful nature. They have gifts that make them influential with children; yet they have been eliminated from contact with those whom they were originally called to guide and inspire. They are now executives, and they render certain involved clerical services. Some of them conduct investigations into the courses of study, resulting more than seldom in a condition less favorable than the previous status of the curriculum. Heavily endowed with genius for communicating information and awakening the enthusiasm of children, they are called upon to perform details of administration of a marked impersonal character, thus losing coveted opportunities to translate their own thrilling life experiences into superlatively fine subject-matter for the eager minds of the young. Truly great teachers are all too rare, and it is emphatically a vicious form of educational waste to demote upward a divinely gifted instructor just because the position "above" carries with it increased authority and remuneration. Greatness in teaching is not a matter of race, sex, color, age, quantity of training or membership in conspicuous, scientific associations. It is a gift of the gods, too uncommon and invaluable to be pushed aside for the commonplace compensations of the system. It should be conserved and encouraged to grow, receiving continuously the most excellent professional training available—not for mere promotion's sake, but for the purpose of enlarging the instructional reach of a genuinely superior teacher.

When shall we begin to seek out and make available to the masses of children the inspired classroom leadership of our most radiant teachers? When shall we make it the highest reward of the profession to remain at one's instructional post and be allowed to arouse and direct the learning life of children under circumstances most favorable for educational achievement? How wise it would be to delegate more of the administrative duties of principals and superintendents to those who lack the divine fire so dearly treasured by children and so seriously needed in the classroom.

The NRA experiment in social cooperation is demanding the best we have—men and women of character and personality. Its success will necessitate intelligent discussion in school and home of the industrial, commercial and political issues involved in the recovery movement. We have tackled a pretentious national project—more complicated, difficult and challenging than the programs being enacted in other countries. With us education is not mere propaganda and compulsion for circumscribed forms of thought; it is something more than the memorizing of certain censored sections of general information. With us education is assigned the responsibility of developing youth for vigorous leadership and loyal followership in the consummation of an exceedingly intricate national experiment. Our schools are being called upon to give us men and women of enlightenment, able to meet emergencies and make correct adjustments at strategic points. Our children are allowed and required to become familiar with human enterprises the world over, and they are given the most authentic information anywhere available. To accomplish these ends we must have exceptional instruction and the most brilliant classroom teachers that can be secured. This is an unusual opportunity to weed out the unfit and to see that the supremely well-prepared teachers are in continuous action. This is an aspect of educational economy that must not be neglected. It is equally as important as deciding which subjects are the most indispensable when curtailments and retrenchment are in order. It is not efficient to use the less capable performers when the more talented teachers are preoccupied with contributions less convincing in their value.

And, finally, there are too many teachers of education. Two thirds of the present number would suffice. The other third should be teaching our youth in the public elementary schools, public and private secondary schools and junior colleges. If they are worthy of their present hire, they should be employed with daily demonstrations of expert instructional procedures. Our boys and girls should receive the immediate advantages of their superior abilities, and apprentice teachers should be the direct beneficiaries of their stimulating illustration of sound methods of instruction. Much of our teacher-training is too roundabout, and far too many men and women are engaged in it who are concerned with a type of research and subject-matter foreign to the pressing issues of the modern classroom. Many of our ends are now merely glorified means, and we seem to be losing sight of the major motive of the very important business of training teachers—which is, and always will be, to make accessible to the school children of America the very best teaching talent that can be provided.

CARROLL D. CHAMPLIN
THE PENNSYLVANIA STATE COLLEGE

AN OPPORTUNITY MISSED

IN going to the Century of Progress Exposition I was particularly interested in examining the educational exhibit. Of course, the whole exposition was highly educational or better informational. But I wanted to see the exhibit of education itself. When I reached the exposition I readily found it in the Hall of Social Science. It presented certain impressive facts as to the growth of education aided by graphics and dioramics at their best, but there was no exposition of plan or organization, modes, method or material, aside from an illustrative school conducted for a limited time during the summer and a set of small colored photos, rather inconspicuous because of size and location, showing various types of work and some slight hints as to modes of conducting them. Altogether the exhibit was very inadequate, giving the impression of a makeshift and extremely limited display—not a general or comprehensive exhibit at all. Even the director was frank to confess its inadequacy.

Aside from the meager display in the Hall of Social Science several universities had valuable and interesting displays of special activities in the Hall of Science.

All this was very different from the prominence given to education by extensive and impressive exposition in previous world's fairs, beginning at least as early as 1893.

No greater opportunity to give account of itself, its achievements, its significance and its fundamental constructive character has ever been given to education. Over every building that displayed the genius and the amazing progress of the nation's leading enterprises one could easily imagine an interrogation point symbolizing the question, Whence? But there was no answer anywhere.

It is perfectly proper to say that some "self-made" men of genius have done marvels in discovery and accomplishment. But it is more to the point to say that without doubt most discoveries and accomplishments have come through people educated in our schools. At any rate it takes many educated people to follow out the work of geniuses and not only give it intelligent application but make improvements that of themselves argue genius.

It is greatly to be regretted that education could not have seized the opportunity to make itself felt as never before and give itself the prestige it greatly needs in these times of stress and crucial test.

Another opportunity looms in the coming repetition of the Chicago exposition. Let the question mark, that may again be imagined as hanging over every typical group of achievements in the exhibits, find answer and interpretation in some hall in which education will show itself generously and comprehensively by well-planned displays of its organization and aims, its results and its modes of achieving them. Or, if it does not choose to have one general building, let each great department of human interest have a space set aside showing the bearing of education on that department. Education can magnify and enforce itself phenomenally if it accepts such a challenge. I shall look forward with solicitude to see the issue.

F. F.

SPECIAL CORRESPONDENCE

STUDENT ENROLMENT AT THE UNIVERSITY OF PARIS

A REPORT from the University of Paris, according to a correspondent of the *Journal of the American Medical Association,* indicates a large increase in enrolment during the current academic year, and the resulting inadequacies of lecture halls and other facilities have caused the authorities much concern. Not so long ago the influx of students was viewed with pleasure at the university, but the numbers of students have now become so large that it is almost impossible to provide satisfactorily for all who have registered or who seek to register.

The total number of students, men and women, matriculated on the basis of scholarship, is 35,365, as compared with 33,821 the previous year, which signifies an increase of 1,544. The number of foreign students, which in 1932 was 7,504, declined in 1933 to 7,496. The number of women students has increased from 9,252 in 1932 to 9,809 in 1933. The studies that attract the most women are those pertaining to law and belles-lettres, in which faculties in 1933, respectively, 305 and 352 more women students were enrolled than during the previous year. Scientific studies attracted 100 fewer women students in 1933 than in 1932 in the field of medicine, and 61 fewer in the pure sciences.

With regard to the total number of medical students enrolled in the French faculties, the minister of public instruction has furnished statistics that show an increase since the war. The roster of students enrolled in the faculties of medicine in January, 1914, was 8,533, of whom 1,368 were foreigners. These figures include men and women students studying for the degree of doctor of medicine, for the title of public health officer and for the diploma of dental surgeon. The number of students enrolled in the faculties of medicine, at the end of December, 1932, was 19,220, of whom 4,285 were foreigners. These figures include men and women students studying for the degree of doctor of medicine, for the diploma of dental surgeon and for the diploma of midwife.

The number of foreign students at the Faculté de médecin de Paris, which in 1932 was 3,232, rose in 1933 to 3,516, an increase of 184. It is this fact that disturbs the French students most, and even the French physicians; for these foreigners, for the most part, instead of returning to their native country, succeed in circumventing the laws and in practising medicine in France, where there is a plethora of physicians, many of whom find it difficult to earn a respectable living.

QUOTATIONS

ADULT CRAVING FOR EDUCATION

No activity developed under the federal emergency relief administration has evoked a more remarkable public response than that of the civil works educational service. Primarily designed as a means of providing relief for unemployed persons eligible to teach, it has demonstrated that the adult demand for education is far in excess of what was anticipated even by persons foremost in the adult education movement.

When the CWES project was under preliminary consideration it was thought that the major problem would be to find pupils enough to engage the efforts of those enrolled as teachers. The contrary is true. In Chicago and throughout the state classes are being enrolled and applications for teachers are being made at a rate which outruns the available funds. Approximately 50,000 students have been registered in Cook county. The demand comes from young persons of college grade, and from thousands of older persons whose early schooling was scant, or whose foreign origin is a handicap because they lack mastery of even elementary English. Eagerness is manifested for vocational instruction, commercial and industrial, as well as for academic teaching.

What is happening in Chicago and Illinois is said to be typical of the response in other populous cities and states. Educators are watching this experiment in adult education with keen interest. Theories long advocated are being put to test on a countrywide scale, and many believe that a demonstration is being made which will profoundly affect educational policy in the future.

Dr. George F. Zook, federal commissioner of education, frequently has declared his belief that, in an age of rapid change, educational opportunity must be available throughout adult life, if the individual is to be able to adjust himself effectively to altering conditions. The social importance of such adjustment needs no argument. Educators generally agree that it is a fundamental requisite to social stability. Not alone reeducation vocationally, but reorientation to political and economic problems, is held to be vital.

In seeking to relieve the pedagogical unemployed, the government has tapped a latent adult craving for instruction that may refuse to be satisfied with mere emergency provision.—*The Chicago Daily News.*

REPORTS

THE CARNEGIE FOUNDATION FOR THE ADVANCEMENT OF TEACHING

The twenty-eighth annual report of the Carnegie Foundation for the Advancement of Teaching, issued during February, discusses, among other topics, the appointment of a federal cabinet member for education, intercollegiate athletics, college admissions, the educational effectiveness of the college, the unified control of higher education and the finances of the foundation.

The proposal to create a Department of Education in the Federal Government with a secretary in the cabinet and with large appropriations to be expended in the various states, is opposed by Dr. Henry S. Pritchett, president-emeritus, as a grandiose scheme certain, if passed by Congress, to demoralize the public schools.

The cry to equalize educational opportunity throughout the Union is a tempting plea for the educational orator. There is nothing in this plea. It would be both impossible and unwise to undertake to equalize educational facilities. . . .

Thousands of public-school teachers would, under such a dispensation, be in hot pursuit of their congressmen. What this sort of pressure would do to the public treasury would make the advocates of the soldiers' bonus seem modest in comparison. The plan to regiment education from Washington is not only contrary to the spirit and letter of our Constitution, but contrary to the fundamental conception upon which education in every state should stand, namely, sincere and thorough work by the pupil in a school provided by a self-respecting state and community.

If some community, however small, will back away from the traditional and organize its schools on the basis of intellectual sincerity, plan to teach a few things well, get away from text-book methods, and teach children to use the text-books as reference books and to do their own thinking—if some community will do this, it will hasten the day when the elementary school will give a new spirit of sincerity to the secondary school and to the college. Such a transformation may save us from financial bankruptcy due to educational inflation.

Returning to the attack launched by the foundation in recent years against the commercialization of college athletics, Dr. Pritchett writes that "football is an excellent game for college boys when played as a game. It is grossly demoralizing when developed into a commercial show for the public."

To make a hundred thousand dollars by exploiting students before the public is no part of the work of a college that stands for intellectual ideals. To-day professional football teams are fast becoming commercial rivals of the colleges. They play, of course, a more skillful and more interesting game, including among their players many ''scholars'' graduated at the colleges—a new vocation for the college graduate. But the banishment of commercialism from the college will come only when the college itself offers an intellectual life that appeals more strongly to its students than the glamor of commercial shows financed in the name of the college and fostered by a demoralizing publicity.

The late Dr. Henry Suzzallo, president of the foundation until his death in September, 1933, joins in the report with Dr. William S. Learned, of the foundation staff, to criticize the so-called "Carnegie unit," widely used for admission to American colleges. The "unit," which was defined about 1907 as representing a "a year's study in any subject in a secondary school, constituting approximately a quarter of a full year's work," has now served its purpose, according to these writers. "With changed conditions and sharper and more wieldy tools, such expedients become obsolete. They should undoubtedly give place to more flexible, more individual, more exact and revealing standards of performance as rapidly as these may be achieved. The foundation looks with favor upon any and all means of judging qualifications for college admission which recent widespread experiment, scientifically and practically appraised, reveals as distinctly better than previous methods."

"The American college degree, on its present four-year credit basis of award, possesses but a small fraction of its potential significance in terms of assured intellectual competence," writes Dr. William S. Learned, staff member of the foundation.

The sooner institutions that make a business of education frankly divert their recognition from hollow forms to a just and substantial appraisal of the student at whatever level, the sooner will education be able to justify the extensive demands that it makes on society with a contribution that it can in some real sense guarantee.

There are to-day ample means whereby a college can ascertain with great definiteness just what a student brings with him. Better still, a word from the colleges to the schools below would shortly result in the consistent story of a growing mind over a period of years. Here the college would find, in clear and comparable terms, the relative power and grasp of a pupil in many fields; it could gauge at once his persistence, retention, breadth of curiosity, and inner motivation not as revealed in a single, hectic examination, but as measured normally, without pressure, as his native ability displays itself.

In discussing the professions and their organization, Dr. Alfred Z. Reed writes as follows:

We certainly ought to regard the term ''learned profession''—the proper field of university activity—as a developing concept. Our new country—

our land of courageous innovations—ought to be able to bring within the university sphere callings which in other countries traditionally stand outside. That it has done so is not to be regarded as an unfortunate break with the past. Rather, it is evidence that we do not intend to let an inherited mechanism restrict the free development of social and economic activities. We prefer to adjust the educational system to modern conditions. Not only is it futile to rail at American colleges and universities because they break with tradition. It is equally futile to condemn particular so-called institutions of higher learning for not conforming even to the requirements of pure reasoning—for not fitting in with well-grounded ideas as to what higher learning ought to be. We should not be the slaves of words. In the future, as in the past, the terms "university," "learned profession," will doubtless often seem to some of us to be misused. Perhaps, once, it would have been worth while to try to protect these honored expressions from being exploited.

The report points out that at present there is a considerable tendency "toward singleness of control of state public higher education in the United States. Until recently, the states of the Union with few exceptions have approached their problem of higher education through the creation of a separate board for each publicly controlled institution. Developments in recent years in thirteen states have looked toward partial or complete unification of educational offerings. In at least two states consideration of the problem has involved institutions controlled privately as well as publicly. . . .

"In so far as these tendencies improve the quality of the education available to all the people of a state, they will effect a salutary change in the life of the nation. If they can be furthered, while at the same time the cost of our higher education, paid by all the people, is reduced, they will be doubly welcome."

Salient facts concerning the financial resources, receipts and expenditures of the foundation for the year ended June 30, 1933, are as follows:

Face value, all investments, $31,409,589.

Face value, permanent funds, $18,251,000.

Proportions of investments of permanent funds: in bonds, 98.64 per cent.; in stocks, 1.36 per cent.

Income received from all investments, $1,506,518.

Current rate of income, 4.81 per cent.

Received from Carnegie Corporation of New York and disbursed for educational research projects, $106,250.

Paid on account of retiring allowances and widows' pensions, $1,717,327.

Paid on account of administration and publication, $96,476.

Paid on account of the foundation's research activities, $36,092.

Facts concerning the retiring allowances and widows' pensions of the foundation for the year ended June 30, 1933, are as follows:

Total expenditure for retiring allowances and pensions, $1,717,327.

Increase over year ended June 30, 1932, $44,402.

New allowances and pensions begun, 123.

Retired teachers receiving new allowances, 71.

Average amount of new allowances, $1,586.

Widows receiving new pensions, 52.

Average age of 71 teachers retired during 1932–33, 68 years.

Average service of 71 teachers retired during 1932–33, 37 years.

Total allowances and pensions in force, 1,064.

Total allowances granted 1906–33, 2,077.

Total expenditure, retiring allowances and pensions, 1906–33, $25,370,122.

EDUCATIONAL RESEARCH AND STATISTICS

HOW UNIVERSITY STUDENTS PREPARE FOR NEW TYPES OF EXAMINATIONS

AMONG the considerations which must not be overlooked in evaluating the relative advantages and limitations of different types of examinations or examination procedures is the effect of the procedure or type of test upon the attitudes of the students and their methods of study. For example, the annual giving of uniform objective tests to high-school students in a number of secondary schools followed by a comparison and judgment of the individual pupils and schools is certain to bring about changes in the attitudes of students towards various types of subject-matter, highly prejudicing them in their study activities against such as may not be tested by means of written examinations, *e.g.*, appreciations, tastes, attitudes, interests and objectives other than factual information and subject-matter skills.

It has been frequently stated that the use of new-type examinations tends to invite students to concentrate upon the temporary acquisition of an unassimilated mass of the more important isolated factual details. Students frequently inquire of college instructors whether the examination will be "new-type" or "old-fashioned" admitting that they study differently for different types. It was for the purpose of discovering how common this differentiation in study methods for different types of examinations was and what was the nature of the differences in study procedures that this point was included in an investigation of students' reactions to different types of examinations and marking procedures.[1]

The basic data reported in this communication were the replies made by 316 students,

[1] Data on other phases of investigation will be reported in an article to appear soon in SCHOOL AND SOCIETY.

TABLE I

METHODS OF STUDY EMPLOYED IN PREPARING FOR OBJECTIVE EXAMINATIONS AND FOR SUBJECTIVE EXAMINATIONS

		Class				
		Sophomores	Juniors	Seniors	Graduates	Totals
a. Read and review generalities and trends	Objective	15	47	13	9	84
	Subjective	35	147	30	20	232
	Combined	50	194	43	29	314
b. Try to remember the words of the book on numerous points	Objective	29	117	30	20	196
	Subjective	8	20	4	3	35
	Combined	37	137	34	23	231
c. Learn tables and minute details of the material covered	Objective	33	138	22	18	211
	Subjective	7	16	7	1	31
	Combined	40	154	29	19	242
d. Attempt to draw several important conclusions from tables	Objective	14	50	12	9	85
	Subjective	36	134	28	20	218
	Combined	50	184	40	29	203
e. Read notes on text and lectures carefully, but without picking out details to be memorized	Objective	19	62	12	6	99
	Subjective	31	134	20	20	205
	Combined	50	196	22	26	304
f. Learning groups of facts in logical summary (such as causes of American Revolution)	Objective	25	103	18	12	158
	Subjective	28	91	24	14	157
	Combined	53	194	42	28	315
g. Try to understand underlying relationships	Objective	20	45	6	8	79
	Subjective	33	144	30	22	229
	Combined	53	189	36	30	308
h. Formulate personal opinion regarding materials involved	Objective	4	10	1	4	19
	Subjective	36	162	30	23	251
	Combined	40	172	31	27	270

chiefly juniors, in the College of Education of the University of Minnesota to the following question, "Which of the following methods of study do you use in preparing for an objective examination? Which for a subjective?" Following the question were the eight methods of study listed in Table I.

A summary of the replies is found in Table I, in which for purposes of comparison, data were given separately for sophomores, juniors, seniors and graduate students. As judged by their practise as stated, these students believe that in preparing for an objective examination it is good study procedure to:

(1) Learn tables and minute details of material covered—70 per cent. believe this to be a good method.

(2) Try to remember the words of the book on numerous points—60 per cent. employ this practice.

(3) Learn groups of facts in logical summary—more than half report this approach, (an equal number consider this to be good advice in studying for subjective examinations).

(4) Give little attention to formulating personal opinion regarding materials involved, only 6 per cent. suggest this method.

For a subjective examination these students believe it is wise to:

(1) Know what you think about the content of the course, or formulate personal opinion regarding material involved—mentioned by 93 per cent.

(2) Read and review generalities and trends, try to understand underlying relationships—77 per cent. suggest this procedure.

(3) Attempt to draw several important conclusions from tables—65 per cent. follow this plan.

(4) Read notes on text and lectures carefully, but without picking out details to be memorized—67 per cent. use this method. One third believe this method good in preparing for objective exams also; but, no matter what kind of a test it is, 55 per cent. learn groups of facts in logical summary.

Some of these answers are probably influenced by the way the question was asked. Without question, the replies were also conditioned by the objective examinations with which they had had experience. These were not uniform for all the students of the various major curricula and of the various years spent in the university. Very few indicated that the same study methods were used irrespective of the type of examination, although one can hardly believe the line is that sharply drawn.

Rather sharp differences between methods used in preparation for the two types of tests are readily noted. Chief among these are the following:

Methods employed commonly in preparation for subjective examinations but by a distinct minority for objective examinations are (1) "Read and review generalities and trends," (2) "Attempt to draw several important conclusions from tables," (3) "Formulate personal opinions regarding materials involved," and (5) "Read notes on text and lectures carefully, but without picking out details to be memorized."

Methods employed commonly in preparation for objective tests but only by a distinct minority for subjective examinations include: (1) Learn tables and minute details of the material covered, and (2) try to remember the words of the book on numerous points.

In the preparation for each type of examination there is a fairly common tendency, employed by about half of the students replying, to "learn groups of facts in logical summary."

Separate analyses of the data for various year-classes yields little of interest, except that what is true of the entire group seems to be true of each class. The nearest approach to an exception may be found in the tendency of the sophomores to give relatively more attention to trying to understand underlying relationships. This must be explained largely in terms of curricular differences rather than in terms of learning with experience. These sophomores are all in special curricula—physical education, home economics, industrial education, art and music.

By way of general conclusion, then, it is obvious that the type of examination does influence methods of preparation for it and that the objective type focuses attention upon details and exact wording, while the subjective type apparently favors methods involving organization, perceiving relationships and trends, and personal reactions.

HARL R. DOUGLASS
MARGARET TALLMADGE
UNIVERSITY OF MINNESOTA

SCHOOL AND SOCIETY

WITH WHICH ARE COMBINED THE EDUCATIONAL REVIEW, ESTABLISHED IN 1891, THE TEACHERS MAGAZINE, ESTABLISHED IN 1878, AND THE SCHOOL JOURNAL, ESTABLISHED IN 1874.

EDITED BY J. McKEEN CATTELL, R. D. LINDQUIST AND W. H. COWLEY

EDITORIAL COMMUNICATIONS SHOULD BE ADDRESSED TO THE EDUCATION BUILDING, THE OHIO STATE UNIVERSITY, COLUMBUS, OHIO

Volume 39 SATURDAY, MARCH 17, 1934 Number 1003

CLIO AND THE TEACHER;[1] OR, THE PLACE OF HISTORY OF EDUCATION IN THE EDUCATION OF TEACHERS

By Professor THOMAS WOODY

THE UNIVERSITY OF PENNSYLVANIA

EVERY profound disturbance of society produces reverberations immediate and remote. In highly organized groups the effect is apt to be much more sharply felt than in simple ones. Education, by which a society seeks to control and direct its course, is inevitably disturbed along with other institutions of society. All eyes are turned upon it: witness the critical fifth century in Athens, the French Revolution, the first quarter of the nineteenth century in Germany and the Bolshevik Revolution. Though the cataclysm of world-wide war, followed by the American economic collapse, has produced no revolution as yet in our own society (despite all cries to the contrary) it has (1) sharpened existing criticisms of education and (2) has brought many more or less novel criticisms to bear upon it. There is wailing and gnashing of teeth; there is running hither and thither, which reminds the observer of animals lost in a maze from which they find no escape. This disturbed condition pervades American education, affecting it at the lowest and highest levels.

One might suppose that, in the circle of those whose business it is to direct institutions of learning, and educate the personnel of the teaching profession, serene vision would be found. But this is far from the truth. The periodical literature of twenty years past is filled with evidence to this effect. Since 1929, when the disturbance of our world reached a climax, this evidence of uncertainty has sharply increased. To-day, it is most evident in the discussion of "What to teach future teachers?" "How to teach them?" "How should the subject-matter of their course be organized?" "Should their professional preparation be primarily practical apprenticeship?" "Should theoretical education be stressed more, or less?" "Should they be prepared simply to perform the tasks indicated by a job analysis?" "Should they be required to 'take' courses at all?" "Should there be systematic courses, or simply work upon 'important problems'?" To the first of these questions the following remarks are addressed.

What professional studies should be

[1] A paper read at the round-table conference for teachers of history, principles and philosophy of education, National Society of College Teachers of Education, Cleveland, 1934.

stressed in the preparation of future teachers? "Let us determine by a job analysis," some say. "Let us ask those who have been on the job a few years to tell us what they have found necessary and useful in their previous training," says another. These sources of information are not without value, but they are neither all-inclusive, nor infallible, with respect to the actual technique of teaching and administering a school system, though analysis of the job ought to be a useful indication of some of the things the future teacher should get in her preparatory studies. But with respect to the teacher's larger functions in the school, the community and the state (for the teacher must not blot out the citizen), job analysis falls short. The judgments of recently graduated alumni, too, being the products of a most imperfect training, unsupplemented by continued, broad and profound study, are apt to lead astray.

It may well be that human history itself gives a more judicious answer to the vexed question of what to teach teachers than interested persons and laborious job analyses are able to do. At least, one can measure and probe the various present suggestions by comparing them with what has been known for centuries.

To-day, the preparation of teachers is a conscious process, and all agencies of education serve as instrumentalities of government. Government and politics have as their object the promotion of the good life. This was not always so. Early societies had no clear idea of the power of the educational process. The first teachers were born to the task, stumbled into it or came to it by some other means than conscious selection. Their preparation was by apprenticeship, through which a fund of knowledge and a skill in approved technique were gained. There was no thought of conscious control or redirection through the educative process. We may allow this preparation of the teacher, which included in a simple form what to-day would be called organization, school management, method and practise teaching, to be represented by a straight line ————. This was the plateau of primitive experience. It represents society's educational habits, at the time when men were just beginning to work effectively as social units. Many things came to pass, new instruments were invented, the task of teaching became immeasurably more intricate and difficult, but still the educative process was qualitatively much the same: A process of faithful memorization, so far as ideas were concerned; a process of physical and emotional habituation, with respect to the physical being. Writing and books which contained the most sacred knowledge of a people, which were the content of their education, do indeed imply that a new social level has been reached. But a critical study of education as a social process, a critical educational philosophy, has scarcely begun. The preparation of the teacher now requires a great factual knowledge of books of the past, but not a critical and selective appraisal of them with respect to future betterment of education and society. The practise of teacher preparation up to this point may be represented by a curve ________/‾‾‾‾‾‾‾‾, which has a second plateau.

Thousands of years passed by. Nations, even world states, rose and fell. Still, critical reconstruction on the basis of present and past knowledge had not begun; no clear vision had appeared in the minds of scholars with respect to improving their present state. Revolutions and rebellion did occur, indeed, but these were blind reactions against systems which knew not the law of inevitable change and looked to the future only as an endless present.

At length, a versatile people, beset by confusing, kaleidoscopic changes in their society, made a contribution to a critical educational philosophy, became leaders in the reconstruction of human experience, attempting to lay down fundamental principles upon which government, politics and education for the good life might be rationally established. From this time on, in the western world, whenever human societies have gained their majority, educationally, they have had recourse to theoretical studies in the preparation of their teachers.

more, he is an educational statesman. In our society he must be an independently thinking, wisely judging citizen first; add to this a knowledge of a subject and skill in methods of imparting it, and he becomes a teacher in a satisfactory sense. The graph of the development of teacher preparation, at this point, has become a little more complex:

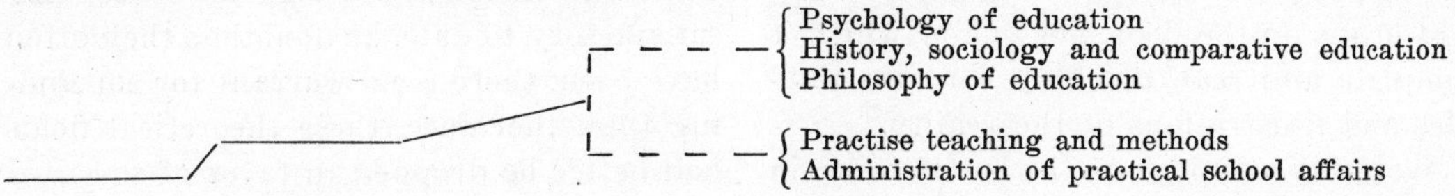

The teacher's work, having the good of society as its object, as has been generally accepted, must be based on a knowledge of the three chief things with which he must deal: man's nature, the nature of society and the nature of truth itself, *i.e.*, to enable us to distinguish between opinion and what has general validity. The range of knowledge of these three fields was narrow at the beginning, but it has increased. Great or small in amount, perfect or imperfect as to quality, it is obvious that, at any time, the educator's work must be conditioned by his understanding of these fields of knowledge. Present societies, in which education has become a definite instrument of social control, can not afford to ignore any one of these fields in the preparation of its teachers. To-day, these fields of knowledge are fairly covered by our designations (1) biology and psychology, (2) history, sociology and comparative education, and (3) philosophy of education. Naturally, instruction in these three main fields of theoretical study of education draws upon the contributions of many tributary fields. We may designate this stage of development of teacher preparation as quite novel: no longer is the teacher merely a classroom personage, prized simply for skill in teaching a subject, nor for technically efficient administration of a school; he is that and

Administration and methods, formerly represented by the practical technique gained through an apprenticeship to teachers, have been elevated to a new level as a result of new insights gained through psychology, biology, history, philosophy, and so on; but, one must add, they have by no means taken into careful account all that these theoretical studies have to offer. Particularly, it may be said that our conception of method (so far as general practise is concerned) is still ill-fitted to attain the objectives of political democracy. Theoretical studies must still run ahead of practise and light the way.

Compare this outline of historical development of the conception of the preparation of teachers and educational statesmen with our immediate situation and certain tendencies of the day. Faced by immeasurably greater problems than were ours before, we find an increasing tendency to turn new teachers upon details of teaching technique, administration, measurement of achievement, extra-curricular activities, school organization, national, state and local machinery of education, classification of students, curriculum adjustment, school buildings, adult education, vocational education, extension schools, country schools, school finances, health education, scientific supervision, the science of education, the professional training of teachers. And these detailed subjects, branches of the total educational field, are given to the future teacher, at the very beginning of preparation, as an "Introduction to Education." Imagine teaching a mechanic to know an automobile by first introducing him to all its parts in a heap on the floor or, to keep the analogy closer, let us imagine that there are some twenty odd heaps on the floor, not one of which is complete and real, but only contains samples and illustrations of the reality.

Would it not, perhaps, be better to begin with the whole method, by seeing education in the large, seeing it as the instrument man has used throughout his existence, once blindly, then more intelligently, to improve himself individually and as a group? Would it not be better to master as a whole the psychological approach to education, furnishing as it does the foundation for method, and much of the basic information that, along with history and sociology, must be taken into account by educational philosophy? Would it not be better to gain a philosophical grasp of what we are to do, before we master the technique of doing it? And then, by all means, follow this up with the nicest possible knowledge and skill in the performance of the acts pertaining to administration of school and classroom and the actual instruction of youth. Putting last things first is capable of defeating the very purpose of education, so far as democratic society is concerned. It is first of all important that we be able judges of direction, ways and means, essential and non-essential; to judge what will harmonize with our socio-political ideals and what will not; to know what are the greater and what the lesser evils. If we put technical skill first, who can tell what master it shall serve?

As democracy demands that its teachers be critical, wise judges first, and narrow technicians afterwards, schools of education, if they would serve truly, must put a scholarly knowledge of fundamental fields first; must not be led astray by thinking that a half-year introductory smattering of every branch of professional studies is an adequate preparation for technical specialization. They must face the fact that if the results of a study of educational philosophy, educational history and sociology and educational psychology have been unsatisfactory to date, as doubtless they often have been, there is no warrant for concluding that, therefore, these theoretical fields had better be dropped in favor of so-called practical studies. One is not designed to crowd out the other. In place of such a conclusion, it would be more correct to say: "Our failure, probably, does not set aside the judgment of history and of contemporary societies. Our failure suggests that, probably, we have not devoted the time to these fields that we should have; that we have pursued them like children looking for curios, rather than in a philosophical spirit; that we have interpreted these fields narrowly, not broadly; that they have yielded little value to our students, because they have been handled frequently by persons almost wholly unprepared to teach them." Who among you does not know at least one teacher who has "taught" "philosophy of education" and "history of education," without having studied them in a single course? Who does not know tens of teachers who began to give instruction in these and other fields with only the reading of a text-book in a single course for a foundation. Low scholarship, I venture to surmise, is the basic cause of failure to prepare teachers better. For this, in general, the system is to blame, not the individual teacher.

The weaknesses of scholarship are fundamental and far-reaching in their effect. In the past, due to the fact that professional studies for teachers were a new field, this weakness may charitably be excused. To-day there is no excuse for it. What in general must be undertaken? First, there must be a definite order of studies, beginning with the general and theoretical and concluding with the practical; second, an adequate limit of time must be allowed to do a scholarly job (this will eliminate flimsy introductions, containing something of everything which the future teacher will ever live to know about the subject); third, the easy assumption that anybody who has studied some education, and has had a little experience, can teach history of education, philosophy of education and educational sociology, must be set aside, for it is better that these things be untaught than taught badly. These I think of not as an order of studies, a number of hours or an array of scholarly knowledge, that are in and of themselves sacred; instead, they are only to a certain extent aids to, and guarantees of, a systematic preparation, which must be carried on until an able grasp of fundamentals has been achieved.

It is probable that most among you will not be inclined to question the legitimacy of psychology and sociology. Philosophy of education, too, would find many friends among you. With respect to history of education, it may be admitted that its opponents are numerous, there being many who would allow it only an incidental and grudging attention, if, indeed, they would give it any at all. Partly because it has many detractors, and partly because it does occupy a strategic place in the education of the citizen-teacher, it is proposed here to examine the functions of educational history, which are of value in the preparation of our teachers. Chief attention is given to the unique functions of educational history and study of contemporary systems other than our own—values which can rarely be derived from other sources.

First among the functions of educational history is the cultivation of a healthy, scientific skepticism with respect to the educational world around us and the establishment of a critical basis for judging the kaleidoscopic present. Nothing has been more characteristic of American education in the past hundred years than the tendency to run after every new word and phrase, make a fetish of it, proclaiming it a cure-all. At no time have our teachers possessed sufficient scientific skepticism to cause them to examine carefully, try out experimentally and reserve judgment until the novelty proves its value, or perhaps proves upon comparison with the past to be no novelty but only an old idea masquerading under a new name. The student of history meets these "novelties" under many guises and in many places. That which deceived a people as a great new idea in a certain century is, quite obviously, an old one to him who looks back from the vantage point of the historian. That which deceives so many to-day with its advertised title, "progressive," "revolutionary," etc., is seen by a careful observer of past education for what it really is. Not long ago a spokesman of the "new education in Europe" addressed an enthusiastic audience, a great part of which appeared to be convinced that the speaker had personally discovered these things recently, which were in reality a part of a movement hundreds of years old. So far, it appears, there is no way of gauging these "novelties" which appear, save by the historical yardstick. Every teacher in democracy's schools, and, indeed, every adult citizen, ought to have developed a basis for critical evaluation, that they may not be imposed upon. It would, moreover, be a first-rate service to the present bearers of so-called "new" and "progressive" ideas, and to democratic education in general, if they were always challenged by teachers who knew ancient history well enough to distinguish between old and new. To-day a book is laid upon my desk, claiming attention as the "latest thing." There is no new material, new insights or ideas or organization to be found in it. But its chapters are called "Units of Instruction." The economic value of such skepticism, both as to money and human effort, is obvious. A well-informed person does not buy every "novelty" the merchant chooses to display.

History is to the social science student as the telescope is to the astronomer. It brings near that which is remote, magnifies the total picture many times, permits him to see the interconnection of economic, religious, social and political factors with the educational process, and shows change taking place in one direction or another, in spite of determined efforts to prohibit it. At length, new elements appear in this stream of social life flowing under the lens. Education appears as an agency of conscious control. No longer is society so completely dominated by its physical environment. It is able to modify its condition intentionally. Considering its past, its present, and reconstructing the picture in accordance with its ideal aspirations, here and there a society is seen moving forward towards previously unsought goals. In an autocratic society, the teacher is the servant of the sovereign will, whatever it may be. Being only the servant of this autocratic will, it is not so indispensable that he understand the total educational process. It is enough that he be an effective inculcator of official doctrines, which constitute the established faith. In a democratic society, the teacher is the servant, too, of a collective will, but, at the same time, in some degree, he participates with others in choosing ends and means. Of all people, in such a society, the entire body of teachers should be preeminently qualified to judge critically both ends and means. Those unprepared for this critical judgment may select, or allow to be selected, means which can only defeat the ends of democratic education. Sharing this larger function, then, it is of utmost importance for teachers to understand the types of factors, material and ideal, which have conditioned education at all times. To no source, save the Book of Changes, can we turn for light. Without this knowledge of history, philosophy of education itself is blind.

History of education functions as guidance. Society of the present moment has arrived at a definite point in its development. We wish to go forward, not backward; to improve our lot, not to make it worse. We know now that education can be used constructively, creatively, and need not perform simply the function of conservation. But, without history, how can we know which direction is forward? Without history we must suppose ourselves ignorant of whence we have come, the experiments we have tried, the ideals which once guided us, the defeats we experienced and the successes as well. Without historical knowledge, it is no exaggeration to say that we can have no sense of direction, and can not even know where we are. Without knowledge of where we are, and in which way the next step forward lies, we constantly deceive ourselves into believing that we have progressed further than we have, and that we are now moving forward, when, in reality, we may be slipping back. We should think ill of a medical doctor who practised the dark magic of the savage medicine man, declaring it to be the latest word in medical science; but, to-day, due to a failure of critical, historical analysis among us, due to a failure to compare critically our present position with the past, it is no unusual thing at all to find savage practises extolled by schoolmen of democracy as the proper means to educate free men. To those who believe in the improvability of society and who look forward to the emancipation of men, history functions, then, as guidance, providing points of reference. For those who hold such faith in future progress to be mere delusion, history can, at least, teach humility with respect to present attainments, can show the untamed savage and the belief in magic still masquerading, under the cloak of "civilization," in our schools.

Historical study of education as a function of government reveals it to us as a process of growth, of evolution. By historical analysis of the great drama which has been unfolded, we are able to see social *mores*, educational traditions, political and economic systems as social habits, formed by a group in similar fashion as individual habit is formed. And as the elimination, or correction, of bad individual habits and the formation of correct ones causes the individual curve of learning to rise to a higher plateau, so it is evident that a society in similar fashion, but more slowly and with greater pains, has profited by new insights, which, in the course of generations and epochs, placed it in some respects beyond its former existence and above its contemporaries, who had no such insight or vision, or, if they had it, refused to profit by it. Whether it be accomplished intelligently or not, whether it lead to improvement or not, it is obvious to the student of history that social change is inevitable. The law of social growth, maturity and decay appears as clear to the careful student of society, who has watched it over thousands of years, as does the process of physical growth and decay to the student of fish and flowers. One may ask, then: "Why bother with it; do not the flowers wither and decay?" Indeed, they do. And, throughout the past, human societies have grown, achieved almost unlimited power, have decayed and been covered with dust. Change is inevitable in the biological and the social realms. The difference between them, and this is of greatest consequence, is that human capacity for modification and redirection is immensely greater than that of lower forms of life. Breed and select swine with all the care one may, they are still possessed of the same manners, the same piggishness. But history shows that human societies, as well as individuals, can be made, to a certain degree, benevolent or treacherous, cruel or kindly, friendly or hostile, selfishly individualistic or socially inclined, worldly or otherworldly. Society, in other words, can add nothing to the stock of human intelligence possessed by its members of any generation, but it can determine, to a remarkable degree, and always has determined, blindly or with foresight, the direction this intelligence will take, the ends it will serve; and it has also capitalized the emotional tendencies in man, determining in one age that they support one set of practises and, in another, that they make war upon them.

Now it has been, still is, and probably always will be, true that human nature finds satisfaction in things as they are. Even those who suffer under present circumstances are often very obviously averse to the uncertainty of change. But change comes inevitably. All our will can not turn it back; but, by intelligent control, it can be directed.

There are two irreconcilable views of this tendency to change—the autocratic and the democratic. Autocracy, throughout times past, appealed to divine kinship and authorization for evidence of the validity of its determination to prohibit change. The autocrats of the world, failing to recognize the law of nature, the unity of man with the rest of his world, and, misinterpreting wilfully or merely ignorantly the voice of God, set themselves haughtily in defense of the sacred present.

Modern democratic political philosophy arose in association with the philosophy of naturalism. Modern democracy, looking upon the necessity and inevitability of change, in the ordinary course of nature, regards it not with fear, hatred and intolerance, conniving to thwart it, but seeks only to control and direct change in the way productive of the greatest common good. There is no sacred present moment to be held fast. Democracy is a way of living, not the end of it. As a means, it is preferable to other ways of living only if, and in so far as, it provides greater freedom for man in thinking and acting, makes possible readier adjustment of the life of its individual members to the conditions around them, than is possible under other systems. In such a society, education can play a creative rôle, in addition to its inescapable function of conservation. The teachers of democracies must realize this conception of change, inevitable in nature and in the social body, and the creative function of education in controlling the evolutionary process. If they do not, they serve not the ends which the democratic philosophy of life has fixed upon as valuable, but those of some master, or clique of masters, who arise, from time to time, in every society and strive to control it for their selfish ends. These cliques are numerous in the United States to-day. Their claims for sympathy and support of schoolmen are clothed in fair raiment. Against special interests and special pleading of these factions the only safeguard lies in a firm grasp of the significance of our democratic philosophy of life and education; and this is impossible without a knowledge of the past from which it evolved and against which it was a protest.

That educational history performs a supplementary function, completing the circle of knowledge of man's past, is obvious. Since man first left a pictorial record, or kept chronology by knotting cords, he has enriched and extended the mind of each generation by pointing to a past as well as the present. When he became able to use a flexible, written language, histories became complex. The histories of Herodotus and Diodorus and the geography of Strabo are mixtures of wonderful mysteries and sober facts: That the gods determined the outcome of a battle, and that the lizards fried in the hot sun as they crossed the streets of ancient Susis at noonday; that the Greeks triumphed at Salamis, and that the ants of India were smaller than dogs though bigger than foxes; all these, and many other miscellanies, the early historians and geographers committed to their pages. Thucydides began to write more critical, scientific history. To-day there is scarcely a science, whether it be of government, of law, of psychology, of medicine, of theology, of engineering, which does not have its appropriate history. Each one of these is a valuable, indeed indispensable, supplement to the other. To a knowledge of human society each must make, and does make, its contribution.

Education, whether we regard it from the standpoint of individual happiness or social utility, is the most inclusive and most difficult of man's tasks. To it all other sciences bear tribute; through education they minister to man. In its history, their histories are synthesized. As the record of man's first efforts to make life bearable, as a record of his actual improvement of his natural heritage, and, as a preparation for an understanding of his present aspirations with respect to his next step forward, educational history performs a function which no other study can. Were this function alone to be considered, the history of man's educational endeavor should be taught to all our youth, for it is more meaningful to the ordinary citizen than the history of military affairs, law, politics, medicine or any other single isolated phase of human culture.

All of us, whether as teachers or not, enter the theater of social life late; the drama has long been in progress; the present scene is meaningless without some knowledge of the one preceding it, and the ones before that. Even to listen with understanding requires this knowledge. How much more indispensable is it for those citizens of democracy who must play a part. In a theater, one does not fail to snatch up a libretto, that he may appreciate to the full the new play he is about to see. Human societies, too, when they have become conscious arbiters of their own destinies, employ the libretto of the past, in order that the new generation may not only understand the significance of its culture, but may play an intelligent part in the furtherance of it.

History's cultural significance to the student is, obviously, not to be denied. If the modern world thought it had time for culture, it would take time for history. But, to-day, leading a life of idolatry before the golden calf of "practical efficiency," that which can be realized immediately and conveniently measured, the whole world seems to say with the poet: "Anything but histories." Diversion, too, it has been admitted, is provided by history. But who has time for diversion by the wayside of life, when it is loudly proclaimed that a crown of laurel awaits those who win the race? Still, I am at once so bold and backward as to allude to history, and recommend it, as diversion. Now entertainment, recreation of the mind through history, though it was deprecated by Thucydides, perhaps in lieu of an apology for the fact that his own history made no pretense of "listening" as well as that of other writers of antiquity, and though it is not the primary purpose of history of education, may with some justice be defended as of distinct value to teachers, whose lives are often drab enough without being subjected exclusively to more prosaic and more practical studies. Moreover, Clio in diverting mood is often most instructive. Nothing could be more delightful and amusing than Lucian's instruction as to "The Way to Write History," which, though composed for entertainment, is not without value to the staid historian. Indeed, one might ask, who has set forth the essential qualifications of the historian better than he? "There stands my model, then: fearless, incorruptible, independent, a believer in frankness and veracity; one that will call a spade a spade, make no concession to likes and dislikes, nor spare any man for pity or respect or propriety; an impartial judge, kind to all, but too kind to none; a literary cosmopolite with neither suzerain nor king, never heeding what this or that man may think, but setting down the thing that befell."

The inspirational function of history of education has been mentioned often, and always, it seems, overrated. It is true, of course, that a study of great men and great dramatic movements is inspiring; but it is also true that history is filled with comedies of error, which tend to balance the beam and leave little reason for valuing history for its inspirational contribution. The follies and errors men and societies have fallen into seem likely to be as instructive to us as their wisdom; perhaps more so. Besides, what is taught primarily for inspirational value will have to be carefully selected for that end. By this process of selection, the essentially true relationships of historical facts tend to be obscured, and even ignored. In fact, historical educational sociology is pushed into the background, while educational biography and a history of technical, pedagogical innovations, almost wholly disassociated from economic, political and social background, take its place.

So far as inspiration is concerned, we scarcely need to examine the past laboriously in order to find it. Men will drink it in from the present, with far greater ease and understanding. Great leaders are all around us. Let us not blind ourselves by thinking that for inspiration we must go to the Pestalozzis, the Platos and other great leaders of the past. If we do go to them thus directly for inspiration, we shall probably end by taking them uncritically, whereas what we need is critical examination of ideas, a separation of the wheat from the chaff, whether it was harvested three thousand years or three thousand minutes ago. By this it is not meant that inspiration, derived from educational history, is of no value, but that seeking inspiration should not be the end of our study. All studies, pursued zealously and with understanding, undoubtedly furnish inspiration to their devotees—one gains it from physics, another from chemistry and another from law. This valuable, incidental derivative from the history of man's education is not to be denied. To sense the vital power of an idea long ages after its originator gave it birth; to observe the well-nigh imperishable character of a culture; to gain an understanding of man's increasing mastery of the material world; to see how, so far, he has failed to master his social world, save for brief periods, and in isolated groups; all these lead us to contemplate in the soberest temper the problems which lie before us to-day. And if, facing this task, the words of one of the greatest teachers come to us, let us not scorn the inspiration—no, not even in this most practical of all practical worlds:

> Neither must we cast a slight upon education, which is the first and fairest thing that the best of men ever have, and which, though liable to take wrong direction, is capable of reformation. And this work of reformation is the great business of every man while he lives.

THE CASE FOR THE PUBLIC SCHOOLS[1]

By WILLIAM J. SHRODER
PRESIDENT, BOARD OF EDUCATION, CINCINNATI, OHIO

I HAVE been asked to present some views because I have had "experience as a business man and as a member and president of a board of education." Therefore you must anticipate that my approach, and possibly my conclusions, may differ radically from those of the professional educator. You must understand that I claim neither authority for, nor popular acceptance of, the views presented.

Preliminary to the consideration of the public schools themselves, let us consider their relative position in the entire scheme of American life. To consider them as an agency which can be separated from other important parts of the social plan would be a primary error. We must look upon our national life as a unit, with all the great social forces which take part in its making interrelating and reacting upon each other. The ideal should be so to coordinate the play of these activities as to attain the one object of human life—the welfare, contentment and spiritual satisfaction of all the people. The functions of the public schools must be related to and coordinated with the industrial, cultural, recreational and religious life of our citizens, if it is to play its part in making life more complete and more satisfactory.

Quantitatively there can be no question of the importance of education, in which the public schools are of major moment, in the making of our people. Approximately 30,000,000 individuals, or almost one fourth of our entire population, are engaged in formal education as pupils or teachers. Many pupils spend a period equal to one fourth of their productive lives in school, while an appreciable percentage spend from one half to again as much in what we call higher education.

Were it not for its subsequent application, I would not bore you by repeating

[1] Address before the fourth general session, Department of Superintendence, Cleveland, Ohio, February 27, 1934.

that education for all the people is one of the basic conceptions of American government. Almost from the beginning it has been deemed essential to the preservation of democracy. It was felt that this form of government could not survive unless the people were able to choose between true and false leaders and that this choice could be made possible only by educating the masses so that they might read, write, think and decide with a degree of intelligence which could be attained only through general education.

Theoretically, higher education was for the development of leaders, elementary education for the development of intelligent followers. The fact that leadership is frequently found among those who have not had the advantage of higher education and that many who have had this advantage do not make even reasonably sound followers does not necessarily invalidate the theory; it may merely indicate that many who by reason of their qualities were entitled to higher education were by mischance of fate denied their opportunity, and that many have received this opportunity who could make no use of it after it had been given to them. In the main, the theory has held good in experience, in that a disproportionate number of leaders in all lines have been from among those who have enjoyed the privilege of education beyond public-school years.

Our conception of how much education is needed to insure the safety of a democratic form of government necessarily changes with the life of the people. As this life becomes more complex and more difficult, the number of people for whom natural endowment, with a minimum of formal education, suffices to meet the strain becomes less, and the need for reenforcement, through additional and diversified training, becomes greater. The traditional "three R's" are inadequate in helping the majority of the people to face life and to adjust themselves to it.

Let us examine a few of the fundamental economic and social changes of the past fifty years. When families lived in separate houses—horizontally—home-life provided, through the household duties in which every one participated, a training in social adjustment which was in large measure lost when people began living in apartments—vertically. When the Bible ceased to be a book for daily reading and became Sunday literature (to compete with the Sunday supplement among numbers of people), the precepts and example of a just social life were withdrawn from the daily living of many. When space became so closely occupied with houses that nothing but the streets remained for wholesome play, and then they too were made unsafe by speeding traffic, opportunity not only for health-building exercise, but also for character-building training in fairness, honesty, cooperation and clean competition was taken from many of our youth. When the small individual business, in which the children followed the parent, gave way to big business, and at the same time the apprentice system, under which the youth could learn a trade, was practically discarded, opportunity for training for a living, as well as training for life, was minimized. When automotive machinery reduced the number of men and women required by industry (and this brings us to to-day), not only is the age when young people are welcomed into industry deferred, and the age at which workers are forced out of industry reduced, but the hours of those actually employed are being lessened to the point where there are more leisure than working hours in the waking day.

Also, during the period under examination, there has been progress in the recognition, diagnosis and treatment of physical and mental ailments. A civilization which was rich in opportunities arising from undeveloped resources financially could afford to ignore the human wreckage resulting from a laissez-faire attitude, but to-day the public is increasingly conscious of the cost of neglect. Partially because of more sensitized feeling, but largely from enlightened selfishness, the people are demanding that every effort be made to adjust the handicapped—those chronically ill, crippled, deaf, blind, mentally deficient or with warped personalities—to independent adequacy in community life.

Which of the great agencies of civilized existence would be expected to assume the responsibilities arising from these many changed conditions? The religious institutions could neither be financed nor organized to handle these problems. From the beginning the homes were inadequate to meet these situations. Industry was both unwilling and unable to function in these fields. Obviously these problems did not belong to the fields of music and the arts. The government alone could be looked to to meet the need, and of all the branches of government that of public education was alone in a position, by enlargement and change of its organization, to attempt on behalf of all the people to satisfy these changed demands.

What are some of the changes resulting from this undertaking? The schools in some measure take the place of the home in developing proper social attitudes, the place of the church in developing ethical standards and the love of social justice, the place of industry in training for a living and the place of natural recreational opportunities in developing sound health and those moral standards which we include in the term "sportsmanship." In addition thereto they must afford educational and cultural opportunities for training not only the child but also the adult for the constructive use of increased leisure.

Science has demonstrated the value of research, and changed conditions have suggested its application to education. Industry, always convinced by increased profits, has accepted research as a means not only of determining basic facts but also of increasing efficiency in operation. It is therefore somewhat surprising to find industrialists attacking research in education as a "fad" or "frill" at a time when complete understanding is more essential to the common welfare than ever before in the history of our people. Educational research, as I see it, must be directed not only to the physical equipment, the substance of the curriculum and the essentials of teaching, but also, through applied psychology, to the needs, capacities and possibilities of the pupil. Mass education, disregarding individual differences, will no longer satisfy a people who are asking that they and their children be prepared to meet life as it is. Educational research must challenge old practises based on old assumptions. For instance, it must determine the vocabulary most useful in life. It must determine the most efficient ways of teaching reading, to develop both speed and understanding. It must find out what the differences are in the way in which people of different degrees of mentality learn. It must ascertain causes of difficulty in certain subject-matter and the best method for overcoming these difficulties. It must perfect the means of determining capacity for learning, and then attempt to so place the pupil as to develop him to his utmost.

When we realize that public-school children range from the feeble-minded to the exceptionally endowed, from the permanently crippled to the almost perfect, from those of warped character and attitude to those of fine personality and social adjustment, we recognize that these fundamental differences in children demand not only facilities for classification, but also such differentiation in educational opportunities as will permit the individual child to develop to the limit of his own capacity.

This evolution in public-school responsibility has necessitated fundamental changes in all three basic school requirements—physical facilities and equipment, curriculum and teacher qualifications. Meeting public requirements will never be a closed book. Additional lines and chapters must be written as social and economic changes demand. This is just another way of saying that the public educational system must be continuously tied up with social needs. Where this has not been true in the past, it must be made true. As far as one can foresee, the indications are that public education, as it meets these demands, will become more costly as well as more valuable to the country.

These considerations should make it clear that criticisms of educational costs based on comparisons with other periods, be they ten, twenty or fifty years ago, have no validity. It would be as logical to make comparisons of vehicular transportation costs, or of costs in any other field where the changes have been so radical as to make the matters compared not merely of different species, but truly of different genus.

Let us examine what is taking place in such districts as have most nearly met the needs arising from economic and social changes. Differentiation in the opportunities offered requires more classes and more specialized facilities and equipment. It also imports a more difficult type of school administration, and consequently more highly qualified school principals to guide activities. Obviously the small school can afford neither the physical equipment, the number of teachers nor the qualified personnel. The change from the small to the large unit, whether in rural or city districts, is not based upon educational theory, but on necessity which will not be denied. The large unit or centralized school involves a greater average distance from the homes of the children, and this in turn creates the problem of transportation. Both large schools and transportation costs have been criticized as unnecessary developments of public education. These critics force upon the schools the decision of either continuing these expenses or of denying to our children a fair opportunity for an adequate life.

When we come to the consideration of the content of public education as expressed in its curriculum, we should be frank in admitting that part only is tested and proven, that some is experimental and that much is traditional and possibly of doubtful value. The public is in part responsible for the retention of the obsolete in the curriculum. Conservatism of school people must also share this responsibility. Lack of understanding of the significance of changes in the world at large, both by school and lay people, must bear its full share. An additional factor of considerable importance should not be overlooked. Quite logically elementary education is directed to meet high-school continuation. In turn, high schools must attempt to qualify their pupils for higher education. The rigidity of college entrance requirements controls a large part of high-school curricula and thus indirectly imposes a certain rigidity on elementary school activities. Since this is superimposed on courses designed to meet the major obligation of the public educational system to provide for the overwhelming majority who do not enter either general high schools or college, it is not surprising that the curricula of the public schools are criticized, and with some justice, for including a bit of this, that or the other, without coordination, and with little practical or cultural value. It is not surprising that those not expert in education overlook the beauty of the forest because they see much of the underbrush and dead trees.

The mere statement of where the responsibility lies gives some indication of the steps necessary for improvement. Educators must be the interpreters of new needs in the life of the people and, through enlightening the public, must secure its support for necessary adaptations of the schools. The *status quo* is more comfortable and arouses less objection and criticism than does creative change. School positions are of long tenure, and their major activities are somewhat removed from the planes of everyday life. These conditions breed ultraconservatism and tend to cloud the vision to changing needs. A consciousness of this danger should result in conditioning these very natural attitudes toward a more flexible and progressive conception of curricular needs.

How to bring about an understanding of the significance of fundamental economic and social developments so as to promptly adapt school activities to new needs is a serious problem. It is possible that the solution requires the creation of state or federal bureaus, with highly trained and specially qualified personnel, to interpret both economic and social evolutions, and with sufficient authority to direct such curricular modifications as may be demanded. Whatever the solution, I am convinced that the public schools must get more promptly in step with contemporary life.

I know that I am trespassing on a technical field when I discuss college entrance requirements. However, the effect of their pressure on the public educational system is so serious as to justify the expression of lay thought, however unqualified.

While I do not consider my suggestion radical, it is so far from accepted tradition that I offer it with considerable hesitancy, and in the form of a question. Why can not students be admitted to college on the basis of their capacity and the adequacy of their preparation in the fields in which they have shown interest and desire for thorough knowledge? Would not that be as fair a test of whether or not they are college material as the present entrance requirements? If the answers were affirmative, the elementary and secondary schools would be free to develop a variety of curricula meeting the needs of all types of pupils and without inadequate required courses which add little or nothing to their preparation for life.

Let us now consider the effect on teacher qualifications of the new demands on public education. It should be quite obvious that the average teacher who was entirely adequate to the needs of his time in a simpler society could not meet present requirements. The preparation necessary for individualized instruction is entirely different from that sufficient for mass instruction in a uniform way. In the earlier days high-school graduation was sufficient qualification. Later an added two-year normal school course was considered adequate. To-day teaching has become one of the great professions, requiring a broad cultural background in addition to specialized knowledge of subject-matter. It requires understanding of social, psychological and economic materials. It utilizes a technique based on research and practise. It is not only a profession, but a profession with a scientific background. It is also an art, requiring practise for its attainment. In addition to his science and art, the teacher must have character and personality. We have seen how the school has been compelled to take over part of the training of the child which in a less complex social organization belonged to the home and to the church. Its obligation has progressed from that of developing intelligent voters to that of preparing children for a living and for life. All the technical qualifications attainable would not qualify the teacher for this purpose. To produce character one must have character. To effectively mold the lives of others we must have personality to win and to hold the approval and the affection of those we are attempting to influence. Not only must the teacher start with these qualifications, but he must have a professional attitude toward his own work; must be anxious at all times to devote his means and his energy toward continuous improvement. A teacher who is no better twenty years later than he was at his start should never have been a teacher. The need for constant adjustment of education to the changing world imports the obligation of the teacher to keep himself abreast of these changes.

How then are we to secure such teachers? Doubtless many will teach because they love teaching more than any other pursuit. But even those who are doing the work they crave must live. In order to do their work effectively they should be reasonably free from financial worries and should be able to maintain themselves on a standard which their professional position implies.

They must have sufficient free time and sufficient free money to continue their professional improvement. Unquestionably they are willing to make some financial sacrifice to live the life they love. It never should be necessary for teachers' compensation to compete with commercial compensation. However, the salary schedule must be sufficiently high to attract to and maintain in the service of public education teachers with adequate professional and personal qualifications. Those of us past fifty can remember the day when even city schools paid teachers a mere pittance. As recently as the world war the pay of most teachers was merely a contribution to the family expense, not sufficient for independent maintenance. That to-day an effort is being made to recognize the teaching profession not only by the professional requirements but also by professional pay is to the credit of our people. However, this is the main cause of the increased cost of public education. No demand for percentage reduction of educational costs can be made without affecting teachers' pay. It is therefore hopelessly inconsistent, and either ignorant or in bad faith, for critics of school costs to demand heavy reductions along with maintenance of pay. In one breath they say, "We value our teachers; we expect them to be thoroughly qualified; we approve of the national recovery program for maintaining the income and spending capacity of the people; we do not want salaries reduced"; and in the next breath they say, "You must reduce school costs 30 per cent.," when merely superficial examination would show that the entire cost of the schools, exclusive of educational personnel, is not 30 per cent. of the total.

What, then, are we to do in the present situation? If the functions of public education are to be enlarged not only by the needs of the age group now in the schools, but also by the necessity of retraining for other industries adults who have lost their places in economic life, and to serve adults who require training for the constructive use of their increased leisure, where are we to find the necessary support? Some are advocating centralization of educational responsibility in the state. Others are looking forward to federal support. If there is any way of avoiding these alternatives, the way should be found. While doubtless such centralization would be of advantage to the poorer and more backward sections of the country, it would be distinctly to the disadvantage of the urban communities which must care for more than 50 per cent. of the people. If these alternatives are to be avoided, it can be done only by directed, continuous and intelligent effort toward creating public understanding of the functions, methods and plans of the public schools. I believe that when the people understand how much they have at stake, they will demand sufficient financial support to insure the efficient operation of public schools. This would be propaganda, but it is propaganda in its best approved form. It must be free from selfish interest and must be not for the benefit of the school people, but for the benefit of all the people. If the million teachers of this country will first fully inform themselves, and then use every means at their disposal for informing the public, the cause of public education will be safe.

EDUCATIONAL EVENTS

THE NAZI TRAINING OF GERMAN STUDENTS

UNDER the new organization of students imposed by Chancellor Hitler upon German universities all undergraduates are being required to submit to military training in Nazi storm detachments and to a one-year term of manual labor. The new organization, known as the Federal Corporation of Students at German Universities, is being directed by Dr. Oskar Staebel, a Nazi leader. His activities are under the direct supervision of Dr. Wilhelm Frick, Minister of the Interior, a member of Hitler's cabinet.

The imposed constitution of the student organization provides that the task of the student corporation is "to educate students through obligation to storm detachment service and labor service, and by political training to become German men conscious of the national honor and trained to bear arms and give responsible and selfless service to the people and the state."

The German student corporation also will see that the German academic youths remain in contact with the plain people, instead of forming a snobbish and exclusive caste as has been charged against them in the past. Hence, their obligation to do manual labor for a year.

The constitution also charges the student corporation with the duty of "linking German students in the Reich and those beyond its frontiers together and fostering worthy relations with student bodies abroad and with foreign guests at German universities." An officer in the superior school of the storm detachments is intrusted with the task of giving military training to the students, while their political education is to be undertaken by a National Socialist German Students' League.

The German student corporation was formed in 1919 as a union of all German university students. Recognition of it as a legal student body was withdrawn by the state in 1927 because of its anti-republican attitude. Nazi undergraduates gained control of it for the first time in 1931, and, last year, it was recognized formally by the Hitler government as the only authorized university students' organization.

TEACHERS' SALARIES AND THE COST OF LIVING

REED COLLEGE has recently published a bulletin entitled "Women's Wages Compared with the Living Costs and General Community Standard, 1914–1932," demonstrating that teachers' salaries have continuously decreased, while the cost of living has increased. This study, based on statistics gathered by the Women's Bureau of the U. S. Department of Labor and supplemented by a study of the budgets of 629 grade teachers in Portland, Oregon, has been compiled by Miss Jessie M. Short, assistant professor of mathematics at Reed College, who has drawn the following conclusions:

(1) Despite marked wage increases during the World War period (1914–1920, since throughout those years economic effects of the European conflict were dominant), wage-earners were worse off in actual buying power than they were before the war and than they have been since; for although wages increased during the war period, the cost of living increased much more rapidly. From 1916 to 1920 wage-earners were subject to a positive disadvantage in buying power—their "real wage" or actual buying power was, on the average, about 12 per cent. less than it was in 1914.

With wages in 1920 up about 88 per cent. above the 1914 level, wage-earners were no better and no worse off than they were before the war began, for the cost of living had likewise risen 88 per cent. Since 1920 wages have increased quite steadily up to 1930 (when unemployment began to make wage statistics of dubious value) and during the same period the cost of living fell steadily, giving wage-earners a positive and rather great advantage in buying power.

(2) Comparison of the lot of Portland public school teachers with that of wage-earners generally in all industries during the same 18 years leads to three rather striking conclusions: First, the disadvantage in buying power to which wage-earners

generally were subject during the war period was experienced by teachers in an immensely greater degree; for when wages were increasing and the cost of living was soaring, the salaries of most of the Portland public school teachers were reduced 10 per cent. Second, while wage-earners in 1920 regained buying power equal to that of 1914, teachers did not make the same recovery until mid-year, 1931. In 1920 living costs had increased to 188 per cent., wages to 188 per cent., and the average salary of high-school and grade teachers to 124 per cent., each as compared with 1914. Third, after 1920 wage-earners (and likewise the employer group) enjoyed a great positive advantage in buying power which lasted ten years; but the slight advantage which came to teachers in 1931 was cut short a year later by 24.5 per cent. reduction in pay, which again put them at a positive disadvantage in buying, as compared with their buying power in 1914.

(3) Since the majority of teachers are women, they are quite commonly regarded with the same discriminative attitude that is taken toward gainfully employed women generally. Single women work to support themselves only, and married women work for "pin money" to spend in addition to their husband's incomes, it is often said, in accordance with the traditional notion that women are the home-makers and men are the providers for the home.

A wealth of evidence gathered by the Women's Bureau of the United States Department of Labor controverts these ideas completely and clearly establishes the fact that when married women work, in nearly all cases their total earnings go to the support of their families. A survey of a representative group of Portland public school teachers (629 women) shows rather conclusively that, on the average, each supports the equivalent of one total dependent.

This last conclusion has been reached by showing that 334 people were totally dependent on the earnings of 236 teachers, and that 612 people were partially dependent on the earnings of 326 teachers in the group. Thus, on the earnings of 629 teachers in the whole group, 946 people, aside from the teachers themselves, were wholly or partially dependent for support.

THREE NEW DOCTORATE DEGREES AT COLUMBIA UNIVERSITY

THREE new doctorate degrees in law, medicine and education have recently been authorized by the trustees of Columbia University. Acting upon the recommendation of the university council, they have established the degrees of doctor of medical science, doctor of the science of law and doctor of education. The Faculty of Medicine, in petitioning the council, asserted that the degree of doctor of medical science was needed to identify competent practitioners in the specialized branches of clinical medicine and to protect the public from doctors who, without adequate training, claim to be specialists. The new degree, replacing the degree of master of science now conferred in graduate medical fields, involves "the successful completion of a training of not less than three years after one year's hospital internship, and original work in graduate medical studies as shall be prescribed by the Faculty of Medicine.

The School of Law will award the degree of doctor of the science of law, instead of doctor of law, for advanced professional study. This change is made to distinguish the highest degree in law of Columbia University from the doctor of law degree awarded by many American schools as a first degree in law.

Teachers College will confer the degree of doctor of education instead of doctor of philosophy on students who undertake a course of professional preparation instead of educational research. All three degrees are intended to mark more sharply the difference between research work leading to a Ph.D. degree and advanced professional study. The trustees also sanctioned the award of a certificate in landscape architecture through University Extension.

It was stated in the petition of the Faculty of Medicine that "no phase of medical service and education is more important, both from the interests of the public and of the profession, than that of the proper training of specialists. At the present time, the public is confused by the large number of doctors who claim to be specialists, whereas in reality there is a serious shortage of properly trained experts to meet the needs of the country. The preparation necessary for proficiency in the highly technical aspects of the various fields of surgery, for example, requires a comprehensive preparation in the basic medical sciences as well as a long period of experience under the supervision of expert surgeons. What is needed particularly in the graduate medical program is a degree which will permit identification of the individual as qualified by a university grade of training in one of the specialized fields of clinical medicine."

The Faculty of Education presented its conviction that Teachers College can serve American education more effectively if the administration of professional education be separated from that of educational research. "The usual course of training for the degree of doctor of philosophy puts great emphasis upon individual study, relatively less upon formal course requirement, and centers most of its effort upon the dissertation," according to this faculty's petition. "This is ideal when the student plans to engage in work in which research will play a great part. But in most professions, other than that of university scholar and research workers, the need is not what the student can do 'to' the subject. Rather it is what the student can do 'with' the subject. We are concinced that we can strengthen our work and serve American education better if we separate the two functions completely. The establishment of the proposed degree, doctor of education, will separate the administration of professional education from that of educational research."

PRECEPTORIAL AND TUTORIAL PLAN AT COLGATE UNIVERSITY

DR. GEORGE BARTON CUTTEN, president of Colgate University, announced on March 10 that the entire class entering the university in the fall of 1934 will be trained under the preceptorial, tutorial and tutorial seminar plans of instruction. The preceptorial plan is now in its third year. The first year it was tried out with thirty-five students, all freshmen. Last year it was extended to ninety, and this year to half the freshman class, or 150 men. Tutors have been working with many of the sophomores, and the tutorial seminar plan has been used for the upper-class men. The entering class next fall will have the benefit of the different plans during four years in college. Dr. Cutten makes the following statement:

The preceptor is not a coach to help the freshman cram for examinations. He is not expected to teach him outside the classroom the things that his confrères are supposed to be teaching him inside the classroom. His concern is not primarily with the courses which the freshman is taking or the subjects which he is studying. His first concern is with the freshman's mind, how it is developing and what it needs to accelerate and steady its development.

The preceptor is the one member of the faculty whose appointed function is to consider the freshman as a whole. He is deputed to set before the youth the vision of his education as a unified process of development and not as the aggregate of an allotted number of subjects or courses, or, worse still, as the arithmetical sum of a series of credit units. . . .

Just what form the individual conferences take depends largely upon the personalities of the preceptors. Through regular consultations among the members of the preceptorial staff and the comparing of experiences, certain broad lines of procedure are laid down, subject always to change as experience may suggest. Standardization of method is not only difficult but undesirable.

While the essence of preceptorial conferences is intimacy, freedom, informality, there is always a "subject before the house." The perennial matter always under consideration, tacitly if not in so many words, is the student and his intellectual development as a whole.

The freshman preceptorial system is an essential part of the Colgate plan, which has been recognized by a grant of $30,000 a year for four years from the Carnegie Corporation of New York to put it into full operation. Addition of new instructors now and more next fall is making the broadening of its scope possible.

THE MOVING PICTURE HABITS OF HIGH-SCHOOL STUDENTS

THE National Council of Teachers of English has completed the first phase of its experiment in studying the moving picture habits of American high-school students and in determining whether these habits can be significantly improved through the medium of the English class. William Lewin, chairman of the photoplay appreciation committee of the National Council of Teachers of English, reports that 68 groups of students were included in the experiment.

These were distributed in California, Colorado, Florida, Georgia, Illinois, Indiana, Kansas, Michigan, Minnesota, Montana, New Jersey, New York, Pennsylvania, Tennessee, Virginia, West Virginia and the District of Columbia. In all, 36 progressive teachers, 1,851 representative pupils, 31 junior and senior high schools and 28 cities were considered statistically. The cooperation of 57 theaters was enlisted, and, in spite of the economic depression, free admissions totaled approximately 14,000.

At the outset of the experiment 72 per cent. of the pupils included in all groups stated they had never in their lives, so far as they could remember, prepared a theme or a talk on a photoplay. In spite of the fact that adolescents go to the "movies" on the average once a week, three quarters of them report that their educational needs and interests in this field have never been touched by the schools.

The committee found that the most common habit of high-school students in relation to selecting a photoplay to see is to discuss it with a member of the family. About 70 per cent. report this habit. A majority of adolescents ordinarily read what a critic says about a picture before they decide to see it. About half of them usually also discuss the question with a friend. Do they consider whether the story is by a good author? Nearly half of them do. Do they consider who produced and who directed the picture? About one in three considers the producer and one in five the director. The last thing they ever think of in selecting a picture is to ask a teacher about it.

The experimental teachers set up in each experimental school two groups of pupils matched in age, grade, intelligence, home background and general appreciation of photoplays. Arrangements were then made to have both groups go in a body, with permission of their parents, to see the same series of photoplays in a local theater. After seeing each photoplay one group consistently got instruction in appreciation, while the other group merely continued to see the pictures without discussion or instruction of any kind. The activities of the instructed pupils were based on new units of photoplay appreciation prepared for the Curriculum Commission of the National Council of Teachers of English.

Even before the publication of the monograph which will present the full report of the committee, the following recommendations are being widely adopted:

(1) That units of instruction be introduced into the nation's schools, with a view to improving, by mass education, popular standards of taste and judgment in relation to photoplays.

(2) That courses in methods of teaching photoplay appreciation begin to be included in the curricula of schools of education.

(3) That further experimentation be arranged with a view to formulating children's standards, in harmony with those of teachers, for judging photoplays.

(4) That a committee of English teachers regularly preview selected current photoplays and prepare suggestions as to which productions may well be discussed in the classroom.

(5) That critical discussion guides be developed for the study of selected screen plays.

PROGRAM FOR TEACHERS-IN-SERVICE IN CAMDEN, NEW JERSEY

THE professional committee of the Teachers Association of Camden, N. J., under the leadership of Dr. Leon N. Neulen, superintendent of schools, has cooperated with the administration of the city school system in formulating a comprehensive five-year program for the education of its teachers-in-service. According to a report from Dr. Walter N. Myers, of the Camden High School, the professional committee proposes that each year of the five a major theme should be inaugurated, and that this point of emphasis should be broad enough to meet the needs of all levels of the school system.

The policy and planning committee formulated the following possible themes or problems, one of which is to be studied each year. The first of these has already been adopted for the current academic year: (1) The cultivation of specific character traits through school experiences; (2) new orientations in education for participation in a changing social order; (3) the direction of pupil experiences in accordance with the laws of learning, and the direction of pupils in the techniques of effective study; (4) the adjustment of school experiences to the needs and capacities of Camden children; (5) the determination of the causes of pupil failures and the making of necessary adjustments.

The committee outlined the several implications of each major theme, and the following proposals, both preventive and curative, have been suggested:

(1) That an investigation be made in each school of those character traits which are most appropriate to its needs, and that a proper program be organized to develop these. That the organization of this program utilize the life situations that are peculiar to that school locality, and at the same time discover the rôle that tempera-

mental differences play in the formation of character traits.

(2) That a survey be made of the social environment which forms the background of the character traits revealed by school experiences, and that a composite character program be organized which will develop the cultural and creative phase of school experiences.

(3) That a study be made of the psychological and physiological foundations of character traits desirable at various school ages, and that a wholesome guidance program be made with a view to preventing maladjustments.

(4) That this knowledge be used to form a constructive program of extra-curricular and leisure time activities.

(5) That measurements of character growth be initiated as a foundation of corrective school experiences.

(6) That a study be made of the cause and effect of failures and their relationships to the development of character.

Of the possible factors contributing to the education of teachers in service, the policy and planning committee determined the following eleven agencies and activities as properly belonging to the implications of the first theme, which deals with character education: Library helps and bibliography; teachers' meetings and round table; reading circles; school survey work and social service; research and experimentation; educational clinics and mental hygiene; visual education; contributions to educational literature; the press; the public forum, and radio education.

To assist the policy and planning committee in the appointment of the special committees of these eleven agencies and in the enrolment of volunteer groups, two means were employed. First, a confidential personnel card was supplied to each teacher and administrative officer, on which he was invited to record complete academic and professional information. Secondly, each teacher who wished to participate in the several activities of the first year's theme was invited so to signify on a special form.

EDUCATIONAL NOTES AND NEWS

Professor Arthur Cutts Willard, acting dean of the College of Engineering of the University of Illinois, has been elected president of the university. He succeeds Dr. Harry Woodburn Chase, who resigned a year ago to become chancellor of New York University.

Lewis W. Francis has been elected president of the Packer Collegiate Institute of Brooklyn, N. Y., to succeed the late Frank L. Babbott.

Dr. James Alexander MacLean, president of the University of Manitoba, tendered his resignation on March 9, to take effect at the close of the current academic year. Dr. MacLean, who has reached the age limit of sixty-five years, gave that as his reason for resigning.

John Wilber Lowes, who became last fall special financial assistant to President Conant, of Harvard University, has been appointed to the newly created post of financial vice-president of the university. Mr. Lowes will take over the work formerly conducted by Arthur Lovett Endicott, controller for the past eight years, who has been granted an indefinite leave of absence because of ill health.

Dr. Dorothy Canfield Fisher and Louis John Taber, master of the National Grange since 1923, have recently accepted invitations to address the Citizens' Conference on the Crisis in Education, which will be held on April 5 and 6 in Columbus, Ohio. Speakers already announced include Mrs. Franklin D. Roosevelt, Paul V. McNutt, Glenn Frank, William J. Bogan, Robert Maynard Hutchins and Newton D. Baker.

Dr. Harold Willis Dodds, president of Princeton University, has been elected to honorary membership in Phi Beta Kappa.

Dr. Leon C. Marshall, professor of law in the Institute of Law of the Johns Hopkins University, has been appointed by President Roosevelt to the National Labor Board.

Dr. H. Gordon Hayes, professor of economics at the Ohio State University, has recently been appointed chief economic adviser in the U. S. Bureau of Foreign and Domestic Commerce.

Dr. James Rowland Angell, president of

Yale University, left with Mrs. Angell on March 14 for Colorado, California and Hawaii. During the trip they will be the guests of several Yale clubs at annual alumni meetings.

DR. HENRY C. SHERMAN, Mitchill professor of chemistry at Columbia University, has been awarded the William H. Nichols Medal of the New York section of the American Chemical Society. The Nichols Medal, founded in 1902 to stimulate original research in chemistry, was given to Dr. Sherman for his work showing that "chemistry, through nutrition, may raise the level of positive health and increase the average length of life."

DR. GREGORY PAUL BAXTER, professor of chemistry at Harvard University, has been awarded the Theodore William Richards Medal, which is bestowed biennially by the northeastern section of the American Chemical Society to scientific men who have attained outstanding eminence in the field of pure chemistry.

DR. EWEN GILLIS, professor of pharmacy at the Ohio State University, has been awarded the Ebert Gold Medal for an outstanding contribution to pharmaceutical literature during 1933. His essay is entitled "Phytochemical Investigation on *Hydrastis canadensis*."

EIGHT faculty members are among the ninety candidates recently elected to membership in the Columbia University chapter of Sigma Xi. They are Dr. Henry A. Bartels, Professor George B. Karelitz, Dr. Henry W. Raudenbush, Jr., Professor Frank A. Ross, Dr. Arthur T. Rowe, Dr. Edward Singer, Dr. M. Russell Stein and Professor Daniel E. Ziskin.

DR. GUY M. WINSLOW, president of Lasell Junior College at Auburndale, Mass., and president of the New England Junior College Council, has been elected vice-president of the American Association of Junior Colleges.

DR. ARCH T. ALLEN, state superintendent of public instruction for North Carolina, recently called a conference of fifty-six organizations of state-wide character and twenty institutions of higher learning within the state for the purpose of making changes in the public school system. The initial plan evolved by the conference calls for a two-year study of the curriculum. Each organization has named a committee to recommend construction changes, which will be considered at another general meeting to be held within the next six months. Principal speakers, besides Dr. Allen, were Governor J. C. B. Ehringhaus and Dr. Frank P. Graham, president of the Greater University of North Carolina.

MRS. HOWARD E. MACGREGOR, head of the music department of Simpson College at Indianola, Iowa, has been granted the degree of master of organ music by the University of Michigan. Mrs. MacGregor is said to be the only woman who has ever received this degree from the university.

PROFESSOR ALBERT DEF. PALMER, chairman of the department of physics at Brown University, and Professor Albert B. Johnson, of the department of Romance languages and literature at the same institution, will retire at the end of the current academic year.

PROFESSOR HENRY B. DATES, for twenty-nine years head of the electrical engineering department of the Case School of Applied Science, has been named by President William E. Wickenden as director of the new evening division of the school, which will open in September. Professor Clyde A. McKeeman has been appointed assistant director, and Professor Willard E. Nudd, registrar.

DR. SAMUEL ALAN CHALLMAN has been appointed director of the Minneapolis Child Guidance Clinic, succeeding Dr. Herbert E. Chamberlain, who resigned last year to direct a similar clinic at the University of Chicago.

PROFESSOR C. R. MELCHER, formerly dean of men at the University of Kentucky and head of the German department, who was retired from active duty at the university last June, has been appointed acting professor of German at Centre College at Danville, Ky., following the resignation of Professor E. A. H. Fuchs of that college.

DR. P. A. WADIA, dean of the Faculty of Arts and professor of economics, political science and philosophy at Bombay University, will arrive in the United States early in April, according to an announcement made by the Institute of International Education, where he will make his headquarters. Dr. Wadia is planning a lecture tour of the leading American colleges and universities.

DR. PAYSON SMITH, commissioner of education of Massachusetts, has announced that the annual state conference of principals and supervisors of elementary schools will be held at the Massachusetts State College from April 4 to 6. The program will include addresses by Dr. Charles H. Judd, director of the School of Education of the University of Chicago; Dr. Mark A. May, of the Graduate School of Education of Yale University, and John Lund, superintendent of schools at Newton, Mass.

DR. P. A. PARSONS, head of the sociology department at the University of Oregon, will serve as chairman of the annual Commonwealth Conference to be held at the university from March 19 to 24. Marshall N. Dana, regional adviser of the Northwest area for the Public Works Administration; Frank Bane, director of the American Public Welfare Association, and Frank Branch Wiley will address the conference.

DR. WILLIAM MATHER LEWIS, president of Lafayette College, has been appointed by the American Friends of Lafayette to serve as chairman of the committee on educational institutions in regard to the observance of the one hundredth anniversary of the death of General Lafayette. The anniversary, which occurs on May 20, will be celebrated in the schools and colleges on either May 18 or 21.

JAMES ALEXANDER NUGENT, superintendent of schools in Jersey City, N. J., was awarded Knighthood in the Order of St. Gregory the Great on March 7, when Pope Pius awarded promotions to fifteen ecclesiastics and conferred honors upon four laymen of the Diocese of Newark, N. J.

PROFESSOR HUNTLEY M. SINCLAIR, of the department of economics at Washington University, St. Louis, has resigned from the faculty and will soon return to Canada. Professor Sinclair, who came to the university in 1926 from the University of British Columbia, has announced his intention of running for election to the Canadian Parliament.

ROBERT B. BROWNE has been appointed by Acting President Arthur H. Daniels, of the University of Illinois, to serve as acting head of the extension courses by correspondence which have recently been established at the university.

ARTHUR WILD, formerly a reporter on the *Chicago Daily News*, has been appointed by President Conant of Harvard University to serve as secretary to the university for information. Mr. Wild succeeds William I. Nichols, who was in charge of the university's information department from September, 1932, until January, 1934.

DR. ALLEN SINCLAIR WILL, organizer and director of the department of journalism at Rutgers University and associate professor in the Pulitzer School of Journalism at Columbia University, died on March 10 at the age of sixty-five years.

DR. ERNEST SCOTT, professor of pathology at the Ohio State University and son of William Henry Scott, formerly president of the university, died on March 4. Dr. Scott was in his sixtieth year.

MRS. ELISE SEYFARTH MUSTOR, assistant director of the educational clinic of the College of the City of New York and former state director of special education in Wyoming, died on March 8. Mrs. Mustor was fifty-two years of age.

MISS MARIA BOWEN CHAPIN, founder, trustee and former head mistress of the Chapin School in New York City, died on March 8, at the age of seventy years.

THE REVEREND PATRICK M. COLLINS, prefect of studies at St. Peter's College, Jersey City, died on March 5.

LIEUTENANT-COLONEL WILLIAM C. MICHELL, formerly supervising principal for high schools of Toronto, died on March 9 at the age of sixty-five years.

THE Drexel Institute Gift Fund, sponsored by the alumni of the college, has been established, and the money will be used to found the Matheson Memorial Book Fund, in honor of the late Dr. Kenneth G. Matheson, president of Drexel Institute from 1922 until his death in 1931; to support the student scholarship fund; to support the *Drexel Alumni Review*, and to contribute to other projects approved by the fund committee of the alumni and the board of trustees of the college.

THE will of Mrs. Annie Allegra Longfellow Thorp, youngest daughter of Henry Wadsworth Longfellow, who died in Cambridge on February 28, leaves $2,000 each to the Tuskegee Normal and Industrial Institute, Tuskegee, Ala.; the Calhoun Colored School, Calhoun, Ala.; the Berry Schools, Mount Berry, Ga., and the Pine Mountain Settlement School, Pine Mountain, Ky.

A MONUMENT to Woodrow Wilson will be erected in Princeton, according to plans made public on March 3 by Rolf William Bauhan, Princeton architect and member of the Federal Public Works of Art Committee. Officials of the Borough of Princeton, working with this committee, are furthering the project with the cooperation of the New Jersey State Highway Commission. Plans for the monument, designed by Mr. Bauhan and Jean Labatut, critic in architectural design of the School of Architecture of Princeton University, envisage a sixty-foot pyramidal shaft twelve feet square at the base. The four chief phases of Mr. Wilson's life—as president of the university, as governor of New Jersey, as President of the United States and as advocate of the League of Nations—will be depicted in bas-relief on panels on the four faces of the base. Above the panels will be massed flags of the nations, carved in low relief. The site for the shaft is near the monument commemorating the Battle of Princeton, fought in 1777.

THE will of the late Mrs. Minnie P. Huber, widow of former Lieutenant-Governor Henry A. Huber, provides for the establishment of a loan fund at the College of Agriculture of the University of Wisconsin. The fund, to be known as the Henry A. and Minnie P. Huber Scholarship Fund, is estimated at $35,000 and is available to students from Dane County, Wis., who are interested in the study of agriculture and farm management.

NEW YORK STATE will soon award twenty-five scholarships of $250 each to men and women qualified to become teachers of trades in the public schools of the state. Those who pass the examination given by the vocational and extension education divisions of the State Education Department will receive ten months' training in the industrial teacher training class of the State Teachers College in Buffalo and will be licensed for life to teach trades in the public schools. College graduates are not eligible for the scholarships.

THE trustees of Williams College have accepted a gift of the 1,800 acre estate of Mrs. M. Theresa B. Hopkins, daughter-in-law of Mark Hopkins, formerly president of Williams College. Mrs. Hopkins has given the estate, valued at $100,000, as a memorial to her husband.

SYRACUSE UNIVERSITY and Goucher College will receive $1,000 each under the will of the late Professor Joseph H. Mosher, of the College of the City of New York. Professor Mosher died on February 6.

A UNITED PRESS dispatch reports that science is the most popular subject with Turkish students. Out of a total enrolment of 3,154 at the new university in Istanbul, 1,147 are studying science, with 1,133 choosing law, 887 literature and 374 medicine.

THE National University of Mexico has been named beneficiary of a $50,000 trust fund provided before his death by the late Dwight W. Morrow. A statement issued through J. P. Morgan and Company on February 15 publicized the gift which has been transferred to the Bankers Trust Company of New York as permanent trustee. The money, according to Mr. Morrow's will, shall be used by the university for the purchase of books for its departmental and national libraries.

THIRTY-EIGHT signatories have been obtained to a new convention for facilitating the international circulation of educational films drawn up at a conference convened by the League of Nations. The main purpose of the convention is to abolish custom duties and accessory charges in respect of the importation, transit and exportation of educational films of an international character, and to free such films from taxes other than those to which films made inside each specific country are subject. Every film, including any form of sound reproduction supplementary to it, for which exemption from custom duties is to be claimed, will have to be submitted to the International Educational

Cinematographic Institute, which will issue a certificate on accepting the film. The presentation of the certificate will ensure free passage of the film. Any dispute as to whether a particular film should be classified as educational may be settled by friendly arbitration between the countries concerned, and the International Institute may act in an advisory capacity for this purpose. The convention does not debar any signatory nation from censoring films in accordance with its own laws, or from prohibiting or limiting importation of films for reasons of public security or order. It allows signatories the right to prohibit or restrict importation for reasons "based on the necessity for defending its market against invasion by films of foreign origin." The International Institute is to publish periodically a catalogue of all films for which a certificate has been issued. The convention is due to be ratified by the signatory nations, and other nations may accede to it, if they so desire, after April 12, 1934.

THE League of the British Empire, London, reports that the world crisis has naturally affected the interchange of teachers, but, in spite of the difficulties which had to be overcome, 61 exchanges between teachers of Great Britain and in the overseas Dominions were effected in 1933. This year for the first time an exchange with Newfoundland has been made, the other teachers coming from all parts of Canada, South Africa, Australia and New Zealand. In cooperation with the authorities and teachers concerned a way has been discovered to overcome the fluctuation in currency, thus enabling those who might otherwise hesitate to embark on the venture in these uncertain times to take advantage of the scheme. The majority of teachers taking part are from the elementary schools, but there is an ever-growing number of secondary teachers overseas awaiting the opportunity of exchange. Teachers continue in the pay of their own service, so that the year spent overseas counts for increment and the purposes of the superannuation acts.

THE United Press reports that cornerstones for ten new public school buildings have recently been laid in Rio de Janeiro. According to Dr. Pedro Ernesto of the Federal District, a program calling for the expenditure of nearly $1,000,000 has been inaugurated to reorganize the public schools in Rio de Janeiro. The program is being financed by the issue of 7 per cent. municipal bonds.

DISCUSSION

WHAT NEXT IN EDUCATION?

THE history of education, it has been said, is nothing more nor less than the history of those big movements that have marked our educational development. Within the memory of most people interested in education to-day the following have been launched: The testing movement, the curriculum revision movement, the junior college movement and the junior high-school movement. Previous to these were others among which might be enumerated, the academy movement, the battle for free public schools, the battle against sectarian control, the high-school movement and the normal school movement. To-day this question is being asked frequently, "What will be the next big movement in education?"

It should be noted that new movements never arise spontaneously but always in response to a felt need. When Horace Mann, acting as secretary of the State Board of Education in Massachusetts, saw and pointed out the needs of education the movement for free public schools was started. When Harper, Folwell and Tappan saw the need for extending the secondary school upward, the junior college movement was born. When the need for extending the secondary school downward became clear, the junior high school movement came into existence. In other words, necessity has determined the nature of the movements education has experienced.

If there is one need to-day greater than another it is in the field of administration. Our administrative techniques have developed rather haphazardly and with little directed control. As each new movement sprang up, it brought with it certain administrative implications. Many of the administrative problems that have arisen in this manner have never been clearly defined, and many have never been satisfactorily solved. One reason for this is that each movement has greatly eclipsed the minor problems which arose in its wake and became a part of it.

We have been so busy, in the past, experimenting with and theorizing about new movements that we have had little time left for perfecting administrative techniques. We have solved some of the most pressing problems and have permitted the others to accumulate. In many cases we have failed even to recognize and define some of these minor problems. We have gone ahead doing the essential things, solving those problems that demanded immediate solution and postponing the solving of others less pressing, until to-day, as a result of the present economic depression, we are faced with a horde of unsolved administrative problems, the solution of which years ago might have tended to mitigate the dire educational cataclysm we are now experiencing. There is a need to-day for the expenditure of effort in the solution of these problems we have postponed for so long. In addition, the present financial condition has brought with it a multitude of new problems that are pressing for immediate solution. Conditions change, new movements come and go, and with it all administrative techniques must be constantly refined if education is to make the progress it should.

It has been said that when a new movement is first recognized it is already well under way. It may be that the next big movement has already been launched and is on its way toward recognition. A summary perusal of the recent literature in the field of educational administration and a comparison with that of ten or even five years ago, gives the impression that it is increasing—if not in quantity, certainly in quality. It has been said, and probably correctly, that all the later movements in education are but a part of one big movement, the scientific movement. In other words, these so-called movements are but manifestations of the development of a scientific attitude in education. This scientific trend is to be observed in an examination of the recent literature in the field being discussed.

It is only in recent times that something more than a modicum of the scientific attitude has become observable in this field. Now, for the first time, has educational administration begun to make use of principles scientifically developed in other related fields. First, probably, it began to borrow from the field of accounting. Then it began to reach out into the fields of law, political science, public finance and business management. As yet, however, it has merely tapped these sources and has but barely scratched the surface. Much work remains to be accomplished in this connection. These related fields must be carefully searched for principles that are applicable to educational administration. These must then be mastered and translated into the field of education. In other words, the field of educational administration must be critically examined, and its techniques must be refined in light of principles borrowed from other related fields. Then will it become scientific. Who knows but that this attempt to make educational administration scientific will be recognized as the next big movement in the field. If the existence of a felt need is any criterion, then this must come soon. But it will not come spontaneously, traveling under its own momentum. It will come as an answer to a long-felt need.

LEE O. GARBER

MINNESOTA STATE TEACHERS COLLEGE, MANKATO

NEW LIGHT FOR BLIND ALLEY JOBS

IN the future no position can be called a blind alley job. Holding the commonest job will not prevent a man's making something of his life. The new era will see few great fortunes, for we shall cease our worship of genius. Already factory and mill jobs are more attractive than the small managerial positions of the past decade. Store workers, truck drivers and janitors are enjoying privileges greater than those once allotted their bosses. The holder of the small job has ceased to be the football of employers. Against the abuses of pay and hours we have the arm of the NRA. Since the recovery codes have admitted the common job to the best of our occupational society, the blind alley job need cause our vocational counselors no further concern.

The new era has enriched the simple job. In

the place of the sweatshop and child labor the NRA has established respectable wage minimums and decent hours of labor. While the ill wind of the country's depression has brought much harm in its wake, it has put new foundations under a large part of American society. To-day men are clinging to small jobs instead of casting their lot with precarious and uncertain attractions. Strange as it may seem, fast-moving America is taking time to appreciate the advantages of the average life.

In contrast with the rise of the common job is the career position's decline. The NRA specifically exempts from its benefits executive and managerial positions. Overseers, salesmen, managers and professional men must paddle their own canoes. And the paddling becomes steadily harder. Competition, increased standards and higher costs of preparation are everywhere noticeable. The *Boston Herald* recently stated that Boston already had three times as many lawyers as the city could support honestly. An article in School and Society for December 16, 1933, reports decreased enrolments in the professional schools. Engineering enrolment has steadily declined since 1930. It is fortunate that we are voluntarily appreciating the small job at a time when opportunity in the career field is falling.

This decline has led to the passing of the fetishes of pay and promotion. The experiences of their fathers have prompted young people to evaluate the job situation more thoroughly. They are thinking less of the vagaries of fortune and more of a secure competence. They are thinking beyond the job into the possibilities that life may offer with it. Of 412 college preparatory public high school pupils recently questioned, 368 rated security as being the most important of twelve job elements. Pausing on the mountain side, we are agreeably surprised to find that all the grandeur is not reserved for the peaks.

The coronation of the common job is an encouragement to honesty and right living. At last the laborer and the vice-president can live within their means. We can now enjoy a simple way of life without shame or reproach. The milk man can be paid and we shall wear the old clothes a little longer. We shall not be forced, in keeping up with the Joneses, to turn in the old car until we can afford the exchange. Just as nature never planned us all to grow to six feet, so she never intended us all to be leaders. We Americans have lived the better part of our lives overlooking and despising the common comforts and joys of an average life, while we have fretted and schemed for higher things. In the new day, with confidence and respect, we can put our buckets down where we are.

Henry L. Farr

Manchester, Conn.

SPECIAL CORRESPONDENCE

TRANSLATING AUTONOMOUS FUNCTION INTO INTELLIGENT AND RATIONAL PURPOSE

I wonder whether readers of the issue of School and Society for December 9, 1933, recognized the diametrical opposition between the two leading articles, by President Robinson, of the College of the City of New York, and Professor Wheeler, of the University of Kansas. On the face of things, this might appear as an opposition between the intellectual positions of an administrator and a classroom teacher. But the difference of position stems from deeper sources than these, as the creative work and attitudes of such an administrator as Chancellor Capen, of Buffalo University, plainly illustrates. It is traceable to a difference of postulates regarding the nature of human life and experience.

The one writer assumes that the current human reality is an assemblage of more or less discrete cultural and nationalistic groups or parts which must gradually and insensibly merge, by sheer momentum, into an organic or social whole; and at the same time he illogically insists that each of these, as a sovereign entity, should cultivate and consolidate its own disparateness. The other, if he had referred to man's group and cultural dispersion, could have assumed that humanity is nevertheless one whole and that the historical disparateness of each part is primarily an accident and incident of the features of its earthly habitat, as biological knowledge abundantly testifies, just as he does assume that the apparently disparate organs and functions of the psychological organism are accidents and incidents of abstractive observation. Professor Wheeler would hold that the getting together again of the Humpty Dumpty, the species *Homo sapiens,* is to be achieved by apposite ideation or conception, by translation of this ideation into ideal or purpose and by intentionally creative activity under guidance of this purpose.

Santayana rightly tells us, "Peoples can not love one another unless they love the same ideas." It is by trying to propagate a set of universalistic ideas of humanity, and by trying to live and to realize such a set of common ideas, that humanity is to grow back into a social unity, which the terrestrial and cultural conditions of its living have heretofore prevented.

What, then, is to be that set of ideas? It is to be found by a study of man as an organic species—as a subject-matter of the biological sciences, linked up with the modern physicists' conception of the cosmos as a process creating its own further continuance of existence. In other words, it is the nature of man, as of the other organic species, and indeed of all other strains of reality, processally to support and continue the existence of his species. It is the natural and proper function of successive generations, of individuals, local groups and institutions, to live and exploit themselves as supporting instrumentalities of a species life that is potentially immortal.

What is needed above all else, in all educational activities, is the translating of this function into a concept, idea or ideal, as a guiding purpose of human life or existence. We may rightly assume that we human beings, of whatever race, are naturally so constituted that, knowing of each other's existence, the only way by which individuals may enjoy full organismic unity, sanity and health is by positively entertaining, championing and living this supreme concept of the meaning of individual, group and institutional life. The remaining ideas of the set may be derived by developing the implications of this concept, each of the implicated and derived ideas serving also as a persuasive invitation to its realization.

President Robinson is still living and exhibiting the Euclidean, Newtonian, Aristotelian, mechanistic and authoritarian thought patterns of the nineteenth century. He regards the activities of life, culture, civilization as being of the nature of a push or drive from behind, and an administrator—a "ministerer unto," and thus properly an instrumentality to his group—as an authoritarian manager or driver of men into these activities. He would regard a stimulus as a drive to action, as the old Roman use of the word implied, and as modern psychological theory assumed, at the time when the word was imported into our psychological vocabulary.

Professor Wheeler would regard the organism, and especially its effectors, the "forward" end of its reaction apparatuses—if such divisive abstraction may for the nonce be permitted—as an organization of energies, which the stimulus releases. Ideally, he would not stand for a government of either men or law—each a mechanistic and inhibitive means of control, but rather for individual self-government, by action of ideas of humanistic ends to be achieved. And so he would be a universally humanistic pragmatist—a life, or species pragmatist, rather than a more narrowly utilitarian one, devoted to the conservation of outgrown particularist instrumentalities already abiding in the racial life as so many vestigial organs.

This does not mean that education as such should be a work of propaganda and indoctrination. But it does imply the possibility and need of a universally humanistic orientation and motivation of those to be educated. And it implies that the ideals which should guide the educative process, and in turn serve as the means of this orientation, should be propagated —else how shall they be spread so as to prevail? And who will suggest a more universal, a more humanistic, and therefore a more apposite set of ideas, that would be humanly preferable? Knowing the function that the carriers of the species life have heretofore been left autonomously to subserve, let us translate knowledge of this function into purpose, whereby these carriers may raise themselves into their full potential stature as civilized men and women.

O. O. NORRIS
MICHIGAN STATE NORMAL COLLEGE

QUOTATIONS

THE CARNEGIE UNIVERSITIES TRUST FOR THE UNIVERSITIES OF SCOTLAND

At the annual meeting of the Carnegie Trust for the Universities of Scotland it was mentioned that during the last four completed academic years the total number of students attending the Scottish Universities has been approximately 12,000 each year, with only a variation of about 1 per cent., and it was doubtful if any further increase would be wholesome. Principal Sir Thomas Holland, however, stated that in Edinburgh there were some 500 or 600 students from over-seas, who went back to their own countries when they had finished their studies, thus diminishing the risk of unemployment. In medicine there were 200 fresh students every year, but most of these went away, and it was believed that they all obtained employment. The Trust still pursued the principle of paying the fees of necessitous Scottish students, and during the past year the amount repaid by former beneficiaries had been £1,702. With regard to research the chairman, Lord Sands, said that chemistry, particularly organic chemistry, presented the most openings to-day. The Trust received more applications from men exceptionally well qualified in chemistry than from any others. During the past five years, out of fifty-seven chemistry scholars there had been seventeen physical chemists. In organic chemistry the fifteen Fellows to whom awards had been made published over thirty papers, which were said to constitute a very substantial contribution to current advances in this subject. Attention was drawn to the important researches at St. Andrews on the chemistry of sugars and terpenes. At the laboratory of the Royal College of Physicians, Edinburgh, which was supported by the Trust, eighteen workers had been engaged in research during 1932–3, and a fresh and promising line of research on industrial diseases had been started in cooperation with the Factory Department of the Home Office. During the thirty years of the Trust's operations the total number of awards for scientific research had been 2,982, and the total publications received had numbered 227 volumes and 2,002 other original contributions. The expenditure on research for the first quinquennium, 1908–13, had been £27,754, rising to £69,268 in 1928–33, with a gross total of £250,772 for the period of thirty years.—*British Medical Journal.*

REPORTS

THE ANNUAL REPORT OF THE GENERAL EDUCATION BOARD

In the annual report for 1928–1929, the development of the policies of the General Education Board was traced from the foundation of the Board in 1902. In that report the intention was announced of maintaining for the time being the policies in force since 1924 in three major fields—college education, public education (mainly in the South) and Negro education. In the field of college education, the board until recently has continued to cooperate in carrying out promising plans for the improvement of the quality of undergraduate work through changes in curriculum and in methods of teaching and administration. But during the last years, grants in this field have been for the most part to ensure the continuation of projects in jeopardy because of loss of support.

With the change in economic conditions, the General Education Board, in common with other agencies devoted to public welfare, has been considering how its resources may best be used in the solution of the problems of personal and social adjustments to which the depression has given emphasis. Toward this end, it was determined to undertake a review of the major aspects of educational endeavor in the United States. Though the conclusions to which this survey pointed have not yet been fully developed in the activities of the board, it has approved plans for the improvement of general education, for research in the field of child development and for more intensive work in certain restricted fields in the South.

Under these headings, it is proposed in the report for 1932–33 to give assistance for the training of teachers and research workers to meet the needs of each program, as well as for other essential factors. In the field of general education, it is hoped that such grants as that made to the Fieldston School will assist in reorganizing and enriching the curriculum. Similarly, such grants as that made to Teachers College, Columbia University, and to the Progressive Education Association may prove instrumental in providing materials to facilitate an insight into the problems of the day and their implications for the future. Other grants, such as those to the Brush Foundation and to the Merrill-Palmer School in Detroit, will forward the study of individual development that will contribute to the educational program of adolescents.

Grants during the 1932–33 for public education, for the most part in the South, were relatively small. Emergency grants were made in some cases to maintain work previously supported by appropriations from the board, and to a number of Negro institutions that experienced difficulty in obtaining funds for current expenses. Grants to Negro universities and medical schools reflect the board's continuing concern in the development of centers of higher education for Negroes. Other appropriations for medical education were restricted to those necessary to ensure the continuance during the depression of enterprises carried on under expiring appropriations. Appropriations listed under "Other Projects" in the table of contents also represent, mainly, obligations that grew out of an earlier program that is now being superseded by the plans under development.

The appropriations made by the board in 1932–1933 amounted to $2,423,303.56, all chargeable to income.

The total of appropriations made in this year is less than that of any of the three years immediately preceding. In each of those years, in addition to the use of the entire income, large appropriations from the principal of the board's funds were made, many of which were payable, provided the donees satisfactorily met conditions regarding the raising of supplementary sums. Owing to the increasing difficulties of raising funds for educational purposes due to the severe economic depression and the greater amount of appropriations made in the past three years, the outstanding appropriations of the board at the opening of the year 1932–1933 aggregated $32,516,574.85, of which $21,139,496.09 was chargeable to principal and $11,377,078.76 to accumulated income. Pending requests for payment, accumulated income had been temporarily invested. At the time these appropriations were made, the market value of the securities owned by the board was much higher than it had become by July 1, 1932. The effect of the depreciation was greatly to reduce the margins of free funds in excess of outstanding obligations. This fact and the further fact that it was difficult to convert securities into cash in large amount without further depressing their market value, led to the decision that it would be best to reduce the rate of appropriations until the securities of the board had regained some of their former value, and to keep its assets liquid for meeting payments on appropriations as they should become due.

This decision was opportune, not only because of the financial considerations but also because it gave the officers time and opportunity to continue their study of educational conditions, to which reference is made above.

EDUCATIONAL RESEARCH AND STATISTICS

WHAT COLLEGE STUDENTS BELIEVE THEY THINK ABOUT CERTAIN TYPES OF EXAMINATIONS

A group of advanced students at the University of Minnesota, who had become interested in the various European plans of instruction and in the experimental colleges throughout the United States, were particularly concerned with some of the difficulties facing administrators and professors. One of the large problems causing student comment and faculty study was the examination system.

Because the faculty of the College of Education were especially interested, it was possible to formulate a questionnaire on the subject and have it presented to students in the larger classes in education at the University of Minnesota. This questionnaire was worked up from points brought out by student group discussions. The material was revised and much assistance was given by interested faculty members. Three hundred students, practically all the members of the large third-year sections, answered the questionnaire thus presented. The results are facts only in so far as they are facts concerning what students believe they think.

I. OBJECTIVE VS. SUBJECTIVE EXAMINATIONS

A bit of information as to students' reactions to objective and subjective examinations was obtained by the first two questions. Definitions of the words "objective" and "subjective" were not given, but in order to avoid misconstruction, the word "preferable" as it was used throughout the questionnaire was defined as "referring to: (1) degree to which it measures important things of the course; (2) degree to which it stimulates good methods and habits of study; (3) degree to which it measures accurately, and hence, fairly, the student's progress in the course."

The first all-inclusive question asked, "In general, what kinds of examinations are preferable? Objective, Subjective." As indicated in Table I, objective examinations were overwhelmingly favored by students of all classes.

TABLE I

TYPE OF EXAMINATION SAID TO BE PREFERABLE

	Objective	Subjective
Class:		
Sophomores	42	2
Juniors	146	30
Seniors	31	5
Graduates	22	3
All	241	40
Major field:		
Mathematics	15	13
Science	55	32
Foreign language	45	21
English	109	73
Industrial and home economics ed.	10	6
History and social studies	87	45
Education	43	26
Commercial education	49	35
Physical education	76	56
Child welfare	40	16
Nursing education	48	23
Arts and music	115	65
Not given	35	16

TABLE II

TYPE OF EXAMINATION SAID TO BE PREFERABLE FOR DIFFERENT TYPES OF COURSES

		Class: Sophomores	Juniors	Seniors	Graduates	Totals
A. Informational type						
History	Objective	32	109	23	16	180
English	Subjective	14	68	16	9	107
Education						
B. Mental skill type	Objective	31	104	30	19	184
Mathematics	Subjective	16	67	9	7	99
C. Laboratory courses						
Chemistry	Objective	37	113	27	23	200
Household arts	Subjective	9	60	11	3	83
Accounting						
D. Special skills type						
Music	Objective	25	80	23	13	141
Art	Subjective	22	94	16	9	141
Physical education						

TABLE III

TYPE OF EXAMINATIONS SAID TO BE PREFERABLE FOR LARGE AND FOR SMALL CLASSES

	For large class (75 or more) Objective	For large class (75 or more) Subjective	For small class (25 to 50) Objective	For small class (25 to 50) Subjective
Class:				
Sophomores	46	1	23	23
Juniors	170	12	84	92
Seniors	36	1	22	16
Graduates	24	3	18	8
Totals	276	17	147	139

The students expressed a preference for objective examinations in the ratio of approximately 2 to 1 for courses in subjects of the "informational or reading" type, such as history, literature and education, and for courses in subjects of the "mental skill" type, such as mathematics and foreign language, and also for courses in subjects of the "laboratory-reading" type such as chemistry, home economics and accounting. For courses in "motor skills," music, art and physical education, neither type of examination was preferred by a significantly greater number. It was interesting to note that there was a tendency for students to be more favorable towards subjective examinations for the fields in which they were majoring than for other fields.

While the undergraduate students favored objective examinations (18–1) for large classes, they were rather evenly divided with respect to small classes. While instructors might well have been expected to be of this mind, it is not easy to explain why the students preferred different types of examinations for different types of class. It may be suspected that their opinions were affected by prevailing practise. Graduate students expressed a strong preference for objective examinations for classes of both sizes.

II. CONCERNING "OUTSIDE" EXAMINATIONS

In several departments of the University of Minnesota, regular examinations are replaced by what is known as "outside exams." This means the examination is to be written up outside of class with the use of books, if desired, but without help from other individuals, students or faculty. Usually the amount of time to be spent on the examination is left to the discretion of the student, and the examination frequently is given out a week or ten days before the deadline date.

TABLE IV

ATTITUDES TOWARD "OUTSIDE" EXAMINATIONS

	Class				
	Sophomores	Juniors	Seniors	Graduates	Totals
Do you like to have an instructor give out an examination to be written outside of class?					
Yes	2	27	8	11	48
No	1	20	3	2	26

Because of this practise, student opinion on the subject was sought. Only 76 of the 297 students answering the questionnaire said they had ever taken such an examination. Of this group 48 liked them, while 26 did not.

Reasons for their attitudes were also asked. Of the 48 who liked this type of examination, the following reasons were listed:

(a) 39 said, "It provides training in practical application of the subject";
(b) 34 said, "It puts emphasis on ability to use books and knowledge";
(c) 31 said, "It permits everyone to do his best."

No other reason was given by more than two students.

Of the reasons given for not liking outside examinations by those who had taken them,

(a) 19 said, "It encourages getting too much help from others";
(b) 15 said, "It is unfair to permit such a variation of time and effort to be put on an exam";
(c) 6 said, "It won't give a wide enough distribution in grades."

No other reason was given by more than four students.

Of the graduate students answering the questionnaire, 13 had taken an outside examination and of this number all but two favored this type.

All these "facts" of student opinion must be interpreted in a very critical attitude. Possibly no two of these answers are based on the same outside examination, and the wide difference between a good and a poor outside examination gives cause for a wide variety of attitudes concerning them.

III. FREQUENCY OF EXAMINATIONS

In trying to discover a student's preference as to how often examinations should be given, it seemed worth while to use the classification of courses by four types. In each of the first three types of courses, "informational," "mental skill" and "laboratory," the majority felt that weekly examinations were "best." In "mental skill" courses, a large minority favored daily tests. For the "special skills" type of course, semi-quarterly or six-weeks examinations were favored, with a good many favoring yearly examinations. Data relative to this point are given in Table VII. There were no differences in opinions between students of different classes, sophomores being distributed in their opinions similarly to those of higher classes.

TABLE V

OPINIONS AS TO DESIRABLE FREQUENCY OF EXAMINATIONS

	Type of Course			
	Informational	Mental skill	Laboratory courses	Special skills
Daily	9	65	8	6
Weekly	140	175	137	49
Monthly	61	28	71	58
Semi-quarterly	76	26	56	112
Quarterly	25	15	25	56
Yearly	11	2	3	16
Total	322	311	300	297

VI. A NEW MARKING SYSTEM

A partial answer to the question of what to substitute in place of examinations as a basis of term marks might be the use of a two-point marking scale (S for Satisfactory, and U for Unsatisfactory). Sixty-two per cent. of the students (184) answering the questionnaire feel that the effect of instituting such a system would be "Students would work more for subject-matter, and less for grades," but only 27 per cent. (80) think "it would lead to ultimate raising of standards for satisfactory work."

TABLE VI

OPINIONS AS TO EFFECTS OF EMPLOYING "S" AND "U" IN PLACE OF PRESENT FIVE POINT MARKING SYSTEM

	Class				
	Sophomores	Juniors	Seniors	Graduates	Totals
A. Students would work more for subject-matter, and less for "grades"	27	116	25	16	184
B. It would lead to ultimate raising of standards for satisfactory work	8	54	13	5	80
C. It would help to substitute desirable cooperation for competition of student against student	8	64	19	8	99
D. It would create an attitude of indifference toward superior achievements	19	59	13	8	99

The interpretation of these replies is not as simple as it would appear from the questionnaire. Probably few of the students answering it gave serious consideration to many of the implications. The strength and the weaknesses of any system are conditioned by the method of its administration. It is possible that some of the distaste for the present system would disappear if requirements of honor points for graduation and other rewards were abolished.

SUMMARY

This study indicates that students in the College of Education at the University of Minnesota:

1. Prefer objective examinations for (a) All types of subjects except those of the motor skill type—art, music and physical education; (b) large classes.

2. Prefer neither objective nor subjective examinations to the other in (a) subjects of the "motor skill" type; (b) small classes.

3. Prefer examinations which they may write outside of the classroom.

4. Prefer weekly examinations within all types of courses except those of the "motor skill" type for which they prefer semi-quarterly tests.

5. Are not averse to semi-quarterly or monthly tests in "informational or reading" and "laboratory-reading" courses and daily tests in the "mental skill" subjects, though for no other type of subject do daily tests seem to be acceptable.

6. Believe that a marking system consisting of only two marks—Satisfactory and Unsatisfactory—would be desirable, though only a minority believe that it would lead to raising standards for satisfactory work.

Perhaps it is wise to interpret the results of the survey in the light of two facts—first, that the students involved in this study are like other human beings in that we may not be certain that they really believe what they have said they believe, and, second, that these opinions are based upon the limited experience these students have had with objective examinations.

MARGARET TALLMADGE
HARL R. DOUGLASS
UNIVERSITY OF MINNESOTA

SCHOOL AND SOCIETY

WITH WHICH ARE COMBINED THE EDUCATIONAL REVIEW, ESTABLISHED IN 1891, THE TEACHERS MAGAZINE, ESTABLISHED IN 1878, AND THE SCHOOL JOURNAL, ESTABLISHED IN 1874.

EDITED BY J. McKEEN CATTELL, R. D. LINDQUIST AND W. H. COWLEY

EDITORIAL COMMUNICATIONS SHOULD BE ADDRESSED TO THE EDUCATION BUILDING, THE OHIO STATE UNIVERSITY, COLUMBUS, OHIO

Volume 39 | Saturday, March 24, 1934 | Number 1004

THE ASSUMPTION OF GRADUATE WORK BY UNDERGRADUATE INSTITUTIONS*

By Dean OTTO HELLER
WASHINGTON UNIVERSITY

THE facts I am about to present can not have much novelty for this audience; therefore, whatever interest my remarks are apt to elicit belongs to the importance of the problem with which they deal, namely, the increase of "graduate work" in institutions not designed and equipped for it, and in many instances not even fully qualified for work of the college grade. It is my contention that this alarming growth should be resolutely checked, lest the development of real university work, which for the moment is unavoidably cramped by economic adversities, be wantonly hindered in addition.

At our annual conferences I have witnessed considerable solicitude, first and last, for the reputation of the Ph.D. degree, while less concern has been evinced over the master's degree, even though its credit is in still greater jeopardy. Largely as a result of our common counsellings, the basic requirements for Ph.D. have been fairly agreed upon, for the time being, among those schools morally entitled to confer it. The master's degree, on the other hand, is still far from a standardized significance. Yet when we consider that this degree is awarded annually to 20,000 persons, more or less, giving them a right to teach in the upper schools and to aspire to the doctorate, we can not well shirk the protection of those values of which it is the widely accepted symbol. For, on the one hand, there will always be a direct connection between how well one can teach and how much one has learned; on the other hand, inferior preparation for advanced graduate work not only puts the individual under a disadvantage, but is likely to dilute the work of an entire group. No amount of intransigency can permanently immunize a teacher against the aggregate influence of his pupils. Ultimately, he will adjust his methods to their capacity. Hence the bonafide graduate school is increasingly exposed to danger in that its standards are automatically brought down by students entering with slipshod preparation. I know I shall be told that the degree can be inexorably withheld from the undeserving, and it is true that in part the earlier educational defects can be patched up. But there always remain irreparable gaps in the educational "background" as a whole, with devastating effects upon the conservation of a highly cultivated species now fast becoming *rara avis* in the olive

* A paper read before the Association of American Universities at Princeton University, October 26, 1933.

grove of Academe. Moreover, in casting up eventually a weak student's chances of graduation, the human nature of the professor, bulging with the bowels of compassion, is always to be reckoned with. Thus a depreciated M.A. prepares the way for an inflated Ph.D., and the recipients of cheap degrees to-day become the givers of cheap degrees to-morrow. I am of the belief that notwithstanding the temporary standardization of the essential requirements, the Ph.D. is not rising to a higher stature.

Naturally, this unpleasant view of things is liable to be challenged with a demand for mathematical proofs. I should be only too glad to lisp my whole sad story in numbers were they to be obtained by some less intrusive path to the data than the all-too-well trodden one of the questionnaire. Certain figures, conducive to a rough quantitative estimate of the situation, have been made available. But considering that educational statistics are by way of becoming one of our chief national industries, the abeyance of their qualitative analysis is to be deprecated. Even so, a timid start toward an objective evaluation of graduate schools or departments has been made on lines laid down by President Robinson of Goucher College in his volume on "American Universities and Colleges," and it is to be expected that a number of investigations now under way will throw some light on the actual state of affairs. It may be that the problem here under discussion is receiving attention right now from the National Educational Council in its comprehensive canvass of graduate instruction in the United States. If so, I do hope that the frightful mess made of the preliminary compilation of data has been unscrambled or thrown overboard. Another investigation of graduate studies, within a more circumscribed scope, is also in progress, in connection with the National Survey of the Education of Teachers, directed by Dr. Walton C. John, of the U. S. Office of Education. Namely, one section of the forthcoming publication will be a report on graduate work in the education of teachers by Professor S. E. Evenden, of Teachers College, Columbia University. Through the kindness of these two gentlemen I am enabled to give in advance some facts as to the number of institutions doing graduate work and offering the master's degree. (The responsibility for possible minor errors in my computation is divided between the overlapping rubrics in the original classification which is intended for the National Survey, and my ineptness in fitting it to a different purpose. On the whole, however, my figures are correct.) The story told by these figures is that there are at this time 76 publicly supported and 143 not publicly supported universities, colleges and kindred institutions, that is, 219, engaged in graduate work leading to the master's degree. In this number the teachers colleges and colleges of education are properly not included, because their graduate students "major" in education alone. But inasmuch as in nearly all of them students may, or must, "minor" in subject-matter fields, teachers colleges can not be altogether eliminated from the total count. Leaving out, then, all teachers colleges incorporated in higher institutions of complex organization, and adding to our list only the fourteen independent institutions of this class, we arrive at a grand total of 233 graduate schools (exclusive of schools offering graduate instruction but not awarding the master's degree). Of this entire number no more than 27 have so far been deemed eligible to membership in this association on the merit of their graduate work. To make matters worse, additional institutions of undergraduate caliber are constantly breaking into the graduate field, and the aggregate enrolment in these pseudo-graduate schools is mounting at an amazing rate. Nor are all the interlopers content to put the period after the master's degree; some offer a further year of work, nay, a few, after a third year of graduate residence, confer the doctorate.

In more than one instance the location of these colleges and universities posing as graduate schools severely tests one's educational geography. The guesser of their whereabouts can not always take a safe chance on the far-flung state of Texas. Nor are they regularly situate *in partibus infidelium,* for I know of at least three such spurious seats of learning in the vicinity of one of our greatest universities. Of course, the main incentive to this prodigious outcropping of graduate schools is given by the misleading idea that colleges functioning satisfactorily within their proper province deserve extra credit for taking a hand in the production of masters of art and the creation of a learned proletariat. A person not gifted with a firm teleological belief in the spontaneous evolution of good out of evil may well ask himself the question, whether this wild and luxuriant growth can safely be left to its own devices regardless of the consequences to the general academic morale. If not, then the inordinate ramification of unsatisfactory graduate work, accompanied by its incessant clamor for recognition, invites an uncompromising attitude. A refusal to accept graduate credits earned in schools of the dubious grade is greatly resented by them and characterized as narrow-minded, stupid arrogance. In the long run, resistance misses its effect. The front door is not the only one through which students can enter some graduate schools of recognized standing. Public opinion is in favor of the laxer practise and sides, as it usually does in any educational dispute, with the view that passes for liberal. The layman is easily persuaded that the social value of all education should be adjudged by its range. Our loose scholastic terminology adds to his obfuscation. Were we more fastidious in labeling our institutions, the very name "university" would warrant a school in conferring master's and doctor's degrees. Under current usage, the moral right to award even the master's degree can be conceded to many a so-called but only partially developed university only in its sufficiently advanced departments of study. Be it readily granted that even a full-fledged university may be notoriously weak in some fields and that, conversely, eminent teachers are sometimes located in smallish or obscure institutions. But the competency of a sporadic teacher is no proof of an institution's fitness for graduate work. By and large, colleges of arts, barring perhaps a dozen notable exceptions, are not designed for advanced specialization in any branch, but for undergraduate work alone. As for the teachers colleges, they were organized for the training of elementary teachers, and should be conducted with that end in view.[1] If they have any legitimate graduate status at all, it can only be in the field of education. I prefer to steer clear on this occasion of questioning the intrinsic value of teachers colleges for the national system of education, and should draw comfort from the ascertained fact that teachers colleges do not permit "majoring" in any other field than education, were it not for the equal certainty that all teachers colleges giving the master's degree offer minors in subject-matter fields. The reason for this

[1] From their ordained purpose they have been so thoroughly diverted that the following statement contained in "The Government of the State of Texas," Part X, p. 16, holds true in most parts of the country: "Teachers Colleges have no necessary function that cannot be served by other colleges." *Cf. ibid.*, p. 9: "Regardless of the statutes, these colleges are giving training to students who are not becoming teachers and many of whom have no intention of becoming teachers."

may be that, broadly speaking, the training in education as given nowadays is better designed for school executives than for teachers; but as there are not enough executive positions to go around, the average B.S. in education must sooner or later show graduate standing in some special branch of teaching. Since almost invariably teachers college graduates seeking admission to regular graduate schools are found wanting in the prerequisites for non-pedagogical subjects, is it illogical to hold that graduate work pertaining to subject-matter fields is not being carried on in teachers colleges with the necessary thoroughness? The forthcoming official survey to which I have made reference should speak out plainly on this point and at the same time show clearly whether a coordinated plan of studies always governs graduate work in teachers colleges, or whether the master's degree sometimes represents random combinations of majors and minors. The report should also point out those places where the master's degree is given for an additional group of undergraduate courses in a single field of concentration, or at the extreme worst, promiscuously assorted *ad libitum.*[2]

Apparently the educationists, with few exceptions, connive by silence in the status of graduate work in teachers colleges, when they do not defend it by the most equivocal of reasons. "So far as the first year of graduate work is concerned," writes Professor Evenden, "the graduate work in the bigger, better teachers colleges is quite comparable to that offered in many of the smaller and less well staffed arts colleges." The pungent irony of the comparison is unintentional. Dr. John is more explicit, and he almost comes to the point when he says: "All of these schools offer graduate work in minor fields outside of education, and it is quite probable that in a number of the smaller ones graduate work is not up to par." But are the full-grown, full-blown schools necessarily the better? Professor Emil L. Larsen, of the College of Education, University of Arizona, after collecting much information concerning the policies and practises of "representative, reputable institutions" as to the master's degree in the field of education, has formed a distinctly low opinion of the work in the minor, *i.e.,* subject-matter courses. Worse than that, his conclusions regarding the major work, *i.e.,* the work in education itself, arc far from complimentary. He estimates that 40 per cent. of the non-public teachers colleges have no credit-prerequirements for graduate work in education.[3] Altogether, the customary ranking of schools by size impresses one as too naïve. In the world of education, too, good things sometimes come in small packages. On the other hand, the greatest injury may be inflicted to the cause of scholarship by schools whose bigness exceeds their distinction.

Special reasons why so many college graduates go to second-rate schools are not far to seek. A great many attend the near-

[2] *Cf.* "The Government of the State of Texas," Part X, p. 5: "Graduate degrees are being offered for what is little more than a year of extra undergraduate work in three of the smaller and most poorly equipped of the Teachers Colleges. This practice should be stopped immediately, since such degrees are deceptive to students who may be led to think they are taking graduate work; the practice cheapens graduate work in the state, and it is so costly that the state cannot embark on a program which would furnish qualified staffs and adequate library facilities for real graduate work."

[3] Other estimates place the number of schools with proper prerequisites as low as 30 per cent., and even in this minority group the prerequisites are not rigidly enforced, and the student is allowed to embark upon graduate work in education as in other subjects when he has had little or no undergraduate work in it. *Cf.* E. L. Larsen, "Major Problems Relating to the Master's Degree in Education," *Educ. Administration and Supervision,* p. 701, December, 1932.

est school because they can not afford to go far from home, or because the school is especially active in "placing" its graduates. Others, it is sad to relate, are students of dubious scholastic extraction, "rejects" *de facto* or *in spe* from standard schools, thankful for a sanctuary where their sins of omission will not find them out; this applies particularly to students who would fight shy of the extra work prescribed by the stricter schools in commutation of undergraduate deficiencies. At more lenient schools the shortage is indulgently blinked at, provided the student seems moderately well grounded in his specialty. In consequence, the master's degree can be earned by fragmentary attainments within a narrow and isolated field. Another contingent is supplied to the graduate student body of these lesser schools by the notorious filial loyalty of the American collegian which makes him willing to cling to the breast of dear Alma Mater for a year beyond the normal limit, regardless of the specific gravity of her milk. Happily for such victims of malnutrition, they remain in lifelong ignorance of their adult infantilism.

The scornful attitude toward the master's degree observed in many university teachers may also be doing its bit to swell the attendance at schools of doubtful quality. This attitude drives away many students who for practical reasons find it convenient or necessary to make that degree en route to the doctor's or perhaps have no immediate intention to transgress those "frontiers of human knowledge" about which we hear so much. This class of students would feel more at home in first-rate graduate schools if the professors refrained from confusing the minds of their students with suggestions about a premature separation of the student body into future research scholars and future teachers, and dwelled, instead, more emphatically on the common objective of both pursuits, namely, increase in professional skill. An inter-academic agreement regarding the purpose of the master's degree might help the student at the outset to discriminate between genuine graduate work and the imitation article. As far as I know, this association has never articulated a joint opinion regarding the requirements for the master's degree. The North Central Association of Colleges and Secondary Schools has shown itself more resolute in tackling the problem; this is the conclusion promulgated by that body: "The Master's degree should represent a year of intensive work based on undergraduate specialization in the same field of at least eighteen semester hours in subjects like English, History, Chemistry, Mathematics, and Foreign Languages, which are open to Freshmen. Requirements in the field of Education should correspond."[4] Although these requirements seem quite rational and many schools try conscientiously to meet them, their enforcement is rendered difficult by the imperfect segregation of graduates and undergraduates; graduate work needs to be disencumbered of all superfluous routine by a comprehensive system of examinations.

The advent of teachers colleges and liberal arts colleges on the preserve of the university has greatly aggravated the difficulty of administering graduate work in the smaller schools in conformity with the most commendable standards. This complex difficulty arises mainly from (1) a latent uncertainty regarding the aims of graduate study; (2) a lack of sharp distinction between graduate and undergraduate work; (3) vacillating policies of admission; (4) illogical alignments of the major and minor fields; (5) the variety of

[4] The file of the *N. C. A. Quarterly* shows that the organization has given much attention to graduate work. For the above quotation *cf.* Vol. III (September, 1928), pp. 170–71.

views on the nature of the thesis; (6) discrepant opinions relative to object and method of the final examination; (7) the uneven previous training of the students. From the resultant muddle, how can the Association of American Universities, as the widely recognized guardian of true university standards, expect to keep its hands off permanently? Is it not for this association to come to the protection of the higher studies both for the sake of efficacious teaching and of creative scholarship? Or shall graduate schools good, bad and indifferent be left to their own devices? Various agencies have been proposed for raising the general level of graduate work, as for instance a separate league of all the graduate schools outside the Association of American Universities, or an all-inclusive federation of institutions engaged in graduate work. That would be setting the fox to keep the sheep. In a huge body like that, our group would form a hopeless minority.

A more practical plan is that repeatedly suggested by Professor Homer L. Dodge, of the University of Oklahoma, who directs one of the largest graduate schools outside the A. A. U., and has shown himself earnestly concerned about the improvement of graduate work in the South. Mr. Dodge advocates the adoption of some scheme of accreditation for deserving schools and acceptance at par of their work for the master's degree. Such a practice on the part of the A. A. U. would be quite consistent with its present treatment of the colleges, but much more difficult to carry out. The evaluation of each separate department of an institution on the score of graduate standing seems logical enough for the larger schools, although their sundry divisions, too, have their ups and downs. In the small schools, however, the reputation of a department may depend on one teacher alone, and consequently be subject to frequent change. At all events, the graduate gearing of a school as a whole is an important factor. A graduate school whose work is merely an extension of the undergraduate has no valid claim to recognition. Statistics bearing on physical equipment, library and laboratory facilities, size, quality, degrees held and teaching load carried by the faculty, etc., do not tell the whole story.

The increasing tendency among students to secure the master's degree from institutions located in or near their home communities, coupled with the increasing importance of the Ph.D. label for appointment to teaching positions, should make this association peculiarly vigilant in the defense of its standards. If our member institutions will not go to the length of outright rejecting graduate credits from undergraduate schools, they should at the very least suspend all credits thus earned until the student has proved himself after a full year of residence. It is a question whether at this critical economic juncture the pursuit of graduate studies, even at first-rate schools, can be encouraged in a spirit of fairness to students. There can be no question that graduate studies under second-rate auspices should be decidedly discouraged. President Roosevelt told the whole country a few weeks ago that we are turning out too many teachers each year. "We have to-day," he said, "a large surplus of so-called qualified teachers—men and women who, even if we had full prosperity, would and probably should be unable to find work in the field of education." The relevancy of the President's comment to the existing overproduction of masters of art and of science is self-evident. Any further unnecessary inflation of the sphere of graduate studies must be viewed as a disservice to the cause of education as well as to that of creative scholarship, and therefore a disservice to society.

A STATE CORPS OF SECONDARY SCHOOL TEACHERS

By M. M. CHAMBERS
DEPARTMENT OF EDUCATION, OHIO STATE UNIVERSITY

IT has now become universally apparent that the states must give increasing assistance to local public-school districts if a decent standard of public education is to be maintained in every county and every district. This obvious necessity is generally discussed exclusively in terms of grants of money from the state to local districts. There are other ways in which the states could support education in the localities. Instead of making the local district a gift of money to be expended for school purposes, the state could instead give to the locality the services of one or more carefully selected and highly competent teachers for its high school. This transaction would not involve the transfer of any funds from the state treasury to the treasury of the local district. It would thus cleanly avoid all the difficulties which are associated with the supervision of the expenditure of state funds by a large number of local fiscal officers, most of whom are untrained for their tasks and some of whom are wholly unfit for the responsibility of handling public money. It would also avoid the controversies and bad feeling which often arise between the state school authorities and local school boards and clerks regarding the handling of school money.

In our present economy, money is the all-important desideratum of the operation of schools or any other social service; but money is only a means to an end, and the principal end to which school money is devoted is that of securing the services of competent and faithful teachers for the pupils in the schools. It has long been agreed that at least two thirds of the operating expenses of schools should be spent for instructional services; and again and again we give lip-service to the maxim that it is teachers and not marble buildings that make a school. Is it necessary that the state's assistance to its constituent communities for school purposes should all be in the form of money grants? Is this the best and only form of assistance which the state can and should give to its local districts?

The proposed alternative is a corps of high-school teachers selected, appointed and paid by the state, and assigned and transferred from time to time to service in high schools throughout the state. The idea of a state corps of teachers is novel in the United States, but by no means uncommon in Europe, where the secondary school teachers of several of the continental countries have long been state officers, paid and assigned to duty by the state. Without jumping to hasty conclusions, it may be said that there are certain obvious advantages in such a status for carefully selected members of the teaching profession. It is well known that the teachers in the secondary schools of France, for example, enjoy a prestige and a professional status far above that of the American high-school teacher of to-day. It is equally well known that European secondary schools almost without exception maintain higher standards of achievement than our high schools. Without pursuing any further invidious comparisons, let us get to the point and ask what is wrong with the position and working conditions of the American high-school teacher and in what way these matters are susceptible of improvement.

For his appointment, our teacher depends upon the judgment of a local board of education or superintendent of schools, after he has met the minimum requirements established by the state certification laws. In large cities appointments are often notoriously dictated by local political considerations bearing no relation to the efficiency of the schools; and in small towns and rural districts the exercise of nepotism and local favoritism, always present, has been greatly intensified during recent years on account of individual and collective financial hardships. The result is that at present it is next to impossible for any applicant who has no local connections to secure an appointment. Our high-school staffs are loaded with teachers, few of whom have any training beyond a bachelor's degree and some of whom have never earned any degree. Meantime hundreds of experienced and ambitious teachers have won master's and doctor's degrees from our colleges and universities and now find the gates of employment virtually closed to them. What a sad anomaly that high-school boys and girls must be deprived of the services of many who are among the most intelligent and enterprising members of the teaching profession! How inexcusable that the bright days of adolescent boys and girls, curious to know the significance of what is going on in these stirring times, should be spent under the tutelage of under-trained and mediocre teachers who hold their positions by virtue of nepotism or the provincial exclusiveness which has resulted from the shock of four years of financial dislocation!

Is the state doing its best for its boys and girls, if it pours public money into the hands of local authorities of short and narrow vision and allows it to be expended in accordance with the same practises which have manifested themselves most strongly during the past four years? In view of the fact that two thirds of the school money should go for teaching services, are not the selection and tenure of teachers matters of supreme importance? If so, who will contend that these matters are not handled in a sorry manner, by and large, by local school authorities, when the subject is viewed from the standpoint of the welfare of the boys and girls of the state as a whole?

The state could make immediately available the services of a class of superior teachers, most of whom are now either ill-paid and unrecognized or wholly without employment, if it would establish a state corps of high-school teachers, appointment to which would be wholly divorced from the petty local considerations above mentioned, and made dependent entirely upon qualifications as demonstrated by adequate training and fitness for teaching. Having established such a corps and recruited it with, let us say, teachers possessing not less than the master's degree and able to demonstrate high proficiency in professional education and in one or more subject-matter fields, the state could then offer their services to local school districts entirely without charge, in lieu of an amount of financial aid equivalent to the salaries of the teachers in question.

The acceptance of a state teacher might be optional with the authorities of the local district; and if any state teacher in service became unhappy in his personal relationships in his place of service, his transfer to another locality, either at his own request or at the request of the local authorities, could be readily accomplished. The tenure of state teachers could be for life during good behavior, or until retired on account of incapacity occasioned by age or other cause. Dismissal from the service for gross misconduct or willful misbehavior tending to destroy professional usefulness should be provided for, with adequate safeguards in the form of notice and hearing before the chief state school authority. Thus the tenure of state teachers would be in no sense dependent upon the whims of any local clique, as the tenure of teachers now so often is. This feature alone would be of incalculable value in making the most competent teachers feel free to do their best work.

The development of a state corps of secondary school teachers could be a gradual process. If in the beginning the personnel of the corps numbered not more than one tenth or one twentieth of the teachers necessary to staff the high schools of the state, the members of the corps could be placed by inviting all city and county school districts to choose an appropriate percentage of their high-school teachers from the state corps. If compulsion were necessary, compliance could be made prerequisite to maintaining their high schools in the Grade A rating of the state department of education. Probably no compulsion would be required, if the state offered the services of members of the state teachers' corps in lieu of an amount of financial aid equal to their salaries; but if the local authorities showed reluctance to accept this form of state aid, they could be easily brought to terms in a great variety of ways. For example, the state might choose to provide that each city or county district must receive a stipulated fraction of its assistance from the state in the form of teaching services, as a condition of receiving any state aid at all.

It seems immediately apparent that great improvement of the quality of the teaching personnel, as well as a unification and stimulation of the whole enterprise of secondary education within the state, could be accomplished by the introduction of this form of state aid to localities. Persons are more important than either money or materials; and it is clear that the state could supply to its high schools a type of teaching personnel which the local authorities are very generally unable or unwilling to supply.

If it is thought that friction might often arise between teachers of the state corps and the constituency of the schools in which they were assigned, let it be remembered that a certain amount of friction always exists; and that a community is not unlikely to benefit from the temporary presence of a non-resident teacher of high qualifications, even though a majority of the natives may so dislike his personality or work as to necessitate his transfer to another field. In other words, evolution upward is sometimes a painful process; and the improvement should not be foregone on account of the fear of temporary unpleasantness which may accompany it.

In short, a proposed state corps of secondary school teachers would give to the boys and girls of the state a type of educational leadership superior to that which is now afforded them. It would enable the state to utilize at once the services of available teachers, with minimum regard for local prejudices and petty greed. It would give to the best educated and most competent teachers of the state a steady employment in the work for which they are fitted. It would give to the cooperating localities a gift from the state more valuable than money—a gift of well-educated, competent, enthusiastic men and women ready to throw their energies into the building of better opportunities for accomplishment, better insight into the problems of the swiftly changing times for the boys and girls of high-school age.

EDUCATIONAL EVENTS

TEACHING METHODS IN THE SOVIET SCHOOLS

THE Soviet school, especially in its elementary grades, has changed almost beyond recognition during the last two or three years, according to the Moscow correspondent of the *Manchester Guardian Weekly*. Before that change, the Soviet educational system is reported to have been wildly, recklessly and uncompromisingly experimental. Discipline was conspicuously non-existent, and the children's organizations often had more voice in the direction of the schools than the teachers. Radically new pedagogical methods were introduced. The teaching of individual subjects was scrapped and succeeded by the so-called "complex" method, under which a class was assigned some general theme, such as a street or a season of the year, and was supposed to study it as a whole, learning a bit of arithmetic here, a fragment of natural science there, a smattering of reading and writing somewhere else. Another innovation was the "project" method, under which an assignment of school work was given to a group of five or six children, who were then supposed to study collectively.

A resolution published by the Communist Party Central Committee in the summer of 1932 pronounced judgment on the defects of the over-experimental school system and was followed by a series of sweeping changes which have made the present-day Soviet school entirely different from its predecessor of two or three years ago. The complex and project methods have been discarded; marks and examinations, hitherto denounced as "bourgeois," have been restored; teaching is by subjects, with emphasis on such basic elementary things as reading, writing, arithmetic, grammar, mathematics and physics; the teacher is the unquestioned authority in the classroom. Unruly children may now be punished with suspension or expulsion, and the pre-war practise of having the class rise when the teacher enters the room has been restored.

The better schools of Moscow and other large towns now differ little from those of Western Europe in discipline and pedagogical efficiency. Education is compulsory for at least four years for all Soviet children, but provincial schools sometimes suffer from lack of trained teachers and adequate buildings, text-books and school accessories, and the enforcement of the compulsory education law is not absolute in mountainous and backwoods regions.

The reversion to more conservative methods of teaching and study has not affected the dogmatically Communist character of the Soviet educational system. The requirement, introduced in 1929, that teaching in the schools must be not only non-religious but pronouncedly anti-religious is rigidly enforced.

Children are supposed not only to absorb the new view-point themselves but also to act as missionaries among their unconverted elders.

THE FINANCIAL SITUATION OF DENOMINATIONAL COLLEGES

THAT many church colleges and private schools are maintaining their services to students in face of great and increasing financial difficulties is revealed by recent reports to the Federal Office of Education. Colleges affiliated with churches (referred to as church colleges) are feeling the effects of economic conditions even more severely than other privately controlled institutions (referred to as private colleges), according to information received from 279 institutions. Almost half the church colleges are in arrears in payments due their faculties in February. Seven private colleges are also unable to complete salary payments to members of their faculties. Thirty-two institutions (30 church, 2 private) each owe faculty members more than $20,000. Nine church colleges and one private college were each in arrears on salaries more than $40,000, in February.

Reasons for the financial difficulties are that church and private colleges are carrying a large number of needy students, accepting notes for tuition; that some have accumulated obligations for salaries and other operating costs; that many have obligations for buildings and repairs which require refinancing; and that many have mortgages, bonds and other miscellaneous debts which are difficult to meet in these times. Only 20 out of 210 church colleges, and only 7 out of 69 private colleges have no students who have not had to give notes for their tuition. In each of 28 church institutions and 15 private institutions, more than 300 students have given notes for all or part of their tuition.

Five church colleges and 6 private colleges each have more than $80,000 in tuition due them from students whom they are carrying through the hardships of the economic situation. Tuition notes to the amount of $10,000 and up are in the hands of treasurers of each of 96 church colleges and 43 private colleges reporting. Although 85 church colleges and 52 private colleges report that they have been able to pay current operating costs, including salaries, many are not so fortunate. Seven institutions are "in the red" on current maintenance obligations to the extent of $125,000 or more; 29 have $50,000 or more outstanding. The Federal Office of Education asked these institutions as to the extent of their capital improvement obligations for buildings and repairs which call for early refinancing. The response from 228 institutions showed that 10 have $500,000 or more in this type of obligation.

Bonds requiring interest payment, mortgages and other debts comprise the fourth source of financial difficulty. Sixty-three church colleges report a total of $10,399,713 in such debts; private colleges, $6,950,000; a total of $17,349,713 for 80 colleges.

The same reports which disclose the serious financial straits of private and denominational institutions tell what the faculties have done to help meet the situation. In 18 church institutions and 3 private colleges, salaries, which were never large, have been cut 50 per cent. or more. Twenty-one of 69 private institutions and 174 out of 210 church colleges reporting have reduced salaries 20 per cent. or more. Only 23 church colleges and 21 private colleges throughout the country have been able to avoid salary cuts.

GIFTS FROM INDUSTRIAL CONCERNS TO NEW YORK CITY SCHOOLS

IT has been pointed out recently in an article in the *New York Times* that New York City's public schools are the beneficiaries of material gifts valued at hundreds of thousands of dollars, principally as a result of the cooperation of industrial concerns in the vocational program of the education system.

The continuation schools and industrial and technical high schools during the last eight years have received equipment valued at $400,000. The printing schools have received the largest share of this equipment in typesetting machinery, presses and other paraphernalia valued at $250,000. Civic organizations, parents' associations, mothers' clubs, students' organizations and individuals, however, have contributed flags, radios, motion picture machines, portraits, murals, statues, trees, and even a rock garden to the schools.

The gifts are accepted by permission of the Board of Education. Gifts of a decorative nature are permitted by the board subject to the approval of the Municipal Art Commission, and installation of equipment must be under the direction of the Superintendent of Schools. The value of the equipment donated to the vocational schools far exceeds that furnished by the Board of Education, according to Morris E. Siegel, director of continuation and evening schools, who declared the printing schools were almost entirely equipped by private concerns.

The practise of donating equipment to these schools started more than a score of years ago, Mr. Siegel stated, when he was made principal of the Murray Hill Evening Trade School. There was no equipment in the school and Mr. Siegel induced employers of his students to aid their education by supplying the practical tools.

The law in 1913 sponsored by industry, labor and social welfare organizations, making attendance compulsory in continuation schools until the age of 17, sent great numbers of children into these schools, and equipment as well as accommodations had to be found.

A system of cooperation by industry grew up and was later sponsored by the Advisory Board on Industrial Education, with the result that large amounts of equipment were donated by industrial concerns, business houses, motion picture companies, merchants and others. The printing industry, aviation and the textile industries, in the order named, have donated the greatest amount of material.

Unemployment conditions recently have added thousands of students to the vocational schools. About 8,000 have been added as a result of the NRA child labor provisions. There are 12,000 students on full time in the continuation schools now, and 35,000 on part time. The industrial high schools have 8,000 enrolled.

STATISTICS ON EMPLOYMENT AND TECHNOLOGICAL ADVANCE

DR. KARL TAYLOR COMPTON, president of the Massachusetts Institute of Technology; Dr. Robert Andrews Millikan, director of the Norman Bridge Laboratory of Physcis of the California Institute of Technology, and Dr. Frank Baldwin Jewett, president of the Bell Telephone

Laboratories, at a joint meeting of the American Institute of Physics and the New York Electrical Society on February 22, presented statistics demonstrating the relationship of scientific inventions to employment, in addresses that have been published in the *Scientific Monthly* for April. Science has created more employment instead of replacing men by machines, as is often charged, according to Dr. Compton, because science has made new industries. A list of some inventions and the number of jobs for which they are responsible follow:

Automobile	2,400,000
Electrical equipment	1,000,000 plus
Motion pictures	389,000
Telephone	357,000
Steamship	217,000
Machine tools	87,000
Refrigeration	72,000
Airplane	50,000
Rayon	41,000

Calling attention to the fact that certain NRA codes tended to limit technological advance, and that only one fourth of one per cent. of the Federal budget is allocated to scientific investigations, Dr. Compton predicted that any further check on scientific research in the United States would result in calamitous competition from foreign countries.

Dr. Jewett, vice-president in charge of development and research of the American Telephone and Telegraph Company, declared that when that company installed dial telephones, no operators were dismissed.

Dr. Millikan pointed to census figures to refute the argument that advancing technology has been responsible for unemployment. In 1880 34 per cent. of the population of the United States was gainfully employed, he asserted, while in 1930, after fifty years of sweeping technological progress, 40 per cent. of the population was gainfully employed.

SUMMER FIELD COURSES OF THE INTERNATIONAL INSTITUTE

THE International Institute of Teachers College, Columbia University, announces a number of field courses in the study of European education to be offered during the summer of 1934. These field courses are organized under the auspices of the Zentralinstitut für Erziehung und Unterricht in Germany, and of the official educational authorities in the various other countries.

The purpose of the field courses in European education is to aid American teachers in the development of a clear, authentic understanding of the objectives and organization of foreign school systems. The courses are so organized that liberal opportunity is afforded members of the groups for intimate contact with many other phases of life and culture in foreign countries, such as music, art, drama, industry, agriculture, commerce and politics.

University credit will be granted, if it is desired, to members of the field courses who satisfactorily complete the requirements of the study group in which they are enrolled, as stated in the Columbia University Summer Session Bulletin of Information.

Dr. Thomas Alexander and associates will conduct the course in German education, providing for visits to important German cities and to all types of German educational institutions. Dr. S. Ralph Powers will organize the course in science and science education in Germany, which the natural sciences division of the International Institute of Teachers College is offering. In view of the fact that the International Congress of Home Economics is to meet in Berlin from August 22 to 26, 1934, there will also be offered a course in home economics; and since the Nationalist Socialist Government is devoting special attention to the development of all phases of rural culture, a small group of American teachers interested in rural life and education will be formed.

A course in French education is also being organized to give American school executives, supervisors and teachers an opportunity to study the rather complex mechanism of the French state educational system. The effects of the direct control of the central government on the school system will be observed through visits to all types of institutions. Two to six points of credit may be earned by satisfactory participation in this course.

The course in English education will offer an opportunity for the study of the English school system by employing the same techniques of study as described for the German and French courses.

EDUCATIONAL NOTES AND NEWS

DR. RUDOLF A. CLEMEN, of Winnetka, Ill., has been named president of Whitman College, the oldest institution of higher education in the State of Washington. Dr. Clemen succeeds Dr. Stephen B. L. Penrose, who is retiring after forty years of service.

THE REVEREND DR. JAMES H. FRANKLIN, foreign secretary of the American Baptist Foreign Mission Society, has been elected president of Crozer Baptist Theological Seminary at Chester, Pa., succeeding the Reverend Dr. Milton G. Evans, who has been president since 1909.

DR. ORLIE M. CLEM, until recently professor of secondary education at Syracuse University, has been elected superintendent of schools at Owego, N. Y. He will also serve as principal of the Owego Free Academy.

ARTHUR D. ARNOLD, superintendent of schools in Passaic, N. J., has been reappointed by the board of education for a three-year term.

MRS. MATTIE LLOYD WOOTEN, assistant professor of sociology at the Texas State College for Women, has recently been named dean of women of the college.

PHILIP M. B. BOOCOCK, master at the Nichols School at Buffalo, N. Y., who graduated from Rutgers University in 1926, has been appointed head master of the Rutgers Preparatory School. Mr. Boocock succeeds William P. Kelley, who resigned on February 1 after serving over twenty years.

ROBERT TREMAINE HALL, head master at the Englewood School for Boys, Englewood, N. J., has been appointed superintendent of the Staunton Military Academy in Virginia, to succeed Colonel LeRoy Sutherland.

DR. ALBERT RUSSELL MANN, provost of Cornell University, has been appointed by Governor Lehman, of New York, to act as chairman of the State Planning Board. The board will work with the governor in making an intensive survey of state agriculture, industry, forests, parks and other social and commercial features of the state, and in developing a systematized program for these projects.

DR. JACOB VINER, professor of economics at the University of Chicago, has recently been appointed special assistant to Secretary of the Treasury Morgenthau.

WILLIAM G. RICE, formerly professor of law at the University of Wisconsin, has been appointed by President Roosevelt to serve as attorney for the National Labor Board. He will represent the board in legal cases arising under the industrial codes.

PROFESSORS WALTER E. SIKES, George L. Maxwell, Robert Hugh McWilliams and G. Eleanor Kimble, members of the University of Denver faculty, have been appointed to the newly organized Crime Prevention Committee of the City of Denver.

PROFESSOR HARRY N. HOLMES, of Oberlin College, has been selected by the Department of State as one of several delegates to represent the United States at the Ninth International Chemistry Congress, which will be held in Madrid, Spain, in April.

PROFESSOR WOLFGANG KOHLER, director of the Psychological Institute at the University of Berlin, where he is also a member of the philosophy department, has been appointed William James lecturer in philosophy and psychology at Harvard University for the first half of the academic year 1934–1935.

DR. PAUL A. M. DIRAC, Lucasian professor of mathematics at Cambridge University, England, and winner of the Nobel Prize in physics last year, has been appointed visiting professor in mathematical science at the Institute for Advanced Study in Princeton for the academic year 1934–1935.

DR. W. H. WISER, who received his Ph.D. degree in the department of rural social organization of the New York State College at Cornell University, with a thesis on "Social Institutions of a Hindu Village in North India," has been appointed professor of rural sociology in the North India United Theological College at Saharanpur, United Provinces, India. This is the first professorship of rural sociology in India.

DR. JUDAH L. MAGNES, chancellor of the Hebrew University in Jerusalem, officially opened the new Einstein Institute of Physics at the university on March 11. The ceremony followed the matriculation of 178 new students, including forty from Germany.

DR. GEORGE NEELY HENNING, professor of Romance languages and dean of the School of Graduate Studies of the George Washington University, and Dr. Thomas H. Healy, professor of foreign policy at Georgetown University, each were awarded the Cross of the Legion of Honor at a ceremony held on March 8 at the French Embassy. The decoration was conferred upon Dr. Henning by Ambassador de la Boulaye in recognition of his contribution to the knowledge and appreciation of French literature. Dr. Healy was recognized primarily for his participation in the activities of the French Institute of Washington, which he helped to found eight years ago.

MRS. GENEVIEVE GARVAN BRADY, chairman of the national board of the Girl Scouts of America and vice-chairman of the national women's committee on welfare and relief mobilization, has been awarded the Laetare Medal, which is bestowed annually by the University of Notre Dame upon some leader of the Catholic laity in the United States, in recognition of merit and as an inspiration to greater achievement.

HENRY METCALFE FISKE, head of the French department of St. Paul's School at Concord, N. H., has been awarded the decoration Les Palmes d'Officier d'Académie by the Government of France. The Palmes Académiques honor, which was established by Napoleon I in 1806 for achievement in educational fields, has rarely been awarded to other than French schoolmen.

DR. ALBERT FITCH, one of the founders of the Pennsylvania State College of Optometry, has received a gold medal from the Distinguished Service Foundation of Optometry for his leadership in optometric education. Dr. Daniel L. Marsh, president of Boston University, made the presentation during the annual convention of the New England Council of Optometrists in Boston.

DR. FRANCIS PRESTON VENABLE, professor of chemistry emeritus, of the University of North Carolina and president of the university from 1900 to 1914, died on March 17. Dr. Venable was seventy-seven years of age.

DR. AUGUSTUS TROWBRIDGE, dean of the graduate school of Princeton University since 1928, died on March 14. Dr. Trowbridge was sixty-four years old.

DR. FRANCIS GARNER MILLER, dean of the School of Forestry of the University of Idaho since 1917, died on March 8, at the age of sixty-three years.

GEORGE HENRY BRINEGAR, assistant professor of education at Illinois State Normal University since 1924, died on March 14.

DR. WILLIAM H. SMILEY, superintendent emeritus of public schools in Denver, died on March 14. He was seventy-nine years old.

CHRISTOPHER GREGORY, superintendent emeritus of schools at Long Branch, N. J., died on March 12.

THE National Conference on the Education of Negroes will be held in Washington from May 9 to May 12, inclusive.

THE Educational Buyers' Association, with representatives from two hundred colleges and schools in attendance, will hold its annual convention at Miami University, Oxford, Ohio, on April 5 and 6. The discussions will be concerned principally with the effects of various NRA codes on college buyers.

THE sixth annual Institute of Government, sponsored by the School of Government of the University of Southern California, will be held at the university from April 2 to 6.

THE Ball State Teachers College at Muncie, Ind., has received $55,000 from the Ball Brothers Company of that city to be used toward the erection of the new Arts Building. The work on the structure has been recently stopped because all bids for the contract exceeded the funds available. The college has on hand $259,000; the Federal Government, through the Public Works Administration, has supplied $95,000, and the trustees will apply to the Federal Emergency Administration for the additional amount.

Two gifts of $50,000 each have been made to Harvard University by Earl Wilson Bemis, retired engineer, of Worcester, Mass. One gift, a memorial for the donor's mother, Mrs. Elizabeth E. Bemis, will help finance a survey now being conducted by the Harvard Astronomical Observatory. The other gift will supplement Mr. Bemis's endowment of $100,000, given last year to the Gray Herbarium.

CHARLES F. LEWIS, director of the Buhl Foundation, has announced that the foundation has granted $25,000 to the Carnegie Institute of Technology for the establishment of a laboratory for research in experimental physics. Professor Otto Stern, who has been studying the structure of the atom by the use of molecular beams, will be in charge of the laboratory.

DR. WILLIAM KIRK WOOLERY, dean of the faculty at Bethany College, Bethany, W. Va., announced on March 8 that every member of the faculty had agreed to donate at least 10 per cent. of his salary to the college for the current academic year.

THE National Education Association reports a membership drop of about thirty thousand between January 1, 1933, and January 1, 1934. On the former date, the membership numbered 207,418; on the latter, 189,173. All states showed a decline in membership except Delaware, Idaho, Illinois, Massachusetts, Mississippi, Missouri, New York and Wisconsin. Membership in state associations declined during the same period from 682,607 to 652,338.

THE state of Georgia, according to the annual report of the state auditor, operated its entire educational system on $6,162,353 in 1933, as compared with $7,352,396 for 1932. The fund was derived from legislative appropriations, amounting to $3,630,141, and from allocated funds supplemented by endowments. The school equalization fund, derived from the one cent a gallon state tax on gasoline, furnished the department of education with $2,244,516.

THE National Committee on Standard Reports for Institutions of Higher Education has recently issued a bulletin, entitled "Suggested Methods and Forms for Use in Unit-Cost Studies in Colleges and Universities." Copies of this report may be obtained by addressing the chairman, Lloyd Morey, at the University of Illinois, Urbana, Ill.

DIPLOMAS have been granted to 130 farmers and villagers of Van Hornesville, N. Y., at the completion of a ten-weeks' course in night school. This experiment in adult education, which cost the school board two dollars a night, has been conducted by Maurice S. Hammond, principal of the school, and fourteen teachers, who donated their services.

DR. H. R. CROSSLAND, professor of psychology at the University of Oregon, and L. K. Shumaker, supervisor of the English bureau, have recently conducted experiments on a group of twenty-four students, segregated because of study difficulties. Of this number, eighteen were found to be "left-eyed," yet were right-handed, rather than right-handed and right-eyed or left-handed and left-eyed, as in normal functioning. In practically every case tests disclosed the presence of a cerebral interference, which made reading and perception of the printed page difficult, due to the fact that the left eye dominated vision. By having the student turn his head slightly or having him move his book a few inches to the right, the right eye was forced to take over its share of the work. Dr. Crossland and Mr. Shumaker maintained that this resulted in an almost instant improvement in learning.

A REVISION of educational activities conducted by American missionaries in foreign fields is urged by Dr. I. L. Kandel, professor of education at Teachers College, Columbia University, in the educational year book of the International Institute of Teachers College. Asserting that educational missions have failed in adapting educational ideals and practises to the local environment and in preparing nationals themselves to assume leadership, Dr. Kandel declares that American educators conducting schools or colleges in foreign lands should adopt a more realistic attitude toward their task. Dr. Kandel cites a recent report of the League of Nations Mission of Educational Experts to China, and lectures by the late Dr. Carl H. Beeker at the University of London, which were devoted to a criticism of American educational missions. "That this view is spreading is indicated in the restrictions which are being imposed on foreign educational missions in such countries as China, Japan, Mexico and Turkey. It means on the whole that educational missions have failed in two directions: first, in adapting educational ideals and practises to the local environment and, second, in preparing nationals themselves to assume leadership."

A SUMMARY of the report given in *Nature* states that education in India in 1930–31 is briefly reviewed by the Educational Commissioner with the Government of India in a pamphlet recently issued from the Central Publication Branch, Calcutta. Statistics of enrolment of students show that the rate of expansion was much slower than in past years, while in the higher stages (post-secondary education) there was a decrease by 5 per cent., from 83,334 to 79,225. The prevailing financial stringency and economic depression coupled with the laxity of discipline engendered by the civil disobedience movement are mentioned in this connection. The number of females under instruction, 2,375,593, shows an increase in all stages and now represents 1.8 per cent. of the total female population, while for males the corresponding percentage is 7.36. The standard of instruction in the secondary stages is said to be slowly rising, at any rate in government institutions. The use of the vernacular as the medium of instruction and examination is increasing and inspectors complain that since the change of medium was introduced the standard of written and spoken English has deteriorated. As regards primary schools, the most striking feature of the returns is the extent of wastage, especially in the first year, the number of pupils in class 2 being 2,124,478 as compared with 5,266,579 in class 1. The need of a clearing house for educational ideas and a medium for the diffusion throughout India of new methods has been felt since the abolition in 1923 of the Central Advisory Board of Education and Bureau of Education, and the government has decided to revive them as soon as financial conditions improve.

A SYSTEM of mass education by radio was inaugurated in Italy on March 10, when Commendatore Giulio Santini, director general of elementary schools, spoke to hundreds of thousands of school children listening in from classrooms over all Italy. Schools, even in the most rural districts, have been equipped with receiving sets to pick up lessons to be broadcast daily from Rome.

ACCORDING to the *Journal* of the American Medical Association, the creation of open-air schools has progressed in Germany. These schools have been established chiefly for weakly children; later, forest schools for healthy children arose. Some of the hygienic advantages of the open-air school, as observed and reported by the krankenkassen, were disappearance of glandular swellings and anemia, tanning of the skin, increase of weight, increase of bodily vigor and improvement in physical appearance, lessened tendency to colds, increase of resistance and of general well being, and strengthening of the nervous system. The work in the open-air schools seeks to inculcate a fondness for a simple, natural and healthy mode of living, independence of action and self-reliance. In addition to the hygienic advantages, their importance lies, therefore, in the attainment of an education that will make for a thrifty, financially sound mode of living in family and state.

ACCORDING to *The Christian Science Monitor*, partly for reasons of economy and partly because the supply of teachers is far in excess of the demand, the training of state teachers in New Zealand is to be suspended. All teachers must pass through a training college, of which there is one in each of four main centers. The government decided some time ago to close the Dunedin and Wellington Colleges and to curtail the activities of those at Auckland and Christchurch. It was also decided to close these two colleges at the end of 1933, and the period during which they will remain closed appears to be indefinite. It was estimated that at the beginning of 1934 there would be a surplus of 966 teachers in the Dominion. The staffs of the closed training colleges are being utilized in the university colleges.

SERIOUS charges against the Japanese are contained in an official report to the Chinese Ministry of Education, according to a recent comment in the *New York Times*. An inspector for the Chinese government has reported that under Japanese orders the teaching of Kuomintang party principles is forbidden in the schools in the towns of the demilitarized zone in Hopei Province between Peiping and Tientsin and the Great Wall. Japanese non-commissioned officers, who frequently inspect the Chinese schools, have prohibited the display of pictures of the late Dr. Sun Yat-sen and have ordered a revision of the teaching of history. The report also charged that the Japanese have promoted an organization called the Society for the Study of the Japanese Language and Protection. For fifty cents a month, one may buy the "protection" afforded by this organization, and abstention from membership is listed as "a reactionary activity for which one may be arrested."

DISCUSSION

THE TEACHER AS MENTAL HYGIENIST

WHEN a truism has been accepted so long that we ignore its implications, it is time to restate the axiom. Most of us agree that the teacher is an important agent in the educative process. Yet educational practise is such that we often violate the corollaries that follow. We change our text-books; we revise our courses of study; we rephrase the aims of our curriculum—but in the classroom, teachers who have not been won over to the new tendencies proceed in the old ways.

It is with the classroom teacher that most of our hope for a new spirit in education, for one conducive to the development of mental health, is to be found. She it is who is in daily contact with the children and thus has the greatest opportunity for influencing the pupils' development. The teacher decides which appeals and motives are to be used, and it is her task to adjust the demands of the school to the personality of her charges. Signs of maladjustment are apparent to her long before they are serious enough to warrant the attention of the school psychologist. Moreover, because of the intimate nature of the teacher-pupil relationship, children are more likely to confide in a sympathetic class teacher than in almost anybody else.

The attitudes of instructors vary from that of the person who is totally unaware of mental hygiene to that of the schoolmaster who acts as an amateur psychiatrist. We may dismiss with a few words the person who is still blind to the possibilities of classroom mental hygiene work. We don't remain neutral in our influence upon the child's mental development merely by ignoring the matter.

The teacher who is willing to help but doesn't know how presents an equally serious, but a more hopeful, problem. Criticism may be directed at some school mental hygiene programs because they venture into fields where expert direction is needed at a time when the educational system is financially able to furnish only good intentions and amateurism.

The first principle to guide educators interested in improving the youngster's chances for emotional stability is that the teacher's chief function is preventive, not remedial. Few school people dare to tell you, officially, how to treat a persistent headache or a defective tooth. Nevertheless, innumerable voluntary advisers feel perfectly confident to discuss complexes and perversions.

It is unwise for the teacher to preempt the place of the clinician. She need not hesitate to call upon the clinic for a picture of the child's development in various traits, an explanation of the conditions found, a study of probable causes, or suggestions of the type of treatment to be followed. These problems necessitate a skill that is far above the level reached even by an interested schoolmaster who is concerned also with other educational problems.

Most teachers can make a distinct contribution by evaluating our educational procedures in the light of the influence on children's personalities. In current educational investigations, results generally are measured by using some sort of objective test. These measuring instruments necessarily ignore the child's personality.

Let us illustrate by considering two suggested plans for drilling on arithmetic fundamentals. Plan A has a daily ten-minute drill period. Plan B involves the use of five two-minute drill periods each day. The standardized tests used to compare results are so objective that they make no provision for studying the effects of the two plans upon the children. It is for the teacher to carry the experiment one step farther and to essay the task of determining the influence of the two plans upon the emotional stability of her pupils. How do the pupils react to the constant demand for speed and high tension work as entailed in the steady use of the two-minute drill periods? Is a habit of concentrated work formed that is carried over to other parts of the day's work? And so forth.

We realize that the answers to these and similar questions do not lend themselves to statistical treatment—that is why they are ignored by most educators. In almost every investigation there are significant questions that the experimenter prefers to overlook because they are not amenable to "scientific" study. But there is a point at which too narrow a conception of scientific method results in the treatment of relatively insignificant details at the expense of those that may have more influence upon the child's mental health. It is here that the class teacher makes her contribution by studying the less objective but the more vital questions of the influence of the experiment upon the child's emotional stability. With the teacher rests the responsibility of asking "How?" when others seem to be interested only in "How much?"

A third responsibility of the teacher grows out of the circumstance that consciously, as well as unintentionally, children imitate her. Not only must she set an example of poise and self-confidence, but she must display a manner of meeting opposition and frustration that is such as to deserve imitation.

An emotionally maladjusted teacher affects the lives of the youngsters adversely. The frustrations of life are not met by the teacher who attempts to compensate for defeat elsewhere by being over-domineering in the classroom. Unfortunately, our social customs deprive the teacher of some means of self-expression available to others in the community. It is doubly unfortunate when this condition leads to the personality that seeks relief by bullying, nagging and giving vent to outbursts of temper, or by the other extreme of being so paternalistic that little opportunity is afforded the child to face his own problems and to take the consequences of his mistakes.

Then, the teacher's interest in the pupils' mental health should control the selection of the motives upon which the work of the class is based and the choice of punishments meted out to pupils who are "different."

Burnham stresses the importance of leaving with the child the responsibility for selecting the plan of procedure. The teacher must make some provision for the development of the student's ability to work on his own initiative.

A fundamental difficulty of motivation as it is used to-day is that so often the appeal is highly individual, rather than social. We must reevaluate our appeals and see where we can emphasize the social development of the child. Learning to cooperate with others and to share in common triumphs and trials is sufficiently important to get the attention of teachers.

Our punishments are often unnecessary or unwise. It is obvious that the child should not be punished for "crimes" for whose commission he is not responsible. Obvious? but ignored. How many youngsters are punished by retardation because they have failed to meet the demands of a course of study totally unsuited to their abilities, their needs and their interests? We shame a child into submission without thinking of the consequences of ill-advised humiliation repeated frequently.

An important duty is that of detecting the early symptoms of maladjustment. Common practise gives undue weight to sins of commission and slights those of omission. To the teacher who is harassed by the million and one details of daily routine, the child who does not interfere with the smooth progress of the group offers no problem.

The person who never violates the mores of the group may, nevertheless, be leading an unhealthy and an unhappy life. We must be alert for youngsters who are always quiet, for those who constantly seek to avoid social activities, for those whose emotional reactions seem out of all proportion to the stimulus, etc. A teacher may have perfect discipline in her class and yet have quite a few children who need sympathetic guidance in assisting them to overcome personality traits that hold the threat of poor adjustment.

Finally, the teacher should be familiar with the names and the addresses of individuals and organizations in the community that can give expert guidance in the treatment of the behavior problem child. After the child has been examined by the expert and the diagnosis has been made by a skilled person, it often remains for the teacher to adjust the school environment so that the opportunity for successful treatment is increased.

Surely there is enough for the teacher to do without venturing into psychiatry. Little is gained from the amateur attempt to read into the child's mind and to "find" complexes and perversions that probably don't exist. It is for the teacher to help the emotional stability of her class by being herself well adjusted to life and by assisting the youngsters with the sympathetic understanding that encourages each to face the problems of the day with confidence, with interest and, we hope, with success.

Harry N. Rivlin

College of the City of New York

A CONSUMER'S CODE FOR RESEARCH

The field of educational and psychological research needs a code for the benefit of the consumers of research material. Students, public-school teachers, executives, business men and the medical profession need access to the results of such investigation. The unfortunate fact is that publication of such results is so illogically scattered through periodical literature as to render it almost valueless to many who would use it if they could.

To illustrate, inspection of my guide card copied from the library file shows a list of 68 publications in which one may find reports of psychological and educational research. Since making this list I have been forced to go outside it three times for such material, once to a magazine of eugenics, once to a magazine of home economics, and once to one of agricultural research.

I pick ten cards at random from my file on character and personality and find them drawn from eight publications. Ten cards from the file on school achievement yield the names of seven publications. Many afternoons spent in the libraries are more taken with searching for material for study than with study itself. The undergraduate class that asks for a text-book is not to be jeered at thoughtlessly as having no interest in learning. It is more probable that they have no interest in spending time from a crowded day in walking back and forth in search of magazines for original material.

Even when the instructor assumes the burden of providing an annotated bibliography the task of learning is sufficiently difficult. But for a student attempting to work independently the search for material is so time-consuming as to be maddening.

To contrast this situation with an ideal one of going to the library and, if one were interested in learning, asking for the *Journal of Research in Learning,* wherein the material would be classified as to its nature, is a bit more Utopian than seems possible, but need not be.

I wish to propose nine steps for the improvement of publications devoted to educational and psychological research.

(1) Classify research in these fields as to scientific relationships and utility.

(2) Assign to magazines of national circulation as much material in a given field as they would normally select from the whole field, combining those left-over, or starting new ones if needed. Restrict each magazine to its own type of material.

(3) Require all research material to be submitted to a board of readers whose duty it would be to classify, edit, abstract and distribute such material.

(4) Sign agreements with graduate schools to submit abstracts of theses written in article form, or to file copies of theses with a central organization to which the board of readers would have access.

(5) Provide translators adequately trained in psychology to make available important foreign research without delay.

(6) Offer to specialized and general magazines abstracts of articles related to their fields or articles overlapping.

(7) Draw up a set of standards to increase value of articles by adequate presentation.

(8) Collect articles which belong in the field of education or psychology but which have wandered for publication into other fields and abstract them completely.

(9) Eventually republish valid research material of the past in all fields, as has been done by Dr. Curtiss for science teaching.

Such a program presupposes the willingness of the cooperating magazines. But the purpose of educators is to educate, and it is difficult to see how they could refuse to cooperate in an enterprise of so much value to those who need educational material.

The foremost advantage of this plan is of

course the time and money saved the consumers of research material. The only possible objection on this ground is that it removes one of the higher hurdles in the path to higher degrees. This ideal of testing the candidate for learning by assailing him with a plague of petty distractions and annoyances has few supporters among real educators, however.

Another obvious advantage is the unlocking of material now unavailable to the average person in unpublished theses, foreign magazines and institutional organs. Theses not worth publishing are probably not worth writing, but the outlet is not always available unless the candidate chooses to write his own article. Catalog statements to the contrary, the average practising Ph.D. probably can not read any language but his own well enough to derive any great benefits from his efforts in foreign fields. Institutional organs are so narrowly circulated and so inadequate compared to national magazines that the institution could hope to win greater recognition by cooperation than by individual efforts.

The realization of this scheme is not impossible. Most educators have at one time or another publicly advocated in other fields the reform I now propose in their own. Psychologists are no fonder of inefficiency than any one else, and from their record should be willing to cooperate. It might be necessary to make copyright arrangements somewhat differently, and perhaps to reciprocate with foreign scientists, which should be a pleasure.

The magazines in these fields are not published for profit. The chief hindrance is probably inertia and tradition. None is insurmountable. I suggest communication among editors to arrange for a conference on the plan.

VICTOR C. SMITH
RAMSEY JUNIOR HIGH SCHOOL
MINNEAPOLIS, MINN.

SPECIAL CORRESPONDENCE

THE CONGRESSIONAL HEARINGS ON FEDERAL AID FOR SCHOOLS

BEGINNING on February 26, the Committee on Education of the House of Representatives of the 73rd Congress devoted three and one half days to hearings on the needs of the schools for emergency aid from the Federal Government for the school year 1934–35.

Dr. James H. Richmond, superintendent of public instruction of Kentucky, and chairman of the National Committee for Federal Emergency Aid for Education, opened the case for the schools and introduced subsequent speakers. It is highly gratifying that not a single person appeared in opposition to federal emergency aid. In addition to state superintendents, commissioners of education or members of state departments of education from eleven states, Dr. Paul R. Mort, authority on school finance problems, and representatives of twelve important lay and professional organizations took part in the hearings. The case for emergency aid for education was ably presented also by six congressmen from five states. The Committee on Education invited Dr. George F. Zook, U. S. Commissioner of Education; Harry L. Hopkins, Federal Emergency Relief Administrator, and Stanley Reed, general counsel for the Reconstruction Finance Corporation, to testify.

The hearings dealt with items 2 and 3 of the six-point program adopted January 6, 1934, by the Federal Advisory Committee on Emergency Aid in Education, a committee called by United States Commissioner of Education George F. Zook, to determine the need for federal emergency aid. The National Committee for Federal Emergency Aid for Education, James H. Richmond, *chairman,* was an outgrowth of the Federal Advisory Committee on Emergency Aid in Education, called by U. S. Commissioner of Education George F. Zook. The latter committee, composed of representatives of thirty-two national organizations, proposed the following six-point program for federal aid:

(1) $50,000,000 to keep schools open during 1933–34; (2) $100,000,000 to keep schools open during 1934–35; (3) a substantial additional appropriation to insure normal operation of schools during 1934–35; (4) federal loans to school districts on the security of delinquent taxes, frozen assets in closed banks, etc.; (5) not less than 10 per cent. of any new appropriations for public works to be allocated for school and college buildings and buildings for other educational enter-

prises, and (6) $30,000,000 to assist students to attend institutions of higher education.

Several bills covering points 2 and 3 directly or indirectly were before the Committee on Education, but the hearings were concerned with the needs of the schools rather than with the merits or limitations of the proposed legislation. Since the time of the public hearings, the committee has held several executive sessions devoted to the question of emergency federal aid for schools during the coming year. Its report is expected within the near future.

The National Committee for Federal Emergency Aid for Education gave the following reasons why emergency federal aid for schools will be needed in 1934–35. Evidence was introduced to substantiate each point.

(1) School revenues in 1933–34 have been seriously reduced.
(2) School opportunities in 1933–34 have been inadequate or lacking.
(3) Federal aid granted this year has been the only means of keeping many schools open.
(4) Enrolments next year will show significant increases.
(5) Property taxes, the chief source of school revenue, will be inadequate in 1934–35.
(6) State school funds for 1934–35 will not offer sufficient relief to depleted local resources.
(7) Further state and local borrowing for school support is impractical.
(8) Reports from most of the states indicate falling school revenues for 1934–35.
(9) Reports from most of the states indicate urgent need for federal emergency aid next year.

On Wednesday, February 28, and Wednesday, March 7, the Reconstruction Finance Corporation Subcommittee of the Banking and Currency Committee of the House of Representatives considered bills looking toward the refinancing of school indebtedness by the Reconstruction Finance Corporation, and the borrowing of money by school districts from the corporation, with frozen assets and delinquent taxes pledged as securities. The committee considered also a bill providing for the lending of money on school warrants held by teachers.

In presenting the case for emergency federal loans to school districts the following points were emphasized:

(1) The demands on available school revenue for current operating expenses will be unusually heavy in 1934–35.
(2) An abnormal share of the school revenue available is required for debt service.
(3) Refinancing a small percentage of the total school debt would bring definite and sorely needed relief to many school districts.
(4) It is proposed that loans be made only on the basis of adequate security.
(5) The proposed use of federal credit is in the interest of public welfare and is in complete accord with the purposes and established policies of the Reconstruction Finance Corporation.

All estimates that have been made thus far indicate that during the year 1934–35 it will be more difficult to finance the schools than it has been during the present year. Unless some measure of federal aid is extended next year, it will be impossible for many of the states to keep their schools open and operating on a reasonably satisfactory basis.

JAMES W. CAMMACK, JR.
National Committee for Federal Emergency Aid for Education

QUOTATIONS

ELIOT ON EDUCATION

WHEN 3,000 children from the public schools of Cleveland sing to an audience of 7,000 superintendents and teachers, and when two high school orchestras at the opposite ends of a hall—a full city block in length—play Bach in antiphonal sequence, these arts can not be thought fads or frills. They belong to the fundamentals in public education. The exhibition would have mightily pleased that great prophet of democracy, Charles W. Eliot, the centennial of whose birth is being celebrated this year.

In what might be called his last educational will and testament he outlined a program of public education. The teachers in session at Cleveland could not do better than adopt it as a platform on which all can stand who look forward to education's more helpful part in a democracy. It is a counsel of perfection, but its words should be written in letters of light as defining the ideal to be made real as far as possible. As Barrie once said of "the equal chance" to be got through education for the children and youth of Scotland, the words "as far as possible" tarnish the splendid hope. He looked forward to the day when "we may be able to cast them out." It is to be hoped that we of America may find it possible to approach more and more closely Dr. Eliot's ideal for all children.

In summary his program was set forth as follows:

1. Enlist the interest of every pupil in every school in his daily tasks in order to get from him hard, persistent and enjoyed work.
2. Cultivate every hour in every child the power to see and describe accurately.
3. Make the training of the senses a prime object every day.
4. Teach every child to draw, model, sing or play a musical instrument and read music.
5. Make every child active, not passive; alert, not dawdling; led or piloted, not driven, and always learning the value of cooperative discipline.
6. Teach groups of subjects together in their natural relations.
7. Put into all American schools universal physical training for both boys and girls from 6 to 18 years of age.
8. Make sure that every pupil has a fair chance to learn the elements of agriculture, dietetics, cooking and hygiene, every boy the elements of some manual trade and every girl the domestic arts. The instruction in hygiene should include the defenses of society against the diseases and degradations consequent upon ignorance, moral depravity, poverty and vice.
9. Make room for the new subjects and for increased instruction addressed to the individual pupil; reduce class work and the size of classes, lengthen the school day and shorten the summer vacation.
10. Keep the atmosphere of every school and family charged with the master sentiments of love, hope and duty. Keep out both fear and selfishness.

This is a large order, but it is one that democracy must undertake for its own sake. There could be no better celebration of the centenary of Charles W. Eliot, the great educational statesman, than the general adoption of this program as a code for the schools. The meeting of the National Education Association in July should devote at least one session to his memory and his testament of education.—*The New York Times.*

EDUCATIONAL BOOKS OF 1933[1]

The attempt has been made to present a complete list of all educational publications appearing in 1933. Many indexes, current educational publications, government lists and publishers' catalogues have been checked as well as the Library of the U. S. Office of Education.

It is interesting to note that despite the sharp decline in the number of books published in many subjects, 808 titles were discovered in education as compared with 831 in 1932, 777 in 1931, 685 in 1930 and 532 in 1929. City and state courses of study have been excluded as well as books on religious education.

The starred titles are those included in the "Sixty Educational Books of 1933," published in the *Journal of the National Education Association* for April, 1933.

There have been many revised editions, including such important ones as: Cubberley, "An Introduction to the Study of Education"; Dewey, "How We Think"; Fargo, "Library in the School"; Frazier and Armentrout, "Introduction to Education"; Murchison, "Handbook of Child Psychology," and Norsworthy and Whitley, "Psychology of Childhood."

As in the 1932 list, "Higher Education" remains the largest group, numbering 120 titles, though most of these titles are in pamphlet form. "Administration" is again the second group in size, with 85 titles to its credit. The present financial situation and its danger to education has drawn forth considerable material that should prove helpful to administrators.

Of the special subject groups, "Art" is by far the most prolific, with many excellent helps for the teacher in this field. Another outstanding group is "Child Psychology," with its title expanded this year to "Psychology of Childhood

[1] Prepared by Mary Rebecca Lingenfelter and Rea J. Steele, Enoch Pratt Free Library, Baltimore, Maryland.

and Youth." "Educational Psychology" had some splendid contributions, with such books as Pressey's "Psychology and the New Education"; Hollingworth's "Educational Psychology," and the like.

A peculiar feature of this year's list is the inclusion of several exceedingly important series, notably: J. E. Anderson, "Century Childhood Library"; W. W. Charters, "Motion Pictures and Youth: The Payne Fund Studies," and F. W. Reeves, "The University of Chicago Survey."

A new group, "Education for the New Social Order," has been added, which includes books on the training of youth for a new society and a wiser use of leisure time. This is the most outstanding challenge to educators of to-day. These annual lists offer an inspiring exhibit of the substantial labors and intelligence that constantly go into the development of America's schools.

LIST OF EDUCATIONAL BOOKS

(1) History, Principles and Philosophy of Education

Abel, J. F. The nations at school—India. A study course and bibliography. 16p. 1933. Amer. Assn. of Univ. Women. $.20.

Adams, Sir John. Externals and essentials. 152p. 1933. Longmans. $1.35.

Bollig, R. J. History of Catholic education in Kansas, 1836–1932. 131p. 1933. Catholic Univ. of Amer. $1.25.

*Butterweck, J. S., and Seegers, J. C. An orientation course in education. 392p. 1933. Houghton. $2.00.

Chesterfield education: the record of four years of experiment and reconstruction. 312p. 1932. (Amer. ed., 1933.) Oxford Univ. Press. $1.75.

Clifton, J. L. Ten famous American educators. 272p. 1933. R. G. Adams & Co., Columbus, O. $1.20.

Cubberley, E. P. An introduction to the study of education, rev. by E. C. Eells. 532p. 1933. Houghton. $2.25.

Doyle, J. J. Education in recent constitutions and concordats. 139p. 1933. Catholic Univ. of Amer. $1.25.

Duggan, Stephen. Critique of the report of the League of Nations' mission of educational experts to China. (Bul. No. 1, series 14.) 40p. 1933. Institute of International Educ. $.25.

Education in India in 1930–31. 81p. 1933. British Library of Information, 270 Madison Ave., N. Y. C. $.10.

Eginton, D. P. A comparison between some principles of education in England and New Jersey. 128p. 1933. Printed by Finlay Bros., Hartford, Conn.

Fitzpatrick, E. A., *ed.* Saint Ignatius and the Ratio studiorum. 275p. 1933. McGraw-Hill. $1.00.

Frankel, R. L. Henry M. Leipziger: educator and idealist. 202p. 1933. Macmillan. $2.00.

Frasier, G. W., and Armentrout, W. D. An introduction to education. 3rd ed. 422p. 1933. Scott, Foresman. $1.80.

*Kandel, I. L. Comparative education. 922p. 1933. Houghton. $4.00.

Kandel, I. L., *ed.* (Ninth) Educational yearbook of the International Institute of Teachers College, Columbia University. The relation of the state to religious education. 497p. 1933. Teachers College, Columbia. $3.50.

Kandel, I. L. The outlook in education; one of the Joseph Payne Lectures for 1932–33. 18p. 1933. Oxford Univ. Press. $.45.

*Kilpatrick, W. H., and others. The educational frontier. 325p. 1933. Appleton-Century. $2.50. (Published also as: Yearbook No. 21 of the National society of college teachers of education. Univ. of Chicago Press. $1.50 paper.)

Marvin, F. S. The nation at school: a sketch with comments. 172p. 1933. Oxford Univ. Press. $1.75.

Matthews, J. C. The contributions of Joseph Baldwin to public education. (Cont. to educ. No. 111.) 184p. 1933. George Peabody College for Teachers. $1.35.

Melvin, A. G. Education for a new era. (Pamphlet, No. 21.) 32p. 1933. Day. $.25.

Morrison, H. C. The evolving common school. (Inglis lecture. 62p. 1933. Harvard Univ. Press. $1.00.

Mulhern, James. A history of secondary education in Pennsylvania. 714p. 1933. Science Press. $5.00.

National Education Association. Department of Superintendence and Research Division. Education discussed in lay magazines, April 1, 1933. (Circular, No. 4.) *Mimeographed.* 11p. 1933. The Association. With subscription to Educ. research service.

National Education Association. Department of Superintendence and Research Division. Education discussed in lay magazines, December 1, 1933. (Circular, No. 13.) *Mimeographed.* 14p. 1933. The Association. With subscription to Educ. research service.

National Education Association. Department of Superintendence and Research Division. Education discussed in lay magazines, February 1, 1933. (Circular, No. 2.) *Mimeographed.* 12p. 1933. The Association. With subscription to Educ. research service.

National Education Association. Department of Superintendence and Research Division. Education discussed in lay magazines, June 1, 1933. (Circular, No. 6.) *Mimeographed.* 12p. 1933. The Association. With subscription to Educ. research service.

National Education Association. Department of Superintendence and Research Division. Education discussed in lay magazines, October 1, 1933. (Circular, No. 11.) *Mimeographed.* 19p. 1933. The Association. With subscription to Educ. research service.

National Education Association. Research Division. Depression and the schools; statement prepared for the joint emergency steering committee. *Mimeographed.* 7p. 1933. The Association. $.05.

Outline of the structure of the educational system in England and Wales. (Board of educ. pamphlet, No. 94.) 46p. 1933. British Library of Information, 270 Madison Ave., N. Y. C. $.22.

Plimpton, G. A. The education of Shakespeare; illustrated from the schoolbooks in use in his time. 140p. 1933. Oxford Univ. Press. $2.00.

Rowland, W. T. Aims of public education in the United States. (Cont. to educ. No. 117.) 167p. 1933. George Peabody College for Teachers. $1.35.

Sanford, C. W. A critical study of certain aspects of infant and common school education, 1810–40. (Abstract of an unpublished thesis.) 8p. 1933. Univ. of Ill., High School Visitors' Office. $.25.

Sarafian, K. A. French educational theorists. 134p. 1933. C. C. Crawford, Univ. of Southern Cal., Los Angeles, Cal. $1.50.

Siegl, M. H. Reform of elementary education in Austria. 145p. 1933. (Thesis.) Columbia Univ.

Stoker, Spencer. The schools and international understanding. 243p. 1933. Univ. of N. C. Press. $2.50.

Taylor, Hoy. An interpretation of the early administration of the Peabody education fund. (Cont. to educ, No. 114.) 166p. 1933. George Peabody College for Teachers. $1.25.

Thompson, M. M. Outline of the history of education. 157p. 1933. Barnes and Noble, Inc., 105 Fifth Ave., N. Y. C. $.75.

U. S. Office of Education. Good references on the education of the indigenous peoples of Mexico, comp. by K. M. Cook and F. E. Reynolds. (Bibliography, No. 8.) *Mimeographed.* 11p. 1933. The Office. Gratis.

Woelfel, Norman. Molders of the American mind, a critical review of the social attitudes of seventeen leaders in American education. 304p. 1933. Columbia Univ. Press. $3.00.

Wright, L. M. Literature and education in early Quakerism. (Univ. of Ia. studies, Vol. V, No. 2,

New series No. 244.) 60p. 1933. Univ. of Ia. $.50.

Wyndham, H. A. Native education, Ceylon, Java, Formosa, The Philippines, French Indo-China, and British Malaya. 264p. 1933. Oxford Univ. Press. $3.50.

Wynne, J. P. Modern theories of the educative process; a syllabus in the philosophy of education. 60p. 1933. The Author, State Teachers College, Farmville, Va. $.60.

(2) ADMINISTRATION AND FINANCE

Aaron, Marcus. Adequate support for public education. 13p. 1933. Board of Educ., Pittsburgh, Pa. Gratis.

*Almack, J. C., *ed.* Modern school administration: its problems and progress. 382p. 1933. Houghton. $2.50.

American school and university: a yearbook devoted to the design, construction, equipment, utilization and maintenance of educational buildings and grounds, 1933–34, sixth annual edition. 403p. 1933. Amer. School Pub. Corp., 470 4th Ave., N. Y. C. $2.50.

Beach, F. F. The custody of school funds. An appraisal of systems of school fund custody with particular reference to New York state. (Cont. to educ. No. 577.) 159p. 1933. Teachers College, Columbia. $1.75.

Bryan, M. De G., and Handy, E. H. Furnishings and equipment for residence halls. 95p. 1933. Teachers College, Columbia. $1.00.

California. State Department of Education. Maintaining educational efficiency during emergency. (Bul. No. 5, 1933.) 26p. 1933. The Department. Gratis.

Carr, W. G. School finance. (School economy series.) 106p. 1933. Stanford Univ. Press. $1.00.

Citizens' Conference on the Crisis in Education. Report of proceedings prepared by the Agenda committee. 112p. 1933. Amer. Council on Educ., 744 Jackson Pl., Washington, D. C. $.15.

Cooper, W. J. Economy in education. (School economy series.) 82p. 1933. Stanford Univ. Press. $1.00.

Dienst, C. F. The administration of endowments; with special reference to the public schools and institutional trusts of Idaho. (Cont. to educ. No. 560.) 131p. 1933. Teachers College, Columbia. $1.50.

Dudley, L. L. The school and the community; a study of local control in the public schools of Massachusetts. (Harvard studies in educ. Vol. XX.) 190p. 1933. Harvard Univ. Press. $2.50.

*Edwards, Newton. The courts and the public schools; the legal basis of school organization and administration. (Social science studies, No. 28.) 591p. 1933. Univ. of Chicago Press. $5.00.

Engelhardt, N. L., and Wallack, W. M. Budget preparation and cumulative record book. Pt. I—Budget preparation book. Pt. II—Permanent continuing budget record. *Mimeographed.* unp. 1933. Teachers College, Columbia. $1.00.

Engleman, J. O. Centralizing tendencies in educational administration in Ohio since 1900. (Kent State College quarterly, Vol. XX, No. 2.) 186p. 1933. State College, Kent, Ohio. $.75.

Godman, Mark. Manual of organization and administration for high schools. (Educ. bul. Vol. I, No. 6.) 164p. 1933. Dept. of Educ., Frankfort, Ky.

Holy, T. C., *comp.* Comparison of school-plant-insurance premiums and reported school fire losses in Ohio cities and counties for 1930–31. 9p. 1933. Ohio State Univ., Bur. of Educ. Research.

Holy, T. C., *comp.* The disposition of school bond issues and special levies in Ohio cities and exempted villages, at the November 7, 1933, election. *Mimeographed.* 8p. 1933. Ohio State Univ., Bur. of Educ. Research.

Holy, T. C., *comp.* The extent of financial proposals to be submitted by Ohio county school districts on November 7, 1933. *Mimeographed.* 9p. 1933. Ohio State Univ., Bur. of Educ. Research.

Holy, T. C., *comp.* Financial data for Ohio cities and exempted villages for September, 1933. *Mimeographed.* 14p. 1933. Ohio State Univ., Bur. of Educ. Research.

Holy, T. C., *comp.* Information on school plant insurance in Ohio. 10p. 1933. Ohio State Univ., Bur. of Educ. Research.

Hull, R. B. School-grounds, their planning and planting. (Extension bul. No. 189.) 19p. 1933. Purdue Univ., Extension Dept. $.04.

Larson, E. L. School finance and related problems in Arizona. (Bul. Vol. IV, No. 1. Social science bul. No. 1.) 85p. 1933. Univ. of Ariz.

Lawler, E. S. A technique for computing the amount of new aid required for state equalization programs. (Cont. to educ. No. 547.) 46p. 1933. Teachers College, Columbia. $1.50.

Lee, C. A., and Viles, N. E. Schoolhouse planning and construction. (Bul. No. 2.) 116p. 1933. State Educ. Dept., Jefferson City, Mo. $1.00.

Maguire, J. W. R. Adequate financing of the Catholic college. (Bul. Vol. XXIX, No. 2.) 15p. 1933. Nat'l. Catholic Educ. Assn., 1312 Massachusetts Ave., N. W., Washington, D. C. $.10.

Martin, R. L., Fern, G. H., and Woods, L. A. Handbook and instructors' manual for public school janitor-engineers. 180p. 1933. Tex. State Board for Vocational Educ. Trade and Industrial Division, Austin, Tex. $.50.

Michigan Education Association. Program making; a handbook for district meetings. (Bul. No. 16.) 74p. 1933. The Association, Lansing, Mich. $.50.

Mort, P. R., and Lawler, E. S. Equalization of educational opportunity and the burden of support for education. *Mimeographed.* 29p. 1933. Amer. Assn. of Univ. Women. $.50.

Mort, P. R. State support for public education. (Nat'l. survey of school finance.) 496p. 1933. Amer. Council on Educ., 744 Jackson Pl., Washington, D. C. $2.00.

National Collegiate Athletic Association. Round table conferences; twenty-eighth annual convention. Pt. I—The athletic budget. Pt. II—Recruiting and subsidizing. 52p. 1933. Frank W. Nicolson, Sec'y., Wesleyan Univ., Middletown, Conn.

National Committee on Standard Reports for Institutions of Higher Education. Suggested forms for financial reports of auxiliary activities and organized activities relating to instructional departments and supplementary suggestions concerning general financial report forms of colleges and universities. (Bul. No. 7.) 63p. 1933. The Committee, G. H. Mew, Sec'y, Emory Univ., Ga. Gratis.

National Conference on the Financing of Education. Report, held under the auspices of the Joint commission on the emergency in education of the National Education Association and the Department of Superintendence, August, 1933. 78p. 1933. N. E. A., Dept. of Superintendence. $.25.

National Education Association. Department of Secondary School Principals. Economies in secondary-school administration. (Bul. No. 48). 32p. 1933. The Department.

National Education Association. Department of Secondary School Principals. Meeting the emergency in education. The present situation, what is being done about it, some suggestions for school administrators. (Bul. No. 46.) 32p. 1933. The Department. $.50.

National Education Association. Department of Secondary School Principals. Proceedings of the seventeenth annual meeting of the Department of Secondary-school Principals, Minneapolis, Minnesota, 1933. (Bul. No. 45.) 350p. 1933. H. V. Church, Exec. Sec'y, 3129 Wenonah Ave., Berwyn, Ill. $2.00.

National Education Association. Department of Superintendence. Meeting the emergency. (News letters, No. 1–5.) *Mimeographed.* p. 14; 11; 11; 24; 14. 1933. The Association. Gratis.

National Education Association. Department of Superintendence and Research Division. Application of the National industrial recovery act to school building construction. (Circular, No. 7.) *Mimeographed.* 12p. 1933. The Association. With subscription to Educ. research service.

National Education Association. Department of Superintendence and Research Division. References to standards proposed for school buildings and equipment. (Circular, No. 8.) 8p. 1933. The Association. With subscription to Educ. research service.

National Education Association. Department of Superintendence and Research Division. Summary and advance pages from the National survey of school finance. (Circular, No. 3.) *Mimeographed.* 8p. 1933. The Association. With subscription to Educ. research service.

National Education Association. Joint Commission on the Emergency in Education. Data on closed schools, short terms and subcode teachers, 1933–34; preliminary report: rural areas only. *Mimeographed.* 8p. 1933. The Association. Gratis.

National Education Association. Research Division. Compensation for injured school employees. (Studies in state educ. administration, No. 12.) *Mimeographed.* 55p. 1933. The Association. $.25.

National Education Association. Research Division. Constructive economy in education. (Bul. Vol. XI, No. 3.) p.57–90. 1933. The Association. $.25.

National Education Association. Research Division. Current conditions in the nation's schools. Bul. Vol. XI, No. 4.) p.95–113. 1933. The Association. $.25.

National Education Association. Research Division. Salaries in city school systems, 1932–33. (Bul. Vol. XI, No. 2.) p.43–55. 1933. The Association. $.25.

National Education Association. Research Division. Salaries paid administrative and supervisory officers. *Mimeographed.* 1933. The Association.
- Tabulation I–B. In cities over 100,000 population. 12p. $5.00.
- Tabulation II–B. In cities 30,000 to 100,000 population. 13p. $5.00.
- Tabulation III–B. In cities 10,000 to 30,000 population. 13p. $5.00.
- Tabulation IV–B. In cities 5,000 to 10,000 population. 10p. $5.00.
- Tabulation V–B. In cities 2,500 to 5,000 population. 11p. $5.00.

National Education Association. Research Division. Salaries paid teachers, principals, and certain other school employees. *Mimeographed.* 1933. The Association.
- Tabulation I–A. In cities over 100,000 population. 28p. $5.00.
- Tabulation II–A. In cities 30,000 to 100,000 population. 46p. $5.00.
- Tabulation III–A. In cities 10,000 to 30,000 population. 45p. $5.00.
- Tabulation IV–A. In cities 5,000 to 10,000 population. 39p. $5.00.
- Tabulation V–A. In cities 2,500 to 5,000 population. 44p. $5.00.

National Education Association. Research Division. The school board member. (Bul. Vol. XI, No. 1.) p.1–40. 1933. The Association. $.25.

New York (State) Associated Academic Principals. Proceedings: 48th annual meeting, December 28, 29, 30, 1932. 109p. 1933. David G. Allen, c/o High School Council of School Superintendents, Boonville, N. Y. $.15.

New York (State) University. Transportation. (Bul. No. 1013. Law pamphlet 8.) 14p. 1933. The Author.

Nicholas, Albert. Salaries in the accredited public high schools in Illinois, school year 1932–1933; prepared under the direction of A. W. Clevenger and O. F. Weber. (Bul. Vol. XXX, No. 23.) 24p. 1933. Univ. of Ill. Apply.

Oklahoma. State Department of Education. Handbook for county and city superintendents of schools. (Bul. No. 134.) 106p. n.d. The Department.

Oklahoma. State Department of Education. A uniform financial procedure for general fund expenditures in Oklahoma schools. (Bul. No. 135). 52p. 1933. The Department.

Pasadena, California. Board of Education. The six-four-four plan of school organization in Pasadena, California: a report to the Board of Education, the patrons, and the staff, by W. M. Proctor. 201p. 1933. The Author. $.75.

Pearman, W. I. Support of state educational programs, by dedication of specific revenues and by general revenue appropriations. (Cont. to educ. No. 591.) 141p. 1933. Teachers College, Columbia. $1.50.

Pennsylvania. Department of Public Instruction. Cumulative pupil personnel records, elementary and secondary schools. (Bul. No. 81.) 23p. 1933. The Department, Harrisburg, Pa.

Pitkin, R. S. Public school support in the United States during periods of economic depression. 143p. 1933. Stephen Daye Press, Brattleboro, Vt. $1.50.

Powell, O. E. Educational returns at varying expenditure levels; a basis for relating expenditures to outcomes in education. (Cont. to educ. No. 573.) 54p. 1933. Teachers College, Columbia. $1.50.

Reller, T. L. State certification for administrative positions: Pt. I—Trend and present status of legal provisions. Pt. II—Analysis of the requirements for certification. 32p. 1933. Univ. of Pa. Division of Educ. Administration. School of Educ.

*Rice, G. A., Conrad, C. C., and Fleming, Paul. The administration of public high schools through their personnel. 723p. 1933. Macmillan. $2.75.

Sahlstrom, J. W. Some code controls of school building construction in American cities. (Cont. to educ. No. 581.) 153p. 1933. Teachers College, Columbia. $1.50.

Seyfried, J. E. The contractual status of California city school superintendents. (Publications in educ. Vol. VII, No. 2.) p.63–144. 1933. Univ. of Cal. Press. $1.00.

Smith, H. L., and Noffsinger, F. R. Bibliography of school buildings, grounds, and equipment, Pt. II. (School of educ. bul. Vol. IX, No. 2.) 182p. 1933. Bur. of Cooperative Research, Ind. Univ. $.75.

Smith, H. L., and Noffsinger, F. B. Bibliography of school buildings, grounds, and equipment, Pt. III. (School of educ. bul. Vol. IX, No. 3.) 130p. 1933. Bur. of Cooperative Research, Ind. Univ. $.50.

Snavely, T. R., and others. State grants-in-aid in Virginia. (Univ. of Va. Institute for research in the social sciences. Institute monograph, No. 15.) 244p. 1933. Appleton-Century. $2.50.

Soper, W. W. Development of state support of education in New York State. (Bul. No. 1019.) 69p. 1933. Univ. of State of N. Y. $.25.

Spencer, E. R. Rural school yard and its beautification. 79p. n.d. Interstate Printing Co., Danville, Ill. $1.50.

Strayer, G. D., and Engelhardt, N. L. Standards for elementary school buildings. Rev. ed. 181p. 1933. Teachers College, Columbia. $1.60.

Swift, F. H. European policies of financing public educational institutions; France. (Publications in educ. Vol. VIII, No. 1.) 179p. 1933. Univ. of Cal. Press. $1.75.

U. S. Office of Education. Centralized purchasing and distribution of school supplies, by Timon Covert. (Circular, No. 112.) *Mimeographed.* 12p. 1933. The Office. Gratis.

U. S. Office of Education. City schools and the economic situation, by E. M. Foster and L. B. Herlihy. (Circular, No. 124.) *Mimeographed.* 24p. 1933. The Office. Gratis.

U. S. Office of Education. The deepening crisis in education. (Leaflet, No. 44.) 15p. 1933. Supt. of Doc. $.05.

U. S. Office of Education. Economies in class and school organization, by M. M. Proffitt and David Segel. (Circular, No. 113.) *Mimeographed.* 9p. 1933. The Office. Gratis.

U. S. Office of Education. Economies through budgeting and accounting, by E. M. Foster and L. B. Herlihy. (Circular, No. 116.) *Mimeographed.* 11p. 1933. The Office. Gratis.

U. S. Office of Education. The effects of the economic depression on education in other countries, by J. F. Abel. (Bul. 1933. No. 14.) 37p. 1933. Supt. of Doc. $.05.

U. S. Office of Education. Larger units for educational administration; a potential economy. (Pamphlet, No. 45.) 43p. 1933. Supt. of Doc. $.05.

U. S. Office of Education. Operation and maintenance of the school plant, by E. M. Foster and L. B. Herlihy. (Circular, No. 115.) *Mimeographed.* 10p. 1933. The Office. Gratis.

U. S. Office of Education. Per capita costs in city schools for 1931–32, by L. M. Comstock. (Circular, No. 73.) *Mimeographed.* 12p. 1933. The Office. Gratis.

U. S. Office of Education. Some effects of the economic situation on city schools by W. S. Deffenbaugh and E. M. Foster. (Circular, No. 79.) *Mimeographed.* 16p. 1933. The Office. Gratis.

U. S. Office of Education. Small city school systems, 1930–1932; comparative data, by L. B. Herlihy. (Pamphlet, No. 46.) 14p. 1933. Supt. of Doc. $.05.

U. S. Office of Education. National Survey of School Finance. Research problems in school finance. 164p. 1933. Amer. Council on Educ., 744 Jackson Pl., Washington, D. C. $1.00.

Waller, J. F. Outside demands and pressures on the

public schools. (Cont. to educ. No. 542.) 151p. 1933. Teachers College, Columbia. $1.50.

Waller, J. F. Public relations for the public schools: a manual based on a study of good practice. 112p. 1933. MacCrellish & Quigley Co., Trenton, N. J. $1.50.

Williams, R. C. Determining per-pupil costs for tuition purposes. (Research bul. No. 13.) 9p. 1933. State Dept. of Public Instruction, Des Moines, Ia. Gratis.

Williams, R. C. Unit levies and costs: school years 1930–1932. (Research bul. No. 11.) 9p. 1933. State Dept. of Public Instruction, Des Moines, Ia. Gratis.

Wrightstone, J. W. Stimulation of educational undertakings: a study of school support in New York cities and villages under earmarked and non-earmarked state subsidy plans. (Cont. to educ. No. 562.) 76p. 1933. Teachers College, Columbia. $1.50.

Young, L. P. The administration of merit-type teachers' salary schedules. (Cont. to educ. No. 552.) 104p. 1933. Teachers College, Columbia. $1.50.

(3) Supervision

Altus, W. D. Study of the status of the county superintendent in Kansas. (Studies in educ. No. 7.) 52p. 1933. Kan. State Teachers' College, Emporia, Kan. $.20.

*Breed, F. S. Classroom organization and management. (Measurement and adjustment series, ed. by L. M. Terman.) 472p. 1933. World Bk. Co. $2.00.

Massachusetts. Department of Education. Supervision of instruction in junior high schools. (Bul. No. 7.) 27p. 1933. The Department. $.10.

Michigan Education Association. Department of Elementary School Principals. Rethinking supervision: a cooperative Michigan project. Sixth yearbook. 158p. 1933. The Association, Lansing, Mich. $1.00.

*National Education Association. Department of Superintendence. Eleventh yearbook: educational leadership; progress and possibilities. 528p. 1933. The Association. $2.00.

*National Education Association. Department of Supervisors and Directors of Instruction. Sixth yearbook: effective instructional leadership; a study of the problem of integration. 183p. 1933. Teachers College, Columbia. $2.00.

(4) Reports, Surveys, Statistics and Legislation

American Bankers Association. Savings Division. School savings banking during the school year of 1932–1933: fourteenth annual report on systems throughout the United States with honor roll and comparative statistics. 31p. 1933. Amer. Bankers Assn., 22 East 40th St., N. Y. C. $.25.

American Educational Research Association. The legal basis of education. (Review of educ. research, Vol. III, No. 5.) p.369–482. 1933. The Association, N. E. A. $1.00.

Brumbaugh, A. J. Authority of boards of education in the administration of pupils and teachers as defined by the courts. Badger. $3.00.

Carnegie Endowment for International Peace. Division of Intercourse and Education. Annual report of the director for the year 1932. 63p. 1933. The Endowment. Gratis.

Carnegie Foundation for the Advancement of Teaching. Twenty-eighth annual report of the president and of the treasurer. 189p. 1933. The Foundation. Gratis.

College Entrance Examination Board. Thirty-third annual report of the secretary, 1933. 196p. 1933. The Board. $.25.

Commonwealth Fund. Fourteenth annual report. 79p. 1933. The Fund. Gratis.

Educational Press Association of America. Committee on Standards. Ninth yearbook. 31p. 1933. The Association, N. E. A. Gratis.

Educational Records Bureau. Committee on the Relation of Elementary and Secondary Schools. Second report. *Mimeographed.* 6p. 1933. The Bureau. Gratis.

Educational Records Bureau. School and College Relations Committee. Second report. *Mimeographed.* 18p. 1933. The Bureau. Gratis.

Franciscan Educational Conference. Report of the fifteenth annual meeting, Marathon, Wisconsin, June 30th, July 1st, 2nd, 1933. (Vol. XV, No. 15.) 177p. 1933. The Conference, Office of the Sec'y, Capuchin College, Brookland, Washington, D. C. $1.25.

George, J. B. The influence of court decisions in shaping school policies in Mississippi. (Cont. to educ. No. 113.) 265p. 1933. George Peabody College for Teachers. $1.50.

Holy, T. C., and others. Survey of the Ohio soldiers' and sailors' orphans' home. (Bur. of educ. research monographs, No. 18.) 178p. 1933. Ohio State Univ., Bur. of Educ. Research. $2.00 cloth; $1.50 paper.

Horack, F. E., and others. First yearbook of school law, 1933. 106p. 1933. M. M. Chambers, Ohio State Univ. $1.00.

Illinois. University. Report of the committee on admissions from secondary schools for the year 1932–1933. (Bul. Vol. XXX, No. 41.) 15p. 1933. The University.

Illinois Vocational Association. A report of the convention at Hotel Sherman, Chicago, November 4 and 5, 1932; ed. by L. J. Lease. (Bul. No. 4.) 64p. 1933. The Association, H. O. Meyer, Sec'y., Tilden Technical High School, Chicago, Ill. $.20.

Institute of International Education. Fourteenth annual report of the director, 1933. (Bul. No. 4, series 14.) 71p. 1933. The Institute, 2 W. 45th St., N. Y. C. $.10.

Johnsen, J. E. Federal aid to education. (Reference shelf, Vol. IX, No. 3.) 213p. 1933. Wilson, H. W. $.90.

Kentucky. Department of Education. Report of the Kentucky educational commission. (Educ. bul. Vol. I, No. 8.) 324p. 1933. The Department. Gratis.

Kentucky. University. Proceedings of the tenth annual educational conference. (Bur. of school service bul. Vol. VI, No. 2.) 90p. 1933. The Author, Campus Bookstore, Lexington, Ky. $.50.

Maurer, Harold. A statistical study of sixty Ohio cities and exempted villages in Garfield Heights, Ohio. *Mimeographed.* 16p. 1933. Garfield Heights City Schools, Office of the Supt., 4900 Turney Rd., Cleveland, Ohio. Gratis.

Middle States Association of Colleges and Secondary Schools. Proceedings of the 46th annual convention, 1932. 110p. 1933. The Association, Dr. G. W. McClelland, Univ. of Pa. $.25.

National Association of Public School Business Officials. Proceedings of the twenty-second annual meeting, Pittsburgh, Pennsylvania, May 16th–19th, 1933. 130p. 1933. The Association, J. S. Mount, Sec'y., Trenton, N. J. $2.00.

National Catholic Educational Association. Report of the proceedings and addresses of the thirtieth annual meeting, St. Paul, Minnesota, June 26–29, 1933. (Bul. Vol. XXX, No. 1.) 664p. 1933. The Association. $.25.

National Conference of Social Work. Proceedings at the fifty-ninth annual session held in Philadelphia, Pa., May 15–21, 1932. 694p. 1933. Univ. of Chicago Press. $3.00.

National Education Association. Booklet of information, 1933–34. 23p. 1933. The Association. Gratis.

National Education Association. Proceedings of the seventy-first annual meeting held at Chicago, Illinois, July 1–7, 1933. Vol. 71. 1000p. 1933. The Association. $3.00.

National Education Association. Weathering the storm: annual report of the secretary including the reports of the directors of divisions, Chicago, Illinois, 1933. 38p. 1933. The Association. $.25.

National Education Association. Committee on Retirement Allowances. Report. *Mimeographed.* 80p. 1933. The Association. $.25.

National Education Association. Department of Superintendence. Official report, 1933. 309p. 1933. The Association. $1.00.

National Education Association. Department of Superintendence and Research Division. School and city current expenses compared, 1931—310 cities above 30,000 in population. (Circular, No. 9.) 11p. 1933. The Association. With subscription to Educ. research service.

National Education Association. Department of Superintendence and Research Division. State school legislation, 1932. (Circular, No. 5.) *Mimeographed.* 8p. 1933. The Association. With subscription to Educ. research service.

National Student Federation of America. Annual report, 1932–33; projected program, 1934. 15p. 1933. The Federation, 218 Madison Ave., N. Y. C.

New York (State) University. Duties of officers of common-school districts. (Bul. No. 1022, Law pamphlet, No. 4.) 30p. 1933. The Author. $.05.

Oregon. Department of Education. Oregon non-high school district law; a manual of suggestions and recommendations for use by boards of education of non-high school districts, school boards of high school districts, high school principals and superintendents, June 1933. 16p. 1933. The Department.

Rhode Island. Department of Education. Survey of public schools of Barrington, Rhode Island, requested by the School committee of the town; report of the Survey commission, 1932. (R. I. educ. circular.) 18p. 1933. The Department, Providence, R. I. Gratis while supply lasts.

Shorewood, Wis. Salary Committee. Suburban school salaries, 1932–33. 24p. 1933. School District No. 4, 1701 E. Capital Drive, Milwaukee, Wis. $.03 postage; Ltd. supply.

U. S. Office of Education. Indexed list of city school reports, 1930–31, by B. Y. Hebb. (Circular, No. 81.) *Mimeographed.* 17p. 1933. The Office. Gratis.

U. S. Office of Education. Laws relating to the releasing of pupils from public schools for religious instruction, by W. W. Keesecker. (Pamphlet, No. 39.) 17p. 1933. Supt. of Doc. $.05.

U. S. Office of Education. Legislative action in 1933 affecting education, by W. W. Keesecker. (Circular No. 85.) 7p. 1933. The Office. Gratis.

U. S. Office of Education. Legislative action in 1933 affecting education, by W. W. Keesecker. (Circular No. 87.) *Mimeographed.* 17p. 1933. The Office. Gratis.

U. S. Office of Education. Legislative action in 1933 affecting education, by W. W. Keesecker. (Circular No. 89.) *Mimeographed.* 15p. 1933. The Office. Gratis.

U. S. Office of Education. Legislative action in 1933 affecting education, by W. W. Keesecker. (Circular No. 122.) *Mimeographed.* 17p. 1933. The Office. Gratis.

U. S. Office of Education. Public education during the past year and prospects for the coming year reported in July, 1933, by 33 states and the District of Columbia. (Circular No. 119.) *Mimeographed.* 41p. 1933. The Office. Gratis.

Williams, R. C. Some facts about Iowa schools; a brief tabular summary of various reports concerning the operation of Iowa's public schools for the biennium ending June 30, 1932. (Research bul. No. 10.) 8p. 1933. State Dept. of Public Instruction, Des Moines, Ia. Gratis.

(5) CONDUCT AND CHARACTER FORMATION

Brown, Marion. Leadership among high school pupils; a study of pupils selected by fellow pupils to positions of leadership in a certain high school. (Cont. to educ. No. 559.) 166p. 1933. Teachers College, Columbia. $1.75.

*Heaton, K. L. The character emphasis in education: a collection of materials and methods. 415p. 1933. Univ. of Chicago Press. $3.00.

Herriot, F. W. Scope and relationship of character building agencies dealing with high school students, Montclair, New Jersey. 223p. 1933. Printed by Montclair Printing Co., Montclair, N. J.

Morgan, A. L., *comp.* Bible readings in character and citizenship. 354p. 1933. Cokesbury. $2.50 cloth; $3.50 De Luxe.

Smith, H. L., and Krueger, L. M. A brief summary of literature on leadership. (School of educ. bul. Vol. IX, No. 4.) 80p. 1933. Ind. Univ.

Stephens, J. M. The influence of the school on the individual. 106p. 1933. Edwards Bros.

(6) PSYCHOLOGY OF CHILDHOOD AND YOUTH

Alschuler, R. H. Two to six. 160p. 1933. Morrow. $1.50.

American Home Economics Association. Annotated bibliography on child development, parent education and family relationships. Rev. ed. *Mimeographed.* 24p. 1933. The Association, 620 Mills Bldg., Washington, D. C. $.10.

American Home Economics Association. List of pamphlets and magazines on child development, parent education and family relationships. Rev. ed. *Mimeographed.* 9p. 1933. The Association, 620 Mills Bldg., Washington, D. C. $.06.

American Home Economics Association. Selected list of books and pamphlets on child development, personal hygiene and sex education, social and personality adjustment, family relationships, and home management. *Mimeographed.*. 15p. 1933. The Association, 620 Mills Bldg., Washington, D. C. $.06.

American Home Economics Association. Trends in teaching child development and family relationships in the high school. *Mimeographed.* 17p. 1933. The Association, 620 Mills Bldg., Washington, D. C. Gratis.

Anderson, H. H. Behavior problems of the normal child. (Extension bul. No. 307.) 16p. 1933. Univ. of Ia. $.10.

*Anderson, J. E., *ed.* Century childhood library. 3 vols. 1933. Appleton-Century.
- Anderson, J. E. Happy childhood: the development and guidance of children and youth. 321p. $2.50.
- Foster, J. C. Busy childhood: guidance through play and activity. 303p. $2.50.
- Stuart, H. C. Healthy childhood: guidance for physical care. 393p. $2.50.

Arlitt, A. H. Adolescent psychology. 246p. 1933. Amer. Bk. Co. $2.25.

Association for Childhood Education. Yearbook; fortieth annual meeting, Denver, Colorado, June 28–July 1, 1933. 48p. 1933. The Association, 1201 16th St., N. W., Washington, D. C. $.25.

Bailey, E. W., and others. Outline for study of children in schools. 248p. 1933. McGraw-Hill. $2.25.

Baudouin, Charles. The mind of the child. Trans. by E. and C. Paul. 282p. 1933. Dodd. $3.00.

Bayley, Nancy. The California first-year mental scale. (Syllabus series, No. 243.) 24p. 1933. Univ. of Cal. Press, Institute of Child Welfare. $.50.

Bayley, Nancy. Mental growth during the first three years; a developmental study of sixty-one children by repeated tests. (Genetic psychology monographs, Vol. XIV, No. 1.) 92p. 1933. Clark Univ. Press. $2.00.

Booth, Meyrick. Youth and Sex. 299p. 1933. Morrow. $2.00.

Caille, R. K. Resistant behavior of preschool children. (Child development monographs, No. 11.) 142p. 1933. Teachers College, Columbia. $1.50.

Cameron, H. C. The nervous child at school. (Oxford medical publications.) 160p. 1933. Oxford Univ. Press. $1.75.

Chadwick, Mary. Adolescent girlhood. 303p. 1933. Day. $3.50.

*Charters, W. W., and others. Motion pictures and youth: the Payne fund studies. 7 vols. 1933. Macmillan.
- Blumer, Herbert. Movies and conduct. 257p. $1.50.
- Blumer, Herbert, and Hauser, P. M. Movies, delinquency and crime. 233p. $1.50.
- Charters, W. W., and others. Motion pictures and youth; a summary. (and) Getting ideas from the movies, by P. W. Holaday and G. D. Stoddard. 2 Vols. in 1. 66p.; 102p. $1.50.
- Dale, Edgar. How to appreciate motion pictures: a manual of motion picture criticism prepared for high school students. 243p. $1.20.
- Dysinger, W. S., and Ruckmick, C. A. The emotional responses of children to the motion picture situation (and) Motion pictures and standards of morality, by C. C. Peters. 2 vols in 1. 122p; 285p. $2.00.
- Peterson, R. C., and Thurstone, L. L. Motion pictures and the social attitudes of children (and) Social conduct and attitudes of movie fans, by F. K. Shuttleworth, and M. A. May. 2 vols. in 1. 75p; 142p. $1.50.
- Renshaw, Samuel, and others. Children's sleep. 212p. $2.00.

Chicago Association for Child Study and Parent Education. Developing attitudes in children; proceedings of the Midwest conference, March, 1932. 156p. 1933. Univ. of Chicago Press. $1.50.

Driscoll, G. P. The developmental status of the preschool child as a prognosis of future development. (Child development monographs, No. 13.) 111p. 1933. Teachers College, Columbia. $1.50.

Drury, S. S. School, home and company. 238p. 1933. Farrar & Rinehart. $2.25.

Freeman, G. L., and Freeman, R. S. The child and his picture book: a discussion of the preferences of the nursery child. 102p. 1933. Northwestern Univ. Press, Chicago, Ill. $1.25.

Furfey, P. H. Understanding your school-age child. (Child welfare Pamphlet No. 18.) Reprinted from Toward understanding children II: a report of the Fifth annual Iowa conference on child development and parent education. 13p. 1933. Univ. of Ia. $.05.

Gale, A. V. Children's preferences for colors, color combinations and color arrangements. 60p. 1933. Univ. of Chicago Press. $1.25.

*Gruenberg, S. M., and Gruenberg, B. C. Parents, children and money; learning to spend, save and earn. 219p. 1933. Viking Press. $1.75.

Hagman, E. P. Companionships of preschool children. (New series, No. 255. Studies in child welfare, Vol. VII, No. 4.) 69p. 1933. Univ. of Ia. $1.00 paper; $1.35 cloth.

Howden, R. A. Child upbringing and the new psychology. 105p. 1933. Oxford Univ. Press. $1.00.

Humphreys, P. A., and Hosey, Gertrude. A workbook in child psychology. 120p. 1933. Smith, R. R. $.60.

Iowa State University. What the University of Iowa is doing for children. (Bul. New series, No. 689.) 21p. 1933. Univ. of Ia. Gratis.

Isaacs, Susan. Social development in young children: a study of beginnings. (Behavior of young children, Vol. II.) 480p. 1933. Harcourt. $4.00.

*Jersild, A. T. Child psychology. 462p. 1933. Prentice-Hall. $3.00.

Jersild, A. T., Markey, F. V., and Jersild, C. L. Children's fears, dreams, wishes, daydreams, likes, dislikes, pleasant and unpleasant memories; a study by the interview method of 400 children aged 5 to 12. (Child development monographs, No. 12.) 172p. 1933. Teachers College, Columbia. $1.50.

Moser, J. G. Simple methods of child training. p.13–78. 1933. Sather Gate Bk. Shop, 2271 Telegraph Ave., Berkeley, Cal. $1.50.

Murchison, Carl, *ed.* A handbook of child psychology. 2nd ed. rev. 956p. 1933. Clark Univ. Press. $5.00.

National Research Council. Committee on Child Development. Fourth conference on research in child development, the University of Chicago, June 22–24, 1933. *Mimeographed.* 181p. 1933. The Council. Gratis.

Norsworthy, Naomi, and Whitley, M. T. The psychology of childhood. Rev. ed. 515p. 1933. Macmillan. $1.80.

Richardson, A. E., and Miller, M. L. Child development and parental education in home economics: a survey of schools and colleges. 125p. 1933. Amer. Home Economics Assn., 101 E. 20th St., Baltimore, Md.

Richmond, W. V. The adolescent boy: a book for parents and teachers. 233p. 1933. Farrar & Rinehart. $2.50.

*Smithies, E. M. Case studies of normal adolescent girls. 284p. 1933. Appleton-Century. $2.00.

Thom, D. A. Guiding the adolescent. (U. S. Dept. of labor. Children's bureau publication, No. 225.) 94p. 1933. Supt. of Doc. $.10.

Tucker, B. R. Adolescence; life's spring cleaning time. 121p. 1933. Stratford. $1.25.

U. S. Office of Education. Educational activities for the young child in the home, by Rowna Hansen. (Circular, No. 86.) *Mimeographed.* 15p. 1933. The Office. Gratis.

U. S. Office of Education. Practical aids for study groups and for individuals interested in child care and training, by E. C. Lombard. (Circular, No. 82.) *Mimeographed.* 9p. 1933. The Office. Gratis.

Wagoner, L. C. The development of learning in young children. 322p. 1933. McGraw-Hill. $2.50.

(7) Educational Psychology

American Educational Research Association. Mental and physical development. (Review of educ. research, Vol. III, No. 2.) p.81–181. 1933. The Association, N. E. A. $1.00.

Beebe, E. L. Motor learning of children in hand and eye coordination with introduction of prismatic deflection. (Thesis.) 25p. 1933. Johns Hopkins Press. $.25.

Benson, C. E., and others. Psychology for teachers. Rev. ed. 490p. 1933. Ginn. $2.00.

Brown, A. E. Workbook in educational psychology. 226p. 1933. Macmillan. $1.35.

Coxe, W. W. Directed study; a review of the theory and an analysis of the practices in New York state schools. (Bul. No. 1025.) 52p. 1933. Univ. of State of N. Y. $.10.

Dewey, John. How we think; a restatement of the relation of reflective thinking to the educative process. Rev. ed. 301p. 1933. Heath. $2.00.

Hamilton, D. W. A workbook in educational psychology. 136p. 1933. Norton. $1.00.

*Hollingworth, H. L. Educational psychology. 540p. 1933. Appleton-Century. $3.00.

Jordon, A. M. Educational psychology. Rev. ed. 522p. 1933. Holt. $2.50.

Kelly, W. A. Educational psychology. 501p. 1933. Bruce Pub. Co. $2.40.

Lehman, H. C., and Stoke, S. M. A work book in educational psychology. 152p. 1933. Prentice-Hall. $.80.

Mace, C. A. The psychology of study. 96p. 1933. McBride. $.80.

Mattson, M. L. Relation between the complexity of the habit to be acquired and the form of the learning curve in young children. (Genetic psychology monographs, Vol. XIII, No. 4.) p.299–398. 1933. Clark Univ. Press. $2.00.

Norem, G. M., and Wiederaenders, M. F. Studies in the psychology of learning. (New series, No. 260. Educ. psychology series, No. 1.) 75p. 1933. Univ. of Ia. $.75.

Patry, F. L. Methodology in the formulation of mental hygiene case studies for teachers and teachers in training. 73p. 1933. Univ. of State of N. Y. $.20.

*Powers, F. F., and Uhl, W. L. Psychological principles of education. 510p. 1933. Appleton-Century. $2.50.

Pratt, G. K. Mental hygiene and the individual child. (Child welfare pamphlet, No. 20.) 10p. 1933. Univ. of Ia. $.05.

*Pressey, S. L. Psychology and the new education. 594p. 1933. Harper. $2.25.

Remmers, H. H. Learning, effort, and attitudes as affected by three methods of instruction in elementary psychology. (Bul. Vol. XXXIII, No. 6. Studies in higher educ. No. 21.) 48p. 1933. Purdue Univ., Division of Educ. Reference. $.50.

Thorndike, E. L., and others. An experimental study of rewards. (Cont. to educ. No. 580.) 72p. 1933. Teachers College, Columbia. $1.50.

(8) Educational Tests and Measurements

American Council on Education. Educational measurement and guidance; report of the second conference under the auspices of the Cooperative test service and the Committee on personnel methods of the American council on education and the Educational records bureau. 148p. 1933. The Author, 744 Jackson Pl., Washington, D. C. $.50.

American Educational Research Association. Educational tests and their use. (Review of educ. research, Vol. III, No. 1.) 80p. 1933. The Association, N. E. A. $1.00.

Arthur, Grace. A point scale of performance tests. Vol. II. The process of standardization. 106p. 1933. Commonwealth Fund. $1.50.

Boynton, P. L. Intelligence: its manifestations and measurement. 466p. 1933. Appleton-Century. $2.50.

Bregman, E. O. The performance of student nurses on tests of intelligence. (Nursing educ. New series, bul. 2.) 32p. 1933. Teachers College, Columbia, Bur. of Publications, Dept. of Nursing Educ. $.55.

Brown, Ralph. Mathematical difficulties of students of educational statistics. (Cont. to educ. No. 569.) 64p. 1933. Teachers College, Columbia. $1.50.

College Entrance Examination Board. Commission of Scholastic Aptitude Tests. Eighth annual report, 1933. 24p. 1933. The Board, 431 W. 117th St., N. Y. C. Gratis.

Dickenson, H. F. Primary and secondary discriminative reactions. (Cont. to educ. No. 116.) 55p. 1933. George Peabody College for Teachers. $1.35.

Educational Records Bureau. Achievement testing in independent schools: a report on the cooperative testing program of April, 1933. (Bul. No. 10.) 46p. and charts. 1933. The Bureau. $1.50.

Educational Records Bureau. Achievement testing in public and independent secondary schools: a report on the cooperative public school testing program of May–June, 1933. (Bul. No. 11.) 67p. 1933. The Bureau. $1.00.

Educational Records Bureau. Handbook for independent schools. *Mimeographed.* 90p. 1933. The Bureau. $1.50.

Educational Records Bureau. 1933 fall testing program in independent schools. (Bul. No. 12.) 66p. and charts. 1933. The Bureau. $1.50.

Findley, W. G. Specialization of verbal facility at the college entrance level: a comparative study of scientific and literary vocabularies. (Cont. to educ. No. 567.) 76p. 1933. Teachers College, Columbia. $1.50.

*Garrett, H. E., and Schneck, M. R. Psychological tests, methods, and results. 235p. 1933. Harper. $2.75.

Harter, R. S., and Smeltzer, C. H. Self-instructional manual in handling test scores. 58p. 1933. Holt. $1.25.

Hildreth, G. H., *comp.* Bibliography of mental tests and rating scales. 242p. 1933. Psychological Corp., 522 5th Ave., N. Y. C. $3.00.

Jones, H. E., and Conrad, H. S. Growth and decline of intelligence; a study of a homogeneous group between the ages of ten and sixty. (Genetic psychology monographs, Vol. XIII, No. 3.) p.223–298. 1933. Clark Univ. Press. $2.00.

Kansas State Teachers College. The all-Kansas state contest. (Bul. of information, No. 115.) unp. 1933. The College, Emporia, Kan. Gratis.

Kansas State Teachers College. A manual of standard tests. (Bul. of information, No. 119.) 34p. 1933. The College, Emporia, Kan. Gratis.

Kansas State Teachers College. Report of the seventeenth every pupil scholarship test, January 10, 1933. (Bul. of information, No. 118.) unp. 1933. The College, Emporia, Kan. Gratis.

Kansas State Teachers College. Report of the eighteenth nation-wide every pupil scholarship test for high schools and elementary schools, April 5, 1933. (Bul. of information, No. 121.) unp. 1933. The College, Emporia, Kan. Gratis.

Kansas State Teachers College. Studies in measurements and standardization. (Teaching, Whole No. 89.) 33p. 1933. The College, Emporia, Kan. Gratis.

Keeler, L. W. Results of the testing program in the branch county public schools and in the Michigan state public school. (Bur. of educ. reference and research bul. No. 147.) 40p. 1933. Univ. of Mich., School of Educ. $.30.

Keeler, L. W. Results of the testing program in the Grass Lake public school. (Bur. of educ. reference and research bul. No. 143.) 38p. 1933. Univ. of Mich., School of Educ. $.35.

Krey, A. C., and Johnson, P. O. Differential functions of examinations. (Bul. Vol. XXXVI, No. 4.) 23p. 1933. Univ. of Minn., Committee on Educ. Research. Gratis.

Milde, P. R. Simple technique for permanent new-type tests. 15p. 1933. The Author, 1707 Bull St., Savannah, Ga. $.25.

Portenier, L. G. Pupils of low mentality in high school. (Cont. to educ. No. 568.) 109p. 1933. Teachers College, Columbia. $1.50.

Porteus, S. D. The Maze tests and mental differences. 212p. 1933. Smith Printing & Publishing House, Vineland, N. J. $2.50.

Roberts, K. E. Learning in preschool and orphanage children: an experimental study of ability to solve different situations according to the same plan. (New series, No. 251, Studies in child welfare, Vol. VII, No. 3.) 94p. 1933. Univ. of Ia. $1.35 cloth; $1.00 paper.

Twentieth annual conference on educational measurements. (School of educ. bul., Vol. X, No. 1.) 98p. 1933. Ind. Univ. $.50.

U. S. Office of Education. National and state cooperative high-school testing programs, by David Segel. (Bul. 1933, No. 9.) 47p. 1933. Supt. of Doc. $.05.

Wood, B. D. Basic considerations in educational testing. 18p. 1933. Educ. Records Bur., Committee on Educational Testing. Gratis.

Woody, Clifford. Results of the testing program in the Ironwood public schools. (Bur. of educ. reference and research bul. No. 146.) 114p. 1933. School of Educ., Univ. of Mich. $.50.

(9) SPECIAL EDUCATION AND EXCEPTIONAL CHILDREN

Cutsforth, T. D. The blind in school and society: a psychological study. 263p. 1933. Appleton-Century. $2.50.

Doll, E. A. The problem of the feeble-minded in New Jersey: the relation of the public schools to the public institutions. (Publication 23.) Reprints from Training School bul. Nov., Dec., 1932, Jan. 1933. 31p. 1933. Dept. of Institutions and Agencies, Trenton, N. J. Gratis.

Dransfield, J. E. Administration of enrichment to superior children in the typical classroom. (Cont. to educ. No. 558.) 107p. 1933. Teachers College, Columbia. $1.50.

Embree, E. R. Julius Rosenwald fund; review for the two-year period, 1931–1933. 47p. 1933. Julius Rosenwald Fund, 4901 Ellis Ave., Chicago, Ill. Gratis.

McCuistion, Fred. Higher education of negroes. (A summary.) 40p. 1933. Southern Assn. Colleges and Secondary Schools, 517 Cotton States Bldg., Nashville, Tenn. Gratis.

MacKane, Keith. A comparison of the intelligence of deaf and hearing children; a study of the reactions of comparable groups of deaf and hearing children to three performance scales and a non-language test. (Cont. to educ. No. 585.) 47p. 1933. Teachers College, Columbia. $1.50.

National League of Nursing Education. Education Committee. Nursing school faculty; duties, qualifications, and preparation. 123p. 1933. The Committee, 450 7th Ave., N. Y. C. $.75.

National Survey of the Education of Teachers. Education of negro teachers, by Ambrose Caliver. Vol. IV. (U. S. Office of Educ. Bul. 1933, No. 10.) 123p. 1933. Gov't. Print. Office. $.10.

New York Institute for the Education of the Blind. Year-book, 1933. Ninety-eighth report of the board of managers, report of the principal general information. 51p. 1933. The Author, 999 Pelham Parkway, N. Y. C. Apply.

Peabody Conference on Education and Race Relations. Education and racial adjustment; report of the second conference, July 21–23, 1932. 63p. 1933. Executive Committee of the Conference, 703 Standard Bldg., Atlanta, Ga. $.10.

Thurmond, Sarah. Comparison of the intelligence and achievement of twelve-year old negro children in the rural schools of Clarke County, Georgia. (Bul. Vol. XXXIII, No. 11c. Phelps-Stokes fellowship studies, No. 12.) 44p. 1933. Univ. of Ga., Division of Publications, Athens, Ga. $.50.

U. S. Office of Education. Annotated bibliography on the education and psychology of exceptional children, comp. by E. H. Martens. (Circular No. 120, sup. to pamphlet No. 23, 1931.) *Mimeographed.* 7p. 1933. The Office. Gratis.

U. S. Office of Education. A background study of negro college students, by Ambrose Caliver. (Bul. 1933, No. 8.) 132p. 1933. Supt. of Doc. $.10.

U. S. Office of Education. Blind and partially seeing children. (Circular, No. 120, pt. 5.) *Mimeographed.* 8p. 1933. The Office. Gratis.

U. S. Office of Education. Crippled children. (Circular, No. 120, pt. 7.) *Mimeographed.* 7p. 1933. The Office. Gratis.

U. S. Office of Education. Deaf and hard-of-hearing children. (Circular, No. 120, pt. 6.) *Mimeographed.* 11p. 1933. The Office. Gratis.

U. S. Office of Education. Delicate children. (Circular, No. 120, pt. 9.) *Mimeographed.* 3p. 1933. The Office. Gratis.

U. S. Office of Education. The education of native and minority groups: a bibliography, 1923–1932, by K. M. Cook and F. E. Reynolds. (Bul. 1933, No. 12.) 57p. 1933. Supt. of Doc. $.05.

U. S. Office of Education. The education of Spanish-speaking children in five southwestern states, by Annie Reynolds. (Bul. 1933, No. 11.) 64p. 1933. Supt. of Doc. $.10.

U. S. Office of Education. Gifted children. (Circular, No. 120, pt. 3.) *Mimeographed.* 6p. 1933. The Office. Gratis.

U. S. Office of Education. Group activities for mentally retarded children. A symposium, compiled by E. H. Martens. (Bul. 1933, No. 7.) 146p. 1933. Supt. of Doc. $.15.

U. S. Office of Education. Mentally deficient children. (Circular, No. 120, pt. 2.) *Mimeographed.* 10p. 1933. The Office. Gratis.

U. S. Office of Education. Negro and the emergency

in education, by Ambrose Caliver. (Circular, No. 123.) *Mimeographed.* 5p. 1933. The Office. Gratis.
U. S. Office of Education. Organization for exceptional children within state departments of education, by E. H. Martens. (Pamphlet, No. 42.) 35p. 1933. Supt. of Doc. $.05.
U. S. Office of Education. Public and private residential schools for delinquent children, 1930–31. (Circular, No. 83.) *Mimeographed.* 13p. 1933. The Office. Gratis.
U. S. Office of Education. Public and private residential schools for mentally deficient and epileptics, 1930–31. (Circular, No. 76.) *Mimeographed.* 16p. 1933. The Office. Gratis.
U. S. Office of Education. Rural elementary education among negroes under Jeanes supervising teachers, by Ambrose Caliver. (Bul. 1933, No. 5.) 57p. 1933. Supt. of Doc. $.10.
U. S. Office of Education. Secondary education for negroes. (Bul. 1932, No. 17, Monograph, No. 7.) 121p. 1933. Supt. of Doc. $.10.
U. S. Office of Education. Socially maladjusted children. (Circular, No. 120, pt. 4.) *Mimeographed.* 20p. 1933. The Office. Gratis.
U. S. Office of Education. Speech defective children. (Circular, No. 120, pt. 8.) *Mimeographed.* 5p. 1933. The Office. Gratis.
U. S. Office of Education. State and private schools for the blind, 1930–31. (Circular, No. 70.) *Mimeographed.* 11p. 1933. The Office. Gratis.
U. S. Office of Education. State and private schools for the deaf, 1930–31. (Circular, No. 75.) *Mimeographed.* 18p. 1933. The Office. Gratis.
U. S. Office of Education. Teachers' problems with exceptional children. Pt. I—Blind and partially seeing children, by Beatrice McLeod. (Pamphlet, No. 40.) 32p. 1933. Supt. of Doc. $.05.
U. S. Office of Education. Teachers' problems with exceptional children. Pt. II—Gifted children, by E. H. Martens. (Pamphlet, No. 41.) 44p. 1933. Supt. of Doc. $.05.
Walker, Wilma. Visiting teacher. (Child Welfare pamphlet, No. 19.) 11p. 1933. Univ. of Ia. $.05.
*White House Conference on Child Health and Protection. Committee on Physically and Mentally Handicapped. The handicapped child; report, W. J. Ellis, chairman. 452p. 1933. Appleton-Century. $3.00.
Wisconsin. State Department of Public Instruction. Crippled Children Division. Care and education of crippled children. (Bul. No. 1.) 77p. 1933. The Department, Madison, Wis.
Woodson, C. G. The mis-education of the negro. 207p. 1933. Associated Pubs., Inc., 1538 9th St., N. W., Washington, D. C. $2.00.
Wright, A. D. The Negro rural school fund, inc. (Anna T. Jeanes foundation) 1907–1933. 177p. 1933. Anna T. Jeanes Foundation, 726 Jackson Pl., N. W., Washington, D. C. Gratis.

(10) Educational Research

*Abelson, H. H. The art of educational research; its problems and procedures. 332p. 1933. World Bk. Co. $2.00.
Campbell, W. G. A form book for thesis writing. 145p. 1933. Univ. of Southern Cal. Press. $1.10.
Joyal, A. E., *comp.* Abstracts of doctors' theses in education at the University of California, 1898 to March 1933. 104p. 1933. Phi Delta Kappa, Haviland Hall, Univ. of Cal., Berkeley, Cal. $.25.
Kentucky University. Theses in education. (Univ. of Ky. Bur. of School service bul. Vol. V, No. 4.) 61p. 1933. Univ. of Ky., The Campus Bookstore, Lexington, Ky. $.50.
Larkin, A. E. Index handbook for education reference and research. *Mimeographed.* 86p. 1933. The Author, 292 North St., Pittsfield, Mass. $.50.
National Education Association. Department of Superintendence and Research Division. Questionnaire studies completed—bibliography, No. 4, 1932–33. (Circular, No. 12.) *Mimeographed.* 12p. 1933. The Association. With subscription to Educ. research service.
National Education Association. Research Division. Index to certain bibliographies available in printed, typewritten or mimeographed form. *Mimeographed.* 45p. 1933. The Association. Gratis.
Seyfried, J. E. Preparing and printing a manuscript. (Educ. series, Vol. VII, No. 1). 62p. 1933. Univ. of N. Mex. $.25.
U. S. Office of Education. Bibliography of research studies in education, 1931–1932, prepared in the library division, by R. A. Gray. (Bul. 1933, No. 6.) 282 p. 1933. Supt. of Doc. $.20.
U. S. Office of Education. List of educational research studies in city school systems, 1931–32, *comp.* by R. A. Gray. (Circular, No. 72.) *Mimeographed.* 63p. 1933. The Office. Gratis.
U. S. Office of Education. Research in secondary schools. (Bul. 1932, No. 17, Monograph, No. 15.) 71p. 1933. Supt. of Doc. $.10.
Witmer, E. M., and Feagley, E. M., *comps.* Beginner's guide to bibliography with examples drawn from the field of education. *Mimeographed.* 16p. 1933. Teachers College, Columbia. $.25.

(11) Teachers and Teaching Methods

Adams, W. H. The placement of students in teaching positions as carried on by higher educational institutions—including normal schools, teachers colleges, colleges and universities. 131p. 1933. Abilene Christian College, Abilene, Tex. $1.50.
American Association of Teachers Colleges. Twelfth yearbook, 1933. 174p. 1933. The Association, C. W. Hunt, Sec'y., 2060 Stearns Road, Cleveland, Ohio. $1.00.
American Educational Research Association. Psychology of learning, general methods of teaching, and supervision. (Review of educ. research, Vol. III, No. 4.) p. 279–368. 1933. The Association, N. E. A. $1.00.
Arkansas. Department of Education. The Arkansas co-operative program to improve instruction; study program. (Bul. No. 1.) 153p. 1933. The Department, Little Rock, Ark. $.50.
Bachman, F. P. Education and certification of elementary teachers. (Field studies, No. 5.) 225p. 1933. George Peabody College for Teachers, Division of Surveys and Field Studies. $.75.
*Breed, F. S. Classroom organization and management. (Measurement and adjustment series, ed. by L. M. Terman.) 472p. 1933. World Bk. Co. $2.00.
*Brown, E. J. Everyday problems in classroom management: a case and problem book. 306p. 1933. Houghton. $1.80.
Burr, S. E. An introduction to progressive education. (The activity method.) 72p. 1933. C. A. Gregory Co., 345 Calhoun St., Cincinnati, Ohio. $.50.
Chamberlain, L. M., and Meece, L. E. The graduate of the college of education and the depression. (Univ. of Ky. Bur. of school service bul. Vol. VI, No. 1.) 38p. 1933. The Campus Bookstore, Univ. of Ky., Lexington, Ky. $.50.
Clark, L. V. A study of the relationship between the vocational home economics teacher training curricula of a group of women's colleges and the expected responsibilities of beginning teachers. (Cont. to educ. No. 586.) 82p. 1933. Teachers College, Columbia. $1.50.
Cole, P. R. The method and technique of teaching. 388p. 1933. Oxford Univ. Press. $3.25.
Conference on the Improvement of Teachers. Northwestern University. Preparation and improvement of teachers. 147p. 1933. Northwestern Univ., School of Educ. $1.25.
*Cooke, D. H. Problems of the teaching personnel. 384p. 1933. Longmans. $3.00.
Crutsinger, G. M. Survey study of teacher training in Texas, and a suggested program. (Cont. to educ. No. 537.) 226p. 1933. Teachers College, Columbia. $1.50.
Davis, F. G. A course in supervised teaching. 123p. 1933. Inor Pub. Co., 30 Irving Pl., N. Y. C. $1.25.
Eells, W. C. Teachers' salaries and the cost of living. (School economy series.) 94p. 1933. Stanford Univ. Press. $1.00.
Foster, Josephine, *ed.* The broadening field of teacher activity: health education record keeping, research, home and school cooperation. 36p. 1933. Assn. for Childhood Educ., 1201 16th St. N. W., Washington, D. C. $.25.
Gabler, E. R., and Frederick, R. W. Methods of teaching in junior and senior high school: a guidebook. 207p. 1933. Inor Pub. Co., Inc., 30 Irving Pl., N. Y. C. $1.55.
*Garrison, N. L. The technique and administration of teaching. 593p. 1933. Amer. Bk. Co. $2.50.
*Hissong, Clyde, and Hissong, Mary. An introduction to the principles of teaching. 260p. 1933. Winston. $2.00.

Industrial Arts Cooperative Service. Mimeographed studies. Type 1.—Units; Type 2.—Direction studies; Type 3.—Reports of use; Type 4.—Source material. (Descriptive catalogue of above unit material.) Published intermittently. 1932–1933. The Author, 519 W. 121st St., N. Y. C. Apply.
Kinder, J. S. Practice teachers workbook. 68p. 1933. Edwards Bros. $1.90.
Kuhlmann, W. D. Teacher absence and leave regulations: some basic facts and principles related to temporary absence of teachers, for use in formulating valid absence regulations. (Cont. to educ. No. 564.) 75p. 1933. Teachers College, Columbia. $1.50.
Lindsay, J. A. Annual and semi-annual promotion with special reference to the elementary school. (Cont. to educ. No. 570.) 170p. 1933. Teachers College, Columbia. $1.75.
Long, F. M. Desirable physical facilities for an activity program. (Cont. to educ. No. 593.) 116p. 1933. Teachers College, Columbia. $1.50.
McCall, W. A., and Crabbs, L. M., *eds.* Teachers' lesson unit series—units on various subjects, published intermittently. 1932–1933. Teachers College, Columbia. $.25 each.
McCuiston, Ed, *director.* The Arkansas co-operative program to improve instruction. (Bul. No. 1, Study program.) 153p. 1933. State Dept. of Educ., Little Rock, Ark. $.50.
Maryland State Normal School. Towson, Maryland. Guide for student teaching. 3d ed. *Mimeographed.* 74p. 1933. The Author. $1.00.
Maryland. Teachers' Retirement System. Sixth annual report of the board of trustees. 32p. 1933. Office of Retirement System, 2004 Lexington Bldg., Baltimore, Md. Gratis.
Mendenhall, J. E., and Mendenhall, M. E. The influence of familiarity upon children's preferences for pictures and poems. (Lincoln school research studies.) 74p. 1933. Teachers College, Columbia. $1.50.
Michigan Education Association. The supply of and demand for teachers in Michigan, book two: report of the committee on teacher training in two books. (Bul. No. 26.) 247p. 1933. The Association, Lansing, Mich. $1.00.
Minnesota. State Department of Education. Statistical Division. A study of unemployed secondary teachers in Minnesota, 1933. 39p. 1933. The Department, St. Paul, Minn.
National Education Association. Department of Superintendence and Research Division. Estimating changes in teacher's cost of living. (Circular, No. 1.) *Mimeographed.* 15p. 1933. The Association. With subscription to Educ. research service.
National Education Association. Department of Superintendence and Research Division. Unpaid salaries of teachers and other school employees. (Circular, No. 10.) 11p. 1933. The Association. With subscription to Educ. research service.
National Education Association. Research Division. Federal pay cuts and their bearing on teacher's salaries; prepared for the joint commission on the emergency in education. *Mimeographed.* 12p. 1933. The Association. $.10.
National Survey of the Education of Teachers. Selected bibliography on the education of teachers, comp. by G. L. Betts, B. W. Frazier, and G. C. Gamble. Vol. I. (U. S. office of Educ. Bul. 1933, No. 10.) 118p. 1933. Gov't. Print. Office. $.15.
New York (State) University. Elementary Education Division. Cooperative room activities. (Informal teaching series, Circular, No. 4.) 17p. 1933. The University. $.05.
Pannell, H. C. The preparation and work of Alabama high school teachers. (Cont. to educ. No. 551.) 118p. 1933. Teachers College, Columbia. $1.50.
Peterson, F. E. Philosophies of education current in the preparation of teachers in the United States. (Cont. to educ. No. 528.) 147p. 1933. Teachers College, Columbia. $1.50.
Philadelphia, Pennsylvania. Board of Education. Division of Educational Research and Results. Individualization of instruction; devices for use within the teaching group. (Bul. No. 272.) 36p. 1933. The Board. $.10.
Prescott, D. A. Training of teachers. (Bul. series 9, No. 8. Studies in educ. No. 5.) 35p. 1933. Rutgers Univ., School of Educ. $.25.
Progressive Education Association. Committee on Social and Economic Problems. A call to the teachers of the nation. (Pamphlet, No. 30.) 31p. 1933. Day. $.25.
Quigley, Samuel. The integration of teaching and learning: a syllabus of the key-course in the teaching and learning processes. 77p. 1933. The Author, 3420 Alta Vista Drive, Chattanooga, Tenn. $.50 single cop.; more than fifty $.35.
Rich, R. W. The training of teachers in England and Wales during the nineteenth century. 286p. 1933. Macmillan. $3.25.
Smith, W. R., OBrien, F. P., and Bayles, E. E. The value of professional training in education; including a review of the A. A. U. P. bulletin on required courses in education. (Bul. of educ.) 15p. 1933. Univ. of Kan. Gratis while supply lasts.
Sperle, D. H. The case method technique in professional training. (Cont. to educ. No. 571.) 92p. 1933. Teachers College, Columbia. $1.50.
Umstattd, J. G. Learning units in secondary school teaching. 77p. 1933. Perine Bk. Co., 1500 Univ. Ave., Minneapolis. $1.00.
U. S. Office of Education. Certificates issued by the Scottish education department, by J. F. Abel. (Circular, No. 66.) *Mimeographed.* 11p. 1933. The Office. Gratis.
U. S. Office of Education. The education of teachers and the financial crisis. (Circular, No. 110.) *Mimeographed.* 36p. 1933. The Office. Gratis.
U. S. Office of Education. Provisions for individual differences, marking, and promotion. (Bul. 1932, No. 17, Monograph, No. 13.) 472p. 1933. Supt. of Doc. $.40.
U. S. Office of Education. Selection and appointment of teachers, by W. S. Deffenbaugh and W. H. Zeigel, Jr. (Bul. 1932, No. 17, Monograph, No. 12.) 115p. 1933. Supt. of Doc. $.10.
U. S. Office of Education. Selective admission to teachers preparation, by C. E. Hagie. (Leaflet, No. 39.) 12p. 1933. The Office. $.05.
U. S. Office of Education. Techniques for teaching large classes, by David Segel and M. M. Proffitt. (Circular, No. 114.) *Mimeographed.* 25p. 1933. The Office. Gratis.
Virginia. University. Extension Department. The unit method of teaching. (Record extension series, Vol. XVII, No. 7. Secondary educ. in Va. No. 17.) 241p. 1933. The University. $.30.
Walser, Frank. The art of conference. 305p. 1933. Harper. $3.00.
Watson, G. H. Success and failure in the teaching profession. 99p. 1933. Teachers College, Columbia.
Yorke, P. C. Educational lectures. 282p. 1933. Text Bk. Pub. Co., 21 Washburn St., San Francisco, Cal. $1.50.

(12) PRESCHOOL, KINDERGARTEN AND ELEMENTARY SCHOOLS

Caswell, H. L. Non-promotion in elementary schools. (Field studies, No. 4.) 100p. 1933. George Peabody College for Teachers. Division of Surveys and Field Studies. $.30.
Conrad, H. S. The California behavior inventory for nursery school children. (Syllabus. Series, No. 244.) 75p. 1933. Univ. of Cal. Press. $.75.
Hill, P. S. Kindergarten child in the new deal. (Radio address.) 4p. 1933. Bradley. Gratis.
Illinois. Western Illinois State Teachers College, Macomb. Typical activities in the first grade. (Quarterly, Vol. XII, No. 4.) 1933. The College.
Instructor yearbook, 1933–34. 96p. 1933. Owen. $.40.
Kansas City, Missouri. Public Schools. Bibliography for elementary schools. (School service bul. Vol. V, No. 3.) 177p. 1933. Dept. of Educ. of Kansas City Public Schools, Kansas City, Mo. $.50.
*Langdon, Grace. Similarities and differences in teaching in nursery school, kindergarten, and first grade. 392p. 1933. Day. $2.95.
New York (State) University. Elementary Education Division. Materials and supplies in unit teaching. (Informal teaching series, Circular, No. 2.) 11p. 1933. The University. $.05.
New York (State) University. Elementary Education Division. Use of textbooks, a fair appraisal of the use of the textbook in the progressive forward-looking elementary school. (Informal teaching series. Circular, No. 3.) 12p. 1933. The University. $.05.
*Retan, G. A. Management and teaching technique

in the elementary school. 370p. 1933. Prentice-Hall. $2.00.
Skeels, H. M. A study of some factors in form board accomplishments of preschool children. (New series, No. 249. Studies in child welfare, Vol. VII, No. 2.) 148p. 1933. Univ. of Ia. Apply.
U. S. Office of Education. Kindergartens in public schools of cities having 2,500 population or more, as of June, 1932, by M. D. Davis. (Circular, No. 88.) *Mimeographed.* 8p. 1933. The Office. Gratis.
U. S. Office of Education. Nursery schools; their development and current practices in the United States, by M. D. Davis and Rowna Hansen. (Bul. 1932, No. 9.) 92p. 1933. Supt. of Doc. $.15.
West, Parl. A study of ability grouping in the elementary school, in terms of variability of achievement, the teaching problem, and pupil adjustment. (Cont. to educ. No. 588.) 70p. 1933. Teachers College, Columbia. $1.50.

(13) CURRICULUM

Secondary Education Board. Report of a study of the secondary curriculum. Rev. ed. 315p. 1933. The Board, Milton, Mass. $.50.
U. S. Office of Education. Procedures in curriculum making. (Bul. 1932, No. 17, Monograph, No. 18.) 99p. 1933. Supt. of Doc. $.10.
U. S. Office of Education. The program of studies. (Bul. 1932, No. 17, Monograph, No. 19.) 340p. 1933. Gov't. Print. Office. $.15.
U. S. Office of Education. Recent courses of study for elementary and secondary schools, comp. by F. C. Fox. (Circular, No. 111.) *Mimeographed.* 36p. 1933. The Office. Gratis.
*Webb, L. W., and others, *eds.* High school curriculum reorganization. 395p. 1933. The North Central Assn. of Colleges and Secondary Schools, The Ann Arbor Press, Ann Arbor, Mich. $1.50.

(14) SECONDARY EDUCATION

Boogher, E. W. G. Secondary education in Georgia, 1732–1858. (Thesis.) 452p. 1933. The Author, Merchantville, N. J. $3.50.
*Briggs, T. H. Secondary education. 557p. 1933. Macmillan. $2.50.
Carley, V. A. Student aid in the secondary schools of the United States. (Cont. to educ. No. 594.) 118p. 1933. Teachers College, Columbia. $1.50.
Draper, E. M., and Roberts, A. C. Study guide in secondary education. 151p. 1933. Appleton-Century. $1.00.
Frederick, O. I. Two standardized check lists for the organization of secondary schools: one for junior high school grades and one for senior high school grades. 64p. 1933. Ann Arbor Press, Ann Arbor, Mich. $1.50.
French, Will. Promotional plans in the high school. (Cont. to educ. No. 587.) 90p. 1933. Teachers College, Columbia. $1.50.
Hawkins, M. A. Frederick Douglass high school—a seventeen year period survey. (Thesis.) 203p. 1933. Univ. of Pa.
Hyatt, O. W. The development of secondary education in Alabama prior to 1920. (Cont. to educ. No. 118.) 168p. 1933. George Peabody College for Teachers. $1.25.
Hylan, J. C. The history of secondary education in York and Oxford counties in Maine. (Bul. Vol. XXXVI, No. 5, Studies, second series, No. 29.) 78p. 1933. Univ. of Me. $.50.
Illinois. State Superintendent of Public Instruction and the University. The recognition and accrediting of Illinois secondary schools. 28p. 1933. The Author. Gratis.
Jordan, Floyd. The social composition of the secondary schools of the southern states. (Cont. to educ. No. 108.) 101p. 1933. George Peabody College for Teachers. $1.50.
Kasuya, Yoshi. A comparative study of the secondary education of girls in England, Germany and the United States with a consideration of the secondary education of girls in Japan. (Cont. to educ. No. 566.) 211p. 1933. Teachers College, Columbia. $2.25.
Moore, M. W. A study of young high school graduates. (Cont. to educ. No. 583.) 78p. 1933. Teachers College, Columbia. $1.50.
Mulhern, James. A history of secondary education in Pennsylvania. 714p. 1933. Science Press. $5.00.
Nanninga, S. P., and Knode, J. E., *editors.* Articulation of high school and college in New Mexico; report of a conference held at the University of New Mexico, July 21–22, 1933. (Educ. series, Vol. VII, No. 2.) 96p. 1933. Univ. of N. Mex.
National Education Association. Department of Secondary School Principals. Abstracts of unpublished masters' theses in the field of secondary-school administration. (Bul. No. 47.) 100p. 1933. The Department.
New York (State) Associated Academic Principals. Constants in the secondary school: report of a sub-committee of the Committee on secondary school problems. 29p. 1933. David G. Allen, c/o High School, Council of School Superintendents, Boonville, N. Y. $.10.
New York (State) University. Selected, annotated bibliography on the general phases of secondary education for use by teachers and supervisors. (Bul. No. 1024.) 24p. 1933. The author. $.10.
Plenzke, O. H. An analysis of the costs of high school tuition, board and lodging, school year 1931–32. 52p. 1933. John Callahan, State Supt. of Educ., Madison, Wis.
*Rice, G. A., Conrad, C. C., and Fleming, Paul. The administration of public high schools through their personnel. 723p. 1933. Macmillan. $2.75.
Trimble, O. C. A comparison of two methods of measuring the high school. (Bul. Vol. XXXIII, No. 9. Educ. reference Circular III.) *Mimeographed.* 16p. 1933. Purdue Univ. Division of Educ. Reference. $.20.
Trimble, O. C., and Remmers, H. H. Measures of educational machinery as high school accrediting criteria. (Bul. Vol. XXXIII, No. 7, Studies in higher educ. No. 22.) 37p. 1933. Purdue Univ., Division of Educ. Reference. $.35.
U. S. Office of Education. Accredited secondary schools in the United States. (Supplement to bul. 1930, No. 24.) 45p. 1933. Supt. of Doc. $.05.
U. S. Office of Education. Articulation of high school and college, by P. R. Brammell. (Bul. 1932, No. 17, Monograph, No. 10.) 96p. 1933. Supt. of Doc. $.10.
U. S. Office of Education. District organization and secondary education. (Bul. 1932, No. 17, Monograph, No. 8.) 208p. 1933. Supt. of Doc. $.15.
U. S. Office of Education. High-school instruction by mail; a potential economy, by W. H. Gaumnitz. (Bul. 1933, No. 13.) 69p. 1933. Supt. of Doc. $.10.
U. S. Office of Education. Interpreting the secondary school to the public, by Belmont Farley. (Bul. 1932, No. 17, Monograph, No. 16.) 113p. 1933. Supt. of Doc. $.10.
U. S. Office of Education. Legal and regulatory provisions affecting secondary education, by W. W. Keesecker. (Bul. 1932, No. 17, Monograph, No. 9.) 114p. 1933. Supt. of Doc. $.10.
U. S. Office of Education. Part-time secondary schools, by G. N. Kefauver and others. (Bul. 1932, No. 17, Monograph, No. 3.) 98p. 1933. Supt. of Doc. $.10.
U. S. Office of Education. Reorganization of secondary education. (Bul. 1932, No. 17, Monograph, No. 5.) 423p. 1933. Supt. of Doc. $.40.
U. S. Office of Education. The secondary-school population. (Bul. 1932, No. 17, Monograph, No. 4.) 58p. 1933. Supt. of Doc. $.10.
U. S. Office of Education. The smaller secondary schools. (Bul. 1932, No. 17, Monograph, No. 6.) 236p. 1933. Supt. of Doc. $.15.
Williams, R. C. Educational programs of smaller graded and high schools. (Research bul. No. 14.) 72p. 1933. State Dept. of Public Instruction, Des Moines, Ia. Gratis.

(15) SCHOOL LIBRARIES

American Library Association. Publicity Committee. Significance of the school library. (Leads, No. 10, September, 1933.) *Mimeographed.* 50p. 1933. Amer. Lib. Assn. $.50.
Brown, C. H., and Bousfield, H. G. Circulation work in college and university libraries. 179p. 1933. Amer. Lib. Assn. $2.25.
Fargo, L. F. Library in the school. 2nd ed., rev. 479p. 1933. Amer. Lib. Assn. $3.00.
Los Angeles City School District. The school library system of Los Angeles. (School publication No. 235.) 212p. 1933. The Author. Apply.
McCrum, B. P. An estimate of standards for a college library; planned for the use of librarians

when presenting budgets to administrative boards. 78p. 1933. Washington & Lee Univ., Lexington, Va. $.55.

*National Education Association. Department of Elementary School Principals. Twelfth yearbook; the elementary school libraries. 576p. 1933. The Association. $2.00.

Plum, D. A. *comp.* Bibliography of American college library administration; supplement, March, 1931–July, 1933. 42p. 1933. Vassar College Library, Poughkeepsie, N. Y. $.50.

U. S. Office of Education. Aids in book selection for elementary school libraries, by E. A. Lathrop. (Circular, No. 69.) *Mimeographed.* 18p. 1933. The Office. Gratis.

U. S. Office of Education. The secondary-school library, by B. L. Johnson. (Bul. 1932, No. 17, Monograph, No. 17.) 110p. 1933. Supt. of Doc. $.10.

(16) READING, WRITING AND LANGUAGES

Boney, C. D. A study of library reading in the primary grades. (Cont. to educ. No. 578.) 70p. 1933. Teachers College, Columbia. $1.50.

Chicago. University High School. Faculty of English Department. English instruction in the University high school. (Publications of the laboratory schools, No. 4.) 178p. 1933. Univ. of Chicago Dept. of Educ. $1.50.

Coleman, Algernon, and Jacques, Agnes, *comps.* An analytical bibliography of modern language teaching, 1927–1932. 296p. 1933. Univ. of Chicago Press. $3.00.

Columbia University. Teachers College. Institute of Educational Research. Division of Psychology. Language learning; summary of a report to the International auxiliary language association in the United States, incorporated. 59p. 1933. Teachers College, Columbia. $1.00.

Entwistle, W. J., *ed.* The year's work in modern language study, by a number of scholars, edited for the Modern humanities research association, Vol. III. 186p. 1933. Oxford Univ. Press. $2.25.

Gates, A. I., and Bennett, C. C. Reversal tendencies in reading; causes, diagnosis, prevention and correction. 33p. 1933. Teachers College, Columbia. $.40.

*Gray, W. S., and Whipple, Gertrude. Improving instruction in reading: an experimental study. (Supplementary educ. monographs, No. 40.) 226p. 1933. Univ. of Chicago Dept. of Educ. $1.75.

Greene, H. A. A criterion for the course of study in the mechanics of written composition. (New series, No. 246. Studies in educ. Vol. VIII, No. 4.) 64p. 1933. Univ. of Ia. $.75.

Hardy, Marjorie, *ed.* Reading emphasis in school activities. 46p. 1933. Assn. for Childhood Educ., 1201 16th St. N. W., Washington, D. C. $.35.

Henley, Faye. Teacher's source book in literature units for elementary grades and junior high school. 60p. 1933. Galena Press, 2709 Northwestern Ave., Indianapolis, Ind. $.50.

Jacobson, P. B. Two experiments with work-type reading exercises in ninth grade. (Univ. of Ia. studies in educ. Vol. VIII, No. 5, New series No. 247.) 85p. 1933. Univ. of Ia. $.75.

Ladd, M. R. Relation of social, economic and personal characteristics to reading ability. (Cont. to educ. No. 582.) 100p. 1933. Teachers College, Columbia. $1.50.

Lee, D. M. The importance of reading for achieving in grades four, five, and six. (Cont. to educ. No. 556.) 64p. 1933. Teachers College, Columbia. $1.50.

Pooley, R. C. Grammar and usage in textbooks on English. (Bur. of educ. research, Bul. No. 14.) 172p. 1933. Univ. of Wis., Bur. of educ. research. $.75.

Robinson, F. P. The rôle of eye movements in reading with an evaluation of techniques for their improvement. (New series, No. 252. Series on aims and progress of research, No. 39.) 52p. 1933. Univ. of Ia. $.50.

Secondary Education Board. Final report of the Committee on modern foreign languages, containing reading list in French. (Secondary Curriculum, supplement 2.) 122p. 1933. Secondary Educ. Board, Milton, Mass. $.25.

*Seely, H. F. On teaching English. 391p. 1933. Amer. Bk. Co. $2.00.

Selzer, C. A. Lateral dominance and visual fusion; their application to difficulties in reading, writing, spelling, and speed. (Monographs in educ. No. 12.) 119p. 1933. Harvard Univ. Press. $1.00.

*Trommer, C. J., and Regan, T. A. Directing language power in the elementary school child through story, dramatization, and poetry. 497p. 1933. Macmillan. $2.00.

U. S. Office of Education. Instruction in English, by D. V. Smith. (Bul. 1932, No. 17, Monograph, No. 20.) 89p. 1933. Supt. of Doc. $.10.

U. S. Office of Education. Instruction in foreign languages, by H. M. Eddy. (Bul. 1932, No. 17, Monograph, No. 24.) 61p. 1933. Supt. of Doc. $.10.

West Allis, Wisconsin. Public schools. Department of Instruction. The teaching of spelling. (Bul. No. 14, Pt. 2.) 8p. 1933. The Department. Gratis.

(17) MATHEMATICS AND SCIENCE

Bond, E. A. The professional treatment of the subject matter of arithmetic for teacher-training institutions. 250p. 1933. Teachers College, Columbia. $2.50.

Bradley, A. D. The geometry of repeating design and geometry of design for high schools. (Cont. to educ. No. 549.) 131p. 1933. Teachers College, Columbia. $1.50.

*Breslich, E. R. The administration of mathematics in secondary schools. 407p. 1933. Univ. of Chicago Press. $3.00.

Buckingham, G. E. Diagnostic and remedial teaching in first year algebra. (Cont. to educ. School of educ. series, No. 11.) 136p. 1933. Northwestern Univ., School of Educ., Evanston, Ill. $1.50.

Christofferson, H. C. Geometry professionalized for teachers. 204p. 1933. Banta. $1.50, plus postage.

Clemensen, J. W. Study outlines in physics: construction and experimental evaluation. (Cont. to educ. No. 553.) 154p. 1933. Teachers College, Columbia. $1.75.

Fagerstrom, W. H. Mathematical facts and processes prerequisite to the study of the calculus. (Cont. to educ. No. 572.) 68p. 1933. Teachers College, Columbia. $1.50.

Hurd, A. W. Cooperative experimentation in materials and methods in secondary school physics. 60p. 1933. Teachers College, Columbia. $.60.

Hurd, A. W. An experiment in the use of a teaching unit in science. 50p. 1933. Teachers College, Columbia, Institute of School Experimentation. $.63.

Jotter, E. V. Forestry and school studies: a correlation for elementary grades. (Official publication, Vol. XXXIV, No. 21.) 128p. 1933. Univ. of Mich. Press. $.25.

Kramer, G. A. The effect of certain factors in the verbal arithmetic problem upon children's success in their solution. (Studies in educ. No. 20.) 106p. 1933. Johns Hopkins Press. $1.75.

Mapes, Charlotte, and Harap, Henry. Six activity units in fractions. (Curriculum laboratory, No. 33.) *Mimeographed.* 19p. 1933. Western Reserve Univ. Press. $.15.

Maryland. State Department of Education. Science in the elementary school: suggested units, grades 1–7. (Md. school bul. Vol. XV, No. 1.) 331p. 1933. The Department. $.50.

Metter, H. L. The arithmetic curriculum since 1860. (Abstract of an unpublished thesis.) 15p. 1933. Univ. of Ill., High School Visitors Office. $.30.

*National Council of Teachers of Mathematics. Eighth yearbook: the teaching of mathematics in the secondary school. 264p. 1933. Teachers College, Columbia. $1.75.

Opportunity for investigation in natural history by high-school teachers. (Reprinted from the Journal of the Michigan School-masters' club.) 127p. 1933. Univ. of Mich. Press. $.50.

Schorling, Raleigh, Everett, J. P., and Shriner, W. O. *eds.* Contemporary guide in the teaching of junior high school mathematics. 122p. 1933. Edwards Bros. $1.20.

Schorling Raleigh, Overman, J. R., and Shriner, W. O., *editors.* Contemporary guide in the teaching of arithmetic: an experiment in cooperative teaching. 126p. 1933. Edwards Bros. $1.20.

Shuler, C. E. The professional treatment of freshman mathematics in teachers colleges. (Abstract of Cont. to educ. No. 115.) 9p. 1933. George Peabody College for Teachers.

Torrey, R. E. Science and its function in education;

with an illustrative commentary based upon the author's General botany for colleges. 93p. 1933. Quarterly Book Dept., P. O. Box 64, Station O, N. Y. C. $.50.

U. S. Office of Education. Instruction in mathematics, by E. S. Lide. (Bul. 1932, No. 17, Monograph, No. 23.) 72p. 1933. Supt. of Doc. $.10.

U. S. Office of Education. Instruction in science, by W. L. Beauchamp. (Bul. 1932, No. 17, Monograph, No. 22.) 63p. 1933. Supt. of Doc. $.10.

Webb, H. A. The high-school science library for 1932–33. Bibliography. (Reprinted from Peabody Journal of Educ. Vol. XI, No. 1.) 10p. 1933. The Author, George Peabody College for Teachers. $.12.

Wells, Harrington. The teaching of nature study. 169p. 1933. State Teachers College, Santa Barbara, Cal. $1.65.

Whitcraft, L. H. Some influences of the requirements and examinations of the College entrance examination board on mathematics in secondary schools of the United States. (Cont. to educ. No. 557.) 115p. 1933. Teachers College, Columbia. $1.50.

(18) Geography and Social Studies

Baxter, Tompsie, and Young, B. M. Unit of work: ships and navigation. 219p. 1933. Teachers College, Columbia. $2.00.

Bye, E. C., *ed.* A bibliography of the teaching of the social studies. Rev. ed. 104p. 1933. Wilson, H. W. $.60.

Gill, W. L. The Gill method of moral and civic training. American citizenship at the beginning of life. 3d book. 64p. 1933. The Author, 501 W. Mt. Pleasant Ave., Mt. Airy, Philadelphia, Pa. $.50.

Greenman, A. T. Making efficient citizens. 148p. 1933. Christopher. $2.00.

Hatch, F. W. Status of the social sciences in secondary schools of Maine. (Bul. Vol. XXXXV, No. 9, Studies, second series, No. 27.) 114p. 1933. Univ. of Me. $.50.

Hughes, A. W. Carrying the mail: a second grade's experiences. 253p. 1933. Teachers College, Columbia. $2.25.

Ireland, N. O. Historical biographies for junior and senior high schools, universities and colleges: a bibliography. 108p. 1933. McKinley Pub. Co. $1.00.

Koopman, G. R., Chairman of Editorial Committee. Helping children experience the realities of the social order: social studies in the public schools of Ann Arbor, Michigan. 307p. 1933. Board of Educ., Ann Arbor, Mich. $2.00 cloth; $1.60 paper.

Lackey, E. E. Introductory geography for teachers' college students (with emphasis on the home region). A method of selecting and evaluating materials for a professional subject-matter treatment. 124p. 1933. The Author, Univ. of Neb. $1.50.

*National Council for the Social Studies. Supervision in the social studies: Yearbook, Vol. III. 260p. 1933. McKinley Pub. Co. $2.00.

*National Society for the Study of Education. The teaching of geography; ed. by G. M. Whipple. 615p. 1933. Public School Pub. Co. $4.50 cloth; $3.00 paper.

New York (State) University. Handbook for rural elementary schools. The social studies group. (Curriculum bul. No. 2.) 235p. 1933. The Author. $.25.

Peck, M. E. Teaching history in high school. 96p. 1933. State Teachers College, Farmville, Va. $.60.

*Pierce, B. L. Citizen's organizations and the civic training of youth. (Amer. historical assn. Commission on the social studies. Report, Pt. III.) 428p. 1933. Scribner. $2.00.

Porter, Marie. Indian records. 13p. n.d. Industrial Arts Cooperative Service, 519 W. 121st St., N. Y. C. $.40.

Sweet, Mayme, and Butler, E. L. Some facts about the Manhattan Indians and their way of living. 22p. n.d. Industrial Arts Cooperative Service, 519 W. 121st St., N. Y. C. $.60.

*Swindler, R. E. Social studies instruction in the secondary schools; with particular reference to the curriculum, the library, the objectives, and the unit system. 348p. 1933. Prentice-Hall. $2.50.

U. S. Office of Education. Instruction in the social studies. (Bul. 1932, No. 17, Monograph, No. 21.) 105p. 1933. Supt. of Doc. $.10.

U. S. Office of Education. Tests in the social studies, by David Segel. (Circular, No. 71.) *Mimeographed.* 12p. 1933. The Office. Gratis.

Weaver, R. B., and Hill, H. C. United States history by units (in two parts). Pt. I—Selection, organization, methods. Pt. II—The units of the course. p. 1–54; p. 55–184. 1933. W. F. Quarrie & Co., Chicago, Ill. $1.50. (Pupils' ed.—Pt. II. bound separately. $.60.)

Welling, Richard. Civics as it should be taught. 15p. n.d. Nat'l. Self-Government Committee, 80 Broadway, N. Y. C. $.10.

Wilson, H. E. The fusion of social studies in junior high schools: a critical analysis. (Harvard studies in educ. Vol. XXI.) 211p. 1933. Harvard Univ. Press. $2.50.

(19) Art, Music and Drama

Eakright, J. B., and Young, B. M. Adventuring with toys; activities of a fourth grade. 242p. 1933. Teachers College, Columbia. $2.00.

Hughes, C. W. Chamber music in American schools. (Teachers College dissertation.) 202p. 1933. The Author, 28 Ralph Ave., White Plains, N. Y.

*Klar, W. H., Winslow, L. L. and Kirby, C. V. Art education in principle and practice. 512p. 1933. Bradley. $2.50.

Littlejohns, John. Training of taste in the arts and crafts; with an account of investigations on children's preferences by A. Needham. 152p. 1933. Pitman. $3.75.

McCauley, C. J. A professional study of public school music. 795p. 1933. J. E. Avent, Univ. of Tenn., Knoxville, Tenn. $3.00.

McConathy, Osbourne, and others. Music in rural education. 290p. 1933. Silver, Burdett. $1.20.

Music Teachers National Association. Proceedings of the annual meeting of the fifty-sixth year, 1932. (Series 27.) 288p. 1933. The Association, Oberlin, Ohio. $2.00.

Opp, P. F. Dramatics in the secondary schools. 1933. Fairmont Printing Co., Fairmont, W. Va.

Perry, E. K. Art adventures with discarded materials. 169p. 1933. Wetzel. $2.00. Teachers and libraries 20% disc.

Ruckmick, C. A., *ed.* Studies in the psychology of art under the direction of Dr. N. C. Meier. (Studies in psychology, Vol. XVIII.) 200p. 1933. Univ. of Ia. $2.75.

Russell, Mabel, and Wilson, E. P. Art training through home problems, ed. by W. G. Whitford. 214p. 1933. Manual Arts Press, Peoria, Ill. $2.85.

School Arts Magazine. Plays and puppet shows in which the parts are played by famous and familiar characters found in school stories and studies. 48p. 1933. School Arts Magazine, 645 Printers Bldg., Worcester, Mass. $1.00.

Secondary Education Board. Final report of the Committee on music. (Secondary curriculum, supplement, 1.) 22p. 1933. The Board, Milton, Mass. $.15.

Sicelogg, M. M., and others. Validity and standardization of the McAdory art test. 32p. 1933. Teachers College, Columbia. $.75.

Stanton, H. M., and Koerth, Wilhelmine. Musical capacity measures of children repeated after musical training. (New series, No. 259. Series on aims and progress of research, No. 42.) 48p. 1933. Univ. of Ia. Apply.

*Todd, Jessie, and Gale, A. Van N. Enjoyment and use of art in the elementary school. 134p. 1933. Univ. of Chicago Press. $1.50.

U. S. Office of Education. Instruction in music and art, by A. E. Pierce and R. S. Hilpert. (Bul. 1932, No. 17, Monograph, No. 25.) 68p. 1933. Supt. of Doc. $.10.

Williams, H. M. Musical guidance of young children. (Child welfare pamphlet, No. 29.) 15p. 1933. Univ. of Ia. $.05.

(20) Vocational, Business and Industrial Education

Bennett, C. A., *ed.* Term papers in historical research in industrial education. *Mimeographed.* 72p. 1933. Ia. State College, Industrial Arts Dept., Ames, Ia. $.75.

California. State Department of Education. Aims and desired outcomes of typewriting instruction in California secondary schools. (Bul. No. 8.) 9p. 1933. The Department, Sacramento, Cal. Gratis.

Chicago. University. Conference on Business Education. Proceedings: School of business, University of Chicago, June 28 and 29, 1933. Reconstruction of business education in secondary schools. 99p. 1933. Gregg Pub. Co. $.50.

Connecticut. State Board of Education. Vocational education in Connecticut. Plans for administration of the Smith Hughes and George Reed Acts, 1932–1937. (Vocational bul. No. 1.) 64p. 1933. Conn. State Board of Educ., Hartford, Conn. Gratis.

Davidson, J. B. A study of the extension service in agriculture and home economics in Iowa by a committee of the staff of Iowa State College, Ames, Iowa. 237p. n.d. Ia. State College, Ames, Ia. $1.00.

Eastern Arts Association. Addresses at general sessions of Washington convention, April 27–29, 1933. (Bul. Vol. XXXIV, No. 2.) 50p. 1933. Burton A. Adams, Sec'y., Technical High School, Springfield, Mass. Subscription $1.50 per year.

Eastern Arts Association. Addresses at home economics sections of Washington convention, April 27–29, 1933. (Bul. Vol. XXXIV, No. 4.) 47p. 1933. Burton A. Adams, Sec'y., Technical High School, Springfield, Mass. Subscription $1.50 per year.

Eastern Arts Association. Addresses at industrial arts and printing section of Washington convention, April 27–29, 1933. (Bul. Vol. XXXIV, No. 3.) 55p. 1933. Burton A. Adams, Sec'y., Technical High School, Springfield, Mass. Subscription $1.50 per year.

Eastern Arts Association. Report of Washington convention, April 27–29, 1933. (Bul. Vol. XXXIV, No. 1.) 39p. 1933. Burton A. Adams, Sec'y., Technical High School, Springfield, Mass. Subscription $1.50 per year.

*Eastern Commercial Teachers' Association. Sixth yearbook; teaching devices and classroom equipment. 422p. 1933. The Association. $2.50.

Everhart, F. M., and Matt, H. D. Books commonly found in industrial arts libraries in Iowa. *Mimeographed.* 9p. 1933. Ia. State College, Industrial Arts Dept., Ames, Ia. $.10.

Graham, Jessie. The evolution of business education in the United States and its implications for business—teacher education. (Educ. monographs, 1933–34 series, No. 2.) 228p. 1933. Univ. of Southern Cal. $1.50.

Harap, Henry, and Grosmehr, H. K. Home economics objectives from studies of home life. (Curriculum laboratory, No. 32.) *Mimeographed.* 38p. 1933. Western Reserve Univ. Press, School of Educ. $.25.

Haynes, B. R., and Graham, Jessie. Problems in business education. 146p. 1933. Univ. of Southern Cal. Bookstore, Los Angeles, Cal. $1.00.

Hunter, W. L. Annotated list of graduate theses and dissertations in industrial-arts education and vocational-industrial education accepted by institutions of higher learning in Iowa. *Mimeographed.* 10p. 1933. Ia. State College, Industrial Arts Dept., Ames, Ia. $.15.

Hunter, W. L., *comp.* Two hundred poems for teachers of industrial arts. *Mimeographed.* 102p. 1933. Ia. State College, Industrial Arts Dept., Ames, Ia. $.75.

Iowa. State Board for Vocational Education. Vocational education in Iowa; a brief explanation of the vocational education program in Iowa as organized under the provisions of the federal and state vocational education acts, showing the nature of the vocational instruction offered, its scope, and how it is financed. (Miscellaneous No. 4.) 17p. 1933. The Board, Des Moines, Ia.

Isaacs, Mervin. Professional accountancy training in collegiate schools of business. 152p. 1933. The Author, 2435 Dickens Ave., Far Rockaway, N. Y. $1.25.

Lynn, J. V. Technique of teaching trades. (Industrial teacher training series, No. 1.) *Mimeographed.* 100p. 1933. Ia. State College, Industrial Arts Dept., Ames, Ia. $.75.

Magill, E. C. The college performance of high school graduates of vocational agriculture as compared with others. (Bul. Vol. XXVI, No. 11.) 40p. 1933. Va. Polytechnic Institute, Blacksburg, Va.

Manual Arts Conference, Twenty-fourth. Special Research Committee, *comp.* Annotated list of 800 graduate theses and dissertations in industrial-arts education and vocational industrial education accepted by institutions of higher learning in the United States. *Mimeographed.* 89p. 1933. Ia. State College, Industrial Arts Dept., Ames, Ia. $.75.

Massachusetts. Department of Education. State-aided vocational and part-time education in Massachusetts. (Bul. No. 1.) 47p. 1933. The Department. $.10.

*Nichols, F. G. Commercial education in the high school. (Century vocational series.) 514p. 1933. Appleton-Century. $3.00.

Strickler, F. J. A fundamental in education. (Text of a paper read before the Eastern Arts Association, Washington, D. C., April 28, 1933.) 16p. 1933. Burton A. Adams, Sec'y., Technical High School, Springfield, Mass. $.50.

U. S. Federal Board for Vocational Education. Agricultural part-time schools; methods of organizing and conducting part-time schools. (Bul. No. 108. Agric. series, No. 27.) Rev. ed. 21p. 1933. The Board. $.05.

U. S. Federal Board for Vocational Education. The earning ability of farmers who have received vocational training; a comparison of the earnings of former vocational students now farming with the earnings of an equivalent group in farming who did not receive vocational training. (Bul. No. 167, Agric. series, No. 43.) 44p. 1933. Supt. of Doc. $.05.

U. S. Federal Board for Vocational Education. Effectiveness of vocational education in agriculture; a study of the value of vocational instruction in agriculture in secondary schools as indicated by the occupational distribution of former students. Rev. ed. (Bul. No. 82, Agric. series, No. 13.) 19p. 1933. Supt. of Doc. $.05.

U. S. Federal Board for Vocational Education. The home project in homemaking education: place, function and value of the home project in the vocational program. (Bul. No. 170, Home economics series, No. 16.) 179p. 1933. Supt. of Doc. $.15.

U. S. Office of Education. Good references on junior business education. (Bibliography, No. 9.) *Mimeographed.* 12p. 1933. The Office. Gratis.

U. S. Office of Education. How school departments of home economics are meeting the economic emergency, by E. S. Whitcomb. (Circular, No. 84.) *Mimeographed.* 9p. 1933. The Office. Gratis.

U. S. Office of Education. A symposium on the new homemaking education. (Bul. 1933, No. 3.) 56p. 1933. Supt. of Doc. $.10.

U. S. Office of Education. Technical and trade schools. (Pamphlet, No. 44.) 23p. 1933. Supt. of Doc. $.05.

Voth, J. J., and Hunter, W. L., *comps.* Objectives of industrial arts education. *Mimeographed.* 75p. 1933. Industrial Arts Dept., Ia. State College, Ames, Ia. $.75.

Warner, W. E., and others. The terminological investigation of professional and scientific terms from the literature of vocational and practical arts education. (Western arts assn. bul. Vol. XVII, No. 2.) 45p. 1933. The Ass'n., Harry E. Wood, Sec'y., 5251 College Ave., Indianapolis, Ind. $.10.

Wisconsin. State Board of Vocational Education. Fourth annual report of the adult trade extension circuit. (Trade and industry series, bul. No. 39.) *Mimeographed.* 47p. 1933. The Board, Madison, Wis. Gratis.

(21) GUIDANCE AND PERSONNEL SERVICE

*Allen, R. D. Case-conference problems in group guidance. (Inor group-guidance series, Vol. II.) 151p. 1933. Inor Pub. Co., Inc., 30 Irving Pl., N. Y. C. $1.55.

*Allen, R. D. Common problems in group guidance. (Inor group-guidance series, Vol. I.) 186p. 1933. Inor Pub. Co., Inc., 30 Irving Pl., N. Y. C. $1.95.

American Council on Education. Committee on Personnel Methods. Measurement and guidance of college students: first report; with an introduction by H. E. Hawkes. 199p. 1933. Williams and Wilkins. $2.00.

American Educational Research Association. Pupil personnel, guidance, and counseling. (Review of educ. research, Vol. III, No. 3.) p.185–278. 1933. The Association, N. E. A. $1.00.

*Bennett, M. E. College and life. 456p. 1933. McGraw-Hill. $2.75.

Choosing a vocation. (Vocational bureau bul. No. IX.) Rev. ed. 3p. 1933. Pictorial Review Co., 222 W. 39th St., N. Y. C. $.05.

Cunliffe, R. B. Trends in vocational guidance. (Bul. Series VIII, No. 10b. Studies in educ. No. 4) 42p. 1933. Rutgers Univ., School of Educ. $.25.
Emme, E. E. The adjustment problems of college freshmen. 125p. 1933. Cokesbury. $2.00.
Lee, C. A. A guidance bulletin for junior-senior high schools. 78p. 1933. Charles A. Lee, Sup't. of Schools, Jefferson City, Mo. $1.00.
Lowrey, L. G., and Smith, Geddes. The Institute of child guidance, 1927–1933. 116p. 1933. Commonwealth Fund. Gratis.
Macrae, Angus. Talents and temperaments: the psychology of vocational guidance. 211p. 1933. Appleton-Century. $2.00.
Stratton, D. C. Problems of students in a graduate school of education. (Cont. to educ. No. 550.) 168p. 1933. Teachers College, Columbia. $1.75.
U. S. Office of Education. Programs of guidance. (Bul. 1932, No. 17, Monograph, No. 14.) 144p. 1933. Supt. of Doc. $.10.
U. S. Office of Education. State guidance programs, by M. M. Proffitt. (Pamphlet, No. 35.) 27p. 1933 Supt. of Doc. $.05.
Virginia. State Board of Education. Division of Trade and Industrial Education. Vocations for women. (Occupational series, No. 11.) 43p. 1933. The Author. Gratis.
Vocational Service for Juniors, New York City. Annual report, 1932. 15p. 1933. Vocational Service for Juniors, 122 E. 25th St., N. Y. C.
Wood, Harriette. The need for guidance programs in privately supported mountain schools, ed. by A. H. Estabrook. *Mimeographed.* 127p. 1933. Southern Women's Educational Alliance, 401–2 Grace-American Bldg., Richmond, Va. $1.00.

(22) HEALTH AND PHYSICAL EDUCATION

American Child Health Association. Health education: a brief bibliography for administrators and instructors of health education in junior and senior high schools. *Mimeographed.* 5p. 1933. The Author. Gratis—single copy.
American Child Health Association. Health education in elementary schools: a brief bibliography for classroom teachers. *Mimeographed.* 5p. 1933. The Author. Gratis—single copy.
American Child Health Association. Some recent contributions to health education. *Mimeographed.* 4p. 1933. The Author. Gratis—single copy.
American Child Health Association. Suggestions for 1933. 30p. 1933. The Association. $.10.
American Child Health Association. Supplementary reading materials for health education, grades I–IX. *Mimeographed.* 6p. 1933. The Author. Gratis—single copy.
American Physical Education Association for the years 1931 and 1932. Committee on Dancing. Dancing in the elementary schools. 134p. 1933. A. S. Barnes. $1.00.
Bennett, T. G. A health program for the children of a county: a study of child health in Queen Ann's county, Maryland, with a proposed child health program for this county, considered from the standpoint of administration. (Cont. to educ. No. 584.) 196p. 1933. Teachers College, Columbia. $2.00.
Calkins, Clinch, *ed.* Youth never comes again. 71p. 1933. Committee on Unemployed Youth, 450 7th Ave., N. Y. C. $.25.
Charters, W. W., and Hindman, D. A. The duties of Ohio public-health commissioners. (Bur. of educ. research monographs, No. 17.) 70p. 1933. Ohio State Univ. $1.00.
Cooper, J. A. The effect of participation in athletics upon scholarship measured by achievement tests. (Studies in educ. No. 8.) *Lithoprint.* 128p. 1933. School of Educ., Pa. State College. $.10.
Fenton, Norman. Organizing a mental hygiene program through child guidance. (Bur. of juvenile research. New series, bul. No. 9.) 8p. 1933. Cal. State Print. Office, Sacramento, Cal.
Foster, J. C. Busy childhood: guidance through play and activity. (Century childhood library.) 303p. 1933. Appleton-Century. $2.50.
Franzen, Raymond. An evaluation of school health procedures. (School health research monographs, No. 5.) 127p. 1933. Amer. Child Health Assn. $1.15—cloth; $.90—paper.
Handbook of suggestion on health education. 111p. 1933. British Library of Information, 270 Madison Ave., N. Y. C. $.17.
Latimer, J. V. A suggested teaching unit for secondary schools on tuberculosis and its prevention. 31p. 1933. Mass. Tuberculosis League, 1149 Little Bldg., Boston, Mass. $.20.
Lindwall, R. E. Intramural activities, their organization and administration in the junior and senior high school. 88p. 1933. The Author, Intramural Supt., Lincoln High School, Monitowoc, Wis. $2.00.
Lloyd, F. S. Safety in physical education in secondary schools. (Educ. series, Vol. IX.) 167p. 1933. Nat'l. Bur. of Casualty and Surety Underwriters, 1 Park Ave., N. Y. C. $1.25.
Maryland. State Department of Education. Spring athletics in Maryland. (Md. school bul. Vol. XIV, No. 1.) 12p. 1933. The Department. Gratis.
Moore, Fred. Child health: a state and national dilemma. (Child welfare pamphlet, No. 16.) 13p. 1933. Univ. of Ia. $.05.
Nash, J. B., *ed.* Physiological health. (Interpretation of physical educ., Vol. IV, School of educ. series, N. Y. Univ.) 308p. 1933. A. S. Barnes. $2 00.
National Collegiate Athletic Association. Proceedings of the twenty-eighth convention held at Chicago, Illinois, December 30, 1933. 126p. 1933. Frank W. Nicolson, Sec'y., Wesleyan Univ., Middletown, Conn.
National Education Association. Department of School Health and Physical Education. Athletics for girls: a digest of principles and policies for administrators and teachers in junior and senior high schools. 14p. 1933. The Association. $.10.
*National Recreation Association. The new leisure challenges the schools; shall recreation enrich or impoverish life? Based on a study made by E. T. Lies. 326p. 1933. The Author, 315 4th Ave., N. Y. C. $1.50—paper; $2.00—cloth.
National Safety Council. Seven days for safety. (Public safety memo., No. 20.) *Mimeographed.* 4p. 1933. The Council, 20 N. Wacker Drive, Chicago, Ill. Gratis.
Quincy Senior High School. A report of progress in corrective and developmental physical education. 30p. 1933. Pleiades Co., Dept. R., Newton, Mass. $.25.
Spencer, M. E. Health education for teachers: a critical study of the pre-service preparation of classroom teachers for the school health program. (Cont. to educ. No. 589.) 118p. 1933. Teachers College, Columbia. $1.50.
Stuart, H. C. Healthy childhood: guidance for physical care. (Century childhood library.) 393p. 1933. Appleton-Century. $2.50.
Thompson, B. L. Fundamentals of rhythm and dance, with an analysis of the rhythmic approach in teaching dance skills. 230p. 1933. A. S. Barnes. $3.60.
U. S. Office of Education. Camps and public schools, by M. M. Ready. (Circular, No. 74.) *Mimeographed.* 9p. 1933. The Office. Gratis.
U. S. Office of Education. Health instruction in grades IX–XII, by J. F. Rogers. (Pamphlet, No. 43.) 22p. 1933. Supt. of Doc. $.05.
U. S. Office of Education. Health work and physical education. (Bul. 1932, No. 17, Monograph, No. 28.) 97p. 1933. Supt. of Doc. $.10.
U. S. Office of Education. Intramural and interscholastic athletics. (Bul. 1932, No. 17, Monograph, No. 27.) 143p. 1933. Supt. of Doc. $.10.
White House Conference on Child Health and Protection, 1930. Committee on the School Child. Summer vacation activities of the school child; report of the Subcommittee on summer vacation activities of the school child, W. H. Kilpatrick, chairman. 82p. 1933. Appleton-Century. $.75.

(23) EXTRACURRICULAR ACTIVITIES

Atkinson, H. M., and Flemming, C. W. Education for constructive social influence through student organizations. (Horace Mann professional book.) 31p. 1933. Teachers College, Columbia. $.50.
Crump, Irving. "Making" the school newspaper. 250p. 1933. Dodd. $1.50.
Eiland, Kathleen. Schooldays program book. 153p. 1933. Fitzgerald Pub. Corp., 14 E. 38th St., N. Y. C. $.60.
Hobbs, M. F. Play production made easy, prepared for the National recreation association. 71p. 1933. Nat'l Recreation Assn., 315 4th Ave., N. Y. C. $.50.

Kansas City, Missouri. Public Schools. American education week, November 6–12, 1933. (Kansas City school service bul. Vol. V, No. 4.) 29p. 1933. Dept. of Educ. of Kansas City Public Schools, Kansas City, Mo. $.10.
National Education Association. American education week, November 6–12; handbook 1933. 29p. 1933. The Association. $.25.
U. S. Office of Education. Nonathletic extracurriculum activities, by W. C. Reavis and G. E. Van Dyke. (Bul. 1932, No. 17, Monograph, No. 26.) 174p. 1933. Supt. of Doc. $.15.

(24) RURAL EDUCATION

American Country Life Conference. Adult education and rural life; proceedings of the fifteenth conference, Wheeling, West Virginia, October 14–16, 1932. 153p. 1933. Pub. by Univ. of Chicago Press for Amer. Country Life Assn., 105 E. 22nd. St., N. Y. C. $2.00.
California. State Department of Education. Handbook for rural parent teacher activities and relationships. (Bul. No. 12.) 109p. 1933. Cal. State Dept. of Educ., Sacramento, Cal.
California. State Department of Education. Teachers' appraisal of rural school supervisors' work in California, by E. E. Redit. (Bul. No. 16.) 32p. 1933. The Department, Sacramento, Cal.
Connecticut. State Board of Education. An investigation of 1st grade entrants in the rural schools of Connecticut, 1928–29. (Rural educ. Bul. No. 1.) *Mimeographed.* 64p. 1933. Conn. State Board of Educ., Hartford, Conn. Free, Ltd. distribution.
Cyr, F. W. Responsibility for rural-school administration; allocation of responsibilities in the administration of schools in rural areas, with special reference to the county. (Cont. to educ. No. 579.) 158p. 1933. Teachers College, Columbia. $1.75.
Experiment in rural reorganization. (Board of educ. pamphlet, No. 93.) 35p. 1933. British Library of Information, 270 Madison Ave., N. Y. C. $.20.
*Landis, B. Y., and Willard, J. D. Rural adult education. 229p. 1933. Macmillan. $1.75.
McConathy, Osbourne, and others. Music in rural education. 290p. 1933. Silver, Burdett. $1.20.
National Education Association. Department of Rural Education. Organization of curriculum for one-teacher schools. 44p. 1933. The Association. $.25.
New York (State) University. Handbook for rural elementary schools. The social studies group. (Curriculum bul. No. 2.) 235p. 1933. The Author. $.25.
Thrun, F. M. Rural school organization in Michigan. (Agric. experiment station, special bul. No. 229.) 32p. 1933. Mich. State College of Agric. and Applied Science, East Lansing, Mich. $.03.
U. S. Office of Education. School administrative units with special reference to the county unit, by W. S. Deffenbaugh and Timon Covert. (Pamphlet, No. 34.) 25p. 1933. Supt. of Doc. $.05.
U. S. Office of Education. Some effects of the economic situation upon the rural schools, by W. H. Gaumnitz. (Circular, No. 80.) *Mimeographed.* 18p. 1933. The Office. Gratis.

(25) HIGHER EDUCATION

American Association of University Professors. Report of the committee on college and university teaching. (Section 2.) 122p. 1933. The Association, 744 Jackson Pl., N. W., Washington, D. C. $.50.
American Association of University Women. Research information service in secondary and collegiate education. 6p. 1933. The Association. $.06.
American College Personnel Association. Report of the tenth annual meeting. 95p. 1933. Mrs. Esther Lloyd-Jones, Teachers College, Columbia. $2.50.
American Medical Association. Councils on Medical Education and Hospitals. Choice of a medical school. 12p. 1933. The Association. $.10.
Association of American Universities. Journal of proceedings and addresses of the thirty-fourth annual conference, held at the state university of Iowa, November 10–12, 1932. 166p. 1933. Univ. of Chicago Press. $1.00.
Association of Land Grant Colleges. Proceedings of the forty-sixth annual convention held at Washington, D. C., November 14–16, 1932, ed. by C. A. McCue. 512p. 1933. C. A. McCue, Agric. Experiment Station, Univ. of Del., Newark, Del. Gratis while supply lasts.
Association of University and College Business Officers of the Eastern States. Minutes of the 12th and 13th annual meetings, 1931–1932. 2 vols. 108p; 110p. 1933. The Association, H. S. Ford, Sec'y., Mass. Institute of Technology, Cambridge, Mass. Gratis.
Association of Urban Universities. Nineteenth annual meeting, 1932; summary of proceedings. 168p. 1933. The Association, C. S. Marsh, Sec'y., 25 Niagara Sq., Buffalo, N. Y. $1.00.
Bennett, H. G. Some implications of the coordination of higher education. (Bul. Vol. XXX, No. 6.) 16p. 1933. Agric. and Mechanical College, Stillwater, Okla. Gratis.
Brown, E. E. A few remarks. 251p. 1933. N. Y. Univ. Press. $2.00.
Bull, George. Function of the Catholic college; an address delivered at the convocation of faculties of Fordham University, May 14, 1933. 11p. 1933. Amer. Press, 461 8th Ave., N. Y. C. $.05.
Burstall, S. A. Retrospect and prospect; sixty years of women's education, with a preface by Sir Michael Sadler. 286p. 1933. Longmans. $3.00.
Campbell, D. S. Problems in the education of college women; a study of women graduates of southern colleges. (Field study, No. 6.) 80p. 1933. George Peabody College for Teachers, Division of Surveys and Field Studies. $.25.
Carnegie Foundation for the Advancement of Teaching. Annual review of legal education in the United States and Canada for the year 1932, by A. Z. Reed. 67p. 1933. The Foundation. Gratis.
Chamberlain, L. M., and Meece, L. E. State performance in higher education. (Univ. of Ky. Bur. of school service bul. Vol. V, No. 3.) 37p. 1933. The Campus Bookstore, Univ. of Ky., Lexington, Ky. $.50.
Chen, W. K. The influence of oral propaganda material upon students' attitudes. (Archives of psychology, No. 150.) 43p. 1933. Archives of Psychology, Columbia Univ., N. Y. C. $.80.
Clark, J. K. Pitfalls along the legal education road. (Law series I, No. 5.) 12p. 1933. Nat'l. Advisory Council on Radio in Educ., Univ. of Chicago Press. $.15.
College admission and guidance: report of a conference under the auspices of the cooperative test service and the committee on personnel methods of the American council on education and the Educational records bureau. (Reprint.) 110p. 1933. Amer. Council on Educ., 744 Jackson Pl., Washington, D. C. $2.00.
College Entrance Examination Board. Bulletin of general information for 1934. (Doc. No. 141.) 28p. 1933. The Board, 431 W. 117th St., N. Y. C. Gratis.
College Entrance Examination Board. Definition of the requirements, December, 1933. (Doc. No. 142.) 97p. 1933. The Board. $.30.
College Entrance Examination Board. Examination questions. (Comprehensive and restricted.) June and September, 1933. 257p. 1933. Ginn. $1.60.
Colorado. University. Abstracts of theses for higher degrees, 1933. (Bul. Vol. XXXIII, No. 16. Studies, Vol. XXI, No. 1.) 92p. 1933. The University. $1.00.
Columbia University. Honorary degrees awarded in the years 1902–1932; appreciations by N. M. Butler. 194p. 1933. Columbia Univ. Press. $4.00.
*Conference of Universities, New York, 1932. Obligation of universities to the social order, prepared under the editorial supervision of H. P. Fairchild. 503p. 1933. N. Y. Univ. Press. $2.00.
Conger, N. A study of the content of professional courses in education in institutions of higher learning in Oklahoma: summary. (Bul. No. 133.) 70p. 1933. State Dept. of Public Instruction, Oklahoma City, Okla.
Cook, R. C., *ed.* Presidents of American colleges and universities. 256p. 1933. Robert C. Cook Co., 296 Broadway, N. Y. C. $6.00.
Crothers, G. E. The educational ideals of Jane Lathrop Stanford, co-founder of the Leland Stanford junior university. 32p. 1933. The Author, DeYoung Bldg., San Francisco, Cal. $.25.
Frasier, G. W. The objectives of higher education in the light of contemporary social needs and trends. 24p. Colo. State Teachers College. $.25.

George Peabody College for Teachers. Division of Surveys and Field Studies. Report on functions of state institutions of higher learning in Mississippi: a basis for the allocation of funds. 73p. 1933. The College. Gratis.

*Gray, W. S., *ed.* Needed readjustments in higher education. (Proceedings of Institute for administrative officers of higher institutions, 1933, Vol. V.) 283p. 1933. Univ. of Chicago Press. $2.00.

Hartmann, G. W. Measuring teaching efficiency among college instructors. (Archives of psychology, No. 154.) 45p. 1933. Archives of Psychology, Columbia Univ., N. Y. C. $.80.

Harvard University. Graduate School of Arts and Sciences. Summaries of theses accepted in partial fulfilment of the requirements of the degree of doctor of philosophy, 1932. 380p. 1933. Harvard Univ. Press. $2.00.

Held, O. C. An attempt to predict the success of university freshmen in their adjustment to scholastic work. 50p. 1933. Edwards Bros.

Hill, D. W., and Kelly, F. J. Economy in higher education: Pt. I—Principles. Pt. II—Administration. 127p. 1933. Carnegie Foundation. Gratis.

Hodous, Lewis, *ed.* Careers for students of Chinese language and civilization, edited for the Committee on the promotion of Chinese studies of the American council of learned societies. 65p. 1933. Pub. by Univ. of Chicago Press for American Council of the Inst. of Pacific Relations, 129 E. 52nd St., N. Y. C. $1.00 cloth; $.25 paper.

Institute of International Education. American field service fellowships for French universities, including record of former fellows, by E. R. Murrow. (Bul. No. 3, series 14.) 62p. 1933. The Institute. $.25.

Institute of International Education. Guide book for American students in the British Isles. (Bul. No. 5, series 14.) Rev. ed. 104p. 1933. The Institute. $.25.

Institute of International Education. Handbook for American students in Italy by H. R. Marraro. (Bul. No. 2, series 14.) 58p. 1933. The Institute. $.25.

Institute of Women's Professional Relations. Fellowships and other aid for advanced work. Cumulative supplement 1930–33. 91p. 1933. Women's College of the Univ. of N. C. $.50.

Institute of Women's Professional Relations. Occupations for college women; a bibliography. (Bul. No. 1, Oct. 1929. Supplement, No. 4, Feb. 1933.) *Mimeographed.* 29p. 1933. Women's College of the Univ. of N. C. $.25.

International Institute of Intellectual Cooperation. (League of Nations.) Holiday courses in Europe, 1933. 60p. 1933. World Peace Foundation, 40 Mt. Vernon St., Boston, Mass. $.50.

Iowa State College. Council on Teaching. Some college teaching problems. (Bul. No. 4.) 16p. 1933. Ia. State Teachers' College, Cedar Falls, Ia.

*Jones, E. S. Comprehensive examinations in American colleges. 436p. 1933. Macmillan. $2.50.

Jones, E. S. Comprehensive examinations in the social sciences. (Supplement to Comprehensive examinations in American colleges by the same author.) 128p. 1933. Assn. of Amer. Colleges. $1.25.

Jones, R. M. Haverford College. 244p. 1933. Macmillan. $2.00.

Jones, T. F., *ed.* New York University, 1832–1932. 459p. 1933. N. Y. Univ. Bk. Store, 81 Washington Sq. E., N. Y. C. $3.00.

Journal of the proceedings of a convention of literary and scientific gentlemen, held in the common council chamber of the city of New York, October, 1830. 286p. 1933 reproduction of the 1831 edition. N. Y. Univ. Press. $2.00 bds.

Kelly, F. J., and McNeely, J. H. The state and higher education; phases of their relationship. 282p. 1933. Carnegie Foundation. Gratis.

Kramer, Stella. A path to understanding. 259p. 1933. The Author, West End Ave. at 92nd St., N. Y. C.

Larson, J. K., and Palmer, A. M. Architectural planning of the American college. 181p. 1933. McGraw-Hill. $2.00.

Leighton, R. W. Studies to determine the relative achievement of students at different potentiality levels. (Studies in college teaching, Vol. I, Bul. 1.) 32p. 1933. Univ. of Ore. $.25.

Mallory, A. E. The significance of plane geometry as a college entrance requirement. (Cont. to educ. No. 110.) 108p. 1933. George Peabody College for Teachers. $1.35.

Melcher, George. The junior college of Kansas City, Missouri. (Kansas City school service bul. Vol. V, No. 2.) unp. 1933. Dept. of Educ. of Kansas City Public Schools, Kansas City, Mo. $.10.

Meredith, W. F. Regulations concerning the acceptance of health and physical education for college entrance credit, state, regional and institutional. 188p. 1933. The Law Abstract Co., Newark, Ohio.

Michigan. University. Bureau of Educational Reference and Research. Abstracts of dissertations and theses in education, 1931–1932. (Monograph, No. 2.) 130p. 1933. The University, School of Educ. $1.00.

Minnesota. University. Committee on Educational Research. Collegiate educational research: report of the Committee on educational research for the biennium 1930–1932. (Bul. Vol. XXXVI, No. 1.) 32p. 1933. Univ. of Minn. Gratis.

Morgan, J. H. Dickinson College. The history of one hundred and fifty years, 1783–1933. 460p. 1933. Dickinson College, Carlisle, Pa. $3.00.

Morrison, R. H. Internal administrative organization in teachers colleges. (Cont. to educ. No. 592.) 193p. 1933. Teachers College, Columbia. $1.75.

Nanninga, S. P., and Knode, J. E., *editors.* Articulation of high school and college in New Mexico; report of a conference held at the University of New Mexico, July 21–22, 1933. (Educ. series, Vol. VII, No. 2.) 96p. 1933. Univ. of N. Mex. $.25.

National Committee on Standard Reports for Institutions of Higher Education. Suggested methods and forms for use in unit-cost studies in colleges and universities. (Bul. No. 8.) *Mimeographed.* 27p. and charts. 1933. The Committee, G. H. Mew, Sec'y., Emory Univ., Ga.

National Survey of the Education of Teachers. Curricula for the education of teachers in colleges and universities: supplementary report, by W. E. Peik. *Mimeographed.* 74p. 1933. U. S. Office of Educ. Gratis.

National Survey of the Education of Teachers. Curricula in teachers colleges and normal schools: supplementary report, by E. U. Rugg. *Mimeographed.* 76p. 1933. U. S. Office of Educ. Gratis.

National University Extension Association. Proceedings of the eighteenth annual convention at Bloomington, Indiana, May 24, 25, 26, 1933, Vol. XVI. 132p. 1933. Ind. Univ. $1.00.

New York School of Social Work. Social case work; an outline for teaching, with annotated case records and sample course syllabi, by a committee of the school; ed. by M. A. Cannon and Philip Klein. 626p. 1933. Columbia Univ. Press. $5.00.

New York (State) Chamber of Commerce. Survey of adult technical education in the New York industrial area. 179p. 1933. The Author, 65 Liberty St., N. Y. C. Apply.

Ohio State University. Abstracts of doctors' dissertations. (No. 11.) 1933. Ohio State Univ. $1.00.

Oxford. University. Handbook to the University of Oxford. 2nd ed. 465p. 1933. Oxford Univ. Press. $1.75.

Pallett, E. M. Studies of student mortality at the University of Oregon. (Studies in college teaching, Vol. I, bul. 2.) 32p. 1933. Univ. of Ore. $.25.

Peters, C. C., and Hartmann, G. W., *editors.* Abstracts of studies in education at the Pennsylvania State College, Pt. III. (State studies in educ. No. 8.) *Lithoprint.* 80p. 1933. Pa. State College, School of Educ. $.50.

Pittsburgh. University. Graduate school. Abstracts of theses, researches in progress, and bibliography of publications, Vol. IX. (Bul. Vol. XXX, No. 2.) 671p. 1933. The University. Gratis to public and university libraries.

Purdue University. Purdue University, 1922–32. 176p. 1933. The University. Gratis.

*Reeves, F. W., director, with ten associates. University of Chicago survey. 12 vols. 1933. Univ. of Chicago Press. $30 a set or sold separately.
Vol. I—Reeves, F. W., Miller, E. C., and Russell, J. D. Trends in university growth. 242p. $2.50.
Vol. II—Reeves, F. W., and others. The organization and administration of the university. 151p. $2.00.
Vol. III—Reeves, F. W., and others. The university faculty. 326p. $3.00.

Vol. IV—Reeves, F. W., Peik, W. E., and Russell, J. D. Instructional problems in the university. 245p. $2.50.
Vol. V—Reeves, F. W., and Russell, J. D. Admission and retention of university students. 360p. $3.00.
Vol. VI—Reeves, F. W., and Russell, J. D. The alumni of the colleges. 126p. $2.00.
Vol. VII—Raney, M. L. The university libraries. 250p. $2.50.
Vol. VIII—Reeves, F. W., and others. University extension services. 173p. $2.00.
Vol. IX—Reeves, F. W., Kelly, F. J., and Russell, J. D. University plant facilities. 154p. $2.00.
Vol. X—Reeves, F. W., and Russell, J. D. Some university student problems. 194p. $2.00.
Vol. XI—Reeves, F. W., Henry, N. B., and Russell, J. D. Class size and university costs. 229p. $2.50.
Vol. XII—Breasted, J. H. The oriental institute. 455p. $4.00.

Reid, W. D. Teaching methods in medicine; the application of the philosophy of contemporary education to medical schools. 111p. 1933. The Author, 510 Commonwealth Ave., Boston, Mass. $1.00.

Remmers, H. H. Exemption from college semester examinations as a condition of learning. (Studies in higher educ. XXIII.) 52p. 1933. Purdue Univ. $.50.

Remmers, H. H. Report on the uses made of the freshman entrance test results at Purdue University. (Bul. Vol. XXXIV, No. 4. Educ. reference circular, 5.) *Mimeographed.* 8p. 1933. Purdue Univ., Division of Educ. Reference. $.20.

Report on functions of state institutions of higher learning in Mississippi: a basis for the allocation of funds. 73p. 1933. George Peabody College for Teachers, Division of Surveys and Field Studies. Gratis.

Robson, B. R. House management problems of fraternities and sororities. 93p. 1933. Teachers College, Columbia. $1.00.

Rollins College. The American association of university professors; a study of its procedure together with some of the experiences of Rollins College in submitting to its "Investigation." (Bul. Vol. XXIX, No. 11.) 27p. 1933. The Author, Winter Park, Fla. $.40.

Seyfried, J. E. Youth and his college career: a discussion of student problems from the viewpoint of the high school graduate and the college beginner. 251p. 1933. Univ. of N. Mex. $2.25.

Smith, V. T. Correspondence between occupations and major specializations of graduates of the University of Illinois of the class of 1923. (Abstract of thesis.) 6p. 1933. Univ. of Ill. $.25.

Sparling, E. J. Do college students choose vocations wisely? (Cont. to educ. No. 561.) 110p. 1933. Teachers College, Columbia. $1.50.

Stephen, Barbara. Girton College, 1869–1932. 202p. 1933. Macmillan. $1.25.

Texas (Denton). North State Teachers College. Cooperative planning for teacher training standards in Texas: Vol. III, proceedings of third Texas conference on teacher training in Texas. (Bul. No. 100.) 165p. 1933. The College. $.10.

Thompson, C. O. The extension program of the University of Chicago. *Mimeographed.* 188p. 1933. Univ. of Chicago Press. $1.00.

U. S. Office of Education. Articulation of high school and college, by P. R. Brammell. (Bul. 1932, No. 17, Monograph, No. 10.) 96p. 1933. Supt. of Doc. $.10.

U. S. Office of Education. Biennial survey of education, 1930–1932. Chapters 1–7. (Bul. 1933, No. 2.) Apply for prices.

U. S. Office of Education. Collegiate courses in advertising, 1932, by J. O. Malott. (Circular, No. 90.) *Mimeographed.* 4p. 1933. The Office. Gratis.

U. S. Office of Education. Collegiate courses in banking and finance, 1932, by J. O. Malott. (Circular, No. 95.) *Mimeographed.* 12p. 1933. The Office. Gratis.

U. S. Office of Education. Collegiate courses in business law, 1932, by J. O. Malott. (Circular, No. 96.) *Mimeographed.* 6p. 1933. The Office. Gratis.

U. S. Office of Education. Collegiate courses in business organization and management, 1932, by J. O. Malott. (Circular, No. 100.) *Mimeographed.* 14p. 1933. The Office. Gratis.

U. S. Office of Education. Collegiate courses in accounting and business statistics, by J. O. Malott. (Circular, No. 94.) *Mimeographed.* 12p. 1933. The Office. Gratis.

U. S. Office of Education. Collegiate courses in foreign trade and foreign service, 1932, by J. O. Malott. (Circular, No. 97.) *Mimeographed.* 7p. 1933. The Office. Gratis.

U. S. Office of Education. Collegiate courses in insurance, 1932, by J. O. Malott. (Circular, No. 98.) *Mimeographed.* 4p. 1933. The Office. Gratis.

U. S. Office of Education. Collegiate courses in marketing and merchandising, 1932, by J. O. Malott. (Circular, No. 99.) *Mimeographed.* 8p. 1933. The Office. Gratis.

U. S. Office of Education. Collegiate courses in realty, 1932, by J. O. Malott. (Circular, No. 101.) *Mimeographed.* 3p. 1933. The Office. Gratis.

U. S. Office of Education. Collegiate courses in secretarial science, 1932, by J. O. Malott. (Circular, No. 102.) *Mimeographed.* 11p. 1933. The Office. Gratis.

U. S. Office of Education. Collegiate courses in transportation, 1932, by J. O. Malott. (Circular, No. 91.) *Mimeographed.* 4p. 1933. The Office. Gratis.

U. S. Office of Education. Cooperative part time courses in business offered by colleges and universities, 1932, by J. O. Malott. (Circular, No. 106.) *Mimeographed.* 2p. 1933. The Office. Gratis.

U. S. Office of Education. Correspondence courses in business subjects offered by colleges and universities, 1932, by J. O. Malott. (Circular, No. 105.) *Mimeographed.* 4p. 1933. The Office. Gratis.

U. S. Office of Education. Directory of collegiate bureaus of business research, 1933, by J. O. Malott. (Circular, No. 92.) *Mimeographed.* 4p. 1933. The Office. Gratis.

U. S. Office of Education. Economic outlook in higher education for 1933–34, by H. G. Badger. (Circular, No. 121.) *Mimeographed.* 19p. 1933. The Office. Gratis.

U. S. Office of Education. Evening classes in business subjects offered by colleges and universities, 1932, by J. O. Malott. (Circular, No. 104.) *Mimeographed.* 5p. 1933. The Office. Gratis.

U. S. Office of Education. Extension classes in business subjects offered by colleges and universities, 1932, by J. O. Malott. (Circular, No. 107.) *Mimeographed.* 3p. 1933. The Office. Gratis.

U. S. Office of Education. Higher education in foreign countries, its history and present status: a list of references, by J. F. Abel. (Circular, No. 77.) *Mimeographed.* 30p. 1933. The Office. Gratis.

U. S. Office of Education. Land-grant colleges and universities; preliminary report, 1933, by W. J. Greenleaf. (Circular, No. 126.) *Mimeographed.* 23p. 1933. The Office. Gratis.

U. S. Office of Education. University and college courses in radio, by C. M. Koon. (Circular, No. 53.) *Mimeographed.* 14p. 1933. The Office. Gratis.

Wellck, A. A. The annuity agreements of colleges and universities. 65p. 1933. The Author, 88 Morningside Drive, N. Y. C. $1.25 cloth; $1.00 paper.

(26) ADULT EDUCATION

American Association for Adult Education. Annual report, 1932–33. 39p. 1933. The Association. Gratis.

American Association of University Women. Book service facilities. 39p. 1933. The Association. $.10.

American Association of University Women. Publications; materials, reprints, and reference pamphlets for branch meetings, adult study groups, open forums, and communal activities. 32p. 1933. The Association. $.10.

*Bittner, W. S., and Mallory, H. F. University teaching by mail; a survey of correspondence instruction conducted by American universities. (Studies in adult educ.) 355p. 1933. Macmillan. $2.50.

Burdell, E. S. An adventure in education for the unemployed; a report and comment on two six weeks sessions of a free school for the unemployed. 45p. 1933. Ohio State Univ. Gratis.

California. State Department of Education. Lessons of practical information with exercises and drills for intermediate classes of adults. (Bul. No. 9.) 47p. 1933. Cal. State Dept. of Educ., Sacramento, Cal. $.10.

Carter, Jean. Mastering the tools of the trade; suggestive material for experimental use in the teaching of English in workers' classes. Rev. ed. 44p. 1933. Affiliated School for Workers, Inc., 302 E. 35th St., N. Y. C. $.25.
Educational opportunities of greater Boston for working men and women. Catalog No. 11, 1933–1934. 157p. 1933. The Prospect Union Educational Exchange, 678 Massachusetts Ave., Cambridge, Mass. $.50.
Herring, J. W. Social planning and adult education. 138p. 1933. Macmillan. $1.25.
*Kotinsky, Ruth. Adult education and the social scene; with a foreword by W. H. Kilpatrick. 208p. 1933. Appleton-Century. $2.00.
*Landis, B. Y., and Willard, J. D. Rural adult education. 229p. 1933. Macmillan. $1.75.
Manwell, E. M., and Praeger, Rosamond. A course for the preparation of lay leaders of parent study groups. (Guidance materials for study groups, No. 12.) 81p. 1933. Amer. Assn. of Univ. Women. $.60.
Michigan. University. Extension Division. Parent education. 44p. 1933. The University. Gratis.
National Congress of Parents and Teachers. Parent-teacher manual; a guidebook for leaders of local congress units. 179p. 1933. The Congress. $.20.
National Congress of Parents and Teachers. Proceedings of the thirty-seventh annual meeting, Seattle, Washington, May 21–26, 1933, Vol. XXXVII. 488p. 1933. The Congress. $2.50 cloth; $2.00 paper.
National Congress of Parents and Teachers. A publicity manual for parent-teacher workers. 87p. 1933. The Congress. $.50 cloth; $.25 paper.
National Education Association. Department of Adult Education. What American leaders say about adult education: thirty-nine representative Americans present their views on the importance of the education of adults, especially during the present crisis. 19p. 1933. The Department. Gratis.
Nelson, T. H., *ed.* Adult education for social needs. (Occasional study, No. 16.) 96p. 1933. Association Press. $1.00.
Nelson, T. H. Ventures in informal adult education, with an introduction by G. B. Cutten. *Mimeographed.* 120p. 1933. Association Press. $1.00.
Noffsinger, J. S., *comp.* Home study blue book. 5th ed. 32p. 1933. Nat'l. Home Study Council, 839 17th St., NW., Washington, D. C. Gratis.
The parent-educator; a series of papers on the problems of parents as educators of their children, Vol. III. 71p. 1933. St. Anthony Guild Press, Paterson, N. J. $.50.
Sorenson, Herbert. Adult abilities in extension classes: a psychological study. 100p. 1933. Univ. of Minn. Press. $1.00.
Stoddard, G. D. What the kindergarten and nursery school have in store for parent and child. (Child welfare pamphlets, No. 17.) 7p. 1933. Univ. of Ia. $.05.
Taylor, N. B. Programs for parents. Rev. ed. 48p. 1933. State Teachers College, St. Cloud, Minn. $.25.
U. S. Office of Education. Report on 206 part-time and continuation schools, by M. M. Proffitt. (Pamphlet, No. 38.) 12p. 1933. Supt. of Doc. $.05.

(27) VISUAL AND RADIO EDUCATION

American School of the Air. Teachers' manual and classroom guide, 1932–33. 79p. 1933. Columbia Broadcasting System, Inc. Gratis.
Arnspiger, V. C. Measuring the effectiveness of sound pictures as teaching aids. (Cont. to educ. No. 565.) 156p. 1933. Teachers College, Columbia. $2.00.
*Devereux, F. L. The educational talking picture. 222p. 1933. Univ. of Chicago Press. $2.00.
*Forman, H. J. Our movie made children. 288p. 1933. Macmillan. $2.50.
George Peabody College for Teachers. Department of Industrial Education. Industrial education films. *Mimeographed.* unp. 1933. George Peabody College for Teachers. $.50 single copy; $.35 ten or more each.
*MacLatchy, J. H., *ed.* Education on the air: fourth yearbook of the Institute for education by radio. 380p. 1933. Ohio State Univ., Bur. of Educ. Research. $3.00.
Merry, R. V. Problems in the education of visually handicapped children. (Harvard studies in educ. vol. XIX.) 243p. 1933. Harvard Univ. Press. $2.50.
Modern trends in education: syllabus for teacher-training course utilizing educational talking pictures, ed. by the Educational research staff. *Mimeographed.* 170p. 1933. Erpi Picture Consultants, Inc., 250 W. 57th St., N. Y. C. $1.50.
National Education Association. Department of Visual Instruction. Visual instruction directory, 1933. 80p. 1933. Office of the Sec'y., 1812 Illinois St., Lawrence, Kan. $1.50.
Rulon, P. J. The sound motion picture in science teaching. (Harvard studies in educ. Vol. XX.) 236p. 1933. Harvard Univ. Press. $2.50.
Sigman, J. G. Origin and development of visual education in the Philadelphia public schools. 249p. 1933. Temple Univ. Press. $1.00.
Tyler, T. F. An appraisal of radio broadcasting in the land-grant colleges and state universities. 150p. 1933. Nat'l Committee on Educ. by Radio, Washington, D. C. Gratis to city, state, and univ. libraries.
Tyler, T. F. Some interpretations and conclusions of the land-grant radio survey. 25p. 1933. Nat'l Committee on Educ. by Radio, Washington, D. C. Gratis to city, state, and univ. libraries.
*Tyson, Levering, *ed.* Radio and education: proceedings of the 1933 annual assembly of the National advisory council on radio in education. 203p. 1933. Univ. of Chicago Press. $2.50.
U. S. Office of Education. The art of teaching by radio, by C. M. Koon. (Bul. 1933, No. 4.) 92p. 1933. Supt. of Doc. $.10.
Wisconsin. University. Bureau of Visual Instruction. Visual aids, 1933–1934; catalogue of educational sixteen millimeter motion picture films (narrow width), offered for loan by Bureau of visual instruction, University extension division. (Bul. series No. 1920, General series, No. 1704.) 69p. 1933. The University. Gratis.

(28) EDUCATION FOR THE NEW SOCIAL ORDER

Adamson, Sir John. Externals and essentials. 152p. 1933. Longmans. $1.35.
Angell, Norman. From chaos to control. (Halley Stewart lecture, 1932.) 208p. 1933. Appleton-Century. $2.00.
*Conference of Universities, New York, 1932. Obligation of universities to the social order, prepared under the editorial supervision of H. P. Fairchild. 503p. 1933. N. Y. Univ. Press. $2.00.
Haggerty, M. E. Children of the depression. (Day and hour series, No. 6.) 25p. 1933. Univ. of Minn. Press. $.25.
International understanding through youth; interchanges and travel of school pupils. (International co-operation series.) 120p. 1933. World Peace Foundation, 40 Mt. Vernon St., Boston, Mass. $1.85 cloth; $1.50 paper.
*Judd, C. H. Problems of education in the United States. (Recent social trends monographs.) 214p. 1933. McGraw-Hill. $2.50.
Kilpatrick, W. H., and others. The educational frontier. 325p. 1933. Appleton-Century. $2.50. (Published also as: Yearbook No. 21 of the National society of college teachers of education. Univ. of Chicago Press. $1.50 paper.)
Lindeman, E. C. Social education: an interpretation of the principles and methods developed by the Inquiry during the years 1923–1933. 233p. 1933. New Republic, Inc., 421 W. 21st St., N. Y. C. $1.00.
Mehnert, Klaus. Youth in Soviet Russia; tr. by Michael Davidson. 270p. 1933. Harcourt. $2.00.
National Education Association. Division of Publications. Selected quotations on the emergency in education as seen by leading citizens and editors; prepared for the joint commission on the emergency in education. *Mimeographed.* 19p. 1933. The Association. Gratis.
*National Recreation Association. The new leisure challenges the schools; shall recreation enrich or impoverish life? Based on a study made by E. T. Lies. 326p. 1933. The Author, 315 4th Ave., N. Y. C. $1.50 paper; $2.00 cloth.
Reeder, R. R. Training youth for the new social order. 248p. 1933. Antioch Press. $2.00.
*Woelfel, Norman. Molders of the American mind, a critical review of the social attitudes of seventeen leaders in American education. 304p. 1933. Columbia Univ. Press. $3.00.

SCHOOL AND SOCIETY

WITH WHICH ARE COMBINED THE EDUCATIONAL REVIEW, ESTABLISHED IN 1891, THE TEACHERS MAGAZINE, ESTABLISHED IN 1878, AND THE SCHOOL JOURNAL, ESTABLISHED IN 1874.

EDITED BY J. McKEEN CATTELL, R. D. LINDQUIST AND W. H. COWLEY

EDITORIAL COMMUNICATIONS SHOULD BE ADDRESSED TO THE EDUCATION BUILDING, THE OHIO STATE UNIVERSITY, COLUMBUS, OHIO

Volume 39 SATURDAY, MARCH 31, 1934 Number 1005

PUBLIC EDUCATION AND THE NATION'S BUSINESS[1]

By EDWARD A. FILENE
BOSTON, MASSACHUSETTS

I CAN not speak to professional educators upon the theory and technique of education. When business men assume to educate our educators, the results are not always satisfactory. They may even educate the educators into an understanding of what a lot of things there are in life which business men do not know.

But educators also are not free from unwarranted assumption. That has recently become obvious. No matter how big a fool a big business man may make of himself before an audience of educators, those educators have usually assumed that he *did* understand business. And we know now that that is not so.

Great financiers wrecked our finances. Power kings turned out to be weaklings. Captains of industry fled from the battle at the first smell of danger and, by cutting wages and curtailing the public buying power, led the grand stampede away from industry and toward unemployment.

It is time, surely, that we business men should be very humble and begin to question our assumption of a divine prerogative to give advice to everybody else. And yet I do not see how business could, if it were in a mood to do so, keep its hands off our problems of education. Nor can I see how education can longer leave the field of business to business men. Business problems are your problems quite as definitely as they are ours. And uneducated as we may be to cope with it, the problem of education is our problem quite as much as it is yours. The time has come when we must think these things through together.

Fifty years' study of the problem of business, and of the social and political problems which have arisen from the evolution of business, has compelled me to see that there is no basic solution for them except in education. On the other hand—and I say it with full knowledge that I am unqualified to tell professional educators what to do—I have been forced to conclude that there is no solution merely in more education of the traditional and customary kind.

No student of business during the past fifty years could fail to note how the whole world was being brought closer and closer together by the advance of trade. But there was no general education in accordance with this great world fact, with the result that the world was torn to pieces in war.

No student of business evolution in

[1] Address before the sixth general session, Department of Superintendence, National Education Association, Cleveland, Ohio, February 28, 1934.

America could fail to note the inescapable tendency within our economic mechanism toward greater and greater cooperation. But our education was not in cooperation. Our education was in hotter and hotter competition and in rugged individualism.

It was evident everywhere that we were living in a new order, but it was equally evident that we were experiencing a new and increasing disorder, and we were not being educated to discover what the trouble was.

We said, for instance, that parents should bring up their children in the way that parents used to bring them up; not troubling ourselves very much to find out why they were not doing so or even if such a thing were no longer possible. We said there should be stricter laws and swifter justice, and thousands of committees and commissions busied themselves promoting this and that reform. But we were dealing everywhere with effects, not causes. Everybody was engaged in repair work, not in reconstruction in accordance with the revolutionary changes through which our world was passing.

In the so-called exact sciences, to be sure, amazing progress was being made; and a new discovery in a chemical laboratory might suddenly result in the total scrapping of huge industrial plants and the inauguration not only of new methods, but also of a new science and a new approach to the whole fundamental problem. In our social, political and educational experimenting, however, we have had no such luck.

We never exchange a going social order for a better one if we can help it. We wait invariably until the old order is completely wrecked, and then our tendency is to keep as much of the old pattern in the new design as possible.

We suffer from corrupt and inefficient government in our cities; but if it is not too utterly corrupt, it is next to impossible to get our citizens to do anything about it. And when they are aroused to elect a reform administration, the reforms are usually so ineffective that there is always imminent danger of the majority voting in the forces of evil again.

It is true that we have experimental schools; and after years and years of discouraging effort, some of these experiments are gradually given an opportunity to make limited demonstrations here and there; but you educators know how slow the process is. Now, why is this process slow? Is it because we have so much time that there is no need for haste? Is it because we are producing such a satisfactory brand of citizenship now that we can afford to let well enough alone? Or is it, perchance, that Americans are naturally so conservative that great changes are not to be expected?

We all know that it is none of these. We have little time. Staggering problems are pressing upon us, requiring a degree of understanding that we have not developed. Our citizens are not only unequipped to cope with these new problems, but are pitifully unable often to maintain standards of ordinary honesty and decency in their municipal and state, and sometimes even in their national governments.

As for conservatism, the average American is not in the least averse to change. Millions of Americans turn in fine, serviceable and efficient automobiles annually because each insists upon having a car with a few new ideas in it. You may criticize that attitude. You may call it flashy. You may call it extravagant. The point is that you can not call it conservative.

But how about the matter of human relations in America and the American's attitude toward them? Our educators will agree, I think, that there can be no more important problem. All morality, all character, all so-called spiritual development can be measured only in terms of human relations and the responsibilities which they entail. But how many Americans, up to March 4, 1933, evinced any particular eagerness for new ideas in that direction?

Have your American schools so advanced in their understanding of human relations as to be able to sell us a better code of human conduct year after year? Have they kept pace, say, with the motorcar industry? Some may think these questions unfair. We can not draw an analogy, they will say, between the development of human character and the development of a machine. The schools, they will protest, do teach good citizenship. They uphold the moral code. They exalt virtue and warn against vice. And if it happens that crime and corruption fill the land, the responsibility lies with the criminal and the corrupt, not with an educational system which has consistently held up the opposite ideal.

In other words, we should judge our educational system by its intentions—not by its results. Well, we will not argue the point. Let us ask, rather, Why do we get such great and such rapid results in the field of chemistry and physics, and why are results so slow and so disappointing in the matter of human conduct and of human character? Is it because we understand the laws of chemistry and of physics, and can therefore teach them accurately and exactly, whereas we do not know the laws of moral and spiritual development and can not be certain as to just what we should teach?

No. The exact opposite is the case. We do not know the laws of chemistry and physics. We know we do not—therefore we have to find out what they are, and therefore we do make appreciable progress.

As to moral conduct, however, we are sure that we know it all to start with. Therefore, we don't have to learn anything. Therefore, no matter how human relations may change, we make little change in our teaching—at least until conditions get so terrible that no one takes the old teachings seriously any longer, and we don't even believe them ourselves. Therefore, we do not make appreciable progress.

One result of this sort of moral education is that many students do not see the point and eventually become bad men, while others readily accept it and become good men. And the result upon society, as a rule, is that many of the good do more harm than the bad.

It has been good men, not bad, who have given us our worst government. It has been good men, not bad, who have led us into wars. It was good men who exploited labor most abominably. It was good men, as a rule, who recently wrecked our financial system and brought millions to the verge of starvation.

These were men of character. If they had been more self-indulgent weaklings, they would never have been exalted to such places of power. They were educated, according to our existing concept of education, both intellectually and morally. You could trust them absolutely not to pick your pocket or to hit you over the head with a lead pipe. They were fine husbands and fathers. They fairly doted on their families, and they denied themselves leisure, often preferring to toil and scheme early and late to make it possible for those families to live like royalty, that is, as royalty used to live.

No, they were not immoral. Some of them did not even break the law. But they broke the country. They were educated, but they didn't know any better. For they were not educated in human relations as they are and had no conception of their responsibilities. They were educated in the code of human relations as they used to be; and their conduct was conduct which used to be all right.

They understood the necessity for sweeping changes in industry; for production had become a matter of fact-finding, and when they found a way to produce more goods with less overhead, they did not hesitate to scrap their obsolescent machinery. But they saw no necessity for any change in man's attitude toward man. That subject had never been presented in terms of fact-finding at all. Those who proposed sweeping changes in this field—that is, changes in keeping with the sweep of events—were looked upon as extremists. It seemed normal and Americans generally were educated to think of it as normal, that in a world where human relations were changing with dazzling rapidity, our attitude toward human problems should change only by imperceptible degrees.

We called this attitude conservatism, although, as we must now perceive, nothing whatever was conserved by it. We can not conserve the values of the past by trying to conserve the formulas of the past. A course of conduct which is normal and constructive in an agrarian age may become abnormal and destructive in a machine age.

"The letter killeth. Only the spirit giveth life." Orthodoxy in morals is the end of true morality; for by overemphasizing those virtues which were once successfully developed, it neglects to call attention to the virtues which most need to be developed now.

Similarly, orthodoxy in teaching is the death of education. Teaching children what to think can not possibly fit them for life in these changing times. We do not know what they should think; for they must deal with things which we know nothing about. We must teach them how to think—how to find out about those things, so that they may apply this new knowledge to the new problems with which they will inevitably be faced.

That way, I am convinced, lies education. With the old approach, much of our education becomes a lie. Naïve ignorance is dangerous enough, but confident knowledge of things that have ceased to be true is more dangerous. The toughest task before the business man to-day is not the learning of business. It is the unlearning of what he was taught was business—what he is positively sure is business because it used to be business.

We may even learn a lot of new truths; but if we simply add them to our ancient superstitions, we are very likely to be sunk. That is how business was so recently sunk. American business men generally had come to see that high wages meant high buying-power; and in the early days of the depression they made more or less effort to keep wages up. That was a wonderful new thing in history, but it didn't work. It didn't work because we tried to combine that idea with a lot of fatal knowledge which we had not yet unlearned.

We tried to keep wages at a certain level, for instance, when, if we had studied all the facts, we would have seen that that level was still not high enough to provide a market for the enormous and constantly increasing output of our machine age. So we couldn't sell and we had to slow production down; and we laid off men and created unemployment and put still further crimps in the public's buying power. And when the public inevitably bought still less, we dropped the high-wage theory as impractical and brought on conditions of panic and paralysis. Now, we did that because we didn't know any better; and we didn't know any better, not because of any natural stupidity, but because we had not been properly educated.

Oh, I know what educators can say. They can say that we business men would not permit the schools to tackle the problem of human relations in the same bold, experimental, fact-finding way in which they tackle the problems of chemistry and physics.

That's true. The schools have turned out

graduates so densely ignorant of the things which most needed to be known that these graduates would not permit the schools to turn out a better product. There is no need, then, of the pot calling the kettle black. Traditional thinking was our common enemy. Neither the best type of business nor the best type of education could, in the very nature of things, result from it. And so, in the course of time, we had a nation with more graduates per square foot than had ever been known before, utterly baffled by the problem of how to keep a people with great surpluses of all life's necessities from suffering individually for the want of them.

I think I can say without even being accused of partisanship, that had it not been for the extraordinary leadership of President Roosevelt, America would very likely have been thrown into some such social convulsion as has occurred in several European countries. And had there been such a convulsion, it would not have been the fault of radical tendencies in America, but of a fixed and firm American tradition which would not permit us to consider and to deal with fundamental changes when those fundamental changes were actually taking place. We had to wait for a collapse.

What, I wonder, would any of us think of a system of physical education, if its graduates uniformly waited for a physical collapse before taking any measures to guard their health? We know that many individuals are thus neglectful, but the course is not advocated and accepted as normal. It is chiefly in the matter of human relations—of the actual structure of society—that we have learned not to expect results from our educational efforts.

This structure is basically economic. It changes as our economic mechanism changes; and if in this period of the greatest and most rapid changes in human history, we do not find out what these changes are and how they relate us to other human beings, we shall be powerless to deal with the human problems which arise.

If these changes were a great mystery and beyond the province of human investigation, perhaps the only hope for society would be to keep its members regimented as far as possible, under high-pressure policing, according to some code of conduct handed down to use from heaven knows where. But our economic structure, complicated as it may be, is no more mysterious than the human body; and the human relations which are determined by it can be and would be understood and dealt with, if it were our educational practise to approach the problem in an objective, fact-finding way.

Now, I do not presume to give you the formula for this new and necessary kind of teaching. You have the formula already and are using it constantly. In the scientific courses—that is, the courses which aim, not merely at the handing down of old knowledge but the digging up of knowledge which has never been known before—students are encouraged to experiment and to make a note of everything that happens. And when they complete an experiment successfully, they are encouraged to apply the principles which they have learned to the perfection of chemical, mechanical and electrical apparatus which, if perfected, will still further change human relations.

But they are encouraged to employ this method in solving the problems of these new human relations. You educators know, better than I can tell you.

It is suggested that they clean up their cities by this method. Or are they not exhorted, rather, to stick to the traditional method—the method by which we periodically throw bad men out of office and elect good men to do the bad things thereafter.

It is suggested that, having learned the scientific method, they try their hands at creating an up-to-date constitution for

America, in place of one which divides us into now meaningless geographical districts and makes it next to impossible for our so-called representatives to achieve a national view?

It is suggested that they find out what are the moral principles governing human conduct in this machine age and that they employ fact-finding for the purpose of constructing a practical moral code? Or are they not urged, rather, to follow the codes which were practical in societies where human relations were altogether different?

We can not make good citizens of those who can not see their actual relation to society, and are not, therefore, conscious of their actual responsibilities. We may make them obedient and law-abiding, and they may even be well-intentioned and kind. But good citizenship demands a positive, constructive attitude toward society, and an understanding of the relationships involved. We can not develop this by telling children to be good, or even by priming them with the formulas of goodness which actually were effective and constructive in the days when human society was put together in very different ways.

What we do get from this attempt to fasten ancient formulas upon modern minds—and calling the process education—is not even the conservatism which seems to be our aim. When we try to teach people what to think, instead of how to think, we get such extremes of conduct as to threaten our social stability.

I refer to the law of pendulum thinking. Now it is possible that you never heard of any law by that particular name. I do not care about that. I do not care what you call it, and if you can give it a better name, I shall not be offended. But the law is obvious and it works like this.

Whenever a society hangs on to a formula as long as it can, and does not change it when, as and if the facts disclose that it needs changing, it eventually lets go of that formula with a violent reaction. It does not go back to some moderate, more rational position. It swings definitely to the opposite extreme; and when this position becomes no longer tenable, back it goes again, away past the point of equilibrium, toward the first or a similar extreme once more.

America has seemingly been saved in the nick of time from such a catastrophe by the sudden introduction of experiment and fact-finding in government and business relations, before the point of desperation had quite been reached. The secret of President Roosevelt's leadership can not be found either in his charming personality or in his exceptional political acumen. Fortunately, he is well equipped with both; and considering the seriousness of the national crisis, we may well rejoice that he is so endowed. Nevertheless, the essential greatness of the President lies in the fact that he has not appealed to tradition or to prejudice. He has not even appealed to "public opinion," for the crisis was one in which government by opinion would not do. He did not say: "This is my platform, and I shall abide by it," or "This is my creed and I shall remain loyal."

What he said in effect was: "This is the trouble; and this is one of the things which we are going to try in seeking to effect a cure. If the experiment is successful, we shall go on with it. If it fails, we shall abandon it and try something else."

The nation is not out of danger yet by any means. Already the voice of the Tory is heard in the land, not with any contention that the President is ignoring the facts, but that he is violating the sacred traditions of pioneer times, when everybody of necessity did business according to his individual hunches and protected his profits with his individual six-shooter.

There is great promise, however, that America will now turn permanently to fact-finding in the arrangement of its economic affairs, and this promise must be of peculiar interest to educators. For with fact-finding accepted as the normal approach to the study of human relations, the schools will be freed to educate in a sense in which they have not been able to educate before.

Education, I understand, means drawing out—the drawing out of the individual mind into a greater and greater awareness—especially awareness of one's relations to the community and the acceptance of the responsibilities which they suggest. But heretofore our schools, even if the business interests had permitted it, could scarcely have initiated their students into an understanding of America with any certainty that the understanding would make for effective loyalty and devotion.

For America, with all its prosperity, was chaotic; and drawing out the mind of youth into an awareness of this chaos, while it might lead some to seek the way of law and order, was quite likely to result in the acceptance of chaos as a fundamental condition of life. Millions at least were so educated—in and outside the schools. The result was cynicism, individualism, irresponsibility—the negation of any purpose and plan, and therefore of any real faith in life.

At last, however, we have the beginnings of an ordered society in this machine age. By fact-finding, we have discovered that it did have a human purpose after all. The function of business, we have discovered, is to get goods to people—not merely to offer goods for sale, but to enable the masses to buy. This, of course, will necessitate a plan; and the plan is being worked out, not according to anybody's utopian dreams but with a direct and scientific approach to the social facts.

Under this plan, whatever its eventual details may prove to be, we know that the masses must have a more adequate share of the wealth that is produced. We know also that they must have leisure, else they can not consume the masses of things which, under science, have become available now. But they must have more than that. They must have responsibility, an awareness of their relation to the whole plan and consequent interest in its success.

All this could not be taught before, because it was never true before. Earnest critics of our social planlessness could proclaim their theories; but so could self-seeking demagogues, while dreary traditionalists chanted their outworn formulas of the past. There might be endless debate, but the economic struggle was so strenuous that few could give attention to the merits of the debate. Under the circumstances, we can hardly wonder that education failed.

But that era, it appears, is over. The day of economic order and of social understanding has dawned. Our opinions may differ widely still, but now it doesn't matter. We are through, I hope, with following opinions; we are now after the facts of everybody's relation to everybody else. Nor will the intense struggle for individual existence divert us now from considering these facts. For that struggle has now become collective, and it is to everybody's individual interest to see to it that everybody else's interest is considered.

That is the meaning of the New Deal. That is the meaning of all these business codes; and those who are viewing the event in terms of particular criticism are missing the point entirely. It may be that this administration, which I have considered so wise, is doing wrong and foolish things. But if so, in the very nature of this fact-finding program, errors will be corrected as they are proven to be errors. Some plan which will take everybody into consideration must eventuate; and it must provide for consumption by the masses of the tremendous volume of wealth which the masses, under science and scientific management, are now able to produce.

Fascism does not provide for that. Hitlerism, based on the archaic theory that might makes right and the end justifies the means, can have no enduring social plan. Nor does communism provide for it; although, to be fair to the great Russian experimenters, we must recognize that it is their ultimate intention to provide for everybody when in the course of time everybody shall have been made over into an unquestioning communist.

In America, however, regardless of our conflicting theories, we may all unite in finding out just what plan will make such ample provision for everybody. Our machine has become so productive that capitalism can not continue unless adequate consumption is provided for, and if, as some contend, capitalism can not continue if there is such adequate consumption, none of us need worry. So long as everybody is provided with wealth, leisure, security and culture, and in the nature of this provision, becomes so definitely and understandably related to the whole scheme that social responsibility may normally be expected, it will make little difference whether we call it capitalism or something else.

Education in this new age will be effective because it will be dealing not with the worn-out axioms of former ages, nor with the other-worldly dreams of those who can find no place in their utopias for the facts of human nature. It will be effective because it will be dealing with actualities. And there is no reason why it should not be as effective in the development of social and spiritual values as it now is in the development of material achievements.

THE EDUCATIONAL PROGRAM OF THE CIVILIAN CONSERVATION CORPS[1]

By C. S. MARSH

EDUCATIONAL DIRECTOR, CIVILIAN CONSERVATION CORPS, U. S. OFFICE OF EDUCATION

FROM the hundreds of letters written by young men in CCC camps I have selected a paragraph. The letter tells the usual story. The boy is a high-school graduate who had hoped to go to college. With no money and no job he roamed the country hungry, hopeless, bitter. He tells of enrolling in the CCC, of his impoverished physical condition, his renewed hope and particularly his joy in his day's work. He says:

> A new confidence has entered my being which has renewed my old hopes so that I am confident that they shall be fulfilled. The CCC has given me the power and confidence of creating things with my own hands. It has helped me create something that shall not only be admired by my generation, but for generations to come. This I have done with my own hands, and each time that I finish a piece of work I have a feeling that must be akin to that of some famous musician as he receives the plaudits of his admiring audience, or some sculptor exhibiting a piece of work to his patron.

A young man who is capable of such development should have a chance to continue his education while in camp. This paper tells you what is being done for him and many thousands more.

The Civilian Conservation Corps is a part of the Emergency Conservation Work program. It was authorized by Congress on March 31, 1933, and approved by the President that same day. Five days later President Roosevelt appointed Mr. Robert Fechner director of the Emergency Con-

[1] A paper read before the Research Section, Department of Secondary School Principals, National Education Association, Cleveland, Ohio, on February 28, 1934.

servation Work, and by executive order designated four departments of the Government, *viz.*, War, Labor, Interior and Agriculture, to work with him in setting up and operating a system of camps.

As stated by Director Fechner:

> The outstanding objectives of this new legislation were the relief of acute distress through furnishing employment to jobless men, the accomplishment of useful work in the forests and parks, the rehabilitation of young men whose morale and health had been undermined by the depression, and the reduction of state relief burdens, through the payment of cash allowances to men whose dependents were in dire need.

The Civilian Conservation Corps proper is composed of 218,000 young men from 18 to 25 years of age, 26,000 war veterans and approximately 45,000 experienced woodsmen. Under separate management, there are Indian camps on Indian reservations, and still others in Hawaii, Puerto Rico and Alaska.

The Labor Department, through a designated agency in every state, selects the men, except the veterans, who are selected by the Veterans Administration; the War Department enrolls the men, transports them to camps, houses, feeds, clothes, cares for them, provides recreation and educational opportunity; the Forest Service in the Department of Agriculture and the Parks Service in the Department of Interior, in the main plan and supervise the day's work of the men, five days a week, eight hours a day.

The enrollee receives a cash allowance of $30 a month, of which the Government, with few exceptions, send $25 to his home. Certain supervisory positions pay somewhat more. We are now in the second six months' camp period, which will close on March 31. The President has approved two more periods; necessary legislation is expected.

With dramatic power Director Fechner has told in the press and over the radio what these camps have accomplished: That in these nearly 12 months since camps were authorized 486,000 men have been enrolled; forest fire losses have been reduced; tree and plant disease curtailed; flood control advanced; soil erosion decreased; in round numbers $100,000,000 total pay has been issued; that the average gain in weight per man has been 7.2 pounds (some have gained as much as 12 pounds); that courage and pride have returned to men in the forests and to their dependent families at home.

When the first camps were set up in the spring of 1933, it was not long before Dr. George F. Zook, U. S. Commissioner of Education, other Government officials and many public-spirited citizens realized that these young men, living together in camps, needed something more in the way of an educational program than the War Department was at that time able to supply; that effective rehabilitation of these young men demanded not only that they be fed and clothed and given honest work to do, but that in their spare time they be given the utmost opportunity to learn about the world in which they live and their relation to it.

Ultimately, in December, 1933, the President, Mr. Fechner, the War Department and the commissioner of education approved the plan which this paper portrays.

The administration set-up for the educational program is as follows: Under the commissioner of education in Washington an educational director of the Civilian Conservation Corps has general supervision of the whole educational enterprise. The War Department operates the camps. Now the War Department divides the United States into 9 Army Corps areas, in each of which is a commanding general. At each of these nine area headquarters we have an educational supervisor or adviser, appointed by the office of Education but responsible to the area commander. This educational adviser functions on the one hand as a member of the commanding general's staff (his adviser on this educational program) and on the other hand as the supervisor of the educational effort in all the camps within the area. There are 1,468 camps. They are located in every state of the Union, except two. In each of these camps is a camp educational adviser, selected and appointed by the Office of Education and responsible to the camp commander. Assisting this camp educational adviser in each camp is one enrollee chosen from the ranks for his fitness to help in the camp program. He is called an assistant camp leader. In addition also to these two men, who give their full time to the camp educational program, there are usually in each camp three military officers and several members of the forestry and parks staff, all of whom are interested in the educational program and most of whom are actively helping to carry it on.

What are we trying to teach these men? Anything they want to be taught. I repeat, anything *they want*. Study is wholly voluntary on their part. In one Army Corps area a January report showed enrolments of men as indicated for these subjects:

Botany	339	First Aid	1,336
Citizenship	473	Personal hygiene	2,136
English	444	Surveying	616
Forestry	2,716	Zoology	168

Also algebra, astronomy, bookkeeping, entomology, geology, history, music, painting, sociology, trigonometry—all these and many more subjects were taught.

In another Army Corps area an analysis of the previous schooling of 47,734 enrollees showed 211 college graduates and at the other extreme 666 with no schooling. If 100 enrollees in this area were taken as a statistical sample they would classify thus:

2 would have had no schooling.
50 would have attended elementary school, 23 of whom would have graduated.
44 would have attended high school, 15 of whom would have graduated.
4 would have attended college.

The study effort in camp must necessarily be informal in many cases. We in the Office of Education think the more informal the better. We are not striving for credits. Here is learning prompted by desire for knowledge. Here are scores of thousands of young men figuratively, and sometimes literally, on the ends of logs; we need thousands of Mark Hopkinses. Have we got them? How would you go about it to pick 1,468 Mark Hopkinses, under pressure of time and with the obligation to take only men who are unemployed?

This is the plan which the Office of Education followed. In each state a committee of three public education state officials was asked to furnish a list of suitable candidates for these camp advisory positions—twice as many names as camps in each state, with the names ranked in order of the merits of the candidates. It was an enormous task, but it was promptly and conscientiously done. Generously these officials gave their time, many of them two solid weeks, interviewing thousands of candidates in order to furnish the lists. From these lists the Office of Education in Washington chose the 1,468 camp advisers.[2] Many hundreds of men who had been city and county superintendents or principals were listed. You will be interested in the degree of training of the men chosen from one state list: 23 were selected, and of these one has his doctor's degree, 15 have their master's degree and each of the remaining 7 has done graduate work beyond the bachelor's degree, mostly in the field of education. You will be heartened to know that every effort has been made to keep this educational enterprise free from political influence. One letter that Commissioner Zook sent to each of these state

[2] Selections made; assignments to camps now in process.

committees contained this sentence: "The President is quite anxious to have these appointments made solely on the merits of the educational training and experience of the candidates, and to keep the appointments free from political influence."

In no instance was a man's political party allegiance any criterion by which the Office of Education measured his fitness. In a very few instances did we know the candidate's political faith. The educational integrity of the enterprise and the educational fitness of the candidate were our sole concern.

The purposes, methods and organized plan of the CCC educational program are outlined in a remarkable pamphlet prepared by the Office of Education, and published by the War Department. It is the guidebook for this whole enterprise, and it contains both an adequate philosophy of adult education and a full complement of suggested procedures for all concerned with the program.

The aims of this CCC camp educational program are stated in the handbook as follows:

(1) To develop in each man his powers of self-expression, self-entertainment, and self-culture.

(2) To develop pride and satisfaction in cooperative endeavor.

(3) To develop as far as practicable an understanding of the prevailing social and economic conditions, to the end that each man may cooperate intelligently in improving these conditions.

(4) To preserve and strengthen good habits of health and mental development.

(5) By such vocational training as is feasible, but particularly by vocational counseling and adjustment activities, to assist each man better to meet his employment problems when he leaves camp.

(6) To develop an appreciation of nature and of country life.

"The program," says this handbook, "will comprise such instruction suited to the needs of any particular camps as may be practicable, it being recognized that conditions as regards intelligence, aptitude and receptability of enrollees, and many other factors, will vary not only in nine corps areas but in 1,500 camps, each having its own problem. The basic thought in providing a program of instruction and in imparting instruction will be that of returning to the normal workaday world, upon completion of the emergency-relief project, citizens better equipped mentally and morally for their duties as such, and with a better knowledge of the Government under which they live, and of all that that Government means."

The handbook also reminds the camp adviser to build upon the existing educational program wherever practicable; to fit himself into the life of the camp; to make the educational program appeal to the men; to realize that his task, having no clear precedents, demands ingenuity; to remember that the study interests grow out of the needs of the men themselves; to utilize fully the intellectual resources among the enrollees.

You will probably wonder if these camp advisers are receiving any special training for this new and different task. They are being brought together at various centers for intensive training in conference sessions. Many of them have never taught adults.

Their imaginations must be quickened. They have to see not only their obligation but also their opportunity to lead these men a step forward intellectually from where they are now; to arouse intellectual curiosity; to make knowledge winsome. These advisers must realize that they can not judge, that in fact no one can judge the success or failure of this enterprise by conventional standards. This educational program will be good because of what it prevents, as well as what it accomplishes.

Once given this point of view, the camp adviser finds out what things the enrollees want to know. He organizes discussion groups, classes, selects text-books, uses magazines, newspapers, pamphlets and moving pictures. He uses not only the camp staff officers and the trained men in parks and forestry services, but where available the better trained enrollees as class or discussion leaders. He has much volunteer service from interested citizens in nearby communities. Nor does he forget the spiritual uplift to be found in music, in dramatics, debates and such activities, and he organizes the boys in groups around these interests. Please keep in mind that among these enrollees are a great many college and normal school graduates, accomplished musicians, experienced actors and men who have held responsible places in community and civic organizations. The camp adviser also establishes relationships with those nearby educational and social agencies that will not only aid the educational program in the camps, but facilitate the return of enrollees into wholesome social and economic life upon their discharge from the camps. Here is the biggest single volunteer adult education enterprise the world has ever seen.

What are our obstacles? Obviously these: Great variety of study interests; dearth of suitable text material for adults; lack of comfortably furnished and adequately lighted discussion and classrooms; lack of ample library books, though each camp has a library; lack of laboratory facilities; fatigue on the part of enrollees after a day of labor; sufficient teach-training of the advisers directed toward this particular task.

What are our advantages? In the first place, enrolment is voluntary. No one has to study anything. Only those who want to learn will continue in a class. Moreover, the men themselves decide what they want to be taught. Then, too, no credits are at stake. For the most part the work is informal and the plan flexible. We shall get ingenious and virile teaching. The teacher or discussion leader who can not hold the attention of a group of men, under conditions which the camp presents, simply is not the right man for the job. He may have been an able administrator, or he may have been an acceptable teacher of formal classes, but if he can not do this job under conditions as they are, he must give place to some one who can. But our great advantage is that here is comradeship in quest of knowledge. Learners and teachers live together under camp conditions. A teacher or discussion leader confronted by a student's baffling question can not well retreat behind a Jovian frown. His success will largely depend upon the extent to which in genuine comradeship he and those who help him can lead these young men along the paths of knowledge.

Can men like you, who have been classroom teachers and principals and superintendents, now undergo a metamorphosis and become under camp conditions not only teachers but counsellors, leaders of discussion groups, sympathetic companions to young men in quest of knowledge? I think they can. You know and I know that if they are real educators in the true sense of the word they will respond to this challenge with results that will be inspiring.

Announcement of this educational plan resulted in an amazing outpouring of cooperative interest. Such organizations as the American Association for Adult Education, the extension departments of state universities, the American Library Association, the National Education Association, various civic and service clubs and the National Student Federation have offered their facilities and their services. Last but not least, to your everlasting credit be it gratefully said that many of you school men, in spite of reduced budgets and curtailed programs, have found ways and means of opening your laboratories and classrooms and shops at night to these boys in nearby camps. By the truck load they come to spend their evenings profitably in the facilities which your thoughtful generosity has provided.

I do not want to close without reminding you once more that the War Department is conducting the camps, and doing the job admirably without military discipline. There are no guard-houses in these camps. The Office of Education is assisting the War Department in an advisory capacity, by selecting the teaching personnel and recommending to the Secretary of War the teaching procedures and materials. But in the end it is the War Department which is responsible for the success of this vast project.

It is a smart army that knows how to make war effectively; judged by that standard, the United States Army is a smart army. But it is a smarter army that, in addition, knows how to carry on some of the great new tasks of peace that have recently come upon us, that does not merely lie in wait for war, but adapting its organization and training and experience to this great peace-time enterprise so conducts it that hundreds of thousands of our young men, bewildered and discouraged in their economic plight, do here find not only employment, but comradeship and recreation and knowledge and hope.

These young men will come back to you, we know, in better physical condition than when they left you; they will come back to you, we hope, more wholesome in spirit for their living in the parks and the forests, with a finer appreciation of all that is implied in good citizenship, with better clarified vocational purposes, with more effective understanding of the social order, with quickened interest in what you are doing and with keener realization of the merits in the great enterprise of public education.

I close now with two paragraphs from a letter written by a young man in one of these camps.

When I joined the CCC I was still all hopelessness and despair. My viewpoint had become so distorted that life and law were all wrong to me, and there seemed no such thing as justice. The long tramp from coast to coast, looking for the job I never found, hadn't improved my temper any. But there is something soul-satisfying about good hard labor, especially when you've ached for something to do for three long years. The CCC became a kind of game—one that kept challenging the best that was in me. It caused me to take stock of my shortcomings and to set up a standard of mental and physical perfection.

The Civilian Conservation Corps has regenerated me mentally, physically and spiritually. It has given me practical knowledge about camp life, plumbing, carpentry, bookkeeping; but more than that, it has taught me to appreciate the good things of life, I have learned to appreciate what Thoreau calls "the beneficence of nature." In the deepening twilight my eyes stray up until they rest upon the last tall pine on the hills, etched against the afterglow of the sun. And as it fades, a flood of memories closes in upon me—memories of the boy who wearily tramped the streets and sought death in the bitterness of despair. Happiness to him was something out of reach, somewhere beyond the stars. I know now the serenity of soul that comes from a busy, well-ordered life. And happiness—well, happiness, is here, not beyond but beneath the stars.

EDUCATIONAL EVENTS

PROPOSED REVISION OF CURRICULUM IN SCHOOLS IN AUSTRALIA

THE educational authorities in Australia are engaged at the present time in revising the study courses for the primary schools, according to a report in the *Christian Science Monitor*. The curriculum now in use is a modified form of the original "new syllabus," which caused much discussion when introduced in 1905. Since then it has undergone revision in 1916, 1922 and 1925.

To meet the social needs of to-day, it is proposed to bring the syllabus up to date, and in this work the administrative heads of the state education department are seeking the cooperation of inspectors, teachers and other interested persons.

Syllabus revision involves the sifting of suggestions and the elimination of obsolete matter, together with supplementation and amendment of existing material. All this is likely to occupy the attention of committees for some time. The principle that "the child's course should be conceived in terms of activity and experience rather than of knowledge to be acquired" is not likely to be challenged, but the acquirement of knowledge will receive its due emphasis.

The opinion has been expressed by an eminent authority that Australia is lagging behind in the social sciences. In the present syllabus the importance of linking up the child's schooling with community life is emphasized. According to an official statement the selection of activities and studies in the new syllabus will be determined not by the needs of adult life, but by the interests and needs of the child as he progresses through school. Only as he is deeply interested in the social and political framework which he sees about him, will his course of study help him to prepare effectively to participate in adult life.

The present requirement that moral teaching should permeate discipline in the manners of the children and in the example of the teacher will be firmly retained. The three traits which will be most emphasized on this side of the new syllabus will be patience to be thorough, concentration to understand and persistence to apply.

THE SPREAD OF COMMUNISM AND FASCISM AMONG BULGARIAN STUDENTS

IT has been stated in recent correspondence published in the *New York Times* that the spread of radical doctrines among Bulgarian students is precipitating a crisis at the University of Sofia. Both communism and fascism are finding many adherents in the university. Frequent and often bloody clashes between rival factions have taken place, which the police have tried to remedy by violence and the university authorities by expulsion en masse of those students, particularly the Communists, who take a leading part in the disturbances. The university is not alone in being rent by extremist factions, however, for the same state of affairs prevails in educational establishments throughout the country and seems to reflect a recent intensification of Communist propaganda.

The reasons for the students' readiness to turn to extremist doctrines are not far to seek. The university has expanded rapidly in recent years, and the ever-growing number of students—6,672 at present—has created a serious problem, for there are not jobs enough for so many young men and girls with a university education. At the present time there are 1,080 students of pedagogy, of whom 430 are ready for their final examinations, yet the teaching profession is already overcrowded and there are no vacancies.

Were this problem confined to university graduates it would not be grave, but there also are thousands of young people who have passed out of the higher schools to face unemployment or unsuitable employment. Many of them have so thoroughly assimilated their knowledge that there has opened between them and their much less educated elders (who had few educational facilities) a great gulf of misunderstanding and resentment. Their parents are slow, coarse, unimaginative, stubborn and raw, deriding their sons' clamor for progress and binding their daughters to the drudgery of the household or the prostitution of the marriage market in the Oriental style.

A SURVEY OF COLLEGE EXPENSES BY THE U. S. OFFICE OF EDUCATION

A SURVEY on college expenses has recently been made by the U. S. Office of Education. Tuition rates twenty years ago were relatively low, the survey demonstrates, and so standardized that for a period of fifty years, few changes had been made.

In 1914–15 rates began to be revised upward, and ten years later many tuitions had been doubled. In 1934 the highest tuition rates, from $400 to $500 per year, were charged in twenty-five colleges and universities. The study shows that a student in 1913 could attend any college by paying from $150 to $200 a year for tuition, but in 1934 he will have to pay two or three times as much. Ten of the twenty-five colleges have increased their tuitions in the past five years, and women's colleges have maintained the highest rates.

Tuitions in the non-tax-supported institutions have changed considerably in the past five years. Among the private and denominational colleges, tuitions have been lowered in 125 on an average of $62 per year, and have been raised in 100 on an average of $49. Thus, for the country as a whole, the decreases were greater in number and in average size than the increases. The chief decreases took place in the coeducational institutions under Protestant denominational control; 101 such colleges reduced their rates on an average of $64 each. Colleges which increased their tuitions are more diversified.

The estimate of what the average freshman spends for tuition, board and room, and all fees and incidental expenses varies from $1,023 in the men's colleges to $438 in state institutions. For 359 institutions averaged together the typical cost is $630 per year. In the publicly supported institutions the average minimum cost is $376. This amount would be sufficient at some fifty-five state colleges, but in thirty-nine other state institutions a student must provide from $500 to $800, especially if he selects one in California, Connecticut, Delaware, Maine, Maryland, Michigan, Minnesota, Pennsylvania, Vermont, Virginia, Alaska or Hawaii.

In the privately controlled institutions, where average minimum costs vary from $600 to $901, a student may get along with $495 at Wabash College for men; $547 at Brenau College, for women, or $270 at Lincoln Memorial University, which is coeducational.

RELATIVE DELINQUENCY OF ALIEN AND NATIVE CHILDREN

THAT the crimes committed by foreign-born adults are fewer than those committed by the native-born is the assertion of Dr. Clifford R. Shaw, head of the department of research sociology of the Illinois Institute for Juvenile Research. In a recent survey published by the institute, Dr. Shaw also advances the opinion that delinquency among the members of the second generation of foreign-born does not occur because of the accident of birth but because of residence in areas of low economic status.

To substantiate the first statement, Dr. Shaw points to one of the conclusions of a report made for the Wickersham crime commission by Miss Edith Abbott, head of the social service administration department of the University of Chicago.

"In proportion to their respective numbers the foreign-born commit considerably fewer crimes than the native-born," the report states, followed by the assertion that "the foreign-born approach the record of the native white most closely in the commission of crimes involving personal violence. In crimes for gain the native whites greatly exceed the foreign-born." The general misconception that crime is found mainly among the foreign-born is partly owing to newspaper publicity in a few outstanding cases, Dr. Shaw thinks.

From studies of juvenile delinquency in seven large cities in the United States it has been found that the ratio of delinquent children of foreign-born parents to those of native-born parents was two to one, but this, Dr. Shaw believes, does not prove that the second generation of the foreign-born have greater criminal tendencies than the native-born.

American-born children in the same area where there was a low economic status were just as delinquent as the children of the foreign-born, the studies show. Furthermore, as soon as these foreign-born children moved out into better neighborhoods their delinquency fell off and approximated that of American-born in the same areas.

THE BENEFITS OF STATE CONTROL FOR NORTH CAROLINA SCHOOLS

DR. WILLIAM JOHN COOPER, of the George Washington University, speaking before the twenty-first annual Schoolman's Week, which convened in Philadelphia on March 14, traced the present system for the distribution of taxes for education in the state of North Carolina.

North Carolina's experiment has been the outcome of a situation in which the state found itself several years ago at the beginning of the depression when the closing of rural schools was threatened, teachers were not being paid and a wide inequality between educational advantages in various localities was apparent.

The constitution of North Carolina, it was stated, placed upon the General Assembly the responsibility of providing by taxation or otherwise for a general and uniform system of public schools. In addition, there has been in the state permissive legislation authorizing local districts, counties and cities, to vote upon themselves special taxes for the operation of the schools on higher standards than those provided by the state. The money thus raised was under the discretionary control of the board of trustees in the city schools or communities in the local tax districts, with no state control for years.

This system resulted in a spotty condition of educational opportunities, and at the beginning of the depression complaints about the local school taxes brought about the authorization of local county committeemen to pass upon and determine the amount of taxes to be levied in these special districts.

The state board of equalization was the next step in this gradual growth of state control. The board was set up to overcome, in part, the wide gap which prevailed between the richer and the poorer counties in the school system.

In the fall of 1931, it became evident that this dual support system of the schools had failed, and the resulting legislation brought about a replacement of local support by complete state support, the substitution of indirect taxes for local ad valorem taxes and the setting up of the whole educational system upon a substantial foundation by a guaranteed appropriation basis which could no longer fail because of the failure of local tax collection. Through the abolishing of district lines and the consolidation of schools which this has made possible, a more economical distribution of schools has resulted. Transportation has been studied and $1,000,000 saved, while 20,000 more children have been carried this year than any year before.

ENGLISH MONOGRAPH IN THE SURVEY OF SECONDARY EDUCATION SERIES

AN unwarranted emphasis upon grammar, drills, technicalities and other matters of form, with surprisingly little concern about the pupil having something to say, are among the outstanding findings set forth in a monograph on "Instruction in English" recently published by the National Survey of Secondary Education of the Office of Education. As pointed out in this report, there is a notable lack of recognition of the major objectives of expression and the methods most effective in achieving those objectives.

Among its other findings, it is stated in the report of the nation-wide study of high-school English, that literature of English authorship takes an overwhelming lead in the classics taught in American high schools. "Silas Marner" ranks first and "Julius Caesar" second. The study reveals that there are 30 classics most frequently used in junior. senior and four-year high schools. The "Idylls of the King," "Ivanhoe" and "The Tale of Two Cities" compete for third place. Five of the titles are dramas, and all of them are Shakespearean. Four of them are novels by George Eliot, Scott, Dickens and Stevenson; ten are long narrative or epic poems; five are short stories; three are collections of essays, short stories and verse; one is an essay; one an oration, and one a combination of story and essay. Eighteen of the 30 titles are from English literature, 7 from American literature, 2 from other foreign sources and 3 from a combination of all.

The monograph, which was prepared by Dr. Dora V. Smith, associate professor in education at the University of Minnesota, in her capacity as specialist in English of the National Survey of Secondary Education, reveals changes that have occurred with reference to English instruction, and describes present conditions, proffering suggestions for further study. There is also indicated a considerable amount of uncertainty surrounding the formal study of grammar. On this study emphasis varies. For example, some courses list 45 principles that should receive attention, while others enumerate as many as 149. There appears to be no agreement as to what grammar is absolutely needed.

In consideration of the problems of administration, the report concludes that "in the junior high school there is a general tendency to reduce the time allotted to English to five hours a week in the ninth grade, and slightly more in the seventh and eighth." This tendency, it is explained, is accompanied by an increasing emphasis of each branch of study in the school on the use of English as it affects its own field as well as an emphasis on a closer relationship of English to all studies. The question is raised as to whether the program of interrelationship is carefully enough defined. It is noted in the conclusion that "study of the programs reveals also a disposition to look upon English as a unified activity with little of the old-time division into elements, such as spelling, language, reading and grammar, taught in different courses by different teachers."

The monograph lays down nine serious problems that should be considered in the future teaching of English in secondary schools: (1) What should be the relationship of high-school English to the general objectives of secondary education? (2) How far does the present program in composition and in literature meet the present or the future needs of adolescent boys or girls? (3) To what objectives other than mere correctness should the composition course contribute? (4) To what extent does the present program in English grammar influence speech and writing? What is its relative importance in an overcrowded program of instruction, (5) Granted that a pupil is of low intelligence and has but a year or two to remain in school, what program of English instruction will contribute most to his future welfare and efficiency? (6) What is preparation for college; that is, what are the *actual* demands of higher institutions? To what extent should they dominate secondary school practise? (7) Is there a common body of literary material with which all pupils should be familiar? (8) What are minimum essentials and on what bases should they be selected? (9) Granted that the major objectives of the teaching of literature are breadth of experience and interests and a habit of lifelong association with good books, what literature content and what methods of classroom instruction are best calculated to achieve these ends?

THE MINNESOTA STUDY OF COMMERCIAL CORRESPONDENCE SCHOOL COURSES

THE University of Minnesota Press has recently released a study relating to the field of adult education entitled, "Commercial Correspondence Courses and Occupational Adjustments of Men," prepared by Charles Bird and Donald G. Paterson, of the department of psychology. This study is based on the records of 294 men who had registered with the University of Minnesota Employment Stabilization Research Institute for the purpose of securing vocational counsel. One hundred and ninety-one of these men were unemployed at the time of their interview while 103 were in an earning capacity, although the report indicates that most of these were in the lower wage brackets.

The study found that the educational capacities and vocational experiences of those examined were in most cases not in line with the type of courses which they had been pursuing and the conclusion was drawn that many students were attempting to pursue correspondence courses for which they had little capacity and in only 28.6 per cent. of the cases had had vocational experience within the field of endeavor. The intelligence tests given, however, indicated that these men had a higher mental age than the grade to which they had attained in the public schools.

Dr. J. S. Noffsinger, director of the National Home Study Council, has prepared an abstract of the study, and he states that the study vigorously condemns correspondence schools on the ground that they have permitted many students to enroll in courses covering certain vocations, when tests indicated that the students had little probability of success therein. The study recommends that vocational and aptitude tests be given adult students before they are enrolled in order to give guidance and eliminate the large "mortality" found within the field.

The study, according to Dr. Noffsinger, was incidental and merely a by-product of a larger investigation, and therefore much of the data on which its conclusions are founded are quite limited and are not above serious question. The fact that the case histories of only 294 persons who presented themselves to the Employment Stabilization Committee formed the basis of the study might invalidate most of its conclusions. Of more than 3,000 registering with the committee, only 9.2 per cent. were found to have taken correspondence courses, while the data for the entire adult population of the country is 16 per cent.

The recommendation that correspondence schools should utilize such vocational tests is definitely at variance with the conclusions of Dr. Irving Lorge, of the Institute of Educational Research, Teachers College, Columbia University, who in February, 1934, released his twelve-year study entitled "The Chimera of Vocational Guidance." Dr. Lorge feels, according to Dr. Noffsinger, that the values of vocational guidance tests are yet unproven.

The type of guidance conducted by the colleges and universities is held in this study to be ideal for the correspondence schools, but Mr. Noffsinger points out that Dr. Brammel, in the Office of Education Bulletin No. 17, 1932, reports that 62 per cent. of 517 institutions of higher learning openly advise students to follow their own interests in selecting their own courses.

In Dr. Noffsinger's judgment the study does not present a complete picture of the field. Its criticism is based on the failure of the correspondence schools to measure the ability or capacity of the student before he enrolls. It fails to recognize the values of interest, ambition and method employed which are most important factors in education of this type.

EDUCATIONAL NOTES AND NEWS

Representative Alfred L. Bulwinkle, of North Carolina, has introduced a resolution in the House of Representatives calling for an investigation of the charges recently made by Dr. William A. Wirt, superintendent of schools at Gary, Ind. Dr. Wirt asserted through an intermediary that the professorial advisers of President Roosevelt have conspired to lead the country into communism.

Dr. Walter F. Dexter, president of Whittier College, has announced his candidacy for the Republican nomination for congressman in the twelfth district of California.

Dr. R. B. von KleinSmid, president of the University of Southern California, has been appointed to the honorary committee of the Motion Picture Research Council of New York.

Louis Bamberger and Mrs. Felix Fuld, founders of the Institute for Advanced Study at Princeton University, have resigned as president and vice-president of the board of trustees. According to the announcement made by Dr. Abraham Flexner, director of the institute, they will continue to serve on the executive committee in *ex-officio* capacities, although they have relinquished all executive and administrative duties.

Cornelius Brett Boocock, head master of the Collegiate School of New York City, has been appointed associate head master of the Haverford School, at Haverford, Pa.

Mr. Galen Jones, assistant superintendent in charge of secondary schools at Tulsa, Okla., has been elected principal of the high school at Plainfield, N. J. Mr. Jones succeeds Mr. Lindsay Best, who has reached the age limit for service and will retire this year.

Dr. Arthur C. Bachmeyer, since 1925 dean of the College of Medicine at the University of Cincinnati, has resigned his position in order to devote more time to the Cincinnati General Hospital, of which he is superintendent. Dr. Bachmeyer's resignation will become effective on September 15.

Dr. Luther Harr, professor of finance at the Wharton School of Finance at the University of Pennsylvania, has been appointed economic adviser and treasurer of the publishing companies of *The New York Evening Post, The Philadelphia Record* and *The Camden Courier and Post.*

Dr. John A. Lester, formerly head of the English department of the Hill School at Pottstown, Pa., and at present executive secretary of the Friends' Council on Education, has accepted membership on the committee on the orientation of secondary education of the National Department of Secondary School Principals. He replaces Burton P. Fowler, who has resigned.

Walter Lippmann will be given the honorary degree of doctor of laws at a special convocation to be held on May 23 at Wesleyan University.

Dr. Robert J. Havighurst, associate professor in science education of the university schools of the Ohio State University, has been granted a year's leave of absence to work with the General Education Board in a study of general education.

David H. Buttrick, of Arlington, Mass., and Abigail Homans, of Boston, have been named by Governor Ely as trustees of the Massachusetts State College to fill vacancies caused by the deaths of Charles H. Preston and Frank Gerrett.

Miss Frances K. Wetmore, supervisor of adult education in Chicago, on March 12 opened a series of classes for the teachers of the 50,000 adults who have recently enrolled for class work under the C. W. E. S.

Claude M. Fuess, head master of Phillips Academy, Andover, Mass., was the guest of honor at a dinner held on March 16 by the New York Alumni Association of the academy. Dr. Harold Willis Dodds, president of Princeton University, and Dr. Ernest Martin Hopkins, president of Dartmouth College, were among the speakers.

Dr. Harvey Warren Cox, president of Emory University, was the principal speaker at the Founder's Day celebration of Randolph-Macon Woman's College, which was held on March 12. The exercises were in commemoration of the late Dr. William Waugh Smith, who as first president opened the institution in 1893.

Jerome D. Greene, who has held for two years the Woodrow Wilson professorship of international politics at the University College of Wales, Aberystwyth, has recently returned to the United States.

Dr. Lee A. DuBridge, assistant professor of physics at Washington University, St. Louis, has been appointed professor of physics at the University of Rochester.

Chancellor George R. Throop, of Washington University, St. Louis, has recently announced the resignation from the faculty of Professor Frank B. Hanson, of the department of zoology, who has been on leave of absence this year with the Rockefeller Foundation. Dr. Hanson will become assistant director of physical sciences with the foundation. Dr. Throop also announced the appointment of Mr. Charles E. Galt as lecturer in civil engineering for the second semester, and of Mr. Tu-Shan Jung, a China Medical Board fellow, as fellow in radiology.

Dr. Frank R. Menne, professor of pathology at the Medical School of the University of Oregon, has been appointed to the editorial board of the *Archives of Pathology*. He will succeed the late Dr. William Ophüls, head of the department of pathology at the College of Medicine of Leland Stanford University.

Walter C. Baker, who graduated in 1915 from Union College, Schenectady, N. Y., has been elected a life trustee of that college. Mr. Baker had just completed serving two years of his five-year term as an alumnus trustee when his permanent appointment was announced.

Dr. Foy Spencer Baldwin, director of research of the National Industrial Conference Board and for twenty years professor of economics at Boston University, died on March 21. Dr. Baldwin was sixty-three years old.

Dr. William Thornton Whitsett, founder of the Whitsett Institute in North Carolina and president of the school from 1888 until 1918, died on March 22. Dr. Whitsett was sixty-seven years old.

Dr. James Archibald Campbell, founder and president of Campbell College at Buies Creek, N. C., died on March 18. He was seventy-two years of age.

Dr. Edward H. Farrington, professor of dairy husbandry at the University of Wisconsin from 1894 to 1927, when he retired with the title of professor emeritus, died on March 22 at the age of seventy-three years.

Dr. George F. McKibben, professor emeritus of Romance languages at Denison University, died on March 23 in his eighty-third year.

William H. Hall, superintendent emeritus of schools in West Hartford, Connecticut, died on March 23. Mr. Hall was eighty-eight years of age.

A map library, which will contain more than 400,000 maps when completed, is being established at the University of Chicago. The project, under the direction of Dr. Wellington D. Jones, professor of geography at the university, has as its nucleus the 50,000 maps already on file in the map division of the university library and will include a collection of master topographic maps, large-scale city maps, various types of maps containing special data and historical maps.

Thirty-six massive volumes, a complete set of the "Grande Encyclopedie," the great French reference work of the eighteenth century, have been given to St. John's College by an anonymous friend of the institution. The books, edited by Diderot, are believed to have belonged to Catherine the Great of Russia.

THE first junior newspaper guild in the United States has recently been formed at the Lee School of Journalism, of the Washington and Lee University.

A QUESTIONNAIRE recently sent out by the School of Education of Northwestern University demonstrated that most of the Protestant ministers in Chicago do not wish children to believe that God sends storms, earthquakes and other disasters to punish people for their sins. The questionnaire, intended by its sponsors to determine the stand taken by pastors in regard to what children of junior high school age should believe, was sent to the 1,039 ministers listed in the directory of the Chicago Church Federation.

REPRESENTATIVES from thirteen colleges and twenty-nine preparatory schools participated in a series of conferences on education held at Harvard University from March 9 to 17. There were twelve meetings, the first of which was held in conjunction with the New England Association of Teachers of English. Problems of interest to educators in the fields of humanism, Latin, French, social studies, science, teacher-supply, secondary education, music, commercial education, student personnel and school committees were discussed at the other meetings.

SINCE its founding in 1915 501,514 students have enrolled in the State University Extension course in Massachusetts. Of this number, 430,000 have taken class work, while 71,000 have studied through correspondence.

THE tenth anniversary of National Child Health Day will be celebrated on May 1. The Conference of State and Provincial Health Authorities of North America, in cooperation with the American Child Health Association, will be in charge of the observance of the day.

THE New York Adult Education Council held its annual meeting on March 12. The principal speakers were Dr. George S. Counts, professor of education at Teachers College, Columbia University; Dr. Harry A. Overstreet, chairman of the executive committee, and Mayor La Guardia.

A TABLET in memory of Andrew Hamilton, eighteenth century lawyer, whose defense of John Peter Zenger helped to establish freedom of the press, was unveiled in Independence Hall, Philadelphia, on March 10, by a committee representing the New York Lawyers' Association.

AN earthquake which occurred in northern Utah and southern Idaho on March 12 split the walls of the Home Economics Building at the Utah State Agricultural College in Logan. No injuries were reported, but college officials stated that the three-story structure would have to be abandoned.

THE fifteenth annual observance of Public Schools Week will be celebrated in California during the week beginning April 23. The purposes of the occasion are similar to those of American Education Week, which is annually observed throughout the nation in November.

FORTY-TWO awards, totaling $36,290, have been made to members of the faculty of Harvard University for research in many fields. The awards are made possible by two funds, one established in 1924 by the late William F. Milton, and the other in 1925 by Joseph H. Clark. Although most of the research will be done in Cambridge, some will be conducted in Colorado, Florida, California, Montana, Santo Domingo, Estonia, France and Italy. The widely varied subjects to be studied include cosmic rays, fossil insects, the modern department store, human personality, choral music, frost, the operation of buildings, the Anglo-Japanese alliance and the character of William James.

A COLUMBIA UNIVERSITY survey shows that, not including emergency government work, 98 per cent. of all architects are unemployed.

THE number of students electing major art courses in the schools of New York City has increased from about 4,000 in 1927 to more than 13,000 in 1933. Forest Grant, director of art for the Board of Education, points out that this increase has occurred despite the fact that these courses are no longer alternative courses and students find it difficult to carry the work in addition to their required studies. The first technical art syllabus which has been printed in New York City since 1911 is now being prepared and will soon be released.

FELLOWSHIPS for research at the headquarters of the Linguistic Atlas of the United States and Canada at Brown University have been granted by the General Education Board to Professor

Claude M. Wise, of Louisiana State University; Professor E. E. Ericson, of the University of North Carolina; Professor S. J. McCoy, of the College of William and Mary; Professor Archibald A. Hill, of the University of Virginia, and N. M. Caffee, a graduate student of the University of Virginia.

A TRUST fund of $10,000, created by the will of the late C. M. Kimbrough, of Muncie, Ind., has been given to the Ball State Teachers College. The income from the fund will be used for assisting students who have no other means of gaining an education.

The Atlantic Monthly and Little, Brown and Company have recently announced a prize text-book contest. They offer a total prize of $4,000, half as an outright prize and half as an advance on account of royalties, to the author of the best text-book or text-book series in the field of senior-high-school English, excluding anthologies. The judges of this contest will be Dr. Thomas H. Briggs, of Teachers College, Columbia University; Clarence Stratton, directing supervisor of English in Cleveland, Ohio, and Ellery Sedgwick, editor of *The Atlantic Monthly*. Details regarding the rules of the contest, which closes December 1, 1934, may be secured by writing to The Atlantic Monthly Press, 8 Arlington Street, Boston, Mass.

"HEALTH through the Ages," by C.-E. A. Winslow and Grace T. Hallock, and "Light and Shade," a pictorial supplement in the form of a chart, have recently been published by the School Health Bureau of the Welfare Division of the Metropolitan Life Insurance Company. The booklet, designed to give boys and girls of high-school age a sense of the agelessness of man's search for health, is to be furnished free of charge for use in junior and senior high school classes on the basis of ten copies to every hundred pupils. The basis for the free distribution of the chart is one copy to a classroom.

PRESIDENT ALBERT LE BRUN of France has sent a vase to Oberlin College, accompanying it with a letter of praise for the school's activities. The institution was named in honor of an Alsatian educator and minister.

STUDENTS of the Peking National University are conducting a vote to determine which of the present faculty members are unpopular, according to a report published in the *New York Times*. The names of the alleged incompetents will be submitted to the chancellor with a proposal that they be discharged. The students also demand student representation in the administrative council of the university, the abolition of monthly examinations and the discontinuance of student attendance records.

THE California State Department of Education has been organizing study groups for the parents of the school children. Under the direction of Dr. Gertrude Laws, of the State Department, more than seven hundred persons have done six successive weeks of study in these groups since September 1, 1933. Beginning on March 1, a series of four discussions was conducted in Sacramento, Stockton, Lodi and Roseville. Parents went to these study centers from a distance of fifty miles.

CHILE'S 18,000 public primary school teachers are submitting to examinations of their competence, the Associated Press reports. Failure to take such examinations will automatically bring dismissal. This is an ultimatum laid down by President Arturo Alessandri in support of his Minister of Education, Domingo Duran, in a controversy recently waged with the School Teachers Association. The examinations have been ordered by Duran as a means of eliminating teachers who have affiliated with communistic or other anti-government movements.

THE Turkish Ministry of Education has recently issued an order that all Turkish secondary schools offer Russian as an elective in modern languages. English, French and German are already included in the curriculum.

THE University of Pennsylvania has received 125 rare volumes from the private library of the late Czar of Russia, together with ethnographic material from central Russia, Tibet and Siberia. The books have been acquired as a result of arrangements which the University Museum has made with leading Soviet museums for the exchange of books, ethnographical and archeological objects and scientific data.

THE eighth Vienna Summer School under the auspices of the Austro-American Institute of Education will be held from July 9 to August 19.

THE International Institute of Intellectual Cooperation has recently announced its intention of publishing an educational bibliography, the object of which is to keep the ministries of national education informed on all important publications appearing in any country and to deal with the national systems of education, their administrative organizations, the fundamental laws governing public teaching and the funds placed at the disposal of the departments or services concerned.

ENFORCEMENT of a recent amendment to the Mexican constitution will give employment to about three thousand teachers, according to Senor Narciso Bassols, Minister of Education. The measure requires haciendas on which twenty or more children of school age reside to maintain adequate schools.

THE *Christian Science Monitor* reports that in his recent address as president of the twenty-second Congress of Educational Associations, Dr. George Dyson, director of music at Winchester College, urged a complete revision of England's educational ideals. Following so closely upon the address of the Prime Minister before the Scottish Educational Congress, in which Mr. Macdonald called for "a thorough survey of the whole educational system," Dr. Dyson's address has created a stir throughout England. The fact that the Congress of Educational Associations embraces fifty-five subsidiary educational groups of all types has added to the force of Dr. Dyson's address. Dr. Dyson pointed out that the English system of education is modeled, in his judgment, on that devised in the fourteenth century which was established to produce "clerks," or administrators for church and state. Such a school, he observed, was and is as purely vocational as are the workshops and laboratories of any large industry. British education, he averred, "neither acknowledges nor trains more than a fraction of human faculty and character . . . and the cumulative effect of the system is ever more serious as time goes on and more modern fashions of life replace the past." Dr. Dyson proposed that a series of secondary schools be established: one devoted to literary and linguistic studies, one to mathematics and the sciences, one to handicrafts and engineering, one to domestic science for girls and one to art.

DISCUSSION

THE RELATION OF MOTION PICTURES TO STANDARDS OF MORALITY[1]

THERE has been a vast amount of acrimonious debate on the question of "morality" in commercial motion pictures, but there has hitherto been almost no actual measurement of the amount of conflict between motion pictures and standards of morality. Indeed, it has seemed impossible to study morality scientifically—that is, by methods of precise measurement. Our first task had to be to develop a means of determining *what* the accepted standards of morality really are. To the sociologist this is not quite so difficult as it seems to the layman. For morality is merely conformity with the *mores,* and the *mores* are the ways to which groups of people have become so accustomed that they take them as "of course the right ways" and are emotionally upset when they find themselves or others doing otherwise.

Our first step was to build up scales briefly describing 326 different incidents (bits of conduct), such as one might encounter in life, arranged in order from very "good" to very "bad." Each of these incidents had a numerical index to show its degree of badness, which indices were developed by a very elaborate statistical process and showed the extent to which a typical individual would be shocked if he saw such incident occurring in real life. With these scales the standards of 18 different social groups were determined from large samples of their members. That is, it was determined how far down on the scale conduct might go and yet be within the approval of a quarter or a half or three fourths of each of the 18 groups and of the society constituted by the groups combined. Then committees of five members each observed 184 motion pictures, rating their scenes quantitatively with the use of these same scales. From the numerical ratings given to the scenes (incidents) as averaged from the five judges, comparison could be made between the level of badness of the incidents in the movie and the level of approval of each of the 18 groups and

[1] Statement before American Educational Research Association, Cleveland, Ohio, February 26, 1934.

of the society constituted by the groups combined. The measures proved surprisingly consistent and valid and showed the feasibility of making studies of the moral qualities of motion pictures by precise measurement.

Of course the incidents of the movies varied widely in moral quality. The author, in his book on "Motion Pictures and Standards of Morality," published by the Macmillan Company, gives in great detail the distribution of these scenes in relation to the levels of approval of the various social groups. But in general it may be said that the movies fall, prevailingly, much below the *mores* in respect to aggressiveness of girls in love-making; that is, girls are much more aggressive in the movies than would be approved in ordinary life. In respect to kissing, many scenes were such as would call forth disapproval from the typical member of society, but, on the average, the kissing in the motion pictures investigated fell only a trifle below the indicated approvals of most of our groups. In respect to democratic practises and attitudes the conduct in motion pictures was, on the average, above the levels to which our sample members of society are accustomed, and hence the scenes were such as to challenge admiration more often than to call forth disapproval. In the treatment of children by parents, which was the fourth phase of morality studied in the investigation, the movies were found at their best; three fourths of all the scenes involving the treatment of children by parents lay above the level of bare approval of our social groups, while 70 per cent. of them were of the kind to challenge not only approval but also the admiration of half or more of our social groups—acts that they would wish to have imitated.

It is also worthy of note that morally "good" acts are more often enacted by characters played up throughout the movie in attractive rôles, while "bad" ones are more often played up in unattractive rôles. It is believed that this has a tendency to make the "good" acts attractive, and thus to get them imitated, and to make the "bad" ones repulsive. But this policy is by no means consistently followed; in vast numbers of cases conduct that we would not wish imitated is exemplified in characters that are made to appear attractive in the movie. This is a policy about which motion picture producers could well afford to take thought.

A study of the relation of the morality of a picture to its "success" suggested that motion picture producers are tragically mistaken when they assume that in order to make a movie successful they must make it as naughty as the censors will permit. Scientific evidence is presented of the existence of a negative correlation between the success of pictures and their degree of offence against morality. That is, producers lose rather than gain by antagonizing morality. Motion picture production is found unbelievably naïve and unscientific in respect to the social adjustments of their output, and the investigator concludes that "a few good social science research men could render as important service in improving motion picture production as research in agriculture has rendered to scientific farming or research in physics to the improvement of the radio and of refrigeration."

CHARLES C. PETERS
PENNSYLVANIA STATE COLLEGE

INSTITUTIONAL TEACHER PLACEMENT

DURING the last decade teacher placement has been definitely recognized and accepted as an essential service of institutions which prepare teachers. The recognition of this educational obligation has resulted in the rapid development of purposes and practises for the guidance and operation of teacher placement. This present article attempts to outline certain of these purposes and practises and to describe recent trends and events of nation-wide significance in the movement.

DEFINITION

By institutional teacher placement is meant the teacher-placement activities of all higher educational institutions which train teachers and similar activities of state departments of education which maintain well-organized bureaus for the placement of teachers. The term includes all teacher placement conducted as an educational and professional service to schools without commercial profit.

PURPOSES

Teacher placement service in any educational institution is conducted solely for two purposes.

Its primary purpose is the improvement of the educational structure of the region served. It achieves this purpose by aiding school officials in their programs for staff improvement.

A secondary purpose of institutional teacher placement is that of aiding competent individuals to secure teaching positions for which they are well qualified. The attainment of this purpose involves both the encouragement and recommendation of competent persons and the discouragement and diversion of the incompetent.

Features

Well-organized and efficient institutional teacher placement service includes the following features of value to school officials:

(1) Extensive information about experienced and inexperienced candidates. All institutional personnel records of alumni and seniors are placed at the disposal of the director of teacher placement for his guidance in the recommendation of candidates. These records include scholarship in terms of marks and range of subjects, extra-classroom activities, intelligence ratings, statements from staff members as to personality and promise, health records and other personal data.

(2) A file of confidential testimonials prepared by school officials under whom the alumni teach. These credentials supplement the above-mentioned personnel data and with it give the employing official a complete case history of each candidate.

(3) Various practises directed toward the greatest possible reliability and validity in the appraisal of candidates, including: (a) The application of a sincerely scientific attitude toward placement; (b) researches to discover and measure traits which differentiate the good from the poor teachers; (c) scrupulous care in transference of data from the originals; and (d) cooperative action by groups of institutions toward greater accuracy in describing candidates.

(4) A follow-up service to keep the institution in contact with the educational needs of the region, to stimulate teachers and to supply data for validating prognostic rating devices.

(5) A range of service which covers all types of educational positions from nursery school teaching to the college presidency and which, in some of the institutional bureaus, supplies, in addition to teaching and administrative workers at all levels, such specialists as psychologists, psychiatrists, research experts, teachers of the subnormal and school nurses.

(6) Service over a wide geographical range. The concept of geographical range has several aspects. In the first place, a superintendent, by communicating with the nearest institutional bureau, may secure candidates from several different states because practically no collegiate institution draws all its students from one state. Many draw students from ten or twelve different states, and a few have every state represented in their enrolment.[1]

Again, through their local connections, students graduating from out-of-state institutions often return home to teach. Also, many students through letters of inquiry sent to various states or to foreign countries eventually locate at distant points as the result of credentials sent by their institutions. Furthermore, through direct requests from school officials, teacher placement offices in some of the larger institutions make placements in fifteen or twenty different states each year, even during times of stress upon local patronage.

Finally, in almost every state there are several well-organized institutional teacher placement bureaus. Any superintendent or any college president who wishes to employ graduating seniors, graduate students or alumni of any particular college or university in America need but to direct a communication to the teacher placement office in that institution to cause the complete personnel system which aids the placement office to operate to meet his specification, either for experienced teachers or for inexperienced candidates.

(7) The practise of supplying experienced as well as inexperienced candidates, as implied above. This policy of supplying both experienced and inexperienced candidates has been followed by many institutional placement bureaus since their establishment, and during recent years increased interest in the problem of placement[2] has caused many others to adopt

[1] C. R. Foster, Jr., and Paul S. Dwyer, "A Study of the Geographic Distribution of Students in Three Hundred Sixty-three American Colleges and Universities," *Rutgers University Bulletin*, July, 1931, *Studies in Education*, No. 1, Rutgers University, School of Education, New Brunswick, New Jersey.

[2] Walter H. Adams, "The Placement of Stu-

the practise. In terms of experience, the registrants in institutional bureaus range from those who have had only practise teaching to those whose experience and ability qualify them to hold the most difficult educational position.

(8) Economy to teachers and schools. The services of institutional placement offices are rendered without financial profit. A recent study revealed that 58.2 per cent. of the 158 institutions which reported data on this phase of the investigation charged no fee at all for placement services. The median fee charged by the other 41.8 per cent. was $2.00.[3] It is extremely doubtful that any institutional placement office in America attempts to make a profit from its fee for placement service.

(9) Up-to-date files for alumni. Many institutional placement offices permit alumni in the field to have testimonials sent to their permanent folders at any propitious time without charge, whether or not they are on the active files for the current year. This practise provides credentials ready for immediate use whenever the alumni wish to seek promotions.

EXTENT

As noted above, Adams found that 86.7 per cent. of the 465 institutions included in his study maintained teacher placement bureaus. At this rate there would be approximately eight hundred teacher placement bureaus in American colleges and universities. In the study of 166 institutions mentioned above, the forty-one university and college bureaus which supplied placement data reported 4,713 placements or an average of 114 placements per institution during 1931. Since the average size of the forty-one institutions was larger than the general average for the country, 114 placements should not be taken as the general average. In the writer's judgment, fifty placements per institution during 1931 would be a conservative estimate of the average. This would make a total of approximately 40,000 placements during 1931 by the eight hundred institutional bureaus in the United States.

With respect to the other type of institutional teacher placement, the bureaus conducted by some state departments of education, Brogan[4] reports that eighteen states had teacher placement bureaus either in the state department or in the state education association in 1930. Returns just received by the writer from the forty-eight state departments of education show that eleven of the departments now operate organized teacher placement bureaus. The eleven states and the dates given for the establishment of their bureaus are: Massachusetts 1912; Minnesota 1913; Maine 1918; Oklahoma 1919; Alabama, Pennsylvania and Vermont 1920; Idaho 1923; Wyoming 1925; New Mexico 1931; and Mississippi 1932. Six other state departments which have operated such bureaus, together with dates reported for establishment and discontinuance, are Iowa 1919–1927; South Dakota 1919–1927; South Carolina ?–1925; Nevada 1923–1927; Virginia 1923–1932; and Texas 1928–1933. The eleven state department bureaus now operating reported a total of 1,600 placements or an average of 145 placements per bureau for 1931. (Mississippi reported for 1932.)

The placement activities of state education associations are not included in the definition of institutional teacher placement given at the outset of this article, but the findings of a recent inquiry are here presented because of the interest they carry. Eight of the forty-six secretaries of state education associations who responded to the inquiry by the writer stated that their associations maintained teacher placement bureaus. (Five of the eight charge commission fees ranging from 1 per cent. to 3½ per cent. of the first year's salary.) The eight states and the years the bureaus were established are: Texas 1918; California 1919; Kansas 1921; Nebraska and North Carolina 1922; Michigan 1924; South Carolina 1927; and Montana 1931.

dents in Teaching Positions as Carried on by Higher Educational Institutions.'' Abilene Christian College, Abilene, Texas, 1933. The per cent. of institutions with placement organizations increased from 73.1 to 86.7 between 1920 and 1931, Table IX, page 30; 79.2 per cent. of the 226 institutions included in the study registered alumni in their bureaus, Table XVI, page 42.

[3] J. G. Umstattd, ''Teacher Placement in One Hundred Sixty-six Educational Institutions.'' The Perine Book Company, Minneapolis, Minnesota, pp. 21 and 22.

[4] Whit Brogan, ''Work of Placement Offices in Teacher Training Institutions,'' Teachers College, Columbia University Contributions to Education, No. 434, Bureau of Publications, Teachers College, Columbia University, New York City, 1930, page 6.

Utah and Arkansas recently discontinued such bureaus after having conducted them five or six years. Six of the bureaus now operating reported placements for 1931, their total being 1,309 placements, of which 938 were reported by one office.

National Organization

In February, 1923, plans for a national organization were laid by a group of directors of college appointment bureaus. At the Chicago meeting of the Department of Superintendence in February, 1924, the group organized as the National Association of Appointment Secretaries and announced as its purpose "to promote and develop the work of the appointment offices throughout the United States, emphasizing cooperation, research, and service," and limiting its membership to "all who are officially engaged in appointment work in educational institutions without commission charge."[5] Annual meetings have been held since 1924 to discuss teacher placement problems and to report research work. As the result of this effort progress has been made toward scientific and efficient service in institutional teacher placement bureaus in all parts of the United States.[6]

State Organization

The directors of teacher placement in educational institutions within given states are actively engaged in developing informal organizations of state groups of institutional teacher placement officers. An alert national organization has clearly defined the problems to be solved in the field of institutional teacher placement. State groups are sensing these problems and are cooperating in their solution. In Nebraska, New York, California, Michigan and Minnesota groups have been at work for two or more years. Directors of institutional teacher placement offices in thirty-one other states have responded favorably to the idea of state groups and are now in various stages in the development of their programs.

[5] Report of the First and Second Annual Meetings of the National Association of Appointment Secretaries, Chicago and Cincinnati, February, 1924, and February, 1925.

[6] The organization is now called the National Institutional Teacher Placement Association.

The two aims of efficiency and economy in teacher placement are uppermost in the purposes of these state organizations. Throughout the entire country, institutional teacher placement directors are concentrating their efforts to attain these two standards to the highest possible degree.

J. G. Umstattd

University of Minnesota

THE EDUCATIONAL SIGNIFICANCE OF THE SCHOOL LIBRARY

In the issue of School and Society for January 27 Mr. George F. Bowerman, of the Public Library at Washington, D. C., invites school officials and educators to a careful reading of the attack he has made on school libraries as a general proposition, in the *Library Journal* for January 1, 1934.

May I have the privilege of extending a like invitation through your pages to a careful reading of the replies to Mr. Bowerman's unwarranted and unprofessional article in the *Library Journal* of February 1, 1934, by Mr. Frank Tolman, Miss Lucile F. Fargo, Miss Helen S. Carpenter and others.

Mr. Bowerman tries to prove that the school library is a menace to education and appeals to the overburdened taxpayer in defense of his own plan of cooperation between the public library and the public schools in Washington, D. C. On the costs of school libraries he quotes certain figures that are credited to Miss Lucile F. Fargo's book, "The Library in the School." Miss Fargo in her reply to the article shows that no such figures appear in her book.

Schools, according to Mr. Bowerman, should not have libraries of their own, but should use the plan of school library service conducted by Mr. Bowerman's library for some years. He states that this plan is the only economical one. But he fails to point out to the taxpayer just how the public—which supports both institutions—saves money by having the public library transport collections of library books to schools and back twice a year at least, when the schools might have the same books as permanent collections in the school buildings under a trained teacher-librarian.

As the aim of modern education is toward letting a pupil find out things for himself after he has been taught how to use tools of information, where can he possibly do this as well as in an adequately equipped school library? If there is one thing that has been proved to be of highest value in every type of school, it is just this new kind of school library. So Mr. Bowerman misses the point entirely and evidently has no adequate knowledge of what is going on in this field anywhere else.

A taxpayer who reads his original article or the excerpt in the issue of School and Society of January 27, 1934, may be considerably confused. It is possible he may say like some poorly informed people, "Why should we have school libraries at all when there are so many public libraries in existence?"

The two institutions are absolutely different in purpose, but there are no real conflicting interests except those manufactured by Mr. Bowerman. The public schools make readers for the public libraries and sow the seed. No public library branch can become actually a part of the school system and retain its usefulness to the adult population it is supposed to serve. What the schools do get from every public library is fine cooperation in every way. Pupils brought up in a school library naturally upon leaving school are readers and public library patrons with borrowers' cards. They are book minded and library conscious.

This is not a time to cut library appropriations or to cripple schools. They have recently had new lines of endeavor mapped out for them, namely, teaching the proper use of leisure time and under the New Deal of working out richer and more diversified courses of study leading to a broader and more wholesome outlook on life.

Does any educator believe this can be done without well-organized libraries in schools where children may be taught how to find information but first may be subjected to the influence of good books, inspirational books during the entire school course?

C. G. Leland,
Superintendent of Libraries

Board of Education
New York, N. Y.

SPECIAL CORRESPONDENCE

THE REPORT OF THE CLEVELAND MEETING OF THE N. E. A.

Two divergent comments concerning Mr. W. D. Boutwell's review of the Cleveland meeting of the Department of Superintendence of the N. E. A. have been received by the editors. They are published herewith in full:

To the Editors of School and Society:

Mr. Boutwell's review of the Cleveland meeting (School and Society, March 10) represents the superintendents as being "irritated" by the fact that "preconvention meetings, addressed by John Dewey, H. C. Morrison, Thomas H. Briggs, and others, gave a color to the meetings quite contrary to the majority opinion of the rank and file of superintendents. . . ." Of the three speakers whom Mr. Boutwell mentions by name, two—Messrs. Morrison and Briggs—made a plea for "sincerity in the present situation." Does Mr. Boutwell charge that the "majority opinion of the rank and file of superintendents," in supporting the "quite contrary" view, glorifies insincerity in the present situation?

Even an outsider has little difficulty in appreciating the irritation of the Department of Superintendence because so many other organizations flock to the city that it chooses for its convention, but I am sure that the superintendents themselves will resent Mr. Boutwell's reference to the organizations as "camp-followers," and will wonder, as I do, why so coarse an epithet is permitted to mar the columns of School and Society, the essential dignity of which has been a source of so much pride to our profession.

Sincerely yours,
(Signed) William C. Bagley,
President, National Council of Education

To the Editors of School and Society:

In the March 10th issue of School and Society is a review of the annual convention of the Department of Superintendence written by W. D. Boutwell. I want to thank you for this very helpful and constructive report. It is the best analysis of the convention I have seen. It is very fair and helpful in its appraisal. His analysis of the good and bad points of the new plan of the discussion group organization is timely and suggestive.

Last March, right after I was elected President of the Department of Superintendence, I presented this plan to Dr. Edmonson and Dr. Carr and later to the Executive Committee. We all realized that a new plan would not work as smoothly as the old one, but we were unanimous in feeling that something should be done to make possible active participation in the convention by its members. That some of the contributions are not particularly meritorious is neither surprising nor significant. I feel that the significant thing is the fact that thousands of members of the Department of Superintendence took advantage of the opportunity to prepare material before coming to Cleveland and to discuss this material after they arrived there.

Thank you again for your fine appraisal of this meeting.

Cordially yours,
(Signed) PAUL C. STETSON,
Retiring President, Department of Superintendence, N. E. A.

QUOTATIONS

THE PLIGHT OF THE SCHOOLS

UNLESS remedial and nationwide action is taken, the present year will find *Three Million Five Hundred and Thirty Thousand* American children being deprived of education.

Proud as this country has been of its ideals of education, and excellent as our schools undoubtedly have been in many states, even normally education has not been a national success. Before the depression set in, there were in the country at large every year two million two hundred and eighty thousand boys and girls, between the ages of 6 and 15, receiving no school instructions.

Depression conditions have continually increased this "normal" number, and—unless something is done—an additional million children will be upon the streets and byways before April first, with perhaps no chance ever after for many of them to obtain school training.

The Hearst newspapers have warned repeatedly of this increasing condition. Only lately we reported that the Federal Emergency Relief Administration was allotting funds to keep a large number of rural schools from closing on March first. But we also said that this emergency action was not enough.

In this gravest of emergencies the Ohio State University has now *assumed national leadership*. Under its auspices a national "citizens' conference on the crisis in education" will be held at Columbus on April 5, 6 and 7.

Not only educators, but eminent men and women in other activities will participate in this conference. It is necessary that the whole citizenship of America be brought to understand what is happening to our schools. And if the Ohio conference helps to bring about such a proper realization, it will be a patriotic service of the first order.

In the past Americans have supposed their school system to be equal to any, and superior to most.

For persons who comprehended the relationship between education and good citizenship, it is something of a shock to be told that the average American school term, throughout the country as a whole, is now fifty to one hundred days shorter per year than the average in European countries.

In years to come American citizens will not be able to compete with Europeans if America does not now keep pace with Europe in education.—*The Los Angeles Examiner.*

SOCIETIES AND MEETINGS

THE CITIZENS' CONFERENCE ON THE CRISIS IN EDUCATION

A NATIONAL meeting of citizens interested in education is being called in Columbus, Ohio, for April 5 and 6. It is being made possible through the cooperation of the Ohio State University. Its program is as follows:

Thursday, April 5

7:30 P. M.

Presiding, George White, governor of the State of Ohio

"The State's Obligation to Its Youth," Paul V. McNutt, Governor of Indiana.

"Balanced Budgets and Unbalanced Lives,"

Glenn Frank, president, University of Wisconsin.

Friday, April 6

10:00 A. M.

Presiding, Walter C. Lindley, judge of the United States District Court, Danville, Illinois

''Education and Rural Community Life,'' L. J. Taber, master of the National Grange.

''Education and Crime,'' Royal S. Copeland, senior United States Senator from New York.

2:30 P. M.

Presiding, George F. Zook, United States Commissioner of Education

''Education and the Future of America,'' John H. Finley, associate editor of the *New York Times.*

''Teachers and Their Proper Preparation,'' Mrs. Franklin D. Roosevelt.

7:30 P. M.

Presiding, Frank P. Graves, commissioner of education, State of New York

''Education and Government,'' Alfred E. Smith, New York City.*

''What Can Parents Do?'' Dorothy Canfield Fisher, Arlington, Vermont.

''Making Men of Boys,'' Newton D. Baker, Cleveland, Ohio.

The Citizens' Conference will be followed by the fourteenth annual Ohio State Educational Conference, which convenes on Saturday morning, April 7, at 8:30. At that time the following 36 sections will meet simultaneously, giving their major attention to what has happened in all branches of education because of the depression:

Adult education
Art
Attendance officers
Biological science
City superintendents
Clinical psychology
Commercial education
County superintendents
Educational tests
Elementary principals
Elementary teachers
English
Exempted-village superintendents
Geography
Guidance counselors
Higher education
High-school principals
Home economics
Industrial arts and vocational education
Journalism
Junior high-school principals
Kindergarten and primary teachers
Latin
Mathematics
Modern languages
Music
Physical education and health
Physical sciences
Religious education
School business officials
School librarians
Social studies
Special education
Teacher education
Village and consolidated-school superintendents
Visual education

* The address by Mr. Smith will be read by the chairman.

At the conclusion of the sectional meetings four general meetings will convene at 10:30, as follows:

I

Presiding, B. O. Skinner, director, State Department of Education of Ohio

''The Administration of School Systems in the Depression,'' Paul C. Stetson, retiring president, Department of Superintendence, National Education Association.

II

Presiding, C. H. Lake, superintendent of schools, Cleveland, Ohio

''The Curriculum and the Depression,'' Charles H. Judd, University of Chicago.

III

Presiding, J. G. Collicott, superintendent of schools, Columbus, Ohio

''Legislation and Finance in the Depression,'' George D. Strayer, Teachers College, Columbia University.

IV

Presiding, James E. Hagerty, Ohio State University

''Crime and Delinquency in the Depression,'' Henry H. Goddard, Ohio State University.

A sixteen-page pamphlet entitled "The Educational Emergency" will be distributed to all who attend either of these conferences. The pamphlet reviews the national situation and includes such topics as these: "The Attack on Education"; "3,500,000 Children Deprived of Schooling"; "School Funds"; "Restricted School Services"; "The School Load"; "Length of Terms"; "The Salaries of Teachers"; "School Buildings"; "Text-books"; "The Teachers' Contribution," and "The Citizens' Contribution."

Individual copies or copies in bulk of this pamphlet may be secured by addressing Dr. W. H. Cowley, at the Ohio State University, Columbus, Ohio.

EDUCATIONAL RESEARCH AND STATISTICS

THE RELATION OF AN ABNORMAL WEEKLY SCHEDULE TO GRADE POINT AVERAGE*

EACH semester students approach college administrators with the request to carry more than the normal amount of work. These requests are usually refused or granted on the basis of the student's former record. If the student has earned high marks the preceding semester, or semesters, he is usually permitted to increase his load; if not, his request is very apt to be denied. The justification for this practise in the past has been the belief that only those students who maintain a high scholastic record can carry additional loads without adverse results. More recently, however, this assumption has not been fully substantiated by careful investigations. Pierson and Nettels[1] studied the scholarship records of a somewhat selected group of high-school pupils and found that those pupils who carried five solids did their work as well as did pupils of the same IQ levels who carried only four solids. Lehman and Stoke[2] showed that in general those college students who increased their loads by the greatest number of hours from one semester to the next improved most in scholarship, and those students who decreased their loads by the greatest number of hours from one semester to the next deteriorated most in scholarship.

The purpose of this study was to ascertain whether or not there is any consistent relation between an abnormal weekly schedule and grade point average attainment on the college level. An abnormal weekly schedule is defined as either above or below the normal number of hours designated by the college as being advisable for a student to carry each semester in that college in order to complete the requirements for the degree in the usual four-year period.

SCOPE OF THE STUDY

The results of the study are based upon the data compiled for 300 students selected at random from the 1927 and the 1928 entering classes in the University of Arkansas. In the analysis of the factual data these 300 students were segregated into two distinct groups:

Persisting Students: a group of 100 students who continued in the university until they received their degrees or who attended irregularly for seven or more semesters and were continuing their work in the fall semester of 1932.

Non-Persisting Students: a group of 200 students who attended the university from three to eight semesters but did not receive their degrees and were not continuing their work in the fall semester of 1932.

TABLE I

GRADE POINT AVERAGE OF 300 STUDENTS GIVEN BY SEMESTERS AND BY TYPE OF LOAD CARRIED

Semester	Below Normal load		Normal load		Above Normal load	
	Number	G.P.A.	Number	G.P.A.	Number	G.P.A.
1	102	1.60	148	2.03	50	2.34
2	114	1.26	91	1.95	95	2.50
3	110	1.29	98	2.21	92	2.60
4	119	1.36	61	2.14	92	2.75
5	103	1.78	42	2.32	49	2.99
6	79	1.70	32	2.52	53	2.96
7	60	2.33	27	2.74	41	3.02
8	53	2.76	19	2.64	32	2.91
Total	740	1.63	518	2.10	504	2.71

* Research Paper No. 343, Journal Series, University of Arkansas.

[1] C. D. Pierson and C. Nettels, "Scholarship of High-school Pupils Taking Five Solids *versus* Those Taking Four Solids." *Educ. Res. Bul.* (Los Angeles City Schools), 7: 2–3, October-November, 1927.

[2] H. C. Lehman and L. M. Stoke, "Is the Heavy Schedule an Incentive to Greater Effort?" SCHOOL AND SOCIETY, 32: 767–71, December 6, 1930.

TABLE II

CORRELATIONS OF STUDENT LOAD PER SEMESTER AND GRADE POINT AVERAGE FOR DIFFERENT QUARTILES IN MENTAL ABILITY

Quartile	Persisting students			Non-persisting students		
	Number of student semesters	r	P.E.	Number of student semesters	r	P.E.
I	242	.31	.04	220	.31	.04
II	268	.23	.05	221	.24	.05
III	211	.32	.04	247	.15	.04
IV	72	.11	.07	290	.24	.03

GRADE POINT AVERAGES OF STUDENTS CARRYING A NORMAL LOAD AND OF STUDENTS CARRYING AN ABNORMAL LOAD

When the students used in this study were segregated by semesters into three catagories according to type of load carried during a particular semester, as shown in Table I, it was found that in general those students carrying the heaviest load made the highest grade point average (G. P. A.).[3] Those carrying a normal load made slightly lower grade averages, and those carrying the lightest loads made the lowest grade averages.

RELATION OF NUMBER OF SEMESTER HOURS CARRIED TO SCHOLARSHIP

Only approximately one half of the students carried the same number of hours for two consecutive semesters. It was also frequently noted that during three consecutive semesters, a student was classified in each one of the three student-load categories mentioned above. The "product-moment" correlation coefficients between student load and grade point average or scholarship, however, indicate a consistent and fairly constant positive relationship.

The total number of semesters attended by the 100 persisting students was 781 student semesters. The correlation coefficient between load per semester and grade point average for these 781 cases was .28 ± .02.

The total number of semesters attended by the 200 non-persisting students during the first six semesters was 932 student semesters. The coefficient of correlation between load and grade point average, using the entire 932 cases, or pairs, was .27 ± .02.

No significant differences were found between the correlations by semesters for the persisting students and for the non-persisting students. In every instance these coefficients indicated a low positive relationship between student load and scholarship, as evidenced by semester marks. Furthermore, this relationship was fairly consistent from semester to semester. A relatively low correlation found during the first semester was due to the fact that one of the variables, student load, is kept fairly constant for entering students.

For twenty-five students it was possible to secure complete data regarding the amount of time spent each semester on outside work and extra-curricular activities. The correlation between grade point average attainment and student load for these students was .12. When, however, the amount of time devoted to outside work and extra-curricular activities was "partialed" out, this correlation was .14. This seems to indicate that when the factor of outside work and extra-curricular activities is kept constant, there is a slightly higher correlation between grade point average and student load.

EFFECT OF CHANGES IN STUDENT LOAD UPON SCHOLARSHIP

Using the average or normal increments of increase in grade point averages at each successive semester level for the 100 persisting students as bases for comparison, it was found that:

(1) Students who increased their load from one semester to the next, in general, increased their grade point average over that of the pre-

[3] A weighted average computed by using the following values for semester marks: A = 6, B = 4, C = 2, D = 0, E = −1 and F = 2.

ceding semester. This increase during the second and third transition periods was practically double the actual normal gains made by the entire group of 100 persisting students during the same periods.

(2) Students who decreased their load from one semester to the next, in general, increased their grade point average over that of the preceding semester. When compared with the entire group of 100 persisting students, this group made more consistent and greater gains than did those students who increased their load for a succeeding semester.

(3) Students whose load remained the same from one semester to the next showed a smaller and at some transition periods even a negative gain in grade point average when compared with those students who shifted to a heavier or lighter schedule load for a succeeding semester.

Relation of Student Load to Scholarship of Students of Different Mental Levels

The 300 students included in this study were distributed approximately equally among each of the four quartiles in mental ability.[4] When segregated into persisting and non-persisting groups, however, a relatively much smaller number of persisting students and a relatively larger number of non-persisting students were found in the fourth or lowest quartile.

The coefficients of correlation given in Table II indicate that on all four quartile levels of intelligence there was a low positive relation between student load and grade point average. In other words, this means that the students in the lower mental ability groups carried the heavier schedule about as well as did those of the upper groups.

Implications

All the correlation coefficients in this study indicated a consistent positive relation between student load and grade point average. Moreover, the fact that these correlations remained positive when such factors as time devoted to extra-curricular activities and intelligence were kept constant, or were "partialed" out, tends to indicate that for all groups the heavier schedule appears to be an incentive to higher scholarship.

The chief implications of this study are that the dangers involved in permitting certain students to carry on abnormally heavy schedule have been unduly exaggerated and that many students undoubtedly can profitably, and with no consequent lowering of grade point averages, carry a heavier load than most college regulations permit.

H. G. Hotz
J. A. Trice
University of Arkansas

[4] All students who entered the university as freshmen in 1927 and 1928 took the American Council Psychological Examination at the time of entrance.

NEW BOOKS IN EDUCATION

Aiken, Janet R. *A New Plan of English Grammar.* Pp. v + 216. Holt. $1.40.

Allen, Richard D., Francis J. Stewart and Lester J. Schloerb. *Common Problems in Group Guidance.* Pp. xix + 186. Inor Publishing Company.

Allen, Richard D. *Case-Conference Problems in Group Guidance.* Pp. x + 151. Inor Publishing Company.

Atkins, Willard E. and Arthur Wubnig. *Our Economic World.* Pp. ix + 411. Illustrated. Harper. $1.68.

Bache, Louise F. *Health Education in an American City.* Pp. xi + 116. Illustrated. Doubleday, Doran. $2.00.

Boorman, W. Ryland and James M. Johnston. *Independent Young Thinkers.* Pp. 171. Christopher. $1.50.

Cohen, Morris R. and Ernest Nagel. *An Introduction to Logic and Scientific Method.* Pp. xii + 467. Harcourt, Brace.

Cole, Percival R. *The Method and Technique of Teaching.* Pp. x + 388. Oxford. $3.75.

Davis, Horace W. *Money Sense.* Pp. xi + 256. McGraw-Hill. $2.00.

Duffus, R. L. *Our Starving Libraries.* Pp. 148. Houghton Mifflin. $1.25.

Graham, Jessie. *The Evolution of Business Education in the United States and Its Implications for Business-Teacher Education.* Pp. xxiii + 228. University of Southern California Press.

Holmes, Harry N. *Out of the Test Tube.* Pp. x + 373. 83 figures. Long and Smith. $3.00.

Kohn, Hans. *Orient and Occident.* Pp. vii + 140. Day. $1.75.

Mills, John. *Signals and Speech in Electrical Communication.* Pp. 281. Harcourt, Brace. $2.00.

Parker, Lockie. *Art and People.* Pp. 126. Day. $1.75.

Price, Guy V. *Optimistic America.* Pp. 297. Western Baptist Publishing Company, Kansas City, Missouri. $2.25.

Russell, Mable and Elsie P. Wilson. *Art Training Through Home Problems.* Pp. 214. 110 figures. Manual Arts Press. $2.85.

Thorndike, Edward L. *Prediction of Vocational Success.* Pp. xviii + 284. Commonwealth Fund, New York. $2.50.

SCHOOL AND SOCIETY

WITH WHICH ARE COMBINED THE EDUCATIONAL REVIEW, ESTABLISHED IN 1891, THE TEACHERS MAGAZINE, ESTABLISHED IN 1878, AND THE SCHOOL JOURNAL, ESTABLISHED IN 1874.

EDITED BY J. McKEEN CATTELL, R. D. LINDQUIST AND W. H. COWLEY

EDITORIAL COMMUNICATIONS SHOULD BE ADDRESSED TO THE EDUCATION BUILDING, THE OHIO STATE UNIVERSITY, COLUMBUS, OHIO

Volume 39 SATURDAY, APRIL 7, 1934 Number 1006

CHARLES WILLIAM ELIOT[1]

THE MAKING OF HARVARD UNIVERSITY

By Dr. JAMES BRYANT CONANT
PRESIDENT OF HARVARD UNIVERSITY

As president of Harvard University, it it my privilege to share in this celebration of the one hundredth anniversary of the birth of Charles William Eliot. Throughout the United States, Harvard men this evening are gathered together to honor the memory of the twenty-first president of the university and his forty years of fruitful service. A numerical statement of the growth of the college and the professional schools during Mr. Eliot's administration is impressive, but perhaps tends to obscure the significance of his work. Harvard grew and expanded because its leader slowly instituted fundamental changes of great value; the increase in the number of students was a consequence but not a direct aim of his policy. It matters little, however, what tests you choose to apply—measured by any standard, Mr. Eliot's achievement was so great as to constitute a refounding of the institution of which he was the head.

He was able to develop Harvard so wisely because he himself had the power of wise self-development. Although in many respects his character seemed inflexible and his principles of granite, yet he had the great gift of sympathetic understanding of new ideas. He slowly assimilated new opinions and oriented himself to take advantage of new developments. How otherwise could he have been Harvard's skilful and successful pilot during those forty years in which the whole aspect of American civilization was so profoundly altered?

To take a specific example, in his later writings he repeatedly affirmed the principle that a university is concerned with extending the boundaries of knowledge. He wrote of the importance of the "scholarly achievements of the teaching staffs"; during the second half of his administration his words and actions bore witness to his earnest desire to promote scholarly work. In 1898, in an address on "The Aims of the Higher Education," Mr. Eliot described the threefold function of a university—"to teach, to accumulate great stores of systematized knowledge and to seek new truth." In regard to the third phase he said:

> A university is a society of learned men, each a master in his field; each acquainted with what has been achieved in all past time in his special sub-

[1] Addresses made on the occasion of the celebration of the centenary of the birth of Charles William Eliot, given in Sanders Theater, Harvard University, March 30, 1934.

ject; each prepared to push forward a little the present limits of knowledge; each expecting and hoping to clear up some tangle or bog on the frontier, or to pierce, with his own little searchlight, if only by a hand's breadth, the mysterious gloom which surrounds on every side the area of ascertained truth. Hence universities are places of research, of diligent inquiry for new or forgotten truth. This function is quite as indispensable as either of the two former. It is indispensable for two reasons: first, because a university which is not a place of research will not long continue to be a good place of teaching; and secondly, because this incessant, quiet, single-minded search after new truth is the condition of both material and intellectual progress for the nation and for the race.

Thus wrote the president at the close of the century. And yet in the inaugural address of 1869 we find no statement of such aims or ideals. At that time the new president apparently envisaged the future of Harvard in terms of professors whose "prime business must be regular and assiduous class teaching." His excellent specifications for a suitable candidate for the faculty were that he must be "a real gentleman and a natural teacher"; there was no emphasis on the possibility that a permanent member of the staff might be a creative worker in his own right. Indeed, the story is told that a few years after President Eliot's inauguration, a young assistant professor, full of joyous enthusiasm, applied for some relief from his long hours of teaching that he might devote more time to his own investigations. After a question or two about the proposed research, Mr. Eliot replied, "I do not see how such work would be of service to Harvard College." Contrast this remark with Mr. Eliot's attitude twenty years later. He was then choosing members of his faculty because of their scholarly promise. He was gladly lightening the burden of routine work and encouraging the professors to devote much of their time and energy to writing and research.

What happened in the interval to change Mr. Eliot's opinions on such fundamental questions? The answer is clear. In 1876, the Johns Hopkins University was formally opened. Daniel Coit Gilman proved that it was possible to have an institution of higher learning in America which was a real university in the sense in which that word was understood in Europe. What he proposed to do and what he actually accomplished impressed his friend, the president of Harvard. Mr. Eliot was an interested observer of the great events which were in progress at Baltimore. He saw and he understood. He reshaped his own course as a consequence. Harvard also became a university.

His task was in many ways much more difficult than Gilman's. At the Johns Hopkins University, a new institution could be built from the beginning; at Harvard University, the traditions of many years must be slowly modified. An ancient but vigorous undergraduate college, vital to the community, must be made the core of the new structure. The change proceeded slowly but was the more permanent because of the patient care with which each new stage was discussed and planned. The final result was possible only because of the president's steadfast courage. He dealt skilfully with a great variety of men whose opinions and character differed widely from his own. He fought boldly and persistently for what he believed to be right, and he almost invariably won.

I have chosen to dwell on this particular aspect of Mr. Eliot's educational work because it illustrates so strikingly the extraordinary elements of his character. In a man of rigid principles and invincible faith, the power of growth is rare. This unusual combination of qualities enabled him to transform his university and deeply influence his country. With gratitude and admiration we pay tribute to his memory.

A GREAT CAREER

By Dr. A. LAWRENCE LOWELL
FORMERLY PRESIDENT OF HARVARD UNIVERSITY

In the popular memory of a great career the result obscures the long labors by which it was achieved, the victory overshadows the conflict; and so it seems that in surveying the great advance he accomplished in the university there is a side of President Eliot's long life that has been dwelt upon too little.

The public impression of his work is one of rapid and widely accepted success, and a speaker here on his ninetieth birthday said that when elected he was at once recognized as a great leader in education. But that leaves out the obstacles, the resistance, the striving, the disappointments, and with them the courage and tenacity required to attain the ends he sought.

Although much of the fruition came later, the foundations for most of what he wrought were laid in the first ten years of his administration; and yet not until he had been president more than twice as long did he win the general admiration of students and alumni; and approbation from other seats of learning came even later still. At his election he received honorary degrees from Williams, Princeton and Yale; the next after this was from Johns Hopkins when he had been in office thirty-three years; and not another until he had resigned. Recognition of his work came slowly, the sequel to a long fight against obstinate dissent.

At a meeting of the club which he had joined towards the end of his administration he said that his life and work had perforce been solitary; for, although he had close friends and many admirers, he stood, like the captain of a ship in a storm, on the quarter deck, apart. He set his course and kept to it regardless of the buffets of the sea.

Whether by nature, or by self-restraint acquired from the conditions under which he worked, he seemed to the outer world austere. Yet one was every little while amazed at his knowledge of former students, their character, what they had done and how they had fared since graduation. Even to a capacious memory such information does not come through intellectual curiosity, or professional attention to the effects of education. It springs from a personal interest in the men themselves, which he must have felt, although he showed it little, even to those whose prospects and careers he kept in mind.

Those among us who have passed the meridian of life can recall the tall, erect, stately figure that stood so often in this place; resolute, unflinching in his pursuit of the goal that guided him, steadfast in his ideals, just to his opponents—too just to harbor resentment—a character masterly in its size and strength.

HOW ONE CHILDREN'S THEATER BECAME SUCCESSFUL

By BEVERLY F. FREITAG
EAST SCHOOL, STONEHAM, MASSACHUSETTS

The great desire to have a Children's Theater took root back in my childhood days. My family did not look with favor on the stage, so my desire to act and my dreams for a theater where children like myself could act and where the audience would really take our work seriously were kept to myself. As I grew older and worked with children in music, dancing and in the school and saw their eagerness for the fanciful and their delight in interpretation, I began to prepare myself for the fulfilment of that great desire. With the help and encouragement of Dr. Everett L. Getchell, of Boston University, and Mr. Clayton D. Gilbert, of The New England Conservatory of Music, I prepared myself to take over the responsibility of a Children's Theater and sought for some experienced person with whom to work—one who had the same ideas as I about the theater.

The success of such a project lies in the hands of its leaders. They should not only be expert in everything pertaining to the stage but should also thoroughly understand the psychology of children and their place in this world of "make-believe," which to them is very real. As a leader possessing all these qualities, having at one time taught in the lower grades, I knew of no one more capable than Dr. M. Goldeth Myers of Boston.

The next step was to present our carefully laid plans to the public by inviting them to a meeting at the school. The pupils in my fourth grade wrote invitations to the 125 parents in our building and enough others to send to all the primary and elementary teachers to put on the board for their pupils to copy and take home. In this way we reached all the parents in the town who would be interested in a Children's Theater and from this group we started our list of patrons.

There are several types of Children's Theaters; one in which adults perform for children—better called a Theater for Children to attend—one in which both adults and children act, and the last, which we attempted, a theater with all children of various ages performing, and under proper guidance and supervision, taking over the entire business of the theater. The purpose of our theater is to provide our children with the wholesome entertainment at their own interest level, to give them an opportunity to express themselves in drama and a chance to learn the intricate workings of the stage. A theater of this type in some respects limits the kind of play to be given, but compensation is made in that many more children are used. One of the chief aims of such a theater is to give a chance to those who otherwise would not have opportunity for self-expression. Instead of drawing upon the few prominent boys and girls who are ordinarily given a major share of school responsibilities we use all children who care to take part by putting them in groups and alternating the players. Pupils taking a leading rôle in one play have a minor part in another, thus allowing every child to experience the thrill of the lead as well as to feel the necessity of perfect cooperation of the minor parts in the making of a successful performance. This means more rehearsals and slower progress, but it also accomplishes the purpose of brightening the lives of many children who otherwise never know the thrill of dramatic expression.

Our success was assured from the start by enlisting the services of Mr. Andrew Flagg, a talented art supervisor in Stoneham, who gave unstintingly of his time and efforts with the pupils to make both settings and costumes lovely. Pupils working on costumes were required to have the clothes correct for the period. This requirement not only called the attention of the children to accuracy of details but also rated the performance higher with the 1 per cent. in the audience who knew the proper costumes for the different periods.

Two plays are cast at the same time, so as soon as one play is over work can begin on the next. In this way a play can be given every five weeks and no child is overtaxed. Under the platoon system in our schools we rehearsed with such difficulty for the first play that we made a tentative plan wherein the high-school students attending school in the morning and the elementary students worked together and the junior high for the majority worked alone, each group presenting a play a month. In this way we had different heights, wider range in quality of voice and older children for the more mature parts in children's plays. The plan worked so well that we are continuing it this second season.

With few exceptions the cast of forty-three in the first play, "Over the Hills and Far Away," were making their first public appearance, and they were so thrilled over being made up to appear before the lights and with their own importance in the rôle that we expected them to burst out of their costumes any moment.

All rehearsals are out of school time, and the children are taken in small groups. For rehearsals that extend after dark, transportation is furnished to the children living a distance from the hall and those living near are chaperoned to their homes. By keeping the welfare of the children in mind, the respect of the parents is gained.

Any new endeavor must go through the crucifixion period, and ours was no exception. If the director knows her work so thoroughly that she can justify her every move, misunderstandings can be straightened out. There were two special meetings of the members after the first play to discuss the points that were good and how weak places could be strengthened and errors eliminated from the next performance.

There is no forcing in coaching these child actors. They go ahead at their own pace as fast as they can be led to see and feel the necessity of the change in their work. By the end of the second performance it was possible to shift the major portion of the back-stage management to the children themselves. Members of the theater entertain with solos, dances and recitations between the acts. Child directors lead the children in the audience in songs to allow the wee ones to stand and relax.

From the first the children felt the responsibility of being courteous to the public and always took great pride in writing and delivering letters of appreciation to those who in even the slightest way assisted us. All materials that are available in the town are being purchased for the theater, thus making about a 90 per cent. patronage.

A Saturday afternoon and evening performance, using double cast for the leads, is proving successful. Tickets are 25 cents for children and 50 cents for adults. Special arrangements are made for large families, and there is always an opportunity for ambitious children to earn tickets. True to its purpose of having only children perform all duties, child ushers dressed in storybook fashion are the first to welcome patrons.

The theater stands all the expense of the productions, so that no child will have to forego the pleasure of becoming a member because of the expense of costumes.

No more apt statement of the aims for which the directors and interested parents are striving can be given than that contributed to us by Mary O. Pottenger, elementary supervisor, Springfield: "Children live and learn through imaginary situations which take on the aspect of reality. Those who play interpret character, live in the experiences of others and grow in insight. Those who form the audience go adventuring with the players in the various situations with good honest emotions. Both groups raise their standards of oral expression through speaking the King's English and hearing it spoken. I am hoping that the Little Theater for Children will continue to grow and exert a fine influence on our boys and girls."

Although the first two plays this year were cast last spring, the work was not begun until the children were well established in their school work. Dorothy Oppen, a junior in high school, is the first student director to assume one half the responsibility of directing a play. She has shown unusual ability in working with children. Our student prompter of the past season has successfully coached a short play with high-school students for an assembly program.

The editor of the *Independent,* a town paper, has given us strong support. Members of the theater have correlated the writing of articles for the paper with their language work, and remarkable results have been obtained from grades as low as the fourth. Unknown friends have been most generous in their columns on the children's work.

As in all walks of life, men carry on work to different degrees of perfection. So it is with dramatics and all phases of stage production. There are those who are interested in it only as a means of enjoyment, for a better appreciation of the theater, a means of perfecting poise, overcoming self-consciousness, or enriching the voice, while there will also be those who eventually will earn their livelihood by it. There is no better time at which to start this training than the impressionable years of childhood. The parents are eager to see their children grow in understanding.

The plays have attracted much favorable comment from prominent educators. Among these are: Dr. Payson Smith, state commissioner of education; Dr. Getchell, of Boston University; Mr. Clayton D. Gilbert, head of the drama department at the New England Conservatory of Music; Dr. Cheney C. Jones, superintendent of Home for Little Wanderers, Boston; Charles Rounds, professor of English at State Teachers College, Trenton, N. J.; Frederick W. Porter, superintendent of schools, Greenfield, Mass.; Mary O. Pottenger, elementary supervisor, Springfield, Mass., and Winifred Ward, instructor at Northwestern University and director of the Children's Theater in Evanston, Illinois.

EDUCATIONAL EVENTS

THE VOCATIONAL GUIDANCE PLAN FOR RUSSIAN CHILDREN

WRITING in the *New York Times* of March 25, Miriam Ziony describes the system of vocational guidance being developed in Russia. The program provides actual experience in many varieties of employment, psychological analyses by counselors and follow-up during the first years of employment. Pupils in the sixth- and seventh-year group take part in actual work in the factory, although they do not receive pay for practical work done there because the factory carries part of the expense of the school. After seven years of elementary training, the student is eligible for admittance into the factory school, which is connected with a particular factory and gives a two-year course in theory and practise in various industries. Half of the time at the factory school is spent in actual work, the other half in academic studies.

A vocational guidance clinic is attached to each factory or, in some cases, to a group of factories. A psychologist is provided for every 450 pupils. These psychologists are required to be graduates of a psychological institute and to have had three years of teaching experience.

The pupil's record, which accompanies him from the central consultation center connected with his elementary school, includes information about his physical health; a record of tests and measurements from the time he entered the first prekindergarten group; a report on the first interview with the school psychologist regarding outside environment—family background, relations with parents and friends, type of books the child reads, type of clubs attended, interest and knowledge of the different professions and occupations.

Individual vocational tests—adaptations of German tests—are used to indicate various traits, such as self-reliance, etc. Material and information on previous school work and the opinions of previous teachers are considered important, and contact is maintained with teachers and schools in the different provinces in the case of children who have come from places outside of Moscow. Objective tests are not as popular in Russia as they are in the United States. It is the function of the guidance clinic to make adjustments in the attitudes and practises of the child, the home and the school. An intensive study is made of the child's interests and capacities. If he is unhappy or unsuited to the work at the factory school, he is redirected through the guidance department to another school for readjustment.

After the first two months at the school the student is required to write a composition in which he gives his impressions of the factory school. Analysis of these compositions by the vocational guidance counselor may lead to changes in method of teaching and even to changes in factory equipment. Contacts are maintained between the counselor and the home in order to give the parents greater insight into the ideals and interests of the younger generation.

A NATIONAL INSTITUTION OF PUBLIC AFFAIRS AT WASHINGTON

UNDER the sponsorship of Secretary of Commerce Roper, a National Institution of Public Affairs is being developed in Washington. The institution is to be a laboratory for leadership in public affairs, and early in 1934 will bring to Washington approximately 120 college students and 20 college professors as the first matriculants.

The students will be chosen through regional or district selection committees, which will designate the students according to the high standards of qualifications finally determined by the advisory board and the educational committee. The college professors will work with the institution as observers, following every detail of the students' training for the purpose of developing better, more effective and more practical educational procedures and methods for college and university teaching throughout the country. The students will not attend classes, but will, in effect, serve actual "interneships" in the Federal Government. Thus, training will be work and practise rather than theory. They will be assigned positions as though on the government pay-roll. Original research, analytical thinking and constructive criticism will be the guiding principles of their training.

"The practical and inspiring value," observes Chester H. McCall, assistant to the Secretary of Commerce, "of bringing more than a hundred of the nation's most talented and forceful students to Washington for two or three months' training, experience and study in the procedures and processes of the Federal Government can not be minimized. This institution should be, in the broadest sense, a laboratory for authentic leadership."

Major emphasis will be placed upon the dynamics of leadership, the human element in public affairs, the formulation of policies and the transformation of those policies into governmental procedures and processes. Within a period of four years between six hundred and seven hundred young people would attend this university of public affairs, each of them thus becoming a potential leader for the years ahead.

The educational committee of the institution comprises the following: Dean Walter James Shepard, president of the American Political Science Association; Dr. Charles R. Mann, director of the American Council on Education; Dr. Walter M. W. Splawn, member of the Interstate Commerce Commission and formerly president of the University of Texas; Dr. Charles E. Clark, dean of the Yale University School of Law, and Dr. Arnold Bennett Hall, director of the Institute for Government Research, Brookings Institution.

A SURVEY ON THE SOCIAL STUDIES

UNDER the sponsorship of the U. S. Office of Education, Monograph No. 21 of the National Survey of Secondary Education, entitled "Instruction in the Social Studies," came from the press on March 30. The monograph was prepared by William G. Kimmel, executive secretary of the investigation of the social studies in schools of the American Historical Association. The findings of the survey are presented in ten chapters and give an analysis of the social studies in the junior high schools of 55 cities and the senior high schools of 43 cities.

The author observes that "courses of study, with few exceptions, reveal the need for considerable improvement in the character and quality of lists of books to be used by teachers and pupils in the social studies. With the growing realization of the bankruptcy of many current concepts in economics, politics and social relationships, the implications for the social studies in the secondary schools are of tremendous importance, and are indicative of the need of a greater measure of responsibility than has ever been assumed heretofore." He observes that the situation requires a thorough reorganization of subject-matter to include more current information.

The monograph includes studies of history, civics, economics, sociology, geography, vocations and homemaking. Examination of social studies programs in junior and senior high schools reveals that American history and some form of civics are favored most as courses for grades 8 and 9, respectively. For the senior high school, courses in world history in grade 10, United States or American history combined in some cities with civics in grade 11, and semester courses in economics, sociology or civics in grade 12, represent a favored program in 13 of the 43 cities studied. The number of subjects other than United States history included in grades 11 and 12 varies widely in different cities. There are differences among senior high schools in the same city.

Only one objective is found, in many instances, while the largest number found in one course is 135. A study of general objectives listed in 60 social study courses by Swindler indicates that social civic efficiency takes first place in frequency of mention. Other objectives often mentioned are participation in civic activities; information as a basis for participation; making the world intelligible to pupils; knowledge of civic rights, duties and responsibilities; ability to think, discriminate, judge; knowledge of social, economic and political principles; knowledge of the past in order to interpret the present; intelligent patriotism, and service and cooperation in society. Still other objectives in the list of 28 include respect for law and institutions; knowledge of moral, ethical and religious principles; worthy use of leisure; vocational efficiency; general culture, and health efficiency.

Nine problems for further study are proposed in the analysis of the objectives underlying social study. To combat these problems the report makes certain recommendations. There is urgent need for thoroughgoing analyses of the assumptions and hypotheses to which the list of objectives is subjected, for investigations of the ranges and depths of social experiences to which pupils are exposed in relation to their mental maturity and ability in different grade levels and for differentiation between those ultimate objectives to be realized after the completion of the courses in social studies and the more immediate.

THE PROPOSED STUDY OF HONORARY FRATERNITIES

At the annual meeting of the National Association of Deans and Advisers of Men, convening at Northwestern University over the week-end of March 30, Dr. Francis W. Shepardson, president of the Association of College Honor Societies, and Joseph A. Park, dean of men at the Ohio State University, proposed that a study be made of intercollegiate honor societies.

Dean Park pointed out that a wide discrepancy exists between membership costs for various societies and that the national treasuries of these organizations are in many cases putting heavy financial burdens upon local chapters. He also pointed out that most existing honor groups were originally founded with worthy purposes and have been properly conducted, but that universities are justified in questioning some societies as to their worth and even as to their right to continue to function on college and university campuses.

"Is it fair to the individual," he asked, "whose achievement has been in one field to be forced by that fact to pay a $25 initiation fee and $5 annual dues, whereas if he had achieved success in another field he might have paid $5 and ended his financial obligations at that point, having in the second case membership in a society more widely recognized than the first?"

Pointing out that the number of college honor societies now runs into the hundreds, Dean Park asserted that "there are in existence on our campuses societies of every possible variety, in recognition of every imaginable interest or difference." He observed that the national headquarters for some of these societies collect from 80 to 90 per cent. of the students' initiation fees, taking in the neighborhood of $10,000 annually from large universities. He estimated that more than a quarter million dollars is contributed each year by American college students for the support of these honorary groups.

Dr. Shepardson's organization, the Association of College Honor Societies, has been approved by the National Association of Deans and Advisers of Men as the proper organization to evaluate honor societies and to attempt to eradicate the evils which have arisen.

THE PROBLEM OF CONTINUATION SCHOOLS IN BOSTON

Because of the NRA codes and their provisions preventing the employment of children under sixteen, Mr. Patrick Campbell, superintendent of the Boston schools, reports that the Boston board of education faces two serious problems—first, how to employ the almost completely abandoned continuation schools and, second, how to deal with the sudden overcrowding of the regular schools.

Continuation school attendance in Boston has, within recent months, dropped from 4,000 to about 400. Mr. Campbell reports that the future of the continuation schools must await legal developments. At the present time, he asserts, the board of education is marking time, since it is unwilling to disestablish the continuation program which still serves a purpose and may in time attract large numbers of students. This would be true if the Massachusetts law were revised to raise the school attendance age from sixteen to eighteen. A movement, sponsored by leading educators and laymen, is already under way in the state to bring about the necessary legislation to make this change in the school-leaving age.

The problem of dealing with the overloading of the high schools presents a serious situation not only in Boston but in all Massachusetts schools. Writing in the *Boston Transcript* of March 31, Agnes Florencia Fennelly raises the question as to "what to do with the suddenly idle children to whom the regular schools are not suited, and the further problem of whether or not facilities ought to be enlarged to take care of children even up to the age of eighteen in view of the probable continuation of unemployment. What is becoming of the boys and girls who leave school at sixteen, bored with the regular high-school curriculum, who are at the adolescent stage and particularly plastic?"

The Massachusetts Federation of Labor has become interested in the problem and has introduced a bill in the legislature which provides for changing the requirement for children under sixteen from attendance at continuation schools to full-time attendance. The education committee of the legislature has, however, reported adversely on the bill, even though it has been strongly urged by Commissioner of Education Payson Smith. Most of the unemployed children below sixteen have returned to school voluntarily, but the remaining group, unless they are required to attend school, are thought to be the probable source of much social delinquency.

The school opportunities for these children, it is pointed out, must be different from those available to the average child. They are most of them impatient with ordinary school subjects, chiefly because of inferior scholastic abilities, and special curriculums must be made available to them. To meet the needs of these boys and girls, Mr. Robert O. Small, director of the Division of Vocational Education of Massachusetts, has organized a school of "special opportunity" for pupils who have left regular school courses. "It appears," he observes, "that some type of full-time opportunity school, different from the regular established vocational schools and from the traditional high or junior high schools, must be worked out to meet the needs of the children who have been put back into the regular schools on full time. These children are cramping the opportunity of the pupils already in the schools. Teachers can deal with those desiring the regular school curriculum, but under these new conditions they are handicapped."

THE NATIONAL STUDENT LEAGUE WAR POLL

A syndicated Hearst newspaper release reports that 129 colleges and more than 30 high schools on April 6 voted under the sponsorship of the National Student League on a resolution "declaring non-support of the government of the United States in any war it undertakes."

The National Student League held its annual convention in Washington on December 26 and is reported to have arranged the date and itinerary of eight field organizers. *Fight,* the official organ of the league, claims, according to the press report, that 22,000 students have voted on the "war resistance" issue in American colleges, 8,000 indicating entire refusal to fight in any war, 7,000 expressing their willingness to fight only in case of invasion, and 7,000 recording their willingness to obey any call to arms. It is reported further that Julian Prager, of the National Student League, discussed the April 6 polling date as follows:

The week of April 6 should be set aside as national anti-war week in the schools. Symposia should be held. Club meetings should be converted into peace meetings. Statistics and other data should be gathered by students and read and discussed.

And on April 6, to duly commemorate the anniversary of the entrance of the United States into the world war, large demonstrations should be held. They must be carefully planned and dramatically carried out.

Also, a resolution declaring non-support of the Government of the U. S. A. in any war it undertakes must be presented and every effort made to pass it.

Although these conferences may draw many students (other than N. S. L.) they are just the first step in an anti-war campaign. The success of a conference or its failure depends upon the ''continuation'' work. Permanent committees should direct demonstrations and struggles to oust the R. O. T. C. if there is one on the campus. Campaigns of protest in support of students of other schools and colleges who have been expelled or suspended for anti-war activity—such as C. C. N. Y., West Philadelphia High School and Manly High in Chicago—should be carried on:

These actions which I have described so far are of purely student nature, but there is another phase of our work which requires just as much, if not more, attention. It concerns our cooperation with the workers in a common struggle.

We realize that the students alone can not stop war. The most potent force in the struggle against imperialist war is the working class, and it is with them and around them that we must build our movement. For this express purpose we have the American League Against War and Fascism. We can and must participate in all their demonstrations, their local conferences, and in all their national campaigns.

EDUCATIONAL NOTES AND NEWS

AT the International Congress of Educational and Instructional Cinematography, to be held at Rome, Italy, from April 19 to 25, the United States will be represented by Professor W. W. Charters, director of the bureau of educational research of the Ohio State University; Cline M. Koon, radio specialist in the Department of the Interior, *chairman;* C. F. Hoban, of the state department of public instruction, Harrisburg, Pa.; Paul B. Mann, Evander Childs High School, New York City; Frederick L. Devereux, Erpi Picture Consultants, New York City, and Carl E. Milliken, secretary of the Motion Picture Producers and Distributors of America.

HERBERT HOOVER has become chairman of the Mills College Council, a national committee of fifty-eight members, formed to extend the influence and usefulness of Mills College, according to an announcement recently made by Dr. Aurelia Henry Reinhardt, president of the college.

SIR ARTHUR STANLEY EDDINGTON, director of the Cambridge Observatory and professor of astronomy at the University of Cambridge, will deliver the annual Messenger Lectures at Cornell University, which begin on April 9. The Messenger lectures, twelve in number, are made possible by a fund bequeathed by Dr. Hiram J. Messenger, who graduated from the university in 1881.

FOLLOWING the publicity accruing to him because of his statements concerning the radical intentions of the so-called "brain trust," Dr. William A. Wirt, superintendent of schools at Gary, Ind., has written a pamphlet entitled "America Must Lose," which will be issued in instalments and is being sponsored by the Committee of the Nation. In a press release Dr. Wirt observed that he seeks to answer some of the questions raised by Secretary of Agriculture Wallace in his recent brochure, "America Must Choose."

DR. LEO WOLMAN, professor of economics at Columbia University, has been appointed by President Roosevelt to serve as impartial member of the Automobile Labor Board, organized to carry out the terms of the recent agreement which averted a strike in the automobile industry. Dr. Wolman is at present chairman of the NRA Labor Advisory Board.

Dr. Kenneth Dameron, of the Ohio State University, has been named secretary and director of research for the newly created national Trade Economics Board. The other members include John Burke, of New York City, who will serve as chairman; Dr. Paul H. Nystrom, of Columbia University; Dr. Walter Eddy, of New York City, and Mr. T. A. Howell, of Richmond, Va. The board will study the economic effects and results of various provisions of the code of fair competition for the retail trade.

Miss Margaret B. Martin has been appointed acting director of the Library School of the New Jersey College for Women for the next academic year. Professor Ethel M. Fair, director of the school, has been granted a leave of absence for that period in order to study at the Graduate Library School of the University of Chicago.

Thomas G. Wagner, superintendent of schools at Croton-on-Hudson, N. Y., has been elected superintendent of schools of the second supervisory school district of Westchester County to succeed Charles H. Cheney, of White Plains.

Señor Salvador Dinamarca, instructor in Spanish at Harvard University, has been appointed consul from Chile for New England. Señor Dinamarca formerly served as chancellor to the consulate at Philadelphia.

Dr. Francis Bitter, research physicist of the Westinghouse Electric and Manufacturing Company, Dr. Joseph H. Keenan, of the Stevens Institute of Technology, and Dr. Robley D. Evans, of the University of California, have been appointed to the faculty of the Massachusets Institute of Technology, as of September 1, Dr. Bitter as associate professor in the department of mining and metallurgy, Dr. Keenan as associate professor of mechanical engineering and Dr. Evans as assistant professor of physics.

Paul F. Gaiser, principal of the senior high school in Vancouver, Washington, has been elected superintendent of schools to succeed DeGaris Reeves, who has resigned after four years of service.

Dr. Arnold E. Joyal, of the department of education of the University of Denver, has been appointed director of a Summer School Executives Conference, which will be held at the university from July 18 to 27, inclusive. The field of school administration and supervision has been announced as the main topic of discussion for the conference.

Dr. Norman L. Torrey, of Yale University, has been appointed professor of French at Swarthmore College. Dr. Torrey will begin his duties at the beginning of the new academic year.

Paul Vellacott, fellow and tutor at Peter House, University of Cambridge, has been appointed head master at Harrow. He will succeed Cyril Norwood, who will leave at the end of the summer term to become president of St. John's College, of the University of Oxford.

Dr. Thomas S. Kepler, professor of English Bible at Mount Union College, has resigned to accept a similar position at Lawrence College.

Professor C. R. Arnold, of the department of rural economics at the Ohio State University, has been chosen as a delegate to the international agricultural economics conference to be held in Germany in August. Professor Arnold is at present on leave of absence from the university to serve as a deputy production credit commissioner in the farm credit administration at Washington.

Dr. Delo C. Grover, acting president of Baldwin-Wallace College, has been elected president of the Ohio Methodist Association. Dr. Grover succeeds Dr. William H. McMaster, president of Mount Union College.

Dr. Edmund Taylor Whittaker, professor of mathematics and astronomy at the University of Edinburgh, and Governor Wilbur L. Cross, of Connecticut, formerly dean of the Yale Graduate School, received the honorary degree of doctor of laws from the University of California on March 23, when the university held its charter day exercises.

Dr. Howard Foster Lowry, professor of English at Wooster College, has been granted a John Guggenheim Memorial Fellowship to study in England the lives and works of Matthew Arnold and Arthur Hugh Clough.

DR. ROBERT M. MACIVER, Lieber professor of political philosophy and sociology at Columbia University, will serve as president of the recently formed American Political Economy League. Dr. Arthur D. Gayer, lecturer in economics in Barnard College, will assume the office of secretary.

DR. JOHN E. WOLFF, professor emeritus of petrography and mineralogy at Harvard University, has been elected a vice-president of the Geological Society of America.

DR. JAMES P. PORTER, professor of psychology at Ohio University, was elected president of the Ohio Academy of Science, at its forty-fourth annual meeting, held in Columbus, Ohio, on March 30 and 31. He succeeds Dr. E. Lucy Braun, of the University of Cincinnati. Dr. Adolph E. Waller, of the department of botany of the Ohio State University, was elected treasurer, and Dr. William H. Alexander, of the United States Weather Bureau, secretary.

PROFESSOR JEREMIAH D. M. FORD, chairman of the department of Romance languages at Harvard University, will receive the honorary degree of doctor of literature from the University of Dublin at the commencement exercises to be held on July 5.

DR. HENRY RAYMOND BRUSH, chairman of the French department of the University of California at Los Angeles, has been made an "Officier d'académie" by the Ministry of Education of France.

PROFESSOR STANLEY L. GALPIN, head of the department of Romance languages at Trinity College in Hartford, Conn., died at Manila on April 1. Professor Galpin was fifty-six years of age.

JOSEPH ROY ELLIS, registrar of freshmen at Yale University since 1920, died on April 1 at the age of forty-nine years.

DR. CHARLES E. CALDWELL, formerly professor of surgery and anatomy at the University of Cincinnati College of Medicine, died on March 24. Dr. Caldwell was seventy-seven years old.

DR. ELON HOWARD EATON, professor of biology at Hobart and William Smith Colleges since 1908 and later head of that department, died on March 27 at the age of sixty-seven years.

DR. BERN BUDD GALLAUDET, associate professor of anatomy at the College of Physicians and Surgeons at Columbia University, died on March 30 in his seventy-fifth year.

DR. CHARLES H. MARTIN, formerly a member of the faculty of the Ohio College of Dental Surgery and one of the organizers of the Cincinnati Dental College, died on March 28 in his sixty-ninth year.

PHILLIPS ACADEMY at Andover, Mass., has received a bequest of $10,000 from the estate of the late Miss Flora E. Isham.

A $2,000,000 building program at Clark University in Worcester, Mass., has been announced by President Wallace W. Atwood. Arrangements to begin the project, which will cover a ten- to twenty-year period, are nearing completion. It is expected that ground for the first building, a gymnasium, will be broken within a year. When the entire project is complete, the campus will be enclosed in a quadrangle modeled after the universities of Oxford and Cambridge.

GILBERT W. MEAD, president of Washington College at Chestertown, Md., has recently compiled statistics on the comparative college enrolments at the close of the Revolutionary War. Washington College was chartered in 1782, expanding the work done for three quarters of a century preceding by the Kent County Free School in Chestertown. In 1781–82, the Kent School enrolled between 150 and 200 students, and the first Washington graduating class (1783) numbered four. Figures received from official sources of the institutions listed show the following registrations in or near 1782: Harvard in 1782 had 141 men—32 freshmen, 44 sophomores, 30 juniors and 35 seniors. Yale in 1782 enrolled about 200. Pennsylvania (the College of Philadelphia) had 31 in the college, 241 in the academy, and between 50 and 60 from outside the college attending medical and scientific lectures. Dartmouth in 1782 enrolled 81. Rutgers in the fall of 1782 had a college of 18 and an academy of 20. Princeton in 1782 enrolled 40. The College of William and Mary has no record for 1782; three students were listed for 1783. Washington and Lee (Liberty Hall Academy) granted no degrees until 1785, at which time 12 were conferred upon students "who had completed the work required prior to the charter," which was granted in 1782. Columbia (King's College) suspended operations from 1776 to 1784 on account of the war. In 1785 there were 27 enrolled. Brown (the College of Rhode Island) suspended from 1776 to 1782 and reopened with 12 students in 1783.

MORE than 1,000 organizations in the country are conducting educational programs for adults which are of "more than local interest," according to the first national survey of adult education in the United States, recently published by the American Association for Adult Education. The study, which is published under the title, "Handbook of Adult Education in the United States," was made possible by a grant from the Carnegie Corporation of New York. The book includes data on projects being conducted by schools, museums, libraries, settlements, clubs, little theaters, parent groups, universities and other educational and social institutions. In addition, education for the unemployed, vocational guidance and vocational education, visual education, correspondence schools, alumni education and workers' education are discussed. Digests of the educational programs of nearly 150 national organizations, many of them with headquarters here, are included.

THE Commercial Education Association will hold its spring convention on Saturday, April 28, at the Hotel Pennsylvania in New York City. The theme of the convention will be "Skills and Their Development through Commercial Education."

THE Chicago Board of Education voted on March 26 to open a city college in September. Three branches are to be organized, and it is reported that this expansion will be managed without increase in the total budget. William J. Bogan, superintendent of schools, presented an estimate to the board, demonstrating how the college could be financed on $209,000 a year and how this fund could be provided from the tentative budget of $70,000,000.

THE New York Branch of the American Psychological Association will hold a conference on April 7 under the auspices of the psychology department of the Washington Square College of New York University. Three sections of the branch will meet simultaneously at the morning session. Professor Carl J. Warden, of Columbia University, will preside at a section on comparative psychology; Dr. Walter R. Miles, of Yale University, will be chairman of a section on differential psychology, and Professor Samuel W. Fernberger, of the University of Pennsylvania, will head the section of experimental psychology. At the dinner meeting of the association, Dr. Joseph Jastrow will speak on "The Contributions of J. McKeen Cattell to Psychology."

Michigan To-morrow, a new student publication at the University of Michigan, reports in its issue of April 2 that the university authorities have refused permission to Father Charles E. Coughlin, of Detroit, to speak on the campus. The student publication announced that the Sigma Delta Chi journalistic fraternity sought approval of their invitation to Father Coughlin, but that Dean Joseph A. Bursley, acting in the absence of President Ruthven, vetoed the invitation.

DR. C. V. BOYER, acting president of the University of Oregon, has announced a conference on higher education to be held on the university campus on May 18 and 19. Three themes will be discussed: Current social movements; the significance of social changes for higher education, and an evaluation of the attempts of colleges and universities to meet the needs of an evolving social order. Invitations to participate in the conference have been addressed to a dozen leading educators and laymen.

THE Oregon Normal School has recently been accredited by the American Association of Teachers Colleges.

THE recent appointment of Robert E. Simon, formerly president of the United Parents Association, Supreme Court Justice James C. Cropsey, Mrs. Nathan Straus, Jr., and Dr. A. A. Berle, Sr., to the committee which will make a survey of the public school system of New York City has been announced by Mayor La Guardia. Dr. Harold G. Campbell, superintendent of schools of New York City, appointed the other three members of the committee early in February, when the Board of Education passed the resolution calling for the survey. They are Dr. William F. Russell, dean of Teachers College, Columbia University; Dr. John W. Withers, dean of the school of education, New York University, and Frederick D. Chambers, auditor of the Board of Education.

DISCUSSION

THE INCLUSION OF SOCIAL SCIENCE

REORGANIZATION of the curricula of American high schools and junior colleges to include a substantially larger amount of social science is daily becoming increasingly necessary. Articles in the newspapers and magazines, speeches by professional schoolmen and by laymen, and resolutions passed by various organizations all demand that a subject hitherto somewhat neglected be given a place in public instruction more nearly commensurate with its growing importance. It has already been pointed out[1] that one of the causes of the present economic debacle is undoubtedly the persistent ignorance of economic laws and that future recurrences of similar cataclysms may be expected as long as this ignorance continues. We may add that "rugged individualism" and the train of evils which follows in its wake can not receive its due quietus until public instruction has fully exposed the situation to the coming generation.

If we read the signs aright, there is little hope that the present generation has fully learned its lesson from the experiences of the past few years. Desperate effort is being made by middle-aged men to regain life along former lines. The stock market is being played avidly, if not in the volume of 1929. Chiseling is taking place, some being brought to light but more proceeding under cover. Men in high positions avoid payment of income taxes. It seems difficult to hope that much can be expected from men who are more or less set in their ways and who are either unable or unwilling to face about and to fall in line with the new trend of thought. Therefore we must turn to the group of young people who are now receiving their training and to the larger group who are about to enter upon their training if we wish to make function ideas of whose truth some of us are convinced. Public education is a slow process, but it is also a sure process. Its efficiency was proved by the German system prior to 1914. If our lack of centralization prohibits a similar uniform aim over the entirety of our country, at least the schoolmen of the forty-eight states can bring about such a result once they are convinced that it is essential and imperative.

[1] SCHOOL AND SOCIETY, April 22, 1933.

One difficulty which stands in the way of giving social science the place in the secondary curricula which it must take is the presence of a number of subjects which already possess the stamp of approval. Notwithstanding the outcry against "fads and frills," when one actually takes up the task of excision, stone walls present themselves on all sides for the reception of unwary heads. Even the taxpayer who now complains against the cost of public education presents objections to the removal of specific subjects of which he personally approves. How then can any room be found in a curriculum already crowded and approved?

I wish to point to certain subjects in the secondary curricula which apparently are receiving an undue amount of attention and which, in my opinion, might profitably be so reorganized that some of the time now given to them could be assigned to a really adequate presentation of social science. I am referring to the curricula of both the high school and of the junior college, though the high school must perforce receive the larger amount of attention as junior college opportunities are not yet open to all our high-school graduates. The subjects which I have in mind are English, foreign language, physical and natural science and mathematics. These subjects at once divide themselves into laboratory and non-laboratory groups, and in the usual school day of eight forty-minute periods a double period is given to a laboratory subject and a single period to a non-laboratory subject. Consideration will not be given to the matter of outside preparation or "homework" required, as we are now looking only into the mechanics of the school program.

The teachers of English certainly can not complain that too little time is given to their subject. Eight years in the elementary school, at least three years in the high school and commonly one year in the junior college yield time from their day to English, and at that the number of graduates who habitually speak and write correct English or who have a liking for the better English and American literature is pitifully scant. The University of California, to mention but one institution, requires each candidate for admission to write a 500-word essay without gross errors in usage, and far too many fail in the test. These candidates for the most part have studied English for twelve years, together with special coaching for the test. It may be that English is too difficult a language to learn, or it is possible that the use of correct English is not necessary. At any rate, if we are compelled to put up with such poor results we need not give so much time to the subject. Why can not the use of the mother tongue be learned in the eight years of the elementary school? If results can not be obtained in that length of time the English department certainly should clean house. We might even go so far as to allow two high-school units for English and at that we can save enough time for at least one unit of social science.

The devotion on the part of secondary students to the study of one or more foreign languages is little short of amazing, especially when the results obtained are considered. Doubtless the childish complex of wishing to jabber in a tongue unknown to those outside of the immediate circle has persisted, or the glory of appearing to be able to read something unintelligible to one's mates has been alluring. The argument, too long unrefuted, of the possibility of foreign travel has availed much in the propaganda of the foreign language departments. I even once saw the printed statement of a college teacher of French to the effect that one might possibly receive a bequest from a French relative and therefore one should be able to read the will in order to make certain that the correct amount of money was being delivered. A 1911 prophecy of the non-payment of French war-debts! Many high schools of only a moderate size maintain instruction in four foreign languages—Latin, French, German and Spanish—and students not infrequently devote four units to one or more of these languages. Here is an opportunity open for the inclusion of another unit of an American citizenship subject.

The physical and natural sciences are demanding a heavy toll of the student's time. A double period per day—one recitation and one laboratory—is required for one unit's credit. At the risk of being dubbed an iconoclast I propose that this double period be reduced to a single period, that the laboratory work be eliminated, and that the instruction be reorganized along the lines of the history of science or of a science survey with experiment demonstration from the desk by the instructor. In the case of college-preparatory students it will probably be necessary to conduct the instruction along traditional lines. In a high school giving instruction in physics, chemistry and biology, the present set-up may call for nine sections per day, or eighteen periods, on the basis of each of three instructors having three double periods in an eight-period day. In the reorganized program there might be one college preparatory section in each of the three sciences, and thus three sections or six periods would be accounted for. The other six sections would then be reduced to six periods instead of twelve, and six periods would be set free for the inclusion of work in social science. This arrangement would have the additional advantage of greatly reducing the expense of science instruction. It is probable that students in the reorganized science work will not secure the detailed technical knowledge which they now have the opportunity of obtaining. I ask whether for non-college preparatory students detailed information and training of this kind is worth securing at the cost of the present ignorance of a subject so vital to the common well-being as are the various divisions of social science? And I might add that I am not and never have been a teacher of social science.

By diminishing the amount of attention now given to English, foreign language and physical and natural science, we have secured time enough for the inclusion of three units of social science. When we consider the wide range of this subject and the kind of instruction in it necessary for students in the secondary schools, three units is none too much. Further flexibility in the program can be obtained by reorganizing the work in mathematics. There is no modern justification for general secondary instruction in this subject, except in the case of college preparatory students, as the applied phases of mathematics may be taught in the technical curricula. The objection may be raised to a curriculum containing four units of social science that it is top heavy. The obvious reply is that it is about time for the pendulum to swing towards social science, for it has swung in the other direction since curricula were first constructed. Many schools have confined their instruction in citizenship to a single year of United States history and civics. Place must now be made in addition for economics, sociology, social psychology, ethics and political science. Much of this work has been confined to the university, and in fact some of it has been given only in the upper division, but that is no reason why acceptable instruction in these subjects can not be given in the high school and junior college. New methods of teaching can be worked out and new texts can be written. Nothing must be allowed to stand in the way of training all our future citizens to take their places in a régime which will call for vastly more from the individual in regard to his relations with his fellows than does the present one.

F. M. FOSTER

EXTENSION DIVISION
UNIVERSITY OF CALIFORNIA

OVER-TEACHING AND UNDER-TEACHING

WITH the approach of cold weather it was necessary to advance the generator of my car in order to keep the battery at the proper strength for winter driving. Upon asking a mechanic how to do it, I was told to loosen a screw on the outside of the generator and to move one brush up or down as needed. With this slightly vague advice I went to my car the next day and after a little experimenting was able to advance or retard the generator with surprising ease.

I, a teacher, had been given an example of effective teaching by that mechanic. He had given me the fundamental directions that I needed and had not mentioned the details which I was able to work out by myself. How different was this method from that of so many teachers who insist upon submerging the learner in a mass of needless details instead of pointing out the few essential facts. How often a teacher shows the pupil a lot of small trees but never gives him a view of the forest.

Most of us believe that a child learns by doing, but why do so few of us have the moral stamina needed to permit the pupil to do what he can? So often the teacher gets most of the practise, while the pupil is permitted to watch and memorize or act like a mechanical dummy that responds when a wheel is turned. It is the unusual teacher who gives only the help that is needed and who is willing to give the pupil a chance to work out the details for himself. Time is wasted by teaching that which requires no teaching.

If some conscientious person remarks at this point that the teacher is supposed to do as much as possible instead of as little as possible, I would like to suggest that it requires a higher intelligence, broader training and more intensive work to discover the fundamental facts, thoughts, operations and difficulties, than it does for a teacher to confuse major and minor facts in a hopeless sea of details which leaves the pupil in a fog of mental embarrassment.

Child and adult need teachers who are capable of climbing to greater heights and who can give them the benefit of enlarged vision and understanding. Time is too precious to be wasted listening to that which we already know when there is so much to learn and so much to do.

WILLIAM A. SMITH

INDIAN MOUNTAIN SCHOOL
LAKEVILLE, CONN.

REPORTS

THE STATUS OF GRADUATE EDUCATION IN THE UNITED STATES[1]

REPORTS of the Graduate School in previous years have emphasized the importance of further limitations of our student body in the interest of more careful selection on admission to the school and more rigorous training for our degrees. . . . The problem of the selection and training of our student body has taken on a new and pro-

[1] From the annual report of Dean E. S. Furniss, of Yale University, for the academic year 1932–1933.

found significance from the forces of social change which characterize the present day. These currents of change in the social order require a reexamination of our ideas regarding the status and function of a graduate school as a component of the institutional structure of society. The problem is presented in its most challenging form by the increasing difficulty of finding positions for graduate students in the vocations for which they have been trained, a condition confronting all the graduate schools of the country whose dimensions in our own experience are indicated by the records of our teaching appointment office. It is obvious, of course, that no sound conclusion regarding the future of graduate education can be based solely upon the present failure of the schools to place all their trained personnel; for this experience has been shared during the past few years by all types of organizations engaged in preparing young people for the occupations of life. Nevertheless, it is equally clear that no institution of this character can justify its existence unless in the long run it subserves the recognized needs of the social order of which it is a part and from which it draws its support, as evidenced by the regular absorption of its outgoing personnel in useful, self-supporting vocations. At present the combined enrolment of the graduate schools of the country is certainly in excess of social needs; and the numbers of students qualifying each year for advanced degrees after prolonged periods of training are not adjusted to current demands for their services. . . .

It seems fairly certain that the period of rapid expansion of institutions of higher education and of research enterprises, both industrial and academic, which in times past provided an ever-increasing demand for the product of the graduate school, has come definitely to an end. This period has been marked by a rivalry among the universities to exhibit their graduate schools as large and growing enterprises distinguished by the increasing number of their students and of the degrees conferred at commencement. The motives have not been altogether shabby. The graduate school is to a large degree custodian of the research interests of a university; and its flourishing condition may be submitted as evidence that the institution of which it is a part has become in reality as well as in name an institution of higher learning, rendering those high services of scholarly investigation which shed luster upon the history of the university in other lands. But it need scarcely be argued that mere size of the student body, or a mounting flood of degrees and diplomas, is never an accurate measure of these services. The strain after size has had many unfortunate results, which are all too apparent in the present condition of the graduate schools of the country. It has diluted the quality of student personnel; it has been favorable to, if not the cause of, the misdirection of scholarly effort toward pedantic or picayunish or narrowly utilitarian ends which has done so much to bring discredit upon the term "research" as applied to the activities of graduate students. The fundamental purposelessness of much of this endeavor is brought to light in times like these when the boom period of social development ends and recession sets in.

The functions of a graduate school are twofold. It is not solely, or even principally, an educational institution; it is as well a community of scholars, composed of members of the faculty and younger research workers, engaged continuously in an endeavor to increase and improve human understanding through their efforts to extend the frontiers of knowledge into the unknown, and to correlate, interpret and make significant knowledge already attained. These activities have no concern with degrees or diplomas or the routine of an educational process, but only with the spirit of inquiry and the search for truth; and as such they represent the highest service a graduate school can render to its university and to the world at large. If reform is demanded by the altered conditions of our age, it is unbelievable that these functions of research and interpretation will be condemned as obsolete; though they may well be improved in response to the demand that scholarly investigation be more concerned with matters of human significance and less with mere pedantry and the sterile manipulation of research techniques. On the whole it is the program of graduate education which is open to challenge, demanding continuous effort at improvement. Fortunately, as I believe, the way of improvement is plain. Clear perception of the fact that graduate education is subordinate and contributory to the investigatory functions of the university will set the standards to be adopted and the procedures to be followed. It is to perpetuate these investigatory functions at their highest and best, both within the specific university and in other institutions to which our students may go, that the graduate school assumes the tasks of an educational enterprise. The student should be viewed as an aspirant for admission to a select fellowship of scholars from the moment he applies for entrance until he has completed his course of training. His fitness for enrolment in the school, his performance by the way, his qualification to receive the hallmark of approval represented by the highest degree in the power of the university to bestow should be subjected to the same measures of appraisal which one would bring to bear upon the selection of society's permanent staff of scientists and scholars. We need have no fear that our social environment will change so profoundly as to remove the need for individuals with the attitude and capabilities of the true scholar. On the contrary, current trends of development in the world about us are of a nature to enhance the social importance of people so endowed and to enlarge their range of usefulness.

Improvement in the quality of our work must begin at the point of selection of student personnel. This requires as an essential first step drastic reduction of numbers admitted to the school and much more searching methods of examining applicants for admission. Without intending to underrate either the relative average ability of the present student group or their standards of performance—for on both counts the record of the year just past compares favorably with that of previous years—it must be stated as a fact that we have in almost every branch of study numbers of students who ought never to have been encouraged to undertake graduate work. These students impress their unfitness for the careers they profess upon all who come into contact with them: by their uncertainty of purpose; by their plodding, unimaginative performance of tasks; by the obvious shallowness and inadequacy of their preliminary training in their special subject and in cognate fields; by personality factors which will handicap them permanently.

EDUCATIONAL RESEARCH AND STATISTICS

HOW MAY PRESENT-DAY EDUCATIONAL PRACTISE BE IMPROVED?

EVER since the beginning of formal instruction, there have been critics within and without the profession. Many of the criticisms have resulted in needed changes in educational procedure. Constructive criticism is the soul of progress. It was with a desire to collect some current criticisms that the writer recently canvassed the field of educational literature for statements which might point the way to better educational practise. From publications of fifty-six authorities in the field of education, 102 representative statements were listed. These were submitted to experienced teachers and graduate students for their reactions. One hundred and fifty-four responded. Each person stated his major academic interest and designated the items (1) with which he agreed, (2) with which he disagreed, (3) which were so ambiguous that he did not understand them, and (4) which were not ambiguous but about which he was undecided.

Do groups with different academic interests agree with one another in their responses to these items? To answer this question, the papers were scored with a credit of one for each item receiving a favorable reaction. Mean scores were obtained for each of three groups: Group I, those expressing major interest in natural science or mathematics; Group II, in languages, literature or art; Group III, in sociology, philosophy or educational administration. Comparisons of the mean scores for these groups showed them to be almost identical. The means were, respectively, 65.67 ± 2.46; 66.00 ± 2.20; and 66.10 ± 2.22. The fact of agreement among these groups suggests that the reactions of the total group of 154 furnish a valid indication of the reactions which would be obtained from an indefinitely large group. In other words, the items upon which there was agreement constitute a list which should be of great interest to every member of the teaching profession.

There were forty-three items which received approval by at least 80 per cent. of the 154 persons responding. Originating as they do from the most outstanding authorities in education, the items should be regarded as very significant for education. Table I gives them in order of rank in agreement. For example, the first had the approval of 152 judges; the last of 123 judges. While we do not have the right to say that all those having the approval of less than 123 judges are unimportant, we do

TABLE I

SIGNIFICANT STATEMENTS OF EDUCATORS IN THE RANK ORDER OF 154 JUDGES

Number approving	Rank	
152	1	How to make the work of the classroom significant for the larger life outside the school is an outstanding educational problem.
151	2½	Education should teach people how to intelligently attack and solve problems of social, community and political life.
151	2½	The school should teach clearly that education is a sustained process continuing throughout life.
150	4	The importance of knowledge lies in its use.
149	5½	No teacher can afford to think of his teaching merely as training in subject-matter.
149	5½	Instead of preparing for life as it now is, education has too often taught only out-of-date and merely conventional subject-matter.
148	8½	Education should be instrumental to the production of that questioning, experimental, creative mind, which is the greatest asset of any civilization.
148	8½	All through education, initiative should come from the pupil as far as possible.
148	8½	From the very beginning of his experience, the child should experience the joy of discovery.
148	8½	It is not necessary for the teacher to be, or pretend to be a walking encyclopedia; his function is to suggest ways of obtaining information.
147	12	Establishing a consuming interest is worth more than information alone.
147	12	Our duty is so to prepare the rising generation to think that they can and will think for themselves.
147	12	The school must cease to consider that its task is to discipline and cram. Rather it must release and invite.
145	14½	Education should deal with social problems of genuine concern to the participants.
145	14½	The schools should study, observe and participate in the contemporary social life.
144	16½	A progressive society must see to it that its members are educated to personal initiative and adaptability.
144	16½	The schools should teach pupils to tolerate the discussion of controversial issues.
143	18	Subject-matter should be used as a means to an end rather than an end in itself.
141	19	The present conventional schools indoctrinate pupils more than they teach them to think for themselves.
139	20½	Pupils make discoveries from their own point of view whenever there is genuine learning.
139	20½	Education should sift out the dead wood of tradition and the lifeless units of false and formal scholarship now found in all school subjects.
138	22	Education should concern itself primarily with mind growth rather than with knowledge storing.
135	23	The greatest happiness comes from creative activities.
134	25	There can be no effective and thoroughgoing reorganization of education unless we envisage our problem from the social point of view.
134	25	Social need and social use—this is the test that must always be applied to curriculum material.
134	25	Education should bring freedom but must recognize an enlightened and sympathetic discipline as a primary and indispensable means of obtaining it.
133	27½	The teacher's major responsibility is that of arousing the pupils to self-instruction.
133	27½	A pupil's individuality and his tendencies should determine in large measure what we should teach him.
131	29½	Education should deal less with traditional academic accumulations having little vital relation to social reconstruction.
131	29½	The aim of education is to produce young people who can think clearly and deeply on permanently worth-while matters.
129	31½	A very important question in education is what subject-matter should be taught and how it should be organized.
129	31½	The schools should finally help our young people to make the shift from external to internal authority.
128	33	A free society has not yet been achieved.
127	35	Youth must cease to be indoctrinated in old-folk ways and myths that stand in the way of a consistently scientific attitude of life.
127	35	Most of our so-called reasoning consists in finding arguments for going on believing as we already do.
127	35	Eradicate the fatal disconnection of subjects which kills the vitality of our present curriculum.
126	38	All thinking is research and is original for him who carries it on, even if everybody else is sure of what he is still looking for.
126	38	The school should be a miniature democratic community in which right living will be the chief subject of instruction.
126	38	The emphasis in education should fall on insight rather than on conformity.
125	41	Strain in school work makes pupils hate their work.
125	41	Education should be thought of as participation in life rather than preparation for living.
125	41	Education should turn out the pupil with something he knows well and something he can do well.
123	43	Educators should cultivate a philosophy of education.

contend that those retained in the list are probably of major importance.

A few ideas stand out because of their repetition in successive statements, although each statement has distinctive meanings not found in any other. The necessity for a very close tie-up between formal education and life is emphasized many times. Education that has little distinct relation in pupils' minds to their living is decried. Knowledge that is directly useful to the individual is highly desirable. If its use is not clearly recognized, it is undesirable. Education as development of the mind—not storage of unapplied information—is definitely stressed. Ability to solve one's own problems and society's problems should be an end result of mind development. Eradication of credulity and the development of insight and a rational attitude in life are paramount. Each individual should develop initiative, self-control and some skill, but, if possible, the ability to create something original. And all these are to be accomplished by means of happy experiences without unhealthful strain.

Is present-day education accomplishing these things to the extent that it may? No doubt it is meeting the needs of some individuals quite well. It is doubtful that it is meeting the needs of the great majority. The complicated and confused state of contemporary life and our social institutions give proof of inadequacy somewhere. There is evident need for further educational experimentation and research in attempts to bring about better conditions. The use of instructional units prepared to bring positive results in the direction of the above statements may be easily undertaken in the various school courses being taught, without it being necessary to throw aside the good practises which inhere in the present system. We need more of the adventurous and experimental attitude. I think we may assign our great progress in science and invention, without doubt, to the use of the experimental method in those fields. Experimental teaching units may pave the way for improved practise. We must have continuous but enlightened experimentation to test out promising curriculum materials and methods.

Lincoln Steffens, in his autobiography, gives a quotation from an official of General Motors which illustrates well the spirit of experimentation: "We don't think any more in business. Oh, we may have our opinions; .... We may think up a theory, but we don't act on theories .... We send a theory .... into the laboratory and .... have it tried out. If it doesn't work, we change .... it. But if a theory, modified, works, we may take it into an engine or a car and put it out for trial on the market, but .... even then, its only a sort of working hypothesis. We go on monkeying with that and other theories and hunches to improve the car on trial."

Educational institutions may well emulate the industrial world in this progressive attitude. If social life is to measure up to the high mark made possible by recent industrial developments, education must point the way. If it knows not the way as yet, the experimental method of attack may be depended upon to eventually find it.

A. W. HURD

TEACHERS COLLEGE
COLUMBIA UNIVERSITY

NEW BOOKS IN EDUCATION

Adult Education in the United States. American Association for Adult Education, New York. Pp. 383. $2.00.

DOWNING. *Introduction to the Teaching of Science.* University of Chicago Press. Pp. 257. $2.00.

EMBREE, SIMON, MUMFORD. *Island India Goes to School.* University of Chicago Press. Pp. 120. $2.00.

HAYES, MOON, WAYLAND. *World History,* Book 1, Book 2. Macmillan. Pp. 912 each. $1.60 each.

Inscriptions Written by Charles William Eliot. Harvard University Press. Pp. 62.

JANZEN, CORNELIUS C. and STEPHENSON, ORLANDO W. *Everyday Economics.* Silver, Burdett and Company. Pp. 510 + xvii. $1.68.

KANDEL. *Educational Yearbook. International Institute.* Teachers College, Columbia University. Pp. 642. $3.50.

MEAD and ORTH. *The Transitional Public School.* Macmillan. Pp. 371. $2.25.

MIRZA. *Son of the Sword.* Viking Press. Pp. 211. $2.00.

MITCHELL, ELMER D. and MASON, BERNARD S. *The Theory of Play.* A. S. Barnes & Co. Pp. 547. $2.80.

NEUBERG, MAURICE J. *Principles and Methods of Vocational Choice.* Prentice-Hall. Pp. 302. $2.25.

NIXON, COZENS. *Physical Education.* W. B. Saunders Co. Pp. 262. $2.50.

SYMONDS. *Mental Hygiene of School Children.* Macmillan. Pp. 321. $1.50.

THOMPSON, MERRITT MOORE. *The Educational Philosophy of Giovanni Gentile.* University of Southern California Press. Pp. 217.

EDUCATIONAL REVIEW

Edited by Nicholas Murray Butler, 1891–1919, Frank Pierrepont Graves, 1920–1924, and William McAndrew, 1924–

MONTHLY SURVEY OF EDUCATIONAL BOOKS

By WILLIAM McANDREW

REAL TEACHING OF READING

MR. GRAY'S[1] and Miss Whipple's monograph on reading in the elementary schools crowns five years of closely studied experimentation in schools selected in a city of 35,000 people, in a town of 8,000, in a village of 300, and in a rural school. The staff of investigators set out to determine ways of improving teaching in harmony with the results of scientific studies, to estimate the difficulties of such improvement, and to measure the improvement of pupils after experiencing the reformed teaching.

As a preliminary step the chief findings of the more than 500 studies that were in print when the investigation began were summarized as affording the basis for teaching procedures to use in the experiment. The exposition of these earlier findings, the manner of organizing and conducting the reformed teaching in the selected schools, the detailed accounts of methods and results makes this book in value to school workers comparable to a compendium of successful methods in surgery for a practitioner's library.

Over toward the end, an inconspicuous account of the difficulties these experimenters encountered could be taken by a Mencken and shown to be a most scandalous arraignment of American public education. One wonders how much the medical or engineering profession could show of this sort of obstacles the teaching army throws into the road over which it is marching.

"Sinister political influences undermining the professional morale of the teacher created wrong attitudes. This condition almost resulted in disaster to certain units of the experiment. The administrative officers were unable to cope with it." If there is a forward-moving superintendent of schools who has none of his work flooded with this backwash let him write a book on how he escaped it and his fortune will be made. "Sinister political influences!" How do they work? The whispering campaign seeps through the corps. "He'll work you to death." "Teachers are breaking under the strain." "This is another fad; as soon as you get it working, along'll come another." Selected messengers get the word to favorite board members. It is rule one with many such to block anything educational that is new. Boards fear change.

The twenty difficulties to be overcome in a systematic improvement of teaching reading will be recognized by supervisors at large as the gullies, ridges, hostile batteries and machine-gun nests in terrain of advance in any school project.

Unwillingness of principals to assume responsibility for the professional leadership of teachers.

Unwillingness of many school officers to cooperate. Either they were too busy with routine, or were self-satisfied or frankly not interested.

Limited knowledge by supervisors and teachers that recent professional literature is revolutionary since the results of research have demonstrated what methods are more successful.

Unwillingness of teachers to adjust out-of-school engagements so that group discussions could illuminate study problems.

Those are some of the interferences these investigators encountered.

But this was offset by some supervisors, principals and teachers who were eager to learn and improve. The interest of the real workers was nursed into enthusiasm and satisfaction. Six pages of this more enheartening positive spirit furnish a high-grade guide to supervision well worth copying upon a handy tablet to use as grace before beginning the work of the day. The actual gains made in these schools, the hints for effective supervision, an abundance of practical comment, make this monograph indispensable.

A REFERENCE BOOK TO READ ENTIRE

WILSON, indexer and compiler extraordinary to the literary, scientific, artistic and industrial

[1] William S. Gray, Gertrude Whipple, "Improving Instruction in Reading." University of Chicago Press. 226 pp. $1.75.

world, issues a magnificent volume[2] as a companion to his "Living Authors." The first thing that strikes you is the clear photographs of the literary folk. There is one picture for each biography. The type and paper are inviting. The "lives" are lively. "She liked to command, editors as well as satellites. The anguish that overwhelmed her at a typographical error in her poems was inconsolable," is a sample from the account of Amy Lowell.

Rene Bazin hated the prevailing type of sex fiction. He made the wholesomeness of the family glow with interest. The perpetual recurrence of adultery in the novel, he said, is due to the intellectual laziness of the author, too indolent to observe the plots in the healthy life about him.

When Max Eastman dines in a restaurant no one passes his table but stops and joins him.

Ed Howe believes both Cellini and Rousseau were liars and is suspicious of Bernard Shaw.

The sketches take care of the dates, facts and lists of works of the authors, give a critical estimate and then go into the personal characteristics so well that instead of being a reference book the volume is something you read for the pleasure of it.

STATISTICS WITHOUT TEARS

PROFESSOR GOOD, School of Education, University of Michigan, condenses into a few pages some elements of statistics with the intent "to induct the novice gently into the subject."[3]

Too large a proportion of mathematical content frightens many who could be benefited by gaining elementary statistical skill. This treatise is simple and brief. It covers approximation, sampling, raw data, frequency tables, discrete scores, graphs, means, medians, deviations, correlation, and much besides.

AKETCHOO

I COMMEND to every teacher a merry treatise on the common cold.[4] The editors of *Fortune,* who also do *Time,* put their compelling style into their accounts of interviews with eminent specialists discussing What is a cold? What causes it? Who catches it? When? Why? What should he do? The things we sniff, suck, gulp, swallow, rub and use, the folks who make them and what they make out of the job are told in a style that holds you as does the grippe.

From all sides a crusade has steadily converged on the common enemy. Fifty per cent. of all disabling diseases start with a cold. The Chemical Foundation has appropriated $187,500 for cold research; and promises $22,500 more; the Metropolitan Life Insurance, $174,000. This company paid over $26,000,000 in benefits as a result of the influenza epidemic of 1918. The American Medical Association's effort to save suckers from wasting money on advertised cures makes an exciting feature of this story. This is a warmer book than its subject suggests.

THE MARCH OF MEDICINE

DR. HAGGARD makes an exquisite book[5] on those forward steps of the healing art that are most likely to interest the common man. The doctor makes Hippocrates, Galen, Paracelsus, Harvey, Lavoisier, Jenner, the Hunters, Rush, Pasteur, Koch, Lister and many other innovators very much alive. The portraits and other engravings are finely reproduced. You will find this a charmingly written bit of the history of civilization.

LOOK TO THE LETTERS

THE beauty or ugliness resulting from one or another spacing of letters in a word is demonstrated by many drawings in Professor Tannahill's treatise on the art of letter arrangement.[6] The same possibilities hang over the location of words on a poster. The talented author with copious illustrations teaches the artistic value of letter shapes, spacing, mass, the beauty of certain posters, monograms, devices, trade-marks, labels, covers and book plates. There are chapters on the teaching of lettering, linoleum-block printing, etc. The book itself is a thing of beauty and a joy. You will wish to bless the author as the same.

[2] Stanley J. Kunitz, Howard Haycraft, Wilbur C. Hadden, "Authors To-day and Yesterday." H. W. Wilson Company, 960 University Avenue, New York. 726 pp. $5.00.

[3] Warren R. Good, "Elements of Statistics." Ann Arbor Press, Ann Arbor. 28 pp. 50 cents.

[4] Editors of *Fortune.* "Our Common Enemy: Colds." Robert M. McBride and Company, New York. 102 pp. $1.00.

[5] Howard W. Haggard, M.D., "Mystery, Magic, and Medicine." Doubleday, Doran and Company, Garden City, New York. 192 pp. $1.00.

[6] Sallie B. Tannahill, "P's and Q's." Doubleday, Doran and Company, Garden City, New York. 119 pp. $4.00.

AMERICA'S TROUBADOUR

Myth-makers have written picturesque sketches of Stephen Foster. Mr. Howard,[7] musician, loves the fantastic tales about the writer of "Old Kentucky Home" and searches diligently for facts that will authenticate them. But when reality overturns the myth he tells the truth. The material this biographer has gathered from letters, print, photographs and talks with living old men and women makes a story that needs no embellishment. The birth of the troubadour on the fiftieth anniversary of the signing of the Declaration, on the same day that marked the death of both Jefferson and Adams, Foster's method of writing his words and music, the composition of two hundred American lyrics of home, the composer's financial competence and later poverty, his chivalry, his fatal craving for drink, his last days in a Bowery lodging house, his death in Bellevue Charity Hospital, are told with authentic detail and numerous anecdotes.

Twenty-five years after Foster's death, Pittsburgh, his native city, began a campaign for a monument in his honor. Ten years later the statue in Highland Park was erected, a public school was named for him, a memorial home was dedicated to mark his birthplace. Pittsburgh is now planning a Foster Hall on land of the university, with a salon for musical exhibitions. Kentucky has a memorial. A granite shaft at the source of the Suwanee River in Fargo, Georgia, commemorates the minstrel. Indianapolis has a bust in Foster Hall.

His songs are sung all over the world. The best of them are more alive than ever. They are genuine folk lore, a true art product. His family never ceased to love him. So it is with almost every home and every assemblage in the land.

PUBLIC-MINDED CITIZEN

Because there is only one side to the question of efficient civil service many Americans find the story of its reform uninteresting. No public issue since the agitation against slavery has been so clearly proved as the need of civil service reform. The necessity of abolishing the evils which have accompanied the spoils system is so obvious that it is hard to see why the people being robbed by the politician are so indifferent. Americans know that large numbers of place-hunters are impairing the integrity and threatening the safety of our government. They know that Canada and England manage the public work much more honestly and efficiently. But the public is bored by the details of the long struggle waged by men like Dana, Foulke, Jenckes, Eaton, Curtis and Schurz. Theodore Roosevelt's six years of service as civil-service commissioner fills a small space in his biographies compared with his brief and breezy record as a Rough Rider. With this sort of observation Professor Perry begins his eighth chapter of the life of one of America's outstanding patriots.[8] Dana had the conviction that a republic may be made the most honest and efficient of any kind of government. He was turned to this reform by a talk with his father one day while on the West-Boston caterpillar bridge. Young Dana made his graduation address at his college commencement in 1874, "Civil Service Reform." You can make this eighth chapter of the Perry book the basis of an address to high school or college students. It is full of adventure. If an informal conversation out of doors on a bridge started so valuable a public service as son Dana rendered, why may not an earnest address to a whole class start some more youngsters into the unfinished task? Dana might seem to have been born with the impulse of public service in him. Whenever I think of him or of Curtis, Foulke, Cole, Folk, LaFollette, Beveridge, or of any of the men who devoted themselves to reform, a sort of laziness inclines me to assume that they were endowed with the sense of duty and courage that drove them into public service. When I read their lives I find them as adverse to sacrifice as the rest of us. But suggestion started them and repetition gave them habit. By suggestion and by practise, education has the chance of developing enough Danas to make this indeed the most honest and efficient of governments. Professor Perry's book is a good tonic for this civic health. It is the life of one who became a devotee of general welfare: school builder, peace promoter, sportsman, city planner, crime preventer, graft suppressor, music patron, mosquito killer, pusher for ballot reform, and an

[7] John Tasker Howard, "Stephen Foster, America's Troubadour." Thomas Y. Crowell Company, New York. 445 pp. $3.50.

[8] Bliss Perry, "Richard Henry Dana." Houghton Mifflin Company, Boston. 265 pp. $3.00.

expert in disregard for personal power or fame.

The trouble with many of the heroes in the reading book is their remoteness. Professor Perry gives you one so close to the problems of to-day that imitation is not impossible. His treatment of his hero is so reasonable, so engaging that a book to be read for sheer pleasure is the result.

MAZZEI OF THE MASCULINE MIND

THE Johns Hopkins University brings out a volume on the life and letters of Philip Mazzei.[9] This Italian merchant, student of agriculture and politics, intimate of Jefferson, Madison and Monroe, became European agent of Virginia. The books published abroad gave such garbled accounts of the American Revolution that Mazzei issued a work, the first accurate story of the United States published out of the country. He went through the French Revolution, became adviser to Stanislaus, King of Poland, and, in old age, retired to Pisa, where he wrote memoirs of his experiences in Virginia and Europe. For Latrobe, architect of the capitol at Washington, he chaffered with Canova and Thorwaldsen for a heroic statue of liberty. He sent marble workers to America to fashion pillars for the national capitol. Jefferson called him well informed and of masculine understanding.

Author Garlick reproduces, in Italian, French and sometimes in Mazzei's difficult English, many letters which this active adopted son of Virginia wrote to prominent men of the day.

EDUCATIONAL RADIO

HERE is a bit of contradiction of the frequent charge that the high schools are utterly neglecting their main duty of informing this generation of the civic defects of the present. The vigorous Thomas Reed, University of Michigan, notes, in the latest volume[10] of the Council on Radio in Education, that the principal users of the "You and Your Government" reprints of discussions on present troubles have been high school and college teachers. The council is continuing its efforts to grade its broadcasts to high school classes.

The present volume carries an informative report by the director with a lively discussion of it by a dozen experts. There are seventeen essays on the various fields of education using the broadcast. There are addresses on radio as a social force, the air as an open forum and other timely topics.

RECREATIONAL RESOURCES

GAMES for the agile and for the shut-ins, tricks, paper-folding, wonders of string, toys and problems fill a book of resources for every teacher who recognizes the refreshment children get from play. The author is a cheery Englishman. This insures a great deal of novelty for the American user. Mr. Abraham[11] draws his own pictures. He is lavish with them. His book has charmed Boy Scout Lord Baden Powell who blesses the author with an introduction recommending this jolly collection for scout leaders everywhere.

CITY LIFE

WHAT American large city do you think has the largest number of theater seats per capita of population? Wrong. It is San Francisco with a seat for every 6.8 persons. Then follow these scores: Los Angeles 7.1; Newark 7.9; Detroit 8.4; Milwaukee 8.6; Cleveland 8.7; Pittsburgh 9.0; Cincinnati 9.4; Philadelphia 10.6; Chicago 10.9; Baltimore 11.8 and your guess, New York, twelfth in the list with one seat to every 12.3 persons. This I get from Gist and Halbert's[12] sociology of cities. It is a text-book with questions, topics and reading references, but, withal, one of the most interesting books for general reading you will come across in many a day. It is the proper study of man. It is an account of a significant movement going on around you whose implications are but dimly realized until disclosed with the clarity and wide observation characteristic of this volume.

Cities of the world now rank according to size in this order: New York, London, Berlin, Chi-

[9] Richard Cecil Garlick, Jr., "Philip Mazzei, Friend of Jefferson." Johns Hopkins Press, Baltimore. 121 pp. Paper, $2.00. Cloth, $2.50.

[10] Levering Tyson, Editor, "Radio and Education." Proceedings of the third annual assembly of the National Advisory Council on Radio in Education. The University of Chicago Press. 201 pp. $2.50.

[11] R. M. Abraham, "Winter Nights Entertainment." E. P. Dutton and Company, New York. 186 pp. $1.75.

[12] Noel P. Gist, L. A. Halbert, "Urban Society." Thomas Y. Crowell Company, New York. 740 pp. $3.50.

cago, Buenos Aires, Philadelphia, Vienna, with Detroit twelfth and Constantinople fifty-second. In the year 1500 the last-named was first; London, 9th, being surpassed by Naples, 3rd; Venice, 4th; Milan, 5th; Lisbon, 6th; and Rome, 8th.

Why cities sprang up, grew and declined; what their different peculiarities are; how and why they have their interior zones; why slums, red-light districts, crime areas, and all; the characteristics of city dwellers, longshoremen, stenographers, political heelers, prostitutes, reformers; the city's food, drink, work and play; its churches, schools and hospitals, social workers; the reconstruction of its society; the future of urbanism are some of the chapters of a really gripping book. It is community civics, geography, history, psychology and economics, at their best.

FINANCE IN UNTECHNICAL LANGUAGE

The banking crisis, the important governmental measures aimed to better economic conditions, the cause and course of panics, the federal deficit, the budget and new accounting methods, business and the new legislation, inflation, managed currency, are treated by the editor of *The Review of Economic Statistics* in every-day language in a compact series of essays.[13] The author, Dr. Hubbard, makes this a book valuable for high-school and college classes in economics.

A SOCIAL STUDY WITH HIGH TONE

It may surprise you—it did me—to learn that economics, frankly so-called, is being taught to children so young as those of the eighth school grade. There is a class of this kind in our neighborhood. They speak as intelligently of its topics and with more interest than they do of grammatical concepts, which they also study. It need startle no one that Doctors Lapp and Ross[14] have made a book for the ninth grade. You will find on reading any of its pages that they are making important public matters clear to children aged under fourteen.

The authors are sure the American teacher can familiarize the younger school children with the problems of taxes, money, employment, budgets, investments, banks and the like. The book strikes me as an excellent proof that this can be done. The tone of it is ideal. It scorns to magnify the individual's appetite for personal advantage. The decent end of life is not what you get but what you do for the general welfare. To be is more important than to have. We have had enough of pig-trough philosophy. The community, state and nation are paying for your schooling that you may be better able to contribute to the public good.

Interest is sustained by the authors through striking use of illustration of common life. The teaching aids are new and decidedly clever.

THE FARMER IS STILL BUNCOED

No great division of human society has ever been lied to and lied about as the American farmer in the last ten years. He has been the victim of more false economic and political information than any other element in the social structure.

The agricultural population has become a definite minority. The framework of our government has been bent from its original conception of protection of society from selfish interests and has become a mechanism through which special groups, getting protection by law, have exploited those less strategically placed. The farmer's interests have been deliberately evaded by those responsible for the direction of national policies.

It is Cassius M. Clay speaking in the pages of a spirited survey of the whole agricultural situation.[15] How the tariff buncoes the consumer and defeats its own proclaimed purpose, how chambers of commerce howl against government in business and coax it farther in, what the great disparity of incomes has done to millions of intelligent and industrious Americans, how pressure groups and interests of small constituencies decide legislation, are described in bright light, not without natural heat. Every aspect of farm relief is analyzed. Constructive measures are outlined. The author writes as a farmer who is broadly informed by study and experience.

[13] Joseph B. Hubbard, "The Banks, The Budget and Business." The Macmillan Company, New York. 147 pp. $1.75.

[14] John A. Lapp, A. Franklin Ross, "Economic Citizenship." D. C. Heath and Company, New York. 305 pp. $1.16.

[15] Cassius M. Clay, "The Mainstay of American Individualism." The Macmillan Company, New York. 269 pp. $2.50.

MONEY-SENSE FOR THE MODEST MAN

PRACTICAL Financier Blodgett[16] writes for the small earners. Therefore the house of Macmillan sends his book for review in a magazine for teachers. Mr. Blodgett proves everything as he goes along and nails his arguments with such sensible fastenings that you can not pry them loose. Teachers stay poor by trying to get rich too fast. This makes them gamblers. Gambling persists only because of the vast majority of losers. I am not, he says, one of those crape-hangers who advise cutting out the movies, cigarettes or wearing shabby clothes and faded neckties. Pay more attention to getting values for your money instead of depriving yourself of things you want. Being in debt $100 is $209 worse than being $100 ahead; for you are paying $6 a year on your debt and losing $3 interest on the $100 that you might have in the savings bank. Hoarding is also losing. Occasionally you hear of born winners. There are such, just as there are born artists and poets. All of them are few. Averages always enter the calculations of an exact thinker.

Saving for rainy days and for age is well enough as far as it goes, but the objectives are too remote. Every observant teacher knows that children work better when the end to be reached is not too far off. To propose $100 in the bank, and then $200, and so on, is infinitely more enjoyable than planning for a competence forty-five years off. This is universal experience. Why should you be blind to it?

Mr. Blodgett shows how to make 10 per cent. on your ordinary purchases. Paying life insurance annually instead of every three or six months is another sure way of making money.

His pages bulge with new ways of increasing income and with old ones made impressive.

I think the book would furnish the school principal and superintendent with material for a refreshing discussion in teachers' meetings. Lord knows our folks need it. For practical truths to form the habits Americans need, it is full of help for the elementary and high-school teacher. A large proportion of college professors whom I know and love should absorb this book for the sake of themselves and their gentle wives.

16 Harvey A. Blodgett, "Making the Most of Your Income." The Macmillan Company, New York. 180 pp. $1.50.

NEGLECTED HUMAN RELATIONSHIP

FORTY years ago Sir William Mather reduced the hours of his factory workers from fifty-four to forty-eight a week. After two years the records showed that production had increased and waste-time grown less. In 1916 the time of munition workers in England was cut from 12 to 10 hours a day. After this, accidents were 40 per cent. of what they had been. English committees and laboratory workers have for years been searching for the cause and cure of industrial fatigue. More than 60 monographs have been printed. The solution of the problem is a long ways off. Research is baffled by it. The disappointing results of experiments in this line at home and abroad fill the opening chapter of Harvard Professor Mayo's work on men and industry.[17]

So-called fatigue has proved itself to be so complex and varied that the word has little scientific value. Reduction of output may be due to physical exhaustion or to boredom because of routine and repetition. Some people are contented in this kind of work; others, unhappy. Professor Mayo gives extended and interesting accounts of experiments in textile factory and electrical shop showing the effect of mental attitude on output. A concern with a highly enlightened plan of all the processes of manufacture, with complete blue prints of supervision and operation, with sanitation as perfect as can be made, endures waste and inefficiency that its managers can neither understand nor cure. The book devotes many interesting pages to this mysterious obstacle to morale. Any supervisor in educational or industrial organization will here find many eye-openers. Chicago is described in relation to its social groups and their capacity for productive industries. Unless there is a normal home from childhood onward the worker in whatever line is handicapped. This defect is to a great extent observable in the failure of supervisors and supervised to understand their work and working conditions. There is a wide-spread sense of personal futility. This is not merely a characteristic of Chicago. It is nation wide. Misunderstanding between employers and workers in every civilized country has persisted for a century without amelioration. The rapid pace

17 Elton Mayo, "Human Problems of an Industrial Civilization." The Macmillan Company, New York. 194 pp. $2.00.

of industrial development uninformed by human research has dispersed collaborate social effort and deprived the workers of social participation and social function. Socialism and communism express the worker's desire for human solidarity. Confidence between workers and employers is absent. Our administrative aristocracy is still the aristocracy of yesterday. It faces the present with outworn weapons. We have too few administrators alert to the fact that it is a human social problem that they face. The universities have not begun to think about the discovery and training of the new administrators.

STUDY OF AMERICAN SOCIAL NEEDS

Rugg and Krueger's study guide[18] is an outline of politics, economics and sociology, including much of controversial matter, which critical persons like to say we teachers fear to touch. The myth of a free press, the real aim of newspaper management, the suppression of facts by government, the lag of educators, the neglect of training citizens to think and to fight—these and an abundance of live topics are put in the form of questions and problems along with lists of modern books in which extended discussions of current perplexities are found.

THE NEXT WAR AND THE U. S. A.

The eighth of Frank Simonds' war books[19] is a postscript to his "Can Europe Keep the Peace?" "Can America Stay at Home?" It is based on the events of the current year: the withdrawal of Germany from the League and from the Disarmament Conference, the economic debacle in Europe and America, the failure of the Treaty of Versailles, defiance by Japan, the Hitler triumph. It is a book that reads swiftly. Its conclusion is that America faces another war in Europe. When America urges a nation to reduce armament that nation considers disarmament a reduction of safety and demands that we assume a share in such a risk. All discussions of European arms must be political and must be accompanied by American commitments.

It is evident that this is a book for study in public schools.

[18] Harold Rugg, Marvin Krueger, "Social Reconstruction." The John Day Company, New York. 140 pp.

[19] Frank H. Simonds, "American Faces the Next War." Harper and Brothers, New York. 82 pp. $1.00.

TOWARD AN ADEQUATE CIVILIZATION

Richard Welling tells me I ought not to miss a day of talking with some one who can throw the right light on what we ought to do towards a better national life. The people worth listening to are busy. I impose on them if I live up to Richard's exhortation. But praise be to publishers, never before in this commonwealth was there such a supply of good talk on timely topics. Comes Harry Overstreet,[20] purveyor of real philosophy to us common men. As in his "Enduring Quest," "About Ourselves" and "Human Behavior," Overstreet is here lucid, persuasive and masterly in argument. He paints the prevailing traditions which are holding the country back. He illuminates the steps already taken to wipe out the present injustices. Taxation, economics, world relations, racial attitudes, planning, health, unemployment, production, proportional representation, the main current problems, are treated with a freshness that makes the book especially satisfying.

He has a red-hot chapter on what education may do in hastening the liberation of mankind.

Most of the repetition, "education will solve the problem," is accepted patter. Education that lets youngsters go out to imitate the lives of glorified money-makers will not solve but aggravate the trouble. There can, as now, be an education which makes a people feel superior to all other nations and so promotes militarism. To say that education will make us over into acceptable human beings is meaningless. American education is interested primarily in the perpetuation of American culture. It is not interested in a culture more adequate than that already realized. It accepts American culture and takes it for granted that children should be fitted into it without friction. It assumes that when students are placed in a classroom they will become social-minded. In fact they remain as individualistic, self-seeking, narrow and local-minded as ever. Teachers have been trained in this education. They serve as effective exponents of the status quo. Their training has been in methods of teaching subjects, not in questioning the maladjustments of

[20] H. A. Overstreet, "We Move in New Directions." W. W. Norton and Company, New York. 384 pp. $3.00.

the social, political and industrial world around us. The business of teaching is critically to examine our civilization and to contribute to its redesign and improvement.

HOLES IN THE NEW DEAL?

EDITOR, historian, author, Professor MacDonald[21] has not been hypnotized into swallowing all the offerings of the present administration. It is of trivial interest, he says, that the majority of the first Brain Trust at the White House were theorists far more than men of affairs. What matters is that, being theorists, they were able in cooperation with the president to put before the country as the real issues an amazing and revolutionary program of economic reorganization and to convince a large majority of the electorate that the program would meet what was vaguely felt to be a national need. Thanks to the spread of socialistic and communist dogma in industrial and intellectual circles, and to the increasing favor with which fascism had come to be regarded, the traditional belief in the inherent virtues of democracy and representative government had been, in large sections of the American people, fundamentally impaired.

Mr. MacDonald sees the policy of the Brain Trust and of Mr. Roosevelt to be a fateful idea.

There was no justification for abandonment of the gold standard by the United States.

The Tennessee-Valley project has stretched the general welfare provision of the Constitution beyond the limit and has aimed a blow at all industry for profit which could, under the theory of the new deal, be regarded as in the field of general welfare. Public works, securities act, home loans, farm credits, railroad control, manipulation of gold, harnessing of industry, subsidizing the farmers and many other recent changes are dissected without anesthetics by this unhesitating surgeon.

According to the researches of Messrs. Harper and Arnett into the social-economic beliefs of school boards and educators, no high-school principal would endanger his position by putting this book into the school library.

ECONOMICS PICTURE BOOK

HOWEVER you may disagree with any of Mr. Mooney's[22] conclusions you will pronounce his primer of economics the most beautiful book in existence on this subject. From the lovely picture on the front of the jacket, representing father, mother, son and daughter gazing at light breaking through the clouds, to the farm and skyscrapers at the back, exquisite photographs and nifty colored diagrams have been used with high talent to carry the text.

Mr. Mooney does not want governmental direction of industry for, admitting all capitalism's past mistakes and blunders, he says it knows better than government how to plan, produce, distribute and perform every industrial function. He welcomes a government that protects every man, woman and child, bestows no special favors and forbids injustice. By means of amazingly clever diagrams the author illustrates the effects of supply, demand, credit, gold and paper currency, the absurdity of tariff obstructions, the balance of trade, the rescue of agriculture, the futility of price-fixing, the evil of shorter work periods, the tragedy of limiting farm products and the success or failure of much besides.

CIVIC GAINS AND LOSSES

THE second and final volume of Mr. Adams' "March of Democracy"[23] is a complete work in itself and for many of us a history of our own times. It covers the period beginning with our civil war and ending in 1933.

Our age of youthful bragging is over. Mr. Adams portrays our merits with enthusiasm, our errors with no justification.

At the end of Grant's first term freebooters had a strong grip on the government. Greeley the opposition candidate was impossible, but it is doubtful that any Democrat could have won. Post-war periods are always times of low public morals.

Arthur made a good president, but there was no demand for his renomination. Boss Platt had said, "Blaine's turn has come."

In Cleveland's last message he said: "The communism of combined capital, the outgrowth of overweening cupidity and selfishness insidiously undermines justice and the integrity of the nation."

---

[21] William MacDonald, "The Menace of Recovery, What the New Deal Means." The Macmillan Company, New York. 401 pp. $2.50.

[22] James D. Mooney, "The New Capitalism." The Macmillan Company, New York. 229 pp. $3.50.

[23] James Truslow Adams, "The March of Democracy," Vol. 11. Charles Scribner's Sons, New York. 438 pp. $3.50.

More than once the retention of the electoral college, no longer a deliberative assembly, has resulted in a weird outcome defeating the candidate for whom the majority of the people voted.

Inconsistent actions of the Supreme Court have afforded basis for popular belief that not legal principles but prejudice and political bias do decide rulings of this high tribunal.

Business does not want honest government. Every business man, even though he desires to be honest, is caught in a system of great or petty graft and bribery.

There are yet living those who believe with Reading-Railway Baer that "the interests of the laborer will be protected by the Christian men to whom God in his infinite wisdom has given the control of the property interests of this country."

Both houses of Congress, for the sake apparently of buying themselves votes, will pan bills of gross damage to the majority of the people.

There are enough of these unpleasant truths set forth clearly in this history to offset the traditional all's-right-with-our-country idea, a notion that many of us took from our school text-books.

A new era is dawning, concludes this historian. The most interesting, the most important and, let us hope, the greatest period in our national life has come.

The simplicity and clearness of Mr. Adams' style, the vividness of his narration, the multiplicity of new and striking photographs, reproductions of paintings and cartoons, will hold the interest of young and old. Its arrangement, its full index adapt it perfectly to use as a supplement in school and college classes. I should want a dozen copies in my school library.

WHAT IS THE NATIONAL INTEREST?

Draw up a bill for Congress to pass. After it has been written compose the preamble saying, "whereas the national interest demands." When many hundred such preambles have gotten into the archives a historian can study them and produce an interesting discussion as to what national interest officially is. Beard and Smith[24] do this in an analytical study of American foreign policy. The result is one of the most engaging books of the season.

No one, heretofore, has explored the nature and implications of the phrase so handily attached to any proposal. If citizens are to support the government which says it is for it, if soldiers are to die for it and foreign policies are to be framed for this avowed purpose what could be more appropriate than to find out what it means? Hamilton used it meaning one thing; Jefferson, another. Private interests engaged in manufacturing for personal profit bring pressure to bear on Congress "in the national interest." The first Roosevelt's conception of the idea had a bewildering variety, but war was a constant ingredient of it. "The clamor of the peace faction," he wrote to Lodge in 1895, "has convinced me that what this country needs is a war." He considered it needful as a stiffening of a people in peril of growing soft.

How the Navy personnel plays the national interest game, how other departments translate it in accordance with their own purposes, how it wobbles when financiers are floating foreign loans, how it got smirched in dealings with Colombia, Nicaragua, Hawaii, the Philippines, Cuba and Puerto Rico, how no steadied interpretation of it has existed in tariffs and trade relations, and how this and that action multiplied inconsistencies, makes, as here told, a great story set in order and confirmed by the review of striking incidents. An old view that if history were not mostly concerned with the personality of rulers, of statesmen, of generals and the events of war it would be too tame to read is upset by this work. Here, canny reasoning has a grip to it. The treatment of events loses none of their picturesqueness. It leaves the reader with a mind well informed on matters of high import to him.

GETTING BEYOND SLOGANS

Intelligent expectation would have been that the American Library Association would have devoted some of its "Reading-with-a-Purpose" series to the new current problems. It has done better. It is bringing out a new battery: "Exploring the Times," attractive twenty-or-so-page booklets each by an authority. The pattern of each of these volumes is that of a simple summary of the problem followed by titles and description of a few books which go

[24] Charles A. Beard, with the collaboration of G. H. E. Smith, "The Idea of National Interest." The Macmillan Company, New York. 553 pp. $3.75.

into the matter more intensively. These are the titles of the essays I have read: "Less Government or More?" by Louis Brownlow and Charles S. Ascher; "Living with Machines," by W. F. Ogburn; "Collapse or Cycle," Paul H. Douglas; "World Depression, World Recovery," by Harry D. Gideonse; "Meeting the Farm Crisis," by J. H. Kolb. Each book gives the author a pertinent biography. You pay 25 cents each for these monographs, any five for $1.00. They are all written with intent to give you both sides and to break up the American weakness for unthinking acceptance of slogans.

THORNDIKE ON REWARDS

A great majority of psychologists, Professor Thorndike[25] tells us, have maintained that the after effects of an attempt at learning do not strengthen it. If this is true your "correct" or "very good" with which you season recitations is a waste of time. In a brief book Dr. Thorndike describes a number of experiments testing the effect of hearing "right" or "wrong" after the effort. You are shown, also, the result of the commendation when immediate and when given after periods of different lengths. Learning may be enhanced by these simple rewards. A punishment may do more harm to learning than it can do good.

The researches upon praise, encouragement, expectation of success, made by this investigator and his pupils, have in them the germs of a revolutionary change in the old punishing habits of teaching. Many of us who had our mistakes in composition smeared with red ink can take a long deferred pleasure in seeing science confirming our ancient doubts.

I remember hearing schoolmaster Donald McNicoll, back in 1880, tell how he got 100 per cent. in arithmetic. "I used," he said, "to give one ferule blow on the hand of each careless arithmeticker for every mistake he made. I found the bairns hating me more than they did their errors. Then I hit on a better plan. I told the lads and lasses before each time of practise with their sums that as soon as everybody had proved all his answers right we'd move back the benches and I'd take down the old fiddle and have a reel. It worked like magic."

I never knew any teacher to adopt auld Donald's method. It was too undignified. Now, as dignified a scientist as the most exacting could require comes with tables, formulas, medians and quartiles to show that the canny Scot was right.

MEASURING PUNISHMENT

Dr. Tuckman, guided by his preceptor, Thorndike, gave his pupils counters representing money. For failures in the lesson he took away counters. When the tests were over he paid the agreed amount of cash for every token not lost through making mistakes. This and closely related tests, together with conclusions, are set out in a complete volume.[26] Whether the punishment for error was merely hearing the word "wrong" or was a failure to receive money or was subjection to an uncomfortable electric shock, a careful summary of the results of learning shows that a punishment may do more harm by occurring than it does good by eliminating the particular error it was inflicted to correct.

WOUNDED MINDS

By turning to the extensive index of the book of Psychiatrist Bassett[27] you will note how much attention this volume pays to matters that are your daily concern. The author devotes many informing pages to teachers, parents, the pre-school child, courses of study, delinquents, counseling and vocational guidance.

The effect of creative recreation in promoting mental health is given much attention in this volume as is the need of the employment of the curative measures of mental hygiene in the activities of the criminal courts and police administration which an indifferent citizenry has left to the care of politicians of none too high intelligence or humanity. This treatise will open your eyes to a great movement hampered by the ignorance, prejudice and apathy of a public which is paying expensive penalties for its complacency.

TIMELY WORK BY OUR OWN

Eleven modest students and practitioners of education have made the twelfth yearbook[28] of

[25] Edward L. Thorndike, "An Experimental Study of Rewards." Teachers College Press, Columbia University, New York. 72 pp. $1.50.

[26] Jacob Tuckman, "Influence of Varying Amounts of Punishment on Mental Connections." Teachers College Press, Columbia University, New York. 45 pp. $1.50.

[27] Clara Bassett, "Mental Hygiene in the Community." The Macmillan Company, New York. 394 pp. $3.50.

[28] Ben G. Graham, chairman, E. W. Butterfield, Walter S. Deffenbaugh, C. Ray Gates, Thomas W. Gosling, George Melcher, John K. Norton, William

the Department of Superintendence, National Education Association, a very present help in time of trouble. There are nine chapters in it, very pertinent to the complex duties of superintendents of school systems of any size. Administration as affected by the structure of government, financial difficulties, laymen's control, increasing professionalism, school efficiency, participation by teachers, economies, informing the public, are handled with a definiteness of procedure and a breadth of view that, even if you didn't know the authors, would convince you of their observant experience and belief in the success of reason. I do not know of any book more immediately valuable to superintendent and principal. Its counsel on situations that are now charged with ill, its calm evaluation of numerous projects which have been strongly urged by enthusiastic proponents are open-minded and at the same time wisely cautious. The controversial points involved in proposals for democratic rule by teachers and in assumption of executive duties by boards of education are treated in a manner that will appeal to every unexcited reader.

The anonymous composer of the foreword opens the book by a quotation from the departed New York Maxwell: "The first primary object of school administration is to secure to every child his natural and constitutional right to an education." The author of chapter III begins his presentation with a similar emphasis on rights. If Dr. Maxwell was ignorant that the Constitution expressed no right of children to an education his friend, Judge Draper, New York State School Commissioner, made the fact plain when, at the Asbury Park meeting of the National Association, he turned to President Maxwell and said: "Education had no place in the Declaration or in the Constitution because it was held to be a matter of private concern and not a function of government at all."

But, eight years ago, Allen Oscar Hansen's delving into the pamphlets of 1787[29] brought out facts that make Dr. Maxwell's claim for education as a child's constitutional right and Judge Draper's assertion that education was held to be no function of government, both untenable. On the contrary, the propositions of Washington, Adams, Jefferson, Madison, Monroe, both Websters, Clinton, Mann, Stephens and of the scores of public men whose arguments set up the public schools, made the duty of preserving and improving the people's government by themselves the reason for taxing everybody to send the children of those who had any to school. The emphasis of the Constitution itself is on duties more than on rights. Dr. Briggs' Inglis lecture at Harvard, four years ago, set out the fundamental purposes leading to the set-up of education at public, not at parental, cost. It was not from love of children nor from concern for their rights but as an investment by the commonwealth for its own political salvation. This was the prime reason repeated by the proponents of the public school. They stressed as an essential core of the scheme that the school should enlighten public opinion on those political-economic matters which are the whole concern of government. Now, in the face of proposals to reduce school support, if we claim that schools have made the political-economic enlightenment of the country the main work, we are so insincere that we fall back on a more emotional claim that the first primary truth is that every child has a natural and constitutional right to be educated at the expense of the whole public. From their utterances elsewhere, at least three of the eleven authors of the report could not be expected to put the satisfaction of the right of children above the obligation to educate them to their civic duties. Current utterances of Owen Young, Boyd Bode, Dean Russell, Director Judd, Professor Moley, Commissioner Cooper, Secretary Ickes, President Coffman, Justice Hughes, Attorney Seabury, Norman Angell, Dr. Cubberley, Professor Bagley, various platforms of the Democratic and Republican parties and the Superintendence Department's resolution on citizenship training, 1932, place as the first object of school management the improvement of general, not children's welfare.

A good rationalizer can argue that the Maxwellian assertion implies all the doctrine stressed from Washington to Welling. In fact by assuming, as is possible, that these eleven apostles whose work is before us admit that civic cooperation is the first primary aim of public school, if they consider this so obvious as not

C. Reavis, Agnes Samuelson, George D. Strayer, David E. Weglein, "Critical Problems in School Administration." National Education Association, Washington, D. C. 383 pp. $2.00.

29 Allen Oscar Hansen, "Liberalism and Education in the Eighteenth Century." The Macmillan Company.

to need mention, the entire report teems with definite tasks that must be performed to realize the great objective. Whether they are discussing graduation exercises, teacher-membership on school boards, adult education, budgets, health, size of classes, fads and frills, taxes, janitors, legislative pottering, libraries, research, parent-teacher associations, salaries, supervision, or teachers organizations, the authors are forthright, practical, progressive and deserving of gratitude for a great piece of patriotic work admirably done and directed toward meeting immediate dangers. This review calls them modest. Their names are not set against their separate chapters. Democratically they work for the team.

The book contains, also, Secretary Shankland's summaries of department work, the constitution, minutes of the 1933 meeting, lists of members and an index.

CUBBERLEY'S BEST BEST

THROUGH the five hundred school years of this continent historian Cubberley marches as in a triumph. His second review of progress in the United States[30] now appearing, fifteen years after its first demonstration that the history of education can be presented with animation and brilliancy, not only makes the past glow with a present interest but shows the best strivings of school service at this moment to be based on definite proposals of statesmen who set a world-example of public education as a necessity of representative government. The passing of pedagogues ashamed to be known as such is indisputably a mark of our day. I doubt that any one man deserves credit for this sanity more than Dr. Cubberley in the volumes he has issued effectively showing the importance and dignity of educational progress in this republic.

Democracy, the author reminds us, postulates education of all citizens. The Constitution said nothing about it. Its framers were schooled in the aristocratic education of a monarchy, but as statesmen they saw the new need. Simultaneously with their drafting of the Constitution they passed the ordinance announcing the perpetual encouragement of schools for the purpose of securing good government. The right of the state to enforce education for general welfare became a fixed idea in New England and spread over the entire Union. Public schools have been established not on an announced declaration that they can teach better than private ones but because it is the inherent right of the people, organized as government, to conduct a type of education looking to the preservation and improvement of representative democracy.

This duty, Dr. Cubberley notes, needs more attention by administrators and teachers. On them rests the burden of the future of free civic institutions and the welfare of national life. What progress we make will be largely determined by how well the school sees national needs and guides its program in accordance.

There are 33 chapters to the book. It runs from the European background through Colonial times to the attitudes engendered by the political revolution of 1776–1787. This leaves thirty chapters given to national development, the battles for free schools, for escape from church control, for high schools, for teacher-training and for professional supervision. There are twenty-eight fine portraits of educational heroes; a hundred and seventy pictures and diagrams.

The Houghton Mifflin Company is issuing a companion volume of readings in education, a collection of source material to which frequent reference by section is made in this text. Selected references are abundant. The propositions from which the free school system sprang are given in the words of the early makers of the republic.

Questions and themes follow each chapter and are in the form that pupils of Professor Cubberley have been promulgating: "evaluate" this, "show why" that, "What would be the result if ———?" "What do schools need to do in order that ———?"

As I compare this work with the author's previous one of the same name it seems to me he has embodied the experience of fifteen years teaching this course, noting improvements from day to day and, on the original plan, building an entire new work. Scarcely a page is the same as in the former book. Even the Colonial period is modified by later researches.

I envy the trainer of teachers who will take them along the professional road with this as a guidebook.

30 Ellwood P. Cubberley, ''Public Education in the United States.'' Houghton Mifflin Company, Boston. 782 pp. $3.00.

SCHOOL AND SOCIETY

WITH WHICH ARE COMBINED THE EDUCATIONAL REVIEW, ESTABLISHED IN 1891, THE TEACHERS MAGAZINE, ESTABLISHED IN 1878, AND THE SCHOOL JOURNAL, ESTABLISHED IN 1874.

EDITED BY J. McKEEN CATTELL, R. D. LINDQUIST AND W. H. COWLEY

EDITORIAL COMMUNICATIONS SHOULD BE ADDRESSED TO THE EDUCATION BUILDING, THE OHIO STATE UNIVERSITY, COLUMBUS, OHIO

Volume 39 SATURDAY, APRIL 14, 1934 Number 1007

THE LIBRARY PROFESSOR AND EDUCATIONAL RESEARCH[1]

By Professor CARTER ALEXANDER

LIBRARY PROFESSOR, TEACHERS COLLEGE, COLUMBIA UNIVERSITY

THE pioneer library professorship and the library consultantship antedating it by a semester, established at Teachers College, Columbia University, in 1932, grew out of a conviction of Dean William F. Russell. This conviction, first set forth in his annual report for 1928, was that the great increase in advanced students at the college, coupled with a demand for the old-time quality of instruction, but at a reduced cost per student, had created a serious dilemma. The only way out, in his judgment, was through a greater and wiser use of libraries and more independent reading by students, or, as he labeled it, "quantity contact with print." To continue in his words:

> A plan must be developed whereby the classes and the library can work closely together; where the teaching process can be started and finished by the instructor and the learning process carried on effectively in the library; where books, pamphlets and periodicals are easily accessible and convenient, where and when they are needed without waste of time or effort; where suggestions and advice can be given in the library as well as in the office of the professor. . . .
>
> There must be bibliographic service of a high order. . . . The desperate need for this service is revealed by the many Doctors' dissertations that are little more than bibliographical tasks.

In furtherance of his idea, the dean took up with the speaker the possibility of a library professorship, but the latter could not then see the possibility of his doing much in that line save with students of educational administration, his specialty for many years. He thought the idea could be carried out successfully if some five or six teaching professors in various fields were gradually attached to the library, but that little could be done by any one professor attempting to cover all phases of education. He offered to do the pioneering in his specialty of administration and train others who would later start to develop similarly additional fields like the curriculum and methods of instruction. Lack of funds, however, prevented the installation of a program that would in time have so large an instructional force attached to the library until there was instituted a large-scale reorganization of instruction. This last involved an energetic attempt to break through departmental lines, to reduce the number of courses, to cut down duplications and to lower the cost of instruction while trying to secure better quality. The

[1] Read in part before Section Q, American Association for the Advancement of Science, Boston, December 29, 1933.

end was that the speaker was assigned to the library in the fall of 1932 as a teaching professor with a specialty in educational administration at all levels, to do what he could for other students as well.

Objectives of the Library Professorship

As the incumbent sees it, his chief objective is an instructional or training one for students of education, particularly those engaged in research. The basic idea is that securing the best results in training students to do educational research requires an approach on instruction by a specialist from the library end as well as from the classroom with its regular instructors in the various departmental fields or grouped divisions. The professor is a member of the general instructional staff assigned to the library end, reporting only to the dean and director of the school of education. Without specific training in librarianship, he has no more responsibility for the policies or administration of the library than any other professor in the college. His function is solely to improve instruction involving the use of library materials and to facilitate educational research through this better use of such materials. His job is to bring students engaged in educational work or preparing to engage in it to have a better understanding of the most profitable ways of doing the library work needed in their researches. His particular concern is to eliminate the great wastes of time and energy heretofore involved in locating and using library materials so that the student may have more time for thinking about the materials, interpreting their contents and putting these to real use. The wastes of concern to the library professor, be it noted, are due to the student's lack of library knowledge or of profitable library experience, not to any original deficiency in library provisions or management.

The Research Index

The first job tackled by the library professor was that of cutting down the tremendous amount of time heretofore consumed by students in trying to find out what researches had been published on a particular phase of education. Doctoral candidates in education need to find this out whenever they start to discover a possible dissertation problem, to isolate one within a given area, to make fruitful interpretations or to avoid duplicating previous studies. Far more would be achieved in educational research if researchers could quickly find out what had been done. They could then put much more of their energy into planning and accomplishing advances. To cut down searching time, the best possible start was clearly the setting up of a research card index.

From the speaker's experience with successive editions of his Educational Research pamphlet, it seemed that the index might well be along the lines of the notes there given for research on any educational topic. After various experiments, the plans were perfected until the index now has over six thousand cards and saves the faculty and students engaged in research at our institution tremendous amounts of time formerly spent in laboriously finding out where to look and in ascertaining what had been done or published. For instance, at any one time, there are hundreds of dissertations under way by students in residence or by former students. Keeping clear of duplicating some of these is always so difficult that the library professor is purposely attached to the Committee on Higher Degrees that he may early know about all dissertations under way. Keeping up this index requires about a third of his time and about two thirds of his secretary's time. He will be glad to write details of this index to any faculty member of another institution desiring to set up an index there. At this time a concrete example will indicate its nature.

Suppose a student in secondary education is interested in finding a good research problem about junior high schools or in prosecuting one already selected in this field. Under that head, the research index will give him within two minutes references with page numbers or data for easy communication with others working in the same field, on such things as the following: A short and well-selected bibliography; the fullest bibliography or several bibliographies that come down to date without overlapping; separate bibliographies on important phases like Articulation, Costs, Curriculum and Methods of Teaching; notes on bringing these bibliographies up to date; names and brief notes on important periodicals and associations; notes on researches and how to trace them for those completed or under way; lists of needed researches; brief theoretical treatments; history of the field; an article or two on present status and one or two on trends. All these will give references bearing directly on junior high schools. If the problem is already a narrow one, for instance, concerned with homogeneous grouping in junior high schools, the index will enable him to locate promptly whatever it has bearing on the problem.

Instruction by the Library Professor

Determining the lines, the nature and the amounts of instruction to be offered by the library professor, constituted a series of baffling problems. In his judgment, little need existed for him to give a brief formal treatment of the mechanics of running down library materials and making formal bibliographies. To begin with, the library consultant held public conferences for this purpose at the beginning of each semester and was available for advice at all times to students, the various library staff members were similarly available in their specialties, and the librarian has always been very alert to issue brief mimeographed or printed helps on the use and possibilities of the library. Should he attempt such a treatment, it would have to be given to several hundred candidates a year, and only the most formal and emptiest of library exercises could be given to any such number at one time. Only one card catalog, or only one of each of the important research index tools is to be expected in the best of educational libraries. To turn scores of students loose at one time on these scarce tools would be preposterous. It could only result in a scandalous waste of the student's time and in wearing out the library tools to no significant end. Moreover, we have too many books on educational research with chapters on library and bibliographic work, to say nothing of excellent separate books on thesis writing, to warrant such a treatment. The student needing only this might better go directly to these books and read up quickly for himself. What the research student really needed, in the library professor's judgment, was training in library methods arising from the needs of actual practise with some research where the student had a strong motive for mastering them. This motive seemed likeliest to spring from the student's need in connection with some research of his very own. Such would be his dissertation or some similar research, or working out a guide to the professional literature in some phase of his major field. It would hardly arise with sufficient force unless it were a voluntary matter with him. Moreover, putting the instruction on a purely voluntary basis would cut down the number of students to be handled by the library professor. Since the library work on separate researches would be largely individual if the best results were to be secured, it could not well be handled by assistants and the library professor's capacity would be limited.

Such considerations produced the decision to try out three lines of instruction during the initial year. The first was a purely voluntary evening short course of about two hours a week for five weeks, repeated every semester, open only to doctoral candidates. These are told plainly that it will be of maximum service to them only when they have fairly well determined on their dissertation problems with their sponsors. The second was an individual instruction course limited to ten students, each of whom would be working on locating and listing the essential sources for some field of at least departmental width, a guide to the literature of Negro education, for instance. The third was individual consultation service for doctoral candidates on their dissertations, when sent to the library professor by their sponsoring professors. Throughout, the idea was that the library professor should stimulate a student to be resourceful in looking up things for himself, and with timely suggestions and just the right amounts of information at psychological moments train him in such resourcefulness. The library professor had no intention of serving him as would a reference librarian.

Voluntary Course for Doctoral Candidates: This has now run for three semesters with very favorable reactions from students and faculty members. It covers when to do library research, setting up a problem for profitable library work on it, scouting and exhaustive library searching, organizing a bibliography and a working index for accumulating library materials, the different kinds of reading needed in research, note-taking and filing. Following each evening is an exercise which the student can do or not as he pleases. If he does it, he receives a written criticism of it and consultations as advisable. Every exercise is wholly on the student's own dissertation with the exception of the skimming one, which is largely on his major field. The attendance was around thirty-five each semester of last year and has run from sixty to eighty this semester. A considerable number of students do the outline of a dissertation exercise, but drop out on the other exercises. The comparatively few doing all the exercises are enthusiastic about the advance on their dissertations for the time put in on the course. The chief reason more students do not do the exercises seems to be that many of them are eager to get help from the lectures before they have settled upon definite problems. Possibly letting a student hand in the exercises without going to the lectures the next semester would help them here. This plan worked well with two students last year.

Individual Instruction Course: The objective of this came from Dean Russell's emphasis on the need for better bibliographic work in education. The plan for attaining this objective came from the library professor's experience in issuing the different editions of his Educational Research pamphlet as a guide to the literature of educational administration. This course was to result in guides to the literature of special fields in education where such guides are needed by research workers. There is, for example, no need of preparing such a guide in educational psychology because of C. M. Louttit's "Handbook of Psychological Literature."[2] The professor told the departmental heads that he would undertake a guide in any field if the right kind of student were sent him, but he preferred to wait a year or more if necessary to secure the right quality of student. Guides to the literature of Negro education[3] and of teacher training[4]

[2] Principia Press, Bloomington, Indiana, 273 pp., 1932.

[3] P. A. W. Cook, "A Guide to the Literature on Negro Education," *Teachers College Record*, 34: 671–77, May, 1933.

[4] John Herrold Lancaster, "A Guide to the Literature on Education of Teachers," *Educational*

were thus completed and published last May. Another guide on the curriculum is in press with the *Teachers College Record.* A fourth on Catholic education was largely done, and considerable progress was made on guides for rural education, music education and commercial education. This year some nine students are working in the course on very diverse guides, one being on prison education. The library professor gives each student mimeographed directions for dealing with the problems involved in getting up a guide, cites him the guides already completed, and then works with him individually from fifteen minutes to an hour as necessary, once a week or once in two weeks. The work is not regarded as completed until the student turns in copy for a guide, practically ready to be sent in to the printer.

Consultation Service: This service on sources of data and how to locate library materials on troublesome points is open to any doctoral candidate who brings a request to this effect from his sponsor or adviser. The object of this restriction is to prevent any possible interference with the sponsor's planning for the student and to save for deserving students, when they really need help, the time and energy that might easily be frittered away on students who were talking about dissertations instead of actually at work on them. Last year, in addition to many incidental cases, some twenty-six doctoral candidates filed such requests for regular consultation service. When a student comes for such a consultation, the library professor as quickly as possible finds out what the difficulties are and makes suggestions for sources, reading, and the like. He makes no effort to teach a student in that brief time what the student could expect to get from the short-course or the individual-instruction course. He gives the student free use of the research index and other aids, but he makes no attempt to develop the student's library research muscles by taking all the exercise himself. Consultations range from ten minutes to two hours, sometimes being continued at luncheon if the problem and the ability of the student warrant.

Course in Library Sources and Methods: From the start, the library professor has had to face a problem that has not so far been satisfactorily solved. This grows out of the fact that our students in general, and our doctoral candidates in particular, often lack knowledge of library resources and special techniques for using these resources, essential for successful prosecution of their researches. There is agreement that this condition exists, but no agreement as to how the lack is to be supplied.

The librarian and her assistants have of course realized this condition for years and have been working on it that long. They have been issuing extremely useful guides to different kinds of library materials.[5] The library consultant, a very successful former school librarian, has been holding a few conferences at the beginning of each semester on our library arrangement, the use of the card catalog, the possibilities of various kinds of reference books and in-

Administration and Supervision, 19: 363–72, May, 1933.

5 Clara Esther Derring, "Lists and Abstracts of Masters' Theses and Doctors' Dissertations in Education," *Teachers College Record,* 34: 490–502, March, 1933; Eleanor M. Witmer, "Educational Research. A Bibliography on Sources Useful in Determining Research Completed and under Way," *Teachers College Record,* 33: 335–40, January, 1932; Eleanor M. Witmer and Ethel M. Feagley, "A Beginner's Guide to Bibliography with Examples Drawn from the Field of Education." Experimental edition, mimeographed. New York: Teachers College, Columbia University, 16 pp., 1933; Eleanor M. Witmer and Margaret C. Miller, "Guides to Educational Literature in Periodicals, Indexes, Abstracts, Bibliographies," *Teachers College Record,* 33: 719–30, May, 1932; "U. S. Office of Education Serial Publications—A Check List with Descriptive Notes," *Teachers College Record,* 34: 302–11, January, 1933.

dexes, and the like. These conferences are extremely helpful and the attendance averages one hundred. She has also given instruction on the use of the library to small groups in various departments, usually one period each. She is specializing in materials for enriched teaching in high school and in showing prospective high-school teachers how to use the library tools and resources they will have available for their teaching. With these students she has all the contacts desired. Excellent results are reported by the students thus reached, but only a small percentage of the whole student body, particularly of the doctoral candidates, has been so reached. Both guides and conferences are naturally largely from a library standpoint, whereas a research student needs in addition to know what a given library tool is good for in various kinds of research and when and how to use it. The library professor some years ago, while in the department of educational administration, used to appear three periods in a combination instrument-of-research course in which he tried to give something of what was needed for advanced students. The numbers of students, around 175 at that time, made this work so formal that it was discontinued.

As a way out of this difficulty, the library professor decided to offer a course repeated every semester on "How to Locate Educational Information and Data." The two hours of class meeting each week cover instruction on the existence and use of the usual library sources and tools, the information being purposely organized so as not merely to duplicate what the student can easily read. Moreover, this information is centered around typical research difficulties with library materials and these same difficulties are used to organize the problems in the exercises which the students must do outside of class. Each student may adapt the exercises to his particular field or to a special problem if he has one.

The students in this course, in the two times that it has been so far offered, seem to be much pleased with the work and almost universally regret they did not have it at the start of their graduate work. But it has had only ten students each time so far. A good many others desired to take it, but as it has not been granted credit for a half-instrument of research, they felt they did not have the time for it. Such credit has so far been refused it by the committee on higher degrees as a whole on two grounds: Chiefly that it does not cover a wide enough range in methods of research, and secondly that it should be required of all doctoral candidates after being stripped to a minimum. The library professor has not been eager to undertake this latter assignment, because with several hundred students in the course of a year required to reach a given state of library knowledge, only the most formal and emptiest of work could be secured, unless many thousands of dollars were spent for additional library tools and indexes, and the library professor worked something like 3 NRA hours for the total per week. To give any individual attention worthy of the name to doctoral candidates, the professor would have to look over the papers himself —no assistant could possibly be of much service on this. If such information is desired of all students, the library professor's idea would be that it should be secured by issuing a list of readings and suggestions for covering them and holding a uniform examination on them several times a year. A student would have to keep taking the examination until he passed it and was certified as having the minimum knowledge. This would be very formal inevitably.[6]

[6] For a detailed treatment of this minimum knowledge and the best ways to secure it, see the chapter on "Library Methods in Educational Research," by Carter Alexander, *Review of Educational Research*, Vol. 4, No. 1, 1934. American Educational Research Association, Washington, D. C.

Such was the situation at the time of reading this paper. Since then, however, instrument-of-research credit to the amount of one half instrument has been allowed in two courses taken with extra work. This extra work consists of demonstrating by a document that the student can focus all his library knowledge effectively upon some specific problem. The granting of credit came as a result of a recommendation from the Student Council, several of whose members had had some of the library work and consultations.

Intersession Library Work

As part of the policy of individual attention to research students, Director Paul R. Mort last summer inaugurated a new type of intersession after the summer session. In this a student who had some definite project, approved by some faculty member, could work independently, file a report and, if the work was acceptable, receive from two to four semester hours of credit, depending upon the time spent and the amount of work done. A few of the faculty involved were around occasionally, although they were not in residence, but this was wholly accidental. The library professor, however, was on duty five days each week as in the summer session, available for guidance and consultation, and he had administrative charge of all intersession students. It was impossible to get the more than sixty students enrolled, together at any one time or in any sort of class. Moreover, this would not have been advisable from the widely different nature of their problems, directed by so many different faculty members, and from their varying stages of advancement. The projects for independent study ranged all the way from discovering and selecting certain modern alphabets and making them available for classroom instruction charts, through developing courses of study for various grades on various bases, to working up the literature of particular fields where orientation or special knowledge was desired, or to the isolation of problems for doctoral dissertations.

The greatest assistance to intersession students by the library professor was of course on problems involving some administrative slants. However, by the use of the research index, and hints and suggestions on clues to students, he evidently gave them enough help for many non-administration students to send him most sincere expressions of thanks. Each week he required of each student a short written report of progress which had in it four items of a mechanical or routine nature, and one requiring a statement of advance in thought, the acquisition of new ideas, and the like, with some concrete supporting evidence. The library professor's part was confined to helping the student on the library phases of his work. The mark for his work was given him by the professor under whom he outlined the project and to whom he submitted his final report.

The isolation of specific dissertation problems was an experiment conducted with two intersession students in educational administration. One was interested in personal relations of school executives and the other in business management of schools, especially purchasing. By assigning them readings, holding individual conferences and requiring written reports and bibliographies of available materials with an outline which they were forced to revise several times until it was satisfactory, the library professor brought these men in two or three weeks to a state of advancement on their problems often not reached by students in their department after several months in the regular session. In fact, they were both given the mark of "A" by the administration professor who sent them into the work and passed upon the results. The amount of time given these men by the library professor was altogether not over five hours each. In this connection nearly half the students of the intersession received a grade of "A minus" or better from the faculty members passing on the papers turned in.

The faculty consider this kind of intersession work very satisfactory for able students, but not for others. Many of the students appreciate the opportunity to work intensively by themselves without interruption. It is planned to extend the intersession provisions the coming summer, when the library professor will offer his "How to Locate Educational Materials and Data" course, and a new one on the isolation of dissertation problems. Any graduate student may enter the former. The latter will be open only to students sent to it for this purpose by faculty members, and each student so sent must bring from a sponsoring faculty member a statement to the effect that the member regards him as of such quality that the member would be willing to sponsor a doctoral dissertation by him. The opportunities for students who desire to work on individual projects will be the same as for this year's intersession.

Service for Field Workers

The newest research service undertaken by the library professor is an experimental offer in the *Teachers College Record* for November, 1933, to any alumnus not taking work at the college and who is an administrator in actual service and a subscriber to the *Record*. The offer is to cite bibliographies and clues for library materials and data on one problem or topic. The idea is to aid eligible school administrators in the field in research on their practical problems. The blank distinctly states that it is not a reference service, that no attempt will be made to answer questions that can be answered by the usual reference department of a library, or to compile or copy bibliographies, and that the correspondence must be reduced to the barest of mechanical features. But every effort will be made to give each eligible inquirer on his one question something like the service he would receive on clues and sources if he made a brief call at the library professor's office. If the number of replies is not too great, a second blank will be printed in February.

Conclusion

Such are the chief activities of what seems to be the first teaching professorship attached to the library of an institution for training in educational research. They have been given in detail because they may be helpful to other institutions in establishing such professorships or in assigning professors for part time in connection with instruction from the library end. It is altogether too early to estimate precisely the results of this pioneer professorship or to predict its exact future developments. Two things about it, however, seem clear. It has so far operated on the principle laid down by Thorndike many years ago: If you want to know whether a person has a given ability, see if he can use it. Also, the students who do the exercises so far developed bid fair to be resourceful and effective on the library phases of educational research, no matter where they may have to work, long after they have left the library professor.

THE IMPORTANCE OF SMALL CLASSES

By ALFRED M. BROOKS
FINE ARTS DEPARTMENT, SWARTHMORE COLLEGE

For ten years I have been a deeply interested onlooker at and, to some extent, a participant in the honors experiment at Swarthmore. I am one of the many who believe that the experimental stage is past, and that the result is a better way of teaching than has been followed in American colleges heretofore. Better, I mean, for those students who are really interested in the things of the mind. This is far from saying that all the best brains find their way into honors work. One often wishes that an exchange of brains between regular classes and honors seminars could be effected. But college faculties, like other expert bodies, have a wholesome prejudice, or is it unwholesome, against swapping horses in mid-stream. It remains for the same wise head and keen minds that have made such a success of the honors experiment to discover, through further experimenting, a better way of teaching the greater number, those not reading for honors, but pursuing the regular course. I would humbly suggest such an experiment be made by substituting small classes for large. There is a strong chance that this would prove that the aristocracy of intellect is not in the honors groups alone, as is too often assumed. Rather, that it does not always make itself known, or get discovered soon enough in the large first and second year classes. At all events it does seem that under the present system of "hand-picked" students, meaning careful selection of tens from hundreds of college applicants, by laborious investigations, tests and "personal interviews" there should be more "honors material" than now comes to light by the spring of the sophomore year; as well as a higher average of really good. Of course, the objection to the small class is its high cost to the college. One answer to this is "cut the whole enrolment of the college in two. Spend as much money on one student as now on two." Halving may not be the right fraction, but it need not take much arithmetic on the part of those who know what the funds are, and the expenses they must meet, to find out how many students, on a small-class basis, could be provided for. To do this would call for courage and wise persistence. But these qualities have never been lacking in the persons who conceived and carried through the honors system, as it now exists. Wherein is this at variance with the essential conception of the advantages of reading for honors? To those who believe in quantity rather than quality the suggestion, it is no more, will be anathema. But to all such the honors plan has always been anathema, and so remains.

I implied at the outset that my participation in the honors experiment at Swarthmore has been small. I profess a subject—fine arts—which, like Latin and Greek, does not attract students in considerable numbers, and is not regarded as "practical" in the way that modern languages, history, the social sciences and economics are regarded. But while my seminars are small it is but fair to say of the students who have elected them through years that they have been, with few exceptions, among the best, judged by the results of their examinations. I say this because at least one first-rate book has been written on the subject of reading for honors by a colleague and not a few distinguished pronouncements have been made from time to time, preeminently those of the prime mover in the matter, the president of Swarthmore College. I do not wish to make my own part appear other than it has been.

I hesitate to say that I have read all the official utterances, but I have read a great many of them and listened to numerous speeches on this subject both at Swarthmore and elsewhere. Further, I have heard much informal discussion of the matter on the part of teachers and students, honor students and others, whose opinions run the gamut between regarding the method as the millennium of education or an unpatriotic, harmful, snobbish aping of procedures long in vogue at Oxford. The latter seems to me idiotic, the former over-enthusiastic. But compared with much earlier college education when the B.A. degree meant little more than the grand total of passing grades gathered here and there much as a rat gathers turnips, no enthusiasm can, in my opinion, be really too great.

That "there is no single, no royal road to knowledge, education, or culture," that "there is no single best way to teach at any stage," is as much the truth as it is a truism. The preceptorial and tutorial systems at Princeton and Harvard, and the honors work at Harvard and Swarthmore, "all are efforts [I quote Dr. Abraham Flexner] to establish close, informal contacts between members of the student body and the instructional staff."

This is faithfully descriptive of the methods named, but not of them only. Such contacts have always been possible, and frequently made, in small classes, wherever and whenever such classes have been allowed, despite the fact that the per capita cost has been a serious, perennial concern to academic heads and all others upon whom the onerous burden of academic financing rests. One of the many good things not generally recognized that have come of honors work is, negatively speaking, the exorcism of the bogey of high cost for small classes because, positively speaking, honors work means small classes on account of their recognized superior value to the student. They mean, automatically, the high price which must always be paid for what is excellent as against the less that buys mediocrity, the certain subversion of all education. A college should be as proud of its small classes in course, as of its equally small honors seminars, provided the teaching be first rate and the students not "snap-hunters." But such hunting is not usually pursued where students foregather in small numbers. It is preeminently a sport for crowds. This in large part explains the relatively high marks of the small class student. Small classes would separate the sheep and the goats well before the end of the freshman year. The kind of training which the students who were then admitted to the sophomore class could be given by the end of the sophomore year would provide such "honors material" as now is rare, to say nothing of raising the work done in course to a quality equally rare at present. The combined results would be a through and through honors college and not, fine as this is, a college with honors in it.

The comparatively recent introduction of what are known as comprehensive examinations is, in a way, another of the good results which has come of honors. Comprehensives are in no far-fetched sense the analogue of honors examinations. Few things are more difficult than to write or give either of these examinations well because they must be such as will elicit from the student the kind of answer that will prove his mastery of his subject, be he in honors or in course; establish his capacity to think, quite apart from displaying his store of facts, for the one has to do with his memory and the other with his mind. This is "the noble, vulgar speech," not philosophical. It is herein that a good memory, devoutly to be worked as well as wished for, often plays tricks with student and instructor. If a student knows that he has a good memory he will be prone to put too much trust in cramming, the cause of many a specious, educational miracle, especially when examination questions are not so skilfully constructed, written or oral, as to preclude these miracles. I believe that cramming, which is closely akin to reviewing and is "intensive reviewing," should be discouraged to the utmost. In this I realize that I am in the great minority.

Again, it is due to a good memory that many a student in the popular subjects, and large classes, gets high grades and, so, the hearty backing of his instructors for entering honors work. Herein lies no small part of that depressing slump which comes not infrequently after such students have been for a while in their honors seminars. The small seminar at an unfortunate time shows up the relative strength of his memory and his mind, the very thing which the small class would have done in season to prevent a regrettable mistake for all concerned which means the student himself, his co-students in the seminar and his instructors. This is the natural concomitant of the large class. It can not be counted the fault of student or teacher. In the small class those close, informal contacts already spoken of simply can not be avoided. The instructor reads every paper and can have repeated discussion with his students. Further, and most important, students who hesitate for many good reasons to ask questions in a large class will do so freely in a small one. The instructor who presides over a large and enthusiastic, or a large and bored class; who has his "readers" and can "get round" at best but once a month will not in the nature of things know much about his students individually. I have sometimes wondered what a statistical mind would discover if it were to set itself to tabulating the results achieved by honors students drawn from large and small classes, respectively. It is fair to assume that it would prove no more than the usual array of statistics proves. But it is unfair to assume that it would throw no light on the reasons for the barely "get-by"-with-honors students, and those who after slowing down their seminars through one or two years return, or are returned to course. Worse yet, those who should be returned and are not. But no system is to be blamed for not working perfectly. It is proof that we think a system is working well, or very well, when we feel convinced that by taking thought it can be made to work extremely well. This is what I believe about the honors system. How to keep out all but "first-raters" is, as I see it, the most important unsolved problem at present.

I shall close with some extensive quotations which seem to me to depict well-nigh ideal examinations, not only of the honors but of the comprehensive type, ideally conducted and ideally taken. They are from a great book on education, school as well as college, which lays no claim to being such and is as generally unknown as it is generally admired by those who do know it—Louis Henri Sullivan's "Autobiography of an Idea," published a dozen years ago by the American Institute of Architects. The first fact to be noted about Sullivan is that while still a boy he had the supreme good fortune to come into the hands of a teacher who taught him the primal fact of all education—how to teach himself, which by the time he was of college age, and had to gather together and systemize his French, mathematics, drawing and history to pass the written and oral examinations for admission to the Ecole des Beaux Arts, meant the ability to "listen with the whole mind, not part of it: with the whole heart, not part of it: to reflect, to discriminate: to observe." His own words shall paint the useful, at-present applicable and brilliant picture.

Several days before the examinations . . . Louis stopped all work, relaxed completely, and in a state of confidence amused himself with the sights and sounds of Paris, and enjoyed a few long sleeps. . . .

The examinations were to be, severally, written, drawn, and oral. . . . The real test for him would lie in the oral examinations (his drawing and his writing he seems not to have questioned at all) which were conducted in little amphitheaters, a professor presiding (outside examiners) and all aspirants free to come and go, as they did in steady stream. . . . The candidate under fire thus was by no means lonely; indeed, he deeply wished to be alone with his inquisitor. . . .

Came Louis's turn for mathematics. For audience he had some twenty strange faces, all rather scared. The examining professor, elderly and of quiet poise, received him most courteously, assuring him "that he need not feel in the least embarrassed, that the inquisition would proceed at a moderate pace, and that Louis was free to solve any problem in any way he liked, *the objective being to discover the extent of his understanding, not his memory.* [The italics are mine.] Then the examining professor settled to the work. For over an hour—Lord knows how long it was—he put Louis through a steady gruelling—always kindly, however—such as Louis had never known, never dreamed of, never believed could be so. . . . Of a sudden he came into his stride, which he held to the end. For after a heart breaking crisis, he suddenly found himself actually *thinking* in terms of mathematics, and, accordingly, lost all fear, relaxed and let his mind go free. From beginning to end he did not make a fluke. At the close the examining professor, who had become quite interested when he found he could increase the difficulties, pressed Louis's hand and said: "I felicitate you, Monsieur Sullivan, you have the mathematical imagination which is quite rare. I wish you well."

Now came the questioning in history, and Louis was equally startled at the method. He was well prepared according to the books, which he had visualized into a moving picture, but he was not prepared for the shock. . . . Louis felt the earth leave him, as the first question came: "Monsieur, will you be kind enough to tell me the story of the Hebrew People?" Then the earth came back, but the question remained immense. . . . So Louis began with the desert tribes, the sojourn in Egypt, the wandering in the desert, carrying the story down to the destruction of Jerusalem, and the captivity. He also sketched the patriarchal age, the prophets in captivity, the final triumph of ritual over inspiration, and righteousness. The charm of this examination lay in the fact that Louis was encouraged by the examining professor to give a pictorial and rather dramatic recital, and the professor's frequent questioning what Louis had said and as to why he thought thus and so. He, for instance, asked Louis what had impressed him most vividly in the history of the Jews, and Louis said: "The emergence and vivid personality of Jehovah, their God."

The next question now followed: "I would like an account of the ten emperors of Rome." Another half hour of talk as Louis covered the ground, from the bookish point of view, and made a few remarks on his own account, which led the professor to say: "You do not seem to be in sympathy with Roman civilization." "No," said Louis: "I feel out of touch with a civilization whose glory was based on force."

Then came the third question: "Monsieur, I see you have a certain faculty, a bit crude as yet, of making word pictures, of discerning something real beneath the glamour of the surface, which is the particular business of the historian to uncover. Now, therefore, as this is to be the last question, do your best and give me an intimate account of the times of Francis First." Louis did this with joy. On account of Leonardo's part in it, he had studied the period with special care and devotion. He had seemed to live in the time and with its people, its manners, its customs, its thoughts, it stood forth for him as a very present picture of the past.

At the close, the examining professor smiled. He said: "The object of these examinations is not to ascertain an array of facts devoid of shaping context, but to discern the degree of intelligence possessed by the candidate; to ascertain his capacity for interpretation, and if he possesses, to any perceptible degree the faculty of constructive imagination—without which pursuit of history is merely so much wasted time."

In all that I have actually known, heard and read of the honors system, and in less degree of the idea of comprehensive examinations; of regular college courses, and honors as meant for the abler student; of advice, and prescription for how to study and instruct in honors work; and of the ends to be aimed at, I have not met, all told, an approximation to Sullivan's clear exposition and grasp of the essence of the idea behind the honors plan as it is now entering upon its second decade in the American college. Sullivan, of course, never heard of honors, and his ideas go back to 1874. But time and nomenclatures have little to do with the inception of ideas though much, seemingly, with their emergence into practical application. I believe —I may be all wrong—that the honors system which has already worked great good to the upper reaches of college education has in it the germ of great good to the lower reaches; that the attainment of this good can come through recognizing the small class as being as much the essential of all the four years of college as the small seminar, for the elect, is now felt to be of the last two years. It should be the right of every student in college, all of whom should be really, not debatably good, else not in college at all. The fact that so many students who are not really good are in college is self-evident. The harm of it lies in the hurt to themselves, and the greater hurt to their fellows.

EDUCATIONAL EVENTS

COMPULSORY PHYSICAL EDUCATION IN THE COLLEGES OF INDIA

The question of compulsory physical education has arisen in the legislatures and university senates of India. The proponents of the physical education program seek to require courses of all students between the ages of 12 and 20. Opponents of physical education point to the expense involved and the diversion of funds from other educational activities.

The issue has been joined recently at Bombay University. In 1930 the university senate passed a resolution favoring the introduction of compulsory physical education at an early date, but in November, 1933, a conference of the principals of the affiliated colleges resolved not to recommend any courses to the senate which would involve subsidies from university funds. Those in favor of developing athletic activities among Indian students urge the desirability of requiring each affiliated college employing a physical director or master of games to organize the physical activities of students. They also propose the appointment of a university physical director to coordinate the work of the entire university and to advise the games masters of the colleges.

The complete program of physical training, sponsored most especially by the Reverend John McKenzie, principal of Wilson College, failed to win the support of his colleagues from the other colleges of Bombay University. The group voted to allow each college to choose its own physical education program, subject to the approval of the university senate. In place of the suggested university physical director the principals voted to appoint a board to advise the university in all matters having to do with sports and games.

The London *Times,* commenting editorially upon the action of the Indian educators, observed in its issue of March 17 that "the discussion went to show that measures of compulsion are not likely to be effective if they are in advance of public opinion. The surest way of progress is that of inculcating the love of organized games which is so marked a feature of English public schools and colleges. Undoubtedly a games master can do much to encourage this spirit, but the teaching staff as a whole can do more."

INTERNATIONAL PEACE AND NAZI GERMANY

That the Hitler government has stopped the educational work of the Carnegie Endowment for International Peace in Berlin was revealed on April 1 in the annual report of Dr. Nicholas Murray Butler as director of the Division of Intercourse and Education of the endowment.

Since 1927, under the Weimar Republic, the European center of the Carnegie Endowment had sponsored lectures at the Deutsche Hochschule für Politik (German School of International Relations) in Berlin. Distinguished economists and professors of various nationalities, including many leading liberals, had lectured there in the interest of world peace. In 1929 a permanent Lehrstuhl Carnegie (Carnegie chair) was established at the school.

Dr. Butler explained on behalf of the endowment that it had enjoyed most friendly relations with the former democratic government of Germany, but that its lectures were stopped immediately after Chancellor Hitler came into power. The reason for this action, he pointed out, presumably was that the whole work of the endowment was based upon free discussion of international relations, so that it was contrary to the aims of the Nazi régime.

The Berlin School for International Relations, at which the Lehrstuhl was established, was taken over by the Nazi Government as an official school. Previously it had been conducted along the lines of the Walter Hines Page School of International Relations at the Johns Hopkins University, and many young German diplomats had attended in order to prepare themselves for their careers.

Dr. Butler observed that the Lehrstuhl had functioned for three years successfully. "The program arranged for 1932–33 was carried through almost completely," Dr. Butler states. "Only the final lecture scheduled for February, 1933, was omitted. At the writing of this report, the Hochschule has been suspended and its quarters are now being used by the German Government for an official school. In view of this fact the Lehrstuhl has not been continued for 1933–34.

"This contact with Germany has been, however, too important to be permanently severed, and Dr. Earle B. Babcock, head of the European center of the endowment in Paris, as well as the director in New York are waiting until some definite word from Germany shall indicate how best the work can be reestablished and continued."

Referring to the visits Mr. Babcock paid to various European countries, Dr. Butler added that the visit to Germany confirmed the feeling that the work there of the European Center should be suspended until some form of cooperation of the division acceptable to German public opinion could be gradually evolved.

THE PROGRAM OF HIGH-SCHOOL ARTICULATION AT YALE UNIVERSITY

YALE UNIVERSITY is inaugurating this spring a program designed to improve the articulation of school and college work. The first step in this program has been the creation of an advisory committee on programs of study, of which Professor H. Emerson Tuttle, master of Davenport College, is chairman, to establish more intimate contacts than have formerly existed with the preparatory schools and with those boys in the schools who mean to attend Yale University. Professor Tuttle will visit the schools, conferring with the masters and with any boy who may care to meet with him, to the end that the course of study pursued by the boy, especially in his last year or two at the secondary school, may prepare him as effectively as possible for the work he may wish to do at the university. Special emphasis will be placed on the possibility of putting the student into sophomore work or advanced freshman work in subjects where his previous school training will make this possible.

The placement of freshmen in advanced courses has been in practise for several years, but the procedure now proposed is designed to stimulate the student in attempting more advanced work in his preparation for the university. According to President James Rowland Angell, the plan is not intended to shorten the four-year course, but rather to make it more significant and intellectually vital. The program will involve the interpretation to the school and to the boy of the offerings of the study programs at Yale, both in the freshman year and later.

A pamphlet entitled "Planning a Course of Study" is now being sent to high-school and preparatory-school students who plan to enter Yale. "It is essential to bear in mind that a college course of studies should, if possible, be planned as a comprehensive whole, extending over the normal four-year undergraduate period," the pamphlet points out. "A good college course is not a series of one-year programs. Since college work culminates in the advanced, upperclass work in some field of concentration, it is the latter which gives purpose and unity to the whole college experience."

Special divisions of freshman year courses in English, history, mathematics, chemistry, engineering drawing and Latin will be formed for first-year men who demonstrate the ability and desire to do more intensive work in one or more of these subjects than is done in the regular divisions. Freshmen who, by excellent grades in the entrance examinations, have made clear that they are properly qualified for advanced work in modern languages will be assigned to advanced courses.

A student may enter a sophomore course in a given subject if he has been especially recommended by the head of his preparatory school as having already covered the work of the freshman course in that subject. He may also, if his school rank indicates that he is likely to secure a high academic rank in his class in college, elect one, or in exceptional cases, two sophomore courses in subjects not offered in the freshman year.

THE NATIONAL SURVEY OF SECONDARY EDUCATION GUIDANCE MONOGRAPH

On March 30 the U. S. Office of Education issued Monograph No. 14 of the National Survey of Secondary Education, entitled "Program of Guidance," prepared by Dr. William C. Reavis, of the University of Chicago.

The monograph reports a study of guidance programs of the school systems in Boston, Chicago, Providence, Cincinnati, Milwaukee, four township high schools in Illinois and the independent Milwaukee Vocational School. From these studies, four general types of organization of guidance programs appear to be in operation: (1) Centralized bureaus of guidance for secondary schools in city school systems, such as exist in Boston, Chicago and Cincinnati; (2) central guidance organizations in city school systems, but with the individual secondary school considered the unit in the program, such as are found in Providence and Milwaukee; (3) centralized bureaus or departments in individual secondary schools, as represented by the Milwaukee Vocational School and the Township High School and Junior College, La Salle, Ill.; (4) central guidance organizations in individual secondary schools, which assign the guidance responsibilities to regular officers and teachers, as represented by the Joliet Township High School and Junior High School, the Thornton Township High School and the New Trier Township High School, all located in Illinois.

The investigation discovered that virtually the same guidance activities are undertaken under the different programs. Chief variations are in methods used in the several school systems and individual schools, and some difference in emphasis on certain phases of guidance activity as vocational guidance, educational guidance or psychiatric social guidance.

In large cities, where there is a centralized guidance bureau, the staff is usually inadequate to provide services needed in all the schools. However, development of the central bureau makes possible occupational research and utilization of the findings in vocational guidance and placement scarcely possible under the other types of programs. It is pointed out, on the other hand, in types of this kind, that guidance activities which belong in individual schools are likely to be neglected unless complementary guidance programs are developed by principals of the schools or are projected by the centralized guidance bureau for individual schools.

There are four conditions which, the report points out, make guidance services by the high school necessary: (1) Character of the demands for modern secondary education; (2) changes in the social and economic order to which the secondary school pupil must adjust himself; (3) the needs of the adolescent for counsel and guidance, and (4) the necessity of avoiding waste in the process of education.

The great increase in number of courses offered pupils is an example of an attempt on the part of schools to meet the various needs of students. One study discloses that in a certain group of schools 53 different courses were offered between 1906 and 1911 in all subject fields. A study, by way of comparison, for the year 1921–30, reveals 306 different courses offered in the same schools. Within twenty-five years, the number of different courses increased nearly 500 per cent.

SUMMER TRIP TO CANADA OF PRINCETON SCHOOLS

President Harold Willis Dodds, of Princeton University, has announced a four weeks' trip to Canada as part of the curriculum this summer of the university's school of public and international affairs. The trip will be made in the Pullman car "Princeton," property of the Princeton Summer School of Geology, and the geology school will join forces with the school of public affairs in making the trip.

The purpose of the school of public affairs in making the trip, which will start on August 1, is to study international relations between Canada and the United States and certain problems in the politico-economic field common to the two countries.

The expedition will include about thirty members, all of whom will travel in the car "Princeton," which has accommodations for cooking, dining and study, as well as sleeping. The school of public affairs is offering four scholarships to students of accredited American universities who wish to make the trip, while the geology school will provide two such scholarships. The scholarships are to be awarded to students who are properly grounded in politics, economics and geology and who have good scholastic records.

The expedition will be under the direction of three Princeton faculty members and one member of the faculty of the University of Toronto. The Princeton professors are Richard M. Field and Erling Dorf, assistant professor of geology, and Leslie T. Fournier, assistant professor of economics. Professor H. A. Innes, of the department of economics at the University of Toronto, has been selected by the president of that university to join the party in Canada.

The politico-economic problems to be studied include the St. Lawrence waterway project, money and currency policies, foreign exchange relations, international investments, methods of unemployment relief and taxation, and branch banking. The School of Public and International Affairs was instituted in 1930.

THE CENTENNIAL CELEBRATION OF PENNSYLVANIA SCHOOLS

One hundred years ago Governor George Wolf of Pennsylvania affixed his signature to the common schools law. In recognition of the event the state and its 2,100,000 public school children in more than 12,000 buildings celebrated Pennsylvania education week from April 1 to 7. The observance started officially with special programs sponsored by the Department of Public Instruction in the Education Building in Harrisburg. It will continue in the schools through the spring and fall months and will culminate in a state-wide citizens' education conference on October 10 and 11, which will be called by Dr. James N. Rule, superintendent of public instruction for Pennsylvania.

Public education in Pennsylvania dates back to the arrival of William Penn in 1682. In his "Frame of Government," he gave definite consideration to education as a public function. The provincial council, at his persuasion, enacted legislation "to the end that poor as well as rich may be instructed in good and commendable learning, which is to be preferred before wealth." But this objective of William Penn's was obtained with varying results. This system, by the early 1800's, led to what became known as pauper schools. Parents were forced to declare themselves to be paupers in order that their children might attend school at the expense of the county. Many parents would not voluntarily assume the stigma of "pauper," and consequently a large number of children did not have the opportunity of attending school. It was reported to the legislature in 1831 that of 400,000 children between five and fifteen years of age, more than 250,000 had not been in school.

In 1829, George Wolf of Northampton County, a former Congressman and an ardent supporter of free public schools, who had been a student and teacher in what became known as Wolf Academy, still standing near Bath, Pa., was elected governor. The foundation act for free schools for all was passed in the spring of 1834, but trouble developed when the districts began to put it into operation. The act was complex, and opposition by the people developed rapidly. Finally, at the instigation of Thaddeus Stevens, a revised law was substituted in 1835. The Constitution of 1874 made definite provision for the education of all children. It prohibited state aid to sectarian schools, gave women equal rights under the school laws of the state, changed the title of the chief educational executive and made him exempt from removal by the governor.

Pennsylvania's school system, like those of other states, now finds itself struggling through financial difficulties. More than 500 school districts have asked for a share of a special aid fund of $5,000,000 provided by legislative action to maintain the state minimum instructional program. While no schools have been forced to close their doors without provision for completing the required minimum term, several hundred high-school pupils in rural areas temporarily have been barred through the inability of their home districts to pay non-resident high-school tuition. State aid for the biennium 1933–35 was cut to $53,000,000 from the $58,200,000 estimated necessary for the two-year period, and the entire reduction must be borne by school districts in appropriations for the coming school year.

COMPETITION AMONG COLLEGES FOR NEW STUDENTS

Addressing the Ohio College Association meeting in Columbus, Ohio, on April 5, President W. G. Clippinger, of Otterbein College, expressed the opinion that the depression has forced colleges and universities into highly competitive "unethical and unfair" practises as a means of increasing student enrolment. He termed student solicitations for increasing college enrolments a "racket" and urged the elimination of excessive expenditures for college publicity bureaus.

Dr. Clippinger pointed out that under the high pressure methods of salesmanship now practised by universities and colleges, the student places himself on the open market and sells himself to the highest bidder. "In past years," he asserted, "the practise of compensating students has been restricted for the most part to athletes, but to-day any students, particularly those of high scholastic standards, are approached."

Dr. Clippinger expressed the belief that cooperative college publicity bureaus should function under a set standard, mutually agreed upon by colleges and universities of Ohio. "In many cases," he remarked, "those colleges offering students scholarships do not reveal the amount of the tuition, which in most cases varies appreciably."

"Of 279 colleges investigated, but 27 were found not to have accepted student notes in payment of tuition, and a certain small college, at present, has $141,000 in open accounts and notes owed to it by students. Five church colleges and six private colleges have $80,000 in tuition due them and another investigation showed that 96 church colleges and 43 private schools are owed $10,000 and upwards each by students," Dr. Clippinger stressed. Colleges should, he suggested, be organized under NRA codes.

EDUCATIONAL NOTES AND NEWS

Dr. Walter Scott Athearn, formerly president of Butler University, filed suit in the superior court of Indiana on April 7 for a $100,000 judgment against the university. The suit alleged that his reputation had been damaged by the unfavorable publicity incident to his dismissal in October, 1933.

Dr. W. H. McMaster on April 8 completed twenty-five years of service as the president of Mount Union College. In 1909 there were 108 students enrolled in the college and 16 members of the faculty; to-day there are 568 students and a faculty of 30. During this quarter of a century the endowment has been raised from $115,000 to $1,500,000.

Dr. Walter J. Shepard, dean of the College of Arts and Sciences at the Ohio State University, has been appointed to the educational committee of the National Institution of Public Affairs, which will open next year in Washington, D. C. Dean Shepard is president of the American Political Science Association.

Dr. Frank W. Thomas, president of the California State Teachers College at Fresno, has been elected president of the Western Association of Colleges and Secondary Schools. He succeeds Dr. Ernest C. Moore, of the University of California at Los Angeles. Dr. Merton E. Hill, of the University of California, has been reelected as vice-president and Mr. A. J. Cloud, chief deputy superintendent of schools in San Francisco, as secretary-treasurer.

Professor O. W. Hoop, of the department of political economy at the University of Tulsa, has been elected police commissioner of Tulsa.

Professor William F. Russell, dean of Teachers College, Columbia University, has sailed for France to complete some researches in French economic history and to study several institutions of higher education.

Dr. Buell Gordon Gallagher was inaugurated on April 3 president of Talladega College, Ala., a liberal arts school for Negroes, which was founded in 1867.

Miss Mary Spellman, a teacher of mathematics in Beaver Dam, Wis., for more than fifty years, has recently been elected mayor of the city.

Dr. James E. Hagerty, chairman of the department of sociology at the Ohio State University, has been elected president of the Ohio Sociological Society. Other officers elected include Professor Charles W. Hertzler, professor of sociology at Baldwin-Wallace College, *vice-president;* Mr. S. C. Newman, Oberlin College, *sec-*

retary-treasurer, and Dr. Frederick E. Lumley, the Ohio State University, *editor* of the *Ohio Sociologist.*

Mr. James H. Hamilton has been appointed to the newly created position of director of admissions at Reed College, Portland, Oregon. Mr. Hamilton will also serve as a member of the faculty in the division of philosophy, psychology and education.

Dr. Robert P. Casey, of the University of Cincinnati, has been appointed chairman of the department of Biblical literature at Brown University to succeed Professor Millar Burrows. Professor Burrows has accepted the Winkler professorship of Biblical theology at Yale University.

Georges Dengler, winner of the Prix Redon, the Grand Prize of Rome and other architectural awards, has been appointed professor of design in the department of architecture of the School of Fine Arts of the University of Pennsylvania.

Professor Kenneth S. Morrow, of the College of Agriculture of Rutgers University, has been appointed professor of dairy husbandry in the College of Agriculture of the University of New Hampshire. He will succeed Professor J. M. Fuller.

Mayor La Guardia, of New York City; Dr. Nicholas Murray Butler, president of Columbia University; Bishop William T. Manning, and John Erskine will speak on May 17 at a dinner celebrating the 225th anniversary of the founding of Trinity School of New York City.

The Haverford College board of managers has announced the appointment of Dr. Frank Whitson Fetter, of Princeton University, as associate professor of economics, and Dr. Cletus O. Oakley, of Brown University, as assistant professor of mathematics. They will succeed Professor D. C. Barrett and Professor L. W. Reid, respectively.

The vice-chancellor of the University of Oxford and the Rhodes Trustees have elected Sir Muhammad Ikbal to be the Rhodes Memorial Lecturer for the year 1935.

Dr. Herbert Wright, professor of international law at the Catholic University of America, has been elected president of the Catholic Association for International Peace.

Dr. and Mrs. Edward B. Haskell, founders and directors of the school for peasant youth which the Near East Foundation has conducted at Pordim, Bulgaria, since 1931, will return to the United States some time in April. Responsibility for the school has recently been assumed by the Bulgarian Government. Dr. Barclay Acheson, executive secretary of the foundation, in announcing the change of administration, stated that the foundation would continue its extension demonstrations in rural Bulgaria, but that the government would also assume direction of health and home-making instruction.

Dean Franklin C. Paschal, of Vanderbilt University, has been elected president of the Tennessee College Association; President James L. Robb, of Tennessee Wesleyan College, vice-president; Professor C. Hodge Mathes, of Eastern Tennessee State Teachers College, secretary and treasurer, and Acting President James D. Hoskins, of the University of Tennessee, and President Ernest L. Stockton, of Cumberland University, members of the executive committee.

Thomas H. Kenworthy, of Springfield, Mass., was elected president of the Massachusetts Elementary Principals' Association at a meeting held at the Massachusetts State College on April 6. Mr. Kenworthy succeeds Miss Effie G. Higgins, principal of the Whittemore School at Waltham.

Lord Leverhulme has been elected president of Epsom College, the London *Times* reports, to succeed the late Lord Burnham.

Professor H. Augustine Smith, head of the department of fine arts in religion at Boston University, has been chosen to head the newly formed department of sacred music at the university.

Wilson Parkhill, assistant head master at the Lawrence Smith School, New York City, has been appointed head master of the Collegiate School. Mr. Parkhill succeeds Cornelius Brett Boocock.

Laurence G. Leavitt has been appointed head master of the Vermont Academy at Bellows Falls, Vt. He has been serving as assistant head master and director of the summer school at Tabor Academy, Marion, Mass. Mr. Leavitt succeeds Dr. John B. Cook, who has recently resigned after 13 years as head master.

Dr. Arthur H. Compton, professor of physics at the University of Chicago and winner of the Nobel Prize for physics in 1927, has been appointed to the George Eastman visiting professorship at Oxford University for the academic year 1934–35.

Dr. Gilbert G. Benjamin, professor of history at the University of Southern California, has been elected a fellow of the Royal Historical Society of Great Britain. Dr. Benjamin, proposed for the fellowship by Sir Charles Grant Robertson, vice-chancellor of the University of Birmingham, has been honored for his research work in English economic history.

Dr. Nicholas Murray Butler, president of Columbia University, and Dr. William Lyon Phelps, formerly Lampson professor of English literature at Yale University, have been named honorary members of the Friends of the Princeton Library Society. Dr. Butler and Professor Phelps are the first to whom this honor has been awarded.

A bust of Dr. John Henry House, founder of the American Farm School in Salonica, Greece, has been presented to the school by Agop M. Agopoff, Armenian-American sculptor, who for three years won the grand prize of the National Academy of Design in New York City. The bust was presented without unveiling because of the Greek custom which forbids a ceremony when the statute's subject is still living.

Dr. William E. Gibbs, formerly professor of physics at the Carnegie Institute of Technology, died on April 3, in his seventy-fourth year.

Harold Murdock, director of the Harvard University Press since 1920, died on April 5. Mr. Murdock was seventy-two years old.

Dr. Joseph C. Myer, dean of the School of Commerce at St. John's University, Brooklyn, died on April 5 at the age of forty-one years.

Dr. Charles Wesley Rolfe, professor emeritus of geology at the University of Illinois since 1917, died on April 5 in his eighty-fourth year.

Sister Mary Angelita, head of the English department of Mundelein College in Chicago, died on April 3, at the age of fifty-six years.

Mr. John E. Morgan, superintendent of the public schools of Wyoming County, Pennsylvania, died on April 6. Mr. Morgan was fifty years old.

Gifts to Columbia University aggregating \$14,417.68 were announced on April 5 by Dr. Frank D. Fackenthal, secretary of the university. The largest amount, \$8,000, was contributed by the General Education Board for the subdepartment of tropical medicine at the College of Physicians and Surgeons.

A group of secondary school educators will meet at Asheville, N. C., from April 16 to April 22, to discuss purposes and functions of secondary education. The group is under the chairmanship of Dr. Thomas H. Briggs, Teachers College, Columbia University, and is being financially supported by the Department of Secondary School Principals of the National Education Association and the Carnegie Corporation for a period of three years.

The latest figures available at the headquarters of the Federal Emergency Relief Administration in Washington show that 52,327 students in 948 colleges are enrolled in part-time work. The Ohio State University, with 930 students, and New York University, with 1,329, are among those institutions with the largest group of students receiving federal aid.

For the first time in five years, the number of women students elected to membership in Phi Beta Kappa at Denison University was less than the number of men.

A study of school conditions in Maine has been begun by the technical staff of the Maine School Commission. This commission, appointed by Governor Louis J. Brann in October, 1933, is headed by Dr. Kenneth C. M. Sills, president of Bowdoin College. The members include Dr. Paul R. Mort, professor of education at Teachers College, Columbia University, who is director of the survey; Eugene S. Lawler, of Teachers College; Harley L. Lutz, professor of economics and taxation at Princeton University, and Clyde R. Miller, director of educational service at Teachers College. The scope of the survey includes all expenditures of funds within the jurisdiction of the department of education, and particularly relates to a study of more equitable sources of revenue for the state school fund, a study of equalization of valuations, and the distribution of all funds on an equalized and mathematical basis.

THE first talking book, a combination electric phonograph and radio set, will be released by the Library of Congress in April, according to a recent announcement made by Robert B. Irwin, executive director of the American Foundation for the Blind. The device, developed in a research sound laboratory by sound engineers and other technicians, is equipped with various controls which allow for variation in speed of reading and in tone and volume. The Electrical Research Products, Inc., the Bell Telephone Company, R. C. A. Victor Company and L. F. Dyer have cooperated in producing the machine. Through arrangements with the Library of Congress, talking book libraries will be established throughout the country, and the records will be loaned free of charge to the blind. The Foundation plans to launch a campaign for $150,000 in order to purchase five thousand of the machines.

SUPERVISORS and teacher trainers in vocational agriculture from thirteen states met in New York City on March 29 for the sixteenth annual North Atlantic Region Conference on Vocational Education in Agriculture. Dr. F. W. Lathrop, specialist in agricultural education of the U. S. Office of Education, led a discussion relating to the technical phases of vocational programs in cooperation with the AAA and the Farm Credit Administration.

A GROUP of Ohio State University students, continuing their campaign against military training, has sought assistance from Congressmen in a visit to Washington. They are being supported in their efforts by the National Council for the Prevention of War. The council has issued a statement to the effect that polls held among students throughout the country have demonstrated them to be opposed to war. The latest poll, they report, was held late in March at Harvard, which demonstrated 229 Harvard students unwilling to take up arms, 515 willing to fight only in case of invasion, and 326 ready to enlist in response to any call of the government. A national poll held last year under the sponsorship of the National Student Federation and the *Brown Daily Herald* showed 8,415 students rating themselves as pacifists out of a total of 21,725 voting. Those who would fight in case of invasion numbered 7,221. Those ready to answer any call to war totaled 6,089.

THE second annual exposition of the University of Detroit will be held on May 3, 4 and 5. Every phase of university life and activity will be on display. Scientific experiments and demonstrations will be conducted in all laboratories. Lectures in the fields of chemistry, physics, biology, philosophy, literature, history, liberal arts, economics, commerce and finance will be delivered each day.

TWENTY-EIGHT of the 72 fraternities on the campus of the University of Illinois have adopted the tutorial adviser system. A faculty member or graduate student, acting as preceptor, lives in each of these fraternity houses. C. H. Frederick, assistant dean of men, reports that a majority of the fraternities which have adopted this system since its inception a year ago have raised their scholastic rank.

AMONG the speakers at the Fifth Annual Institute of Education by Radio, which will be held in Columbus, Ohio, from April 30 to May 2, under the sponsorship of the Ohio State University, will be: H. V. Kaltenborn, of the Columbia Broadcasting System; E. A. Corbett, director of extension at the University of Alberta; Judith C. Waller, of the National Broadcasting Company; C. H. Milam, secretary of the American Library Association; Eugene J. Coltrane, of the National Committee on Education by Radio; Joseph F. Wright, president of the Association of College and University Broadcasting Stations; Frederic A. Willis, educational director of the Columbia Broadcasting System; H. M. Buckley, assistant superintendent of schools of Cleveland; Luther Meyer, radio editor of the *San Francisco Call Bulletin;* Philip G. Loucks, managing director of the National Association of Broadcasters; E. B. Kurtz, head of the electrical engineering department and director of television, State University of Iowa; Morse Salisbury, chief of radio service, U. S. Department of Agriculture; Levering Tyson, director of the National Advisory Council on Radio in Education. The meetings will convene in Pomerene Hall at the Ohio State University, at 9:30 A. M., on April 30, and will be under the general direction of Dr. W. W. Charters, director of the Bureau of Educational Research, Ohio State University.

A FOUR-DAY program of pre-college guidance, designed to give high-school juniors and seniors a foretaste of college activity, has been arranged by the New Jersey College for Women. The program will be presented from April 26 to 29. The high-school girls will live in student dormitories and will attend lectures and small conference groups. They will be addressed by Dr. Ada L. Comstock, president of Radcliffe College, and Dr. Robert C. Clothier, president of Rutgers University.

DISCUSSION

SOCIAL CHANGE IN 1933 AND CHARACTER EDUCATION

"IN my judgment it's a racket." The speaker was a man who has had twenty years of vital contact with adolescents. The words were applied to the program of citizenship education in a large and supposedly progressive junior high school. "Instruction in citizenship, student traffic patrols, student activities galore, student control and self-government, it sounds fine. But there is an excessive and oppressive amount of talk about school citizenship. And student control and self-government are mere words applied to a system which at heart is as inflexible and autocratic as that of the Prussian schools of a hundred years ago. A considerable number of children merely smile to themselves, a few thrive on it, the great majority are restless, jumpy and unhappy without knowing why. School citizenship has become an elaborate rigamarole designed to relieve the principal of disciplinary problems."

Another program, labeled character education and sponsored by a national organization, urges in its literature that adoption of its suggestions will promote a "more orderly and quiet class room." If adopted for this reason, it also is a racket.

These incidents, which could easily be multiplied, raise insistent questions. Why public schools? Why better education? Why the emphasis on social adjustment, on good citizenship, on the development of character? Few teachers ponder these questions, but the guess may be ventured that the answers to them are gradually dawning on those who have had a 10 per cent. cut in salary, and another 10 per cent. cut, and who are now in the process of taking still another cut due to the rising cost of living. The facts of the matter are that the peoples of the world have done and are doing an extraordinarily poor job of living together: a world war; impossible peace treaties; sixteen years of intolerable misery in half of Europe; four years of world-wide distress; and threatened monetary inflation in America, which, if it gets out of control (and all such experiments have gotten out of control in the past), will give us a boom beside which 1928–29 will be child's play and in the end a headache beside which 1931–32 will be comparative comfort.

Behind all this, and closer to home, are the multitude of individual problems of adjustment to the requirements of the immediate face-to-face world; getting along with the boss; cutting expenses to meet income; and living worthily and gracefully with one's family, neighbors, friends and community.

The main business of the schools is the promotion of the art of living together well. We must master this art, not only on the level of immediate face-to-face personal relations, but on the level of larger and larger groups. Among the many features of the modern world which make the mastery of this art difficult to the point almost of despair none is perhaps more important than social change. And no year affords a more impressive and ominous indication of its extent, rapidity and significance than 1933.

On January 23 the thirty-sixth state ratified the twentieth amendment, providing for the convening of Congress on January 3 and the inauguration of the President and Vice-president on January 20.

On January 30 Adolph Hitler became Chancellor of Germany. Late in March Secretary Hull was officially informed that all anti-Semitic activities had ceased on March 26, but on April 1 an even more violent campaign of persecution was initiated. On October 15 Germany withdrew from the League of Nations.

On February 4 the governor of Louisiana decreed the first state-wide bank holiday. Within a month every bank in the United States was closed.

On February 16 and 20 the Senate and House voted to submit repeal of the Eighteenth Amendment to the people. March 22 saw legalization of 3.2 beer. On April 3 the first state ratified repeal of the Eighteenth Amendment. On December 6 the thirty-sixth state ratified repeal. The proportion in favor of repeal in forty-one states for which the votes of the people are available was 75 per cent. The first *Literary Digest* poll completed in 1922 showed only 20 per cent. in favor of repeal. How soon will we have another violent shift of public opinion? Where will it fall?

On March 2 the *New York Times'* average of fifty common stocks fell to $46.85, by July 18 the average touched $98.05. The advance mounted to 109 per cent. in about four and a half months. A comparable advance from the bottom of 1921 required about four and a half years. The volume of transactions on the New York Stock Exchange during May, June and July totaled 350 million shares, the largest three-month total in history, not excepting even the frenzied trading of 1928–29. The speculative fever still runs riot in our blood.

On March 10 President Roosevelt sent to Congress his $500,000,000 Economy Bill, slashing the pensions of veterans and the salaries of government employees. Referring to the deficit of five billion dollars which had accumulated over the three preceding years, he said: "It has contributed to the recent collapse of our banking structure. It has accentuated the stagnation of the economic life of our people. It has added to the ranks of the unemployed." Eleven months later the President estimated the deficit for the first fiscal year of his administration at over seven billion dollars.

On March 27 Japan withdrew from the League of Nations. Her withdrawal followed eighteen months of undeclared war in China and Manchuria.

For March the *Annalist* monthly index of business activity stood at 58.5 per cent. of normal, for July at 89.5, for November at 68.5, up 31.0 points in four months, down 21.0 points in four months. A comparable advance from the low point of the depression of 1921 required twenty-six months, a comparable decline from the peak of 1929 required seventeen months. Virtually a complete business cycle normally requiring from three to ten years was compressed within eight months. Thus, the first serious efforts at national economic planning, one of whose functions is the elimination of violent business cycles, was responsible for the most violent fluctuations in history.

On April 19 President Roosevelt placed an embargo on gold exports. On May 7 the government repudiated its contracts by refusing to pay interest due in gold as provided in its bonds. On May 12 President Roosevelt signed the Farm Mortgage Bill, containing the Thomas inflation amendment. On October 21 President Roosevelt announced the gold purchasing plan of the government. On December 15 the House of Lords ruled that a Belgian company must pay its obligations in gold, as provided in its bonds. Will our own Supreme Court follow suit? What then?

From April 22 to 30 President Roosevelt conferred with representatives of many foreign countries for the purpose of laying a solid foundation for the world Economic Conference at London. On July 3 the world Economic Conference was shipwrecked, and President Roosevelt set his course toward extreme national self-sufficiency. On December 28 the President paid tribute to the internationalism of Woodrow Wilson and announced a new policy of cooperation with South America.

On June 11 the Census Bureau announced that the birth rate for 1932 had fallen sharply to a new low. About 600,000 fewer children were born than in 1921. On the basis of the downward trend of birth rates Whelpton estimated in 1928 that the maximum population of the United States would be about 175 million, to be attained in 1980. But the birth rate fell faster than Whelpton predicted and in 1930 Dublin estimated the maximum population of the United States at 150 million, to be attained in 1970. But the birth rate fell faster than Dublin predicted, and in 1933 Baker estimated the maximum population at 136 million, to be attained in 1950. In 1932 Raymond Pearl had reported that of a group of 2,000 mothers questioned in obstetrical wards by their physicians 35.8 per cent. admitted attempts to prevent conception.

On July 20 President Roosevelt issued a blanket-code to raise wages and shorten hours, while the codes of the NRA were being formulated. The ensuing weeks saw two changes which in normal times would have been characterized as revolutions: Recognition of the right of labor to organize and to bargain collectively, scrapping of the Anti-Trust laws which prohibited trade associations and price fixing.

On August 16 Mr. Morgenthau announced that cotton farmers would be paid a bonus of $110,000,000 to plow under one third of their acreage; nevertheless the total crop was actually larger than in 1932. On August 29 Secretary Wallace announced that wheat farmers would be paid a bonus of $120,000,000 to cut their acreage for the crop year 1933–34 by 15 per cent.; nevertheless, the actual plantings for the country as a whole are estimated to have been cut only 7 per cent. With normal growing conditions the 1934 harvest will be larger than that of 1933. As certainly as the sun rises these farmers and dozens of other groups will want another and another bonus. Thus, we have reenacted a familiar American drama, only in the "good old days" it was our "infant" industries which were clamoring for a higher and higher tariff.

On September 13 the Buy Now Campaign was launched. A quarter of a million people paraded up Broadway, while a million and a half watched the spectacle. Similar parades in other cities officially celebrated the burial of thrift as a virtue. The most cynically pregnant, but insufficiently publicized, wisecrack of 1933 was, "Don't save any money you can't afford to lose."

On October 13 Mr. Hayward, of Dillon, Reed and Company, admitted under cross-questioning that his firm had supported the market for Brazilian bonds while these bonds were being syndicated to the public. On November 23 Secretary Morgenthau announced that government agencies would support the market for government bonds.

On November 16 President Roosevelt announced that diplomatic relations with Russia would be resumed.

On November 26 Governor Rolph said, "If any one is arrested for this job, I'll pardon them all." The number of lynchings in 1933 totaled twenty-eight, as compared with only eight in 1932.

The December issue of *School Life,* official publication of the Office of Education, estimated that "an unskilled factory worker laboring for a year at the *minimum* blanket code rate would receive $728," and predicted that "one out of every three teachers will this year receive for expert services less than $750."

Here, rather than in the measly objective of easing disciplinary problems or of insuring a quiet classroom, are a few examples of the kind of social problems which should provide the motives for better schools, for better education and for the emphasis on social adjustment, on good citizenship and on the development of character.

Frank K. Shuttleworth
Yale University

LEARNING

"Learning is orientation, a single process; it is not several processes put together. . . . Learning is discovery, always discovery. It is not achieved by mechanical methods of exercise and drill."[1]

Yet many of us will testify that we have had to "learn" many of our attitudes and purposeful lines of conduct by slow and laborious processes of thought not at all akin to the dazzling glow of illumination implied in the definition given above. In fact, swift thinking, or what is felt by the person who performs it to be "swift thinking," is under suspicion by psychiatrists. It may be profitable to examine some types of mental performance.

Dr. William A. White, in his "Outlines of Psychiatry," gives a diagram of the "flight" of

[1] Raymond Holder Wheeler, "The Crisis in Education," School and Society, 38: 989, 759, December 9, 1933.

thought of a person in a state of nervous degeneration. It is like this:

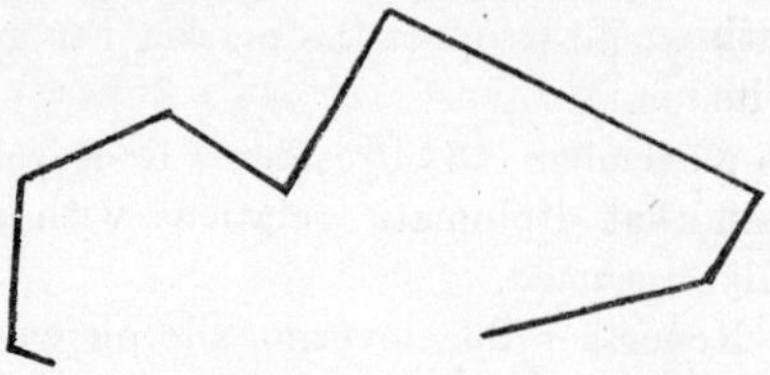

Each straight line represents a sentence, but the whole of a series of remarks has no continuity at all, the connections being entirely superficial ones of the sound of some word or part of a word. The ideas begin nowhere, travel anywhere and reach no point desired or foreseen. This is typical of the thinking of all defectives. Elsewhere in the same volume he says that many of these poor patients will tell you how swift and illuminating are their thoughts. In fact, one of the symptoms of derangement is the assertion of wonderful powers of speed in ideas.

The lowest type of normal thinking might be diagrammed from a speech of Mistress Quickly, which Genung quotes in his rhetoric as an illustration of faulty narrative:

Here a simple story does get told after many backward turns and deflections. But the flow of mere event is interrupted, corrected and revised till the auditor begins to fear that it will never be finished. The separate steps are only stages in a story, but the teller with difficulty assembles them in order and carries them through to the end.

But what a different kind of thinking is required for any of the problems of life, material, mental or spiritual, designing a bridge, or rendering a Supreme Court decision, or making a moral judgment. This noblest and most necessary kind of thinking we might diagram very inadequately as follows:

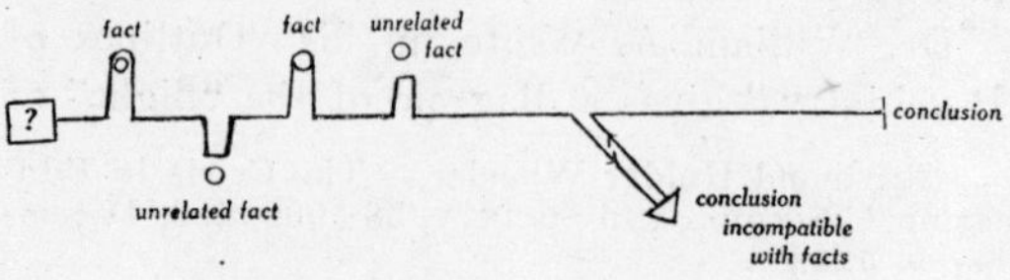

It starts from a definite point, gathers definite related facts, rejecting the ones that are inapposite, travels along a straight line, pursuing every possibility that offers until it is found out of harmony with some of the fundamental conditions of the problem, then it returns to the main line of thought to take up the alternative possibility. In such fashion this thinking process continues laboriously until a satisfactory conclusion is reached. Any problem requires for its solution just these painstaking efforts, a problem in analysis just as much as one in synthesis, a doctor's diagnosis of the patient's symptoms, an astronomer's attempts to solve a mystery of the stars, an engineer's plan for a tunnel, a teacher's presentation of a new and difficult subject to his class.

The laborious quality of this thinking is attested by many of those to whom the world has accorded the palm as its most brilliant thinkers. "Though the dull brain perplexes and retards!" Keats cries in the "Ode to a Nightingale." Shelley stood all one day at the end of a mantelpiece, pencil poised in hand, searching his mind for exactly the right word for his verse of the moment. Vergil spent ten years writing the Aeneid, some nine thousand lines of poetry, hardly averaging three lines a day. When Archimedes shouted, "Eureka! Eureka!", it was because he had striven so long to think of a way to find out how much silver and how much gold the king's crown contained.

Where in our curriculum do we make provision for preparation for this kind of thinking? Yet it is a life need that begins in simple forms even in early adolescence. In fact, the spiritual privacy, which we think it only fair to accord to the maturing boy and girl, compels the adolescent to face some practical questions and struggle silently for their answer. "Why do some of the girls not want to dance with a fellow?", "How does a boy find out what kind of a job he wants?", "How does a girl make the other girls like her?"

Yet if a human being is to live purposefully, consciously, with self-approbation, this is just the kind of "learning" he needs most urgently.

Mildred Dean

Roosevelt High School
Washington, D. C.

SPECIAL CORRESPONDENCE

CONCERNING A DIFFERENCE OF OPINION

To the Editors of School and Society:

I have read the letter in School and Society for March 31, by Mr. C. G. Leland, superintendent of libraries of the Board of Education of New York City. Is a difference of opinion concerning educational methods necessarily "unwarranted and unprofessional?" These are Mr. Leland's terms applied to the article in the *Library Journal,* which he incorrectly attributes to me. It seems to me that this is a case that calls for light and not for heat.

By way of correction, let it be said that the article in the *Library Journal* of January 1 was not written by me but by two members of my staff of high standing in the library profession, Miss Charlotte H. Clark, supervisor of work with schools, and Miss Louise P. Latimer, director of work with children. It was based on 25 years of experience in the administration of the plan for giving library service, apparently with acceptability to all concerned, to the elementary schools and more recently to the junior high schools of Washington.

So many school and library people had studied our library service to schools on the spot and had urged that it be described in print that at my suggestion Miss Clark and Miss Latimer wrote the article. I approved it before its publication, and later through the columns of School and Society commended it to the attention of school people who may not habitually read the *Library Journal.* I still suggest a calm, dispassionate reading of the original article and also of the reply to its critics by Misses Clark and Latimer in the *Library Journal* for April 1, in which they point out some of the apparent misapprehensions of the readers of the original article.

It is not essential to take up the points made by Mr. Leland, since they have all been covered in the original article. One who has been in library work as long as he should, from such professional associations, have gained sufficient knowledge of the fact that there are usually two sides of every question to suggest a tolerant attitude toward those who may hold divergent opinions. It is hardly necessary to be so distressed when a colleague gives expression to beliefs not exactly coinciding with one's own.

George F. Bowerman,
Librarian

The Public Library,
Washington, D. C.
April 7, 1934

SOCIETIES AND MEETINGS

PRESIDENT ROOSEVELT'S STATEMENT TO THE CITIZENS' CONFERENCE ON THE CRISIS IN EDUCATION

President Franklin D. Roosevelt addressed the following communication to the organizers of the Citizens' Conference on the Crisis in Education which was held in Columbus, Ohio, on April 5 and 6:

To the Sponsors of the Citizens' Conference:

May I congratulate the organizers of the Citizens' Conference on the Crisis in Education for calling together leaders in American thought to consider ways and means of solving some of the critical problems that confront the schools of the Nation.

That our educational institutions have suffered much within the past few years is evident. Because of a lack of funds thousands of schools have closed early this year and many have eliminated highly essential services.

Although the effects of the present lack of adequate educational opportunities on our National life may not be noticeable to-day, the time may soon come when direful effects will be apparent. It is, therefore, the responsibility of every American to see that the great strides that we have made in education since Colonial times shall not be lost; it is also his responsibility to see that the schools march forward, that the scope of education become such as to provide educational opportunities for every person from early childhood on into adult life. One group that we need to consider especially are the many youths who are not in school and who are apparently drifting.

I realize the seriousness of the problems that will be discussed at your Conference, but I am confident that after careful deliberation you will be able to formulate a plan of action. My great regret is that I find it impossible to participate in your deliberations upon so important a subject.

I send you my heartiest wishes for a fruitful and epoch-making Conference.

Very sincerely yours,
(signed) FRANKLIN D. ROOSEVELT

A fortnight before the conference convened the following resolutions were addressed to outstanding citizens over the country, and 88 industrial, religious, civic and political leaders endorsed them. The names are listed at the end of the resolutions.

At the concluding meeting of the conference Judge Howard L. Bevis, of the Ohio Supreme Court, presented the resolutions to the 4,000 people assembled in Memorial Hall, and they were unanimously adopted by the conference.

We, the undersigned citizens, observing the serious plight into which our schools have been forced because of the economic situation of the past four years, and sharing the conviction that the schools must be preserved as our basic democratic institution, submit the following resolutions in connection with the Citizens' Conference on the Crisis in Education being held at Columbus, Ohio, April 5 and 6, 1934:

1. We call the attention of the people of the United States to these disquieting facts about our schools and their enforced curtailments of educational services:
   a. 3,500,000 children of school age were on April 1 deprived of all schooling: 110,000 of these children had their educational opportunities taken away from them when 2,000 rural schools failed to open in the fall of 1933. 140,000 were affected at the end of December by the closing of 2,600 schools; and a million more were, on April 1, forced to relinquish their educational opportunities by the closing of 20,000 additional schools. These groups in addition to the more than two million who have no educational opportunities even in normal times brings the total to three and a half million children who are to-day unable to share their traditional right to free education.
   b. Even though the schools of the nation are responsible for 1,300,000 more pupils than in 1929–30, they are this year receiving approximately $563,000,000 less for the education of their charges.
   c. There are at the present time in the neighborhood of 3,000,000 young people between the ages of eighteen and twenty who are out of work and out of school and who are subjected to the influences that turn many of them to criminal tendencies. The United States Department of Justice has found that the majority of the 240,071 criminals whose finger prints were recorded last year were in the neighborhood of nineteen years of age.
   d. It costs in the neighborhood of a billion and a half dollars each year for the people of the United States to incarcerate its 500,000 criminals, while it costs but two million more to educate its 26,000,000 school children.
2. We commend to the consideration of the citizenry of the country the stability, the saneness, the optimism, the patriotism of the American school teacher during these times of stress. Even though a third of the teachers of the nation have been reduced to salaries of less than the $728 a year "blanket code" minimum established by the NRA for unskilled laborers, and even though 40,000 of them are now owed more than forty million dollars in back pay and thousands of others are being paid in warrants cashable at high discounts, the teachers and school administrators of all the states of the union have devotedly continued to serve the rising generation.
3. We urge that every citizen interested in the future of our children and in the destiny of our nation assume personal responsibility to keep in constant contact with the educational situation in his community and with the officers charged with keeping the schools open and effective. In this crisis we must depend upon an aroused public opinion to ensure to the children of the country educational advantages as adequate as those made available in past years to present-day adults. We

must not for a moment forget that education is the bulwark of our democratic society and our surest guarantee for the future.

W. W. Atterbury, president, The Pennsylvania Railroad Company
D. J. Brumley, chief engineer, Illinois Central System
Paul Shoup, vice-chairman, Southern Pacific Company
F. A. Seiberling, president, Seiberling Rubber Company, Akron, Ohio
S. S. Kresge, chairman of board, S. S. Kresge, Inc.
Harold H. Swift, Union Stock Yards, Chicago
James P. Warburg, New York banker
Edward A. Filene, president, Wm. Filene's Sons Company, Boston
F. A. Vanderlip, former president, National City Bank of New York
M. H. Aylesworth, president, National Broadcasting Company
Marcus Aaron, manufacturer, Pittsburgh, Pa.
Mrs. Franklin D. Roosevelt
Mrs. Dorothy Canfield Fisher
Glenn Frank, president, University of Wisconsin
Paul Block, president and publisher, *Pittsburgh Post-Gazette, Toledo Blade, Milwaukee Sentinel*, and other papers
James M. Cox, former governor of Ohio and now owner of Ohio News League
Frank E. Gannett, president, The Gannett Newspapers
George E. Vincent, formerly president, Rockefeller Foundation
Oswald Garrison Villard, former editorial writer and president of the *New York Evening Post*. Now, editor, *The Nation*
Will Durant, author
Harry Elmer Barnes, editorial writer, Scripps-Howard Newspapers
Lewis Mumford, contributing editor, *The New Republic*
Archibald MacLeish, editorial writer, *Fortune*
Walter Damrosch, musical counsel, National Broadcasting Company
Theodore Dreiser, author
John Erskine, author
Sinclair Lewis, author
Edgar Lee Masters, author
Elmer Rice, playright
Reverend Charles E. Coughlin, Detroit
Dr. Harry Emerson Fosdick, Riverside Church, New York
Rabbi Stephen S. Wise, Free Synagogue, New York
Bishop William T. Manning, New York
Rabbi Abba Hillel Silver, The Temple, Cleveland, Ohio
Right Reverend Ernest M. Stires, Protestant Episcopal bishop of Long Island
Right Reverend Walter Taylor Sumner, bishop of Oregon
Reverend Hoyt M. Dobbs, bishop of the Methodist Episcopal Church, Shreveport, La.
Reverend John Haynes Holmes, The Community Church, New York, N. Y.
Reverend Edward Thomas Demby, suffragan bishop, Episcopal Church of the Southwest, Little Rock, Ark.
William Green, president, American Federation of Labor
E. A. Hayes, national commander, The American Legion
Dr. Morris Fishbein, editor, *Hygeia;* president, American Medical Association
Norman Thomas, League for Industrial Democracy
Edwin R. Embree, president, Julius Rosenwald Fund
Lewis E. Lawes, warden, Sing Sing Prison
Sherwood Eddy, secretary for Asia, Y. M. C. A.
Charles Moore, chairman, Commission of Fine Arts
L. J. Taber, master of the National Grange
Margaret Sanger, National Committee on Federal Legislation for Birth Control, New York, N. Y.
Judge Walter C. Lindley, U. S. District Court, Danville, Ill.
Dr. George F. Zook, U. S. commissioner of education
Newton D. Baker, ex-secretary of war
Dr. Frank P. Graves, commissioner of education, New York
Charles D. Hilles, ex-president, Republican National Committee
Hiram Bingham, president, National Aeronautic Association
Mrs. Ruth Pratt, member, Republican National Committee
Homer Stille Cummings, Attorney-General of the United States
George Wharton Pepper, former U. S. senator from Pennsylvania; member, Republican National Committee
Hugh S. Johnson, NRA administrator
H. A. Wallace, Secretary of Agriculture
Louise Stanley, Bureau of Home Economics, U. S. Dept. of Agriculture
Arthur Capper, senator from Kansas
Elbert D. Thomas, senator from Utah

Royal S. Copeland, senator from New York
Morris Sheppard, senator from Texas
James N. Rule, superintendent of public instruction of Pennsylvania
David S. Ingalls, director of public health and welfare, Cleveland, Ohio
John W. Bricker, attorney-general of Ohio
John H. Stahl, Jr., auditor-general of Michigan
Theodore S. Fry, treasurer of Michigan
Paul F. Voelker, superintendent of public instruction of Michigan
B. B. Moeur, governor of Arizona
Edwin C. Johnson, governor of Colorado
Wilbur L. Cross, governor of Connecticut
Henry Horner, governor of Illinois
Paul V. McNutt, governor of Indiana
Clyde L. Herring, governor of Iowa
Alf M. Landon, governor of Kansas
William A. Comstock, governor of Michigan
Floyd B. Olson, governor of Minnesota
William Langer, governor of North Dakota
George White, governor of Ohio
Julius L. Meier, governor of Oregon
Hill McAlister, governor of Tennessee
George C. Peery, governor of Virginia
Clarence D. Martin, governor of Washington
Leslie A. Miller, governor of Wyoming
Alfred E. Smith, former governor of New York

REPORTS

THE REPORT OF THE COMMITTEE ON GRADUATE INSTRUCTION

THE special Committee on Graduate Instruction of the American Council on Education presents its first report in the April issue of the *Educational Record.* The committee, under the chairmanship of Dr. Raymond M. Hughes, president of the Iowa State College, has conducted an inquiry to determine what universities are adequately staffed and equipped for work leading to the degree of doctor of philosophy or doctor of science in thirty-five of the more important fields of knowledge. The method used in the inquiry was to submit the question to vote by a separate jury for each field, selected from well-known scholars in that field. The panel from which the jury was selected was provided in each case by the secretary of the national learned society interested in the field in question.

The attempt was made to secure a jury of one hundred in each field, but the votes actually obtained in the various fields ranged from 21 to 102. A majority vote of the jury was required to place the name of an institution on the qualified list. Institutions whose work in the field was considered most distinguished by the jury were designated in the list by a star. The names of the various juries are given in detail in the report.

According to the report there are in the United States the following number of institutions qualified for graduate work:

Subject	Total	Distinguished
Aeronautical engineering	3	2
Anthropology	7	5
Animal nutrition	8	3
Astronomy	9	5
Bacteriology	17	9
Botany	30	8
Chemical engineering	9	3
Chemistry	37	16
Civil engineering	15	3
Classics	23	9
Economics	22	11
Education	30	10
Electrical engineering	13	3
English	27	8
Entomology	14	5
Fine arts	6	3
Genetics	17	6
Geography	9	4
Geology	21	12
German	22	7
History	26	8
Human nutrition	14	5
Mathematics	26	7
Mechanical engineering	11	3
Mining engineering	14	3
Philosophy	24	7
Physics	25	12
Plant pathology	19	4
Plant physiology	21	6
Political science	24	8
Psychology	31	11
Romance languages	22	7
Sociology	24	5
Soil science	10	4
Zoology	31	11

The 28 American universities which are members of the Association of American Universities all qualify in one or more fields, and in addition the following 35 institutions appear in the various lists: American University, Boston University, Bryn Mawr College, the California Institute of Technology, the Carnegie Institute of Technology, the Colorado School of Mines, Duke University, George Peabody College for Teachers, Iowa State College, Kansas State College, the Massachusetts Institute of Technology, Massachusetts State College, Michigan State College, New York University, Ohio Wesleyan University, Pennsylvania State College, Purdue University, Rensselaer Polytechnic Institute, Rice Institute, Rutgers University, the State College of Washington, Syracuse University, the University of Arizona, the University of Cincinnati, the University of Colorado, the University of Maryland, the University of Notre Dame, the University of Oklahoma, the University of Oregon, the University of Pittsburgh, the University of Rochester, the University of Southern California, the University of Washington, Western Reserve University and West Virginia University.

The committee consisted, in addition to Chairman Hughes, of Iowa State College, of the following members: Karl T. Compton, president of the Massachusetts Institute of Technology; Virginia Gildersleeve, dean of Barnard College; Frank B. Jewett, vice-president of the American Telephone and Telegraph Company; George Johnson, secretary of the National Catholic Education Association; Charles B. Lipman, dean of the Graduate School, University of California; Albert D. Mead, vice-president of Brown University; John C. Merriam, president of the Carnegie Institution of Washington; W. W. Pierson, Jr., dean of the Graduate School, University of North Carolina; Hyder E. Rollins, professor of English at Harvard University; Beardsley Ruml, dean of the department of social sciences at the University of Chicago; Henry Suzzallo, president of the Carnegie Foundation; E. H. Wilkins, president of Oberlin College.

EDUCATIONAL RESEARCH AND STATISTICS

UNIVERSITY AND COLLEGE ENROLMENTS, 1931 AND 1933

DR. RAYMOND WALTERS' enrolment data in SCHOOL AND SOCIETY have been further analyzed for our use at the University of Oregon, and some comparisons are here presented because of their general interest. We have utilized his reports for 1931 and 1933[1] and have determined several two-year trends in United States higher education. Also we have obtained comparative indices of business conditions throughout the nation, as shown by 1931 and 1933 average bank debits—"the volume of business . . . as it is reflected in the turnover of bank deposits."[2] During the two-year period this business activity index has dropped 31.3 per cent. This is a much larger decrease than is shown by college enrolments during the same time. Enrolment data for both years are available for 422 institutions above the junior college level; their total enrolment has fallen from 580,679 in 1931 to 533,062 in 1933, or 8.2 per cent. Whatever may be the factors affecting bank deposits and college enrolments, we proceed to analyze the schools which have lost these 45,000 students in the last two years.

One possible comparison is by type of in-

TABLE I
INSTITUTIONAL TYPE SUMMARY

Type of institution	Schools	Full time students 1931	Full time students 1933	Per cent. change, 1931 to 1933
A. Universities and large institutions of complex organization	95	359,677	331,841	– 7.7
B. Colleges of arts and sciences	269	143,388	135,600	– 5.4
C. Independent technological institutions	38	56,141	47,827	–14.8
D. Independent teachers colleges	20	21,473	17,794	–17.1

1 SCHOOL AND SOCIETY, 34: 783; 38: 781.

2 *Standard Trade and Securities*, 67, 14, 1:1; 71, 12, 2: 1.

stitution, classified as shown in Table I. Evidently specialized, professional schools have lost most as a class, and the smaller arts and sciences colleges the least. Since the older type of school has suffered least, is this a "return to fundamentals"?

When compared by nature of the controlling organization, whether public or private, it is shown (Table II) that the latter schools have lost less. Of course this is partly, perhaps principally, further evidence of smaller losses in smaller schools. But it is rather surprising, considering that student expenses probably are higher in small schools.

TABLE II

CONTROL TYPE SUMMARY

Type of control	Schools	Full time students 1931	Full time students 1933	Per cent. change, 1931 to 1933
1. Public control	107	270,174	244,795	– 9.4
2. Private control	315	310,505	288,267	– 7.2

The same greater holding effect of smaller schools is shown by the comparison of types of student body. Coeducational schools include most of the larger institutions of the country, and these have lost less heavily than those for men only or for women only (Table III).

TABLE III

STUDENT TYPE SUMMARY

Type of student body	Schools	Full time students 1931	Full time students 1933	Per cent. change, 1931 to 1933
a. Men only	73	78,616	74,631	– 5.1
b. Women only	78	42,784	40,868	– 4.5
c. Coeducational	271	459,279	417,563	– 9.1

It has been suggested that schools in large cities retain enrolments better in times of financial stringency than do those in smaller places, because a larger student population can reside at home, with less living expense and because more jobs may be available for student aid. A slight tendency supporting this contention is shown in Table IV; this compares schools in or within fifty miles of cities of at least 250,000 population with schools in all other locations.

TABLE IV

LOCATION TYPE SUMMARY

Type of location	Schools	Full time students 1931	Full time students 1933	Per cent. change, 1931 to 1933
(a) City over 250,000 population	182	314,948	293,783	– 6.7
(b) Smaller city or town	240	265,731	239,279	–10.0

States of the Union are grouped into nine geographical divisions by the government for statistical purposes, and we have computed changes in college enrolments for each of these divisions as well as for each individual state (Table V). Of the forty-nine states (including the District of Columbia), only six showed increases in enrolment during the two-year period; the greatest of these was 9.9 per cent., in Louisiana. The greatest decrease was 27.1 per cent. in Oregon. All the nine divisions registered decreases, of from 1.4 to 15.5 per cent. In general, New England and the Middle Atlantic region held up best, although Louisiana, Utah and Arkansas showed increases in other sections. East and North Central divisions were hit hardest, although the worst state showing was on the Pacific coast (Oregon).

The drop in business activity was much more uniform over all these nine divisions (Table VI); decreases for individual states ranged from 14 to 54 per cent., with most of them close to the U. S. average of 31.3 per cent. Evidently there has been, during the last two years, no invariable and direct dependence of college enrolments on business conditions. In fact, the correlation of the two by states amounts to only r = .22.

TABLE V

GEOGRAPHICAL DIVISION SUMMARY

Division and state	Schools	Full time students 1931	Full time students 1933	Per cent. change, 1931 to 1933
(1) *New England*	*33*	*53,841*	*51,729*	*− 3.9*
Maine	4	3,570	3,249	− 9.0
New Hampshire	2	4,025	4,034	+ 0.2
Vermont	2	1,918	1,890	− 1.5
Massachusetts	18	33,980	32,467	− 4.5
Rhode Island	2	2,936	2,805	− 4.5
Connecticut	5	7,412	7,284	− 1.7
(2) *Middle Atlantic*	*82*	*128,886*	*126,015*	*− 2.2*
New York	40	78,374	79,119	+ 1.0
New Jersey	5	6,379	6,025	− 5.5
Pennsylvania	37	44,133	40,871	− 7.4
(3) *East North Central*	*91*	*133,499*	*114,793*	*−14.0*
Ohio	26	35,874	32,219	−10.2
Indiana	16	21,052	17,461	−17.1
Illinois	26	41,484	35,265	−15.0
Michigan	15	22,408	18,908	−15.6
Wisconsin	8	12,681	10,940	−13.7
(4) *West North Central*	*58*	*73,444*	*64,880*	*−11.7*
Minnesota	9	16,954	15,394	− 9.2
Iowa	13	15,595	13,336	−14.5
Missouri	14	15,729	14,631	− 7.0
North Dakota	3	3,544	2,862	−19.2
South Dakota	4	1,834	1,504	−18.0
Nebraska	5	8,477	7,158	−15.6
Kansas	10	11,311	9,995	−11.6
(5) *South Atlantic*	*71*	*63,611*	*57,684*	*− 9.3*
Delaware	1	743	744	+ 0.1
Maryland	11	8,273	7,999	− 3.3
District of Columbia	6	7,964	6,937	−12.9
Virginia	13	10,749	9,637	−10.3
West Virginia	5	5,677	4,993	−12.0
North Carolina	11	11,801	10,975	− 7.0
South Carolina	13	7,679	7,105	− 7.5
Georgia	8	6,202	5,256	−15.3
Florida	3	4,523	4,038	−10.7
(6) *East South Central*	*21*	*18,164*	*15,348*	*−15.5*
Kentucky	5	5,868	5,095	−13.2
Tennessee	7	6,961	5,743	−17.5
Alabama	6	4,281	3,581	−16.4
Mississippi	3	1,054	929	−11.9
(7) *West South Central*	*23*	*35,230*	*34,746*	*− 1.4*
Arkansas	2	1,863	1,941	+ 4.2
Louisiana	6	8,117	8,923	+ 9.9
Oklahoma	4	9,517	8,735	− 8.2
Texas	11	15,733	15,147	− 3.7
(8) *Mountain*	*20*	*23,907*	*22,413*	*− 6.2*
Montana	2	2,471	2,329	− 5.7
Idaho	2	2,248	2,133	− 5.1
Wyoming	1	1,171	968	− 7.3
Colorado	7	7,618	6,445	−15.4
New Mexico	2	1,325	1,254	− 5.4
Arizona	2	2,651	2,596	− 2.1
Utah	3	5,542	5,842	+ 5.4
Nevada	1	881	846	− 4.0
(9) *Pacific*	*23*	*50,097*	*45,454*	*− 9.3*
Washington	4	11,160	9,953	−10.8
Oregon	6	7,516	5,481	−27.1
California	13	31,421	30,020	− 4.5

TABLE VI

BUSINESS ACTIVITY BY GEOGRAPHICAL DIVISIONS

Division	Per cent. normal (1920–1924) business activity in 1931	1933	Per cent. change 1931 to 1933
(1) New England	91	70	–23
(2) Middle Atlantic	119	80	–23
(3) East North Central	103	63	–29
(4) West North Central	95	62	–35
(5) South Atlantic	102	74	–27
(6) East South Central	92	71	–23
(7) West South Central	84	60	–29
(8) Mountain	94	64	–32
(9) Pacific	101	68	–33

The unique case of Oregon is of special interest to the writer. Why should college enrolment in this state drop nearly three times as much as in its general geographical division or in any of the bordering states, with the greatest percentage decrease of any state in the Union? Business conditions according to our index have dropped but 28 per cent. here, slightly less than the national average. The comparisons of Table VII show that the two state institutions have shrunk much more than the same type of schools elsewhere, while the private schools reported from this state have closely followed national trends in their respective classes. The implication seems unavoidable that the University of Oregon and the Oregon State Agricultural College are now under a special handicap in attracting and retaining students. Recent reorganization and unsettled conditions in the Oregon State System of Higher Education, with resultant difficulty in making adequate high-school contacts, must be blamed to a large degree. Evidently education must search within itself to find reasons for its success or failure, and confidence and other intangible factors may be of prime significance.

TABLE VII

SUMMARY OF OREGON INSTITUTIONS

Institution or type	Type symbols	Per cent. change 1931 to 1933	
Four Oregon arts colleges	B2c(a)	– 7.3	
U. S. average all schools type:	B		– 5.4
	2		– 7.2
	c		– 9.1
	(a)		– 6.7
University of Oregon	Alc(b)	– 27.8	
U. S. average all schools type:	A		– 7.7
	1		– 9.4
	c		– 9.1
	(b)		– 10.0
Oregon State Agricultural College	Clc(b)	– 36.3	
U. S. average all schools type:	C		– 14.8
	1		– 9.4
	c		– 9.1
	(b)		– 10.0

CLIFFORD L. CONSTANCE

UNIVERSITY OF OREGON

NEW BOOKS IN EDUCATION

CALKINS, CLINCH. *Youth Never Comes Again.* Pp. 71. Committee on Unemployed Youth, New York.

Course of Study in Typewriting for Senior High Schools. Bulletin 76. Pp. 80. 41 figures. Department of Public Instruction, Harrisburg, Pennsylvania.

Critical Problems in School Administration. Twelfth Yearbook. Pp. 383. Illustrated. Department of Superintendence, National Education Association. $2.00.

ELLIOTT, EDWARD C. and M. M. CHAMBERS, Editors. *Charters and Basic Laws of Selected American Universities and Colleges.* Pp. viii + 640. Carnegie Foundation for the Advancement of Teaching.

GABLER, EARL R. and ROBERT W. FREDERICK. *Methods of Teaching in Junior and Senior High Schools.* Pp. xii + 207. Inor Publishing Co.

Guide Book for American Students in the British Isles. Pp. 104. Institute of International Education, New York.

KAPLAN, ALBERT J. *A Study of the Behavior Problem Pupil in a Secondary School.* Pp. 187. Temple University.

MITCHELL, LUCY S. *Young Geographers.* Pp. 83. Illustrated. John Day. $1.00.

National Council for the Social Studies. *Fourth Yearbook: The Social-Studies Curriculum.* Pp. 227. McKinley Publishing Co. $2.00.

PARK, NO-YONG. *An Oriental View of American Civilization.* Pp. 128. Hale, Cushman and Flint. $1.50.

Selected References in Education, 1933. Pp. ix + 190. University of Chicago. $0.90.

Suggested Methods and Forms for Use in Unit-Cost Studies in Colleges and Universities. National Committee on Standard Reports for Institutions of High Education.

SWIFT, FLETCHER H. *European Policies of Financing Public Educational Institutions: I; France.* Pp. xvi + 179. University of California Press. $1.75.

Twenty-eighth Annual Report of the President and of the Treasurer. Pp. xii + 189. Carnegie Foundation for the Advancement of Teaching.

SCHOOL AND SOCIETY

WITH WHICH ARE COMBINED THE EDUCATIONAL REVIEW, ESTABLISHED IN 1891, THE TEACHERS MAGAZINE, ESTABLISHED IN 1878, AND THE SCHOOL JOURNAL, ESTABLISHED IN 1874.

EDITED BY J. McKEEN CATTELL, R. D. LINDQUIST AND W. H. COWLEY

EDITORIAL COMMUNICATIONS SHOULD BE ADDRESSED TO THE EDUCATION BUILDING, THE OHIO STATE UNIVERSITY, COLUMBUS, OHIO

Volume 39 | Saturday, April 21, 1934 | Number 1008

SOCIAL THEORIES AND EDUCATION

By JOHN A. KINNEMAN
ILLINOIS STATE NORMAL UNIVERSITY

In these times of economic and social uncertainty there are many educators who claim that all pupils in our schools and colleges should have a background in the social sciences. Furthermore, the educators now contend, and doubtless quite rightly so, that the social needs should constitute the basis for curriculum construction. In casting about for a determination of the current social needs one is impressed by the great variety of social demands which thrust themselves upon the observer. When the educator attempts to satisfy these social demands, he is confronted with the problem of selecting essential criteria on which the curriculum should be draped. There are several principles in the field of social science which the student of education should recognize and, as I see it, should accept as eternal verities. The first of these is the idea of the early sociologists that all knowledge should be unified. This is represented in the thinking of many philosophers and social theorists. I like to take my departure from a Frenchman of a century ago by the name of Auguste Comte, who from 1830 to 1842 published the six volumes of his "Positive Philosophy." It is amazing to know how seemingly modern his conclusions were when he divided all knowledge into five fields. These five fields greatly resembled the framework of the modern junior high school curriculum, as I think the junior high school is correctly conceived. It is also surprising to know how similar his classification is to the much-discussed curricular reorganization of the University of Chicago. The five fields, which Comte suggested as the basis of the curriculum, were mathematics, physics, biology, language and social-physics. I believe Chicago conceives of the curriculum in four divisions—*viz.*, physical science, biological science, the humanities and social science. It is not necessary to comment upon what Comte meant by these terms. By social-physics, of course, he included the materials of all the social sciences, and he himself coined the word "sociology." But the important thing to note is that this man conceived of human knowledge as being rather simply organized, as being organized around a few points of departure rather than around a multitude of present-day subjects.

Other illustrations pertaining to the unity of knowledge could be cited, but I choose another in the experience of James Quayle Dealey in inviting Lester F. Ward to Brown University to lecture. As many people know, Ward had spent almost a lifetime in investigation in geology and botany. He was in fact a renowned scholar in paleobotany. Professor Dealey once told me that when he invited Ward to come to Brown, where he spent the closing years of his life in writing and lecturing, Dealey gave Ward instructions to lecture on the universe. What a subject for study—the universe! Of course, the fine thing about it was that Ward was able to lecture on the universe. He was a great scholar, finely schooled in many fields of learning. He saw the universe as a unit, integrated, inter-related, tied together in all its parts. His was not the attitude of exploiting botany, chemistry, physics, economics or history. His was truly an interpretation of the universe. While I fully realize that it is difficult, maybe impossible, to secure teachers who are familiar with the world's knowledge, nevertheless that should be our ideal. In the failure to achieve that ideal, the next best step should be in the direction of attempting to integrate and correlate the various subject fields. This unity of knowledge is manifest not only from the social theorist, whom the educator should constantly consult, but it is absolutely imperative from the point of view of attempting to comprehend current problems. Suppose we take a few illustrations of current problems, by which we might be able to illustrate the importance of unifying knowledge.

Why are children delinquent? Is the delinquency the product of the physical condition? Is it a product of abnormal psychological reactions? Is it the result of insufficient family income? Is it the result of inadequate and improper training on the part of the parents? Is it the result of poor institutional contacts? Is it the result of insufficient recreation? The fact of the matter is, we know that it is caused by all these and more. The child is delinquent because of the sum total of the forces which surround him. His delinquency can not be explained alone by the sociologist, by the economist, by the psychologist, by the expert in political administration or by the medical doctor. The explanation must come from the combined knowledge of all these experts. For the teachers, it is sufficient to know the general explanations without being experts in any of the fields.

A second illustration might be taken from the field of the broken home and divorce, or a third one might be taken from the field of the factors which cause modern crime. Or, to take an overworked illustration, we might cite the four-year-old depression. Materials from all the social sciences must be employed to explain these phenomena, and the only point I want to make in this connection is that these problems can not be explained in their entirety by restricting our material to a limited field. This reminds me of the incident in which the University of Chicago professor was asked whether he was a physiologist or a chemist. His reply was "I've no idea; I study problems."

A third angle to this problem of unified knowledge is that which is represented in many curricula reorganizations. I do not profess to have an intimate familiarity with many of these, but for the last decade or more rather drastic curricula revisions have been going on at many colleges. The teachers colleges have been gripped by the movement. However, I want to make it clear that the organization of material into new curricula is only half of the job. The other half consists of establishing teaching materials and processes which are commensurate with contemporary needs.

If we are to integrate and unify knowledge, I see no reason why we should not do more of it in the senior high school, the one place where the school curriculum is most in need of revision. We might start with a unification of world history with world literature. So far as unification is concerned, we have done rather an effective job in the exploratory work of the junior high school.

All this means that the teacher, as a

basis for his or her work, will have to have a broad and general familiarity with human knowledge—to the end that knowledge will be unified as far as human ability and departmental envies will allow.

Turning now to the second principle which I should like to lay down, that of the all-important principle of social change, I shall be brief on this phase of the paper, for I have recently set forth some of my views on this principle and published them in School and Society.[1] In this connection, I would say that the student of curricular problems should be familiar with the work of W. F. Ogburn and of F. S. Chapin, especially with the patterns of change which they trace. While authority is not the best rule of evidence, nevertheless, it is rather impressive that President Hoover should have appointed in the summer of 1929 his commission on social trends. Everybody should know what this group of scholars has done in twenty-nine immense chapters, many of which are being expanded into single volumes.

If you want one answer as to what social science people should teach and what teachers should know, my answer would be, "Take the material in Recent Social Trends." That, however, would not constitute a complete answer, but it would constitute a very significant beginning.

Another phase of this subject of change needs to be understood and exploited by the educator, that is, the failure of organized society to make adjustments or adaptations to physical changes. This failure to bring social action into consistency with mechanistic society and the antiquated modes of control is everywhere about us.

By way of conclusion on this matter of change, I should like to emphasize that it is rather difficult to name a single problem which is not a cultural lag, which is not represented in the failure of organized society to adapt its agencies of control to some process of mechanization or to some principle of change. I maintain that if the school is to be used to adapt people to society in which they live, then that school must make its charges aware of the cultural lags which are constantly arising.

On the other side of this question, there is another view-point which must be maintained. And that is the importance of the folkways in our modern society and the necessity of conserving them in an age of change. If we know what the essential folkways are, why not learn them as quickly as possible by the most efficient method? In the conflict between change and the conservation of the folkways, I should like to suggest that there is far greater danger in refusing to make changes than there is in the making of changes. The greatest danger to the control, which I shall soon discuss, is the traditionalism of the school—in its materials and methods, as well as in its management and administration.

Having touched upon two principles which it is imperative for the school to accept, namely, the unity of knowledge and the importance of change, I turn now to the third element, which the school needs to impart, and that is the importance of control. By control I do not mean the prohibition of this or that by suppressive measures; I mean control by way of stimulation to do rather than by way of prohibition not to do. I mean control not in the interests of extreme orderliness and "mousy" quietness, but control in society as a whole in the sense that it implies intelligent direction and planned procedure, and a critical evaluation of our institutions and ideas.

Of course, I should like to have this control grow out of a democratic society. I believe this is the society of the cooperative enterprise. I should like to think that this cooperative, or in my language this democratic, scheme of things should per-

[1] Vol. 38, p. 422, September 30, 1933.

form two functions. It should serve as a tool for control and as an agency for developing the individual. Of course, I am not thinking of control in the classroom. I apply it here as it should constitute a part of all human society, arising out of the human mind and expressing itself in human institutions. If education simply did this much, it would do about all we could expect of it.

In the second place, on this subject of control, the school needs to apprise itself of the importance of setting up control in the interests of life rather than in the interests of property. I wish the American schools could do more in the direction of securing "life, liberty, and the pursuit of happiness." We have a long way to go in order to give to every citizen the economic security which would give him or her, as Dewey puts it, an "opportunity to achieve distinction."

A third aspect of this element of control lies largely in the field of economy and concerns itself with the teaching that we are doing in an era of abundance, which is ramified and shot through with the habits of the economy of scarcity. In some ways that is the most significant and, indeed, the only startling thing that appears in this paper—the conflict between an economy of abundance and the habits of scarcity, which we instill in young people, is one of the paradoxes of the school system. We ought to bring the school system and all society into consistency with an economy of abundance.

A fourth phase of this subject of control should include extensive and intelligent emphasis on what I have chosen to name, for want of better terminology, a knowledge and appreciation of human groups. This must include more than the limited field of geography. It must encompass more than the history of culture and thought. Here I might reflect upon the way in which the public school has manhandled and mutilated the American Indian, but I must move on. It should incorporate some of the material in the field of social customs. Furthermore, to achieve this control we shall have to include well-selected material from literature, and especially literature from all the world, not only English and American, with which we have distorted the minds of American boys and girls.

But it is only by mastering some of the many accomplishments in the civilizations of isolated groups that we shall come to effect a mastery of human relations in this important phase of control. Jewish religious festivals, Catholic Church music and ceremonials, the origin of our Christian and of our American holidays, Negro accomplishments in the arts, a knowledge of the view-point of the American farmer, the American miner, or the American shop girl—these and a thousand other bits of knowledge should give the American citizen a sanity which might stop lynchings, a tolerance which might overcome prejudice —even a range of vision which might minimize our nationalistic phobias. This can be made to apply to French, to English and to German schools quite as much as to American. If the educator is not familiar with Jonathan Scott's monograph on "The Menace of Nationalism in Education," he might develop a familiarity with that at once. And furthermore, if the educator is not familiar with the series of books edited during the last few years by Merriam on the relationship of the schools of various nations to national loyalties, he should proceed to become familiar with them. Among these are Samuel Harper's "Civic Training in Soviet Russia," Gauss' volume on "Great Britain: A Study in Civic Loyalty," others by Professor Jaszi on the old Austro-Hungarian Empire, by Miss Bessie Pierce on the United States in the volume, "Citizens' Organizations and the Civic Training of Youth," and other volumes on other countries by other authorities.

In the fifth place, under this education for control, I should like to leave with you the idea that it must be control of the individual in relation to his contacts with the group, rather than his control merely as an individual. In other words, if any one is in need of reforming, it is the society more than the individual. Here the new school of criminology has a lot to teach the educators. That lies in the fact that a delinquent child can not rise above the group with which he is associated. If this idea of the criminologists ever gets afloat among the educators, we are going to forget much about individual differences quite as readily as we have eagerly embraced the doctrine. If our teaching were socially sound, we would recognize that there are really few differences, but that all of us are creatures of the groups with which we make our contacts. Shaw, in his "Urban Delinquency Areas," in his "Jack Roller," in his "Natural History of a Delinquent Career," has demonstrated this adequately. For any one who wants a super-abundance of proof on this point, I commend to them the work of Shaw and others on the "Report of the President's Commission on Law Enforcement and Observance," commonly known as the Wickersham Commission. To enlarge this a little further, I would like to say that if the federal program fails, it will be a product of a century's exploitation of the idea of "rugged individualism" rather than that of intelligent cooperation.

There is a sixth thought that I want to suggest on this subject of control, and that is the control based on conditions of conduct rather than on the theory of instincts. I wish I could make our child psychology rather simple, and it is a child psychology which is based on a very simple formula of the social psychologist, and I am indebted, as many people are, to W. I. Thomas for his theory of the basic desires of man. He says there are four, namely, desire for new experience, for security, for response and for recognition. On this point, I think even the political scientists and their new school of biographers have much to teach the educators. In this connection, we are indebted to the school of though in America headed by Merriam of the University of Chicago. He sets forth some of his views quite effectively in his "New View-points in Politics," and he has an especially effective chapter on the relations between politics and psychology. The Merriam school of thought, if I may dignify it by such a term, is concerned with the idea of showing, and I think quite rightly so, that many pieces of political conduct can be explained on the basis of certain basic desires. This is illustrated in a number of biographies, which are to some degree psychoanalytic explanations of political conduct. Some of these are Gosnell's "Boss Platt" and Johnson's "Carter Harrison." Further, we might add some of the pen pictures which Merriam has included in his "Chicago." In this connection, I might say that the debunking biographers should be given some approval rather than constant condemnation. The debunkers have approached their problem in order to analyze the conduct of the character about whom they were writing. While we may not approve of their product, we must accept, in part at least, their methods.

Of course, if the school is to exert any direct controls on society, it is obvious that we shall have to organize materials toward that end. Here the arts, so far as the use of leisure is concerned, have great functional value. Music, drama, sports, reading, the humanities—all have unusual utility in this direction. All this is adequately discussed from many angles by many people in many different ways. The tragic fact is that schoolmen, not proficient in the arts and not recognizing their relationship to a rapidly increasing problem of leisure, are conserving the traditional curriculum at the expense of those materials which have functional value in group living. Rainwater, Curtis and Steiner have covered this subject quite well. To me, this problem is so obvious that to touch upon it further is to waste the reader's time.

Here a word of warning is needed. I should like to see a program of control include more than is ordinarily included in the scope of a program of character education. Call it civic education for all I care. Call it education for self-mastery if you like that term. Whatever terminology you give the movement, it eventually becomes one of social control.

Now that we have covered three of these principles, I should like to turn to the fourth and last one, and that is the importance of training people to make rational choices. This can be done in tolerating religions, in purchasing goods, in choosing programs of political actions, in associating with people of another race, in admitting the excellences of some nationalist group, or of some peculiar form of government, and even, to use a recent experience, to enforce an orderly administration of justice.

Sumner and Keller in their material have exploited this idea quite well. Keller in his "Societal Evolution," which was first published eighteen years ago and has since been rewritten and republished, has given us a monumental work on this subject. Chase and Schlink, in "Your Money's Worth," have given the problem a current setting. Mr. Lester F. Ward, already referred to, did much in his day to further this idea. To him the telic factor, as he named the rational, was all-important in society. These ideas of Keller, of Sumner and of Ward run counter to certain modern tendencies in education to the effect that we should train people to train children to feel rightly and correctly. Instead of training them, we had better educate them, and by educating, we enable them to make rational choices. Emotionalized behavior, when under the sway of the intellectual charlatan and quack, is our most dangerous form of behavior. I take that position because training the emotions of people is likely to result in mere sentimental reaction and not in a capacity of people to meet intelligently and critically the situation that is before them.

Of course, I realize that any effort to train people to make rational selections is met by a wide variety of demands made upon them which are irrational. But any semi-literate person might agree that a capacity to think one's way through a problem is much better than a reliance upon black or even white magic. It is for this reason that I prefer the conference room and the committee table to the orator's rostrum and the political showman's antics. James Weldon Johnson summarizes this quite effectively in his recent autobiography when he says "rhetorical oratory is the foundation upon which all the humbug of our political system rests." And he might have added our social system and our economic system as well. This element of training people to make rational selections is, of course, tied up with the element of control, for how can we control in a social sense unless each one of us is capable of furnishing his share of information and criticism? Let me cite one illustration on this point. Do you remember a few years ago when everybody, except the people who thought or who had some social science training, said, "We don't want the dole!" Maybe you were responsible for saying it just once. Of course we then had the dole in a more dreadful form than Britain ever knew it! Some people felt that if they said "we don't want the dole" often enough they would not have to think about a comprehensive plan of relieving and of further preventing unemployment. As Lichtenberger says of Lester Ward in this connection, "He was the spokesman for his generation in the overthrow of the laissez-faire theory." All I can say on this is that it was very nice to attempt to overthrow the laissez-faire theory, but the point is that Ward should have been assisted by many other overthrowers. Maybe a few humanizers, as James Harvey Robinson uses the term, would have helped tremendously. Probably we are just at the beginning of the successful control of the laissez-faire point of view. And until we can use our energies toward making people capable of leading the group life and making the group life the habit, we shall not have overthrown the laissez-faire idea, for the overthrow of the laissez-faire position is control.

This leads me to one additional conclusion on the subject of teaching people to make rational selections. Certainly we do not want to underemphasize the value of a person's emotional reaction. At the same time, there is no doubt a limit to the degree to which normal persons can have rational experiences. As a third, and indeed an important approach, I should like to emphasize the importance of the school giving its charges certain formulae to live by. Ross does this well in interpreting society in his monumental work through the channels of control; Kelsey does it almost as well from the vantage point of physical basis; Giddings did a superb job of teaching in his theories of aggregation; Sumner left nothing to be done in the field of the folkways, as well as in his analysis of all social processes into four categories of maintenance, regulation, perpetuation and gratification.

At our institution we have attempted in the freshman social science work to make the student aware, in the course of twelve weeks, of the implications of the machine age. In another twelve weeks we have oriented him to the complicated life of modern cities, and finally we have spent twelve weeks in an examination of some of the contemporary problems of society. Have we given the freshmen a formula? I hope we have. At least I know that one freshman of last year announced with some awe to an upper-classman that she had learned by Thanksgiving time that we lived in a machine age. I am confident that if she really learned that she learned a lot. But I am equally confident that sociology, or economics, or political science, as they could be conceived, might not have taught her that important truth. I should like to see an educated person in the classroom in the best liberal, although not necessarily in the best liberal arts sense of the term. In addition to that, I should like to have this person know enough about the teaching process to make the work of the school a genuine delight to all who participate.

By way of conclusion, I should like to say that two groups of people should make the curriculum—the social scientists, who know what to teach, and the educational psychologists, who should by this time have evolved methods and techniques of teaching.

THE EDUCATIONAL STATUS OF THE PRESCHOOL CHILD[1]

By Dr. ARNOLD GESELL

DIRECTOR OF THE YALE CLINIC OF CHILD DEVELOPMENT

The Federal Emergency Education Program has served to focus attention on the educational status of the preschool child. State superintendents in 43 states are taking an active part in that portion of the

[1] Address before the Cleveland Convention of the National Education Association at Cleveland, Ohio, February 28, 1934.

program which relates to nursery schools. Recent reports show that approximately 2,000 nursery units have already been organized. The preschool child has, in a national sense, arrived on the educational scene.

In a biological sense the span of human infancy extends from the zero hour of birth to the middle twenties. It takes time to grow. It takes about twenty-four years for an American youth to reach the stature of maturity. You may think of this cycle of growth as a succession of four stages of six years each: (1) the preschool years; (2) the elementary school years; (3) the junior high school years; (4) the pre-adult years.

We are now beginning to see this cycle of growth in its true perspective. Thus far, for sound social reasons, the middle twelve years have received most of the attention of the public school system. These are indeed important years for the transmission of our cultural inheritance, but the demands of society and the findings of science are compelling us to see the educational significance of the preschool years—the fundamental years which come first in the cycle of life and which therefore must have inescapable priority in all social planning.

Public Education and Social Planning

The administration of public education is destined to become an increasingly important factor in social and economic planning. For this reason the whole problem of the educational organization of the first six years of human life constitutes a major challenge to educational statesmanship. The problem must be approached from a broad and a social point of view. Above all, we must not make the mistake of regarding the nursery school as merely another sub-primary addition to our present graded school system—as another stratification which is to be administered like the traditional schoolroom. Our public school system is already over-stratified. We should organize the educational provisions for the preschool years in patterns which preserve the constructive forces of home life and vitalize parental responsibility.

The education of the preschool child must be conceived in terms of growth instead of in terms of instruction or even of training. If we try merely to adapt the prevailing procedures of the elementary school to the needs of the preschool child we shall commit many new sins in the name of education. The educational welfare of the preschool child can be protected only if our policies rest on firm scientific and social foundations.

Five general requirements can be formulated:

(1) We must make an honest and thorough attempt to secure adequate nutrition and systematic medical supervision throughout the preschool years, beginning with the newborn infant.

(2) This developmental supervision should be accomplished as much as possible through individualized guidance of the parents of children.

(3) To build for the future preschool generation, we must provide more adequate pre-parental training for young men and women in their pre-adult years.

(4) We must recognize the psychological aspects of the care of infant and child; discover individual differences early; and base the educational protection of the young child on a respect for these individual differences.

(5) A knowledge of the developmental psychology of the infant is essential to the professional training of kindergarten and primary teachers.

A Cinema Record of Early Child Development

Now, having tacked these theses on the wall, I invite you to look at some cinema records based on normative and naturalistic studies of the normal human infant. These studies, made at The Yale Clinic of Child Development, were designed to delineate the characteristics of early mental growth. From a biological point of view the growth of the mind is as real and as structured as that of the body. We can not weigh the mind in the balances as the nurse weighs the infant on the scales, but the mind is none the less a structured organism. It develops with the same certainty, precision and progressive differentiation which the body manifests during the period of infancy and childhood. The film which you will see makes manifest in a tangible way the early patterning of human behavior. The natural laws which govern this patterning must be our guide in planning for the educational welfare of the preschool child.

The cinema not only makes the patterns of behavior tangible; it condenses time and age into a brief compass. So that we may have a real sense of the meaning of growth, I shall first give you a glimpse of an infant at the tender age of 20 weeks. An infant so young perhaps has no official status in a gathering of this sort. On the other hand, he is not without educational significance. We can not ignore the fact that in a few years he will come under the auspices of the public school. And one may well ask whether the public school can afford to ignore as completely as it now does the antecedent careers of the young children whom it admits. These careers begin with early infancy. Problems of education are both formed and foreshadowed in the first months and the first years of the cycle of mental growth.

So the first chapter of this film will illustrate the behavior day of an infant 20 weeks of age. The second chapter of the film will show you this same infant under the controlled conditions of laboratory observation. This film will picture developmental changes in the patterns of cube behavior in an infant at 24 weeks and again at 28 weeks with a glimpse of 40 weeks. Although cube behavior does not constitute an educational problem, it may serve as an example of the way in which mental growth proceeds. We have found these one-inch cubes very useful in eliciting the maturity and behavior characteristics of an infant. We find, for example, that typically a 12-weeks-old infant will regard a cube which is placed before him on the table top; that a 20-weeks-old infant will contact the cube. At 24 weeks he will grasp it in his palm and at 40 weeks he may grasp it with his finger tips. At 18 months he can build a tower of three cubes; it takes another 18 months before he can combine these three cubes into a simple bridge.

In the film we note the infant's reactions to the two-cube situation. One cube has been placed in his left hand by the examiner, a second cube is placed on the table top before him. His behavior reactions will be shown at normal speed, then at slowed speed and then in dissected, stopped-motion pictures which will delineate the salient movements in his reaction patterns. Then we shall call upon the technology of the cinema and bring these two age levels into immediate juxtaposition. The self-same infant will be coincidently shown at 24 and at 20 weeks in a comparable behavior situation. By this method of coincident projection the cinema resolves the past and future of the infant into a simultaneous present. Thus the increments of mental growth will be made visible.

(The first two chapters of the film were shown.)

The infant whom you have just seen has marks of individuality, and these marks came into early prominence. He shows great physical mobility; he is, in a motor sense, dynamic; he takes great satisfaction in motor activity. He is also alert in the social sense; he has perception of the mood of others and is resourceful in adopting a corresponding mood; but he is not compliant and has in addition well-defined negative reactions and a fairly robust temper. He shows self-dependence, likes to do things himself, insists on participation in motor activity in particular. In manipulation he displays interest in detail, delicacy of touch and a certain kind of mechanical aptitude. All these characteristics are in large measure conditioned by his inherent capacities and inherent growth traits. His deportment is, of course, much influenced by the character of his home management, but it is very important that we emphasize his own original contribution to his behavior patterns. These contributions have manifested themselves through the first year of life and will doubtless project themselves into the future.

We believe that this film gives a truthful hint of the way in which the mind grows in all fields of behavior, not only in posture, prehension and manipulation, but in all realms of intelligence, of social adjustments, of language behavior and even of personality.

For personality grows by the same genetic laws which govern the manipulation of cubes. Without wishing to be dogmatic I would say that throughout childhood, and indeed throughout life, the individual grows primarily by virtue of innate organizing processes. We watch his development, we guide it, we pray for its best interests; but in the last analysis even the infant must do his own growing. To be sure, he profits by experience, he learns, he acquires habits. But he sheds vastly more habits than he ever retains, because if he retained his habits too tenaciously he would not grow at all. Each individual is born with a unique growth potentiality and just as this potentiality stamps his physique and his physical constitution, so does his fundamental psychological growth potency determine his individuality—not in a predestinarian manner, but in a lawful, limiting, moulding manner.

The mind grows. It is subject to the laws and limitations of growth. It is not wholly determined by habit, by conditioned reflexes, by subconscious complexes; it is primarily shaped by processes of maturation which are innate and distinctive for every individual. Let us remind ourselves again that school children grow in the same way that infants grow.

The third chapter of the film will give you a glimpse of a guidance nursery and its simple equipment. The children range in age from 18 months to 4 years. The infant has now developed into a prekindergarten child. The nursery in our clinic is used for the observation and guidance of young children who are referred for minor behavior problems. These problems are taken up individually and each problem is handled on its own merits. Some children are in long attendance at the nursery, some come only once or twice. It is a guidance nursery, operated on a dispensary basis, which makes it possible to bring parent guidance and child guidance into close relationship. A one-way vision screen is used as an aid to observation by the parents. When a mother is concealed behind the screen, invisible to the child, she tends to take a more detached and impersonal view of her problems of child care.

The part-time attendance arrangement makes a guidance type of nursery flexible; and makes it possible to reach a much larger number of parents and children in the course of a year. Such part-time features could be easily incorporated into kindergarten and nursery organization. A nursery-kindergarten center can be so conducted as to insure occasional anticipatory contacts with two, three and four year olds.

Our film concludes with a brief glimpse of a boy of school age who is undergoing a psychological examination. Under ideal conditions such an examination becomes part of his school record and would be continuous with records made during his infancy. The glimpse of this boy of elementary school age should serve to further remind us of the organic relationships between preschool and school years.

(The third chapter of the cinema film was then shown.)

Infants are born into the world with distinctive growth potentialities out of which arise their individualities. In the preschool period of childhood the first and foremost task of education is to ascertain and to interpret individual differences, normal and abnormal. This task can not and should not be undertaken independently from the sciences of medicine.

THE MEDICAL SUPERVISION OF CHILD DEVELOPMENT

The primary responsibility for protecting the life, the health and the early development of the infant lies with the profession of medicine and especially with pediatrics. Through private medical practise and through socialized provisions like the infant welfare center, every enlightened community provides for the periodic supervision of the child's physical growth. This supervision focuses on nutrition, but is giving increasing regard to the psychological factors which underlie mental health. Development is a continuing process which can be supervised only by periodic examinations which will take into account the early behavior characteristics of the individual and recognize the interrelations of physical and mental welfare.

In the next few decades research in the biological sciences will doubtless perfect new and discriminating techniques for the measurement and clinical appraisal of human characteristics, mental and physical. Such techniques will define with greater precision individual differences in body build, constitutional type and biochemical qualities and susceptibilities; physiological efficiencies of separate organs; behavior traits and trends; and above all, the balance or correlation of different functions in the total personality. In some way these techniques, medical and biometric, will be systematically used for the better control of early human growth.

Education will then rest, as it should, on a biological as well as a social basis. The public school system can perform its most fundamental service for the young child only by bringing its functions into alignment with the medical, clinical and public health provisions which constitute the basic safeguards of the child's development.

PUBLIC SCHOOL PROVISIONS FOR THE PRESCHOOL CHILD

And so we return again to the fundamental concept of growth. Once this concept is accepted as a guiding principle in education, the problem of the school beginner vanishes or it takes on such an altered form that it ceases to exist. Forsooth, what is a school beginner? A six-, a five-, a four-, a three-, or a two-year-old child? And when and how should the parents prepare the child for school? And when and how should the school prepare the parent for the child? And who can draw the line between parent education and early childhood education? These questions are all inextricably interrelated and it is for that very reason that the public school must enter more deeply into this rich preschool terrain, which bristles with problems of educational engineering.

There are two solid pathways for immediate approach: (1) parental and pre-parental education; (2) the readaptation of the kindergarten and nursery school.

1. *Parental and pre-parental education.* Adult education has come into increasing prominence since the war and will come into yet greater prominence as an aftermath of the present NRA period of readjustment. There are endless opportunities

for instruction and guidance of parents in the field of infant care and of child training. There is much to be learned in the practical art of child management. Children, however, differ so enormously and so significantly, and they change so rapidly during the period of their early growth, that child management as an art is a limited educational problem. Educational agencies can render most service by assisting parents to acquire a working philosophy of growth and learning, which will give perspective to the everyday problems of children.

From the standpoint of public school policy, pre-parental education is more basic than parental education. We have been a bit squeamish about attacking this great educational problem which concerns particularly the pre-adult years, ignoring the certain prospect that most maturing adolescents will in time become mothers and fathers. If we can in a constructive way reach the attitudes of these adolescents in their latent strength we shall be performing double educational service. We shall be shaping the careers of the adolescents as individuals and at the same stroke shall be erecting safeguards for the healthier development of the oncoming generation.

How can we reach these adolescents, these pre-adults? By a more frank presentation of the elementary facts concerning the cycle of human growth. Biology, in spite of its concreteness, has been studied too much in the abstract as far as human life is concerned. We need a humanized biology, or rather we need an adequate course of instruction in human biology dealing candidly with the origin, physical growth and mental growth of the human child. In this way we can bring into the curriculum a practical type of psychology concerned with the laws of human nature and with the development of the child mind. Such a psychology, far from being over-introspective, would tend to take the adolescent out of himself and enable him ultimately to assume more objective views of the problems of parenthood. Education frankly addressed to the problems of early human development and child behavior would bear fruit in a decade, because in a few years these youths, whether in shop or college, will be fathers and mothers with a more intelligent outlook upon the life cycle of a newborn infant of their own.

2. *The readaptation of the kindergarten and the nursery school.* The problem of preschool education must be envisaged in terms of the entire age span from infancy to the sixth-year molar. We can not educationally organize this vast domain simply by institutional expansion. We can not multiply kindergartens *ad libitum;* we can not multiply nursery schools *ad libitum.* We must reconstruct both of these agencies in such a way that they will reach all the people and contact the whole range of the preschool years. By the device of part-time and differential attendance, by bringing parent and child jointly into the scheme of education, by converting kindergartens and nursery schools into demonstration and guidance centers, the preschool clientele can be enormously increased without undue additions to the budget. There is no reason why the public school system, in cooperation with agencies of public health and medicine, can not make periodic contacts with the two-year-olds, three-year-olds and four-year-olds. These are problems of administration and of social invention. We can not meet them if we cling too tenaciously to the patterns of attendance and regimentation of the traditional primary school. New occasions have brought new necessities and are teaching a new flexibility. Education and growth are inseparable. As soon as the infant is born he is already on the pathway of education. And social planning must reckon with that axiom.

EDUCATIONAL EVENTS

TRADE SCHOOLS AND THE SCHOOL-LEAVING AGE IN ENGLAND

IN England to-day there are over 100,000 children of 14 and 15 years of age who are unable to obtain employment, the *Christian Science Monitor* Bureau reports, and it is calculated that by 1936 the number will have risen to over 500,000. Part of this anticipated increase has been attributed to the high birth rate in 1919. During the period of 1933–34, according to the London *Times,* the estimated number of those who will leave school is about 64,000, compared with 43,000 in 1932–33. The London Advisory Council for Juvenile Employment in a recent report put the prospective exodus for 1934 at 65,000, as against 60,000 in a normal year.

The Labor Party, the National Union of Teachers and a large section of public opinion favor the immediate raising of the school-leaving age from 14 to 15 years. But the government, comments the correspondent, refuses to accept this solution. Instead, it is providing in its new Unemployment Insurance Act for the provision of junior instruction centers for all unemployed youths between 14 and 18 years of age. The London County Council trade schools are representative of this type of institution. The training offered in these schools is planned to fit students to enter industry with the prospect of becoming skilled workers. Also in operation are the day continuation schools, which offer courses to boys and girls from 14 to 18 years, who may attend the schools for a minimum of 6 and a maximum of 15 hours a week. The curriculum has a definite vocational bias, providing preliminary training for commercial and industrial careers. Evening institutes, which exist in every part of London, provide for a continuation of general education and also give special instruction in commercial and technical subjects. The new educational centers will be under the direction of the Ministry of Labor, and will be partially supported from the Unemployment Insurance Fund.

The attitude of the government, points out the correspondent, is not as reactionary as it appears on the surface. The obvious course is the raising of the school age, which, it is claimed, would be little more expensive than the inclusion of the 14 to 15 year-old group in the instruction centers at a cost of £13 each. There are, however, a number of factors upon which the official attitude is based. Owing to the sharp fall in the birth rate during recent years, following a temporary rise after the world war, there will be 500,000 fewer children in school in 1937 than there are to-day, and 1,000,000 fewer in 1946. Consequently, the additional buildings and teachers needed to provide for the 500,000 extra children in 1936 would not be needed after that date. It has, therefore, been deemed wiser to incorporate the temporary unemployed 14 to 15 year-old group in the general provision made by instruction centers outside the state school system.

Attention is called to the fact that the Board of Education is already providing an increasing number of central schools, where the abler children continue their education until the ages of 15 or 16 years. The ablest members of these groups receive scholarships to the secondary schools. Those who leave at 14 belong mainly to a class to which the prospect of earning something toward the upkeep of the home is more attractive than that of further schooling, while to their parents the extra income is a very genuine benefit. The demand for compulsory raising of the school age is accompanied by an equally strong demand for a maintenance grant to the parents in lieu of wages lost in that way. Some of the best teachers in England, according to the correspondent, feel that such a system would deprive the children involved of the best element on their upbringing, the sense of responsibility to the home, and would intensify the tendency to rely on the state.

CHANGES IN THE LONDON EDUCATIONAL PROGRAM

AT the first meeting of the newly appointed Education Committee of the London County Council held late in March, three changes in the educational program for London schools were effected. The first had to do with teachers' salaries, the second with the restoration of funds for children's prizes and the third with summer camps for residential school children.

On the question of the restoration of salary cuts Mr. A. E. Samuels moved as follows:

That the council would welcome the restoration of the cuts in teachers' salaries; that, in view of the fact that the Imperial Exchequer under the National Economy (Education) Order, 1931, secured a saving much in excess of the whole amount of the cuts in teachers' salaries, the Council urges his Majesty's Government to restore at the same time the basis of grants in respect to teachers' salaries to a position not less favourable to the Council than that obtaining prior to October 1, 1931; and that the President of the Board of Education (of Great Britain) be so informed.

In the discussion which followed it was brought out that the cuts were originally imposed as a temporary measure and that ample evidence exists, by public declaration of responsible Ministers of the Crown, that the necessity of reduced remuneration is no longer present. Mr. Samuel's motion passed by a vote of 23 votes to 15.

The committee passed the proposed plan to resume the awarding of prizes to school children on the scale recently curtailed by necessities of economy. The prize fund has therefore been increased from in the neighborhood of five thousand pounds to fourteen thousand pounds. It was also voted to send all children in residential schools to holiday camps in 1934, instead of half the children, as had been arranged. A budget of £10,500 was approved for the purpose, an increase of £3,000 over the original subvention.

THE HISPANIC-AMERICAN INSTITUTE OF THE GEORGE WASHINGTON UNIVERSITY

A Center of Inter-American Studies has been established at the George Washington University according to an announcement made on April 4 by Dr. Cloyd H. Marvin, president of the university.

The center will be administered by a council and staff of instructors composed of ten men and women who have specialized in the field of Hispanic-American studies. This council will be headed by Dr. A. Curtis Wilgus, associate professor of Hispanic-American history at the university. Dr. Wilgus will serve in this capacity as director of the center and will edit its publications, which will include a yearly volume of lectures given in the university's seminar-conference on Hispanic-American affairs.

Included in the membership of the council are Dr. James Brown Scott, secretary of the Carnegie Endowment for International Peace; Dr. Leo S. Rowe, director general of the Pan American Union; E. Gil Borges, assistant director of the Pan American Union; Dr. Constantine E. McGuire, of the Library of Congress; Dr. William R. Manning, of the Division of Latin-American Affairs of the Department of State; Dr. James A. Robertson, editor of the *Hispanic-American Historical Review* and research professor at the John B. Stetson University; Miss Heloise Brainerd, director of the Division of Intellectual Cooperation of the Pan American Union; Dr. Henry Grattan Doyle, professor of Romance languages at the George Washington University, and Dr. Cecil Jones, professorial lecturer on Spanish-American literature and contemporary Hispanic-American culture at George Washington University.

The council will act as a general advisory body with the duty of formulating the program of action for the center. Its specific functions will be to make recommendations concerning the following matters: Courses, projects, lectures and lecturers; the publication of research results; the exchange of university professors and students; the establishment of fellowships and scholarships; the convocation of scholars, the holding of special conferences and the arranging and supervising of radio broadcasts; the suggestion of concrete methods for cooperation with existing agencies having objects similar to those of the center; the taking of any action necessary to encourage and facilitate all forms of beneficial cooperation between scholars in the American states, and the nomination of individuals of merit who should be granted honorary degrees. Besides the members of the council, scholars in other communities will be asked to serve in an advisory capacity, the president's announcement stated, and to assist particularly in directing research in other localities. As requirements arise, further additions to the staff of instruction will be made through council nominations.

For some years the George Washington University has made a specialty of studies in the inter-American field. It was one of the first institutions to establish a chair of Hispanic-American history, and each summer it schedules a seminar-conference on Hispanic-American affairs.

PLAN OF RURAL SCHOOL INSTRUCTION AT THE UNIVERSITY OF NEBRASKA

THE University of Nebraska extension service has developed a plan of instruction by mail whereby the rural school children of Nebraska and its neighboring states may have opportunities to study the same curricula as those provided for city school children.

Under this plan, started five years ago, the university has prepared a wide range of high-school courses, worded so that preparatory students may understand them and designed to hold their interest. In schools which cooperate with the extension bureau, students register for these courses as for any other, and study under the supervision of a teacher. Dr. A. A. Reed, director of the extension service, states that these supervising teachers need not be especially trained in order to direct the studies of the extension service and that, as a result of the method, many economies in the state school system have been effected. Those rural schools which have cooperated with the service, he asserts, have reduced their expenses to such an extent that they have been enabled to keep open during the last few years in the face of the depression.

About 360 students in more than 100 Nebraska, South Dakota and Kansas schools received training this last year in such specialized subjects as advanced art, Latin, science and other subjects which might have been presented inadequately by their own school systems or not presented at all. The extension fund originally obtained a $5,000 grant from the Carnegie Foundation to conduct the experiment. The student charges are: $1.00 for the registration fee, $6.00 for each course and additional costs for books and other equipment.

IMPROVEMENT OF MEDICAL SERVICES FOR THE SCHOOL CHILDREN OF NEW YORK CITY

AN extensive program of medical service to safeguard the physical welfare of New York City's junior high school and elementary school children has been started under the guidance of an advisory committee of fourteen specialists in cooperation with the Board of Education and the Department of Health. The plan, which is being sponsored by Mrs. Rogers H. Bacon, chairman of the health committee of the Advisory Board on Industrial Education, will be outlined in tentative form by the end of May.

Mrs. Bacon has selected Dr. I. Ogden Woodruff, vice-president of the New York Tuberculosis and Health Association, to act as chairman of the committee of fourteen to direct the medical service. The results already accomplished by the Board of Education and the Department of Health in promoting the health of the children of the continuation schools, according to Dr. Woodruff, point to the successful development of a comprehensive plan in which nurses, physicians, teachers and health counselors may be cooperatively enrolled.

The advisory committee selected includes, besides Dr. Woodruff, Dr. E. H. Lewinski-Corwin, secretary of the New York Academy of Medicine, who will serve as secretary of the committee; Dr. John Wyckoff, dean of the New York University and Bellevue Medical College; Dr. Donald B. Armstrong, vice-president of the Metropolitan Life Insurance Company; Dr. Irving Pardee; Miss Mariam T. Sweeney; Dr. Herbert B. Wilcox; Dr. Ernst P. Boas; Dr. Cassius H. Watson, medical director of the American Telephone and Telegraph Company; Dr. Alec Nicol Thomson, executive secretary of the Five County Medical Society; Dr. Grant Thorburn, of the New York Tuberculosis and Health Association; Dr. Conrad Berens; Dr. Alfred Walker, chairman of the dental committee of the New York Tuberculosis and Health Association, and Dr. Edmund P. Fowler, otologist.

The committee will be enlarged to include other members of the medical profession, Mrs. Bacon stated, and at that time, Dr. S. S. Goldwater, Commissioner of Hospitals, will be asked to serve as the representative of his department. Representatives from the field of surgery will also be added.

The committee will have the use of the report of a survey of health conditions in the public schools of the city, which was financed by the Metropolitan Life Insurance Company, working in cooperation with the American Child Health Association, the Board of Education and the Department of Health. When the plan of procedure for the committee is drawn up, it will be presented for execution to Dr. Harold G. Campbell, superintendent of schools, and Dr. John L. Rice, health commissioner.

THE PLAN OF ADMISSIONS AT SIMMONS COLLEGE

PRESIDENT BANCROFT BEATLEY, of Simmons College, has announced that the college has adopted a new plan of admission requirements, to be used as an alternative to the present plan in determining the qualifications of applicants for entrance to the college. Under the old plan, high-school or preparatory school students wishing to enter Simmons College are required to be certified or to pass with a specified grade the examinations of the College Entrance Examination Board in certain predetermined subjects.

While the established plan will continue in effect, applicants for admission to the college in September of this year will be given the opportunity to present their qualifications under the conditions of the alternative plan if they wish. This plan is designed "to provide a means by which a girl of unusual promise may enter Simmons College when her record of work in the secondary school does not conform to the requirements for admission as stated in the catalogue. . . . The candidate for admission under Plan II is required to submit a variety of evidence *which will be judged as a whole* in determining her admission."

The plan is intended to allow greater flexibility in the specific subjects offered by a candidate, and at the same time to lay greater stress on her personal qualifications, such as initiative, adaptability, emotional and social stability, health and personality. Her scholastic record in preparatory school will be carefully examined, both as to subject-matter and as to marks, as well as her rank in the graduating class. She will furthermore be required to take two of the examinations administered by the College Entrance Examination Board—the Scholastic Aptitude Test and the Comprehensive Examination in English, which demonstrates the candidate's ability to use the English language, to think clearly and to make logical use of the knowledge and understanding gained from the reading and studying of books.

The principal and former teachers in the secondary school attended by the candidate will be asked to give their "matured judgment of the general fitness of the applicant to pursue successfully a suitable curriculum in Simmons College." Finally, the candidate will be asked to state in writing "her educational and vocational plans, her reasons for desiring to enter Simmons, and her choice of a school within the college." Whenever possible, the applicant will be given a personal interview at the college.

"Although this alternative method of admission," observes President Beatley, "was established primarily to serve the needs of the girl who has been unable to plan her secondary-school course in terms of the requirements published in the catalogue of Simmons College, the plan provides a flexibility in the relationship of the secondary school and the college which, it is hoped, will be mutually beneficial."

STUDY OF FAMILY LIFE TENSIONS AT CORNELL UNIVERSITY

THIRTEEN elements in family relationships build successful family life, according to the study of the autobiographies of 200 students made recently at Cornell University in a research on family life. These autobiographies, assembled by Miss Mildred Thurow, of the department of rural social organization of the College of Agriculture, represent students from farm, village and city. Their parents come from various walks of life and are of both native and foreign birth. All are from families in which both parents were living with the children in a family relationship.

Chief among the elements conducive to a happy family life, the survey points out, is the lack of friction between the parents and between the parents and children. Families living in rural sections and in small cities have less tension than families in medium-size and in large cities. Families of moderate means, with the parents having joint control of the purse, are, according to the study, better adjusted. Parents having little education are in more frequent conflict than those with more schooling. As the amount of tension between the parents and between the parents and the children decreases, the confidence of the child in his parents and his satisfaction in the family increase.

Agreement between parents on discipline and a minimum of parental discipline are found to contribute to happiness in the home. Other elements adding to the family happiness are the sharing of most of the meals, the celebration of birthdays and holidays as a family, the entertaining of relatives, chums and family friends, and the attendance of the parents together at social functions. One of the greatest factors in avoiding friction between the children themselves is the parents' open affection for the children and for each other. The children's affection for each other increases greatly as the common interests of the family increase. The study concludes that the happiest families are those in which the children and the parents have some amusements and pursuits in common.

THE ADULT EDUCATION UNIT AT NEW YORK UNIVERSITY

A new unit, tentatively called the Division of General Education, which will administer all adult education and other extension activities, has been established at New York University, and will be effective on and after July 1. Dr. Harry Woodburn Chase, chancellor of the university, has announced that the new division will absorb the existing Institute of Education and the University Extension Division. It will be the coordinating and unifying agency for the university functions in the field of off-campus degree programs.

The proposal for the establishment of the unit was made by a committee representing all the schools whose curricula will be affected by it. The members of the committee were Provost Rufus D. Smith, *chairman;* G. Rowland Collins, associate dean of the School of Commerce, Accounts and Finance; Ned H. Dearborn, director of the Institute of Education; Philip James, associate professor of music in the College of Fine Arts; Paul A. McGhee, executive secretary of the University Extension Division, and Thorndike Saville, professor of hydraulic and sanitary engineering. The committee, according to Dr. Chase, will continue to study the problems arising from the establishment of college credit programs in outlying communities and attempt to define the local conditions in a community which must be met before the university commits itself to a college-credit program there.

The division, Dr. Chase pointed out in his announcement, will prepare to contribute to the field of adult education by inaugurating a program which shall represent New York University in this field. While keeping in mind the particular and specific needs of the adult student, it shall offer not only a program of single courses within specific subject-matter fields, but also some program looking toward the orientation of the mature student to the modern world.

Dr. Chase's announcement also stated that there would be organized an advisory committee under the chairmanship of the dean of the School of Education to foster a program of courses of training for leadership in the field of adult education. A sub-committee will be formed in cooperation with the Division of Public Administration at Washington Square College to study and report upon the problem of setting up a program for civil service training, institutes for public service and other non-matriculant activities of a public service and public administrative character.

Under the new plan, all off-campus degree-credit and non-credit work will be conducted through the Division of General Education. At present, the university conducts off-campus college credit courses in Newark and Paterson, N. J., through the university extension division, and courses for teachers in service in forty-five cities and towns in New York, New Jersey, Pennsylvania, Connecticut and Delaware. The instructors for these and other centers which may be established will continue to be drawn from the regular faculties of the university.

EDUCATIONAL NOTES AND NEWS

Dr. Arthur A. Hauck, dean of Lafayette College, has accepted the presidency of the University of Maine, to which he was elected on April 10. Dean Hauck, who has served as professor of history at Lafayette College as well as dean, will assume his new post during the summer. Born in Minnesota in 1893, Dean Hauck was graduated from Reed College, Portland, Oregon, in 1915, and subsequently received the degree of doctor of philosophy from Columbia University. After the world war, in which he served in the army, he was appointed professor of education and associate dean at Antioch College. In 1922 he was elected president of Punahou School at Honolulu, where he remained for six years. Dean Hauck went to Lafayette in 1931 from Vassar College.

Dr. David M. Edwards, pastor of the First Friends Church at Indianapolis, has accepted the position of president of the Friends University at Wichita, Kansas. He succeeds Dr. W. O. Mendenhall, who will assume the presidency of Whittier College at Whittier, Calif.

Three members of the faculty of Princeton University announced, on April 14, their intention of entering the Mercer County, N. J., primary elections to be held on May 15. Dr. Walter L. Whittlesey, assistant professor of politics and member of the Princeton Survey of the New Jersey State Government, recently completed under the direction of President Dodds, will seek the nomination as representative from the fourth district on the Democratic ticket. Dayton D. McKean has announced his candidacy for the state assembly on the Democratic ticket, and Dr. Charles R. Erdman, Jr., assistant professor of politics and a member of the New Jersey Survey staff, will seek the nomination for the assembly on the Republican ticket.

Professor Philip H. Elwood, Jr., head of the landscape architecture department of the Iowa State College, has been appointed national consultant to the Iowa State Planning Board.

The third dismissal of a Butler University instructor, purportedly because of connections with Dr. Walter S. Athearn, former president of the university, was announced on April 16. Dr. Ernest L. Bowman, formerly of the Ohio State University, and for the past two years registrar and examiner at Butler, has been informed that his contract will not be renewed for the next year. Dr. Albert E. Bailey, dean of the evening and extension courses, and Frederick C. Mackey, head football coach, have already been dismissed.

Dr. Margarete Bieber, formerly associate professor of classical archeology at the University of Giessen, has been appointed visiting lecturer at Barnard College for the academic year 1934–35.

Professor Howard G. Brunsman, of the Bureau of Business Research at Ohio State University, has been named statistical adviser to the real property unit in the Bureau of Foreign and Domestic Commerce at Washington, D. C. He will continue his duties at the university while working with the government.

John L. Kerchen, director of workers' education for the University of California since 1922, has been appointed director of the newly established Workers' Education Division of the University of Oregon, the University of California and the University of Washington. The organization has been designed to provide classes in adult education for workers in the three states served by these institutions. The project, part of the emergency education program of the Federal Emergency Relief Administration, will be carried on by the Federation of Labor in the various states, by the Workers' Education Bureau of America and by the universities. The courses offered will be of college and university level, modeled along the lines of those given in labor colleges in England.

Dr. Roland S. Morris, formerly United States Ambassador to Japan and professor of international law at the University of Pennsylvania since 1924, has been elected a life member of the board of trustees of Princeton University.

Philip Newell Youtz, assistant director of the Brooklyn Museum, has assumed the position of director, following the resignation of Dr. William Henry Fox, who has served in that capacity for twenty-two years. Before going to the Brooklyn Museum, Mr. Youtz acted as curator of exhibitions at the Pennsylvania Museum of Art at Philadelphia.

B. Frank Carter, head master of the Stevens Preparatory School at Hoboken, N. J., has been appointed director of the Stevens Academy, which comes into existence with the recently contracted merger of the Hoboken Academy and the Stevens Preparatory School.

Dr. John H. J. Upham, dean of the College of Medicine at Ohio State University, has announced that the board of trustees of the American Medical Society will meet in Cleveland on June 10. Dr. Upham is chairman of the board.

Dr. B. A. Tolbert, dean of men at the University of Florida, has been elected president of the National Association of Deans and Advisers of Men. W. E. Alderman, of Beloit College, will serve as vice-president of the organization, D. H. Gardner, of the University of Akron, as secretary-treasurer, and J. W. Armstrong, of Northwestern University, as editor. The next conference of the association will be held at Baton Rouge, La., in the spring of 1935.

James G. Blaine, president of the Marine Midland Trust Company of New York City, has been named a trustee of Washington and Jefferson College.

Dr. Robert Williams, president of the Ohio Northern University, has recently been elected to the presidency of the Ohio College Association.

Tuskegee Institute honored Booker T. Washington, its founder, when the annual Founders' Day celebration was held on April 8. Dr. Thomas Jesse Jones, educational director of the Phelps-Stokes Fund, delivered the principal address.

Dr. Camille Eugene Werling, head of the French department of the University of Denver, has been granted the diploma of "Officier d'Academie" by the French Government. The diploma will be officially presented to him by Dr. E. B. Renaud, French consular agent, at a faculty meeting of the Liberal Arts College on April 23. The award has been made upon the recommendation of M. Meric de Bellefon, consular general of France at San Francisco.

Dr. Charles Wilson Greene, professor of physiology and pharmacology at the University of Missouri, has been elected president of the American Physiological Society.

Bert Hodge Hill, formerly assistant curator of classical antiques of the Boston Museum of Fine Arts, has been honored by the dedication to him of the April issue of the *American Journal of Archaeology*. The magazine, appearing on the occasion of Mr. Hill's sixtieth birthday, contains articles contributed by his former students and associates.

Miss Annie Earle Slack has received the Cleveland H. Dodge distinguished service medal for her work as director of health and home betterment in Syria.

Dr. Chaim Weizmann, president of the Hebrew University at Jerusalem, Dr. Judah L. Magnes, chancellor of the university, and Dr. Max Schloessinger, vice-chancellor, will arrive in the United States early in May, according to a recent announcement made by Dr. A. S. W. Rosenbach, president of the American Friends of the Hebrew University, to confer with the American members of the university board.

Seven members of the faculty of Kenyon College left on Sunday, April 15, for a week's visit to eastern colleges to observe and study educational methods and organization of other educational institutions. On Sunday, April 22, another group of seven members of the faculty will start on the same mission to different institutions. The first group includes Professors L. B. Walton, W. R. Ashford, P. W. Timberlake, C. T. Bumer, S. R. McGowan and P. M. Titus. The second group includes Professors R. D. Cahall, R. B. Allen, J. W. Blum, M. G. Rigg, W. H. Coolidge, E. H. Johnson and C. L. Cottrell.

President Ray Lyman Wilbur, of Stanford University, has announced the establishment of the Ellwood and Helen Cubberley Trust Fund of nearly $400,000 in the Stanford School of Education. The fund represents the lifetime earnings, largely in the field of educational authorship, of Dean-emeritus Ellwood Patterson Cubberley. It is the intent of the donors, when the principal of the trust becomes valuable enough, to have it devoted to four main purposes: First, to erect a building for the School of Education; second, to endow the chair which Dr. Cubberley held for thirty-five years; third, to add to the Cubberley Lecture Fund, created by a national committee, headed by the late Henry Suzzallo, on the occasion of the dean's retirement last June, sufficient funds to bring that up to $20,000 if the committee has not achieved that end within a reasonable time, and fourth, to provide a special endowment with which to purchase books for the School of Education Library.

The Reverend Dr. William Mangam Lawrence, formerly president of the board of trustees of Colgate University and of the Divinity

School of the University of Chicago, died on April 10. Dr. Lawrence was eighty-five years old.

DR. HENRY DONALD CAMPBELL, dean of Washington and Lee University since 1908 and a member of the faculty since 1887, died on April 10 at the age of seventy-one years.

PROFESSOR HERBERT GRANT CAMPBELL, head of the department of philosophy at Morningside College, Sioux City, Iowa, died on April 8 at the age of sixty-four years.

PROFESSOR F. PAUL ANDERSON, dean of the College of Engineering at the University of Kentucky since 1917, died on April 8 in his sixty-eighth year.

DR. LAWTON BRYAN EVANS, superintendent of the Richmond County, Ga., public schools since 1883, died on April 6. Dr. Evans was seventy-one years of age.

WILLIAM BAUER, associate professor of music at Connecticut College, died on April 14 at the age of fifty-three years.

THE National College Press Association will hold its annual convention at the University of Kentucky from May 3 to 5. Professor Victor R. Portmann, assistant professor of journalism at the university, and Neil Plummer, instructor in journalism, will be in charge of arrangements. "College Newspaper Advertising" and "Faculty Supervision of College Publications" will be the two general topics discussed at the convention.

THE ninth annual meeting of the American Association for Adult Education will be held at the Shoreham Hotel in Washington, D. C., from May 21 to 24. Dorothy Canfield Fisher, president of the association, will address the general session of the meeting on "Goals in Adult Education."

UNDER the terms of a bill signed on April 6 by Governor Ely, of Massachusetts, school committees in all cities and towns except Boston can not dismiss teachers except for stated causes, including inefficiency, incapacity, conduct unbecoming a teacher, insubordination "or other good cause." Under the previous law, a school committee could dismiss a teacher for any reason. No change was made, however, in the provision which allows dismissal because of a decrease in the number of pupils. Boston schools are governed by a separate statute.

MORE than 50,000 educational toys, marking twenty years of progress in American-made playthings, will be displayed at the American Toy Fair from April 9 to 28. The exhibitions will be held at the Hotel McAlpin and at the Toy Center in New York City. Toys that perform industrial and housekeeping tasks will be featured.

AN International Relations Conference for high-school students throughout the state of Colorado will be held at the University of Denver on April 27 and 28. The conference has been sponsored by members of the Colorado Education Association, in conjunction with the Foundation for the Advancement of the Social Sciences of the University of Denver.

THE Second Conference on Business Education will be held at the School of Business of the University of Chicago on June 27 and 28. The general theme for discussion has been announced as "Business Education and the Consumer." The conference will be concerned with two major aspects of the problem. The first section held on June 27 will include contributions of those speakers who have made studies on the "Position of the Consumer"; the second day, June 28, will be devoted to discussions of the "Status and Means of Consumer Education."

THE Iowa State College Experiment Station, under the direction of Professor H. M. Hamlin, of the Vocational Education Department, is conducting a study to determine the relative cost of educating rural pupils in one-room schools compared with the cost of educating them in town schools. The study is being pursued in cooperation with the State Department of Public Instruction and with the assistance of the University of Iowa and the Iowa State Teachers College.

MALNUTRITION is not a factor in the health of the school children of Minneapolis, according to a recent survey made of 100 schools reported in the *Journal of the American Medical Association.* Seventy-seven schools reported absence of noticeable malnutrition, with an occasional case of undernourishment peculiar to the home and family rather than to the economic situation. Fourteen schools reported a noticeable improvement in the nutrition status of the children as compared with the surveys of a year and two years ago. In these schools particular attention was called to the fact that a fair, if not large, percentage of the students are from homes receiving public relief. The officials of these schools attributed the present favorable conditions to the fact of better food selection.

The establishment of a service bureau for education in human relations has been announced by Teachers College of Columbia University. Associated with Teachers College in this movement are Harvard University, Boston University and Temple University. Under the direction of Mrs. Rachel Davis-Du Bois, executive secretary of Teachers College, the service bureau will aid elementary and high-school teachers in arranging programs which present a sympathetic view-point of racial issues and of the various culture groups of the world. The bureau will also be open to adult educational groups and community organizations.

Dr. Joseph Brewer, president of Olivet College, has devised a study plan for the college which will go into effect next September. Under this system, students will attend no classes. Entire mornings will be devoted to private study. Afternoons will be assigned to athletics for both students and professors, and evenings will be given over to discussions, debates and social affairs designed to contribute to intellectual development. Degrees will be awarded to students who pass two comprehensive examinations, which will be both oral and written. In the junior division of the college, President Brewer states, the student will acquire a general knowledge of physical, biological and social sciences, arts and literature, philosophy and religion. He will obtain a reading knowledge of one foreign language and lay a foundation for specialized study. In the senior division the student will study intensively in one of seven schools: natural and physical science, social science, language and literature, philosophy, psychology, religion, education, fine arts or music. He will also acquire a reading knowledge of a second foreign language.

DISCUSSION

EDUCATION OR REVOLUTION?

A pointless controversy is under way. The flagrant question—"Can the schools build a new social order?"—is abroad in the land. Discussions, debates and lectures flagellate the question with ayes and noes. We witness the radical educator writing for current magazines, pamphleteering, agitating that the schools both could and should. We observe the conservative educator marshaling astonishing scholarship to the effect that schools never did and consequently shouldn't. Once more it is the old malady—words, words, words—but there is no agreement about the meaning of those words.

The time has come to arbitrate between the two camps. A better understanding of the whole affair will result from the clarifying of certain subsidiary concepts and a consequent correct use of words. If a humble one is to understand the view of the proponents of the school as an agency of social change he must alter the question to read—"Can education build a new social order?" If educational institutions are to contribute toward the establishment of any new social order those institutions will not be limited to elementary schools. It is absurd to dream of a millennium ushered in by a vanguard of infants. Even those optimists who dream of the perfect society in the elementary school, leading on to the perfect community when children grow up, have forty years to wait for the miracle. In the meanwhile the reforms we advocate to-day will be passé to-morrow. Our incongruous secondary schools can not understand themselves. They would be but a stumbling block in our search for Utopia. Granted that colleges and universities could transform themselves overnight and make the striking contribution to social invention which we might hope for from mature youths, yet this would be but a part. It can never be the school alone which remakes the social order. It must be the school and the church and the lecture platform and the social forum and the newspaper and the magazine and the publishing house and the social settlement and the moving picture and the radio and even the business man, cooperating in one vast community educational effort. If such conscious effort to speed social change be made, the gain will not be wrought by the school, but by education in its widest sense through every community institution.

Another bone of contention between the factions in the current controversy results from a misunderstanding of the dynamic quality of true culture. Both groups seem hazy in their recognition of the fact that American culture, like every other culture, is composed of constants and variables. The proponents of social change via education tend to underestimate the importance of the constants in the cultural heritage. They are hasty to discard, eager to innovate. They become frothy and furious in their eagerness to set up a social order which they know very little about. They would have us topple head over heels in an attempt to get there before we know where we are going. The die-hards, on the other hand, with a philosophy colored by their own "stake" in the current social order, are ever eager to pass on to youth the constants, but shy away from the variables. The middle course is always the best. An education which teaches only the constants moves on like China to an ultimate cultural breakdown. An education which fritters away all its time on the variables rushes to its own destruction. The conservatives, who argue that education has never built a new social order but has always reflected the established one, are thinking only of constants. Education reflects the constants of the social order. The variables if readily admitted, temper undue monopoly of education by a social minority. They may thus facilitate social change. Thus our question becomes not "Can education build a new social order?" but "Can education contribute to the building of a new social order?"

It is beside the point to insist that schools can never initiate a new social order. If education can contribute, let who may initiate. In any social movement causes and agents are obscured. During the Reformation vast social changes antedated the outburst of Luther. It if of no importance to know who initiates social change. There is a common cause behind the actions of society and individuals. Educators and teachers who arrogate to themselves the duty of initiating or causing or being responsible for the new social order are egregiously conceited. Unless there is something basic to both their own efforts and to current social phenomena they beat their wings against air. Let us give up any swollen idea of our own importance initiating a new social order, and let us seek to guide the expression of forces more fundamental than our own conceits.

It is the imminence of social change, not the genius of our pure intellect that is pricking teachers to social effort. Teachers need not decide whether education shall or shall not contribute to social change. It always had and it always will. The question we must answer is a deeper one. Can education during a social crisis speed up its social contribution by a wider emphasis on the variables. No one acquainted with world affairs to-day doubts that we are passing from one social order into another. The issue for teachers and educators and for politicians and bankers is the same. Can education become our ally rather than our enemy? Can education cease from *laissez-faire?* Can education become causative rather than neutral in our social crisis? It is in the interests of all, liberals and conservatives alike, that education receive a new lease of life, that the full dynamic quality of culture be nurtured and released.

Social change may occur in one of two ways. It may occur rapidly by revolution, or more slowly by the conscious and deliberate process of education. That society which steadfastly refuses to welcome functioning variables into its educational institutions is harboring for itself revolution. Revolution is the painful and wasteful method of social change. Education is the sophisticated and common-sense method. In these days which are passing over our heads we must answer one fundamental question. That question is not "Dare the schools build a new social order?" but "Dare education fail to contribute to a new social order already under way?" In periods of dangerous social change, like the present, it is education or revolution.

A. GORDON MELVIN

NEW YORK, N. Y.

WHY THE SMALL BOARDING SCHOOL?

THE public schools have to be organized on a large scale in order to meet the widely varied demands of universal education. There are a few pupils with definite personality traits who become lost in the machine-like methods which must obtain, to some extent, in a large school system. These same pupils, when given individual attention and an environment that is especially suited to their needs, may be expected to attain far better results and hence we have one of the functions of the small boarding school. This school may select its main purpose in education and then equip itself to produce results in harmony with that educational philosophy. Instead of facing the need of universal education, as does the public school, it can select the pupils who need most the special training which the school is especially prepared to give. Its schedule can be adapted to each pupil's need, whereas in a large system many pupils have to be adapted to the schedule. This elasticity of the curriculum is one of the major opportunities which the small school has for meeting individual needs. A pupil who is retarded in one subject may require extra attention for several months and then be able to make rapid progress. Meanwhile he may have been advanced in another subject, and rapid progress there, if permitted by an elastic schedule, may assist in maintaining his morale while working on the difficult course.

The public school represents a long term investment of the taxpayer, and consequently it is responsible directly to the community. This brings the pupils into a very close relation with that particular unit of society in which they are being trained. There are many advantages in this close contact, since the children of to-day are the citizens of to-morrow. However, a democracy has disadvantages which have a profound effect upon its educational system, as has been illustrated by the Scopes trial in Tennessee and the issue over Muzzey's text-books in Chicago. Within many communities we find political, racial and religious factions which sometimes invade the school system and result in repressions, changes in personnel and in the formation of partisan educational policies. The boarding school is dependent upon tuition, or tuition and endowments, for its support and consequently is responsible to its patrons for the results which it returns to them. The personnel of the school, trained in the science of education, becomes the source of the educational aims and methods, and the school is not dependent upon the average citizen for permission to carry out those purposes. It is in a position to obtain the desired equipment which will facilitate the attainment of its objectives and to apply the best methods known in training the pupils. It can carry on research as wisdom dictates and apply the results or not as their values warrant. The boarding school may be built in a geographical environment favorable to the peculiar purposes of the school.

In many modern homes the parents find it difficult, because of business location and various interests, to devote sufficient time and study to their children outside of school hours. Often there is a resulting danger that the uncontrolled outside influences may react against the training which the school gives, and thus the education of the child is seriously handicapped. It is difficult to develop an integrated personality if there are conflicting influences at work on the pupil. It is a great advantage to the school to have the pupil's entire day within its control. The work of the classroom is important in preparing for entrance examinations, but the concomitant learnings which are not confined to the classroom and study halls are of the utmost importance in the development of a successful life. The worthy use of leisure time can be attained by actual practise during leisure time. The boarding school can offer the opportunity for some worthy use of free time and then give the pupil interpretative instruction when he can use it most effectively. Every child can not be successful in all things, but every child should be enabled to achieve a worthwhile success in at least one useful activity. The value that musical training, ability with the hands, excellence in some sport, friendship with books or a special interest in nature may have for child or adult is sure and unmeasurable.

According to the U. S. Office of Education, of every 1,000 pupils in the fifth grade, 610 enter high school, 260 graduate from high school, 160 enter college and 50 graduate from college. These statistics can not be viewed with satisfaction by those who are responsible for the education of children. Certainly one important duty stands out clearly—the need of greater care in choosing the right school for the child.

WILLIAM A. SMITH
INDIAN MOUNTAIN SCHOOL
LAKEVILLE, CONN.

SPECIAL CORRESPONDENCE

THE EDUCATION OF YOUNG CHILDREN IN ENGLAND

DESPITE the retrenchments which have had to be effected in English education as a result of the economic situation, but which have at no time been as serious as in this country, the last few years have been used to reconsider the reconstruction of the educational system when economic recovery has been assured. The main lines of this reconstruction have been laid down in three reports issued by the Consultative Committee of the Board of Education. Each of these reports incorporates the best opinions of experts and laymen and brief surveys of practises in other countries than England. It is important to note in reading these reports that the Consultative Committee presents its considered opinion after carefully sifting the views presented by a large number of "witnesses." In other words, the reports present not necessarily the most advanced theory on the subject under inquiry but the best that is practicable on the basis of the evidence submitted by those who are in close touch with the system as it is.

The Consultative Committee has worked backwards in its consideration of the problems of reconstructing the educational organization. The first problem which was referred to it arose out of a wide-spread demand for secondary education for all. The first subject of reference, undertaken in 1924, was concerned with the full-time education of children over 11 in schools other than the traditional secondary schools. The result of this investigation was the famous "Report on the Education of the Adolescent," which was issued in 1926 and which recommended the raising of the age of compulsory attendance to 15 and the organization of four-year courses for children over 11, adapted to the abilities of different groups and paralleling secondary education proper. This report immediately led to the investigation of the type of education best suited to the needs of children between the ages of 7 and 11 and resulted in the publication of the "Report on the Primary School" in 1931, which constitutes an outstanding contribution to the literature of primary education.

There still remained two other problems for investigation to round out the organization of the educational system for all children of school age. One of these is the coordination of the type of post-primary education recommended in the "Education of the Adolescent" with the existing secondary school; this problem was referred to the Consultative Committee last year and is now the subject of investigation. The other problem is concerned with the education of young children on which the Consultative Committee issued its report in November of last year under the title "Infant and Nursery Schools."[1] In quality and comprehensiveness this report ranks with its predecessors.

The report on "Infant and Nursery Schools" deals with the history of this branch of education, the physical development of children up to the age of 7, the mental development of children up to the age of 7, the age limits and organization of the infant stage of primary education, the medical supervision, education and training of children below the age of 5, the training and teaching of young children in infant and nursery schools, the staffing of infant and nursery schools and the training of teachers for service in them, the premises and equipment of infant and nursery schools and a summary of principal conclusions and recommendations. As important for students of education as the main text are the appendices, which include a memorandum on the anatomical and physiological characteristics and development of children between the ages of 2 and 7, a report on the emotional development of children up to the age of 7 plus, short descriptions of nursery and similar schools and notes on the provision

[1] All the reports mentioned are published by His Majesty's Stationery Office, London, and may be obtained in this country through the British Library of Information, New York.

for the preliminary education and training of children below the age of compulsory attendance in certain European countries and in the United States.

The Consultative Committee recommends that the present requirement of compulsory attendance from the age of 5 be retained and that children be promoted from the infant to the upper stage of primary education not later than between the ages of 7 and 8. Since the infant school stands between the nursery and the upper stage of primary education the transition from one branch to the other should be eased, a recommendation similar to that of the American kindergarten-primary organization. Signs of retardation should be detected as early as possible, without, however, establishing special classes for retarded children in the infant schools. Out of this suggestion there follows naturally the recommendation that simple forms of school records should be kept.

In considering the physical growth of children emphasis is placed on the importance of looking for signs of malnutrition and investigating dietaries, providing facilities for sleep not only for children below five but also for some above that age, on the early detection of defects of vision and hearing, and again on keeping records of physical development, medical history and home conditions. Hence provisions for the medical inspection and treatment of young children should be extended beyond the existing regulations. In general, schools of open-air design are recommended as the best safeguard against the spread of infectious diseases. Indeed, the importance of an open-air environment is stressed from the point of view both of mental development and of the curriculum.

The discussion of the mental development is followed by a consideration of the training and teaching of children under the age of seven. The Consultative Committee is of the opinion that the nursery school is a desirable adjunct to the national system of education and that nursery classes should be provided for children below the age of five who attend infant schools. "The fundamental purpose of the nursery school or class is to reproduce the healthy conditions of a good nursery in a well-managed home, and thus to provide an environment in which the health of the young child—physical, mental and moral—can be safeguarded. The training of the nursery stage must be a natural training, not an artificial one. Its aim is not so much to implant the knowledge and habits which civilized adults consider useful, as to aid and supplement the natural growth of the normal child." The home has the responsibility of making the training of the nursery school effective.

The work of the infant school must provide for the child's healthy growth, physical, intellectual, spiritual and moral, through teaching based on the open-air activities and interests of the children, offering opportunities for speech training, rhythm in movement, singing, acting and constructive work of various kinds. The curriculum of the infant school should include (a) religious instruction; (b) natural activities, including physical training, open-air life, rest and play; (c) expression training, including speech, dancing and singing, handwork and drawing; and (d) formal instruction in the 3 R's, which should be begun when the child, whether he be three or six years old, wants to do so. As far as possible an instructive environment, including apparatus and an adequate supply of suitable books, should be created whereby the child is put in a position to teach himself, but "individual work" of this type places upon the teacher the responsibility of keeping regular records of progress. The teacher must enjoy freedom in planning and arranging her work if the danger of lapsing into mechanical routine is to be avoided.

The teachers of infant schools and nursery classes should, where practicable, be certificated teachers and where these are not available they should be under a certificated head teacher or be assisted by a visiting expert teacher. Superintendents of nursery schools should have three years of training with specialization in the care of very young children. Recommendations are made on courses of training for teachers of children under seven and for "helpers" for nursery schools and classes. Into the details on premises and equipment, which are discussed in the final chapter, it is not necessary to enter here except to refer again to the emphasis on the open-air character of the infant school: "The essential conditions of fresh air, sunshine and light will best be secured by what may be described as semi-open-air buildings." The nursery school building should not be "institutional" in character, but should consist rather of open shelters with a liberal space for a garden-playground.

It is characteristic of reports issued by the Consultative Committee that in general they reflect the best practise which has already been proved to be attainable. There are already many nursery schools, nursery classes and infant schools of the type recommended in the present report; the aim of the report is to make ready for the next advance which experiments have already shown to be practicable. The three reports of the consultative committee—on "Infant and Nursery Schools," the "Primary School," and the "Education of the Adolescent,"—together present in outline a picture of the system of English education as it will be developed within the near future.

I. L. Kandel

Teachers College
Columbia University

REPORTS

THE GUGGENHEIM FOUNDATION LIST OF FELLOWSHIPS

Trustees of the John Simon Guggenheim Foundation have announced fellowship awards to six artists, nine writers, two composers of music, two workers in the arts of the theater, and twenty-one scholars studying in as many different fields of knowledge. This brings to $1,200,000 the total grants of the foundation to assist American scholars and artists to carry on research and creative work, and the total number of awards so far is 577. Grants to Latin-American scholars will be made in June.

Literature

Conrad Potter Aiken, poet and novelist.

Miss Kay Boyle, poet and novelist.

Leonard Ehrlich, author, granted a renewal of the fellowship awarded a year ago.

Albert Halper, novelist and short story writer.

Younghill Kang, native Korean, now English instructor at New York University; fellowship renewed.

Alexander Laing, of Hanover, N. H., poet and novelist.

George Milburn, of Oklahoma, novelist.

Isidor Schneider, poet and novelist.

Tom Tippett, former professor of economics in Brookwood Labor College at Katonah, N. Y., who plans a volume dealing with the coal industry in the United States.

The Theater

Miss Angna Enters, of New York, a dancer. She will go to Greece to study ancient Greek art forms.

Charles Norris Houghton, graduate of Princeton University. He has done work in New York and Baltimore.

Music

William Grant Still, who will work in this country.

Professor Douglas Moore, of Columbia University.

Art

Peggy Bacon, a satirist in the graphic arts.

Frank Mechau, of Denver, Colorado, a painter of western scenes.

Francis Criss, to study fresco painting in Italy.

Rosella Hartman, N. Y., to study the lithographer's craft in Paris.

Maurice Glickman, a sculptor.

Howard Cook, of Springfield, Mass., has been granted a second fellowship. He is in Springfield doing a mural painting under PWA auspices.

Literary Research

Dr. J. Douglas Bush, professor of English at the University of Minnesota, for a critical study of English poetry.

Dr. Howard F. Lowry, professor of English at the College of Wooster, for studies on Matthew Arnold and Arthur Hugh Claugh.

Sterling Dodd, of Harvard University, for studies on Athenian public documents in Greece.

Dr. Geoffroy Atkinson, professor of Romance languages at Amherst College, for a study of the French renaissance.

Dr. Rudolf M. Riefstahl, of New York University, for research in Islamic ceramics in Italy.

Dr. Ernest Nagel, instructor in philosophy at Columbia University, for studies in symbolic or mathematical logic.

Biological Research

Dr. Michael Heidelberger, associate professor in biological chemistry at Columbia University, for research at the University of Upsala, Sweden, on the molecular weight of thyroid globulin.

Arthur Loveridge, now in Kenya on a fellowship, for the continuation of his studies of the vanishing vertebrate fauna of tropical East Africa.

Dr. Harold Kirby, Jr., associate professor of zoology at the University of California, for studies of Protozoa living in termites in South Africa.

Dr. George Oswald Burr, associate professor of botany at the University of Minnesota, for research in photosynthesis in European laboratories.

Dr. Allan Lyle Grafflin, instructor in anatomy at Harvard, to study kidney structures of fishes.

Physical Research

Dr. Robert B. Brode, professor of physics at the University of California, to make European investigations into heterocyclic compounds containing nitrogen.

Dr. Frank H. Spedding, instructor in chemistry at the University of California, to study solids at low temperatures.

Dr. Francis William Bergstrom, assistant professor of chemistry at Stanford University, to study heterocyclic compounds containing nitrogen.

Dr. Kenneth T. Bainbridge, assistant professor of physics at Harvard University, for research on molecular physics at the University of Cambridge, England.

Dr. Arnold Dresden, professor of mathematics, Swarthmore College, for the preparation of a book on the calculus of variations.

Historical Research

Dr. Grace Lee Nute, curator of manuscripts of the Minnesota Historical Society, for research abroad for biological material.

Dr. Fulmer Mood, renewal of a fellowship to continue his research in early American colonization.

Dr. Lowell J. Ragatz, associate professor of history at George Washington University, renewal of a fellowship to continue his studies into the social and economic situation of the French Antilles during the 17th and 18th centuries.

William Henry Chamberlin, a newspaper man, a renewal of his fellowship for the writing of the history of the Russian revolution from 1917 to 1921.

Dr. Frank Tannenbaum, a renewed fellowship to continue his studies of agrarian problems of Peru and Argentina.

THE FELLOWSHIPS OF THE AMERICAN COUNCIL OF LEARNED SOCIETIES

Appointment of twelve research fellows in the fields of the humanities for the academic year 1934–35 was announced on April 7 by the American Council of Learned Societies.

The holders of the fellowships, who already have obtained the degree of doctor of philosophy, will engage in research and study in the United States, England, France, Germany, Italy, Greece, Turkey, Palestine, China and Japan. The fields in which the fellowships lie include ancient, medieval and modern history, archeology, paleography, linguistics, musicology, literature and oriental art.

The appointments are as follows:

Dr. Solomon Katz. A literary, inscriptional and archeological study of ancient Bithynia, first as a client kingdom and later as a province of the Roman Empire.

Dr. A. O. Sarkissian. Research in the intellectual background of Armenian nationalism, with special reference to the dissemination of European ideas among the Armenian people during the nineteenth century. Work will be carried on in libraries in Venice, Armenia, Jerusalem and Istanbul.

Dr. John W. Stanton, instructor in Oriental history at the University of Michigan. Research in China in the history of the foreign relations of the Chinese Empire from the seventeenth to the nineteenth century, with particular reference to Russia.

Dr. Procope S. Costas, research associate in the University of Chicago. Study in Germany and Greece of the history of the Greek language since classical times.

Dr. Charles F. Voegelin. Further study of the Shawnee language as a part of a general investigation of the Algonkain languages and the Eastern Woodland culture of the American Indian.

Dr. Milan S. La Du, research assistant in Princeton University. Work in Romance paleography, centering in an examination of Manuscript *A* of the *Roman d'Alexandre.*

Dr. Walter T. Pattison, assistant professor of Romance languages at Wesleyan University. A study of the poetry of the troubadour Raimbaut d'Orange, together with work in paleography and Provençal literature in Paris.

Dr. W. L. Schramm, research associate in the State University of Iowa. A study of various types of English verse, to be carried on by means of phonophotography in the laboratories of the State University of Iowa. It is proposed to apply a technique evolved from the study of music to an examination of the nature of metre, pitch patterns and phrasal rhythms in poetry.

Dr. Harcourt Brown. A study of the Huguenot Henry Justel (1620–1693) and his influence in the history of science. Work will be carried on in Italy, France and England.

Dr. Eleanor B. von Erdberg, Fogg Museum of Harvard University. A general study of Oriental art in the collections of China and Japan, and further training in the Japanese language and in Japanese methods of research in the fine arts.

Dr. Henry A. Myers, assistant in the Department of English, Cornell University. A historical study of the attempts to formulate a law of events in poetry and in philosophical systems.

Dr. W. Oliver Strunk, chief assistant in the division of music in the Library of Congress. Musicological research, chiefly in Germany, in the sources and development of the early style of Joseph Haydn.

EDUCATIONAL RESEARCH AND STATISTICS

A SURVEY OF THE REQUIREMENTS FOR THE DEGREEE OF DOCTOR OF EDUCATION

In 1930 Dr. Walter S. Monroe, in the report of a survey[1] of the requirements for the doctor of philosophy degree in education, mentioned six universities granting the degree of doctor of education and made a few comments concerning their requirements for this degree. An examination of the offerings of institutions today reveals that this number has risen to nineteen.[2] Such an increase warrants a study of the requirements for the doctorate in education.

Monroe mentioned as the most significant differences in the requirements for the latter degree as contrasted with the former the elimination of the language requirement, the requirement of professional experience and "a concept of the thesis as an organization and application of existing knowledge rather than as an original contribution."[3] He noted that for the doctor of philosophy degree some institutions were modifying the language requirement and accepting a thesis of the type just mentioned, in lieu of the usual "original contribution" to knowledge. A detailed contrast of the aims and requirements for these degrees is not the purpose of this study. Some light will be thrown on the matter, however, by (1) considering the administration and aims of the doctor of education degree; (2) bringing into relief the distinguishing characteristics of the two degrees as specified by the schools themselves; and (3) analyzing the requirements for the degree of doctor of education.

The administration of the degree is of great importance. At Harvard its control by the Graduate School of Education with a separate professional faculty "is dictated by the fact that no other faculty at the University faces squarely toward the needs, problems, and opportunities of the schools, especially the public schools."[4] At Johns Hopkins it is administered by the School of Higher Studies in Education, the establishment of which made graduate work in education "in part a university unit parallel to the school of higher studies of the faculty of philosophy." In taking this action, the trustees of the university were regarded as expressing "their recognition of the distinctive position of public and private schools in present-day life, of the institutional need for the specific training of school officers and teachers, and of a more intensive and systematic study of educational problems."[5] Similar independence of the school of education in the administration of the degree is found at Indiana, Stanford, Temple, Southern California, Rutgers, Oregon, Boston University, Buffalo and George Washington. On the other hand, at California, Oklahoma, Pennsylvania State, Washington, Western Reserve, Pittsburgh, North Dakota and Boston College, the degree is administered at least partially by the graduate school.

The program for the doctorate in education at Harvard has as its desired outcome "the advancement of knowledge and insight in education," its chief purpose being "to produce studies of genuine value to the profession."[6] The program of each individual is designed to follow "the lead of the lines of thought and

[1] W. S. Monroe, "A Survey of the Requirements for the Doctor of Philosophy in Education." School and Society, 21: 655, May 17, 1930.

[2] West Virginia University no longer offers the doctor of education degree.

[3] W. S. Monroe, *op. cit.*, p. 656.

[4] National Society of College Teachers of Education *Yearbook*, No. 19, p. 110.

[5] "The New Degrees at Johns Hopkins University." School and Society, 29: p. 508, April 20, 1929.

[6] Harvard University *Official Register*, Vol. XXX, No. 30, p. 17, June 22, 1933.

investigation" which he has chosen in the solution of an educational problem, and permits "concentration upon the technicalities of educational research without reference to traditional academic requirements."[7] The degree is a research degree more definitely than a professional one. Temple reserves the degree for students who show "unusual competency for scholarly research."[8] Rutgers confers the doctor of education degree in recognition of "high attainment in the constructive study of educational problems, or upon demonstrated ability to pursue independent research in some aspect of education."[9] The degree is "designed to mark that limited number of educators who are to do original constructive thinking and experimentation"; it is not primarily "a craftsman's degree."[10] Buffalo grants the degree on the basis of "high scholarship . . . as evidenced in several ways." Its aim is to select and assist students "who by their previous study and experience in Education give promise of making a contribution to the underlying knowledge or practises of Education, or to both."[11]

Boston University, Indiana, California, Oregon, Oklahoma, Pennsylvania State, Pittsburgh, Stanford, Johns Hopkins, George Washington and North Dakota, on the other hand, all consider the degree as a "professional" one. California states that it differs from the doctor of philosophy degree "as the practitioner's interest differs from that of the pure scientist."[12] Oregon seeks to provide, through the doctor of education degree, a more sequential course "to prepare men and women for immediate service in administrative and advanced teaching positions."[13] At Stanford "the theory of the Ed.D. is that it stands for scholarship and for the ability to organize and apply knowledge in teaching and administration" in contrast to "the theory of the Ph.D." which "stands for scholarship and for ability in research. . . . Except in the case of instructors in education whose primary function is research, the Ed.D. is truly *the professional degree*."[14] In the majority of instances it was found that the doctorate in education is considered as professional in character; in some, as a research degree; and in a few, as either one or the other.

Stanford, Southern California, Oklahoma and Oregon provide for two types of doctor of education degrees. Stanford has the administrator and the master-teacher types; Southern California, the master-teacher and the administration-supervision and counselor types; Oklahoma, the teacher and the administrator types; and Oregon, the school administrator and the high-school principal types.

An analysis of the requirements for the degree reveals that California, Indiana and Johns Hopkins specify a reading knowledge of foreign languages only when the student's thesis makes it necessary. Southern California and Stanford have this requirement for the administrator type of degree and require one language of all those interested in the master-teacher type. Western Reserve and Boston College require proficiency in the reading of German and French; Temple permits substitutions of other languages or subjects for French and German if the thesis warrants; Boston University allows the substitution of educational statistics for either French or German; Washington stipulates one foreign language and the ability to use educational statistics. Oklahoma calls for proficiency in two of the following: educational statistics, methods of research, French, German and Spanish. Pittsburgh requires certification of proficiency in two of the following: French, German, advanced statistical method, mental measurements and either a master's thesis or a formal paper describing some phase of school practise. Harvard, North Dakota, George Washington, Pennsylvania State, Buffalo, Oregon and Rutgers do not specify languages. In fifteen of the nineteen institutions studied the doctor of education degree may be awarded without an examination in any language or languages.

[7] National Society of College Teachers of Education, *op. cit.*, pp. 110, 114.

[8] Temple University *Bulletin*, Vol. 15, No. 15, p. 45, June, 1933.

[9] Rutgers University *Bulletin*, Series 7, No. 10, p. 225, April, 1932.

[10] Rutgers University, ''The Degrees of Ed. M. and Ed. D.'' *Special Announcement of the School of Education*, June, 1930.

[11] University of Buffalo *Bulletin*, School of Education, July, 1933.

[12] University of California *Bulletin*, Vol. 25, No. 12, p. 11, May, 1932.

[13] University of Oregon *Catalog*, 1933–1934, p. 151.

[14] National Society of College Teachers of Education, *op. cit.*, pp. 144–145.

Of the nineteen universities and colleges granting the doctor of education degree, Indiana, Boston College, Buffalo and Western Reserve make no mention of experience. Washington, Temple and Pennsylvania State require successful educational experience. George Washington places special emphasis on the candidate's success as a teacher, supervisor, administrator or writer. North Dakota requires "a demonstration of practical educational ability in actual school situations"; Harvard and Boston University require a minimum of one year of satisfactory experience; while Stanford, Oklahoma and Rutgers specify at least two years. Johns Hopkins and Southern California require at least three years' teaching or administrative experience previous to taking the preliminary examination, while Pittsburgh states that the applicant must have at least six years of such experience. At Oregon a candidate must offer three years of professional experience, all of which must follow the completion of a standard normal school or college course, one year of which must follow admission to candidacy and be approved by the candidate's committee; and evidence that the experience indicates "ability, leadership, expertness and growth." At California professional success is a part of the "major" and must have been manifested during four years of professional experience, at least one of which follows admission to candidacy and meets the approval of the candidate's committee.

A thesis[15] is required by all institutions, though the importance attached to it varies widely. Harvard regards it as the most important single requirement for the degree and desires "research results of general and lasting value." The thesis may be a "contribution to knowledge" or a "constructive result of importance and value" in which knowledge already available is handled effectively. Oregon, on the other hand, places emphasis upon the mastery of professional subject-matter rather than upon original research. It does, however, accept a thesis of either of the types specified by Harvard. Other institutions which accept either type of thesis and which state this requirement in the same or in almost the same words employed by Harvard are Rutgers, Indiana, California, Southern California, Stanford and Buffalo. Johns Hopkins requires the successful completion of "an original investigation or a verification or extension of existing knowledge based directly upon schoolroom contacts." Boston University, Boston College, Western Reserve and Temple specify a "contribution to knowledge" or a "distinctive contribution to knowledge." Oklahoma requires a "distinct contribution" in the field selected. North Dakota looks to the thesis for evidence of "skill in research and survey methods." Washington desires that the work show high scholarly attainments and independent thinking. Pennsylvania State expects a demonstration of ability to attack an educational problem with originality and independent thought. Pittsburgh and George Washington wish the thesis to be definitely practical.

The differences indicated by these descriptions are perhaps much less real than they may appear to be. Variations in terminology account for much that appears to distinguish one institution from another in their thesis requirements. There is probably some difference of opinion concerning what constitutes a "contribution to knowledge" or "an original contribution" and what represents only an "organization, application or extension of existing knowledge." These various types probably represent a difference in degree rather than in kind and shade one into the other so gradually that to distinguish among them in a scientific fashion would be extremely difficult, if not impossible, involving, as it would, a determination of the point at which an extension of existing knowledge becomes a contribution to knowledge.

The publication of the thesis in full is required by Southern California and Temple. This practise is usual also at Johns Hopkins, Indiana, Washington and Oklahoma. In these latter institutions, however, exceptions are sometimes made, as when the thesis is exceptionally long. In such a case, the printing of an abstract is required. Indiana accepts the thesis in mimeographed form. George Washington and North Dakota require the printing of an abstract of the thesis. In the case of these two and the remaining institutions, two to five type-

15 The term "thesis" is used throughout this study. Eleven institutions require a "thesis" and the remaining eight a "dissertation."

written copies of the thesis must be deposited in the office of the institution.

All the colleges and universities granting the degree of doctor of education, with the exception of Johns Hopkins, require the student to have a baccalaureate degree from a recognized institution before beginning the work which leads to the doctorate. Johns Hopkins requires either a satisfactory bachelor's degree or the completion with distinction of two years of college work. The student who does not have the bachelor's degree must devote at least four years' full-time study for the higher degree. A few institutions specify the number of semester hours in various subjects which must have been included in the work for the bachelor's degree. Such specifications concerning undergraduate work in education vary greatly among institutions. At Harvard a bachelor's degree which includes "a large amount of undergraduate work in education may not be accepted for admission or may be accepted only if supplemented by graduate study or other evidence of preparation for graduate specialization in Education."[16] At Stanford candidates "who have devoted a large portion of their undergraduate time to courses in Education, and others with inadequate basic training,"[17] must build up their training in fields outside that of education. On the other hand, Oklahoma and Southern California require twelve hours or units of undergraduate work in education, and California eighteen undergraduate units in education as a base for graduate study in the subject. The regulations in the case of most institutions are found somewhere between these two extremes, and make no mention of undergraduate work in education as a requirement for graduate study.

While many institutions specify that time limits are of secondary importance, they generally indicate that at least three years of full-time graduate work or its equivalent are necessary to meet the requirements for the degree. Exceptions to the three-year rule are four years at Johns Hopkins for individuals admitted without a bachelor's degree and two years at California, Harvard and Buffalo. Course requirements during these years vary widely. Of special interest are the specifications in terms of academic subject-matter for the master-teacher type of degrees at Stanford, Southern California and Oklahoma. Stanford and Southern California specify the completion of one year's advanced study in the academic field to be taught, while Oklahoma stipulates that approximately one half the candidate's work be taken in the general field in which he expects to teach.

The results of a college scholastic aptitude or psychological test determine in part admission to candidacy for the degree at Pennsylvania State, Harvard, Stanford, Southern California and George Washington. A preliminary or qualifying examination is given by Indiana, Pennsylvania State, Harvard, Washington, Southern California, Western Reserve, Oklahoma, Pittsburgh and North Dakota. California and Oregon require both a qualifying and a preliminary examination.

Another type of examination frequently found is the general or comprehensive type, which takes the place, in some cases, of the preliminary examination, although a few institutions require both. A general examination is given at Boston University, Rutgers, Pittsburgh, Harvard, Stanford, Washington, Johns Hopkins, George Washington and Buffalo. The preliminary and general examinations frequently serve both as a measure of the mastery of the student's special field and his understanding of education in its broader aspects.

This description of examinations is an inadequate representation of the real nature of the achievements to be attained in qualifying for the doctor of education degree. It needs to be remembered that each institution has a set-up somewhat of its own and that examinations bearing the same name may vary widely in different institutions.

The type most widely mentioned in the catalogs and descriptive pamphlets studied is the final or oral examination. Seventeen institutions specify that it be oral, while one provides for either written or oral. Seven state that it shall be chiefly on the thesis. Most of the others mention the thesis and related problems or the thesis and the major and minor fields as the scope of this examination. Harvard has been

[16] Harvard University *Official Register*, *op. cit.*, p. 77.

[17] Stanford University *Bulletin*, Fifth Series, No. 155, pp. 91–92, June 1, 1933.

included in the list of institutions requiring an oral examination, but deserves special mention because the examination is given not when the thesis is completed, as is the general practise, but "as soon as the candidate has the material of his thesis well enough in hand to be sure of the exact definition of his problem, the sources of his data, his method of treatment, and the possible or probable bearings of his results."[18] Another variation from general practise is the Doctoral Conference of Buffalo, which serves as a test of the candidate's ability and insures contacts with students and faculty. Buffalo is the only institution which does not require a "final examination" for the doctor of education degree.

The distinctions between the doctor of philosophy and the doctor of education degree are more marked in some institutions than in others. To the writer the danger of cheapening the doctor's degree appears to be found, not in the type or in the name of the degree, but rather in the standards of the institutions and faculties concerned. In recent correspondence with an officer of one university the fact was brought out that for the doctorates of education and philosophy in the institution in question so many exceptions were granted that much of the work for both was highly inferior.

The study here presented does not reveal a lowering of standards, as was feared by Dr. Freeman in 1931.[19] There appears to be very little evidence of "the substitution of ordinary experience in teaching or administration for some of the customary university work"; in fact, the experience specified appears to be rather an addition to the requirements for the doctor of philosophy degree. The degree of doctor of education allows a greater amount of specialization and individual variation in work in a number of institutions. Stanford University states that "in difficulty of attainment the degrees of Ph.D. and Ed.D. are not especially different; it is the type of difficulty that is different."[20] And this appears to be true of the degrees at many institutions.

If the transfer of the administration of the doctor of education degree to the schools of education has been for the "purpose of escaping some of the requirements which are laid down by the graduate faculty,"[21] some institutions must feel that such escape is desirable and imperative for the finest development of the graduate study of education. What is needed, therefore, is the establishment and maintenance of higher standards for both degrees to the end that more adequately qualified educational leadership may be provided.[22]

THEODORE L. RELLER
UNIVERSITY OF PENNSYLVANIA

[18] Harvard University *Official Register, op. cit.*, p. 95.

[19] National Society of College Teachers of Education, *op. cit.*, p. 157.

[20] Stanford University, School of Education, "Conditions of Candidacy for Advanced Degrees in Education at Stanford University," p. 14.

[21] National Society of College Teachers of Education, *op. cit.*, p. 158.

[22] According to an announcement in SCHOOL AND SOCIETY (39: 1003, 337–338, March 17, 1934), Teachers College, Columbia University, will also grant the degree of doctor of education.

NEW BOOKS IN EDUCATION

COMFORT, MILDRED H. *Happy Health Stories.* Pp. 158. Beckley-Cardy Co. $0.70.

FAULKNER, HAROLD UNDERWOOD and KEPNER, TYLER. *America: Its History and People.* Pp. 850. Harper. $2.20.

FAUNCE, W. H. P. *Facing Life.* Pp. 210. Macmillan. $1.00.

HARDESTY, CECIL DONALD. *Problems and Practices in Housing the Junior-College Program in California.* Pp. 153. University of Southern California Press.

HEPNER, HARRY WALKER. *Human Relations in Changing Industry.* Pp. 671. Prentice-Hall, Inc. $5.00.

HORTON, LILLIAN KNAPP. *Language for Living in a New Land.* Pp. 229. The Stratford Co. $1.25.

JOHNSEN, JULIA E. comp. *Federal Aid to Education.* Pp. 213. The H. W. Wilson Co.

JONES, EDWARD S. *Comprehensive Examinations in the Social Sciences.* Supplement to the December, 1933, Bulletin of the Association of American Colleges. Pp. 128. Association of American Colleges.

LEONARD, MARIA and PALMER, MARIE FREEMAN. *Building and Balancing Budgets.* Pp. 82. L. G. Balfour Co.

MCGUIRE, SAMUEL HARRISON. *Trends in Principles and Practices of Equalization of Educational Opportunity.* Pp. 115. George Peabody College for Teachers.

PALMER, ARCHIE M. and HOLTON, GRACE. *College Instruction in Art.* Pp. 62. Association of American Colleges.

RICHARDSON, M. W. *et al. Manual of Examination Methods.* Pp. 177. University of Chicago Bookstore.

SCHLEMAN, HELEN B. *Group Golf Instruction.* Pp. 80. A. S. Barnes and Co.

SMITH, DAVID EUGENE and GINSBURG, JEKUTHIEL. *A History of Mathematics in America before 1900.* Pp. 209. The Open Court Publishing Co.

SCHOOL AND SOCIETY

WITH WHICH ARE COMBINED THE EDUCATIONAL REVIEW, ESTABLISHED IN 1891, THE TEACHERS MAGAZINE, ESTABLISHED IN 1878, AND THE SCHOOL JOURNAL, ESTABLISHED IN 1874.

EDITED BY J. McKEEN CATTELL, R. D. LINDQUIST AND W. H. COWLEY

EDITORIAL COMMUNICATIONS SHOULD BE ADDRESSED TO THE EDUCATION BUILDING, THE OHIO STATE UNIVERSITY, COLUMBUS, OHIO

Volume 39 SATURDAY, APRIL 28, 1934 Number 1009

ACADEMIC TRAINING FOR SOCIAL WORKERS[1]

By HELEN I. CLARKE

UNIVERSITY OF WISCONSIN

ABOUT a year ago, an article by the above title appeared in SCHOOL AND SOCIETY. The author, Mr. Linus W. Kline, of Skidmore College, had been interested for some time in curricula designed to prepare students for social work. He had found that there was a great variance between the amount of academic and technical training offered and advocated by certain colleges and universities and the amount required of social workers by the civil authorities in towns, cities and counties and, he might have added, by private agencies. Because he observed so great a divergence in the standards advocated by schools of social work and those required by social agencies, he decided to undertake a study of the extent to which colleges and universities are offering training for social work. "Since we hear only of graduate schools and schools not organized on a college basis, the question arose as to whether any courses in social work are provided for undergraduates and the question seemed all the more pertinent in view of the fact that there are so many non-college social workers and others with only the bachelor's degree in social science."[2] He starts with two theories, that social work is not a profession and that graduate work is superfluous, since social work largely involves routine and the tasks requiring skill are done by specialists outside of the field. He proves both contentions to his own satisfaction.

The writer of this paper does not consider it her function to answer all Mr. Kline's statements concerning whether or not social work is a profession or the need and desirability of graduate professional education for social work. Rather only a few of his outstanding points will be emphasized, his general method of research criticized, and then some of the aims and hopes of social workers and teachers of social work outlined.

It is impossible to evaluate some of Mr. Kline's statements until a word is said about his research methods. In a recently published paper, "Social Work and Social Statistics," Miss Edith Abbott, dean of the Graduate School of Social Service Administration, University of Chicago, called attention "to certain questionable uses of social statistics that might be avoided if the data were more intelligently secured and scientifically interpreted by a trained social worker competent to understand their significance."[3] Certainly a compe-

[1] Linus W. Kline, "Academic Training for Social Workers," SCHOOL AND SOCIETY, 37: 941, 18–27, January 7, 1933.

[2] *Ibid.*, p. 18.

tent social worker would never have used the schedule that Mr. Kline employed to gather the data which he wanted. Any one at all familiar with the educational resources for training in social work would know that answers to several of Mr. Kline's questions must be inadequate and inaccurate and that several of them could not be answered at all by the persons to whom they were sent or by those who must necessarily answer them. For example, Mr. Kline asks deans and directors of Vocational Bureaus in institutions not offering social work training the following:

I. 1. Have you graduates with the bachelor's degree whose course in college did not include special training for social work but who are now filling positions in that field?
   a. About how many in the last ten years have accepted such positions?
   b. How many have since graduation taken special courses in social work?
2. To express the comparative success of graduates in "a" and "b" cross out the word approximately describing the range of success of a given group and place above the word thus crossed out the number of graduates having that degree of success:—
   "a" failed mediocre good superior
   "b" failed mediocre good superior

There is no institution in the country which could answer either of these questions with any accuracy; certainly deans or directors of vocational education could not. Even the most efficient commercial placement bureau could not answer questions requiring knowledge of the subsequent activities of those individuals whom it places. Conclusions drawn from the answers to such questions as these must necessarily have very little meaning. The question can well be asked: Why did Mr. Kline go to the trouble of sending this type of questionnaire to nearly 500 institutions? Part of the answers could have been obtained from catalogues and bulletins and part from officers of the Association of Schools of Social Work. Some could never be answered accurately enough to justify trying to get answers.[4]

The questions asked of institutions having social service courses in operation are better drawn, although the one (II, 8) asking for the range of success in social work of those having the degree of bachelor of arts, master of arts and doctor of philosophy is entirely futile.

Statistics are necessary to the social worker, but, just as important, the social worker is necessary to statistics, for facts, figures and data are important only as the facts, figures and data themselves are reliable.[5] Mr. Kline through his study, which is full of inaccuracies, has given to social workers one of the very best reasons why they should be equipped to study the implications of their own field.

As a result of his study, Mr. Kline reaches some interesting and sometimes fallacious conclusions. He learned that institutions not now having facilities for educating social workers are not as a whole interested in creating departments of applied social science nor in the training of social workers and that of the few institutions which are so interested, the undergraduate college is as willing as the graduate school to organize such courses. These are familiar facts to those who are participating in the education of social workers. It is not the aim of teachers of social work greatly to increase the number of schools of social work; rather it is their hope that there be a small number of outstanding institutions offering a high quality of work largely given in graduate years. It is unfortunately true that most universi-

[3] Edith Abbott, "Social Welfare and Professional Education," p. 131.

[4] Mr. Kline received 207 responses, distributed as follows: 24 unfilled but signed schedules; 29 letters unaccompanied by schedules; 10 returns from junior colleges; 14 marked catalogues; 130 schedules more or less completely filled out.

[5] Abbott, *op. cit.*, p. 173.

ties and their administrators have little appreciation of the value of social work education and that frequently they believe undergraduate training is a sufficient preparation; but gradually educators are coming to realize that the content of social work courses can be as great and challenging as that in any other subject.

Mr. Kline learned further from the answers to his schedules that 38 institutions offer training for social work of which 30 grant the bachelor's degree for majoring in courses preparing for social work and 20 confer the master's degree. "If 500 be taken as a conservative number of the standard colleges and universities of the country, it appears that 7.6 per cent. of them have been offering training in social work about 6.6 years and that the majority of degrees granted are the bachelor's." Because of discoveries of the above type he feels justified in drawing such inferences as, "The maturity and training represented by a graduate degree is as valuable in social work as it is in teaching the fifth and sixth grades, for instance, yet it has never been urged under the past and certainly not under our present economic order that such teachers should have graduate degrees." It appeared to him both a superior and model arrangement that graduating students with an integration of courses bearing on social work could immediately secure positions upon graduation. This type of situation in turn leads him to observe, "One does not witness, for obvious reasons, army and navy, engineering, law, medical and theological students leaving school to enter upon their special vocation prior to receiving their professional degrees." Mr. Kline's reasoning seems to be: The demands of social agencies and the requirements of the subject are not such as to require graduate work; a profession requires graduate work; ergo, social work is not a profession.

He finds a decided lack of agreement between the several institutions in the content of courses termed pre-professional and professional and he interprets "the variety of divergent views on the content of the social work curriculum as additional evidence that the work at present is not a technical profession but rather a general or lay occupation based upon a knowledge of a wide group of social sciences." He finds that the group of professional courses includes:

Principles of case work
Case field work
Problems of dependent and delinquent children
Probation and paroles
History of social work
Medical social work
Administration of social work.[6]

According to Mr. Kline the professional courses are decidedly specific—"specific in the sense that spelling a word, unlocking a time safe, or preparing the papers for an old age pension is such." It is almost superfluous for a social worker to comment on how little must the writer of such a statement know of the content of professional courses in social work and of the opportunity for intellectual challenge in the "occupation" of social work.

Mr. Kline believes that an adequate preparation for social work under our present cultural and economic conditions is furnished by the bachelor's degree earned by majoring at least two years in the social sciences, followed by an apprenticeship with pay and under the guidance of a social work office.

> The futility of academic training beyond the undergraduate years is emphasized by the fact that in whatever zone the social worker may be engaged the technical and professional problems that may arise pass at once for solution to men and women technically and professionally trained: the dietitian, the psychometrist, the physician, the

[6] Mr. Kline's lists of courses indicate a lack of acquaintance with the language of the social worker, *e.g.*, "probation and paroles," "case field work."

judge and lawyers, and too, the civic official skilled in solving neighborhood problems, are all alike just in the offing. In fact, it appears highly injudicious to found graduate schools for applied social science in which to train social workers. No one urges the founding of graduate schools of university rank in which to train probation officers, detectives, insurance agents, salesmen and elementary school teachers. . . . Academic training of the graduate rank would seem necessary for those who expect to teach the social sciences or who desire to do original and constructive thinking in this field.

Because the majority of social workers have not had graduate training in social work, (true), because most social agencies do not now require graduate training, (true), because after all social work is an occupation which itself has no specialized skills but calls upon other occupations and professions to render the needed skills, (untrue), for these reasons Mr. Kline concludes that graduate equipment is unnecessary for other than those who wish to teach the social sciences or to do original and constructive thinking.

Mr. Kline's conclusion that only teachers and those who wish to do original or constructive thinking are to be expected to undertake graduate training for social work is particularly challenging. Can we answer Mr. Kline as follows: It is the hope of all persons genuinely concerned with their profession, whatever it may be, that a growing number of participants will be stimulated to engage in original and constructive thinking. In order that there may be both skill in performance and an imagination trained for discovery, carefully planned undergraduate and graduate preparation for any profession is needed. Social workers faced with the present most astounding economic and social conditions are needed to direct the community's thinking toward the implications and meanings of these conditions and toward some partial solutions. Social work has numerous outstanding leaders who are directing thought and action. The world needs more of such persons; through the opportunity for contact with challenging minds in both field and classroom, it is hoped and expected, by outstanding persons in the profession of social work, that greater leadership can be offered the community to aid in directing its manifold and overwhelming problems. It is a narrow point of view indeed which maintains that instead of preparing more and more people for constructive thinking by educational opportunity we shall offer that opportunity only to those who know already that they can and will do original and constructive thinking. Graduate professional training seeks to reach both groups.

Let us turn our attention now to the standards of education and preparation for social work advocated by persons intimately connected with this profession. Whatever may be their ideals of education for social work, both those teaching social work and many of those actively engaged in social work agree that they are concerned with a profession. For our present purposes we are accepting as a fact that social work is a profession and as such there must be clearly defined educational standards for its performance.

In the past the only credentials needed for entrance into social work were interest and some maturity. Experience was the teacher. The apprenticeship method of directed activity has continued, until comparatively recently, to be the paramount means of training. In 1898 Miss Mary Richmond, actively engaged in social work, secured the first organized classes for greater preparation for this field of activity. Out of this experiment have developed the schools of social work. To-day there are 26 institutions which are members of the American Association of Schools of Social Work, organized in 1919. Members of this association have exerted great influence upon active participants in social work to raise the standards of entrance into the field. In 1921 was organized the American Association of Social Workers, one of whose purposes was to define the minimum requirements for entrance into social work; it now has a membership of some 6,000 persons. An analysis of the standards of these two organizations will give us some conception of the aims and expectations of social workers who consider their activity a profession.

The 26 institutions which are at present members of the Association of Schools of Social Work have various standards concerning (1) qualifications for admission into classes, (2) the length of the training period, (3) the content of the course of study, (4) the relationships between the social sciences and social work, (5) the amount and kind of field work to be required, and (6) the place of research in the curriculum. The association has within its membership at least three different types of institutions. First, there are those which have no inherent connection with a college or university and which mean to attract primarily the graduate student, although by no means are these the only registrants. Second, there are those which are an integral part of a college or university and which primarily draw from the undergraduate body of students. Third, there are those which are connected with a college or university and which are essentially graduate schools. The advantage of close connection with a university is apparent when it is realized that such an institution has a great variety of courses open to the students in the school of social work, usually a good library, and in turn a greater opportunity for adequate research. The trend in thinking of the schools is away from the independent school and from exclusive undergraduate training with subsequent apprenticeship. The development is toward affiliation with an institution of higher learning and to one or two years of graduate work with some field work offered during this period but with the major emphasis upon the content of classroom work and original research.

The present requirements of an institution for admission to membership in the Association of Schools of Social Work are higher than for those which have been members for some time. They are essentially:

(1) An organic grouping of relevant courses into a special curriculum for the stated purpose of professional education for social work.
(2) A director to control admission requirements.
(3) A faculty composed of full time and part time instructors with the equivalent of at least two full time instructors.
(4) An annual budget of not less than $10,000, and an assurance of permanency for at least three years.
(5) A curriculum which covers two full academic years, at least one of which must be graduate.
(6) A course of study which includes the minimum curriculum of the association.
(7) A program of field work under the educational control of the school, not less than one third nor more than one half of the curriculum to be devoted to field work.

Institutions which apply for membership may be separate from, affiliated with or constitute a part of a larger educational institution. At least 90 per cent. of the students accepted by the school who enroll in courses for which credit is given toward a degree or a diploma must have secured two years of academic credit beyond high school. This requirement makes possible the enrolment of an adult special group up to 10 per cent. of the total, who are not to be excluded from social work because they have not been able to enter college. Before a graduate degree can be secured, at least one year of graduate work is necessary; a certificate can be gotten in some instances upon the completion of certain specialized work which may comprise a combination of undergraduate and graduate courses and a specified amount of field work experience.

There is more or less common agreement

among the schools that, as an ideal, entrants into social work should have at least one year of special graduate work. As a matter of fact the schools recognize that many excellent individuals will enter social work with no graduate training, even with no undergraduate training; that these same persons will derive their training from supervised experience and sometimes from enrolment in professional courses for which they have not had adequate preliminary training. Certainly it can not be expected that social agencies will insist upon college graduates with postgraduate training until the resources for providing this kind of education are available. The Association of Schools of Social Work is therefore requiring that all institutions in the future admitted to its fellowship shall provide opportunities for graduate education.

For some time the association has had a curriculum committee, which has recommended the following courses for classroom instruction which are to be required by June, 1935, before a professional certificate can be issued:

		Semester credits	Quarter credits
	1. Case Work Undifferentiated	3	4
	2. Medical Information	3	4
	3. Psychiatric Information	3	4
Two courses required from this group	4. Child Welfare	3	4
	5. Specialized Case Work	3	4
	6. Group Work	3	4
Two courses required from this group	7. Field of Social Work	3	4
	8. Public Welfare Administration	3	4
	9. Community Organization	...	...
One course required from this group	10. Social Statistics	...	...
	11. Social Research	1	2
	12. Social Insurance	...	...
	Total	22	30

There are special committees at work on the content of these several courses.

It is clear that the schools of social work are moving in the direction of requiring five years of college or university education with one of the five years devoted to special courses in social work; of placing the emphasis upon the content of scientific courses without too much emphasis upon field work but with carefully supervised and directed field work; and of insisting upon research and original inquiry. Whether Mr. Kline thinks graduate work is or is not necessary for social work, the fact remains that the schools of social work have arrived at the place where the curriculum is planned so that graduate work is not only available, but expected. As more persons with graduate training are made *available* to social agencies, more persons with graduate training will be *demanded* by social agencies.

The most outstanding professional organization of social workers is the American Association of Social Workers. Like the Association of Schools of Social Work, it has changed its standard for admission since its inception. Full membership requirements now include the following qualifications:

(1) Completion of at least two years in an approved college.

(2) Five additional years of education, technical training, or employment in an approved agency. This requirement may be satisfied in either one of the two following ways:

(a) Graduation from an approved college plus one year in an approved school of social work, plus two years of employment in an approved agency.

(b) Five years spent in some combination of: attendance at an approved college, attendance at an approved school of social work, or employment in an approved agency, provided, however, that the applicant has satisfactorily completed:

(1) 20 semester hours of social and biological science in an approved college or school of social work.

(2) 24 semester hours of approved technical social work courses.

(3) 300 hours of supervised field work.
(4) Two years of employment in an approved agency.

(3) Graduation from a four year college plus completion of a two year course in an approved school of social work fulfils requirements 1 and 2.

It seems clear that standards of professional education for social work and standards of admission into the field are advancing together. It is equally clear that at the present time there are many more people doing social work than meet the requirements of either the professional schools or the profession itself. The federal census for 1930 for the first time includes a special category "Social and Welfare Workers." Something over 31,000 are listed under this classification, to which number should be added those otherwise classified, making a total of about 36,000 holding social work positions at the time the census was taken. If to the 6,000 members of the Association of Social Workers are added those who are members of other social work organizations, it is estimated that about one third of the 36,000 persons engaged in social work qualify according to the standards of professional groups.[7]

Many more people than 36,000 are undoubtedly engaged in social work to-day because of the increase in staffs of public relief agencies. Large numbers of these persons will eventually drop out of social work; many will wish to stay in the profession. Schools and agencies both will have a tremendous task equipping these remaining persons according to the now recognized standards of performance. The schools of social work, most of them, are offering opportunity for a high type of classroom study, field work and research. The agencies are not yet able to demand workers who, upon completion of the experience qualifications, will be eligible for membership in the professional organizations; there are not enough of such persons available, but increasingly these agencies are seeking out persons with professional education before they accept upon their staffs those without approved scientific preparation.

It is evident that, with the enunciation of standards by social workers and by those concerned with adequate educational preparation for social work, both groups will have little sympathy with individuals who proclaim social work an occupation without professional characteristics. "An occupation," says Miss Abbott, "should be called professional when it is undertaken *pro bono publico,* when it has a special intellectual content, and when it requires special intellectual discipline and instruction before it can be entered upon."[8]

Social work has become a profession, but like other professions it must go through the stages of convincing some of its own performers as well as the community that such is the case. When it was commonly considered that the teacher's function was to teach the three R's, very elementary preparation obtained in a "normal" school was enough. With an appreciation of the fact that teaching was a much more challenging matter than just that, there was a shift from training to "education" in the "teachers colleges" and in other educational institutions. Law has gone through the stage of being an occupation requiring only "reading" in a law office with directed practise to one requiring not only three years of professional study, but preliminary college work, and in some institutions a bachelor's degree is required before admission into the professional school is permitted. The same situation has prevailed in medicine. Within these professions there are varying standards of *pre*-professional preparation, but each profession now has basic material that is commonly accepted by all educational institutions as

[7] Walter M. West, "Social Work as a Profession," Social Work Year Book, pp. 492–496, 1933.

[8] Abbott, *op. cit.,* p. 76.

indispensable for practise. Social work is arriving at the stage where certain common preparation is to be required. There is dispute as to the kind and amount of pre-professional education needed; there is a diminution of debate as to the nature of professional courses which are basic preparation for the profession.

Social work has two main objectives: (1) The adjustment of individuals and groups to their environment. (2) The improvement of conditions which make adjustment difficult for many reasons.[9]

Mr. Lurie in a recent *Survey* article observes that several decades ago social work was deeply concerned with the second of the above points; then came a period of concentration on psychological adjustment; now we are reverting to the starting point.[10]

Within the last two decades and until the last three years, many social workers had forgotten that social work had any other approach to problems than through case work procedure. Social work is not merely providing individuals with material goods and the means for obtaining or maintaining good health; nor is it merely attempting "to meet the common problems of sexual adjustment, personal hygiene and domestic economy." Social work includes interest in the adjustment of the individual to himself and his environment; but it also includes interest in the community—in the social and economic conditions over which individuals as such have very little control. The social worker must concern himself, perhaps predominantly for awhile, with the organization of social forces; he must identify himself with social movements and their implications; he must become more intent "upon the solution of social problems and less of a technician skilled in adapting individuals to the status quo."

Can any one seriously doubt that preparation to meet such a challenge requires professional education?

The basic requirement of any profession is skilled service; the stature of the leaders in any profession largely determines the quality of service rendered. Leadership expresses itself in two ways: in the formulation of new and constructive ideas and in the application and administration of these ideas. Social work needs more persons thus qualified. Only as there are educational facilities for acquiring basic knowledge of the manifold aspects of social work and for providing opportunities for supervised practise can the highest quality of leadership be developed. Professional schools of social work with high standards of instruction available to alert young persons increasingly willing to continue their education into the graduate years are indispensable if we are to afford the quality of leadership necessary for significant service.

[9] Sydnor Walker, "Social Work and the Training of Social Workers," p. 69.

[10] Harry L. Lurie, "Case Work in a Changing Social Order," *Survey*, lxix: 2, 61–64, February, 1933.

THE REPORT OF COMMITTEE Q AND PROFESSIONAL REQUIREMENTS IN EDUCATION

By Professor WALTER R. SMITH

UNIVERSITY OF KANSAS

IN an era of social turmoil, economic chaos and governmental uncertainties it was inevitable that the schools should come in for their share of critical ferment. At no time in our history has there been greater need of educational vision and perspective than at present. Yet in our hour of need we must depend for leadership upon a teaching personnel inadequately educated, and with a professional training far below that of many leading nations or that we offer in other types of professional service.

With school conditions critical enough to make obvious to every one the need of leadership and a trained teaching personnel, it would seem to be an appropriate time for undertaking a crusade for higher standards of professional education. Yet the March, 1933, Bulletin of the American Association of University Professors, through a report of Committee Q, voices a plea for a reduction in the number of hours of professional education required for a certificate to teach in the secondary schools. Such a document, coming from a distinguished group of scholars, should not go unchallenged. It represents a point of view maintained by a considerable portion of our academic subject-matter teachers and hence embodies a threat to professional standards.

Fortunately the danger in this attack upon professional standards is minimized by two things, first, the purely academic view-point of the committee making the report and, second, the defects of the report itself.

Even a casual reading of the report of Committee Q will reveal its academic perspective. Secondary teachers are dealt with purely as subject-matter specialists—every conclusion being based upon instructional skill. No hint is allowed to escape that these teachers may be called upon to meet other than classroom problems. In the larger mimeographed report numerous references suggest a belief that teachers are born and not made—as if the inheritance factors were more numerous in teaching than in other professions or complex vocations. A special questionnaire is sent to private school principals without a corresponding inquiry being sent to public school principals. Invidious comparisons are drawn between teaching skills, and subject-matter organization, in academic subjects and professional subjects. At all times the assumption is made that teachers should be required to take a greater number of college departmental credits at the expense of the small number of professional credits now obtained.

Further analysis of the report reveals it to be merely a new phase of the age-old effort of the college to dominate the work of the high school. One of its preliminary statements runs as follows: "The committee believes that at the present time the public secondary school system is controlled to a large extent by those definitely committed to heavy professional requirements. It is of the opinion that this fact must be kept clearly in mind and that inquiries should not fail to challenge the right of continuance of such control." Thus in the beginning they challenge the right of those now in control of our high schools to continue—their overt sin being a belief in the value of the professional training now required. Their interpretation of "heavy professional requirements" is shown in the report to be the state average of seventeen semester hours—a little more than a half year of professional work added to a twelve-to sixteen-year period of general education concerned largely with training in subject-matter. To any one possessing a dim vision of a school system manned by a well-educated personnel, selected and trained to render as specialized types of service as we expect of physicians, lawyers and ministers, this "interpretation" is as humorous as it is disturbing.

The report is based upon two sets of questionnaires. One of these was sent to principals of private secondary schools and the other to high-school teachers. Its sweeping generalizations are based upon replies from 83 of the 2,760 private schools in operation in 1930, and from 391 high-school teachers. In the nine states from which the high-school teachers were selected there were in 1930 a total of 81,969 high-school teachers employed. The sampling was, therefore, .47 of one per cent. But the chief conclusion reached, that 12 hours of professional training is "ample," was based largely upon the replies of only 131 of these teachers—a sampling of .16 of one per cent.[1]

The inadequacy of such a sampling is in striking contrast with that used in a study made for the North Central Association of Colleges and Secondary Schools in 1923. At that time questionnaire replies were received and tabulated from 845 high-school principals. By a large majority these principals voted in favor of increasing the 11 hours of professional training then required to 15. Possibly the results of this study had something to do with the sending of the questionnaires to the principals of private schools, responsible for training about 8 per cent. of all secondary students, rather than to high-school principals, who are concerned with the education of the other 92 per cent.

Drawing conclusions from inadequate data, however, is but one of the weaknesses of the report. A review of their own tabulations does not warrant the assumption that 12 hours of professional work is ample for the beginning teacher. The questionnaire asked the number of hours high-school teachers considered "adequate," presumably minimum, and the number considered "profitable." Tabulations of the replies showed the mean number of hours considered adequate to be 15.1, and the number considered profitable 19.6—. But this tabulation was apparently unsatisfactory. By excluding the replies of those with A.M. and Ph.D. degrees and using only the A.B. group, and by eliminating the upper 10 per cent. (15 replies favoring more than 21 hours) a mean of 13 hours was obtained. Then by simple arithmetic one hour was subtracted to obtain the twelve hours recommended. Had the committee used an equally justifiable technique, and eliminated the cases recommending less than 10 hours, a mean of 16.7 hours would have been secured. Also, if the committee had chosen to emphasize the opinion of the better trained administrative group, they could have underscored a mean of 17.8 hours considered as "adequate" and 22 hours as "profitable." Possibly these returns explain the committee's challenge of the right of those now in charge of our high schools to remain in control. As a final notation from the questionnaire figures it should not be forgotten that the mean number of hours designated by the entire group as profitable was 19.6—. which was 7.6 more than the committee considered "ample."

A further evidence of the pre-judgment of the committee is found in the fact that no mention was made of other means for the improvement of teaching service than reduction of the amount of professional credits. Schools of education are rather frank in admitting their shortcomings in the field of teacher preparation. Had the committee been equally frank they might have recognized two other means of meeting any dissatisfaction teachers may have with regard to their professional training. One of these would be the vitalizing and improving of existing courses, and the other would be the addition of new courses better adapted to meet teachers' needs. Either of these types of professional advancement might well be advocated without imperiling our inadequate and universally deplored teacher-training standards.

As a further basis for bolstering up its demand for more departmental credit hours at the expense of present profes-

[1] These figures are taken from a Special Bulletin of the University of Kansas, School of Education, published in February, 1934, which contains a more extensive analysis of the report of Committee Q.

sional requirements, the committee made an attack upon the quality and teaching of the professional courses now offered. One of the inquiries was concerned with the amount of duplication in professional courses as compared with academic courses. As was expected, and as is inevitable, the returns indicated that there has been a greater amount of duplication in the educational courses—a difficulty schools of education have been struggling with for a decade. The writer came into education from the social sciences, against which he had heard the same charges since his school days.

A certain amount of duplication can not be escaped in writing or teaching in a new and complex and rapidly growing field of knowledge. Not merely education and social science but English, domestic economy, physical education and other new departments and professional schools suffer from overlapping fringes in principles, problems and terminology. Only time and long experience can carefully delimit the boundaries of each of the courses in a complicated discipline where principles unfold in a wide variety of applications. Nor can time and experience accomplish this result without reducing the content to a static form. Incidentally, it is widely recognized in schools of education that the chief complaints of duplication come from students without experience in teaching and without enough interest in professional problems to appreciate the implications of principles whose terminology is repeated in different courses in treating different problems or to emphasize different points of view. Without doubt considerable progress is being made in differentiating the field of various courses in education, even as it is being made in the newer academic departments. Sharp demarcation, however, is an accompaniment of fixed subject-matter and hence can not be expected in fields with constantly expanding materials accruing from new researches into ever-varying problems.

The inquiry into the effectiveness of teaching in educational courses was as follows: "Did you find that teachers of 'professional courses' were more skilful and generally successful than teachers in the regular academic departments?" Quite naturally the replies indicated that they were not. It may seem strange, but teachers of education, so far as the writer has heard, have never claimed such superiority. There is no reason to expect teachers in any professional school to be better instructors than those in academic departments. In fact, there are several reasons why the reverse might be expected. Professional teachers must deal with unstandardized, relatively new and fluctuating materials. Neither time nor practical experience repeated through generations have evolved a stabilized content or methodology. Their efforts must be divided between the problem of selecting and organizing the most valuable current materials and that of finding the most effective methods of presentation. On the other hand, academic teachers deal with a carefully sifted, relatively fixed content. Their attention can therefore be concentrated more fully upon student motivation and methods of instruction. A teacher of mathematics or English is handling a type of subject-matter in which he has had twelve to fifteen years of training. By way of contrast, the teacher of some branch of law or medicine or education is lucky to have had that many credit hours in the particular subject he is teaching. Moreover, since their fields are rapidly expanding, a large proportion of professional teachers are expected to save a considerable share of their energies for research work.

A further review brings into prominence the generally recognized fact that effective teaching is a complicated achievement, compounded of interest in teaching, knowledge of subject-matter, native capacity, ability to deal with people, willingness to sweat and knowledge of teaching arts. It is folly to expect 12 hours, or even 17 hours, of professional training, a large share of which is devoted to other than instructional problems, to revolutionize the nature and habits and teaching qualities of a prospective high-school teacher. All that can be hoped for is a reasonable stimulus to motivation, to a critical awareness of the need for educational change, to improved selection and organization of subject-matter and to a more thorough acquaintance with the various methods of meeting instructional and other problems. This contribution would naturally be more decisive in standardized academic courses where teaching problems are less recondite than in new subjects but should not be without value, in lesser degree, in handling the more or less inchoate and changing professional courses. It should be frankly avowed, however, that if the uncritical acceptance of static subject-matter and more expert handling of traditional methods of imparting factual material be accepted as the basis of judgment, most teachers of courses in education would scarcely be disturbed by the strictures of academic literalists.

In the previous discussion we have been concerned with the report of the committee dealing with the narrow field of subject-matter instruction. It would scarcely be fair to professional education to close without insisting that mere classroom teaching is only one of the major educational problems with which they are expected to deal. At least three others deserve emphasis.

Every type of professional school aims not only to train practitioners but to develop an attitude of critical open-mindedness, experimentation and research. Schools of education are so new and must deal with such a variety of complicated problems that this function is conspicuous. As our civilization has struggled toward democracy new population elements have been incorporated into the school clientele. Compulsory attendance laws have required that all, rich and poor, strong and weak, normal and unnormal, be admitted to our schools. Public sentiment has decreed that an ever-increasing percentage of these be carried into the secondary schools. The needs of such a heterogenous and rapidly growing student body make experimentation imperative. Revaluation of aims and objectives, revisions of curriculum content and readjustments in equipment and method must be continuous. To short cut the processes of trial and error in making necessary changes requires research. With the scientific movement still in its infancy valuable results have already been achieved in improving the teaching of the fundamental subjects, such as reading, arithmetic, civics, etc., in equipment, units of organization, student guidance and discipline. Quite obviously it would be of little value to train a few scientific workers in graduate schools without giving to the rank and file of teachers enough insight into the methods and results of research and experimentation to enable them to appreciate and apply new discoveries in practise. Even the members of Committee Q would doubtless admit that training in this field is the function of professional rather than academic courses.

A second major problem of professional education overlooked by Committee Q is that of developing educational leadership. It is axiomatic that every institution and social group must provide leaders for both its internal and external relationships from within its own ranks. If the school is to have wide-awake and broadly intelligent leaders it must provide specialized training for them. In our day the school is a public enterprise with large political and financial responsibilities. No other institution has wider social ramifications or permeates more fully into all phases of our complex social order. Hence it needs professionally trained leaders, educational statesmen who are familiar with all the problems, financial, social and public, involved in the organization and direction of a tax-supported, politically managed and technically complicated school system.

To meet such demands professional training can not be confined to the teaching process. It must include such subjects as school legislation, taxation and finance, professional organization and ideals, the interrelationships of the school with the home, with local community enterprises and with other institutions of state and national scope, in addition to a variety of technical problems that can not be covered in academic courses. Furthermore, this training, if it is to be effective, can not be confined to a selected few. It must reach all teachers to the extent of familiarizing them with the existence and general nature of these larger problems in order to guarantee the consolidated following necessary to make leadership effective. To assume that mere college graduation, or even more extensive academic education, can provide the sort of technical and general leadership required is to assume the impossible.

A third fundamental of professional education which Committee Q failed to mention is the need of training teachers to adjust themselves and their work to the changing demands of a progressive society. Above all other institutions the school has an opportunity, in fact duty, to prepare the oncoming generation to bring about improvements in the social order. If it is to accomplish this mission it must be manned by teachers whose training has made them critically aware of the shortcomings of the present school régime and the various avenues of prospective improvement. Further, if teachers are to inspire in their students a questioning attitude with reference to the political, economic, social and cultural problems which afflict our muddled era, they need to be trained to revise and handle curricular materials in a liberalizing way.

It must be confessed that liberalism has not been characteristic of teachers in the past. Instead they have been noted for conservatism—docility rather than virility. It is not altogether improbable that the nature of academic materials and training has been largely responsible for developing in prospective teachers this *laissez-faire* attitude toward current problems. Thus has arisen a distinct need for a professional training that will stimulate teachers to a more open-minded and aggressive attack upon controversial issues. That such a mission is to some extent being fulfilled is indicated by a study of professorial attitudes in connection with the National Survey of Secondary Education. Ranked on a scale leading from extreme conservatism to extreme liberalism the teachers of education group showed the most liberal attitudes of any professorial group. No contribution to our current school régime could surpass in significance that of stimulating prospective teachers to make such progressive changes in content and method as are necessary to cultivate in students a forward-looking and critically active interest in the newer problems of current civilization.

As a concluding thought it may be well to recall that schools of education were not founded by accident. They grew directly out of the shortcoming of the colleges and existing secondary schools in performing one of their main tasks, that of preparing teachers. A large share of their graduating classes entered teaching but were proving inadequate. Had purely academic work been considered satisfactory the problem could easily have been met by raising scholastic requirements. But the public realized that something else was necessary. Hence normal schools were established to offer professional training and met the need so effectively that they grew with amazing rapidity. Their success created a demand for teacher-training departments, or schools of education, in our colleges and universities, and the expansion of two-year normals into four-year teachers' colleges. Thus the whole development of teacher-training work grew out of the failure of academic institutions to give adequate preparation to the teachers they were sending out. It would therefore seem rather ungracious for representatives of academic departments to be over-critical of the efforts of teachers colleges to do the work which they themselves had failed to do. It is cause for congratulation that few of those engaged in the professional training of teachers are entirely satisfied with the work being done. Hence they are sincerely struggling to bring about progressive improvements. Meantime an emasculation of professional courses by reducing the number of hours required for a secondary teacher's certificate in favor of a return to a larger number of academic credits would be a distinctly reactionary move not likely to meet with public favor, nor to improve teaching results.

EDUCATIONAL EVENTS

THE ANNUAL MEETING OF THE BRITISH NATIONAL UNION OF TEACHERS

THE annual conference of the British National Union of Teachers convened at Brighton on March 31 and continued during half of the following week. The London *Times* reports a series of important problems under discussion, ranging from salary considerations to the social implications of teaching as they affect the malnutrition of school children and the old-age pensions.

One of the chief topics had to do with the school-leaving age. The government has proposed to meet the problem of its 100,000 unemployed children of 14 and 15 years of age by providing in its new Unemployment Insurance Act for the establishment of juvenile instruction centers. That the national union does not agree with this remedy is evidenced by the fact that the conference carried, practically unanimously, a resolution urging Parliament to pass without further delay a bill to raise the school-leaving age to 15. Amendments urging that the age limit should be 16 and calling for adequate maintenance during this extended period were rejected after appeals by members of the executive committee that the conference concentrate on the main principle without raising other issues that might arouse political and industrial opposition.

A resolution calling upon the board of education to abandon the child-teacher ratio of 50, as recognized in Circular 1327 for infants and junior schools, in favor of the 40 children to a teacher ratio which it accepts as suitable for senior schools, was proposed. The union agreed with the Consultative Committee, which in its report on infant and nursery schools found "no justification for the view that it is easier to deal with large classes of younger children than with large classes of older ones," and recommended that both for primary and for infant schools the classes should not contain more than 40 pupils. After further discussion, an amendment substituting "30" for "40" was accepted, and the resolution was unanimously approved.

The question of the restoration of the 10 per cent. cut in teachers salaries was the chief topic of discussion at the closing meeting of the conference. The following resolution was passed: "The exceptional circumstances which created the national emergency of 1931 having passed away, this conference calls upon the government to redeem its pledges given during the crisis by making provision in the forthcoming budget for the discontinuance of the 10 per cent. cut imposed on teachers' salaries as one of the temporary economy measures adopted to meet the budgetary deficiency at that time."

The teachers' demand has been strengthened by the decisions of 65 local education authorities. Of 665 local authorities who cut the salaries of their municipal officers, 323 by the end of January this year had terminated those cuts, and 85 others had since modified them.

THE ESTABLISHMENT OF A LIBRARY OF BOOKS BURNED IN NAZI GERMANY

A movement has been begun in France and in England, which may be extended to the United States, to found a "German Library of Burned Books." The proposal provides for the formation of a collection, first in Paris, of copies of all the works which under the National Socialist Government in Germany have been destroyed, censored or suppressed. This collection will be the basis for the establishment of a library which German refugees are willing to make available, works regarded as indispensable for the study of the Nazi movement, and a large amount of material gathered from hundreds of small archives in various European cities to which the refugees fled after leaving Germany.

The first meeting of the provisional committee for the foundation of the library, the London *Times* reports, was held late in March at the home of the Countess of Oxford and Asquith in London. Dr. Alfred Kantorowicz, secretary for the library in Paris, at that time presented a report of what has already been accomplished. Shortly after the rise of the Third Reich, Dr. Kantorowicz declared, the German émigrés realized the necessity for collecting material relating to the developments in Germany, and there came into existence in Paris, London, Zurich, Prague and other cities hundreds of small private archives, independent of each other. This scattered material has been assembled, Dr. Kantorowicz continued, and the central archives that were established have been increased and supplemented and have been made available to a large number of scientists, writers and journalists. The archives contain more than 200,000 documents, newspaper clippings, letters, laws and speeches covering the sphere of the social changes in Germany in 1933 and 1934.

A comprehensive offensive has now been launched, Dr. Kantorowicz felt, to save and preserve the cultural contributions of Germany to the evolution of humanity during the eighteenth, nineteenth and twentieth centuries. The library will be established in Paris, on premises accommodating 15,000 volumes with room to expand the work. Immediate plans include its inauguration on May 10, when speeches will be made by French and German scientists and writers. The inauguration will be accompanied by an exhibition illustrating the upheaval of the German press.

The provisional committee has been charged with the responsibility of gathering financial support from English sympathizers and with determining the advisability of transferring the proposed exhibition to London, late in May, after its showing in Paris.

THE POLITICAL PLEDGE REQUIRED OF MEXICAN TEACHERS

It is reported by the Catholic press that an attempt is being made by the National Committee for Educational Reform in Mexico to bar all religious influences in Mexican schools and to confine the schools' teaching to laic or socialistic tenets. This is being done by means of a pledge circulated by the committee among the teachers of the country, which, according to the report, binds teachers to support the entire program of the National Revolutionary Party and to oppose anything which will interfere with that program.

Meanwhile the protest of Catholics, led by the National Union of Fathers of Families, against sexual education in the official schools continues to receive the support of non-Catholic opponents of the measure. At a meeting just held at Saltillo, Coahuila, attended by more than a thousand people, a prominent Mason and a Protestant woman, a teacher, declared that they were in accord with the union in its campaign against sexual education. A meeting at Parras, also in Coahuila, called for the purpose of appointing a municipal committee representing the National Union of the Fathers of Families, was addressed by Elias Ramirez, president of the Socialist League. Such a project, Señor Ramirez said in outlining the sexual education project, could have been proposed only by Narciso Bassols, secretary of public education.

Although the circular sent out by the National Committee for Educational Reform does not state that in signing it a teacher is pledging support of the National Revolutionary Party and it might be contended that the signature was demanded only as an acknowledgment, yet church authorities contend that the letter is so worded as to constitute a pledge, no matter what the actual or implied intention of the committee.

RECENT DEVELOPMENTS IN THE CHILD LABOR CONTROVERSY

DECLARING that the proposed child labor amendment to the Federal Constitution is much more objectionable and dangerous than the eighteenth amendment, 68 prominent New York men and women have joined the newly formed New York State Committee Opposing Ratification of the Child Labor Amendment. The committee, headed by Elihu Root, Dr. Nicholas Murray Butler and William D. Guthrie, has announced its intention of cooperating with similar committees in other states in a nation-wide attempt to block the amendment, which has been ratified by twenty states. As its first action, the committee submitted to the state legislature a pamphlet prepared by Mr. Guthrie, the vice-chairman, and on April 18 the Judiciary Committee of the State Senate defeated the resolution of Senator Albert D. Wald to ratify the amendment.

Members of the committee base their opposition to the amendment on the belief that such a measure would grant to Congress unlimited powers and that it would encroach upon states' rights. They foresee failure by Congress to administer these powers. All education, according to the argument of the pamphlet, would come within the implied and incidental power of the amendment to "limit, regulate, and prohibit." Mr. Guthrie asserts that if Congress should prohibit all physical labor of youths between 16 and 18, it would have to take steps to avoid the vices of idleness by requiring occupation either through school attendance or through military training and discipline. It is the contention of the committee that the amendment also would give Congress the power to regulate labor of children in the household or on the home farm. The pamphlet charges that effective enforcement of the amendment would "require a vast army of federal functionaries, field officers, police and detectives, necessarily greatly in excess of the number found insufficient to enforce the Volstead act and its amendments."

Dr. John Dewey, professor emeritus of philosophy at Columbia University, in an interview published on April 20 in the student newspaper of Columbia College, declared his approval of the proposed amendment. He contends that opposition on the basis of states' rights is unjustified. Under the present conditions a state without child labor regulations has a competitive advantage over other states with such regulations, he points out, and since manufacturing and industry operate on national rather than on state lines, regulation should proceed on the same basis.

A statement urging ratification of the measure, signed by the Non-Partisan Committee for Ratification of the Federal Child Labor Amendment, was also sent to the legislature. This statement argues that the amendment is properly drawn as a grant of power to Congress and avoids the difficulties inherent in the prohibition amendment. It points out that "the eighteenth amendment was a direct prohibition. Its great defect was that it embodied in the Constitution a legislative policy on a controversial subject, leaving no road open for the exercise of legislative judgment. Unlike the eighteenth amendment, the child labor amendment contains no prohibition or regulation of the employment of children in the amendment itself. It merely gives to Congress authority to legislate in this field, and any law passed can be changed by a simple majority at any session of Congress."

Legal opinions are cited in this committee's argument in answer to the assertion of the opposition that the amendment if ratified would lead to federal control of education. The statement points out that "labor, as used in labor statutes, has always had a specific meaning, and has been construed by the courts to be limited to the common usage of the term. No case has been found where the ordinary tasks of the household or the study of children in school have been held to be *labor* within the terms of the statute."

THE THIRTY-FIFTH SUMMER SESSION OF COLUMBIA UNIVERSITY

THE thirty-fifth Summer Session of Columbia University will be held from July 9 to August 17, according to an announcement made by Dr. John J. Coss, director of the school. The majority of the 1,000 courses offered will deal with social responsibility as a governmental, educational, sociological, scientific and cultural question.

A detailed study of the public-school system, likewise stressing social responsibility, will be undertaken. Every field of elementary, intermediate and higher education will be covered. A conference on educational plant planning, with special reference to modern community development, will be conducted by the department of educational administration on July 20. On August 10 educational workers in correctional and penological institutions will convene.

George Soule, editor of the *New Republic,* will present the economics of the recovery program. He will discuss the methods used by the administration in seeking recovery, their relation to economic theory and the reasons for expecting their success or failure. Mr. Soule will also give a seminar on the theoretical background and varying programs of economic plannings in the United States.

In general economic theory, Dr. Morris A. Copeland, professor of economics at the University of Michigan and executive secretary of the Central Statistical Board at Washington, will conduct a seminar. Professor Charles F. Remer, of the University of Michigan, will survey the field of public finance, and will deal with such topics as governmental expenditure during the depression and the widening scope of governmental activities.

Labor policies enforced under the NRA and those which have characterized the past in American history will be contrasted by Professor Carter Goodrich. Professor Ivan Wright, of the University of Illinois, will give a course in the financial practises of corporations and their public relations. Professor John M. Chapman will direct courses on the Federal Reserve system and banking reform, and on money and currency, including proposals for price stabilization and currency conditions in the leading nations.

In the department of government and public law, a course in the process of government in the United States will be presented by Professor Schuyler C. Wallace. Professor Benjamin B. Kendrick, of the Woman's College of the University of North Carolina, will lecture in the department of history on American industrialism and imperialism, and on the South since 1850.

Dr. Clarence A. Berdahl, professor of political science at the University of Illinois, will deal with international organization, the League of Nations, the World Court and international law. A sociological analysis of some recent social movements, particularly the Hitler movement, will be made by Dr. George A. Lundberg, formerly director of research in the Columbia Council for Research in the Social Studies.

In the field of psychology, a series of lectures on social organization, social structures and social agencies will be introduced by Professor Floyd H. Allport, of Syracuse University.

PROPOSED REVISION OF CURRICULUM AT HUNTER COLLEGE

A curriculum reorganization has been proposed for Hunter College in New York City, and the results of a questionnaire issued to the 301 members of the teaching staff of the college show that 85 per cent. of them are in favor of the change. Professor Philip R. V. Curoe, chairman of the committee on curriculum revision, on April 21 made public a report on the results of the questionnaire.

According to the returns, 241 of the 283 who answered the questionnaire favor a revision of the existing major-minor system. The proposed revision provides for the establishment of a field of concentration consisting of twenty-four credits in one subject and twelve credits of "related enrichment" outside this subject. The field of enrichment would be substituted for the present allied minor courses and would be chosen by the student and passed upon by the department of concentration.

The hypothetical curriculum, which accompanied the staff questionnaire, suggested that the college set up a few concentrations somewhat more strongly vocationalized than those now offered. The majority of the staff endorsed this proposal, but some respondents suggested that some degree other than the bachelor of arts should be awarded for completion of the college work involving such vocationalized study.

In the more specific details, 96 per cent. favored a science prescription. Although some members recommended a heavier mathematics requirement for science than for other majors, 62 per cent. did not approve of grouping mathematics and the sciences and setting up a requirement for the whole group.

Only 49 per cent. expressed the opinion that art or music should be among the prescribed subjects for all students. Free optionals were favored by 90 per cent. of the staff. Eighty-one per cent. also recommended the advisability of a continuing, organized guidance program, but only 44 per cent. would grant college credit for orientation courses.

The staff endorsed the prescribed work in English literature, composition and speech and physical education and hygiene. Professor Curoe reported a recurrent suggestion that American literature be given a more prominent place in the survey courses. Grants of exemption from college work on the basis of work done in high school were disapproved by the majority of the staff members.

DOCTORATE IN THEATRICAL HISTORY AT YALE UNIVERSITY

THE degree of doctor of philosophy in the fields of theatrical history and dramatic criticism will be inaugurated next year in the Yale Graduate School, according to an announcement made by the university recently. The Yale School of the Fine Arts, through the Department of Drama, of which Professor Allardyce Nicoll is chairman, now offers the degree of master of fine arts. The doctorate degree will offer further opportunities to those students who wish to devote themselves to the historical study of the theater.

In spite of the vast interest which the theater has aroused in men's minds from the days of Aristotle to the present, the announcement states, and in spite of the enormous library of theatrical books already written, comparatively few attempts have been made to coordinate and stimulate historical study of the stage as a whole. The new course of study which the university will inaugurate is designed to provide more unified and practical investigation into such historical material. The work of the department of drama, which includes courses in playwriting, production, stage design and lighting, will not be altered by the institution of the courses leading to the degree of doctor of philosophy. Believing that adequate investigation into theatrical problems may be attained only through a practical knowledge of stage practise, the faculty have decided that the Ph.D. course should include work in the branches of activity already organized, together with courses in historical method and in allied subjects, such as literature or art. Students who have pursued the courses for such a degree, therefore, will be qualified to undertake the duties of teaching posts combining instruction in literature and dramatic direction.

The faculty, in establishing the degree, also expressed the desire to stimulate research. For the next session, accordingly, a special course is being organized for this purpose. Since the theater is an art-form peculiarly transitory, only the scripts of plays and such illustrative material as has been preserved in the form of engravings, drawings or original scene and costume designs may be assembled as a historical record. An attempt to collect, to analyze exhaustively and to catalogue the whole of this illustrative material will be begun next September. The department hopes to gather a comprehensive set of photographic reproductions which shall be adequately catalogued, interrelated and described in detail. Already 600 separate items have been collected.

EDUCATIONAL NOTES AND NEWS

DR. GEORGE F. ZOOK, U. S. Commissioner of Education, stated on April 21 that he would announce soon his acceptance or his refusal of the presidency of the University of Iowa, which has been offered him by the board of trustees of the university.

PROFESSOR MELVIN L. ENGER, a member of the faculty of the University of Illinois since 1907 and head of the department of theoretical and applied mechanics since 1929, has been elected dean of the College of Engineering to succeed Dr. Arthur Cutts Willard. Professor Enger also becomes director of the engineering experiment station. Professor Frederick B. Seely, of the department of mechanical engineering, has been named head of the department of theoretical and applied mechanics to succeed Dean Enger. Dr. R. D. Carmichael, acting dean of the Graduate School, and Dr. M. T. McClure, acting dean of the College of Liberal Arts and Sciences, have been promoted to full deanships.

Dr. William Jasper Kerr, chancellor of the Oregon State System of Higher Education, has announced his resignation, to be effective as soon as his successor can be chosen. Dr. Kerr served as president of Oregon State College from 1907 to 1932, of Utah State College from 1900 to 1907 and of Brigham Young College from 1894 to 1900.

B. L. Stradley, university examiner for the Ohio State University, has been elected president of the North Central Association of Colleges and Secondary Schools.

The Reverend Dr. Herman Brezing has resigned as president of the Wagner Memorial Lutheran College to become director of the Wartburg Orphan Farm School at Mount Vernon, N. Y.

Thomas N. Barrows has been elected dean of Lawrence College at Appleton, Wis. Mr. Barrows has resigned his former position as director of Woodmere Academy at Woodmere, Long Island, N. Y.

Dr. John Hasbrouck Van Vleck, who now holds a research professorship in physics at the University of Wisconsin, has been elected associate professor of mathematics and physics at Harvard College. The president and fellows of the college also have announced the appointment of Alfred Rehder, curator of the herbarium of the Arnold Arboretum of Harvard University since 1918, as associate professor of dendrology, and Leonard Opdycke, as assistant professor of fine arts.

Professor Charles A. Robinson, Jr., of the department of classics at Brown University, has been appointed annual professor at the American School of Classical Studies in Athens for the next academic year.

Simmons College has announced the appointment of three special lecturers for next year in the writing and editing program of its School of English. Harland R. Ratcliffe, of the *Boston Evening Transcript,* will conduct a course in the elements of journalism; Robert N. Linscott, of the Houghton Mifflin Company, a course in book publishing, and James R. Killian, editor of the *Technology Review,* a course in magazine journalism.

Dr. William Hamilton Kirk, professor of Latin at Rutgers University from 1900 to 1925 and since then professor of classical languages, and Dr. Walter Russell Newton, professor of the German language and literature since 1905, will retire from active service on the faculty of the university on June 30. President Robert C. Clothier has announced that Dr. Kirk and Dr. Newton will receive the rank of professor emeritus.

Professor Paul Hazard, of the College of France, and Professor Jan J. L. Duyvendak, of the University of Leiden, have been appointed as visiting professors for the academic year 1934–35 at Columbia University.

Dr. Samuel Flagg Bemis, professor of history at the George Washington University since 1924, has been appointed lecturer on history in the division of history, government and economics at Harvard College for the first half of the academic year 1934–35. Dr. Bemis will join the faculty of Yale University in February, 1935, as professor of diplomatic history and, in the Graduate School, he will be in charge of training specialists in the development of American diplomatic history.

Professor Effie J. Taylor, president of the National League of Nursing Education and professor of psychiatric nursing at Yale University, has been appointed dean of the Yale School of Nursing.

Professor Frederick H. Koch, founder of the Carolina Playmakers at the University of North Carolina, and Lynn Riggs, playwright, will serve on the faculty of Northwestern University for the summer session.

Dr. Joseph M. Carriere, professor of Romance languages at Northwestern University, has begun a study of the dialect now spoken by the descendants of the Acadians of Nova Scotia and will attempt to trace from what French province the Louisiana Acadians originally came. At the close of the current academic year, he will leave for Louisiana to devote three months to the study.

The American Physical Education Association and the Mid-West Society of Physical Education, meeting jointly from April 18 to 21 in Cleveland, honored the following men and women as those who have done outstanding work in physical education: Dr. Clifford L. Brownell, Columbia University; Dr. Louis Raymond Burnett, director of health and physical education for the Baltimore public schools; John E. Davis, U. S. Veterans' Hospital, Perry Point, Maryland; Miss Margaret N. H. Doubler, University of Wisconsin; Dr. William L. Hughes, Columbia University; William R. LaPorte, University of Southern California; Dr. George A. May, University of Michigan; William G. Moorhead, Pennsylvania state department of instruction; Floyd A. Rowe, director of public welfare in the Cleveland public schools; Dr. Rebecca Stoneroad, physician for the public schools of Washington, D. C.; Dr. Frederick A. Woll, College of the City of New York; Frederick W. Marvel, Brown University, and Dr. John F. Bovard, University of Oregon.

Dr. Philip J. Noel Baker, formerly professor of international relations at the University of London and member of Parliament, has received the Henry E. Howland Memorial Prize. The award of $1,500 was presented to Professor Baker on April 23 at Yale University.

Miss Margaret V. Freyburger, instructor of journalism at the San Diego, Calif., high school, has been awarded a gold key by the Columbia Scholastic Press Association. This is the highest award given in the United States to a faculty adviser of a school publication.

Rutgers University has received $2,500 under the terms of the will of the late Ernest R. Ackerman, of Plainfield, N. J., who died on October 18, 1931.

A fund of $300, raised by Cornell undergraduates in memory of Hans Wagner, Cornell alumnus killed while fighting for Germany in the world war, has been allotted to Dr. Kurt Lewin, associate professor of psychology at the university, for child psychology research work. Collection of the fund was begun in 1931, when the university's memorial to its 264 former students killed in the war was dedicated. Wagner's name was omitted from this list.

Professor Joseph H. Weber, head of the department of education at Valparaiso University, died on April 12 at the age of forty-four years.

Dr. Isaac Joachim Schwatt, professor emeritus of mathematics at the University of Pennsylvania, died on April 18 at the age of sixty-eight years.

The Reverend Francis Duffy O'Laughlin, secretary of the board of trustees of Fordham University and former head of the physics department at the university, died on April 17 in his sixty-fifth year.

The Reverend Thomas E. Fairchild, assistant to the president of Boston University since 1917 and director of its summer school, died on April 19. He was forty years old.

Lyman Chalkley, professor emeritus of law at the University of Kentucky, died on April 21 in his seventy-third year.

Dr. George Philip Krapp, professor of English at Columbia University since 1910, died on April 22. Dr. Krapp was sixty-one years old.

Mrs. Frances Haldeman Sidwell, coprincipal with her husband, Thomas W. Sidwell, of Sidwell's Friends School in Washington, D. C., died on April 15 in her seventy-third year.

The John Adams Lectureship for the University of California at Los Angeles has recently been created by the regents of the university. A similar lectureship has been established at the University of London, where Sir John Adams, formerly professor of education at the University of California at Los Angeles, is professor emeritus. Dr. Andre Lobanov-Rostovsky, assistant professor of history at the University of California, has been chosen to deliver the first of a series of annual addresses provided for by the lectureship.

Seven hundred members of the staff of the University of Washington have had restored to them about 50 per cent. of the salary reductions of April, 1933. The reductions at that time, averaging 32 per cent., were described by the U. S. Bureau of Education as the most drastic made by any state university in the country. The board of regents, in announcing the salary restoration, declared that the savings effected during the last year have made this action possible.

The first report of the New York State nursery school program, made public on April 15 by the works division of the Temporary Emergency Relief Administration, disclosed that 1,400 children are being cared for in the fifty-eight emergency nursery schools throughout the state. The children, whose parents are receiving public relief or are compelled to live on exceedingly small incomes, range in age from two to four years. The schools, the majority of which have been in operation for two months only, were started by the Civil Works Service and later transferred to the Bureau of Child Development and Parent Education of the State Department of Education.

The Oklahoma City board of education has announced increased salaries for school teachers, supervisors, clerks and building and ground staff members for the next fiscal year. Day Fezler, board president, has stated that the increase will amount to about 7 per cent. Approximately 1,500 teachers and other workers will be affected.

Student associations at the University of Oregon and the Oregon State College can not legally collect compulsory fees from their student members, according to a recent ruling made by Attorney-General I. H. Van Winkle. Students at the two institutions had paid $15 a year for the privilege of belonging to the association. A group of students at the university, in protest against the fee, appealed to the board of higher education that it be made optional. This request was denied, so the students presented their appeal to the attorney-general.

A tutorial plan to individualize the education of superior students of the College of Liberal Arts and Sciences at the University of Illinois has been proposed and will become effective when it is officially approved by the University Senate and the Board of Trustees. The plan will give juniors and seniors with high averages during their first two years an opportunity to pursue a part of their work under a tutorial adviser rather than to follow the formal classroom instruction. Students under this tutorial system will be given a comprehensive examination by a faculty committee at the end of the senior year.

The College of Liberal Arts at Northwestern University, through Dean Addison Hibbard, has announced a number of changes in its curriculum requirements. The principal change is the abolition of mathematics as a specific requirement for either of the two liberal arts degrees. Another change provides that only three specific requirements are necessary for a degree instead of six. The requirements are English, a foreign language and either Latin or Greek for a bachelor of arts degree. For a bachelor of science degree, the requirements are English, a foreign language and a natural science or mathematics.

The fifth annual School Administrators Conference will be held at the George Peabody College for Teachers at Nashville, Tenn., from April 30 to May 2, inclusive.

Seven colleges have been dropped from the accredited list of the North Central Association of Colleges and Secondary Schools on recommendation of its board of review. The colleges dropped include the University of Detroit; Xavier University at Cincinnati; Rochester Junior College at Rochester, Minn.; McKendree College at Lebanon, Ill.; Ashland College at Ashland, Ohio; Regis College at Denver, Colo., and the College of the Ozarks at Clarksville, Ark. The association also has delegated authority to the board to reinspect Colorado College, the University of Denver and Butler University and to expel these from the accredited roster at its discretion. Until the action of the board, these three colleges remain on the approved list.

The Associated Press reports that more than 200 college professors have been appointed to serve with the Roosevelt administration during its first year. The National Recovery Administration has the largest number of professors, fifty-nine, serving in its departments, and the Department of Agriculture is second with fifty-six.

The Library of Congress now has in its possession 1,000,000 separate films of books and manuscripts. Most of the films, which are on moving picture reels, were made at libraries throughout Europe during the past two years. Dr. Thomas P. Martin, of the manuscripts division, states that the library also has several million photographic copies of scholars' raw material. The films do not move on the screen, but are thrown on by a device much like the old lantern slide. A 35-foot reel, at sixteen pages to a foot, thus contains pictures of 560 pages, more than double the average size volume. Films are made with a small camera, and cost only 3 cents a page. Printing costs 15 cents a page. An 8-column page is contained on a film $1\frac{1}{8}$ by $1\frac{5}{8}$ inches and reproduces excellently when reenlarged to its original size.

The Mecklenburg archeological collection, valued at $10,000 and containing the only scientifically excavated material taken out of the region at the northern end of the Adriatic Sea, has been purchased by the Peabody Museum of Harvard University.

The *Concordiensis,* the semi-weekly student newspaper of Union College, has advocated a reversal of the usual process of examination and has prepared a list of questions for the members of the faculty. Declaring that it is the professor who makes the college and that a college is only as strong as its worst professor, a recent editorial in the paper demanded that each member of the teaching staff determine his own status by answering the following questions: Does he find his greatest interest in his students and in intellectual pursuits? Does he seek to enlighten his students, rather than to make them recite fundamentals? Does he try to introduce them to life and thought, not coach them to pass examinations? Does he put himself forward as a dispenser of truth, not as an ingratiating vaudeville actor? Does he give the student all that he has of scholarship, wisdom and understanding, despite their supposed immunity to such? Does he stimulate the mind of the student to suggest ideas and to correlate the loose ends of information? Is he enthusiastic, alive, free from all dull pedanty and dogma? Is he striving to be a personal friend of the student, a guide, and an inspiration?

An annotated list of 900 books compiled at the New York Public Library, under the auspices of the American Library Association and the American Association for Adult Education, was published on April 18 and will be distributed in emergency classes, Civilian Conservation Corps Camps, and other federal and state educational projects. Distribution of the book, which has been issued under the title, "Books of General Interest for To-day's Readers," has been made possible by a grant from the General Education Board. Miss Doris Hoit, of the New York Public Library, has compiled the list under the direction of Franklin Hopper, chief of circulation and chairman of the American Library Association's board on the library and adult education. A feature of the list is a symbol following each entry, which indicates the degree of simplicty of the book. The classifications are "simplest wording, fairly simple wording and more difficult wording."

Louis Marin, French Minister of Public Health and Physical Education, has formed a commission, the *New York Times* reports, which will be charged with studying all questions connected with preparatory military instruction. The group contains many military officials, with Marshal Hubert Lyautey as honorary president and General Albert Niessal, former member of the Superior War Council, as the active president. M. Marin's move, the dispatch comments, is in line with Marshal Phillippe Petain's contention that because Germany, Italy and Switzerland are training their boys to prepare them for military service, France, as a measure of national defense, should do likewise.

The Chinese Ministry of Education reports the registration of 103 institutions of higher learning. There are 41 universities, 13 of which are national institutions, 9 provincial and 19 private. There are 3 national independent colleges, 13 supported by provinces and 18 by private organizations. The technical colleges number 30, of which 2 are national. A census of students reveals, according to the *New York Times,* that 16,487 are studying law and political science, 10,066 literature and philosophy, 4,231 education, 2,156 commerce, 4,084 engineering, 3,930 natural science, 1,800 medicine and 1,413 agriculture and forestry. Investigation of the occupations of the parents of students reveals that the fathers of 668 students are laborers, while only 473 students are the offspring of military officers.

DISCUSSION

A DEARTH OF TEACHERS FOR THE HANDICAPPED IN THE MIDST OF A GLUT OF UNEMPLOYED TEACHERS

THE committee on special education of Section III, Education and Training, of the White House Conference on Child Health and Protection found need for considerably over 100,000 properly qualified special-class teachers in order to provide about 3,000,000 mentally and physically handicapped children in the schools of the nation with the type of remedial and developmental instruction required to mitigate or correct their handicaps and to transform them from liabilities into social and economic assets.[1]

How many physically and mentally handicapped children are now enrolled in special classes throughout the schools of the country and how many teachers are now employed for the instruction of these children? Based on such facts as the committee on teacher training was able to discover, the number of handicapped children of all kinds in special classes in 1929 was less than 225,000, which is not equal to 10 per cent. of the children in need of skilled instruction in special classes or of efficient corrective treatment, while the number of special-class teachers was considerably less than 7,000,[2] which falls short of 7 per cent. of the estimated requirement. To-day there are probably fewer special-class teachers than there were in 1929. Moreover, it was obvious from the information that could be secured that only a minor proportion of these teachers could be certificated as adequately trained special-class teachers under the standards recommended by the committee, namely, one year of technical training in addition to the completion of the regular course of study for regular grade teachers.[3]

These few facts are rehearsed here for the purpose of emphasizing three considerations of basic importance for the preservation of the brain power of the nation and the development and conservation of all types of talent and levels of ability, and for the purpose of alleviating personal and economic distress in the teaching profession.

(1) Retaining the vast army of seriously maladjusted children in the regular grades is often equivalent to sheer educational neglect. Sometimes this policy can only be described as educational maltreatment or malpractise, not only because of the neglect or the mistraining but also because of the mental and emotional twists and personality maladjustments and distortions that often result from the attempt to force these deviating children into a common mold, or to conform to the demands of curricula which are maladapted to their individual needs. The results of this process of mistraining or inefficient training is eventual social and economic derailment of many youths. Society ultimately will have to pay the penalty for its neglect in double measure for the support of courts, jails, reformatories and almshouses. The obligation to provide skilled developmental, remedial and diagnostic instruction and treatment for handicapped children reduces, in the final analysis, to a matter of enlightened self-interest on the part of the state, rather than to a matter of charity or benevolence or even of constitutional right, important as is the latter consideration.

(2) The establishment of a sufficient number of special classes in the public schools of the country to provide for the needs of all types of handicapped children would absorb most of our unemployed teachers. Although the national government and the individual states have spent many billions of dollars on national projects for the purpose of unemployment relief, the efforts they have exerted in behalf of unemployed teachers through CWA or emergency relief programs or special grants sinks into insignificance. Supplying essential educational relief to the underprivileged, disabled and maladjusted children in the schools will restore about 100,000 teachers to the payrolls, and, incidentally, supply openings for a large

[1] "Special Education, The Handicapped and the Gifted," pp. 3 *ff*, 533 *ff*, 1931. It has been estimated that 3,000,000 of the 10,000,000 handicapped children reported by the conference are so handicapped as to constitute problems for special or differential instruction.

[2] *Ibid.*, p. 554.

[3] See *op. cit.*, pp. 559–579, for the schedule of courses recommended for teachers of mentally retarded, behavior, deaf, hard-of-hearing, blind, partially seeing, speech defective, crippled and lowered vitality cases, and for visiting teachers. See also J. E. Wallace Wallin, "The Baltimore Plan of Training Special-Class Teachers and Other Workers in the Field of Special Education," *The Elementary School Journal*, 1931, 607–618.

number of jobless psychologists, psychometrists and psychoeducational examiners.[4]

(3) With immediate need for 100,000 special-class teachers or teachers skilled in various types of corrective educational treatment (*e.g.,* such as is required by speech defectives and hypacoustics) and only the minority of special-class teachers now in service adequately trained, the special education departments in schools of education would have to be greatly augmented in order to afford adequate facilities for teacher training in the field of special education. The results of this needed expansion would be to provide further openings for the unemployed in the higher ranks of the teaching profession.

Is it not time that this important segment and these particular phases of our public educational program be accorded the attention they deserve? This army of Forgotten Men of the schools has been almost completely ignored in all the weekly educational radio talks that have been broadcast to the nation for over a year for the express purpose of safeguarding the schools against the ravages of the economic depression and of laying solid foundations for a large frontal advance in future, although the vital relations of these problems to the public weal have been brought directly to the attention of the sponsors of the radio programs. Moreover, little consideration has been devoted to the educational needs of the handicapped in the publicity broadcasts that have filled the journals and the daily newspapers during this period of economic dislocation.

A wide frontal attack on the problem of "education in the national recovery" will prove lopsided, abortive or fallacious which does not include in its purview and bring to public attention adequate consideration of these problems which are so vital for the conservation of the social and mental health of the body politic.

J. E. W. WALLIN

WILMINGTON, DELAWARE

THE NEW DEAL AND THE SCHOOLS

THE Public Works Administration came upon us about nine months ago, holding $3,300,000,000 in its hands for the initiation or completion of much-needed public projects. It found our cities, counties and states unprepared. Very few of them had any plans for significant public improvements, and very little of the money has yet been spent. Last November came a new offer of $400,000,000 as a free gift to be spent in almost any sort of a public improvement that would put people to work. Again it found the country as a whole unprepared. But only the people who were ready with some sort of a plan got the money.

From the record of the city-planning congresses that are held each year, it would appear that city planning consisted in making a plat of the city, that it was concerned with the width and direction of the streets, the arrangements of parks, of business, industrial and residence sections and the like. The last few months have made it plain that there is a type of social and educational planning that is quite as much needed and that it behooves every sort of an organization that would make progress to have its next few immediate steps outlined and ready. Within the past year we have had organized a National Planning Board, several regional planning boards and many state and county planning boards. The logic of the situation applies to the schools at least as much as to cities as a whole or counties as a whole. It has been possible during the last three months, as it will be during the next two, to secure almost any sort of a school improvement for which an adequate plan is presented.

In this county, the county superintendent, Miss Haas, called in the school directors from the 140 school districts of the county. Each district made a list of the improvements needed at its school. The combined budget of needs was presented to the officers of the CWA and an appropriation of $75,000 was made for the work. One hundred fifty men, mostly carpenters and painters, have been working since November putting these schools in condition. Thus far sixty sanitary toilets have been installed, cellars have been dug for furnaces at a number of schools. Many interiors have been painted. Several schools have been reroofed. In some the windows have been changed to the left side to avoid cross lighting. I do not know how far similar plans have been carried out in other counties, but apparently it has been possible in all.

There is one improvement that would apply to three quarters of our city schools, which is peculiarly appropriate for a CWA job, because

[4] For a plea in behalf of jobless psychological testers and examiners, see the writer's note in *The Psychological Exchange*, 1934, pp. 199 *f.*

it is practically all work, with very little expense for materials. I refer to the improvement of their playgrounds. Any good-sized city school should have at least an acre near the school that can be used at any time. This means that the ground should be excavated to a depth of eight or ten inches, underdrained and filled in with five to seven inches of coarse cinders or broken stone and rolled down. On this should be placed about three inches of fine crushed rock or loamy soil with a top dressing of stone grits or fine gravel. Such a ground will not get muddy and can be used immediately after a heavy rain. Often the gas or electric plant will install the cinders and even roll them down for nothing.

The Department of Agriculture has announced its intention to withdraw 50,000,000 acres of farm land from cultivation. Last year it spent $200,000,000 to get farmers to reduce their acreage in corn and wheat and cotton and to kill their surplus hogs. It did not work very well, for where one farmer agreed to reduce his acres of wheat or corn, very likely his neighbor, anticipating a rise in price, put in just as much more. There has been no other government project that has caused so much criticism. From the beginning this has been spoken of as a temporary expedient. It is very expensive and there is no permanent result, as the work has to be done over again each year.

Recently the department has announced a different policy. It plans to buy rather than rent some fifty million acres of marginal land, which is now ruining the farmers who attempt to cultivate it in order to get it permanently out of agriculture. $25,000,000 has been set aside as a beginning, with the statement that this might be increased to $350,000,000 if it worked out satisfactorily.

The average rural school probably has less than half an acre of ground. It should have at least two acres. The consolidated school should have not less than twenty and forty acres if possible with a picnic grove, farm and athletic fields both for the school and the community. It would seem to be a better proposition for the department to add these extra acres to these country schools than it is to hire farmers to let a part of their acres grow up to weeds. I do not know that the idea has occurred to Secretary Wallace, but it should appeal to him. If the school people would let it be known that they wanted this land, it is quite likely that he would as readily devote it to such fundamental rural life uses as to let it go back to the wilderness.

HENRY S. CURTIS

ANN ARBOR, MICH.

SPECIAL CORRESPONDENCE

DIVISIONAL ORGANIZATION AT UNION COLLEGE

IN the midst of the worst depression in the history of the country and faced with drastic curtailment of funds, Union College has launched an educational program that in many respects is unique among American colleges, unique not so much because of the originality of the ideas underlying it as because of the sheer boldness of its attack on the educational frontier. The core of the program is the merging of the numerous departments into four main divisions of human knowledge, each division controlling a curriculum of its own which is closely correlated with the curricula of the other divisions. Promulgated because of the pressing need for greater economy, it is, in the firm belief of those who are sponsoring the change, a distinct advance in educational procedure.

Now as to the particular form which divisional organization has taken in Union College. Eighteen departments have been merged into four divisions: Languages and Literature, Social Studies, Mathematics and Science, and Engineering. Each division is charged with the responsibility of preparing and operating its own curriculum, with primary concern for students especially interested in its particular kind of work. These curricula are not acted upon by the general faculty. They are subject to approval, however, by a committee composed of the president, the dean and the chairmen of the divisions. In this way correlation is obtained without the long delays and the acrimony entailed by protracted arguments in meetings of the general faculty.

An idea of what this means can probably best be obtained by examining the curriculum of one of the divisions. Let us take that of the Division of Social Studies. (It must not be assumed of course that all the divisions have organized their curricula in exactly the same way.) There are two general divisional requirements. Each student must pass an examination before the end of his sophomore year which shall demonstrate his proficiency in the correct use of English, and also a similar examination demonstrating a reading knowledge of either French or German. Each freshman is required to take two social studies courses—introduction to social institutions and the history of western civilization. The first course deals primarily with the origins of social institutions, such as industry, capital, property, government, war, religion, marriage and the family; the second course deals with their historical development in western civilization. In addition to these courses one course in science is required. Any freshman who succeeds in passing achievement tests in language or in English may complete his schedule with sophomore electives.

There are three social studies courses in the sophomore year, of which one, a course in methods and problems, is required of all. All are required to take either elementary economics or comparative government and may take both. If a student has completed his English and foreign language requirements, he may complete his schedule with electives.

Of course there is more than one way to construct a curriculum in the social studies. Union College only claims to have found *a* way, a way that is based upon certain fundamental ideas—in other words, to have a planned curriculum.

If at the conclusion of his sophomore year a student has really grasped the significance of two fundamental concepts, he is considered to be adequately equipped for advanced study in the division. Those concepts are the evolutionary development of human institutions and the scientific method of studying social questions. The freshman work is built around the first idea and the sophomore work around the second.

The Union College freshman will begin his work in social studies with an attempt to find out where social institutions came from and how they came into being; and then will trace their slow painful development through the history of the western world, since that is the civilization which most nearly concerns him.

It has been customary for college departments of economics, political science and history to send their students to the laboratory sciences for their methods of reasoning. Modesty is an engaging virtue, especially in college teachers, but isn't this going a little too far? In learning to make a pie it would seem unnecessary to go in search of sand and glue when flour and lard were at hand. Method is obviously best learned in the handling of the material to which it is to be applied. The student can best learn the scientific method of studying social questions by getting to work on social problems.

Recognizing the tremendous importance of the scientific method of studying social questions and further recognizing that the best place to develop this method is in the social studies themselves, the division has built the sophomore curriculum around this second fundamental idea. A course in methods and problems in the social studies is required of all sophomores. In addition either comparative government or elementary economics must be taken, and both may be. These three courses are organized as a unit. Instructors in the methods course draw material from the other two courses (though they are not limited to these two fields) always with method primarily in mind. Instructors in the other two courses draw upon the methods course in the study of the problems they take up. Each of these courses is essentially a problem course rather than the traditional survey introductory course. The instructors in the three courses function as a group, each aware of what is being done and what is being planned by the others.

The junior-senior part of the curriculum has been worked out not with the thought that the student must have certain information before undertaking advanced study—that, for example, he must have had American government to study public administration, or elementary economics to study the labor movement—but with the belief that if he has a real grasp of two fundamental ideas—the evolutionary development of human institutions and the scientific approach to social questions—he is adequately equipped to begin advanced study in any field of the social studies. Consequently, the four courses required in the freshman and sophomore years constitute the only prerequisite.

Within a specified period during the spring of his sophomore year each student member of the division, in consultation with his adviser, selects a major program. A major consists of four of the eight[1] courses in the junior-senior years, to be taken within the division and forming a planned course of study. There are three types of major programs, known respectively as (1) topical majors, (2) field majors, (3) free majors.

For some time educators have felt that the subject major does not meet the needs of all liberal arts students. Specialization has been encouraged to a point where it must, in some cases, have been detrimental. Because there was no alternative some students have been forced to specialize who by interest or aptitude were fitted for a broader course of study. The purpose of the topical major is to provide a reasonable alternative for this type of student. A broad cultural objective is set up, the curriculum is organized to meet that objective, and individual courses are subordinated to it. For example, one objective set up is an understanding of American civilization. Courses especially useful in meeting this objective have been introduced into the curriculum, courses in American literature, American thought, the historical development of ideas and customs and political, religious and economic institutions.

The fact that the subject or field major has not met the needs of all students does not mean that it should be discarded. It has too well proved its worth for those especially interested in one field and qualified to study in that field intensively. One serious weakness of this type of major, however, has been that it is too highly departmentalized, giving the students the idea that there are distinct lines of demarcation between the various fields of knowledge. It has also been quite uneconomical in that each department has felt that it must offer enough courses to meet the major requirements. In our divisional organization of the social studies curriculum a sharp cut has been made in the number of courses and yet the scope of each field major has been greatly enlarged. Instead of merely crossing off ten or fifteen courses from the existing outfit, we assumed that all existing courses were abolished and began to build from the ground up. In working out the advanced courses two ideas were paramount. It was thought that as far as possible overlapping materials should be eliminated. It was also thought that each course should meet as many different needs as possible. For example, the economics department had been offering a course in economics reform, political science a course in political theory, and philosophy a course in social philosophy. Instead of these *three* courses the division now offers *one* course in social and political philosophy, designed to meet the needs of students particularly interested in any of the three fields. Other instances might be given, but this one is enough to show how the underlying ideas have been put into practical effect. Many fewer courses are being offered, but the scope of the major has been greatly enlarged, greater coordination has been brought about and the curriculum has been enriched largely because a *plan* underlies the program.

In addition to the topical major and the field major, provision is made for a free major. Any student who wishes to work out a course of study falling outside the two options mentioned above is, with the approval of his adviser, permitted to follow it. This provision is made for the sake of the able student who knows definitely what his objective is. Undoubtedly only the exceptional student would be in a position to do this kind of work; but in all our planning this exceptional student must not be forgotten, for what we do for him is in many respects the most important phase of the college's entire program.

It is not thought by any means that the educational millennium has been reached in the program just described. Neither is it forgotten that all the machinery in the world will be of no avail without adequate human resources. An able faculty and an able student body are more important than even the perfect curriculum. But we had to revise our educational machinery because of financial stringency, and it is our hope that in so doing we have made changes which tend in the direction of educational improvement.

E. E. Cummins

Union College, N. Y.

[1] Only four courses are required in each of the junior and senior years for the A.B. degree.

REPORTS

THE ANNUAL REPORT OF THE CARNEGIE FOUNDATION ON LEGAL EDUCATION

ANNUALLY the Carnegie Foundation for the Advancement of Teaching publishes a review of legal education in the United States. The report for 1933, issued during the second week in April, gives particular attention to the relationship of professional education to undergraduate instruction and the learned profession.

In this report Alfred Z. Reed takes the position that educators ought not to define the term "learned profession" too narrowly. "Our new county—our land of courageous innovations—ought to be able to bring within the university sphere callings which in other countries traditionally stand outside. That it has done so is not to be regarded as an unfortunate break with the past. Rather, it is evidence that we do not intend to let an inherited mechanism restrict the free development of social and economic activities. It is futile to rail at American colleges and universities because they break with tradition."

But it is proper to approach this educational work critically. "There are three groups who ought to be, and in most cases are, specially interested in finding their way through the educational labyrinth. There are the authorities who are immediately responsible for the conduct of particular universities. There are the sources to which they must look for financial support—state legislatures on the one hand; foundations and individual benefactors on the other. There are finally the young men and women, and their families and personal advisers, who try to make an intelligent choice among the many educational opportunities that are open to them." How to do this "is a task that can not be delegated to practitioners associations or coordinating associations." Each group must rely, finally, upon their own judgment.

Two fruitful principles are, however, suggested. "In the first place, professional work, in the group of universities that we have in mind, should embrace all those callings—neither more nor less—in which (as originally was true only in the case of theology, law and medicine) a substantial body of higher learning already exists, or is in the process of being accumulated. In the second place, even though a particular calling satisfies these criteria, and preparation for it is properly offered by a school that moves on the university plane, it does not necessarily follow that this school should be admitted to the educational brood that is cherished under any particular university wing. Are we sure that simply banding together numerous professional schools, under the aegis of a single greatly expanded university, will give us what we want?" A university of this sort is likely to be "an unwieldy aggregation of units, formally connected with one another but not possessing the self-conscious unity of a living whole. Our modern enormously diversified scientific and economic activities have perhaps brought with them this consequence. In place of the ancient concept of 'a university,' dedicated to the advancement of knowledge and the learned professions, it should now be our aim to develop distinct types of universities."

It is difficult to bring together like-minded men who are dispersed over an enormous geographical area. "This seems to be the explanation for the plague of associations of various sorts that infests American higher education. So great is the number of associations of all sorts, within and without the universities, that coordinating associations have perforce arisen, designed to pool the activities of their constituent or associated members and prevent interested parties from being bewildered by the organization maze. Up to date, the coordinating movement, so far from simplifying, has introduced additional complications into an already overorganized educational system."

The article on "Learned Professions and Their Organization" discusses also the relationship and mutual pressure exerted by three organized forces—practitioners associations, the state and educational institutions. "Diversification of economic activities" or "specialization" must be distinguished from the "fraternal association" or "organic union" of those who practise these activities. "As contrasted with the natural fluidity of the specializing impulse, organizations are relatively rigid, and constitute a stabilizing social force. For a time, this may be an advantage, but it is also a danger. Sooner or later, the lines of organic division cease to coincide with those of the developing economic pattern. Practitioners associations constitute an artificial element that is quite as likely to require reformation itself as it is to serve as our guide to professional betterment. England and America now contain an enormous number of these practitioners associations."

Discussing the question of licensing of individual practitioners, the report states that, "a third system of governmental control over occupations is that of issuing licenses to individual practitioners." This system "first appears in connection with the legal profession in England. Transplanted from England into its American colonies, not only did it long continue in the United States to be the only system in force for the legal profession, but it was extended to many other professions and occupations as well. On the other hand, in England itself, this device has been used most sparingly for other professions, and in the early part of the nineteenth century it was abandoned even for the legal profession." A recent attempt to institute a "self-governing bar" in this country has come into conflict with our established practise of judicial control. Even under a forthright licensing system, each profession, "while regarded in the eyes of the law as a unit, is composed of individuals who more and more tend, as a matter of fact, to pursue a great variety of occupations, many of which have little in common with one another." Inevitably, therefore, selective associations will be "organized in profusion. Whatever be their defects in individual instances, they do much to remedy the artificiality of the antiquated classification that forms the basis of most legally organized professions."

QUOTATIONS

THE PROBLEM OF DEGENERACY

SUPERINTENDENT OF SCHOOLS BOGAN has been inspired by the Zietlow tragedy to form a committee of nine leading psychiatrists to make recommendations for improving the method of dealing with abnormal or subnormal children. This step will be welcomed even by citizens whose memory of similar efforts does not give them much hope of early and practical results. From time to time crimes like the Zietlow case horrify the community, and we have a flurry of protest and proposals of reform. Little has resulted, and it is not in lack of appreciation of the scope and difficulty of the subject that we suggest that more might have been accomplished if less had been attempted, or at any rate proposed.

This is not to say that comprehensive reform should not be laid out by competent men. But public feeling, upon which the accomplishment of legislative and administrative changes largely depends, is unhappily of brief duration, and every program of adequate scope, if it is really to get anywhere, must be taken almost step by step. This is irksome to the impatient theorist and ardent humanitarian, but it is an imperative condition of progress.

We hope therefore that the recommendations of the new committee will include not merely a general scheme but some practical proposals which can be concentrated upon for immediate results. Some concrete betterments actually accomplished will do more to keep public interest alive and thus insure further progress than any effort to create by exhortation a public sentiment strong and persistent enough to carry through a comprehensive plan.

No doubt this sentiment ought to exist, for the facts respecting degeneracy are appalling. But public knowledge of them is scant, and such publicity as has been given them from time to time is soon forgotten. Meanwhile sentimentality has been turned into a murderous racket, distorting the proper application of parole, weakening or preventing the establishment of adequate safeguards for the normal and innocent part of our communities. Dangerous defectives, as Mr. Loesch indignantly and justly protests, are treated with too much leniency in so-called humanitarian courts.

The spectacular crimes warn us often, but they are only one and perhaps the least important aspect of the evil, which is said to be increasing and threatens the health and sanity of modern nations, including our own. While we are quarreling over political and economic forms we would do better to give more heed to this undermining of the foundation of civilized society.—*The Chicago Tribune.*

EDUCATIONAL RESEARCH AND STATISTICS

THE ORAL EXAMINATION: ITS VALIDITY AND RELIABILITY

THE oral examination is, at least apparently, not only acceptable but decidedly creditable as an educational practise. Nearly all graduate schools require it for the doctor's degree; most of them require it for the master's degree; and some of them require it for the professional degree.[1] Also, schools with "honors" systems tend to require it as a part of the program of comprehensive examinations ordinarily administered in these cases.[2]

But, even so, the oral examination, quite as apparently, stands in need of experimental evaluation. Jones thinks that it "is, and distinctly should be, considered incomplete by itself and still on trial."[3] Wood takes the position that it "suffers from all of the weaknesses and ills (narrowness of the functions measured, subjectivity, relative unreliability, etc.) of the essay examination, but in a more acute and less curable form."[4] Barnes and Pressey argue, from experimentally determined facts, that it "should not continue to be uncritically accepted."[5] And cases of similar points of view could be multiplied almost endlessly.[6]

Actually—tradition, common practise and general impression to the contrary notwithstanding—just what the oral examination measures is not known, and furthermore, whether it measures anything consistently is a question. The validity and the reliability of this device require specific determination.[7]

[1] Examine the current catalogues for a random sampling of the institutions of higher learning.

[2] *Cf.* Edward S. Jones, "Comprehensive Examinations in American Colleges." Macmillan, New York, 1933.

[3] Jones, *ibid.*, p. 228.

[4] Ben D. Wood, "The Structure and Content of the Comprehensive Examination for College Sophomores." Institute for Administrative Officers of Higher Institutions: Proceedings, Vol. 3, p. 197, 1931, Univ. of Chicago Press.

[5] Elinor J. Barnes and S. L. Pressey, "The Reliability and Validity of Oral Examinations," SCHOOL AND SOCIETY, 30: 1929, p. 722; and also, S. L. Pressey, L. C. Pressey and Elinor J. Barnes, "The Final Ordeal," *Jour. Higher Educ.*, 3: 261–264, 1932.

[6] Try your colleagues, or almost any one who has had experience with the oral examination.

[7] *Cf.* Barnes and Pressey, *op. cit.*, p. 722.

AN EXPERIMENT

In an attempt to get at this problem, the oral examination was investigated under standard conditions. It was tried out as a final examination, in order that the conditions of motivation would be normal.

Twenty-five upperclass and graduate students in a course in applied psychology[8] were involved as examinees. Early in the semester, the class was told that the final examination in the course would be oral instead of written. Later, the students were instructed (1) to select what they individually considered to be a major subject in or aspect of applied psychology, and (2) to prepare for thorough examination in the direction of the choice made. And finally, late in the semester, the whole examination procedure was explained to the group.

Three staff members did the examining. The writer (*T*) served as chairman of the committee, while Dr. G. C. Brandenburg (*B*), head of the department of education and professor of education and psychology, and Dr. H. H. Remmers (*R*), director of the division of educational reference and professor of education and psychology, kindly assisted in the work.

The procedure was standard, except for the time element. Each examinee was called before the committee at an appointed time and place, questioned along definite lines for a period of only twelve minutes,[9] and summarily dismissed.

During and at the close of each examination, the examiners rated (independently, of course) the examinee as to: (1) judgment in the selection of a subject or topic, (2) ability to state facts exactly, (3) ability to elaborate a topic, (4) method of preparation, (5) background of knowledge, (6) theoretical and practical insight, (7) ability in the refutation of arguments, (8) quality of vocabulary, and (9) relative standing among students in general. A specially constructed rating scale, consisting of nine line-graphs (one for each of the traits and one for the general estimate of relative standing), each scaled to one hundred points, was used in the rating.

[8] A course offered by the writer.

[9] Ordinarily the time spent in questioning the examinee is much longer than this.

TABLE I

Reliability Coefficients for the Ratings

Examiners	Measures*	1. Judgment in the selection of a subject	2. Ability to state facts exactly	3. Ability to elaborate a topic	4. Method of preparation	5. Background of knowledge	6. Theoretical and practical insight	7. Ability in the refutation of arguments	8. Quality of vocabulary	General estimates of relative standing	Composite ratings—Averages of the trait ratings
B and *R*	r	.296	.135	.432	.257	.644	.603	.521	.409	.333	.712
	P.E.$_r$	.123	.132	.109	.125	.079	.086	.097	.112	.119	.066
B and *T*	r	−.231	.028	.402	.199	.492	.342	.299	.428	.404	.489
	P.E.$_r$	.127	.134	.113	.130	.102	.119	.123	.110	.113	.102
R and *T*	r	.380	.419	.349	.528	.796	.128	.216	.529	.225	.611
	P.E.$_r$	.115	.111	.118	.097	.094	.132	.128	.098	.127	.084
Average	r	.128	.194	.394	.328	.644	.358	.345	.445	.321	.604
	R†	.306	.419	.661	.590	.845	.625	.612	.714	.586	.821

* Based on the twenty-five cases.
† Reliability coefficient for the combined ratings—obtained by substituting the value 3 for n, and the average r for r in the Spearman-Brown prophecy formula.

A comprehensive, objective examination—which was given just two weeks before the end of the semester—was used as a validating criterion.

The Reliability of the Obtained Ratings

Reliability coefficients for the ratings were determined by the standard method. First the ratings assigned by one examiner were correlated with the ratings assigned by another. This was done until all possible combinations of the examiners were exhausted. Then the correlations for the different pairs of examiners were added and averaged. Finally the Spearman-Brown prophecy formula was applied, with n = 3 (there being three examiners) and r = the average r in each case.

The results are presented in Table I. Here it will be observed that the correlations in general tend to be low. But it should be pointed out that the values in all cases, except the values in the last row, indicate the reliability of the ratings for a single examiner, from which point of view the correlations are observed to be relatively high; especially those for the composite ratings. The values presented in the last row indicate the reliability of the combined ratings for the three examiners. Here the reliability coefficients, except the first two in the row, indicate reliabilities that closely approximate the statistical requirement for validity in group comparison. The reliability coefficient for the composite ratings (the last value in the row) actually approximates the reliability generally considered as a minimum for individual diagnosis. As a matter of fact this reliability is higher than that of the objective examination used for purposes of validation (see footnote in Table II).

It is interesting to note, also, that the reliability coefficients for the general estimates (which estimates are, ordinarily, the only values used as a basis of judgment in the oral examination) tend to be low as compared with the coefficients for the composite ratings. With the ratings of the three examiners combined, the reliability of the general estimates barely meets the minimum statistical requirement for group comparison, whereas the reliability of the composite ratings nearly reaches the minimum required for individual analysis.

THE VALIDITY OF THE OBTAINED RATINGS

In order to obtain some indication of the validity of the ratings, the composite ratings for the twenty-five examinees were correlated with the scores they made on the objective examination.

The correlations thus determined are presented in Table II. These validity coefficients speak for themselves. They appear to be low; and, as a matter of fact, they are relatively low as validity coefficients go. Even if they were corrected for attenuation they would still be low, except perhaps in one case, namely, that in which *T*'s composite ratings are correlated with the objective examination scores. But, in this case, it must be remembered that *T* was the instructor of the class examined and rated, and that, therefore, his judgments were in all probability influenced (though unwittingly) by his knowledge of the relative standing of the examinees as members of the class. The validity coefficient for the combined composite ratings, when corrected for attenuation, is only .624.[10]

Obviously, then, the ratings and the scores on the objective test represent different functions. But just what function or functions the ratings represent is a question. Presumably the examiners succeeded in doing what they tried to do; namely, rate the ability of the examinees to use knowledge under conditions of challenge; and it goes without argument that knowledge and the use of knowledge are distinctly different things.

CONCLUSION

Now, admittedly, these data are based on a very limited sampling. But, even so, they indicate that at least under certain conditions the oral examination is as reliable and perhaps just as valid (though maybe in a different direction) as the ordinary objective examination. If the oral examination were always definitely planned, carefully prepared for (by both the examiners and the examinees) and systematically administered, it might not be so objectionable as a measuring device.

OTIS C. TRIMBLE

PURDUE UNIVERSITY

[10] This corrected validity coefficient would have turned out to be somewhat higher, perhaps in the neighborhood of .80, if the reliability coefficient for the objective examination (which coefficient was substituted in the attenuation formula) had been determined by the equivalent-forms method instead of the split-test method (*cf.* H. H. Remmers, "A Possible Experimental Error in Determining the Overlap of Two Correlated Variables," *Jour. Gen. Psychol.*, 9: 459–461, 1933). But even then the validity coefficient would be relatively low. And besides, the uncorrected validity coefficient is probably spuriously high because of *T*'s tendency to rate on the basis of foreknowledge.

TABLE II

VALIDITY COEFFICIENTS* FOR THE RATINGS

(1) r—between *B*'s composite ratings and the objective examination† scores	.421 ± .111
(2) r—between *R*'s composite ratings and the objective examination scores	.306 ± .122
(3) r—between *T*'s composite ratings and the objective examination scores	.639 ± .080
(4) r—between *B*, *R* and *T*'s combined composite ratings and the objective examination scores	.494 ± .103

* Based on the twenty-five cases.

† The reliability coefficient of the objective examination was found (by the split-test method) to be .764.

NEW BOOKS IN EDUCATION

COLE, WILLIAM E. *The Teaching of Biology.* Pp. xiv + 252. 7 figures. Appleton-Century. $2.00.

HAIDER, CARMEN. *Do We Want Fascism?* Pp. xii + 276. Day. $2.00.

HENRIQUES, ROSE L. *The Approach to Club Music.* Pp. xii + 91. Oxford University Press. $0.50.

MCKEE, PAUL. *Reading and Literature in the Elementary School.* Pp. xi + 592. *Language in the Elementary School.* Pp. xi + 482. Houghton-Mifflin. $2.00 each.

SEAVER, CHARLES H. *Civics of Today.* A Workbook for the Study of Changing Community Services and Organization Local, State and National. Pp. xii + 244. Sanborn. $0.60.

Teacher and Public. A Handbook of Interpretation for Teachers. Eighth Yearbook. Pp. 240. 22 charts. 19 tables. Department of Classroom Teachers, National Education Association.

TREVELYAN, G. M. *The Mingling of the Races. Being Book One of the History of England.* Pp. 192. 7 maps. Longmans, Green. $1.35.

WOODBURN, JAMES A. and HOWARD C. HILL. *Early America.* Pp. ix + 470. Illustrated. Longmans, Green. $1.20.

SCHOOL AND SOCIETY

WITH WHICH ARE COMBINED THE EDUCATIONAL REVIEW, ESTABLISHED IN 1891, THE TEACHERS MAGAZINE, ESTABLISHED IN 1878, AND THE SCHOOL JOURNAL, ESTABLISHED IN 1874.

J. McKEEN CATTELL AND ALFRED L. HALL-QUEST

EDITORIAL COMMUNICATIONS SHOULD BE ADDRESSED TO THE EDITORS OF SCHOOL AND SOCIETY, 3941 GRAND CENTRAL TERMINAL, NEW YORK, N. Y.

Volume 39 SATURDAY, MAY 5, 1934 Number 1010

THE NEW GERMAN NATIONALISM AND EDUCATION

By Professor I. L. KANDEL

TEACHERS COLLEGE, COLUMBIA UNIVERSITY

I

THE reform of German education in the light of the National Socialist Revolution is proceeding apace. Although little has yet been done to reorganize the administrative system in detail, it is already evident that the tendency will be in the direction of centralization, not within the states as in the past but through one authority for the Third Reich as a whole. But details of administrative reorganization are after all relatively unimportant. The most important aspects of an educational system are the spirit in which it is conducted and the aims which it seeks to promote. Much will be heard of the new spirit of solidarity and the community of ideals which National Socialism has already produced; a great deal will be made of the equality which overrides class distinctions and which inspires every German to address his neighbor as *Kamerad,* although not a whisper will be heard of liberty and fraternity; the new spirit in the peasant class and the reorganization of rural education will be pointed out without a hint as to the political and economic motives underlying them; both the reform and expansion of physical education on a universal basis will be hailed as the mark of national regeneration, without a suggestion of its ultimate purpose; and compulsory labor service, especially for the intellectual classes, will be signalized as a characteristic effort of the Hitler régime to promote mutual understanding between the intellectual classes and the workers.

Those who still retain some faith in liberalism, democracy and world peace must look below the surface of these reforms, if the real aims of the Third Reich are to be understood. Those who hail the Nazi Revolution as the renaissance of the German spirit fail to mention the fact that the solidarity and unanimity have been secured and are maintained by force, that Germany from one end to the other is a military camp, even though it is not armed, and that the cult of hatred and revenge exercises a far greater influence than the cult of positive ideals. Hatred is inculcated against the suspected enemy within and the former enemy without from the earliest childhood up with such venom and barbarism as the world has not yet witnessed. There must be spiritual degeneracy somewhere if as early as the elementary school period children are taught to hate other children, whether Jews, Socialists or Communists; there must be something warped in a mentality that recommends that fairy tales should be used to spread such hate—that the wolf in "Little Red Riding Hood" and in "The Wolf and the Seven Little Goats" is the Jew in disguise, and that the witch in "Haensel and Gretel" represents the French! Man's inhumanity to man is as nothing compared with the tyranny of children against children, which is directly encouraged and which irretrievably sears the souls of its victims.

I can hardly be accused of lack of sympathy for Germany in the post-war period. In my "Comparative Education," the writing of which was completed in August, 1932, I wrote:

> The great danger which today menaces German education is that the high ideal, which was set for it in the Constitution (Article 148), that it should be conducted "in the spirit of German national character and of international conciliation"—*Bildung zum Deutschtum* and *Bildung zur Humanität*—may be thwarted by conditions imposed upon the country by forces over which it has no control. A nation driven in on itself, with its future mortgaged for several generations to external powers, and without hope, torn by internal dissension, can hardly be expected to cultivate an educational ideal based on aspirations of friendship and peace within and without.

That new education of Republican Germany which was beginning to be a model for the world the Nazi régime has set out deliberately to destroy. Not only those teachers who were active in it but all teachers who are suspected of pacifism or of international leanings have been removed, and the rest are threatened with reprisals if they do not conform. To make doubly sure, the system of preparing teachers is being revised; a new institution has been opened at Lauenburg on the Polish border for the training of rural school teachers, a step which, according to a statement of the Ministry, "may well have besides the cultural-political eminently important consequences for frontier economics and national politics. The first decisive advance to the East has been made by the Prussian Ministry of Education." Three new institutions have been established at Plön, Köslin and Potsdam for the preparation of leaders who are to be the new evangelists and stalwarts of the revolution.

In the preparation of teachers and in the school curricula the much decried provision of the Constitution that education should be conducted "in the spirit of German national character and of international conciliation" is replaced by new subjects—*Wehrkunde, Wehrwissenschaft, Wehrsport** (*Wehr-* meaning military defense), *Grenzlandkunde, Auslandkunde, Volkskunde* and *Rassenkunde*. Suspicion of the teachers, inherited from the republic, has, however, led the authorities to lay greater stress on the educative activities of the *Hitlerjugend* than of the schools proper.

The teachers are everywhere made conscious of their new duties in the new social order. They have had, of course, to surrender those notions of democracy and professional leadership for which they have struggled in Germany since 1848. The *Allgemeine Deutsche Lehrerzeitung* quotes an order of the Minister of the Interior of August 5, 1933:

> Since the National Socialist Government has taken upon itself the exclusive administration of the State, it is the Government which defends the interests of its employees. In consequence demands and representations of Government employees and of their organizations, addressed to the authorities, and in particular to the Ministers, relative to salaries, re-classification and service, are not only superfluous but inadmissible, and will in future not be accepted. All representations which criticize superiors, and therefore the administration, which alone is responsible, are forbidden. Personal demands must pass through the administration.

* The banning of Ewald Banse's book, "Germany Prepares for the Next War: A Nazi Theory of 'National Defense,' " was for foreign consumption.

And again in his "Neubau des Deutschen Schulwesens" Dr. W. Hartnacke, commissioner of education in Saxony, warns the teachers that their conversion to the new ideology must be sincere and wholehearted. This radio address concludes with the words:

In the light of recent information I take this opportunity to state that the Ministry of Education can have confidence only in those teachers' associations of which not only the executive officers, but also every individual member is willing to give assurance in writing that he has adopted without reserve the principles of a consciously national and Christian education. The national Revolution is not satisfied with the mere outward semblance of a change. Those capable of no greater change than that cannot expect to be called upon as co-workers. The new German school demands a whole German teacher who finds in the principles of Christian philosophy the motive and power for unselfish devotion to its cause. It will know how to find such men and with their help to build the new German school.

Germany is, of course, entitled to have whatever type of government and education she chooses, but the world which has to live with her has a right to know what the aims of both are. What does the emphasis on loyalty and self-sacrifice, on the study of the nation's heroes, on the nation's heroic past mean? What is the significance of the inculcation of quiescent obedience to the authority of the *Führer*? And it is to be noted that whenever the heroes and the *Führer* are mentioned, there is never included the name of a single leader in art or music, science or literature, or of any one who has made any contribution to the welfare of humanity!

It is possible now to put together a definite picture of what Naziism means for the world. I have already (in an article on "Nationalism, Patriotism and Education in Germany," which appeared in *The Kadelpian Review*, January, 1934, pp. 157 *ff.*) published a translation of the "Suggestions for History Text-books" which were issued on July 20, 1933, and which will color all text-books to be used after Easter, 1935. It is not necessary to repeat here the falsification of history, of the Nordic and Germanic theories, of the race theory and so on. The same ideas are conveyed by the material which is translated and presented below. Whatever the official pronouncements on the desire for peace and on disarmament may be, here is first-hand evidence of the kind of militaristic indoctrination and war propaganda which is going on in the schools with techniques, in comparison with which the propaganda and indoctrination of the Imperial period were infantile. For, more than ever, the whole of German life has become a school and there is no aspect of it—social, political, economic, scientific, literary, esthetic—which has not been *gleichgeschaltet* or coordinated with the fundamental purposes of National Socialism.

II

The following quotations were selected and published in the *Feuille Mensuelle d'Information,* October–November, 1933, of the *Fédération Internationale des Associations d'Instituteurs:*

Objectivity in the teaching of history is only one of the numerous fallacies of liberalism. It is not man in general who studies history but a German, a Frenchman, an Englishman, etc. The "man" of liberalism is only an artificial creation. In reality he does not exist; there are only men who belong to a definite nation or race.

We will never approach history impartially but as Germans. . . . We care nothing about an insipid enumeration of "objective" facts; we want a historical science for Germans. . . . We do not want to know anything about the fantasy of a general humane education. We want to train true Germans.

Nationalist research in history is Pan-German, that is to say it considers the Austrians as Germans of Austria. They are not a people allied to us but part of our people. The *Anschluss* is not a problem for study but a task to solve.

The German Swiss and the Dutch are also members of the great community, of the German *Reich;* their history is the history of Germany, and the immediate duty of Germany is to continue the task of the Roman Emperors and to establish a great Germany, one and indivisible. German destiny has for its sphere the territory between the Rhine and the Vistula, between the Alps and Vienna. It is by imbuing ourselves with this idea of Pan-Germanism that we will understand the significance of the separation from Switzerland and Holland, the interdiction of the *Anschluss* with Austria, the separation from East Prussia. Only those who see danger can avoid it.—*Die Deutsche Schule,* September, 1933.

The war instinct is inborn in our young generation. It finds expression in the war games of children, in the penchant for battles and in the preference for literature which deals with wars and victory.

The training of the military spirit has two aspects: one side physical and the other moral. Moral training consists of awakening and encouraging the war instinct and the love of liberty; physical training is given by pre-military preparation whose end is the training of soldiers. The two aspects in the development of youth are indispensable and inconceivable, the one without the other.—*Berliner Lehrerzeitung,* August 17, 1933.

To the spirit is allied the idea of force which is but the expression of a powerful instinct for preservation; the two are intimately bound together. And if we wish to express this relation symbolically, we turn to the educational program of Mussolini: the Book and the Musket. The book is the symbol of moral education and the musket the symbol of the militaristic spirit.—*Allgemeine Deutsche Lehrerzeitung,* August 19, 1933.

The *Allgemeine Deutsche Lehrerzeitung* has carried the following quotations on the front pages of the issues for the dates mentioned:

The taste for militarism must be inculcated in children; they must be told this at every opportunity that every man of noble birth must be a soldier.—Frederick the Great; in the issue for September 2, 1933.

Rigorous discipline is desirable at a given time. . . . The same discipline imparts the qualities needed by the soldier and the scholar; in fact there is no competent scholar who does not possess the instincts of a good soldier. What should a rigorous school teach?—Obedience and command.—Nietzsche; in the issue for September 23, 1933.

I know that we Germans will be victorious in the next war; it is the will and the way of God. Simply because it is our turn, no one can resist our health within and our young strength. . . . But such a nation whose hour sounds, must arm itself within and without . . . in such a way that it will lead us to victory and to power. Who could then be the heart and head of Europe?—Gustav Frenssen; in the issue for October 14, 1933.

III

The *Zentralinstitut für Erziehung und Unterricht,* which was established in 1915, became under the republic the center for the collection and dissemination of information on the new education. One of its functions was to maintain an exhibit of books and school work dealing with and illustrating the progress of education. Last October this exhibit was cleared out as a symbol of all that was hateful and suspect to the new régime—its emphasis on individualism and personality, its democratic notions, its liberalism and its suspected entanglements with pacifist and international movements. A new exhibit more in accord with current aims and purposes was brought together; its character is described with that fervor which characterizes all recent educational literature in an article by Dr. M. A. Hedwig Fitzler on "National Socialist Literature—The Exhibit at the *Zentralinstitut für Erziehung und Unterricht,*" which appeared in *Das Deutsche Frauenwerk,* October, 1933, pp. 25–28.

The exhibition rooms of the *Zentralinstitut für Erziehung und Unterricht,* which is under the Ministry of Education, has housed, since October 10, an extraordinarily interesting display of National Socialist and national (*völkische*) literature. These, starting from the days of the World War, lead through the disgraceful humiliation of Germany to the awakening of the Nation, to the rise of the Brown Army until the final victory of the National Socialist idea and its penetration into state and law, economics and labor, education and national culture. It is, of course, impossible within the limited assignment of a general report to present even a half-way complete list of the works exhibited or to discuss them in any way.

Here it is only possible to follow the leading idea which dominates the exhibition and to take some book or other from the case and indicate its value and through it the aim and purpose of the exhibition.

The very first group of books before which we stand leads back to the dreary days of the World War. In Werner Beumelburg's *Sperrfeuer um Deutschland,* that unique monument to the Unknown Soldier, the epoch-making four years glow about us like a stream of lava. Out of the austere book, Ernst Jünger's *Der Kampf als inneres Erlebnis,* stares the face of a man who experienced all the gamut of the emotional life released by the War. The *Kriegsbriefe gefallener Studenten, Langemark* with Magnus Wehner's Preface, *Skagerrack* (Friedrich Kühlwetter), *Scapa Flow* (Admiral v. Reuter), *Totenkreuz in Flandern* (Dietr. Volker), *U-Boot im Fegefeuer* (Freiherr v. Spiegel) testify to the heroism of a nation. The strongest war book, however, Hans Zöberlein's *Glaube an Deutschland* is, in the words of our leader, the ''Legacy of the Front'' (*Vermächtnis der Front*).

Then the Siberian trilogy of Edwin Dwinger (*Die Armee hinter Stacheldraht, Zwischen Weiss und Rot. Die sibirische Tragödie 1919–20, Wir rufen Deutschland*) with its shattering naked realism leads through all the hell of imprisonment in the Tsarist Empire as it disintegrates and ends in Bolshevism into the darkest years of the post-War period in Germany to resound in a proclamation of an indestructible will to live, which seeks and finally recognizes the road to the reconstruction of the nation.

Germany's deepest humiliation finds its pithy expression in the *Fibel zum Versailler Diktat* (Heinr. Siekmeyer), in *Versailles—Deutschlands Fessel* (Benno Kettner), and in the National Socialist Monthly, No. 6, *Wir Klagen an!* From the bloody frontiers in the East and West, in the North and South, from the misery and suffering of our sacrificed brothers and sisters, there arises a unanimous appeal through the works of Beumelburg (*Deutschland in Ketten*), Rolf Brandt (*Schlageter, Leben und Sterben eines deutschen Helden*), Grimm (*Die Franzosen an Rhein und Ruhr*), Hanns Jobst (*Schlageter*), A. Pfaff (*Der Young Plan*), and Wilhelm Ziegler (*Abrüstungsbetrug in Versailles*). The effects of the Versailles Treaty, the economic and moral misery, the struggles of despair in German territory, the stranglehold of unemployment are described by von Salomon (*Die Geächteten*), Joseph Goebbels (*Michael*), Richard Euringer (*Die Arbeitslosen*), and Gregor Strasser (*Kampf um Deutschland*). The Frenchman, René Martel, in his book *Deutschlands blutende Grenze,* arouses the conscience of the world, probes into the deep wounds which cut right through Central Europe, and loudly demands the restoration of Germany's Eastern frontiers to make life tolerable.

Necessity is the road to happiness—the recognition of this by Goebbels' *Michael* is the common recognition of Germany's destiny; it compels the awakening of the nation led by the National Socialism of Adolf Hitler (see esp. Eugen Schmahl, *Der Aufstieg der nationalen Idee;* Ernst Boepple, *Adolf Hitlers Reden*). *Mein Kampf* becomes the Bible of the German people. As the world disintegrates National Socialism erects the pillars of the Third Reich. The Brown Army arises (Heinr. Hoffmann, *Das braune Heer*). *SA marschiert* (Wulf Bley). In *Kampfen und Glauben* (Eve Maria Wisser) German youth sees its destiny and its task (*Schicksal und Aufgabe der deutschen Jugend*). How Hitler's spirit inspires German youth is reflected in the terrible conflicts in the soul of the German proletarian youth *Quex* (K. A. Schenziger), to which an unsurpassable tribute is paid in Hans Heinz Ewers' *Horst-Wessel-Buch.*—Biographies of the leaders of the new Germany make up the fifth group of the exhibition. Besides Johannes Stark's *Adolf Hitlers Ziele und Persönlichkeit* mention must be made of Erich Czech-Jochberg's three works: *Unser Führer; Adolf Hitler und sein Stab; Hitler, Reichskanzler.* F. W. Schaafhausen describes *Hindenburg, Vater des Volkes* as the representative of pure Prussian tradition, who recognizes only loyalty to his people. The genius for propaganda and the personality of Minister Goebbels are sketched by Wilfried Bade. Barth and Martin Sommerfeld attempt to picture Hermann Göring, the Fighter; F. Th. Hart draws a sketch of Alfred Rosenberg, while Edgar v. Schmid-Pauli (*Die Männer um Hitler*), Klaus Ekkehart (*Die Reichstatthalter*) and Wilhelm von Müffling (*Wegbereiter und Vorkämpfer für das neue Deutschland*) describe the careers of the men about the leader and his lieutenants.

In these men about Adolf Hitler there matured the nature, principles and aims of the National Socialist German Workers Party (sixth group of books), whose program Gottfried Feder (*Das Programm der NSDAP* and *Der deutsche Staat*) and Alfred Rosenberg (*Wesen, Grundsätze und Ziele der NSDAP* and *Das Wesensgefüge des Nationalsozialismus*) have described clearly and sharply in incisive language for the German people: Race philosophy and state construction; foreign politics and economic ethics; world outlook, religion and politics; renaissance of mortality;—such are the stout pillars on which the will, the power and the soul of National Socialism are building the Third Reich[1] and which the principles of political Education of the Germans (seventh group) must develop with all the speed and urgency possible. Ernst Krieck (*Nationalpolitische Erziehung, Die deutsche Staatsidee, Völkischer Gesamtstaat, Der Staat des deutschen Menschen*), the creator of the national socialist philosophy of education, and the optimistic strength of the books of Moeller van den Brock (*Jedes Volk hat seinen eigenen Sozialismus, Der politische Mensch, Das Dritte Reich, Das ewige Reich*) are here the spokesmen together with Alfred Rosenberg (*Mythos des 20 Jahrhunderts*). Bries de Heckelingen presents in 100 striking quotations a *Wegweiser durch die nationalsozialistische Literatur*. In F. Büchner's *Was ist das Reich?* the profound ideas of Eugen Diesel and Hans Grimm find expression. The problems of political economy and social politics of the national future lead Fr. Burgdörfer in *Volk ohne Jugend* to demand an open road for a great nation's will to live.

Der Völkische Gedanke in der Vergangenheit by M. R. Gerstenhauer leads us through the spirit of Johann Gottlieb Fichte (*Reden an die deutsche Nation*) and Gustav Freytag (*Bilder aus der deutschen Vergangenheit*) to Prussianism (eighth group) whose "style" derives its unconquerable strength as a world principle from its thoroughgoing non-plebeian laws of existence.[2]

The ninth group of the exhibition directs attention to the struggle for room for existence on which this German Prussianism has been compelled to enter through the absurdity of the so-called peace terms. The misery of millions of tortured individuals in the East compels the mobilization of all material and spiritual forces in order to secure a German solution (see Albert Brackmann, *Polen und wir;* Heiss-Ziegfeld, *Deutschland und der Korridor*) on the soil which gave proof of the great colonizing effort of the German people in the Middle Ages (see Karl Hampe, *Der Zug nach Osten;* E. Randt, *Die neuere polnische Geschichtsforschung;* H. Rauschning, *Die Entdeutschung Westpreussens*). Historical as well as international considerations of the most objective accuracy demand a correction of the great injustice of Versailles in the West (see Fritz Klövekorn, *Das Saargebiet;* Karl Linnebach, *Die gerechte Grenze im deutschen Westen;* Aloys Schulte, *Tausend Jahre deutscher Geschichte am Rhein*), and in the South-East and South (see Jos. Papesch, *Fesseln um Oesterreich;* Hans Lukaschek, *Das Schulrecht der nationalen Minderheiten in Deutschland;* Wilhelm Rohmeder, *Das Deutschtum in Südtirol; Sprachenatlas der Grenzgebiete des deutschen Reiches;* Otto Boelitz, *Das Grenz- und Auslandsdeutschtum*). A change is also demanded in the distribution of the colonies which we once won with far greater expenditure of national strength than the other nations (see Hans Grimm, *Volk ohne Raum* and *Der Oelsucher von Duala*).

The groups from ten to sixteen objectify the introduction of the National Socialist idea into physical education (The Idea of Defense, 10), into the working classes (The German Worker, 11),[3] into the peasant class (12), into law (13), into economics (14), into biology and race theory (15). These groups furnish the fundamental arguments for Antisemitism as the duty of the nation-conscious individual (16).

The review closes with three extraordinarily important collections of works on Labor Service (17), on School and University Reform (18),[4] and on *Deutschkunde* (19).

It is these last groups which in the selection of the books on racial and national knowledge, saga and fairy-tales forcibly impress on heart and mind the variety and lofty character of Germanic culture. With pious devotion we lay down Wilhelm Teudt's *Germanische Heiligtümer*. With profound self-consciousness we leave the works of Karl Theodor Strasser (*Die Nordgermanen, Wikinger und Germanen, Sachsen und Angelsachsen*), and the book on Germanic world conquest and founding of states which Will Vesper has described in his *Harten Geschlecht*.

Among the magazines *Das Deutsche Frauenwerk*, as the organ of women leaders, and *Deutsche Jugend im Gelände* are particularly noteworthy.

[1] See on this Hans Glisow, *Die Seele des dritten Reiches;* Eugen Hadamowsky, *Propaganda und nationale Macht;* Heinrich Hoffmann, *Der Triumph des Willens;* Max Frauendorfer, *Der ständische Gedanke im Nationalsozialismus.*

[2] Moeller van den Brock, *Der preussische Stil;* Wilhelm Stapel, *Preussen muss sein;* Herbert Blank, *Soldaten. Preussisches Führertum von Waterloo bis Ypern;* Schinkel, *Preussischer Adel;* O. Spengler, *Preussentum und Sozialismus.*

[3] Especially, H. Stellbrecht, *Der deutsche Arbeitsdienst; Deutsches Studentenwerk: Wo findet die deutsche Jugend neuen Lebensraum?;* Annemarie Willucka, *Freizeiten für jugendliche Erwerbslose.*

[4] Special mention must be made of: Fr. Hiller, *Die "Deutsche Schule," Entwurf eines nationalsozialistischen Schulprogramms;* Philipp Hördt, *Grundformen volkhafter Bildung;* Karl Eckhardt, *Die Landschule;* Ernst Krieck, *Die Erneuerung der Universität;* Ad. Rein, *Die Idee der politischen Universität;* Ziegler, *Praktische Kulturarbeit im Dritten Reich.*

The books, the magazines, and the pictures from the great days of Frederick the Great to the victory of Adolf Hitler, which have been brought together in this first exhibition of national (*völkische*) literature call out to every German man and women:[5] Go and see! Take and read!

EDUCATIONAL EVENTS

THE ANGLO-AMERICAN INSTITUTE OF THE FIRST MOSCOW UNIVERSITY

Dr. I. Vanya Sollins, director of the Anglo-American Institute of the First Moscow University, announced on April 28 that the institute will offer a variety of courses in education, combined with supervised travel in the Soviet Union this summer in order to provide American educators an opportunity to observe educational methods in the new Russia. The program, Dr. Sollins pointed out, will carefully adhere to the agreement made between Maxim Litvinov, Russian foreign minister, and President Roosevelt, when the Soviet Union was recognized. Final plans will be announced early in May after a meeting of leading American educators with Alexander Troyanovsky, Russian Ambassador to the United States. To the end that the Soviet authorities may learn the American reaction to the new Russian educational system an American national advisory council of the institute has been created with the following members:

Harry Woodburn Chase, chancellor of New York University; William F. Russell, dean of Teachers College, Columbia University; John Dewey, professor emeritus of philosophy at Columbia; George S. Counts, professor of education at Teachers College, Columbia University; I. L. Kandel, professor of education at Teachers College; John W. Withers, dean of the School of Education, New York University; Harvey W. Zorbaugh, of New York University; Robert M. Hutchins, president of the University of Chicago; Ernest H. Wilkins, president of Oberlin College; William Allan Neilson, president of Smith College; Frank P. Graham, president of the University of North Carolina; Stephen Duggan, director of the Institute of International Education; W. W. Charters, director of the Bureau of Research, the Ohio State University; Robert L. Kelly, secretary of the Association of American Colleges; John A. Kingsbury, secretary of the Milbank Memorial Fund; Susan M. Kingsbury, professor of social economy and social research, Bryn Mawr College; Paul Klapper, dean of the School of Education of the College of the City of New York; Charles R. Mann, director of the American Council on Education; H. W. Tyler, general secretary of the American Association of University Professors, and Thomas Woody, professor of the history of education, University of Pennsylvania.

The institute will open on July 15 and close on August 26. Dr. Stephen Duggan, director of the Institute of International Education, is now in Moscow arranging for accommodations for the American students.

THE ONE-HUNDREDTH ANNIVERSARY OF TEACHER TRAINING IN NEW YORK

May 2 marked the one-hundredth anniversary of the state legislative action in New York creating provisions for the training of teachers for the common schools and granting state aid to academies for this purpose. This action was the beginning of the permanent policy of state-supported teacher training in America. Prior to May 2, 1834, the academies in New York had attempted to train teachers. Mr. William M. French, writing in *The New York Times*, notes that as early as 1821 the regents of the University of New York reported that "it is to these seminaries that we must look for a supply of teachers for the common schools, as well as for the occasional rise of humble merit from obscurity." The regents at the time were opposed to the Prussian normal school plan, which had been described in America as early as 1825. Instead the regents urged that "the academies should become the nurseries of instructors for common schools, leaving it to the interest of individuals to prepare themselves for the business of teaching." Not until 1844 was the first normal school established in New York. The eight academies selected for teacher

[5] The "woman and National Socialism" has not yet been considered as a separate group in the exhibit. At the suggestion of the writer of this report, however, literature on the subject has already been requested, especially the straightforward work of Paula Siber von Groote, *Die Frauenfrage und ihre Lösung durch den Nationalsozialismus*, and the excellent journal, *Die deutsche Frauenfront*, now *Das Deutsche Frauenwerk*.

training received subsidies of $400 each; others were added later.

When the new plan of training teachers was established the regents required all entrants to pass an examination showing themselves "scholars in the higher branches of English education." But inasmuch as the tests were given by the principal of the academy, the stringency of the test was not highly selective. When the regents in 1882 required a certificate of common-school graduation, enrolments in teacher training classes dropped from 2,514 in 1878–1879 to 1,043 in 1882–1883.

The program of training at first did not differ substantially from the rest of the academic courses. Often prospective teachers were not segregated from the other students. Higher English, mathematics, classical languages, mental and moral philosophy, evidences of Christianity, logic, "book chemistry" and occasionally a modern language were the subjects often studied. But in the nineties more specialized courses were introduced. Reviews of common school fundamentals were now required. School management, science of education, methodology, history of education and a little observation and practise, all of them taught by one instructor, became the "professional" courses. In the nineteen-twenties training for teaching in the rural schools of the state resulted in a new stage of professional education with the more comprehensive teachers college coming into view, and the adjustment of the normal school program to the demand for more technically trained teachers, not only for the common schools, but for the secondary schools as well.

LETTER FROM THE NEW YORK STATE COMMISSIONER OF EDUCATION TO TRUSTEES OF THE COMMON SCHOOL DISTRICTS

THE following letter has been addressed by Dr. Frank P. Graves, president of the University of the State of New York and Commissioner of Education of New York, to the trustees of the common school districts of New York State:

School patrons throughout the State of New York have convened this evening in regular annual meeting to determine the educational plans which shall guide the conduct of the schools for the coming year.

The facilities for education within the various communities of the State can never greatly exceed the desires nor far outstrip the thinking of local school patrons. Let us be of single mind and purpose this evening in the discharge of our duty, that in each district of our State a school program may be promoted for the best advantage of the children, the community and the State. Let no child become the loser in school opportunity by the insincere purposes or selfish action of his elders.

Many communities have maintained high educational standards for their schools during these times of economic stress. Frequently this has been accomplished only by higher local taxation. I congratulate these many districts on such evidences of sacrifice and effort, indicating their high esteem of public education.

I regret to report, however, that educational standards have not been maintained in all instances. In many of our schools the educational program has undergone a severe pruning. Instructional service too frequently has been measured by its cheapness rather than by its true worth to children. Many schools are sorely in need of instructional equipment and supplies now depleted by overzealous economies.

I can render no better advice than to urge you to engage competent teachers and to provide them with adequate instructional equipment so that lost ground may be regained and new gains securely held.

More than ever before in the history of the State the various units of government are under the scrutiny of commissions, committees and individuals. It has been widely charged that many of the common school districts are among the most costly of our small units of government. This problem should receive your careful thought, study and action.

The effectiveness of the central rural school district in meeting the problems of small and poor districts has repeatedly been demonstrated. I again recommend that you study the possibilities offered you under this form of organization.

I urge you to call freely upon your district superintendent and the State Education Department in the various problems that confront you, in order that each district in the State may maintain high educational standards.

GIFT TO THE PRINCETON INSTITUTE FOR ADVANCED STUDY

DR. ABRAHAM FLEXNER, director of the Institute for Advanced Study at Princeton, according to *The New York Times,* announced on April 24 that an anonymous gift of $1,000,000 had been received by the institute to facilitate the organization of the school of economics and politics, which was decided upon some time ago.

The gift was announced at the annual meeting of the trustees of the institute and will be added to the initial endowment of $5,000,000 given by Louis Bamberger and Mrs. Felix Fuld at the time the institute was established by them in 1930.

At the meeting Mr. Bamberger and Mrs. Fuld were made life trustees of the institute with all the powers of the regular trustees.

Dr. Frank Aydelotte, president of Swarthmore College, and Dr. Florence R. Sabin, of the Rockefeller Institute for Medical Research, were reelected trustees, their terms having expired. Professor Oswald Veblen, a member of the institute staff, was made a member of the corporation and was elected a trustee of the institute.

Officers were elected as follows: *Chairman,* Alanson B. Houghton; *Vice-chairmen,* Herbert H. Maass and Walter W. Stewart; *Treasurer,* Samuel D. Leidesdorf; *Assistant-treasurer,* Ira A. Schur; *Secretary,* Frank Aydelotte; *Assistant-secretary,* Esther S. Bailey. Dr. Flexner was reappointed director of the institute.

The Institute for Advanced Study was established in 1930, but up to now only the school of mathematics, which was opened in October, 1933, has been functioning. No definite plans have been announced regarding the opening of the new school of economics and politics.

Dr. Flexner reported that during the first working year of the institute the school of mathematics had five professors, each of whom had an assistant, and that there were enrolled twenty-three workers, all of whom previously had received the Ph.D. degree and almost every one of whom was on leave of absence from a college or university to carry on original research and personal cooperation with a member of the staff.

Among these are mathematicians from Vienna, Edinburgh, Copenhagen, Chicago, Johns Hopkins, Michigan, Cincinnati, the California Institute of Technology, Rice Institute, Bryn Mawr and other institutions of learning.

Professor P. A. M. Dirac, of the University of Cambridge, Nobel prize laureate for 1933 in mathematical physics, will spend the coming year at the institute as visiting professor.

The Institute for Advanced Study closed officially for the current year on May 1, but certain members of the staff and some workers will continue their research work indefinitely.

OPPORTUNITY FOR PRODUCTIVE SCHOLARSHIP AT HARVARD UNIVERSITY

As a preliminary step to providing younger faculty members of Harvard College with sufficient opportunity for productive scholarship and research work, President James Bryant Conant has ordered a detailed survey of the time demanded by teaching, laboratory instruction and tutoring from full-time instructors and from assistant professors on their first appointment in the Faculty of Arts and Sciences. In his annual report Dr. Conant wrote:

> Sufficient time should be allowed for writing and investigation; a satisfactory balance must be struck between teaching and research.
>
> In the future as in the past, our teachers must be scholars who are extending the frontiers of knowledge in every direction. I hope there will never be a separation of our faculty into those who teach and those who carry on creative work.
>
> No line should be drawn between teaching and research. Our strength in the past has lain in the fact that the spirit of scholarship has pervaded our teaching and our scholars have seen the importance of perpetuating the ideals of scholarship as well as advancing knowledge in their own specialty.
>
> Harvard must endeavor to draw to its staff the most able investigators and teachers of the world.
>
> We have at Harvard unusual advantages for scholarly work: libraries, museums, laboratories and special institutes.
>
> In some fields we can provide opportunities for investigation which are unequalled in this country. It is clearly our first duty to see that our permanent staff is composed of those who can use these facilities most effectively and wisely. We must provide every opportunity for the ambitious, brilliant young scholar to come to Harvard and demonstrate his worth.

President Conant's survey begins with the mailing of the following letter to about one hundred instructors doing full-time work under the Faculty of Arts and Sciences:

> Could you let me have before May 1 a statement as to the number of hours of teaching and laboratory instruction and tutoring your present program demands of you each week? It would be a great help also if you could include in the letter some estimate as to the number of hours which you give each week in preparation for tutorial conferences, laboratory exercises and class meetings.
>
> I am asking for this statement at the request of President Conant, who is eager to make a survey of the time demanded by university duties from the instructors under this faculty. He and I are both eager to make sure that programs of instruction do not demand so much time of instructors that they are prevented from finding leisure for their own research work.
>
> We wish to have every man, so far as it is possible, given a sufficient opportunity for productive scholarship, and as a first step in estimating the problem, the president feels that he needs statements of the sort I am suggesting in this letter from each of the instructors who are offering instruction under the Faculty of Arts and Sciences.

CHOOSING-A-CAREER CONFERENCE

IN Newark, N. J., there will convene on June 26, 27 and 28 the first Choosing-a-Career Conference for college students. Among those who will address the conference will be Leonor F. Loree, president of the Delaware and Hudson Railroad; Colby M. Chester, president of the General Foods Corporation; Percy Straus, president of R. H. Macy and Company; S. L. Rothapfel (Roxy); Edward L. Bernays, organizer of the Edison Golden Jubilee; Amelia Earhart; Roy Chapman Andrews, acting managing director of the Museum of Natural History; James P. Warburg; Elizabeth Hawes, fashion stylist, and Nancy McClelland, interior decorator. Among the careers to be discussed will be advertising, automotive industry, building, government, insurance, journalism, publishing, shipping, steel, beauty culture, secretarial work, literature, magazine photography, radio broadcasting, restaurant management, social service and the theater.

The advisory board includes Frank Aydelotte, president of Swarthmore College; Robert C. Clothier, president of Rutgers University; Margaret T. Corwin, dean of the New Jersey College for Women; Albert Beecher Crawford, director of the department of personnel study at Yale University; George B. Cutten, president of Colgate University; Harvey N. Davis, president of Stevens Institute of Technology; Livingston Farrand, president of Cornell University; Christian Gauss, dean of the college, Princeton University; Herbert E. Hawkes, dean of the college, Columbia University; Henry N. MacCracken, president of Vassar College; William A. Neilson, president of Smith College; Marion Edwards Park, president of Bryn Mawr College; Ellen Fitz Pendleton, president of Wellesley College; Josiah H. Penniman, provost of the University of Pennsylvania; Rufus D. Smith, provost of New York University; Mary E. Woolley, president of Mount Holyoke; Karl T. Compton, president of the Massachusetts Institute of Technology; Daniel L. Marsh, president of Boston University; Ada Louise Comstock, president of Radcliffe College, and Ralph C. Hutchison, president of Washington and Jefferson College.

SUMMER MEETING OF THE DEPARTMENT OF VISUAL INSTRUCTION

CONCURRENTLY with the meetings of the National Education Association, the Department of Visual Instruction will be held in Washington, D. C., on Monday and Tuesday, July 2 and 3. Miss J. Elizabeth Dyer, who has charge of visual instruction in divisions 1–9 of the District Schools in Washington, is local chairman of the committee on arrangements. The sessions will be held in the afternoon and evening. Present announcements state that the general program will consist of a class demonstration in the teaching of fifth-grade geography; a demonstration of techniques for making miniature habitat groups for science, geography and history; a demonstration of techniques for making homemade slides in color; techniques and standards for poster making; the integration of visual-sensory aids in classroom procedure; and an exhibit of the realia used in the Washington, D. C., schools. The foregoing program is planned for Monday afternoon, July 2. The evening program will be devoted to discussions of the relation between motion pictures and the morality of youth, and the probable trends in the field of motion pictures. Mr. John A. Hollinger will lead the latter discussion. At the Tuesday luncheon Mr. C. F. Hoban will give his report as delegate to the International Congress of Educational Cinematography, which has recently closed in Rome. The afternoon session on Tuesday will provide discussions of the relation of films to the radio in the classroom; the educational values in commercial films; the use of films in character education, and the prevention of delinquency. Among those who will appear on the program are: Grace Courtney, of Pittsburgh, Pa.; John Orth, of the American Museum of Natural History; W. T. R. Price, of Scarborough, N. Y.; Wilbur Emmert, of Indiana, Pa.; Lillian Hetherstraw, of Drake University, Des Moines; C. M. Koon, of the U. S. Office of Education; Rita Hochheimer, of New York City; Howard M. LeSourd, of Boston University.

THE AMERICAN COUNCIL ON EDUCATION

THE tentative program of the seventeenth annual meeting of the American Council on Education, to be held on May 18 and 19, has been issued.

The meeting will be held in the building of the National Academy of Sciences, Washington, D. C., and the general topic of the conference will be "Pioneer Adventures in Education."

The tentative program follows:

FRIDAY, MAY 18

Morning Session, 10:00 A. M.

Chairman, Dean William F. Russell, Teachers College, Columbia University

Minutes and Reports.

"Crime and a Revised National Policy in Education," Honorable Royal S. Copeland, United States Senate.

"An Experiment in the Washington Schools," Frank W. Ballou, Superintendent of Schools, Washington, D. C.

"Techniques of Educational Experimentation," W. W. Charters, the Ohio State University.

"Education in the Tennessee Valley Experiment," Fred W. Reeves, Tennessee Valley Authority.

"Emotions in the Educative Process," Daniel A. Prescott, Rutgers University.

Director's Report—"Integration," C. Riborg Mann.

Afternoon Session, 2:00 P. M.

Chairman's Address, William F. Russell, Teachers College, Columbia University.

"Citizens' Councils for Constructive Economy," Howard P. Jones, National Municipal League, New York.

"The Educational Advisory Committee of the New York State Economic Council," Frank E. Spaulding, Yale University.

SATURDAY, MAY 19

Morning Session, 9:30 A. M.

"The Year's Work in the Council's Committees":

"The Problems and Plans Committees," S. P. Capen, University of Buffalo.

"The Committee on Standards," Raymond Walters, University of Cincinnati.

"The Committee on Education and Government," John K. Norton, Teachers College, Columbia University.

"The Committee on Fundamental Factors in Achievement," Cloyd H. Marvin, George Washington University.

"The Cooperative Test Service," H. E. Hawkes, Columbia University.

"The Committee on Graduate Instruction," R. M. Hughes, Iowa State College.

"The Emergency Committee on NRA," Cloyd H. Marvin, George Washington University.

EDUCATIONAL NOTES AND NEWS

DR. LE BARON RUSSELL BRIGGS, professor emeritus of oratory and rhetoric at Harvard University, formerly dean of Harvard College and president of Radcliffe College, died suddenly on April 24, in his seventy-ninth year.

DR. PAUL SHOREY, professor of Greek at the University of Chicago for the last forty-two years, died on April 24. He was seventy-six years old.

DR. WILLIAM HENRY WELCH, recognized leader of the medical sciences in the United States, professor emeritus of the history of medicine in the Johns Hopkins Medical School, previously professor of pathology, first dean of the school and director of the School of Hygiene and Public Health, died on April 30 in his eighty-fifth year.

DR. Q. A. W. ROHRBACH, professor of education and director of courses in educational administration at the University of Pittsburgh, has accepted the presidency of the State Teachers College at Kutztown, Pennsylvania.

Dr. Eugene A. Colligan was installed as fourth president of Hunter College on May 4. Laurence L. Cassidy, chairman of the administrative committee of the college, presided, and Mark Eisner, chairman of the Board of Higher Education, inducted Dr. Colligan into office. Bishop William T. Manning delivered the invocation, and Monsignor Michael J. Lavelle the benediction. Among those expected to attend the exercises were Mayor Fiorello H. La Guardia, Comptroller W. Arthur Cunningham, United States Senator Royal S. Copeland, Dr. James M. Kieran, president-emeritus of the college; Dr. Nicholas Murray Butler, president of Columbia University; Chancellor Harry Woodburn Chase, of New York University; Thomas Stockham Baker, president of the Carnegie Institute of Technology; Robert C. Clothier, president of Rutgers University; Dean Virginia C. Gildersleeve, of Barnard College; Dean Herbert E. Hawkes, of Columbia College, and representatives of more than 100 other colleges and universities from throughout the country.

Dr. John Henry MacCracken, associate director of the American Council on Education, formerly president of Lafayette College, is one of eight alumni on whom Meritorious Service Awards will be conferred at commencement by New York University. Recipients of the awards were guests on April 23 at a dinner given by the hundred alumni who had previously received this award.

Professor Dixon Ryan Fox, of Columbia University, president-elect of Union College, Schenectady, N. Y., spoke at the annual senior dinner of Brothers College of Drew University on May 4.

Dr. James McC. Landis, member of the Federal Trade Commission, formerly professor at the Harvard Law School, was the guest of honor at the annual Phi Beta Kappa dinner at Princeton University, on April 20.

Dr. Arthur Stanley Eddington, Plumian professor of astronomy and director of the observatory at the University of Cambridge, spoke at a luncheon given in his honor by the English-Speaking Union of the United States, at the Astor Hotel on April 28. Dr. Eddington is Messenger lecturer for 1934 at Cornell University.

Dr. Harold G. Campbell, superintendent of the schools of New York City, gave the principal address on April 28 at the annual luncheon of the Alumni Association of the School of Education of New York University. Chancellor Harry Woodburn Chase, Dr. John S. Roberts, associate superintendent of schools, Dean John W. Withers, of the School of Education, and Dr. Campbell were the guests of honor.

Miss Katherine L. Brown, now seventy years old, who retired last February after having taught at Public School 147, New York City, for fifty years, was honored on April 28 by the members of the faculty with a luncheon at the Hotel Astor.

Professor Neil P. Bailey, of the University of North Carolina, has been appointed head of the department of mechanical engineering at the Iowa State College. He succeeds Professor W. H. Meeker, who has been a member of the faculty since 1891; Mr. Meeker will continue as professor in the department.

Professor Atlee Lane Percy will succeed the late T. Everett Fairchild as assistant to President Daniel L. Marsh, of Boston University. He will also serve as director of the 1934 Summer Session.

Dr. Rodney J. Mott, formerly of the University of Chicago, was recently appointed head of the department of political science at Colgate University.

Mlle. Marguerite Mespoulet, professor of French at Wellesley College, has been appointed an associate in the French department of Barnard College for the academic year 1934–1935.

Dr. Charles E. Chapman, professor of Hispanic-American and Californian history at the University of California, has been appointed visiting professor at the summer school of Northwestern University. He will lecture during June and July on "Hispanic-American History" and on "European Expansion."

Professor William Herbert Hobbs, head of the department of geology of the University of Michigan since 1906, will retire at the close of the summer session after serving for twenty-eight years. Dr. Hobbs reaches the retiring age of seventy years on July 2.

DR. THOMAS M. CAMPBELL, Marcus L. Taft professor of German language and literature at Wesleyan University, who recently received a call to become head of the department of German at the University of North Carolina, has decided to remain at Wesleyan.

THREE of the members of the faculty of the Pennsylvania State College will teach in the service of other institutions during the coming summer session. Dr. Robert P. Carroll will lecture at the University of Maryland; Dr. Carroll D. Champlin will exchange positions for the summer with Dr. J. Orin Powers, of the George Washington University, and Dr. Charles C. Peters will exchange positions with Dr. Percy E. Davidson, of Stanford University.

DR. IVA LOWTHER PETERS, formerly dean of women at Syracuse University, is making a survey of educational innovations and a study of a model curriculum for women.

PROFESSOR R. G. CAMERON, of the University of Perth, returned to Australia during March after seven months spent in visiting educational institutions in Canada, the United States and a number of countries in Europe, including Soviet Russia.

DR. GLENN FRANK, president of the University of Wisconsin, delivered an address on April 14, under the auspices of the San Francisco Liberal Forum, at the International House of the University of California. The lecture was entitled "The Sword over Education." Dr. Frank was introduced by Dean W. W. Kemp, of the University School of Education.

DR. WILLIAM W. COMFORT, president of Haverford College, on April 11 delivered an address on "Links and Chains" at Cornell University, before a joint meeting of Sigma Psi, Tau Beta Pi, Phi Beta Kappa and Phi Kappa Phi. Dr. Comfort, who was head of the department of Romance languages at Cornell from 1909 to 1917, was introduced by President Livingston Farrand.

PROFESSOR PHILIP J. NOEL BAKER, of London, formerly Parliamentary secretary to the Secretary of State for Foreign Affairs, who was presented with the Howland Memorial Prize cup of Yale University on April 20, will give the first of two Dodge Lectures on "The Responsibilities of Citizenship," speaking specifically on "Current European Problems and the Next War."

THE fourteenth annual session of the National University of Mexico summer school will open this year on June 27 and continue until August 18, according to an announcement by Dr. Pablo Martinez del Rio, director. The school administration will sponsor a series of six weekly excursions to archeological and historical sites near the university.

THE Committee on Cultural Relations with Latin America has announced that the ninth annual seminar in Mexico will be held in Cuernavaca and Mexico City from July 10 to 30. During the last eight years nearly 1,000 citizens of the United States have attended the seminars.

THE Psychological Institute of the University of Vienna will hold its third annual summer school in psychology for American students from July 9 until August 9, 1934. The courses, which are taught in English, include the following: Language and personality, Karl Buehler; childhood and adolescence, Charlotte Buehler; biographical methods, Charlotte Buehler; Viennese tests for children, experimental psychology, business and social psychology. The University of Kentucky is again supervising these courses and will grant six semester-hours university credit for the work done in Vienna. For further details address the Educational Director, Dr. Henry Beaumont, University of Kentucky, Lexington, Kentucky.

AT a conference of elementary teachers held at Teachers College, Columbia University, on April 28 discussion centered on ways and means of coordinating various educational agencies serving the elementary school children of the United States. Professor J. R. McGaughy, who presided, called attention to the educational services rendered by the church, the school, the street, moving pictures, radio, libraries, museums, recreation and settlement work. He expressed the belief that the schools should cooperate with all other agencies for the total planning of education. Without such cooperation the existing competition, and waste of money and energy may result in the neglect of "important areas of the child's development" by all the agencies. Those participating in the panel discussions were Professors Jean Betzner, John L. Childs, Gerald S. Craig, Frank W. Cyr, N. L. Engelhardt, Roma Gans, Patty S. Hill, Milo B. Hillegas, L. Thomas Hopkins, J. R. McGaughy, Lois C. Mossman, E. C. Osborne, Mary M. Reed, Edward Reisner, Agnes Snyder, Florence Stratemeyer, all of Teachers College.

A conference on the teaching of social studies in high school, sponsored jointly by the Mississippi Valley Historical Association and the social studies section of the Missouri Teachers Association, was held at the University of Missouri on April 28. The speakers included C. H. McClure, of the State Teachers College, Kirksville; Professor H. R. Anderson, of the State University of Iowa; E. J. Urch, of the Senior High School, University City, and Claude H. Merideth, of the High School at Kirksville.

A series of weekly student forum meetings, for the discussion of international problems, have been arranged at the University of California at Los Angeles. The subjects discussed include national disarmament, economic nationalism *vs.* internationalism; the League of Nations; fascism *vs.* communism; America's recent relations with Cuba; newspaper propaganda and British-American trade conflicts. Members of the faculty who will lead the discussions include Dr. H. Arthur Steiner, assistant professor of political science; Dr. M. W. Graham, professor of political science; Professor Ordean Rockey, chairman of the department of political science; Dr. C. H. Titus, assistant professor of political science; Dr. M. P. González, assistant professor of Spanish; Professor F. A. Shuckman, lecturer in political science, and Professor G. W. Robbins, assistant professor of economics.

The first semi-annual meeting of the National Council of Business Education, organized in Cincinnati in December, 1933, was held in Boston on March 30. Dr. J. C. Wright, assistant commissioner for vocational education, U. S. Office of Education, was the speaker of the evening. In his address Dr. Wright outlined what he believed to be the major problems of leadership in business education. Open discussion followed the report of the Committee on National Policies in Business Education, which was presented by the chairman, Dr. Edward J. McNamara, High School of Commerce, New York City. Because of the fact that he was expecting to travel extensively during the next year, Mr. Clay D. Slinker, who had been elected president of the National Council of Business Education, resigned. Dr. Paul S. Lomax, New York University, as vice-president, automatically succeeded to the office of president. Miss Ray Abrams, Samuel J. Peters Boys School of Commerce, New Orleans, Louisiana, was elected to fill the vacancy thus created in the vice-presidency. Plans were formulated for the work of the council for the coming year. The next meeting is scheduled to be held in connection with the National Federation of Commercial Teachers in Chicago in December.

Applications for the position of supervisor of secondary education in the Indian Field Service, Department of the Interior, must be on file with the United States Civil Service Commission at Washington, D. C., not later than May 28. The entrance salary is $4,600 a year, subject to a deduction of not to exceed 10 per cent. until June 30, 1934, and of not to exceed 5 per cent. during the fiscal year ending June 30, 1935, as a measure of economy, and also to a deduction of 3½ per cent. toward a retirement annuity. A further deduction of $400 a year will be made for quarters, fuel and light. Applicants must have been graduated with a degree from a college or university of recognized standing, and must have had not less than two years of graduate work in the field of education. In addition, they must have had four years of successful, full-time paid experience in educational work, not less than two years of which must have been in educational administration or teacher training, and two years in experimental education involving work on curricula.

The Association of Indian Students Abroad has recently announced an Indian student congress which will be held in Vienna next summer. The offices of this association have been transferred from London to Vienna, and Subhas Chandra Bose, former mayor of Calcutta and secretary of the Indian congress, has been elected president. The principal task of the congress will be to maintain contact between those Indian students living abroad and those living in India.

THE South African Education Conference of the New Education Fellowship will meet at the University of Capetown in Capetown from July 2 to 13, and at the University of Witwatersrand, Johannesburg, from July 16 to 27. The general topic of discussion will be the adaptation of education to meet the rapidly changing needs of society, with special application to South Africa. The American speakers will include Professors John Dewey, Edmund de S. Brunner, Mabel Carney, I. L. Kandel and Harold Ordway Rugg, of Columbia University, and Miss Helen Parkhurst, principal of the Dalton School, New York City.

AN Associated Press dispatch reports that about 50 per cent. of last spring's salary reductions were restored to the staff of the University of Washington on April 15. About 700 persons gained by the increase, which was retroactive to April 1. The reductions last April averaged 32 per cent.

DISCUSSION

THE FUTURE CONTROL OF SCHOOL AND SOCIETY

THE present situation in regard to the control and editorship of SCHOOL AND SOCIETY is explained in the following letter, addressed on March 24 to the secretary of the National Education Association:

You will remember our conversation of several months ago in regard to the future of SCHOOL AND SOCIETY. As I probably told you at that time, at the end of the present year I shall have edited *Science* for forty years and SCHOOL AND SOCIETY for twenty years.

It is obvious that I can not continue to edit these journals for an indefinite period, and I have arranged that when I cease to control *Science* it shall become the unencumbered property of the American Association for the Advancement of Science, apart from an annuity for Mrs. Cattell. The contract was drawn up by Dean Pound of the Harvard Law School.

The relations between the American Association and *Science* have been somewhat unusual, but have worked out very well both for the association and for the journal. When *Science* more than thirty years ago was made the official journal of the association, though remaining my property, there were 1,200 members; there are now about 19,000 members and about 130 affiliated societies. Through its comparatively large circulation, the journal has obtained a large amount of advertising, so that it has become profitable and a valuable property.

As I told you, I want to make some analogous disposition of SCHOOL AND SOCIETY, so that it may be maintained as a national weekly journal of education with its present standards and, of course, in the hope that it will become each year a better and more useful publication. The end of the present year seems to be a natural time to make this arrangement in view of my twenty years of editorship.

I have given consideration to various plans, of which two seem to be the most promising. The one is to give the journal to the National Education Association if it cared to accept it with the provision of an annuity for Mrs. Cattell. As you suggested, it might be placed under the control of the National Council of Education. It could be sent to members of the National Education Association who make this request as an alternative to the association *Journal*. This would, I think, greatly strengthen the membership of the National Education Association in the direction of higher education and social interests. It would also be possible for all members of the association to receive the *Journal* of the association and to let them subscribe to SCHOOL AND SOCIETY at half-price.

SCHOOL AND SOCIETY ought not to be a liability to the association, but an asset. In recent years the publication has been conducted at a profit which has averaged about $2,000. Even during the past two years, when most periodicals are being conducted at a loss, there has been a small profit. This has partly paid for the value of the time given to it by Mrs. Cattell and me.

The individual subscription list is small, but there are at present 2,600 libraries on the list. Prior to the depression there were 3,200. This is one of the largest library circulations of any magazine published. The advertising is at present practically of no value—about $800 last year. But if the subscription list were considerably increased the receipts from advertisements might be as large as in the case of *Science*. In the recent prosperous period they were about $50,000 a year.

A second plan that would accomplish essentially the same purpose would be to give the journal to a special organization that would be incorporated for this purpose. This organization might be affiliated with the N. E. A., holding its annual meeting at the time of the meeting of the Department of Superintendence, and supplying the journal, say, for half-price to members of the N. E. A. and to them only. Such a holding company would have greater independence and power of initiative and would spend all profits on improving the journal, which would not be assured if it were the property of the National Education Association. This proposed corporation might have similar relations with other educational associations (such as the National Society for the Study of Education, the Educational Research Association and the Phi Delta Kappa fraternity) which would join with the N. E. A. in nominating the trustees. Members of these organizations would also receive the journal at half-price. It would have as trustees from ten to twenty of those workers in education who would be most likely to be interested in maintaining and improving a journal of this type. You indicated that you might be willing to be one of the trustees under such an arrangement.

This organization might be in the form of a membership association called, say, "The American Society for the Advancement of Education," the members of which would receive SCHOOL AND SOCIETY at a reduced rate. In that case, profits from the journal might be used for committee reports, surveys, and the like, as, for example, is done for explorations by the National Geographic Society, which by combining a nominal membership in a society with a magazine has attained a membership far above a million.

The problem of the future of SCHOOL AND SOCIETY has been emphasized during the last few days, as the Greek letter fraternity, Phi Delta Kappa, would like to acquire the journal. I had a conference of seven hours on Monday with three members, a majority, of its executive committee.

I said that I would not make over SCHOOL AND SOCIETY to a Greek letter fraternity excluding women and Negroes, but that I should be glad to consider letting them join a holding company from which their members might obtain SCHOOL AND SOCIETY at a reduced rate. They now have the matter under consideration and will make a definite proposal in the course of a few days.

I should rather see SCHOOL AND SOCIETY owned by the National Education Association than by Phi Delta Kappa. Should a special organization be formed, I should rather see it affiliated with the National Education Association than with the Phi Delta Kappa. I am consequently anxious to know what your attitude would be and whether you regard it as desirable to take the matter up in an official way.

I am sending copies of this letter to several of those who have expressed an interest in the fate of SCHOOL AND SOCIETY.

To this letter the secretary of the National Education Association replied on April 9 as follows:

I have delayed answering your letter in order that I might have an opportunity of talking the matter over with some of our faculty. I have seen some of them but they seem to doubt the wisdom of our arranging to take on another journal at this time. It will be sometime before I could have a chance to take the matter before our Board of Directors, but in view of the expressions that have come to me so far, I would doubt the wisdom of presenting the matter to them.

The Phi Delta Kappa fraternity offered to purchase SCHOOL AND SOCIETY, but was unwilling to join on equal terms with other educational associations in forming a board of trustees that would own and control it. While these negotiations were in progress, and in order that the present editor might meet other engagements, the managing editorship was temporarily undertaken by Professor R. D. Lindquist, president of Phi Delta Kappa, and Professor W. H. Cowley, both of the Ohio State University. The journal has now been returned to its permanent office, 3941 Grand Central Terminal, New York City, and Dr. Alfred L. Hall-Quest has consented to become one of the editors.

It is now proposed to proceed with the plan that the present editor has always regarded as the most desirable. This consists of forming a board of trustees representing our leading educational associations, which would own the journal and arrange for its policies and editorship after the present editor relinquishes control. Such a plan has been approved by those whose judgment in educational administration is most highly esteemed and will have their cooperation. It is hoped that there will be thus assured the permanence and continuous improvement of a national weekly journal of education.

J. MCKEEN CATTELL

THE FUTURE OF PHI BETA KAPPA

THE recently issued appeal of the Phi Beta Kappa Foundation for an addition of a million and a half dollars to its present endowment of $267,587 is based, of course, upon assumptions with regard to the future of American colleges. These assumptions require scrutiny. For social changes that are now going on are bound to modify profoundly our whole system of education. What is to be the relation of this old honor society to these changes in the great society and in education? No one will deny that in the 119 colleges in which Phi Beta Kappa has chapters it has consistently resisted low standards and given prestige to certain excellences. If it has overweighted the marking system as a measure of scholarship; if it has overweighted also the classical tradition with respect to culture; if often the coveted key has fed a superiority complex in both undergraduates and alumni, nevertheless Phi Beta Kappa is a synonym for a difference that is actual and important. The key means at least that talents have been put to use rather than hidden in a napkin. That is, granted the alternatives that the college world has felt to be important, Phi Beta Kappa has in the main chosen the better part.

But what if these alternatives themselves should be outgrown? The rise of profounder issues might make the old ones seem less important. Yes, the old incitements to genuine excellence in scholarship might be found to support social distinctions other than those of scholarship. The colleges certainly are a part of, not apart from, our tangled social world. The strains that are indexed in such words as wealth and poverty, unemployment, economic privilege, social classes, freedom and democracy are by no means absent from the classroom, the laboratory and the professor's writing table. What, then, is the social philosophy that underlies the desire of the Phi Beta Kappa Foundation to be more efficient in its promotion of scholarship and culture? A social philosophy of some kind is there. Though it be only tacitly or even unwittingly assumed rather than professed and defended, its influence may not be less—it may even be greater on this account. A time is upon us when every type of education should be explicitly recognized as expressing and confirming one sort of social goal as against other and competing sorts. In particular, we should no longer talk about culture as though it could have standards or content independent of economic assumptions.

The Phi Beta Kappa Foundation could make no greater contribution to culture just now than by admitting that its past glorification of the scholar has contained within itself an unmentioned sanction for social relations, even economic relations, that now are proved to be unsound. The "scholarship graced and guided by breadth of culture" of which the foundation speaks will be either good or bad, according to the degree of its economic realism and the direction of its economic ideals. The cultural life, as it was conceived by Plato and practised by his academy, was realistic enough to understand that it was dependent upon slave labor. Is any trace of a corresponding parasitism to cling in the future to the Societas Philosophica (see the reverse of the Phi Beta Kappa key)? Let the foundation say openly what sort of economic base the scholar of the future should claim for himself.

Apparently the foundation still believes that scholarship and culture are things *per se,* always the same and understandable from within themselves. But such belief is illusory. Actual scholarship and actual culture always are *ad hoc* —they are phases, that is, of more inclusive social purposes and undertakings. Not only is science or learning necessarily a cooperative activity of many minds; this activity concerns, not all possible objects of knowledge equally, but selected objects, and aspects of these objects, that are regarded as important. The motives for this selection often are obscure, being the interests that happen to be taken for granted; but the whole of learning is affected thereby. Thus it comes to pass that scholars who do not subject these motives to critical judgment permit their scholarship to become automatically an adjunct of the social *status quo,* whatever it is. Thus it comes about, also, that every institution of learning is, and has to be, a social-pressure institution.

Everybody realizes that elementary and secondary schools exert such pressure; hence, universal anxiety with respect to the control of them. Hence, also, the recent "Call to the Teachers of the Nation" by a committee of the Progressive Education Association. It is worthy of note that this proclamation, arising out of our social emergency, summons teachers not only to a choice of social goals, but also to more rigorous scholarship, more inclusive appreciation of personality and the widest possible diffusion of culture. Why should not Phi Beta Kappa issue a parallel challenge to the colleges? It would, indeed, summon them to adopt a new social purpose which conventional scholarship might brand as extra-academic; but perhaps this purpose would be, in fact, more deeply academic. For it would require the scholar to be scientific with respect to social factors in his thinking—factors hitherto controlled by assumption if not by prejudice; it would require a discipline of the human spirit that is not much in evidence upon our campuses, and it would engage scholarship, at last, in the task of making culture a prerogative of the whole people. Whoever finds it droll to suggest that Phi Beta Kappa, of all agencies, should issue such a summons might well consider whether his amusement implies that the educational philosophy of this honor society is already senescent. Greater miracles than this have occurred.

GEORGE A. COE,
Retired

TEACHERS COLLEGE
COLUMBIA UNIVERSITY

A MODEST PROPOSAL

MR. ALLEN is to be congratulated on his timely proposal (in his SCHOOL AND SOCIETY article for February 24) to add the reference librarian to the liberal arts college teaching faculty. At the same time it is fair to ask just what the regular teacher will be expected to do after this new type of librarian has performed the many duties assigned him.

Briefly, Mr. Allen allocates to his "bibliogogue": (1) Knowledge of a special field; (2) library attendance; (3) answering students' questions; (4) faculty status and responsibilities; (5) preparation to teach and actually "have one section of a course"; (6) acquaintance with the respective departments' points of view; (7) familiarity with the material offered by the department; (8) as a result of this familiarity ability "to answer much more satisfactorily (than the professors?) the questions of the students after lectures that present points in which they become interested or which they fail to understand. Such familiarity would eliminate the confusion that is often caused when the idea is garbled . . ."; (9) responsibility for bibliographic instruction; (10) authority to make assignments and see that they are handed in on time; and in short, teach the students!

Now, I submit that all these duties are precisely the function of a *teaching* faculty. I recall further that privately endowed colleges, like Mr. Allen's and mine, dependent upon the shrinking incomes of deflated stocks, are unlikely, in spite of NRA trends, to employ two men to do one job. Consequently, the issue squarely before us is, Who shall do the teaching in the liberal arts college, the librarian or the professor?

I hope I shall be pardoned for presuming that the anonymous "speaker at the Chicago convention of the American Library Association," referred to by Mr. Allen two or three times in the beginning of his article, is the present writer. At that meeting I suggested that contemporary college reform was daily rendering classroom teaching steadily superfluous and that inevitably supervised reading periods would replace lecture-recitations. The nature of the program prevented me from amplifying my views, and as a result a paper entitled "The Library Arts College" will be presented for the association's next meeting at Montreal in June. At that time a detailed plan, including library building designs, study courses, instruction methods and other features developed over a period of several years and already exposed to practical criticism, will be described.

For the present discussion, however, the question remains, What shall be done with the non-teaching professor, whom Mr. Allen has gently eased out of the liberal arts college after leaving him nothing but the "necessary outside activities"?

The answer is "Research." Research and teaching are not necessarily complementary in one man. For every researcher who can teach, at least two will be found who can not. Therefore, why not separate the jobs? We hope there are yet a few survey plums and traveling companionships for the investigator to ferret out, another set of denominational colleges with ills to diagnose. For him establish advanced institutes on one hand, and for young America create teaching colleges on the other. And while the drudge in the latter enterprises will never enjoy the educational glory of a set-up for correlation coefficients, he will at least, some day, receive annuities in recognition of giving low-brow Johnny a feeling for the beautiful.

LOUIS SHORES

GEORGE PEABODY COLLEGE
FOR TEACHERS

BASIC ENGLISH AGAIN

PERHAPS the most devastating criticism that can be leveled against simplified language projects is that they are more often argued about than used. Nevertheless, may I comment briefly concerning an article in SCHOOL AND SOCIETY for February 17, 1934, on "Basic English"?

The article in question does not argue either for or against the scheme but lists instead some sixteen words used in a previous contribution in Basic, which, it is claimed, are not permissible under the rules of Basic English. Such purism seems due largely to a misunderstanding of the purposes and nature of Basic. This system aims merely to furnish what, under existing world conditions, would provide the easiest and most workable universal medium for the exchange of ideas and information.

Accordingly, in addition to the basic 850 words and the small special vocabularies for the various technologies and sciences, the names of places and persons are left unchanged. Words which already have an international currency are not excluded. Why should they be? And compounds of the basic words which by their nature and context would be intelligible are allowed. These are the grounds for using such names as the "Tower of Babel" (which was carefully capitalized), such universals as "résumé" and such compounds as "outdo." I regret to say that two entirely illegitimate words, "dictionary" and "information," did creep in. "Word book" and either "facts" or "knowledge" should have been used. Possibly "the debabelization of the earth" or "the nations of the earth" is to be preferred to the "debabelization of mansort"!

As one who is guilty of several printed attempts at the use of Basic, I can testify that a most troublesome feature is to keep out familiar but non-Basic words. In this connection it may be of interest to mention the fact that, in his "The Shape of Things to Come," H. G. Wells includes Basic as one of the many factors which lead to English becoming the major element in the world language of the future. But with surprising penetration he goes on to say that "on the whole it was more difficult to train English speakers to restrict themselves to the forms and words selected than to teach outsiders the whole of Basic."

And as an experimental biologist and hence potential beneficiary of such a *lingua franca,* may I express the most earnest hope that at the earliest possible date some workable compromise or fusion or coordination be evolved between the systems developed in England by Ogden and in Canada and this country by West and Swenson. Perhaps any such integration must appear to the originators as an uncouth hybrid, but otherwise will not the whole fair enterprise crash into a dozen Volapüks and Idos?

G. B. MOMENT

GOUCHER COLLEGE

REPORTS

HOW THE DEPRESSION AND ITS CONSEQUENCES HAVE AFFECTED TEACHERS COLLEGE STUDENTS

AT the San Jose State Teachers College, a California coeducational institution, a study has been made of the effects on students of the depression and its consequences. A questionnaire couched in the "true-false" form has been given to 239 students, 162 women and 77 men. This includes the seniors present on a given day, 161, and 78 juniors. For the sake of homogeneity, those over twenty-five years of age (about 10 per cent. of the original total) are excluded. The age range is, then, from nineteen to twenty-five, inclusive, with decided modes at twenty-one and twenty-two. Since the depression hit California rather late, these students have had opportunity to feel its "before and after" effects.

The questionnaire contains seventy-one items, covering financial, vocational and mental effects, with a final part intended to discover interest in current affairs. Various precautions have been taken to insure accuracy of information; for instance, essay type reports have been requested as well, and certain items of the questionnaire are such that they can be checked against others. The questionnaire is too long to give here, but significant findings will be reported. The investigator's principal concern is with mental effects.

Nevertheless, since the amount in one's pocketbook usually has a decided influence on one's mental outlook, we should give due consideration to the financial aspect. The questionnaire asks for judgments as to the amount of money the students now have to spend in comparison with pre-depression days. The percentages appear below:

40 per cent. of men and 50 per cent. of women ''somewhat less''
36 per cent. of men and 25 per cent. of women ''much less''
20 per cent. of men and 22 per cent. of women ''about the same''
4 per cent. of men and 3 per cent. of women ''more''

General living expenses have been cut down, of necessity, by about three quarters of the men and two thirds of the women. Very nearly 12 per cent. of both sexes say they have been deprived of some real necessities. Pleasures have had to be given up by approximately 80 per cent. of both sexes; and 16 per cent. of the men and 6 per cent. of the women say they "have been obliged to give up *many* pleasures." It is not surprising to find that the big majority of the entire group "have learned to be more economical."

Most of the men (92 per cent.) and a large proportion of the girls (86 per cent.) state that their "parent's (or guardian's) income has been lessened." In over half of the cases, the "parents have had to make real sacrifices." Forty-three per cent. of both sexes say that their parents "have contributed to the support of relatives outside the immediate family, or of friends." Thirty per cent. of the men students and 20 per cent. of the women "have had to borrow money to come to college," and the same percentage expect to borrow for their future education.

We learn that these young people have often had the discouragement of not being able to find jobs when they wished them, for 64 per cent. of the men and 57 per cent. of the women say that they "have wanted to earn more money but found it hard to get employment." Nevertheless, 20 per cent. of the men and 11 per cent. of the girls "have become entirely self-supporting because of the depression and its consequences"; and 12 per cent. of the men and 2 per cent. of the women have even "contributed to the support of relatives."

It will be observed that the men have had rather more financial struggling to do than the women. This has been found to be true in other studies made of students in this college. The men are more often, or more completely, "on their own," as they put it. Perhaps the girls are somewhat more sheltered by their parents; perhaps they do not so often feel the same necessity for undertaking a college education under such handicaps. For them, work is scarcer and not so well paid.

Practically all these young people had decided on a vocational objective, and not a great many have had to change it because of the depression; only 11 per cent. of the men and 7 per cent. of the women. No doubt this is because the great majority who come to a teachers' college do so with teaching as an objective, and, if they can remain in college, naturally keep the same objective. The tales of changed objective come from those who had planned other, and more expensive, types of careers, and, being frustrated, are turning to the teaching profession.

Certain other vocational facts come out. Nine per cent. of both sexes are "all upset in their vocational plans because of the depression and its consequences." Twenty-seven per cent. of the men and 11 per cent. of the women have had to delay their vocational objective, the greater proportion of men being probably a consequence of their greater financial difficulties. Very few men—only 3 per cent.—are attending college because they could not get jobs; but 31 per cent. of the women so report. A good many of the latter are getting further teaching credentials because employment was not available to them. Men candidates for elementary and junior high-school positions are much fewer and much more in demand, since school authorities constantly evince a desire to have a more balanced distribution of the sexes.

Now let us turn to mental effects. In the first place, the questionnaire brings out the fact that 85 per cent. of the men and 82 per cent. of the women feel that the depression and its consequences have made them more serious in their thinking. In some ways this has been a good thing, but in others, bad. On the loss side, they report excessive worry, loss of hope, confidence and ambition, the development of bitter, cynical, disillusioned attitudes and introverted, unsocial tendencies. Let us cull some expressions from their descriptive accounts: "Worry beyond belief," "heartache and worry," "dismay and turmoil in my mind," "so worried I didn't hear what was being said in the classroom," "worried because I can't afford glasses and dental work," "lost my former ambition and hope," "lost confidence," "somewhat disillusioned," "despondent most of the time," "contemplated suicide," "bitter toward life," "more cynical and unsocial and not aggressive any more," "the younger generation is cheated," "life is less interesting and exciting," "my increasingly introverted attitude."

From the questionnaire it is learned that because of the depression and its consequences, the students "have felt depressed and anxious" in the following proportions:

42 per cent. of men and 52 per cent. of women ''sometimes''
13 per cent. of men and 16 per cent. of women ''often''
2 per cent. of men and 2 per cent. of women ''most of the time''

But it is cheering to find that 43 per cent. of the men and 30 per cent. of the women declare that there has been "little or no effect" on their peace of mind. However, when asked if life has "sometimes seemed not worth living" owing to depression effects, 16 per cent. of the young men and 9 per cent. of the girls answer in the affirmative.

Questions are also put to them as to whether they are worrying about employment in the future. Two thirds of both sexes say that the depression has made them worry about their chances for future jobs; and 78 per cent. of the men and 64 per cent. of the women declare they worry lest they will not get the kind of work they want. For the men, these figures seem not altogether consistent with those just given above. Why should they report being "depressed and anxious" to a less extent than the women and yet plead guilty to more worry about their future? The writer has talked over the matter with the men and finds that what many of them are trying to express is that the present crisis has not "gotten them down" (genuinely anxious), but that they feel very much concerned (but not genuinely anxious) about their futures.

As to the good mental effects of the world's economic upheaval, the investigator would like first to quote one young lady's interesting generalization: "It has made me snap out of a high-school attitude toward life, be more serious, and wonder what things are all about—but I think on the whole it's a good effect." Careful examination of the replies shows that "on the whole it's a good effect" about five times as often as it is bad. The bad is sometimes mixed with the good, but there is this strong preponderance of favorable report. Of course some have been little affected mentally, either one way or the other, but this group is less than half as numerous as that which has benefited.

For one thing, the world's plight seems to have developed altruism. Ninety-three per cent. of the women affirm that because of the depression and its consequences they "would like to help other people more." The men appear to be not quite so unselfishly concerned, for the percentage of men so inclined drops to 74. This is one of the more conspicuous differences between the replies of the men and women. Be that as it may, it is clear from both questionnaire and supplementary replies that the present crisis has aroused in both sexes great sympathy for other people and strong desire to help them—not only parents (frequently mentioned) and friends but others as well.

Furthermore, attention has been turned beyond the more immediate human circle to national and world events and problems. Half the women and a slightly greater proportion of the men are found by the questionnaire to be "much interested in current world events and problems"; the rest are "somewhat interested," with the exception of about 2 per cent., who have "very little interest." National affairs have even more attraction, for 70 per cent. of both sexes are "much interested in current events and problems in this country," with again about 2 per cent.—the same persons—"very little" interested and the rest "somewhat" interested. In these questions on current affairs the students are not asked to judge whether their interest is due largely to the depression or to other factors, such as a maturing outlook; but it is significant that they very often cite the former cause spontaneously.

Ninety-six per cent. of the men and 73 per cent. of the women declare they like to read about national and international events and problems when they can. Fifty-eight per cent. of the men and 69 per cent. of the women are satisfied, on the whole, with the form of government the United States has always had. The rest of the group (42 per cent. of the men; 31 per cent. of the women) would like to have socialism, though in many cases they specify their preference for a modified variety. Other forms of government are not considered, being, apparently, either not acceptable or not understood. President Roosevelt's conduct of national affairs is approved, on the whole, by 81 per cent. of the men and 85 per cent. of the girls; while 76 per cent. of the former and 90 per cent. of the latter are in favor of the NRA program in the main. There is evidently some discrimination between the President's performance and his pet instrument, the NRA. Sometimes the students have remedies of their own to propose for the nation's ills—"reform of officials," "a movement toward breeding a super-race," "a corporate state," "more carefulness for others," "forget about wine, beer, etc., and think about honesty." One despairing youth says mass suicide is the only real remedy. Over half of both sexes say (on the questionnaire) they "look forward to trying to help settle some of the world's perplexing problems." Social injustice arouses comment.

Very nearly all the students have given the subject of war serious consideration, and only 14 per cent. of the men and 18 per cent. of the women are undecided where they stand on the question. Approximately half of the entire group think "war is unjustifiable and should be abolished completely"; and the rest are about equally divided between the belief that "only defensive war is justified" and that "both defensive and offensive wars are sometimes necessary and justifiable." Sex differences are negligible in this series of answers.

To these gains in sympathy and broadened interest have been added others, which show best in their own descriptive terms, *viz.*: "Stimulated to economy and hard work," "stimulated to the worth-while experience of earning toward my expenses," "obliged to learn to be a bank clerk which was a fortunate and gratifying experience for me," "obliged to become more independent and self-reliant," "compelled to use my powers of reasoning more," "encouraged to think more clearly, more broadly," "more able to face life and facts," "more able to endure," "content with less," "now able to find enjoyment in books and music without spending money," "appreciative of my privileges," "more appreciative of what my parents have done for me," "appreciative of true character and real values," "life seems more interesting and richer." On the whole, then, the mental gains exceed the losses, and many of these students are likely to be, as one of them puts it, "better citizens because of this experience."

DOROTHY HAZELTINE YATES
OAKLAND, CALIF.

EDUCATIONAL RESEARCH AND STATISTICS

SOME RESULTS SECURED IN PERSONNEL WORK IN A TEACHERS COLLEGE

IN a teachers college, personnel work naturally centers in scientific efforts to discover, interpret and apply data concerning students so that their professional development is both measured and aided. Research is carried on to determine the significance of various kinds of records and to suggest the use of such records in the guidance of students. Sufficiently complete data were available from the N. Y. State College for Teachers at Albany to indicate in statistical terms some values and limitations of several kinds of scores. Since such scores are constantly scrutinized for their general usefulness, they may have more than local interest and importance.

As has repeatedly been true in comparable studies, the correlation-coefficients are too small or low to use for predictive purposes; but their comparative sizes indicate the relative contributions of various scores to a general estimate of students' adequacy. The kinds used[1] included scores on a standardized intelligence test (reported hereafter as I scores), those secured from an inventory of neurotic and emotional tendencies (E scores) and those representing answers on a measure of social traits (S scores), as well as academic averages, health grades and practise teaching grades.

Among a number of correlations figured by the product-moment formula, the largest coefficient secured was that of +.631 ± .029 (195 cases) between freshman I scores and senior I scores on another form of the same test. Less consistency was found between freshman and senior E scores, for which the same inventory was repeated, yielding a coefficient of +.587 ± .037 (141 cases). Most of the other coefficients which seem to be statistically significant involve academic measures of some kind. They probably show the definite degree of relationship because of the many variables which are involved, but not separately measured.

These coefficients are:

+.561 ± .032 (204 cases) between academic averages for the first semester and for the last two years in college.

+.525 ± .035 (202 cases) between academic averages for the first semester and Regents Averages.

+.471 ± .038 (189 cases) between freshman I scores and Regents Averages.

+.429 ± .040 (190 cases) between academic averages for the first semester and freshman I scores.

+.368 ± .040 (215 cases) between academic averages for the last two years and Regents Averages.

+.359 ± .043 (190 cases) between academic averages for the first semester and freshman reading and comprehension test scores.

+.334 ± .044 (190 cases) between academic averages for the last two years and freshman I scores.

The r's of +.429 and +.334, given above, indicate that I scores may be of slightly more help in the guidance of freshmen than of seniors. The reading and comprehension test scores mentioned were those of a single section of the intelligence test. These were separately studied, because it had been noted that in many instances they were more indicative of students' ability for professional training than were I scores. Still more important than the actual score of either kind was the relation between the two kinds of scores.

Scores of different sizes and ranges were made comparable by conversion to a scale of ten representing tenths of a class, 1 always meaning the lowest tenth, 10 the highest. Judicious noting of discrepancies between various converted scores of a student, taking into account the kinds of scores which yielded the most significant correlations, furnished a better basis for predictions of the student's success than did separate scores in relation either to correlations or probability-tables.

To determine as nearly as possible the independent influences of five kinds of variability, the multiple R for practise teaching was computed from the regression equation, indicating the degree to which E scores, health scores, reading and comprehension scores from the intelligence test, Regents Averages and S scores contributed to an estimate of practise teaching. This work yielded a multiple R of .467 for

[1] The intelligence test used was the Ohio State University Psychological Test (forms 11 and 15). E scores were secured from Personal Inventory Revision B_2, designed by Donald A. Laird and published by *Hamilton Republican*, Hamilton, N. Y.; and S scores from Morris Trait Index L, published by the Public School Publishing Co., Bloomington, Ill.

practise teaching, showing that the above-mentioned kinds of data are insufficient for adequate prediction of success in practise teaching, but that they are more useful when combined than if taken separately.

First semester academic averages yielded a higher correlation (though it was only +.352 ± .050—144 cases) with senior practise teaching grades than did any other one kind of measure. The next most significant coefficient was that of +.304 ± .051 (144 cases) between health grades and practise teaching, which was raised to +.363 when other variables were partialed out. The same technique also raised the r of +.213 between Regents Averages and practise teaching to +.236.

One serious difficulty which confronts the educator when he tries to understand and to control conditions in a scientific way, is that he does not know how constant certain important relationships may be. Even when he tries to determine which kinds of scores show the greatest change from freshman to senior year, he is confronted by the fact that results from different classes vary. Similarities between classes, however, are more frequent than differences. Correlations between freshman I scores and Regents Averages for four classes were: +.471 ± .038 (189 cases), +.393 ± .031 (349 cases), +.476 ± .031 (295 cases) and +.418 ± .033 (282 cases)—all statistically reliable and yielding an average r of +.44.

Since many institutions took part in the Cooperative College Sophomore Testing Program, the following correlation-coefficients have more than local interest:

+.410 ± .046 (152 cases)	between local academic averages and Cooperative English and general culture scores omitting general science.
+.313 ± .050 (152 cases)	between local academic averages and Cooperative total English scores.
+.266 ± .051 (152 cases)	between local academic averages and Cooperative general culture scores.
+.256 ± .051 (152 cases)	between local academic averages and Cooperative vocabulary scores.

The last-named coefficient is interestingly similar to that of +.250 ± .051 (152 cases) between academic averages the first semester and vocabulary scores from one section of the intelligence test.

That first semester grades have definitely predictive value for the success of students in their first full year is shown by the coefficient of +.836 ± .013 (278 cases) between these two sets of academic averages. It is also of general usefulness to know that method of computing academic averages seems not to be a highly significant factor.

In general, the data would suggest that:

(1) Although different classes within an institution may show individual characteristics, as do different institutions, careful interpretation of data secured from one group yields conclusions that are helpful suggestions concerning other groups.

(2) It is highly desirable to collect intelligence test scores which can be more fully interpreted in relation to important sectional scores, such as reading and comprehension, and in relation to emotional and social scores, even though the latter are still highly ambiguous.

(3) The interrelation between scores is far more important for predictive and guidance purposes than are the mere scores themselves. They alone of their kind, even compared to some norm, may be seriously misleading.

(4) Practise teaching grades are at present very valuable for certain indications they give in a general way, but prediction of success in teaching and selection of the best candidates for the profession can not be materially and scientifically advanced until we develop more definite criteria of good teaching (perhaps of each of several kinds!) and more objective means for measuring degrees of success achieved.

ELIZABETH H. MORRIS

NEW YORK STATE COLLEGE FOR TEACHERS, ALBANY

NEW BOOKS IN EDUCATION

HINES, HARLAN C. *Introduction to Educational Psychology.* Pp. xxix + 381. Illustrated. Van Nostrand. $2.20.

MILLS, HERBERT E. and others. *College Women and the Social Sciences* Pp. xv + 324. John Day. $2.50.

EDUCATIONAL REVIEW

Edited by Nicholas Murray Butler, 1891–1919, Frank Pierrepont Graves, 1920–1924, and William McAndrew, 1924–

MONTHLY SURVEY OF EDUCATIONAL BOOKS

By WILLIAM McANDREW

THIS REVOLUTION

FROM an economist who, as government investigator, has wide knowledge of the inside of industry and business comes an analysis of causes and changes affecting the nation's material condition.[1] The author, Professor Arthur Adams, is enough of a realist to throw overboard the standard policy of hands off business and to see the need that the people, organized as government, regulate and control the forces that are impoverishing them. Here is the line of his presentation—how booms bring depression, what share the world war had, technology and the decrease in purchasing power, high profits and low wages, failure of economic laws, changing business policy, absence of recovery forces, Hoover policies, public relief, gold standard, inflation, price stabilization, farm relief, public works projects, industrial control, foreign trade, government and business in the future.

Dr. Adams is not concerned with condemning or defending any political party or policy. He tells plainly what he thinks the present measures are likely to bring and the reasons for his beliefs. The industrial revolution permitted the accumulation of enormous private fortunes and has resulted in a situation in which 85 per cent. of us are dependent on daily wages for our daily bread. The competitive forces in wage-earning have more and more favored the employers. The only way to establish equilibrium is by our control of business through our government. This is the new revolution we are now in. This is a calm, plain-speaking book.

OBERLIN'S IMMEDIATE PRESIDENT

YOU would need to be very cold-blooded to avoid enthusiasm in reading a little book by the president of Oberlin College.[2]

In a series of eleven short talks delivered to students, a virile teacher cuts loose from the dear old college platitudes and says, "Here, you, why do you suppose this college was set up? Why do men make it generous gifts? Is it for you? Nonsense! A college is for mankind. Those of them you touch and will live with are in a sorry state, just now. The trouble is economic, political."

In short thrusting sentences Mr. Wilkins tells his collegians what they must do.

You are obligated to exercise your voting rights on every voting day your whole life long. To fail in this is to confess yourself careless as to what will befall your neighbors and yourself, careless of curing the stupidity and injustice of the present order.

An educated man's vote is given meaning by a previous study of the candidates and their policies.

National leadership is essentially possible for a college man and for his college as a college.

If you are to be truly national, you must be more.

Internationalism is forced on us whether we will or no.

An internationalism of intelligence and good will is implied in your college diploma.

The college man must vote while he is still in college. The time to start a habit is at the first opportunity. Then, keep it alive without a break.

How shall you prepare to vote intelligently? By reading, by listening, and, certainly, by discussion. Read your local newspaper. Read, too, one on each side. Ask people, not whom to vote for, but why.

Government truly is endangered. Unintelligence and surrender to the demands of privilege debilitate it. These things are poisoning life for millions of you.

You need a high intelligence not only in what is commonly called politics, but in social economics.

You think that the college man counts little in politics if he stands alone. Very well, don't

[1] Arthur B. Adams, "Our Economic Revolution." University of Oklahoma Press, Norman. 197 pp. $1.50.

[2] Ernest Hatch Wilkins, "A Platform for Life." Oberlin Printing Company, Oberlin, Ohio. 118 pp. $1.00.

be left to stand alone. Organize. Make group decisions, petitions, protests. Conspire together for what you believe is wise and right.

The direct talks of the Wilkins book are upon the college as a national institution, political opportunities and duties, grounds for supporting a political party, America voting, toward peace, a bonfire of vanities, and so on.

In youth and age I have read and heard 1,876,549,300, more or less, addresses of college presidents. I remember only three occasions, besides this one, that escaped the appearance of conformity to custom, of an effort to show erudition, of a disinclination to be too forthright. The striking feature of this book is its tone, as of an intelligent observer outside of college saying without hems or haws what the country needs from the educated man. You may say that Dr. Wilkins has adopted the advice Moses got from his father-in-law, Jethro: "Thou shalt teach them laws and ordinances and the work that they must do."

THE NEED OF MIDDLE-CLASS POLITICS

PROFESSOR HOLCOMBE,[3] of the chair of government, Harvard University, has a new volume in the social-action books of the Norton Company. It is a survey of contemporary American politics. It discusses the passing of the old party strategy, the prospects of proletarian dictatorship, the fascist alternative, the function of and a program for the middle class.

From the change of the country, once predominatingly rural, to an urban population, Dr. Holcombe computes the probabilities of party changes. The farmer influence has been a middle class one. The better paid white-collar workers and the professionals make up the middle class in the cities. In prosperous times there is among these a tendency to accept capitalist policies. The Republican party was originally devoted to the average citizen. The middle class always mitigates the struggle between the proletariat and the capitalist groups. It asserts the supremacy of community interests over those of every kind. What the middle-class program may be is here worked out in detail. Professor Holcombe's discussion involves the possibilities of Marxism and of fascism in America and leads into illuminating criticisms of these movements, as experienced in Russia and Italy.

The conclusion of the matter is that as we become used to urbanization urbane politics will be class politics. The middle class should not shrink from the obligations of its position. Middle-class politics in this urbane age is as American as Corn-Belt politics was in the age that is passing away. No urbane state can be as well governed as one dominated by the middle class. This is the faith that should sustain us through the coming of the new party-politics.

[3] A. N. Holcombe, "The New Party Politics." W. W. Norton and Company, New York. 148 pp. $1.75.

HUGHES' FORWARD-LOOKING CIVICS

SCHOOLMASTER HUGHES has three civic textbooks to his credit—two are half-year courses, one is for a full year. He now adds a workbook.[4] He is all for the newer idea that citizenship is not a body of information to be memorized. What is needed, he insists, is intelligent thinking. The study must abound in projects that aim at high ideals. He lures the youngsters into discussing what citizenship obligates and requires, what community spirit is, how you must behave to be a good citizen. Mr. Hughes' economics text is full of the same urge to know, to reason and to do. The three books are profusely pictured. I have not seen any workbook that is more effectively personal. We are not, says the school to the boy, so much concerned with getting you to know what others think as we are to have you reach conclusions on what the welfare of the farmer, etc., etc., means to you and to others. Most of the Hughes workbook material are questions, "What do you think?" He dares invite responses as to attitudes of labor and capital and to other problems which the careful school-man says are loaded with dynamite. Hughes seems not afraid of controversial topics.

My land! First thing you know somebody will make up a school course in which high-school pupils will be asked: "How fair are the employers to the men in your town?" "What instances of unselfish patriotic action, done by what official of your city government, can you describe?" Then the ghosts of the Founding Fathers will peer in a-smiling and say, "This

[4] R. O. Hughes, "Civic Training." 396 pp. $1.20. "Economic Citizenship." 361 pp. $1.20. "Work-book in Citizenship." 292 pp. 80 cents. Allyn and Bacon, Boston.

is what we promised public education would do if the people would be willing to be taxed for it."

NEW MAGRUDER CIVICS

MESSRS. ALLYN AND BACON offer every year a revised edition of Professor Magruder's civics. The last issue,[5] the 1934 book, gives an account of the efforts of New England to meet the deficiencies of the town meeting, of the snobbishness of Americans in the Philippines, of court privileges to the rich which the poor can not get, of the monopoly of public utilities, of the failure of council-mayor types of city government, of unemployment and other current problems of democracy. Professor Magruder prints on his title page: "It is the duty of government to make it easy for the people to do right and difficult for the people to do wrong." Before beginning the text he urges that each student should be encouraged to subscribe for a weekly magazine of political events and to study and report upon local political conditions. The book is rich in pictures, diagrams, projects and questions. It covers the Federal Constitution and those of the states, courts, parties, elections, finance, education, social problems and foreign relations.

PREVIOUS EFFECTS OF INFLATION

INFLATION takes many forms. Government debt is the most insidious; bank credit, the most volatile. Greenbacks may be less destructive than unlimited borrowing. The lessons of France, Germany, Austria and other countries can teach us much. In financial fluctuations it is the poor who suffer most; the middle class is almost annihilated in the first place; the workers and the farmers always suffer in the long run. These are conclusions from a short, well-balanced book[6] by Dr. Dulles, of the University of Pennsylvania, an economist with high talent for making complex matters simple and clear. The account covers the crisis of 1933, the circumstances which lead to inflation, detailed experience of France, the failure of high prices to bring prosperity.

This is a good book for the use of classes in economics and for debating societies.

[5] Frank Abbott Magruder, "American Government." Allyn and Bacon, Boston. 773 pp. $1.80.

[6] Eleanor Lansing Dulles, "The Dollar, The Franc, and Inflation." The Macmillan Company. 106 pp. $1.25.

ORGANIZATION FOR COMMON DEFENCE

DEAN HAGGERTY[7] contributes to the "Day-and-Hour" series of the University of Minnesota's studies of current problems a forthright proposal for aggressive organization of persons concerned for general welfare. In comparison with the attacks of industrial groups the organized schoolmasters are feeble. The most of wealth is held by the few who represent a small per cent. of the children of the nation. Dr. Haggerty urges combinations to revise taxation and to save the best things America has.

THE ANCIENTS AS EXAMPLES AND WARNINGS

PROFESSOR MOREY'S second history of the old world is written with the collaboration of High-school Master Countryman.[8] It proceeds from early man through the break-up of the Roman Empire. In selecting from the mass of archives the authors tell us that the events which bear on human progress are the only ones included. What benefits through positive advance, what warnings from failures, the Egyptians, Medes and Persians, Greeks and Romans, can teach the present Americans should be stressed in a school text-book. Thus the strength and weakness of Greek political life is gone into at length. There is not so much of the effort in this text to develop the cultivated gentleman as to broaden the civic value of the intelligent citizen. The Roman story is of the economic distress of the common people, farmers ruined by mortgages, masses crowding into the cities and supported by the dole, politicians buying the offices, contractors waxing rich on graft, patriots worsted by demagogues, dictatorships weakening the power of popular government; slavery, greed, plunder, luxury and war driving a great empire to its doom.

Every chapter is supplemented by a synopsis and by exercises. Maps, portraits, restorations, biographical sketches and chronological tables abound.

END TO CLASSROOM DREAMING

DISCUSSION tests, measures of achievement, anti-cramming discipline, cure of classroom

[7] M. E. Haggerty, "Children of the Depression." University of Minnesota Press, Minneapolis. 25 pp. Paper, 25 cents.

[8] William C. Morey, Irving N. Countryman, "Ancient Peoples." American Book Company, New York. 646 pp. $1.84.

dreaming, food for discussion, practise in forming opinion, with other aids to correct study habits in the field of history and the social sciences, are embodied in a new project by Alice Gibbons, of the East High School, Rochester, New York.[9] A majority of the tests are of new-type order. Essay-type tests are included so as to give practise in organizing ideas. The study guide is on the unit plan, involving the completion of maps and the use of means for preventing the sorting of history into separate compartments. The study-skills essential to the mental life of the citizen of to-day, the questioning habit, the creative effect of discussion are emphasized.

A tolerant and critical understanding of the world, says Author Gibbons, must come from the schools or their work is in vain. Long tested in the author's own classes, this scheme of lessons gives the teacher the means of seeing every pupil come at least to an essential minimum of mastery, while the extra exercises provide against the tedium of brighter pupils so often held back by the slower members.

MAKING MY MIND MIND ME

AFTER at least sixty years, containing many annoyances from laziness in myself and others, I am edified by Professor John Morgan's assurance that simple cures are at hand. This professor of psychology in Northwestern University, author of much cheerful matter on making the most of life, has written a book on self-application of mental hygiene.[10] He writes for students and ordinary people aged between 18 and 100.

One learns to loaf by loafing, says our professor. The cure for laziness is not to have it. Go to work and keep working until you have to drag yourself away. This is good old doctrine. Ernest Fenellosa, after residence among the Japanese, said they were free from fear and worry because they got rid of those devils by getting rid of them.

Dr. Morgan has some stiff passages on overwork. It is an imaginary evil. Teachers who complain of it are barking up the wrong tree. The cause of their trouble is not work but something that puts them in a wrong attitude toward it. The essence of play is not that useless things are being done but that the doer is enjoying them. The intrinsic effect of work really is enjoyment. If pleasure is not realized it isn't work that is to blame. It is you.

In easy conversational style this genial psychologist tells you how to end your mental conflicts, how to master fear, what to fight for, how to battle, ways to gain emotional maturity, to make your mind grow, to overcome personal handicaps, to conquer your depressions and to get along with people.

PRACTICAL PREACHING

THE REVEREND DR. POWELL'S[11] persuasive lead toward personal religion is a running comment on his experiences, quoting from great and from every-day people with whom he has worked, and demonstrating that it is eminently possible to get on better with folks and thus to enjoy life more than we do. Dr. Powell has preached cheery doctrine from the Atlantic to the western coast. He tells of success with the ailing, of the need of rethinking in regard to missions, of people who personalize their faith, of present unchristian business, industry and politics, and what you should do to make your share of the world go on right.

REASONABLE EDUCATIONAL REFORM

So universal are the facts and conclusions of Mr. Marvin[12] that the most of his sketch and comments dealing with educational problems in England reads like an appraisal of our own school system. A favorite historian and essayist, he is one of the most easily read and continuously satisfactory authors whose work comes to this review shop. He is appreciative, critical and tolerant. His admiration for teachers is warm, his vision of what they may do much better is reasonable and distinct. He is surprised that so few attempts have been made to describe education simply with the general public in mind and to give the man on the sidewalk a fair estimate of the real good which education has done for the population.

[9] Alice N. Gibbons, "Test Book in the Origins of Contemporary Civilization, a Foundation Course in Social Science." 117 pp. 44 cents. "Directed Study Guide." 225 pp. 80 cents. "Teachers' Manual." 75 pp. 28 cents. Ginn and Company, Boston.

[10] John J. B. Morgan, "Keeping a Sound Mind." The Macmillan Company, New York. 440 pp. $2.00.

[11] Lyman P. Powell, "The Better Part." Bobbs-Merrill Company, Indianapolis. 212 pp. $1.50.

[12] F. S. Marvin, "The Nation at School." Oxford University Press, 114 Fifth Avenue, New York. 173 pp. $1.75.

During the last century the State everywhere has organized a complete and elaborate system of schools and institutions fitting into one another and serving a multitude of ends, but the teaching itself has been obscured by a network of administrative regulations forming a large part of a mystery. The essential thing: what education performs for the mind, is the main theme of the present book.

There are influential groups asserting that the schools are not giving our money's worth, the mass of the population is not so well educated as it was fifty years ago. Others criticise government for limiting the growth and improvement of schools. We are spending much on education, almost a half of what we pay for drink. Education has been deemed necessary by all modern states. The statistician shows that, with the increase of schools, public health has been enormously improved, crime in almost all countries has decreased, the general state of society is marked by higher intelligence, common sense and good will.

We are weak in essential enquiry into the result of teaching as found in the taught. As soon as one has acquired the necessary consciousness let a student or a common man ask himself: "How far am I an educated person? What is an educated person? So far as I am one, to what do I owe it? What more might be done to extend the process?" The answers to be of value must be honest. They should consider the country as a whole. One must ask how far in his lifetime has the average man kept his body in a state of healthy activity. The average physical condition of people over middle age, the crowded hospitals, sanitariums and nursing homes, the actual deaths from preventable disease do not suggest encouraging ratings for this examination.

On the esthetic side there is much to ask. School and college have not made a brilliant success in this line or how can we explain that the majority of our contemporaries are content to live in hideous areas of modern towns and feast their eyes on the monstrosities of modern newspapers and cinemas? That this should go on and grow while eye and ear are open to all the beauty and delight of nature in sky and sea with the songs of birds, the shapes and colors of trees and flowers waiting to be enjoyed, is the strongest indictment of modern education.

Disappointment at Results

Our memory is less vivid and less trained—because less relied upon—than it was with our ancestors, the reciters of Homer's lays. Personal memory is weaker because the written word is always at hand to replace it, with the result that in our declining years few of us are able to console ourselves with the recital of fine poetry learned when we were children.

The fetish of examinations engenders a false sense of finality in the work of schools and colleges. The more cheerful aspect of appraisal is a hope that some vital seed will, if cultivated, take root, spread out and grow. It is the growing quality, not the mere sowing, that is essential. The self-examiner may be well pleased if he will take down his Vergil now and then, but it must be to make new discoveries and cover fresh ground. For the majority the lines of growth lie elsewhere.

From the millions of children who were in school the proportion of those who make good with what they were taught is woefully disappointing. When a few millions of self-examiners are developed the nation may hold up its head.

When Mr. Marvin discusses the state as parent, equal education for all, the private school, caste and merit, examinations, general aim, instruments helping to achieve it, seats of learning, universities, technical training, neglected agricultural and lack of efficient business education, nationalism, world relations, he does it with a breadth and vision more than admirable.

What he says of weakening of home teaching as the state does more, the civilizing effect of cooperative sports, the effect of literacy on health and reform, the failure of teaching to create a taste for other than the cheap newspaper output, the growth of orderly conduct in the masses as results of their attendance at school, the persistence of parents who choose a school for social reasons, the need of problem-methods in teaching if we are to develop a thinking citizenry, is deftly and persuasively presented.

Surely education when consciouly and skilfully directed can cure the general callousness of the people toward beauty and art. There must be a revolution affecting Latin and Greek for they have lost their supreme value in the human heritage. The creative spirit can be better invoked. It can be done with ease and with great satisfaction to the learners. World affairs must be more extensively taught. Mr. Marvin develops all of these and other proposals with persuasive reasons. His criticism has no sting in it nor offense of too certain propaganda. The book is a model of the sweet reasonableness esteemed by the old masters who taught the art of persuasion to the good life.

SCHOOL MANAGEMENT ON BASIC PRINCIPLES

Instead of a common way of building comments on schools as they are, Professor Otto,[13] Department of Education, Northwestern University, begins with basic principles derivable from the civic needs of the country, from the known facts of the learning process, and from the conclusions of the psychological laboratory. From these he advances to what and how the pupils should do and to the duties of the administrator as dependent on this.

It must be recognized, says Dr. Otto, that there is too wide a gap between the American School and American life. As long as prosperity lasted the public did not criticise much. Now, the school program is confronted with the most criticism it has ever had. Why has the school not trained people to guide more intelligently our civic-economic progress? What ought the school to be doing, now, to guard against economic and political disaster in the future? Mere administrative makeshifts without a fundamental clarity of purpose will accomplish little.

The persistence with which Dr. Otto keeps the large objective in sight is good teaching by him. "The elementary school child must be advanced in sensing his share in the social, civic and industrial responsibilities of the democracy."

An encouraging note appears in the Koos table of percentages showing the relative importance given to different objectives by writers from 1912 to 1923. Civic-social responsibility ranks highest, 82 per cent.

But, when any one spends a day in a public school looking for teaching directed toward political-economic responsibilities he wonders at the gap between what is there done and what educational writers say should be done. President Eliot once said teaching is fifty years behind its literature. Werrett Charters, more sanguine, says ten. A training class using Dr. Otto's book can deliver some human yeast-bearers into some classrooms in two or three years. Their opportunity they say is small. Our author reiterates the fact that the school principal is the key log in this civic-economic-educational jam. The book is rich with daily devotional exercises for your morning preparation.

One of the many sturdy features of the book is its forswearing of any coddling for the schoolman. Educational management is a great, a complex, a hard job as Dr. Otto portrays it. In one place he enumerates 174 distinct duties assembled from only ten principals telling what they do.

Slowly enough the public is being educated to realize that a school manager, in variety of duties, in reliance on scientific findings, in value of services is not inferior to the head of a bank, railroad or hospital.

This volume, in scope, in clarity, in reliance on definite findings of research, merits place in the front rank of hand-books for efficient school direction.

[13] Henry J. Otto, "Elementary School Organization and Administration." D. Appleton-Century Company, New York. 651 pp. $3.00.

DEFINITE SCHOOL ECONOMY

Where does the money paid as taxes go? First, the largest amount for government debts; second, two and a half billions a year for schools; next heaviest payment, for highways. Everywhere, slices have been cut off the school funds. Retrenchment can be made by those who levy the taxes but economy can be practised only by those who have charge of the school system. Thus does William John Cooper[14] begin his concise summary of what intelligence, planning, and administration the school people must use rather than mope in bewilderment during these sorry times. Dr. Cooper uses the extensive experience and observation he has developed as town and state superintendent and as national commissioner. His economy measures are based on obvious facts which he reviews. His presentation is singularly lucid and practical.

[14] William John Cooper, "Economy in Education." Stanford University Press, California. 82 pp. $1.00.

KEEPING THE PUBLIC POSTED

PRESIDENT WILBUR'S school economy series continues with a breezy review of the ways used to keep people interested in education.[15] The author, Dr. Farley, is the cheerful journalist who manages public relations for the National Education Association. He has used his own and others' experiences so as to make clear the necessity of an informed public if education is to avoid stagnation. He treats of the organization of school publicity, of the avenues usable, of principles and practises. He does this in a style that makes a readable book valuable to every school superintendent. The importance of the material and the way Dr. Farley has arranged it makes this a first-class text-book for courses in school administration.

MEASUREMENT UP TO DATE

FOR the last words on educational management try the addresses of the last conference of the appraisers.[16] The subjects discussed are: Pupil attitudes as changed by teaching; logical learning in college; social change affecting public schools; effect of marks in physical training; measuring the high school; appreciation of literature; disability in reading and arithmetic; school sites.

SCHOOL MONEY

RESEARCHER CARR'S[17] up-to-date study of school funds places major emphasis on the most crucial issue—the relation of the state to the support of education. He presents current trends and needs, relating them to fundamental principles of government, economics and education. He discusses the North Carolina plan as well as developments in New York, Utah and elsewhere.

HOW SHALL WE GET AND KEEP GOOD TEACHERS?

THERE has been little evidence to show, say Investigators Deffenbaugh and Zeigel,[18] in their contribution to the Cooper-Koos National Survey of Secondary Education, what methods are the most effective in obtaining competent teachers. The smaller community is seriously handicapped by lack of tenure, remuneration and advancement. The teacher should be encouraged in his effort to better himself elsewhere. This is good for the teacher, but God help the children whose school boards are content with the perpetual turn-over while maintaining a training ground for the larger cities. Get behind the movement for state aid. In more than half the boards studied the choices of teachers are made from only persons who apply. There is too little effort to search for the best. The Deffenbaugh-Zeigel study covers the case of both elementary and high-school teachers. It considers the determination of the number needed, higher qualifications, location of desirable talent, collection of reliable facts regarding prospective teachers, retention of those of high quality. The survey covers twenty-eight selected states.

KEEPING SCHOOL WITHIN THE LAW

PROFESSOR EDWARDS, Chicago University's specialist in school law,[19] will get the thanks of superintendents and school boards for the carefully indexed compendium of court decisions—581 large pages of them—he has published. He makes clear the fundamental principles underlying the relation of the state to education, he cites cases and principles applicable to practical organization and management of schools. At the foot of each page are the cases in which the decisions applicable were rendered. Whether the author is discussing the powers and duties concerned with finances, contracts, elections and records, or liability for negligence, or dismissal of teachers, or pensions and wages, or discipline of teachers or of pupils, he is touching on troubles that have beset superintendents over and over and that may jump into your path any day. To know where to find the authentic solution, to have a manual on your desk an ever-present help, must do much to strengthen a notoriously worried profession. For the first time such an aid has been organized on the basis of administrative experience.

THE WHOLE HOME-ROOM PROBLEM

BOOKS by Harry McKown which have been reviewed here—"Extra Curricular," "Clubs,"

15 Belmont Farley, "School Publicity." Stanford University Press, California. 118 pp. $1.00.

16 Eight Authors, "Twentieth Annual Conference on Educational Measurements." Bureau of Cooperative Research, University of Indiana, Bloomington. 98 pp. 50 cents.

17 William G. Carr, "School Finance." University Press, Stanford University, California. 105 pp. paper, $1.00.

18 W. S. Deffenbaugh, William H. Zeigel, Jr., "Selection and Employment of Teachers." Superintendent of Documents, Washington, D. C. 115 pp. 10 cents.

19 Newton Edwards, "The Courts and the Public Schools." University of Chicago Press. 591 pp. $5.00.

"Assemblies" and "Commencements"—have all been characterized by a description of actual doings in the most noted schools of America. The author's comment on various usages and his urge that they be employed with a conscious aim to realize the best attainable philosophy of education are in his latest book[20] strongly evident.

He begins with a startling array of opinions on the failure of the scholarship motive for public-school education. He urges a high-school program based on more successful contribution to the social, economic, political needs of the community. He says that experience shows it is stupid to contend that the mental development, still held to be in so many cases the purpose of high school, insures the discharge of duty toward the public. How the home-room organization and conduct can be made to realize undreamed-of service in this direction is set forth in a series of thorough chapters of supreme importance and practicality.

He has made a handbook that will furnish the school principal with ideas and models.

SANDUSKY'S SANDY

I CAN remember my father, sixty years ago, reciting verses about "the man of Ross" who held every man his brother. Sandusky High School has a civics teacher of this name.[21] He publishes an appeal to his brother taxpayers to save democracy by increased support of education. He argues in strong everyday style. He is rich in racy illustration. He calls the financiers "moon men" because they never show the other side. He punctures slogans. He tackles the tax problem. He argues for the junior college. He sees the public school as the battle ground in this revolution.

EDUCATIONAL TONIC

PROFESSOR KILPATRICK, ten years after its first appearance, has revised and enlarged his source-texts on educational doctrine and practise.[22] It gives easy access to many short and ordinarily inaccessible writings on educational purposes. Conflict and contradiction must appear when so many men are heard. Be warned against easy acceptance. Knowing Professor Kilpatrick, you will expect ample counsel from the good and great on social obligations, regard for others, right and wrong, the good life, democracy, progress and ideals. You will not be disappointed. The spirit of the extracts, their directness and brevity, are such that you can find quick solace in them for the disappointments of unlucky days, if you have any. There are selections which the compiler intends for your wrath, some for your laughter, most for your daily growth. There is an index of subjects and one of authors. The book distils good sense, persuasion, too, the real majesty of education and satisfaction at being in the procession.

FOR SCHOOL AND COLLEGE DRAMATICS

FOR the National Council of Teachers of English, Milton Smith, New York Teachers College author of books on the school theater, has done a thanks-deserving work in listing and describing hundreds of available plays.[23] He furnishes an alphabetized list of full length plays and of those consisting of one act. He gives a synopsis of each, tells how many and what kind of actors are needed, what royalty, if any, must be paid, and other information in aid of selection. The dramas are classified as Greek and Roman, Medieval and Elizabethan, and Modern. Charles Allen, illustrator, has enlivened the text with many pictures of costumes, settings and so forth.

The book is a great time-saver.

DISGRACED AND NEGLECTED

ANOTHER of those monumental volumes of the White House Conference comes from the D. Appleton-Century Company.[24] It is concerned with a blot on America's escutcheon. It formulates a declaration of principles and a program for the care of orphans, dependent children at home and in school, babies born out of wedlock, causes of child dependency, opportunities for prevention, accidents, unemployment, poverty, sickness, mothers' aid, legislation, problems of the Negro, Mexican, and Porto Rican popula-

20 Harry C. McKown, "Home-Room Guidance." McGraw-Hill Book Company, New York. 447 pp. $3.00.

21 James Ross, "The Cost of American Democracy." Published by the author. Sandusky, Ohio. 85 pp. 40 cents.

22 William Heard Kilpatrick, "Source-Book in the Philosophy of Education." The Macmillan Company, New York. 535 pp. $2.25.

23 Milton Smith, "Guide to Play Selection." D. Appleton-Century Company, New York. 174 pp. $1.25.

24 Homer Folks, Chairman and Committee of Investigators, "Dependent and Neglected Children." D. Appleton-Century Company, New York. 448 pp. $3.00.

tion in the United States, agencies, courts, and laws.

Child protection, as we know it to-day, began in 1822 when "Humanity" Martin got his first law enacted by the British Parliament. As late as 1874 New York had to seek legal protection for children under the law for the prevention of cruelty to animals! In 1875 Henry Bergh and Elbridge T. Gerry chartered the Society for the Prevention of Cruelty to Children, the first such society in the world. Other cities, other countries, followed this example. The trend of the movement has been to do more than punish offenders. Emphasis is placed more and more on prevention. There are 443 of these protective societies in the United States, 201 of which are active enough to answer the White House inquiry for facts. Animal protection receives more help than the other. Organized child protection service is woefully inadequate to meet the needs. Depression, increase of illegitimate births, larger percentage of them among native-born than with immigrants, other causes, make the situation more serious than ever before. The compilers of this book summarize the pressing present needs in eight terse recommendations.

FIND THEM EARLY

AMONG the hundreds of children under school age studied by the Institute for Juvenile Research the beginning of disturbances in behavior which become serious difficulties in school were discovered. Psychologist Kawin[25] writes a monograph on the service the nursery school renders, the value of clinics, the education of parents in child care and summaries of adjustment of problem cases. She gives the results of special researches, tests for the younger children and a report of the preschool work of the Institute of Juvenile Research, of which she is director. A reprint, paper binding, of typical case studies, descriptions of nursery schools and clinics is available, 96 pp. at $1.00.

CIVILIZATION ROUND THE WORLD

KNAPP-FISHER is the author who wrote the popular outline of world history for boys and girls which is a scholarly account understood and enjoyed by young readers. He achieves a similar success in a new venture.[26] It is geography, history, people, government, civilization, life told with lively simplicity.

"Civilization began," says this narrator, "when two men agreed to work together on something which neither of them could do alone." The author, without preachiness, is a delightful missionary of this idea all through his sprightly descriptions of people, their customs and laws.

EARLIER JUVENILE PICTURE BOOKS

YOU may see many delighted thrills if you put among the available books in your school library Philip James' pictorial volume.[27] He writes an informative essay on the pioneer makers of children's books and follows it by 145 of the old pictures, seven of them in colors. Beginning with Comenius you have beautiful engravings of the eighteenth century, Robinson Crusoe, Sandford and Merton, Dick Whittington, Goody Two Shoes, the Mohawk Primer, the Rollo Books, Cock Robin, Mother Hubbard, the Colored Grammars, Rhymed Alphabets, and many others.

Among the artists represented are Kate Greenaway, Walter Crane, John Constable, the Cruikshanks, Caldecott, Edward Lear, Sir John Tenniel and the Bewicks. You'll need an extra copy for your art teacher.

GETTING ABOUT

SHIPS, steamers, railways, trains, roads, bridges, automobiles, balloons and aircraft glide through Mr. Webster's bright book or stand up for admiration.[28] He has made an attractive reader of these things for elementary grades. His manner is decidedly interesting. He has helped himself generously by descriptive pictures made expressly for this text.

A NEW AND LIVELY PROJECT

HERE is a cheery suggestion from the Lincoln School of Teachers College, Columbia University. The Parent-Teachers Association has printed a book telling what their city has to enliven your leisure time.[29] It lists hundreds

25 Ethel Kawin, "Children of Preschool Age." University of Chicago Press. 340 pp. $3.50.

26 H. C. Knapp-Fisher, "The Modern World: A Pageant of To-day." E. P. Dutton and Company, New York. 447 pp. $2.50.

27 Philip James, Edited by C. Geoffrey Holme, "Children's Books of Yesterday." Studio Publications, 131 4th Avenue, New York. 128 pp. Paper, $3.50; Cloth, $4.50.

28 Hanson Hart Webster, "Travel." Houghton Mifflin Company, Boston. 441 pp. $1.08.

29 Parent Teachers Association, "Spend Your Time." Teachers College Press, Columbia University, New York. 74 pp. $1.00.

of attractions, historic, dramatic, musical, artistic, literary, scientific, civic, industrial, commercial, scenic and recreative.

It strikes me that, even in the seemingly most barren locality blessed with a school, the preparation of a book, by children, parents and teachers, on the worth-while things near us would be an enlivening project cultivating observation, appreciation and community spirit. It could be illustrated, bound, repeated year by year, and kept in the archives. It ought to have some spirited chapters on town improvements needed and how they can be made.

SEX TALKS BY A PHYSICIAN

A MAGNIFICENT service to education is rendered by the American Medical Association in the issue of five handsome books by a talented physician writer and dealing with sex problems.[30] They carry the endorsement of the Bureau of Health and Public Instruction and are written by a teacher. It is personal and direct talk to boys and girls. I have already reviewed "In Training" in these pages. It is particularly for boys. "The Story of Life" is for both. High-school girls are addressed in "How Life Goes On and On," "Romance" is marriage information. "Diseases" is a correction of terrifying errors rife in the minds of thousands of supposedly intelligent people. The authority and the purpose behind these salutary booklets, the tone of the writing, their skilful handling of important themes schools have been afraid, too long, to touch, are warrant for getting the set into your school library. You know how eagerly they will be read.

UNHYPNOTIZED PROPOSALS FOR COLLEGE

THERE is plenty of erudition in President Frasier's short summary of what higher education is obligated to do.[31] The writer's direct manner of squeezing out of famous discourses on education the elixir suitable for the present distresses banishes dullness from his use of quotations.

Literary culture? It would be a glorious thing to instill. After many years of trial, says Dr. Frasier, you find that the old classics, so carefully taught, leave the graduate with no taste for them. He doesn't read Shakespeare. The educational graybeards of the college entrance board tell the high schools what to teach. The prescribed masterpieces are too musty to create reading habits in youth. The required science with its laboratory note-books is a waste of time. Everyday life is ignored.

The high-school curriculum, says Dr. Frasier, quoting President Butler and Harvard Dean Holmes, is dominated by college committees. It is meaningless educationally to the extent that it is influenced by college demands. The college curriculum is largely a persistence from the dark ages. The ignorance of college students as to the functions and care of the human body is appalling. There are colleges that still require their students to mull over algebra and Latin. God help these youngsters!

If the booklet did not name its author you would never believe it written by a college president. It seems like proposals of what not to do and what to do for young men and women spoken as a thinker would plan it if not hypnotized by previous presidential addresses.

AMERICAN GOVERNMENT FOR COLLEGIANS

"I SHALL do my best," promises Professor Johnson in a preliminary note at the beginning of his college text-book on American government,[32] "to humanize the subject." Promise fulfilled! From "the foundations" through "the New Deal" the book discusses problems in the style and language of a professor more desirous of interesting students than of displaying erudition. The author is no dogmatist. He buttresses conclusions with ample footnotes designating authority, book and page. The modernity of his references gives the work distinct timeliness.

Here is Professor Johnson's terse comment on one feature of school finance—the poorer districts have not property enough to raise taxes for adequate schooling. The larger unit, the state, needs to help. Who objects to this?

30 Truman B. Rice, M.D., "How Life Goes On and On," "The Story of Life," "In Training," "The Age of Romance," "The Venereal Diseases." American Medical Association, Chicago. About 40 pp. each. 25 cents the copy.

31 George Willard Frasier, "Objectives of Higher Education." Colorado State Teachers College Publications, Greeley. 24 pp. 25 cents.

32 Claudius O. Johnson, "Government in the United States." Thomas Y. Crowell Company, New York. 696 pp. $4.00.

The taxpayers in the richer communities. They say each township should educate its own children. This is a similar protest to the old one that each family should educate its own.

On knowledge of the anatomy of government Professor Johnson says it is not enough. Political hygiene must be added. You must know how much more there is to government than its written words. You must know its real processes and its trends. The essential thing is to keep an open mind. All life, to quote Justice Holmes, is an experiment, even the Constitution of the United States.

THE NEGRO IN COLLEGE

A NATIONAL survey of the social, economic, cultural, academic and intellectual status of Negro students in colleges and universities comes from the United States Office of Education.[33] The investigator-author believes Negro schools should make a more careful study of their students. He finds many facts of importance that should be considered by administrators and to produce decided changes in management.

THE BOOM IN ADULT EDUCATION

A FEELING that the crises of the times are too urgent to wait for another generation is pushing adult education faster than ever. Sixteen experienced students of adult service appear in a handy volume[34] issued by the American Country Life Association. Arts, religion, statesmanship, politics, economics figure in the farmer's movement for self-improvement. He is studying the means of preserving his right to live, cooperative merchandising, credit, industry and marketing. What is being done, what needs to be done, are both given extended attention in this informative book.

PALMER, WYETH AND THE ODYSSEY

SIX years ago the Houghton Mifflin Company brought out a sumptuous translation of the Odyssey at five dollars. In view of continuing demand and reduced incomes of us middle-classers, they are putting out an edition at half price. I don't see anything cheap in the new book.[35] The paper, type and binding are luxurious. The pictures are splendidly done. Professor Palmer, America's beloved man of letters, has been translating classics into beautiful English for years. In this epic he gets into a more direct and simple expression than has hitherto been judged admissible, but he maintains the dignity and beauty of the original.

Here is a bit. "And after the fair robed Nausicaa and the maidens had washed the clothes they spread the linen carefully on the shore where the water washed up the pebbles on the beach. Then, bathing themselves and anointing with oil, they presently took dinner on the river bank and waited for the clothes to dry in the sunshine. And when they were refreshed with food, the maids and she, they then began to play at ball, throwing their wimples off."

I think our present-day youngsters will not tire of Professor Palmer's speech as I am afraid I did of the more formal Worsley, whose Odyssey in my school days was found pretty heavy. Do you care to see the English clergyman and the Harvard professor side by side?

Worsley: "Thitherward sailing through the night we sped. Yea, some divinity the swift ships led through glooms not pierceable by power of eye. Round us the deep night air swung listless, dead." Palmer: "Here we sailed in, some god our guide, through murky night. There was no light to see, for round the ship was a dense fog. No moon shone out from heaven. It was shut in with clouds."

Artist Wyeth, painter of historic murals, illustrator of twenty classics, has sixteen glorious full-page pictures here in colors.

This is a book to fill the mind with rich memories.

AUDIENCE IS FEMININE

A MAN in a crowd thinks differently from the man alone. Women are not so. Each woman is the embodiment of the traits of the crowd. She, all by herself, is much more like a crowd than a man is. A man when alone must be convinced; you must reason with him. The woman is persuaded through her emotions rather than by appealing to reason. From this, when you stand before an audience, you may conclude that whatever would persuade the individual woman will persuade the audience.

This startling tip is from Professor John

[33] Ambrose Caliver, "A Background Study of Negro College Students." Superintendent of Documents, Washington. 132 pp. 10 cents.

[34] "Adult Education and Rural Life." University of Chicago Press. 153 pp. $2.00.

[35] George Herbert Palmer, translator; Newell C. Wyeth, illustrator, "The Odyssey of Homer." Houghton Mifflin Company, Boston. 314 pp. $2.50.

Pelsma's new work on speaking.[36] The author, professor of public speaking, Kansas State Teachers College, Pittsburg, develops the platform art from the basis of effect on an audience. Its size and nature must set your style. Professor Pelsma is a good teller of stories and is effective with them in clinching his point. Every person of ordinary intelligence, he says, can become a good reader and speaker. How? The book is the detailed and persuasive answer, covering the techniques of reading, conversation, sales talk, debate, platform service and radio broadcasting. Authority Gislason is not keen for the written and memorized speech; Authority Pelsma is. There you are. If you could put them on the same platform each could use from his own book the directions for debating and when it was all over you could say to either, as did Dominie Robert, answering James VI, "Your argument is conclusive but I hold as I did lang syne."

VERBOMANIA

Professor Huse, of the University of North Carolina, protests[37] from the top of Chapel Hill that the moronic quality of the everyday American is too dangerous to be neglected longer. This simple creature is subject to word magic. It lures him into buying what is bad for him, to throwing away his vote, to dissipating the natural strength of his mind, to talking and believing nonsense. He is hypnotized by words spoken or printed.

Learning to read is the most important act of education, almost synonymous with it. The problem of reading, like the problem of life, is to get free from the intellectual tyranny of the crowd, free from convention, free in belief and action, loose from the sounds and prestige of words. The reading which the schools teach is the conversion of symbols into sounds or into inner speech. The majority of people never learn to read in any other sense. The problem of intelligent reading is to retain consciousness, not to fall into hypnotic suggestibility.

In defense of this thesis, Dr. Huse writes a highly informative book full of interesting anecdote and pungent argument. He has disturbing chapters on verbomaniac education, the fairylands of advertising and eloquence, academic minds and criticism. He is grave and gay, caustic and sympathetic, scientific and popular, abounding in illustrations from your everyday experience.

THE WORK-BOOK HAS REACHED THE LIBRARY

Librarians and teachers will be grateful to Professor Lewis and Miss Lesser[38] for a time-saver in the form of a pupil's work book aimed at enjoyment of reading, improvement of study and familiarity with library facilities. The authors have a keen sense of entertainment. The youngsters who are put through the tasks will have much pleasure in solving the puzzles and mastering techniques of literary investigation. Each must name book-using skill he intends to develop. He is to make a card catalogue for himself, open new books so as not to injure their anatomy, make a graph of his own thirty details of personal and social traits and learn why a dictionary page has two columns. Ostensibly a guide for using books, it is a mental gymnasium giving practise in work habits. It is a course in English, in history, geography, science, manners and morals. It is consistent in its purpose and will achieve it unless the teacher babies the pupils by omitting some of the harder problems he never himself solved.

A BEDEVILED VIKING: STRINDBERG

Another of the "Great Lives" in the Macmillan series of short biographies, now reaching the number of twenty-four, is the turbulent career of Johan August Strindberg.[39] Here are sixty years of adventurous life: school teaching, medical studies, quarrels with professors, playwriting, painting, starving, newspapering, telegraphing, assisting in libraries, adoring other men's wives, attempting suicide, issuing Strindberg books that Strindberg announces should never have been written, attacking contemporaries, hating Ibsen, opposing the movements for women's rights, outlawed as a blackguard, obsessed with a persecution complex and working prodigiously on a time schedule upon books, plays and essays which have brought Sweden to

[36] John R. Pelsma, "Essentials of Speech." Thomas Y. Crowell Company, New York. 344 pp. $2.00.

[37] H. R. Huse, "The Illiteracy of the Literate." D. Appleton-Century Company, New York. 273 pp. $2.00.

[38] E. E. Lewis, Goldie D. Lesser, "Adventures with Books and Libraries." American Book Company, New York. 196 pp. 40 cents.

[39] G. A. Campbell, "Strindberg." The Macmillan Company, New York. 143 pp. 75 cents.

acclaim him as her greatest writer and a mighty force in the world of letters. He, when a child, told a religious woman he would rather be a genius than one of God's chosen. He had his wish, along with a brutal and vindictive life full of rancor, bitterness, vice and tragedy. Mr. Campbell's account uses Strindberg's autobiography as the main source and makes you pretty fully acquainted with a bewildering personality.

PHELPSIANA

In Professor Phelps's[40] anthology of prose he takes things, not because it is commonly believed they should be in a selection of prose writings, but because he personally enjoys reading them. He has made a book not for instruction but for delight. It is not a text-book, though a teacher who cares more for literature than for statistics can use it with profit. It is 718 pages of entertainment, edification and culture in the words of more than 100 authors from Solomon to Ring Lardner, with conversational comment by this much beloved teacher.

It is a good companion for the train-trip, for the night season, for the half hours a day that can make the cultivated man

A COUNSELLOR FOR READERS

Mr. W. E. Simnett's "Books and Reading," published in England in 1926, met so cordial a reception in its various editions that an American publishing house[41] asked Librarian Drury, of Nashville, to adapt it for American readers. It contains bright talks on the pleasures of reading, the habit, methods, the use of libraries, adult education, how to form a private library and fourteen chapters of surveys of literature. These discuss books of all sorts each after its kind. It is a valuable handbook for librarians and teachers.

CONRAD AS A TEXT IN ENGLISH

Professor Cushwa[42] has selected from the works of Joseph Conrad those parts in which the appeal is fairly universal. From Conrad's fiction the selections are those in which skill in narration is preeminent. The author's life and personality are shown in extracts from his autobiography and letters. Professor Cushwa, who, by the way, has a chair of English in Phillips Exeter Academy, adds questions, topics for discussion and further study, references, a glossary and recommendations for other readings.

SINCLAIR LEWIS AS A SCHOOL TEXT

Harcourt, Brace and Company offer "Arrowsmith"[43] with suggestions for study, a biographical sketch and questions leading to an independent appreciation of the author and to an estimate of his talent. Along with direct inquiry to the student as to what he thinks of this or that characterization, the editor has brought in many comments of literary critics in such a way as to lead to the discussion she wishes.

This venture is a fine answer to the criticism that the usual high-school literature is far off the field of books that are read by Americans not in school.

SCIENCE IN FASCINATING STYLE

A bar of magnesium light enough to be carried by one man will support an automobile. It is one of the lightest of metals by itself or alloyed with others. Its use in aviation and in building makes its production sought in rapidly increasing quantities. Its manufacture has been a long series of trouble. Only one American company has outlived the failures of experimentation in producing magnesium. Problems piled up, until solving them was generally abandoned. In Germany a process was devised that was commercially profitable. The product was exported to the United States in such quantities as to threaten American attempts to manufacture the metal. But one company here hung on and is now producing magnesium 99.9 per cent. pure. Its price has tumbled from $5.00 a pound in 1915, to $1.00 a pound in 1924, 48 cents in 1930, to 30 cents in 1931, when over a million pounds were made. Dr. Mantell's book[44] abounds with interesting facts like this. He is a consulting engineer in Pratt Institute, Brooklyn. He is one of the authors of the Williams and Wilkins series of one-dollar books devoted to describing the progress of science up to the immediate present. They cover astronomy, an-

40 William Lyon Phelps, "What I Like." Charles Scribner's Sons, New York. 718 pp. $2.75.

41 Francis K. W. Drury, "What Books Shall I Read?" Houghton Mifflin Company, Boston. 327 pp. $2.50.

42 Frank W. Cushwa, "An Introduction to Conrad." Doubleday, Doran, and Company, Garden City, New York. 436 pp. $1.25.

43 Barbara Grace Spayd, Editor, "Arrowsmith by Sinclair Lewis." Harcourt, Brace and Company, New York. 489 pp. $1.00.

44 C. L. Mantell, "Sparks from the Electrode." The Williams and Wilkins Company, Baltimore. 199 pp. $1.00.

thropology, automobile engineering, bacteriology, biophysics, chemistry, communication, animal life and social growth, entomology, evolution, eugenics, geology, medicine, industry, mathematics, mining, physics, aviation, electricity and psychology, one volume to each.

Dr. Mantell gives in plain words for the untechnical reader the story of electrical power in the production of metals, the harnessing of Niagara, aluminum, carborundum, copper, stainless steel, chromium and other modern metals. The combination of scientific exactness with the fascination of human adventure and persistence gives the books of the series unique attraction for readers, young and old.

GENERAL SCIENCE AND THE SOUND CINEMA

The idea of using motion pictures as an aid of teaching is attractive. It is novel, it seems progressive. But in these hard times we must have better reasons. Mr. Rulon experiments with it and checks with careful testing.[45] His book, besides showing a superiority of 20.5 per cent. of results with the sound-pictures over the efficiency of general-science teaching without them, contains so much on methods of teaching as to be a valuable addition to any junior or senior high-school library.

ART FOR CHILDREN

In one of his popular lectures the school people's favorite, Lorado Taft, demonstrates a reason why many other nations have a refined artistic taste more universal than ours. The children see artistic creations in greater abundance. Master story-teller Hillyer[46] worked for several years, trying his lessons on the children of the Calvert School until he had a history of art they understood and enjoyed. The Appleton-Century Company has issued these as a book of supreme beauty. Each period of painting, sculpture and architecture is covered in short, spicy chapters with engaging animation. More than half the book is concerned with the art of the present epoch. The pictures are beautifully reproduced and are generously abundant.

ON THE RATING OF DRAWINGS

Among the Johns Hopkins University studies in education I notice an ingenious work-out of a scale for measuring free-hand drawing, the work of two researchers.[47] Using art merchants, art graduates, artists and art teachers as raters of drawings from a dozen cities the investigators reasoned out their conclusions, which you will find of significance pertinent to the direction of public schools. A wealth of fertile observations on drawing in school enlivens the monographs.

BECOMING A MUSICAL NATION

At some teachers' conventions I have met Sigmund Spaeth. He is a favorite on their programs. He is both a trained musician and a speaker who is able to make us amateurs understand what have been to us previously the mysteries of music. In his latest book[48] he writes as he talks. He introduces you to music that has proved its permanent value and to many pieces that have won wide popularity. He pays most attention to music that is heard from the radio or is available in records. There is no point in trying to create interest in what is inaccessible. He generally disregards biographical details. They are not music. The appreciation of a work has no more to do with the life of the composer than the enjoyment of baseball has to do with the private affairs of Babe Ruth.

Enjoyment of music is primarily, he says, an instinct that can be stopped by turning the matter into too hard a task. The study of how others have increased their appreciation may give you the art of listening with zest.

In the last few years music-appreciation classes have permeated even the one-room schools in the far corners. The everyday classroom teacher is called upon to turn on the record and help the children listen with the best advantage. The important questions asked in the lesson are, "Do you like this piece?" "What do you like about it?" "Why?" Spaeth's help to worthwhile answers is generous and sane. He treats of time, rhythms, melody, harmony, tone color, form, the patterns of musical composition,

45 Phillip Justin Rulon, "The Sound Motion Picture in Science Teaching." Harvard University Press, Cambridge. 236 pp. $2.50.

46 V. M. Hillyer, E. G. Huey, "A Child's History of Art." D. Appleton-Century Company, New York. 443 pages. $3.50.

47 Linus Ward Kline, Gertrude L. Carey, "A Measuring Scale for Free-Hand Drawing." Representation. 101 pp. $2.00. Design and Composition. 82 pp. $1.75. Johns Hopkins Press, Baltimore.

48 Sigmund Spaeth, "The Art of Enjoying Music." Whittlesey House. McGraw Hill Book Company, New York. 451 pp. $2.50.

songs, operas, instruments and other things, genially, brightly, understandingly. Sic semper Spaeth.

THE WOUNDED AND SLAIN OF THE FOOTBALL FIELD

A HEAD coach, joining with an orthopedic surgeon,[49] finds the death toll of fifty players in one year paid by football to be alarming. The book of these two experts is concerned with prevention and treatment of injuries. The authors stand solidly for football played for fun. They consider the grind, the bumps and the bruises worthwhile education for the youth of the country in the art of how "to take it" and "to hand it out" in a sportsmanlike manner. The majority of football coaches, according to our authors, have never seen a football fatality.

The contents include training and physical equipment, therapy, types of injury: three damages to the head, four to the face, nine to eyes, ears and throat, six to neck and cervix, nine to shoulder, seven to arm and elbow, and so on, ninety-eight in all, with discussions upon the degree of injury. There are hundreds of pictures of actions on the field, with the danger of each explained. There is a glossary, statistics of injuries, a table showing the number of hurts and number of days lost as the result of each kind of play.

There are five pages tabulating the fatalities of 1931, 2 giving the names of the dead, the match, the play, the treatment and the number of days lived after the injury.

THE PRESSING PROBLEM OF THE MOTION PICTURE

THE PAYNE-FUND investigation of motion pictures[50] has brought out four more of the attractively printed and bound books of their series.

[49] Marvin A. Stevens, M.D., Winthrop M. Phelps, M.D., "The Control of Football Injuries." A. S. Barnes and Company, New York. 241 pp. $3.00.

[50] Ruth C. Peterson, L. L. Thurstone, "Motion Pictures and the Social Attitudes of Children," with Frank K. Shuttleworth, Mark A. May, "Social Conduct and Attitudes of Movie Fans." 217 pp. $1.50. Herbert Blumer, "Movies and Conduct." 257 pp. $1.50. Herbert Blumer, Philip M. Hauser, "Movies, Delinquency, and Crime." 233 pp. $1.50. Perry W. Holiday, George D. Stoddard, "Getting Ideas from the Movies," with W. W. Charters "Motion Pictures and Youth." 168 pp. $1.50. The Macmillan Company, New York.

The Peterson-Thurstone investigation, with the cooperation of a score of superintendents and principals and with the aid of a dozen theater managers, selected films for the purpose of testing their influence on children's attitudes toward the Germans, war, gambling, crime, Chinese, capital punishment and the Negro. The results are given by diagrams and statistics.

Shuttleworth and May, by means of ballots, question blanks and other tests tabulate the social attitudes and conduct of children who frequent the motion picture houses and of those who do not.

The Blumer study takes up the influence of movies on children's play, manners, dress, fright, spirits, grief, control, sex emotions and ideals of life.

Holiday and May test the retention of specific information given by different films, plot and incident, as tested for different ages and sexes. They suggest school utilization of different facts found.

Blumer and Houser tested hundreds of school children, also men and women in prisons and reformatories. They assured anonymity so as to secure as honest responses as possible. They show the per cents. of respondents who attribute their criminal careers to suggestions received from motion pictures. They reproduce statements of how the desires for easy money, luxuries, wild parties, excitement, sex gratification, etc., were stimulated by the screen. The frequency with which men take girls and women to "hot" motion-picture exhibitions so as to debauch them afterward is astounding, as are the "confessions" of high-school and college students. The investigators avoid letting indignation show in their reports. It is all very statistical, with per cents. and caution against assuming more than the evidence contains.

Summarizing the series, Dr. Charters explains the organization of the research, the selection of the sociologists, psychologists and school men as investigators. His outlines of all the studies are illuminating; his conclusions, decidedly important. The sex-stuff, the crime, the excitement, all too common on the screen, are not good for school children. The exhibitors do not grasp the child problem. They show pictures indiscriminately to an audience consisting of minors and adults. But the pictures are made for grown-ups. Theoretically the adult is a free agent. But children must be protected. The motion-picture audience contains two children to one adult. Exclusion of children is clearly out of the question. Institutions which would produce pictures for children in special theaters or on special days in regular hours is one solution, perhaps.

Publishers of books have shown that "juveniles" pay. The Payne-Fund studies do not furnish solutions. They state the facts. These are nothing less than tragic. They will stimulate discussion and should provoke action. Good Lord! Are we the people to see science in photography debauching the generation and invention bringing munitions to the point of world annihilation in war?

WHO THAT HATH EYES TO SEE

A REFRESHING sprightliness marks the new Appleton-Century book on eyesight.[51] This is one of this house's popular health series, now grown to 23 volumes. Some startling facts are given in this work. School easily is responsible for defects of vision that hamper people all their lives. Clear and ample presentation by the authors explain why this sad fact is true and how the present generation of superintendents, architects and teachers may avoid continuing the serious damage heretofore done.

With explanatory diagrams the authors explain why the eye in childhood and youth is more likely to become deranged than later. There are unusual chapters on eye happiness in the home, the eye and energy, the eye a health barometer, the eye and personality, woman's eyes, fooling and pleasing with the eye, etc. Even the best make-up for the upper eyelid, depending on what your complexion is, is not omitted.

WHEN YOU TALK IT OVER

MR. WALSER, who has had to get things done through agreements of many minds, writes a book on group discussions.[52] He treats of these when composed of persons who think alike or not at all, of talk when minds are in conflict, when school classes consider plans, when employers meet workers, when women draw up protests, etc. He advises on planning, managing and getting harmony. This present revolution, the question of government getting justice for all, the function of conference in these disturbing times, are treated at length.

MIND THE LIVING ROOM

A CURIOUS, rather startling, but when you come to study it, pretty reasonable basis for estimating your social status by the sort of living-room you maintain is elaborated in Stuart Chapin's recent booklet[53] on measuring your grade in the social scale. The living room correlates so closely with your various factors of social importance that a measurer is fairly accurate if he looks no farther. What is in it, how clean and in what repair the contents are, also other tell-tale things of this room, are estimated here in a style so reasonable and accurate that you will again feel wonder at the progress measurement is making. The living room tells what you are. I wonder whether this idea might not be expanded to the possibility that fitting up a living room to the standard of a cultivated person and keeping it so might help you to become more refined. You know some good-natured housewives who should be consigned an hour a day to such a room.

MEASURING THE MEASURER

ANOTHER interesting Minnesota contribution to the same field is a scale for estimating social case workers.[54] This is a rate-sheet on courage, honesty, tact, adaptability, patience and other qualities analyzed into very interesting particulars and compiled from the judgments of a large number of persons responsible for social service. Superintending a system, managing a school, teaching a class, are social services, aren't they? After reading the recent survey by Messrs. Deffenbaugh and Zeigel on your lack of essential knowledge of the qualifications of teachers you hire and retain, this Minnesota scale will give you some superior suggestions.

[51] Olive Grace Henderson, Hugh Grant Rowell, M.D., ''Good Eyes for Life.'' D. Appleton-Century Company, New York. 202 pp. $2.00.

[52] Frank Walser, ''The Art of Conference.'' Harper and Brothers. 305 pp. $3.00.

[53] F. Stuart Chapin, ''Measurement of Social Status.'' University of Minnesota Press, Minneapolis. 16 pp. 25 cents.

[54] University of Minnesota, ''Leahy-Fenlason Scale for Social Case Workers.'' Minneapolis. 3 pp. 10 cents: $2.00 per hundred.

SCHOOL AND SOCIETY

WITH WHICH ARE COMBINED THE EDUCATIONAL REVIEW, ESTABLISHED IN 1891, THE TEACHERS MAGAZINE, ESTABLISHED IN 1878, AND THE SCHOOL JOURNAL, ESTABLISHED IN 1874.

J. McKEEN CATTELL AND ALFRED L. HALL-QUEST

EDITORIAL COMMUNICATIONS SHOULD BE ADDRESSED TO THE EDITORS OF SCHOOL AND SOCIETY, 3941 GRAND CENTRAL TERMINAL, NEW YORK, N. Y.

Volume 39 SATURDAY, MAY 12, 1934 Number 1011

EDUCATION AND THE PREVENTION OF CRIME[1]

By Dr. ROYAL S. COPELAND

U. S. SENATOR FROM NEW YORK; CHAIRMAN U. S. SENATE COMMITTEE ON CRIME

ANY member of the United States Senate would be flattered by an invitation to speak to this group. I say this because the National Education Association is representative of what in many respects is the most important profession practised by men and women.

We have chosen in America to turn over to the school teachers not only those duties which are naturally theirs, but also many of the functions which should be performed in the home. We have come to expect the teacher to instruct our children in manners, personal hygiene, social etiquette and the household arts. We expect the teacher to give by precept and example that moral and ethical training which in other times was imparted by the home and the church.

Certain recent experiences of my own have given me a growing belief that America must lean still more heavily upon the school teacher. As chairman of a committee appointed by the United States Senate to investigate crime, it has been my duty to listen to the testimony of hundreds of witnesses. What we have learned centers upon one point—the necessity of preventing juvenile delinquency. To accomplish this, the schools can do more than all other agencies within public control.

The importance of what I shall have to say to you is emphasized by the statistics of crime. In the United States to-day the average age of the criminal is 23 years. The largest age group is found at 19 and the next largest group at 18. The seeds of moral delinquency, sown and grown during school age, develop into evil plants, the fruits of which are publicly displayed by boys and girls long before maturity of their minds and bodies.

In saying these things to this particular group, I am not unmindful that the members of your association have long been concerned over the problems which crime presents. I am aware of the serious thought you have given this subject and am acquainted with your research bulletin on "Crime Prevention through Education," published in 1932, and your "Tenth Yearbook on Character Education," published in the same year.

I am depending on your wide background of knowledge to fill in an outline of the facts for which I have but brief space. I must trust your trained imaginations to supply the details, depending upon

[1] Address before the General Session, Department of Superintendence, National Education Association, Cleveland, Ohio, February 28, 1934.

your proven patriotism and loyalty to perfect and carry out some such plan as the one I shall propose.

First let me present a brief statement of fact: From several sources, apparently authoritative estimates of the cost of crime, it appears to total approximately one fourth of our national income. This sum, as is pointed out in your bulletin, exceeds by at least three times our total expenditures for education. We can agree, I believe, that the cost of crime in money and in reduced morality of the people is devastating beyond computation.

You know better than I how much the situation has been aggravated by recent publicity given the activities within the law of certain metropolitan bankers, utility heads and business executives. Such infractions of the moral law reported by the press are dramatic presentations which must have undermined the public morale and the morals of many individuals. Your minds will quickly jump to acts within your own knowledge, where perhaps there may have been smaller monetary losses, but which are equally distressing examples of that lack of the sense of trusteeship and general public spirit which should characterize men of affairs. The anti-social conduct of persons operating within the law, ruthlessly exploiting the economic resources of the public, has inflamed the minds and emotions of criminals and of weaklings. Recognized as one of the major causes of our economic condition, those acts have added to the general social unrest.

In short, the factors that have acted to promote criminality have been added to of late because of economic conditions and what the average man believes is the chief cause of our economic distress. No matter how we approach the problem, we surely must agree that the menace of anti-social behavior and actual crime is greater than ever before.

Where does crime begin? The answer to that question will determine what we should do about it. While there are many causes, no doubt, yet there will be no dispute of the thesis that the perfect home should develop the perfect character. Most of us regard character building as the primary responsibility of the home. But, if I may jump to my conclusion on this point, I am forced to recognize that there is no immediate hope of greatly improving the home conditions of those who may later follow criminal careers. To accomplish this end is a long range process.

We think of the church as having a heavy responsibility in character building. But as regards this, I can criticize no church except my own. For any except my own denomination, I have no right to comment upon the adequacy of its character building program or to make recommendations for the extension of its work. I will say of my own denomination that I believe there is much more it should be doing. But whatever the churches may do in the future, we can not turn to them for an immediate and major attack on the problem of crime. I pause only long enough to express confidence that the church will lend support to a well-planned program of prevention.

This brings me to the schools. It is an old custom, familiar to you, to carry to the doorstep of the school all the problems that can not be solved in the home or elsewhere in the community. To blame the schools and the teachers appears to be one of the diversions of the American people. But it is not in this spirit that I approach the subject under discussion.

I could devote my available time to reviewing the forces which have tended to transfer from the home to the school almost the entire responsibility for the welfare of children. To you this is a well-known story. But when I turn my thoughts to what the schools can and should do in the matter before us, I have been wondering how the public would respond to a new plan. What would happen to a proposal that the public schools assume the responsibility for a basic crime prevention program?

In face of the alarming facts about crime and the growing anti-social conduct within the law, may not the public be wondering what has happened and why? How many are inquiring how such a state of affairs has come to pass in a country that has so liberally supported schools for the express purpose of insuring good citizenship?

Personally, of course, I do not place upon the American public school system primary responsibility for this crisis. But what shall we say in reply to those who charge the public schools with a share of the blame?

The report and a digest of the hearings of our Senate subcommittee will soon be off the press and they contain pointed discussions of this question. I want to refer you to this report for comments on the merits of the public school record of past performance. Whatever may be your own conclusions, I know you are ready to face the issue of your future responsibilities in this field, and of course it is the future alone that we can do anything about, whether in the line of your duty or mine.

One of the questions I want to ask you to-day is this: Does the habit of appraising the results of schools in terms of intellectual achievement and manual skill have anything or everything to do with our trouble?

To define clearly what I mean I want to make reference to two recent publications: First, the committee of the American Association of University Professors, in its report issued last May, stated that the purpose of college teaching is to "induce self-propelled intellectual activity on the part of the student." The second reference is to a report of the Commission on the Social Studies, entitled, "A Charter for the Social Sciences in the Schools," drafted by Charles A. Beard. This is intended to emphasize the value of scholarship and skill in scientific method as a primary dominating objective. This point of view is epitomized on the 99th page of the report, which I quote:

"All the way through the schools the process may be followed, *ever sharpening the mind* [the italics are mine] by increasing the complexity of the situations about which questions are asked and of the materials necessary to correct answers, rising steadily in the complexity and abstraction of the subjects considered."

The words "character," "conduct," "behavior," "attitude" and "emotions" do not appear in Beard's index. His discussion of character and the process of character building are limited to a few sentences in the closing pages of his 117-page "Charter." These two reports, financed by large foundations, seem to represent the point of view of orthodox leadership of our higher educational institutions.

Is it proper for me to ask: Have not educators tended to define the job of the schools in terms of developing tool skill and of mastering content? Have they not placed remarkable emphasis upon "sharpening the minds" of those who are to be the lawyers and the executives of the future, as well as the minds of the average run of us who pass through the school system?

Has not the habit of appraising the results of schools in terms of intellectual achievement and manual skill tended to produce a citizenry with sharpened wits and skilled craftsmanship, rather than a realizing sense of social obligation and good citizenship? Has not our attention been too sharply focused on mastery of the scientific method to the exclusion of the personal and social needs of the masses of our children?

Let me turn from this questioning process a moment to say this: Sometimes the scientist becomes so engrossed in what he sees in the microscope that he fails to lift his eye from the instrument to gaze upon the wide world about him. Other scientists may become so militant as regards their theories that they engage in wordy battle to worst their opponents. So many of these contests are going on at the same time that those of us who are onlookers are worn out in our efforts to see the whole show. Our brains no longer function as they should and we begin to suffer from a sort of creeping paralysis. In consequence, we become incapable of accurate estimate of the value of the theories proposed.

I have asked what I intended to be pointed questions regarding problems which to me as a layman are not being solved by the intelligentsia—and I use that word with perfect respect. But in all candor, I believe they are shooting over the target.

We must take society as it is. Our program of education must be suited to the requirements and capabilities of each boy and girl, according to individual need. In view of this self-evident truth, it may be fortunate that the many and no doubt brilliant suggestions of educational literature have met no more than languid and ephemeral intellectual acceptance. Far be it from me to criticize, but in humility of spirit I contend that there is something in education more vital than sharpening the mind.

Undoubtedly many ideas in education, now considered too advanced, will find a place in the practise of the schools of the future. It is to be expected that there should exist some lag between the time of general acceptance of a policy, program or principle and its complete incorporation into practise.

Even though the program I present today may be approved by you, it will take time to appraise its value. But certainly as regards past objectives, has there not been an excessive lag in the field of education? Even though this exists in public education, it is also true in home training, in parent education, in the efforts of the church, and in the work of character-building agencies. But these last institutions are outside your field. Certainly your desire is to define the objectives of teaching and to realize them as soon as possible.

I want to refer next to the 1932 Bulletin No. 17, Monograph No. 13 of the U. S. Department of the Interior, Bureau of Education, entitled "Provisions for Individual Differences, Marking and Promotion." This monograph reports a study covering the efforts of the secondary schools to break away from traditional practises and to adjust their programs to individual needs. This report appears to indicate that there is a tremendous desire to do something about the problem of the differences in individuals. But in this report I have found grounds to warrant another question. It is this: Have not the standardizing agencies of the past and the rigid requirements for college entrance made well-nigh impossible real progress in meeting the needs of the average student?

My attention was recently called to an interesting innovation made by Superintendent Herbert S. Weet and inaugurated just before his retirement from the public schools of Rochester, N. Y. Dr. Weet has been active in your body for so many years that I am confident he is known and loved by all of you.

Dr. Weet has provided for two groupings, (a) in accordance with individual ability and (b) a marking system which undertakes to recognize five major areas of desired results, including character building and habits. I note, however, that in his system promotion is decided solely on the marks in tool subjects, such as spelling, arithmetic and geography.

I hope no one will read into my remarks the slightest inclination to criticize any teacher, any parent, any social worker or any clergyman for the emphasis placed upon the scientific method, upon objective thinking or other methods of procedure. Anything I might say is necessarily no more than the general opinion of a layman anxious to be helpful. My purpose is to stimulate your interest and to cause you to focus your attention upon what I personally regard as important—a restudy of the objectives of education.

Perhaps the examples I have given are sufficient preface to a preliminary concrete suggestion dealing with a way in which the public schools can help in a major attack on the prevention of crime. The suggestion calls for a thorough-going application of a particular one of the many generally accepted proposals, with which you are familiar, a proposal which, because of the lag I have mentioned, has not yet been adopted into universal practise.

Nearly ten years ago Dr. Ben D. Wood, of Columbia University, proposed the adoption of a continuous record card for general use in the public school system. The plan for a continuous record has been promoted by various agencies, including the American Council on Education. Many individuals have urged its adoption.

Professor Wood early proposed that the school record should include, not only the classroom grades, but also a behavior record, so designed as to disclose the blossoming character of the child. Such a behavior record has been demonstrated and greatly improved in the practise of the Rochester Athenaeum.

If the system is used, as I believe it should be in every community, the public schools will have placed every child under expert observation. The child who shows anti-social tendencies may then be given special attention and such treatment as the individual case requires. Under this system, prevention of crime can be undertaken in time to produce results. You can readily imagine the far-reaching effects if the character-building agencies of the community collaborate energetically with the schools in helping suspected pre-delinquents to achieve normal adjustment.

Of course, it is not enough merely to start upon another campaign of record-making. Attics and basements are filled with "reports" and material which its fond authors thought to be of such importance that it might sometime be studied, formulated and made of practical use. Holding the same idea, the United States Government is erecting what is called the "Archives Building." It occupies an entire square on Pennsylvania Avenue in Washington. This is to be used to store papers, some of them valuable no doubt, but many of them worthless trash.

If the behavior reports were to be filed in cabinets somewhere, in order that a statistically inclined person might use them some time, I should not be interested. Such reports are invaluable, provided their significance is immediately recognized. If a pupil in the schools has habits of thought or tendencies which may become anti-social in their nature, there should be instituted at once an inquiry to determine what is wrong and what if anything can be done about it.

To this end, there must be set up in connection with every school system a means of immediate treatment of the child who appears to need it. Surely in every community there are enough general medical practitioners, dentists, psychiatrists, specialists and surgeons, also trained psychologists and social workers, who will gladly examine the child and give the school authorities the needed help to determine a course of action.

The thought I have in mind is that the behavior card will carry a warning that there is danger along the path of progress of this particular pupil. It may be a red light, indicating the necessity to "stop, look and listen." If it serves to attract attention to the need of treatment and, if as a result of collaboration with these scientific consultants, the child is returned to mental and physical health, our first purpose has been accomplished.

But important as the use of the behavior record will be with the problem child, its use is vastly more important with all the rest of the pupils. My good friend, Dr. Eugene A. Colligan, president of Hunter College, has supplied me with an excellent manuscript relating to teacher guidance in conducting character education in the public school system of New York. These guides suggest a thoroughly sound program of day-to-day instruction.

In taking over the guidance of a new pupil, however, the teacher is at great disadvantage without a history of the child's behavior in the earlier grades. As I view the problem, behavior records promise to do for the practise of the teacher in the field of character building what records have done for the doctor in his practise. Except in case of emergency, no surgeon would think of operating unless he had studied the case records of the patient. The reports of what the attending physicians have found in the past will help the surgeon to do a good job and perhaps be the determining factor as to what shall be undertaken.

These references to the behavior record system pave the way for another question: Is it possible to do vastly better in character building than we are now doing?

If you answer in the affirmative, there remains the question as to how we shall break through the restraints that have stood in the way of progress in this field. How must we go about our task if we are to make full use of the available knowledge and experience at our command?

As a first movement in a major attack let us secure from the public a new mandate. Let us have new specifications of the results expected from public education or a restatement of objectives. I believe that in drawing these specifications there must be written in large letters certain primary conditions. We expect results in character and in everything that is essential to good citizenship, rather than results measured chiefly in terms of facts learned or in terms of pure intellectual activity or sharpened minds. If you agree with me, I am prepared to join with you in an effort to win general acceptance of a public policy redefined in such terms as I have stated.

The National Government may assemble facts which will be helpful in the formulation of a general policy in education. Let it be borne in mind, however, that the states never delegated to the Federal Government any legislative or administrative authority in the field of education. Under our states rights doctrine, the acceptance of a new policy and of action under such a policy must be left to voluntary cooperation.

In order to have an agency to coordinate such volunteer efforts and to assist in the work of our Senate Subcommittee on Crime, we have formed an advisory body known as the Education and Law Conference. The plan of organization of the conference assumes that its members will all be voluntary, non-official, unpaid workers.

We are in process of organizing an advisory committee and several technical committees. Through these we hope to carry on the work of the conference. The members of these technical committees will be selected from experts known to be free to actively participate in the work of the conference. For example: Professor Ben. D. Wood has accepted the chairmanship of our committee on records and Professor W. W. Charters the chairmanship of our committee on instructional materials. Other committees will be organized as the plan proceeds.

If we agree upon the wisdom of such an organization, we need to consider a second step. Sane practical measures must be taken to develop in practise a full expression of a new American policy in education. Such measures should be evolved as will not interfere with present-day essential educational practise and without reduction in efficiency in providing the pupils with the tools of literacy. It is particularly important in these days of economic stress, too, not to unduly increase the cost of the schools. But the desired results can not be attained unless the plan is so stated as to catch the imagination of every community and command its respect and voluntary cooperation.

To make a clinical test, to use the words of my profession, and to demonstrate the type of development proposed, Dr. Ballou, superintendent of the Washington schools, is arranging to initiate the proposed plan in the District of Columbia. This will involve evolution in many areas. You can see that he must face problems in administration, records, individual instruction, materials of instruction, training teachers in service, adult classes and evening classes. In community contacts there will be a new relationship to the movies, the press, the facilities for recreation, the Church, the Juvenile Courts, children organizations, and many more.

In the furtherance of Dr. Ballou's development, the American Council on Education and the Education and Law Conference have set up a joint committee for the coordination of community effort in making this development a success. Under this arrangement the technical committees of the Education and Law Conference serve in an advisory capacity only. The local joint committee functioning as a committee of the American Council has assumed the responsibility for all operating activities.

I have given you the details of this set-up because I want you to see how we are proposing to face, not only the local conditions, but the deep-rooted traditions of states rights and local autonomy. The most that may be claimed for the Federal Government in such a matter is that it is the function of the Congress to do what it can for the people under the General Welfare Clause of our Constitution.

Our experience with prohibtion has reminded us that it is futile to attempt to modify the practises of our people in major activities through constitutional amendment and federal legislation. Just as the operation of bringing about temperance in America rests upon the educational agencies of our country, so the building of character and good citizenship is more dependent upon volunteer cooperation than upon laws.

It has seemed necessary for the success of Dr. Ballou's project to seek general public approval of his plan and also the approval and cooperation of the colleges and universities in the district, the churches, the so-called character-building agencies, the welfare agencies and all the rest of the agencies which you know from experience affect operations of the public school system. I hope the procedure proposed for the District of Columbia will be followed in each state. A new deal in education must grow from the seeds of progressive ideas and ideals which have been so generally planted locally by you and other leaders in the past.

The agencies of informal education must have a large place in any consideration of this subject. For example, the newspapers, motion pictures and the radio make a daily impression on the majority of our people. That the combined influence of these agencies is growing more constructive requires only a comparison of the releases of a decade ago with those of the present. Here, as in other areas of education, the path of progress is through cooperative study and action, and I hope these agencies will join in using for this purpose the Education and Law Conference.

Because I place such complete dependence upon voluntary cooperation, I have concluded there is needed only one general legislative enactment by the Congress. In consequence, I have introduced in the Senate a bill which is intended to serve two purposes:

First, it is intended to establish privilege status in the courts for teachers and their behavior records of the Ben Wood type—records which I hope will eventually be established for every child of school age in this land.

And second, I hope this bill will establish, so far as the Federal Government is concerned, the professional status of the teacher as parallel with and comparable in its dignity and authority to that of the doctor and clergyman.

If this proposed act meets with your approval, I trust you will join the movement to see that it is also written into the statutes of the forty-eight states. Support of such legislation assumes that you are ready to support my major thesis, which is that we must redefine the desired objectives of education.

If you do support this thesis, I repeat:

We must secure, from the public, support for a restatement of what should be the American policy as to the desired results of education in terms of character and citizenship, as well as content. We must secure from higher educational institutions an emancipation from the requirements for college entrance in so far as they in fact interfere with the legitimate efforts to achieve results in terms of a newly defined public policy. If this policy is adopted, the colleges themselves may well go through a period of soul searching as to the possibility of their own need of readjusting their practises.

To these ends I bespeak your voluntary cooperation, both in the general support of the Education and Law Conference and in the work of its education committees, in fostering joint projects initiated in the spirit of the proposed District of Columbia project. If by this means we can make a successful attack upon juvenile delinquence, the next generation will bless us for our efforts. If we succeed in deepening the public spirit of our students and developing that high sense of trusteeship which will stand the test during the competitive actions of later life, we shall have saved the nation from a repetition of the alarming disclosures of vicious conduct in high places. We shall have had a large part, too, in giving to America the leading place in moral as well as technical education.

LAISSEZ FAIRE VERSUS PLANNING IN EDUCATIONAL RESEARCH

By Dr. GEORGE W. HARTMANN
PENNSYLVANIA STATE COLLEGE

A PARADOXICAL situation confronts us in current educational research activities. On the one hand, we have developed or borrowed a reasonably systematic methodology of investigation which is capable of being applied or adapted to almost any type of problem; yet on the other, we utilize the most haphazard of ways for singling out the problems worthy of such techniques. There is law and order in the manner of solving issues and only irrational chance in determining the ones to be solved. We have at our disposal beautifully organized means for the accumulation and treatment of data, with the most paltry of devices for establishing significant topics to serve as points of departure. In short, our technology is admirable, but our philosophy is contemptible.

At present only two policies are commonly

used by research directors in guiding graduate students toward thesis or dissertation problems. According to one procedure, the hopeful amateur is smilingly invited to indicate his field of interest and encouraged to formulate his own "spontaneously" developed ideas, while the professor in charge limits himself to pointing out the inherent difficulties or practicability of the various suggestions which are "student-originated." This scheme has all the advantages of a democratic and progressive type of education. It credits the student with a high measure of intellectual maturity and potentiality, and permits a nice adaptation to individual differences on the basis of strong personal interest. This method also bears the benediction of most educational psychologists and is eminently suitable to the traditional American spirit, for it seems to represent the easiest way of cumulating those "small advantages" which we prize so highly. Its chief danger lies in the dissipation of research effort upon petty and mediocre issues which may accidentally have loomed large in the professional background of the candidate.

The second method is more dictatorial in nature. The major professor, fully aware that his students come ill-equipped to deal with a first-rate research topic, and having a lot of "hunches" of his own which he would like to see developed, simply assigns problems to his pupils. In extreme cases it would be better to say that the problems are imposed on the recipients, much in the spirit of an executive issuing orders to his subordinates. At best, the student is permitted to choose from among a number of possibilities, any one of which would be equally acceptable to the director in charge. This policy has the great merit of cutting the Gordian knot when the student appears devoid of any capacity to find and state his own problems, no matter whether this inability be due to inexperience or to a fundamental lack of originality. Like most dictatorial methods, it gets things done, but often at the price of much emotional resistance and the possible stifling of independent thought.

It is here contended that neither of these policies is calculated to further the most pressing need of contemporary educational research —the coordination of investigative efforts about some central issues with the accompanying closure of the gaps in our present structure of knowledge. *Laissez faire* is dead or discredited in our political and economic system, but it continues to flourish like the green bay tree in our scientific enterprises. Our schools and laboratories pour forth a veritable flood tide of inductively-established documents, most of which are prepared in complete independence of each other. To be sure, they may eventually be classified under common captions by indexing and abstracting services, but this kinship is largely arbitrary and external and rarely marked by any true inner relationship. The reason for this is that they are assembled and sorted after they have been completed instead of being organically developed as a whole. We have evidently a technique for prosecuting any particular research as such, but we have not as yet perfected either the spirit or the machinery for planning a group of research studies in advance, so that each finished performance will fit in logically and organically with the rest of the total structure.

There is strong reason for believing that this third scheme must soon be adopted if educational research is to be saved from the endless multiplication of trifling and ephemeral studies. Such a stage may well have been necessary historically if the science of education was ever to possess what little real substance it now has, but the fruitfulness of this policy appears to have been diminishing for some time. We have followed a program of expediency and opportunism in our research activities with a crazy-quilt of material as a result. There is less acute need now for additional detailed facts as such than for a pattern which will consolidate and give significance to those we already have. Save for a few outstanding exceptions—such as the Payne Fund Motion Picture Series, the Character Education Inquiry and the now famous "Nature and Nurture" Yearbook of the National Society for the Study of Education—most of our studies have lacked a broader framework of reference and hence have failed to dovetail with each other. Yet it is only by following the example of the models just mentioned that a serviceable educational science can be developed.

The tradition that scientific research is a free-lance career dies hard, despite its incompatibility with the realities of the day. We still cling with superstitious veneration to the idealized picture of the scholar playing his lone hand, even though institutionalized and publicly subsidized investigations dominate the research scene. Scientific workers, like other good citizens, have been fully aware of the social values they create and of the corresponding obligations which they have had to assume. But it seems that now more than a vague sense of well-intentioned endeavor is needed, and that in educational researches particularly the philosophy of the curriculum-builders could well be applied to the techniques of investigation themselves. Specifically, this would not just mean more and better research, but above all, researches which hang together in an integrated fashion. Not only should a common thread run throughout a series of related studies, but if one experiment, figuratively speaking, possesses a convex character it must be supplemented by a concave experiment if a well-organized body of knowledge is to be produced. Since this last desideratum is the real goal of investigative effort it should be definitely provided for at the very inception of a group of projects.

Directors of graduate students' investigations might well profit by an attempt to remodel their advanced seminars on the principle that cooperative intellectual endeavor not only increases the "research drive" as such, but enhances the worth of the ends to be attained. If a given venture is to appeal to the imaginations of several students, each of whom is to be engaged on some natural subdivision thereof, it must have reference to fundamental human considerations and not merely reflect the private whimsy of a dominant and aggressive leader. Many progressive elementary schools with their so-called "activity programs" have provided on the child level an illustration of that organized pursuit of a common objective which seems to be needed now on the adult plane. For example, a group of primary-grade children and the teacher of arts and crafts decide to paint a mural on the theme of family and home life. The plan is large enough in scope to occupy them for weeks and months so that an attractive division of labor takes place after the general approach has been discussed. One child paints a kitchen scene (perhaps merely filling in the sketches traced by the instructor), another works on a garden segment, another decorates the border, etc. The result is unity, coherence and a satisfying totality of experience—qualities which are often distressingly absent in our graduate set-up. At one institution last year, a professor had his students working on the following motley array of problems: The increase in vocabulary size during the college years, sensory transposition in the white rat, flicker thresholds in young children, the value of historical fiction as auxiliary reading in a high-school social studies program, etc. This is typical of the jumbled material which a busy and harassed research director supervises, and although it may be a tribute to his versatility, its ultimate social utility is probably less than that of a well-coordinated group of studies centered about a common nucleus, such as a series of a dozen experiments designed to appraise the merits of "contract" instruction in representative fields. As a research policy a method which views each study as an independent unit is cursed by the fact that it opens up more gaps than it closes.

In kindred fields of science there are numerous examples of such coordinated endeavor. The Mendeléeff periodic table has been a godsend to systematic chemical research for over a generation by providing at any given moment a clear-cut picture of what had been achieved and the "holes" which still remained. Think of what the concept of evolution meant to Darwin and how almost all his extensive publications were devoted to examining the evidence in favor of this view; or consider how Morgan has spent a fruitful life in determining the rôle of the genes and chromosomes in heredity. The famous Würzburg school of imageless thought is a brilliant example of integrated psychological investigation: Külpe set the keynote with his hypothesis that non-sensory elements exist in consciousness, and a series of a dozen brilliant pupils offered the positive confirmation of this view in a variety of related fields. Yerkes, the distinguished animal psychologist, has made his own and his pupils' work hang together by a genetic string, for their joint studies have covered the adaptive and learning behavior of almost every species of organism from amoeba to anthropoid ape. The sixteen volumes of the

Psychologische Forschung contain several hundred compact inductive studies, all of which serve as the foundation stones upon which modern Gestalt theory rests. They constitute splendid testimony not only of the value of specialization, but of the even greater value of harmonized research efforts. Perhaps the impressive finality of the edifice of mathematical thought to-day is in no small measure due to the systematic exploration of all the implications of a problem situation—whenever a *proposition* had been demonstrated, its numerous *corollaries* forthwith fell in line.

Here, then, is the line of development which the administration of educational research in America will probably find it wise to follow. It will diligently avoid any semblance of imposition of a topic from above as well as the tendency to follow too literally the personal preferences of the individual student by merely regulating his fancies when they become too unrealistic. In place of these obsolescent devices, it will move to substitute a system of group or cooperative planning of an extended research program wherein the work of each member falls into its prescribed niche. Continuity rather than discreteness will be its watchword. So far our educational activities have been hit-or-miss shotgun forays into the territory of the unknown; henceforth, we must have mass invasions moving toward the deliberately arranged conquest of key positions.

EDUCATIONAL EVENTS

HIGHER EDUCATION FOR WOMEN IN COLOMBIA

THE University of Cauca at Popayan, Colombia, a *New York Times* special correspondent reports, has opened its doors to women for the first time in its history. The university is the first Colombian institution of higher education to take this step. Courses leading to the professional degrees in dentistry, social hygiene, pharmacy and nursing will be offered to the Colombian women, who have no political rights under the constitution and who, until the present time, have been barred from the universities by social tradition and by lack of accommodations. In recent years, there has been a strong movement of public opinion toward the higher education of women, and the initiative of the University of Cauca is likely to be followed by other educational institutions.

Dr. Jeremias Cárdenas, the new rector of the university, who recently returned to Colombia from the United States, has started a series of lectures designed to acquaint the prospective women students with college practises before the professional courses begin in October. A two-year preparatory course will be required of girls who have graduated from acceptable private high schools before they are admitted to the professional courses. The preparatory courses will include the studies generally made at liberal arts colleges, with elective classes in painting, music and other cultural subjects.

Other new developments to be inaugurated when the academic year begins next October are the establishment of university extension courses designed to foster adult education; cultural missions that will travel the countryside; and free traveling libraries and lectures in rural districts, dealing chiefly with agricultural subjects. Dr. Cárdenas is now working on a plan to establish a permanent exchange of scholarships and fellowships for American and Colombian students and teachers.

THE CHILD LABOR COMMITTEE AND THE RICH FEDERAL CHILD LABOR BILL

AN official statement given out by the National Child Labor Committee states that the committee strongly disapproves of the Rich Federal Child Labor Bill (H.R. 6184) introduced in Congress on January 3 and now in the Labor Committee of the House of Representatives, and will oppose this measure should it be reported out.

The Rich bill prohibits the employment of any person under 18 years except children 14 years and over during vacation periods; it applies to every person in the United States who hires another person for any purpose or for any length of time; it sets up a uniform minimum wage for all employees in all types of work; and carries unworkable provisions for administration and enforcement by the United States Secretary of Labor.

The statement continues:

Such standards and requirements are wholly unreasonable and are palpably absurd. While it is not possible to say what was in Congressman Rich's mind in introducing this bill, it could not have been better designed if framed by the opponents of the Federal Child Labor Amendment, to alienate support from that measure by giving the impression that those interested in protecting children would advocate such ridiculous legislation.

None of the national agencies interested in child labor legislation was consulted in the drafting of the bill and did not know that it was to be introduced. Mr. Rich, Republican Congressman from Pennsylvania, who introduced it, has never before, so far as we have been able to learn, shown the slightest interest in advancing child labor legislation. He is president of a large woolen mill and, we understand, active in the Manufacturers' Association of Pennsylvania.

Those opposing the amendment have commented widely upon the Rich bill, stating that it was introduced "in anticipation of ratification of the Federal Child Labor Amendment" and implying that it has the approval of the proponents of the amendment. Various newspapers have editorially assumed that those working for the amendment are backing the bill. The National Child Labor Committee, however, believes that the bill, instead of illustrating the type of legislation desired by the proponents of the amendment, seems rather to illustrate the tactics of the opposition to the amendment.

SURVEY OF THE SCHOOLS OF NEW YORK CITY

Members of the State Department of Education have begun a survey of the personnel of the New York City school system as part of the investigation being conducted by State Commissioner of Education Frank P. Graves, according to *The New York Sun*. The report on the personnel survey will constitute Part III of the Graves investigation into the New York schools.

Dr. Graves has already submitted two reports on his survey. The first recommended, among other things, the abolition of the Board of Superintendents and centralization of authority in the Superintendent of Schools. The Board of Education has accepted this recommendation, and is sponsoring a bill to put the proposal into effect.

Part II of Dr. Graves's report covered the pedagogical efficiency of the city schools, and showed that New York City children, while slightly behind others throughout the country as to grade, are ahead in achievement for their age.

The personnel survey, it is expected, will be broad in its scope. The State Department representatives met recently with Superintendent of Schools Harold G. Campbell and members of the Board of Examiners to outline a program.

According to present plans, the survey will cover the eligibility requirements for teaching and supervisory licenses in the city schools, the methods used by the Board of Examiners in selecting teachers, the teaching efficiency of selected members of the teaching corps, the regulations of the Board of Education regarding sabbatical and other leave of absence, with or without pay, and similar matters.

The State Department representatives surveying the city schools are Assistant State Commissioners J. Cayce Morrison, George M. Wiley and Lewis A. Wilson and their staffs. Cooperating with them are Superintendent Campbell, Deputy Superintendent John E. Wade, Associate Superintendent William E. Grady and Eugene A. Nifenecker, director of the bureau of reference, research and statistics.

It is expected that several months will be required for the completion of the survey.

ART EDUCATION EXPERIMENT AT CAMBRIDGE

According to *Museum News,* the Germanic Museum, Cambridge, Mass., Charles L. Kuhn, curator, has been conducting, in collaboration with the Museum of Fine Arts, Boston, and A. F. Burke, art director of the Cambridge schools, an experimental course in art history and appreciation for eighth grade children. Mrs. D. B. Tanner, of the Museum of Fine Arts, is in charge of the course, which consists of meetings on Saturday mornings at the Germanic Museum and trips to the other museums in Cambridge and Boston.

At the Saturday meetings an illustrated lecture is given on some phase of art history. This is followed by a motion picture, the theme of which is the same as that of the talk. During the week following, the children are taken by special buses to the Museum of Fine Arts or to the Fogg Museum, where they are shown original works of art related to the Saturday meeting. For example, the first lecture was on Egyptian art. The film shown was entitled "Egyptian Life, Ancient and Modern" and compared the activities of the modern Egyptian peasants to the peasant scenes in the ancient tomb paintings. During the week, the children were conducted through the Egyptian collections of the Museum of Fine Arts.

The Saturday morning talks and motion pictures—most of the films are produced by the Metropolitan Museum—give the children historical background and familiarize them with the style of the art of some particular country. The ground thus having been broken, the children are in a position to see the original objects with new understanding. The purpose of the course is not to give a condensed history of art but rather to demonstrate a simple and comprehensible method of approach to the art of the past and of the present. The attendance has been well over a thousand.

THE NATIONAL NEGRO EDUCATION CONFERENCE

THE work of the National Negro Education Conference sponsored by the Office of Education that met in Washington, D. C., from May 9 to 12, was in charge of fifteen committees headed by specialists in each field. The conference was under the general chairmanship of Commissioner Zook and the direction of Ambrose Caliver, specialist in the education of Negroes.

The names of the committees follow: (1) Home Life; (2) Vocations; (3) Citizenship; (4) Recreation and Leisure Time; (5) Health; (6) Ethics and Morals; (7) Elementary Education; (8) Secondary Education; (9) Collegiate Education; (10) Rural Education; (11) Adult Education; (12) Public Education; (13) Private Education, and (14) Financial Support of Education.

The immediate aim of the conference was to study certain fundamental problems which are peculiar to the education of Negroes, because of their social and economic status, and to focus the attention of thoughtful people on the educational issues involved in the development of a bi-racial culture.

The purpose of the first six committees is to study education in its relationship to the various life activities through which individuals function. The purpose of Committees (7) to (11) is to consider both the general and special methods, materials and machinery by means of which education at the various levels may contribute to the development of the knowledge, skills, appreciations and ideals needed in each of the activities treated by the first six committees. These committees will study also the special problems in effecting greater coordination among the different levels of education to the end that the education of Negro children may be treated more nearly as an integrated process and a unified whole. The Committees on Public and Private Education and Financial Support will consider special problems and functions of each of these large divisions, canvass ways and means of effecting greater cooperation between them and among the different institutions within each division, and, in general, point the way toward greater cooperation and coordination in the organization, administration and financing of education for Negroes.

THE INSTITUTE FOR ADMINISTRATIVE OFFICERS OF HIGHER INSTITUTIONS

THE Institute for Administrative Officers of Higher Institutions will be held in the Lounge of Judson Court, the University of Chicago, 1035 East 60th Street, on July 11, 12 and 13.

A most cordial invitation is extended to administrative officers of all higher institutions, including liberal arts colleges, universities, teachers colleges and junior colleges, to attend. Principals of high schools are also very cordially invited to participate in the institute. Arrangements have been made for visitors to attend the institute, to visit classes and to enjoy other university privileges without the payment of fees.

The central theme will be "A New Definition of General Education." The chief topics which will be considered follow:

WEDNESDAY, JULY 11

''Critical Issues Involved in Defining General Education,'' Robert M. Hutchins, president of the University of Chicago.

''Nature, Scope and Essential Elements in General Education,'' Henry M. Wriston, president of Lawrence College, Appleton, Wisconsin.

"The Relation of the Humanities to General Education," Howard Mumford Jones, professor of English language and literature, University of Michigan.

"The Relation of the Natural Sciences to General Education," Richard E. Scammon, dean of medical sciences and professor of anatomy, the University of Minnesota.

THURSDAY, JULY 12

"The Relation of the Social Sciences to General Education," John M. Gaus, visiting professor of political science, the University of Chicago.

"Significant Trends in the Curriculum at the Junior College Level," Leonard V. Koos, professor of secondary education, the University of Chicago.

Experimental Programs of General Education in Colleges and Universities

1. "The Colgate Plan," Eugene G. Bewkes, professor of philosophy, Colgate University, Hamilton, New York.
2. "The General College, the University of Minnesota," Malcolm S. MacLean, Director of the General College, the University of Minnesota.

FRIDAY, JULY 13

Experimental Programs of General Education Involving both the High School and Junior College Level

1. "The Pasadena Reorganization," John W. Harbeson, principal of Pasadena Junior College, Pasadena, California.
2. "The Joliet Experiment," W. W. Haggard, superintendent, Joliet Township High School and Junior College, Joliet, Illinois.
3. "The Tulsa Experiment," Will French, associate superintendent, Tulsa Public Schools, Tulsa, Oklahoma.
4. "The Four-Year College, the University of Chicago," Chauncey S. Boucher, dean of the College, the University of Chicago.

"Summary of the Conference," George A. Works, dean of students and university examiner, the University of Chicago.

For additional information, address William S. Gray, Department of Education, The University of Chicago.

SPECIAL CONFERENCE ON PROBLEMS OF BUSINESS ADMINISTRATION IN COLLEGES AND UNIVERSITIES

A SPECIAL conference, concerned with problems of business administration, will be held at the University of Chicago, on July 9 and 10, immediately preceding the annual Institute for Administrative Officers of Higher Institutions. This conference will center its attention to some extent on the recommendations of the National Committee on Standard Reports for Institutions of Higher Education. The work of this committee has been practically completed, and its final report is almost ready for publication; preliminary reports have already been issued and the recommendations adopted by numerous colleges. This conference provides an opportunity to become better acquainted with the suggestions of the National Committee as they affect accounting, reporting and other problems of business administration.

The conference will be under the direction of John Dale Russell, department of education, the University of Chicago, and Lloyd Morey, comptroller of the University of Illinois and chairman of the National Committee on Standard Reports for Institutions of Higher Education. An important feature of the program will be a clinic on accounting and reporting problems, to which administrative officers are invited to bring problems pertaining to the application of the recommended procedures to their own local systems. Stress will be laid on accurate reporting in the newly adopted accrediting procedure of the North Central Association of Colleges and Secondary Schools.

Further details of the plans for this conference may be obtained from John Dale Russell, Department of Education, The University of Chicago.

COURSES AT THE SUMMER SESSION OF WESTERN RESERVE UNIVERSITY

THE Summer Session of Western Reserve University is offering a special series of lectures and courses on Current Problems in Labor and Industry, in Population Trends, in Agriculture, in Government, in Currency and in The Far East.

Visiting lecturers in these fields include:

Sumner H. Slichter, professor of business economics, Harvard University Graduate School of Business Administration.

Whiting Williams, writer, lecturer and consultant

on labor, industry, personnel and management problems.

Warren S. Thompson, director, Scripps Foundation for Research in Population Problems, Miami University.

Oliver Edwin Baker, senior agricultural economist, Bureau of Agriculture and Economics, U. S. Department of Agriculture.

D. W. Brogan, London School of Economics and Political Science.

Thomas H. Reed, professor of political science, University of Michigan.

Frederick A. Bradford, associate professor of economics, Lehigh University.

Lewis B. Williams, chairman of the board, Federal Reserve Bank, Fourth District.

George Hubbard Blakeslee, professor of history and international relations, Clark University.

No-Yong Park, lecturer on Oriental affairs.

Among other new courses are "Famous New Deals in American History," "The Historical Backgrounds of the New Deal," "The Rise of Modern Russia," "American Relations with the Far East."

COUNCIL OF THE FACULTY OF HARVARD UNIVERSITY

IT is announced from Harvard University that a new council of sixty members of the Faculty of Arts and Sciences, elected by the faculty, will meet frequently with President James Bryant Conant, beginning next autumn, to discuss questions facing the new administration. The creation of such a council and the rules for its election were approved by the Board of Overseers at their last meeting.

In the annual report of President Conant he pointed out that:

Where the faculties are small they function well as legislative bodies; where they are much larger than one hundred, their size, for many reasons, makes the transaction of business difficult. Therefore, in the larger faculties more and more work is being done by administrative boards or committees. This is a very efficient system but tends to debar from discussion a large number and keeps the president from being in close touch with the general sentiment. It would seem worth while for the larger faculties to consider the possibilities of having a council of about sixty members elected on some representative plan. If provisions were made for rotation in office in this body, essentially all the members of the larger faculties would serve in the course of a few years. Such a council might then function as all faculties did a generation ago and the smaller faculties do to-day.

Dean Kenneth B. Murdock said in part:

The exigencies of the times and the beginning of a new administration must both produce an unusual number of major questions on which the advice of the faculty will be valuable to the president and governing boards. Unfortunately, the present size of the faculty makes it very difficult to get useful discussion of such questions.

It seems clear that to have the faculty because of its size or the apathy of its members lose its influence would be unfortunate, and equally clear that general discussions by men able truly to represent the whole faculty would be of the greatest value. It is to be hoped, therefore, that in the near future the faculty may at least consider what means can be devised by which it can become, as it was at least in the earlier years of Mr. Eliot's administration, a useful deliberative and advisory body. This position it inevitably began to lose toward the end of Mr. Eliot's term of office because of its growth in numbers, and it has lost more and more as its numbers have continued to grow in each successive year.

The following rules have been approved by the Overseers:

1. Method of Election of the Council.

One representative shall be elected by each of the following departments of the faculty by such method as the department may determine: Semitic languages and history, Indic philology, classics, English, Germanic languages and literatures, Romance languages and literatures, fine arts, music, physics, astronomy, engineering sciences, chemistry, biology, geology and geography, mineralogy and petrography, history, government, economics, sociology, anthropology, mathematics, philosophy and psychology. The precise composition of the voting body of each department for this purpose shall be determined by the dean of the faculty and the chairman of the department. The representatives so elected shall nominate a group composed of twenty per cent. of the membership of each of the following ranks—professors (at present 128), associate professors (at present 45), assistant professors (at present 60), instructors on three-year appointment (at present 58) and representing so far as possible the membership of the faculty with reference to the size of the various divisions. Lecturers (at present 10) will be classed with the different ranks in such fashion as the dean of the faculty shall determine. From the list of those nominated the faculty shall elect by mailed ballot one half the number nominated from each rank, the details of procedure to be determined by the president and the dean of the faculty. In case of a tie between two or more of those nominated the issue shall be decided by lot. The representatives elected by the various departments, together with those elected by the faculty, shall form the council of the faculty. These elections shall ordinarily be held during the first two weeks of the college year. *Ex-officio* members of the council shall be the Dean of the Faculty of Arts and Sciences, the the Dean of Harvard College, the Dean of the Graduate School of Arts and Sciences, the Dean of University Extension, the Dean of Freshmen, the Chairman of the Committee on Admission and the Secretary of the Faculty. The president shall be a member and shall preside over the council.

2. Membership in the Council.

All elections to the council shall be for the period of one year. No member of the faculty shall be elected by the faculty to membership in the council for more than two one-year terms in any period of five years.

THE RETIREMENT OF THE CHANCELLOR OF THE OREGON STATE SYSTEM OF HIGHER EDUCATION

Dr. W. J. Kerr, for the past two years chancellor of the Oregon state system of higher education, announced his desire to retire from his present office when a successor may be obtained, in a formal statement to the state board of higher education at a recent meeting in Portland.

The plans of the chancellor, who before his appointment as head of the system of higher education in Oregon was for twenty-five years president of Oregon State College, were made known at the end of a summary statement reviewing the progress of the unification movement under the single board for the five years ending on July 1. Dr. Kerr said:

When, on September 6, 1932, in a period of emergency, I accepted the responsibilities of the chancellorship, it was with no thought of continuing in the office indefinitely. It was assumed that with the cooperation of the faculties and the support of the board, the unified organization could be effected within a reasonable time and a stable policy established, insuring to future higher education in Oregon coordination, harmony and a sound basis for further development.

Since these conditions now prevail, with prospects for steady and continued advancement, I feel justified in announcing to the board, in accordance with my original intention, my desire to retire from the chancellorship when a successor to the office may be obtained.

While taking no direct action, the board recognized the desires of Dr. Kerr in a statement which said that the retirement request came as an unexpected problem even though the members realized that it was the chancellor's desire to relinquish the heavy responsibilities of the chancellorship when conditions would permit. It pointed out that Dr. Kerr had dealt with the important problems of reorganization in a spirit of tolerance and justice, and by taking the far view as well as the near view, had shaped the course of higher education toward objectives that bear the stamp of educational statesmanship. "The board receives with regret your request for retirement from the chancellorship," the statement concludes, "but depends upon your loyalty to higher education and your spirit of service to the state not to contemplate release until a suitable successor is obtained—a man broad enough in educational training and experience to comprehend in his understanding and his sympathies the entire scope of higher education in Oregon."

Chancellor Kerr will round out forty-nine years of college administrative work—forty of which he has been a college president—at the end of this school year. He began his administrative career at the University of Utah and served as president of Brigham Young University and then of Utah State College before taking the presidency of Oregon State College in 1907. He continued as president of Oregon State College for the next quarter of a century building it to a point where it is recognized as one of the three greatest land grant institutions in the country.

With the reorganization of the state system of higher education in Oregon in 1932, Dr. Kerr agreed to become the first chancellor of the system.

EDUCATIONAL NOTES AND NEWS

The doctorate of laws was conferred on May 2 by Indiana University on Dr. Ellwood Patterson Cubberley, at exercises commemorating the one hundred and fourteenth anniversary of the founding of the university. Dr. Cubberley, who recently retired as head of the School of Education of Stanford University, graduated from Indiana University in 1891.

Dr. Edward L. Thorndike, professor of psychology and director of the Division of Psychology of the Institute of Educational Research at Teachers College, Columbia University, has been elected a trustee of Wesleyan University.

Roland S. Morris, formerly ambassador to Japan, candidate for the Democratic nomination for U. S. Senator from Pennsylvania, professor of international law at the University of Pennsylvania, was elected a charter trustee of Princeton University at a meeting of the board on April 12. Mr. Morris is president of the Woodrow Wilson Foundation, a member of the advisory board of the Princeton School of Public Affairs and president of the American Philosophical Society.

Dr. Walter A. Jessup, who recently resigned as president of the State University of Iowa to accept the presidency of the Carnegie Foundation for the Advancement of Teaching, took office on May 1.

Dr. Earl S. Rudisill, of York, Pennsylvania, has been appointed president of Thiel College to succeed Dr. E. Clyde Xander, who resigned last October. Dr. Rudisill will be inducted into office on commencement day, June 6. The president-elect is a graduate of Gettysburg College and Theological Seminary. He received his A.M. degree at the University of Pittsburgh and his Ph.D. at the University of Pennsylvania. He has taught in both these institutions.

President Frederick B. Robinson, of the College of the City of New York, has been elected a Chevalier of the Legion of Honor of France. Dr. Robinson received the medal and scroll at a luncheon given in his honor in Washington by the French Ambassador, M. André Lefebvre de Laboulaye, on April 26.

Professor A. G. Bovee, of the University High School of the University of Chicago, has been awarded the Palmes Academiques. This award is made because of his contributions to the study of French civilization in the United States through his books entitled "Aventures Par La Lecture," "Une Aventure En Français," "Vocational Opportunities for the Foreign Language Student" and "A Basic French Vocabulary."

Dr. James G. Needham, professor of entomology and limnology at Cornell University, was the guest of honor of the Cornell alumni of the University of Tennessee at a dinner given during a recent visit to the South. A hundred persons attended the banquet, at which Dr. Needham made the address.

One of the three gold medals of the National Institute of Social Sciences, New York City, has been awarded to Dr. Walter Bradford Cannon, George Higginson professor of physiology at the Harvard Medical School. The medal will be presented to Dr. Cannon by Dr. John A. Hartwell, director of the New York Academy of Medicine, at the annual dinner of the institute, which will be given on May 10.

Dr. John E. Anderson, director of the Institute of Child Welfare, of the University of Minnesota, has been given the eighth annual book medal awarded by *The Parents' Magazine* for the most helpful books published during 1933. The award went to Dr. Anderson for his editorship of the three-volume Century Childhood Library.

The Howland Memorial Prize of Yale University was formally presented to Professor Ragnar Östberg, the Swedish architect, at a ceremony held in the Yale Gallery of Fine Arts on May 7. The prize carries with it a medal, which was presented by President James Rowland Angell. Professor Östberg responded with a brief address. At the same time an exhibition of Dr. Östberg's drawings was opened in the Gallery. The Howland Memorial Prize, awarded "in recognition of marked distinction in the field of literature or fine arts or the science of government," was established in 1915 by the late Charles P. Howland, '91, who was professor of international relations; Miss Frances L. Howland, of New York City, and Dr. John

Howland, Yale, '94, in memory of their father, Judge Henry Elias Howland, Yale, '54, of New York City. Professor Östberg, while in this country, will also receive the gold medal of the American Institute of Architects. It will be presented to him in the White House by President Roosevelt.

DR. ALBRECHT GÖTZE, of the University of Marburg, has been appointed visiting professor of Assyriology and Babylonian literature at Yale University, and Dr. Carl J. F. Skottsberg, professor of botany at the University of Upsala, Sweden, has been appointed Bishop Museum visiting professor of botany. He will give instruction and direct research at the university in the problems of the Pacific area under the terms of the agreement by which Yale and the Bishop Museum of Honolulu are affiliated. It is also announced that Erwin R. Goodenough, associate professor of history, has been promoted to be professor of the history of religion.

DR. NED H. DEARBORN, since 1929 director of the New York University Institute of Education, has been appointed acting director of the recently established Division of General Education. The appointment is effective immediately. The division will absorb the existing Institute of Education and the University Extension Division and is expected to play a leading rôle in the field of adult education. All outside degree-credit work will be administered by the Division of General Education in cooperation with the university schools and colleges concerned. At present Dr. Dearborn, through the Institute of Education, administers courses for teachers in forty-six cities of New York, New Jersey, Pennsylvania, Connecticut and Delaware. The University Extension Division conducts college credit courses in Newark and Paterson.

PROFESSOR FRANK W. GARRAN, of Dartmouth College, has been elected dean of the Thayer School of Civil Engineering to succeed Raymond R. Marsden, who is on leave of absence this year.

THEODORE A. DISTLER, director of admissions and student personnel at the University Heights division of New York University, has been elected dean of Lafayette College. He will succeed Dr. Arthur A. Hauck, who recently resigned to become president of the University of Maine.

PROFESSOR ERNEST MERRITT will retire from administrative work as head of the department of physics at Cornell University at the close of the present academic year. Professor R. C. Gibbs has been appointed chairman for the year 1934–35.

DR. JAMES HAUGHTON WOODS, professor of philosophy at Harvard University, a member of the Harvard faculty for the past thirty-four years, will retire next June to become professor emeritus.

DR. OSCAR M. SCHLOSS has resigned as professor of pediatrics at the Cornell University Medical School and as pediatrician-in-chief of New York Hospital to resume private practise as a pediatrician. He is to remain with the medical school as professor of clinical pediatrics and with the hospital as attending pediatrician. He also will continue his research work at the hospital. Dr. Samuel Z. Levine, now associate professor and attending pediatrician, has been appointed acting pediatrician-in-chief and acting professor of pediatrics.

DR. HAROLD W. FOGHT, until his resignation in February president of the University of Wichita, Kansas, vice-president of the National Education Association in 1924–25 and 1926–27, has been appointed, subject to approval by President Roosevelt, superintendent of the Burke Navajo Vocational School at Fort Wingate, New Mexico. Dr. Foght will succeed James Arentson, who will resume the position of supervisor of vocational education for the Indian Bureau.

DR. K. P. R. NEVILLE, registrar of the University of Western Ontario, London, Canada, has been elected president of the American Association of Collegiate Registrars.

PROFESSOR THOMAS ALEXANDER, of Teachers College, Columbia University, has been appointed chairman of the Committee on Courses for the Training of Teachers of the National Society of College Teachers of Education. This committee will analyze the findings of the National Survey of the Education of Teachers, and from this and other sources will propose one or more programs for the education of teachers.

DR. GRACE M. FERNALD, associate professor of psychology at the University of California at Los Angeles, who for the past six years has conducted a clinical school for children at the summer session of the University of Oregon, will during the summer direct a small clinical school at the University of California at Los Angeles in connection with a special course in clinical psychology.

HAROLD J. COOLIDGE, JR., assistant curator of mammals at the Museum of Comparative Zoology, has been appointed director of the newly established Harvard Film Service. It has taken over the equipment and many of the films of the University Film Foundation, which was set up in 1928 and thereafter carried on as an independent service under an agreement with the university, which encouraged its operation.

DR. RICHARD E. SCAMMON, dean of medical sciences at the University of Minnesota, was appointed recently chairman of the state planning board following the resignation of Professor Morris B. Lambie, of the department of political science at the university. Professor Lambie is the present head of the state board of relief and was unable to devote time to both positions.

LINDSAY BRADFORD, vice-president of the City Bank Farmers Trust Company, and Joseph P. Chamberlain, professor of public law at Columbia University, have been elected members of the Board of Trustees of the Russell Sage Foundation. With the addition of these two new members, the board consists of Lawson Purdy, vice-president; Lindsay Bradford, Joseph P. Chamberlain, Johnston de Forest, Frederic A. Delano, John H. Finley, John M. Glenn, Mrs. Frederic S. Lee, Mrs. Finley J. Shepard and Harold T. White. Mr. Purdy is treasurer, and Mr. Glenn is secretary. Shelby M. Harrison is general director of the foundation.

DR. FREDERICK P. KEPPEL, president of the Carnegie Corporation, will give the Graduate School Convocation address at Brown University on June 16. His subject will be "The Relationship of the American Foundation to American Scholarship."

CHANCELLOR ERNEST H. LINDLEY, of the University of Kansas, was the chief speaker at the Centenary Convocation Exercises at the University of Delaware on May 12. His subject was "The State University and the State." President Walter Hullihen, of the university, spoke on "One Hundred Years of Higher Education in Delaware."

DR. FRANCIS PENDLETON GAINES, president of Washington and Lee University, Lexington, Virginia, will be the speaker at the commencement exercises closing the ninety-sixth session of the Medical College of Virginia to be held on May 29.

THE REV. DR. WILLIAM FREDERICK SLOCUM, president emeritus of Colorado College, formerly chairman of the board of the Carnegie Foundation for the Advancement of Teaching, a Congregational minister for more than fifty years, died on May 1. He was eighty-two years old.

DR. THOMAS CARR HOWE, president emeritus of Butler University, Indianapolis, died on May 4. He was president of the university from 1908 until his resignation in 1920.

ISRAEL UNTERBERG, president of the Jewish Education Association since its founding in 1921, died on May 1 at the age of seventy years.

LILLIAN M. ELLIOT, late principal of the Harlem Evening High School for Women in New York City, died on April 29.

ISAAC BROWN GARDNER, emeritus principal of the New York School for the Deaf, died on April 23, at the age of sixty-five years.

A BUST of the late Dr. Sidney Mezes, fourth president of the College of the City of New York, was unveiled during the Charter Day exercises in the office of the president.

DR. LUCY L. W. WILSON, principal of the South Philadelphia High School for Girls, who recently received the Philadelphia award of $10,000, has contributed this amount to a scholarship fund for girls.

AT the meeting of the National Academy of Sciences held in Washington on April 23, 24 and 25, members were elected as follows: Vannevar Bush, professor of electrical engineering and vice-president of the Massachusetts Institute of Technology; Herbert Spencer Gasser, professor of physiology, Cornell University Medical College, New York; Edmund Newton Harvey, professor of physiology, Princeton

University; Dennis Robert Hoagland, professor of plant nutrition, University of California; Ernest Orlando Lawrence, professor of physics, University of California; James Flack Norris, director of the research laboratory of organic chemistry, Massachusetts Institute of Technology; John Howard Northrop, biochemistry, member of the Rockefeller Institute; Charles Palache, professor of mineralogy, Harvard University; Thomas Milton Rivers, pathology, member of the Rockefeller Institute; Edward Sapir, Sterling professor of anthropology and linguistics, Yale University; Elvin Charles Stakman, plant pathologist, U. S. Department of Agriculture; Harry Shultz Vandiver, associate professor of mathematics, University of Texas; Norbert Wiener, professor of mathematics, Massachusetts Institute of Technology; Sewall Wright, professor of zoology, University of Chicago.

THE twenty-seventh annual meeting of the American Home Economics Association will be held in New York City, from June 25 to 29, with the Hotel Pennsylvania as headquarters. The central theme, "The Consumer in the New Economic Order," will be discussed by representatives of industry, business, government agencies and consumer groups as well as by members of the association. The chairman of local arrangements for the meeting is Miss Edith Barber, 36 West 9th Street, New York City. Permanent headquarters of the association are at 622 Mills Building, Washington, D. C.

THE College Entrance Examination Board has appointed a commission to revise the Entrance Board Examination in history. Members of the board are: James P. Baxter, III, Harvard University; Edmund E. Day, Rockefeller Foundation; Harold W. Dodds, Princeton University; Claude M. Fuess, Phillips Academy, Andover; Carlton J. H. Hayes, Columbia University; Tyler Kepner, High School, Brookline, Mass.; William L. Langer, Harvard University; Wallace Notestein, Yale University; Edward P. Smith, State Education Department, Albany, N. Y.; C. Mildred Thompson, Vassar College; George Van Santvoord, Hotchkiss School; Conyers Read, *Chairman,* University of Pennsylvania, and Evelyn P. Braun, secretary, Box 16, Bennett Hall, University of Pennsylvania. The commission hopes to obtain the assistance of secondary school teachers. The chairman of the commission accordingly urges every one who has any ideas on the subject of revising college entrance examinations in history to communicate with him at Bennett Hall, University of Pennsylvania, Philadelphia, Pennsylvania. It will be pertinent in this connection to consider history in its broadest sense and to raise such questions as the desirability of including within the scope of history the related cultural and social studies.

THE Geneva School of International Studies will open its eleventh annual summer session in Switzerland on July 30, closing on August 31. Each summer since Professor Alfred Zimmern conducted his first seminar in 1924 during the League of Nations Assembly, 150 to 200 students, representing thirty-five to forty nations, have enrolled. Among the lectures will be a series by Professor Zimmern on "The Philosophy of International Relations." Professor J. H. Richardson, of Leeds University, England, will lecture on "Economic Democracy; an International Survey," and Professor Ross McFarland, of Columbia University, on "Recent Social Changes in Russia."

DISCUSSION

A PROPOSED SYMPOSIUM ON THE TRAINING OF TEACHERS FOR THE SECONDARY SCHOOLS

ONE of the most devastating committee reports that has appeared during a long period of time in the field of higher education, at least in its implications, is the report of Committee Q of the American Association of University Professors on "Required Courses in Education."[1]

Curiously, this challenging report, compliance with whose recommendations would result in the virtual decimation of the faculties of

[1] This report was submitted in December, 1932, and published in abbreviated form in the March, 1933, Bulletin of the American Association of University Professors, pp. 173–200.

college departments or schools of education or of teachers colleges which train for the secondary field, has been almost completely ignored so far as can be judged by open discussions in the educational journals or in the meetings of professional organizations concerned with teacher-training work.[2] Is this due to the fact that professional teachers of education in colleges, universities or teacher-training institutions consider the report to be of no consequence or to be an ex-parte one,[3] and therefore a biased document which is not deserving of recognition and which should be allowed to suffer the fate that befalls so many perfervid, exaggerated, partial reports which are consigned to oblivion even before they reach the dusty shelves of the alcove?

Or do educators consider the findings and conclusions of this committee to be irrefutable and that present certification requirements and set-ups of education courses can not be defended or vindicated upon the basis of demonstrated merit or upon the basis of the attested results of a program of professional education that has steadily developed with irresistible surge as the result of the growing application of the methods of scientific research to the solution of educational problems? Is silence to be construed as tacit agreement with the findings and recommendations of this trenchant report and as admission that continuous scientific study has little to contribute to education on the secondary level (or on any other level)?

Does academic training *ipso facto* produce expert teachers? Are we justified in assuming that expertness can be acquired in our modern highly complicated secondary school field (or in any other field) merely by pursuing the traditional content courses offered in the liberal arts colleges, with, perhaps, a modicum of "professionalized subject-matter" added as a permissible supplementary but not essential ingredient?

Do educators generally accept the conclusion "that instruction in subject-matter is the prime essential in training secondary teachers," and that a "maximum of twelve semester hours is ample to cover that part of professional training which can be regarded as essential for the beginning teacher who has a bachelor's degree from a standard college or university, and who qualifies for teaching an academic subject," said training to "involve practise teaching and methods" and "courses in psychology or educational psychology"? Are school men agreed that "some of the general courses" should not be offered until the novitiate has had "two or more years of experience"?

Is it self-evident that native teaching ability, good common sense and the acquisition of scholarship through the pursuit of subject-matter courses in the liberal arts department are the essential conditions of becoming a successful secondary school teacher or school administrator?

Will the report of Committee Q be accepted by the colleges, universities, schools of education and certification bodies as the "gospel truth" so far as concerns training for secondary school positions and superintendencies, as a pronouncement from the group of professorial leaders that must be accorded the supremacy of an unassailable and immutable decree that should be put into immediate effect to save the schools from an army of incompetents whose incompetency is largely due to excessive requirements in professional courses, and as the final, inexorable verdict of the Court of Higher Learning, beyond which there can be no appeal to any other court of parallel, coordinate or higher jurisdiction? And is this report but the precursor of other similar reports dealing with the elementary, normal school and college fields?

The inescapable consequence of an affirmative answer to these queries would be the virtual extermination of one of the outstanding educational structures erected during this "century of progress."

We should like to suggest that SCHOOL AND SOCIETY set aside a limited amount of space in each of its issues for a symposium on the ques-

[2] A paper was presented by the chairman of Committee Q of A. A. U. P. on "A Liberal Arts View of the Training of High School Teachers and Administrators" at the first annual meeting following the A. A. U. P. report of the National Society of College Teachers of Education, the professional organization that should be most vitally concerned with this report. But the discussion was immediately terminated when pointed questions were propounded from the floor regarding certain obvious implications of Committee Q's report.

[3] Apparently all the eight members of the committee are professors of academic subjects in liberal arts departments in large state and private universities.

tion of teacher-training, open alike to academic and professional educators, for a cool, frank, unprejudiced and critical examination of all the facts and issues involved in the light of all the functions which a modern system of schools should discharge: mental, physical and social training in accordance with individual needs; the development of knowledges and skills in subject-matter; the development of scholarship, insight, understandings, appreciations, attitudes and habits of response; the development of desirable personality traits; the prevention and overcoming of personality maladjustments by the regimentation of all the processes of the school in accordance with the principles of mental health and mental and physical hygiene; remedial and diagnostic instruction for the remediation of specific or general disabilities or defects; the stimulation of the creative "impulse" and development of talent and leadership; the furtherance of a constantly expanding and improving system of education from the primary to the graduate levels, as against smug, self-satisfied complacency with a stationary conventional or traditional program of education largely confined in its purview to scholarship achievements; programs of emotional and personality development as against highly intellectual régimes; etc.

If we assume that a progressive, comprehensive program of public education is required for the adequate preparation of our youth for wholesome, efficient participation in the complicated activities of our American life, which is constantly becoming more complex, must we not also assume that many techniques can be employed for putting this whole program across, and that some of them are efficient, some less efficient, some indifferent and some very ineffective? Can the prospective teacher acquire effective techniques for putting across not only instruction in subject-matter but all the other elements of the program by the pursuit primarily, if not exclusively, of academic content courses?

The above questions, and other similar questions and implications, should be given consideration in the proposed symposium. A series of brief, pithy, searching, constructive contributions, conducted in a dignified manner, free from doctrinaire presuppositions, but sensitive to the comprehensive program of education demanded by the requirements of the cultural, social, industrial and economic conditions of the America of to-day and the America of to-morrow, should prove illuminating, clarify and validate our thinking on a highly complex problem in the light of its multitudinous factors and phases, and lead to the acceptance of a common ground of theory and practise with respect to preparation for the profession of teaching.

Can we ever hope to make a profession of teaching, comparable to the legal, dental, medical and engineering professions, without substantial requirements with respect to technical training and substantial agreement regarding the basic elements of this program of professionalized preparation?

J. E. W. Wallin
Wilmington, Delaware

DICTATORSHIP AND DEMOCRACY IN EDUCATION FROM A TEACHER'S VIEW-POINT

In 1917 and 1918 probably the average citizen believed that the United States had entered the war "to make the world safe for democracy." The assumption was that the day of autocracy was drawing to a close and that a new era was at hand.

In 1934 we are facing a different outlook. Instead of a triumphant democracy and a defeated autocracy there is in Europe the spectacle of dictators with more power than pre-war monarchs ever thought possible. Many people in the United States are wondering to what extent we have given up representative government in favor of an administration strangely suggestive of a dictatorial pattern. We are surrounded by alphabetical commissions which appear to be capable of manifesting heretofore unbelievable interest in the personal affairs of individual citizens. This changing political and social outlook can not but affect the educational program in the schools. Will the schools prepare for the efficiency of an autocratic government or will they prepare for the less efficient, more complicated and idealistic democracy, the preservation of which was once considered a worthy reason for entering the most devastating war in history?

Schools are generally organized with one individual at the head who is responsible to those who appoint him to run the institution. Heads of schools vary from the absolute dictator type, whose methods are efficient and show favorable results quickly, to the leader who attempts to build up within his system a group of individuals developing a sense of responsibility and an ability to cooperate with others in contributing to the general welfare. The head alone can not determine the exact extent to which he will go in either direction. Those who appoint him influence his methods by the nature of the demands put upon him. Those who work under him influence his methods by their willingness and ability to reflect his policies. Generally it is easier to adopt an autocratic system.

Perhaps the greatest difficulty in building a democratic school system is the development of mutual guidance within the system. It is so much easier for the head to direct the teachers and for the teachers to direct the pupils. If pupils are to be trained for representative government they should be given a voice, not the steering wheel, in controlling and directing their school society. This implies that suggestions should be encouraged to flow not only from the head downward to the teachers and to the pupils, but also upward from pupils to teachers and from teachers to the head. A wholesome interchange of ideas between pupils and teachers gives the pupils the advantage of the greater experience and training which the teachers have. On the other hand, the teacher receives the original and frequently ingenious ideas that only youth can give. Criticism to be valuable should be directed towards an end which may benefit the group or which may benefit the individual without detracting from the welfare of the group.

Mutual guidance finds its most important expression in the interchange of ideas between teachers and between teachers and the head. The concentration of responsibility that the head assumes places him in a more difficult position than that of other members of the faculty. This normal difference in position need not interfere with the very necessary integration of policies which apply to the school. In fact, it should provide a clearing house for conflicting ideas and thus result in progressive development instead of aggressive static. In some systems this healthy opportunity is lacking because the artificial barriers of dictatorship interfere with the give and take of teamwork.

There is a grave danger in interpreting the suggestions made by others. Criticism prompted by the most idealistic motives is sometimes misinterpreted and it does not take many such mistakes to make a shell hole in any system. This hazard of misunderstanding can be eliminated to a great extent by first recognizing its importance and then developing a distinct policy of avoiding the danger. Any suggestion may be ambiguous if we look at it long enough or if we assume the possibility of hidden meanings. For those ideas which have not been made clear or which are not valuable and practical there is always the privilege of acceptance and relegation to a file for the time being. Time often takes care of a poor idea and a good idea will probably recur. Meanwhile the freedom of utterance has been recognized and inhibitions may have been avoided.

In conclusion, let me suggest a similarity between the present policy of the national government and that of many school systems. Our democracy has been sufficiently flexible to provide for the use of limited dictatorship methods in cases of emergencies which can be met most effectively by such methods. At the same time its fundamental character remains unchanged and the emergency tactics may be discarded after they have served as tools of representative government. In like manner school systems may cling to their ideals of democracy and yet make use of occasional imperial procedures when conditions demand their temporary application.

WILLIAM A. SMITH

INDIAN MOUNTAIN SCHOOL
LAKEVILLE, CONN.

SPELLING REFORM

THE function of alphabetic writing is to represent the sounds of the spoken language. Originally the spelling of English was entirely phonetic, but through a variety of causes it has become conventionalized on the basis of words as such, the symbols sometimes representing sounds quite satisfactorily. Single sounds, however, are represented by a variety of symbols, and many symbols represent a variety of sounds. Perhaps the most absurd incongruity is the representation of the sound of *r* by *lo* in *colonel.*

It is, therefore, impossible to teach spelling logically and systematically. What should be an easily acquired tool subject becomes a futile burden to teacher and pupil, absorbing a year of school life, with unsatisfactory results. Much of the condemnation of the schools comes from business men on this score, notwithstanding the fact that spelling is better taught to-day than formerly.

Efforts toward reform have been only partially successful. Howell in the seventeenth century successfully advocated the dropping of many silent letters, such as the final *ge* in *dogge* and *re* in *warre.* Webster attempted some general reforms in the first edition of his dictionary, but conservative opinion forced him to retract, and the effect of his effort was negligible.

One obstacle to successful reform is the lack of agreement among reformers as to what form the changed spelling should take. There are those who hold to the doctrine of least disturbance, which contemplates the omission of silent letters, and the selection of present letters or combinations of letters in accordance with the frequency with which they appear in present spelling. This would regularize the representation of sounds so that the ideal of the philologist—one symbol, one sound; one sound, one symbol—would be attained without disturbing the native character of our spelling, but would require combinations of letters to represent some of the sounds. This is the scheme of the Simplified Spelling Board.

A second plan is the rigid application of the principle of one symbol for each sound, and would involve the creation of ten or more new characters, the number of these depending on the whim of the inventor and the analysis of existing sounds.

Obviously, the former plan is the one more likely to be adopted, but without financial backing and without agreement among competent scholars the question is purely academic.

D. C. Croissant
George Washington University

SPECIAL CORRESPONDENCE

SCIENCE AND EDUCATION IN NAZI GERMANY

When the story of the behavior of the teachers of Germany in the new national revolution is told, it will be pieced together from a thousand tales like the one with which I shall deal. In this story we see the national socialist ideology reflected in the *Journal of Mathematical and Scientific Instruction* (*Zeitschrift für mathematischen und naturwissenschaftlichen Unterricht aller Schulgattungen*). This journal, which was founded in 1869 and is now in its sixty-fourth year, is devoted to the betterment of mathematical and scientific instruction in the German higher schools. A reading of recent numbers of the *Journal of Mathematical and Scientific Instruction* supplies evidence for the belief that the National Socialist movement in Germany is carrying some of the German teachers outside of the confines of their particular fields into the wider activity of making their own special work contribute specifically to the building of the new Germany. Of the science teachers who are represented in this particular journal, the mathematicians and physical scientists see their chief contribution as that of developing the military capacities of their students, while the biologists are emphasizing *Völkerbiologie* and *Rassenkunde* as cornerstones of the new German education.

I do not mean to imply that the articles in this journal represent the attitude of the majority of German science teachers. This journal is only one of several dealing with science teaching, and I have seen none other that supports so enthusiastically the purposes of Hitler. But these articles have been written by men who have influence and command a hearing in Germany. No. 7 of the journal which appeared in October, 1933, contains in front of the table of contents the following statement:

> This journal has worked for more than 60 years in the service of mathematical and scientific instruction. It will now place itself fully and completely in the service of national reconstruction and national education and it will take up with special vigor those tasks which the reconstruction of German school affairs in pedagogical and material respects assigns to the teacher and the educator. Therefore the subject-matter of this journal will

be expanded from the mathematical-physical to the entire realm of the mathematical-scientific, and biology as the science of organisms will be especially stressed.

The first article in this number of the journal is entitled "The Revival of the New German Schools through the Spirit of Biology." The author, Dr. H. Wolff of Lübeck, says that the old humanism of the schools with its dependence upon the Greeks must disappear along with the "feminizing" and "atomizing" pedagogy of the past. In its place must be put the faustian-nordic ideal and a new philosophy of life, the foundations of which have been cast in Hitler's "My Battle" and Rosenberg's "The Myth of the 20th Century." "The school of the future has only one duty: to spread and strengthen this philosophy of life (*Weltanschauung*) and to develop characters which are motivated for and capable of carrying on the gigantic struggle for the sacred inheritance and the germanic-nordic expression of our culture and homeland."

Dr. Wolff continues by saying that the study of biology, provided biology is sufficiently developed beyond its present rather narrow boundaries, will be instrumental in developing this new philosophy of life.

We base the new world-view scientifically upon the elementary law of life of each organism: Species and environment must stand in inner agreement with one another. Every kind of plant or animal and every human race and every racially-defined nation which has not yet lost its identity in a characterless racial chaos has its characteristic form and being. Even in the smallest organ, even in every cell there is a definite and peculiar configuration and a unique life-rhythm. Every living thing makes definite demands on its environment and is diversely sensitive toward foreign influences and enemies. The German Folk, whose feeling for life is that of the nordic race, is peculiarly fashioned, and is, for example, highly sensitive to intermixture and infection from the Jewish race. We must neither let ourselves be robbed of the right to mold our environment according to our will, nor allow our blood and thought to be adulterated. . . . No one can doubt that this folk- and race-defined theory of life, rooted in the *mythos* of honor and freedom, is as scientifically accurate as it is noble. But many may voice doubts concerning its practical fruitfulness; for "Only that which is fruitful is true." However, it is actually from this theory that we may expect the most valuable stimulation. A few examples will show that we have good ground for this expectation. In religion, for example, we abjure every way of thinking and teaching that contradicts the religious perceptions of our great god-seekers, from Ekkehard to Fichte and Lagarde. The Old Testament is thus condemned, and also all literal superstition, miracle belief and implicit faith, and in addition the internationalism in missions, religious practice (negro bishops!), and marriage, which weakens our national teaching.

Again the biological theory gives us the solution of various political and eugenic problems.

Since we recognize the struggle for existence and the necessity for rigorous selection, pacifism is to be rooted out as cowardly and false to life. The Jewish problem is a problem of the parasitism of a folk in other national bodies. . . . The nordic-charactered man is the chief good of the nation and on the strength of his race depends the fate of the western world. With the retreat away from the Emancipation of Women, with the decision for a masculine-featured state of warlike and war-capable men and with reverence for Motherhood we are making smooth the way back to a life of procreative, fruitful tone such as the chaos of democracy threatened to obliterate.

The kind of biology which helps to develop the philosophy of life sketched in this paper is to become the "core of the school of the future." And in the next number of the journal there is a description by Dr. Schwarz, also of Lübeck, of a biology course he has developed in an *Oberrealschule,* which he believes approaches Dr. Wolff's demands.

Another paper which appears in the same number of the journal is by E. Tiedge, entitled "Mathematics and Sciences in the Service of National Education." Even though his chief purpose is to show that mathematics and the exact sciences are needed in the development of the new German spirit, he yields first place to biology.

Biology has secured an uncontested position in the national education. Its teaching that all life depends upon the ordering of parts and processes and their subordination to the needs of the whole organism establishes the organic world-concept of folk and fatherland as realities that have higher value than the desire and fate of the individual man. Biology through heredity theory and racial studies provides the foundation of a far-sighted population-policy and therefore should be the corner stone of popular education. A people grows out of the blood and soil and upsurging forces of its native landscape. Our forefathers held counsel and worshipped deity under the towering trees of the forest. They lived in and with Nature, which gave them much intuitively that we to-day must gain cognitively, but which we can make good use of in our education concerning Folk and God.

Tiedge goes on to say that mathematics and exact sciences have been very important in the development of the new Germany. Even the great leader, Adolph Hitler, owes much of his success to his use of airplane and microphone. If Germany's leaders during the war had been as ready to use technical devices as Hitler is, the war would certainly have come out differently. During the war, "the predominantly defensive use of technology corresponded in no way to the German offensive spirit." The development of science and technology has gone hand in hand with the development of German culture. The study of exact science and mathematics will help to develop the old Prussian ideal of truth and faithfulness even in the smallest things. The new physics helps to develop the proper religious attitude. In the hard, iron age which awaits the German people the nation can win its proper place only if science and technology are bound up with the will and power to war.

The order of the day demands of us . . . a selection of teaching materials which furthers the well-being of the State. That material and scientific knowledge must be stressed which is valuable in the building of a firm political order and a strong people which feels and wills as a unit. After the loss of the war and the boundless misery of the post-war period we can fulfill our task as a people only if we maintain the Folk and the Nation at the focus of our thought and action and education. Like our whole life, the schooling and culture of German youth must respond to the motto: All for Germany.

This paper was presented at the annual meeting of the German Mathematical Association before the Imperial Union of German Mathematical Societies, on September 20, 1933, and according to the report which appears in our journal it was received with "spirited applause in a crowded auditorium." A detailed account of the paper appeared in the newspaper *Fränkisches Volk* for September 21, 1933. The Imperial Union sent copies of this number of the paper to mathematicians and to all government offices.

The editor of the *Journal of Mathematical and Scientific Instruction,* Dr. W. Lietzmann, of Göttingen, published an article in the September number of the journal entitled "Mathematical Instruction in Military Science." In 1917 he was appointed to visit the western front to find out and assemble the mathematical and scientific material which would be valuable as a foundation for military training, and to prepare it as part of a revised course of study for all German schools. This plan was not carried through, but the author feels that the time has now come for the introduction of such material into the school courses. There is a very definite preoccupation with military preparedness on the part of several writers of mathematical and physical articles which have appeared in this journal recently. Also No. 7 of *Unterrichtsblätter für Mathematik und Naturwissenschaften* contains five articles on the bearings of various sciences on military science and preparedness, and two more on the relations of science to the new national education, out of a total of ten articles.

R. J. HAVIGHURST
OHIO STATE UNIVERSITY

QUOTATIONS

DEAN LE BARON RUSSELL BRIGGS OF HARVARD UNIVERSITY

IT may seem, though it is not, an anomaly that the death of Dean Briggs, perhaps the most typically local Yankee figure associated with Harvard for a long span of years, has been regarded, if the comments of the press reveal the fact of the matter, as a national loss. So indeed it is, and for the simple reason that his essential quality had the distinctive American flavor that we associate with Lincoln. If Lincoln had possessed a little more Latin, and had produced a book of charades, he would have liked nothing better than to print on its title-page "*Dulce et decorum est desipere in loco.*" If a friend had written to him about the best charade in the book, Lincoln might have answered, like Briggs, "I could name several of which each has a way of becoming the worst." If Lincoln had become a college dean, in succession to a somewhat unapproachable official, one can readily imagine his saying, "Hereafter I hope the man will seek the office and not the office the man"; and, again, "I had rather be fooled a dozen times than be unjust once." A more "literary" Lincoln, but still a Lincoln, might well have written, moreover, in a Dean's report: "It is melancholy to see able-bodied youths the victims of diseases which permit all pleasures and forbid all duties; it is almost equally melancholy to see how they spell the names of the diseases with which they are perfunctorily afflicted."

These are but straws of suggestion, but they can hardly fail to recall something in Briggs which won for him, in his more restricted field, the same kind of affection and admiration that came to Lincoln from all the world. There is now, by no means for the first time, a strong impulse to make Harvard more than ever before a national university. It has often been said that the New England colleges and schools hold their place in the country at large by virtue of their very identification with New England, a region for which a certain respect remains mingled with certain occasions for ridicule. The Yankee figure of Dean Briggs puts it all into human terms, of which the upshot is that your most typical New Englander may also be a most typical American. His type, alas, is none too common in any single region, for personalities like that of Dean Briggs are rather the gift of heaven than the product of any special conditions. Let us hope only that under the conditions of a changed world their occasional appearance will not cease to be possible.

The truth is that every college faculty needs a "character," preferably with the qualities of Dean Briggs—a man whose sayings are quoted, whose personality may be quaint, yet one who commands respect and wins love. In this restricted space it is impossible to suggest all that he did for the cause of good English—established before him by Edward Tyrrel Channing and Adams Sherman Hill in the Boylston Professorship—for sound standards in athletics, for friendly, human academic relationships. Who else in our time has more abundantly enriched the Harvard tradition of the scholar and the friend?—*Harvard Alumni Bulletin.*

EDUCATIONAL RESEARCH AND STATISTICS

CERTAIN ASPECTS OF LECTURE, READING AND GUIDED READING

THE question of the relative effectiveness of lectures when compared with other methods of presenting topics to college students is one of long-standing interest, and the wide use of the lecture system makes the question an important one. In recent years a number of significant reports have been made in this field by Bane,[1] Spence and Watson,[2] Scheideman and Knight,[3] Eurich,[4] Hudelson,[5] Downing,[6] Duggan[7] and Douglas.[8] An inspection of these reports shows that the differences between the results of the various methods of presentation are generally small and unreliable with the measuring techniques available. Most of the writers conclude that over a period as long as a semester or a quarter many important differences in the results of two methods of presentation would not

[1] C. L. Bane, "The Lecture in College Teaching," Badger, Boston, 1931.

[2] R. B. Spence and C. B. Watson, "Lecture and Class Discussion in Teaching Educational Psychology," *Jour. of Ed. Psychol.*, 19: 454–462, 1928.

[3] N. V. Scheideman and F. B. Knight, "A Comparison of Two Methods of College Instruction," SCHOOL AND SOCIETY, 25: 672–674, 1927.

[4] A. C. Eurich, "Reading Abilities of College Students," Col. Problems Series, University of Minnesota Press, 1931.

[5] E. Hudelson, "Problems in College Education," University of Minnesota Press, Chapter 32, p. 417.

[6] E. R. Downing, *School Review*, 33: 688–697, 1925.

[7] S. P. Duggan, "Lecture Systems in American and European Universities," *Int. Inst. Ed. News*, 32: 7, 2–3.

[8] H. R. Douglas, "Controlled Experimentation in the Study of Methods of College Teaching," University of Oregon, Pub. 1: No. 7, 1929.

be adequately measured. In the interests of better controls, the experiments reported below were limited to six 50-minute periods, during which strictly the same topics were presented in various ways.

The Experimental Procedure and Results

During the last six years a series of classroom experiments have been made by the writer at Columbia University, the College of the City of New York and the University of Michigan.[9] Most of the 648 students used were from the writer's classes in elementary psychology.

The procedures followed the regular class schedules, with a minimum of interruption. Small classes averaging 29 students were used throughout. Students were told that they would have four or six fifty-minute periods of experimental study, one per week. In each period twenty-five minutes were used for the presentation of a topic either by reading or by lecture, and fifteen minutes for a test of what had just been presented. The students were told what procedures they would be asked to follow and they were asked to reserve judgment until after the experiment concerning their satisfactions in these procedures. From one to six weeks after the presentation the students were given another test, using identical forms to measure delayed retention. They were not told of this delayed test in order to prevent additional uncontrolled study.

The students were approximately 85 per cent. college sophomores, 10 per cent. juniors, and 5 per cent. were seniors and special students. At two institutions all the students were men, and at the third approximately 35 per cent. were women and 65 per cent. men. It is believed that they represented a fair sample of the sophomore literary college students in these institutions. They seemed, with few exceptions, pleased to cooperate in the experiment, and they apparently gave better than usual attention to the presentations because they expected an immediate test.

The topics chosen were similar to those given in the elementary psychology course, but they were not found in the texts available to the students. Each topic was presented in approximately 2,500 words which included an introduction of about 500 words, an account of experimental procedures and results of about 1,700 words, and a summary of about 300 words. The titles of the topics were as follows:

(1) "Phenomenal Memorizing as a Special Ability," by H. E. Jones.[10]
(2) "Auditory Sensitivity of the White Rat," by W. S. Hunter.[11]

The following were prepared by the writer for this experiment:

(3) "Physiological Aspects of Emotions."
(4) "Transfer of Training."
(5) "Conditioned Responses."
(6) "Neural Basis for Behavior."

For silent reading each student was given an 8-page booklet set in 8 point Ionic linotype, containing but one topic. The students indicated their rates of reading by marking the places in the booklets where they were reading when numbers were called to indicate one-minute intervals. When presented orally the speaker placed the few diagrams which appeared in the booklets on the blackboard and followed the wording of the booklet very closely. He spoke from notes at the rate of approximately 100 words per minute. After several preliminary practises this was done with considerable ease and accuracy by the writer, who gave all the oral presentations for the sake of uniformity. These lectures probably differed from the average college lectures in being shorter, better organized and more uniform in rate and manner of delivery.

Tests were desired which would measure accurately and as analytically as possible the changes in information and skills which took place during the presentations. In order to secure measures of a large number of facts and relationships, short test items were composed of the True-False or Completion varieties, so that the subjects spent very little time in writing.

[9] This work was made possible by the interested cooperation of Professor R. S. Woodworth, Professor Harry Overstreet and Professor W. B. Pillsbury. It was aided by a grant from the University of Michigan Research Fund.

[10] H. E. Jones, "Phenomenal Memorizing as a Special Ability," *Jour. of Applied Psych.*, 10: 367–376, 1926.

[11] W. S. Hunter, "Auditory Sensitivity of the White Rat," *Jour. of Animal Behavior*, 4: 215–222, 1914.

In order to avoid much guessing students were asked to indicate whether they were sure or doubtful of their answers by checking an S or D for each item. In order to roughly distinguish two sorts of learning patterns, two kinds of questions were included, "information" and "inference." The "information" questions were constructed so that they could be answered directly from a single line or two of the text. The "inference" items depended upon a comparison between two or more parts of the text. They seemed to require more complex thinking processes and they were more difficult to answer than the "information" items. While there is no sharp dividing line between these two kinds of items, they probably involve different emphases. Each True-False test contained fifty items, of which thirty-five were designed to be information items and fifteen inference items. A sample of each follows:

Information:

T F S D The Russian psychologist found a final differentiation of tone of four vibrations per second by the salivary reflex in dogs.

Inference:

T F S D The learning process is, according to K. S. Lashley, largely a process of inhibiting certain neural connections.

The reliability of these tests as shown by the correlation of odd-even item scores was on the average .45, which is raised by the Brown-Spearman formula to .62. This coefficient compares favorably with current subject tests, E. P. Wood[12] and standard reading tests, Current and Ruch,[13] of similar length using similar groups. The reliability is also indicated by the repetitions of the tests. Correlations were found when tests were repeated after intervals of one week, to range between .47 and .86, mean .65. These figures probably show as great constancy of measurement as can be expected with this kind of narrow sampling of material and students.

[12] E. P. Wood, "Improving the Validity of College Achievement Tests," *Jour. Ed. Psychol.*, 18: 18–26, 1927.

[13] W. F. Current and G. M. Ruch, "Further Studies on the Reliability of Reading Tests," *Jour. of Ed. Psychol.*, 117: 476–481, 1926.

The validity of the tests was guaranteed somewhat by their construction. The writer composed them and submitted them for suggestion to two or three instructors who were familiar with the material. After some rewriting the tests were then given to small groups of students who pointed out other ambiguities. In final form they were given to a group of 28 students who had not read the topics, and the average of this group was 9 per cent. correct without guessing. In spite of these precautions there is room for improvement in both the choice of items and their construction, but the tests represent a fair sampling of the information presented and its most common interpretation.

The following methods of presentation have been included at various times:

(1) Lecture without note taking; students requested not to take notes.
(2) Lecture with note taking; students requested to follow their usual practise in taking notes.
(3) Unguided reading; without note taking.
(4) Unguided reading; with note taking.
(5) Guided reading; without note taking. Here the students were given the mimeographed test sheets along with the booklets and asked to mark the questions correctly.

In comparing these types of presentation the method of equivalent groups was followed. The groups were carefully equated on the basis of age, sex, schooling and general mental tests. In some experiments the types of presentation were rotated to eliminate possible differences in sampling. Thus in comparing the relative effectiveness of lectures and silent reading six topics were used with two equivalent groups of approximately 125 students each. One group was given Topics 1, 3 and 5 by lecture and Topics 2, 4 and 6 by reading. The other group was given Topics 1, 3 and 5 by reading and 2, 4 and 6 by lecture. In other experiments each group was given all topics by one method of presentation to see if there might be some practise effect from the repetition of procedures. A more technical description of some of the methods, subjects and tests may be found in articles by Greene,[14,15] and unpublished data in the writer's files.

[14] E. B. Greene, "The Relative Effectiveness of Lecture and Individual Reading as Methods of

The results shown in Table 1 may be summarized as follows:

(1) *Lecture vs. silent unguided reading:* The immediate test results showed that the average student did as well from the lectures as from

TABLE 1

RESULTS OF VARIOUS PRESENTATIONS ON IMMEDIATE AND DELAYED TESTS

		Per cent. correct of total possible score			
		Immediate test		Delayed test	
	N	Mean	S.D.	Mean	S.D.
Lecture:					
Notes taken ...	129	57.8	5.6	46.3	4.2
Notes used on delayed test	114	59.2	4.9	54.7	4.7
Without notes	77	58.2	5.3	47.0	3.9
Unguided reading:					
Notes taken ...	106	56.9	8.7	46.4	7.7
Without notes	104	53.1	9.5	41.2	6.9
Guided reading...	118	83.2	9.7	64.1	6.9

the reading with no reliable differences on any topics. When the students were divided and compared on the basis of their reading ability, as shown by Part I of the Thorndike College Entrance Examination, some large differences appeared. The highest quarter of the group in reading ability tended to do much better after individual reading than after lectures, while the opposite was true for the lowest quarter. The good readers averaged approximately 215 words per minute and the poor readers 97 words per minute. The lecture thus tended to hold back the best readers and accelerate the presentation for the poor readers on these particular topics. Statistically the chances are about one in five thousand that a student in the highest quarter of readers would do as well after one of these lectures as he would after reading for himself. Three quarters of these students indicated more satisfaction from their own reading than from these lectures.

College Teaching,'' *Genet. Psychol. Monog.*, 4: No. 6, 1928.

[15] E. B. Greene, ''Effectiveness of Various Rates of Silent Reading of College Students,'' *Jour. of Applied Psych.*, 15: 214–227, 1931.

Approximately five sixths of the poor and of the average readers indicated a preference for the lectures as a method of presentation. The reasons for these preferences were ascertained. While they do not adequately analyze the processes, still they may throw considerable light on them. The reasons given by students for preferring individual reading were principally:

(1) Reading was much faster than speaking; allowed more time to go over interesting or new parts of topic.
(2) Reading more active, more concentrated.
(3) No losses through temporary inattention.
(4) Visual impression more effective.
(5) Lecturer and audience distract from learning.

The reasons given for preferring the lectures were:

(1) Presentation of the lecturer more entertaining.
(2) Slow reader, not enough time allowed to read.
(3) Auditory impression more effective.

The results did not show that either method of presentation favored any particular test item or group of items. On delayed tests the amounts forgotten were nearly the same for both types of presentation where no opportunity had been given for reviews. The average dropped from approximately 57 per cent. correct of the total possible score to 46 per cent. correct. The highest and lowest quarters of the group seemed to drop in nearly the same proportions.

(2) *The lecture vs. guided reading:* During the guided reading periods the students were given the tests along with the booklets and asked to answer the questions. They read the questions first, then looked for the answers in the booklets. This activity of searching and evaluating the material presented seemed much more lively than either the lecture or unguided reading procedures. Students who had hitherto sat passively now sat up straighter, complained about poor lighting and showed other signs of getting to work.

The results on immediate tests show that the average student got approximately 57 per cent. correct after the lectures and 83 per cent. after the guided reading. On the delayed tests the former dropped to 46 per cent. and the latter to 64 per cent. Best readers tended to show a little greater relative difference between the two procedures than the poorer readers, but the proportions of change were very similar.

The results also showed a marked difference in the correct answers for "inference" items. On immediate tests the lecture resulted in approximately 15 per cent. correct of total inference items, and the guided reading, in 76 per cent. correct; on delayed tests 10 per cent. and 62 per cent., respectively. This indicates that the inference items were retained slightly better than the information items after the guided reading procedure, but not after the lecture. The students estimated that the guided reading was more effective than unguided reading or lecture in 91 per cent. of the cases. The reasons given for preferring the guided reading were:

(1) Greater interest because a more questioning approach was made. More challenging.
(2) More satisfaction because you know when you have the right answer.
(3) More active than other methods.
(4) More definite directions.

(3) *The effects of note taking during lecture and unguided reading:* The notes taken by students were collected and carefully scored according to a carefully standardized scale.[16] When allowed, approximately 53 per cent. of all students took some notes during the unguided reading and 72 per cent. during lectures. Somewhat more detailed notes were taken during lecture than reading periods. If 20 words per minute is taken as the average rate of writing, the average student spent approximately 19 per cent. of the lecture periods and 16 per cent. of the reading periods in writing notes as well as listening or reading.

The results show very regularly that on immediate tests groups which were not allowed to take any notes did as well as groups which were encouraged to follow their usual practises in note taking. This was also true of delayed tests when the notes were not available for reference or review. Furthermore, in a group allowed to take notes, the excellence of note-taking proved to be of little aid on an immediate test, for the product moment correlations between grade of notes taken and scores on immediate tests averaged approximately .16.

One group of 114 students was allowed to refer to their notes on the delayed test. Of course, the students who had taken detailed notes benefited much more than those who had not. The average delayed test without aid from one's own notes showed approximately 46 per cent. correct, and with notes 54 per cent. correct. The improvement due to notes was principally in "information" items, rather than "inference" items, indicating that the notes were not clear or detailed enough for the kinds of comparison required by the "inference" items. The results of using notes are still far below the average delayed test results (roughly 64 per cent. correct) from guided reading. Statistically, there is about one chance in five thousand that any student will do as well from lecture or unguided reading with the aid of notes as he will from guided reading, on either immediate tests or tests delayed for 4 weeks.

In explanation of these results it is urged that there are very large and important differences in method. Also, the students seemed to work considerably harder during the guided reading than during the lecture or the unguided reading. This was an almost unanimous report of both students and instructors. Most of the students also reported more interest and more reasoning activity. In trying to analyze learning processes one is baffled by a lack of knowledge of the essential mechanisms of learning and the varied results of experimental attempts. From nearly all theoretical points of view, however, learning takes place more rapidly and more permanently if there is a particular tension or desire which gives intensity or concentration to the act. Furthermore, in situations, such as a topical presentation of experimental procedures, the organization of the items or generalizations into more meaningful patterns is probably a most important act of learning. Little seems to be retained without this "organizing" activity over a long period of time (Greene,[17] Powers[18]) unless it is continually

[16] *Op. cit.*

[17] E. B. Greene, "The Retention of Information Learned in College Classes," *Jour. of Ed. Res.*, 24: 262–273, 1931.

[18] S. R. Powers, "Diagnostic Study of Subject Matter of High School Chemistry," Teachers Col-

used or relearned. The guided reading seems to demand this activity of comparison and organization to a much larger extent than the others.

It would not be urged that the guided reading as used here is ideal in the choice of questions. With more careful consideration of objectives, better materials could undoubtedly be prepared.

It may also be argued that this guided reading method affords too much guidance, and that a student should be left to discover important relationships for himself. This, of course, must differ with the students and the particular course, but in so far as a course does seek to develop techniques or evaluation, some guidance is helpful. The guided reading seems to offer by far the most efficient method of concentrating on course objectives such as the acquisition of specific information and comparison of various relationships.

Summary and Conclusions

This study has made comparisons between three methods of presenting material to college students; lectures, unguided reading and guided reading, with and without notes. It was found on both immediate tests and tests after from one to four weeks that the results of the guided reading were very superior to either the results of the lecture or the unguided reading. The differences were in all cases large and reliable. This superiority was greater in items which required inferences from more than one part of the topic than in items which required only specific information. Roughly, the gain of the guided reading method over either of the others was 50 per cent. for information items and 500 per cent. for inference items. It is thought that these differences were due to the more active comparisons made during the guided reading and the greater interest shown. On the delayed tests the "inference" items were retained a little better than "information" items. These results indicate that for this situation there is not as much as one chance in five thousand statistically calculated that any student from these groups would do as well after either lecture or unguided reading, as after the guided reading periods.

The comparison of lecture and unguided reading procedures showed that the average student did equally well after either presentation, but that the good readers did considerably better after their own reading than they did after the lectures, while the poor readers did better after the lectures than after their own reading.

During some of the lecture and unguided reading periods students were allowed to take notes in their usual manner. These notes were collected and scored according to a fairly reliable scale. There was a tendency for a larger percentage of students to take notes during their lectures than during their own reading and the notes taken during lectures were more detailed than those taken during reading. On immediate and delayed tests the effect of note-taking was negligible when students were not allowed to use their notes for review. When allowed to inspect their notes during the delayed tests the group averages improved considerably, from approximately 46 per cent. to 54 per cent. of total items, but not to the level of averages from the guided reading periods of 64 per cent. correct.

These results are fairly conclusive for the particular students and presentations reported, but they should not be used as a basis for sweeping generalizations concerning the relative worth of all lectures and guided study plans. A large number of extremely significant and interesting studies must be made in order to evaluate differences in rate of presentation, effectiveness of individual lecturers, complexity of topics and demonstrations, training in listening, reading and note-taking. In addition, the total situation must be considered in such matters as availability of printed material and traditional practises.

Edward B. Greene
University of Michigan

lege, Columbia University, Contrib. to Ed., 149: pp. 49–54, 1924.

NEW BOOKS IN EDUCATION

Gardner, Ernest A. *Greece and the Aegean.* Pp. 254. Illustrated. McBride. $2.50.

Loomis, A. K. and others. *The Program of Studies.* Pp. x + 340. National Survey of Secondary Education Monograph No. 19. U. S. Government Printing Office.

Tuttle, Harold S. *A Social Basis of Education.* Pp. x + 589. Crowell. $3.00.

SCHOOL AND SOCIETY

WITH WHICH ARE COMBINED THE EDUCATIONAL REVIEW, ESTABLISHED IN 1891, THE TEACHERS MAGAZINE, ESTABLISHED IN 1878, AND THE SCHOOL JOURNAL, ESTABLISHED IN 1874.

J. McKEEN CATTELL AND ALFRED L. HALL-QUEST

EDITORIAL COMMUNICATIONS SHOULD BE ADDRESSED TO THE EDITORS OF SCHOOL AND SOCIETY, 3941 GRAND CENTRAL TERMINAL, NEW YORK, N. Y.

Volume 39 | SATURDAY, MAY 19, 1934 | Number 1012

EDUCATION, A SOCIAL TOOL[1]

By Chancellor HARRY WOODBURN CHASE

NEW YORK UNIVERSITY

MUCH current popular discussion of education in the United States seems to go forward on the same sort of assumptions that were made by the older economics about the material with which it dealt. There was, you remember, an abstraction known as the "economic man," who was supposed to behave in strictly logical ways, and one built up a system on the assumption that he would so behave. When he insisted on misbehaving economically, it was a sad commentary on him and his judgment, but not, of course, on the theories, which were logical and therefore necessarily correct.

In somewhat the same way, a great deal of conversation goes on about American education, which seems to assume that education is an abstract process existing in a vacuum, and not, as it is, an existing and established social institution, a system with a great variety of social urges and pressures, which has assumed a pretty definite pattern and which is subject to control by a great number and a wide range of social forces operating both from within and from without its own boundaries.

It has seemed to me, therefore, that, especially at a time like this, we need more insistent and more realistic study of education from, if you please, the institutional point of view; from the standpoint of an analysis of the educational system as a social institution, subject to social forces and controls, subject to general social laws, sharing in part in the common social psychology of established institutions generally, and distinguished in part by certain concrete social pressures and controls that are characteristic of itself. After all, our thinking about what education can and should do or leave undone must rest, not alone on an agreement as to what is desirable, but on an understanding of the character of the structure which conditions and limits what is possible.

Such a point of view is, of course, not new to any thoughtful observer of education. It has been stated many times, and it is ignored at his peril by any educational administrator, who must deal with concrete situations that arise out of such a background. And yet it is a point of view which I am convinced needs more careful analysis and wider recognition. To take a single illustration, there is a general consensus of opinion that secondary education in this country, especially the last two years of high school and the first two years of college (which are properly included in

[1] Fifth Annual Davies Lecture, delivered before the Institute of Arts and Sciences, Columbia University, New York, April 18.

secondary education), needs radical revision. There is even fairly general agreement as to what the main lines of that revision should be, and yet, with regard to the system as a whole, very little happens. Why not? The answer, and therefore the answer as to how to make something happen, can not be given without an analysis, from the institutional point of view, of the social characteristics, forces and controls which operate and have operated to give the existing system of secondary education its established form and structure.

What, therefore, I want to do to-night is to take one illustration of this general point, to say something about the characteristics of education in this country at one level, as an established social institution. I take, naturally, the field with which I am most familiar, that of higher education. What are some of its common institutional traits?

In the first place, let me point out that our institutions for higher education do actually form a highly compact system, welded together by strong forces which operate on that system as a whole, and render it, in temper, highly orthodox and conservative. The Office of Education in Washington recognizes something like five hundred colleges and universities in the United States, and the addition of teachers colleges, normal schools, technical and professional schools of various types probably brings the number close to a thousand. Within this group, and especially within the group of colleges and universities, the pressure toward conformity is exceedingly strong, so strong in fact that only a handful of institutions or of departments within institutions are in a position to ignore it and go their own way. These pressures arise both from within the system itself and from without. They are so strongly marked that more than one educational institution, founded to report new ideas and procedures, has found itself gradually becoming conventionalized and forced into the common mould. Let us first consider a few of those operating from within.

The system as a whole, for example, is still dominated by entrance requirements stated in terms of fifteen units of work completed in secondary schools with periods of such and such length, with a given content and with particular patterns and interrelations of subjects that are assumed to possess some mysterious virtue. The standardizing agencies of the country, which have rendered a valuable and necessary service, have, at the same time, up until very recently, themselves been dominated almost altogether by the idea of fixing a definite pattern to which institutions should conform. An institution, in order to be accredited, must have so many books in its library, such and such a proportion of Ph.D.'s on its faculty, a given amount of endowment or its equivalent, such and such requirements for its degrees and all the rest of a long line of standards of such character. These have sometimes operated in a curious fashion. I recall when I was in the South being visited by a representative of a small college which was anxious to be admitted to the Southern Association, and which therefore found it necessary to increase the number of volumes in its library. This representative came into my office and asked me if the university faculty could not make some donations of books to her college. I asked her what kind of books she wanted, and her reply was that it was a matter of no importance whatever, that they had to meet the standards of the association of a certain number of volumes and that was all they were interested in.

The tendency to fall into this common mould has been reinforced by the fact that graduate students, trained in the larger universities, have gone out through the country carrying with them a definite stamp, by the fact that the same text-books are widely used and the same curricula set up. The growth of the influence of learned societies again has produced a sense of professional solidarity that has involved common outlooks and view-points. Any one who has had experience with the way in which curricula are made in most institutions is familiar with the fact that the first procedure of a curriculum committee is to get a large assemblage of catalogues from other institutions and to try to determine from these, not what is the best practise fitted to the individual needs of the institution, but what is the standard current practise of institutions in general. Thus it is that of the hundreds of colleges and universities in America only a handful have conducted significant educational experiments. The system as a whole is conventional, traditional and orthodox. In this it does not differ altogether from other social institutions. Its mass is only slowly permeated by new educational ideas. It changes with difficulty and with reluctance. Furthermore, such resistance to change is reinforced by the existence of fixed interests within the institutions themselves. Changes in curricula which involve changes in the status of departments within institutions, invoke, as everybody knows, a high degree of resistance.

The introduction of newer fields of knowledge brings out the protest on the part of older established interests that the standards in these newer fields are inferior. Newer types of objective tests and examinations spread very slowly in actual use because they disturb the traditional ideas of what examinations ought to be. I recall a department head that had followed the movement toward objective tests in his field with a great deal of interest, who told me that he had a complete collection of such tests in his files and that they were no good. I asked him if he had ever tried them out and he said that that wasn't necessary, because he knew from looking at them that they were not in line with the established principles of teaching in his field. I have, I confess, been somewhat amused by some of the statements that have been made that colleges and universities are hotbeds of radicalism. I believe that any one who has had experience with them and who has seen the extraordinary difficulty with which changes come about in them could scarcely share in such a feeling.

Now, like all social institutions, higher education is also subject to strong pressures from without. These pressures are, naturally, in the direction of reinforcing the existing *mores* and therefore contribute to the orthodox and stable pattern of the system as a whole. Illustrations are obvious and numerous. If the community, or the sustaining body, is ultra-conservative in its religious beliefs, the biologist finds himself in trouble, and his teaching may even be interfered with by law. If sentiment is militaristic, an institution which is averse to military training finds itself in difficulties. Tensions and pressures from public opinion in the field of the social sciences are, and promise to be, very great. With certain even more fundamental results of social pressures from without I shall deal in a moment.

I have not attempted to do more than illustrate the types of influences which have been at work, within and without, to contribute to the extreme conventionality of our American system of higher education.

But the most important effects of social pressures from without on our institutions are concerned with a very real change in the social functions of our whole system of higher education. This change has been in the making for a long time, but it has proceeded at a highly accelerated pace during the last generation. To put it briefly, higher education as a system has become our chief instrument for facilitating individual migration to higher social and economic levels, and, largely in consequence, it has reflected, more and more, the American philosophy of the value of economic success, of which, indeed, it has come to be considered as the chief agent.

Let us consider these points for a moment. The traditional conception of higher education in America assumed that the students who availed themselves of its opportunities were, on the whole, those who were economically and socially privileged. Going to college for most of these students did not involve a change in the social and economic class to which they belonged before and after their college experience. The years of higher education were, it is true, informally pointed toward laying the basis for training for a small and limited group of professions. But essentially the years of college were years devoted to general culture, to the acquisition of backgrounds rather than to techniques. Now all this is changed. I am speaking, you understand, once more of the system as a whole. The foundation and growth of the state and municipal universities, the development of junior colleges, the growth of colleges and universities, whose main task is that of popular education, have not been accidental. Such a development, which has resulted in an increase of 600 per cent. in thirty years in the enrolments of colleges and universities, has been in response to an essential change in the conditions of American life. Immigration, the growth of cities, the passing of the frontiers, the increased complexity of our economic life, these things have meant more and more that the road to opportunity is visualized as running through the college campus.

Opportunity, in the public mind, has come to be regarded as being made possible but by prolonging and vocationalizing the period of preparation for life. In response to this tendency we have tremendously increased the area of our professional training. The schools of agriculture and mechanic arts that were founded in the early sixties and seventies as a result of the Morril Act were undoubtedly conceived in the beginning as intended to do work of more of a semi-professional character for students who could not avail themselves of college and university education. Gradually, however, both those that were separate institutions and those which were parts of state universities came to regard themselves as distinctly professional schools. There began schools of engineering, forestry, nursing, library schools, schools of education, dentistry, pharmacy, medicine, law, commerce, business and so on. The law student no longer reads law in an office. Less and less does he attend proprietary schools. He goes to college for his pre-law work, and the law school he attends is in most instances an integral part of a university organization. Preparation for medicine has evolved from the doctor's office through the proprietary school to the university with standards for professional work which involve not only the medical school itself but the pursuit of a specified curriculum during the pre-medical training. The university, in short, has been a sort of center of gravity which has attracted one agency after another of vocational training, and the college has been dominated by the necessity of preparing for these vocational opportunities.

As a result of this situation the vocational motive now dominates our system from the moment of entrance to college straight on through the graduate work of our universities. Liberal arts colleges must plan their curricula in terms of pre-professional requirements, or else professional schools take charge of the student from the moment of his entrance. Medicine and law, for example, have preferred to use the liberal arts colleges as service schools; engineering has generally followed the other course. In either case, the student is vocationally minded from the start.

No better illustration of what I am trying to point out can be found than the history of the development of the Ph.D. in our graduate schools. It has become, as we all recognize, just as definitely the trade label for admission to the staffs of colleges and universities as the M.D. for entrance to the medical profession. The original idea that it should be conferred only on the completion of a piece of really original and significant research, irrespective of the time element involved, has perforce yielded in practise to the completion of a three-year technical and specialized curriculum, which still includes, to be sure, a thesis that is supposed to show ability in research. But no one would, I suppose, argue that even the majority of the recipients of the degree are capable of pursuing important original research, and, furthermore, in certain fields the difficulties of finding research problems of any real significance which are within the grasp of any but the very exceptional graduate student are becoming more and more apparent. Yet the whole system is so thoroughly organized for specific vocational ends that practise has altogether overwhelmed theory. Schools of education, which have sometimes been accused of vocationalizing the degree, are in this respect no greater sinners than the humanities and the sciences.

So it is that our system of higher education has come to reflect the fundamental characteristics of American life. First, it has become the organ of an unstable society, in which people want to get on and up and in which parents are willing to make enormous sacrifices that their children may do so. Second, it has become geared into the machinery of economic success, and has played a larger and larger part as an instrument of that success.

On the whole, this vocationalizing of the system has come about with a curiously divided attitude on the part of faculties themselves. In the case of the Ph.D., for example, the discussion has had far more to say about older and newer subject-matters than about the altered conception of the degree as a whole; there has been large failure on the part of departments like the humanities and the pure sciences to recognize what was happening in their own fields. To take another illustration, liberal arts faculties have, on the whole, welcomed the definition of requirements for pre-medical students on the part of the medical profession, a definition which, until recently, has made a really liberal education for pre-medical students who were not college graduates almost impossible. On the other hand, they have as a rule opposed the attitude of state boards of education with regard to specific requirements for the training of teachers. Yet both these pressures have been based, at bottom, on precisely the same philosophy.

On the whole, it seems a fair generalization, subject, of course, to many exceptions and qualifications, that our system of higher education performs the social function which it does perform to-day more because of outside than of inside pressures and influences. It has been shaped, in other words, more largely by the desires of students, of parents and of public opinion generally, in its main objectives and purposes, than by those of its faculties.

Furthermore, where the influences of faculties from within have been strong, they have usually been, for obvious reasons, in the direction of conservatism. Consider, for example, the situation in our liberal arts colleges, both those which exist as independent units and those which are parts of universities. May I remind you once more that I am speaking of general tendencies in our system as a whole, not of individual cases. I do not believe that liberal arts colleges can lay their present haziness with regard to what they should be doing wholly at the doors of the vocations. They have, rather, not been sufficiently clear as to their own possibilities to be able to insist on the importance, with the vocational framework, of a reinterpretation of their own task in the light of changed conditions. One ventures, naturally, at this point, into the region of personal opinion. For my part, I am convinced that the central task of liberal arts colleges must derive from the attempt to put people into touch with contemporary civilization. I do not mean to disregard the past, from which the present derives. Nor do I mean to assume that they should attempt a fixed and static adjustment in a rapidly shifting world. I mean, rather, that their graduates need to look out on modern life with some understanding and appreciation and with certain attitudes and values. But, in most instances, there seems to exist neither this nor any other central principle of unification for the efforts of teachers and students. Curricula are disjointed and largely in water-tight compartments. The predominant influences which have created the situation seem to be two. First, there is the implicit assumption on the part of the specialist that subject-matters are specialized and that they should be taught from the beginning very much as though all beginning students were taking their first feeble steps toward the doctorate. In my judgment, for example, much of the elementary instruction in the natural sciences in our liberal arts colleges is wasteful, emphasizes too much laboratory technique, is over-specialized and fails to give the student any real sense of fundamental scientific conceptions of the view-point of science itself and of the importance of that view-point in the modern world. Courses in biology, for example, based on the idea of attempting, not to make students biologists, but to give them a biological slant on life, are altogether too few.

Second, there is still great over-emphasis on the importance of the formal subjects for the general student. Much teaching of foreign languages, for example, goes on mainly as mental exercise, resulting neither in ability to speak the language nor in appreciation of its literature.

Whether most liberal arts colleges are too much in the grip of existing tendencies to make a thorough reconstruction possible is debatable. In case they are not, since it is becoming more and more clear that the social function they should perform must be done somehow, we may look probably for the creation of quite new types of institutions that will undertake this task. Inertia and tradition and the satisfaction of vested interests do not stand forever in the way of important social needs. If the emerging junior college proves in these respects more responsive to social needs, liberal arts colleges face, I suspect, difficult days, unless they resolutely attempt, not further patching away at existing curricula, but the sort of reconstruction which makes of them colleges which are both liberal and devoted to the arts of life.

Now to return once more to the general functions of higher education. No one, I suppose, can be blind to the fact that a task is beginning to emerge which is destined to assume great importance. Some one has rather cynically remarked that many of us send our children to college because we don't know what else to do with them. This, so to speak, custodial function of higher education on the undergraduate level has always been in evidence, of course. But it bids fair to assume a greatly increased importance in view of the growing recognition of the fact that scarcity of employment is not an immediately curable fact in our society. To reduce it to its lowest terms, jobs for young people who have finished high school are scarce and will remain scarce. Society is faced with the question of what it will do with its young people up to the age of maturity. The only constructive answer to that question is that of education. It seems fair to look, therefore, as this responsibility is increasingly realized, for a prolongation upward to the period of popular education. Inevitably, such a result will increase still more the present vocational set-up of our system. Whether it will be narrowly vocational or something more is a question of great importance. Here lies a great opportunity for the liberal arts colleges, if they are wise enough to avail themselves of it.

In all that I have been saying to-night, some of you will probably feel that I have neglected a large amount of constructive leadership on the part of men and institutions. That is true. I have been concerned, rather, to discuss the system of higher education as an existing and established institution, welded together into an orthodox pattern, conservative and conventionalized, geared into the machinery of economic success, and the most important agent in contemporary society for the forwarding of industrial opportunity, with a growing custodial function as social needs push upward the limits of popular education. This, I confess, seems to me a fairly accurate analysis of the situation as a whole.

What, then, lies ahead? Let me say, first of all, that I believe that both those who fear and those who hope that our system of higher education is a possible agency of social and economic reconstruction are doomed to disappointment. It is too cumbersome, too traditional, and, above all, too highly set in the direction of the provision of opportunity for the individual to make the system as a system so function. It will, I venture, continue to express the prevailing American philosophy, and only in case that philosophy should itself alter would its own motivation alter, and that only slowly and with considerable lag.

Nor do I look for any marked change in its strong vocational set-up. It is true that there is heavy unemployment among college and university graduates; but, after all, what other agency does American civilization to-day provide for the still strong upward urge? Only in a more highly stratified and more stable society would one look for a marked departure from the set. Naturally, with more intense competition, guidance, selection and higher standards will play an increasing rôle, but these things do not modify the dominant tendencies.

But I will not venture further into the field of prophecy. I will merely venture this concluding opinion: That our system of higher education, considered as a whole, is to-day one of our most definitely motivated, least flexible and highly static of our social institutions.

OUTSTANDING WEAKNESSES OF HIGH-SCHOOL FRESHMEN[1]

By Dr. GUSTAVE A. FEINGOLD

PRINCIPAL, BULKELEY HIGH SCHOOL, HARTFORD, CONNECTICUT

THE mass invasion and the overcrowding of the secondary schools, which began in boom times, has been greatly intensified by the impossibility of dropping from the rolls the incompetent pupils who are entering in these depression times. Consequently, the problem of how to handle the misfits in the high school is more baffling

[1] Address delivered before Section Q of the American Association for the Advancement of Science, Cambridge, Massachusetts, December 29, 1933.

now than ever before. To cope with this situation as it exists in Hartford, Connecticut, and as it must exist in other communities where the 8–4 plan is in operation, a questionnaire on the outstanding weaknesses of high-school freshmen was addressed to more than one hundred high-school teachers. They were asked to name in order of importance the weaknesses of lower freshmen when they first enter school; which of these weaknesses are a real hindrance to their studies; what suggestions they can offer in the way of overcoming the difficulties; and to comment specifically on whether the freshmen know how to prepare home assignments, whether they are properly equipped in the use of the English language and whether they are receiving adequate training in enunciation and oral reading, so that when they are called upon to recite other members of the class may be able to benefit from their recitations.

A tabulation of the replies from the 101 high-school instructors, representing the departments of English, mathematics, science, history, foreign languages and business, shows that the lack of knowledge of fundamentals—such as grammar, spelling, vocabulary and arithmetic—is considered as the most outstanding weakness of the ninth grade pupils. The other weaknesses listed in order of rank are: Inability to comprehend the printed page; poor study habits; lack of concentration; self-complacency or too easily satisfied with mediocre results; too great dependence on the teacher, manifested in a lack of self-reliance and initiative; inability to follow instructions; and, finally, inability to speak distinctly when called upon to recite. Other weaknesses mentioned are such as the lack of a sense of values or relationships; failure to use ordinary instruction aids, such as notes and dictionaries; and failure to use model examples and illustrations.

In reply to the question, "Which of the weaknesses are a real hindrance to the pupils in their first-year high-school work?" fifty-five teachers declared categorically that all the weaknesses mentioned are a hindrance. Some felt, however, that the lack of fundamentals was responsible for more failures than any other single cause; while others declared that the inability of the pupils to understand what they read or to follow directions was the second greatest cause of high-school mortality.

In reply to the question on how the difficulties mentioned might be overcome, the high-school teachers recommend that commencing with the seventh grade pupils should be trained specifically for their high-school studies and responsibilities. Departmental instruction should be introduced in the seventh grade so as to cultivate self-reliance and the ability to glean information out of books. Especially should the child be imbued with the understanding early in life that school is not play and that many unpleasant things, including the mastery of the fundamentals of grammar, sentence structure and arithmetic, have to be endured before success can be attained. Especially should the habit of home work and the ability to read clearly and distinctly while standing and facing the class be developed in the children before they enter high school. The high-school teachers further recommend more concentration on a few fundamental subjects, rather than the spreading out over a wide field, which seems to be the increasing tendency in the elementary schools.

There is also a general complaint that the pupils who have been entering high school in the past half dozen years are deplorably deficient in initiative and courage. This has been noticed by faculty advisers in extra-curricular activities, as well as by classroom teachers. To state the matter in the words of one of the faculty advisers: "The lack of initiative on the part of many pupils is disheartening. They seem to feel that they are beginning something that they will never finish and thus put a minimum of effort on their work."

This is rather a crushing indictment of the so-called Progressive education movement which is creeping into the public schools. The goal of Progressive education is to develop initiative by giving free rein to the special abilities of young people. But in doing this it also develops a distaste for duty performed at personal sacrifice. It does it at the expense of failing to train them how to stick to a task even when it is painful and when the ultimate result is so far removed that it can not be foreseen by them. Finally, it does it at the expense of failing to equip them with the essential tools of life, the early handling of which may produce swollen hands, perhaps, but which are nevertheless necessary in training young people how to get along with confidence, enthusiasm and some degree of success among their fellow men. The failure to inculcate the few necessary fundamentals overwhelms the high-school freshman with a sense of utter helplessness and with an inferiority complex which is crushing to his spirit and to such native ability as he may possess.

Let no one overlook the fact that our degree of self-expression is directly proportionate to the things that fill our minds, the things that can readily shape themselves on our tongues. How can we expect high-school freshmen to perform simple operations in elementary algebra or to discuss intelligently what they read in text-books, when they find themselves incapable of handling the rudimentary operations of arithmetic or to grasp the meaning of simple expressions or even to pronounce correctly ordinary English words?

The inability of high-school freshmen to recite with sufficient clearness to make themselves understood by other members of the class or to grasp the meaning of the printed word is attributed to the fad of silent reading which spread through the elementary schools of the country some dozen years ago. The tremendous falling off in the numbers pursuing foreign languages in the high schools—it has been 40 per cent. in the last ten years—may be attributed in part, at least, to the tying of the tongue brought about by silent reading. Everybody knows that the ability to analyze words into their component parts is the most essential requisite in the beginning of foreign language study. And this ability is neglected in silent reading.

There is no lack of persons who would place the blame for poor pronunciation upon the home rather than on the elementary school. Their claim is that many more children from foreign homes now enter high school than ever before. These people should be reminded, however, that if the argument is to be fair it must hold in both directions; and in that event they must concede that there are an equal number of cases where credit for the good habits of speech should likewise be attributed to the home rather than to the school. In view of the fact, however, that children now attending public schools are more homogeneous than any schools population since the '80's, owing to the complete cessation of immigration since 1914, are we justified in attributing educational shortcomings to the home rather than to the school? We must not forget that virtually all children in this country now under eighteen years of age were born in the United States and that their habits of speech, such as they are, were started in our own kindergartens.

To illustrate how poorly equipped grammar-school children are when they first enter high school, I need only refer to the results of a test in English usage recently given to 270 freshmen five weeks after they were admitted to high school. The vehicle used was the O'Rourke Test. The average intelligence of the 270 lower freshmen was I.Q. 100; their average mark on the English test was 40.8 on a scale of 100. Only 23 per cent. of them passed the test. Their achievement quotient was 82.1. The same test given to 354 upper freshmen, who were six months older than the others, and whose average I.Q. was 104, yielded an average mark of 49.4; with an achievement quotient of 90. Fifty-one per cent. of these passed the test, as compared with 23 per cent. of the lower freshmen. Apparently, after six months of enrolment and study in the high school, more than twice as many were able to pass the minimum requirement and all of them showed an absolute improvement of almost 20 per cent.

If we ask what is the fundamental cause of the inadequate preparation with which grammar-school children enter upon their high-school work, we are driven to the conclusion that it lies in the wrong point of view which the grammar schools seem to take of their function in the educational scheme. It appears that some educators still follow the antiquated theory that the purpose of the grammar school is to prepare for active life, and so the children are given a smattering of everything from the intricacies of stocks and bonds to esthetic dancing, as their preparation. It is significant to note that the high school does not presume to load the minds of even its most capable pupils—those who are taking the college preparatory course and who in time might become the bankers, the engineers, the doctors, the city and state officials—with such worldly problems and social graces. The goal that the high school sets up for these pupils is to give them a thorough preparation in elementary mathematics, in one or two foreign languages, in English and in one or two sciences—trusting that they will manage to pick up a little more knowledge about the affairs of life after they graduate from the secondary school.

It was quite proper to prepare elementary school children "for life" when not more than 50 or 60 per cent. of them used to enter high school and when not more than 30 per cent. of these remained in high school long enough to secure a diploma. But with conditions as they are now, and as they will continue to be in our increasingly regulated machine age, 95 per cent. of the grammar-school graduates are admitted to high school, and of these some 75 or 80 per cent. receive the high-school diploma. Does it not seem reasonable, therefore, to demand that the emphasis of grammar-school instruction should be placed primarily upon preparation for the secondary school?

Now, what does this involve? It involves, in the first place, the establishment of at least two curriculums in the elementary school, beginning with the seventh grade. In the second place, it involves a really scientific program of homogeneous grouping, starting with the primary grades.

If the grammar school is to fall in line with modern educational trends, it must adopt one curriculum preparing specifically for the high school; and another preparing for further development of the individual on a horizontal plane. The former curriculum should embrace all pupils who, by the time they have completed the sixth grade, have given unmistakable proof of their ability to go on with high-school studies; while the latter should be designed for all children who do not show such promise by the end of the sixth grade. Generally speaking, this group would be made up of children with I.Q.'s below 90.

There is no good reason why this type of pupil, who is incapable of book learning beyond the sixth-grade level, should be compelled to mark time in the seventh and eighth grades, and then suddenly be catapulted into the high school with the expectation that the spelling, the reading, the civics and arithmetic of the sixth grade will be provided for him for four more years. To be sure, there are some educators who would make of the public high school a waiting station on the way to the coalyard, the car barn and the wash tub. But these good people forget that education for the masses is one thing, and education for the morons is an entirely different thing; and that it is illogical to maintain that the high school should remain "high" and at the same time provide education for the mentally low. How generally is it known, I wonder, that in at least one large city in New England the State Board of Education makes it obligatory for the high schools to accept and "educate" pupils whose I.Q.'s are too low for admission to the trade-school supported by that same board.

If it is claimed that intensive training in the arts and crafts can not be introduced in the seventh and eighth grades because a certain irreducible minimum of academic subjects must be taught to grammar school children, it should be remembered that an equally irreducible minimum of mathematics, foreign language, science and literature must also be taught to high-school pupils. And this can not be done if an increasing number of youths whose mental development has stopped at the sixth-grade level have to be housed in the high school. Why should any boy be allowed to graduate from high school without a rudimentary knowledge of plane geometry or elementary chemistry or physics? Surely, this type of knowledge is just as essential in our technological age as the knowledge of how to repair a motor car or to match the wallpaper in the house. The most surprising thing about those who would spread out the elementary school education until it embraces almost everything that man has created, including the automobile, the radio, the moving picture, the electric washer and beauty culture, is that they forget that all these things were created and incorporated into American life by a generation which was brought up almost exclusively on the "Three R's." Apparently, the "Three R's" do not in themselves militate against the development and enjoyment of a technological life. No, it would seem best that the singleness of purpose of the secondary school should color the efforts of the elementary school rather than that the kindergarten practises should permeate the whole of our public school educational policy.

Another defect which illustrates the lack of integration between the two branches of public education, and which unquestionably redounds to the injury of the child, is the almost total lack of male instructors in the American elementary schools. For instance, the writer discovered that in such a large and prosperous city as Hartford, not more than seven male classroom teachers of academic subjects out of a total of eight hundred instructors were employed in the elementary schools. Why? Is the child in the eighth grade so terribly much more immature than when he reaches the ninth grade as not to require the point of view of a male instructor? Does he undergo such a complete change of body and mind and outlook when he passes from the eighth to the ninth grade that the community should boast that it spends only $94.00 a year on his primary training and close to $175.00 a year on his high-school education? The whole scheme is silly on the face of it. Here again, the adoption of the point of view that the elementary school is preparing for the high school and not for "life" would result in better coordination among the two types of institutions.

It is quite likely that the lack of initiative among high-school freshmen, so bitterly complained about by high-school teachers, is due to the fact that they are constantly exposed to none but feminine influences in the elementary schools. We must not lose sight of the fact that the boys of well-to-do parents who are being sent to private schools in increasing numbers are almost entirely under the direction of male teachers. Is there no danger that the citizen of to-morrow, who is in the public school of to-day, will grow up to be a spineless, weak individual because of his failure to come in contact with virile men teachers in his formative years, while his more fortunate playmate, whose father is able to afford the expense, will be trained not only for leadership but also how to acquire it? If the public is too poor to pay salaries for male instructors in the elementary schools, then it must not be astonished to see its children become the hangers-on and blind followers, while the chosen places in private and public life fall into the hands of the economically privileged few.

Let no one think that the conditions described here are peculiar to the school systems which operate under the 8–4 plan only. While they are somewhat minimized in communities where the junior-high-school system exists, it is nevertheless true that most of them are merely deferred one year, and instead of cropping out in the ninth grade, they appear in the tenth grade. The writer is aware that it is not the fashion these days to speak of the more substantial values of education. It is much easier to win the general applause by pleading for more art and crafts, for more music and home-making, more typewriting, plumbing and beauty culture in the public schools. The only mistake that such pleaders make is that they overlook the fact that the very individuals who are incapable of comprehending the rudiments of elementary mathematics, foreign languages and science are equally inert to the deeper meaning of art and music, English and history—yes, and even the scientific aspects of beauty culture.

Our study then leads us to the following conclusions:

(1) That greater emphasis should be given in the elementary school to the teaching of the fundamentals of English and arithmetic.

(2) That there should be more assignment of home work in the elementary school, especially in the seventh and eighth grades, so as to develop self-reliance and the habit of getting information out of books.

(3) That there should be less emphasis on silent reading and more on oral recitations in the elementary school, so as to develop the ability of clear, distinct self-expression and to overcome the extreme shyness and timidity so manifest among high-school freshmen.

(4) That the instruction of the seventh and eighth grades should be patterned along the lines of the ninth-grade requirements, so that the gap between the elementary and the high schools should be less bewildering to the children.

(5) That there should be established two distinct curriculums in the grammar school, commencing with the seventh grade—one known as the "high-school" curriculum, designed for those who give unmistaken proof of ability to pursue high-school studies; and the other known as the "general" curriculum, designed for those who are capable of only horizontal development beyond the sixth grade.

(6) That there should be a larger number of properly trained and adequately compensated male instructors in the elementary schools to enable our children to grow up with well-rounded, wholesome attitudes.

We are driven to the view by this investigation that before you can apply knowledge to life, you must possess some degree of knowledge about life, and that it is fantastical to assume that either the grammar schools or the high schools can by themselves and of their own accord prepare for "life" with anything like finality. For the life of the individual is a constantly unfolding process, requiring his constant adjustment to his environment both in his early and later years; and the utmost educators can do is to equip him with a few fundamental tools, to teach him how to use these tools effectively and to develop in him an open attitude of mind favorable for the further acquisition of knowledge and skills in the arena of life.

EDUCATIONAL EVENTS

EDUCATION AND UNEMPLOYMENT IN ENGLAND

THE Archbishop of York's Committee on Unemployment has issued two of a series of pamphlets under the general title of "A Challenge to Christians." The second of these pamphlets, "The School-leaving Age and Juvenile Unemployment," is written by Mr. R. H. Tawney. It is summarized in the London *Times* as follows:

Mr. Tawney argues for the immediate raising of the school age. He says that the educational case put forward by the Hadow Committee for raising the age of compulsory school attendance won general acceptance and is still unanswered; and the arguments of the report have now been reinforced by others more tragic. Even if all young people found employment immediately on leaving school, the proper place for children of 14 would be the school, and not the factory, but "when the economic situation is such as to lend support to a policy which is essentially sound, it is proper that due weight should be given to that consideration." Owing to the increase of the birth rate in the years immediately following the war, the number of boys and girls of 14–18 years of age in 1935 will exceed the number in 1933 by 115,000, in 1936 the increase will be 306,000, and in 1937 it will be 443,000. "The last figure is actually larger than the total number in the age group 14–15 in the present year; the effect of the increase, in fact, is as though a whole new age group were added to the four between 14 and 18. After 1937 the tide will turn, but it will not recede to the former level. It is thought that even in 1940 the number of juveniles available for employment will still be 167,000 above that of 1933."

The question to which Mr. Tawney offers an answer is: "How can the unemployment of boys and girls be ended, except in individual cases of exceptional bad luck, and ended for good?" The answer is: "Continue till 15 the normal progress of education." There would then be held back from employment 438,000 children this year; 405,000 next year; 398,000 in 1936; 372,000 in 1937; 350,000 in 1938; 349,000 in 1939, and 342,000 in 1940. This action would be beneficial to the children retained in school and would make openings in industry for more than all the juvenile workers between 15 and 18.

Mr. Tawney discusses the practical difficulties of the change, and the question of cost. He points out that the net cost will depend on the savings on unemployment benefit now paid to persons who would be reabsorbed into industry when children are not available; on evening schools, and on courses for unemployed juveniles, the last of which has been estimated to require £1,130,000 for 100,000 children. Consequently, the estimate of the Board of Education in 1930 that the cost of retaining the additional age group at school, with maintenance allowances, would be £6,250,000 is out of date. Mr. Tawney maintains that "the decline in the juvenile population gives us an unusually favorable opportunity of effecting an educational and social reform which is long overdue. It would be criminal to allow that opportunity to slip."

THE THIRD INTERNATIONAL CONFERENCE ON PUBLIC EDUCATION

THE Swiss Federal Department of Foreign Affairs has invited all governments to be represented at the third International Conference on Public Education which will open at Geneva on July 11. The agenda for the conference includes the following items: (1) Reports of the Ministries of Public Instruction on the Educational Movement in 1933–1934; (2) The Raising of the School Leaving Age; (3) Admission to Secondary Schools; (4) Economics in the Field of Education. It is hoped by those sponsoring the conference that the features and problems peculiar to education in each country will have in common characteristics sufficient to provide a basis for discussion and planning of value to each country represented. To this end it is proposed that the conference have at its command an authoritative documentation on the educational movement in each country during the school year which will have closed at the time of the conference. The International Bureau of Education, therefore, has invited all the Ministries of Education to send a report summarizing the principal achievements in education during the school year 1933–34. These will later be reproduced in the "Annuaire international de l'Education et de l'Enseignement, 1935."

Because of their special timeliness the Executive Committee of the International Bureau of Education believes that the conference might well examine certain of the questions which have been the object of inquiries and reports by the bureau. Among these the inquiry into the occupations of children leaving school before the authorized age deserves further consideration. The bureau has received replies from fifty countries relative to the question of raising the school-leaving age. This question will receive major consideration at the International Labor Conference in 1935. Because this whole matter of compulsory school age limits has far-reaching effects on unemployment throughout the world the Executive Committee of the International Bureau of Education believes that the problem should be studied in advance by the Ministries of Public Instruction in each country.

The overcrowding of universities and colleges has affected acutely the question of the conditions of admission to secondary schools. Forty countries have supplied the Research Division of the bureau with information bearing on the problem, and the replies have been analyzed by the director of the inquiry and his staff.

Thirty-one countries have replied to an inquiry concerning economics in the field of education. The report, drawn up by the Research Division, which will serve as a basis for the work of the conference, has already appeared. It contains a general summary of the problem and a study by countries based on data furnished by school administrations.

THE RESIDENTIAL COLLEGES OF YALE UNIVERSITY

A statement issued by Yale University summarizes the progress of the residential colleges established a year ago.

Some 1,740 undergraduates applied for the 1,249 available places and for the first time in Yale's history, seniors, juniors and sophomores from the Sheffield Scientific School, Yale College and the Yale School of Engineering are living side by side. The physical as well as artificial boundary lines which once separated the undergraduates in the various schools have been eliminated and an early result has been the election of students in Yale College to the honor societies in the Scientific School.

A second immediate result has been the great increase in the number of students participating in athletics. 1,572 undergraduates this year played in fall and winter inter-college sports, against 476 who were active last year in class athletics. The nine college football teams this fall attracted 256 students, whereas only 61 played on their class teams in the previous year. All the college teams had a schedule of eight games. Some 160 students are now playing on their college baseball teams, and large numbers are out for tennis, golf and crew. William H. Neale, secretary of Inter-College Athletics at the university, believes that at least 2,000 students will have taken part in inter-college athletics this year, all these in addition to the regular teams.

With the aid of a fund given by Mr. Edward S. Harkness, '97, who made the residential colleges possible, self-supporting students in the colleges are assisting in the administration of these units, and others are earning part of their expenses in positions which are intrinsically interesting and worthwhile, and in which manual drudgery is at a minimum. As a result of the bursary scholarships set up by Mr. Harkness, and of gifts to the Alumni Fund, the self-supporting student group, instead of being excluded from the opportunities of the colleges, as some had feared, are relatively better off than before.

Spontaneous organizations and cultural activities have sprung up in the colleges. Debating, discussion groups, with faculty or guests drawn in—publications, orchestral music, informal singing and dramatics—are some of the activities, and more are planned for next year. The associate fellows of the colleges, men of prominence in their respective fields, have been of much assistance, and visit the colleges from time to time for discussions and consultations.

The masters and fellows agree that the chief task now is that of building the colleges more completely into the educational fabric of the university. With each college there is associated a group of fellows who represent important divisions of the educational field and who are chosen for their personal and scholarly qualities as men around whom individualistic and intensive work of the tutorial variety may readily develop. Many of these men, however, now carry a full teaching load, and can not be relieved in order to give more time to the students in the colleges. The university plans to assimilate into the colleges and develop as rapidly as possible the tutorial procedure already existing on a modest scale in connection with the "honors work."

THE HARVARD PRIZE FELLOWSHIPS

In his address at the thirty-fifth meeting of the Associated Harvard Clubs at Hot Springs, Va., on May 12, President James B. Conant announced that beginning next autumn the university will install its prize fellowship plan with from five to ten selected school boys from the group of states including Ohio, Indiana, Illinois, Michigan, Wisconsin and Minnesota. These students will enter as freshmen. Dr. Conant said:

In the three months this spring since our plan was announced we have had 233 applications and many more queries from the six states. More than one hundred and fifty applicants said that they would require the entire one thousand dollar stipend in order to be able to go to college; these are boys of high scholastic standing, many of them of great potential value to the country, an indication of the vast need for more large scholarships.

In determining the fellowship winners the committee will place emphasis on originality, ambition and initiative. The question arises whether or not we can correctly appraise the worth of these school boys.

There is a great deal of evidence showing that we can select young men of real ability before they enter college. Most of our other scholarship winners of the past have become high ranking students in college and prominent in extra-curricular activities; they have gone on to become outstanding men in the world of affairs and in teaching and research.

At present it is extremely difficult for a student to work his way through college. It seems to me a mistake to make a young man of intellectual promise spend long weary hours doing non-intellectual tasks to help himself through college. It taxes . . . his physical strength and may break his morale. It is a social waste.

We hope to have eventually such scholarship funds that ten per cent. of each entering class may be taken care of by scholarships sufficient to carry the very promising men through college.

Harvard College of the future, barring drastic revolutions, should have about 50 per cent. of its student body composed of sons of what may be called the Harvard community who, on the whole, will not need financial aid. There will be no danger of forcing these men out of the college by providing opportunity for the new fellowship men. I do not intend to turn Harvard College into a group of highly selected students, all of whom are carried by means of large fellowships.

In seeking to develop this fellowship plan, we should note that many potential leaders are to-day lost because of the fortuitous circumstance that they are not able, for financial reasons, to complete their higher education. Not only doctors, ministers, lawyers, teachers and research workers reap benefit from our universities. Those going out into the world of affairs gain greatly from the opportunities which colleges and universities provide. We need in our present troubles all the brains that can be brought to bear on our problems and we need to have these brains widely and broadly trained and educated. No one can tell in what walk of life our new freshman prize fellows will eventually be found.

SCHOOL CONDITIONS IN OREGON

The exact financial condition of teachers in the schools of Oregon—outside of Portland—has been investigated through a state-wide survey by Dr. C. L. Huffaker, professor of education at the University of Oregon. The results prove that the depression has caused a serious shrinkage both in the income of individuals and in the number employed.

Dr. Huffaker's survey included both teachers and principals. It showed that in 1925–26 a total number of 1,101 teachers and 208 principals were employed in schools of the state outside Portland. The peak was reached in 1928–1929, when the number was 1,286 teachers and 216 principals. This year the number of teachers fell to 1,191, and the number of principals to 212.

In 1925–26 salaries for men teaching in schools of less than five teachers averaged $1,511 per year. This rose to $1,533 in 1929–30, but for the present year fell to $1,023. In schools of six to 10 teachers the 1925–26 average was $1,655, in 1929–30 was $1,750, and this year is but $1,281. Men teachers in schools employing over 10 teachers received an average of $1,681 in 1925–26, in 1929–30 were paid $1,719, and for this year they will get an average of $1,323.

Women teachers in 1925–26 received an average salary of $1,269 in schools of less than five teachers; $1,328 in schools of six to 10 teachers, and $1,354 in schools of more than 10 teachers. Present average salaries for the first group are $895, for the second $908 and for the third $1,140.

Men principals in schools of less than five teachers averaged $1,951 for 1925–26, and only $1,417 for this year. Those in schools of from six to 10 teachers received an average of $2,286 in 1925–26, and $1,886 in 1933–34. In schools of over 10 teachers earnings fell from an average of $2,342 in 1925–26 to $2,017 this year. Women principals were receiving an average of $1,614 in 1925–26, and now get but $1,127.

RADIO EDUCATIONAL PROGRAMS

A GROUP of educators recently met in Washington, D. C., to consider the fundamentals that should underlie American radio policy. The five fundamentals considered were:

1. Variety sufficient to satisfy the tastes of all groups of effective size should be provided, but matter detrimental to the welfare of listener groups should be eliminated regardless of commercial profit.
2. Responsible minorities should not be debarred from broadcasting privileges because of their size.
3. Impressionable thoughts of children must be protected against insidious, harmful and degenerative influences.
4. The best obtainable of culture, entertainment, information and statecraft should be given place on the air.
5. Discussion of live, controversial issues of general public concern should be encouraged. They should not be denied a hearing because offensive to advertisers or other groups.

Dr. Jerome Davis, of the Yale Divinity School, a member of the group, discussed the relatively small amount of time given to education in the radio programs. Great Britain devotes twenty-three per cent. of the time to its radio educational program; the United States one half as much. Mr. James A. Moyer, extension director of the Massachusetts Department of Education, listed among the causes for the failure of college radio programs the following: lack of any sense of showmanship, too much "academic" self-consciousness, too many inferior lecturers, inadequate financial support. Other speakers at the conference expressed the belief that the government should undertake more effective supervision of all radio broadcasts. The conference resulted in a report to be laid before President Roosevelt. The following members of the conference signed the report:

Dr. Arthur G. Crane, president of the University of Wyoming; Harold B. McCarty, director of the Wisconsin State Radio Station; James Rorty, writer and advertising specialist; Armstrong Perry, of the National Committee on Education by Radio; Walter E. Myer, Civic Education Service; Dr. Tracy F. Tyler, National Committee on Education by Radio; the Reverend Charles A. Robinson, St. Louis University; Dean W. G. Chambers, Pennsylvania State College; Dr. W. W. Charters, the Ohio State University, and Dr. Jerome Davis, Yale University Divinity School.

COMMISSION ON HIGHER INSTITUTIONS OF THE MIDDLE STATES ASSOCIATION OF COLLEGES AND SECONDARY SCHOOLS

A MEETING of the Commission on Higher Institutions of the Middle States Association of Colleges and Secondary Schools was held at the University of Pennsylvania on May 10. The function of the commission is to prepare an approved list of colleges which meet the required standards and whose work may be accepted by graduate and professional schools.

Two institutions were added to the approved list: the Newark College of Engineering, and, to the list of junior colleges, Williamsport-Dickinson Seminary, Williamsport, Pennsylvania. In addition, the status of a number of colleges on the list was reviewed on the basis of reports and inspections by members of the commission.

The commission reaffirmed its stand that no college offering athletic scholarships would be considered worthy of a place on the approved list. It was reported that the president of each college on the list had stated in writing in October last that it was living up to this requirement in letter and spirit. The acting chairman was instructed to send to each college on the list, during the spring, a letter reiterating its stand and explaining a number of points in regard to which questions have been raised. The position of the commission is that athletic ability should not count either for or against the awarding of scholarships; that athletes who hold scholarships should be required to maintain academic standing equivalent to that required of non-athletes; and that the ratio of scholarships awarded to athletes should not exceed the ratio of athletes to the entire student body.

After the death of Professor Adam Leroy Jones, of Columbia University, who had been chairman of the commission since its organization, Wilson Farrand, head master of the Newark Academy, has been appointed acting chairman.

RECOMMENDATIONS FOR THE REORGANIZATION OF THE CURRICULUM OF NEW YORK HIGH SCHOOLS

DURING the year the high-school principals of New York State, in cooperation with the superintendents of schools, presented definite recommendations relative to the reorganization of the high school curriculum whereby the requirements for high-school graduation might be readjusted and made much more flexible. These recommendations received the full approval of Dr. Frank P. Graves, Commissioner of Education, and were unanimously approved by the Board of Regents.

These recommendations which are presented as a guide in curriculum organization are as follows:

1. That the high school curriculum include English in each year, health education in each year, social studies in the ninth year and also in the twelfth year (in each year where conditions will permit), also that guidance form a part of the program either through direct instruction or through indirect group and individual conferences. These subjects should constitute what may be called the constants.

2. That the value of sequential work be recognized. To this end the program of each pupil should be so planned that his own interests and abilities may be challenged. It is therefore recommended that each pupil follow through a three-year sequence in one of the following fields: social studies, science, mathematics, foreign language, music, drawing, commercial subjects, or arts and crafts, including practical or industrial arts.

3. That each pupil also carry a two-year sequence in some field other than that of the three-year sequence.

4. That the additional units necessary to complete the 15-unit program in the four-year high school, or the 12-unit program in the senior high school, be free electives. The complete program offered in any particular school should be determined in terms of the size of the school, the fundamental arts and interests of the community, and the adolescent groups whose needs are to be served.

5. That the junior high school (or grades 7, 8 and 9 in the six-year secondary school) include in its curriculum English, social studies, science, mathematics, health education, drawing, music and practical arts. There should be a partial or complete departmental organization. The school should give recognition to individual differences in capacities, tastes and abilities in the organization and technique of class work. There should be a definite and effective plan of pupil guidance.

CONFERENCE ON CURRICULUM AND INSTRUCTION FOR ADMINISTRATORS AT STANFORD UNIVERSITY

ADMINISTRATORS and teachers will be offered the opportunity to become informed of new developments in educational psychology and particularly of social changes in connection with the necessity for a reconstruction of the present school curriculum in a six-day conference at Stanford University lasting from June 25 to 30. Attention will be devoted by the entire conference group to the basic problems fundamental to a consideration of education on all levels in all fields. These introductory presentations will be analyzed and supplemented by a panel formed of specialists in each group. The panel will include Dean Grayson N. Kefauver, Dr. John C. Almack, Dr. Reginald Bell, Dr. Richard T. La Piere, Dr. Theodore J. Kreps, Dr. Harold C. Hand, Dr. Jesse B. Sears, Dr. William M. Proctor—all of Stanford; Dr. Paul Hanna, Teachers College, Columbia University; Mr. Walter R. Hepner, chief of Division of Secondary Schools, California State Department of Education; Dr. C. C. Peters, Pennsylvania State College; Dr. William B. Featherstone, Los Angeles City Schools.

For those members interested in the curricula

and instruction in their own specific fields, additional group sessions will be afforded, in which the participants may examine their programs in light of the challenges growing out of the general sessions. Although criticisms of the existing offerings will be considered, chief stress will be placed on the projection of an improved program. Provision for the following groups will be made: superintendents of schools, secondary-school administrators, elementary-school administrators and general supervisors, kindergarten and primary teachers, intermediate elementary teachers. The subject groups will include teachers in junior high schools, senior high schools and junior colleges.

For the duration of the conference, all text-book companies in the United States will be represented in a text-book exhibit. The exhibit will be readily available for all members, who should find it a valuable means of reference.

Attendance at the conference may be with or without credit; if registered without credit, the registration fee will be $5.00; if registered for two quarter units of credit, the registration fee will be $12.00. Dormitory facilities will be made available at the rate of $1.50 per day for single rooms, or $1.00 per person per day with two in a room. Persons desiring such accommodations should write requesting same prior to June 18 to director of the Curriculum Conference, School of Education, Stanford University, California. Those planning to attend the conference should notify the director, so that proper arrangements can be made. This notification should be made even though room reservations are not requested.

OCCIDENTAL COLLEGE SUMMER SCHOOL FOR WORKERS

The Occidental Summer School for Workers will hold its second session at Occidental College, Los Angeles, from July 9 to August 4. The school, the only one of its kind in the West, is sponsored by the California Association for Adult Education, the State Department of Education, the Extension Division of the University of California, the State Federation of Labor, the Young Women's Christian Association, and a committee of colleges in California. It is coeducational and students live on the campus in the college dormitories.

The courses given include labor economics, history of the American labor movement, literature, the writing and speaking of English, American history, social psychology, dramatics, gymnasium and swimming. A weekly forum on problems of N.R.A.; a seminar on race relations; concerts, and trips to libraries, museums and galleries make up the extra-curricular activities.

The instructors are: William F. Adams, University of California at Los Angeles; Miriam Bonner, former instructor, Bryn Mawr, Vineyard Shore, and Southern Summer Schools for Women Workers in Industry; Albert Croissant, Occidental College; Anne E. M. Jackson, Extension Division, University of California; Allen Kenward; John L. Kerchen, Director of Workers Education for Extension Division of the University of California and State Federation of Labor; Marjorie Lucas, Occidental College; H. J. Voorhis, Voorhis School, California; Lucy Wilcox Adams, director.

The Occidental Summer School for Workers has been selected by the Federal Emergency Education Administration as one of ten centers in the United States for the training of unemployed teachers in the field of workers education, and maintenance for about thirty teachers will be provided. The regular classes will be used as laboratories of observation and study, and courses in teaching technique and discussion leadership, the organization of workers' classes, and studies of conditions among workers in California will be offered. Further information can be obtained from Mrs. Lucy Wilcox Adams, 311 California State Building, Los Angeles, California.

THE SUMMER TERM AT NEW YORK UNIVERSITY

The Summer Term of the Washington Square College of New York University will begin its sessions on June 26, two weeks earlier than usual, to allow for a full twelve-week series of liberal arts courses. The new plan will enable students to complete the full summer schedule of work by September 4. The new term will be divided into three six-week sessions with the middle session overlapping the first and final sessions. Students who wish to attend only six weeks may enroll on June 26, July 7 or August 6. Charles P. Barry, director of the Summer Term, announces that more than one hundred liberal arts courses by one hundred and twenty-five instructors will be offered. The regular entrance requirements will prevail and will be enforced "in order to establish the identity of the summer term not as a 'special' session but as a coordinate semester of the college year." Mr. Barry believes "that a student may successfully study during ten and one half or eleven months of the year if he so desires." Two visiting professors will augment the regular faculty of the summer session. Dr. E. M. Hulme, professor of medieval history at Stanford University, will teach courses in "European Thought and Culture" and "The Renaissance and Reformation" during the middle six-week term. Dr. H. S. V. Jones, professor of English at the University of Illinois, a specialist in literature of the Renaissance, will teach a course on "Non-dramatic Literature of the Sixteenth Century" and a graduate course in "Non-dramatic Literature of the Tudor Period" during the middle session.

Sixteen new courses will be given in English; three in French, history and public speaking; two in German, and one each in biology, economics, philosophy, sociology and Spanish. There will be courses also in chemistry, geology, government, Italian, mathematics, physics and psychology. Among the new courses will be current economic problems, book reviewing, the English language to-day, the social revolt in American literature, contemporary trends in American literature, convention and revolt in poetry, the English drama, romance and satire, the English Bible, contemporary English and American essayists, Negro folk song, contemporary English and American poetry, main currents in the modern novel, the age of Johnson, lyric poetry of the classical period and modern European drama and its influence on America.

THE INSTITUTE OF PUBLIC AFFAIRS AT THE UNIVERSITY OF VIRGINIA

Eleven round-table discussion groups on national and international problems of timely interest are being arranged for the eighth Institute of Public Affairs, which is to be held at the University of Virginia during the two weeks beginning July 2.

Dr. Charles G. Maphis, founder and director of the institute, has planned for six of these open conferences to be held during the first week of the Summer Session and five during the second week.

Round-table groups for the first week, July 2 to 7, with the leaders, are as follows:

''Money'': leader, Dr. Wallace McClure, president of the Academy of World Economics in Washington.

''The Good Neighbor Policy with Latin America'': leader not yet selected.

''County Government and State Planning'': leader, George W. Spicer, of the political science faculty, University of Virginia.

''The Function of the Church in Modern Life'': leader, Dr. John McDowell, moderator of the General Assembly of the Presbyterian Church in the United States.

''Democracy *versus* Dictatorship in Europe'': leader not selected.

''Home Ownership and the Country Church'': leader, Dr. Henry W. McLaughlin, director of the country church activities for the Presbyterian Church.

For the second week, from July 9 to 14, the round tables and leaders are the following:

''Current Conflicts in the Far East'': leader, Grover Clark, of Columbia University, expert in Far Eastern affairs.

''An Evaluation of the Work of the NRA'': leader, Spencer Miller, Jr., secretary, Workers' Education Bureau of America.

''Protestants, Catholics and Jews'': leader, the Reverend Everett Clinchy, director of the National Conference of Jews and Christians.

''Management Versus Regulation in Government'': leader, Dr. Thomas H. Reed, professor of political science, University of Michigan.

''Religious Education'': leader, the Reverend Minor C. Miller, secretary, Virginia Council on Religious Education.

EDUCATIONAL NOTES AND NEWS

Dr. Tyler Dennett, professor of international relations in the newly established School of Public and International Affairs at Princeton University, was elected on May 12 by the trustees president of Williams College to succeed Dr. Harry A. Garfield, who resigned last October and who will retire next month. Graduated from Williams in 1904, Dr. Dennett served for a brief period as a Congregational minister after receiving a diploma from Union Theological Seminary in 1908. Following several years' work in journalism he accepted an invitation from Mr. Charles Evans Hughes, then Secretary of State, to engage in editorial and administrative work in the Department of State, first (1924–1929) as chief of the Division of Publications and editor, then, during the following two years, as historical adviser. In 1931 Princeton University called him to his present position. Dr. Dennett's biography of John Hay, published in 1933, received the Pulitzer Prize last week for the year's best work in American biography.

PRESIDENT GUY H. WELLS, of the South Georgia Teachers College, has been elected president of the Georgia State College for Women at Milledgeville. He succeeds Dr. J. L. Beeson, who became professor of chemistry at the college in 1897 and has served as president since 1928.

DR. MARVIN S. PITTMAN, professor of teacher training at the Michigan State Normal College at Ypsilanti, has been elected president of the South Georgia Teachers College at Statesboro.

DR. WINFIELD A. HOLCOMB will retire in June as principal of the Geneseo State Normal School. In accepting his resignation the Board of Regents of the University of the State of New York adopted the following resolution: "That the resignation of Dr. W. A. Holcomb as principal of the State Normal School at Geneseo be accepted with regret and that the Board of Regents tender its hearty thanks and congratulations upon his successful administration of the Geneseo school and upon the completion of a half century of faithful service in the teaching profession."

DR. E. E. HUBERT, professor of forestry at the University of Idaho, has been appointed acting dean of the School of Forestry. He occupies the vacancy created by the death on March 8 of Dean F. G. Miller, for seventeen years head of the school.

VISITING professors for the University of Pittsburgh 1934 Summer Session include: Dr. LeRoy A. King, University of Pennsylvania, educational administration; Dr. R. R. Aurner, University of Wisconsin, commercial education, and Miss Mabel Snedaker, University of Iowa, elementary education.

THE presentation of the gold medal of the American Institute of Chemists to Dr. James Bryant Conant, president of Harvard University, will be made at the annual meeting of the institute on May 21. Dr. Conant's contributions to the science of chemistry include the establishment of the chemical structure of many complicated organic compounds.

DR. MARCEL AUBERT, professor of the history of art in the School of Fine Arts of Yale University, and associate fellow of Berkeley College, has been elected to the Institute of France in the Academy of Inscriptions. Dr. Aubert is Officer of Public Instruction, Chevalier of the Legion of Honor, member of the Commission des Monuments Historiques, and director of the Société Française d'Archeologie. He has received the honorary degree of doctor of letters from the University of Paris.

DR. HARLOW SHAPLEY, director of the Harvard College Observatory, was the principal guest at a dinner of the Harvard Club of Cambridge, England, on May 8.

THE faculty of the State Teachers College at Buffalo recently gave an anniversary dinner in recognition of the completion of fifteen years service as head of the institution by Dr. Harry W. Rockwell. Greetings were extended by Dr. Hermann Cooper, representing the New York State Education Department; by Dean Julian Park, representing the University of Buffalo, and by Inez Parker, president of the College Alumni Association, and a testimonial signed by all members of the faculty was presented to him. The principal address was delivered by Dr. Charles Hubbard Judd, chairman of the department of education of the University of Chicago, on "The Future of Teacher Training in the American Educational System."

DR. JOSEPH P. O'HERN, deputy superintendent of schools at Rochester, New York, will retire at the end of the present school year.

JOHN LUND has resigned from the superintendency of schools of Newton, Mass. He will be succeeded by Julius E. Warren, now superintendent of schools in Lakewood, Ohio.

AT the recent annual convention of the American Association of Collegiate Schools of Business, convening at Washington University, St. Louis, Mo., Dean Henry F. Grady, of the University of California, was elected president.

DR. A. S. W. ROSENBACH has been elected president of the Shakespearean Society of America, to succeed the late Professor Ashley H. Thorndike, of Columbia University.

PROFESSOR EARL LEV. CRUM, of Lehigh University, was elected president of the Classical Association of the Atlantic States at the twenty-seventh annual convention held recently at Misericordia College, Wilkes-Barre, Pa.

PATRICK T. CAMPBELL, superintendent of the Boston public schools, has been reelected president of the Boston Latin School Association.

AT the annual meeting on May 12 of the Association of Consulting Psychologists in New Brunswick, N. J., Dr. Percival M. Symonds, of Columbia University, was elected president to succeed Dr. Louise E. Poull, psychologist at the Children's Hospital, Randalls Island, New York. Dr. Henry E. Starr, of Rutgers University, was elected *vice-president;* Dr. Warren G. Findley, of Cooper Union, *secretary,* and Miss Gladys G. Tallman, of the Neurological Institute, *treasurer.*

PRESIDENT NICHOLAS MURRAY BUTLER and other officers of the Carnegie Endowment for International Peace were reelected at the recent annual meeting of the board. Peter Molyneaux, editor of the *Texas Weekly* of Dallas, and Thomas J. Watson, of New York, a member of the advisory board of the foreign office of the Irving Trust Company and the advisory committee of the Chase National Bank, were elected trustees.

DR. WILLIAM H. F. WARTHEN, for ten years director of the Bureau of Child Welfare, Baltimore, has been appointed assistant commissioner of the City Health Department, succeeding the late Dr. John Frederick Hempel.

DR. H. GORDON HAYES, of the department of economics of the Ohio State University, will be in Washington, D. C., on leave of absence for the spring and summer quarters, as chief of the Division of Economic Research of the U. S. Department of Foreign and Domestic Commerce.

GEORGE H. EDGELL, professor of fine arts at Harvard University, dean of the Faculty of Architecture, a trustee of the Boston Museum of Fine Arts since 1927, and a member of the committee of the museum from 1931 to 1933, has been appointed curator of the Department of Paintings of the museum. Professor Edgell will divide his time between Harvard University and the Boston Museum.

PHILLIPS BRADLEY, professor of political science at Amherst College, has been appointed a member of the executive board of *Social Science,* as a representative of the American Political Science Association. He has recently been serving as collaborator in the office of the economic adviser of the Department of Agriculture in Washington.

AT Columbia University Frank H. Bowles has been appointed acting director of admissions. Mr. Bowles has been in charge of the office since the death of Dr. Adam Leroy Jones. Talbot Faulkner Hamlin has been appointed librarian of Avery Library, and Irving W. Raymond, assistant to the dean of Columbia College. Mr. Hamlin received the degree of bachelor of architecture at Columbia in 1914 and has since been a member of the faculty of University Extension. He is a member of the Avery Advisory Committee. Professor Raymond is a member of the department of history.

DR. WILLIAM T. BAWDEN, managing editor of the *Industrial Education Magazine,* will return to the Kansas State Teachers College for the 1934 summer session, where he will conduct graduate courses in industrial education.

DR. HARRY WOODBURN CHASE, chancellor of New York University, will be the speaker at the commencement exercises of Lafayette College on June 8.

DR. CHRISTIAN GAUSS, professor of modern languages, Princeton University, and dean of the college, will be the commencement speaker at Smith College on June 18.

DR. CHARLES DE GARMO, president of Swarthmore College from 1891 to 1898, and from 1898 until his retirement in 1914 professor of the science and art of education at Cornell University, died on May 14, at the age of eighty-five years.

DR. ALBERT RUSSELL ELLINGWOOD, professor of political science and assistant dean of the College of Liberal Arts at Northwestern University, died on May 12 at the age of forty-six years.

THOMAS WILLIAM CHURCHILL, formerly president of the New York City Board of Education, died on May 6. His age was seventy-one years.

HARRY H. ZEISER, superintendent of schools in Wilkes-Barre, Pa., since 1918, died on May 8. He was sixty-two years old.

DR. GUSTAVE STRAUBENMULLER, formerly associate superintendent of the New York City schools, a member of its public school system for fifty years until his retirement in 1931, died on May 13 at the age of seventy-three years. Entering upon his career in the New York schools as a special teacher of languages in 1880, Dr. Straubenmuller became assistant superintendent of schools in 1895 and associate superintendent in 1906. He served as secretary of the teachers pension system for many years. Following the retirement of the late Dr. William H. Maxwell he was acting superintendent of schools from 1916 to 1918. He developed the vocational schools, classes for the blind and deaf, for anemic and tubercular children, extension work in speech improvement, school gardens and fire-prevention work. Through his efforts appreciation of art was introduced into the school work. He established the first textile high school, and was a leader in the establishing of junior high schools, training schools for teachers and continuation schools, and in furthering research studies of various phases of school organization.

DR. LAWTON B. EVANS, superintendent of schools at Augusta, Georgia, died on April 6. A correspondent writes: "Dr. Evans graduated from Emory College in 1880 and received the Master's Degree in 1881 from the University of Georgia. He had been City Superintendent of Schools at Augusta since 1882. He was a trustee of the Carnegie Endowment for International Peace. For over half a century he had actively participated in the affairs of the Department of Superintendence and of the National Education Association. Those who were associated with him loved him because of his spirit of humanity, his great culture and his ability to lead."

MRS. KATHERINE M. GIBBS, founder of the Katherine Gibbs schools of New York, Boston, and Providence, R. I., died on May 10. Her age was seventy-nine. More than ten thousand girls were graduated from the Gibbs business schools. Mrs. Gibbs believed in a comprehensive business education, including technical and broadly cultural courses.

THE National Committee of the Motion Picture Research Council, of which Mrs. August Belmont is president, includes the following members from New York: Dean Virginia Gildersleeve, of Barnard College, Columbia University; Dean William F. Russell, of Teachers College, Columbia University; Ethel Stringfellow, head mistress of Miss Chapin's School; Dr. Edward L. Thorndike, of Teachers College; Florence Hale, editor of the *Grade Teacher;* Dr. Eduard C. Lindeman, of the New York School of Social Work; Dr. Paul R. Mort, of Teachers College; Mrs. Evelyn W. Adams, head mistress of the Buckley School, and Dr. William C. Bagley, of Teachers College.

AT the annual meeting of the American Philosophical Society held in Philadelphia on April 19, 20 and 21, the following members were elected: Dr. Detlev W. Bronk, professor of biophysics at the University of Pennsylvania and director of the Eldridge R. Johnson Foundation for Research in Medical Physics; Dr. Willa Cather, New York, N. Y., novelist; Gustavus Wynne Cook, Wynnewood, Pennsylvania, president of the South Chester Tube Company; Dr. Wilbur L. Cross, New Haven, governor of Connecticut; Dr. Cass Gilbert, New York, N. Y., architect; Dr. Edward S. Harkness, New York, N. Y., railroad executive; Horace Howard Furness Jayne, director of the University of Pennsylvania Museum; Dr. Alfred Vincent Kidder, Andover, Massachusetts, chairman of the Division of Historical Sciences of the Carnegie Institution of Washington; Dr. John Livingston Lowes, professor of English, Harvard University; Dr. Frederick G. Novy, professor of bacteriology and director of the Hygienic Laboratory of the University of Michigan; Dr. Conyers Read, professor of English history, University of Pennsylvania; Dr. Jesse S. Reeves, William W. Cook professor of American institutions and chairman of the department of political science, University of Michigan; Owen J. Roberts, Washington, D. C., associate justice of the United States Supreme Court; Dr. George Sarton, lecturer on the history of science, Harvard University, and editor of *Isis;* Dr. Deems Taylor, New York, N. Y., musician.

AT the request of the National Council of Parent Education the Smith College School for Social Work announces a seminar on "The Application of Mental Hygiene to Problems in Parent Education." Dr. Frederick H. Allen, of the Philadelphia Child Guidance Clinic, and Dr. Muriel W. Brown, of the National Council of Parent Education, will lead a series of discussions which will center around such major problems in the field of parent education as the nature of adult learning, the rôle of leader in the leader-group relationship, and the principles involved in the selection and use of content material for parent education—all from the mental hygiene point of view. This seminar will be open to a limited number of parent education workers and members of other professions whose work includes parent education; previous training and experience in some aspect of parent education work are necessary prerequisites. The school reserves the right to select among the applicants.

EIGHT hundred students and faculty advisers from New York, New Jersey, Pennsylvania and Connecticut took part on May 5 in the fourth annual Industrial Arts Exhibition and Conference, sponsored by the Department of Vocational and Industrial Arts Education of the School of Education of New York University, with Frederick W. Landers as chairman of the exhibit. The participants, representing elementary, vocational, trade and high schools, showed samples of every important industry in the country, those of woodworkings, ceramics, metal and wrought iron craftsmanship and electricals being featured. Samples of aeronautics, art fiber weaving, art metal, boat club models, bookbinding, design, drafting, jewelry, machine shop and printing were also shown. Rudolph Schumacher, Jr., American coppersmith, and Frank Gigle, specialist in pewter spinning, gave demonstrations in their respective fields. Dr. Ralph E. Picket, chairman of the Department of Vocational and Industrial Arts Education, and C. L. Searles, director of education of the Western Electric Company, addressed the conference.

DISCUSSION

THE CONTRIBUTION OF PHYSICAL EDUCATION TO THE NEW EDUCATION

A CHANGING civilization is demanding a changing education to meet the problems of the new America and the new day. A new education is asking for a new physical education that will prepare youth physically to meet the problems of a rapidly and fundamentally changing world. There is a new physical education here with emphasis on the noun *education;* the word *physical* is an adjective to describe a kind of education. The terms physical culture and physical training are passé. The end is not to build strong men nor to train varsity champions. Physical education is a way of education; it is a unit in the administration of education that aims to prepare and to train growing boys and girls with aptitudes, skills and habits that will make for a physically educated citizenry. In 1890 the emphasis in physical education was on drill, calisthenics and gymnastics; in 1900 the emphasis was placed upon high-powered athletics; in 1910 the stress was placed upon play and recreation; in 1920 we had the health education movement, and in 1930 the emphasis is now placed upon education. A modern physical education program, to-day, includes all these five elements, namely, (1) the building of strong, healthy bodies, (2) the development of character education by the way of sportsmanship through sports, (3) the preparation and training in play and recreational habits and attitudes, (4) the training in health habits for wholesome living, and (5) having educational aims and objectives that bring about physically educated boys and girls. In brief, a modern physical education system now combines the best of these five historical movements.

The modern physical education program has five major objectives. They are of real importance and aim to meet the five major problems of American life to-day. These five objectives are: (1) The development of bodily strength and organic vigor; (2) the development of neuro-muscular skills; (3) the development of healthful habits of living; (4) education for the wise use of leisure time through wholesome recreation; (5) the training for citizenship through character education.

The modern physical educator aims to accomplish these five objectives through programs that are educationally progressive, physically wholesome, mentally stimulating, emotionally satisfying and socially sound. Physical education leadership to-day plans activities that will develop attitudes, skills and habits that will bring definite accomplishments in these directions. A real, well-balanced and rounded physical education program to-day is composed of plays, games, sports, athletics, rhythms, gymnastics, aquatics, correctives and health education.

To-day there is great need for the development of bodily strength, physical vigor, organic power, neuro-muscular skill, nerve stability and emotional balance. Our present civilization is making it most difficult for boys and girls to-day to keep physically strong and well. Tomorrow it will be more difficult for boys and girls to be physically strong and well. We must stress the word *physical*.

The five objectives stated above are closely related to the present problems facing this country. Physical education has a tremendous contribution to make to the five pressing problems facing America.

First, the mechanical machine is playing havoc with the human machine. Men are cracking under the strains and stresses of modern living; the machine dominates both his play and work life. There are three new American diseases which we did not have before 1900. These are (1) physical breakdowns, (2) mental breakdowns and (3) nervous breakdowns. Notice the word *breakdowns*. This is due to our high-speed, high-tensioned, artificial, standardized ways of living. It is also due to our mechanized, industrial, machine age. So there is need for an education that will build for organic power and physical strength. Just as we have mental education, so we must have body education in order to meet the problems of the new America.

Second, there is a vital need for the training of neuro-muscular skills. This machine age is robbing children, in fact all of us, of the use of their muscles and neuro-muscular skills. The machine does the work of the world. The old crafts are gone. Inventions and labor-saving devices do the creative work of the world; fatigue has disappeared from labor. No longer does man use his big muscles, his arms and his legs that meant for physical strength and nervous stability in the past. Man no longer controls his tools; the tools control him. Man is a mere robot; a machine attendant; a puller of levers and a pusher of electric buttons. Once man used his whole body in his work—his arms and his legs—pulling on ropes, wielding hammers and axes and pushing weights. They took care of the health of the vital organs of the body—the heart, lungs, liver, kidney and stomach. Until recently the vital, neuro-muscular skills by which men lived and survived were developed in both our play and work life when we were active participants. We can not develop our neuro-muscular skills in our work life. We must develop them in our play life; otherwise they become atrophied. The only way, in this artificial, mechanical world, that boys and girls can develop those neuro-muscular skills once developed by our fathers in their work life is through physical activities—by games, sports and athletics. By sitting at his work and riding in his automobile and going to the movies and sitting in big stadia, man is losing control and power over his bodily action. His bodily controls and reactions are slowing up. That is why we are having so many accidents. There are many reasons why we must have neuro-muscular skills, but the one for safety is becoming more apparent.

Third, there is great need for training in health habits. With the passing of the open spaces, with the rapid growth of cities, the removal of people from the soil, taking fun and creation out of their work, man is now living a highly artificial life. So we have the diseases of modern civilization that did not exist thirty years ago, when most grown-up folks, living out-of-doors, did the labor of the world, traveled four miles an hour and slept like logs after twelve hours of work Our present civilization is affecting the anatomical structure and the physiological growth of human beings. The first of the seven cardinal principles to-day is an important one—education for health.

Fourth, perhaps the biggest problem facing America to-day is education for leisure. It will be as important to educate for leisure to-morrow as it was to educate for labor yesterday. Avocational education will become as important as vocational education. We have seen the rapid decrease of the work week and the steady increase of free time. Free time is dangerous time. People do not get into trouble when they work or sleep, but the problems of court, church and community arise from free hours. Shall these free hours become wholesome leisure hours through recreational avocations? There are 168 hours in the week. Our grandfathers worked 82 hours in the week, 14 hours a day, for six days; our fathers worked 72 hours, 12 hours a day, for six days. The young men and women in our schools to-day will only work 30 hours out of the 168. Counting their hours for sleep and meals, the boy and girl of to-morrow will have twice as much free time as they have work time. All education has an obligation, but physical education has a big part. Why? Because of this machine age and labor-saving devices, it will become necessary for men to find recreation in the out-of-doors through sports, games, camping, hiking, gardening and nature study.

Fifth, however, the greatest problem facing this country is good citizenship. It is probably more important than economic recovery. The wide-spread disregard for law, racketeering, kidnapping, is to me America's most pressing problem to-day. We must educate youth in habits of good citizenship, integrity, control of temper, good will, fair play, clean living and right action. We need more sports, not for sports sake, but for sportsmanship's sake. Just as spelling is a tool of learning for the appreciation of literature, so the basketball should be a tool of learning in the habits of clean living and fair play. Character education can not be developed through lip service; it can not be learned by recitations. It must be practised in life situations. Dame Nature has given us plays, games and sports through which life situations are reproduced and in which boys can be taught those fundamental rules of good sportsmanship. Namely, play the game, play fair, keep faith with yourself and your team mates and be courteous to your opponents.

In summary, there are five great powers that physical education as a way of education can formally and informally train and prepare for:

(1) Building organic fitness for to-day and to-morrow through activities definitely selected to build strength, vigor and capacity.

(2) Inculcating health habits for to-day and to-morrow by not only giving the knowledge, but by providing ways and means for wholesome living in practise.

(3) By developing physical abilities and controls; by providing a wide, rich program of many activities that develop neuro-muscular skills.

(4) By generating within the hearts of boys and girls recreational habits and interests that they will carry over into their adult hobbies and avocations.

(5) By definitely training for behavior through sportsmanship and in this way build for character and better citizenship.

JAMES EDWARD ROGERS,
Director
NATIONAL PHYSICAL EDUCATION SERVICE
NATIONAL RECREATION ASSOCIATION

WHO'S AFRAID OF LOWERING ENTRANCE REQUIREMENTS?

WHAT the late Dr. Adam Leroy Jones said on admission requirements[1] in his annual report to the president of Columbia University deserves the attention of the colleges and the secondary schools. Dr. Jones thought that the decrease in enrolment in colleges and the attendant financial pressure will bring about a lowering of qualitative standards and the giving up of specific subject requirements. "The tendency is one," he said, "which in effect practically eliminates secondary school training as a prerequisite for college work." This, he thought, would mean, in most colleges, the debasement of the baccalaureate degree.

The tendency to lower qualitative standards, "to adjust college curricula to the needs of a body of students who may have had little or

[1] SCHOOL AND SOCIETY, 39: 996, 123–125, January 27, 1934.

no preparation in common and no instruction in any subject beyond the barest rudiments" and the tendency to give up specific subject requirements surely antedates the present depression of financial support for education. The question of the value of specific subject requirements has been long debated. Attempts to answer the question objectively have brought forth a considerable number of studies and a preponderance of evidence that intelligent students get along in college and that unintelligent students do not get along, regardless of the distribution of the subjects studied in high school. The recent financial pressure has helped to break down the opposition, which was more inertia than anything else, so that an educationally sound trend could begin to make headway.

Stanford University was compelled to limit the number of women to 500 because when Stanford had only 1,000 students somebody thought that there should never be more women than men and set the limit at 500, but the depression made it possible to remove this limitation. Perhaps the depression has done a similar good deed in removing the opposition to change in admission requirements.

Attempts to adapt college curricula to the varying needs and intelligence of students should not be looked upon as educational retrogression. Rather, is it not true that standardization is the "big bad wolf"? The experiment at the University of Minnesota, which provides a special school for misfits, is a good example of an attempt to adapt the curricula to the student who might not ordinarily be thought of as college material, and is generally looked upon as a progressive adjustment.

Even debasement of the bachelor's degree need not be abhorred, if debasement means pushing it down to a lower level, say to the end of the junior college, and making it the symbol of the completion of secondary or general education. This type of debased bachelor's degree is surely not a stranger in the world of educational thinking.

Dr. Jones would probably have agreed with most that has been said. We suspect that he had observed a tendency among institutions which are not in the habit of taking the lead in educational planning to profit financially by seeming to join the movement to liberalize entrance requirements when, actually, they are merely lowering standards. This type of behavior is to be feared and merits criticism.

Roy W. Bixler

University of Chicago

SPECIAL CORRESPONDENCE

NEW FEATURES IN THE STANFORD SCHOOL OF EDUCATION

During the past two years the faculty of the Stanford School of Education has been studying, analyzing and reconstructing the program of training for professional workers in education. Changed conditions in society and in schools make periodic examination of the training program desirable. In order to maintain the high level of education well adapted to the needs of students being served, it is necessary from time to time to make fundamental changes in the program. Similar programs of evaluation and change are also being undertaken by other schools of education in the country. The experiences in these institutions have been considered by the faculty in its deliberations. While the Stanford program differs from the developments in these other institutions in certain important respects, some of the features may be found in one or more of the other institutions. The more important features of the Stanford program will be canvassed in this statement.

Increased Stress on Basic Training in Social Studies and Psychology

Students are limited in their understanding of educational problems if they lack understanding of social conditions and human nature. They may be able to grasp the suggestions of other people as to what program of training is appropriate, but they do not possess the basis for creative critical thinking, an essential in graduate study and in high-level professional activity. The educational program should be closely articulated with contemporary social conditions and the school should be coordinated with other social agencies in achieving individual and social betterment. When educational workers lack these social understandings, the educational program is not likely to be a powerful social force; in fact, they may adopt policies that impede social progress. Knowledge of the nature of the learner is no less important. All educational procedures are adopted to serve the individual and society through the individual. The conception of education as a process relatively external to the learner with curriculum and instruction set up with little regard to the learner, is not tenable. His interests, his goals, his experiences and his problems must be the focus of attention. Effective recognition of the characteristics of the individual and expertness in dealing with his problems require basic psychological training.

The modified program of training guarantees recognition in these fields of study in several ways. The requirements for the undergraduate major in education leading to the degree of bachelor of arts include work in the social studies and psychology as well as in education. The requirements for establishing graduate status in the school of education place stress on the work in these two fields. The program of training leading to the degree of master of arts, master of education, doctor of education and doctor of philosophy require recognition of these supporting fields of study. The program of training for these advanced degrees gives about half of the time to the field of concentration, and the second half is given to the associated fields. For example, if a student is training to be a superintendent of schools, about half of his time will be given to a specific treatment of the problems met by the superintendent, and half will be given to courses in educational psychology and psychology, educational sociology and sociology, and history of education and history. This broader training is believed by the faculty of the school of education to be essential for one who is responsible for leadership in education.

Integrated Program in First Year of Graduate Study in Education

Programs of training in education have universally involved a series of courses in the different fields. Students take courses in history of education, educational psychology and educational sociology, with the thought that they would retain the understandings these courses developed and apply them later to the courses dealing with the curriculum, methods, guidance or administration. These applications frequently were not made by the student because he may have taken the applied courses before the basic courses, giving attention to the educational problems before canvassing the content of these preliminary courses. In other cases, considerable time elapsed before the applied courses were taken, resulting in forgetting much of the preliminary training before the final applications were made.

These maladjustments will be corrected in the integrated program of study. Two thirds of the student's time will be given to an integrated program of training to be taught cooperatively by a group of faculty members consisting of an educational psychologist and educational sociologist, a specialist in history of education and specialists in the curriculum, administration and guidance. Each will bring to bear on the problem under consideration the material insight gained through his scholarship in his special field. This program differs from the program at Yale University, where all the time of first-year graduate students is given to the "general seminar." In the Stanford program, two thirds of the time is given to this integrated course leaving the remaining third for other courses and allowing for some supplementary specialization.

Second and Third-Year Graduate Study on Seminar and Independent Study Basis

The number of advanced courses has been reduced and the program has been organized in larger blocks. Beyond the first year of graduate study, the program of training provides for seminars in the major fields. Students may enroll in these seminars for from two to ten units of credit and carry out a program of study partly on an individual basis and partly in cooperation with the seminar group. Each of these seminars will run throughout the year. There will be a seminar in educational psychology, educational sociology, general educational administration, elementary education, secondary education and higher education. There will be a thesis seminar to be taken by all students working towards the Ed.D. and Ph.D. In addition, any student may study along a special line on an individual basis under the guidance of a staff member. This program provides for adaptation to individual differences and places the responsibility on the student to utilize the staff and the faculties of the university in developing mastery in the field of his special interest.

Increased Freedom of Student under Guidance

The spirit of the new program is one of increased freedom for a student to define his professional objective and to project a program which will best prepare him for it. The faculty will aid in interpreting the opportunities in the different fields of educational work and the training needed for each. There is a minimum of specific course requirements. The faculty has laid down certain general principles with opportunity for the student to project his own program with the aid of the staff. The faculty is finally much interested in the demonstration of scholarship in the field of special interest when the program is completed. This policy has led to the elimination of certain specific requirements. The detailed curriculums for the master's degree have been dropped; each student projects his own program with the counsel of the staff member responsible for program of training in his special field. The requirement of three consecutive quarters for the doctor's degree has been dropped; the faculty will approve a program which gives promise of developing the desired degree of mastery. The faculty is chiefly concerned with the development of a high level of scholarship on the part of candidates for the doctorate, and it does not enforce a uniform program of study leading thereto. Other examples might be given, but these will serve to illustrate.

New Master of Education Degree Based on Two Years of Graduate Study

One year of graduate study is not sufficient training for many of the professional positions in education. The program for the Ed.D. and the Ph.D. is beyond that now required for many positions and beyond the interests of many persons who are desirous of continuing their training beyond the master of arts. The two-year program of training is appropriate for many lines of work. The two-year professional degree is not new to the Stanford campus. Degrees of master of engineering and master of business administration have already been established. Harvard University has also set a precedent for a two-year graduate program for the degree of master of education. Persons with a degree of master of arts may continue their training for a second year and secure the degree of master of education, and persons planning to work later for the Ed.D. or Ph.D. may meet the requirements of the Ed.M. without loss of credit. It is the belief of the faculty that this degree and the program projected for it will render an important service.

Increased Cooperation with Other Divisions of the University and Palo Alto City Schools

The program of training in curriculum and instruction on both the teacher-training and graduate levels is being strengthened by the addition to the staff of persons who are adequately trained both in education and in the subject-matter of a teaching field. These specialists teach in the Palo Alto High School and serve as chairmen of the committees of teachers responsible for the improvement of the program of instruction in their teaching fields. At the university they will be responsible for courses dealing with the curriculum and instruction in their fields of specialization. In addition, they will cooperate in the general courses on the curriculum. These persons are being selected cooperatively by the Palo Alto superintendent of schools, the head of the subject-matter departments concerned at Stanford and the dean of the school of education. This cooperative program makes it possible both for the Palo Alto schools and the university to secure better prepared staff members in these fields than could either one operating alone. The splendid cooperation given by all persons participating in this program is deserving of special mention.

Grayson N. Kefauver,
Dean of the School of Education
Stanford University

QUOTATIONS

PRESIDENT DENNETT OF WILLIAMS COLLEGE

SELECTION of Tyler Dennett to be president of Williams College is of more than local or purely academic significance. The college to the headship of which he is now summoned has a long and fine tradition, no part of which is more outstanding in these years of educational flux than its steadfast clinging to its old and approved ideals. It has not sought to put on university trappings. While its courses of study have inevitably been broadened and made more elective, there has been no real departure from its inherited standards of intellectual discipline. For years it was a small college by necessity. It has remained one by preference. Some time ago a questionnaire was sent to all living alumni of Williams, asking their opinion about the most desirable number of students. That they should be kept at 1,000, or preferably lower, was the overwhelming preference shown by the response. This was taken as an assurance that the college would continue to afford the best early training in democracy by allowing students to rub elbows with each other, and measure comparative mental and moral qualities, through association in a class not too large for every student to know all his mates. It was also a promise that the work of teaching would almost wholly be done by full professors in direct contact with the different groups of young men.

Although Professor Dennett is himself a son of Williams, he bears none of the marks of collegiate inbreeding. His experience has given him a wide background. With men and public questions in many fields, national and international, he has had a close and fruitful acquaintance. His studies of Far Eastern affairs, together with his distinct and valued service for a time in the State Department, naturally led to his appointment as Professor of International Relations at Princeton. From that university he will by a strange coincidence pass as did his predecessor, President Garfield, to Williams.

His accession to its presidency has given satisfaction to all friends of the college. The congratulations which have poured in upon him are evidently more than personal. They imply a sense of the great opportunity opening before him. Williams College is still identified in memory and legend with the shining and venerable name of Mark Hopkins. No one will expect a man of this feebler-thewed generation to bend the bow of that Ulysses. But those who know President Dennett are confident that he will prove worthy of the heritage upon which he is soon to enter.—*The New York Times.*

IN the selection of Dr. Tyler Dennett to succeed Dr. Harry Augustus Garfield as president of Williams, the college trustees have taken the position that only a man of distinguished scholarship and long training in education may properly direct affairs in a liberal arts college. The so-called "business administration" which other colleges have chosen recently, it was felt, not only was unnecessary, but actually detracted from the emphasis upon scholarship which has been a Williams tradition.

As was Dr. Garfield, Dr. Dennett is both an alumnus of Williams and a faculty member of Princeton. His brilliant record as historian and 1934 Pulitzer prize winner, together with his years of service in the Department of State, have already brought him unusual prestige. His appointment indicates that, although Williams has long held fast to the classics, the college is more than willing to have an acknowledged leader in the field of social sciences as its president.

Dr. Garfield retires after twenty-five years with Williams and twelve as head of the Institute of Politics. As another Williams alumnus, MacGregor Jenkins, describes him in a forthcoming book, "Sons of Ephraim Williams," Dr. Garfield has been "high in aim, consistent in purpose, fruitful in accomplishment." He will take with him into retirement the gratitude and esteem of all alumni and friends of Williams.—*New York Herald-Tribune.*

SURVEY OF GRADUATE SCHOOLS

HARVARD has more graduate departments of distinction than any other university in the country, in the opinion of a large number of famous specialists whose views were canvassed recently by the American Council on Education and reported in the April number of the *Educational Record.*

The University of California and the University of Wisconsin, in the judgment of the same authorities, have the largest number of "adequate" graduate departments.

Princeton leads the entire country in the ratio of "distinguished departments" to "adequate departments." Figures for the leading institutions:

University	Adequate departments	Distinguished departments	Percentage distinguished
Princeton	17	14	82.3
M.I.T.	11	9	81.8
Chicago	26	21	80.8
Harvard	29	23	79.3
Columbia	28	21	75.0
California	31	21	67.8
C.I.T.	11	7	63.6
Yale	26	16	61.5
Cornell	27	16	59.3
Wisconsin	31	17	54.8
Michigan	27	14	51.8
Johns Hopkins	23	10	43.5

Omitting M.I.T. because its work is limited entirely to the sciences, Princeton, Chicago, and Harvard share the honors *in the opinion of the scholars consulted;* these are the institutions which are placed first, fourth, and second, respectively, in the *Weekly's* recent survey of National Research Council fellowships.

The present survey by the American Council on Education is open to criticism on several grounds: it was in the form of a questionnaire; it was based on the opinion of individuals and could not be subjected to scientific proof; in certain cases less than 50 per cent. of the individuals answered the questionnaire. The *Weekly,* therefore, does not present these facts as establishing the worth of the institutions concerned, but only as providing a statement of fairly representative scholarly opinion on that subject.

For each of the thirty-five most important fields of knowledge, the American Council on Education obtained from the secretary of the national learned society in that field a list of 100 well-known scholars distributed among the various special branches of that field. To each of these scholars the A.C.E. sent a list of all U. S. institutions offering work for the doctorate in that field, and a list of the graduate teaching staff. He was asked to check those which had staff and equipment adequate to prepare candidates for the doctorate; and to star the departments of highest rank, roughly 20 per cent.

Institutions checked on a majority of the returned ballots were pronounced "adequate" by the A.C.E.; those starred by a majority were placed in the "distinguished" group.

Princeton facilities and faculty in the following fields were pronounced distinguished: Astronomy, Chemistry, Classics, Economics, English, Fine Arts, Geology, Mathematics, Philosophy, Physics, Politics, Psychology, Romance Languages and Zoology. Three fields were pronounced "adequate" but not placed in the starred group: Genetics, German, History. Each Princeton department, in other words, was approved except Oriental Languages, a field not included in the A.C.E. survey, and Engineering, in which Princeton does not offer the doctorate.

Princeton can not compete with Chicago, Harvard and the great western universities in the number of fields in which it is adequate; but, in the judgment of the men consulted, Princeton has avoided more successfully than any other institution the tendency to spread out too thin.—*The Princeton Alumni Weekly.*

EDUCATIONAL RESEARCH AND STATISTICS

THE OPINIONS OF HIGH-SCHOOL PRINCIPALS REGARDING COLLEGE "REQUIRED" COURSES

New plans of admission to colleges and universities, especially the new plan without examinations under the highest-seventh rule, imply a growing reciprocity between the high school and the college. One of the frank aims of the plan without examinations is to open the college (using this term to include universities) to applicants from distant (Western) states where students are not prepared for College Board Examinations. In other words, this liberalized admissions plan, whatever its other virtues may be, is a consequence, in part, of the need of the colleges for more students. Growth in elasticity of college entrance rules is paralleled by an increasing elasticity of college and university requirements for graduation. The latter type of "liberalism" has taken a number of forms. One device consists in the reduction of the time requirements for graduation introduced at the University of Buffalo, the University of Chicago, at Rollins College and elsewhere.[1] Another arrangement excuses students from class attendance, as is the case at Rollins College and Bennington College. A curriculum free from "required" courses seems to be the favorite device for adapting the college to the student's wishes. At Wells College, under the direction of the curriculum committee, a questionnaire was sent to the principals of about 650 high schools (I use this term to include preparatory schools) with a view of ascertaining the attitudes of high schools towards the required courses of the colleges and universities. It is the aim of this paper to report the main results of this inquiry.

VALIDITY OF THE QUESTIONNAIRE

Replies were received from 347 schools, but the following data are based on 332 replies, since a number of letters were too late for tabulation. A "sample" may be considered of sufficient size when the addition of further cases does not alter average results materially. Computation shows that if we take the results of but three fourths of the letters (249 instead of the 332), the averages deviate less than one per cent. from what they are for the total group. So far as numbers are concerned, the questionnaire is therefore based on a sufficient number of cases. It is also true that the reliability of a sample does not increase in direct proportion to the size of the sample, but increases as the square root of the sample. Hence, the size of the sample should be determined, not solely by the size of the group under investigation, but by the consideration that the absolute size of the sample must be above an unreliable minimum.

THE GROUPS INVESTIGATED

Letters were sent to representatives of five groups of schools, as follows: The North Central Association, The Middle States Association, The New England Association, the Wells Schools and the so-called "Progressive Schools." Letters were sent to the various states comprising the area of the large associations in proportion to their number of accredited schools. The variation in the number of accredited schools in the various states is surprisingly large. Thus, in the North Central Association, which extends into 20 states, Illinois has 368 accredited schools, and Wyoming has but 30. In the Association of the Middle States and Maryland, Delaware has but 4 accredited high schools and Pennsylvania has 72. To the extent that the matter could be accurately determined, letters were sent to Catholic schools, non-Catholic private schools, public schools and college or university preparatory schools in proportion to their actual number. The Wells Group consists of some 160 preparatory schools that have supplied Wells College with students during the past four years.

THE QUESTIONNAIRE

The questionnaire consisted of six questions, some of them calling for the opinions of principals, others asking the principals to report the attitudes of high-school students. Our primary interest concerned the reactions of the young women who had some thought of going to college, and no letters were knowingly sent to boys' schools.

The first question calls for the principals' opinion regarding the advisability of a free option in the college freshman year, that is, the advisability of having one course left to the student's choice, perhaps with advice. We had anticipated that a large majority of the principals would favor such an option. Actually, such an option was favored by 53 per cent. of the principals, while 34 per cent. voted against it. The principals of private high schools regard a freshman option with more favor (65 per cent.) than do the principals of public schools. The principals of the Middle States Association were exceptional in that a slight majority of them considered the freshman option unwise.

Questions two, three, four and five are all concerned with the desirable and undesirable course requirements. The principals are asked to list the college courses which they would consider as desirable and as undesirable require-

[1] "Changes and Experiments in Liberal Education," Thirty-first yearbook of the National Society for the Study of Education, pp. 161, 162, 227, 1932.

ments, in a college giving a cultural (not professional) education. A "requirement" was defined as a course required of all students regardless of their major fields. The two remaining questions asked the principals to mention courses which they have heard high-school students mention as desirable or undesirable college courses.

The principals mentioned desirable requirements more than twice as often (694 times) as they mentioned undesirable requirements (333 times). Students were reported as mentioning desirable requirements 382 times and undesirable courses 317 times. Courses that are mentioned with high frequency as "undesirable" tend to be mentioned with high frequency as "desirable" in other letters. Thus, mathematics, the most unpopular requirement in the list, is still considered as a desirable requirement by 10 per cent. of the principals, which is a better figure than is accorded to many courses. Our complete tables give the status of some 30 courses. In the brief table below, we report the judgments on outstanding subjects. The table gives the frequency, in percentages, with which the principals (first two columns to the left) judge courses to be desirable or undesirable requirements. The two columns of figures to the right give the corresponding figures for

TABLE I

PRINCIPALS' AND STUDENTS' DESIRABLE AND UNDESIRABLE REQUIREMENTS

	Principals		Students	
Subjects	Und.	Des.	Und.	Des.
(1) Botany	.3	.0	.0	.0
(2) Chemistry	1.2	1.5	3.3	.6
(3) Economics	.9	16.2	1.2	6.9
(4) English	1.5	53.5	4.8	21.0
(5) French	1.2	2.7	.9	3.0
(6) German	.3	1.8	.6	1.2
(7) Greek	5.7	.9	2.4	.0
(8) History	.9	27.0	3.3	14.1
(9) Latin	14.4	2.7	12.9	.3
(10) Music	.0	6.6	.3	3.6
(11) Philosophy	.9	10.5	.6	2.4
(12) Sociology	.0	7.2	.9	4.5
(13) Physics	3.0	3.0	2.1	.3
(14) Psychology	.3	12.3	1.5	5.4
(15) Zoology	.3	.0	.6	.0

high-school students, as reported by the principals.

English is by far the most popular requirement, and mathematics, Latin and Greek are the most unpopular. However, none of the judgments, whether favorable or unfavorable, are overwhelming. If but 14 per cent. of principals and students regard Latin as an undesirable requirement, this rejection is mild compared to the anathema heaped upon Latin by the "liberalists" in modern education. The abbreviated table above embraces the most pronounced judgments. The questionnaire bespeaks a pronounced indifference of the high schools regarding college "required" courses.

The last question asks the principals to indicate the frequency with which high-school girls ask six typical questions regarding the colleges: (1) Questions regarding entrance requirements, (2) questions regarding the fields of training offered by the college, (3) questions regarding the ability and "hard work" required to get "through" the college, (4) questions regarding the freedom of choice of courses, (5) questions regarding the location of the college, and (6) questions regarding the costs of education in the various colleges. The principals were asked to estimate the frequency with which these questions are asked in terms of a scale giving five grades of frequency, ranging from "very infrequently" to "very frequently." The returns indicate that no question appears to be asked with the low or the high frequency permitted by the key. Nevertheless, the question regarding the freedom of choice of courses was asked with the least frequency, and the question regarding entrance requirements was asked with the greatest frequency. This result would seem to contradict the idea entertained by some college officials that the high schools are showing a tendency to discriminate colleges on the basis of the freedom of their choice of studies.

C. OLIVER WEBER

WELLS COLLEGE

NEW BOOKS IN EDUCATION

BOWERS, ETHEL M. *Recreation for Girls and Women.* Pp. xxii + 425. Barnes. $3.00.

BUELL, RAYMOND L., *Editor. New Governments in Europe.* Pp. ix + 440. Nelson. $2.50.

SHARMAN, JACKSON R. *Introduction to Physical Education.* Pp. viii + 317. Barnes. $2.00.

SCHOOL AND SOCIETY

WITH WHICH ARE COMBINED THE EDUCATIONAL REVIEW, ESTABLISHED IN 1891, THE TEACHERS MAGAZINE, ESTABLISHED IN 1878, AND THE SCHOOL JOURNAL, ESTABLISHED IN 1874.

Volume 39 SATURDAY, MAY 26, 1934 Number 1013

THE AMERICAN COUNCIL ON EDUCATION

By Dr. RAYMOND WALTERS

PRESIDENT OF THE UNIVERSITY OF CINCINNATI

THE American Council on Education has entered upon "a new deal in education." Limited to problems of higher education since its foundation in 1918, the council is now extending its activities to include the entire educational field. To guide its work on this broadened basis, the council has elected as director Dr. George F. Zook, who, simultaneously with his acceptance, announced his resignation as United States Commissioner of Education.

This whole development, which was consummated at the annual meeting of the council held at Washington on May 18 and 19, was made possible by large grants from educational foundations. From the General Education Board the council is to receive for its general support "an amount not to exceed $300,000 over a five-year period or longer, beginning on July 1, 1934," and, in addition, $9,000 for the current budget. From the Julius Rosenwald Fund, for support of the work of the Problems and Plans Committee during the next two years, the council is to receive $20,000. From the Carnegie Corporation the council is to receive $15,000 for general support, $5,000 for a continuation of the study of unitary differential traits, and $1,500 to complete and distribute the study of the Modern Foreign Language Committee. From the Josiah Macy Junior Foundation, the council receives "a grant of $5,000 a year for two years for a study of the relation of emotion to the educational process, and an additional grant of $1,500 toward the expenses of a summer conference."

Unheralded before the meeting, these gifts caused pleased gasps among the eighty or more institutional delegates at the morning session of May 18, when the chairman of the council, Dean William F. Russell, of Teachers College, Columbia University, referred to them as copies of the report of the executive committee were passed out. A statement concerning the discussion which led up to the grants and concerning the enlarged scope of the council was given at the same session by Director C. Riborg Mann. In his report entitled "Integration," Dr. Mann declared that "only integrated individuals can produce an integrated world. This is the challenge of America to her schools."

> If our schools decide to accept this challenge and make American education a vital force in creating a new world, it is clear that cooperation on a national scale is an indispensable necessity. Such national cooperation requires a national center of coordination. For several years we have been trying to decide how that center should be organized, operated and financed. Now it appears that the American Council on Education most nearly meets the requirements of such a center. Therefore the challenge to the schools is a challenge to this council to accept leadership in a new deal in education.

Dr. Mann traced the steps by which those within and without the council reached the present plan, which provides, by constitutional amendments, for opening "institutional membership to a broader range of institutions" and for "extension of council activities into the entire field of education." Referring to the special interests involved in the various national organizations in the field of education, Dr. Mann maintained that "a council composed of, say, a hundred delegates of national associations and three hundred delegates of individual institutions is a much safer group for consideration of educational questions." He continued:

> The American school system is the most nearly folk-made of any system of education in the world. . . . We in America have kept the development and control of schools independent of political government. With us, schools are agencies created by the people to help them achieve their aspirations. In other countries, schools are agencies created by government for such uses as government may choose to make of them.
>
> The perpetuation of this American system requires leadership which is so fully aware of the basic requirements of popular sovereignty that it can not permit our folk-made schools to become the instruments of indoctrination for any group or class. Only thus can we keep the social purposes and specific processes of education in close harmony with the aspirations of the people.

Dean Russell, who was reelected chairman of the council for next year, touched upon the broad problem of the council and of education for the future in his chairman's address at the afternoon session of May 18. He said, in opening, that the general topic for this meeting as announced was "Pioneer Adventures in Education" but that, "with the perversity of the average college professor," he had taken as the title of his paper "An Old Adventure in Education." With entire detachment Dean Russell pictured the effect of the depression upon two schools of thought. One school looks back into the past, finds that there have been numerous other depressions and concludes that each time we recover and surge on to greater heights. A second school is made up of "pioneer thinkers" whose study of history leads them to quite different views. They conclude that "some sort of external control must be closed upon man, upon his work, upon his life; and it is to provide this that we find the dictatorship of industry, such as is found in Communism and Fascism. The fact that one has its origin in the revolt of the middle class, the other in the proletariat, does not disturb the essential similarity of the two movements." Dean Russell's close was as follows:

> There are two kinds of waves on the ocean, the ordinary waves that we see, and the huge waves, the results of which are the tides. Let us not confuse the little waves with the big. The new social order, as I see it, will not be the result of the activities of the present. It will be the result of the combined efforts of the thinkers of the past two hundred years. . . . It is a big movement. It is a long movement. It has momentum. And shortsighted indeed will be American schools if they fail to teach their pupils their proper place in the succession of social reformers, and stupid indeed will they be if they fail to appreciate and be thankful for their heritage.

In a brief address at the morning session of May 19, Dr. Zook said that he "appreciated tremendously the confidence and the honor the council has extended" in electing him director. When he came to Washington a year ago he had no thought other than of a considerable period of service as United States Commissioner of Education; and that, in general, he did not approve of short terms. The influence which led him to resign was, Dr. Zook went on, the conviction that the American Council on Education, on its new basis of activity, seemed to present "a wonderful opportunity for service in formulating fundamental policies in education now so needed." The forward step of including the whole of education in its province was the factor which most moved him. Dr. Zook praised the achievements of the preceding directors,

Dr. Samuel P. Capen and Dr. Mann, and said that "the names of these two men will live in American education because of their efforts in this council. I hope, with the cooperation which I am sure awaits me, that the American Council on Education may make an increasingly great contribution to American education."

PAPERS BY SENATOR COPELAND AND OTHERS

The opening paper at the morning session of May 18 was by Senator Royal S. Copeland, whose title was "Crime and a Revised National Policy in Education." Referring to the testimony presented before the Senate Committee on Crime, of which he is chairman, Senator Copeland declared that the primary lesson gained is that "anti-social conduct looms as a greater national menace than ever before in our history." He asked, "Is there any single agency under public control other than the schools to bear the responsibility of training in the qualities of citizenship essential to modern cooperative living?"

Senator Copeland appealed to the American Council on Education for "support in character education of a research program . . . built upon a better record system than is yet in customary use. . . . We medical practitioners took a long step forward when we adopted the practise of keeping complete records of the condition and progress of every patient. My emphasis on the use of continuous behavior records is due to the conviction that without them children will not be dealt with properly, no matter how competent the teachers may be."

Do we not owe it to society and to our nation to see to it that no one receives a credential and the implied endorsement of one of our institutions unless he has established a behavior record to justify its receipt. The granting of a degree should represent a vote of complete confidence in the character, sense of service and public spirit of the recipient. . . . These times demand of every institution that it check objectives to see that qualities of citizenship and character have an adequate place in plan and practise.

Senator Copeland asked for the collaboration of the American Council on Education with the Education and Law Conference, associated with his Senate committee; and later, upon motion of Dr. Mann, the council voted to cooperate with the conference.

Superintendent Frank W. Ballou, of the schools of Washington, D. C., sketched the program for an experiment in character education in the public schools of Washington, to be started next September. The experiment will be based upon a definition of the purpose of education as including "the ideals of social justice, cooperative living, and the privileges and responsibilities of good citizenship, in addition to present intellectual achievements and manual skills." Superintendent Ballou said that "one school for white children and one school for colored children for each rank will be selected for the experiment as follows: two elementary schools; two vocational schools; two junior high schools; two senior high day schools; two senior high night schools."

In the absence of Professor W. W. Charters, of Ohio State University, his paper on "Experiments in Character Education" was read by Dr. John Henry MacCracken, associate secretary of the American Council on Education. "Improvement of character and personality must be a cooperative project, experimental in design and persistent in application." The paper stressed the advantage of "a spearhead organization. This means in effect that operations should be begun with a few units, a number small enough to be handled with substantial effectiveness." A program must evolve out of the local situation; in cooperative projects there is no place for ready-made plans. The efficient administrator will not be committed to any one formula; he will use everything. An impartial view of results is essential. Many projected programs of character development have been found to be detrimental or useless when their effects have actually been measured. "Over a period of years an expanding program will evolve if the objective of the program is socially appealing, if the administration has been effective, and if cooperation has been sustained."

How training in vocational fields and an adult education program are being carried on among the people in the Tennessee Valley was related by Dr. F. W. Reeves, director of personnel and social development of the Tennessee Valley Authority.

Professor Daniel A. Prescott, of Rutgers University, told of the approach to the study of "Emotion in the Educative Process" now being undertaken by a committee of the American Council operating under a subvention from the Macy Foundation.

Mr. Otis T. Wingo, Jr., executive secretary of the National Institution of Public Affairs, told about the project of this newly established organization to bring to Washington next February college students and graduates from all parts of the country who will participate in the institution's "training in the practical and human elements of government and politics." The institution is a body which is non-partisan and non-political, "privately financed and apart from political or governmental control in any way." Scholarships covering tuition and living expenses for two months will be awarded on the basis of "strong scholastic standing, a demonstrated interest in politics and government, and qualities of character and ability, particularly those having to do with leadership."

At the afternoon session of May 18, Mr. Howard P. Jones, of the National Municipal League, New York, reported on the support given to education during the depression by Citizens' Councils for Constructive Economy; and Professor Frank E. Spaulding, of Yale University, outlined the work of the Educational Advisory Committee of the New York State Economic Council.

BUSINESS MEETING OF THE COUNCIL

Professor Doak S. Campbell, of the George Peabody College for Teachers, as secretary, read the minutes of the 1933 meeting of the council.

At the business meeting at 3:30 P. M. on May 18, President Frederick B. Robinson, of the College of the City of New York, as chairman of the nominating committee, when the resignation of Dr. Mann had been read, presented the following:

RESOLVED, That Dr. C. R. Mann be, and hereby is, appointed director emeritus of the American Council on Education; that he be provided with appropriate space in the offices of the council and adequate stenographic help; that his salary be, and hereby is, fixed at $7,500 per annum for the first three years of service as director emeritus and $6,000 per annum for the next four years; that thereafter a suitable retirement allowance for life be provided for him as a first charge against the financial resources of the council.

This resolution was unanimously adopted. Dean Russell read a letter from Dr. MacCracken presenting his resignation as associate secretary of the council. The letter closed as follows:

It has been a great privilege to have had the opportunity of working in such close association with Dr. Mann the past four years, and I can not but regret that this goodly fellowship must end. It is a satisfaction to know that the council, in whose creation I had some part, is assured of essential financial support for several years ahead and may look forward to making increasingly valuable contributions to American welfare in the fields of educational research and educational statesmanship.

Dean Russell quoted from his letter in reply, telling how highly the members of the council value the contribution made by Dr. MacCracken and their satisfaction that he will continue as a member of the problems and plans committee and the committee on the study of emotions.

Tributes to Dr. Mann and Dr. MacCracken were given by various members present.

Dr. Zook was appointed director of the American Council on Education "for a period of five years at a salary of $18,000 a year, with no obligation as to retiring allowance." His election is effective on July 1, and he is to take office on September 1.

Officers were elected as follows:

Chairman: Dean William F. Russell, of Teachers College, Columbia University.

First Vice-Chairman: Dr. Sidney B. Hall, of Virginia, of the National Education Association.

Second Vice-Chairman: Dr. W. D. Cutter, of the Council on Medical Education and Hospitals, American Medical Association.

Secretary: The Reverend George Johnson, of the National Catholic Education Association.

Executive Committee Members: President Edward C. Elliott, of Purdue University, and President Cloyd H. Marvin, of the George Washington University.

Reports of Council Committees

"The Year's Work in the Council's Committees" was the topic at the morning session of May 19. Reports were presented as follows.

The Problems and Plans Committee, by the chairman, Chancellor S. P. Capen, of the University of Buffalo.

The Committee on Standards, by the chairman, President Raymond Walters, of the University of Cincinnati.

The Committee on Education and Government, by the chairman, Professor John K. Norton, of Teachers College, Columbia University.

The Cooperative Test Service; the report of the chairman, Dean Herbert E. Hawkes, of Columbia College, Columbia University, read by Dr. Mann.

The Committee on Fundamental Factors in Achievement and the Emergency Committee on NRA, by the chairman of both committees, President Cloyd H. Marvin, of the George Washington University.

The Committee on Graduate Instruction, by the chairman, President R. M. Hughes, of the Iowa State College.

There was a long and lively discussion of the report of the committee on graduate instruction which was published in the *Educational Record* for April. (A summary of this report was given in School and Society for April 14.) While granting some mistakes in details, defenders of the study maintained that it is a creditable piece of work which, as a first effort in recording the opinion of selected juries as to graduate departments, has usefulness. Other members declared that, not only in details but in fundamental method, the report is faulty. Others insisted that it is bad policy for the American Council on Education, after having kept out of the field of accrediting for so long, to go into it now; and that there is no more fundamental reason for such action in regard to graduate schools than for other levels of education.

The council finally voted to receive the report of the Committee on Graduate Instruction; and further passed a resolution that "the matter of promulgating and publishing a list of institutions approved for graduate work be referred to the executive committee for study and report."

SOCIAL BETTERMENT THROUGH ART[1]

By President ERNEST H. WILKINS

OBERLIN COLLEGE

The suggestion made to me that I speak upon the theme "Social Betterment through Art" and my acceptance of that suggestion indicate that there are two of us, at least, who believe that social betterment is possible and desirable, and that art may have a significant share in such betterment.

[1] An address delivered at the biennial meeting of the Music Supervisors' National Conference, Chicago, on April 9, 1934.

For that double belief, indeed, one might expect from this audience a unanimous support—unless there be among you some pessimists who, though admitting that social betterment would be desirable, doubt that it is possible. So much general agreement may reasonably be assumed, in any case, that my task is not to propose and to defend a novel thesis, but rather to explore with you a region of thought which your minds have already found congenial.

The idea of social betterment implies, at the least, a discontent with society as it is and the belief that "something ought to be done about it." But the idea of social betterment, if so developed as to be worthy of your consideration, implies far more than that. Few of us would be willing to maintain that our present society is already all but perfect and that a little careful tinkering would finish the job. The idea of social betterment, as I understand it, strikes much deeper. It implies that society is by its very nature a living organism rather than a static institution. It implies the inevitability of change; but it does not assert that change will necessarily be for the better. It implies the possibility of a long and ultimately glorious evolution, but it does not preclude the possibility of disaster. Against the background of historical retrospect and astronomic prospect it implies that we stand not at the culmination of the human era, but rather at its beginning; and that the measure of betterment possible to our descendants is not the final illumination which lies beyond maturity, but rather the whole span of growth which lies beyond this our infancy. It implies that our task is immediately critical and infinitely important: immediately critical because we face the possibility of social disaster; infinitely important because, though the influence of any one of us be small, the centuries through which that influence may in some measure continue are unnumbered.

The betterment of which we are speaking is not individual, but social; not lyric, but symphonic. The ministry of art has usually been considered as a ministry to individuals: to many individuals, indeed, but still to individuals as separate esthetic perceivers. Our present and somewhat less familiar concern is with the ministry of art to men and women not as isolated persons, but as "members one of another," seeking both to live now in spiritual neighborliness and to work toward a cooperative society in which fulness of life may flow with mutual enhancement from the whole companionship to its every member, and from every member to the whole companionship. And we may think of art not only as a glowing element in such fulness of life, but as an instrument for the achieving of such companionship.

If we do so think of art, we are surely led to give to that brief word the broadest possible interpretation. Art as the diversion of the few may be defined as narrowly as you will: art as a ministry to all must itself be in some true sense universal; must be not a lake, but all lakes and all oceans; must be not a wind, but all winds and all serenities.

There are two ways, at least, in which we may rightly enlarge the more familiar concepts of art. In the first place, let us be sure that we do not limit our thought to music alone, or to music, architecture, sculpture and painting alone, or to music, architecture, sculpture, painting and literature alone. Let us rather extend our thought to the inclusion of all artistic effort whatsoever, whether major or minor, "fine" or humble, familiar or novel, creative or re-creative, durable or evanescent—whether its very character as art be primary or subordinate.

Specifically, and in full accordance with

the recent catholicity of Dr. Keppel[2] and of John Dewey,[3] I should welcome fully into the guild of art all those who, with purpose and with plan, seek to achieve the production of beauty in etching, engraving, illustration, photography, woodworking, the drama, the cinema, the dance, the clavilux, pageantry, the making of musical instruments, reading aloud, the weaving of textiles, the making of clothing, ceramics, metal work, the craft of the silversmith, jewelry, basketry, the illumination of manuscripts, the printing and the binding of books, furniture, the fittings and implements of the household, the making and the keeping of the home, the making of the means of recreation, the arrangement of flowers, gardening, landscape architecture, the building of roads and bridges, city planning, the preparation of exhibitions and the endless varieties of commercial design.

In the second place—and here again I am following John Dewey—we may well think of art as signifying not merely and not primarily the art product—not merely and primarily the statue, the fresco, the church, the poem, the sonata, the vase, the table, the garden—but as a twofold experience linked by the art product: the long creative experience of the artist and the perceptive experience of those to whose consciousness the art product is offered. For art hath not its perfect work until that which has been created is received and absorbed by those who have eyes to see and ears to hear. The process of receiving and absorbing is part and parcel of the art process; and those of us who enter into it with loyal energy may claim comradeship with the makers who, of their vitality, have given us means for our own inner enrichment.

[2] F. P. Keppel and R. L. Duffus, "The Arts in American Life," New York, McGraw-Hill Book Company, 1933.

[3] John Dewey, "Art as Experience," New York, Minton, Balch and Company, 1934.

Art conceived with such inclusiveness of range, with such completeness in respect to process, is clearly not a thing esoteric or occasional, but an experience continuous with life; and is therefore such, in its very nature, that it may rightly and naturally serve for social betterment.

If we are to move effectively toward social betterment, we should have specific goals in mind. Perhaps we may best discover such goals by asking and answering the question: What would be the main characteristics of a really good society?

My answer to that question is based on the belief that health and education are prerequisite to good social living in any field, and that the main fields of social living are five in number, namely, home life, the field of earning, citizenship (very broadly understood), leisure, and philosophy and religion (very broadly understood).[4]

Against the background of that belief, I propose for your consideration these seven characteristics as essential to a really good society:

(1) The general maintenance of physical and mental health.

(2) Ample opportunity to learn, at all ages.

(3) The prevalence of living conditions ideal in setting and in human relationships.

(4) Opportunity to earn enough, and with satisfaction in the work itself; together with an approach to equality in economic status.

(5) Cooperation in the planning and the achievement of the common welfare, local, national and international; together with security from crime, injustice, violence and war.

(6) Ample opportunity for the pursuits of leisure, including activities in the fields of art, avocation and recreation.

(7) Ample opportunity for the development of philosophy, conceived as the endeavor to understand life as a whole, and of religion, conceived as the willing and cooperative consciousness of the interrelations of all life, and of the creative spirit

[4] This belief and its implications for higher education are developed in my book, "The College and Society," New York, The Century Company, 1932.

which moves through all life, together with the activities which follow from such consciousness.

If, then, we are effectively to undertake social betterment, we should move consciously toward goals such as these.

In such striving, what is the place of art?

The order of my thought would call for a review of the seven characteristics, one by one, with a discussion in each case of the possible service of each of the many phases of activity included in the whole wide realm of art, bearing ever in mind the fact that the art process includes both creation and perception. You will realize that the carrying out of such a plan would mean not seven paragraphs, but seven chapters; not seven chapters, but rather seven volumes. The thinking and the writing of those chapters, those volumes, I must bequeath to you.

In the remainder of my address I should like to take just one of the several arts, and to suggest, not completely at all, but merely by instances, something of the service which that art might render in each of the seven movements which seem to me to represent the seven main phases of social betterment.

My own participation in the art of music is perceptive and not creative; but it has been and is so vital to me that I venture to take music as my representative art and to indicate briefly certain lines which your own completing thought might follow as to the possible service of music in social betterment.

(1) *The general maintenance of physical and mental health:* The fact that music has therapeutic value has long been recognized. Surely its positive value in the maintenance of mental health is even more significant than its curative value. In so far as any one, young or old, can enter into the experience of musical performance, in so far he gains some sense of creative power and of cooperating significantly with his fellows. And to the listener, music may bring reenforcement of vitality when the spirit needs to be aroused and given confidence, or rhythmic calm when the spirit needs gentleness and repose.

(2) *Ample opportunity to learn, at all ages:* The language of music should be learned, both for understanding and for utterance, as normally and as generally as the language of speech. In the first school years each child should be given opportunity to make music by voice and by instrument, preferably by a variety of instruments; the foundations should be laid for the perception of the larger musical rhythms and relationships; and all true initiative in composition should be encouraged. At every level in school, college and university, opportunity for further musical education should be present, with such emphases and adaptations as the maturity of the student may suggest. Adult education, whether remedial or continuant, has in the understanding of music one of its most promising fields.

(3) *The prevalence of living conditions ideal in setting and in human relationships:* No home is complete without its own music; no home, it may be said, even now, is complete without the reception of music set vibrating by distant masters. The best home music, from the point of view of social value, is the ensemble, vocal or instrumental, in which several members of the home, with the occasional companionship of friends, participate.

(4) *Opportunity to earn enough, and with satisfaction in the work itself; together with an approach to equality in economic status:* In this field, perhaps, music as a vocation has, on the whole, more to receive than to give. But there are possibilities in the use of music in connection with the maintenance of satisfactory conditions of work—especially if, as I foresee, periods of rest are to play a larger part in the industrial day than they do now. The

availability of music to all should make for contentment in an economic democracy.

(5) *Cooperation in the planning and the achievement of the common welfare, local, national and international; together with security from crime, injustice, violence and war:* Positive suggestions as to the service of music in this field could easily be multiplied. I bring you at this point a challenge of a different order. Social betterment calls for security from war. Has music no responsibility for the prevention of war? Music has lent itself in the past to the propagation of the war-like spirit; has led parading millions to their death. Will it so lend itself again? War seizes on every reenforcement, every sanction, it can find. It has seized in the past on the Christian ministry; but thousands of Christian ministers are more conscious now than they were twenty years ago of the implications of chaplaincy. Are musicians conscious now of what war asks of them? I do not myself take the extreme pacifist position, for I believe that there may still arise conditions the continuance of which would be even worse than war. But I believe that war should come only as an utterly last resort; only after far more drastic efforts of prevention than the governments of the world have as yct dared to make. And I believe that governments should know that they can not count on the common support unless they have made such efforts. Music has power: let it not be lightly used. Music has no moral right to obscure the real nature of war: no martial music tells the whole truth unless it ends in a dirge.

(6) *Ample opportunity for the pursuits of leisure, including activities in the fields of art, avocation and recreation:* This, by definition, is music's primary and familiar place. There is no end to the possibilities of the development of music as an enrichment of leisure. Its importance and its opportunities will, of course, increase directly with the increase in leisure resulting from the shortening of the working day and the working week.

(7) *Ample opportunity for the development of philosophy, conceived as the endeavor to understand life as a whole, and of religion, conceived as the willing and cooperative consciousness of the interrelations of all life and of the creative spirit which moves through all life, together with the activities which follow from such consciousness:* Music has more to give than it has yet given toward the understanding of life as a whole. Music is itself a phenomenon of such extraordinary vitality that no philosophy is complete which does not account for its might and its mystery. The experience of music is in itself a clarifying experience: the thinker into whose consciousness there come frequently the stimulation and the refreshment of music is the more adequate for his high task.

Music and religion have gone ever hand in hand. There is that in the nature of each which is incomplete without the other. Religion needs music not merely for its maintenance, but for its growth. Religion is growing, casting off much that is aged, gaining much that is youthful. Music is always in danger of confirming that which is aged in religion rather than that which is youthful. There is an incongruity in any service in which the words of the preacher are those of a forward-looking social gospel and the hymns or the anthem revert to an obsolete theology. The difficulty is rather with the hymnodist than with the musician; but the musician as composer or director may at least give every possible encouragement to the poet who keeps pace with the forward efforts of the modern church. Yet music in essence, like religion in essence, is neither youthful nor aged, but eternal. Music, like religion, is conscious of the interrelations of all life; music, like religion, voices the creative spirit which moves through all life.

It is, indeed, because music partakes of the nature of religion that we may rely on music to play an increasing and ever nobler part in the unending task of social betterment.

EDUCATIONAL EVENTS

INTERNATIONALISM IN EDUCATION

WRITING in the *News Bulletin* of the Institute of International Education, for May, Charles D. Hurrey reports that all the countries of South and Central America are represented by students in the colleges and universities of the United States. From the Latin America area 1,000 students are this year enrolled in 211 different institutions. The University of Louisiana leads with 62 of these students, Columbia ranking second with 48. Among the most popular courses are engineering and medicine, but many students are taking work in teacher training, business administration and dentistry.

Puerto Rico has the largest number of representatives, 228, and Mexico is a close second with 212. Argentina, Jamaica, Trinidad, Uruguay and Venezuela show a slight increase over their representation in 1932–1933, the present number for these countries being 74 as compared with 54 last year.

The League of Nations Handbook, 1931, 1932 and 1933 shows that 17 countries of Europe offered during these years in 119, 135 and 155 summer schools courses with enrolments of 17,506, 15,655 and 14,071 for each of the three successive years. Germany had the largest number of schools, but the enrolments in France over the three-year period far exceeded those in any other country, with 6,302 in 1931, and 4,440 and 3,964, for the following two years. Mexico had two summer schools in 1931 with a total enrolment of 525, and in 1933, three summer schools with 189 students. Puerto Rico, however, with only one summer school during each of the past three years, had the following attendance: 1,240, 1,490 and 1,549 for each of the three years.

The total number of Americans attending European summer schools declined from 2,969 in 1931 to 1,900 in 1933. The largest number enrolled in French schools. In Latin America and Hawaii the number of 1,116 American students enrolled in 1931 was reduced to 1,038 in 1933. Hawaii attracted far more students than Mexico and Puerto Rico combined.

THE UNIVERSITY OF JERUSALEM

THE Hebrew University of Jerusalem has received from anonymous donors a $200,000 trust fund for the purpose of creating a department of research into the causes and possible cure of cancer. The work will be under the direction of Professor L. Halberstädter, now in charge of cancer therapy at the Rothschild Hadassah Hospital in Jerusalem, and formerly in charge of the department of radiobiology of the Cancer Institute of Berlin. He will be assisted by Dr. George Goldhaber, of Berlin.

Dr. Judah L. Magnes, chancellor of the university, who is now in this country for conferences with the American members of the Board of Governors, reports, also, a grant to the university by the Palestinian government for the purpose of assisting its efforts to prevent and control malaria, at the research station at Rosh Pinah in the Huleh swamp. The government, likewise, is aiding the university in its work to eradicate fowl pox and field mice. This is the first government aid the university has received.

At the reception tendered to him and to his associate at the Waldorf Astoria on May 16, Dr. Magnes announced further that $100,000 will be spent by the university over a period of three years to provide for about twenty displaced German scholars. Thereby the university will care for a larger number of expatriated scholars than any other institution of learning except the University of Istanbul. Additional sums have been granted by Mrs. Felix M. Warburg, the Rockefeller Foundation, the New Century Club of Boston, the Academic Committee for the Aid of Displaced German Scholars and the American Jewish Physicians' Committee. An anonymous gift of $50,000 to be used in removing the indebtedness on the Institute of Chemistry building was also announced. The structure includes a new wing which houses the department of microbiology. In March of this year the Einstein Institute of Physics, devoted principally to research in spectrography, was opened.

The university, which is located on Mount Scopus, was opened nine years ago. While the Hebrew language, Jewish history and literature are emphasized in the program of studies, a comprehensive curriculum in the sciences is being developed.

Among those who welcomed Dr. Magnes and his associate at the reception were Professor John Dewey, who extended a greeting on behalf of American academic scholars; Dean Christian Gauss, of Princeton; Dr. Edmund Sapir, of Yale; Dr. G. Canby Robinson, of Cornell; Dean Paul Klapper, of the College of the City of New York; Dean Marshall S. Brown, of New York University; Dr. Frank P. Graves, New York State Commissioner of Education, representing Governor Herbert H. Lehman; Professor Richard Gottheil, of Columbia, who was the first director of the American School of Oriental Research in Jerusalem.

In the course of his address at the reception Dr. Dewey referred to the University of Jerusalem as eminent in its contributions to "health, agriculture and industry." Commenting on the university's "broad and humane spirit," Dr. Dewey said:

I like to recall the fact that while the troubles between the Moslems and the Jews were most acute in Palestine the work of this university in eradicating malaria from the Arabic parts of the country went on undisturbed. I like to think of the fact that one of the projects its faculty of humanities is carrying on is a concordance of Arabic classic poetry, and another is a critical edition of the works of the most important Moslem historian. I like to think that in its library of a quarter million volumes there is an unrivaled collection of Islamic literature.

For these things are typical of the broad and humane spirit that rules the university. Of all the agencies anywhere in the world that are operating for the moral disarmament of the animosities and prejudices that divide the world into hostile groups, I know of none that is doing more, with the scope of its resources, than the Hebrew University in Jerusalem.

NEW YORK CITY'S "PAYLESS FURLOUGHS"

THE New York City Board of Education announced on May 18 its new policy affecting the cuts in salary of administrative officers, teachers, mechanics and custodians of buildings. Referred to as "payless furloughs" the new policy involves a salary reduction over a period of six months, during four of which the personnel will be on duty. The reductions during the remaining two months will be made on checks covering the vacation period of June and July. Teachers' salaries are paid on a twelve months' basis. Mechanics, however, work on a *per diem* schedule, and they are the only employees actually furloughed.

The furloughs will not affect teachers or other employees whose annual salary is less than $1,200, and will vary in proportion to salary in the higher brackets. Thus, a teacher receiving from $1,200 to $1,500 will have a 2 per cent. reduction, or $24, while salaries of $6,000 will be reduced by 8 1/3 per cent., or $500. The salary cuts will be effective on checks due June 30, and a sixth of the total reductions will be deducted during each of the succeeding six months. The furloughs were ordered by the State Legislature as part of Mayor F. H. La Guardia's economy program. They will save $5,270,000, the bulk of the saving coming from the $3,000 brackets with 4½ per cent. reduction. The schedule of cuts follows:

Annual Compensation From	To	*Terms of Furlough	†Percentage
$1,201	$1,500	7	2
1,501	2,000	9	2½
2,001	2,500	11	3
2,251	2,500	13	3½
2,501	3,000	15	4
3,001	3,500	17	4½
3,501	4,000	18	4¾
4,001	4,500	19	5
4,501	5,000	20	5¼
5,001	5,500	21	5½
5,501	6,000	22	6
6,001	and over	1 month	3⅓

* Calendar days or one month.
† Percentage of compensation to be deducted.

THE GENERAL FACULTY CODE AT THE UNIVERSITY OF TEXAS

AT a recent meeting of the general faculty of the University of Texas a definite policy was adopted in the form of a code of ethics to be observed by members of the faculty and employees of that institution in the matter of their relations with members of the legislature and other state officers.

The code provides that all matters pertaining to the administrative affairs of the university in which state authorities are involved shall be performed solely by the president and the Board of Regents. It prohibits any faculty member or any employee from initiating or promoting through individual members of the legislature or other state officers any policy relating to the university. It also would be violation of the code for any member of the faculty or employee of the institution to seek to secure advancement in salary or promotion by direct or indirect lobbying.

Should any member of the university staff receive an invitation from a member of the legislature or other state officer to discuss matters affecting the university, it is made the duty of such a staff member to inform the president of the nature of such discussion. The code by this means seeks to prevent legislation or other state administrative acts that would be in the nature of individual or departmental discrimination.

The code was formulated by a committee appointed by President H. Y. Benedict after he had circularized the faculty asking for nominations. The five who received the largest number of nominating votes were Dr. A. F. Brogan, *chairman*; Dr. E. C. Barker; Dr. W. J. Battle; Dr. B. F. Pittenger and Dr. R. W. Stayton.

APPOINTMENTS AT COLUMBIA UNIVERSITY

At Columbia University Professor Joseph Hudnut has been appointed as dean of the school of architecture, and Dr. William C. Rappleye, now dean of the faculty of medicine, as dean of the faculty of dentistry, the appointments to become effective on July 1. Benjamin A. Hubbard, of New York City, has been appointed as director of non-athletic student activities at Columbia College. Mr. Hubbard has served for thirteen years as graduate treasurer of the King's Crown board of governors. This board, which has controlled undergraduate non-athletic activities at Columbia since 1913, was discontinued on May 7 of this year. In its place President Butler was empowered to appoint a director of non-athletic activities and five members of an advisory committee of nine. The new organization thus created by the trustees corresponds to the plan that now controls the athletic activities of the university. Mr. Hubbard will be assisted by an advisory committee which will include three officers of the university, two alumni to be appointed later, two undergraduates named by the student board of Columbia College and two undergraduates elected by the student body.

Professor Hudnut succeeds Dr. William A. Boring, who retires on July 1. Dr. Hudnut after practising his profession of architect in New York City became professor of architecture at the University of Virginia and director of the McIntire School of Fine Arts. From this position he was called to Columbia University in 1926 as professor of the history of architecture. During the current academic year he has been serving as acting dean of the School of Architecture.

Dr. Rappleye succeeds Dr. Alfred Owre, whose resignation becomes effective on July 1. He has been acting dean of the School of Dental and Oral Surgery during the absence of Dean Owre.

In addition to the foregoing appointments Dr. Enard Cathcart, now practicing medicine in Detroit, Michigan, has been named associate dean of the Faculty of Medicine to succeed Dr. Frederick T. Van Buren, who resigned. Dr. Cathcart is a graduate of the University of Michigan, and in 1921 received his medical degree from the same institution.

Fifteen appointments have been made to the faculty of the university's School of Journalism. Of these one is a full professorship, one an assistant professorship and thirteen, instructorships. Dr. Douglas S. Freeman, editor of the Richmond (Va.) *News Leader,* will serve as professor during the academic year 1934–1935. Reginald Coggeshall was appointed assistant professor. Dr. Freeman will offer a new course in "News of the World," a present feature of the Richmond *News Leader*. The second-year class of the school will be organized as a news staff and will summarize and interpret international affairs, the program to be correlated with work in the Graduate Faculties of Columbia University. Dr. Freeman will continue his editorial connections in Richmond, a post he has filled for twenty-one years.

Mr. Coggeshall has been associated with the Boston *Herald,* the Associated Press and the New York *Herald*. For three years he was assistant to President A. Lawrence Lowell, of Harvard University, and for one year as assistant to Professor Bliss Perry at Harvard. More recently he has taught journalism at the University of Oregon and the University of Minnesota. In his new position he will organize a course in foreign correspondence.

THE SEMINAR-CONFERENCE ON HISPANIC AMERICAN AFFAIRS

Under the auspices of its recently organized Center of Inter-American Studies, the George Washington University will open its third annual Seminar-Conference on Hispanic American Affairs in Washington, D. C., on Monday, July 2. The conference will continue for six weeks until August 10, with lectures and discussions scheduled daily.

Emphasis will be centered upon the "A. B. C. Powers"—Argentina, Brazil and Chile, with lectures by Dr. A. Curtis Wilgus, director of the center, and distinguished experts from other American universities.

Following Dr. Wilgus's introductory lecture on July 2, Dr. J. Fred Rippy, of Duke University, will lecture on "Modern Argentina," from July 2 through July 13. From July 16 to July 27, inclusive, Dr. Isaac J. Cox, of Northwestern University, will lecture before the conference on "Modern Chile." Professor Percy A. Martin, of Stanford University, will give the concluding ten lectures in the conference from July 30 through August 9, on "Modern Brazil."

This will be the third consecutive summer that the George Washington University has conducted a Conference on Hispanic American Affairs as a feature of its summer sessions. The first conference, in the summer of 1932, brought together the largest group of experts in the field ever assembled, and dealt with every phase of Central and South American history and culture. In the second conference, held last summer, the emphasis was centralized on the Caribbean area, with particular attention to American diplomacy, and to the history of Mexico, Central America, the West Indies and northern South America. Members of the faculties of nine American and Latin American universities, as well as officers of the Pan American Union and other agencies concerned with Latin America, participated as lecturers.

The lectures delivered before these conferences are to be printed each year by the George Washington University Press. The first volume of this series, containing twenty-three lectures delivered during the summer of 1932, recently appeared.

EDUCATIONAL NOTES AND NEWS

Dr. George F. Zook resigned on May 18 as United States Commissioner of Education, effective on July 1, at which time he will become director of the American Council on Education. He will be succeeded by John Ward Studebaker, superintendent of schools at Des Moines, Iowa. Beginning on September 1 Mr. Studebaker has been granted a year's leave of absence by the Des Moines Board of Education, after which he will return to Des Moines. Three weeks ago Dr. Zook declined an invitation to become president of the State University of Iowa.

Jerome Davis Greene, formerly secretary to President Eliot, later trustee and secretary of the Rockefeller Foundation and recently for two years Woodrow Wilson professor of international politics at the University College of Wales, Aberystwyth, has been appointed secretary to the corporation of Harvard University. He succeeds Francis Welles Hunnewell, who will resign at the close of the present academic year.

Donald W. MacKay, state rural school supervisor of New Mexico, has been elected president of the Eastern New Mexico Junior College. Mrs. Grace Corrigan, who retired as rural school supervisor in 1933, has been reappointed. Since February she has occupied the position of Educational Relief Director for the State Department of Education. Floyd D. Golden, since 1928 superintendent of the Portales public schools, was recently appointed dean. He will, however, continue his work as superintendent.

Dr. William Fogg Osgood, Perkins professor of mathematics, emeritus, at Harvard University, has accepted an invitation to join the department of mathematics at the National University of Peking. He expects to sail early in August.

Dr. Jacob Gould Schurman, president of Cornell University from 1892 to 1920 and later ambassador to Germany, celebrated his eightieth birthday on May 22.

Dr. Thos. W. Gosling, who recently retired as superintendent of schools at Akron, Ohio, to accept the position of director of the Junior Red Cross at Washington, was tendered on his departure from Akron a farewell banquet by more than five hundred school teachers of the city.

Alfred W. Abrams on April 1 received the congratulations of his colleagues and friends upon the completion of twenty-five years successful service as head of the Visual Instruction Division of the New York State Education Department. Under his guidance the work of the division has been increased and broadened. More than a million slides were lent to schools in 1933, and screen pictures have become a part of classroom instruction and a basal means of developing the regular curriculum.

St. Lawrence University, Canton, New York, will at commencement confer an honorary degree on Dr. George A. Plimpton, member of the firm of Ginn and Company, chairman of the board of trustees of Amherst College.

Birmingham University on May 9 conferred the honorary degree of LL.D. on Dr. A. D. Nock, Frothingham professor of the history of religion at Harvard University.

The annual fellowship in landscape architecture of the American Academy in Rome has been awarded to Alden Hopkins, of Chepachet, R. I. The fellowship, which is of the value of $1,450 for each of two years, beginning next October, includes free residence and studio.

Dr. M. G. Neale, president of the University of Idaho, was elected president of the Inland Empire Education Association at the thirty-sixth annual session held in Spokane. A. T. Peterson, superintendent of the Billings, Montana, schools, was elected vice-president.

Superintendent W. E. Englund, Ely, was elected president of the Minnesota Council of School Executives at its recent annual meeting held during Schoolmen's Week. J. John Halverson, Excelsior, was named vice-president.

Paul W. Chapman has been appointed dean of the Georgia College of Agriculture, relieving H. P. Stuckey, who continues as director of the station.

Dr. Alfred C. Redfield, professor of physiology, has been appointed director of the Biological Laboratories of Harvard University, a post created to make more effective the consolidation of the departments of botany, zoology and general physiology into a department of biology.

At Columbia University Dr. Harold C. Urey, associate professor since 1929, has been promoted to a full professorship in the department of chemistry. Professor Urey recently received the Willard Gibbs Medal of the Chicago section of the American Chemical Society for his discovery of "heavy water."

Samuel Cahan, for ten years professor of journalism at Syracuse University, has presented his resignation and will return to active journalistic work. Last summer Professor Cahan was a member of a commission named by Governor Herbert H. Lehman to investigate the costs of education. In 1926 he was one of a group of business and professional men who studied conditions in Russia.

Richard M. Gummere, Haverford, Pa., head master of William Penn Charter School, Philadelphia, president of the Headmasters' Association, has been named chairman of the committee on admission of Harvard College. Since the death of Henry Pennypacker last November, the office has been filled by Arthur F. Whittem, dean of special students and director of university extension, as acting chairman.

Miss Hannah M. Egan, who has served as acting dean, has been appointed dean of Hunter College. Miss Egan's appointment follows a period of controversy between representatives of the students and the Board of Education regarding her policies as acting dean.

Silas Gaiser, for the last two years superintendent of schools at Milton, Oregon, has been elected superintendent of the Salem schools. Mr. Gaiser was formerly superintendent at Sidney, Montana, where he served for nine years.

He has been president of the Montana Education Association and was a representative of the state at the White House Conference on Child-Welfare.

DR. CHAS. E. MCCORKLE, who has been residing on a farm near Sidney the past year, was recently elected superintendent of the Shelby County, Ohio, schools. He succeeded H. R. Taubken, who resigned to accept a position with the Federal Reformatory at Chillicothe. Mr. McCorkle was previously superintendent of schools at Morgantown, West Virginia, and at Kenmore and Ironton, Ohio.

JOHN H. FINLEY, superintendent of schools at Paulding, Ohio, has been chosen as county superintendent in Paulding County to succeed A. F. Ptak. Mr. Ptak has been head of the county system since 1929. To succeed Mr. Finley as head of the Paulding schools, the board of education has promoted O. W. Buchanan, a high school instructor in Paulding for the past six years.

CONTINUED leave of absence for the next academic year has been granted by the University of Michigan to Dr. Joseph R. Hayden, professor of political science, who is serving as vice-governor of the Philippine Islands.

BECAUSE of ill health, Dr. Jere M. Pound has been forced to ask for a year's leave of absence from his duties as president of the Georgia State Woman's College, Valdosta. During Dr. Pound's absence Dr. Frank R. Reade, of the Georgia School of Technology, will serve as executive dean.

DR. CARTER ALEXANDER, professor of library work at Teachers College, Columbia University, will give a course in educational administration during the first term of the 1934 summer session at the University of Texas. The course will emphasize source materials in education and methods leading to their maximum use in the library and in the field.

DR. B. F. PITTENGER, dean of the School of Education at the University of Texas, will deliver a series of lectures at a conference of school administrators to be held at Texas Agricultural and Mechanical College from June 13 to June 15. His lectures will deal with school finance in Texas.

DR. HARRY WOODBURN CHASE, chancellor of New York University, spoke on "Education for a Changing World" on May 15 at the annual meeting in New York City of the Phi Beta Kappa Alumni in New York.

THE commencement address at Goucher College will be delivered by Dr. Edgar Johnson Goodspeed, professor of Biblical and patristic Greek and chairman of the department of the New Testament at the University of Chicago.

PRINCE ANDRE LOBONOV-ROSTOVSKY, of the faculty, delivered on May 16 the first annual address under the newly created John Adams Lectureships at the University of California at Los Angeles, speaking on the theme "The Realities of International Cooperation." The John Adams Lectureship in this country and in England was founded to "foster the understanding between British and American workers in education." It provides for an annual lecture to be given by a member of the faculty of the University of California at Los Angeles.

DR. FRANK L. MCVEY, president of the University of Kentucky, has been appointed to the advisory committee of the Institute of International Relations, Nashville, Tenn. The institute, whose purpose is to foster international understanding and good will, will sponsor an all-day program of lectures and study classes with round-table discussions and public lectures in Nashville, July 1 to 11. Among those who have already agreed to take part in the institute are Dr. William Y. Elliott, head of the department of government, Harvard; Dr. Fong Foo See, Shanghai, China, founder of the Shanghai Press; Otto Fischer, Stuttgart, Germany, chairman of the advisory board of the "Deutsche Bank," and Dr. Herbert Schofield, English scientist and engineer, and president of Loughborough College, England.

DR. MATHER ALMON ABBOTT, head master of the Lawrenceville School, New Jersey, died on May 17 at the age of sixty years. Born in Halifax, Nova Scotia, Dr. Abbott completed his college education at King's College, Windsor, and his work for the master's degree at Oxford. He had received honorary degrees from Yale and Princeton. From 1897 to 1916 he taught Latin at the Groton School. During the following three years he filled an appointment as professor of Latin at Yale University. In 1919 he succeeded the late Dr. S. J. McPherson as headmaster of the Lawrenceville School.

THE REV. DR. ROBERT ORVILLE MATTHEWS, president of Lincoln Memorial University at Cumberland Gap, Tennessee, from 1923 to 1928, died at Toledo, Ohio, on May 17.

THE REV. GEORGE F. STROHAVER, dean of the College of Arts and Sciences at Georgetown University, died on May 18. He was forty-eight years old.

ALFRED A. JONES, for the last thirty years a teacher of music and of commercial law at the James K. Paulding High School, New York City, died on May 8, at the age of sixty-three years.

MISS ELEANOR MCMAIN, pioneer welfare worker and director for thirty-eight years of Kingsley House, died suddenly on May 13.

ALBERT LE ROY BARTLETT, superintendent of schools in Haverhill, Mass., from 1888 to 1897, commissioner of public safety from 1912 to 1914, and mayor during the following two years, died on May 13, at the age of eighty-one years.

THE annual conference on educational problems, which has been part of the Montana State University's summer session for the past two years, will be held at Missoula again this year, from July 9 to 12. Well-known speakers from outside the state will attend and participate in the programs. Among those who expect to be present are Dr. M. G. Neale, president of the University of Idaho, who was for years professor of education at the University of Minnesota and later dean of the school of education at the University of Missouri; Dr. N. D. Showalter, state superintendent of public instruction of the State of Washington and former president of the State Normal School at Cheney, and Lewis C. Tidball, dean of Gray's Harbor Junior College. Other speakers will be Dr. Sheldon E. Davis, president of the State Normal College; Dr. Lynn B. McMullen, president, Eastern Montana State Normal School; Elizabeth Ireland, state superintendent of public instruction. Programs will be held each morning and afternoon. The meeting is under the direction of Freeman Daughters, dean of the School of Education.

THE College of Paterson, a non-profit, private college, will open September of this year, with registration commencing June 1, in the city of Paterson, N. J. It is expected that this college will fill an important need of the northern part of the state, since many students will be able to take advantage of the local facilities to live and work at home and to attend a higher institution of learning at low tuition. The courses offered will seek to prepare students for work in textile and dye chemistry, aeronautical engineering and accounting; training will be provided for entrance to professional schools, and adults in the community will be reached for occupational and avocational needs. A staff of experienced men and women has been organized to direct the institution, taken largely from Eastern institutions. Included in this group are: Henry Cremer, *president;* Lawrence Saltzman, *dean;* Fred Levin, *bursar,* and Robert Conklin, *registrar.*

BARNARD COLLEGE has accepted a gift of $30,000 from the Women's Organization for National Prohibition Reform to establish a fellowship to be administered by the faculty. The fellowship will be awarded annually to a woman graduate of a college or university of recognized standing in this country, who has shown special ability in the field of political science and special promise of future usefulness in public service. The fellowship will be used for a year of graduate study at any approved college or university, and may be continued for a second year.

E. R. SQUIBB AND SONS, New York, have established research fellowships in various institutions throughout the United States. The fellowships, valued at $1,800 for the first year, and not more than $2,200 in subsequent years, will be awarded in medicine, biology, chemistry and physics. Applicants must hold the degree of doctor of medicine, or doctor of philosophy or an equivalent. The fellowships will be administered through the biological laboratory of the company at New Brunswick, New Jersey.

THE $25,000 gift to the Long Island College of Medicine from the Misses Jennie A. and Cornelia Donnellon has been utilized, according to their wishes, in the purchase of their former residence adjoining the college and in equipping it as a student recreation center. The basement has been converted into a cafeteria; the first floor consists of lounge rooms and card room; the second and third floor of study and game rooms.

IF the necessary $250,000 can be raised Auburn Theological Seminary will be moved to Rochester, New York, where it may share in the use of the Colgate-Rochester Divinity School buildings, thereby greatly reducing its overhead which at present has resulted in a total deficit of $200,000. Efforts will be made to raise the required sum through the presbyteries of New York State.

IT is reported that a recent questionnaire submitted to the faculty of Princeton University resulted in a vote of 91 to 59 against compulsory chapel and of 84 to 66 against the continuance of the Reserve Officers Training Corps.

THE organization of a new University Alumni Council at the University of Pennsylvania was announced by President Thomas S. Gates in an address to the students during the annual Class Day exercises on the second of a three-day program of graduate and undergraduate activities. The new organization, according to *The Christian Science Monitor,* is composed of six men, three chosen by the university and three by the trustees of the General Alumni Society. They will act as a clearing house for suggestions relating to the mutual welfare of the university and its graduates, and will assume a definite responsibility in carrying out those suggestions. Representing the university in the new council are Judge J. Whitaker Thompson, an alumni trustee of the university; Dr. George W. McClelland, vice-president of the university in charge of undergraduate work, and Frederick L. Ballard, also an alumni trustee of the university. The General Alumni Society is represented on the council by Ralph Morgan, Robert T. McCracken and Homer R. Sullivan.

DURING April fourteen members of the faculty of Kenyon College visited Swarthmore, many of whom made side trips to Haverford and other colleges. According to the correspondent who sent us this information, "the authorities of Swarthmore gave the Kenyon groups every possible opportunity to observe their system. Kenyon College is already making some use of a seminar method vaguely resembling that employed at Swarthmore and there is a movement afoot to systematize and extend the plan. It is hoped that it may become an annual practise to send a considerable number of the faculty to see other colleges in operation." The visit to Swarthmore was financed by Mr. Wilbur L. Cummings, of New York, a trustee of Kenyon College.

DISCUSSION

MORE CURRENT HISTORY

IN SCHOOL AND SOCIETY for February 10, 1934, the writer presented the responses of 155 college students to a questionnaire that called for the identification of 24 places, persons or terms prominent in current news. The returns indicate that our undergraduates have a decidedly sketchy knowledge of the important men and movements of our day. Thinking to supplement that study with one somewhat more systematic, we have given to a group of 164 unselected college students another questionnaire asking for the identification of 15 persons whose names are of current importance in newspapers, and 15 places that are similarly significant to current history. The papers are scored according to correct answers, 30 (which no student attained) being a perfect score. An answer that indicated a partial but not satisfactory knowledge of the given person or place was allowed one-half credit. The scores are widely distributed, the lowest being 3.5 (indicating 26.5 errors out of a possible 30), and the highest being 27 (only three errors). The most disconcerting fact is that the median score is only 13.5. In other words, the average student in this group can properly identify fewer than half of the names in the questionnaire.

When the questions were presented, the students were directed not to give their names but to indicate sex, age, college class and the size of the high school from which they graduated. A study of the scores shows no appreciable difference between those of men and those of women.

Among the men, those under 20 show a median score of 14; those from 20 to 25, 13; and the few over 25 a score of 13.5. In the case of the women, both those under 20 and those between 20 and 25 have a median score of 13, while the few older women (most of whom have had some years of teaching experience) show a median score of 16.5. The scores by classes seem to indicate progress until we come to the seniors, the median scores being: freshmen, 13; sophomores, 13.5; juniors, 15; and seniors, 13. Scores seem to vary inversely with the size of the high school, which is a practical index of the size of the student's home community. Those from high schools of fewer than 250 students show a median score of 14; those from schools of 250 to 500 have a median of 13.5, while those from the large high schools of over 500 have the lowest median score, 12.

The list of persons whom the students were asked to identify is given below, with the number of correct answers for each:

Alfred E. Smith	148	Robert M. LaFollette, Jr.	61
William Sunday	147	Henry Morgenthau, Jr.	55
Katherine Hepburn	138	Lucrezia Bori	47
David Lloyd George	110	Henry Pu-yi	31
Charles E. Hughes	108	Mikhail Kalenin	17
William B. Yeats	81	Arthur Capper	16
Leopold III	80	Carlos Mendieta	14
Gaston Dumergue	69		

The places to be located brought the following correct responses:

Peiping	133	Kiev	43
Little America	131	Muscle Shoals	37
Cape Town	120	Danzig	23
Winnipeg	120	Iraq	23
Valley Forge	106	Cracow	12
Copenhagen	96	Angora	10
Downing Street	72	Seoul	5
Montevideo	65		

Ever since his disillusioning discovery that there were freshmen in one of America's greatest universities who did not know the location of India, the writer has been relatively fortified against such revelations as have been found in these two studies of college students and current history. Probably a large number of the students who show a lamentable ignorance of current affairs could pass quite creditably a similar test in the better known characters and locations of ancient history or of the earlier history of their own country. Doubtless even a busy student might make better use of newspapers and current magazines than he does, but it should not surprise us that when he turns from his text-books to the newspaper he seeks the sport pages and the comic sheet. Possibly the fault is in a curriculum that while properly emphasizing the ancient and medieval sources of our civilization does not give sufficient time to the impact of social ideas upon the days in which we live.

A colleague of the writer suggests that this questionnaire is really a test of interests and that the reason that Billy Sunday and Katherine Hepburn stand so high in the scores is that students are really interested in religion and motion pictures. He suggests a questionnaire on leaders in athletics. Certainly many students would rank high in such a test, but others would be as lost among the athletic records as these are among the names of Angora and Seoul and Capper and Mendieta. There is another possibility for a profitable questionnaire of this type. It would give the names of the writers of catchy songs and best-seller novels, of athletes and actors and other tremendously popular people of the twentieth century, and also those of the really most significant men and women of the same period. Ruling out such strictly contemporary favorites as Mae West, would not the chances of being remembered be with the real contributors to civilization?

E. LEIGH MUDGE

STATE TEACHERS COLLEGE
EDINBORO, PA.

X-RAY FILMS OF SPEECH-ARTICULATIONS AND THEIR UTILITY IN TEACHING

LATE in December 1927, with the collaboration of a Berkeley roentgenologist, I began to make systematic series of 8 by 10 x-ray films in order to discover and study the characteristic articulations of the most important pure vowels, also of a few continuant consonants, typical of English, French, Spanish and (much less comprehensively) of three or four other "world languages." Specially devised apparatus enabled me to preserve the same angles and distances and thus to repeat for verification any given position. All my 500 or more films reveal (of course in only two dimensions, and in what may conveniently be called a sagittal median plane) the varying positions of the tongue, soft palate and larynx, at the peak or most significant instant, in an exposure lasting about one twentieth of a second, in their production of this or that single vowel or consonant. For each individual, each sound must be recorded radiographically at least twice. All successful films are then traced for comparison by superimposition, etc.

Much though such anatomical presentments can not reveal (for example, the degrees of transverse curvature), to the scientifically minded linguist, to the laryngologist and to others, they obviously disclose unquestionable facts of genuine importance which can not be learned otherwise.

If a film is successful, it makes the tongue stand out brightly, like a photograph of the crescent moon on a dark night; even that slender appendage, the uvula, usually reveals its precise position, with that of the soft palate; likewise other important parts involved in speech-articulations.

Although there are often very marked anatomical variations in different individuals, relatively, for a given sound, their articulations are the same essentially, and for one individual are generally identical. That is, like articulations produce like sounds and are never chaotic, as has been incorrectly concluded from certain ill-controlled experiments in this field.

To the experienced observer, every well-made film (or a proper tracing of it) outlines not only the invariable nasal passages but, more usefully, the two variable resonance-chambers, upon whose size and form the quality that identifies each speech-sound so largely depends. For each, there is a characteristic cavity in the mouth and, behind the mouth, a corresponding cavity whose back wall is formed by the ever clearly visible triple constrictor muscles of the pharynx. In an orderly manner these two resonance-chambers change their reciprocal relation as one proceeds through the acoustic series, beginning with the "high-back" vowel [u], as in "f*oo*d," and ending with the "high-front" vowel [i], as in "f*ee*d." They vary typically and uniformly also for the continuant consonants [f, v, l, m, n, r, s, z, etc.].

Sixteen films, arranged systematically in my illuminated viewing-boxes, thus tell a most instructive story, which is true. In this respect, they differ markedly from certain pre-x-ray "Vowel Charts." By a teacher who understands them, they can be profitably utilized (in reproductions) whenever the anatomy or physiology of speech must be considered. Precisely what technique might work best in a pedagogical utilization of x-ray speech films is a subject not within the limited scope of this present brief statement in SCHOOL AND SOCIETY, but I venture to add that their first effect on pupils who enjoy discovery is often that of a stimulating fascination.

RICHARD T. HOLBROOK
UNIVERSITY OF CALIFORNIA

SPECIAL CORRESPONDENCE

AN EDUCATIONAL EXPERIMENT THAT WORKED

SOME thirty-three years ago, the ancient town of Hadley, situated in the fertile alluvial plain of the Connecticut Valley in Western Massachusetts, was facing problems—economic and social—due to an increasing number of settlers from Poland. These newcomers were industrious and thrifty and made a success of farms which had failed to pay under the management of Yankee owners. Moreover, in many cases the old stock was dying out as the result of small families and the migration of the younger element to larger communities.

The issue was how to merge these immigrants, differing from the American element in race, temperament, religion and standards of living. Unless some solution of this problem was found, the community was likely to become as "a household divided against itself."

Fortunately, Hadley, in dealing with this question, had a capable and intelligent leadership that has been an effective influence in making the adjustment to new conditions. Dr. Frank H. Smith, a son of the town, graduate of the local high school and of Amherst College, where he is now medical officer, sensed the impending changes. Dr. Smith has been for many years a member of the board of trustees of Hopkins Academy—the town high school. In the fall of 1907, at a dinner to commemorate the death of Governor Edward Hopkins, whose bequest led to the establishment of the academy, Dr. Smith took occasion to note the failure of the school to attract and hold the young people. He showed that in the ten years from 1897 to 1907 the enrolment in the academy was less than half what it should be and that of the boys entering only 13.5 per cent. remained till the fourth year. He said the Hopkins Fund could double its grant to the high school. While recognizing the value of the courses leading to college, he raised the question as to whether practical subjects should not be added as a means of bringing more pupils into the school.

Among other things he said:

> Unfortunately, we can not cram learning into an unwilling mind. We can not assume to be our "brother's keeper" and say that he ought to accept what we offer in our high school as the very best possible for his children. We may believe it is and the best philosophers and wisest teachers may uphold us in our belief. If our brother doesn't see it in the same light he won't send his children and he can't be made to do so. Such people must be reached by some method which will at least attract their children, even though the attractive thing may not be the most valuable pedagogically. . . . If a bright colored sweater with the letters H. A. on its front is all that is needed to turn the scale in favor of spending a little more time in school, shall we not do well to have sweaters in the curriculum. . . . The need which I have outlined is the ground, I believe, from which is springing up with rapid growth, all around us, the clamor for a more practical education.

While Dr. Smith did not refer specifically to the Polish families, then in the pioneer stage of settlement in the town, he doubtless sensed this factor as one of great importance.

A year later, in October, 1908, the trustees of the Hopkins Fund voted to appoint a special commission to consider the educational needs of the town and to recommend to the board a plan for the best use of its income in connection with property about to be secured. This property, situated in the center of Hadley village, consisted of a sizable parcel of land, with space for playgrounds and athletic field and plots for teaching agriculture. The school was to be housed in a large frame building, providing Assembly Hall, classrooms, laboratories and workshops for projects in wood and metal. A barn was to be transformed into a gymnasium and a theater. A cottage could be adapted for home-making courses. Later, a residence with garage was erected for the principal. Recently, there has been added an annex to accommodate the overflow of pupils from the main building. The estimated value of this plant is about $30,000.

The special commission, as appointed, consisted of William Orr, then principal of the Central High School, Springfield, Mass., Dr. John M. Tyler, head of the department of biology, Amherst College, and Dr. Rufus W. Stimson, at the time director of the Smith Agricultural School at Northampton. Dr. Frank H. Smith, of the trustees, and Franklin E. Heald, principal of the academy, were members *ex officio*.

The report of the commission was presented to the full board of trustees on January 19, 1909, and was adopted unanimously. Eight days later, the trustees proposed to the school committee that the property would be fully equipped for school use by the following September, provided that the town continued its appropriation for support and put in force the findings of the commission. Naturally, such a radical departure, especially as it involved drawing on the capital of the Hopkins Fund and an increased grant from its income, called for both courage and foresight. At the January meeting of the board, the members, for the most part thrifty, hard-headed Yankee farmers, were a bit hesitant till one of their number put the issue tersely in these words: "Wall, as near as I can figure, this 'ere town is to be largely Polish in thirty years, and I kind of reckon the town it is going to be depends on the way we treat these Poles." Homely but sound philosophy! The report of the commission, printed as a pamphlet of 33 pages, is a definite contribution to educational policy.

As it will be twenty-five years next September since the new plan was put into operation, there has been ample time to test the workings of the program and its value to the boys and girls and to the community. From the reports of the school committee and other data it is possible to assess the results with accuracy:

1. *Enrolment:* In 1909 when the beginning

was made in the new order the register had 41 names (14 boys and 17 girls). Principal J. P. Reed states that in 1929 there were 139 pupils in the academy (62 boys and 77 girls) and on January 1, 1934, 206 (92 boys and 104 girls). In these twenty-five years the roll of the school has increased five times; ten times faster than the population of the town.

2. *Response of Polish Families:* Of the enrolment in 1929, 70 per cent. was Polish in origin; in 1934, 75 per cent. An interesting and significant item is that the Hopkins Academy Soccer Team in the fall of 1933—undefeated champions of western Massachusetts—had thirteen out of 16 players from Polish homes. Here are some of the names: Mushenski, Jekanoski, Matuska, Punska.

3. *Tenure of Principals:* Prior to 1908, the principals of the academy served only for a year or two. In most cases this position was held by recent college graduates, who wished to earn some money for further study, or who looked upon the Hadley School as a stepping-stone to more important or lucrative positions. Principal Heald, who did much to organize and direct the school along new lines, was in office from 1908 to 1914. His successor, James P. Reed, will have completed a term of service of twenty years in June, 1934. Such permanence in the head of the school gives continuity in policy, conserves the lessons of experience and makes for steady progress. Again, as the principal identifies himself with the life of a comparatively small community, such as Hadley, he increasingly exercises a helpful influence among his former pupils and on the people. This longer tenure is due to the job being worthwhile, to the better salary paid and also to the provision of a comfortable home. Such a post as that of the head of Hopkins Academy calls for the best in a schoolman.

4. Other large values that can not be expressed in terms of statistics are inherent in the Hopkins program. Thus the academy, as now constituted, in addition to its functions in general education and practical training, is a social center where pupils, past and present, meet on a ground of common interests. Such a focus is all-important in a community undergoing such a rapid transition in population from that of the early New England type to one in which the Polish element, with its marked differences in traditions, temperament, religious beliefs and ritual of worship, predominates. During such a change a community is in danger of losing its unity and may split into factions. Hadley appears to be meeting this test with gratifying success. Certainly, it offers a cheerful contrast to other and larger places, in which alien "strangers within the gates" have become segregated into racial and religious groups, exploited by scheming politicians and bosses to the detriment of the common weal.

During the quarter of a century in which this "New Deal" in education has been in operation the town has prospered. In 1905 (State Census) the population was 1,895. In 1930 it was 2,682. This figure shows a falling off since 1925, when there were 2,888 inhabitants. This decrease may possibly be due to the decline in general business. The town clerk estimates that 1,800 of the residents are of Polish extraction. Apart from the appeal to the pupils, the courses in manual training, farming and home-making must have a beneficial effect on standards of living. For obvious reasons it is impossible to assess such results.

Definitely cultural courses are included in what is known as the "Non-Latin" course. As the charter requires and in loyalty to the purpose of Governor Hopkins, ample provision is made for pupils who wish to prepare for college. Now that the Polish settlers are moving out of the pioneer stage their children are in larger numbers seeking the advantages of college. Thus, in the junior class at Amherst there appears the name of John Charles Kulikowski, of North Hadley.

There remain to be considered the methods used by the trustees to assure the success of the experiment. A careful survey was made of conditions in the school and community. Based on the needs thus disclosed, definite objectives were outlined. Advantage was taken of the advice of competent counselors on the commission. Dr. John M. Tyler, professor of biology at Amherst, set forth the importance of fitting the program to physiological factors in adolescence. This quotation shows the sane and wholesome way in which Dr. Tyler stated this phase of the problem:

The aim of physical training is primarily a

healthy body as the servant of a sound and vigorous mind; and, the promotion of growth in immature pupils. Careful study has shown that the grammar school years and the first year of the high school cover a period when the body is changing very rapidly in all its organs. The girl is fast becoming a woman; the boy, a man. These changes are more rapid in the girl than in the boy, and usually more marked.

In both sexes they result in a large amount of waste being thrown into the blood, clogging the action of all the organs. This waste must be removed and the growth and repair of organs must be carried on. But the trunk and vital organs are small, compared with the size, and especially the length, of the arms and legs. The waste of tissue threatens at this age to exceed the income of the body. Hence between the ages of eleven and twelve and sixteen or seventeen in the girl and a little later in the boy there is more disorder than at any other age or period of school life.

Professor Tyler outlined the procedure to be followed in meeting such physiological changes, in promoting a normal growth of the pupil, keeping in mind adjustments to the environment and requirements of rural life. He emphasized the opportunity of making the school an athletic and social center.

He stressed the value of games:

Open air play is generally the best form of exercise for our pupils. The game can not be replaced by work in the school garden or any form of manual training. "All work and no play makes Jack a dull boy." The game is needed to stimulate alertness, vigor and keenness; to refresh and recreate the pupil; to give poise and grace to the body.

It fell to Dr. Rufus W. Stimson to outline projects in gardening and other farm activities and home-making courses. Based on his suggestions, a four-year program—the "Non-Latin" course—was added to the curriculum of the academy. Graduates from this course would be fitted to enter agricultural colleges and normal schools. Dr. Stimson suggested methods of cooperation between home and school:

The garden introduces a new vegetable, the cooking school learns how to cook it. The girls get up a Thanksgiving dinner, or better they learn the economics of buying and planning for the family for a considerable period of time. The problems which arise at home will be excellent material for discussion at school. In some schools girls serve lunches or part of lunches.

The school should benefit by the experience of farmers and housekeepers and as the result of the interchange of ideas the reverse should be true.

Principal Orr, who began his teaching as the head of Hopkins Academy, prepared the scheme of the general curriculum intended to meet the needs and interests of pupils of a scholastic bent of mind. This course contained subjects in preparation for college and was dovetailed into the "Non-Latin" program so as to avoid unnecessary duplication of classes. Economy in cost of instruction was secured by alternating subjects, as chemistry one year and physics the next.

An important part of the report was made by Principal Heald and Dr. Smith, who were intimately acquainted with local conditions. Data were compiled on town and school population, interests of pupils and parents, intentions as to vocations, records of graduates and the financial resources of the fund and of the town. There was no purpose to make "bricks without straw," *i.e.,* dollars and cents. Fortunately, amounts available from local sources were supplemented by grants from state and Federal Government. (The new departure at Hadley coincided with the growing realization everywhere of the need of a type of rural education adapted to country conditions.)

It may be of interest to summarize the receipts and expenditures for the school year from January 1 to December 31, 1933.

Expenditures

Teachers	$ 8,900.00
Supplies	633.88
Janitor	420.00
Transportation	1,947.77
Fuel	701.47
Maintenance of buildings (exclusive of fund)	197.81
	$12,800.93

Receipts

Town	$ 7,114.45
Hopkins Fund	2,000.00
State grants	3,174.93
Federal grants	511.55
	$12,800.93

The Hopkins Fund dates from 1657. An English merchant and man of affairs, Edward Hopkins of London, came to New England in 1637, and settled in Hartford, Conn. He became prominent in the Colony of Connecticut, where he was governor on five different occasions. He was successful in business ventures.

Governor Hopkins returned to England in 1653 and was so engrossed in public service that he could not return to the Colonies, as had been his purpose. He died early in 1657.

His will provided that, after several personal bequests were paid, the residue of his estate in New England was to be placed in the care of trustees, who were charged to carry out the wishes of Governor Hopkins, namely, "to give some encouragement to those foreign plantations for the breeding of hopeful youths both at the grammar school, and college, for the public service of the country in future times."

One of these trustees, William Goodwin, while the estate was in process of settlement, came to Hadley. Largely through his influence a part of the bequest was awarded to Hadley in 1664, a date which has been fixed as the beginning of the Hopkins School. However, it was not until 1816 that the academy was incorporated.

As near as can be ascertained the sum coming to Hadley was 308 pounds. Gifts from the town and individuals made small additions to this amount. At times the fund suffered reverses, but under wise management reached a total of $140,000 some years ago. It has felt the effects of the fall in security prices but still amounts to many times the original sum.

William Orr

Amherst, Mass.

QUOTATIONS

NEGLECTED CHILDREN

The children of the United States of America must now be used to seeing themselves described as those "whose faces are turned toward the light of a new day and who must be prepared to meet a great adventure." It would be interesting to learn whether they know what this means, or what impression, if any, the reiterated description has made upon them. For there has been time: they have not been the same children. The White House Conference of 1909, with its portentous production of platitudinous resolutions in the form of "The Children's Charter," appears to have initiated the attitude and suggested the description. Ten years later a second conference confirmed the opinions of the first. And now, as the result of a third conference held eleven years later still, and as the outcome of the labors of hundreds of persons combined in associated committees over a period of a quarter of a century, we have the official publication of a large volume on *Dependent and Neglected Children*,[1] which reechoes the description of American children and reconfirms the opinions previously expressed. Following a general report adopted by the executive committee in plenary session, the book contains an abundance of subsidiary reports, resolutions, addresses and memoranda; the whole material, with copious bibliography and index, occupying 448 pages. It may be doubted whether this repeated enunciation of truisms, after immense labor and at great expense would be tolerated by the White House under conditions more recently established there.

Such, however, appear to be the now recognized American methods and procedure, and it must not be supposed that they are entirely without some useful or suggestive results, though, in the main, the conclusions set forth are essentially the same as those reached long ago in this country by less laborious and more common-sense effort. One may ask why the word "dependent" appears in the title. Is it not of the very essence of childhood to be dependent? One may ask, again, whether it is really necessary or helpful to keep repeating the statements that children of decent parents and deserving mothers should be kept at home, that every child should receive the best medical attention, and that local child-caring agencies should cooperate? Yet there are scores of conclusions and recommendations of this kind set out at the end of the various sections into which the report is divided. One can only suppose

[1] *Dependent and Neglected Children.* White House Conference on Child Health and Protection. Section IV. London: D. Appleton-Century Co. 1934. (12s. 6d. net.)

that they are the result of "the opportunity to develop and harmonize different points of view on policies and methods" which the committee claims is "one of its major contributions to the field of child welfare."

Nevertheless, if there is no very practical or concrete outcome easily apparent from the whole business, the wide and complete survey over a great field may serve to bring home to an intelligent but not very thoughtful community the shortcomings of its provision for child care, the general need for effort and the main directions in which effort is needed, and the nature and extent of the progress that has been made since the year of the original White House Conference. Those, too, who in our own country are urging the enactment of a new method of preventing procreation in the case of persons who, they believe, are unfitted for parenthood, may well have their attention called to the comprehensive tabulation and review in this volume of the numerous causes of child neglect in the home other than backwardness of mind in a parent.—*The British Medical Journal.*

REPORTS

THE FINAL REPORT OF THE COMMISSION ON THE SOCIAL STUDIES

THE conclusions and recommendations of the Commission on the Social Studies, sponsored by the American Historical Association, have been issued in a series of instalments of its final report, which was published by Charles Scribner's Sons on May 21. The entire report will comprise fourteen major and several supplementary volumes. Basing its conclusions and recommendations upon a very large number of special studies and researches and prolonged deliberation and reflection during the past five years, the commission "is convinced by its interpretation of available empirical data that the actually integrating economy of the present day is the forerunner of a consciously integrating society in which the individual economic actions and individual property rights will be altered and abridged." The report recognizes throughout the transitional character of the present epoch and the tensions that mark the conflicts attending transition.

Describing these tensions the report refers to

> privation in the midst of plenty, violations of fiduciary trust, gross inequalities in income and wealth, widespread racketeering and banditry, wasteful use of natural resources, unbalanced distribution and organization of labor and leisure, the harnessing of science to individualism in business enterprise, the artificiality of political boundaries and divisions, the subjection of public welfare to the egoism of private interests, the maladjustment of production and consumption, persistent tendencies toward economic instability, disproportionate growth of debt and property claims in relation to production, deliberate destruction of goods and withdrawal of efficiency from production, accelerating *tempo* of panics, crises and depressions attended by ever-wider destruction of capital and demoralization of labor, struggles among nations for markets and raw materials leading to international conflicts and wars.

The report reviews existing achievements that may serve as resources in the necessary effort to "ward off the dangers of goose-step regimentation in ideas, culture and invention, of sacrificing individuality, of neglecting precious elements in the traditional heritage of America and the world, and of fostering a narrow intolerant nationalism or an aggressive predatory imperialism." Whatever new directions may be chosen, however, the American people "should respect and safeguard the right of the individual to be free from excessive social pressures on his personal behavior, mode of living, cultural satisfactions and avocations, and religious, economic and political beliefs." The new social philosophy will demand, the commission believes, broad understanding and tolerance among the diverse races, religions and cultural groups which compose the American nation. To this end "nationalism should be infused with enlightenment, reason, and, by making the wisest and most effective use of domestic resources and by conceiving of foreign trade as the exchange of commodities of mutual benefit rather than as an expression of national power, economic imperialism should be checked.

The commission is convinced that the emerging economic order "will involve the placing of restraints on individual enterprise, propensities and acquisitive egoism" in all the avenues of

American life. And it believes that in the light of these probable restraints the implications for education are clear and imperative:

(1) The efficient functioning of the emerging economy and the full utilization of its potentialities require profound changes in the attitudes and outlook of the American people, especially the rising generation—a complete and frank recognition that the old order is passing, that the new order is emerging, and that knowledge of realities and capacity to cooperate are indispensable to the development and even the perdurance of American society; and (2) the rational use of the new leisure requires a cultural equipment which will give strength and harmony to society instead of weakness and discord.

If education meets its obligation, as thus interpreted, the ideals of American democracy and cultural liberty will be realized through

the recognition of the moral equality and dignity of all men; the abolition of class distinctions and special privileges; the extension to every individual, regardless of birth, class, race, religion, or economic status, of the opportunity for the fullest development of his creative capacities, his spiritual qualities, his individuality; the encouragement of social inquiry, inventiveness, and tolerance; the protection of all liberties essential to defense against the exercise of brute power; the development of resistance to appeals to racial and religious passion and prejudice.

All this involves the preparation of the rising generation "to enter the society now coming into being through thought, ideal, and knowledge, rather than through coercion, regimentation, and ignorance."

The report offers detailed suggestions affecting the content and method of the elementary and secondary programs of study. In the elementary school the emphasis should be placed, as recommended by the commission, on the

making of the community and the nation, although materials bearing on the development of world-society and culture would by no means be excluded. The approach would begin with a study of the immediate neighborhood in which the child lives, a study that would involve a comprehensive survey of the locality in all its major activities, together with its remote origins and more immediate history. The preponderant method would be pupil participation in social projects of rich variety. In the secondary school the central theme would be the development of mankind and the evolution of human culture, together with broad courses in the several fields of the social studies. Much attention would be given to comprehensive reading lists in historical and social literature, including newspapers, magazines, great historic documents, classics of social thought, as well as to achievement of familiarity with the methods and instruments of inquiry in the social sciences, with historical criticism, analysis, verification, and authentication.

Critical toward intelligence testing and skeptical toward the new-type tests the report expresses the conclusion that the "social results of the program of instruction recommended by the present commission will be tested, not in the classroom by teachers, but in the arena of social and political life and by the long sweep of history."

In the section on "Reform of Normal Schools and Teachers Colleges" the report advocates social science instruction that is marked by "scholarship, courage, and vision." In the field of teacher training the commission proposes a program based upon far-reaching revisions of present practises:

(1) A drastic curtailment in the number of courses—often thin, arid, and duplicating—offered in the principles and methods of education; (2) an insistence that persons engaged in training teachers in various branches of learning shall, first of all, be competent scholars in these fields; (3) the abandonment of the conception of a distinct ''science of education'' and the reunion of education with the great streams of human knowledge, thought and aspiration—empirical, ethical and esthetic.

These proposals imply further that the old division between colleges and universities, on the one side, and normal schools and teachers' colleges on the other, must be abolished and the two institutions of thought and training united. The weaker normal schools and teachers' colleges should be closed, while the remainder should become centers, not of pedagogy as traditionally conceived, but of knowledge and thought devoted to the organization and conduct of education as a focal point in the evolution of culture. Social science departments in the colleges and universities, besides discharging their other obligations to society, should turn their attention to the preparation of teachers and to the organization of materials of instruction for use in the schools.

In summary, an institution for the preparation

of social science teachers should be a center for introducing young men and women to a realistic knowledge of the trends, tensions and conflicts of American society in its world setting, for bringing them into close and living connection with all the great systems of social thought—ancient, modern and contemporary—and for revealing to them the magnificent potentialities of science in the realization of the finest dreams of mankind.

In its consideration of the status of the teacher the report names six requisites that, it is believed, will equip the teacher for the heavy social responsibilities that the new society will impose upon him. Summarized, these requisites are: A more intensive and extensive program of preparation; economic security; favorable working conditions; the teacher's abandonment of that "seclusion, aloofness or indifference which too often has been his habit"; sufficient measure of freedom in teaching to enable the teacher "to introduce his pupils to a thoroughly realistic and independent understanding of contemporary society—its tensions, its contradictions, its conflicts, its movements, and its thought"; and an increased number of teachers who will aspire to positions of influence and leadership in the local community, the state and the nation.

The commission in its report champions a national protective organization in which members of the profession of teaching might pool the thought and proposed policies pertaining to national education, and through which the individual teacher might be protected "in the exercise of his rights, the enjoyment of his privileges and the discharge of his obligations to society." Such an organization would protect the teacher "against the assaults of ignorant majorities, heresy-hunting minorities, and all self-constituted guardians of public morals and thought" and provide for "the review of controversies, thus arising, by trained specialists competent to pass judgment upon the scholarship, subject-matter, and manner of presentation in question." The commission believes, however, that a completely integrated national system would be "beset by grave dangers, involving overstandardization, regimentation, and discouragement of local initiative and experimentation." Instead of "coercive and detailed legislation emanating from the Federal Congress" the commission hopes that the "optimum degree of integration may be achieved"

through the friendly cooperation of state and nation, the spread of knowledge, the nation-wide circulation of educational journals, the training of leaders in centers of learning, the removal of all barriers to the free interchange of teachers among the different sections of the country and the development of a professional organization which would embrace practically the entire teaching staff of the United States and would concern itself increasingly with the formulation and execution of the educational policies of the nation. Broad principles for the operation of the schools might be established by national legislation, with the responsibility for administration reserved to local agencies in cooperation with the organized teaching profession. But whatever the ultimate disposition of the problem, the teachers should recognize the necessities growing out of the emergence of an integrated economy and proceed at once to the preparation of a policy of adaptation in harmony with the ideals of American democracy and cultural freedom.

The report makes it clear that two social philosophies are now struggling for supremacy: individualism, with its attending capitalism and classism, and collectivism, with planned economy and mass rights.. Believing that present trends indicate the victory of the latter the Commission on the Social Studies offers a comprehensive blue-print by which education may prepare to meet the demands of a collectivist social order without submerging the individual as a helpless victim of bureaucratic control. The report is signed by twelve members of the commission. The four dissenting members believe the report to be extremely radical. The names of the members of the commission follow:

Charles A. Beard, retiring president of the American Historical Association.

Dr. Isaiah Bowman, director of the American Geographical Society.

Ada Comstock, president of Radcliffe College.

George S. Counts, professor of education, Teachers College, Columbia University.

Avery O. Craven, professor of history, University of Chicago.

Guy Stanton Ford, dean of the graduate school, University of Minnesota.

Carlton J. H. Hayes, professor of history, Columbia University.

Henry Johnson, professor emeritus of history, Teachers College, Columbia University.

A. C. Krey, professor of history, University of Minnesota.

Leon C. Marshall, Brookings Institution, Washington.

Jesse H. Newlon, director of Lincoln School, New York.

Jesse F. Steiner, professor of sociology, University of Washington.

The four members who refused to sign are:

Frank W. Ballou, superintendent of schools, District of Columbia.

Edmund E. Day, director of the social science division, Rockefeller Foundation.

Ernest Horn, professor of education, University of Iowa.

Charles E. Merriam, chairman of the department of political science, University of Chicago.

EDUCATIONAL RESEARCH AND STATISTICS

THE DOLLAR AND REAL INCOMES OF TEACHERS, 1889–90 TO 1933–34

I SUSPECT that certain findings of this study will prove disturbing to the tens of thousands of teachers who have been protesting against cuts in teacher's salaries. The facts of the matter are that from the peak of prosperity as represented by the school year 1928–29 through three years of depression the real incomes or purchasing power of teachers' salaries actually rose 13.8 per cent. During a comparable period from the calendar year 1929 to 1932 the real incomes of wage workers were cut 46 per cent.

Certain other findings and their inferences for the immediate future should prove profoundly disturbing to the hundreds of thousands of teachers who have been patiently living through the depression. The facts of the matter are that the country as a whole has been climbing out of the depression ever since the summer of 1932. From the school year 1931–32 to 1933–34 the real incomes of teachers have been cut 30.2 per cent. During a comparable period from the calendar year 1932 to February, 1934, the real incomes of wage workers have increased 27.8 per cent. Further, the implications of the data in the light of certain rather obvious facts about the present economic and political situation point to a very slow recovery and possibly some further deflation of the real incomes of teachers over the next three to five years.

The essential facts upon which these observations are based are presented graphically in the accompanying chart (see Table I and accompanying notes for sources of data and details). The pair of curves at the top of the figure show the trend of the cost of living. The cost of living for teachers is indicated by the solid line and is in terms of school years. The cost of living for wage workers is indicated by the dash curve and is in terms of calendar years. The last point on the curve for teachers is 85.8. That is, teachers now need only $85.80 to buy

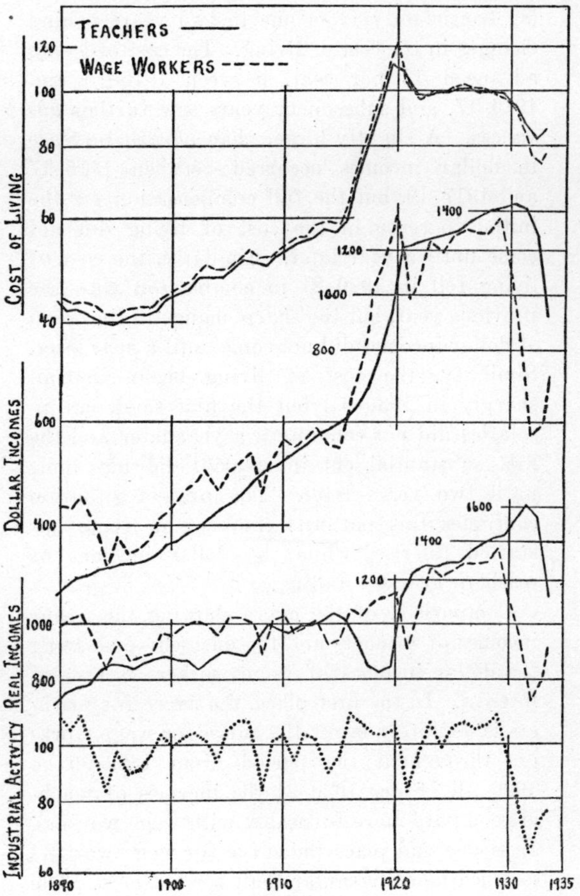

FIG. 1

the goods and services which would have cost on the average $100 in the ten-year period from 1921 to 1930. In the nineties $40 to $45 had the same purchasing power as $100 in the decade 1921 to 1930.

The second pair of curves shows the trend of dollar incomes. Again teachers are represented by the solid curve in terms of school years, while the dollar incomes of wage workers are represented by the dash curve plotted to calendar years. Beginning with $308 in 1889–90 the average annual dollar incomes of teachers rose steadily to $634 in 1916–17, then more rapidly to $1,201 in 1920–21, and then more slowly to a peak of $1,440 in 1930–31. The first decline appeared in 1931–32, and subsequent cuts, plus an allowance of 8.2 per cent. for unemployment, reduced the 1933–34 average to $934. Comparison of this curve with that showing the cost of living shows that dollar incomes of teachers lag consistently from one to two years behind changes in the cost of living. The cost of living advanced 13 per cent. between 1915–16 and 1916–17, and subsequent years saw further advances. A slightly larger than normal increase in dollar incomes occurred between 1916–17 and 1917–18, but the full compensation for the initial increase in the cost of living did not come until a year later. Similarly, the cost of living fell in 1920–21 in comparison with the previous year, but the sharp change in the trend of dollar incomes did not come until a year later. Similarly, the cost of living began to fall sharply in 1930–31, but the first small cut in salaries did not come until a year later and the first substantial cut in salaries did not come until two years later. The present situation continues this pattern: the cost of living has started to rise, while the dollar incomes of teachers are still falling.

Comparison of the curve showing the dollar incomes of teachers and the dash curve showing the dollar incomes of wage workers is also of interest. In the first place, the curve for teachers is definitely below the curve for wage workers throughout the period from 1889–90 to 1920–21. Since 1920–21 the incomes of teachers compare more favorably with wage workers. In the second place the curve for wage workers is much more irregular than for teachers. The irregular fluctuations of the dollar incomes of wage workers, which are deflated for unemployment throughout, are due largely to fluctuations in the business cycle. In the third place the dollar incomes of wage workers do not exhibit the lag in relation to changes in the cost of living which is characteristic of the dollar incomes of teachers.

The third pair of curves shows the real incomes of teachers and of wage workers. Real incomes represent the purchasing power of dollar incomes when allowance is made for the cost of living. In 1889–90 the dollar incomes of teachers averaged $308. But the cost of living was low, hence $308 would purchase as much of what teachers buy as would have required $720 in the period for 1921 to 1930. The chart shows that real incomes rose rapidly from $720 in 1889–90 to $845 in 1894–95, a period in which the cost of living was falling. In the eight years which followed, teachers actually lost ground in spite of steady increases in dollar incomes, due to the fact that the cost of living rose somewhat faster. From 1902–03 to 1914–15 dollar incomes rose somewhat more rapidly, the cost of living rose somewhat less rapidly, and real incomes mounted from $833 to $1,049. In spite of continued increases in dollar incomes the spectacular rise in the cost of living during the war put real incomes down to $817 in 1918–19. Substantial increases in dollar incomes and a drop in the cost of living resulted in a huge gain in real incomes, which reached $1,220 in 1922–23. Continued increases in dollar incomes and a fall in the cost of living raised real incomes to a peak of $1,609 in 1931–32. A subsequent cut of 10.6 per cent. in dollar incomes was softened by a further drop in the cost of living, so that even in 1932–33 the real incomes of teachers were still 8.6 per cent. above the level of 1928–29. The last very severe cut in dollar incomes was aggravated by a rise in the cost of living so that real incomes for 1933–34 fell to $1,124.

For comparative purposes the dotted curve at the bottom of the chart shows the level of industrial activity in terms of calendar years. It is apparent that the fluctuations in the real incomes of wage workers parallel the fluctuations in the business cycle, whereas no such correspondence appears between the real incomes of teachers and the business cycle.

With this description of the data as a background we turn to the major problem. What factors determine the real incomes of teachers over short periods of time? In the first place, and contrary to popular opinion, the real incomes of teachers have been influenced very little by depressions in the level of industrial activity, due in part to the tendency of the cost of living to fall during such periods. Thus, during the four major depressions of the last forty-five years the real incomes of teachers increased on the average at the rate of 7.5 per cent. per year. It is periods of rising industrial activity and of prosperity, with the accompanying tendency of prices to rise during such periods, which hold back the real incomes of teachers. On the average during such periods the real incomes of teachers decreased at the rate of 2.5 per cent. per year. The present situation conforms to past experience and is exceptional only in that the initial recovery period, instead of holding back real incomes, has witnessed a sharp deflation. The contrast between teachers and wage workers at this point is extreme: the correlation between the year to year changes in the real incomes of teachers and the changes in industrial activity is actually slightly negative, whereas in the case of wage workers the correlation is strongly positive .893.

In the second place, and paradoxically enough, changes in the trend of dollar incomes constitute a relatively unimportant factor in determining changes in real incomes. Of course, if dollar incomes were arbitrarily cut in half, real incomes would also be cut in half. But such things simply don't happen. There is a tremendous inertia in the trend of dollar incomes; even the most strenuous efforts of teachers to obtain larger than the traditional increases in the war period did not prevent real incomes from falling 21.8 per cent.; even the most strenuous efforts of taxpayers to cut salaries in the period 1929 to 1932 did not prevent real incomes from rising 13.8 per cent. It results that changes in the trend of dollar incomes exerted a substantial influence on real incomes in only two out of the forty-five years: between 1919–20 and 1920–21 the momentum for higher salaries which had been gathering strength during the preceding years resulted in an increase of 29.4 per cent. in dollar incomes and this plus a drop in the cost of living was translated into an increase of 33.1 per cent. in real incomes; between 1932–33 and 1933–34 the momentum for lower salaries which had been gathering strength during the preceding years resulted in a decrease of 23.6 per cent. in dollar incomes, and this plus a rise in the cost of living was translated into a decrease of 27.8 per cent. in real incomes. Eliminate these two years, and the correlation between the year-to-year percentage changes in dollar and in real incomes is zero. In contrast, the similar correlation for wage workers is .866. This is not to depreciate the importance of dollar incomes. They constitute an essential factor in the situation, but when the cost of living begins to move, all the king's horses and all the king's men can't move the dollar incomes of teachers fast enough to catch up.

It follows from this analysis that the cost of living and the lag in dollar incomes are the important factors in determining changes in the real incomes of teachers over short periods of time. As the cost of living falls, the real incomes of teachers rise; as the cost of living rises, the real incomes of teachers fall. In contrast, the cost of living is a very minor factor in determining the real incomes of wage workers. If anything, the real incomes of wage workers rise slightly in spite of rising costs of living. It is the level of industrial activity which is the determining factor in the real incomes of wage workers.

The implications of these data for the immediate future are unfavorable for teachers and favorable for wage workers. It requires no special foresight to predict that the cost of living will rise during the next three to five years. The only question among competent observers concerns the nature of the rise: how long it will last, how far it will go, how gradual or violent it will be. While rising costs of living can be counted upon to bring higher dollar incomes eventually, nevertheless, even moderately rising prices will restrain any trend to higher real incomes among teachers. The probabilities favor a return to normal industrial activity. Each increase in the level of industrial activity should be reflected promptly and fully in increased real incomes for wage workers and eventually in larger dollar incomes for teachers. A third factor to be considered is the possibility that economic ignorance and political opportunism will shove us into the whirlpool of paper money and wildcat inflation. While it is barely conceivable that wage workers might maintain their real incomes in this eventuality, it is certain that the process would prove extraordinarily painful to teachers.

In evaluating the plain inferences of the historical record a number of minor favorable factors in the outlook for teachers need to be taken into consideration. In the first place the cuts during the current school year have been most severe and their very severity argues for some rebound upward. In the second place the current sharp drop in real incomes is due in part to an allowance for unemployment which, given a strong industrial recovery and a slow and controlled rise in prices, should shortly disappear from the picture. In the third place, it should be easier in the immediate future to obtain increases in dollar incomes than it was during the war period. These factors may turn the balance from unfavorable to favorable. In any case, however, the outlook for the real incomes of teachers over the next three to five years is much less promising and many times more hazardous than the outlook for wage workers.

TABLE I

Cost of Living, Dollar Incomes, and Real Incomes of Teachers and of Wage Workers, 1890 to 1934

Year	Cost of living 1921–30 equals 100		Dollar incomes deflated for unemployment		Real incomes in terms of 1921–30 dollars		Average number of days in school year	Industrial activity averages of monthly data
	Teachers	Wage workers	Teachers	Wage workers	Teachers	Wage workers		
(1)	(2)	(3)	(4)	(5)	(6)	(7)	(8)	(9)
1890 ...	42.8	44.1	308	436	720	989	134.7	111.5
1891 ...	41.8	42.8	316	435	757	1016	135.8	106.7
1892 ...	41.9	43.3	323	450	771	1039	136.3	112.0
1893 ...	41.4	42.4	326	402	788	949	137.6	97.0
1894 ...	40.2	41.1	334	343	830	835	138.4	83.2
1895 ...	39.9	41.1	337	384	845	934	139.5	97.0
1896 ...	40.5	42.0	342	363	844	864	140.7	88.8
1897 ...	41.0	42.4	342	369	833	870	141.8	90.5
1898 ...	41.1	42.4	350	374	851	882	142.7	96.4
1899 ...	41.8	43.3	357	414	853	956	143.4	104.1
1900 ...	43.2	44.9	372	428	862	953	143.7	99.5
1901 ...	44.2	45.8	379	453	856	989	144.2	102.5
1902 ...	45.4	47.1	388	474	854	1006	145.2	104.4
1903 ...	47.2	49.2	393	490	833	996	146.2	101.1
1904 ...	47.4	48.8	409	466	862	955	148.3	93.7
1905 ...	47.3	48.8	424	494	897	1012	149.4	105.2
1906 ...	48.5	50.4	435	510	898	1012	151.1	109.6
1907 ...	51.1	53.4	453	534	887	1000	152.2	109.7
1908 ...	50.3	51.3	475	451	943	879	153.7	82.5
1909 ...	49.8	51.3	495	516	994	1006	155.6	101.2
1910 ...	52.0	54.3	510	562	980	1035	156.5	103.2
1911 ...	53.9	56.0	522	540	969	964	157.4	94.8
1912 ...	54.6	56.4	543	563	995	998	157.6	105.3
1913 ...	56.0	58.1	559	584	998	1005	158.3	102.5
1914 ...	57.0	59.0	578	544	1014	922	158.7	89.4
1915 ...	56.3	57.7	588	540	1045	936	159.5	96.7
1916 ...	59.2	63.2	607	667	1026	1055	160.1	113.3
1917 ...	66.9	75.9	634	783	948	1032	160.4	108.6
1918 ...	80.8	92.4	682	1014	844	1097	160.8	103.9
1919 ...	94.3	104.7	771	1167	817	1115	161.3	103.9
1920 ...	111.0	121.3	929	1375	837	1134	162.0	105.5
1921 ...	108.5	104.3	1201	998	1107	957	162.9	82.4
1922 ...	99.6	97.1	1225	1032	1230	1063	164.4	96.5
1923 ...	98.5	99.2	1249	1249	1268	1259	166.2	109.5
1924 ...	99.6	99.2	1261	1192	1266	1202	168.0	99.7
1925 ...	100.0	101.8	1279	1269	1279	1247	169.1	106.9
1926 ...	101.2	102.2	1300	1302	1284	1273	169.7	109.3
1927 ...	100.2	100.6	1349	1282	1346	1274	170.4	106.5
1928 ...	99.5	100.1	1375	1281	1382	1280	171.3	107.8

TABLE I—(*Continued*)

COST OF LIVING, DOLLAR INCOMES, AND REAL INCOMES OF TEACHERS AND OF WAGE WORKERS, 1890 TO 1934

Year	Cost of living 1921–30 equals 100		Dollar incomes deflated for unemployment		Real incomes in terms of 1921–30 dollars		Average number of days in school year	Industrial activity averages of monthly data
	Teachers	Wage workers	Teachers	Wage workers	Teachers	Wage workers		
(1)	(2)	(3)	(4)	(5)	(6)	(7)	(8)	(9)
1929 ...	99.7	99.7	1410	1357	1414	1361	172.1	112.7
1930 ...	99.0	95.9	1420	1119	1434	1167	172.7	94.3
1931 ...	94.2	86.4	1440	829	1529	960	....	79.9
1932 ...	87.7	77.4	1411	569	1609	735	....	64.2
1933 ...	82.2	74.8	1262	598	1535	799	....	71.9
1934 ...	85.8	78.3	964	735	1124	939	....	76.2

SOURCES AND DERIVATION OF DATA

Column one, years. The data for wage workers and for industrial activity are in terms of calendar years. Data for teachers are in terms of school years; thus, 1890 refers to the school year 1889–90.

Column two, cost of living for teachers. These indices were computed by weighting the components of the U. S. Bureau of Labor Statistics index as follows: Food 21.6 per cent., clothing 13.9 per cent., rent 13.6 per cent., fuel and light 4.5 per cent., house furnishings and furniture 4.9 per cent., and miscellaneous 41.5 per cent. These percentages are averages based on budgets of teachers in five cities, as reported by Eells[1] and in Bridgeport, Conn. The author is indebted to Miss Katherine L. Fitzpatrick for the Bridgeport figures, which permit division of the general percentage for "housing" as given by Eells into the more specific categories. Note that, contrary to the procedure of Eells, miscellaneous costs do not include an allowance for savings, investments and insurance. In the first place, the index of miscellaneous costs as computed by the Bureau of Labor Statistics does not purport to cover these costs. In the second place, the argument of Eells that insurance costs are inflexible is only superficially correct, since an $8,500 policy will now provide the same protection as a $10,000 policy in 1929. The data of the Bureau of Labor statistics weighted as indicated above provide indices for forty-one months from December, 1914, to June, 1933. December, 1933, figures are not available at this writing. With the indices for forty-one months as bench marks, indices for the intervening months were calculated from the monthly figures of either Douglas[2, 3] or the National Industrial Conference Board. The resulting monthly indices for the months September of one year to August of the next were combined to obtain yearly averages which coincide with the school year. Components of the National Industrial Conference Board were similarly weighted and spliced to the above series to bring the data to February, 1934. The index for 1933–34 is the average of the five months from September, 1933, to February, 1934. The cost of living for wage workers as computed by Douglas in the years prior to 1915 was adjusted to school years by adding one fourth of the index for one year to three fourths of the index for the next year and the resulting figures spliced to the indices computed from the data of the Bureau of Labor statistics to extend the series back to 1889–90. The whole series is set on a base of 1921 to 1930, equalling 100.

Column three, cost of living for wage workers. The index of the cost of living for wage workers from 1890 to 1928 was derived from the figures of Douglas[2, 3] to which were spliced the indices of the National Industrial Conference Board. The 1934 figure is for the month of February.

Column four, dollar incomes of teachers. Average annual salaries of all public school teachers, including kindergarten teachers, principals and supervisors, but excluding superintendents, have been published irregularly by the U. S. Office of Education from 1914–15 to 1929–30. The 1931–32 average was obtained by correspondence with the Office of Education. Averages for the years 1930–31, 1932–33 and 1933–34 were taken from reports of the Research Division of the National Education Association.[4] The 1933–34 average seems unduly low, but the Office of Education has used this figure in a recent bulletin.[5] Average

[1] Walter Crosby Eells, "Teachers Salaries and the Cost of Living." Pp. 94. Stanford University Press, 1933.

[2] Paul H. Douglas, "Real Wages in the United States, 1890–1926." Pp. 682. Houghton Mifflin Company, 1930.

[3] Paul H. Douglas, and F. T. Jennison, "The Movement of Money and Real Wages in the United States, 1926–28." Pp. 57. University of Chicago Studies in Business Administration, 1930, Vol. I, No. 3.

[4] "Current Conditions in the Nation's Schools."

salaries for the remaining years of the period 1914–15 to 1933–34 were estimated by the author on the basis of reports of from nine to thirteen state departments of education. Average salaries for the years 1931–32, 1932–33 and 1933–34 were deflated .4 per cent., 2.6 per cent., and 8.2 per cent. to allow for unemployment among school teachers. These percentages are the averages of two estimates. In the first estimate the trend in the number of teachers employed from 1925–26 to 1930–31 was projected to 1933–34. In the second estimate the trend in the number of teachers was calculated on the basis of one teacher to 29.29 pupils. Subtracting the number of teachers in service from these estimates indicates that between 9.8 per cent. and 6.6 per cent. were unemployed in 1933–34 (for pupil and teacher data see reference No. 4). When the Bureau of Education began the calculation of average annual salaries it extended the series backward by dividing the total expenditures of public schools for salaries of teachers, principals, supervisors and superintendents by the total number of teachers. This procedure, however, introduces a slight discrepancy in the series. This discrepancy has been corrected by deflating salaries computed by this method by 4.8 per cent., so that the 1914–15 average is identical with the more carefully determined figure, which relates to all teachers not including superintendents.

The resulting average annual salaries show an increase from $240 in 1889–90 to $1,440 in 1930–31. These figures, however, greatly exaggerate the upward trend of salaries. Three factors conspire to make the salaries of the nineties unduly low. In the first place, the school year averaged only twenty-seven instead of thirty-four weeks. In the second place, it was formerly the custom to pay teachers, particularly in rural areas, a salary plus board and lodging. In the third place, the relatively larger proportion of men, the longer summer vacations, the relatively high wages for labor and the absence of summer schools during the nineties resulted in no inconsiderable proportion of teachers relying on out-of-school work for a large part of their total income. These factors are no longer operating. Adjustment for these factors was made as follows: Annual salaries were divided by the number of school days as recorded in column eight to give daily wages and the result multiplied by 172.7 (the number of days in the 1929–30 school year) to give the figures in column four. The adjustment which has been applied accomplishes the following things in a single operation: It gives a good picture of the probable total incomes of teachers throughout the period 1889–90 to 1933–34; it corrects for the lengthening school year; the resulting trend is precisely the same as the trend of daily, weekly or monthly wages; and the resulting data give a truer comparison with the earnings of wage workers than would either the original salary data or the daily, weekly or monthly data.

Column five, dollar incomes of wage workers. Average annual dollar incomes of wage workers in manufacturing and transportation to 1927, deflated to allow for unemployment, were taken directly from Douglas.[2, 3] The Federal Reserve Board indices of factory payrolls were used to extend the data to 1933. The 1934 figure is for February and is based on *The Annalist* index of factory payrolls, which is adjusted for seasonal variation and which shows that February payrolls were 22.9 per cent. above the average of 1933 on a seasonally adjusted basis. The errors involved in splicing these two series are small, as may be shown by estimating dollar incomes based on factory payrolls from 1919 to 1926 and comparing the resulting figures with the independent data of Douglas. On the average for these eight years dollar incomes based on factory payrolls differ from the dollar incomes as determined by Douglas by only 2.9 per cent.

Columns six and seven, real incomes. Real incomes are dollar incomes divided by the cost of living.

Column eight, average number of days in the school year. These figures are the moving averages of three years centered. This smoothing is necessary to eliminate the influence of a few erratic fluctuations in the reported number of days in the school year.

Column nine, industrial activity. These figures are averages of monthly indices, as compiled and published by *The Annalist*.[6] The 1934 figure is for February.

FRANK K. SHUTTLEWORTH
YALE UNIVERSITY

Research Bulletin of the National Education Association. Vol. XI, No. 4, November, 1933.

[5] "The Deepening Crisis in Education." The Office of Education, Leaflet No. 44, 1933.

[6] "Economic Changes in the United States, 1854–1933; The Sequence of Fluctuations in Five Main Indices." *The Annalist*, 43: 96–97, 274, 349, January 19, February 9 and February 23, 1934.

NEW BOOKS IN EDUCATION

MOTT, FRANK L., Editor. *News Stories of 1933.* Pp. 336. The Clio Press. $2.25.

STONE, JOHN C., CLIFFORD N. MILLS and VIRGIL S. MALLORY. *Unit Mastery Mathematics.* Book I. Pp. v + 314; Book II. Pp. v + 432; Book III. Pp. v + 469. Illustrated. Sanborn. $0.96, $1.00, $1.20.

SCHOOL AND SOCIETY

WITH WHICH ARE COMBINED THE EDUCATIONAL REVIEW, ESTABLISHED IN 1891, THE TEACHERS MAGAZINE, ESTABLISHED IN 1878, AND THE SCHOOL JOURNAL, ESTABLISHED IN 1874.

Volume 39 | Saturday, June 2, 1934 | Number 1014

THE FUNCTION OF THE CHURCH COLLEGE IN PRESENT-DAY EDUCATION[1]

By Professor FREDERICK E. BOLTON

UNIVERSITY OF WASHINGTON

In ancient days it was the church that inspired learning in order that the benighted might see the spiritual light of salvation. It was religious fervor that produced the greatest book of all the ages; a book which is a classic in expression, a beacon throughout the ages, not only in religion but in morality and conduct. During the black intellectual night of the middle ages the church and religious zeal kept aflame the torch of learning and were the only spurs that caused men to grope for something higher than the brute instincts dominating that pagan age.

The founding of the land of the Stars and Stripes was due primarily to the desire to find a realm of religious freedom. Various bands of religious worshipers established shrines in different sections of the new colonial world—the Pilgrims in Massachusetts, the Friends and Lutherans in Pennsylvania, the Catholics in the Carolinas and Maryland, and the Church of England or Episcopalians in Virginia.

Every colonial institution of higher learning owes its origin to religious zeal. Beginning with Harvard in 1636, which became the Unitarian stronghold, there soon followed Yale, the mother of all Congregational colleges; William and Mary in Virginia, and King's College, now Columbia, both forerunners of Episcopalian institutions. Princeton is the mother of Presbyterian colleges, while almost every state has its Wesleyan College, the name indicating the great founder of Methodism. Every city and countless sequestered rural nooks have their Catholic colleges, convents and monastic institutions, training teachers and others in the established orders of their faith.

Among the greatest more recent factors, not only in religious leadership, but equally in secular education, we must not fail to note the Baptist University of Chicago, the Catholic University of America in Washington, D. C., Brigham Young University, Provo, Utah, and the great trio of Methodist institutions—Northwestern University at Evanston, Ill., Boston University and the University of Southern California, at Los Angeles.

Colleges founded by the apostles of all the great religious denominations have been established by the pioneers in every state in the Union. So zealous and so vigorous have the churches been in the planting of educational institutions that at the present time, even with all the provisions made for state institutions, more than half of all the army of students—a million strong—pursuing higher learning are in church-founded organizations.

Even in the establishment of public edu-

[1] Presented at the meeting of Independent Colleges, Spokane, on April 2, 1934.

cation, the underlying and expressed motive was the desire to spread Christianity; this was true in the Colonies. It was specifically expressed in the Ordinance of 1787, which states that "Religion, morality, and knowledge, being necessary to good government and the happiness of mankind, schools and the means of education shall forever be encouraged."

Those church colleges have led the way; they have conserved the best in education and in civilization. While state institutions through purely intellectual zeal have sometimes forgotten spiritual values, the church schools have served as a stabilizing factor, ever holding aloft the idea of the superlative value of the eternal verities of life. Even some of the parent church schools that have become wealthy and unwieldy have been dazzled by purely intellectual and material values, but the small church colleges have held steadfast and have clearly visioned the fundamental values upon which all civilization rests.

Such has been the contribution of the small denominational colleges; such is their commission to-day.

You do not need to have a layman recount these achievements of the church colleges. They are full well known to you. It may be a matter of gratification to you, however, to know that they are understood and appreciated by a layman whose entire school days and professional career have been spent in state institutions, where religious instruction is taboo and even forbidden by law in most states.

But with this distinguished record of achievement the church college must not regard its mission ended. At no time in history has it been more needed than today. With other institutions absorbed in intellectual and scientific achievements, with the church itself handicapped in its spiritual ministrations, some institutions must be maintained that will still have for their chief aim the sound interpretation of all that has been wrought in science, philosophy, history, politics, commerce and industry, and the selection of those factors that will make for the betterment of mankind. That is the function of the church college to-day.

As I conceive the paramount function of the church college, it is the unique mission to keep to the front the real and fundamental meaning of all education. Right now that meaning is needed as never before. Altogether too easy and alluring is the idea that education is merely to sharpen men's minds and to fit them to outwit all others for their own individual advancement. That is the common interpretation of vocational and professional education. Thus viewed, the boy through a trade is expected to acquire some superior skill, the lawyer shrewdness and legal tricks, and the salesman a compelling line of argument to bewilder resisting clients to buy inflated bonds or over-boomed real estate.

Now, we well know that the world is full of men with intellectual alertness and possessed of skill or even professional training who are not desirable neighbors or worthy citizens. Not a few of such help to keep our police busy and our jails crowded. Not all crooks and criminals are feebleminded. If all criminals who ought to be in jail were behind the bars the intellectual level of the jail population would be rather high. Many escape because of shrewdness or because of sufficient wealth to employ shrewd and unscrupulous lawyers. Some one has said, "It takes as much brains to pick a lock as to make one." The difference between the one who makes a lock and the one who picks a lock is wholly one of attitude—the lock breaker being one who is anti-social, one who believes that society owes him a living without honest work.

Former President Coolidge said, "It is not only what men know, but what they are disposed to do with what they know that will determine the rise or fall of civilizations."

Ruskin wrote: "Education does not

mean teaching people what they do not know. It means teaching them to behave as they do not behave. It is not teaching the youth the shapes of letters and the tricks of numbers and then leaving them to turn their arithmetic to roguery, and their literature to lust. It means, on the contrary, training them into the perfect exercise and kingly continence of their bodies and souls.''

Never before in the history of the world has there been such need for sanity and balance in the conduct of individuals and of nations. Never before have the allurements of Mammon been so enticing. Never before have men the world over been quite so obsessed with a belief in material power. With their new-found freedom men have often become intoxicated with a belief in their own individual power and worth and have come to scorn the rights of society.

Never before in the history of the world has there been such need of cooperation and coherence of groups, societies and nations. All Europe is a volcano ready to burst forth in another cataclysm. India is in rebellion, Russia is building up a great standing army. China is in the throes of a horrible, devastating internal death struggle and has been reduced in population by a hundred million in the last few decades. Never before in the history of the world have such colossal armies and navies been in formation as at this very moment.

What are the greatest needs in the world to-day? Not roads and bridges, not transportation, not means of communication, not food and shelter. Not even physical health and sanitation. Not plough-shares or factories or automobiles or even aeroplanes. Important as are these products of the mine, the farm, the factory, of science and invention, something far more important is demanded.

Creature comforts are so abundant, science has so successfully unlocked the secrets of the earth, the air and the atoms composing them, that everybody in the world could enjoy the greatest physical comforts—if—if everybody willed that everybody should! But with all these opportunities within our grasp H. G. Wells has said that civilization is a race between education and catastrophe. What did he mean? Simply that the mind of humanity is being so directed that science slowly evolved by man is used in fierce competition by each half of humanity in the attempt to exterminate the other half. Instead of encouragement and assistance; obstacles, theft, perversion of the laws are used to thwart justice. Even all the force of a pent-up Dante's Inferno are concentrated in the diabolical bombs, poison gas and other enginery of modern warfare. Twenty million keen-eyed, strong-limbed, buoyant youths in four short years sacrificed on the altar of Mammon! All Europe to-day is a seething cauldron ready to engulf two score million more. The Orient is threatened with decimation, not by starvation, but by the bayonet thrust in the hands of assassin brothers, of kindred blood but mad with jealous hatreds.

What kind of education did Mr. Wells mean? More science, more inventions? Hardly, when science is used to invent tenfold swifter means of forceful subjugation, coercion and extermination. More knowledge of trade and commerce? Not when all the knowledge of these is used but to whet the greedy appetites of unscrupulous plutocrats who grind down the helpless men and women that turn the wheels of industry and keep moving the marts of commerce. Even the innocent children are still employed in the dwarfing, deadening factories, their lives ebbing away; sacrificed to fill the coffers of unfeeling molochs.

India's starving millions are not wasting away because of lack of training for work. That, they could easily secure if permitted. The real causes are political oppression which stifles all incentive to labor, the toll exacted by those who exploit a fettered nation; or the age-old superstitions and ignorance which have perpetuated insanitation and filth and have debased the millions in that benighted country.

China's toiling masses are not without vocational skill; many possess it to an uncanny degree. They are not without diligence; the hobo unwilling to work is practically unknown among them. The real cause is that their grinding labor is not recompensed. Those more economically fortunate, largely in other lands, fill their coffers with the unearned profits on goods produced by Chinese skill and science. I need but mention silk and opium to convince.

It is not lack of skill or the will to work that explains the squalor, disease and degradation of the sweat-shop districts of our metropolitan centers, nor the pallid faces and pithless arms of the children of the cotton factories; nor the forlorn appearance of our mining districts and the often sullen, rebellious population of the steel mills and the denizens of the stockyard districts. We are told that "white slavery is recruited from girls who cannot earn living wages in the knitting works," in some of our great department stores and in multitudes of factories.

This recital is not intended to produce class antagonisms, but merely to show the paramount problem if the world is to be made safe for democracy. The oppression is ofttimes unintended and but reflects age-long tradition's sway. The unfortunates also frequently remain oppressed simply because the voice of ambition has never stirred them to achievement. Only the development of the chivalrous instinct on the part of the strong to succor the weak and the will on the part of the weak to become strong and helpful can ever save a struggling, battling world from complete destruction. Democracy means not merely rights and privileges but duties and obligations as well.

What the world needs are new attitudes, new sympathies, new friendships, new understandings of the integral part which each one plays in the weal or woe of civilization.

The way was pointed out nearly twenty centuries ago, but the lesson is yet but half learned. There is also danger that, like the newly rich who can not survive prosperity, we may become intoxicated with the apparent success of our experiment in civilization just begun and dash our chariot upon the rocks of destruction. We may see only the alluring signboards of rights, privileges, personal gain and luxury, and be blinded to the beckonings of duty, obligation and social amelioration which we must likewise follow if we would drive to safety and ultimate satisfaction.

This lengthy statement is made to drive home, if possible, the tremendous need for some new objectives in education—education for character and citizenship—and these are largely matters of attitude.

On a recent Memorial Day President Hoover, standing on the identical spot where Lincoln delivered the immortal Gettysburg speech, said, "The things of the spirit alone persist. It is in that field that the Nation makes its lasting progress. To cherish religious faith and the tolerance of all faiths; to reflect into every aspect of public life the spirit of charity, the practise of forbearance and the restraint of passion while reason seeks the way; to face with courage and confident expectation the task set before us, these are the true glory for this nation. They will lead us to a life more abounding, richer in satisfactions, more enduring in its achievements, more precious in its bequests to our children—a life not merely of conflict, but filled with the joy of creative action."

President Franklin D. Roosevelt, outstanding pioneer of the New Deal, pleads for social justice whereby men may live and work together in a world in which mutual welfare rather than individual gain shall be the watchword and the rule of a New Day.

Well might we all take unto ourselves the words of Lincoln in that prophetic address: "It is for us, the living, to be dedicated here to the unfinished work which they who fought here have so nobly advanced. It is rather for us here to be dedicated to the great task remaining before us—that from these honored dead we take increased devotion—that we here highly resolve that these dead shall not have died in vain—that this nation, under God, shall have a new birth of freedom and that this government of the people, by the people and for the people, shall not perish from the earth."

We believe and expect that students nurtured in institutions founded upon Christian principles will develop attitudes of honesty, integrity, fairness and good will; that they will strive to promote happiness and prosperity; that if they become leaders of the youth no action will tarnish their good name; if they enter the great professions they will be examples of the highest ethics; if they engage in commerce or trade, fair dealing shall be their guide; if public life shall call them, public welfare shall submerge all personal ambition or emolument. In whatever capacity, be it the humblest and most obscure, or the most exalted in the gift of nations, their lives should be characterized by purity of motive, honesty, unselfishness, toleration, generosity and devoted service.

The type of problem which education should face is suggested by an article in the February *American Magazine,* entitled "A Young Man Speaks His Mind." This youth, signing himself "J. W.," purporting to be eighteen years of age, asks for a single practical reason why he should be honest. He plans to be a lawyer, but says only dishonest lawyers can succeed. He says his father and mother have been honest, "but see what failures they have been." On the other hand there is "Mr. J., who used to keep a store in the same block with Dad. He is rich now, and retired. He and his family have servants, fine clothes, and fine cars. They travel." He tells how Mr. J. got ahead by shrewd, dishonest practises. He says:

> Mr. Editor, I want to make money. This life is all I'm sure of and I want to enjoy it. I want money to spend for comforts and pleasures. And I'd like to buy some comforts and pleasures for Dad and Mother, too. Furthermore, I don't want to be old and stiff before I have money to spend. That's where dishonesty really comes in. I think I can make money quicker. . . . I've watched until I know how to be a respected crook, and it's simple. Anybody can do it. . . . It looks to me as if it doesn't make much difference whether you are honest or dishonest, because people don't seem to care about honesty. Neither do they care about dishonesty unless they consciously suffer by it. . . . So one good reason, please, Mr. Editor, why an ambitious young man should be honest. It's got to be a real, practical reason, too. And don't talk to me about great men having been honest. I don't want to be great. I want to be comfortable.

If this youth's attitude is representative, the very foundations of civilization are undermined and only a complete revamping of education can forefend against its complete collapse. To accomplish this the church colleges must assume the leadership.

In this unique work committed to you no phase is more important than the training of teachers; in fact, I believe it is the most outstanding function of the church college to-day. You are not only to interpret education to all your students, but a goodly percentage of them are to go out and carry the message to countless others in the lower schools.

In pioneer days it was the special work of the church college to train missionaries for foreign fields. Now, they are still to train missionaries, but not so much for foreign fields. The young heathen of today who need your ministrations are in our own commonwealths. They need not enlightenment in material things or in worldly ways. They are abundantly sophisticated. They need especial help in understanding the common rights of man and in the inculcation of the plain homely virtues of honesty, truthfulness, tolerance, duty, justice and sincerity.

For consecrated teachers with these qualities the demand is great and continually increasing. More and more are parents asking for leaders of their boys and girls, guides who can be trusted to instill in their plastic minds not only scientific truths, but principles of right living as well.

There are many parents who do not attend any church yet who do not wish their sons and daughters guided by sophisticated and worldly-wise teachers who are cynical regarding every moral law and who openly sneer at all religion.

There are many school board members who may themselves smoke like a factory chimney, but who do not wish their daughters to be trained by a cigarette smoking flapper.

Unique and noble is the work of the teacher of children if imbued with principles of Christian living. Daniel Webster realized the pivotal place in civilization occupied by the teacher and left us the following gem:

> If we work upon marble, it will perish; if we work upon brass, time will efface it; if we rear temples, they will crumble into dust; but if we work upon immortal minds, if we imbue them with principles, with the just fear of God and love of our fellow men, we engrave on those tablets something that will brighten all eternity.

Arthur Guiterman has paid beautiful tribute in the following lines to one of America's greatest teachers—Mark Hopkins—and his equally illustrious pupil, James A. Garfield:

Mark Hopkins sat on one end of a log,
  And a farm boy sat on the other.
Mark Hopkins came as a pedagogue
  And taught as an elder brother.
I don't care what Mark Hopkins taught—
  If his Latin was small or his Greek was naught—
For the farmer boy he thought, thought he,
  All through lecture time and quiz,
"The kind of man I mean to be
  Is the kind of man Mark Hopkins is."

Theology, languages, medicine, law
  Are peacock feathers to deck a daw
If the boys who come from your splendid schools
  Are well-trained sharpers or flippant fools.
You may boast of your age and your ivied walls,
  Your great endowments, your marble halls,
    And all your modern features—
Your vast curriculum's scope and reach,
  The multifarious things you teach—
    But what about your teachers?
Are they men who can stand in a father's place,
  Who are paid, best paid, by the ardent face,
When boyhood gives, as boyhood can,
  Its love and faith to a fine true man?

No printed word nor spoken plea
  Can teach young hearts what men should be.
Not all the books on all the shelves
  But what the teachers are themselves.
For Education is Making Men:
  So is it now, so was it when
Mark Hopkins sat on one end of a log
  And James Garfield sat on the other.

EDUCATIONAL EVENTS

THE NEW NATIONALISM IN MEXICO

THE Mexican Ministry of Interior has launched a general movement by governmental agencies to prevent further alleged defamations of Mexico, her people and her customs. As reported in the *Herald-Tribune* of New York, the Ministry of the Interior contemplates a bill to be introduced at the approaching session of Congress and designed to control the production and distribution of motion pictures which might in any way give offense to the Mexican people. It is understood that the new legislation will provide ways and means for controlling, among other things, the operation of foreign motion picture firms in Mexico. The measure, it is believed, will provide for a plan resembling prevailing American codes for the Mexican motion picture industry to supervise its own productions with a view to preventing offenses against "ethics, dignity or historic truth."

Aron Saenz, Governor of the Federal District which includes Mexico City, has issued a statement lamenting "the decadence of Mexican artistic and theatrical spectacles," and intimating that efforts will be made to create a fund for aiding enterprises that promote nationalistic Mexican motion pictures. Governor Saenz, in declaring that the great cities of the world have sought for some time to safeguard "the national aspect of the people's artistic and spiritual existence," expressed the government's determination to declare war against "the invasion of things foreign-called artistic without being so—which are corrupting and weakening our public taste, though, in fact, it attained unquestionable refinements." He expressed the opinion that Mexican "collective psychology is being foreignized to an alarming degree. The motion picture, radio and other amusement agencies are slowly but vigorously absorbing the distinctive soul of our race."

This foreign influence, Governor Saenz believes, is leading to decadence of Mexican music and architecture. "Neither snobbism nor chauvinism must be our rule, but general progress must be admitted within our own culture and within our geographic panorama."

PART-TIME SECONDARY SCHOOLS

A MONOGRAPH on part-time secondary schools has been recently issued by the National Survey of Secondary Education.

After increasing steadily for a number of years, continuation school enrolment in the states decreased for the first time from 1928 to 1930. The total continuation school enrolment in 1930 was 310,000 in 282 schools. Between 1920 and 1930, evening school attendance practically doubled, and amounted to 1,000,000 students in 664 schools.

The monograph, prepared by Grayson N. Kefauver, Victor H. Noll and C. Elwood Drake, constitutes one of 28 special reports now in process of publication which will give complete findings of the three-year study.

The survey was conducted under the auspices of the Federal Office of Education, by authority of Congress, with Dr. William John Cooper, who was then United States Commissioner of Education, as director. Dr. Leonard V. Koos, professor of secondary education in the University of Chicago, was associate director. The major burden of directing and handling the survey was entrusted to Dr. Koos.

Part-time continuation schools give four or more hours a week to students in the day time, while evening schools serve them late in the day or in the early evening. The objectives of the evening schools relate chiefly to vocational education where these schools receive aid from the Federal Government.

Approximately 70 per cent. of the continuation schools considered in the report are receiving some aid from the Federal Government. These schools have larger enrolments than those which do not receive Federal aid. There is a great variety in the types of courses offered. For the 312 schools selected for the investigation, there were reported 341 different subjects. Studies in the field of industrial arts and academic subjects constitute the majority. Home economics, dress-making, English, typing and woodwork are most commonly offered. Thirteen per cent. of the schools are making provision for part-time cooperative training, about half of the time to be spent on the job itself and the other half in school pursuing subjects related to the job. About a third are housed in separate buildings in contrast to a fourth of those not federally aided. About one half of both types carry on their work in the high-school buildings. Thirty-five per cent. have a full-time principal compared with 23 per cent. of the latter group. Most class periods in the two types of schools are 60 minutes long. Many of the schools are making an effort to relate vocational training to the needs of the community. Some follow-up work is carried on after students are placed. However, most of the schools keep little data concerning their pupils. From the investigation of the characteristics of the students, it was found that the median age of continuation pupils is 17. Ninety per cent. of the students had completed the eighth grade in the regular school, which is the most common dropping-out point. One third of the boys and two thirds of the girls dropped out after completing this grade.

Slightly more than half the boys after leaving school entered either the transportation and communication field or the labor field for their first jobs. Nearly two thirds of the girls entered the personal service field, first, and next went into miscellaneous jobs of the manufacturing and mechanical industries. Boys were employed about 36 hours a week at a median wage of about $12.00, while girls worked, on an average, 30 hours a week for $6.24. After two or three years of attendance in continuation school, students are still generally in the same field of work.

THE LAS VEGAS CONFERENCE ON INDIAN EDUCATION

THE United States Indian Service recently called together representatives of five western states to meet in the city of Las Vegas, Nevada, for the purpose of considering important matters having to do with the education of Indian children in the southwest area of the United States.

The most important phase of development at the conference grew out of the announcement during the conference that the Johnson-O'Malley Bill, formerly the Swing-Johnson Bill, had passed the national Congress.

A brief summary of the topics discussed at the Las Vegas meeting is as follows:

1. The federal government and its responsibility for Indian education;
2. The definition of an adequate educational program for Indians;
3. Interstate relationships in connection with certain problems of Indian education.

A brief review of the statement on public schools and the federal Indian service, together with congressional measures affecting the Indian, is presented as follows:

1. The federal government, through its Indian service, is not attempting to saddle any additional burden upon the states or the Indians but rather to do a better job for the Indians (and also for the whites) by combining available resources of the federal government and the states in the strengthening of local facilities for education and community development.
2. Reduction and elimination of federal Indian boarding schools is an important step in this process not only because multiplication of these institutions has had unfortunate social and educational effects, but also because one of the chief reasons the federal government has not been able to give adequate attention to local community work for Indians is that the boarding schools have absorbed an overwhelming share of the financial resources available for education.
3. So far as possible the Federal government in its Indian education work should be dealing directly with the state educational authorities rather than with the local schools. It is recognized however that diversity of conditions in the various states prohibits any standardized application of this principle. As fast as the states develop needed types of child care for rural populations, including Indians, the Indian service will cooperate with the state rather than maintain separate facilities, provided of course, the welfare of Indian children is safeguarded and participation of Indians in school and community life is assured.

Two recent modifications in the regulations covering public school tuition are as follows:

1. Payment of tuition for Indian children shall not be made for use by public school districts for any obligations except those of the current year and assurance to such effect must be given by school districts or counties.
2. The right is reserved to refuse or reduce tuition payments for Indian children to any school district maintaining less than the highest state standards in respect to professional preparation of teachers, school equipment and supplies, text and library books, construction and sanitation of buildings.

BARD COLLEGE OF COLUMBIA UNIVERSITY

THE name of St. Stephen's College, undergraduate unit of Columbia University at Annandale-on-Hudson, N. Y., has been changed to Bard College in honor of John Bard, who founded the institution seventy-five years ago.

The new designation, according to a statement made by President Nicholas Murray Butler, is linked with the early history of Columbia University, John Bard having been related to Samuel Bard, who was a member of the first Faculty of Medicine, in King's College, as Columbia was originally known, and who became president of the College of Physicians and Surgeons in 1811. Bard Hall, residence for men at the Medical School, erected through a gift of Edward S. Harkness, is named in memory of Samuel Bard.

With the approval of the Columbia University Council, a new educational program in the liberal arts and sciences "more closely adapted to the individual needs and abilities of young men" will go into effect next fall. To inaugurate this program the Carnegie Corporation has made a grant of $10,000.

Seven new members of the faculty will be appointed and more selective entrance standards will be established. Professor Donald G. Tewksbury, of Teachers College, Columbia University, will continue as acting dean. Greater financial resources to enlarge educational facilities and to pay adequate salaries to teachers will be sought.

The new program, according to a statement made by Dean Tewksbury, will permit and encourage the student to build his own curriculum around his own particular talents, needs, and purposes, as shown at entrance and during the early years of his college course. The materials of the curriculum will be arranged in five fields: natural sciences and mathematics; ancient and modern humanities; philosophy and religion; fine arts, music and drama; social studies and history. Three fundamental principles govern the plan. First, the student's approach to his college work should be made through the individual abilities, interests and purposes which he has discovered and demonstrated during the years of his previous educational experience. Second, these motivating elements in the life of the individual should be the center around which he should proceed to build his own curriculum. And third, his college education, following the lines of expanding interest and enlarging purpose, should culminate in a broad cultural outlook.

Through changes in the charter of the college, made recently by the Board of Trustees and sanctioned by the New York Legislature, the college becomes "Episcopal by tradition and influence rather than by control." The Church is to be represented on the Board of Trustees "by appropriately elected representatives rather than by majority representation." These representatives will be charged under charter provision with the maintenance of the primary religious tradition of the college. While the preparation of young men for the ministry is to be retained as an integral and important part of the work of the college, it is proposed to place emphasis upon the broader religious purposes of the institution.

FELLOWSHIPS IN THE GRADUATE SCHOOL OF ARTS AND SCIENCES AT HARVARD UNIVERSITY

A greater number of large fellowships for students in the Graduate School of Arts and Sciences at Harvard University has been provided by a regrouping of small scholarship funds. This is in accordance with the plans of President Conant, announced in his annual report, that the number of large fellowships be increased, both in Harvard College and in the graduate schools.

Beginning with the academic year 1935–36, $6,000 from the income of the Edward Austin Fund will be used in the Graduate School of Arts and Sciences as a lump sum for Austin Fellowships of amounts varying from $400 to $1,200, and $14,400 from general funds will be used in a similar way. This will provide seventeen fellowships of the maximum amount, if necessary, and more fellowships if the individual recipients require less than the maximum award. Graduates from other colleges will be equally eligible with those from Harvard College.

President Conant has frequently advanced the idea that fellowship funds can be more wisely used if the awards are large enough to cover, when necessary, all normal expenses of a year at Harvard. The graduate student, especially, it is felt, needs to have his time entirely free for the pursuit of study and research.

A part of the plan in connection with the new fellowships in the Graduate School is that the man who receives one of these fellowships and maintains a high record may be reappointed for a second and a third year, and so be able to study continuously for higher degrees. President Conant emphasizes the need for awarding fellowships for more than one year to superior students, with certain safeguards to prevent abuses of such a system. A number of the new fellowships will be awarded to men for their first year of residence.

President Conant's first step in establishing large fellowships was the recent introduction of half a dozen thousand-dollar fellowships for entering freshmen from six Middle Western States—Ohio, Illinois, Indiana, Michigan, Wisconsin and Minnesota.

THE SECTION OF EDUCATION OF THE AMERICAN ASSOCIATION FOR THE ADVANCEMENT OF SCIENCE

SECTION Q of the American Association for the Advancement of Science will hold its summer meeting at the University of California on June 19, 20 and 21.

The preliminary program is as follows:

Tuesday Morning, June 19

Relationships between Eye Structure and Reading Difficulties. Peter L. Spencer, associate professor of education, Claremont Colleges, California.

Visual Defects as Factors Influencing Achievement in Reading. L. P. Farris, principal of Oakland High School, California.

Experiments in the Improvement of Reading. Grace Fernald, associate professor of psychology, University of California at Los Angeles.

Investigation of Reading Difficulties on the College Level. William Mason Danner, Jr., research assistant in psychology, Stanford University.

Tuesday Afternoon, June 19

Work of the American Association for the Advancement of Science Committee on the Place of Science in Education. Otis W. Caldwell, *chairman,* Institute of School Experimentation, Teachers College, Columbia University, New York City.

The Effect of Reading on Spelling in Secondary Schools and Colleges. Luther C. Gilbert, lecturer in education, University of California.

Learning Difficulties in Arithmetic. Velma Wood, graduate student, University of California.

An Investigation of Ability in the Reading of Experimental Literature in Education. Wynn E. Olson, graduate student, University of California.

Wednesday Morning, June 20

The Harvard Growth Studies. Edward Lincoln, assistant professor of education, Harvard University, Cambridge, Massachusetts.

Questions Concerned with the Validity of Mental Age Concept. Hubert Armstrong, assistant director of child welfare, Oakland, California.

Certain Physical and Physiological Aspects of Adolescent Development. Helen B. Pryor, research associate, Institute of Child Welfare, University of California.

Wednesday Afternoon, June 20

Study of Elements in Leadership. Floyd Caldwell, instructor in education, State Teachers College, Chico, California.

Factors Related to Leadership on the High School Level. Marion Brown, dean of girls, University High School, Oakland.

Social and Educational Adjustment of the Under-Age Students in a University. Noel Keys, associate professor of education, University of California.

Extent of Freedom and Responsibility Given Students in Different Types of Schools. Grayson N. Kefauver, dean of the School of Education, Stanford University.

Thursday Morning, June 21

Application of Science to Guidance. Truman L. Kelley, professor of education, Harvard University.

The Factor of Interest in Guidance. Edward K. Strong, professor of psychology, Stanford University.

College Students of High Intelligence in a Personnel Program. C. Gilbert Wrenn, assistant registrar and director of vocational guidance, Stanford University.

EDUCATIONAL NOTES AND NEWS

DR. HARRY WOODBURN CHASE will be installed formally as chancellor of New York University on the morning of June 8, at the one hundred and second convocation. Dr. Chase had been previously successively professor of psychology and president of the University of North Carolina and from 1930 until his election chancellor of New York University, president of the University of Illinois. Dr. Chase succeeded Dr. Elmer Ellsworth Brown, who had been chancellor of the university since 1911.

THE American Association for Adult Education at its meeting in Washington, D. C., on May 23, elected Dr. Edward L. Thorndike as president for the ensuing year. Dr. Lewis A. Wilson, assistant commissioner of education of New York, Mrs. Eugene Meyer, Dr. George F. Zook, Alain Locke, professor of philosophy at Howard College, and Malcolm G. Wyer, dean of the School of Librarianship at the University of Denver, were elected vice-presidents. Dr. Charles A. Beard, Dr. Harvey N. Davis, president of Stevens Institute, and Dr. William Neilson, president of Smith College, were reelected.

DR. A. LAWRENCE LOWELL, president emeritus

of Harvard University, will give an address on "War and the League of Nations," at the two hundred and ninety-fifth commencement of the university.

DR. ALFRED SHERWOOD ROMER, professor of vertebrate paleontology at the University of Chicago, has been elected professor of biology at Harvard University.

ALFRED V. DE FOREST, research engineer, has been appointed associate professor of mechanical engineering at the Massachusetts Institute of Technology.

DR. ALVIN JOHNSON, director of The New School for Social Research, has announced the appointment of five additional members to the Graduate Faculty of Political and Social Science (the University in Exile), for the academic year, 1934–1935. Those appointed are: Albert Salomon, professor at the Pedagogical Institute, Cologne; Hans Staudinger, economist and formerly Secretary of State for Prussia; Erich Hula, formerly lecturer on international law at the University of Cologne and recipient of a three-year traveling fellowship of the Rockefeller Foundation; Alfred Kahler, formerly director of the Bokhochschule Harrisleefeld in Schleswig-Holstein, and Fritz Lehmann, specialist in banking and business economics. More than fifty lecture and seminar courses will be given by the Graduate Faculty during the coming academic year. All the original members of the faculty will continue their work except Professor Hermann Kantorowicz, who will go to the London School of Economics.

DR. JAMES HENRY BREASTED, director of the Oriental Institute of the University of Chicago, was awarded on May 26 the fine arts medal by the American Institute of Architects for "distinguished achievement in adding to the world's knowledge in the fine arts, and in particular for his work in archeology in Egypt over a long period, for his "sympathetic understanding of human relationships and for his particular appreciation of arts of a great period." Dr. Livingston Farrand, president of Cornell University, was among those elected to honorary membership in the institute.

DR. CARL E. SEASHORE, professor of psychology and dean of the graduate college at the University of Iowa, was honored for the seventh time on May 22 with an annual commemorative concert given in recognition of his contributions to the study of music. Dr. Seashore plans to retire as dean of the Graduate College in 1935. He asked to be relieved of administrative work this spring in order to devote more time to research, but was persuaded to continue the deanship for another year. Dr. Seashore, who has been connected with the university since 1897, has been head of the department of psychology since 1927 and has served as dean for twenty-six years.

THE completion of fifty years continuous service by Dr. William Shaffer Hall as professor of mathematics at Lafayette College was celebrated on May 28. When Professor Hall began teaching at Lafayette the faculty numbered twenty and the student body, 250. In the eighties Professor Hall had charge of three departments—mining engineering, graphics and technical mathematics. He did most of the teaching in each department. To-day fourteen men are needed for this work.

C. G. MONTEFIORE resigned on May 15 the presidency of University College, Southampton, England. For about 27 years he has been associated with the council of the college. He became vice-president in 1908, and president in 1913. Lord Mottistone, Lord Lieutenant of the county, was elected president, and the appointment of Mr. Montefiore as vice-president was ratified.

FROM Mexico City comes the announcement that Dr. Narciso Bassol, Minister of Education, has resigned. As reported in the *New York Herald-Tribune* Dr. Bassol's resignation follows a long-standing controversy between the Church and the State, the latter, under the presidency of Abelardo Rodriguez, sponsoring what the president has referred to as "the spiritual liberation of our nation." Dr. Bassol in his letter of resignation placed direct blame for educational disturbances upon the Mexican clergy and affiliated organizations.

THE REV. DR. HENRY SLOANE COFFIN, president of Union Theological Seminary, sailed on May 26 for England, to receive the honorary degree of LL.D. from St. Andrew's University in Scotland. Amherst College conferred upon Dr. Coffin the same degree in 1927.

THE Association of Colleges and Universities of the Pacific Southwest has elected the following officers for the year 1934–1935: Dr. James Jaqua, president of Scripps College, *president;* Dr. Robert A. Millikan, California Institute of Technology, *first vice-president;* Dr. Emory S. Bogardus, University of Southern California, *second vice-president;* Charles T. Fitts, Pomona College, *secretary-treasurer.*

DAVID R. PORTER, a secretary of the National Council of the Young Men's Christian Association since 1907, will become head of the Bible department at Mount Hermon School at Northfield, Mass., beginning in September. He will be associated with the Bible department of Northfield Seminary and the Northfield Summer Conferences.

DR. MARGARET KIELY, principal of the Bridgeport Normal School, has been elected to the Board of Trustees of Teachers College, Columbia University, as representative of the women members of the Alumni Association.

PROFESSOR GAIL DENSMORE, of the University of Michigan, will conduct a new course in radio announcing in the autumn. The course will include studio management, the building of original programs and instruction in script writing and diction.

PROFESSOR JULIUS TANDLER, of the University of Vienna, will arrive in New York on June 14 to deliver two lectures on anatomy at the New York University School of Medicine. Professor Tandler was formerly a socialist city councilor of Vienna, and upon his return to Vienna from China after the civil warfare last February, was arrested, but was later released, and retired on pension.

DR. SOLOMON LEFSCHETZ, Fine professor of mathematics at Princeton University, has accepted an invitation from the government of Soviet Russia to represent the Institute for Advanced Study, Princeton, at the International Mathematical Conference to be held at Moscow in June and July.

LEAVES of absence at Columbia University have been granted as follows for the academic year 1934–35: Crawford F. Failey, assistant professor of biological chemistry; Edward M. Earle, associate professor of history; Walter B. Pitkin, professor of journalism; David Snedden, professor of education, and Richard P. McKeon, assistant professor of philosophy. For the spring session, 1935, Otis W. Caldwell, director of the Institute of School Experimentation and professor of education, and Julius Goebel, professor of law. The following promotions have been made: Mabel Carney, professor of education; Gerald S. Craig, associate professor of natural sciences; Erling M. Hunt, associate professor of history; Helen E. Judy-Bond, associate professor of household arts; Clarence Linton, associate professor of education; Elizabeth D. McDowell, associate professor of speech; Lois Coffey Mossman, associate professor of education; Sarah M. Sturtevant, professor of education; Percival M. Symonds, professor of education; Mary DeGarmo Bryan, assistant professor of household arts; Frank W. Cyr, assistant professor of education, and William R. Odell, assistant professor of education.

DEAN JAMES B. TRANT, of the College of Commerce of the Louisiana State University, has been selected as a member of a southern committee, appointed by the Southwestern Social Science Association, to carry on research in the social sciences. The committee is to be made up of two groups, one representing the states east of the Mississippi and the other those west of the Mississippi. Other members in the southwestern group in addition to Dean Trant are Professor C. O. Brannen, University of Arkansas; Professor Raymond D. Thomas, Oklahoma A. & M. College; Professor S. D. Myres, Southern Methodist University; Professor Frank Carney, Baylor University, and Professor J. J. Rhyne, University of Oklahoma.

THE new staff of the *Modern Language Journal,* published by the National Federation of Modern Language Teachers, was announced in the May issue as follows: Managing editor, Dean Henry Grattan Doyle, George Washington University; assistant managing editors: Professor John Van Horne, Italian, University of Illinois; Professor Josef Wiehr, German, Smith College; Professor Benjamin M. Woodbridge, French, Reed College; Professor Wilfred A. Beardsley, Spanish, Goucher College; Professor James B. Tharp, experimentation and methodological research, School of Education, Ohio State University; Professor

Grace P. Young, bibliography, Indiana University. The new business manager is George W. H. Shield, of Los Angeles, Calif. The appointment of an editorial advisory board, consisting of all former managing editors of the *Journal,* has been announced as follows: Professor E. W. Bagster-Collins, Columbia University; Professor Algernon Coleman, University of Chicago; Professor J. P. Wickersham Crawford, University of Pennsylvania; Professor Bayard Q. Morgan, Stanford University, and Dr. Charles H. Holzwarth, principal of the West High School, Rochester, N. Y.

Professor George Byron Roorbach, professor of foreign trade in the Harvard Graduate School of Business Administration since 1919, and special adviser to the State Department on foreign trade, died on May 23, at the age of fifty-six years. From 1909 to 1914 Dr. Roorbach served as instructor of geography at the University of Pennsylvania. His services as a government expert began in 1918.

Miss Anna Frances Whitmore, founder and for forty-seven years principal of the Newark, N. J., Seminary for Girls, died on May 22. She was eighty-three years old. Miss Whitmore founded the Newark Seminary in 1881 and continued as its principal until her retirement in 1928.

Professor James Young Simpson, who occupied the chair of natural science of New College, Edinburgh, since 1904, and was lecturer at the School of Theology in Edinburgh since 1919, died on May 20, at the age of sixty years. Professor Simpson was Terry Lecturer at Yale in 1929.

The corner-stone of the Mary Harkness House, presented to the Connecticut College for Women by Mrs. Edward Harkness, of New York, was laid on May 26. The new dormitory will be built of granite and limestone in simple classic design similar to the other buildings on the campus. It will house seventy-five students.

The Third Pan-Pacific Women's Conference will be held in Honolulu, beginning on August 6 or 8 and continuing until August 22. Representatives to the conference, it is expected, will come from Canada, the Fiji Islands, Australia, Japan and China. At present membership in the Pan-Pacific Women's Association includes thirteen charter member countries. The organization was established in 1930 as a result of the deliberations of the first and second Pan-Pacific Women's Conferences held in Honolulu in 1928 and 1930 under the auspices of the Pan-Pacific Union. The forthcoming meeting was scheduled for 1933, but economic conditions throughout the world made it necessary to postpone the sessions until the current year. The organization sponsors an international council composed of representatives of Australia, Canada, China, the Fiji Islands, Hawaii, Japan, Korea, New Zealand, the Philippines, American Samoa, United States and England. The headquarters are at the Pan-Pacific Club, Honolulu.

The General Education Board has granted to Mount Holyoke College a sum not to exceed $375,000 for the extension of the Williston Memorial Library. This sum will represent seventy per cent. of the cost of the enlargement and reconstruction of the library and will be deeded to the college on condition that it furnish the remaining thirty per cent., and that the total cost of the reconstruction be limited to $550,000. The college already has on hand $67,000 to meet the first of the foregoing conditions.

DISCUSSION

STATEMENT CONCERNING THE REPORT OF THE COMMISSION ON THE INVESTIGATION OF HISTORY AND THE OTHER SOCIAL STUDIES OF THE AMERICAN HISTORICAL ASSOCIATION

The following statement covers in general my reasons for not signing the report on "Conclusions and Recommendations" of the Commission on the Investigation of History and Other Social Studies of the American Historical Association.

On the one hand, in my judgment, the report is destructively critical of current educational practises which the commission did not adequately investigate and dispassionately appraise; on the other hand, the report does not present a reasonable definite, constructive program for the improvement of instruction in the social studies, which program, in my judgment, should have been the main feature of the report.

The final volume on "Conclusions and Recommendations," in my judgment, does serious injustice to the scientific movement of education as described in the chapter on "Tests and Testing." This chapter is not based on any thoroughgoing investigation of testing in general or on any conclusions reached in the discussions of the commission. The vigorous protests made by me and some of my colleagues against the chapter have been to a large extent ignored in the final revision as published. Moreover, the chapter itself is not based on conclusions and recommendations developed in the volume prepared by Messrs. Krey and Kelley and scheduled to be published by the commission.

In my judgment the destructive criticism of the teacher and methods of teaching and teacher training institutions is bound to arouse antagonism rather than to promote unity and improvement in American education.

The chapter on "Selection and Organization of Materials of Instruction" is a disappointment. In my judgment it should have been the heart of the volume and should have included a vital statement in specific terms outlining subject-matter now being taught and the changes and improvements in subject-matter which the commission thinks should be made. This the chapter does not do. The discussion is so general that frequently one can not determine whether the discussion has to do with elementary schools, the secondary schools, or colleges and universities.

As a member of the commission and superintendent of schools, it was my hope that the final volume would be the basis on which constructive improvement of teaching the social studies might be based. In my judgment the report is inadequate in this respect.

Recently I asked Mr. George J. Jones, head of the department of history and the social studies in the junior and senior high schools for white pupils, to read the galley proof of the final volume and give me a memorandum showing the specific suggestions that have been made in the volume for the improvement of instruction in the social studies which could be followed in the public schools of Washington. I also asked Mr. Jones to give me a brief statement of his opinion of the report.

The specific recommendations taken from the volume of "Conclusions and Recommendations" of the commission by Mr. Jones cover less than two typewritten pages. Even some of these recommendations of the commission do not represent constructive helpful proposals of which use can be made by supervisory officers in the public schools throughout the country.

The following are quotations from Mr. Jones' analysis of the volume of "Conclusions and Recommendations":

> About five years ago I talked with a member of the Commission who deplored the chaos and lack of uniformity in the social science field throughout the country. I told him that I was not so pessimistic. * * * *
>
> It seems to me that able scholars after five years' study and five years of consultation with teachers should give us specific recommendations for our program. Instead these scholars say the programs "*should be made by competent teachers in the social sciences in consultation with able scholars.*"
>
> This sort of thing will bring on the very chaos which a member of the Commission thought existed five years ago. A report of this kind glittering in generalities will be of little use to the vast majority of social science teachers in this country.
>
> The report is a sad disappointment to me. For two years I have withheld the printing of our social science courses (grades 7 to 12 inclusive) waiting for the report of the commission. I expected that there would be definite recommendations. I will now give the manuscript for the courses to you about June 15th and I might say that after studying the recommendations not one change will be made in the manuscript for the course of study. The reading of the manuscript has reassured me, however, in my stand against "fusion" and in my plans to emphasize the study of international problems and to teach American history in its world setting.

FRANK W. BALLOU

WASHINGTON, D. C.

THE PHILOSOPHY OF PHI BETA KAPPA

THE challenge to Phi Beta Kappa given by Dr. George A. Coe in SCHOOL AND SOCIETY for May 5 is somewhat veiled. If it is what I hope, it is already being met; if what I fear, it must be ignored even at the risk of appearing droll and senescent.

If Dr. Coe means that Phi Beta Kappa should summon the colleges "to more rigorous scholarship, more inclusive appreciation of personality and the widest possible diffusion of culture," that challenge is already squarely faced. The needed endowment is largely for this purpose. Many chapters have revised their standards and methods in this direction. Recommendations of the Phi Beta Kappa Senate to the Eighteenth Triennial Council, which meets at the University of Cincinnati on September 10, 11 and 12, include proposals to raise standards, to emphasize the liberal or cultural motive in education, and to encourage the use of other criteria of scholarship than the accumulation of course grades. The Phi Beta Kappa quarterly magazine, *The American Scholar,* embodies this liberal emphasis and seeks to diffuse "culture" as far as properly lies within the society's province. Even a cursory survey of the articles published in recent numbers will show that Phi Beta Kappa is awake to the need for more careful thinking in the realm of social and economic philosophy.

It is desirable, of course, that the scholar should be "scientific with respect to social factors in his thinking"—or at least as scientific as the subject matter permits; for after all, the building of a society like the development of a personality is perhaps as much an art as it is a science. "Scholarship graced and guided by breadth of culture" means that scholars should have a good general understanding of the natural and social world in which they live. Phi Beta Kappa will continue to encourage scholars who work in the social and economic fields as she encourages scholars in other fields.

If Dr. Coe means, however, that Phi Beta Kappa should summon college teachers to a choice of some more or less particular social goal or economic theory, such as Socialism or Fascism, he too would seem, as he says is true of other scholars, to permit "scholarship to become automatically an adjunct of the social *status quo,*" namely, a general uncritical demand for change, which seems to be the present *status quo.* It would be uncritical for Phi Beta Kappa to abandon its exclusive interest in the quality and method of mind which makes a student scholarly. The content of his scholarship is not the society's concern. Scholarship as such can hardly be called "good or bad, according to the degree of its economic realism and the direction of its economic ideals." Scholarship for its own sake, so-called, would seem to have even more justification than art for art's sake. Without such, for example, Einstein would not have had at hand the indispensable non-Euclidean geometry. It would be contrary to the deeper and more permanent interests of society to tie scholarship to any particular social philosophy or to any social philosophy at all, to say nothing of economic ideals.

The charge of parasitism also seems to lack the realism demanded. Parasitism may, from another point of view, be cooperation. Is the scholar of this type any more parasitic than the artist? Has not untrammelled intellectual curiosity real social value in the long run? The *status quo,* present pressing human needs, must not lead us to sacrifice blindly the more permanent values. Phi Beta Kappa needs only to be careful, it seems to me, to hold true to its ideal —"There shall be no discrimination because of such characteristics as sex, race, color, residence, or religious, political, economic, or other belief." The scholar must of all things be free. The scholar can recognize no summons, no proclamation, and remain a scholar, whether he resides in Russia, Germany or America. His loyalty is to truth—including, to be sure, the truth about slavery and economics, but also the truth about countless other realms of interest, some of them happily unconcerned with the abolition of slavery or other social evils, except perhaps ignorance and boredom. Phi Beta Kappa gives recognition to scholars. Phi Beta Kappa does not give recognition to economic and social philosophies.

WILLIAM ALLISON SHIMER

SPECIAL CORRESPONDENCE

EDUCATION IN THE PRISON WITHOUT WALLS

THIS paper presents the fundamental facts of a specific project in education which is being carried on at the Federal Penitentiary at McNeil's Island in the state of Washington. The data have been gathered from personal observation on the part of the writer, interviews with the supervisor of education and from published and unpublished reports of the institution.

The school at McNeil's Island was started in 1929 by certain inmates, who organized a group of men within their own cells for the purpose of evening study. Other inmates became interested, and permission was granted by the warden, Mr. Finch R. Archer, to promote this work on a more extensive basis. Accordingly, one man, an inmate, was designated to spend his entire time promoting the interest in education and carrying on educational activities. No classes were organized. The instructor spent his time going from tier to tier and from cell to cell, giving such instruction as was possible under the circumstances. All instruction was carried on through the bars. This experiment met with such a favorable response among the prisoners that two additional inmates were assigned to this work. From this small beginning initiated by the inmates, with the cooperation of Warden Archer, the present school has developed until it requires the services of a civilian supervisor and ten full-time and ten part-time instructors on the teaching staff. These instructors are all inmates of the institution.

Professor J. Herbert Geoghegan, the supervisor, was chosen to take charge of the school in the autumn of 1931. At the time of his selection for this position, Mr. Geoghegan was a member of the teaching staff of the department of sociology at the University of Washington. He graduated from this university in 1922 with a major in sociology, having been elected to Phi Beta Kappa in his junior year. In 1923 he received his master's degree from the same university. Between the time of Mr. Geoghegan's graduation from the university and his election to the teaching staff of the department of sociology, his activities carried him into such related fields of social activity as: Pastoral work as a minister; organized study classes in railroad construction camps; study classes among loggers and mill workers; study classes for foreign-speaking groups in sawmills; educational work in army camps during the world war. He was elected in 1927 to the House of Representatives of the Washington Legislature, where he served on various committees dealing with educational and social problems of the state.

The first step in the procedure of the school is to determine the prisoner's educational status. The manner in which this is done is indicated in a statement of the supervisor. "On the twelfth day after his arrival at the penitentiary each prisoner is given the following educational tests: The Otis Arithmetic Reasoning Test, form A; the New Standard Language Usage Test, form V, and the New Standard Reading Test, form W. For special cases the new Stanford Achievement Test both for the intermediate and the higher grades is used." These tests serve to "locate" the man educationally and to check on his statements concerning his previous training.

After these tests have been completed and the prisoner's status has been at least temporarily defined, the general plan of the school system at the penitentiary is explained to him by the supervisor of the school. He is presented with a catalogue of courses offered and is invited to enroll as a student. While the facilities of the school are open to every inmate, no pressure is brought to bear upon any person to compel him to participate in any part of its program. It is made clear to every man that no discrimination is to be shown against those who do not enroll in the school, neither are there to be any special favors offered to those who do enroll. To quote Mr. Geoghegan, "The prisoners are given absolute liberty of choice in this matter."

The prisoners who choose to enroll are permitted to take any course or courses which the preliminary tests and other available information indicate they are qualified to pursue. Certain restrictions, however, should be noted here. The offense for which a prisoner has been committed must be taken into consideration. Should a particular type of training be such as to make this person more adept in the performance of the act for which he is now "serving time" he is excluded from that particular training. Implicit in this rule is, of course, more than merely the making of the prisoner more adept at his particular offense. It has in mind an attempt toward reorientation of the person in a new social group.

The courses range from the most elementary number-work to calculus; from simple sentence construction to short-story writing; from manual arts to psychology and philosophy. The ages of the inmates as of February, 1933, range from 17 to 71 years. The modal age is 31 years and represents 5.8 per cent. of the entire prison population at this time.

Of still more significance is the wide range in the educational status of the prison population as determined by the methods described above. Of the prison population on the above date 5.6 per cent. were illiterate; 8.2 per cent. were of university grade; the remainder of the population was distributed between these two extremes.

It must be borne in mind that the penitentiary is not primarily a school. Each prisoner must perform some type of work for eight hours each day and the school work is done in what might be termed spare-time, or after work and recreation have been provided for. To meet this situation there has been developed a system which represents a combination of the Oxford tutorial system and the home study method used by the extension departments of a number of universities. Under this system class work is reduced to a minimum. The teachers are, in reality, tutors.

The student works on his assignments at his own rate of speed, the work being done in the evenings or other spare time while in his cell. The tutor makes the rounds of the cell blocks, going from cell to cell giving such instruction as the different students require. When a lesson assignment is completed by a student it is taken by the tutor and graded and returned to the student by the tutor, who, if the student wishes, reviews the assignment with him in order to clear up points of error. This routine continues until the course has been completed.

It should not be inferred from what has been said that there is no classroom instruction. Classes are held in the main dining-room four nights each week from 6:00 until 7:15 o'clock. On other evenings the tutors visit the cell blocks in the manner previously described.

The teaching staff is made up entirely of "inmates." The supervisor is the only civilian employed. The instructors are chosen by the supervisor from the general prison population. All those chosen are men well qualified academically for the position. In fact, most of them are experienced teachers, and all have had, in addition to their academic training, special experience in the field in which they are teaching.

A report of the school for the first calendar year of the administration under the present supervisor (December, 1931, to December, 1932) shows a remarkable interest for a school in which work is purely voluntary. During this year the number of students enrolled increased from 360 to 653, or over 81 per cent. Of still more significance is the fact that the percentage of the inmate population enrolled in the school increased from 39.47 per cent. to 69.32 per cent. The number of courses for which these students were registered increased from 653 to 1,164 or over 78 per cent. This report indicates that these students were not merely registered for courses, but were actually at work. The lesson reports completed and turned in for correction increased from 1,839 to 6,727, or 265 per cent.

The comparative report for February, 1932, to February, 1933, emphasizes still more the growing participation of the inmates in the actual work of this school. This report indicates that the lesson reports turned in for correction increased 521 per cent. and an ever-increasing number of men are availing themselves of the opportunity for personal interviews with the supervisor and members of the teaching staff.

At this point we must turn to the consideration of some factors that elude any statistical analysis or objective measurement, yet nevertheless are very pertinent to the success of this venture. This factor is that undefined attitude existing between supervisor and student body. It must be borne in mind that the work in the school is wholly optional on the part of each individual. No person is offered any remuneration in the way of early parole consideration or other ulterior advantage as an inducement to membership. Even the advantages of "making good" when released from the institution are not used as an argument to secure enrolment. The steady growth in enrolment in the absence of any compulsion or suggestions of ulterior advantages to be gained seems to be indicative of the presence of "interest" which is held up before every class in the psychology of method as the *summum bonum*. This interest is secured not by artificial devices, many of which might be offered in a situation like this, but through an organization of the educational program in accordance with the fundamental interests and needs of these men.

While the choice of classes remains with the individual, the director has arranged for an advisory system whereby each student's educational problems are made the subject of a conference between the director and the student. In the background of the program of the school is the conscious and deliberate effort to organize the training of each individual so as to give him the best possible opportunity to make a satisfactory adjustment when he returns to civilian life.

The question may well be asked, "What will be the result of this in the rehabilitation of the criminal?" The answer can not be more than a prophecy. This particular experiment has not been in operation for a sufficient length of time to justify any prediction of final results as to social rehabilitation of the men involved. Our whole American philosophy of education would seem, however, to demand at least a hopeful anticipation of favorable results from an educational program placed upon a high academic plane and accepted so enthusiastically by such a large percentage of the population of a penal institution.

R. R. MARTIN
UNIVERSITY OF WASHINGTON

QUOTATIONS

SCIENCE AND INTELLECTUAL LIBERTY

A LITTLE more than a year ago, a number of scientific workers and scholars formed themselves into an Academic Assistance Council with the intention of helping university teachers and investigators "who on grounds of religion, political opinion or race were unable to carry on their work in their own country." The Council consists of forty-two members, representative of all sides of British intellectual activity, and its first annual report, which has just been issued, is a document worthy of careful study.[1] Upon the Council's records are the names of 1,202 scholars and scientific workers who have been displaced. Of these, rather more than a quarter, 389, have been permanently or temporarily—in the majority of instances only temporarily—enabled to continue their work, 178 in the British Isles, 211 abroad. There remain 813 so far unsuccoured.

Although the Council does not confine its aid to those of German origin, nearly all these distressed intellectuals have come from, or still suffer in, Germany. It might seem, then, that the Germany of to-day is not a very kindly soil for the cultivation of science and scholarship. Prof. J. Stark, president of the Physikalisch-Technische Reichsanstalt, Berlin, has, however, been at some pains to demonstrate both in our correspondence columns and also in a pamphlet entitled "Nationalsozialismus und Wissenschaft"[2] that, far from seeking to diminish scientific freedom, it is the mission of the National-Socialist Government to free German science from the influences which were strangling it.

It is necessary first of all to realize the distinction in the German political mind at the present time between *Germanen* and *Juden*. To *Germanen* has been vouchsafed the gift of seeing things as they really are, with the result that practically all *Naturwissenschaft* is regarded as the creation of the Nordic-German branch of the Aryan peoples. The *Juden*, on the other hand, are entirely centered on them-

[1] The Academic Assistance Council. Annual Report, 1st May, 1934. (London: c/o Royal Society, Burlington House, London, W.1.)

[2] Zentralverlag der N.S.D.A.P. München, 1934.

selves, can not, or rather will not, see things as they really are, and only respect facts which can be made subservient to their own ends. They are consequently quite incapable of making any great discoveries in *Naturwissenschaft*. It is true that Heinrich Hertz made an important discovery, but then Hertz had a Germanic mother. We might also mention names, such as those of Jakob Henle and Paul Ehrlich; whether anatomy and immunology are not *Naturwissenschaften* at all, or the pedigrees of Henle and Ehrlich have been insufficiently scrutinized, we do not know. The result of the moral and intellectual limitations of the *Juden* has been, not only that they have devoted themselves to unreal theorizing, but also that little Jewish coteries have succeeded in strangling genuine German science. One of these *jüdische Wissenschafter-Konzerne* founded by Klein and Hilbert no doubt discouraged that stern objectivity which should characterize Nordic-German mathematics; another, controlled by Einstein and Sommerfeld, tampered with physics; a third, the Haber-*Konzern,* has strangled physical chemistry. What *Konzern* has suppressed Germanic biology is not disclosed. Anyhow, we are apparently led to the conclusion that, instead of discovering anything important, Germany has been simply putting on the market dogmatic theories, such as Einstein's theory of relativity.

It may be difficult for the English reader, recalling the often painful elaboration of genuine Germanic humor, not to suppose that "Nationalsozialismus und Wissenschaft" is a facetious essay, but the consequences of its acceptance in Germany are too plainly evident. No one can suppose, however, that this kind of "reasoning" will be taken seriously long. Even the Committee of Public Safety was not wholly composed of Barères: more temperate counsels will prevail in Germany in good time. Meanwhile, however, a good deal of "sand" is being thrown into the intellectual machinery of the world.

One function of the Academic Assistance Council has been to enable serious workers to escape from an atmosphere of noise and truculence and to continue their researches. The reports of what has already been done by grantees show the success of the policy. One (a mathematician) "has finished an exceptional piece of work which will make a considerable sensation when it appears and add greatly to his status." Another (a physiologist) has done work which, the referee thinks, "may well be revolutionary." Another (an art historian) "has been doing quite invaluable work"; and so the story goes on.

These are the products of a single year's work and of comparatively trifling expenditure. Were we only concerned for the credit of Great Britain and the enrichment of its intellectual life, we might almost pray that the present vogue in Germany would be long. It would be difficult indeed to invest capital at a more usurious rate of interest—we are securing some of the best intellects in Europe, perhaps permanently. However, we all hope that the restraint of German intellectual activity will not continue; but common prudence must warn us that, for some years to come, much of the burden of maintaining the intellectual life of Europe will have to be borne by us. The Academic Assistance Council estimates that £25,000 a year for the next two years will be necessary to enable it to continue and consolidate its work. In 1931–32, according to the return of the University Grants Committee, the expenditure in Great Britain on salaries (including payments for superannuation) of teaching staff in university institutions of Great Britain was £2,856,216. The annual sum required by the Academic Assistance Council is less than one per cent of this. While it would be preposterous to suggest that the whole of the burden can be, or should be, borne by the academic staffs of British universities, and reasonable to expect that enlightened men of wealth will contribute to this deserving object, it does at least appear that the Council is not asking for a sum beyond the means of those who value science and scholarship to supply.

We doubt whether an appeal more worthy of support than this has ever been made to the educated public. We have the ordinary appeal to decent human sympathy which the story of oppression makes, but beyond that is the appeal to our imagination. The individuals suffering at present will pass away and be forgotten: the revocation of academic freedom in Germany will no more be forgotten than the revocation of the Edict of Nantes.—*Nature.*

EDUCATIONAL RESEARCH AND STATISTICS

AMERICAN GRADUATE SCHOOLS

MARKED changes have occurred in the relative standing of the leading graduate schools of American universities during the past decade, according to an analysis of the judgments of more than two thousand outstanding scholars which have just been made public. The state institutions have made rapid strides upward at the expense of the older privately endowed institutions, which held much higher rank ten and twenty-five years ago. The special committee on graduate instruction, which was appointed by the American Council on Education in 1932, has just made its report.[1] The chairman was President R. M. Hughes, of Iowa State College, who made a comparable study in 1925.

METHOD USED BY THE COMMITTEE

In preparing a list of American graduate schools "offering adequate facility for work in the various fields," the committee used the following procedure. A list of 50 fields of knowledge in which it seemed possible to study graduate work was prepared, although the report as finally made covered only 35 of these fields. A list of the 50 fields was sent to the dean of the graduate school of every institution known to be offering work for the doctorate. The dean was requested to check the fields in which graduate work for the doctorate was offered, to indicate the number of doctorates conferred during the last five years, and to submit a list of the graduate faculty in each field. From the reports of the deans, supplemented by study of catalogs, lists of institutions offering graduate work for the doctorate in each field were prepared, complete so far as the information at the disposal of the committee could make them.

The secretary of the national learned society in each field was requested to provide a list of 100 well-known scholars distributed, as far as possible, among the various special branches of the field. The lists of scholars secured varied from 109 in psychology to 25 in civil engineering, but averaged over 88 for each of the 35 departments studied. To each of these scholars was sent a list of all the institutions offering work for the doctorate in his field, with the names of those composing their respective staffs. Each scholar was requested to check those institutions which in his judgment had an adequate staff and equipment to prepare candidates for the doctorate; and to star the departments of the highest rank, roughly the highest 20 per cent. Replies were received from 2,018 of the 3,090 men of whom this request was made, or from over 65 per cent. The percentage of replies varied from 85 per cent. of the mathematicians and 84 per cent. of the civil engineers to 44 per cent. of the mechanical engineers. The results of these judgments were summarized by departments, and those institutions accorded a star by the majority voting in each field were placed in the starred group; those checked by a majority of the judges, but failing of a majority of stars, were placed in the group of those adequately staffed and equipped.

The report of over 40 pages contains for each field the following information: Names of the judges, list of starred and adequate institutions, information concerning number of institutions offering work for the doctorate and number of doctorates conferred. No summary, however, is made for institutions as a whole. It would seem that such a valuable body of material, representing the best judgment of more than two thousand outstanding scholars in all the principal fields of graduate study, warrants further analysis and study. It is the object of this paper to undertake such an analysis and to make significant comparisons with a similar study made a decade earlier.

INSTITUTIONS ADEQUATELY EQUIPPED

In introducing each of the 35 lists of institutions the committee uses the following phraseology: "The jury named above has, by a majority vote, approved the following institutions as adequately staffed and equipped for work leading to the doctorate in [Name of field], starring those which it considers most distinguished." A total of 62 different universities and technical schools is represented in the various lists. The first 45, all those which were selected in three or more fields, are summarized in Table I.[2]

[1] R. M. Hughes, chairman, "Report of the Committee on Graduate Instruction," *The Educational Record*, xv: 192–234, April, 1934.

[2] In the report of the committee, Harvard Uni-

It appears from Table I that California and Wisconsin are tied for first place on the basis of adequate staff and equipment, each being so rated by a majority of the judges in 31 of the 35 fields of graduate study, but California is given first place because it is "distinguished" in more fields than Wisconsin.

Twenty of the group of 45 institutions are publicly controlled. The first 15 on the list (of which 7 are publicly controlled) are judged to be adequately staffed and equipped for the doctorate in over half of the 35 fields studied. Four of these, Harvard, California, Chicago and Columbia, are "distinguished" in over half of the 35 fields. Twenty-eight institutions are "distinguished" in one or more fields, 19 of them in two or more fields.

The column "unweighted rank" is determined by the number of departments in which the institutions are judged to be adequately staffed, as shown in the first column. (Ties in this ranking are settled, where possible, by reference to the second column.) If, however, weights be used (somewhat arbitrarily) by assigning a weight of 2 to each field in which an institution is judged distinguished and a weight of 1 to each field in which it is adequately equipped but not distinguished, the result is the weighted rank as given in the last column. On this basis, Harvard and California are tied for first place, with Columbia third and Wisconsin fourth. On the whole, however, little difference would result in relative ranks whichever method were used. The 11 institutions in the upper quarter of the table would all remain in the upper quarter, Illinois making the greatest shift down-

versity and Radcliffe College are treated as a unit in all fields except three of those involving engineering, since no staff members offer instruction in Radcliffe College who are not also members of the faculty of Harvard University. This Harvard-Radcliffe unit is reported as Harvard University only in the present analysis. Institutions judged to be adequately staffed and equipped in two fields were Boston University, the George Peabody College for Teachers, the University of Arizona, the University of Oklahoma and the University of Oregon; those equipped in one field were American University, the Carnegie Institute of Technology, the Colorado School of Mines, Kansas State College, Ohio Wesleyan University, Rensselaer Polytechnic Institute, the University of Colorado, the University of Maryland, the University of Notre Dame, the University of Rochester, Washington State College and West Virginia University. The only one of this group of institutions which was starred was the University of Rochester.

TABLE I

HIGHER EDUCATIONAL INSTITUTIONS JUDGED TO BE ADEQUATELY STAFFED AND EQUIPPED FOR WORK FOR THE DOCTORATE IN SPECIFIC FIELDS IN 1934

Institution	No. of departments adequately staffed and equipped	No. of departments in which most distinguished	Unweighted rank	Weighted rank
*University of California	31	21	1	1
*University of Wisconsin	31	17	2	4
Harvard University	29	23	3	1
Columbia University	28	21	4	3
Cornell University	27	16	5	6
*University of Michigan	27	14	6	8
*University of Illinois	27	4	7	11
University of Chicago	26	21	8	5
Yale University	26	16	9	7
*University of Minnesota	25	9	10	10
Johns Hopkins University	24	12	11	9
Stanford University	23	4	12	13
*Ohio State University	22	4	13	14
University of Pennsylvania	21	5	14	14
*University of Iowa	18	2	15	17
Princeton University	17	14	16	11
*University of Missouri	16	0	17	19
Northwestern University	14	1	18	21
New York University	14	0	19	22
*Iowa State College	13	3	20	19
*University of Texas	12	1	21	23
Massachusetts Institute of Technology	11	10	22	16
California Institute of Technology	11	7	23	18
Bryn Mawr College	11	1	25	25
*University of North Carolina	11	1	25	25
Washington University	11	1	25	25
*Indiana University	10	0	27	27
Brown University	9	1	28	27
*University of Cincinnati	9	0	29	29
Duke University	8	0	30	30
University of Pittsburgh	8	0	30	30
*Pennsylvania State College	7	0	32	32
*University of Kansas	7	0	32	32
*University of Nebraska	6	0	34	35
*University of Washington	6	0	34	35
*Purdue University	5	1	36	35
Catholic University of America	5	0	38	38
*Michigan State College	5	0	38	38
Western Reserve University	5	0	38	38
Rutgers University	4	1	40	38
*University of Virginia	4	0	41	41
Clark University	3	1	42	41
Rice Institute	3	0	44	44
Syracuse University	3	0	44	44
University of Southern California	3	0	44	44

* Publicly controlled institutions.

ward from fourth to eleventh place and Chicago shifting upward from eighth to fifth place. Further down the list, Princeton would tie for eleventh place when ranked on a weighted basis, with 14 departments distinguished out of the 17 in which it is judged adequate. The only other striking shifts would be of the Massachusetts Institute of Technology with its 10 out of 11 departments judged as distinguished, and the California Institute of Technology, with 7 out of 11 of its departments similarly judged.

CHANGES IN A DECADE

In January, 1925, President Hughes, the chairman of the present committee, read a paper before the American Association of American Colleges, entitled "A Study of the Graduate Schools of America." The procedure which he used at that time was so similar to the committee report now under consideration as to justify comparison of the two sets of results. To secure the 1925 data, from 40 to 60 leading college and university professors in each of twenty different departments of study were asked to rank the principal graduate schools of the country in the order of their standing as most desirable places for graduate study in their respective departments. Replies were received from about half of the men asked, varying from sixteen in geography to forty-seven in psychology. The departments ranked were astronomy, botany, chemistry, classics, economics, education, English, French, geography, geology, German, political science, history, mathematics, philosophy, physics, psychology, sociology, Spanish and zoology. A total of 32 universities were mentioned in one or more departments. As in the present report, however, President Hughes did not summarize in any way the findings for institutions as a whole. Such a summary was made by the present writer.[3]

It is interesting to note that the 16 leading institutions at that time, those which were ranked in at least 10 of the 20 departments studied, were exactly the same institutions which occupy the first 16 positions in Table I. Perhaps this may be taken as indirect evidence of the comparability of the two studies. The order, however, shows some very interesting and significant changes. These are exhibited in Table II.

TABLE II

COMPARATIVE RANK OF 16 LEADING GRADUATE SCHOOLS IN 1925 AND IN 1934

Institution	Rank 1934	Rank 1925	Change in rank: Publicly supported	Change in rank: Privately supported
*University of California	1	10	+9	
*University of Wisconsin	2	7	+5	
Harvard University	3	2		−1
Columbia University	4	3		−1
Cornell University	5	9		+4
*University of Michigan	6	8	+2	
*University of Illinois	7	11	+4	
University of Chicago	8	1		−7
Yale University	9	5		−4
*University of Minnesota	10	13	+3	
Johns Hopkins University	11	6		−5
Stanford University	12	14		+2
*Ohio State University	13	15	+2	
University of Pennsylvania	14	12		−2
*University of Iowa	15	16	+1	
Princeton University	16	4		−12

* Publicly supported institutions.

The most striking and significant fact here indicated is the marked increase in rank of the publicly supported universities in comparison with those on private foundations. Each of the seven publicly supported institutions on the list raised its rank in the short period of nine years. The changes of California from tenth place to first, and of Wisconsin from seventh place to second are particularly striking for such a short space of time. On the other hand, seven of the nine privately supported institutions lost in rank. The only two to advance their positions were Cornell, by four places, and Stanford, by two places. Chicago, which held first place in the 1925 study, has dropped to eighth place; Princeton has dropped from fourth to sixteenth; Johns Hopkins has dropped from sixth to eleventh. In 1925 Chicago and Harvard

[3] Walter Crosby Eells, "A Study of the Graduate Schools of America," SCHOOL AND SOCIETY, xxiii: 535–36, April 24, 1926

were practically tied for first place; in 1934 California and Wisconsin have this distinction.[4] Is primacy in graduate work passing rapidly from the privately supported institutions to those publicly supported?

Adequacy in Special Fields

In Table III are listed the 35 fields of study which were included in the committee's report, and information on the adequacy of the departments offering work in these fields as judged by a majority of the more than two thousand leading specialists who cooperated in the study.

Table III shows that although there is an average of over 32 institutions offering work for the doctorate in the different fields (varying from 7 in aeronautical engineering to 67 in chemistry), an average of less than 19 (or 58 per cent.) of these were judged to be adequately staffed and equipped for the purpose, and an average of less than 7 were judged as really distinguished. The most significant information of Table III, however, is found in the last column, which gives the percentage of institutions in each field which were judged to be adequately staffed and equipped for the doctorate. It shows a variation from 42 per cent. of the institutions offering work in economics which are so equipped to the anomalous situation of 120 per cent. in political science! In the latter field there were only 20 institutions reported as offering work for the doctorate, but the judges felt that there were 24 that were adequately equipped for it.

TABLE III

Adequacy of American Graduate Schools in 35 Special Fields, 1934

Field	Institutions offering work for doctorate	Institutions adequately staffed and equipped	Institutions most distinguished	Per cent. of total institutions adequately equipped
Chemistry	67	37	16	56
Education	61	30	10	49
Zoology	59	31	11	53
History	55	26	8	47
Economics	53	22	11	42
Physics	52	25	12	48
English	49	27	8	55
Psychology	49	31	11	63
Mathematics	48	26	7	54
Botany	45	30	8	67
Philosophy	45	24	7	53
Sociology	44	24	5	55
Geology	39	21	12	54
Classics	38	23	9	60
Romance languages	37	11	7	59
Bacteriology	37	17	9	46
German	33	22	7	67
Plant pathology	32	19	4	59
Plant physiology	27	21	6	78
Entomology	23	14	5	61
Genetics	22	17	6	77
Electrical engineering	22	13	3	59
Political science	20	24	8	120
Mining and metallurgical engineering	19	14	3	74
Civil engineering	19	15	3	79
Chemical engineering	18	9	3	50
Human nutrition	18	14	5	78
Geography	18	9	4	50
Mechanical engineering	17	11	3	65
Soil science	15	10	4	67
Astronomy	14	8	5	57
Anthropology	12	7	5	58
Fine arts	11	6	3	55
Animal nutrition	9	8	3	89
Aeronautical engineering	7	3	2	43
Average	32.4	18.9	6.7	

The computations in the last column may be summarized as follows: In 6 of the fields in which American graduate schools are offering work for the doctorate, professional judges of these fields feel that less than half of the institutions are adequately staffed and equipped for it; in 25 of the 35 fields they feel that less than two thirds of the institutions are adequately equipped; in only 6 of the fields do they feel that over three fourths of the institutions are so equipped.

Average Doctorates per Institution

A final significant analysis may be made by comparing the number of doctorates reported as conferred in the five-year period from 1928 to 1932 with the number of institutions offering work for the doctorate. This is done in Table IV.

[4] It is interesting to compare these two rankings of American universities with one made by Cattell in 1910, based upon the number of the first thousand leading American men of science found in each. His first five in order were Harvard, Chicago, Columbia, Johns Hopkins and Yale. His first ten included only three state universities, Wisconsin, Michigan and California, which ranked seventh, ninth and tenth, respectively. (See *Science*, n. s., xxxii: 683, November 11, 1910.) This determination, however, was based entirely upon the sciences and so is not strictly comparable with the more comprehensive 1925 and 1934 studies.

TABLE IV

TOTAL AND AVERAGE DOCTORATES PER INSTITUTION IN 35 FIELDS, 1928–1932

Field	Doctorates conferred, 1928–32	Institutions offering work for doctorate	Average doctorates per institution, 1928–32
Chemistry	1,434	67	22
Education	1,300	61	21
German	995	33	30
English	603	49	12
History	599	55	11
Economics	535	53	10
Physics	483	52	9
Psychology	453	49	9
Zoology	382	59	6
Mathematics	329	48	7
Botany	274	45	6
Philosophy	271	45	6
Romance languages	256	37	7
Geology	251	39	6
Sociology	226	44	5
Political science	210	20	10
Bacteriology	154	37	4
Classics	153	38	4
Plant pathology	138	32	4
Chemical engineering	133	18	7
Human nutrition	103	18	6
Entomology	99	23	4
Genetics	69	22	3
Soil science	63	15	4
Geography	58	18	3
Plant physiology	56	27	2
Electrical engineering	55	22	3
Animal nutrition	52	9	6
Mining and metallurgical engineering	41	19	2
Astronomy	38	14	3
Anthropology	31	12	3
Fine arts	21	11	2
Civil engineering	15	19	0.8
Mechanical engineering	15	17	0.9
Aeronautical engineering	0	7	0

The leading fields for graduate study are seen to be chemistry, education, German, English and history, in the order named. The doctorates in these 5 fields alone during the 5 years under consideration were half of the total of 9,895 conferred. Chief interest, however, attaches to the last column of the table which shows the average doctorates per institution in the five-year period. This varies from 30 in the relatively small number of institutions offering the doctorate in German to 0 in aeronautical engineering. By fields of study the average number of doctorates per institution is: Over 20 in 3 fields; from 10 to 19 in 4 fields; from 5 to 9 in 12 fields; from 0 to 4 in 16 fields.

On the basis of these figures the question may be raised whether the opportunities for work leading to the doctor's degree are not far more numerous than necessary or desirable for best results. It should be remembered that these figures are averages only. Unquestionably the number of doctorates is much greater than the average in the outstanding institutions; it follows therefore that the number must be correspondingly smaller than the average for many of the others. It should be remembered, too, that these averages are for a five-year period. Each entry in the last column of Table IV should be divided by 5 to secure the annual average per institution. If this is done it is found that there are only 7 of the 35 fields in which the annual average per institution is as great as 2 doctorates.

Should there, perhaps, be a greater concentration of graduate work in a few centers, even more adequately staffed and equipped than at the present time, rather than the increasing diffusion of such opportunities in a large number of different centers? Do we really need and can we adequately staff and equip without excessive cost, 52 institutions for doctoral work in physics or 49 in psychology with an average annual output of less than two doctors each? Or can we afford to staff and equip 44 institutions for sociology, 38 for the classics or 37 for bacteriology with average annual outputs of one doctor or less for each institution? Or 59 in zoology with an average annual output of slightly over one doctor each?

The report of the American Council's committee on graduate instruction with its carefully compiled judgments of over two thousand specialists in the principal fields of graduate work is worthy of closer study than it may receive because its findings, while presented *in extenso,* are not summarized and analyzed so as to make some of their implications readily apparent. The method used by the committee has its limitations, as the report itself is careful to point out, but until more valid measures of excellence are devised, it is deserving of careful consideration by those concerned with the administration of our graduate schools.

WALTER CROSBY EELLS
STANFORD UNIVERSITY

EDUCATIONAL REVIEW

Edited by Nicholas Murray Butler, 1891–1919, Frank Pierrepont Graves, 1920–1924, and William McAndrew, 1924–

PEOPLE, PERFORMANCE AND PUBLICATIONS

By WILLIAM McANDREW

Bravo, Cleveland!—One need not go very deeply into the study of history to find that the value of education as a government function ranked second to none when the Constitution was adopted. Along with everything that could effectively be left to the states, it was omitted from the federal agreement. But Washington officially designated public education as "of primary importance." Franklin, Adams, Jefferson and Monroe gave it no less stress and Madison insisted that "it is a certain and a vital desideratum." The Continental Congress enacted that schools should forever be encouraged. Their treatment by government in 1933–34 stretches to preposterous thinness every conception of the idea of primary importance, certain or vital or desideratum or perpetual encouragement.

Who keep tariffs in the class of things of primary importance? Manufacturers. Who hold justice to workers there? Labor unions. Who make certain and vital the need of government aid to transportation? Railway, shipping and aircraft investors. In my long life with teachers I have seen them change from almost complete ignorance of their responsibility for keeping the American idea of government support of education alive. I have seen fear and dislike of this duty change to a healthy recognition of it and in some cases to an effective and formidable force. Thirty years ago a small group of Cleveland teachers met such timidity in their colleagues that they abandoned an entirely justifiable petition directed toward an improvement of the condition of the schools. But, yesterday, the public school workers in that seat of educational disturbance published the declaration that railroads, banks, farmers and manufacturers are a deep concern to the federal government, but the public school is the backbone of American civilization.

The failure of railroads, farmers, banks and manufacturers is a major catastrophe, they declared, but the collapse of schools is worse. There are no words to depict the hopelessness of our country, should this happen.

In every recovery education is the last to get relief. The rise of prices, a recovery sign, cuts down the living of teachers and that for them is the opposite of prosperity's return.

Accordingly, the Cleveland public-school laborers in the vineyard asked at the eleventh hour to be put into the scheme of federal aid.

On that day, on a railroad train a member of the city government of that Ohio metropolis, a boyhood friend of mine, remarked, "They ought not to do that."

"Why not, Tom?"

"They're playing politics."

"Not so, old dear, they're trying to make politics work."

Whereupon I quoted large mouthfuls of our Allen Oscar Hansen's researches showing that the American schools were, by the most wonderful statesmen of history, set up expressly as a department of politics and consecrated thereto.

Did you ever notice that the most violent critics of teachers for going into politics are politicians?

How do you compare with Jersey?—They have just had a notable convention in Lakewood, New Jersey. I listened all one afternoon to designated members of the Ocean County Teachers Association give opinions as to what are the most needful things for us to do right now. These people had been organized into what they call a "panel." It had held meetings and sifted out what it considered the most timely themes for the county convention. The result was a care in preparation by the speakers (no papers read), and a warmth of attention by the other members that were a refreshing contrast to many educational meetings. After each presentation, chunks of controversial dynamite were tossed at the speakers. Even the state inspector was treated to these missiles and, smiling, caught them with practised skill. There was a most courteous assassination of some beloved old educational traditions. Somebody cornered with a very pertinent question the genial Bair, superintendent of the Lakewood schools. His answer was of a kind that would be true in most schools of the United States, I think, but which a few years hence would excite wide-eyed wonder. He said, "For forty years I have been visiting classes in civil government, civics, problems of democracy or whatever name is used, and not once did I hear discussion of any civic question that really concerns the community the school is in."

Marriage as a misdemeanor.—To those professors in teachers colleges and in university departments of education who are perplexed to find unploughed fields of research for Ph.D. candidates the status of married women as teachers is recommended. It offers profitable exploration of history, psychology, physiology, law and the statistics of success and failure in teaching. With the wealth of material that can be gathered and coordinated, with the welter of repeated assertions founded on prejudice or fancy, the question has been futilely debated in newspapers for, to my knowledge, more than forty years. It remains so misty that Mrs. Franklin D. Roosevelt, invited to address the country-wide citizens conference at Ohio State University, made it a main theme of her speech. Who knows that France and other nations are wrong in their claim that marriage improves a woman's teaching—and a man's. Who can defend the tremendous human waste in subjecting the rising generation to the 'prentice hands of young girls required by school board rules to leave as soon as they have learned better how to teach? What becomes of the respect for education if boards of education officially brand the mature woman school teacher with what no small number of Americans regard as a name of contempt? Who consistently believes that public schools are here to prevent husband and wife both from receiving pay? Here is something that needs research.

Not shooting into the air.—Many a time have guessing critics alleged that the schoolmaster never examines the target after shooting. George Bowman, Stuart Courtis, R. C. Hall and Paul Rankin made one good denial in their appraisal scheme for National Education Association conventions. Their four-page enquiry of superintendent members of the association is follow-up extraordinary. Did you consult with teachers and board members to find out anything they wished you to pick up? Did you prepare to take part in the discussions? Rate each of the eleven features of the last convention on a scale of five grades of value. What features did you later discuss with your educational family? What changes were made in your schools as a result of the convention? These are some of the pertinent points pricked into the skins of the members. A reminder sent out a month before the next convention ought to get farther into the general realization of why conventions are.

There is no capitalism.—Teachers unpaid, statisticians reporting the number of families in dire poverty as contrasted with the abundance of goods in America, may find the declarations of Dr. Nicholas Murray Butler before the American Woman's Association a good center for discussion by civics classes. There is no such thing as capitalism, insists Dr. Butler. It is a debating term adopted by Karl Marx. It is an accident. The real controversy is between liberty and compulsion—whether you will be free to do or will be compelled to do. Fundamental principles of American government are now, he says, everywhere derided and treated with criticism and scorn. These criticisms, Dr. Butler said, can be answered only by calm and reasoned argument and by efficient performance.

This will lead you in your lessons in problems of democracy to discuss the connection of equality, justice and general welfare with Teapot Dome, tariff and investigators of the Hughes Life Insurance Committee, the Walsh Utilities Committee and the Pecora disclosures of banking.

What is the date of the dark ages?—Here is an item to save until the history class is busy with the medieval period. Wilber Glenn Voliva, overseer of Zion Colony, Illinois, closed the schools recently, carrying out his threat to crack down if his school-board candidates were not elected. They were not. For the first time in the history of Zion his three men were defeated. An order was posted closing the schools. They have an attendance of 1,300 children. Voliva's theory that the world is flat is taught. The teachers have not been paid for a year. This is a news paragraph distributed by the Associated Press.

Connecticut courtesy.—Danbury and its high-school principal, Roscoe Bassett, must be added to those who know the etiquette of an educational meeting. I saw group after group walk from the door and fill the front seats. When the speaker was introduced he had the entire audience as close to him as the seats permitted as if to say courtesy begets proximity.

MONTHLY SURVEY OF EDUCATIONAL BOOKS

EDUCATIONAL MAELSTROM

NINETEEN men and women contribute to the fourth yearbook[1] of the National Council for the Social Studies. Some of them are half freed from the chrysalis state induced by academic tradition and the requirements of college entrance boards. Some, like Messrs. Keohane and Hill, of the laboratory schools of the University of Chicago, would have us ponder whether the bad way to which the country has come may not be due in part to the fact that the generation now in control has been obliged to struggle with problems while having no understanding of modern society. Most high-school graduates, remark these two contributors, are deficient in comprehension of their civic and economic surroundings and responsibilities. Collapse of economics, inadequacy of politics, rapid change in social affairs, argue for a reorganization of curriculums for a wide dissemination of social intelligence. In the Chicago outline the methods of political parties, patronage, the boss, pressure groups, abuses of democracy and attempted reforms are stressed.

The yearbook makes distinctly valuable reading for every teacher. All sorts will find kindred spirits among the contributors. There are the bewildered souls, the philosophers who cherish so many doubts regarding each new proposal that the safety of teaching ancient history allures them.

There are courses of study, objectives and techniques of teaching as professed by many cities. All through is the conviction that society is in much worse straits than ever before, that education must bestir itself. There is, says Professor Wilson, president of the Council, a maelstrom of proposals and counter proposals in the social studies.

Let us rejoice. Out of such comes advance. Consider what perfect agreement did for the study of Greek in the high schools.

[1] Howard E. Wilson, president and editor, "The Social Studies Curriculum." The McKinley Publishing Company, Philadelphia. 227 pp. $2.00.

AN ENGROSSING ACCOUNT OF UNION

THE college text on American government, by Professors Lien, Washington University, and Fainsod, Harvard,[2] is enriched by specific instances of efforts of a changing country to interpret its ancient constitution to fit present needs. Developing its theme from four apt quotations from Penn, Jefferson, Lincoln and Wilson, the book proceeds through discussions of the population, national government, state, municipal and local control, popular sovereignty and world relations. A Constitution steeped in the philosophy of individual rights and framed in a belief that the government which governs least is the best has had to be adjusted to the needs of a growing people. This task with its consequent criticisms has fallen on the Supreme Court. Cheers and groans follow its decisions. The question is more and more seriously raised of completely abolishing the system of a judicial review and leaving the interpretation of the Constitution entirely to Congress and the President.

There is a superb chapter on popular sovereignty and another on obstacles to successful democratic government. Apathy of the citizens, their ignorance, their feeling of the hopelessness of individuals to combat traditional abuses, their hope in a hero, delay the improvement of government. The founders proposed education as a preventive of stagnation. Throughout the book the political obligations of the school are stressed.

The people have the power. They must be instructed in politics. All the people must be trained with a sufficient knowledge of the issues at stake to enable them to vote intelligently.

[2] Arnold J. Lien, Merle Fainsod, "The American People and Their Government." D. Appleton-Century Company, New York. 629 pp. $3.25.

They must be imbued with a sense of personal responsibility for the way government is run. The democratic way of life is to take care that the avenue of economic opportunity is kept open to all. The cardinal principles of the Declaration and the Constitution—equality in rights to life, liberty and happiness, equal duties involving union, justice, tranquillity, defense, general welfare and changing the government—must be preserved unimpaired. With all its disappointments democratic government continues to make progress. It contains faith in the innate good will and capacity of mankind and the promise of a happier life created by themselves for all people. It is this dream, this faith in the nobility of the common man which gives democracy a vitality that survives disillusionments.

To keep this spirit alive, to forward means of its realization, education was taken over by the republic from private or religious agencies.

Civic education awakening the voter to his responsibilities is a duty inherent in a democratic society. Every voter must be informed on political issues and the qualifications of candidates. The standards of a citizen are a product of the education and training he received. Citizenship is not a condition of only adults. Minors have their civic duties to perform. The schools must give them practise in community service. The ways of cooperative government should be practised by children in school. The teachers should entrust real problems to them and guide them in management.

These quotations are selected from many such sprinkled through the pages. There is no sour criticism in any of the chapters and no patriotic slop-over. The whole treatise is flavored with reasoned optimism. Its style is lucid, engrossing and convincing. It is a great work.

SOCIOLOGY FOR HIGH SCHOOL

The discrimination shown by Professors Beach and Walker, of Stanford, in their selection of social problems probably comes from an extended questioning as to what are the present vital issues and from an observant experience in holding the interest of young students.[3] Education, as is meet in a public school, is given attention as obligated to aim at the general welfare. It must lead the generation to observe the changes needful and to cooperate in getting them made. School must train its beneficiaries so that they will think critically and not believe merely because a statement is printed or is spoken by some one of prominence. Schools are challenged to give democracy a better trial and consciously to aim at effective citizenship. It is not enough to know. You need practise. Therefore, the school must provide exercise in cooperative government.

Human nature, group life, American culture, immigrants, Negroes, wage-earners, the family, poverty, crime, planned society, the function of science, are presented. Topics for study and discussion are plentifully listed. Hints for pupils and teachers abound. It is a first-class working text for high school.

BLAZING CIVICS

On the heels of Richard Welling's revolutionary "Civics as It Should be Taught" comes from a new source a constructive booklet devoted to political misdemeanors and constructive measures now under way to correct them.[4] Ellis Chadbourne, the author, wrote a book on "The Defense of Modern Youth" which Fannie Hurst and Harry Elmer Barnes crowned with fragrant laurels. In the present detailed exposition he shows why the youth movement, well known in other countries, should here enlist and concentrate energies wasted on trivialities or worse and should direct them to something really worth while: a better immediate living area, a better city, a better commonwealth.

Mr. Chadbourne cites the case of five New York elementary school principals—Elizabeth Haas, Simon Hirsdansky, Eugene Gartlan, William Henwood and Amelia Scherer (I know these good people, I used to work with them and still affectionately admire them)—who have sponsored a boys' club for community service. Their part of the city had the worst law-breaking record. Since the formation of the club no child has been committed for delinquency.

Mr. Chadbourne thinks that the gagging or punishing of teachers for their protest of criticism against unfairness in school administration ought to be stopped by law. He notes with satisfaction the recent set-up of a student forum

[3] Walter Greenwood Beach, Edward Everett Walker, "American Social Problems." Stanford University Press, Stanford University, California. 391 pp. $1.58.

[4] Ellis Chadbourne, "New York Blazes the Way." Citizens Movement, 10 E. 40th Street, New York. 46 pp. 25 cents.

in the city-owned Hunter College for girls with the aim to study municipal affairs.

Boards of education, he says, need educating. The New York board he considers a political group, sunk in routine with no progress or vision. Political influence and favoritism reign supreme.

The booklet describes one after another the glaring defects of government in the city, the measures under way and proposed by Mayor La Guardia and his administration to move toward a model of management, and urges teachers, students and school managers to organize and help. This sort of cooperation is what the old founders of public education said they had in mind. It has wandered far, thinks Mr. Chadbourne. So direct a diagnosis of the city's diseases may even be scorned from the classrooms. Such observers as Lincoln Steffens, Frank Kent, Charles Taft and John Chamberlain show that New York crookedness is typical not only of other cities but of towns, villages and rural governments. Mr. Chadbourne's booklet, therefore, has a wide market.

PERSONAL ECONOMICS

YOU have brains, pleads Law-counselor Davis.[5] Use 'em. If you look on your economic life as dependent on yourself you will develop a money sense and remove yourself from the hazards which beset the mass. Write the income you should command at the periods ending at your thirtieth, fortieth and fiftieth birthdays, computing these figures from the general average. Look out. You will naturally want more than you will naturally get. The book gives tables to show what this average is. Mr. Davis treats of acquiring money, knowing where it goes, honesty, why it pays, punctuality, order, system, personal budgets, discretion, appearance, buying your things, baits and lures, waste of instalment buying, how to lose, saving, investing, bank accounts, life insurance, marriage economy, speculation, the balanced life. President Hutchinson, of Washington and Jefferson College, appalled by the lack of the simplest fundamentals of personal economics among students, asked Financier Davis to write a book for youngsters. This is it. Dr. Hutchinson says he is mightily pleased with it. It decidedly is sound sense and admirably suited for high-school and college use.

CLEAR TRAIL

EVEN a journal like the *Saturday Review of Literature,* taking all learning as its province, intimates that economics and politics are dull. With persistent voices insisting that duty requires us schoolmasters to keep abreast of this kind of literature an author such as Princetonian Professor Kemmerer[6] is a boon companion. That is to say, he is a benefaction good to linger with. This former currency expert and financial adviser to China, Colombia, Chile, Ecuador, Bolivia, Poland, Peru and the Philippine Government offers an elementary discussion of the important facts and underlying principles of the present money problems of the United States. Albeit much of the book was written by the author for articles in *The New York Sun* it is easy-running and directly informative reading. The gold standard, the present paper one, gold purchase, inflation, deflation, greenbacks, silver, commodity dollar, Germany's experience, debtor, creditor and the way back to stability are short, comprehensive and lucid chapters.

In my early teaching days anybody who was entangled in his accounts or in a problem of measurement no longer, as his father used to, came to the schoolmaster for help. Finders of fossils did, and disputants over grammatical correctness. A large company of respectables, leaders in our own schoolmastery guild, are pushing us into the duty of wide knowledge of public affairs. Noah Webster, top-notch student of government in his day, demanded that teachers should be experts in government, political economy and matters of public concern. Professor Kemmerer blazes a clear trail to that road.

YOU'LL GET WHAT YOU WANT

ANOTHER work[7] of simple exposition of the complexities of the currency question comes from Professor Edie, formerly of the chair of finance, University of Chicago, now in business.

The American people, over a period of time, will get the kind of dollar they fundamentally

[5] Horace W. Davis, "Money Sense." McGraw-Hill Book Company, New York. 256 pp. $2.00.

[6] Edwin Walter Kemmerer, "Money." John C. Winston Company, Philadelphia. 197 pp. $1.50.

[7] Lionel D. Edie, "Dollars." Yale University Press, New Haven. 293 pp. $2.50.

desire. But they must formulate a conception of what they want. So begins this presentation of theories, experiments and facts. You want, says this expounder, a dollar that commands confidence at home and abroad. For this we must have a balanced, ordinary budget and avoidance of excessive spending. Our paper currency must not be depreciated by issue of unbacked currency. Banking must be held to a sound relation to the production, income and price-level of the nation. Gold must be the primary base of the monetary structure. The stabilization of the domestic value of this metal is essential. A price level above that of the days when the banks closed in 1933 and not so high as in the boom of 1929 is essential. There must be a balance of prices fair to both agriculture and industry.

Elaboration and illustration of these propositions make the Edie book. Its history of modern government finance, its exposition of needed action are clear and intended for the man on the sidewalk.

WHAT THE RISING GENERATION SHOULD KNOW

JOHN MCCONAUGHY, a man's man if ever there was one, writes of public affairs in a way that grips the younger generation as it does those who are getting the brunt of national calamities. In a history of the political and financial pirates[8] who have milked the country from its earliest days he presents doings much more vital to an understanding of where we are than can be found in the usual school texts. No great American involved in the plunder of the people whether in the earlier or later days of the Republic is here whitewashed. Jefferson scotched the intent of the money makers to buy titles of nobility as can be done in England, but now this distinction must be obtained from foreign rulers or from dispensers of college degrees. Jackson warned the Congress that the rich are ever bending the government in favor of their selfish purposes. The first Roosevelt found a tendency of Americans, awed by the huge profits of public plunder, to adore big business. Civil-war profiteering, coal steals, railway plunder, corporation contributions to both political parties at the same time, tariff manipulations, all the continuing stabs into equality, liberty, justice and general welfare are told as history.

These are things that have been withheld from school boys. These are evils which, unchecked, have brought America to its present absurdity of want amidst plenty. These are facts to be known and understood by every ward of public education. To know, to preserve, to improve upon American ideals the Continental Congress in 1787 decreed: Schools and the means of education shall forever be encouraged for good government and the happiness of mankind. McConaughy's history of bad government is as essential for school study as is pathology for a course in medicine.

THE GREEKS AS DEMOCRATS

GREEK PROFESSOR BONNER,[9] University of Chicago, makes Athenian democracy with its clubs, tricks of the law courts, briberies, investigating committees, frame-ups and campaigns for justice and reform a picture surprisingly modern, albeit of the life of twenty-four centuries ago. The ordinary citizen was glad to hold office for the pay if for no other reason. To get a quorum, officers, at times carrying a long, freshly painted rope, would march across the marketplace sweeping the loiterers into their places for meeting. You will find the book an attracting account of the people, their lawsuits, politics, citizenship, liberties, literature, religion and imperialism.

The research involved in a work of this kind, the careful citation of authority, will command your respect. No less will you admire the talent which gives this erudition the interest of a history of our own times.

REQUIRE IT FOR COLLEGE ENTRANCE

RHODES SCHOLAR LINDLEY,[10] serious, vigorous, entertaining, knows The New Deal outside and in. He was the *New York World's* assignment to cover Franklin Roosevelt as governor and later as presidential candidate. He is a

[8] John McConaughy, "Who Rules America?" Longmans, Green and Company, New York. 338 pp. $3.00.

[9] Albert J. Bonner, "Aspects of Athenian Democracy." University of California Press, Berkeley, California. 199 pp. $2.25.

[10] Ernest K. Lindley, "The Roosevelt Revolution." The Viking Press, New York. 325 pp. $2.50.

Herald-Tribune's Washington writer. His rapidly moving book is a lively history of large events, well knit into a national history and vivid with pen pictures of the men now in the public eye. My young high-school friends are passing my copy from hand to hand and say that this account of the important doings of our own times is the kind of history they wish they were studying in school. Good land! Why aren't they? Guess the reason the principal gives: "Not time enough, considering college entrance requirements."

MAKING HISTORY BLOOM

To give a zest of reading to your students of history I recommend a new Bobbs-Merrill book, "They Had Their Hour."[11] What is it? Sixteen rattling stories: the unintended landing of the Pilgrims at Plymouth instead of farther south, the questionable propriety of continuing to call Captain Kidd a pirate, startling scientific adventures of Benjamin Franklin, forgotten facts appertaining to Paul Revere, and an assortment of picturesque episodes likely to make the school boy's American history shrub as attractive as a Christmas tree. Author James with his biography of Sam Houston won the Pulitzer prize. His "Andrew Jackson" moved Bernard de Voto and the New York and Boston papers to ecstasies. The present volume is made up from authentic sources studied by the author in the course of gathering material for his published biographies. Result: true stories as fascinating as the clevcrest fiction.

TO SUPPLEMENT HISTORY

AMONG the school and college students with whom my life has been spent, the most have had but fleeting glimpses of a nearby world of thought where fundamental protest has been the breath of life. The odd persons here and there who emitted a philosophy of objection were, to my circle, cranks, Quixotes, nuts, brain-storms, March hares, belfry-bats, labeled by the student paper and, for the rest of their course, made fun of. The boy who read Henry George, I remember, got one vote for our class presidency. Here is a history[12] of reviled political and social objectors from Conrad Bersel to John Dewey. The fascination of this book may be due in part to the startling similarity between the cries for justice rising out of every earlier epoch of our history and the still unanswered protests against a failure to realize the promises of the fundamental pronouncements of the national beginnings. But the felicity of expression, the selection of events, the characterization of participants, the absence of preaching, would make this book a prize-winner at any time. It is a human panorama, distinct, authentic, colorful.

Groups of idealists and serious thinkers pass through these pages repeating the political and social prophecies of the founders of the Union, making small headway among the enticing calls of boundless opportunities for wealth. Robert Owen, Frances Wright, Charles Fourier, Bronson Alcott, Edward Aveling, Tennessee Clafflin, Victoria Woodhull, Daniel De Leon, Friederich Engels, Ferdinand Lassalle, Karl Marx, Eugene Debs, Henry George, Father McGlynn, Henry Mencken, Morris Hillquit, Elizabeth Gurley Flynn, Emma Goldman, Samuel Gompers, Tom Mooney, Upton Sinclair, Scott Nearing, Norman Thomas, hundreds more of the army of rebellion say their best and their worst in these pages without praise or blame from the pair of experienced managers who have set the stage for the immense pageant. It is a tremendously informative book. You finish it a sadder and a wiser man.

THE MACHINE VS. THE NOBILITY OF MAN

PROFESSOR JASPERS, of Heidelberg,[13] will not take it as a matter of course that human life is the supply of mass-needs by rationalized production with the aid of technical advances. The financial-industrial mess has engendered an awareness of ruin and a dread of life. The new system making the world an apparatus to supply the material necessities of life annihilates what it has no place for. Will gets itself translated into the state. The state uses force to preserve its unity. War is not a conflict of human beings but a technical struggle of the machines of states. We turn to youth, expecting it to restore what the world has lost. But youth are demanding the right to produce for

[11] Marquis James, "They Had Their Hour." The Bobbs-Merrill Company, Indianapolis. 324 pp. $2.75.

[12] Lillian Symes, Travers Clement, "Rebel America." Harper and Brothers, New York. 392 pp. $3.00.

[13] K. Jaspers, "Man in the Modern Age." Henry Holt and Company, New York. 243 pp. $2.50.

themselves what their teachers no longer possess. Already, they are having a say in the ordering of the school. When the state uses education for the moulding of character in accordance with the purposes of those who are in control of government we have unity in education and paralysis of mental freedom.

On the decay and the possibilities of the mind, on culture, the press, art, science, philosophy, sociology, anthropology, Marxism, Professor Jaspers cogitates deeply.

His themes and his thought make rapid reading of him wasteful and absurd. His consideration of what mankind can become batters against the barriers set against selfhood. He exposes the perversions of liberty. The sophist is perpetually on hand, but the hero is no longer seen. There is struggle but no fighting front. Shall the developer of his selfhood retire from the world? Companionship in it awakens all that is human in self.

This book is a searching analysis of an age becoming the slave to machinery. It is a constructive suggestion for saving the man's nobility now in danger of suffocation.

UNAFRAID OF DISAGREEABLE QUESTIONS

We had two young professors in the university at Ann Arbor whom we called moderns, John Dewey and James Tufts. I remember they wrote a book together, "Ethics," which some of the old fellows of those days thought an improvement on the much older teaching of the sainted Dr. Crocker, a predecessor. A dip into the works of each of these men will set you to thinking there must be something in philosophy to keep an addict young or something in these two that gives philosophy a virility of youth. The new Tufts' book[14] tackles the dilemma of the changing ideas of fairness, politics and morals.

What is social morality? What do you, the American citizen, care for? What is happening to the old attitude toward work? Why these suicides? Whence this sex wave? What are the standards of business, industry, the wealthy and the poor? Do you see the outcome of the conflict between traditional government and the forces of change? Can you see abatement of the lawless strong, the young delinquents, the crooked officers? What convictions have you in the matter of commercialized gambling, prostitution and drunkenness? Are these live questions? How extensive a proportion of the brains of the country are considering them with the ardor and intelligence that some high-class minds are, for instance, deciphering pieces of clay dug from the mud of ancient rivers, or are rationalizing from rocks and gravel the story of the birth of the world, or are collecting from different periods man's idea of God?

Sociologist, economist and philosopher, Tufts gathers and sifts the views of able minds on the questions of politics, of right and wrong listed a few lines back. It is the function of education, he pleads, to make supreme a loyalty of men and women to the common good. The school is an agency of democracy which has enlarged liberty, opened the door for equality and ministered to the prosperity of all people. It needs now, more than ever, to take up these new questions.

I find this book easy to follow, deliberate in its judgments, unhesitant in dealing with disagreeable things and untainted by despair.

LIVING IS A HAPPY ART

Editor Breitigam[15] of the *New York World-Telegram* sits cheerily in front of his typewriting machine and rattles off an optimistic lot of good sense on personality, self-mastery, right and wrong, energy, leisure and laziness, health, sociability and other matters men and women are forever eager to learn. The old Greek dogma that life is an art guides the Breitigam meditation. His themes are important; his style is engaging. He is good for the old and especially for the young.

THE SCHOOL AS DEMOCRACY

Professor Tuttle's[16] text-book for intending and practising educators does not touch the social order incidentally but boldly tosses to one side a plenitude of vocational, cultural and

[14] James Hayden Tufts, "America's Social Morality." Henry Holt and Company, New York. 326 pp. $2.40.

[15] Gerald Breitigam, "Dare to Live." The Falcon Press, 330 W. 42nd Street, New York. 229 pp. $2.00.

[16] Harold Saxe Tuttle, "A Social Basis of Education." Thomas Y. Crowell Company, New York. 589 pp. $3.00.

child-centered aims, unless the activities of achieving them are directed to a more perfect national and world union, justice, peace and general welfare. "The final aim of education is nothing short of the aim of society itself: civilization, the best for the human race."

He develops a striking line in the pursuit of happiness. Subjective satisfaction has been too much considered as though its chief source were in the esthetic field. The arts have been looked on as the outstanding realm for refined enjoyment provided by school. Freedom and democracy yield high satisfactions. Emphasis of school should be conspicuously thrown on this field of human values rather than limiting such training to poetry, music and art. Culture must be inclusive of democracy, rich in abiding happiness.

Professor Tuttle takes up in detail the activities of school, regular and extra curricular. He stresses their civic possibilities. It is not enough that these pursuits be considered to have in themselves these civic effects. What is the teacher for? The civic motive must be kept clear and active. Education's recent history has enough of the accounts of student government and honor systems whose experimenters say the trials have failed. If anywhere they have succeeded that is the most convincing proof that failure is unnecessary. It may be that the direction has failed where failure is reported. Democracy requires the organization of a school in such a way that the child develops initiative and responsibility in accordance with group interest. Participation in determining conditions of learning is a duty of the school to give its members not as a privilege but as an education in cooperative democracy.

TEN THOUSAND VIEWS OF TEACHERS

AMONG us it would be hard to find one more free of the chilling traditions of schoolmastery than Frank (well-named first and last) Hart, University of California professor of education. He has compiled, analyzed and put into readable form[17] ten thousand estimates of teachers furnished by high-school seniors. It is a remarkable revelation no less from the composites of the best-liked teacher, the one esteemed least of all, and others of varying traits, than from the sound and rarely thought-of implications brought out by the author that the effort at teaching may count for little if the learner is not receptive. Rare is he who learns much or well from an unwanted source.

Quotations will not give you the feel of the book. They would be bricks from the house. Professor Hart's concluding chapter is corking. Every trait in his good and in his horrible teachers are attainable or avoidable by an ordinarily intelligent person. Memory takes me back forty-six years when I had the courage to submit blanks (not so good as the one in the Hart volume) to my high-school class and found myself in reputation somewhat better and worse than I thought I deserved and smarting under what I thought were snippy slanders. All the same, a testing of oneself at the close of every term by means of the Hart diagnosis ought immensely to increase the value of teaching.

HIGH SCHOOLS OF LESS THAN 1,000 PUPILS

SUCH problems as the national surveyors deemed peculiar to the smaller high schools are considered in a special monograph.[18] I find it full of good reading, no matter what the size of your school. It is interesting to note the introduction of new subjects—problems of democracy, economics, sociology. Mathematics shows little change. For each subject dropped, two were added. Latin, the report says, is going from enough schools to indicate a trend. Ancient history is falling out notably. The instances of greater community service of high schools, as recorded in this report, are worthy of special attention and praise.

HIGH SCHOOL AND THE UNFIT

DR. BILLETT'S publication[19] in the great Cooper-Koos appraisal of American high schools covers some of the most frequently criticized features of teaching. Forty years ago the

[17] Frank W. Hart, "Teachers and Teaching." The Macmillan Company, New York. 285 pp. $1.50.

[18] Emery N. Ferris, W. H. Gaumnitz, P. Roy Brammell, "The Smaller Secondary Schools." Superintendent of Documents, Washington, D. C. 236 pp. 15 cents.

[19] Roy O. Billett, "Provisions for Individual Differences, Marking and Promotion." Superintendent of Documents, Washington, D. C. 472 pp. 40 cents.

high schools found the handling of individual differences an easy matter. You recognized only two sorts of children—those who were fit for high school and those who were unfit. The first class you fed one diet and kept of them those who digested 70 per cent. of it. The unfit were no responsibility of yours. They took your food, found it indigestible and left. Some schools were strong enough to put them out. With no adequate development as children these youngsters faced the problems of adults. This was so generally accepted as a normal working of a survival of the fittest that when, in 1902, a committee of teachers of the Washington Irving High School, New York, issued a manifesto that it is the business of high-school teachers to lure into school, and to serve, all children over fourteen years old, whether fit or unfit, the *School Review,* secondary education mouthpiece of the country, published a composite reply by many teachers pronouncing the Washington Irving doctrine an absurdity. How we have changed, remarks Dr. Billett. America has encouraged the trend of secondary education toward the goal of serving all the older children in the country. Under continued onslaughts the high-school barriers have been broken down. The students are no longer a selected group. Every kind is in. Out of this fact springs the need of desire, intelligence and organization devoted toward preventing this multitude from going to waste. Dr. Billett works out the implications in a masterly study of the whole problem. What is the literature on the problem? What are the successes of the segregating and grouping plan? What are the outstanding schools in these kinds of organization? What is the specific procedure in each?

In the daily management of work you have the Morrison plan, the Dalton, the Winnetka and others fully described here and appraised.

In his treatment of marking and promotion Dr. Billett shows that tradition has been subjected to corrective experiment and alteration in many details, while "my status, right or wrong" is no dead slogan, yet.

THE UNEMPLOYED COLLEGE INSTRUCTOR

Professor Umstattd, University of Minnesota, contributes a study[20] of the number of degree holders expecting college instructorships in the several fields of study, the number given appointments, and the increase of supply over demand.

COLLEGE PUBLICATION SAVING MONEY

Pennsylvania State College is issuing education studies[21] that reproduce the typewritten originals directly in print and are bound by ingenious wire stitching. The print is not too small for even my old eyes, but the college furnishes reading glasses if you wish. The printing process reproduces tables and diagrams at reduced cost. The crisp volume I have covers conclusions on the melody method, effect of foreign birth on success in American schooling, mechanical ability in general science, guidance and twenty-four investigations that even Abraham Flexner would praise.

GRAMMAR AND A NEW FREEDOM

If Professor Pooley had done for the teaching of American history what he has performed for instruction in grammar Chicago's 100 per cent. Americans would have burned his book.[22] It's a knockout. Without sarcasm, jibe or ridicule, it leaves a picture in your memory of a great army of teachers laboriously holding children to a slavery to things that aren't so. Professor Pooley quietly subjects the eternal verities repeated in the school language-texts to deadly comparison with the usage of authors of recognized mastery.

"It's me" is anathema to the teacher; perfectly good English for one who knows language. School grammar teaches "it snows" as the regular present tense. You never, in your life, heard any one say it. Many honest idioms that have led a moral life does Dr. Pooley clear of the slander that writers of school grammar have smeared upon them. His array of expressions such book makers use in the same text that on some other page condemns these forms as

[20] James G. Umstattd, "Supply and Demand of College Teachers." University of Minnesota Press, Minneapolis. 41 pp. Paper, 50 cents.

[21] Charles C. Peters, George W. Hartmann, "Abstracts of Studies in Education." 79 pp. 50 cents. John Andrew Cooper, "The Effect of Athletics Measured by Achievement Tests." 21 pp. 10 cents. State College, Pennsylvania.

[22] Robert C. Pooley, "Grammar and Usage in Text-books on English." University of Wisconsin Press, Madison. 172 pp. Paper, 75 cents.

wrong is startling. His citations of this sort of pedantry in sixteen commonly used texts is delicious. Here is a compact little essay full of specific suggestions for sanity and sense in the teaching of English. You'll love it.

THE LIBRARY LEARNING FROM THE ERRORS OF SCHOOL

PROFESSOR BUTLER'S[23] half dozen brilliant essays are as valuable to teachers as to the librarians for whom they were written. They are the first of a series to be issued from time to time by the Graduate Library School of the University of Chicago. What Dr. Butler says of the nature and methods of science, of the history of library science and of practical considerations is distinctly valuable to school workers. His essay, "The Sociological Problem," touches us sharply. Educational activities, he observes, are suffering a distortion. Occasional and fragmentary attempts to meet a new demand have worked the educational scheme away from a well-integrated adequate objective. This objective is preponderatingly civic social service. No civilization can maintain itself unless the necessary portion of each generation are versed in the knowledge which, as Washington worded it, gives enlightened force to government. Knowledge for its own sake has no esthetic or ethical value to society. Society must consider the costs and results of education. Modern education's enthusiasm over techniques and method slights the interests of society.

In our earlier epoch when a youth left college he was already a man because he possessed the knowledge for adult life. In our day he is still a boy. This is not because education or the youth has deteriorated. It is due to the violent changes in society itself. This enormously magnifies the task of education. Cumulative knowledge has outrun the curriculum. The two used to be more nearly identical.

No one can claim that the almost universal requirement of Latin should be continued. It was suitable for an old-fashioned humanistic society. Libraries suffer from the same adherence to tradition. A lovable old fogy of prominence will, on a library board, get its money wasted on a collection that used to be a gentleman's library when the member was a boy.

One can not argue that the great masterpieces produce a change in society. A master is so original that his language fails to reach the multitude. What really effects the change is the work of interpreters of the master. Schools did not change the thought of the world in the direction of the views of Galileo or Luther or Darwin. The world changed and education came trailing after. Popular science works are not to be spurned.

This little book is full of yeast to expand your thought. Chapter III on reading is a treasury.

[23] Pierce Butler, "Introduction to Library Science." University of Chicago Press. 118 pp. $1.50.

LIBRARIANS' AIDS

THE American Library Association has issued an 87-page booklet "Reference Books, 1931–1933," by Isadore Gilbert Mudge and Constance M. Winchell, listing works in various languages and classified according to title and field. A summary accompanies each title. This guide is priced at $1.25. The association has published, at 35 cents, an introductory manual of classification, 22 pp., by Margaret M. Herdman, of the School of Library Science, Louisiana State University.

THE FORGOTTEN WOMAN

WHEN I was twenty-one (dear me, fifty years ago), I landed on Mackinac from a thirty-foot sailboat on which I was chaperoning five of my high-school boys for a six-weeks cruise. In the store were books of Constance Fenimore Woolson stacked by the cord for the tourist trade. I bought "Anne" and "Castle Nowhere." By lantern-light under the sleeping tent we hung from the boom every night; also by daylight under pine trees in Georgian Bay or on the banks of the Saint Mary's I read these gentle tales and shared the conviction of those days that here was the perfection of the novelist's art. No woman with rarer qualities, said Mr. Stedman, or more decided gifts is among us. Henry James thought no writer surpassing her in close observation and ability to translate outward appearances into their moods.

Last week I captured two big volumes of "Picturesque America," the old Appleton enterprise done by artists who set up their easels for it over the country. Reading the text, prosy enough, I come to a chapter sparkling with life. I turn to the table of contents and find its author, Constance Fenimore Woolson. Dear lady, I meet no one who reads her. For a generation a deep neglect has erased her from the ken of all except a few special students. Such is a professor of English in Temple University, Dr. Kern.[24] He has made a pilgrimage to Mackinac, the Great Lakes places figuring in her stories, the Ohio uplands, the Southern plantations, the European scenes of her various books. He has scoured public libraries east and west, gained access to autograph collections, interviewed old people and read the one hundred and seventy-seven Woolson stories and sketches which he lists. His life and letters of Miss Woolson retells many of her narratives, gives his own and her contemporaries' criticism of her work and wonders that the best of it is now so widely forgotten.

I have no old man's archeological appetite. An old book, because old, has no charm for me. But Dr. Kern's bright and scholarly volume sent me to the attic where the rising generation of our family puts all but the bright-backed books. I have brought down our Woolsons. They are as delightful as in the 1880's. She is as able a literary pioneer as Bret Harte or Edward Eggleston. Mark Twain was no more admired than she. Dr. Kern claims for "Anne," "East Angels," and "For the Mayor" the right to permanence. Her ballad "Kentucky Belle" is still a stirring tale, well told. Her hope was to be buried on her beloved island in the straits between Lakes Michigan and Huron. This has so far failed of fulfilment. The women's literary clubs in Michigan may well devote a meeting to this well-beloved artist and inquire as to the feasibility of putting her tomb where she wished it to be.

STORIES OF YOUR GRANDFATHERS

READING in the *Atlantic*, in *Scribner's*, *The Forum*, *Collier's*, *The Saturday Evening Post* and I know not where else for the past ten years I have felt the good-story appetite aroused when I saw the name of young Edmonds. Always I got the shears and paste ready for adding another treasure to the scrapbook. Walter D. Edmonds, R. D. (Reader's Delight) is the Dickens of the exulting blustering swaggering years beginning in 1820 when the waterways thrust out from the eastern states and pulsed prosperity into the middle west and sucked wealth to the Atlantic shores. Three volumes[25] of canal sagas by this Booneville boy are now in the bookstores. He caught the old skippers, cooks, drivers, lock tenders and repair men before they passed out. His home town is in the canal country. The dialogue of his stories is racy with the speech of a pioneer tribe gone forevermore. "Erie Water" is a vibrant novel of the planning and digging of the ditch and of the day when Lake Erie water was let through the open gates with the firing of cannon so spaced on the tow path and Hudson shores that the shot fired in Buffalo, heard by the next gun, was relayed boom by boom to little old New York. "Rome Haul" is the odyssey of a farmer boy who became skipper. "Mostly Canallers" is made up of enlivening "shorts," adventurous tales of Ohio travelers, weird lock tenders, shanty men, wandering preachers, bad folks, ghosts, freak boats, money-makers, easy marks, warehousemen, peddlers, horse-traders, weddings, bornings, girls, wives, old women, panoramas of the human comedy and tragedy afloat and ashore.

Edmonds is a delicious recounter. His cabin breakfasts make your mouth water. His canal basins at night, his boats gliding through woods or dells or marshes or plains have the fascination your grandfathers felt when they sat under the awnings on the decks of the packets and saw the world slowly enough to let the beauty of it filter into them.

REMARKABLE CONDENSATION OF KNOWLEDGE

WONDER and admiration rise as the new Doubleday-Doran encyclopedia[26] is examined and studied. Its purpose is to answer immediate questions that come up in intelligent con-

[24] John Dwight Kern, "Constance Fenimore Woolson, Literary Pioneer." University of Pennsylvania Press. 198 pp. $2.50.

[25] Walter D. Edmonds, "Erie Water." 506 pp. $2.75; "Rome Haul." 347 pp. $2.50; "Mostly Canallers," 467 pp. $2.50. Little, Brown and Company, Boston.

[26] Della Braddy, Lawrence H. Dawson, Richard Friedenthal, "Facts." 4 vols. Doubleday-Doran and Company. 1950 pp. Exclusively by subscription. $19.50.

versation. Its aim is quick reference. Its condensations, the compilers declare, are not secured by leaving out facts but by elimination of unnecessary words and by abbreviating terms. By ingenious means more than 30,000 articles, 3,000 pictures, maps and diagrams are tucked into four snug stoutly bound volumes. Among the twenty-seven chief contributors are economists, lexicographers, encyclopedists, historians, scientists, authors, musicians and newsmen.

Have a sample? RELATIVITY. ("Special" theory 1905: general, 1915: Einstein). Based on 2 experimental facts: (1) absolute motion thr. space cannot be detected or measured. (2) Velocity of light is same whatever velocity of source relatively to observer. Some consequences: Mass varies with velocity—proved experimentally. Light subject to gravity a) deflected in passing through field; star image displaced owing to attraction of sun; b) spectrum lines displaced toward red in strong gravitational field. Proof doubtful. Time varies with velocity, likewise demensions. Ultimate picture of universe is a structure in space of 4 dimensions, space-time being one of these; matter causes a curvature or working (worked space) wh. is the gravitational field: thus time and space are equivalent (Lorentz-Minkowski.)

Here's another: TECHNOCRACY. Word coined, 1919 by Wm. Henry Smyth, Calif. engnr. and invntr. to descr. system of govt. in wh. energy, not price, is the basis of the econ. structure; arose fr. a suggestion of the late Thorstein Veblen in 1919, later incorp. in his *The engineers and the Price System,*) that a survey be made of the available energy and raw matls. and man-power in U.S.; rcd. wide publicity late in 1932.

The simple and readily translated shorthand enables these four volumes to cover biography, history, the arts, sciences and the whole field of knowledge, ancient and modern, usually requiring ten or twelve fat volumes.

PICTURES IN ARITHMETIC

IN the matter of holding the interest of children the old lag of arithmetic disappears in Professor Upton's program for teaching the younger children.[27] He has made a text-book for the first grade. His problems and number stories are based on the play, games and natural interests of little children. His stories, poems and directions confine themselves to the vocabulary of primary readers. He works in accordance with accepted rules of habit formation. He plans for individual differences in children. He offers a suitable work book to go with this text. A book like this could well be used as a demonstration to parent teacher meetings that the advance of teaching is amazing.

ILLUMINATING SUPERVISION OF HIGH-SCHOOL MATHEMATICS

LET there be acclaim when a college professor of mathematics avers that entrance requirements prevent improvements in high-school teaching, that the large number of failures in secondary school mathematics is a disgrace, that youngsters retain a small amount of mathematical knowledge and skill. Dr. Breslich, University of Chicago, sets down these things in his third book on high-school teaching.[28] The other two were expressly for teachers. This one is for heads of departments, supervisors, principals and superintendents. I find his psychology and practical suggestions direct and efficient. If you undertake to direct teachers you must know what they are doing, what particular part needs improvement, how to get them to see it without humiliation and how to mend it. The functions of a supervisor, his class visits, his records, his conferences, his term plans, his tests, his ways of getting teachers to work with conscious intent to secure those changes in pupils' minds for which mathematics is employed, specific illustrations taken from various parts of the high-school course, the whole matter covered so clearly that I whom the Lord endowed with no mathematical instinct can understand and enjoy it, make this a notable masterpiece.

INADEQUACY OF SCIENCE

WELL toward the close of his survey of present science[29] Mr. Sullivan sums the modern

27 Clifford Brewster Upton, "First Days with Numbers." American Book Company, New York. 160 pp. 40 cents.

28 Ernest R. Breslich, "The Administration of Mathematics in Secondary Schools." University of Chicago Press. 407 pp. $3.00.

29 J. W. N. Sullivan, "The Limitations of Science." The Viking Press, New York. 307 pp.

revolution in science as an overturn of the Newtonian outlook which dominated the scientific world for nearly two hundred years. Science has become self-conscious and comparatively humble. Eminent men of science are insisting that it gives us but a partial knowledge of reality. If the universe of science is accepted as a reality it makes of man an entirely accidental by-product of a huge, mindless, purposeless, mathematical machine. There are men of science who find such a conclusion disconcerting. The discovery that science no longer compels us to believe in our own essential futility is greeted with acclamation even by some scientific men. This change in the scientific outlook has taken place suddenly. It is not sixty years since Tyndall in the Belfast address claimed that science alone is capable of dealing with all man's major problems. It is only twenty years since Bertrand Russell asserted that only on the firm foundation of unyielding despair can the soul's habitation safely be built.

Scientists recognize that the old claims were exaggerated. Their negation of beliefs incapable of mathematical proof seemed, to perhaps the majority of thoughtful men, to have darkened life. It is not, therefore, surprising that the new interpretation of science by such men as Eddington and Jeans is welcome.

Mr. Sullivan treats of the expanding universe, the mystery of matter, the web of reason, the scientific accounts of origins, the nature of mind and the values of science. He reviews the conclusions of Whitehead, Millikan, Lamarck, Haldane, Jeans, Eddington, Einstein and other investigators. The developing scientific outlook owed, heretofore, its main features to the predilections of the mathematician. He assumed that only the quantitative is the real. Although mathematics has been the most valuable tool for scientific investigation it is no longer universally believed by scientists that nature is necessarily mathematical. Although adopting different routes, there are scientists who arrive at the same conclusion: that the ultimate nature of the universe is mental. "The stuff of the world," as Eddington puts it, "is mind stuff."

The reason science has hitherto formed a closed system is that the terms of science are defined in terms of one another.

Mr. Sullivan has produced an ideal humanization of science. This book is a selection of the Scientific Book Club and is recommended by the Book-of-the-Month Club.

SCIENCE FOR LITTLE TOTS

BEHOLD an attractive, beautifully illustrated science book[30] for first-grade children. To get seasons, weather, animals, plants, sun, moon and stars into the approved vocabulary of first-grade print is a feat of skill. This trio of authors has done the feat supremely well.

JOHN ADAMS, FRONT VIEW

FOR twenty-six years Chevalier Chinard, Johns Hopkins professor of French literature, holder of degrees from Chatellerault, Poitiers, Bordeaux and Paris, has been teaching and writing in the United States. His "Thomas Jefferson," hailed by Claude Bowers and Charles Beard as a contribution of the first order, is now followed by a biography of John Adams.[31]

This is a distinctively handsome example of book-making, beautifully illustrated with portraits. Professor Chinard combines the patience of a delver into forgotten manuscripts with the mastery of clear-flowing English. His selection of experiences in the childhood, youth and manhood of his New Englander, demonstration of their effect in building the character of the great Federalist, produce a masterly character study. "The Education of John Adams" is a chapter of singular freshness and charm. As in his "Jefferson," Professor Chinard is not carried into adulation nor tempted to shock any hero-worshiper by piling up accounts of frailties. Honest John is also painted, warts and all. Meet a conceited, sincere, obstinate, irascible, vindictive, pardoning, lovable old dear. A reading of this book is an enjoyable review of epoch-making history, so well does the author maintain the scenery of concurrent events.

The long overplayed story of lasting animosity between Jefferson and Adams is given a happy quietus by liberal quotations from affectionate letters from each.

30 Wilbur L. Beauchamp, Gertrude Crampton, William S. Gray, ''Science Stories, Book One.'' Scott Foresman and Company, Chicago. 144 pp. 60 cents.

31 Gilbert Chinard, ''Honest John Adams.'' Little, Brown and Company, Boston. 359 pp. $3.75.

HEROIC AMERICAN FAMILY

WITH the affectionate badinage with which members of American families jolly one another, with dignified quotations upon their services to their country and the world, Lyman Beecher Stowe portrays his twelve Beecher relatives.[32]

In these days of schoolmaster's strivings for character training a book like this, with its gripping human interest, its connection with national problems, its unexaggerated stories of civic courage, is a godsend. Catherine, Henry Ward, Harriet and Thomas are especially dear to the American schoolmaster. The whole dozen exemplify that public-mindedness which is due for the great revival, now. The entertaining author, without preaching, makes preachers companionable persons. These Beechers he presents as amusing, lovable and outrageous, playing an untiring part in turning religion from theoretical philosophy to sturdy world-service. This book you will earmark for school and college libraries.

JEFFERSON FOR BOYS[33]

HERE is a spirited story, beautifully illustrated, full of human quality, depicting the great democrat as a frontier boy, learned in wood craft and Indian lore, going off to get an education, getting into college, devouring national philosophy, prying into science, learning how to discuss, dancing with the girls, playing the fiddle, courting, reading law, and so coming of age. You see him in the House of Burgesses and joining in the compact of the Virginia rebels. Amateur architect, he lays out picturesque Monticello, discomfits her other suitors and carries away as bride to his new home the charming Martha Skelton, a widow of twenty-three. For the Virginia protesters against the galling exactions of the mother country he drums up resolutions so well buttressed with justice that Burke quotes them in a speech to Parliament. The British government lists the young Virginian as a dangerous subject along with John and Samuel Adams, Hancock and Henry.

The story of the great Declaration as told here is striking, as is "the inner revolution," the forward leaps in government secured by Jefferson in his native state, his work as military governor and his mission to France.

The humor of the contention of two parties upon the etiquette of ceremony is not missed nor the fundamentals of the quarrel between the aristocratic Hamilton and the democratic representative of proud Virginia. He won his fight for a decimal system of money; he lost it for weights and measures. His presidency, his retirement, his work for a public school system, his establishment of the University of Virginia, his perpetual experimenting in the new sciences are told with an animation sure to hold the interest of young readers, as do the adventures of Edison and the earlier Roosevelt.

It is a book the history teachers will want in the school library.

GUIDANCE EFFECTIVELY OUTLINED

STUDY the last census. Group the occupations into production of raw materials, manufacturing, transportation, buying and selling, clerical, professional service, personal service and public service. Study the qualifications, wages and work conditions of the people engaged in these separate services. Use your best arguments and persuasions to break down the exaggerated preference of youth for white-collar employment; make clear the unpromising outlook now ahead. Bring in cheery suggestions, poems and facts, tell the whole story as if you had a group of lively youngsters in front of you. Sprinkle new photographs of work through the manuscript, try the whole thing in as many junior high schools as you can, improving it day by day. Then get it into comfortable types and a real strong binding. This is what a University of Michigan professor of vocational guidance, collaborating with teachers in Detroit, has done.[34] The spirit of it is excellent. Its teachable quality is highly effective. It is intended for seventh, eighth or ninth school years. You had better distribute it over

[32] Lyman Beecher Stowe, "Saints, Sinners, and Beechers." The Bobbs-Merrill Company, Indianapolis. 450 pp. $3.75.

[33] Gene Lisitzky, "Thomas Jefferson." The Viking Press, New York. 358 pp. $2.50.

[34] George E. Myers, Gladys M. Little, Sarah A. Robinson, "Planning Your Future." McGraw-Hill Book Company, New York. 419 pp. $1.50.

the three of them, for its contents should get permanent lodging in the youthful mind.

INHERITANCE AND TRAINING

CLINICAL Psychologist and Researcher Schwesinger[35] assembles the scientific evidence which has accrued in the past ten years and offers a study in the genesis of psychological characteristics. Previous publications have emphasized the hereditary basis of development. This work is devoted to a better understanding of the influence of environment. As, since the world began, the wise have had much controversy whether nature or nurture weighs the most, the author of the present large volume marks every step of the way with references to original source material. The main chapters are upon measurement of intelligence and personality, studies of the heredity-environment problems, conclusions.

With this author as an experienced guide you may traverse in an orderly manner the pieces of country you have viewed separately as you have gone into books and articles of Burnham, Freeman, the Watsons, the Allports, Thorndike, Pintner, Newman, May, Kretschmer, Kelley, Gesell, Elliott, Cattell, Burks and others of the quiet idol-breakers who have been patiently building the causeway of solid fact into the marsh of guess and assumption. What the measurers have found in the different mental powers of twins raised in different homes, how adopted children differ from their family, numerous such facts as these make the book particularly interesting. But the hope that keeps teachers going, the belief that, of whatever parents the boy was born, we can make him better than if he were left alone, is the big human idea that makes this study of tremendous importance.

CHARACTER TRAINING TO-DAY

LEISURE! leisure! The magazines and serious books are warning us that science and engineering are pushing it on us faster than we can provide for taking up the slack. One of the forthright tacklers of the problem is Kenneth Heaton.[36] The live school town of Pontiac, Michigan, thinks so much of him and his specialty that she maintains him in the public school system as director of character education. The University of Chicago published a book by him called "Character Building through Recreation." In his newer volume he returns to the main theme and again gives the extra curriculars a large charter as developers of essential qualities more needful than those derivable from the teaching of Latin and geometry. It is a book of materials and methods. The author recasts the seventeen statements of character aims as given in the tenth year book of the National Education Association superintendents. He substitutes fourteen marks of the person who has good character. He analyzes the regular curriculum for its character possibilities, propping them with many valuable suggestions. When he shakes loose from this prevailing attachment to the *status quo,* he gets into a free gait, guiding us profitably through school misconduct by children, the techniques of turning misdeeds into character training. He brings out the power of well-guided discussions of conduct by children and warns of the formalities that shrivel such exercises to dry husks. On research in school, on practise, dramatization, stories, clubs, individual guidance, organization of school in accordance with character objectives, on counselling, on grouping, he cites types of projects from the whole country and stresses the conscious purpose necessary in their use. He rejects the cautious praise of pupil participation in management found in many appraisals in current educational articles. He will not call it extra curricular. It is an essential entity of effective organization. It is not a scheme to help the principal; it is not to be used to get a pupil membership saying and doing what the boss suggests. He summarizes in eight sturdy paragraphs the principles basic to a school citizenship plan.

So we see, again, how the writers on educational purposes needed to-day are putting more emphasis on other than the subject studies, more on what we were brought up to call leisure time.

35 Gladys C. Schwesinger, ''Heredity and Environment.'' The Macmillan Company, New York. 484 pp. $4.00.

36 Kenneth L. Heaton, ''The Character Emphasis in Education.'' University of Chicago Press. 415 pp. $3.00.

SCHOOL AND SOCIETY

WITH WHICH ARE COMBINED THE EDUCATIONAL REVIEW, ESTABLISHED IN 1891, THE TEACHERS MAGAZINE, ESTABLISHED IN 1878, AND THE SCHOOL JOURNAL, ESTABLISHED IN 1874.

Volume 39 — SATURDAY, JUNE 9, 1934 — Number 1015

UNIVERSITY AND COLLEGE FINANCES DURING THE DEPRESSION

By JOHN C. CHRISTENSEN

CONTROLLER AND ASSISTANT SECRETARY, UNIVERSITY OF MICHIGAN

I

THE administration of our colleges and universities is being put to a severe test during the depression in trying to maintain high standards of instruction within reduced income. This situation has caused most administrators to turn a searching eye upon their own institutions in an effort to discover where economies may be made. As long as prosperity was supposed to be "just around the corner," temporary makeshifts enabled many institutions to reduce expenditures and thereby to maintain balanced budgets.

Although some of the devices used in reducing expenses may be of permanent value, most of them were probably of a temporary nature. In preparing material for a discussion of this subject before the annual meeting of the Association of University and College Business Officers in 1932, I secured information from fifty or more universities and colleges concerning the means adopted to reduce expenditures during the depression. From these reports I compiled as a summary of my investigations the following list and although these items have been given considerable publicity in various publications, I shall enumerate them here:

(1) Increase the load of the faculty by not making appointments to vacancies.

(2) Rearrange courses so as to enlarge the size of classes or to give certain courses only once a year or at longer intervals.

(3) Non-appointment to positions on annual appointment, after the expiration of the present year.

(4) Reduce equipment expenditures to a minimum, and in some cases abolish the purchase of library books, except continuations.

(5) Reduce compensation for extension lectures and work in connection with correspondence courses.

(6) Eliminate extra pay for summer sessions by requiring the faculty to teach during the summer session without extra compensation and arranging vacations in alternate years or otherwise.

(7) Reduce expenditures for research when chargeable to general funds.

(8) Reduce appropriations for publications, except when provided out of special funds.

(9) Reduce expenditures for travel.

(10) Reduce clerical help and office expense to a minimum.

(11) Reduce maintenance and operation of buildings to a minimum, doing only the absolutely necessary repairs to keep property from deteriorating.

(12) Eliminate certain activities which, while desirable, are not directly concerned with the instruction of students, such as publicity bureaus, university press publications, etc.

(13) Curtail the construction of new buildings and other plant extension items, unless specifically provided out of special funds.

Inasmuch as the foregoing proposals were listed in an effort to outline a few items which could be considered before resorting to indiscriminate salary cuts, the list should be considered from that angle. It now seems that the future of financing higher education will probably be a serious problem for at least a few years to come. Consequently, a study of university and college finances during the depression should take into account reforms intended to be permanent.

II

The principal sources of income of our colleges and universities are student fees, investments and gifts, and in the case of publicly supported institutions, public appropriations. There are few institutions which have not suffered from reduced income from one or more of these sources. The problem would solve itself if income could be augmented, but in most cases it is undoubtedly futile to expect relief from this source in the immediate future. In some instances, particularly tax-supported institutions, it may be possible to secure increased income during the next few years if we can secure reforms in our taxing systems. Some institutions may find it possible to increase student fees, while in others it may be necessary to reduce these fees in order to make the institutions available to greater numbers. Likewise, income from gifts is likely to be greatly reduced during the next few years. It seems, then, that the prospect of increasing income is dubious, and therefore the solution of the financing problem is largely one of reducing expenses.

III

In endeavoring to reduce expenses of operation, there is presented to us a field for thorough study and reorganization. It is undoubtedly true in many institutions that the period of prosperity through which we passed prior to the collapse of 1929 brought about many hastily prepared educational programs, some of which were of questionable value or may have duplicated in part what was already offered by the institution.

It is therefore important to consider the scope of each institution. Do we have too much duplication between institutions in a single city? Or a single state? Just now it is reported that two of our larger universities are considering a consolidation. The questions which arise in this discussion are these: Can the city support two law schools, two medical schools, two schools of business administration, as well as other duplications? What is going on in this city has been considered in various communities in America, and in some cases real efforts have been made to define the scope of the various institutions in such communities. It has even been suggested that the various institutions of higher education in a single city be combined into a greater university in which all institutions, including engineering colleges, medical, law and dental schools, as well as schools of business administration, education, etc., would be coordinated for greater and better work in each field. This may be accomplished without actual corporate consolidation through agreements similar to those now in effect in one of America's largest universities. It would then seem that a study of the scope of each institution is a matter of importance in university and college financing.

IV

A detailed examination of courses and curricula may reveal serious duplication within the institution itself and it may show that many courses are offered in which few students enroll. Students say that subject-matter of courses is repeated under various names. Whether this criticism is justifiable or not is a matter for study by those familiar with the content of courses, but undoubtedly it is true in some cases. For example, there may be duplication between various courses in English literature, public speaking, rhetoric and journalism, in psychology and educational psychology, or in such science courses as botany and plant breeding. The division of the faculty into so many departments, divisions, schools and colleges is responsible for much of this duplication.

It may be found, also, that certain courses are offered from year to year with very small enrolment. This may result from the desire of an instructor to present the subject of his own narrowly specialized study for the doctorate. There may be a real demand for such work, but if not watched carefully, the catalogues and announcements will become cluttered with courses for which there is little demand. A study of courses with relation to curricula and the scope of the institution may be a source of reducing expenses and at the same time increase the effectiveness of instruction.

V

In most institutions, and especially in the larger colleges and universities, there is an ever-increasing item of expenditure for research. Nothing should be done to curtail genuine research, provided funds are available. However, all that is called research is not always genuine research, and therefore a study of the institution's educational program would also involve an investigation for this purpose. That institution is fortunate which has special and adequate funds for research projects, as thereby the expenditures for this line of activity can be controlled automatically and without infringement on the general funds of the institution. But even here good management would see that research funds are expended to the best advantage in promoting fundamental discoveries.

VI

Closely related with the study of courses and curricula and research would be a thorough-going investigation of the quantity and quality of educational equipment and its uses. Although the smaller colleges may have little duplication in equipment, even here a careful investigation may reveal the need for a rearrangement of the use of existing equipment. In our larger institutions, with their subdivisions into departments, there may be considerable duplication of equipment, while some may be found which is seldom used.

All will realize that if our institutions are to do satisfactory work there must be constant improvement and additions to equipment; however, it may be necessary to have control over expenditures for this purpose so as to make equitable distribution of funds for equipment to the several departments and divisions of the institution. This control must be exercised with due understanding of, and sympathy for, the instructional and research activities of the institution. The temporary policy of eliminating entirely the purchase of equipment, as has been necessary in some colleges, can not continue over a long period of time.

What is true of educational equipment for laboratory and other teaching units is equally true with reference to the library. The curtailment in the purchase of books during the past few years will seriously hamper the work of our colleges and universities if continued over a long period. The needs of the library, as well as the teaching and research units, must be considered carefully in any study of the economical operation of our institutions.

Likewise, the purchase, storage and use of supplies through well-arranged and well-managed stockrooms may prove economical in institutions which have not already centralized and systematized the handling of supplies.

VII

During the early years of the depression, faculties were kept intact as far as possible by dropping the younger members who were on annual appointment and by not filling vacancies. Such a procedure, while the most desirable from a humane point of view, will eventually bring about stagnation in the faculty. It is an exceedingly slow process to build up a high-grade faculty—something which the average layman may not realize—and this fact makes it important that the institutions look at this problem from a long-range point of view. The economies which may be effected by limiting the scope of the institution, by curtailing courses and curricula, as well as other economies, should have as their goal the strengthening of the faculty. Salaries of faculty members should be kept as high as is possible in order to maintain the quality and stability of the faculty and also to attract to the teaching profession young persons of ability. It may be far better to increase the size of classes within workable limits and readjust laboratory periods than to lower the quality of the faculty.

VIII

The usual organization of our colleges and universities into departments of instruction and the grouping of these departments into schools and colleges has probably led to duplication not only in equipment but also in courses and curricula. In order to remedy defects in this matter, some institutions are grouping departments of instruction into divisions of related subject-matter. This divisional arrangement is comparatively simple in the traditional college, in which the departments of instruction are all administered by a single dean. In the larger universities this grouping is somewhat difficult if lines of authority of the departments of instruction are to be maintained. Various solutions have been suggested and it may be that committees on curricula in which the various schools and colleges and departments concerned are represented may serve as a means of arranging the subject-matter of courses in such a manner as to avoid duplication as far as may be possible. This new plan of divisional organization has been put into effect in some of our larger institutions, of which we may give as an example the four divisions of biological sciences, physical sciences, humanities, and social sciences in the new organization plan of the University of Chicago.

IX

That the administration of our larger universities is a matter of concern is illustrated by the fact that in several institutions plans for reorganization have been under consideration during the past few years. These plans have been brought about by the realization that our institutions have expanded beyond their administrative organization. In some institutions temporary provision has been made by the addition of administrative officers to handle new activities without a complete study of the entire administrative machinery. As a result there are perhaps few institutions of large size in which improvements could not be made. What is true of the large universities may also be true in the small colleges, and it is very important, as part of any study leading towards the economical administration of our institutions, to make an investigation of the entire administrative organization. Is there duplication between the offices of the academic deans, the deans of men and deans of women, the registrar, the alumni office and the placement bureau? Is there clear understanding as to the relation of athletics to the faculty and the business department? Are the university press and other publishing agencies coordinated with other divisions of the institution? Is the business organization functioning throughout the institution or are there a number of independent business organizations without definite responsibility for business matters? Is the institution administered through committees, especially in the faculty organization, where administrative officers would be more satisfactory? On the other hand, do administrative officers fail to consult committees when such consultation and advice would be expedient? The committee administration of one large university, at least, has been subjected to a thorough investigation with the recommendation that the number of committees be reduced and administrative work done previously by committees be assigned to administrative officers. A modern university or college is not a Sunday-School picnic but a going concern which should be handled by officers authorized to make final decisions within certain limits. It is a strange anomaly that scientific institutions may be decidedly unscientific in administration.

X

The business department of every well-managed institution must be the center of the administration of business affairs if the institution is to function properly. The care of funds and investment thereof, the collection of current income, accounting, purchasing, disbursements, the operation of dormitories and the operation and maintenance of buildings and grounds, as well as the supervision of new construction and any other business activities, are items of considerable magnitude in most of our institutions, and in proportion to its size are equally important in the small college. Methods of business management and accounting in our universities and colleges have undergone decided improvement during the past twenty-five years but there are still many institutions in which modern methods have not been introduced.

The investment management is a vital part of every endowed institution, and whether investments are made directly by the institution, through its investment committee or through the agency of trust companies, the business organization of the institution should be competent to advise in regard to this matter. In the routine administration of the business of the institution a competent business manager should be the right hand of the president in business affairs, and if there is complete understanding between the two, the business manager should be the clerical assistant of the president in the preparation and administration of the budget, as well as in ordinary routine business matters. No institution should pass through a period of depression without an efficient business department.

XI

There is a direct relation between the expansion of plant and the use of general funds of the institutions for the operation and maintenance of buildings and grounds. Monumental buildings, expensive to maintain and operate, have in some instances become a serious drain upon the resources of the institution. Wise administrators have endeavored to remedy this matter to some degree at least by securing endowment for the maintenance of new buildings. During a period when there must be retrenchment in operating expenses, it seems important to watch carefully every expansion program, whether it be in buildings and lands or in educational matters.

Before projecting new buildings, a study of existing buildings should be made. A survey of the use of buildings will frequently surprise administrators by demonstrating concretely that the most economical use is not being made of the physical plant. It may become necessary as a measure of economy to readjust class and laboratory periods so as to use buildings to a greater extent instead of expending funds for new buildings.

XII

The temporary program suggested at the beginning of this article mentioned the possibility of postponing repairs to buildings except those absolutely necessary to keep buildings from deteriorating and of reducing the expense of maintaining and operating buildings to a minimum. This might do for a period of three or four years but not for a longer time. The time will come when extensive repairs will have to be made unless the plant is kept continually in good condition. As a necessary move of economy, administrators should study carefully what must be done to keep buildings from deteriorating, and all painting, roof repairs and other items which were postponed during the early days of the depression must receive attention. It seems wise to prepare a schedule which would take care of the necessary plant maintenance items from year to year over a period of five years or more rather than hastily to curtail all repairs, without carefully considering the consequences, in order to bring the institution through a temporary emergency.

XIII

Thus far, attention has been given primarily to the matter of keeping expenses of institutions within the income, but of equal importance is the matter of keeping the cost of education within the ability of the student to pay. This must be considered in fixing the amount of tuition. The ability to pay will vary in different localities and in different institutions, depending upon its constituency and general financial support. The amount of tuition which should be reasonable has been a matter of discussion for a number of years, and privately endowed colleges and universities have sometimes suggested that the student should pay his proportion of the direct cost of education, that is, the salary of the faculty and other instructional costs, and that the remaining expenditures be met from endowment fund income, gifts and other sources. On the other hand, tuition fees in publicly supported institutions have been governed to a large extent by the policy of the institution in offering to citizens an education within the reach of all who are willing and able to benefit therefrom. As a rule, publicly supported institutions have not attempted to fix tuition fees in relation to the cost of education, but their fees vary greatly in different states and in some cases have been fixed at a figure roughly midway between free tuition and the high tuition of corresponding privately endowed institutions.

It is evident that if higher education is to be made available to those who can benefit most from such education, either the fees must be kept low or there must be liberal assistance in the form of scholarships to those of limited means. Tuition fees, then, must be fixed in such a way as to meet two desiderata, to provide as much income as may be possible for operating expenses and at the same time to open the facilities of the institution to the class of students it desires.

But the cost of tuition is only a part of the expenses of the student, because living expenses, as a rule, exceed the usual tuition charges. It is therefore important to consider in connection with tuition the administration of scholarship and aid funds and student loan funds, as well as the living expenses of students.

XIV

With the increasing cost of tuition at many of our institutions and the avowed policy in many to require the student to pay the direct cost of instruction, the need for scholarships becomes increasingly pressing. In reality, the modern scholarship award has become a means for assisting needy students in gaining an education and, if properly administered, it should be a distinct benefit in enabling students of all classes to attend our better grade of colleges and universities. There is then need for increased scholarship funds in most institutions to meet the present emergency of our citizens, and also as part of a permanent program in extending the benefits of education. However, the provision of scholarships will never be an entirely successful method of meeting the cases of needy students, as no machinery has yet been devised which will make scholarship awards to all those who can benefit most from what any institution offers. It seems that in our scheme of education, there should always be some institutions with low tuition which would be available to those who are unable to pay higher rates or who are unsuccessful in securing scholarship awards.

Student loan funds should also be available, and if these funds are carefully administered, they will assist in educating students in perpetuity. The student loan fund has the advantage of making the student pay for his own education, but it is doubtful if students loan funds alone will enable all worthy students to secure the benefits of higher education. It seems to me that a combination of scholarship and student aid funds, with ample loan funds, would be the best method of assisting needy students to get an education. There should also be centralized administration of these funds so as to avoid duplication in awards.

XV

To reduce the living expenses of students, including the cost of books, laboratory material and other incidental expenses, is just as important as the reduction of tuition in determining the cost of education to the student. Institutions operating dormitories and dining halls may help to solve this problem by operating such units at the lowest cost possible for good service. Some institutions are operating cooperative dormitories in which the students do the major part of the housekeeping, thereby reducing costs. In others, cooperative boarding clubs have been organized which have reduced board to a minimum. Cooperative purchasing in fraternities, sororities and boarding clubs is not uncommon, and this, too, assists in reducing living expenses. Cooperative book and supply stores have in some cases been of great value in keeping down the personal expenses of students. It seems then that institutions may do a distinct service to students by encouraging and directing cooperative efforts which tend to make it easier for them to get an education and by operating institution-managed dormitories and dining halls with the distinct purpose of furnishing students with high-grade service at low cost.

XVI

In the foregoing discussion an attempt has been made to suggest items to be considered in a thorough-going study of higher education in an effort to operate within income, and at the same time keep tuition and living expenses within the ability of the students to pay. Nothing has been said about limiting attendance. This question is receiving serious consideration in many places and probably will become a fixed policy in some privately endowed colleges and universities and, to some extent, in those supported from public funds.

It is hoped that what has been said will be of interest to the layman as well as the professional educator. All who are interested in the advancement of higher education know that we can not continue operating to the highest efficiency during a period of decreased income without a definite policy in mind. At the same time, persons with financial means, as well as legislative bodies, can do nothing better than to give liberally to our colleges and universities to keep them going until general financial conditions are improved, because even with increased economy in operation there will be few institutions which could not use to advantage additional income for operation.

SOCIAL DYNAMICS AND THE YOUNG CRIMINAL[1]

By Dr. LAWRENCE A. AVERILL
HEAD OF THE DEPARTMENT OF PSYCHOLOGY, STATE TEACHERS COLLEGE, WORCESTER, MASS.

TWENTY years and more ago, the mode criminal was an adult individual somewhere in the vicinity of middle life. Increasingly during the past two decades his age has been reduced until at the present time it is under thirty years. This is bad enough, but it is even worse when one studies the crime statistics and discovers hundreds of thousands of persons entering careers of crime while still in their 'teens. Arrests for crime committed between the ages of fifteen and twenty years are distinctly on the increase, and at the still lower juvenile level some two hundred thousand boys and girls pass through the juvenile courts of the United States each twelvemonth. There is no more disconcerting series of sociological facts confronting the American public to-day than this steady penetration downward of criminal behavior into the ranks of middle and late adolescence. It appears that successful identification with crime is coming more and more to be conditioned upon the youthfulness of the participant. A career of crime in these days of rapid-fire guns, of swift automobiles for pursuit and escape, of radio and police teletype, and the like, requires a quickness of reaction, a keenness of sense-organ and a strength and agility of muscle that are possessed typically only by younger persons. The elderly or middle-aged crook is by way of becoming extinct, forced out of business by the advance in the technique of his art, on the one hand, and on the other by the advance in the efficiency of police methods and intelligence. Modern crime demands in its perpetrators youth, coolness, daring, cleverness, precision and a colossal cold-bloodedness.

In this paper one can but refer briefly to some of the less frequently discussed but none the less insidious psychological causatives inherent in the American social scene which make attractive to the young person adventurings in crime and waywardness.

Prominent among the factors that lead thus into delinquency and crime is a lost loyalty to home. It matters little whether the home be a broken home or whether it masquerades as a sickly substitute—and America to-day has far too many of both types—when the steadying influence of his home is withdrawn or has never been experienced, the young person feels a sense of incompleteness, of loneliness, of recklessness and ruthlessness that is in more or less direct ratio to the degree of insecurity that characterizes the home situation. In such a state of mental conflict, he is ready for any sort of adventure that will supply lethal substitute experience for the emotional satisfactions which his environment can not afford. Delinquency offers such adventure in plenty. The pleasurableness which lawlessness affords is an agreeable antidote to the unhappiness and loneliness which the insecure young person has known. The excitement and exhilaration of crime bring with them a kind of vicarious satisfaction and a degree of happiness that go far to make up for the incompleteness of the family life. The dangers of detection supply a thousand thrills; the planning and executing of escapades sharpen the wits and fill the hours with

[1] Address delivered before the Section of Psychology of the American Association for the Advancement of Science, Harvard University, December 30, 1933.

dash and glow; the comradeship in crime offers a new loyalty and a new security. The community of planning, storing, sharing, keeping secret, etc., yields the young delinquent some feeling of identification with the welfare and life of others, some flattering notion of his own importance and indispensableness to the gang group. The road to crime, in other words, for legions of young persons is a road into which they flee in order to drown their unhappiness.

Even though the home experiences of young persons are not made unpleasant through conflicts and insecurities, there is too frequently a drabness and commonplaceness about them which contrasts sharply with the tinseled world that beckons scintillatingly beyond the home. The heart of the young person beats synchronously with the restless heave and throw of that strangely inscrutable thing we call life. The lure of the bright lights and the gay throngs can not be resisted by young persons whose organisms are a-tingle with their pulse and throb. To listen to meal-time after meal-time discussions of the hardness of the day's work, the meanness of employers, the inhumanness of bosses and foremen, the sheer drudgery of existence, the impossibility of making both ends meet; to be in intimate contact with tired mothers, worn-out fathers and quarreling younger children; to be chided with well-meant diatribes upon the conduct of young people and the certainty of no good end coming to most of them; to see always the same faces, hear the same voices, participate in the same small talk—these are unbearable, and impel many a youth to seek distraction and forgetfulness elsewhere. Inevitably many of them are swept into delinquency. Some of them run away from home to join the vast throng of migrant juvenile wanderers, now estimated to be two hundred thousand strong; some of them seek the great cities with their lights and gaiety; some follow will-o'-the-wisp ideas of becoming actors and actresses; some of them are absorbed by gangdom and the underworld; some ask for nothing more harmful at the outset than adventure, mystery, enchantment, companionship and understanding that are denied them in their homes. Too often the foot of the rainbow holds for them not the pot of gold of their dreams but sadness, disillusionment and delinquency.

The following brief epitomization of one of my case-studies must suffice to illustrate the home hazard as a causative of crime adventurings. Arni, now 20 years of age, never had any real childhood. Being the oldest girl in a family of nine children, she had the responsibility of caring for the younger ones as well as doing most of the housework. Her mother is notoriously lazy and has been content to allow the major care of the entire family to rest upon the frail shoulders of Arni. Throughout her grammar-school days, Arni was compelled to go home immediately after school to help with the family washing or the ironing or to scrub the floors or prepare the meal or do other housework which the mother ought in all conscience to have done herself. Rarely did the child ever finish her tasks before nine or ten o'clock at night. Leaving school at the legal age, Arni became still more the drudge of the family. The only way in which she could satisfy her craving for sociability and companionship lay in making late evening sorties from her home to join some band of revellers. As was to be feared, she got in with the wrong crowd, and in consternation her mother made the discovery that at sixteen Arni had been indiscreet. In a fit of fury, she had the girl placed in a reformatory. After the expiration of her term, Arni and her baby were dismissed from the institution to face life alone. Arni secured employment as a mother's helper in a home where there was neither solicitude nor care for her welfare. Again she drifted into fast company, and a second time she became a mother. Arni now has a new position in domestic service, and is trying to care as well as she can for her two little babies. To the social worker she expresses deep concern for their welfare, and appears to have learned a harsh lesson from all that she has suffered.

The passion for adventure that will bring one into the limelight is another of the dominant psychological urges that drives many young persons into careers of crime. Indeed there is good evidence that much of the crime committed by adult lawbreakers, if it is not actually inspired by the thirst for public limelight, is at least by reason of the notoriety achieved made far more attractive and satisfying to its perpetrators. Public officials and the public press too often cater directly to this urge to crime by the unfortunate publicity which they give it whenever and wherever it occurs. It is inevitable that the secrecy with which one must surround his wrongdoings, the stealth and cleverness with which he must prosecute them and the thrill he experiences from finding his escapades heralded in bold headlines, all combine to give to crime and delinquency to those persons, young or old, who devote their energies to asocial forms of conduct something of the thrill of a fascinating game of wits. The elimination of its heroic aspect is likely to become one of the most cogent preventives of crime. As it is, the conduct of criminal investigation degenerates frequently into little more than an attempt by reporters to discover some feature in a crime that will make good publicity material. The perpetrator smiles in his beard and enjoys the whole vaudeville hugely.

The notoriety that attaches in the popular mind to crime is extremely flattering to those who gamble in it. Any one who has ever been a spectator at a trial to which wide publicity has been given, and has noted how milling crowds of curious and thrill-seeking human beings will pack courtrooms and court-premises, and how not infrequently the culprit under indictment, especially if he be young—or if *she* be young—plays the rôle of hero or heroine, can appreciate the strong urge to delinquency a young person may feel as he plays with the idea. There have been not a few instances in the recent history of our American courts when half-hysterical spectators have forced their way to the prisoner's side and have embraced and wept over some culprit until he himself no doubt was half persuaded that he was being made an innocent martyr to the harsh cause of justice. This turning of the spotlight of human attention and interest upon a delinquent youth is hardly to be thought of as a deterrent to further misdoings.

The appeal of easy wealth and acquisition becomes for many young persons the starting-point whence they gravitate into crime. The multiplication in the modern age of opportunities to buy and spend has necessitated new attention to the gaining of money with which to buy the desired commodities and pleasures. The lure of the show-window and of the market-place and of the emporium of pleasure is a powerful one, especially for the adolescent individual. The circumstance is made worse by the rather wide-spread opulence which, even in times of financial stress, he encounters all about him, intensifying in him the passion to possess for himself. Much of this opulence is ill-gotten. The young person reads of lotteries that yield the "lucky" mints of money; he hears of gaming and gambling which are reputed to enrich one in a single evening; he sees the spectacle of "playing the market" and "cleaning up" in some deal; he sees accounts of hold-ups and robberies and kidnapings and "rackets" which net their perpetrators fabulous amounts; he gets wind of illicit businesses which flourish when legitimate ones go to the wall; he listens to embittered conversations alleging the dishonest or questionable methods by which great fortunes are builded, and the impossibility of an honest man's getting anything more than a bare living—in short, on every hand he is met with facts, conditions or allegations which he interprets as making wealth extremely desirable and the methods of its acquisition of negligible importance. We seem, in truth, to have plunged headforemost into an age that is ruthless in the means which it employs to acquire the things it wants. To work for what one gets, at a reasonable rate of return for effort expended, is by way of becoming unpopular. To "work" somebody or something for it is far easier. The adolescent, typically not yet inured or habituated to work, and impatient of slow and steady methods of progress, readily allies himself with those who aspire to get something for nothing, or for very little. Consequently, one finds a wide trail of crime and waywardness which its youthful blazers mark out in response to a strong urge for easy acquisition and for possession without earning.

Ross, 16 years of age, has been recently committed to a reformatory. For several months a so-called "bedroom burglar" had been entering homes in widely scattered sections of the city in which Ross lived. Small articles of jewelry appeared to be his particular specialty. Some of these were of only modest worth; others were quite valuable. The police suspected that the same person was responsible for all the breaks, and they haunted the pawnshops in the hope that they might apprehend him. Finally, after successfully eluding them for weeks, Ross was caught in the act of disposing of a valuable ring. Everybody was amazed that the burglar turned out to be Ross, for his family was an eminently respectable one, and Ross himself had never for a moment been suspected of any form of delinquent behavior. It developed in the course of the investigation of the lad's burglaries that he had been activated principally by the idea of having a great deal more money for a good time than he was given by his parents or than he could earn for himself. The relative ease of burglarizing appealed to him, as did also the readiness with which small articles of jewelry could be safely disposed of. The adroitness with which he spread out his sales among a considerable number of receivers of stolen goods and his naiveté in raising his loans afforded him complete protection for weeks. His popularity with his set during this time was very great, due to his constant supply of ready money and his generosity in spending it, no one having the slightest suspicion that he was getting it dishonestly.

In an age of gangster domination, there is scarcely any impetus to delinquency stronger than that afforded by the attractions of gang life. The underworld in our great cities, and to a degree in our lesser, is controlled by gangs composed of both sexes and all ages. The turnover in personnel of the gang is recruited from the ranks of youth who have themselves had some experience of crime through membership in juvenile gangs. Springing up like mushroom growth, lacking good leadership and offering a broad field of expression for the natural spirit of adventure that characterizes youth, many of these juvenile gangs are ready breeding grounds for those vicious and asocial traits that culminate in the professional gangster and racketeer. The evil influences of the unsupervised juvenile gang have been among the most powerful factors in the production of delinquents and criminals and in the feeding of underworld gangs and dives.

The case of Anthony is in point. Anthony, at the age of 19, was sentenced to a term of 20 years in state's prison. He was the leading influence in a vicious gang. His family, immigrants in the second generation, has good intelligence and is respectable and law-abiding. His brothers and sisters have clear records. Anthony was attracted to a gang of young fellows, of whom, because he was more bold and daring, he became shortly the leader. Though held under police suspicion for some time, Anthony's gang got into no difficulty until the perpetration of the crime for which their leader was committed to the penitentiary. Armed to the teeth, Anthony and his pals, on a stormy night, held up a motorist on the state highway, robbed and bound him and then made off in his automobile. Another motorist discovered the crime and spread the alarm. The police were soon on the trail of the speeding automobile, and after pursuing it for more than a hundred miles finally overtook it. The young bandits attempted to defend themselves with their guns, and in the battle which ensued one of them was killed outright, while a policeman was shot and severely wounded. Anthony was captured, recognized as the leader and "brains" of the gang, tried and sentenced to half a life-time in prison.

The blatant exaggeration of sex in an age which is peculiarly sex-ridden incites large numbers of young persons to delinquency and immorality. The sex *motif* plays a far more prominent rôle in the drama of human life than it can safely be permitted to do. Our moving-pictures fairly reek with sex, holding up to ridicule many of those notions regarding it which centuries of racial and social experience have taught to be essential. Much of our modern literature is permeated through and through with sex. Our advertisements, our news-stand literature, our divorce scandals, our adult looseness and promiscuousness all tend to throw sex into distorted perspective.

There is no reliable evidence of the extent of illicit sex indulgence among adolescents. There never has been. Alarmists and cynics like to insist that high-school boys and girls are consumed with it. They point out that the opportunities for sex experience and the ease with which its biological consequences may be prevented were never so glaring. More sanguine observers point to the innumerable physical outlets which young people to-day have for their energies, and discount the notion that illicit practises are any more common than they ever were. Certainly the saner attitude toward the whole matter of sex which is prevalent among parents and educators to-day has served to remove much of the mystery that has always enshrouded it, and has raised it from the limbo of the evil and the vile to which it has all too commonly been assigned in past generations. Still, the dangers are undeniably disconcerting. Only a relatively small number of young persons ever receive any planned or reliable sex information. Some of them learn a little from their parents; some mislearn more from their comrades; some "pick up" all they ever know at second-hand from the gossip of the street corner and the gutter. Few receive any satisfying and elevating information at the time when they critically need it. Consequently, too many yield ignorantly to the impulse and learn only in bitterness and humiliation afterwards. Curiosity to examine the forbidden and the mysterious animates some; abnormal arousal by contact with the salacious and the pornographic instigates others; loss of control through thoughtless intimacies motivates still others. An adult generation that allows its Frankenstinian amusements and its own weaknesses, irregularities and example to imperil the welfare and the future of its youth merits the full force of that Scripture which assigns the millstone as the lesser punishment.

Marion is a young mother at 16. She

grew up in a home of good breeding and good standards. She received no sex instruction from her mother. In fact, no mention seems ever to have been made to her of this subject, save at the time of the establishment of the menses, when some carefully veiled reference was made by her mother to the fact that when she grew older she would understand how this monthly phenomenon all worked into nature's plan. Being not particularly inquisitive, Marion asked no further enlightenment. At fifteen—it appears in all ignorance and innocence—Marion permitted a young friend to become intimate with her. Shocked beyond measure, Marion reproached her mother bitterly, and was in turn bitterly reproached and forbidden continued membership in the family. In a friendly home for girls who were shortly to become mothers, Marion learned for the first time from a kindly matron the story of life. Carrying her baby bravely with her, Marion went back into the community, broken and humiliated. Whom shall one blame: Marion, her mother or the age? And what is to prevent *ad infinitum* repetition of tragedies like Marion's?

In fine, what sociological or psychological preventives of any of the excursions of the adolescent into delinquency and crime are distinguishable? Without hazarding a final answer to this baffling question, one may at least draw from the evidence certain significant conclusions, among which are the following:

(1) Prevention of the enormous social wastage which is seeping off into delinquency and juvenile crime must to a considerable degree be conditioned upon universal education for parenthood, guidance for leisure time activities, training in home-making, censorship or supervision of "movies" and books, provision of adequate playgrounds and neighborhood enterprises and the general reorganization of the community for adolescent welfare. Few of these important phases of education have been yet even envisaged by our American communities.

(2) A considerable amount of the motivation to crime will be removed when press and police officials learn to grant to crime in general a minimum of publicity, and to remove from about the head of the felon that halo of distinction with which modern court and journalistic procedures tend to invest him.

(3) For a philosophy of life and conduct which postulates a ruthless acquisitiveness and a devil-may-care individualism, there is extremely pressing need of a substitute philosophy which will restore to the minds of those grown up and those growing up, alike, a sense of the value—even of the sanctity—of honest work and honest effort, and of the extreme fallacy of the doctrine which encourages one to enjoy before he has earned.

(4) The continuing existence of the gangster and the racketeer not only preys upon legitimate business and terrorizes our citizenry, but—and far more disastrous ultimately than these things—it is diverting the energies and the ambitions of too many adolescents from constructive young citizenship into the labyrinthine channels of crime.

(5) The flagrant appeal to sex which is being made by our amusements and our miscalled literature to-day may conceivably yet be our moral and spiritual and perchance even our social and racial undoing. Human experience has never yet subverted the fundamental doctrines of the Pentateuch, and there is no trustworthy evidence in modern biological or sociological science that the basal mores can be flouted with impunity by a people destined for survival.

EDUCATIONAL EVENTS

TEACHERS' SALARY CUTS IN ENGLAND

THE London *Times* reports that letters from the Prime Minister and the President of the Board of Education on the subject of the restoration of salary cuts were considered at a recent meeting of the executives of the National Union of Teachers. Both these communications were in reply to a letter sent by the union to Mr. Macdonald, in which a hope was expressed that the Government looked on the remission to be given this year as an instalment, and as constituting promise that complete relief will be afforded those who suffered in 1931 before concessions of other kinds are granted in future budgets. The Prime Minister wrote:

None of my colleagues approached the problem of "cuts" because they were forced to do it, nor did they do so in a grudging way. The government had to call for a general sacrifice in order to prevent the financial foundations of the state being shattered, and every one of us regretted that the necessity to do so should have arisen and determined that, when circumstances arose to permit of restitution, restitution would be made. The size of the balance on the right side in last year's income and expenditure must not mislead you; but even that balance was inadequate for complete restoration. We must see what another year will bring forth, and that will depend upon some uncertain influences of an international, and not national, character. The pledges which we gave, much less to the public than to ourselves, as to what our action should be if we were successful in restoring trade we still impose upon ourselves. All representations, especially when made so fairly and reasonably as you have made yours, you can depend will be most sympathetically considered.

Lord Halifax, the president of the Board of Education, to whom the letter from the National Union of Teachers was shown, sent a reply in addition to that of Mr. Macdonald, because in view of "the very temperate and reasoned tone" of the letter he was reluctant to do no more than send a bare acknowledgment. He wrote:

Your executive does not repeat the suggestions of discriminatory treatment or unfulfilled assurances which have emanated from less responsible quarters, and I need not, therefore, say more than that the measure of relief given to teachers was as great as was consistent with parity of treatment of the various classes affected by the emergency measures of 1931.

I can quite understand that many of the teachers represented by your union would have preferred relief in income-tax allowances to the reduction in the standard rate of income-tax. You are familiar with the reasons which the chancellor adduced in opening his budget for the course which he decided to take; but, apart from those reasons, I am not sure that, taking a long view, the reduction this year in the standard rate may not be found ultimately more advantageous to the teachers than any relief in allowances, since the stimulus which it is hoped that that reduction will give to the expansion of trade and employment should enhance the possibility of giving further relief in the future to those classes (including teachers) which suffered from the emergency measures of 1931.

Your executive can rest assured that it will always be my concern to see that the teaching profession receives a full measure of consideration and justice in relation to other classes of the community.

UNDERGRADUATE SCHOLARSHIPS AT YALE UNIVERSITY

THE corporation of Yale University at a recent meeting enacted modifications of the scholastic qualifications for undergraduate scholarship aid. Heretofore the requirements for this privilege have been defined in terms of students' general average, which has resulted in some inequalities as among different classes or schools. In order to place these standards on a more uniformly comparable basis for all undergraduates, they will henceforth be expressed in terms of students' relative standing within their respective classes instead of on the basis of any particular grade.

The new regulations are as follows:

1. That qualifications for a so-called A grade tuition scholarship (carrying a stipend of $250 gift and $300 loan) be changed from the present basis of a minimum average of 85 (on a scale of 100) to standing in the upper tenth of a student's respective class.

2. That scholastic qualifications for a regular B grade scholarship (bearing a stipend of $150 gift and $300 loan money—full tuition) be changed from a minimum scholastic average of 75 to relative standing not below the middle of a student's respective class.

3. That students ranking somewhat below average (but not below the third quarter) of their respective classes be considered eligible for a full loan grant covering their tuition (analogous to the awards now made some students with a general average below 75 (or C+), but not below 70 (or C).

Up to this time 831 applications have been filed with the Bureau of Appointments for next year's scholarships by members of the classes of 1935, 1936 and 1937. The number of awards available to members of these classes next year is about 500. As these figures indicate, competition is so keen that not even all of these meeting the new standards of qualification will receive grants. However, it was in view of this general situation and the great demand for financial assistance that it was considered fairer to all applicants to establish the new bases of formal scholarship qualifications, so that each student will compete with his own class as a unit, instead of seeking a definite numerical average which may not represent the same high calibre of achievement in all classes.

LEAVES OF ABSENCE FOR RESEARCH WORK AT HARVARD UNIVERSITY

ASSISTANT professors and instructors at Harvard University are given greater opportunity for research work through rules voted this week by the Harvard Corporation. Assistant professors, who previously had to wait six years after appointment to that rank in order to obtain leave of absence for research, may now, as a special privilege, be granted leave, with salary, for important projects of research three years after such appointment. Instructors, who previously were granted no leave of absence for research, will now be given leave for research during their third or subsequent year of service in that grade, if, in the opinion of the President and Dean of the Faculty of Arts and Sciences, the nature of their research work warrants such leave.

President Conant said in his annual report that faculty members should be given "sufficient time for writing and investigation; a satisfactory balance must be struck between teaching and research." He urged that "our teachers must be scholars who are extending the frontiers of knowledge in every direction."

The new rules are:

1. Leave of absence for a half-year with full salary may be granted to assistant professors in their first term and to full-time instructors on three-year appointments or during their third or subsequent year of service in that grade, provided that they are engaged in important projects of research which would be furthered by such leave.

2. An individual who has been granted leave of absence for purposes of research will not again become eligible for such leave until two full years of residence in the grades of instructor or assistant professor have intervened.

3. In case leave of absence for purposes of research is granted to an assistant professor, his eligibility for subsequent sabbatical leave of absence will be determined by his years of residence following his leave of absence for purposes of research, and his years of residence prior to his leave of absence for purposes of research will not be counted in determining his eligibility for sabbatical leave.

4. Application for leave of absence for purposes of research may be made to the dean of the Faculty of Arts and Sciences and will be acted upon by the president and the dean of the Faculty of Arts and Sciences.

President Conant said in his report:

Learning must be advanced as well as perpetuated. Indeed, in the last analysis it is only by advancing learning that it is possible to perpetuate it. When knowledge ceases to expand and develop, it becomes devitalized, degraded, and a matter of little importance to the present or future. The community loses interest, and the youth of the country responds to other challenges. Able young men enlist in an enterprise only if they are persuaded that they, too, may contribute by creative work. A zest for intellectual adventure should be the characteristic of every university. In the future as in the past, our teachers must be scholars who are extending the frontiers of knowledge in every direction. I hope there will never be a separation of our faculty into those who teach and those who carry on creative work. No line should be drawn between teaching and research. Our strength in the past has lain in the fact that the spirit of scholarship has pervaded our teaching and our scholars have seen the importance of perpetuating the ideals of scholarship as well as advancing knowledge in their own specialty.

A NEW SCHOOL OF PUBLIC AFFAIRS AT THE AMERICAN UNIVERSITY

PLANS have been completed for the inauguration of a new School of Public Affairs at the American University, Washington, D. C.

The first session of the school will be held from June 25 to August 17 and will be conducted as an Institute for the Study of the Emergency Agencies of the Government. Dr. Arnold Bennett Hall, director of the Institute of Government Research of the Brookings Institution, will serve as advisory counsel and Dr. G. A. Graham, of the Princeton School of Public and International Affairs, will serve as visiting dean. Arthur S. Flemming, executive director of the United States Society, has been appointed director.

Establishment of the School of Public Affairs was announced at the installation of Dr. Joseph M. M. Gray as chancellor of the university on March 3. At that time President Roosevelt, who delivered the principal address, stated that he was "especially happy in the announcement of the establishment of this School of Public Affairs. I can assure you," the President continued, "of the hearty cooperation of the administration in all of its branches."

The administrative officials of the school will be assisted by five visiting professors, all experts in the field of the social sciences.

The broad problems of government underlying all the emergency agencies of the government will be emphasized. Primary attention will go to round-table discussions to be participated in by governmental administrators, legislators, members of the various governmental advisory boards and others who may not, at the present time, be actually engaged in governmental activities. In addition to these round-table discussions the work of the institute will be so organized that students will have every possible opportunity actually to see the government in action.

The purpose of the institute is to provide the nation with a laboratory for the social sciences, available to students of government everywhere, and conducted under the best possible auspices.

Juniors and seniors enrolled in accredited institutions of higher learning and majoring in the social sciences; graduate students in the same field; social science instructors in both high schools and colleges, and persons not actively engaged in academic work but desirous of enlarging their fund of information on current developments, who have pursued a certain amount of work in the social sciences, have been invited to participate in the program. It is possible for students to earn six semester hours' credit as a result of the eight weeks' work.

THE TRAINING OF COUNSELORS AT THE SUMMER SESSION OF THE UNIVERSITY OF PITTSBURGH

COURSES specifically designed to prepare persons for counseling positions in schools and social agencies are being given during each of three terms of the 1934 University of Pittsburgh Summer Session.

A wide variety of offerings is to be found in the session, which runs from July 2 to August 10. Dr. P. W. Hutson will give a course in secondary school counseling, and Dr. A. M. Goldberger a course in materials for occupational counseling. An allied course in Student Personnel Administration will be given by Miss Thyrsa Amos, dean of women. Dr. Alfred G. Dietze, of the department of psychology, will offer four courses of interest to counselors. These are: mental adjustments, problems of personality, superior children and abnormal psychology.

In the department of sociology three courses are being offered. Dr. David B. Rogers will give a course on the urban community and one on community organization, and Dr. M. C. Elmer will teach methods of social investigation.

In the pre-two-weeks session, from June 18 to June 29, courses on the guidance function will be offered by Dr. Hutson, and on major social problems by Dr. Walter A. Lunden. The post-two-weeks session, from August 13 to August 24, will give students an opportunity to take a course in social control under Dr. V. C. Wright.

Students who are interested in qualifying for a counselor's certificate in Pennsylvania may take the following courses: Education 210, The Guidance Function in Education, during the pre-two-weeks session; Education 426, Materials for Occupational Counseling; Education 427, Secondary School Counseling, and Psychology

164, Superior Children, during the six-weeks session from July 2 to August 10. Such a program would enable the student to obtain eight of the eighteen credits required. In addition, other allied courses could be studied which would give the counselor or prospective counselor a wide and varied background for his work.

PROGRAM OF ADULT EDUCATION AT TEACHERS COLLEGE, COLUMBIA UNIVERSITY

AN advanced program in adult education, covering a wide range of subjects, has been inaugurated at Teachers College, Columbia University, under the direction of Dr. Edmund de S. Brunner, professor of education and head of the adult education department.

Coordinating the college with the community, realistic courses in adult education have been introduced, with a view towards broadening the entire adult field. Thirty individual projects are under way, conducted largely by graduate students working for their doctor of philosophy degrees. The projects cover the whole field of adult education, taking into account various phases of present-day life.

Dr. Brunner cites the growing importance of adult training in the new era coming under the New Deal as significant. More leisure time and more intelligent treatment of increasingly complex legislative problems demand a far greater degree of understanding by the citizens of this country. Hence it is essential to get a complete picture of the adult education field, the educator points out.

Dr. Lyman Bryson, formerly of the University of California, and director of the California Association for Adult Education, has been appointed visiting professor, as part of the general program to enlarge the adult field. While at Teachers College he will conduct a course in "Discussion Methods in Adult Education." Projects now under way by graduate students include the following:

1. *Determination of a Minimum Area for a Rural Library System,* carried on by Elsa Berner, a librarian, with the aid of a special seminar group and a number of leaders in library work, education and allied fields.

2. *The Library-adult-elementary Education Study.* This project is in charge of Mrs. Elizabeth C. Morriss, of the staff, and Miss Edna Phillips, a librarian, who have secured the assistance of a number of CWS workers.

3. *The Educational Possibilities of the NRA Organization in Mount Vernon, N. Y.* Christian E. Burckel, director of the local NRA, is in charge of this study, with the assistance of eight investigators and several office workers.

4. *The Workers' Education Project,* made by Halo Chadwick, of the staff of the Affiliated Schools for Workers. It includes observation of existing workers' education groups and the setting up of new groups.

5. *Criteria for Building or Selecting Materials for Adult Study Groups.* This study centers about the methods of presentation of materials for study.

6. *A Project in Parent Education,* being undertaken in an underprivileged area in the Bronx, in which are three public schools in close proximity, was selected for an experiment to discover new means of interesting parents in the school.

7. *The Utilization of a Residence for Young Working Women—the Alma Mathews House—as an Educational Center.* This project was conceived by Miss Margaret Forsyth. The property is owned by a denominational missionary society, the managers of which are cooperating in the project.

8. *A Study of the Uses of Music in Adult Education* aims to discover what type of organization will satisfy the needs of musical interests in an adult community.

9. *An Experiment in Informal Education among Young Industrial Women Workers* will be carried out by Miss Frances Parry.

CONFERENCE ON THE PROBLEM OF UNEMPLOYED YOUNG PEOPLE

A SPECIAL conference was held in Washington on June 1 and 2 to discuss possible plans to bridge the gap between school and employment. Dr. George F. Zook, Commissioner of Education, who called the conference and who served as chairman, stated that:

> It is estimated that there are in this country at the present time about 4,000,000 young people between the ages of 14 and 18 who are not enrolled in high schools. Some are excluded from industry by code limitations. In the college age level, seven are out of college for every one in college. The fortunes of nearly 12,000,000 young men and women who are not now in school or college are at stake. Not less than 3,000,000 in the age group from 18 to 20 alone are not only out of school but out of work. This situation is bad for boys and girls and it is bad for our Nation.

Three groups of problems were considered. Those centering in employment of youth; those centering in education and guidance, and those centering in better use of leisure time.

Addresses were made by Courtenay Dinwiddie, general secretary, National Child Labor Committee, New York, on education; by Helen Heffernan, supervisor of rural and elementary education, California, on education and guidance, and by Eva Whiting White, president of the Women's Education and Industrial Union, Boston, on leisure time activities.

EDUCATIONAL NOTES AND NEWS

AT its commencement exercises on June 5, Columbia University conferred honorary degrees on three university presidents elected during the past academic year. The degree of doctor of science was conferred on Dr. James Bryant Conant, president of Harvard University, and the degree of doctor of letters on Dr. Harold Willis Dodds, president of Princeton University, and on Dr. Harry Woodburn Chase, chancellor of New York University.

THE doctorate of laws was conferred at the commencement of Syracuse University on June 4 on Dr. Livingston Farrand, president of Cornell University.

THE University of Wisconsin will confer honorary degrees upon leaders in the fields of education, engineering, music and public affairs at its eighty-first annual commencement exercises on June 18 as follows: Martha McChesney Berry, founder and director of the Berry schools for mountain boys and girls at Mount Berry, Ga.; Dr. Karl Young, professor of English at Yale University; Dr. Karl Taylor Compton, president of the Massachusetts Institute of Technology; Robert B. Goodman, director of the Subsistence Homestead division of the U. S. Department of the Interior; John Alden Carpenter, American composer, Chicago; John L. Savage, chief designing engineer of the U. S. Bureau of Reclamation, Denver, and Dr. Albert R. Mann, provost of Cornell University.

THE University of Pennsylvania will confer at its commencement exercises to be held on the morning of June 20 the degree of doctor of laws on Dr. Ralph Dorn Hetzel, president of the Pennsylvania State College, and of doctor of letters on Dr. James Noble Rule, superintendent of public instruction of the Commonwealth of Pennsylvania, and on Dr. Edwin Cornelius Broome, superintendent of schools in Philadelphia.

THE doctorate of laws will be conferred by the Ohio State University on Dr. Charles H. Lake, superintendent of the Cleveland schools, at the commencement to be held on June 11.

DR. ROBERT CLARKSON BROOKS, professor of economics at Swarthmore College, received the degrees of doctor *honoris causa* of the Faculty of Law in connection with the celebration of the centenary of the University of Berne.

THE degree of doctor of letters was conferred on May 16 by the University of Manchester on Dr. H. J. C. Grierson, professor of rhetoric and English language at the University of Edinburgh and on Dr. G. M. Trevelyan, Regius professor of modern history at the University of Cambridge.

THURSTON J. DAVIES, secretary of the Graduate Council and supervisor of sports at Princeton University, was recently elected president of Colorado College. He succeeds Dr. Charles Christopher Mierow, who has been president since 1925. Dr. Mierow for the past year has been on leave of absence and working at the American School of Classical Studies in Rome.

DR. CARMON ROSS, of Doylestown, president of the Pennsylvania State Education Association for 1934, has been appointed president of the State Teachers College at Edinboro. Dr. Ross leaves Doylestown after serving there as supervising principal for twenty-nine years. He succeeds C. C. Crawford, whose resignation as president will become effective on September 1.

THE REV. JOHN F. O'HARA, who was appointed vice-president at the University of Notre Dame last July, has become acting president to fill the term of the late Rev. Charles L. O'Donnell.

COLONEL AMOS W. W. WOODCOCK was installed as president of St. John's College,

Annapolis, at the commencement exercises on June 6.

A portrait of Dr. Marion Edwards Park, president of Bryn Mawr College, painted this spring by Charles Hopkinson, a gift of the class of 1898, was presented to the trustees of the college on June 3.

Dr. Hans Zinsser, professor of bacteriology and immunology at the Harvard Medical School, will go to the University of Paris for the second half of 1934–35 as exchange professor from Harvard University, and Dr. Jules Blache, professor of physical geography at the University of Grenoble, will be exchange professor from France at Harvard for one-half year, as yet undetermined, in 1934–35.

Dr. Eugen Rosenstock-Hussy, professor of the history of law and of German law at the University of Breslau, and Dr. Paul Kluckhohn, professor of German language and literature at the University of Tübingen, have been appointed Kuno Francke professors of German art and culture at Harvard University for next year. Dr. Rosenstock-Hussy will lecture during the first semester and Dr. Kluckhohn during the second.

Miss Helen Wood, of Newton Highlands, Massachusetts, has been appointed director of the School of Nursing at Simmons College, Boston. The appointment coincides with a reorganization of the school from a school of public health nursing to one in which emphasis is placed on the undergraduate preparation of nurses, to meet the changing demands in the professional nursing field. Work in public health nursing will be continued under the direction of Miss Marjory Stimson, who has served as acting director of the school for the past two years.

Dr. Phillip Justin Rulon, instructor in education at the Graduate School of Harvard University, has been promoted to an assistant professorship.

The commencement speaker at Park College, on May 28, was Chancellor E. H. Lindley, of the University of Kansas.

President William Mather Lewis, of Lafayette College, will deliver the address at the commencement of Blair Academy, on June 11.

Frank Bane, director of the American Public Welfare Association, will give the commencement address before the University of Oregon graduating class on June 11.

Dr. W. B. Bizzell, president of the University of Oklahoma, visited the Iowa State College on the occasion of the annual honors-day program on May 24. At the convocation he spoke on "The Quality of Learning," and at the banquet, held under the auspices of the chapter of the American Association of University Professors, he spoke on "The Changing Intellectual Climate."

Rev. Melbourn Evans Aubrey, general secretary of the Baptist Union of Great Britain and Ireland, will deliver the baccalaureate sermon at Carleton College on June 10. On June 11 the commencement address will be delivered by Dr. Phillips Endecott Osgood, rector of Emmanuel Church, Boston.

Dr. Howard McClenahan, '90, director of the Franklin Institute, Philadelphia, will make the graduation address at Centenary Junior College, Hackettstown, N. J., on June 11. The baccalaureate service will be held on June 10, at which Bishop Francis John McConnell, of New York, will preach the sermon. In the evening there will be a special vespers at which Dr. George F. Zook, U. S. Commissioner of Education, will speak.

A memorial meeting in honor of the late Dr. William H. Welch, formerly dean of the medical faculty, director of the School of Hygiene and Public Health, and professor of the history of medicine at the Johns Hopkins University, will be held in connection with the Berkeley meeting of the American Association for the Advancement of Science. The principal address will be made by Dr. Ray Lyman Wilbur, president of Stanford University and formerly dean of its medical school. Dr. Welch was president of the association in 1906.

Congressman Clarence E. Hancock, a Wesleyan alumnus, Republican representative from the thirty-fifth New York district, will join the faculty of Wesleyan University as Frank B. Weeks visiting lecturer in government for six weeks next fall.

The nomination of Professor Claudius T. Murchison, of the University of North Carolina, to be director of the Bureau of Foreign and

Domestic Commerce has been sent to the Senate by President Roosevelt. If the nomination is confirmed he will succeed Professor Willard Thorp, whose nomination was withdrawn under Senatorial pressure.

Dr. Joseph Eugene Rowe, who resigned the presidency of Clarkson College in June, 1932, and who has since that time been engaged in research in the social sciences at the Johns Hopkins University, has been appointed a member of the Board of Veterans Appeals for Maryland.

Dr. Lawrason Brown, of Saranac Lake, N. Y., was recently appointed a member of the New York State Board of Social Welfare.

Roger Shaw, foreign editor of *The Review of Reviews,* has been elected a member of the board of trustees of Rollins College.

Dr. Ernest Fisher, professor of real estate management in the School of Business Administration of the University of Michigan, has been named an administrative member of the Code Authority for the real estate brokerage industry. Professor Fisher, sole representative of the government, is one of twelve members of the Code Authority, which will control operations of the real estate brokerage industry of the country.

Dr. John M. Brewer, associate professor of education in the Harvard Graduate School of Education, has been elected president of the First Church of Christ, Scientist, succeeding Mary C. Ewing, of Brookline.

The new members of the Joint Commission on the Emergency in Education of the National Education Association and of the Department of Superintendence are President Lotus D. Coffman, of the University of Minnesota; Blanche McCarthy, National Education Association director for the state of Wisconsin and teacher at the Appleton, Wisconsin, High School, and Superintendent A. J. Stoddard, of Providence, R. I.

Dr. Julian Alvin Carroll Chandler, since 1919 president of the College of William and Mary, died on May 31 at the age of sixty-two years.

Father Charles L. O'Donnell, for six years president of Notre Dame University at South Bend, Indiana, died on June 4. He was in his fiftieth year. He was elected eleventh president of Notre Dame in 1928.

Dr. Irvah Lester Winter, professor emeritus of public speaking at Harvard College since 1925, died on May 30, at the age of seventy-eight years.

Dr. Prosser Hall Frye, professor of English at the University of Nebraska, with which he had been connected since 1896, died on June 3, at the age of sixty-seven years.

The National Commander of the American Legion has announced that the National Fidac Jury of Award will consist of: Gen. L. R. Gignilliat, superintendent, Culver Military Academy, Culver, Indiana, *chairman;* Dr. Lindsey Blayney, dean of Carleton College, Northfield, Minnesota; Dr. John J. Tigert, president, University of Florida, Gainesville, Florida; Dr. Thomas H. Healy, Georgetown University, Washington, D. C.; Louis Johnson, past national commander of the American Legion, Clarksburg, W. Va. Past Commander Johnson and Dean Blayney are also members of the International Executive Committee of Fidac. This jury will decide to which three American educational institutions shall go the three medals, offered annually for the highest service rendered in that year to the cause of international peace. The Fidac is an international organization consisting of eight million veterans of the allied armies in the war and is dedicated to the advancement of better international understanding.

For the first term of the summer session of the University of Texas, visiting teachers will include: Dr. William Campbell Binkley, professor of history from Vanderbilt University; Dr. R. A. Tsanoff, professor of philosophy from the Rice Institute; Dr. L. A. McGee, extension instructor from Southwest Texas State Teachers College; Dr. Paul P. Young, associate professor of history from Southwestern University. Professor Carter Alexander, of Teachers College, Columbia University, will teach in the department of educational administration; Bonner Frizzell, N. S. Holland and S. R. LeMay, school superintendents from Palestine, Breckenridge and Athens, respectively, will teach in the department of educational administration;

J. M. Foote, of the Louisiana State Department of Education, will teach educational psychology, and G. W. Gotke, school superintendent from Brownsville, Texas, will teach in the department of the history of philosophy of education.

A CONFERENCE of supervisors and teacher trainers of vocational agriculture from sixteen states was held recently in the Office of Education for the purpose of formulating plans whereby teachers of vocational agriculture throughout the United States may cooperate more closely in emergency programs set up to aid farmers. Representatives of the Agricultural Adjustment Administration, Farm Credit Administration, Soil Erosion, Subsistence Homesteads, Federal Emergency Relief Administration, the National Grange, American Farm Bureau Federation, Civilian Conservation Corps, and Federal Office of Education met with the conference to explain the significance and plan of operation of projects they represent.

THE first American Youth Congress, a conference of 500 leaders called together from every state in the union by the Central Bureau for Young America to present their versions of "What Youth Wants and What it has to Offer," has been invited to hold its meetings at New York University on August 16, 17 and 18.

AT the annual meeting of the Trustees of the Woodrow Wilson Foundation, held on May 18, it was voted unanimously to award the sum of $4,000 to the Institute of International Education. The tribute to the work of the institute which accompanied the award reads: "The Institute of International Education is recognized by an award because of its record of accomplishment during the past fifteen years. It has thoroughly studied and intelligently implemented plans for the realization of that most difficult accomplishment—a better understanding among unlike peoples. It has done this through wide correspondence, personal consultations and the perfecting of working relations between the educational institutions of the United States and its neighbors. These relations are sustained in part through visiting professors, the promotion of the teaching of foreign languages in our schools and colleges, and the granting of exchange fellowships. The headquarters of the Institute has become an educational embassy of permanent value to the American people."

THE final accounting of the estate of the late B. Duke has been made by his executors. The funds set aside for educational and charitable purposes are those bequeathed to the Duke Endowment Fund, and will be used to further the work of Duke University, in North Carolina, and of hospitals, orphanages and other philanthropic institutions. The total amount of more than $42,000,000 includes a $10,000,000 specific bequest made by Mr. Duke. In addition the fund will receive two thirds of the residuary estate, of which Miss Duke's share is one third. This residuary estate was listed in the final accounting at $42,227,909.21, on which income of $7,057,202.68 was given as having been collected, making the two thirds share of the fund more than $32,000,000.

THE will of the late Dr. William H. Welch bequeaths to the Johns Hopkins University all his medical, scientific and literary books, a rare collection of medical portraits and pamphlets, all to be dedicated to the Institute of the History of Medicine and the School of Hygiene and Public Health of the university. One fourth of the residue of his estate is bequeathed to the university.

THE executive committee of the Oregon State Teachers Association has recently pledged its support to the two-year emergency sales tax, which has been adopted by the State Legislature and which will be voted upon at the elections to be held on May 18. By resolution the committee condemned Oregon's system of taxing, which, they stated, has "placed the burden of school support on a small group of public-spirited taxpayers by pyramiding taxes."

THE University of Redlands will offer annually competitive scholarships for four years to the ten highest ranking freshmen, five men and five women, after their first year of work. This plan will be established at the beginning of the academic year 1934. The scholarships will be available for a period of four years if the student maintains a position in the upper one fifth of his class. Eligibility stipulations for a competitive scholarship require that the freshman must have ranked in the upper one fifth of his graduating class in high school.

DISCUSSION

SHOULD THE COLLEGE BOOKSTORE BE OPERATED AT A PROFIT, AND TO WHAT SHOULD THE PROFIT BE APPLIED?

THE original assignment given to me for discussion is a little more explicit—"Should the College Bookstore Be Administered by the Institution on a Cooperative or Profit Basis? If the Latter, to What Should the Profit Be Applied?" In securing information for this subject, a questionnaire was sent to approximately one hundred managers of bookstores that are members of the National Association of College Stores and to the business managers of colleges belonging to our association. Sixty-one replies were received. As these replies were from every type institution and all kinds of stores, I feel that they represent the true condition in college store operation and organization throughout the U. S. Mr. Claude Reaves, Jr., manager of Birmingham-Southern College Bookstore, was of great assistance to me in obtaining and compiling the answers contained in the questionnaire.

Ten of those replying represented stores that were privately owned. Ten were operated on some form of cooperative or non-profit basis. The balance were operated by the institutions for profit. There is a wide difference of opinion as to the kind of store that is considered cooperative. Some seem to think that a store is cooperative when the profit is used to aid student activities, keep up a student union or contribute to student loan funds. I should think that no store should be considered cooperative that does not return to individual students a dividend at the end of each year based on the amount of purchases made. This definition will be used in the discussion to follow.

After a careful survey of the answers received, I find that the only successful cooperative store is the one operated on the cooperation association plan as is used at Harvard, Princeton and the University of Texas. Here the store operates on a profit basis and the profits are distributed to those who join the association on the basis of purchases made during the year. The criticism of this type store is the fact that only those students who buy membership into the association participate in the earnings. (At Harvard it seems that only about 67 per cent. of those eligible for membership join the association.) Their dividend last year was 9 per cent. If all students eligible had joined the association, a dividend of only 6 per cent. could have been paid. However, if they had depended upon the earnings received from the sale of merchandise, this dividend could not have been paid. Income from other sources amounted to approximately 33 per cent. more than the net profit on merchandise sold. In order to be able to return a dividend, a store must do a volume of business of not less than $150,000 annually. Therefore, cooperative operation of the stores in colleges represented by this group is out of the question, so I believe it would be wise for me to use the remainder of my time in discussing a successful college store operated for profit.

It is true that state laws in some states require that all text-books be sold at cost. This would prohibit some stores from operating at a profit, but with few exceptions all college stores should be operated at a profit and all articles sold at list price or with a mark-up commensurate with sound business practice. These should be operated on a business-like basis with the proper charges for rent, heat, lights, janitor service, depreciation, etc. A store that does this can not give a discount on books. One person writes:

> It was decided to give a 10 per cent. discount on all purchases as an experiment for one term. At the end of one term the practice was discontinued because it was found that the store would lose money. The average commission on sale of books is 20 per cent., figuring in transportation, this would cut it to about 16 per cent. Very few stores can operate under most favorable circumstances on an overhead of 20 per cent. On textbooks it was obvious that a discount of 10 per cent. could not be maintained unless prices were raised in other sections of the store.

In a survey made by the National Association of College Stores it was found that the average overhead cost for cooperative stores was 18.7 per cent., of institutionally owned stores 14.2 per cent., and of privately owned stores 11 per cent. A great amount of bookkeeping and detailed work is necessary in a cooperative store, which naturally raises the overhead cost. The only item that students can rightfully expect the college to furnish at a discount, if possible, is text-books, and with the small profit which is allowed, it is impossible for this to be done. If a student were to receive a dividend of 10 per cent. on text-book purchases over a period of a year, the average dividend, I do not believe, would exceed $2.50. I maintain that profits expended as a whole for student enterprises are of more value than this small amount returned to individual students. One manager of a successful store writes, "Profits can not be made on text-books, so why create a false impression in the minds of faculty and students?"

Stores operated for profit tend to better management and give better service and also keep peace with local merchants. So long as a college store does business on a sound basis, taking their rightful profits, I do not believe there will ever be any criticism from local merchants.

A college store doing any amount of volume can be operated at a profit, I believe, if the following suggestions are followed: When the volume is not over $10,000 per year, the store should be under direct operation of the college business manager or treasurer and he should pass on all orders or purchases made. He should figure costs and mark-up on all merchandise. Under him should be two students, preferably a senior and junior. Their salary should be very small, not exceeding $75 per semester. In addition to this they should receive a percentage of the net profits. Inventory should be taken once each month and a profit and loss statement drawn up. This should be checked carefully by the college business manager. All bookkeeping should be handled separately from the institution but in the same office if possible.

As soon as the volume reaches $10,000 a full-time manager should be employed to direct and operate the store. If your volume amounts to this much you will not obtain the best results until a full-time manager is put in charge. (I may state here that I learned from the questionnaire that stores managed by men showed a higher percentage of sales and profits than those managed by women.) This manager also should share in the net profits of the business. This tends to cause him to watch every detail. He should be capable of keeping his own books, but all checks should be signed by the person to whom he is responsible. As the business increases, students may be used part-time and should always be paid in money and not in tuition, room or board. With a pay day coming once each week or each month, a student realizes more clearly that he is receiving pay for the work which he is doing. The full-time manager should be allowed to discharge any student when he isn't performing his duty satisfactorily and should always be consulted before his assistants are employed.

The most important items to be watched carefully by the manager are: (1) Number of books ordered; (2) to return promptly all unsold books possible for credit; (3) never pay students more than 50 per cent. for used books (second-hand book concerns only pay them about 20 per cent.); (4) keep students' good will; (5) keep student help on the alert to sell other things than those called for by the students; (6) know your stock and keep it clean and in order. If these items are closely watched there will be a profit in the management of your store.

In the majority of cases the profits from bookstores are used to finance some student activity. Some use the profit to purchase books for the library. I see no reason why the institution can not feel free to use this income in any manner it sees fit.

Until such time as it is possible for a truly cooperative store to be successfully operated, by all means operate your store for profit, charging list price and a fair mark-up on all merchandise sold. "This," as one man writes, "will not give the students, in their most formulative period, the impression of communism or socialism but Americanism."

N. M. Yeilding

Birmingham, Ala.

THE ADMINISTRATION OF NEGRO EDUCATION IN THE NORTHERN ELEMENTARY SCHOOL

The extent to which northern school districts find it desirable to provide separate facilities for the education of Negro children makes an interesting study in contrasts. Any adequate treatment of this subject requires a statement of procedure in cities of considerable colored population. A clue to these urban centers of large Negro populations is found in the last census report. The trends traced here represent an investigation of thirty such cities in nine states. Several factors contribute to an understanding of current practise. An appreciation of the forces which have created this concentration of Negro population in industrial centers is essential. A canvass of state laws bearing on the segregation of the Negro is necessary. And finally, the matter of the employment of colored teaching personnel, which is closely associated with the maintenance of separate schools, may well be considered here.

The past decade has witnessed an unprecedented migration of the Negro from the agricultural South to the industrial centers of the North and the Middle West. This northern movement has extended across the entire breadth of the South, as these people have moved into sections which gave promise of higher wages and better living conditions. A belt of states stretching from New York and New Jersey on the Atlantic seaboard to Missouri and Kansas in the Middle West has received much of this exodus. Most cities of relatively large Negro population, exclusive of the South, lie in this region. Concentration of large numbers of Negroes in these urban localities has brought with it many problems. Adjustment to city living has been difficult for those accustomed to a freer and less exacting life. The meeting of two racial groups has always been attended by difficulties. This is especially true when they meet as economic competitors contending for a limited amount of employment. They have inevitably fallen heir to the most dilapidated sections of the city. Public neglect and a status on the bottom of the economic scale have combined to make their district the center of crime and disease. This is the social situation with which the school administrator deals.

State laws condition and limit the administrative practises of school districts. As such, they are a factor to be considered in examining current practise. State regulations fall roughly into three classes: Those which would seem to prohibit segregation; those which make provisions for separate facilities permissible, and those that require such practise. Of the nine states investigated, the majority were of the first type, although some fell in each of the three classifications. While the wording of the statutes of the various states differs, the following extract from Pennsylvania school law is typical of regulations of the first class. "It shall be unlawful for any school director, superintendent or teacher to make any distinction whatever on account or by reason of the race, or color, of any pupil or scholar who may be in attendance upon, or is seeking admission to any public school maintained wholly, or in part, under the school laws of this Commonwealth." As we move westward we find states with permissive types of legislation. Indiana has regulations of this type. Their statute says in part that "the trustee or trustees of such township, town or city may organize the colored children into separate schools of the township, town or city; having all the rights, privileges, and advantages of all other schools of the township, town or city. . . ." In some midwestern states we find mandatory segregation operative. Here the state law specifically provides "that separate schools shall be provided for white and colored children." Any mere statement of state law fails to give a true picture of prevailing practise, however. As might be expected, local sentiment and court interpretations provide a wide range of variation. This will be considered in the following discussion of current practise in the various school districts.

Of the cities studied, a rather even division was found between those localities that provide separate schools and those that do not. In most cases practice seems to be quite independent of state law. It is common to find separate schools maintained in districts within a state whose statutes say there shall be no distinction made because of race or color. Judicial precedents are not consistent. Courts have held that the provision for separate facilities is no infringement of the legal rights of the colored children and their parents. Other interpretations have abrogated the decisions of boards of education to provide separate schools. Neither does the relative number of Negro inhabitants, in itself, determine administrative practise. One city in a given state often provides separate schools, while another of equally large colored population does not. Local practise in states that make segregation permissible or mandatory is easily understood. The situation in states whose statutes would appear to prohibit segregation is not so easily explained. The situation that is forced on the Negro is the one which is apt to be troublesome, especially when state law does not specifically sanction the procedure followed. Many all-colored schools have evolved as a natural result of the development of the district. This, no doubt, accounts for their frequent existence in states of the first type. The Negro population of a city tends to concentrate in a given area. When, as a result of this, a school's enrolment becomes 80 to 90 per cent. colored, the white children begin to move out. At this time a corps of colored teachers may be put into the school. In a year or so all the white children will have left in all probability. If transfers are not refused to either Negro or white children, the situation takes care of itself. Most Negroes are satisfied with such an arrangement and are content to attend their own school. In the larger cities of the North the practise of providing equal facilities is universal, regardless of prevailing state rules and local practise regarding segregation. It often happens that the colored child attends the older and less desirable schools, but this is a result of their residence in the older and more outmoded sections of the city, and is in no sense a racial matter. In matters of teacher training, salary, length of term and other items of this kind, identical provisions are made for both races.

Colored teaching personnel is the almost inevitable accompaniment of separate schools. There were no exceptions to this found in the large sampling of northern and midwestern school districts studied. It is rare, however, to find Negro teachers employed in mixed schools in small and medium-sized cities. It is quite possible to find cases where as much as 96 per cent. of the enrolment are colored and yet no colored instructors employed. The larger cities frequently, but not always, use Negro teachers in their schools of mixed enrolment. Where this is done, the number employed is much smaller than the percentage of colored enrolment would seem to warrant.

CHARLES PREDMORE

WASHINGTON SCHOOL
PLAINFIELD, N. J.

THE NUMBER OF DOCTORATES CONFERRED IN GERMAN—A CORRECTION

MY article, "American Graduate Schools," in the last issue (June 2) of SCHOOL AND SOCIETY was based upon the official report of the Committee on Graduate Instruction of the American Council on Education as published in the journal of the council, the *Educational Record.* A copy of the article was submitted to President Hughes, chairman of the committee, in advance of publication. A statement received from him after the article had gone to press states that the original report was in error in its statement of the number of doctorates conferred in German. Instead of 995 for the five-year period, it was only 75. The average number of doctorates per institution in German, therefore, as reported in Table IV of my article should be 2.3 instead of 30; and the total number of doctorates in the thirty-five fields under consideration was 8,975 instead of 9,895.

WALTER CROSBY EELLS

STANFORD UNIVERSITY

SPECIAL CORRESPONDENCE

FOUR-YEAR COURSES AT THE MARYLAND STATE NORMAL SCHOOLS

THE Maryland State Board of Education at its meeting held on Friday, May 25, decided to increase the length of the courses offered at the three state normal schools for white students to cover a period of four years. The action was taken upon unanimous recommendation of the county superintendent of schools, the state elementary school supervisors and the normal school principals. The county students who enter the normal schools in September, 1934, will enroll for the four-year course leading to the degree of bachelor of science in elementary education. Upon the request of the school commissioners of Baltimore City a three-year course will continue to be offered at the Towson Normal School for the preparation of teachers of Baltimore City.

The considerations which led to the action of the State Board are as follows:

The work of the elementary school teachers in imparting knowledge, forming habits and molding character is as important as the task of any other group of teachers, and the group of pupils with which the elementary school teachers work is by far the largest section of the school population. Their training should, therefore, be equal to that which has long been required of high-school teachers—four years beyond high-school graduation. The growing complexities of modern life make it essential that the teachers have wide knowledge of subject-matter, vision of the possibilities of children's interests, and a knowledge of the sources of more information and of community resources for the children's contacts. Teachers must be able to express themselves with clarity, accuracy and force in spoken and written English. They need to be intelligently concerned with the problems of contemporary life and social institutions and must teach with a view of world betterment. They must be able to accept new attitudes in science.

The additional year will be used to give a broader subject-matter background in elementary subject-matter fields including the social studies, literature, science and probably economics to be added in the sophomore year. The related subject-matter will enlarge both the teachers' and indirectly the pupils' horizon and will enrich and make much more valuable the elementary school course offered in Maryland. The professional work in the normal schools, including practise teaching, will not be increased.

The recent lengthening of the normal-school courses from two to three years has resulted in marked improvement in the poise, maturity and cultural background of the graduates, and the addition of a fourth year will enable the schools more nearly to meet the demands made of the present-day elementary school teacher. Leading thinkers in teacher training are agreed that four years are necessary for equipping elementary teachers, and the more progressive states, including those bordering on Maryland, have already raised their standards to this point.

It is believed that a better student personnel will be attracted to the normal schools by the longer course. As a rule, the stronger high-school graduates wish to study for at least four years after leaving the high school and wish to qualify for degrees. In these respects the normal schools will now offer opportunities comparable with those of the liberal arts or other professional colleges and a prestige will be given to elementary school teaching which it has not known before and which will attract the thoughtful and able high-school graduate. Some who might have used the two- or three-year course (inexpensive alike in time and in money) as a stepping stone to another profession will be less likely to consider devoting four years to preparation for a task in which they will engage for only a short time. The profession will thus be relieved of teachers whose primary interest does not lie in their school work, and the overcrowding in the profession will be advantageously reduced. Furthermore, graduates with four years of special preparation rather than three will more likely be successful beginning teachers and the turnover in the schools, always a drawback to the most effective work, will be lessened.

The fact that there is now an oversupply of candidates for elementary school teaching makes the present an auspicious time to lengthen the normal-school course, since there will probably be no shortage of qualified teachers during the transition period. Moreover the students in the normal schools as well as the county superintendents are enthusiastically in favor of the change, and some of the present students who will doubtless return for the fourth year will form an excellent group with whom to inaugurate the new course.

The graduates of the four-year courses with a rich background of subject-matter will constitute a strong group from which to recruit teachers for junior high schools as this type of school gradually develops in the larger centers.

No increase in the normal school budgets is necessary for the immediate adoption of the four-year course.

The state normal school which trains teachers for the colored elementary schools and which is located at Bowie will increase its course from two to three years, beginning with the students entering in September, 1934.

Albert S. Cook,
Maryland State Superintendent of Schools

THE REORGANIZATION OF THE GERMAN SECONDARY SCHOOLS

AFTER the world war the German secondary schools were reorganized in many useful ways. Permanent gains were the creation of the six-years' secondary schools (*Aufbauschulen*), the abolition of the preparatory schools, the foundation of experimental schools, the reformation of the education of teachers, etc.

The very fact that the movement of Hitlerism has received its strongest support from the middle classes indicates that the secondary schools have been the centrums of Nazi propaganda. Consequently, the secondary schools of Germany have been accepted by the new Hitler régime without making many of the needed changes. The pupils who had forgotten their educational duties because of the political agitation in favor of Hitler were passed with satisfactory grades by instructions from the new government. This was legalized by the official Prussian decree of May 5, 1933, stating: "All school punishments, imposed on the pupils from January 1, 1925, for the deeds done for patriotic reasons, are abolished. The expelled students will be allowed to enter the particular class upon passing an entrance examination."

Another Nazi provision concerning the secondary schools is the law of April 25, 1933, which provides for all the schools, with the exception of those with compulsory attendance, a *numerus clausus* regarding the real need of the graduates of these schools for public tasks. It concerns not only the new students but also the students already registered. A limitation on the number of students was imposed for the year 1933; superfluous students were to be excluded, although the law does not state distinctly the basis for exclusion. Quite obviously, however, the law is directed against the Jews, except the children of the Jews who had fought for Germany during the world war and the children of the Aryan-Jewish couples, married before Hitler's coup. The execution of the law is left to the ministers of education of the individual German lands, who are to decide the details for the execution of the principle of *numerus clausus*. The excluded pupils are not allowed to continue studies in any school of the same type and can not enter any university.

Further provisions concern the increase in the total number of educational hours and the establishment of English as the leading foreign language in all secondary schools. The latter provision shows especially how the German schools are influenced by political considerations. After the world war Germany was swept by an anti-French wave, and the French language everywhere was replaced by English. After the first decade, however, French began to replace English, but with the arrival of Hitler, the anti-French tendency reappeared.

There have also been introduced into all the secondary schools more detailed courses in German ancient history (*Deutsche Vorgeschichte*). The history courses have a systematic discussion regarding the unjust and deteriorating results of the Versailles treaty. The Prussian Ministry recommends as a text-book G. Hanke's "Die Kriegsschuldfrage in der deutschen Schule." In addition, the students are advised to enter patriotic societies and organizations, and so that they may be constantly aware how the individual neighbors of Germany are armed, maps of European armament (*Rüstungskarte Europas*) are displayed in prominent places in every school.

The rise of nationalism has been accompanied by a return to religion, especially in the Protestant parts of the Reich. The Saxon Ministry of Education ordered on April 22, 1933, that all pupils, even those without a confession, must study religion. In addition, each day is begun with a prayer, and the week with a religious ceremony for the whole school. Another decree provides for the removal of any questionable politico-religious books from the professorial and student libraries by the director of the school. Concurrently pictures and monuments, especially of the democratic leaders of Republican Germany, must be abolished. Special attention is paid to the memorial days, which commemorate the signing of the Versailles treaty and the memory of the professors and pupils who had died during the world war, as well as those who had died for the victory of Nazism.

The same spirit is dominating the most important periodical of the German teachers in secondary schools, the *Monatschrift für höhere Schulen*. For example, number three of volume thirty-two is devoted to the question of eastern

Germany and the way that this all-important problem of Germany is to be made known to the German youth (*Der deutsche Ostraum als Frage der Nation*). The main ideas are as follows: It is foolish to assume that the secondary school is not to mix in politics. Political activities concern every class of society, and the individual trying to avoid politics (*der politische Privatier*) excludes himself from the state. Because political life is a struggle, every individual must be trained for it; such training must be given to him by the secondary school, the aim of which is to teach the student to understand the problem of Germany. The Imperial Germany understood the German problem too narrowly, and avoided the question of the Germans behind the borders. The "Weimar Democracy of Lies" (*Trugdemokratie*) was so afraid of the rest of Europe that it was limiting the expressions of true German nationalism in the schools. The political education of the German youth must not only influence the whole of Germany, but also the Germans living abroad, showing to them the unity of blood and soil. The most natural way of expansion for Germany is to the east. For that reason the German students must be instructed in this possibility and learn about the Slavs. It is a difficult task, because the chaotic and nihilistic soul of the Slav is quite hard for the German to understand. But this chaos is also an advantage to the Germans, because the Slavs do not know how to run their own state. The hate of the Slavs is the hate of the born slaves against the born masters (p. 185). The Germans do not want to Germanize the Slavs—this would spoil the purity of their race—but to lead them.

This is just a bare outline of the details which indicate the direction in which the German secondary educational system is drifting.

JOSEPH S. ROUCEK
PENNSYLVANIA STATE COLLEGE

QUOTATIONS

THE CUBBERLEY TRUST FUND

THE recent annual report of the president of Stanford University announced an important addition to the Ellwood and Helen Cubberley Trust Fund. The fund was established some years ago with a gift of $25,000 from Dr. and Mrs. Cubberley. Following Dr. Cubberley's retirement last summer, the Cubberleys made an additional gift of $367,199.25, making a total of nearly $400,000.

The Cubberley Fund is to be used to support the program of the School of Education. The particular purposes to which it will be applied were listed by President Wilbur as follows:

> The intent of the donors, if the trust fund becomes sufficiently valuable, is eventually to have the principal of the fund devoted to four main purposes: (a) the erection of a building at Stanford University to house the School of Education; (b) to endow the chair which Professor Cubberley has held for the past 35 years, under the title of the Cubberley Professorship of Education; (c) to add to the Cubberley Lecture Fund, created by a national committee and presented to the university on June 6, 1933, sufficient funds to bring the principal of the Lecture Fund up to $20,000 in case the national committee is not able to do this within a reasonable period of time, and (d) to provide a special endowment to purchase books for the School of Education library.

Those of us who were privileged to study with "Dad" Cubberley and to know both him and Mrs. Cubberley will recognize in this gift expression of the same loyalty, devotion and social idealism they practised and taught during their 35 years at Stanford.

During this period of service, the Cubberleys contributed to the development of an outstanding program of professional training. Even though now retired from active service, the Cubberleys are able through this gift to give permanent support to this program. New possibilities are opened up for the Stanford School of Education by the funds thus made available.

All persons who learn of this gift, even though not aided directly in their professional activities, will be inspired to a higher devotion to their professional task. One can search the pages of histories of education, but no more noble example will be found than the Cubberleys.—GRAYSON N. KEFAUVER, dean of the School of Education, Stanford University, in *The Sierra Educational News*.

TRUSTEE–FACULTY RELATIONS

WHEN the Institute for Advanced Study, in accordance with its charter, last month elected Oswald Veblen, a member of its faculty, to be also a member of its board of trustees, it advanced one more step along the road American education has been following for the last two decades. Legislative-executive relationships are always delicate, but seemingly nowhere more easily thrown out of adjustment than in educational institutions. In 1915, in the belief that certain important rights and interests of teachers were being flagrantly disregarded in many institutions, the American Association of University Professors was organized, and there were other indications that the teachers were ready to put up a good fight. In some cases they had to.

Meanwhile, a few presidents and trustees determined to seek other ways of adjusting differences. Princeton, under the leadership of President Hibben, was one of the earliest to provide for faculty review on questions of academic freedom and tenure; and to organize trustee-faculty conference committees to consider questions affecting both bodies. To-day nearly every university has a committee of this sort, or, as an alternative to it, an arrangement whereby certain faculty members sit with the board of trustees. Cornell is an example in the latter category.

Until last month, however, none of these faculty representatives had a vote. At California Institute of Technology the faculty has perhaps as much power as anywhere else, but even there the faculty does not actually vote at trustees' meetings (the institution has no president, his duties being discharged by an administrative committee of eight—four faculty members and four trustees).

Now, however, the Institute for Advanced Study in Princeton has gone the whole way and elected a faculty member with full voting powers. This action is to be commended as a gesture of friendliness toward the "society of scholars," but it should be noted that the Institute charter says only three faculty members may be included among the fifteen trustees. One fifth of the membership will hardly give the faculty a representation more effective than that now provided in dozens of universities by an energetic president who realizes, as President Dodds has demonstrated he realizes, that his most important function is that of liaison officer between the trustees and the faculty.—*The Princeton Alumni Weekly.*

SOCIETIES AND MEETINGS

THE ASSOCIATION OF AMERICAN COLLEGES

THE Association of American Colleges recently sponsored a very successful joint conference of colleges, trust institutions, life insurance and the bar at the Bellevue-Stratford Hotel, Philadelphia. More than 250 persons were present, many of them from a considerable distance, for the purpose of discussing and approving ways and means of assisting higher education through furthering gifts and promoting endowments under wills and trust agreements and by means of life insurance. The conference, which was conducted under the auspices of the association, was arranged locally through the painstaking efforts of Mr. Leroy A. Mershon, of Philadelphia.

The president of the association, President William Mather Lewis, of Lafayette College, presided at the meeting. Following an introductory statement by President Lewis, papers on "Past Methods of Securing Endowments" were presented by George A. Brakeley, administrative vice-president of the University of Pennsylvania, and Archie M. Palmer, associate secretary of the Association of American Colleges.

The question of what the colleges can do on the campus and in the field to meet their separate and collective needs in order to accord with changed conditions were discussed by three speakers. Thomas A. Gonser, assistant to the president of Northwestern University, spoke on the topic, "Making the Alumni Organization Effective for Better Financial Support"; Felix A. Grisette, director of the Alumni Loyalty Fund of the University of North Carolina, on "Present Day Efforts to Supplement State Appropriations"; and Charles J. Miel, general manager of the University of Pennsylvania Fund, on "What the Individual College or University Can Do to Promote the Interest of its Alumni and Friends in Providing for Their Institution out of Their Estates."

The afternoon session was opened by President Homer P. Rainey, of Bucknell University, with a paper on "How Can the Cooperation of Trust Institutions, Life Insurance and the Legal Profession be Made Effective?"

Gilbert T. Stephenson, vice-president of the Equitable Trust Company of Wilmington, Delaware, and ex-president of the Trust Division of the American Bankers' Association, explained what the trust institutions can do; John A. Stevenson, chairman of the executive committee, Association of Life Agency Officers, and Professor Solomon S. Huebner, of the Wharton School of Finance and Commerce of the University of Pennsylvania, discussed what life insurance can do; and Robert T. McCracken, a member of the Philadelphia Bar, discussed what the bar can do.

Leroy A. Mershon presented suggestions as to the first steps in making effective cooperation between the various groups represented at the meeting, and Robert L. Kelly, executive secretary of the Association of American Colleges, gave a summarization of the high lights of the conference.

President John S. Nollen, of Grinnell College, chairman of the committee on resolutions, made a report as to definite procedure, which was uanimously adopted. The report provided for the organization of a financial and fiduciary institute, subsequently named "The American Institute for Endowments." The *Bulletin* of the Association of American Colleges will be the official organ of the Institute, carrying reports of current developments in this field.

The May issue of the Association *Bulletin* is devoted to the Proceedings of the Philadelphia Conference and to current expressions of vitality in the colleges as reported by their officers and teachers. The latter have contributed generously of their personal experience in curriculum building, in leadership training, maintenance of spiritual values and art appreciation. They have reported the latest developments in improved articulation of high school and college, and have indicated how, in spite of many difficulties, both students and colleges are paying their bills.

"Comprehensive Examinations in the Social Sciences" by Edward S. Jones, of the University of Buffalo, a supplement to the earlier volume, "Comprehensive Examinations in American Colleges," has been published since the annual meeting, under the auspices of the association's Commission on Faculty and Student Scholarship. As a handbook of suggestive data for the growing teacher, this 128-page monograph is meeting a real demand.

"College Instruction in Art," by Archie M. Palmer, of the Association office, and Grace Holton, assistant professor of art, New Jersey College for Women, is a concise but readable report of more than eighteen months' painstaking investigation of college offerings in the fine arts, excluding music. The project was undertaken upon recommendation of the Commission on College Architecture and College Instruction in Fine Arts and was subsidized in part by the Carnegie Corporation. With the pressure upon higher education to train for the wise use of leisure, enjoyment and worth-while avocations, a new emphasis is given to art courses for the layman, such as many liberal colleges may aspire to offer.

A report of the College Music Study of the Association of American Colleges, directed by Randall Thompson, a brilliant young American composer and teacher, will be published in the fall. This report is sponsored by a special committee, of which President E. H. Wilkins, of Oberlin College, is chairman, and was made possible through a subvention of $25,000 from the Carnegie Corporation. It will be an important and stimulating contribution to the larger purpose and function of art education on the college level.

The executive secretary of the Council of Church Boards of Education, assisted by a research staff, is engaged in the production of a new edition of the "Handbook of Christian Education." This book will contain statistics of approximately 800 Protestant church-related colleges and universities, junior colleges, theological seminaries, training and secondary schools, a comprehensive list of Protestant teachers of Bible, religion and religious education; the latest standards of the accrediting agencies; the names and addresses of about 1,500 religious workers with students in institutions of higher learning. The book will be completed in the early summer.

Due to a request from Oxford University, for clarification of the confused degree situation, the Association of American Colleges is preparing data as to the present meaning of the Ph.B., B.L. and other unusual baccalaureate degrees conferred by American colleges, to be submitted to a committee of specialists in higher education.

The Association staff is also collecting data as a background for a possible study of the extent to which achievement and scholastic intelligence tests function in the actual workaday program of the college student and teacher. It is of vital importance that the colleges should know what degree of coordination exists between scientific knowledge and learning and teaching procedure where the matter has been subjected to thorough investigation.

Many state college associations and individual colleges in almost every state, on their own initiative and stimulated by the office of the Association, are expressing appreciation to the FERA of the successful operation of the student aid plan during the present semester and requesting a continuance of the same program for the next academic year. A multitude of most striking human interest stories are being furnished the officers of the FERA.

R. L. K.

REPORTS

ASSISTANCE TO EXILED GERMAN SCHOLARS IN GREAT BRITAIN

THE first Annual Report of the Academic Assistance Council, formed in Great Britain in 1933 to assist university teachers and investigators "who on grounds of religion, political opinion or race were unable to carry on their work in their own country," contains much matter of general interest to American men of science. The purposes and convictions which led to the formation of the council are stated by it as follows:

> Behind the activity of the council lies the ambition to protect the tradition of academic freedom in which Western culture has developed, and to preserve the scholars in whom the tradition is maintained. It is convinced that the world of scholarship is a kingdom of its own which dare not admit subjection to temporary political dictations, and that the universities must be preserved as communities of free learning. The council clearly realizes that its work will be permanently successful only if the universities and learned institutions of the world can be enlarged to incorporate the services of those scholars and scientists who are being driven from European universities on account of their religion, political opinion or race. The reorganization of the University of Istanbul, which has created posts for thirty of the displaced German teachers, and the invitations which have reached the council from South America, India and China, show that the redistribution of university teachers is possible and practical. This diffusion will require an alteration in the economic support of the universities; in those countries which wish their universities to continue as free institutions, the public will have directly to contribute towards their support and extension, by new endowments or scholarships. The university teachers of Great Britain have shown their appreciation of the problem by contributing generously to the funds of the council and in certain cases voluntarily taxing themselves a part of their salaries.

The council received during the year in subscriptions and grants from various sources £14,-250, out of which maintenance grants at the rate of £250 for married persons and £182 for single persons have been given directly to 49 scholars, to enable them to continue their research in British universities; other agencies, in cooperation with the council, have provided similar grants for 90 additional displaced university teachers. A total of 178 have been placed in salaried positions in British educational or research institutions—the four largest groups being 31 at Cambridge, 17 at Oxford, 17 in University College, London, and 16 at Manchester—and the council has also assisted in obtaining for those whose needs have been brought to its notice 211 positions in other countries. As "showing the size and nature of the problem" the council gives as the total number of teachers and investigators in universities or institutions of similar rank who are definitely known to have been displaced, 1,202. The council reports that its funds are now almost exhausted, and asks for the sum of £25,000 per annum for the next two years to enable it to continue and consolidate its work.

Appended to the report are twenty-five "extracts from reports on work being conducted by German scholars working in England on grants from the council," which give striking evidence of the value to science of the researches whose continuance has thus been made possible, and also of the tragic position in which many such scholars and their families would have been left if such assistance had not been afforded.

Copies of the report may be obtained from the general secretary of the Academic Assistance Council, Mr. Walter Adams, Rooms of the Royal Society, Burlington House, London, W.1.

A. O. L.

VOCATIONAL OUTCOMES OF A LIBERAL COLLEGE[1]

REED COLLEGE has just published a bulletin on the vocational choices of its graduates; the data cover 701 of the total alumni list of 748. Probably the most significant fact reported is that more than half of those reported on have gone on to graduate study. The average of this item for twenty-two liberal arts colleges recently reporting was 32 per cent.

Quite naturally the largest definite vocational group is that of the teachers—79 men and 92 women, total 171. The marked feature here is the large number teaching in colleges and universities—49 men and 18 women. High-school teaching claims 25 men and 70 women. To these might be added librarians, 10 (women), making the grand total 181.

The next largest group is a quasi-vocation—housekeeping, 150 women. This is at first glance a startlingly small proportion of the 366 women included in the report; the shock is mitigated by several considerations: The college is young, with its largest classes but recently graduated; a considerable but not determined number of women listed under other vocations are married; and college graduates in general are slow in marrying.

The next largest group come under the rather broad term of "business"—64 men and 30 women. To this might be added: Insurance, 9 (men); executive directorship, 6 men and 3 women; this would make a grand total of over a hundred in business and related fields.

Medicine comes next with 22 men; 16 women are in work "related to medicine." Really many more go to medical study from Reed College, leaving college before graduation; Reed College does not grant its degree to these students, as is done in some cases. Exact figures are not available, but not far from 50 students (nearly all men) belong in this group. This would raise the total number for this vocation to about 88.

Scientific outcomes, in addition to medicine, are: Chemistry, 9 men; engineers, 6 men; research, 4 men, 8 women. Grand total in "science" group, 115.

The next large group is social service, 34—women, 23, men, 11; then government (chiefly diplomatic service), 19—men, 15, women, 4; law, men, 14. Journalism has 11—8 men and 3 women. The ministry has 7 men. Total in "social" group, 85.

Then a considerable number are reported as now engaged in graduate study—26 men and 19 women, total, 45. The majority of these will eventually be added to the teaching and research groups.

In summary: Education, 171; housekeeping, 150; business, 103; medicine and other science, 115; social, 85; graduate study, 45. This is a picture of the vocational outcomes of one liberal college.

EDWARD O. SISSON

REED COLLEGE

[1] Abstract of Reed College Bulletin, Vol. xiii, No. 1 (January, 1934) with comments.

NEW BOOKS IN EDUCATION

CRAIG, ALICE E. *The Junior Speech Arts.* Pp. xiv + 470. 34 figures. Macmillan. $1.40.

DONNELLY, FRANCIS P. *Principles of Jesuit Education in Practice.* Pp. xiii + 205. Kenedy. $2.00.

MURSELL, JAMES L. *Principles of Education.* Pp. xii + 505. $2.75. *A Workbook in Principles of Education.* Pp. iv + 140. Norton. $1.25.

STRONG, L. A. G. and MONICA REDLICH. *Life in English Literature.* Pp. xii + 547. Illustrated. Little, Brown. $1.72.

ULLMAN, B. L. and A. W. SMALLEY. *New Progress Tests in Latin.* Pp. v + 122. Illustrated. Macmillan. $0.40.

WILLETT, GEORGE W. *Philosophy and Practices in High School Administration.* Pp. 244. Christopher Publishing House. $3.00.

SCHOOL AND SOCIETY

WITH WHICH ARE COMBINED THE EDUCATIONAL REVIEW, ESTABLISHED IN 1891, THE TEACHERS MAGAZINE, ESTABLISHED IN 1878, AND THE SCHOOL JOURNAL, ESTABLISHED IN 1874.

Volume 39 SATURDAY, JUNE 16, 1934 Number 1016

A TECHNIQUE FOR COLLEGE TEACHING

By Professor ROSWELL H. JOHNSON

UNIVERSITY OF PITTSBURGH

THE recent report on college teaching by a committee of the American Association of University Professors failed to supply what some of us had anticipated—a technique for college teaching in the classroom. Therefore, I venture to offer my conclusions as to methods which are based on my student experience in seven universities and on my twenty-one years of college teaching.

It is a truism that no one technique can be best for all college courses and for all grades of students. For instance, the fundamental mathematics, modern language, composition, fine arts, laboratory, project and autonomous courses require peculiar techniques. Yet there still remains, roughly, half of the curriculum which could be taught by a common method. It is for this half of the college courses that the following proposals are offered. Illustrations are selected from a large variety of courses.

There is one technique for stimulating helpful student activity outside of class and there is another technique for presenting class material in the most effective way. Of the various ways to interest outside activity, we list the following devices.

(1) The term paper. This is the expression used for a long, individual study. It seems best to require only one such paper in a course, in order that the quality of that one may be higher. There are two general types of term papers. The better type, possible with certain students and in certain courses, is a piece of minor research that is actually novel. For instance, one might be the student's own family tree or the drafting of sections of a model state constitution or a comparative study of the attitudes of a class of students towards races, religions, etc.

The less valuable but sometimes necessary type of term paper consists mainly of compilation or the abstracting of material, such as a sketch of the history of the student's home town, when the history has already been fully written up. Good term papers should not be rigid abstracts nor long lists of quotations. The student should be encouraged to recreate and to record personal reactions and especially personal experiences that are illustrative. Of course, adequate documentation should be taught, but when excessive stress is laid on that element, the tendency is for the student to question the worth-whileness of his work. He suspects it is either "busy work" or a form of exploitation by the instructor. The student should always be made to feel that his work has value, and he does invariably feel that it has, when he has made some worthwhile original observations and hypotheses.

The instructor should try to have as many of the term papers of the first type as is possible. Nor should he be dissuaded by the thought that the student might not do the job as well as would be possible later. It is not the quality of the product so much as the value of the doing to the student that counts most.

It is well to give students the chance to suggest their own subjects before any list is made public. After the list is posted, the students should still have the opportunity to make their own choice. If his choice does not appear to be a good one, the instructor helps him to develop another topic, if possible, somewhat related to the one he had earlier chosen.

It seems best not to mention the matter of term papers till about the third or fourth meeting of the class. Any student who has not selected his subject, by the time that the term is a quarter passed, should have his subject assigned to him by the instructor. The papers ordinarily should be due a month before the end of the course, so that adequate use may be made of them in class. Some of them may be read to the class, but frequently, especially in large classes, it is better for the student to give a talk with the paper as a basis.

(2) Intermediate papers. Two types of intermediate papers are here suggested. There is the biographical sketch of the outstanding contributors in the field covered by the course. These topics, though written, should be given orally in class. The second type comprises tabulations, frequency graphs or correlation tables, such as the legal age for marriage in the various states, a frequency curve of the size of state legislatures, or a correlation table of population in relation to the size of legislatures. All intermediate papers or topics should be scattered throughout the course so that they would not pile up at the end.

(3) The keeping of current time-series graphs. Thus, a class member may keep a time-series graph currently, throughout the course, on the price of gold or the ratio of stocks of a certain studied industry compared to the whole volume of stocks. Where space permits, such graphs should be kept on the classroom wall.

(4) Assembling the necessary data, so as to bring up to date the graphs or tables used in the text-book.

(5) The problem. This device under the name of "challenges" has been used with marked success by Professor Edward A. Ross in classes in sociology, a field where it had seldom been used before. Professor Ross prepares in advance a list of problems, some of which are considered at each class period. There is considerable variety in the types. Occasionally they involve the student's consulting and reporting on some article. Such problems are usually assigned to only one or two students, but most of the problems are assigned by rows. Thus, in a classroom with four rows, Row A will get problems 1 and 5, Row B problems 2 and 6, and so forth. For the most part each problem will call for a 50 to 100 word answer, to be written in advance but nevertheless given orally in class when called for. The remaining students in each row report any deviation in findings or opinions. Then the discussion is before the whole class. The value of this plan, which is discussed in the preface to Dr. Ross's revised "Outlines of Sociology" depends mainly on the professor's skill in devising the problems. The best, of course, are those that force the student to think through a problem or those that evoke from his own experience data bearing on the problem. Some problems should be asked of the whole class, for example, "How many brothers and sisters have you had and how many did each of your parents have?" In a problem like this, statistics are built up in the class on the basis of these reports. "What grounds for divorce do you think should be legally listed?" With this problem also a table of the returns may be prepared.

Examples of problems of this sort may

be found in Professor Ross's "Outline of Sociology," Revised, Thompson's "Population Problems" and in Popenoe and Johnson's "Applied Eugenics," second edition. In fact, during the last year or so several books have appeared with this problem feature, which might well be a feature of nearly all college text-books.

There are, of course, the old-time problems, too, that provide practise in the technique that is to be learned, especially useful in scientific method or appraisal courses. The problem for each student may use the same data. The danger of parasitism is, however, so great that it is well to have some of the data varied as between students. An easy way to do this is to have one or more of the variables a function of the seat number. For example, "What is the probable error of a phalanx . . . where the number of cases is 50 plus 3 times your seat number?"

Recently paper-bound "work-books" have been developed for some courses in psychology and in education. Typically they consist of detachable sheets with space for the problems and answers to the questions. Most of those the writer has inspected are useful, but where the questions merely call for quotations, such work books are not worth while. The work book is less valuable as a written lesson to hand in than as a basis for discussion. During the class hours, the sheets of the work book should be in the student's hands.

(6) Students should be made to feel free to break into discussion, especially to ask for the meaning of words not understood or when an explanation may have been inadequate. Students should recognize that an interruption for the sake of adding illustrative material or to express dissent is better postponed either till the end of the division under consideration, when the lecturer will call for discussion, or till that part of the next class meeting when just such contributions are in order. Occasionally it happens that some one student is prone to be too loquacious or too disputatious for the good of the class. It is best to talk privately with such a student, rather than to rebuke him in class, lest by such a rebuke the instructor might inhibit too much the less voluble members.

(7) Formal oral recitation, used as a means of scoring, should be avoided. The probable error in oral recitation so greatly exceeds that in written work on uniform questions that oral recitation proves to be a very poor measurement. It is also deadening to class interest in contrast to the zeal evinced when Ross's problem method is used. In that method, which is not intended for scoring, the answer has been thought out with care and therefore has more interest. Yet occasionally in class a short, quick question on the part of the teacher is a useful device to arouse a student with flagging attention or to enlist the class's help in supplying an example.

(8) Written tests. The instructor needs to watch the class to see if there is enough internal incentive for the students to do the required reading or other work. Where the incentive is happily found to be adequate, written tests may be omitted. But where there is evident need for some additional incentive, occasional written tests become an essential. They are most effective when short, frequent and unannounced. The results should be posted on the bulletin board in the order of excellence of the cumulative tests to date.

(9) No college teacher in his effort to develop student self-activity should swing to the extreme of entirely omitting lecturing. To be sure, college lecturing should be informal. That is, it should be interspersed with questions from students and with class discussion. But, nevertheless, the lecture must nearly always remain an important element in a college course. I remember attending a course by the famous Hollander, Hugo de Vries, on the mutation

theory. The course was made up almost wholly of lectures, and every student, I think, so wished it, in spite of the fact that Dr. de Vries had recently published similar material in a book. We wanted a maximum *from him,* and were willing to look out for the reading and studying by our own devices.

However, it is true that one of the chief factors that determine the right amount of lecturing in a course is whether or not the class is using a recent text written by the instructor for the express use of the class. Obviously, where there is such a book, lecturing is of minimum advantage and should deal mainly with presenting what has happened since the publication of the book.

The art of lecturing to college classes is not taken seriously enough by instructors. All aspirants for college teaching would do well to take a course in public speaking and to participate in debating. The following defects seem to be the most conspicuous in the public speaking of college teachers.

(a) Sometimes the instructor adheres too rigidly to his outline and is too loath to permit digression. It is better to provide the students with a typewritten outline, so that the lecturer need give less attention to the skeleton structure, captions, etc. Digression, within reason, may then be indulged in with less confusion to the student.

(b) There is the opposite fault of undue rambling, which is all too common.

(c) The difference in the instructors' speed of presentation is surprisingly varied. Where too slow, boredom results, and where too fast, the student is unable to follow the argument. Furthermore, with a too rapid style the lecturer nearly always sacrifices clearness and enunciation.

(d) Faulty enunciation is especially to be avoided in college teaching, because of the large amount of new and technical nomenclature.

(e) Teachers should remember that students hear so many lectures that mannerisms and stereotypes become more than usually annoying and should especially seek to eliminate these faults.

(f) Yet earnestness in a teacher is much to be preferred to meticulous poise, the latter tending to bore students. Expressiveness is important, and it is best attained by earnestness. Earnestness should not carry one into excessive subjectivity nor to undue appeal to the emotions nor too ardent an advocacy.

(g) The pronunciation at least of all technical nomenclature should be flawless and new technical words that are not simple should be written on the board that the students may visualize the spelling.

(10) Many courses are helped by the free use of objects, diagrams, maps, slides, graphs, demonstrations and experiments. This is largely a "counsel of perfection" as many of the deficiencies in this regard are due to limited appropriations and facilities.

(11) In the choice of examples and of evidence, preference should be given to those which tie up most closely with the student's interest, yet the choice should be from a wide field. Thus, some features of social psychology can be illustrated from the field of college sports, movies and newspapers.

The college teacher should bear in mind the well-known "human interest" of the journalist. An illustration arising from an experience is to be preferred to a wholly descriptive illustration. It should be used where it is most effective and does not reduce the aptness of the illustration. Thus, an economic geologist, in teaching about famous ore deposits, brings in something of interest about the discoverer or the leading investigator of the deposit.

(12) Should the instructor be fortunate enough to possess the gifts of wit and apt expression, he will find his teaching effectiveness greatly enhanced.

(13) A text-book, sometimes two in suc-

cession, should nearly always be used. It need not be employed throughout the course. There may be omissions and there will always be additions. The value of the text-book lies in the fact that the student can utilize it during hours that can not be used for work in the library or at times when the assigned book is not available. The ideal is for the author to write the text for his own course. This is most easily done by starting with mimeograph outline sheets, at first distributed from time to time, but in later years assembled and sold as a syllabus. The editions should be kept small so that, with each new edition, the contents may be revised. A text-book which has grown in this way with pragmatic adaptation makes the best text-book.

It goes without saying that neither instructor nor student should ever treat the text as absolutely authoritative. The instructor should make clear his own changes in view-point since he wrote his book or, if the book is by another, he should explain the differences between it and his own views clearly. It is far better to have the student a little confused with "I don't know which to believe" than to have him get into a habit of mental rigidity. The student is entitled to know whether the opinion is one in which "sides are taken" by well-trained men in the field or whether the instructor's view represents a minority among the specialists or whether it is unique.

(14) The matter of text assignments is best controlled by the early preparation of a schedule by the instructor which would keep the balance between weeks as he desires. But this control sheet should not be handed out. The assignments are best announced each time, giving the instructor opportunity to depart from time to time from his control schedule. The purpose is to try to keep the text work in the classroom as nearly as possible abreast of the outside preparation. The class may properly lag a little behind the text-book assignments, except where there is so abstruse a point that the mere reading of the book, without aid of blackboard or model, is likely to be inadequate. An example of this situation is found in geology classes studying the nomenclature of faults, where a demonstration by models is almost imperative.

(15) Collateral reading should be assigned unless the text itself is too long for the course. The principal reason is to help the student get a different view-point from that of the text and the instructor. There are three main systems of outside reading which are not mutually exclusive. The first is possible where a "source book" is published.

Where there is no source book, there are occasionally classic passages or articles that all in the class should read. In case of an important short passage, this may well be given on a mimeographed sheet. Either with or without a source book, depending on the amount of ground to be covered in the given time, it is an excellent plan to have each student assigned to report on a different book, unless the class is too large. In the latter case, one book may be divided between several class members. One particular advantage of this method is the enriching of the class discussions, since each student then has both another author's and his own view to report, whenever these views are significantly different.

In addition a bibliography with some definite passages cited should be given out for those who are ambitious to read more than the assigned work.

(16) An active bulletin board is excellent in many courses. Clippings of articles, illustrations and graphs are posted by the instructor, and students are invited to bring in such items, subject to editing. Latin classes have made large use of this method, but it deserves wider use. The "wall newspapers" in the Soviet Union carry this method through all levels of the schools and into the factories.

(17) Sometimes the first chapters of the

text-book are unduly abstruse and do not engage the interest of the student. The order may then be changed or there may be other good reasons for a change. But whenever such changes are made, unless very simple, a mimeograph outline should be distributed to prevent any confusion arising from the new order.

(18) Mimeograph sheets should be used very freely as well as maps, graphs, bibliographies, problem lists and outlines, when the resources of the institution permit. In general, it is never wise for the teacher to dictate material for the students to write in their notebooks. If there is occasion for this, it would be better done by mimeograph, unless the passage is very short. It is also an abuse of the student's time, attention and energy to have him spend much time copying from the blackboard. Mimeographed sheets are ordinarily letter size, and because of this the students should be asked to use a letter-size notebook. There are instructors who require a formally organized notebook handed in by the student at the end of the course. Doubtless there is some value in this method, but it is not here recommended, as it has a bad effect on the morale of the student. It would be better to get the values in some other way not so damaging to the rapport between teacher and student.

(19) Teachers should avoid overcrowding a course with material. It is well to remember that as the years pass the active teacher is constantly adding to his course. To be sure, some of these new data sometimes simply replace old material, for example, new census data. More frequently a clear addition is made. One of three choices the instructor must then make, (a) enlarge the course by increasing the number of class hours, (b) have it "bud" a new shorter course or in most cases (c) cut out some of the old material. The instructor should recognize that there is a "struggle" for the admission of the best material into his course, and the victory should go to the material most fit for the student's purpose. Otherwise he will make the mistake of overweighting the course at the expense of effective learning. Probably one of the best places to curtail is in the ever-increasing list of names and dates.

(20) Another profitable method is the use of the trip, notably in such subjects as botany, geology, social psychology and industrial engineering. Our main concern in this discussion is with the technique of the field trip and also with the range of subjects to which it may be applied. Too frequently the field trip is not considered at all because there is but little occasion to use it. There are many courses in which a few field trips, or at least one, might be used to great advantage. Thus students in social psychology might well see a prize fight, or zoology students attend a poultry show or a county fair, students in economics might visit the stock exchange, or a sociology group would profit greatly by a visit to an institution for the feeble-minded and a divorce court, as just a few instances.

As to technique, the most common devices in connection with the field trip have been the preparation of an herbarium in botany classes, the mapping and collecting of fossils for geology students and a written report in industrial engineering.

One technique that is especially recommended in connection with field trips that thus far has not been much used is the questionnaire. When the questionnaire is well drawn some of the questions will call for close observation on the part of the student, some will call for inferences and a few of the questions may well call for the listing and classifying of the student's observations, with the construction therefrom of a frequency polygon, a time series graph or a correlation table and graph.

The field trip may well merge into individual field problem assignments, where assignment is made to certain individuals to make certain observations for instance on the electric car, or to make specified observations which will evoke the student's inferences. Of course all such individual field assignments are reported in class.

(21) It is often possible to give one's students a wider viewpoint in the field under consideration by inviting an outside speaker to address the class on his own direct experiences. The students generally enjoy and profit by such an experience, especially in asking questions of such a man. The heads or other functionaries of institutions are often pleased to be invited. Then too one may find a visitor in the city, who could be called on to good advantage. Lastly it is sometimes well to call in a professor from another department or from another nearby university to talk upon a specialty.

(22) In discussing the art of presentation, one thinks especially of the information conveyed to the student. Let us next consider what can be done, in addition, toward cultivating scientific habits of thought on the part of the students.

(a) By the instructor being meticulously logical both in presenting and in discussing material. However, excessive "documentation" of all the premises used will clog the line of thought.

(b) By the instructor holding the student to strict account in his reasoning before the class, yet encouraging the student to use his own observations as data for reasoning.

(c) The instructor should fully realize that while figures of speech and the selection of examples are useful and needed, both are dangerous sources of fallacy. Actual cases of fallacies appearing in this way should be called to the student's attention. In fact, the teacher should be on continuous watch to explode fallacies, or better yet, to lead the students to do so.

(d) In the attempt to teach successfully there is the danger that the instructor will over-simplify. He is likely to treat effects as the direct results of a simple cause, whereas usually there is a network of multiple, interacting factors. The teacher has a difficult task to avoid simplifying more than is necessary for the particular stage of the student's progress.

(e) There is a temptation for some instructors, in the name of objectivity, to show the evidence on one side of a controversy and then the other and to leave in the student's mind the impression that one side is no stronger than the other and that it is no great concern what opinion he holds. Students should be taught to feel strong discontent with such academic apathy. It may be on the matter under discussion that there are no adequate data yet for satisfactory analysis. The question to be considered in that case should be "What investigation is needed to enable one to make a judgment?"

(f) This earnestness of attitude should nevertheless accompany the equally important quality of open-mindedness. It should be evident to the students that the instructor takes his attitude, because, from the data on hand, it seems the proper one to him and also that he would welcome more substantiated data, whether or not it would necessitate a change of view.

(23) Important as it is to help students seek after and recognize truth, may not society properly ask something more of the teacher? Should he not, in so far as possible, direct the attention of his students, by the proper selection and use of material, to the applications of the course subject to the student's life and especially to the increase of human welfare? At this point a difficulty arises from ambiguity as to what is human welfare. The instructor may well show what the general mores indicate at the time as the goal of human welfare in the field being studied, but he

should indicate what the most competent specialists teach as well, otherwise progress would be unduly delayed.

One useful means for improving one's college teaching is to be on the watch for promising new pedagogical devices and to give them a fair trial. In general, the greatest need for the instructor is to avoid too much subjectivity. When he himself attends lectures or hears papers read at the scientific meetings, it is well for him to realize the analogy between that and the situation in his own classroom. Then he may speculate as to whether or not he himself may not be guilty of the same faults as the speakers before him.

THE SEA OF ADOLESCENT STORMS

By L. L. LOVE

ACTING JUNIOR DEAN, THE OHIO STATE UNIVERSITY

SIT with me for a day in a high-school counselor's office and listen to the questions and the stories of the boys and girls who come, one after the other, to talk over their problems and difficulties. Listen to the tales of worry over failure to make friends, of inability to do successful school work, of misunderstandings with parents, of conflicts between science and religion, of disappointments in the extra-curricular life of the school. Some discuss love affairs or desire help in choosing a vocation. Others have financial problems with all their attendant ramifications. Personal appearance, racial prejudices, sex problems, ethical conduct, student-teacher incompatibility—all these at one time or another pass in review, often with several of them inseparably linked in the same individual.

After you have listened for a time, I should like to have you tell me if there is any real and vital educational significance, any responsibility which the school should not avoid in these problems and crises. I should like to have you tell me, too, whether or not intelligent and scientific aid to the individual in arriving at satisfactory solutions to these difficulties is not fully as important as learning the binomial theorem or the conjugation of an irregular Latin verb or the chemical reactions in the process of photosynthesis. I should like to have you say if reasonable grounds do not exist for the belief that such help may often be even more necessary than academic work if the individual is to make his best adjustment to life.

You doubt that these boys and girls will discuss with a stranger their doubts, their fears, or that they will ask frank questions about matters of grave personal concern to them? Wait until evening and let the events of the day answer for themselves. They will, of course, talk freely only if they believe that they really can secure help with their problems and that their confidence will be respected. There is nothing psychic or supernatural about these conferences; instead they are made as scientific as possible by use of all available or obtainable information such as school records, intelligence and aptitude tests, social and academic adjustment schedules, self-analysis blanks, personality inventories and other devices. But here comes the first boy.

He is a fine-appearing sixteen-year-old junior. He says he wants to talk about "some things that are so important to me right now that I've just got to have some help." He mentions grades. I start to look up his score on the intelligence test. "Oh, yes; you'll tell me I made a high score on that test and that I could get high grades if I would only try. That's what

I've always been told.'' And the tears begin to suggest themselves in the corners of his eyes.

Can school grades alone be the cause for this emotional upset or are they merely symptomatic of other difficulties? In school activities he holds several responsible positions and performs their attendant duties in a conscientious and effective manner not usually found among high-school students. He also carries a paper route. Bit by bit the situation comes to light. Here is a boy in whom not one factor but an accumulation of many of them have caused stresses and strains from which he is seeking release. His health has never been good. His parents are fine people, but they do not understand him. They are strict religionists and compel him to attend several religious services every Sunday. He thinks he has become an atheist, but is deeply troubled over the development of a life philosophy and the part that religion should play in it; because his school grades are low, he is not allowed to tinker with model aeroplanes, a hobby which he once very much enjoyed.

But that is not all. The girl in whom he has been interested for the past year has dropped him and now shows preference for his best friend. In common with many others he is very much worried over a sex problem—needlessly in his case. School problems, home problems, girl problems, health problems, sex problems, time problems, recreational problems—all have resulted in an intense inferiority complex. Does he not need careful counsel and help?

You would hardly guess this next girl to be Jewish, but she is. Grandfathers on both sides of the family were rabbis. Her mother was something of an opera star in her day, and the girl herself has a brilliant mind. She is the only child of well-to-do parents. They have a lovely home in one of the best residence sections of the city. She has been in this school a little over a year, but has almost no friends of either sex. Failure to make her mark socially has upset her emotionally to such an extent that she has become hypercritical both of herself and of others. You have probably noted her peculiar and disconcerting mannerisms which have hindered her adjustment. The numerous exclusive cliques with which this school is cursed have magnified her difficulties. She has been forced to remain without the pale. Vocation will probably never be a problem for her, but what steps can be taken to help her make desirable personal adjustments?

Boys like this next one offer little in the way of a problem. He is president of the student body, in all respects a fine outstanding boy. He is eighteen, has enough mental ability to succeed in any field and has made an almost perfect record in high school. He would ''rather study than eat.'' Chemical engineering is his vocational choice, made only after careful study of the field. He is going to college in the fall and must make his own way. The only thing which is puzzling him is this: Shall he join an outstandingly good fraternity which is rushing him or should he forego this opportunity since he must be self-supporting?

Here comes an immature fourteen-year-old boy who will graduate next spring. Such a pale, anemic youngster, so nervous that he can not sit still, can hardly be in good physical condition. Those thick-lensed glasses have probably resulted from the fact that he reads six or eight books each week on chemistry and related fields. He is the only child of old and poverty-stricken parents, who live on a small, isolated poultry farm. Mentally he is a potential genius; socially he is a moron; physically he is a weakling. Every effort has been made to convince his parents that he should remain in high school another year so that he might learn to live with people as well as to absorb information from books; but they are blinded to other considerations by pride in their son's scholastic achievements. What can be done to help this boy strike a reasonable balance between academic success on the one hand and physical and social development on the other?

The next girl's problem is entirely one of vocational choice and training. She will graduate in the spring. She is a strong, normal, healthy, reasonably attractive country girl who came to the city to work her way through high school. She is having difficulty in choosing between two fields—high-school teaching and nursing. She must make her own way entirely, but feels that if college training is the thing she needs she can accomplish it. And if she should decide upon nursing, should she take two years of college before entering training?

This rather lethargic boy who just stepped in is a freshman whose sister came in yesterday to talk about him and to arrange for me to see him to-day. He is as large as you or I, yet he is barely fifteen. It seems that last semester he failed three subjects and received a bare passing grade in the fourth. Lack of mental ability is often the explanation in such a case, but it does not apply here. According to the scholastic aptitude test which he took, his intelligence is such that without great difficulty he should have earned the highest grades in all his courses. He says he tries hard and has become discouraged over his lack of success.

Several factors contribute to his difficulty. First of all he has grown so fast that by the time he has gone to school all day and delivered groceries in the evening he has no energy left for study. He is intensely interested in anything mechanical, particularly in aeronautics, but this school offers no opportunity to explore in that direction. Much of his leisure time is spent in reading mechanical magazines and in "tinkering," but no connection exists between these interests and his school work. Only the traditional college preparatory courses are offered here. While he was in elementary school the work was so easy for him that he did not need to study to get fair grades. As a result he developed such slovenly study habits that now he has no idea how to study efficiently and effectively.

Would transfer to the technical high school straighten out his difficulties? How much mental and physical effort should we expect him to put forth while growing so fast? Can we make arrangements to train him in the techniques of study? The boy is blessed with an understanding father who is willing to cooperate in any way possible.

The next girl is eighteen years old, of German extraction and the oldest of several children. She started in the commercial high school but found it impossible to carry the work satisfactorily, and so she transferred here. In this general high school she is carrying the first semester of English for the fourth time. Last semester she failed everything but general science, and she barely passed that. As far as ability to get information out of books is concerned she is in the lowest one or two per cent. of high-school students. Yet she says she likes school and wants to continue!

Her father operates a small farm, and she enjoys such work better than any other occupation with which she is familiar. But her father, she says, has no use for her and has driven her away from home. She "hates" cooking and sewing. What outlets are there for her through science, she inquires. Her general appearance certainly gives no promise of an early marriage! What should such a girl do?

The boy who follows is one of the worst stammerers I have ever seen. Despite this and the fact that he is descended from the riff-raff of the town, he is well liked both by teachers and students. He gave one of the gamest exhibitions of running I have ever seen a few days ago when the coach sent him in to act as pace-setter in the half mile race of an important meet. He hopes eventually to become a newspaper man, due principally to the suggestion of an English teacher who says he has a rare spark of genius for writing. But did you see his face light up with hope when I suggested to him that there was a chance that his speech defect might be cured? No one had ever before told him that such a possibility existed. Every other consideration has become secondary to a consuming desire to rid himself of a condition that has for years made him miserable.

About a year ago I talked to the boy who has just come into the room. At that time he was very much discouraged because of his poor scholastic record. He was aimlessly drifting through school. He liked mathematics and history and was much interested in "why the wheels go round." A few suggestions were made to him last year: First, he was given definite instructions on how to improve his study habits; second, several occupational fields were discussed with him and ways of getting further information about them suggested; third, he was urged to investigate the feasibility of transfer to a technical high school. A remarkable change has occurred in a year's time. I can hardly believe he is the same boy. The uncertain, doubtful, hesitant attitude of twelve months ago has changed to a confident, happy outlook on life. He now wants to become a mechanical engineer, and although he has only average mental ability he seems likely to succeed.

This has been rather an extraordinary day. I am willing to grant that not every day does one meet with such a wide variety of problems as these boys and girls have presented. But the day is unusual when some situation different from the more obvious and expected vocational or educational problem does not appear. One never knows what situation will next present itself.

Out of the thousands of conferences similar to these to-day have come questions covering the whole range of educational, vocational and personal problems that perplex adolescents. Here are some samples: How can I get any social development when my parents won't even let me walk home from church with a boy? How could I get work in a cow-testing association? What does a year at college cost? How can I stop my mother from running around with men? Should I take my father's offer to set me up in the hardware business?

Since high school is so hard for me is it worth while to try to get through college? Is there any chance for a woman in electrotherapy? Should a boy who is late in reaching adolescence go to college at sixteen or seventeen? How do you get into the Government Forest Service? How can I study science and still believe in the Bible? Doesn't it take more courage to commit suicide than to live? Does it cost less to go to a small college than to a large one? If sex is a normal thing why don't people act like it was?

Are correspondence courses in electricity any good? Can business college training be transferred toward a regular college degree? Should a Protestant girl enter a Catholic hospital for nurse's training? How can I learn to concentrate? Are there any tests that will tell me what I am fitted for? Should I take up medicine just because my folks want me to? Should I go to a large college or to a small one?

Since my mother is insane do I dare to marry and have children? How is the best way to learn to be a chef? After I finish high school should I stay out a year and work or go on to college right away? Will bookkeeping machines crowd out regular bookkeepers? Does a professional boxer make anything if he is just an ordinary "palooka"? What things in life are most worth while?

And thousands of others. No one person, of course, no matter how thoroughly trained and competent he may be, can hope to answer all of them. He can answer many factual questions directly or put the individual in touch with reliable sources of information, but when the problem involves choice between two or more alternatives the counselor must be forever on his guard against making the decision himself. His chief functions are to see that the person understands his own problem and to help him get all information necessary for its intelligent solution.

How frequently do the various kinds of problems occur? After talking individually with about four thousand of these students, most of them seniors, I find that about seven questions out of every ten are concerned in one way or another with vocations. Nearly half of this group of questions, however, make specific inquiry about training for some occupation, so they may just as well be called educational as vocational. Nearly one fourth of the total involve general educational problems having to do with such things as college choice, entrance, cost, courses and so forth. Many are interested in trade schools and apprenticeship. Some, even as late as the senior year, wish help in improving their adjustments to high school.

Personal adjustment questions make up about 10 per cent. of the total. This is probably conservative as an estimate of the actual number of such problems which students have, owing to the very natural hesitancy of an individual to discuss his most intimate problems with another. It is surprising that the highly intelligent students have more personal adjustment problems than do those with less mental ability.

Why many of these problems should still be problems, particularly in the senior year of high school, is a question that has constantly recurred to me throughout the two years in which these conferences have been taking place. There seems to be but one answer—that some of the institutions which make up our society have failed in some degree to function effectively for these boys and girls, otherwise more of these questions would have been answered satisfactorily in earlier years.

No personnel program, no matter how effectively conceived and executed, would eliminate all problems. New problems constantly occur and old ones recur. The human equation can not be controlled mathematically; but the almost appalling nature of many of the problems indicates that more should be done to aid the individual to solve them. More important still, the occurrence of many of them should be forestalled before they ever become problems. We must give adequate attention to the prevention of maladjustment before serious social and emotional as well as academic and vocational problems develop.

If the home, the church, industry, other social institutions do not perform for young people the functions that might conceivably be allocated to them, it becomes the duty of the school to do whatever is necessary to make a well-rounded and satisfactorily adjusted individual. The school is responsible for doing more than it has in the past to forestall the occurrence of, or to resolve after occurrence, many of the problems of those enrolled.

On the surface of the moon astronomers have christened one area the Sea of Storms, because of its disturbed appearance. Perhaps no period of human existence can more certainly be called the Sea of Storms than adolescence. These adolescent storms, now waxing, now waning, sometimes intense, sometimes scarcely creating a ripple, have as their generating forces the processes which Hollingworth calls becoming psychologically weaned, achieving self-support, developing a heterosexual attitude and acquiring a point of view on life. Menninger's description of the storms of the college student aptly applies to the high-school student as well when he says:

There are problems of athletic ambition and disappointment. . . . There are problems of love affairs dealt with in the immature fashion to be expected at this age, but also with an intensity which the unsympathetic may easily underestimate. There are problems of jealousies and envies inside and outside the family, conflicts with parents, special antipathies to subjects and instructors, religious problems, curricular problems, physical problems real and imaginary, life-work problems, racial problems, sexual problems, economic problems—in fact, all the problems that older people have, plus a great many more.

As bodies of water often appear safe and calm, but have dangerous reefs, shoals, cross currents, undertows under the surface, so also has the Sea of Adolescence. If ever the individual needs a pilot to help him steer a course it is when he is passing through the adolescent Sea of Storms into the safer and calmer waters of adulthood. An effective student personnel program in every high school will go far toward helping chart the course.

EDUCATIONAL EVENTS

VACATION COURSES AT THE UNIVERSITY OF GENEVA

THE University of Geneva offers its forty-third annual summer vacation courses for modern French, for the benefit of foreign students, from July 5 to October 12. This year the courses include: A general course in French language, literature and culture from July 5 to 31; a special course in French language, literature and culture for teachers of French, from July 16 to August 15, and an elementary French course in 2 series, from July 5 to 31, and from August 3 to 29.

In the general course are included practical instruction in vocabulary, grammar, translation, phonetics and diction; lectures on French stylistics; descriptive and practical phonetics and literary recitals, also lessons on a variety of cultural topics. In the beginners course the students are grouped in small classes, according to their native language, and they will be given ten lessons per week by experienced teachers. Their studies will be devoted to French vocabulary, grammar, spelling, pronunciation, phonetics, exercises in phraseology, conversation, etc. Vacation courses for modern French will also be held at Lausanne and Neuchâtel.

At Lausanne, which is situated on the Lake of Geneva, vacation courses are available in two series of three weeks each, from July 16 to August 25 and from August 30 to October 10, respectively. At Neuchâtel, two university summer courses for modern French will be held from July 16 to August 9, and August 13 to September 5, respectively.

The fees for any of these courses at Geneva, Lausanne or Neuchâtel are very modest and the Swiss Railways and the Postal Motor Coach services will grant a special reduction of 30 per cent. on tickets issued at the Agencies of the Swiss Federal Railways or Tourist offices abroad. This reduction is granted for the summer season, *i.e.,* from June 15 to October 15, on condition that the visitor stays at least 7 days in Switzerland.

In addition it may be pointed out that the Swiss Railroads grant a special rebate of 50 per cent. on single or return second and third class tickets to foreign students between the ages 16 to 25 provided that they are registered in a foreign university, and that they subscribe to at least one series of a vacation course.

Extensive preparations are made by Swiss university cities for the general entertainment of foreign students. There will be musical and literary soirées, as well as regular excursions. Wednesday afternoons are generally devoted to hikes in the city's environs, with each one having a goal of its own, such as an old church, a medieval château, a picturesque village or near-by point of view. Saturdays are usually devoted to longer trips into the Alpine regions. Participation in these outings is not obligatory, but their cost will be kept at a low figure.

STATE AID FOR PUBLIC SCHOOLS IN 1933

THE National Education Association has drawn up the following summary of state legislation enacted during the year 1933:

Alabama pledged net proceeds from new personal and corporation income taxes to refund state obligations that include $11,000,000 for education.

California raised from state sources revenue formerly required for school support from county sources.

Indiana kept all schools open by providing that county school corporations shall receive three fourths of the proceeds remaining from a new tax on intangibles after 10 per cent. is paid to the state general fund.

Iowa strengthened its teacher certification laws, differentiating certificates according to training and position.

Michigan set aside for equalization purposes 10 per cent. up to $15,000,000 of the balance from a new gross retail sales tax, after $31,700,000 is set aside for other state purposes.

North Carolina provided a $16,000,000 annual appropriation to operate schools for eight months on state standards.

Ohio apportioned 96 per cent. of the revenue from a tax on intangibles among schools.

Pennsylvania took steps to provide $5,000,000 for financially embarrassed school districts, through tax on alcoholic beverages.

South Carolina assumed for a six-month term the cost of public school teachers' salaries. The state also earmarked for school purposes $893,000 of the proceeds from the personal income tax.

South Dakota earmarked for school purposes 50 per cent. of the gross revenue from a new gross income tax.

Tennessee authorized a bond issue from which the state paid to counties approximately $8,000,000 owed them for schools.

Virginia restored to the school budget $150,000 to prevent school closings up to the January, 1934, meeting of the General Assembly.

West Virginia adopted a county-unit system of schools, consolidating all magisterial, subdistricts and independent districts under county boards of education.

THE UNEMPLOYMENT PROBLEM IN PENNSYLVANIA

DR. JAMES N. RULE, state superintendent of public instruction for Pennsylvania, writes in the May issue of the *Public Education Bulletin* that this year Pennsylvania secondary schools graduate more than 60,000 boys and girls. Possibly one fourth of this group will continue their work in higher institutions next fall. A small percentage of them will find employment. A still larger group will join the ranks of the unemployed.

He continues: "There is a distinct need in Pennsylvania for types of educational activities and opportunities, both on the vocational and the avocational level, that will extend our present program of adult education. It is reported that in one of the large industrial cities in the country an agreement has been reached to employ no one who is under twenty-one years of age. Conditions in industry practically have determined that this situation will prevail in most of our communities. Present educational and recreational facilities are neither adequate nor adapted to meet the needs of our young people. So that their needs may be understood more clearly, the following suggestions are made:

1. Every community in the Commonwealth should organize cooperative committees to consider the problem of unemployed youth, and youth about to leave or be graduated from school. This committee may well be made up of business men, school teachers, supervisors and administrators, social leaders and representative youth in the community.
2. Efforts should be made wherever possible to develop recreational programs and enterprises which will provide wholesome, creative activities for groups of unemployed young people.
3. As a part of the community survey an effort should be made to see if it is not possible to organize cooperative enterprises, handicraft centers, and projects of some type to engage the interest and abilities of these young people, at least temporarily.
4. Much has been accomplished in the way of developing morale-building programs. Youth itself can be of tremendous help in this respect. Summer camps, organized on a cooperative basis and providing for a low cost maintenance, will be helpful.

THE MICHIGAN TRAINING SCHOOL FOR YOUNG EXPLORERS

THE organization of a training school for young explorers, interested in adventure and the scientific methods of modern exploring, with uncharted wilds of the Yukon as the first "laboratory," will be initiated at the University of Michigan under the direction of Professor Ralph L. Belknap, of the department of geology and director of the last University of Michigan Greenland Expedition. It is proposed to develop an American group of young explorers, similar to the Oxford Arctic Club, which is a recognized scientific organization in England.

Professor Belknap points out that it is a popular idea that exploring, except in the Antarctic regions, is a business of the past, but the fact is that large areas exist in many parts of the world of which we have no real knowledge other than the report of their existence by some who have traveled rapidly across country. This was the case with Greenland until recent years, when scientific men of several nations became interested in the weather of that continent as an influence on transatlantic flying.

The new explorer, it is said, will differ from the traditional adventurer who traveled largely for sport, curiosity, personal profit or vague scientific interest. He will be a man fairly expert in several sciences at least. Instead of dashing across country he will travel slowly, mapping the land, studying its plant, animal and human life, with particular care given to accurate estimates of natural resources and geological and meteorological conditions. Probably the work will be carried on increasingly by fairly large expeditions, like that of Admiral Byrd, so that the members of expeditions will be in a position to achieve more really important results for the advancement of knowledge, than the old-fashioned pioneer adventurer.

The party which will enter the Yukon this summer will consist of Professor Belknap; George Tennant, cook of the first Byrd expedition, and, probably, Dr. Peter Heinbecker, of Washington University, St. Louis, who has made medical studies in Labrador and Greenland, and about twenty "students."

Establishing a base camp above Dawson, the expedition will travel northward into territory ideally suited to learning the technique of exploration. A little gold panning is planned, but practical geography, geology, nature study and photography will be given most attention. It is also planned to study how glaciers eat backward into mountain valleys and to make tests of the thickness of the glacial ice.

APPOINTMENTS FROM NEW YORK STATE TO THE FACULTY OF THE SUMMER SESSION OF COLUMBIA UNIVERSITY

ACCORDING to an announcement recently made by Dr. John J. Coss, director of the Columbia University summer session, which opens on July 9, more than fifty representatives of labor, the clergy, the arts, business and the schools, colleges and universities of the State of New York are included in the faculty appointments.

Among these are:

Dr. Edmund B. Chaffee, director of the Labor Temple, New York City, who will participate with Kirby Page, editor of *The World To-morrow,* and Professor Daniel J. Fleming in a course in ethical issues in modern society at the Union Theological Seminary. C. Ivar Hellstrom, minister of religious education at the Riverside Church, New York City, will give a course at the seminary on "The Church's Educational Task." Dean L. A. Weigle, of the Yale Divinity School, and Professor H. S. Elliott, of Union College, will also collaborate in this course.

Carl L. Becker, John Stambaugh professor of history at Cornell University, will give a course on political and social conditions in France prior to the Revolution and the intellectual movement in the eighteenth century. Dr. Nathaniel Schmidt, professor emeritus of Semitic languages and Oriental history, also of Cornell University, will direct a study of the Roman empire.

Bruce Bliven, editor of *The New Republic,* and Joseph Wood Krutch, dramatic critic and associate editor of *The Nation,* will join with four other scholars in a symposium on outstanding movements in the literature of the present day. A class in "Newspaper Practice," directed by Robert E. Garst, of *The New York Times,* will be organized as a newspaper staff with the instructor as the editor in charge, and the essentials of writing advertising copy will be outlined by William I. Orchard, of Batten, Barton, Durstine and Osborn, Incorporated. Otto W. Fuhrman, consulting typographer and director of the Division of Graphic Arts, New York University, will consider printing as an art and compare it with other forms of artistic expression in a course on the history of bookmaking.

Miss Amelia Grant, director of the nursing service of the New York State Board of Health, and Miss Jessie T. Prisch, of the State Normal School, New Paltz, will give instruction in nursing. Courses in the School of Library Service will be given by Miss Amelia H. Munson, of the New York Public Library; Miss Edna B. Bayer, librarian of the Benjamin Franklin Junior-Senior High School, Rochester; Miss Linda H. Morley, librarian of the Industrial Relations Counselors, Incorporated, New York City, and Charles F. McCombs, superintendent of the Main Reading Room, New York Public Library. In music, courses will be given by members of the Juilliard School.

Other instructors will include Floyd H. Allport, professor of psychology at Harvard University; Dr. Joseph M. Feld, of Brooklyn College; Edward W. Mammen, of the College of the City of New York, and Dr. Varney Clyde Arnspiger, director of research of the Erpi Picture Consultants.

THE SUMMER QUARTER OF STANFORD UNIVERSITY

ACCORDING to a correspondent, Stanford University plans a Summer Quarter faculty for 1934–35 which is representative of widely varied academic circles. From Europe, Angel Gonzales-Palencia is bringing Spanish culture and his special knowledge of Arabic; Camillo von Klenze, of the University of Munich, is teaching both during the spring and summer; Felix Bloch, the German physicist, will lecture at the university for a two-year period; G. Marston Haddock, director of the Leeds School of Music, England, will be a lecturer in public speaking.

Professor William Leonard Crum, of Harvard University, formerly editor of the *Harvard Review of Economic Statistics,* will lecture in the department of economics. From Yale University, the head of the department of history, Professor Ralph H. Gabriel, will give courses relating to the social and intellectual history of the United States.

The department of sociology will hear Professor Roderick D. McKenzie, of the University of Michigan; lectures in mathematics will be given by Professor Dunham Jackson, of the University of Minnesota. Professor Peter H. Odegard, from the Ohio State University, is giving during the spring and summer months the courses usually directed by Professor T. A. Barclay, who is now on leave. Professor William Savery, of the University of Washington, will lecture in philosophy.

Among lecturers in the School of Education are Charles Clinton Peters, director of educational research at Pennsylvania State College; John Alexander McGeogh, professor of psychology at the University of Missouri; Walter R. Hepner, chief of the Division of Secondary Education for the State of California; Lucia Bush Mirrielees, professor of English at the University of Montana; Alvin C. Eurich, assistant professor and assistant director of educational research at the University of Minnesota, and Paul R. Hanna, associate director of research, Lincoln School, Columbia University.

SCHOOL EXECUTIVE CONFERENCE AT THE UNIVERSITY OF DENVER

IN recognition of the fact that many school executives find it impossible to remain away from their work for the full duration of a regular summer session, and that others are not able to remain in Denver during a full six weeks' period, the University of Denver this year is inaugurating a Summer School Executives Conference under the direction of Dr. Arnold E. Joyal, who will serve as director. The conference will be administered by the department of education at the university, and will be held during the last week of the first summer session and the first week of the second session; that is, from July 18 to 27, inclusive.

The purpose of the conference is to provide an opportunity to obtain an intensive study of the recent information in the field of school administration and supervision in a short time and with minimum expense. The conference will be organized with two sessions daily for each of the ten days of its duration. The morning session will extend from 9:00 to 12:00; the afternoon session from 1:30 to 3:30. Thus, there will be twenty meetings of the group. At each of these meetings, some one single important topic of special interest to the group will be discussed. A different instructor will present each of the twenty topics which have been selected.

The faculty will be made up of regular members of the summer session staff and other especially qualified school men in the state who have been invited to participate. The conference will be on a non-academic basis. There will be no academic credit granted for attendance, although a certificate of attendance will be issued to those who desire it. There will be no examinations. Participation in the discussion will be purely voluntary. The total cost of the conference will be $11.00, one dollar of which will pay for a syllabus and selected bibliography.

The topics which have been selected for discussion were built up by a survey of the interests of typical school men in the field. Every attempt will be made to keep the subject-matter and discussion on a practical basis. Each instructor will devote a part of the session to a discussion of the special problems brought out by the conference.

The following is a provisional list of instructors: Helen Allphin, supervisor of intermediate grades, Denver Public Schools; H. M. Corning, superintendent of schools, Colorado Springs; C. L. Cushman, director of research and curriculum, Denver Public Schools; Guy Fox, assistant director of research, Denver Public Schools; Charles E. Greene, assistant superintendent of schools, Denver; Frederick M. Hunter, chancellor of the university and professor of education; Granville B. Johnson, professor of physical education; Arnold E. Joyal, assistant professor of education; Inez Johnson Lewis, state superintendent of public instruction; Percy Locey, professor of physical education; G. L. Maxwell, associate professor of education; Lawrence W. Miller, professor of psychology; W. B. Mooney, executive secretary, Colorado Education Association; W. F. Templin, county superintendent of schools, Las Animas County; A. L. Threlkeld, superintendent of schools, Denver; R. J. Walters, dean of the College of Liberal Arts and professor of education; Gilbert S. Willey, professor of education; Ernest A. Zelliot, associate professor of education.

HONORARY DEGREES CONFERRED BY COLUMBIA UNIVERSITY

AT its commencement exercises Columbia University conferred nine honorary degrees. In making the awards to those most immediately concerned with education, President Nicholas Murray Butler said:

DOCTOR OF SCIENCE

ERNEST WILLIAM BROWN—Native of England, schooled at Christ's College, Cambridge; outstanding mathematician, honored time and again on three continents for highly important contributions to lunar theory and to celestial and general mechanics; who can soothe Othello when he cries: "It is the very error of the moon; she comes more nearer earth than she was wont, and makes men mad." Professor of mathematics at Yale University since 1907.

JAMES BRYANT CONANT—Born and bred in Massachusetts and trained at Harvard College, to which he is giving his life as man of science and now as chief administrative officer; early reaching highest distinction for research in the field of organic chemistry, and as president of Harvard University, twenty-third in a noteworthy succession of truly great men in a truly great post.

DOCTOR OF LETTERS

HARRY WOODBURN CHASE—Of New England stock and birth, graduated from Dartmouth College and Clark University; turning to educational philosophy and administration, and rendering noteworthy service in succession at Clark University, at the University of North Carolina and at the University of Illinois; now our neighbor and friend as chancellor of New York University, which has a full century of accomplishment to look back upon.

HAROLD WILLIS DODDS—Of Pennsylvania stock, pursuing studies at Grove City College, at Princeton and at the University of Pennsylvania; gaining experience as an academic teacher at Purdue and Western Reserve University before going back to Princeton; experienced in public affairs and administration as adviser to several South and Central American governments; just now chosen to be president of Princeton University to take up the noble task which in our own time has been borne with distinction by McGosh, by Patton, by Wilson and by Hibben; rejoicing in the good will and happy friendship of us all.

DOCTOR OF LAWS

CORDELL HULL—Trained in the liberal arts and in the law in his native state of Tennessee; quickly entering upon public service and earning an enviable reputation as, successively, member of the Legislature of the State of Tennessee, Judge of the State Court, member of the House of Representatives and a Senator of the United States; chosen by the President at this critical moment to counsel and to guide in the formulation and conduct of our international relations, which constitute the most important problem before this country and before the world; looking facts steadily and courageously in the face, and giving the counsels of true progress toward peace and prosperity for our own people and for all people.

John Maynard Keynes—Climbing the ladder of scholarship and discipline at Eton and at King's College, Cambridge; quickly and closely associated with public policies, national and international, as trusted economic adviser and counselor; one of the most brilliant economic minds of our time, engaged in the well-nigh hopeless task of trying to make our fellow men informed in respect to what affects them most directly; one who prefers intelligent planning of human affairs to the attempt without either guiding principle or courageous understanding, to "muddle through" changing social, economic and political conditions as these are so constantly presenting themselves in new and difficult forms.

EDUCATIONAL NOTES AND NEWS

Dr. L. P. Sieg, professor of physics, dean of the College and of the Graduate School and acting dean of the School of Education at the University of Pittsburgh, will assume the presidency of the University of Washington, at Seattle, on August 1.

The Rev. Dr. Fred P. Corson, of Baldwin, New York, superintendent of the Brooklyn South District of the New York East Conference of the Methodist Episcopal Church, was elected president of Dickinson College, at the annual meeting of the board of trustees on June 8. Dr. Corson, who is thirty-eight years old, succeeds Dr. Karl T. Waugh, who resigned last June. Dr. J. H. Morgan, president of the college from 1914 to 1928, and again from 1931 to 1932, has been serving as president for the past year.

Dr. Tyler W. Dennett, who will become president of Williams College upon the retirement this month of Dr. Harry A. Garfield, was guest of honor on June 11 at the Williams Club of New York City. The board of governors of the club, headed by Judge Charles C. Nott, Jr., gave Professor Dennett a dinner, and the alumni of Williams welcomed him afterwards.

The Rev. Dr. Earl S. Rudisill was installed as president of Thiel College at Greenville, Pennsylvania, on June 6.

Dr. Joseph A. Serena has resigned as president of Bethany College, West Virginia. Dr. Serena, who was president of the Southeast Missouri State Teachers College at Cape Girardeau, became president of Bethany College last September.

Middlebury College conferred at commencement on June 11 the degree of doctor of laws on Dr. A. Lawrence Lowell, president emeritus of Harvard University..

Boston University conferred on June 11 the degree of doctor of literature on Dr. George F. Zook, U. S. Commissioner of Education and director elect of the American Council on Education. The degree of doctor of the humanities was conferred on Dr. James Bryant Conant, of Harvard University, and on Dr. John Lawrence Seaton, president of Albion College. Dr. Zook gave the commencement address.

At the one hundred and thirteenth commencement of the George Washington University the doctorate of laws was conferred on John Lloyd Newcomb, who was recently installed as president of the University of Virginia, and on President Arthur Cutts Willard, of the University of Illinois. The award to the two college presidents was made in observance of the fiftieth aniversary of the founding of the School of Engineering.

The degree of doctor of laws was conferred by the University of Nebraska at commencement on Dr. Walter B. Pillsbury, professor of psychology at the University of Michigan.

Dean Frank W. Nicholson, who has been associated with Wesleyan University for forty-three years, has retired with the title of professor emeritus. He will be the guest of honor at the annual meeting of the Alumni Association on June 16.

TRIBUTE was paid Dr. A. C. Rothermel, retiring president of the State Teachers College at Kutztown, when all teacher college presidents of Pennsylvania attended a special assembly at the college on May 18. It was the first time the presidents of all State Teachers Colleges had assembled at one of these institutions to honor its president. Dr. Rothermel retires at the close of the current college year following forty-eight years of active service in the public schools of Pennsylvania. For the past thirty-five years he has been president of the college.

A DINNER in honor of Dr. John R. Murlin, director of the department of vital economics at the University of Rochester, was recently given by members of the staff, graduate students and other associates, in celebration of the sixtieth anniversary of his birth. A morocco-bound volume of letters of greeting from many of his friends was presented.

DR. ALEXANDER VASILIEV, professor of ancient history at the University of Wisconsin, has been elected a member of the Academy of Sciences at Belgrade, Jugoslavia, in recognition of his contributions to the field of Byzantine history. Professor Vasiliev is now on leave of absence in order to make a further study of Byzantine civilization.

THE Venezuelan Government has conferred upon Dr. A. Curtis Wilgus, director of the Center of Inter-American Studies of George Washington University, its medal of honor of public instruction in recognition of his scholarship in the field of Hispanic-American studies, and contributions to cultural relations between the countries of the Americas.

PROFESSOR WILLIAM A. LAMBETH, of the University of Virginia, has been decorated with the cross of Commendatore of the Crown of Italy. It is the third time that the Italian government has decorated Dr. Lambeth in recognition of the efforts he has made to bring about a better understanding of Italy in the United States.

JOHN KIRKLAND CLARK, lawyer of New York City, was elected president of the New York Alumni Chapter of Phi Beta Kappa at its recent annual meeting.

DR. HAJO HOLBORN, who since 1931 has occupied the Carnegie chair of modern history and international relations at the Berlin School of Politics, has been appointed visiting professor of history at Yale University.

DR. WILLIAM A. YEAGER, who for the past four years has been assistant director of the Teacher Division of the Pennsylvania State Department of Public Instruction, has been appointed professor of education and director of courses in educational administration at the University of Pittsburgh. He will begin his work with the six weeks' summer session on July 2. Dr. Yeager will fill the position left vacant by the resignation of Dr. Q. A. W. Rohrbach, who becomes president of the state teachers college at Kutztown, Pennsylvania.

THROUGH recognition by the Juilliard Foundation of Music, New York City, the University of Denver will have a professorship of music, beginning in September. Miss Lucille Wilkin, who is a graduate of the Juilliard School, who studied under Madame Olga Samaross while there, has been appointed by the board of trustees to be the first professor.

HORACE S. FORD, bursar at the Massachusetts Institute of Technology for twenty years, has been appointed treasurer and a member of the corporation. Delbert L. Rhind, assistant bursar, succeeds Mr. Ford and Wolcott A. Hokanson, chief accountant, has been made assistant bursar.

DR. HOWARD F. LOWRY, of the department of English of the College of Wooster, has been appointed general editor and educational manager of the Oxford University Press in America. Professor Lowry was recently elected a Guggenheim fellow for 1934–35. Active association with the press will not begin until early in 1935. Dr. Lowry will be in England engaged in literary research from the close of the college year until the beginning of the second semester. He will continue his work in the college, teaching two courses during the college year.

HENRY RUTZ, of Milwaukee, who has been teaching classes for workers in industry in eight principal cities this winter under the program of the School for Workers of the University of Wisconsin, has been named State Supervisor of Workers' Education.

DR. EDWIN W. KEMMERER, Walker professor of international finance at Princeton University, sailed on June 3, *en route* to Turkey, where he will act as adviser to the Turkish Government in its currency and banking problems.

DR. GUY E. SNAVELY, president of Birmingham-Southern College, sailed on June 2 from New York, to spend two months in Europe.

LEAVE of absence for three months has been granted to Clarence E. Walton, assistant librarian at Harvard University, to investigate the organization and special problems of European libraries.

JUSTICE HARLAN F. STONE, of the United States Supreme Court; Marvin Bristol Rosenberry, chief justice of the Wisconsin Supreme Court; Newton D. Baker, and Dean Roscoe Pound, of the Harvard Law School, will deliver the principal addresses on June 15 at the formal dedication of the new building of the University of Michigan Law School.

DR. DAVID ALLAN ROBERTSON, president of Goucher College, Baltimore, delivered the address at the commencement exercises of Mary Baldwin College on May 29, taking as his subject "Commencements." On June 5 he spoke at the commencement of Randolph-Macon College for Women on "Tourists and Explorers." On June 11 he will make the annual Phi Beta Kappa address at the University of Virginia on "Universities in Memoirs," and on June 13 the commencement address, "Foreign Criticism of American Universities" at the University of Buffalo.

DR. CLARENCE C. LITTLE, managing director of the American Society for the Control of Cancer and director of the Roscoe B. Jackson Memorial Laboratory at Bar Harbor, Maine, formerly president of the University of Michigan, gave the commencement address at the Child Education Foundation Training School, New York City.

DR. ROBERT C. CLOTHIER, president of Rutgers University, gave the baccalaureate address at the commencement exercises of the New Jersey College for Women.

AT the seventy-first annual commencement of Kansas State College at Manhattan on May 31, Dr. W. E. Wickenden, president of Case School of Applied Science, delivered the address on "Making Terms with the Machine."

PROFESSOR WILLIAM ROBERT SHEPHERD, Seth Low professor of history at Columbia University, died in Berlin on June 7. He was sixty-two years old. Dr. Shepherd reached Berlin on June 1 expecting to lecture at the University of Berlin on June 5. On account of his illness his lecture was read by Professor Schoenemann. Two years ago Dr. Shepherd was appointed visiting Carnegie professor at the University of Vienna, where he lectured on the influence of American institutions on the life and thought of Europe. For this work he was awarded the gold medal of honor of the government of Austria.

A CONFERENCE of the New York State division of the North Atlantic section of the American Association of University Women was held at Vassar College, Poughkeepsie, from June 14 to 16. The speakers included President Henry Noble MacCracken and Dean C. Mildred Thompson, of Vassar; E. C. Lindeman, of the New York School of Social Work, and Dr. Marion Edwards Park, president of Bryn Mawr College.

DR. JAMES T. SHOTWELL, director of the Division of Economics and History of the Carnegie Endowment for International Peace, has announced plans for a survey of the economic, social and political relations of the United States and Canada. Relations of the two countries will be covered from the time their people were fur traders and forest rangers down to the present. Parts of the Canadian-American survey have been under way for two years, and will occupy the next two years. Results will be announced late in 1934 and again in 1935. There will be large working staffs in both countries.

SENATE BILL 3487, known as the Industrial Credit Bill, which provides for loans from the Reconstruction Finance Corporation to industrial corporations, has been amended in the House to provide for loans to school districts to be made up to January 31, 1935, to pay teachers' salaries due and unpaid up to June 30, 1934. This amendment, known as the Sabath amendment, will provide not to exceed $75,000,000 in outstanding loans at any one time for this purpose. An unsuccessful attempt was made on the floor of the House to have this amendment provide loans to school districts and school boards of education for the refinancing of school district indebtedness as well as the paying of teachers' salaries. Since the original bill had already been passed by the Senate, the amended bill has been returned to the Senate for concurrence on the amendment. A motion was made in the Senate to refuse to concur and a conference committee was appointed to meet with the conference committee of the House. This committee will probably decide what disposition is to be made of this amendment.

AN Associated Press dispatch reports that unemployed teachers in many states soon will attend classes financed by the Federal Government to study methods of giving instruction to industrial workers. Georgia, Iowa, Pennsylvania, Tennessee, Illinois, Wisconsin, North Carolina and California have been allotted $5,600 each for such short-course institutes. Most of the classes will be attended by teachers from surrounding states. The first training center was opened at Atlanta University on June 2, with thirty unemployed Negro teachers from Georgia, Alabama, Mississippi, Louisiana, Texas, Florida, Tennessee, North Carolina, South Carolina, Maryland, Virginia and Kentucky. The second center opened at the State University of Iowa on June 11, with students selected from Iowa, Missouri and Kansas.

ACCORDING to *The Christian Science Monitor*, M. D. Collins, state superintendent of the schools of Georgia, reports that with federal approval of a $2,000,000 grant to the rural schools of the state all such schools are enabled to remain open for the fall term. This grant benefits more than 12,000 Georgia teachers, in addition to the 1,000 teachers on the CWA pay roll already serving in vocational and special adult instruction in various counties. About three fourths of the school systems of the state will be aided with this federal expenditure. A number of counties had already exhausted their school funds and many of the schools had been closed. These can now be reopened.

The Oregon Education Journal reports that through its tax system, 98 per cent. of the school funds of the State of Oregon are derived from a direct property tax. Last year the tax delinquency averaged 43.77 per cent. for the state. Returns from the first quarter payments in twenty-two counties indicate that the delinquency will be as great this year. It is estimated that fully half of the amounts received in March were full year payments. This year they received 3 per cent. discount for paying in full in March. When winter comes the treasuries will again be empty. The school district warrant indebtedness is now $6,000,000, almost half the cost of maintaining the schools last year.

As a first step in a plan which contemplates giving more intellectual independence to students, greater flexibility of schedule and more concentrated periods, the faculty of Vassar College voted on May 21 to abolish hygiene as a required 2-hour course for freshmen, substituting a few required lectures on health. President MacCracken's semester course in education is to be replaced by not more than seven orientation lectures given by the president to assist the freshmen in choosing their major fields. By the new plan a freshman's time will be divided as evenly as possible among four courses in the general groups at present offered—arts, language, social and natural sciences.

ACCORDING to the *Western Journal of Education*, the California Council of Education, under President W. E. Givens, has decided to submit for adoption by the people of a plan for the reorganization of the State Board of Education. Herbert Healy, of Kern County, chairman of the reorganization of the state department committee, proposed the resolution providing for an elective board and the appointment of a director of education, the term of office to be ten years for members of the board and the director to serve at the pleasure of the board.

THE Westchester Institute of Fine Arts has acquired the property in Tarrytown, New York, formerly occupied by the Castle School for Girls. The institute is sponsored by 100 well-known artists. Courses in art, music, drama, literature and dancing will be included in the expanded curriculum. Situated on a site of fourteen and a half acres the school can accommodate 200 resident students and more than

1,000 day students. Charles A. Birch-Field is at the head of the group sponsoring the institute, and the Westchester Galleries, which are an affiliate of the institute, will be housed in the school.

A NEW pension system and group insurance plan will become effective at Princeton University beginning on July 1. President Dodds states that the new plan will guarantee more liberal retiring allowances, and larger members' pension and widows' pensions although the maximum amount will be $4,000. All faculty members above the rank of instructor participate in the plan, which calls for contribution of 5 per cent. of each faculty member's salary, this sum not to exceed $400. The university will set aside each year a like sum. These joint contributions will cease when the accumulations are sufficient to provide for the maximum total pension to which the faculty member is entitled. The new pensions are applicable only to members of the faculty who retire after 1940. Any faculty member retiring at the age of sixty-eight, in the next six years, will receive a pension of half his regular salary during the last year of his active service, the sum not to exceed $3,250. If a member dies, leaving a widow, the university will guarantee a pension for the remainder of her life of half her husband's pension, the minimum annual payment to be $1,500.

BEGINNING with the entering class next fall grades will be eliminated in the compulsory course in physical education required of all freshmen at Dartmouth College. "Passed" and "Failed" will be substituted. The present policy of accrediting this course and various compulsory recreational activities toward graduation will be abandoned, beginning with the next incoming class. The new plan reduces the required number of semester hour credits from 122 to 120. The present standard of 220 points will continue. Accordingly the general scholastic average necessary for graduation will be slightly raised from 1.818 to 1.833 and a possible perfect average of 4.0. Professor Harold R. Bruce, chairman of the committee on educational policy, in commenting on these changes, pointed out that Dartmouth was one of the few colleges in America which granted academic credits for recreational work.

CORNELL UNIVERSITY announces that beginning next autumn the College of Arts and Sciences will offer an undergraduate course in all the major arts and related subjects. The new program will emphasize three points: a requirement of introductory and advanced work in esthetics; a distribution of required and elective courses in literary art, including dramatics, music, drawing, painting, sculpture and architecture; a selection of advanced courses in the major divisions of art. The traditions and products of artistic endeavor, principles of criticism and the recognized canons of good taste will be emphasized.

DISCUSSION

NEEDED: A NEW PATRIOTISM

THE activities of our national government have increased steadily from the beginning. They have increased very rapidly during the last year. A good many of us believe that this movement is to continue. But when we think of it, we are aghast at the inefficiency and corruption of our state and municipal governments and the amount of politics that enters into national appointments. No one can claim that our municipalities are either as well managed or secure the same loyalty that our better corporations do.

In some way we as teachers have failed to give the youth of America a feeling of membership and responsibility such as must come if we are to become in fact a great cooperating community or corporation in which the good of all is also the good of each.

It has generally been held that the creation of loyalty and patriotism was largely a function of the teaching of history and the bestowing of honors. We may well ask ourselves if we can expect to develop the peace-time virtues, the feeling of cooperation and responsibility for the public welfare through a history which devotes two thirds or three fourths of its pages to war. Is there any reason for holding up these wars perpetually to the public gaze? The sooner they are forgotten the better. Does the soldier represent the ideal for America to follow in the years to come?

It has been our custom in the past to regard patriotism as nearly synonymous with army service. If we may judge from the monuments that have been erected to "Our Heroes" of the world war, it was quite unnecessary that this service should have been voluntary. Apparently the soldier became a hero and a patriot through army service, even though he came into the army through a forced draft. The volunteers in the American army of 1918 represented only a small portion, outside of the officers. The army itself was a mere cross-section of American life. Those who entered training were no more and no less patriotic than those who remained at home. Undoubtedly there is something to be said for army service as a method of creating loyalty to the army and the flag. There is much to be said for the attitude of the public toward the soldier after his return to civil life. If you always treat the returned soldier as a patriot, if you eulogize him as such on the Fourth of July and erect monuments to him in every town and place his name on rolls of honor in high schools and city halls, the suggestion may mean much. We always tend to live up to what the public expects of us.

But it must be said of army service in general that it has little effect in developing loyalty to the country's welfare in time of peace. The powerful lobbies ex-soldiers have maintained in Congress to work for public funds and positions have been more feared than any other lobbies. Their insistent demand for the immediate payment of the bonus, not due till 1945, in a national crisis such as this, when most teachers, health officers and other public officials have voluntarily accepted a reduction in pay in order that these various governing bodies might not go bankrupt, has shown that the veteran is made of the same clay as the rest of us. If we look at the struggle for better government in our cities, we do not find returned soldiers particularly conspicuous.

Of course the idea that any one drafted into the army becomes a hero and a patriot thereby is ridiculous on the face of it. The custom of placing "honor rolls" of soldiers in public buildings and lionizing the veteran in public life is not merely grossly unjust to those who served just as devotedly at home, but it tends to perpetuate the ideals and animosities of war, to hold before the youth of the country an obsolete ideal of patriotism, that harks back to a time when war was man's chief business and the very existence of the tribe often depended on this service being instantly and voluntarily given.

While the willingness to serve in the time of a national emergency may be necessary, it is not an occasion in which we are likely to fall short. The drums and bugles, the marching columns, the public press and the draft will care for that. Placing the soldier before the youth of America as an ideal tends only to divert public attention from the issues of the moment which are honesty and efficiency in office and a general devotion to the public good.

Even if the soldier ideal were an adequate ideal of patriotism for young men in the twenties, it would still be a very inadequate ideal to hold before the country at large. It does not apply to men under twenty or over thirty nor to the women of any age. War can never be more than an incident in the life of America. We hope it will not come again in this generation. It is foolish to give so much emphasis to an ideal that applies to so small a section of the population, and one that is so seldom if ever needed.

America needs an ideal of patriotism which applies at all times to all, to boys and girls, men and women alike. That ideal is quite obviously devotion to the public good. It means honesty and efficiency in office. It means willingness to serve where service will be most helpful. It means that the duties of citizenship will not be entirely neglected at the polls. It means that every citizen will enlist to fight corruption in office with as much fervor as he would enlist against a foreign foe.

What shall we say of the murders, racketeering, kidnappings and corruption in our American cities, of the inefficient and wasteful methods by which they are run? These bribe-taking politicians are the real traitors to the American people, a hundred times more guilty than the deserter in time of war. If we deem the latter worthy of death, what shall we say of the politician who practically licenses the racketeer to commit murder?

There are more murders committed in Chicago every year than there are in London in fifty, and where 95 per cent. of Chicago's criminals go free, about 95 per cent. of London's criminals are convicted and punished. It is not that we are less competent to deal with the criminal in this country or that the problem is more difficult, but because the forces of crime are allied with the political machine and our indifference. Our war ideals do not serve. We need a type of patriotism that will make such an alliance so abhorrent to the public conscience that it will sweep out of office and into the penitentiaries such officials.

If this is to come to pass, we must begin down in the grammar school and continue through the universities to hold before the youth of America a broader ideal of citizenship and patriotism. We must build fewer monuments to ex-soldiers and erect more to those who in time of peace have rendered notable service. We must proclaim even in our Fourth of July orations that there are other fields beside battlefields on which a citizen may serve.

There are many things that the community could do better and more cheaply for us than we can do them for ourselves, if we can secure honesty and efficiency in public office. But all progress in government and in community life are halted by this thus far insuperable barrier. Big business has learned how to be efficient. It has discovered new and better methods of doing work. It has carried on continuous research and made great improvements in its product. It has developed great economies in production and marketing. Government is the biggest business of all and the most wasteful and incompetent, because we have not thus far been able to put into it the same sort of devotion that big business has always had.

We have made school children hate our Benedict Arnolds and deserters in time of war. Can we give them the same contempt for the dishonest public official? Can we develop in the youth of America an enthusiasm for public service in the spirit of the missionary and the crusader that will be a real religion of humanity? This is the central need and ideal behind all representative government and all public education; but thus far it seems to have been overlooked. This ideal will not be achieved by lionizing the soldier as our best example of patriotism. The willingness to serve in time of war is a mere by-product of the broader ideal.

HENRY S. CURTIS

ANN ARBOR, MICH.

WHY AN ACTIVITY PROGRAM?

RECENTLY I had occasion to present in one minute the "main" argument for an "activity program," defined as a program in which the learners have considerable freedom of choice as to the activities they engage in and the projects they pursue. Since extreme brevity sometimes helps to clarify issues, the attempted condensation is here set down:

If we grant, as we must grant, that,

(1) *We learn to do what we do by doing it*—in other words, that learning consists largely in the reduction of the amount of effort, waste motion and outside help required for a given action—and that,

(2) *The ability to evaluate and choose one's own objectives wisely and to pursue them steadily is an important and an improvable ability*—in other words, that the power to evaluate, initiate and sustain action, with minimum help and effort (*i.e.*, with maximum skill), may be and *should* be developed—then, we must grant that,

(3) Any program which provides (as an "activity program" provides) an opportunity for children to learn to evaluate and choose their own objectives, and to initiate and pursue their own projects, by allowing, encouraging and helping them to do so, is a program of great value to the child and to society.

JOHN N. WASHBURNE

SYRACUSE UNIVERSITY

SPECIAL CORRESPONDENCE

MORE BOOKS AT LESS COST

THE English department of Evanston Township High School some two years ago found itself squeezed between two forces. On the one hand, there was its curriculum evolving and expanding to meet the requirements of the newer concepts of English education, and on the other there was the continued pressure from the public to reduce the cost of text-books to the individual student. No escape was possible through the school library, for its finances too had been given over to the common enemy of man in Cook County.

The solution of the problem was simple enough, for it rested upon an exceedingly simple fact. The novel, book of essays or anthology of poetry purchased by a student for his own use ran its course as class text and then was relegated to whatever place students have for storage. Except for the remaining large anthologies of literature in the courses, almost no book was active for more than an eighth of the time, most of them much less than that. Common ownership and continuous use were therefore the way out.

The administration authorized a fifty-cent fee to be collected each fall from each student enrolled in the English courses. The fund thus accumulated proved adequate to purchase all books and supplies desired for use in the new scheme of things and to establish the nucleus for new purchases in each following semester.

With the class size averaging close to 30, books were bought in "sets" of 30, 60, 90 and 120, depending entirely upon what use was to be made of the particular book and therefore upon the length of time each class was to have it. It was later found desirable to buy 33 for the class section to provide for absentee books, "make-up" work and small losses. Sixty-five volumes of Montague's "Right off the Map," for instance, sufficed the somewhat smaller junior class for a rapid reading of that book. For a longer unit in the poetry, 135 volumes of Untermeyer's "Yesterday and To-day" equipped some 700 freshmen. A little arithmetic with the number of teaching days in a semester and the number of class sections to be provided for will solve each problem as it arises.

The booking routine becomes a matter of an hour or two a day for a mature student working, for instance, for his tuition. The load is heavier at some times than at others, but foresight in the scheduling can largely eliminate this unevenness. Faculty supervision and assistance are needed at times of peak load and in the planning of the schedule before the beginning of each semester. The student assistant makes the deliveries and collections; the faculty director makes out delivery and collection sheets and now and then helps with the inspections. The books are scheduled through one semester at a time, with the intention that each student shall have a text for his personal use as long as there is need of it. Cataloging procedure does not differ from customary library routine, save that duplicate cards permit a double charge, one against the pupil and one against the teacher responsible for a particular set. Special mimeographed forms for delivery, collection and assessment notices have also been prepared.

The justification of an idea is its fruitfulness. The purpose of this scheme was to provide new materials for the English courses and to save money for the students. The figures that follow, based on two years of operation (the last four months of the present year of 1933–1934 estimated from the schedule) give a fair, though not a meticulous, analysis of the situation.

Total books purchased	2,156
Average cost per book	$0.965
Total circulation (two years)	18,696
Average use-per-book	8.67 times
Average cost-per-use	$0.111

The student would have paid an average retail price each of $1.20 for these books as personal texts. Had the program been expanded on these terms (in this case of course impossible) the sum difference, minus the cost of old materials replaced by new and less the fees paid in, would have totaled about $18,000.

Two to three hundred volumes, most of them bought at second hand, have finished their usefulness at the end of two years; the rest have one, two, three or more years before they will have to be replaced. Therefore, true costs can not be estimated, except in the case of those volumes which have stopped whittling down that all-important cost-per-use figure.

It is especially important to note that the use of these books reduced the number of student-purchased texts remaining in the English curriculum, lowering that cost in most courses from 25 to 50 per cent. Because of the second-hand book trade, totals are impossible to estimate with accuracy. The plan is particularly economical in the replacement of massive, expensive, partly used anthologies of literature.

The objections to the system are obvious.

The teacher must handle the material when it is scheduled to her, and there is a routine of passing and collecting books once in several weeks. A closely knit chronological course of study will suffer from this rotation; an informal extensive reading program will not. The student does not own the books he uses in this way. He may not mark them, but that limitation is not an unmitigated evil. Review and "make-up" work are rendered complicated, and some teachers feel that examinations on such texts are not valid. It is a situation, however, in which money talks with a very loud voice, and there are no inconveniences attached of sufficient importance in these parlous times to refute its argument.

KENT W. FRANCIS

EVANSTON TOWNSHIP HIGH SCHOOL

QUOTATIONS

TEAM WORK IN THE EDUCATIONAL EMERGENCY

THAT higher education in America faces a crisis of the gravest magnitude is now conceded by a majority of educational students and observers. Enrolments in practically every college and university in America, whether state, denominational or privately endowed, have decreased materially during the last three years, despite the ever increasing crop of high-school graduates.

Along with the drop in enrolment and in many instances much worse has been the drastically reduced operating incomes. Even those institutions with the largest endowments, because of the decreased earning power of investments of every type, have felt the unpleasant pinch of decreased income.

In view of such difficulties it was not surprising that higher education looked with envious eyes on the millions and billions which the Federal Government was making available for the financial assistance of practically every type of American endeavor. And yet, generally speaking, no college or university has sought aid from the Federal Government for itself as an institution. Their concern has been for the individual student.

The fairness of such student aid would seem to be unquestionable. The need was obvious. Personal and family financial difficulties were keeping hundreds of thousands of capable and worthy students away from college doors and driving them into the ranks of unemployment with all its social dangers. The educational process, thus halted even for a year or two only, would likely never be resumed.

And yet there was no evidence of interest on the part of the Federal Government. Congressmen and senators, with their natural tendency to keep an alert ear for public sentiment, saw no signs of concern for the difficulties of higher education or college students on the part of the people as a whole. The result is that to date no legislation of any kind has found its way through Congress which will in any way benefit college students.

It is true that the Federal Emergency Relief Administration has made available relief funds for college students, but entirely as a relief measure. During March, April and May the relief administration paid out about one million dollars a month of such aid to approximately 70,000 students in 1,200 colleges located in every state in the Union. About $25,000 per month of this aid came to North Carolina and $3,600 per month came to the university at Chapel Hill. Obviously this money was a great help to those students who received it, and every student and college so aided is grateful to Administrator Hopkins, but it should be borne in mind that these students would have been forced out of college and into relief jobs back home at a higher rate of compensation had this aid not been made available. They were aided as needy individuals rather than as college students.

It thus becomes rather apparent that the government is not concerned over the welfare of colleges or even students within those institutions. This unusual fact has justly caused great concern among university administrators and alumni throughout the country. Why is it that colleges which have striven so desperately during generations to contribute materially to the social security of the state find themselves so little appreciated? Why is it that higher education is made secondary to other governmental functions in times of financial distress? These questions properly are challenging the thinking of people interested in the welfare of higher education.

The answer in many instances seems to be that institutions must more and more arrange their curricula to meet the changing conditions of the times. They must train for a more competent general citizenry as well as for leadership. Many leading state universities are rapidly taking such steps.

The university is fully aware of its responsibilities in this respect. A complete revision of the curriculum is now being carefully studied. Although the plan has not yet reached the completed stage, the alumni of this institution may rest assured that President Graham and his advisers are fully aware of the fact that it is an obligation of the university to keep pace with a rapidly changing social world as it trains for citizenship.

Meanwhile alumni ought to share a large responsibility in guiding our colleges through the crisis. They are vitally concerned. They are the consumers of education. They pay the bill either as contributors or as tax payers. They should be anxious that its product suit their needs. They should be free to suggest and help. They above all people should appreciate its value and interpret those values to the public. At best the job to be accomplished requires perfect team work on the part of both alumni and administration.—*F. A. G. in the North Carolina Alumni Review.*

A "FLUID" SCHOOL

IF flexibility of curriculum is the outstanding mark of modern education, New York City soon will boast an ultra-modern high school. The Board of Education proposes to open a school on the upper East Side whose curriculum will be more than flexible; in the words of Dr. John L. Tildsley, acting chief of the high school division, it will have a "fluid" program of studies. "It will be all things to all boys," he explains, summarizing in a sentence the new trend in secondary education.

"High school" once was a term applied to a college-preparatory institution. The modern high school regards preparation for higher education as but one of its functions. It welcomes all youth, whether the purpose be further academic study, vocational training—or no particular training whatever. It is quite possible now to graduate from a high school, not only in this city but elsewhere in the state, and to receive a diploma without being able to enter college. The Board of Regents has altered its regulations to make this possible, holding that the high school must extend its program to meet the needs of pupils "whose interests lie in other fields than the so-called academic subjects." Any curriculum that will help make better citizens, apparently, may be incorporated in the modern secondary school.

The proposed new high school in this city is to be built upon such a "fluid" conception of education. It is to be an experimental school. It will "seize upon any interest discovered in a boy and then endeavor to build his education on the basis of this interest." Since the school is to be situated in a section largely inhabited by people of Latin racial stock, Dr. Tildsley plans to have its curriculum emphasize music, the arts and the crafts, without making it an out-and-out trade school. Courses will be added as rapidly as possible; ultimately the plan calls for classes in auto mechanics and aeronautics.

Here is a program which is all-inclusive. It is so different from that of the traditional high school that Dr. Tildsley has invited teachers in established schools who are sympathetic with the experiment to volunteer for its faculty. He does not seek the "conventional teacher who has preconceived and inhibited ideas as to what is proper for a high school to teach." Such teachers doubtless would be unhappy in the proposed school. They would be overwhelmed by the fluidity of the courses.

While plans for the proposed school are being perfected it might be a good idea for educators to devise a new term for what is now generally called a high school. Most people persist in thinking of such a school as a college-preparatory institution, and they express adverse criticism of young men and women who, appearing as high school graduates, lack the intellectual training customarily expected of students ready for college. "Secondary school" won't do for the new-style educational venture, for that also is associated with college preparation. Perhaps "youth school" or "adolescent school" would do. Either of these terms would fit an institution that sets out to be "all things to all boys."—*The New York Sun.*

REPORTS

GOVERNOR LEHMAN'S COMMITTEE TO STUDY THE COST OF PUBLIC EDUCATION

A committee to study the costs of public education in the State of New York, which Governor Herbert H. Lehman appointed in July, 1933, has recently submitted its report to the governor. Charles C. Burlingham has served as chairman and Professor George D. Strayer, of Teachers College, Columbia University, as director of studies. In his letters of commission to the group, Governor Lehman asked that the committee seek to "determine whether further economies or savings can be made without lessening the standards of education." The report discusses the history and background of New York public education and devotes the following section to "Changes Since the War and up to the Depression":

One of the most significant changes during the period from the close of the war until the effects of the depression began to be felt was the extraordinary increase in expenditures for schools by the state and the localities and the accelerating rate of this increase. In 1920 the reported total expenditures for public elementary and secondary schools in New York State were $108,596,912. In 1931–32 the total had reached $377,231,098. The total outstanding bonded debt for school buildings in New York City increased from $257,519,041.60 in 1926–27 to $354,004,357.78; and in New York State (exclusive of New York City) from $162,155,956 in 1926–27 to $278,474,591 in 1931–32.

What have these additional expenditures purchased?

(1) In 1920 there were 207,556 pupils in high schools; in 1931–32 there were 572,874, an increase of 365,318 pupils, or 176 per cent. In 1920 there were 1,575,546 pupils in elementary schools; in 1931–32 there were 1,761,282, an increase of 185,736 pupils, or 11.8 per cent. These changes in the numbers of pupils attending school greatly increased the cost. Since it costs more to educate a pupil in a high school than in an elementary school, the rapid rise in secondary school enrolment has greatly increased school costs.

(2) From 1920 to 1930 the number of high schools in the state increased from 759 to 943, and the enrolment in each was greatly expanded.

(3) Since 1920 the length of the school term has increased from an average of 36.6 weeks to an average of 38 weeks in 1930–31.

(4) In 1920 the aggregate value of school houses and sites was $274,000,000; in 1930–31 it had increased to $857,000,000.

(5) From 1926–27 (the earliest date for which data are available) to 1931–32 the bonded school debt in New York State has increased from $419,674,997 to $632,478,948.

(6) In 1920 the number of teachers employed in the schools of the state was 54,165; in 1931 the number employed had reached 77,488, but the ratio of teachers to pupils remained almost constant.

(7) From 1920 to 1931 the average annual salary of all teachers in the state, exclusive of New York City, has increased from $1,322 to $1,845. In New York City during this period the increase was from an average annual salary of $2,770 to one of $3,363. For the state at large, including New York City, the average annual salary increased from $1,892 in 1920–21 to $2,408 in 1930–31.

(8) From 1920 to 1930 the proportion of teachers holding college graduate certificates doubled. Similar gains were made in the proportion of teachers holding other certificates of the higher grades. If quality of teaching is increased by training, there were better teachers in 1930 than in 1920.

(9) Since 1920 there has been a marked improvement in the rural schools.

(10) In 1926–27 only 12,000 pupils were transported to schools; five years later, in 1930–1931, the number exceeded 35,000.

(11) Since 1920 many special services have been supplied by the schools. In 1930–31, 71.8 per cent. of all pupils in cities and villages were given health examinations, and 58.4 per cent. of all defects discovered were treated or corrected. While the proportion of attendance officers to pupils remained about the same from 1920 to 1932, the number of health specialists, librarians, visiting teachers, guidance officers and playground teachers increased.

(12) From 1920 to 1930 children enrolled in kindergartens in the cities increased in number from approximately 14,000 to 16,000, while those in junior high schools increased fivefold,

in summer elementary schools threefold, in trade and vocational schools fourfold and in summer high schools from none at all to more than 9,000.

(13) Since 1920 there has been a large increase in the number of special teachers, such as teachers of health and physical education, industrial arts and home economics.

(14) Since 1920, there have been large increases in enrolment in continuation schools, evening schools, summer schools and recreational activities.

The report entitles the following section, "Changes During the Depression": The full effects of the depression were slow to reach the schools. Some of the money raised from taxes in 1929 was still being spent in 1931. Furthermore, school boards and school executives, in common with many other people, believed what they were told, that the depression was only a temporary setback, that "normalcy" would soon return and that all would be well in a short time. Although each year the number of pupils was increasing, by 1931 school boards saw that they would have to cut expenses. It was becoming increasingly difficult to collect taxes from real estate, and the school year 1932–33 showed the first sharp retrenchment. It must be remembered that there were more high-school pupils and more elementary school pupils in 1932–33 than in 1931–32.

A detailed study has been made of various items of current expense for the period 1929–30 to 1932–33 for cities, villages under superintendents, other villages and central rural districts. Data for 1932–33 were not available for other rural schools, so that the expenditures in this area are not included in the study. Their inclusion would have added approximately $20,000,000 to the total current expenditures for each year reviewed. The study shows that school costs rose from the 1929–31 period until 1932, and then, from 1932 to 1933, fell back to the 1929 level. About $17,000,000 less was spent for current expenses in 1932–33 than in any previous year. The cost per pupil in average daily attendance for current expenses dropped from $144.97 to $131.48. The drop was greater upstate than in New York City. If the schools in the areas studied had made the same expenditures per pupil in 1932–33 as 1931–32 for current expenses only—that is, had made no cuts—the additional expense would have been greater by more than $24,400,000.

The schools have made these cuts in every part of the budget. The estimated costs for the current year are well below the 1929 level. The rate of these decreases is accelerating, that is, they are even greater this year than last. There are cases in which school systems are caring for twice as many pupils as they were in 1929–30, with reduced teaching staffs.

HOW THESE REDUCTIONS HAVE BEEN EFFECTED

(1) Classes have been generally increased in size during the past two years. If New York were to have maintained the same pupil-teacher ratio in 1932–33 as it had in 1929–30, it would have needed 6,784 more teachers.

(2) Teachers salaries have been reduced. Salary costs per pupil have been reduced from their highest points by 8.64 per cent. in the cities, 14.74 per cent. in the villages under superintendents, 21.99 per cent. in other villages and 23.01 per cent. in the central rural districts. In the state, exclusive of New York City, contract salaries have been reduced through outright cuts and "voluntary contributions" an average of approximately 10 per cent., varying from no reduction at all to as much as 33 per cent. The practise of requiring contributions is more common this year than last, and its use is general, even in the smaller villages. Where salaries have not been directly cut, school boards commonly require contributions, and often the two practises are used in combination. Contributions have been used in many cities as a means of reducing salaries of teachers below legal minima. New York City has cut salaries an average of 6.5 per cent., and for several years teachers have voluntarily made substantial contributions to the School Relief Fund.

(3) Salary costs have also been reduced by decreasing the sick leave allowances and employing substitutes. In New York City since 1932 the Board of Education has rather consistently used substitutes on substitute pay to fill regular positions.

(4) Schools have discontinued services. In a study of 55 of the 59 cities of the state, it has been found that 7 have eliminated evening and Americanization classes; 5, kindergarten; 12, summer schools; 5, music; 4, home economics; 10, special subject supervision; 6, elementary

school supervision; 4 have made one or more principals responsible for all supervision; 6 have discontinued recreation and playground service; 2 have discontinued library service, and 7 have eliminated medical and dental service. The same is true of villages. In addition, a few localities have discontinued such services as special classes, continuation schools, art, modern languages, manual training, text-books, school supplies and transportation. Some of these cuts are warranted by the emergency. In the main they are the result of a counsel of despair.

(5) Detailed studies of the ways in which New York City, Buffalo, Rochester and Syracuse have reduced school costs show total reductions in 1934 budget allowances for the General and Special School Funds in New York City and in estimated current expense budgets for Buffalo in 1933–34 and in Rochester and Syracuse for the calendar year 1933, as follows: New York City, \$22,164,865.09; Buffalo, \$1,406,086.16; Rochester, \$1,726,908.87, and Syracuse, \$728,380.17. These figures do not show total differences between current budgets and corresponding ones for some previous year, but instead show total reductions from costs that would have occurred had various economies and retrenchments not been made. Percentage reductions are as follows: New York City, 14.49; Buffalo, 12.15; Rochester, 21.28, and Syracuse, 17.43.

These savings have been effected by reduction or elimination of a large number of services included in the current expense budget. In many cases they represent true economies; in other cases essential services have been curtailed or abandoned. In addition to the economies listed in the preceding section, important positions have been abolished, institutions for the training of teachers have been closed, and the upkeep of buildings and equipment has been unduly cut or postponed.

EDUCATIONAL RESEARCH AND STATISTICS

INTELLIGENCE TESTS IN AMERICAN COLLEGES

IT had been suggested from several quarters that the intelligence of the student body of our universities and colleges has been increasing since the onset of the depression years. An Ohio College Association bulletin[1] indicates that this situation has been observed generally in the colleges of that association. Following up this suggestion, the author sent the following questionnaire to 162 colleges which use intelligence tests other than those of the American Council on Education:

1. Do you use an intelligence examination for entering freshmen?
   Yes........ No........
2. Have you used the same intelligence examination or different forms of the same intelligence examination during the years 1930, 1931, 1932, 1933?
   Yes........ No........
3. Have you noticed any significant increase in the average scores of the entering freshmen?
   Yes........ No........
4. If so, how much? ....
5. Have you noticed any significant difference in the location of the first Quartile and the third Quartile during these years?
   ....

Remarks: ....

One hundred and twenty-three colleges and universities responded to the questionnaire. With the results of this inquiry, data were included from 70 additional colleges which used the American Council Test during the years 1930, 1931, 1932 and 1933, appearing in the *Educational Record* for April, 1931, 1932 and 1933, and from 45 more colleges of the Ohio College Association, as reported in Bulletin No. 91.[2]

Table 1 indicates the number of colleges reporting by means of the above questionnaire, as well as the American Council group. Definite gains, losses, those not giving tests, those reporting no variations and those which changed their tests during the last three years are indicated.

An investigation of Table 1, which is a summary of the report on the American Council Tests and the results of the questionnaires to colleges using other intelligence tests, indicates that out of 193 colleges reporting a population of 466,472, 112 institutions reporting popula-

[1] The Ohio College Association Bulletin No. 91, page 2017.

[2] The Ohio College Association represents a membership of 45 institutions, with a student population of 58,575 in 1931.

TABLE 1

COLLEGES AND UNIVERSITIES REPORTING ON INTELLIGENCE TEST SCORES

	By questionnaire	A. C. E.	Total	Per cent.	Student population
Number reporting	123	70	193	100	466,472
Number with definite gain	44	68	112	58	237,656
Number with definite loss	0	2	2	1	625
Number with no variation	29	0	29	15	88,297
Number giving no test	21	0	21	11	49,225
Number having no available data	29	0	29	15	90,669

tion of 237,656, or 58 per cent. of the institutions reporting, declare that definite gains have been observed in the intelligence test scores. Those institutions reporting a population of 625, or 1 per cent. of the institutions reporting, indicate definite losses, while 29 institutions reporting a population of 88,297, or 15 per cent. of the institutions included in the study, report no variation in general trend of intelligence test scores; 29 colleges or 15 per cent. have no available data; and 21 colleges or 11 per cent. do not give tests, can not report definite gain or loss and, therefore, with those having no data, are not further included in the ensuing table.

There is a question as to the equivalence of the successive editions of the American Council Test. The 1931 median, together with the lower quartile and upper quartile (*Educational Record,* April, 1932, page 14), indicates that the scores are much higher than for the previous year. The assumption, therefore, is that the 1931 test is easier than the 1930 test. This proposition, however, is based upon the further assumption that the true intelligence levels are consistent from year to year and that the variation is to be explained in the character of the test itself. These results were quite unexpected, as is indicated in the same study, page 15.

These facts indicate that the 1931 edition is somewhat easier than the 1930 edition. This difference in difficulty was not at all expected. The tests, with the exception of the analogies test, had been carefully equated in difficulty. . . . The 1932 edition will be somewhat different from previous editions, but it is hoped that gross scores will be directly comparable to those of former years. The changes will be only minor changes in the form to facilitate scoring.

The objective of equivalence, however, met with some disappointment to the authors, quoting the *Educational Record* of April, 1933, page 11:

For several years, the successive editions of the Psychological Examination have been comparable in difficulty, but a few changes in the 1932 test have resulted in scores not directly comparable to last year's edition. The difference between the gross score norms for the 1931 and 1932 gross scores does not, however, represent the difference in difficulty between the two examinations. This is because of a selective factor in the colleges sending in records.

Equivalent scores in the 1931 and 1932 editions indicate, at the fiftieth percentile rank, 12 points in favor of the 1932 edition. These differences are interpreted as accounted for in the test itself on the assumption that the true intelligence level for each year is the same. This supposition is without defense, and no evidence is offered for its justification.

Reports of the Ohio College Association Bulletin No. 91, page 2017, are to the effect that "evidence has been discovered pointing to the existence of an increasing quality of intelligence of the freshmen of the Ohio colleges over the past three years." The correction in the norms for the year 1933–34, as compared with 1930–31 on the same test, is between 11 and 13 percentiles. These increments of gain would seem to indicate that the situation in the Ohio College Association is much the same as that in the institutions reporting, as indicated in Table 1. This would then change the picture as indicated by Table 2. This would seem to augment the evidence toward the indicated trend.

There have been many reasons advanced to explain this upward swing of the average intelligence test scores. Some have suggested that the guidance program in the secondary schools

TABLE 2

COLLEGES AND UNIVERSITIES REPORTING ON INTELLIGENCE SCORES INCLUDING THE OHIO COLLEGE ASSOCIATION

	Total	Per cent.	Student population
Number reporting	188	100	385,153
Number showing gain	157	83.5	296,231
Number with definite loss	2	1	625
Number with no variation	29	15.5	88,297

is beginning to show practical results. For some years the principals of the high schools have been encouraged to urge the brighter students to attend college. Additional selective agencies, such as colleges offering scholarships based on results of scholarship contests, have secured for colleges more students of superior intelligence. Some institutions maintain cooperative dormitories, selecting exceptional students for these privileges. It has been suggested that the possession of cash for fees in times of depression is selective of the better parental intellects, and so of offspring. Some school men feel that the students are becoming more "test-wise." Our elementary and secondary schools are using more objective tests, and thus the students are becoming more familiar with the requirements of examination performance. A recent small decline in the student population throughout the United States has resulted in raising the probability of the elimination of the lower division students. It has also been rather timorously suggested that intelligence of this college generation is superior to that of those past. It appears that all or many of these reasons may operate. Further investigation of this problem seems necessary, if we are to discover the significance of this rather dramatic increase.

Many of the explanations already advanced seem in themselves inadequate. Unless a thorough-going study is made of the situation, it will be difficult to eliminate any one of the proposals until more evidence is brought to light. From this inquiry, it seems significant that such a small percentage of institutions give no intelligence test. A rather large number of institutions seem to have no settled testing program, as indicated by the fact that they change tests from year to year and report that haphazard methods of using tests prevent them from having data available for use, such as required by this inquiry.

SUMMARY

A significant majority of the colleges and universities reporting show important advance in the average intelligence test score of their student body in the last four years.

An insignificant number of colleges and universities report loss in the average intelligence test scores during 1930–31–32–33.

No single explanation attributed to the above findings seems justifiable at the present time.

Evidence is given to the effect that a comparatively small number of colleges in the United States are not using an intelligence testing program.

A considerable number of institutions giving an intelligence test do not appear to have the program stabilized or well managed.

The trend demonstrated in this inquiry shows need for more research on the problem. If the major trend is substantiated by such future research, important educational outcomes are to be expected.

Interest in this problem is manifested by the fact that a large percentage of the colleges and universities responded to the questionnaire on the first notice.

W. H. THOMPSON

MUNICIPAL UNIVERSITY OF OMAHA

NEW BOOKS IN EDUCATION

DOUGLASS, HARL R. and CHARLES W. BOARDMAN. *Supervision in Secondary Schools.* Pp. xvi + 564. Houghton Mifflin. $2.75.

ENGLEHARDT, FRED. *Minnesota Public Schools.* Pp. viii + 155. Educational Test Bureau, Minneapolis.

GOODSELL, WILLYSTINE. *A History of Marriage and the Family.* Revised edition. Pp. xx + 590. Macmillan. $3.50.

HAGERTY, JAMES E. *Twentieth Century Crime.* Pp. iv + 222. Stratford. $2.00.

LUMLEY, FREDERICK H. *Measurement in Radio.* Pp. vii + 318. Ohio State University. $3.00.

STEVENSON, GEORGE S. and GEDDES SMITH. *Child Guidance Clinics.* Pp. vii + 186. Commonwealth Fund, New York. $1.50.

Studies in College Examinations. Pp. vii + 204. University of Minnesota.

TRETTIEN, AUGUSTUS W. *Arthur Trent: Choosing a Career.* Pp. 312. Stratford. $2.00.

SCHOOL AND SOCIETY

WITH WHICH ARE COMBINED THE EDUCATIONAL REVIEW, ESTABLISHED IN 1891, THE TEACHERS MAGAZINE, ESTABLISHED IN 1878, AND THE SCHOOL JOURNAL, ESTABLISHED IN 1874.

Volume 39 SATURDAY, JUNE 23, 1934 Number 1017

INAUGURAL ADDRESS OF THE CHANCELLOR OF NEW YORK UNIVERSITY[1]

By Dr. HARRY WOODBURN CHASE

No man has ever had a more gracious welcome to a university post than that which you have given me. I do not refer alone to these formal ceremonies, deeply as I appreciate what has been said on this platform. Behind them lies the fact that we have known each other, that we have worked together, for a full year. My distinguished predecessor in this office, whom we welcome here to-day so heartily, has spoken of the unfailing support of those concerned with the university. To me these are no empty words. To the council and to the faculty of New York University, to her alumni and students, I should like to make public acknowledgment of the fine cooperation with which you have worked with me during these months.

A deep sense of the promise and power of this institution has been growing in my mind. As it swings into the second century of its existence, may it maintain that spirit of fearless pioneering in which it was conceived; that courage which has illustrated its whole career and that sense of responsibility to community and nation which has given character to its work.

I accept, therefore, this charge which you have laid upon me, as a challenge which affords a most significant opportunity. To this task I pledge you my unremitting efforts.

[1] Delivered at the one hundred and second commencement on June 13.

There is in the world about us to-day such a clamor of dissenting voices, such a fundamental confusion and conflict of ideas and ideals, that the task of universities is no simple one. The background against which their operations are set is not merely one of economic depression. Tragic as the effects of the depression have been and are, large as they loom in the center of the picture to-day, it is becoming more and more apparent that the fundamental struggle in which humanity is engaged is not merely one of overcoming material inadequacies and dislocations. It involves, far more importantly for the future, a series of conflicting and widely differing attempts to formulate a way of life for humanity itself. We are witnessing, if you please, a conflict of philosophies, and the outcome of that conflict has immense importance for human destiny.

I can perhaps best illustrate what I mean by reminding you of a set of attitudes and ideas that, a generation ago, seemed destined to win their way, with constantly diminishing opposition, throughout the western world. These were identified with the world-wide movement toward democracy and liberalism that had come increasingly to captivate the minds of men.

John Morley has an illuminating page in his "Recollections" in which he attempts to define the inner essence of nineteenth century liberalism. Back of all its expressions, he points out, lay an attitude of mind that rooted in a sense of the importance, the dignity, the worth, of the individual. He was the center of the picture. Society existed for him, not he for society. His gradually growing freedom, the increased sense of the importance of his life as a life, higher standards of comfort and a growing variety of satisfactions that were within the reach of more and more men and women over large areas of the earth—these things were important in themselves, as ends that should be striven for. But they were important for other reasons. For, as most of us read history a generation ago, it was with a deep belief, a rather blind belief, if you please, in the reality of progress. We were progress-conscious. I remember once being rather startled by a brilliant volume that pointed out that the very conception of progress had only been in men's minds for a few generations. We believed in it, and we thought that we found in history ample warrant for believing that the possibility of progress itself depended on an attitude that had regard for the individual. As a generation that knew a little about biology, we were impressed by the importance of variations in the evolution process, and we extended the analogy to human society.

Freedom, in other words, was not only a satisfaction to the individual. It was a condition of the advance of civilization. And, because we believed in these things, we believed in the importance of popular education, as an instrument both for developing the capacities of the individual and for maintaining the continuity of human progress.

You and I are to-day citizens of a world in which this whole philosophy has been thrust out of the mind of nation after nation. The movement toward democracy and toward human freedom, toward that sense of the dignity and worth of the individual to which Morley referred, has not only been definitely checked, it has suffered catastrophic reverses. State after state has come to seek efficiency and security through subordination and regimentation of the individual to centralized and despotic authority. Education in such states has become frankly a means of indoctrination and propaganda. The individual life finds itself constrained by a ceaseless external discipline. The rights of minorities are suppressed. Freedom of discussion, the right to differ, the right to plan one's own life—these things cease to exist for millions upon millions of the earth's population.

This is not merely a question of what has happened to the liberalism of a generation ago. It is more significant even than that. We seem rather to be witnessing the ebbing of a tide of human thought that had been flowing more and more strongly since the Renaissance—a tide that was washing away, one by one, the obstacles that circumscribed the development of individual men and women. This attitude appeared in many forms. Intellectually, it meant the right to free inquiry into all things. Religiously, it appeared as the right to choose one's own faith. As a political theory, it meant what we mean by democracy, under whatever governmental form it appeared. Socially and economically, it expressed itself in wider provision for individual opportunities, in an ampler life for more and more people and in the development of universal education.

But I need not go on. That attitude, it is clear, is now on the defensive. It is scarcely satisfying to me to reply that all this has to do with what is happening in Europe, and that this is America. America, after all, has not been guaranteed eternal democracy by divine fiat. There are no international barriers against the contagion of ideas. It is not impossible to regiment the American people. Great sections of them have been regimented more than once in our history. And when we are regimented, we can be violent and cruel.

The history of what happened to the South during reconstruction, the course of the Ku Klux movement a decade ago, are two reminders of that fact. The problem is one of destiny for us as well as for our neighbors. It is whether we can find a way of life that is both free and workable, whether the intricacies of our modern social and economic order are so beyond the power of free men to deal with that we must sacrifice all the significance of the individual life to maintain a going social order. Must all this striving for human progress end in such dreary futility as Aldous Huxley has portrayed with devastating irony in "This Brave New World"?

Do not misunderstand me. All of us are aware to-day that we can not make a twentieth century society function by following in detail the eighteenth century formulas of Jefferson and of Adam Smith. The problem is far less simple than it appeared even twenty years ago. But at the heart of it lies the significant choice: Shall we set out arbitrarily to create a social order and then indoctrinate and drive individuals into subordination to it, or shall we center our efforts on the making of men and women who are themselves competent and disposed, as free agents, to do what should be done?

For myself, I confess, there seems but one possible answer. Civilization and human progress must depend in the long run, not on dictatorship, not on social and economic prescriptions, not even on laws, but on the quality of men and women.

John Milton said long ago that the first step in the decay of a commonwealth took place "when men cease to do according to the inward and uncompelled actions of virtue, caring only to live by the outward constraint of law." That is the point. It makes a vast difference whether we seek to locate the springs of action outside or inside the individual. Discipline we must have wherever there is freedom, but there is no real substitute for inner discipline and self-control.

These things are not only of importance to the individual himself. They have to do with the future of the human race. There is perhaps no lesson which history teaches more plainly than that pressure toward conformity, on the one hand, and the advance of civilization on the other, stand in inverse ratio to each other. Is it possible that we should so soon forget, for example, how slowly the beginnings of free inquiry into nature were able to make themselves felt in a world that believed that the only sound science was that which conformed to the teachings of Aristotle? Regimentation in any area involves a philosophy which is the denial of the basic conditions of progress. Civilization advances in proportion as free inquiry is possible, free discussion and the clash of ideas are permitted, minority opinions can be uttered without fear, and the individual life is regarded as a thing of dignity and importance in itself.

Universities are the organized instruments of society for the advancement and the transmission of knowledge. Because of this, what they do or leave undone is of immense significance for the outcome of this conflict. This is clear enough to those who believe in regimentation. In such states, freedom of learning and teaching, like freedom of the press, ceases to exist. For those who believe in human freedom, on the contrary, there can be no more important task than that of safeguarding the freedom of institutions of learning. This is a primary condition of the advance of civilization in the modern world.

It is not the business of universities to be instruments of indoctrination and propaganda. It is not their mission, on the one hand, to evolve theoretical Utopias and then to condition people for participation in them. Nor is it, on the other hand, their mission to become apologists for the dogma that whatever is, is right. Their concern is rather to open and develop the minds of men and women; to give them understanding, knowledge of the truth, appreciation of the processes by which it is arrived at, so that, as open-minded, informed, free people, they may look at and take part in life as intelligent, reasonable human beings. In proportion as universities can really succeed in accomplishing these things over the years, the question of finding a free and workable way of life is one which will be solved in the only way in which it can possibly be solved in the long run, namely, through sufficiently wide-spread knowledge and competence to make its solution possible through the methods to which free peoples are accustomed.

I have spoken of the necessity for freedom in our universities. It is equally important that universities must not forget the obligation which that freedom implies. In a word, that obligation seems to me to be that of maintaining the scientific temper. Especially, at such a time, should that obligation rest heavily upon those within the fields of the social sciences. In these fields it is not yet always easily possible to dislocate knowledge from dogma, to maintain that detachment from personal and temperamental preferences and dislikes which is the essence of the scientific point of view. I do not mean that in other fields of science these complications are always absent; I do mean that in the fields of social science they are especially insidious, and the objective, impartial attitude especially difficult to maintain. If the study of society is a science, then it should be carried on from the scientific point of view.

Universities, in a word, can properly be neither apologists nor agencies of propaganda. Their concern is with knowledge, and with the illumination that it brings to men. So, and so only, do they, in the end, best serve a free society because they strive to develop freely inquiring and adequately informed human beings.

INVENTION AND SCHOOL ARITHMETIC

By Professor H. G. GOOD
THE OHIO STATE UNIVERSITY

EVEN animals seem to have a number sense. The bee builds her cell in the form of a hexagonal prism, although she may not know what a regular hexagon is nor that its side is equal to its radius. If only she would take the trouble to develop an articulate language, preferably the English, we might be able to speak with more exactness of what she "knows." And we understand but little more of the origin of number in the human race. Perhaps it arose from the rhythmical nature of organic and conscious processes; perhaps, as James Ward thinks, from the intuitive perception of small groups as patterns.[1] "The herdsman could recognize that one of his sheep was missing without being able to count his flock, and even his dog could do the same, the needs of the two in this respect being quite on a par."[2]

Leaving the question of origins and coming to matters of fact, early counting for practical purposes was of concrete things, and consisted first of all in setting up a one-to-one correspondence between the objects and the selected counters, as the fingers, pebbles or tallies. This part of the counting process can be accomplished by

[1] "Mind," xxix: 137.

[2] David Eugene Smith, "History of Mathematics," 2 vols., Boston, Ginn and Company, I: 6, 1923.

observing that there are as many persons as chairs when all chairs are occupied and no one is standing; or, in a serial manner, by laying one cover for John, another for Ruth and so on until there is one for each of the family and guests. In these operations, without using either tallies or number-names, we yet establish the numerical equality of two collections. The second half of the process of counting consists of the use of the successive members of an ordered series with which to set up the correspondence; and the most convenient ordered series is that of the number-words or numerals. The former of these steps may have been taken before the development of language; the latter presupposes the invention of a numeral series and a certain capacity for abstract thought. All the rest of arithmetic is based upon and most of it is evolved out of the simple process of counting.

Counting is itself a kind of measurement, for by finding "how many" we secure an estimate of "how much"; but it is directly applicable only to commodities composed of convenient, fairly uniform, discrete units, to herds of cattle but not to land or even to wheat. Eggs are regularly sold by number; but in the case of land or gasolene, standard units are selected and "applied" to the commodity. When the applications are counted the measure is expressed as a number. These two inventions, counting and measuring, are the bases of that practical use of number from which much of school arithmetic has grown.

The need to measure with exactness has led to many inventions which have had the greatest influence both upon arithmetic and upon that larger complex which we call civilization. The measurement of time is one of the most urgent needs of man in society where cooperation is expected. Nature provides an obvious time-unit and even savages count the days before a feast by means of knots or beads on a string. Such a crude calendar is used by removing a bead each day until the expected event is to occur. The making of a real calendar depends upon the determination of the year, which is an astronomical problem. Egypt in 4241 B. C. introduced a civil calendar of 365 days; and this, if history means the record of datable happenings, is the beginning of history, for this is, so far, the oldest dated event.[3] Perhaps nothing can give so sharp a contrast between civilization and its absence as the fact that to many savages a delay of only a day or two is acceptable performance. In other measurements the ancient culture peoples were even more successful. The engineers who built the Great Pyramid about 2900 B. C. were in error by less than two thirds of an inch in a base line of 765 feet and deviated from a right angle at the corners by only twelve seconds.[4]

From early times commerce was married to arithmetic; and the Sumerian tablets of 2800 B. C. contain accounts, bills, receipts and other business "papers." The invention of the coinage about 700 B. C. was of importance to business and in the collection of taxes also to politics. But we need not pursue these topics, since we merely wish to remark that arithmetic is not only itself an invention but is closely related to other inventions in commerce, politics, the arts and the whole range of civilization.

Another set of facts would lead one to conclude that arithmetic as a racial achievement has been developed not only through practical demands but also through mysticism and through theoretical and scientific inquiries. In a previous paper on "Invention and the Map"[5] it was

[3] J. H. Breasted, "Ancient Times, a History of the Early World," p. 45. Boston, Ginn and Company, 1916.

[4] Smith, *op. cit.*, I: 43.

[5] SCHOOL AND SOCIETY, xxxv: 583–588, April 30, 1932.

shown that philosophy and exploration co-operated in producing the general conceptions and the exact knowledge of the earth which are necessary for accurate mapping. Arithmetic also has this dual ancestry. It, also, was created by philosophers and scientists on the one hand; and on the other, by common men seeking answers to their everyday questions: How many? How far? What time of day? Although painfully acquired by the race, this mathematics may be simple enough; and indeed its social usefulness is directly proportional to its simplicity. To be useful it must be widely disseminated; and to be widely disseminated it must be simple.

We have referred to the probable connection between counting and the rhythms of nature, inorganic and organic. Primitive men and the older culture-peoples attached magical virtues to seven or ten or the swastika and to other selected numbers or forms, whence number-lore or numerology. The Chinese investigated the mysteries of the magic square.[6] Among the Hebrews the "science" of numbers was called *Gematria.* Like the Greeks they used the letters of the alphabet to represent numbers, and therefore it was possible to sum up the "values" of the names of persons. To their Christian successors "Nero" equalled 666, "the number of the beast." The Greeks derived the number of an animal, as a horse, from a geometrical outline of its form with dots.[7] This practise may be compared with that of finding the shapes of animals in the constellations. We still retain in our common arithmetic from these excursions into mysticism such words as "figure"; and "square" and "cubic" as applied to numbers. Pythagoras and his followers developed an extensive theory of odd, even, perfect, triangular and other numbers. This is the actual origin of number theory, an important branch of pure mathematics. Euclid and Nicomachus are the main sources of our knowledge of Greek number theory. Through compends ascribed to Boethius and Bede this theory was introduced into the schools. Bede also included work on the *computus* or the calculation of the church calendar. And this was the arithmetic taught in the medieval schools and universities and continued far into the Renaissance. It was intended for scholars and the clergy, not for artisans or merchants, was of course in Latin and contained little of computation.

Practical arithmetic followed a different line of development. Its fate was very literally in the hands of the common people, for it was carried on by a finger symbolism, a device made necessary by the lack of a convenient number system, by the illiteracy of the people and by the fact that trade was carried on between peoples of different races. The finger-symbolism used in bargaining was fairly independent of spoken language.[8] For number records they used physical devices, such as notches on a stick or knots on a string. Examples are the quipus of the Incas and the tally-sticks which were used by the Bank of England from a time when many of its clients were illiterate down to 1826.[9]

From early times, calculation was most systematically carried on by means of the abacus. It was used in the East, including China, in Greece, in Rome and, as Capella shows, was familiar to western Europe as

6 Vera Sanford, "A Short History of Mathematics," p. 4. Boston, Houghton Mifflin Company, 1930.

7 Louis Charles Karpinski, "The History of Arithmetic," p. 18. Chicago, Rand, McNally and Co., 1923.

8 David Eugene Smith, "Rara Arithmetica . . .", illustrations of finger symbolism, pp. 57, 138. Boston, Ginn and Company, 1901.

9 Charles Dickens ridiculed this system in an address in 1855 on "Administrative Reform." The address may be found in the "National Library Edition" of Dickens, xix: 463 *ff.*

early as the fifth century. Pebbles or calculi were used as counters in early times, whence our word "calculate." Minted *jettons* or casting-counters of bronze, silver or gold, many of them stamped with elaborate designs,[10] were used later, and from the manner of placing these upon the lines of the abacus we have the phrase, "casting accounts." Long after the Arabic numerals came into use, this manual arithmetic was still practised, partly from old custom and partly because it could be used by the illiterate. Recorde's seventeenth century text refers to the ignorant as "those that can but cast with counters," and not reckon with the pen in Arabic characters. Many of the books, including this one, taught both methods. Although the manual arithmetic was not a part of the classical education of that time, yet a school book dialogue of the early sixteenth century begins as follows:

> Is there any Body here that understands Arithmetick? For what? To cast up exactly how many Grammarians there are of us. That may be done without a counting-table, we may count upon our Fingers.[11]

As a means of saving labor the Hindu-Arabic numerals are one of the great inventions of the world. The principle of position or place-value and the use of the zero are its essential features. The idea of place-value occurred to several peoples, the Babylonians, the Hebrews, the Mayas. And the Mayas even had a symbol for zero, but they do not seem to have made much use of it in calculation.[12] The fruitful use of these inventions, which like the alphabet are now familiar to every one and are therefore by almost every one dismissed as unworthy of attention, was made by the Hindus. The Hindu numerals reached Bagdad, where about 800 A. D. an Arab scholar, al-Khowarizmi, wrote an arithmetic employing them.[13] From his name came the word *algorism,* which was widely used to indicate the new form of calculating.

In the twelfth century the arithmetic of al-Khowarizmi was translated into Latin by various scholars who had studied in Spain. But the first European to prepare a full, independent and practical arithmetic using the new instrument was Leonardo Fibonacci of Pisa (1202), "the greatest and most productive mathematician of all the Middle Ages."[14] And a whole row of Latin algorismi date from the fourteenth and fifteenth centuries.

In the history of arithmetic as of letters the Renaissance begins a new period; and the results were as original. The arithmetics of the Renaissance were practical, mercantile works for the counting-house and for the Rechenmeister's practical school. The line-abacus survived for a time, but gradually the new algorism with Hindu-Arabic numerals won the day. The invention of printing spread the new instrument in all quarters. It is to be noticed particularly that as it was developed not by scholars but by practical men so it was also spread first and most widely among the common people; and that it forms a striking exception to Sir Henry Maine's dictum —"Except the blind forces of nature, nothing moves in this world which is not Greek in its origin."[15] Common arithmetic is neither a natural force nor a Greek creation.

The Renaissance in arithmetic as in let-

[10] F. P. Barnard, "The Casting-Counter and the Counting-Board," 353 pp. and 63 plates. Oxford, 1916. *Passim.*

[11] N. Bailey, "The Colloquies of Erasmus," 2 vols. London, 1878.

[12] Florian Cajori, "A History of Mathematical Notations," I: 4, 21, 43 *et passim.* 2 vols. Chicago, Open Court Publishing Company, 1928.

[13] Smith, "Rara Arithmetica," p. 7, but the question is not settled. See also Cajori, *op. cit.,* p. 46, and the references there given.

[14] Smith, "History of Mathematics," I: 214.

[15] Sir Henry Sumner Maine, "Village Communities . . ." [and other papers], p. 238. New York, Henry Holt and Company, 1876.

ters began in Italy, which was the great trading country of that time. The anonymous work of Treviso (1478) was the first to be printed. Pietro Borghi, six years later, printed at Venice an influential text. Neither of these writers would have anything to do with the Roman numerals, the medieval theory of numbers or the abacus; and both wrote in Italian. The natural course of trade was from the East to Italy, thence north through Nuremberg and Augsburg, then spreading out fan-wise to the Hanse towns, to France, Holland and England; and arithmetic followed the lines of traffic. The practical German text of Johann Widman (1489) explains the operations with integers and fractions, compound numbers and proportion and for the first time introduces into a printed book the signs of plus and minus. The rapidity of the spread of the new art, in contrast with its slow development from 800 to 1450, may be gauged from the fact that Professor Smith found in the Plimpton Library of New York 450 titles which were printed before 1600.

The early books tended to present the mechanical operations and a multitude of rules and special cases. Instruction was given in private reckoning schools which grew up to meet the demand or one might say the emergency. Ignored by church and state, each of which regarded them as accessories of business rather than schools in the usual sense, these institutions came to have a powerful influence in creating the common or people's school. Nuremberg had possibly fifty reckoning schools in the sixteenth century, and they flourished in all trade centers. The teachers organized themselves into a gild, admission to which was controlled by an apprenticeship and by an examination, both written and oral. One of the questions which has a historical interest reads: "What is a number? How is the 1 classified and what characteristics has the null?" Other questions dealt with vulgar fractions, simple proportion, progressions and roots.[16]

The next step in the history of arithmetic was in the direction of simpler processes, especially in multiplication and division. Stevin gave the first systematic discussion of decimal fractions in the sixteenth century, and Napier's invention of logarithms was published early in the seventeenth. The latter instrument, partly because of theoretical difficulties and partly because it is not needed before, is usually reserved for secondary education, although the use of the slide-rule can be taught to young children.

No one before Comenius understood, so well as he did, the function or realized so fully the importance of the common school. He announced the cardinal principle, often ascribed to Locke, that everything should as far as possible be presented first to the senses. In his "School of Infancy" he suggested this sensory beginning for arithmetic. His disciple, Andreas Reyher, attempted to apply these ideas in Saxe-Gotha, and the good duke of that little state, by Reyher's advice, provided for a thorough course in arithmetic. He even proposed that teachers should study the subject! Francke made similar beginnings. But in many elementary schools down through the eighteenth century the subject was not taught at all or taught incompetently by ciphering-book and other mechanical methods. Francke and the Württemberg ordinance of 1729 mention the blackboard, another invention of great importance in the teaching of arithmetic. Wall boards were not unknown in the Middle Ages, but were little used. In the United States the blackboard does not appear until the nineteenth century, and Barnard as late as 1839 says that its value

16 C. Jänicke, "Geschichte der Methodik des Rechenunterrichts" in *Gesch. d. Meth. des deutschen Volksschulunterrichtes* (C. Kehr), III: 22. Gotha, 1888.

as a teaching instrument was little realized.

The transformation of the new arithmetic from a special, technical, purely commercial pursuit into a phase of general education and culture for all the children of the spreading common schools took place in the last two centuries. And a great struggle it was. It was in Germany that the pedagogy of the subject received the earliest and most systematic attention, and Christian Peschek (1676–1747) was one of its first exponents. How early progress was made in this field is shown by the Braunschweig ordinance of 1737, which in its arithmetic outline demanded the use of objects, small numbers, concrete questions, the explanation of multiplication as repeated additions and of division as repeated subtractions and in general the teaching not only of processes but also of reasons. Then came the Philanthropinists with new apparatus, wall-charts, flash-cards with patterns of dots, marked splints for the teaching of fractions and much else. Kant expressed the opinion that they were the only teachers of his day who had the freedom to develop new methods. They were the "Progressive" educators of the latter eighteenth century; and A. H. Niemeyer before the end of that century wrote—Pupils should find their own rules; skill and understanding go hand in hand; and both numbers and problems should be taken from actual life. All this before and without Pestalozzi. In arithmetic-methods, at least, Pestalozzi devised nothing valuable that was essentially new. He did help to stir the dry bones and to spread better methods already in use in favored schools. After him and partly because of him, arithmetic took its place beside reading as one of the essentials of a common school education.

The first attempt to introduce the Pestalozzian arithmetic into the United States was made by Joseph Neef, but neither his "Sketch of a Plan of Education Suited to a Free People" (1809) nor his various schools made any impression. Quite otherwise was it with Warren Colburn's "Intellectual Arithmetic" (1821). This popular little book introduced a vogue of mental arithmetic which lasted for more than fifty years.

After it came to be understood that arithmetic should be introduced through concrete objects, teachers and especially school equipment makers devised a large body of plastic and graphic materials to aid the young child. Many patents on such devices have been issued in the United States and a much larger number in Germany. As a matter of fact all the materials needed can be found in the schoolroom and the kitchen cupboard or can be made without much trouble in the school shop. One such implement may, however, be singled out for special mention. In 1813 soldiers returning from Napoleon's Russian campaign brought back to France a form of the abacus which they had picked up. This new-old device was introduced into the schools and has proved to be one of the simplest and most practical aids to an elementary notion of number. Thus, again, an old device on which the race cut its arithmetical eye-teeth has proved valuable in introducing the newest members of the race to our most highly developed concepts. Perhaps there is something in the culture-epoch theory, after all. But one does not need to go far for arithmetic equipment. To play a game equal sides may have to be chosen, the score has to be kept, materials may have to be measured or counted, a field may have to be laid out or a board constructed. It was from such situations that the race discovered its arithmetic; it is in such situations that the child rediscovers the same need. This genetic principle is also the source of motivation in the study, and both ideas have been stressed in the last generation by educational writers.

We have seen that Stevin gave a concise account of decimal fractions, an account which Karpinski says would hardly need to be changed in a single letter if it were written to-day.[17] So useful did decimal fractions prove themselves in calculation that a German teacher, Zöllner, spoke of the "sin of our forefathers in introducing common fractions at all." After all, quarters and thirds are convenient, and even with our decimal coinage it has been found desirable to mint half-dollars and quarter-dollars. Decimals and the metric system are the most recent additions to school arithmetic, and the latter is not even yet quite recognized as a necessary topic in English and American schools.

The latest step in the teaching of arithmetic was taken by Stone, Courtis, Thorndike and their confrères in the last twenty-five years. Of this work in the psychology of arithmetic and in the construction and use of scales and tests we have not space to speak now.

[17] Smith, "History of Arithmetic," *op. cit.*, p. 133. Stevin's "La Disme" is translated in "A Source Book in Mathematics," by David Eugene Smith, pp. 20–34. New York, McGraw-Hill Book Company, 1929, "La Disme" is the antecedent of our "dime."

EDUCATIONAL EVENTS

A UNIVERSITY CITY FOR ROME

According to the London *Times,* in the program of activities planned by Fascism in support of culture and learning the construction of a great university city in Rome occupies a leading place.

On November 4, 1930, a decree of the head of the Italian Government gave over the property of the area adjoining the Polyclinic to the University of Rome. A body of experts was appointed to make a survey of conditions and draw up an estimate of expenditure entailed by the construction on this site of as many university faculties as were scattered all over Rome. The figure was announced as 70,000,000 lire. A convention was signed by cultural institutions in April, 1932, to raise the funds required. The act also set the date of opening of the new premises on April 21, 1935.

Signor Marcello Piacentini, a member of the Royal Italian Academy, was appointed architect, and at the suggestion of Premier Mussolini he appointed a body of young collaborators, to each of whom he assigned a share of the work, reserving for himself the supervision of the whole and the planning of the central buildings to house the Rectorate.

The area allotted is square in shape, with sides about 550 yards long. It is flanked by another stretch of land to be eventually occupied by the students' hostel and the university playgrounds and gymnasium. The site is to be walled in to ensure seclusion and silence, and the actual buildings are to occupy only one sixth of the total area.

The ground-plan of the university city is linked up with Greco-Roman and Renaissance traditions. There will be 12 buildings in symmetrical formation along two main roads, which form a large open space where they cross. The fore part of the central building will be 15 stories high. The rear part, which is lower, will be chiefly taken up by a great lecture hall to accommodate 3,000 persons.

SUMMER SCHOOL ENROLMENT AND COST

America's summer school population has increased nearly four times in less than 20 years, according to a statement made by Dr. Walter J. Greenleaf, of the Office of Education.

Nineteen years ago there were only 83,234 students enrolled to take some sort of college work in institutions of higher learning throughout the United States. Last summer's estimated enrolment in colleges and universities was 319,000.

The peak summer school enrolment in the United States was reached in the year 1932, when 414,390 persons took some sort of college work.

Summer school enrolments in colleges and universities from 1915 to 1932 are as follows:

1915	83,234
1916	89,438
1918	78,059
1920	132,849
1922	220,311
1924	278,125
1926	340,461
1928	382,766
1930	388,006
1932	414,390
1933 (estimated)	319,000

Summer schools are for the most part self-sustaining, and the student pays full costs since no appropriations are provided for carrying on such work. Often persons are admitted as auditors to summer-school courses or to occasional lectures without credit upon payment of the regular tuition fee. They receive certain privileges of the campus, buildings and summer events. At small additional cost excursions are frequently arranged during the summer session to acquaint students with local points of interest and historical landmarks.

For the six weeks' summer session, tuition rates range from $17 to $100, with the most usual charge from $30 to $40. If laboratory courses are elected there will be an additional fee of a few dollars.

Board and room for six weeks will range this year for those studying during the summer from $30 to $100, according to the institution and its location. Charges are probably less in the Middle West than on the east or west coast.

THE HARVARD UNIVERSITY SUMMER SCHOOL

DR. KIRTLEY F. MATHER, director of the Harvard University Summer School, gives in the *Harvard Alumni Bulletin* details in regard to the coming session, which opens on July 2 and closes for the regular classes on August 11. With the cooperation of the Institute of Pacific Relations, there will be offered two intensive courses in the Russian language for a period of twelve weeks, from June 25 to September 15. These courses are primarily intended for advanced students with some experience in research, who desire to acquire a knowledge of Russian as a tool for investigation in their respective fields.

Professors George Z. Patrick, of the University of California, and Samuel H. Cross, of Harvard University, assisted by two Russian lectors, will be in charge.

Among the visiting instructors this year, three are coming to the Summer School for the first time. Dr. Charles A. Ellwood, professor of sociology at Duke University, will conduct two courses, "Introductory Sociology" and "Social Pathology and Social Programs," with field trips to social agencies in the vicinity of Cambridge. James Edward Peabody, recently head of the department of biology at the Morris High School, New York City, will give a new course in education, "The Teaching of Biology in Secondary Schools." Dr. Robert Ulich, visiting lecturer on comparative education, formerly counselor in the Ministry of Education, Saxony, and professor of philosophy in the Higher Technical School, Dresden, Germany, will lead the study of "Social Policy and Education."

Other members of the faculty include: Dr. Albert Schinz, professor of Romance languages at the University of Pennsylvania; Roy Dickinson Welch, professor of music at Smith College; and Dr. Kenneth J. Conant, associate professor of architecture; Dr. A. Hadley Cantril, Jr., instructor in psychology; Dr. Frederick W. C. Lieder, associate professor of German; Dr. Kirsopp Lake, professor of history; Dr. Marshall H. Stone, associate professor of mathematics; Dr. Paul J. Sachs, professor of fine arts, and Dr. Payson S. Wild, Jr., instructor in government—all of Harvard University.

Among the new courses of special social significance are, "Agricultural Policies and Problems" in the department of economics, and "Recent Trends in American Government" in the department of government. The department of physics is offering a course on "Light," and the department of psychology one on "Child Psychology."

Associate Professor Kirk Bryan is to direct field work in geology in the Jemez Mountains of central New Mexico. The party will gather in Albuquerque. The first camp will be in the pine forest near La Cueva for the study of the great crater and the volcanic rocks of the Valles Mountains. The second and some of the later camps will be on the west flank of the Nacimiento Mountains, where 10,000 feet of upturned sedimentary rocks afford opportunity for the study of structure and stratigraphy. The last two weeks of the course will be devoted to an extended trip, 1,200 to 1,500 miles, to view and study the broader aspects of the geology and geomorphology of the region.

THE INSTITUTE OF PUBLIC AFFAIRS AT THE UNIVERSITY OF VIRGINIA

An effort to evaluate the work of the NRA will be made during the eighth Institute of Public Affairs at the University of Virginia in a round table discussion group under the leadership of Spencer Miller, Jr., of the Workers' Education Bureau. This group will meet daily during the second week of the institute, from July 9 to 14.

Donald Richberg, general counsel for the NRA; David Cushman Coyle, member of the reviewing board of the Public Works Administration; William Green, president of the American Federation of Labor; Dr. Leo Wolman, chairman of the Labor Advisory Board, and Dexter Keezer, director of the Consumers' Advisory Board, are among those who have accepted invitations to take part in these discussions.

The NRA will be considered from the political and economic point of view at the opening meeting on July 9 when Mr. Richberg will be one of the speakers.

Gerard Swope, formerly a member of the NRA Industrial Board, and George Houston, president of the Baldwin Locomotive Works, have been invited to speak on July 10 when industry and the NRA will be discussed.

Labor and the NRA will be the subject on the program for the Wednesday meeting. Mr. Green and Dr. Wolman have agreed to speak on that day and Miss Mary van Kleeck, director of the department of industrial studies of the Russell Sage Foundation, has been invited.

The consumer under the NRA is to be discussed on Thursday. Mr. Keezer will be one of the speakers and F. J. Schlink, president of Consumers' Research, and Mrs. Herbert Lederer, of the Women's Division of the NRA in New York, may also be on this program.

Mr. Coyle and probably Dr. Leon Henderson, director of research of the NRA, will be the speakers on Friday, July 13, when trends in the recovery program are to be considered. There will be a general discussion of the entire program of the NRA at the closing session on Saturday morning.

Mr. Richberg on July 9 and Mr. Coyle on July 13 will be speakers before evening public meetings.

CONFERENCE OF EDUCATIONAL WORKERS IN CORRECTIONAL INSTITUTIONS

A conference in which educators, penologists, psychologists, psychiatrists and others will participate will be held at Teachers College, Columbia University, on August 10. This conference has been called for the purpose of studying the educational problems of correctional institutions. Meetings will be held in the morning and a luncheon-meeting will gather later at the Men's Faculty Club of Columbia University, at which Warden Lawes, of Sing Sing Prison, will describe "How a Warden Looks at Education," and Mr. Sam A. Lewisohn will discuss "The New Deal in Prison Policies." For the afternoon round tables have been set up at which the following topics will be discussed:

"The Place of Mental Hygiene in the Prison and Reformatory School."

"Relationship of Classification of Prisoners to Educational Programs in Prisons and Reformatories."

"The Rôle of Health and Physical Education in Programs for Delinquents."

"The Administration of Education in Prisons."

"Relationships of Correctional Institutions to Community Social Agencies."

The evening meeting will consist of speeches by Mr. Calvin Derrick on "Ways and Means of Improving Educational Programs in Prisons and Reformatories," and by Dr. William E. Grady on "The Relationship of the Program of Public Education to the Problem of Delinquency."

The program for the conference has been prepared by Governor Lehman's Commission for the Study of the Educational Problems of Penal Institutions for Youth, which is composed of laymen, workers in penological institutions and educators.

HONORARY DEGREES CONFERRED BY NEW YORK UNIVERSITY

During the commencement exercises of New York University the honorary degree of doctor of laws was conferred upon Dr. Elmer Ellsworth Brown, who is chancellor emeritus of the university; Harold Willis Dodds, president of Princeton University; James Bryant Conant, president of Harvard University; James Rowland Angell, president of Yale University, and Thomas William Lamont, banker and partner of J. P. Morgan and Company, and the degree of doctor of music was conferred upon Lawrence Tibbett, baritone of the Metropolitan Opera Company.

In conferring the doctorate of law on the four college presidents Chancellor Harry Woodburn Chase said:

JAMES ROWLAND ANGELL

James Rowland Angell: In recognition of the splendid service you have rendered to the cause of American education, for your friendly interest in this university, and in token of our admiration for you as a man, as an administrator, and as an educational statesman, we now confer upon you the degree of Doctor of Laws of New York University.

JAMES BRYANT CONANT

James Bryant Conant: You have already achieved international recognition in the world of scholarship. Called to the presidency of America's oldest university, you have already shown that sane, keen and penetrating originality of mind as an executive that has distinguished you as a scholar. With a hearty Godspeed to you in your new career, I confer upon you the degree of Doctor of Laws with all its rights and privileges.

HAROLD WILLIS DODDS

Harold Willis Dodds, the distinguished university which you serve has found in her own faculty a leader whose election has been hailed with unusual acclaim—an acclaim based on a recognition of that solid achievement which has distinguished your career. We greet you as neighbor and friend, and it is with genuine pleasure that I now, by virtue of the authority vested in me by the council of New York University, admit you to the degree of Doctor of Laws.

ELMER ELLSWORTH BROWN

Elmer Ellsworth Brown, my friend, New York University, that you have loved and served with all your heart for a quarter of a century, offers you to-day this tribute of her appreciation. You have wrought well through all these busy years. It is with the wish of every one of us for long and happy and useful years for you that, by virtue of the authority you have so graciously surrendered to me, I now pronounce you an honorary alumnus and a Doctor of Laws of New York University.

THE RETIREMENT OF PRESIDENT AMES OF THE JOHNS HOPKINS UNIVERSITY

PRESIDENT JOSEPH SWEETMAN AMES, of the Johns Hopkins University, announced at the commencement exercises of the university on June 12 his intention to retire at the end of the next academic year.

President Ames's retirement will terminate an official connection with the university that has lasted continuously for fifty-one years. He was enrolled as a student in 1883. His name appeared in the list of the graduating class of 1886; as a fellow in 1887–88, and as an assistant in physics in 1888–91; it appeared on the list of graduate students granted the degree of Ph.D. in 1890. Dr. Ames became associate in physics in 1891, associate professor in 1893, professor in 1899, provost in 1926–29 and president in 1929. When he assumed the presidency five years ago he announced privately his intention of retiring at the end of the academic year during which he reached the age of seventy years.

Dr. Ames is the fourth president of the Johns Hopkins University, the others being Daniel Coit Gilman, Ira Remsen and Frank J. Goodnow. He was a personal friend and colleague of each of them. His term of service with the university comes within seven years of covering its entire history. The recent commencement was the fifty-eighth for the university and the fifty-first for Dr. Ames.

Dr. Ames has guided the university through one of the most difficult periods in its history. His assumption of the office of president coincided almost exactly with the beginning of the depression; and the history of the Johns Hopkins, like that of every other endowed institution, has since been a story of shrinking income. Nevertheless, with the cooperation of the faculties, expenses have been reduced without sacrificing essential service.

THE EIGHTH PRESIDENT OF WESTERN RESERVE UNIVERSITY

THE eighth president of Western Reserve University is Dr. Winfred G. Leutner, who was elected by the board of trustees on June 12 and who was inaugurated the following morning in the presence of the faculties and the graduating class of the university and of representatives of Ohio colleges and universities who had been invited to attend the installation of "a president." Since last December, when Dr. Robert E. Vinson resigned because of ill-health, Dr. Leutner has been acting president. He has served the university for twenty-nine years, as teacher, dean of Adelbert College from 1912 to 1925 and dean of administration since 1925.

When informed that he had been officially chosen, Dr. Leutner said:

> Election to the presidency of a great institution such as Western Reserve University would be, to any man, a challenge. I have been associated with the board of trustees, faculty, graduates and students for a good many years. Under these circumstances my election to the presidency has special, personal meaning, for my associates must often have seen my work when it was not at its best. They and the other old friends in Cleveland and elsewhere have been more than kind in their expression of confidence. My principal effort and my great hope will be that I may continue to deserve their friendship and support to the end that Western Reserve University and its affiliated colleges may go on to greater strength and greater achievement in the interest of the great community in which they are located.

Tribute to Dr. Leutner was paid by Mr. Newton D. Baker, chairman of the board of trustees, both in his announcement of the election and at the installation. He expressed "great satisfaction and confidence" in the new president and pointed out that Dr. Leutner's "lifelong connections with the university and his lifelong residence in Cleveland are great assets for a university which wants to serve a great city which needs to be served."

In his inaugural address, President Leutner referred to the serious financial difficulties which face Western Reserve as a result of the depression and acknowledged contributions of about $150,000 from alumni, faculty, students and friends toward meeting the current deficit.

EDUCATIONAL NOTES AND NEWS

Dr. John Lloyd Newcomb was installed as president of the University of Virginia on June 12. He succeeds the late Edwin Anderson Alderman, who was the first president of the university. Since the death of Dr. Alderman, Dr. Newcomb has served as acting president.

Professor J. Nelson Norwood has been named president of Alfred University. He had been acting president since the sudden death last autumn of Dr. Paul E. Titsworth, who had been president only for a short time.

Dr. Gordon Keith Chalmers, professor of English at Mount Holyoke College, has been elected president of Rockford College, Illinois. He will succeed Dr. William Maddox, who died last August.

Dr. Dexter Merriam Keezer has been appointed president of Reed College, Portland, Oregon, to succeed President Norman F. Coleman.

Dr. Shelton J. Phelps has accepted the presidency of Winthrop College, the South Carolina State College for Women at Rock Hill. He will assume his new work at the end of July. Dr. Phelps has been professor of school administration at George Peabody College for Teachers since 1919; director of instruction, 1927–1931; dean of the graduate school, 1931–1934. The retiring president, Dr. James P. Kinard, has been given the title of president emeritus in recognition of more than forty years service to Winthrop College. He will continue as an active member of the faculty.

Dr. Arthur A. Hauck will take up his work as president of the University of Maine at the opening of the summer session on July 3.

Recipients of honorary degrees from Yale University conferred at its commencement on June 20 include the doctorate of laws on James Bryant Conant, president of Harvard University, and on William Lyon Phelps, Lampson professor of English literature, emeritus, Yale University; the doctorate of letters on Claude Moore Fuess, historian and author, principal of Phillips Academy, Andover, and on Charles Cutler Torrey, Sterling professor of Semitic languages, emeritus, Yale University; the doctorate of humane letters on Robert Bartholow Harshe, director of the Chicago Art Institute; the doctorate of divinity on John Baillie, Roosevelt professor of systematic theology, Union Theological Seminary; the doctorate of science on Frederick George Keyes, professor of physical chemistry research, the Massachusetts Institute of Technology.

The degree of doctor of letters was conferred by Temple University, Philadelphia, on June 14 on Dr. Robert C. Clothier, president of Rutgers University. Edward W. France, director of the Philadelphia Textile School, received the degree of doctor of humane letters.

President Gilbert W. Mead, of Washington College, Chestertown, Maryland, was awarded the honorary degree of doctor of letters at the one hundred and nineteenth commencement of Allegheny College, Meadville, Pennsylvania. President Mead is a graduate of the college in the class of 1911.

Professor William R. Westhafer, head of the department of physics and dean of the College of Wooster, received the honorary degree of doctor of laws from the Ohio Wesleyan University on June 4.

The doctorate of laws was conferred by Niagara University on June 12 on Brother Adolphus Patrick, president of Manhattan College, New York.

Dr. William A. Wirt, superintendent of schools at Gary, Indiana, received on June 11 the degree of doctor of laws from DePauw University, of which he is an alumnus.

Colgate University, Hamilton, New York, conferred the degree of doctor of science on June 11 on Guido F. Verbeck, superintendent of Manlius School, and on William F. Langworthy, retiring professor of botany at the university.

The fellowship honor award of the American Physical Education Association has been given to Dr. William G. Moorhead, of the Department of Public Instruction, Harrisburg. The award is made to members of the society for leadership in and contributions to the field of health and physical education.

Dr. Robert J. Bonner, chairman of the department of Greek at the University of Chicago, has been elected an honorary member of Phi Beta Kappa by the Beta of Illinois chapter. Dr. Bonner was the speaker at the association's annual dinner, at which forty-nine students at the university became members in recognition of their scholastic achievements in the college.

Dr. Q. A. W. Rohrbach, professor of education at the University of Pittsburgh, was recently the guest of honor of the Phi Delta Kappa Chapter of the university. Dr. W. W. Patty, national vice-president and professor of education at Indiana University, was the principal speaker. Dr. Rohrbach leaves Pittsburgh this month to take up his work as president of the State Teachers College at Kutztown.

Dr. John Dewey, professor emeritus of philosophy at Columbia University, has been appointed visiting professor in education at the Johns Hopkins University for the first term, and Dr. Thomas Woody, professor of the history of education at the University of Pennsylvania, has been appointed visiting professor for the second term.

Professor Thomas Nixon Carver, professor of political economy at Harvard University, will teach during the next academic year at the University of California at Los Angeles, as visiting professor of economics in the newly established Graduate School of Arts and Sciences. He will conduct two seminar courses, one on general economic theory and the other on monetary theory.

Dr. Leopold von Wiese, professor of political economy and sociology at the University of Cologne, has been appointed Carl Schurz professor at the University of Wisconsin during the first semester of the next academic year. Professor von Wiese will be on temporary leave of absence from the University of Cologne, and will teach several courses in "Systematic Sociology" and "Recent Social Developments in Europe."

Miss Grace Abbott, chief of the Children's Bureau of the Department of Labor since 1921, retires on July 1 to become professor of public welfare in the School of Social Service of the University of Chicago. She will also become editor of the *Social Service Review*. Miss Abbott succeeded the late Julia Lathrop as head of the Children's Bureau in 1921.

DR. PAUL M. WHEELER, of the Johns Hopkins University, has been made head of the department of English at Winthrop College, South Carolina.

AT the Johns Hopkins University Dr. Allen W. Freeman has been appointed dean of the School of Hygiene and Public Health for three years from July 1. He succeeds Dr. Wade H. Frost, professor of epidemiology. Dr. Edward W. Berry, professor of paleontology, has been reappointed dean of the College of Arts and Sciences for a term of five years; Dr. Frederick S. Dunn has been appointed executive secretary of the Page School, in the absence of Mr. MacMurray. Other appointments include Dr. Edward H. Hume, Noguchi lecturer; Dr. Pasteur Valery-Radot, of Paris, Thayer lecturer in the School of Medicine, and Dr. Julius Lewy, formerly of the University of Giessen, visiting professor in the Oriental Seminary for the first term; Dr. Alan C. Woods, formerly associate professor of ophthalmology, has been appointed acting professor of ophthalomology, and Dr. Ludwig Edelstein, formerly of the University of Berlin, associate in the history of medicine.

DR. IVEY FOREMAN LEWIS, professor of biology at the University of Virginia, has been elected dean of the university, and Dr. George Oscar Ferguson, Jr., professor of psychology and education, assistant dean of the College of Arts and Sciences, has been made dean. Dr. Gordon Thomas Whyburn, associate professor of mathematics in Stanford University, has been elected professor of mathematics, and Dr. Albert Eugene Carey, since 1927 assistant in experimental pathology with the Rockefeller Institute for Medical Research, associate professor of pathology.

DR. JOHN S. BRUBACHER, associate professor of the history and philosophy of education at Yale University, has been promoted to a professorship.

DR. GEORGE J. RYAN, president of the Board of Education of New York, has accepted an invitation from the Italian government to visit educational institutions and universities in Italy. Dr. Ryan is a Papal Marquis, is an officer of the Crown of Italy and holds the Italian Gold Medal for his work in education.

DR. MORRIS B. LAMBIE, professor of political science at the University of Minnesota and relief coordinator for the state, has been invited by the American Municipal Association to spend a large part of the coming year attending economic conferences in various European capitals. For a number of years Professor Lambie has directed the program of the League of Minnesota Municipalities.

DR. GEORGE E. VINCENT, formerly president of the Rockefeller Foundation, was the commencement speaker at Connecticut College, New London.

DR. FRANK PIERREPONT GRAVES, president of the University of the State of New York and State Commissioner of Education, was the speaker on June 12 at the commencement exercises at Lehigh University.

PRESIDENT ROBERT M. HUTCHINS, of the University of Chicago, delivered the commencement address at the George Peabody College for Teachers, on June 8. His subject was "An Intelligible System of Education."

DR. ROBERT CLARKSON CLOTHIER, president of Rutgers University, gave the address at the commencement of the Junior College of Connecticut, Bridgeport, on June 13.

DEAN FREDERICK E. BOLTON, of the University of Washington, Seattle, was the chief speaker at the recent conference on elementary education arranged by the State Normal School at Monmouth for school executives and teachers of Oregon. About a thousand were in attendance. Dr. Bolton delivered two addresses at the general assemblies on "America's Biggest Big Business" and "Some Paramount Objectives under the New Deal." He also spoke at the Phi Delta Kappa-Pi Lambda Theta banquet on tendencies toward centralization in education.

As a memorial to Dr. John Grier Hibben, fourteenth president of Princeton University, the alumni will endeavor to raise funds to endow twenty memorial prize scholarships. An endowment of $25,000 will be required for each scholarship. The annual stipend will be $1,000, more remunerative than any scholarship now in existence at Princeton.

ALUMNI of the College of William and Mary returned on June 9 to pay tribute to Dr. J. A. C. Chandler, president, who died on May 31. Dr. Chandler was to have celebrated his fifteenth anniversary as head of the college, and the alumni reunion had originally been planned as a celebration for that event. A bound book of 200 letters of appreciation and congratulations from prominent men and women alumni was to have been presented to him by his oldest son, Herbert G. Chandler.

DR. JAMES BRYANT CONANT, president of Harvard University, delivered the address to the senior class of Stevens Institute of Technology at the commencement exercises on June 9.

AN Economic Conference was held from June 18 to 22 at George Peabody College for Teachers, at which fundamental factors and principles essential to the understanding of the present economic, industrial and agricultural situation in America were presented through lectures and round table discussions. Speakers at the meeting included Dr. John T. Madden, dean of the School of Commerce and director of the Institute of International Finance, New York University; the Honorable Jesse Jones, chairman of the Reconstruction Finance Corporation, and General Hugh S. Johnson, National Recovery Administrator.

THE American Educational Research Association will meet this summer for the first time in conjunction with the National Education Association. The meeting will open in Washington, July 5, at 2 P. M., in the lecture room of the National Academy of Sciences. The program includes papers on "Motion Pictures," by W. W. Charters, director of the Bureau of Educational Research, Ohio State University; on "The Use of the Radio," by Tracy F. Tyler, secretary and research director of the National Committee on Education by Radio; on "Personality Records of Children," by Ben D. Wood, associate professor of collegiate research, Teachers College, Columbia University, and on "Standardized Tests," by J. Cayce Morrison, assistant commissioner for elementary education, New York State Department of Education.

THE American Council of Learned Societies offers in 1935 grants in aid of research and postdoctoral fellowships for training and research in the humanities for which application must be made by December 15. The grants are in two categories: small grants, not exceeding $300, and larger grants, not exceeding $1,000. Applicants for grants must possess the doctorate or its equivalent, and must be actually in need of the desired assistance and unable to secure it from other sources. The grants are made for specific purposes (other than living expenses or in lieu of salary), such as travel, photostats, secretarial assistance, etc., in connection with projects of research actually under way. The fellowships have a basic stipend of $1,800, to which allowances for travel, expenses of research and other purposes may be added. Applicants must have the doctorate, must not be more than thirty-five years of age, and must have demonstrated unmistakable aptitude for constructive research. Further information can be obtained from the American Council of Learned Societies, 907 Fifteenth Street, Washington, D. C.

ANNOUNCEMENT has been made by the University of Denver, through its Department of Speech and Dramatic Arts, of twenty scholarships in dramatics and twenty scholarships in debate to be given to outstanding high-school juniors. These awards are for a four-weeks period, from June 27 to July 25, 1934, at the university for the purpose of fostering speech work in the high schools and encouraging the development of worthy talent in dramatic arts among high-school students. Arrangements will be made for students to attend several dramatic performances produced at local theaters for both entertainment and practical instruction. Debate students will receive thorough instruction in the latest methods of debate and will work on the question, "Federal Aid to Education."

THE National University Extension Association announced at its meeting in Chicago on May 18 a number of correspondence courses designed to explain to the average citizen the meaning and implications of the New Deal. W. S. Bittner, secretary of the association, states that university extension departments during the past year have made a special effort to develop courses intended "to adjust the thinking of adults to the changes going on in industrial and social life." Practically all university extension departments now offer courses on economics and political science with emphasis on international relations, the New Deal, the NRA, currency, taxation and problems related to unemployment. Likewise, courses on art, appreciation of music, contemporary literature and similar subjects are now available. Mr. A. M. Harding, president of the association, states that registration in courses coming under the latter group are increasing. New types of courses in vocational guidance are being developed by several extension departments.

One hundred presidents of American colleges recently signed a letter and sent it to President Roosevelt, protesting against war, and urging the immediate passage of drastic anti-war legislation. The following quotations from the letter are taken from the *Christian Science Monitor,* for May 18: "An act empowering and requiring the President of the United States to declare a complete embargo upon trade between this country and any belligerent nation in the event of hostilities in any part of the world." "An act prohibiting the use of the armed forces of the United States either for the collection of debts owed to Americans by foreign nationals or their governments, or for the protection of American property owned abroad." "An act prohibiting the manufacture, purchase or sale of firearms, and of ammunition of every description, within the United States, or in foreign trade between the United States and other countries, except by the Federal Government of the United States or under license and complete control by the Federal Government." Five other suggestions deal with the flotation of war bonds, removal of the possibility of great profits for munition makers in the event of war, adherence of the United States to the World Court, steps toward joining the League of Nations and the offer of cooperation with the League in the meantime.

The Ironwood, Michigan, Board of Education has announced increased salaries for teachers of the grades, high school and junior college for the next school year. Arthur E. Erickson, superintendent of schools, is reported to have stated that the increases will be from 8 to 15 per cent., averaging about 10 per cent.

DISCUSSION

WHAT CORRELATION IS THERE BETWEEN EDUCATION AND VOCATION?

A young man came into my office recently and gave me the high sign of a Massachusetts Institute of Technology graduate. I recognized him as a graduate of five or six years' standing of the cooperative course in electrical engineering, who had taken his cooperative work with the Boston Elevated Railway. I returned his salute and asked him what he was doing and how he was getting along.

He was in the life-insurance business, vice president in charge of agency organization and sales promotion, a director and a member of the finance committee. I laughed and said jokingly: "Well, you are exhibit A of a wasted engineering education. You take a five-year course full of higher mathematics, advanced scientific theory and laboratory technique. You spend sixteen months qualifying as motorman, conductor and inspector, grub away in the car shops, work over traffic studies and timetables, experiment on the acceleration and control of trolley cars and trains; then you become a life-insurance agent. That's my idea of a wasted education."

"You're dead wrong, professor," he came back. "It's just the right education for the job. I needed a stiff course in mental training. I had to learn to think hard and long and straight. That's just how an engineer has to think, and I got the knack and habit of thinking this way by studying electrical engineering for five years. I learned to get the facts and to distrust opinions. Man! I'll never forget the call-down one of the fellows got when he used a statement in a popular magazine as an authority to back up an argument. I learned from the Lab. that there are ways of getting facts if you really go after them. As for the time I spent on the Boston Elevated, man, that was one of the most valuable parts of my education. I mixed with all kinds of men—lumpers, craftsmen, engineers and superintendents. I learned the way the other fellow thinks and what his viewpoint is likely to be on all sorts of subjects. I learned a lot from every one of those Boston Elevated men. Yes, sir, the whole course is an ideal training for my insurance work. Why do you suppose they made me vice president instead of keeping me working as one of their agents? It was just because I had the advantage of a kind of education that the other fellow had missed, which made me able to do things he couldn't do."

This young man's story is a rather striking one, but it isn't by any means unique. In fact, it more or less typifies the attitude held by scores of other engineering graduates who have found their life work outside of the vocational compartment statistically labelled "Engineering."

The usual method of arriving at a figure to designate the extent of correlation between engineering education is to make a survey of engineering graduates and classify them according to whether or not they are in engineering work. In 1923 such a survey was made by Eta Kappa Nu, which is an honorary fraternity of electrical-engineering students and graduates. The distribution of its alumni among the various occupations ought to be fairly typical of the general distribution of electrical-engineering graduates. A questionnaire was circulated to 1,714 electrical-engineering graduates, of whom 844 replied. These were listed as to whether they were in electrical engineering, other engineering or non-engineering. The results of this kind of tabulation were published by the Society for the Promotion of Engineering Education in 1929, and showed that 61.4 per cent. of the graduates remained in electrical engineering, and that 83.5 per cent. were in some kind of engineering. This leaves only 16.5 per cent who were in occupations outside the engineering classification. It is interesting to note that the graduates of later classes tend to stick closer to electrical engineering than the graduates of the earlier classes and that a smaller percentage of them are in the non-engineering field. Based on these statistics alone, we might be tempted to draw the conclusion that in the electrical-engineering courses as a whole there is about a 60 per cent. correlation between electrical-engineering education and the vocations which the graduates enter.

An interesting study was made of what the 61.4 per cent. were doing who remained in electrical engineering. Nearly half (42.9 per cent.) went into the technical group, and 17.8 per cent. were in operation and maintenance. There was also a decided shift among the older graduates from these two groups into the administrative group. This is to be expected. Administrators are ordinarily drawn from the older graduates. There is also a similar shift among the older classes to the commercial group.

Of the 16.5 per cent. who went into non-engineering work, over half are in administrative work, while among the older graduates this ratio is a little more than two thirds. A logical conclusion from this study would be that an electrical-engineering education is effective in giving a young man the broad fundamental training in habits of thought which fits him for administrative responsibilites, even though his duties are not connected with engineering details.

Later, in June, 1932, the *Journal of Engineering Education* published the results of another study. This included graduates of civil, electrical, mechanical and other engineering courses in land-grant colleges, and covered the records of 9,334 graduates. In this study graduates classified as being in engineering work included the professional engineers and all others in occupations closely allied with engineering, such as teaching in the engineering field. According to this classification, it was found that 62.3 per cent. of all the graduates remain in engineering work. There was the same drift among the older graduates away from the engineering field into other responsibilities. These figures corroborate the figures concerning electrical engineers.

The apparent conclusion from such statistics is that the correlation between the education and vocation of a graduate in engineering is only about 60 per cent. But this kind of statistical study is an exceedingly artificial way of testing the correlation between education and vocation. The assumption is made that correlation exists only when a graduate in engineering goes into a vocation that has the tag

"Engineering" tacked on to it. This is making the limits of the correlation altogether too narrow. A much fairer criterion of correlation would be to try to answer the question, "To what extent does a given college course fit a man for the job; first, as to habits of thought and action, second, as to the factual knowledge needed for the job?" The college course that does this best has the closest correlation.

Now concerning an engineering education, it has sometimes been said that the engineer gets his mental training and scientific methods of attack almost entirely from scientific material, that is, the facts and theories of mathematics, chemistry and physics, and therefore he enters his vocation ignorant of the great mass of knowledge and philosophy which constitutes the study material of courses in law, literature, economics and political and industrial history. But let us investigate the facts. Consider, for instance, the course in electrical engineering at M. I. T., the curriculum with which I am most familiar. To be sure, the great backbone of the curriculum is a series of subjects dealing with theoretical mathematical physics, but this backbone is augmented and buttressed all through the first two years by courses in English and in political and industrial history and in the senior year by the seminar course in biographies of the scientists. There are two courses in political economy, and at least two general studies from a long list, including psychology, humanics, international law and American foreign policy, as well as numerous courses in literature and history. In the cooperative course, two of the required subjects are business law and business organization.

Just considering subject-matter alone, what better array of facts and knowledge could a man bring to his vocation than that represented by a study of such a curriculum? Imagine a conference among four leaders from four outstanding professions, say a lawyer, an economist, a financier and an engineer. Each must be a specialist in his own particular field, but each should have a broad knowledge of the fields of the others in order to effectively work with them. I am willing to wager that the engineer would know more about the fields of the other three professionals than all the three others would know about his. I believe I can confidently state that the graduate of an engineering school is more likely than a graduate of any other professional school to have the advantage, not only of having had a superior mental training in the analysis of facts, the drawing of concrete conclusions and in the actual doing of the job, but also of bringing to his task a larger mass of facts and information pertaining to the problem than the graduates of any other professional school. We read, and hear it said over and over again, that we live in an engineering world. Modern civilization is built upon the discovery and application of scientific facts and scientific methods. If this is so, then the factual side of one's education should consist of the knowledge of scientific and engineering facts, theories and methods. It is this kind of material that makes up by far the greater part of the material contained in a modern engineering course, and while we recognize that the prime purpose of an engineering education is not the acquisition of knowledge and facts, but rather the training of a man to think straight, nevertheless it is true that the very information which he acquires in the process of receiving his training is of such a nature as to be of the very greatest possible use to him. In other words, the engineering course, as now developed, gives the graduate habits of thought by which he is enabled effectively to tackle modern problems, and at the same time gives him a mass of information of such nature that it is bound to be of maximum use in his chosen vocation, almost regardless of what that vocation may be.

But there is another correlation, the nature of which is rather hard to put into words. It is the correlation between the spirit of a man's education and the motives which later should govern not only his vocation but his whole life. If it is important that the factual material and the thought processes acquired at school should be directly applicable to a man's vocation, it is far more important that those mental attitudes and ideals be instilled in the student, the application of which in the practice of his vocation will have a beneficent effect upon society. More tritely, when a man's whole life work has been summed up, the world should be a better place to live in as a result of his having lived in it and worked in it.

The unselfish devotion of science and engineering to the constant bettering of mankind's condition is too well recognized to need elaboration. Young men who receive their education in this atmosphere bring to their vocations, however diverse they may be, this traditional spirit of service. Of course, some graduates have caught more of it than others, but few take four years of engineering training without acquiring some of it. What the world needs at present is more men with these ideals of science and engineering, and it needs them in every vocation. So, whatever vocation he may enter, if the engineer is true to his educational ideals, he brings to it the very element most urgently needed by that particular vocation.

Thus, when we take as our criteria the power and habit of straight thinking, the acquisition of the most useful body of knowledge, the inculcation of high ideals, we are compelled to arrive at the conclusion that there is a most gratifying correlation between the education of the modern engineer and almost any vocation that he may choose as his life work.

W. H. TIMBIE

MASSACHUSETTS INSTITUTE
OF TECHNOLOGY

PRESIDENT ROOSEVELT'S VOCABULARY

AT the present time molding public opinion looms important. Millions of people in a few minutes and at one time over a nation-wide radio network listen to the same message. Social and political leaders are readily taking advantage of this vehicle of communication. The general population has become accustomed to hearing these leaders. President Roosevelt's voice is familiar to millions. He has been called the "Radio President."

For the educator it becomes a significant problem to isolate some of the specific characteristics of those who have been so influential in directing public opinion. What are these attributes that may be more or less significant to those who must formulate educational programs? Obviously language is a basic attribute.

The many investigations which psychologists and educators have conducted on vocabularies make it possible to approach the study of this phase of Mr. Roosevelt's language. Results of this study are briefly summarized in the table to aid the reader in following the analysis.

Occurrence of words[1] in general reading	Franklin D. Roosevelt		
	Inaugural address	Radio address Oct. 22, 1933	Lincoln's Gettysburg address
	Per cent.	Per cent.	Per cent.
500 most common words	67.8	72.9	77.7
1,000 " " "	74.2	80.6	85.5
2,000 " " "	82.9	87.9	90.7
3,000 " " "	86.8	91.1	94.0
4,000 " " "	89.5	93.0	94.0
5,000 " " "	92.0	94.3	98.5
10,000 " " "	97.0	97.2	99.3
15,000 " " "	98.0	97.8	99.6
20,000 " " "	99.5	98.0	100.0

An examination of the figures in this table shows that about 70 per cent. of the words in the inaugural address and in the radio address (portraying national conditions) occur among the first 500 most common words found in general reading material. In each of these addresses 74.2 per cent. and 80.6 per cent. of the vocabulary, respectively, fall in the first 1,000 most common words. These thousand most common words cover 85 per cent. of the vocabulary in the written material of college students[2] and 85.5 per cent. of the vocabulary in Lincoln's Gettysburg address.

In the first 5,000 most common words are included 92.0 per cent. and 94.3 per cent. of the vocabulary in Roosevelt's two addresses and 98.5 per cent. of the vocabulary in Lincoln's Gettysburg address. This number is nearly the maximum writing vocabulary of college students and provides 90 per cent. of the vocabulary in books of fiction.[3]

The October radio talk by President Roosevelt shows his successful attempt to confine himself to more commonly understood words. The

[1] E. L. Thorndike, "Teacher's Word Book," 1932.

[2] P. A. Witty and M. Fry, "The Vocabulary Content of Composition Written by College Students," *Jour. Educ. Res.*, 19: 135–138, 1929.

[3] P. A. Witty and L. L. LaBrant, "Vocabulary and Reading," SCHOOL AND SOCIETY, 31: 268–272, 1930.

vocabulary in this talk is more simply couched than his inaugural address. The Gettysburg address is a picture of even greater simplicity of vocabulary. It is interesting to note that during student days at Harvard Mr. Roosevelt participated quite actively in the college paper and served as editor.

The results of this experiment leave open the question as to whether simplicity of vocabulary is the principal factor determining the effectiveness of President Roosevelt's messages in reaching the average man. Supplementary consideration should be given to the style and diction, to the personality of Mr. Roosevelt's voice and to his rôle as a public personage.

RICHARD S. SCHULTZ
THE PSYCHOLOGICAL CORPORATION
NEW YORK, N. Y.

SPECIAL CORRESPONDENCE

EDUCATION AND CULTURE CONTACTS

YALE UNIVERSITY offers from July 30 to September 8 as its fourth summer seminar in education a study of the general topic, "Education and Culture Contacts." A cosmopolitan faculty of internationally recognized distinction will come together under the direction of the department of education of the Graduate School to present to a carefully selected group of students the opportunity to study and discuss the social, religious and educational problems which arise in areas where different races and cultures come into contact with one another.

From the time that civilizations began to fringe one another, the problems resulting from the overlaying of cultures have been apparent. The establishment of the first trade routes, bringing together peoples of greater cultural differences, complicated the situation. To-day, in a world knit closely together by the devices of modern science and invention, the problems have become extraordinarily complex and difficult. The ultimate analysis and solution of these problems would prove an effective approach to the realization of world peace and concord. For this reason the seminar should be timely and of general interest.

Although credit is not a controlling factor of the seminar, arrangements can be made for the taking of examinations and securing of credit if the student so desires.

The members of the seminar will consist of directors of education, superintendents, supervisors, inspectors of schools, principals and teachers at training colleges and secondary and elementary schools, government officials, missionaries, social workers and others interested. Among the number will be twenty officials and representatives from the West Indies, twenty-five officials of the General Education Board and a number of men and women actively engaged in the field of culture contacts in both this and other countries.

The cooperation of the Carnegie Corporation of New York and the General Education Board has made it possible to offer to men and women of distinction in the various fields covered a limited number of fellowships covering the cost of membership in the seminar and board and lodging in the Hall of Graduate Studies. A limited number of tuition scholarships are also available to missionaries on furlough and others not in permanent employment. The members of the seminar are fortunate in having at their disposal the beautiful Hall of Graduate Studies at Yale where the meetings of the seminar will be held. They will also have recourse to the Sterling Memorial Library, the Penniman Memorial Library of Education, the Penniman Reading Room and new and important books and magazines, not only in education, but in related subjects. The resources of the Peabody Museum and of the special anthropological library will also be available.

The general topic, "Education and Culture Contacts," is subdivided into eight series of lectures and discussions. The method to be followed is the "lecture-discussion" type, which is used extensively at Yale and has proven very successful. The period of discussion following the lecture proper will give to the members of the seminar an opportunity to raise questions and advance contributions and opinions. In addition there will be special discussion groups and formal and informal evening lectures.

A brief résumé of the lectures to be given and their content is as follows: Professor Alfred R. Radcliffe-Brown, professor of anthropology at the University of Chicago and formerly professor of social anthropology at Capetown and Sydney, will give a series of lectures on "Comparative Sociology," including an analysis of the cultures of different peoples into such elements as health, family life, government, law, agriculture, industry, religion and recreation, with emphasis on those elements which chiefly concern the educator.

Mr. Arthur I. Mayhew, secretary of the British Government's Colonial Education Committee, London, will lecture on "Education in the British Colonies." Mr. Mayhew's lectures will include a summary of English influence on the education of India from 1800 to 1920; a discussion of education and culture contacts in Ceylon, Malaya, Hong Kong and Palestine; English educational aims, methods and results in the British dependencies, in tropical Africa and in the western Pacific; a comparison of the educational processes of assimilation and adaptation as carried out in India, the Far East, the West Indies, Africa, and elsewhere; and an analysis of the desirability and possibility of cultural unity in education and methods of preserving distinctive characteristics of widely varying civilizations and cultures.

Dr. Thomas Jesse Jones, educational director of the Phelps-Stokes Fund, New York, and well known for his surveys of education in Africa and the Near East, will present "The Essentials of Education"—an outline analysis of civilization and its educational implications.

Dr. Charles T. Loram, Sterling professor of education at Yale and chairman of a newly organized subdepartment of race relations, will lecture on "Education and Cultural Contacts in South Africa." Dr. Loram will deal with the cultural changes which are taking place among the South African natives as a result of contact with western civilization, and their implications for education.

Dr. W. Carson Ryan, director of education, U. S. Indian Service, Washington, has as his topic "The Education of the American Indian." These lectures will deal with the social and economic status of the American Indian, the present situation in Indian education and the reforms begun and contemplated.

President Francis Cho-Min Wei, Central China College, Wuchang, China, will discuss "Education and Culture Contacts in China." Mr. Wei's lectures will include a consideration of the conflict of cultures in China and an outline of the ancient and modern educational systems, with suggestions for the development of a system in keeping with China's needs to-day.

Dr. Frank Tannenbaum, who is at present undertaking a study of social, economic and educational conditions in South America and Cuba, will present "Education and Culture Contacts in Mexico and Latin America." He will give a survey of the present situation, together with an outline of the educational system in Mexico, with special reference to rural education in which Mexico has made significant progress.

Dr. Thomas J. Woofter, Jr., of the department of sociology at the University of North Carolina, will deal with the "Education of the American Negro." These lectures will consist of an analysis of the social and economic position of the Negro and the ways in which education is attempting to meet those needs.

Among those who have been invited to give lectures and take part in the conferences are: Dr. W. W. Alexander, director, Interracial Commission, Atlanta, Georgia; Professor Charles Johnson, Fisk University, Nashville, Tennessee; Professor U. W. Leavall, George Peabody College for Teachers, Nashville, Tennessee; President Frank E. Midkiff, Kamehameha Schools, Honolulu, Hawaii; Dr. Anson Phelps Stokes, chairman of the Phelps-Stokes Fund.

It is to be noted that each lecturer, due to his close contact with the field with which he is dealing, will be able to present to members of the seminar his own first-hand knowledge and experiences of the problem.

Professor Charles T. Loram, who is the director of the 1934 summer seminar, will be glad to answer all inquiries and send a prospectus of the seminar to all those who are interested.

CHARLES T. LORAM,
Director of the Summer Session

COLORADO HIGH-SCHOOL STUDENTS AS A MODEL HOUSE OF REPRESENTATIVES

Two years ago the Ecclesia Club, a social science discussion group at the Adams State

Teachers College, sponsored a model Colorado constitutional convention for high-school students of the San Luis Valley in southern Colorado. This project proved so successful that the club decided this year to conduct a project along similar lines. Instead of a constitutional convention it was decided to have a model Colorado House of Representatives. The participants were to be as before high-school students with the guidance of the club members.

The model House of Representatives convened on April 16. An attempt was made to give all the atmosphere of a regular legislative chamber. Desks were arranged in semi-circles about the platform of the speaker and the press table. At the rear and along the sides sat spectators, consisting of non-participating students, collegians and faculty members and a number of townspeople. Behind the speaker was draped a large United States flag and the flag of Colorado. Adjoining rooms to the legislative chamber were arranged for committee meetings.

The Ecclesia Club sent out instructions and bibliographies weeks before the assembly, and the high schools were asked to conduct elections for their representatives. However, many found this impractical, although it would have lent a realistic touch. There was a fear among many that the best qualified would not be chosen.

The students came to the model House of Representatives knowing what districts they were to represent, the committees on which they were to serve and some of the principles which would be discussed. They registered on arrival, and all those not acting as Representatives were seated on the sides of the legislative chamber.

At ten o'clock the session was opened with the invocation by the assembly chaplain. After brief remarks of welcome the clerk read the official announcements and the assembly got under way. A temporary speaker was chosen and a permanent clerk designated. A committee on credentials was selected, who made its report, and a college student representing a judge of the supreme court administered the oath to the members. This was followed by the election of a permanent speaker, who had the clerk read the message of Governor Johnson. The governor went to no little effort in preparing a message for this model House of Representatives and laid down a constructive program of work that was adhered to quite closely by the youthful legislators.

At eleven o'clock the assembly adjourned to committee sessions to discuss proposed measures which were dropped in the basket at the speaker's desk at the beginning of the session. The committee meetings proved to be full of excitement. The number of committees was reduced to five in order to get a large enough group for discussion in each committee, they were: (1) Education, (2) Counties and County Lines, (3) Finance, (4) Appropriations, (5) Amendments. It was later found that other committees had to be appointed in order to discuss all the proposed measures, but these five remained the major ones throughout the session. Full discussion was permitted on all measures before the committees, and most of them held hearings to permit different interests to present arguments for and against the measures.

Lobbyists and pressure groups of all kinds attempted to influence legislation in the committee sessions and any other time they could get the ear of the members. Blank telegrams were filled out and carried in to the different legislator as well as piles of petitions on many of the subjects under discussion. Pages were scurrying to and fro, and the whole atmosphere was that of a legislative body working at top speed in order to draft solutions to some of the problems of the state.

Like most legislative bodies there were many more bills introduced than could be handled in the session, so most of them died in the committee rooms. However, when the voted hour of adjournment rolled around in the evening, the assembly found itself unable to pass many of the important measures up for the third reading, and they ordered the clocks to be stopped until they could partially complete their task.

There was no lack of realism in the assembly, down to the removal of a radical from the floor by the sergeant-at-arms. The students were given as much of the local color as possible without destroying the seriousness of the work by the Representatives. A mimeographed sheet was run off several times during the day which kept all the members familiar with what was going on in all the committees. The legislators were in the constant atmosphere of the urgent problems of the state. Arrangements were made for groups who were working on the same committee to eat together.

Needless to say, these students learned much in the way of parliamentary procedure in the one day, but procedure was sacrificed many times in order to have full discussion of the problems under consideration.

The students and faculty advisers were so pleased with the experiment that they have requested the Ecclesia Club to again have a conference of high-school students. The apparent success of this project and the one tried several years ago, a model Colorado constitutional convention, has prompted the club to lay plans for similar conferences in the future to be held annually. It will be the policy to try a number of different projects, of local, national and international interest.

LASHLEY GREY HARVEY
ADAMS STATE TEACHERS COLLEGE
COLORADO

QUOTATIONS

ENGINEERING AS A FINE ART

DR. JAMES BRYANT CONANT, president of Harvard University, speaking on June 9 at the sixty-second annual commencement of Stevens Institute of Technology said that "members of two professions are certain to survive the worst of political and economic storms—the engineer and the doctor." President Conant said in part:

It has been well said that a man who knows exactly where he is going never gets there. This is particularly true of one's education. I take it that it is because of this impossibility of seeing the ultimate goal that we rejoice in an opportunity to applaud when each runner passes a certain post.

Many of you will probably find your permanent life work in applied science. You will practise some form of engineering or become connected with some business venture through your scientific training. I can not claim to speak to you to-day as a full-fledged engineer or an applied scientist but I have now and then spent some time on the technical problems which arise when science and industry meet. I may perhaps qualify as an ex-amateur, and as such rather than as a college president you will permit me to say something about the responsibilities which lie on the shoulders of the engineering profession.

In the first place, it seems quite clear that whatever sort of a social and economic order lies ahead of us, society will demand the luxuries and conveniences afforded by modern technology. Taking a long range view, and for the moment the most pessimistic one possible, it would seem to me that members of two professions were certain of surviving the worst of political and economic storms—the engineers and the doctors. . . . The engineers will be in a peculiarly important position of influence. Much may depend on the way they look at life, and their ideals and standards may have a determining effect on society at some not very distant date. If we want certain things preserved in this world it is to you gentlemen and your successors that we may have to look for their preservation.

The monks in the dark ages preserved the remnants of one civilization to enable another to come to life. Perhaps, in some measure at some time, the scientist and engineer may have a similar opportunity to transmit to posterity the studies we now call the humanities. This is the responsibility that lies heavily on the shoulders of engineers and scientists and those who educate them. I believe the men of applied science will prove themselves worthy of the challenge to whatever extent it is presented. I believe to-day in many institutions we are educating men who understand not only their technical professions but also the needs and aspirations of the human spirit. . . .

The significance of science, so it seems to me, is not to be found in an evaluation of its practical results or an enumeration of the shortcomings of the present industrial age. The significance of science to civilization is exactly like the significance of a Greek temple or a Greek drama. It must be regarded as one of the marvelous products of the human spirit which will have a meaning for man as long as he continues on this planet. Perhaps we might liken the growth of modern science to the building of a medieval cathedral. It is the work of many hands and has arisen slowly and to some extent irregularly. . . .

May I illustrate the way in which science represents a collective enterprise running over many years by an example drawn from my own particular branch of the subject? A few years ago a German chemist, Hans Fischer, succeeded in synthesizing the red coloring matter of the blood, known as hemin. . . .

Now, it seems to me that the appreciation of scientific achievement has a cultural value comparable to that which comes from an understanding of poetry or art. The educational problem, however, of inculcating the basis for this appreciation is very difficult. I believe that the hidden springs of action of the artist and the scientist are essentially the same. The material success which has followed the application of science to industry has partially hidden the true nature of scientific endeavor from the lay public and perhaps even from the scientist himself. This is particularly true of applied science. I imagine that in some subsequent age when our technological marvels have lost their novelty the great scientists and engineers of our day will be thought of not so much as distributors of material benefits but rather as inspiring examples of the creative intelligence of the human race. They will be classed with the philosophers, the writers and the artists, and their work will be judged by similar standards.

From my experience with a great variety of technical men in universities and in industry, I feel sure that the zest of their work lies in the pure joy of its creativeness—in the thrill of overcoming the perpetual challenge which inanimate nature seems to present to the human brain. In this spirit, gentlemen, you will approach your own work. This is the spirit which has made possible all advances in knowledge. It is but another aspect of the imaginative vision which has inspired poets, painters and composers. The scientist is the most recent recruit to the ranks of creative workers. He must realize his kinship. He must be catholic in his appreciation of the present and humble in his judgment of the past. We may hope that art, literature and philosophy, if necessary, can be carried through a period of turmoil by the technical man who has had a liberal education and realizes to the full its implications.

REPORTS

A NEW CONCEPTION OF ACCREDITING STANDARDS

THE new program for the accrediting of higher institutions adopted by the North Central Association of Colleges and Secondary Schools at its annual meeting in April comes after three years of diligent search for an answer to the question, "What comprises a good institution of higher education?"

In common with other accrediting agencies, the North Central Association has been for several years the object of criticism both within and without the educational profession. The standards have been assailed as rigid, mechanical and minimal; the agencies as repressive and discriminatory.

That the old standards grew from a definite need for protection from "diploma mills" and various unethical practices, few of their critics have denied; that in their growth they had become inelastic and to some extent mechanical, few of their staunchest supporters failed to admit.

Out of the need for a more pliable method of evaluating an institution's excellence came the appointment of a Committee on Revision of Standards by the North Central Association. Within this committee a smaller group in charge of the study have sought by surveys of 57 cooperating institutions of various types to evolve criteria which would more truly indicate the value of an institution. Aided by financial support from the General Education Board, the association was able to undertake a study of sufficient scope as to furnish a basis for an entirely new accrediting program.

One of the most striking features of the new plan is the complete elimination of "standards" in the old sense. Instead of standards, a statement of policy has been adopted embracing 19 provisions, but without the word "standard" occurring once. However, it is not the mere elimination of the word which is important; it is the elimination of the idea. There is to be no more "standardization" in the North Central Association.

Another basic change, closely related to the foregoing, is a new recognition of the necessity for individuality in institutions. Instead of attempting to force all into a common mold, the new plan allows each institution to develop its program in terms of its own objectives. Accrediting in the future is to be based, not on the degree of conformity to definite requirements, but on the degree to which the announced objectives are successfully achieved. The entire "pattern" which the institution presents as an institution of higher education will be considered.

In order to objectify the institutional pattern, a so-called pattern map has been devised which will show at a glance the percentile position of a particular institution, as compared with all other institutions, with respect to eighty-one characteristics. These characteristics are grouped under eleven major headings, such as faculty, library, student personnel service, and administration; and represent those characteristics which have been shown by research to be indices of excellence.

The percentile ratings will be based on criteria contained in the new statement of policy. In formulating these criteria, most of the criticisms which have been made of the old standards have been avoided; the new are general rather than specific, flexible rather than rigid, human rather than mechanical, maximal rather than minimal.

As an example of the type of criteria to be used, that on the subject of finance is here quoted because of the fact that the old endowment standards have been especial sources of irritation in the past. The new policy of the North Central Association on finance is as follows:

> The institution should provide evidence of financial resources adequate for and effectively applied to the support of its educational program.
>
> The items of information to be considered in determining the adequacy of the financial support are the expenditure per student for educational purposes; the extent to which the institution is dependent on student fees; the stability of the financing, as indicated by the amount of income per student from stable sources, and the avoidance of burdensome indebtedness; and the procedures in financial accounting and reporting. Necessary adjustments will be allowed for contributed services of instructors and administrative officers in Catholic institutions.

Due to the necessity of obtaining an increased amount of information concerning institutions being considered for accreditment, the new plan provides for a more detailed and extensive inspection than has been true in the past, except in case of surveys. The old one-man, one-day inspection is being abandoned in favor of an inspection by at least two persons who will spend at least two days at each institution. The inspectors will be provided with detailed schedules, so that data secured at all institutions will be comparable. While it is realized that it will be advantageous to have the same inspectors visit as many institutions as possible, there is no intention of creating a permanent inspectorial staff.

No change has been made in the actual organization of the association for accrediting. The reports of the inspectors, together with the pattern maps and any other information available will be presented to a committee of seven, called the Board of Review, which since 1927 has had delegated to it the preparation of the accredited lists of higher institutions. The recommendations of this board are presented in turn to the Commission on Institutions of Higher Education and the Executive Committee.

However, this new concept of accreditment, which discards all minimal standards and judges institutions in the light of their own objectives and in terms of those characteristics which this study has shown to be indices of excellence, is such a radical departure from prevailing methods that the results will be of interest to all who are concerned with problems of accrediting.

President L. D. Coffman, of the University of Minnesota, was chairman of the general committee. The following persons were in charge of the study: Dean M. E. Haggerty, University of Minnesota; Floyd W. Reeves, Tennessee Valley Authority; John Dale Russell, University of Chicago; D. H. Gardner, University of Akron; Douglas Waples, University of Chicago, and George F. Zook, U. S. Commissioner of Education.

H. M. DOUTT

UNIVERSITY OF AKRON

TESTIMONY BEFORE THE SENATE COMMITTEE INVESTIGATING CRIME

FOR some months the Subcommittee of the Committee on Commerce of the United States Senate has been investigating crime and so-called "rackets" with a view to their suppression. The subcommittee, under the chairmanship of Senator Royal S. Copeland, has been taking testimony from a large number of individuals, representing the legal profession, law enforcement officers and educators. A digest of the hearings has recently been published by the United States Government Printing Office and is available for the use of citizens.

The following excerpts from the report are of special interest to educators:

THE STATUS OF CRIMINALS

Charles L. Chute: The great bulk of crime in this country is a youth problem, and its beginnings are nearly always found in misdirected childhood.

Irving W. Halpern: Crime to-day is the chosen field of youth, and the predominance of youthful offenders among those charged with crime has long been a subject for concern. . . . Young men, desirous of obtaining . . . those luxuries and amusements which their limited earning power in legitimate enterprise can not supply, have steadily drifted into the criminal ranks. The lure of easy money is constantly dangled before them by criminal associates and others with whom they come in contact. . . .

Howard W. Ameli: The real menace in our country to-day is the alarming increase in the number of our youthful criminals, who have not had or who have disregarded the opportunities for education in the trades, professions and business. Statements have been made to the effect that a large percentage of our criminals who have been imprisoned are under the age of 25 years. Youths of the age of 20 furnish the highest ratio; the next are boys of ages ranging between 18 and 19.

Dr. George Kirchwey: A few years ago we made a study of the total intake of our court of general sessions for a year, investigating particularly the 3,000 men who were arranged for the first time for a felony in that court . . . how many of them do you suppose had in childhood been in the Children's Court? Ninety-two per cent. of them had been. . . . What we are destroying in our present system is not only childhood but perhaps the most precious elements in our childhood, the courage, the daring, the capacity to do great things.

Henrietta Additon: As I was leaving the office this morning I received this report of a case, referred by a school: a boy, twelve years old, with the Irish name of Jerry, and a boy with a nice Italian name are accused of extorting two cents a week for protection from the younger children of the schoolyard. . . . We had a group of boys over in Brooklyn. We found that they were going into the small groceries and saying to the owners, "You give us so many sandwiches." They would make up the sandwiches and the boys would take them and say, "All right, thank you." The owners would say, "Where is the money?" The boys would say, "Well, we will come back and break up your windows, but if you give us the sandwiches and apples we will see that no other boys come in and bother you."

Senator Royal S. Copeland: Let me give you, in a word, what the division of investigation of the United States has discovered in this year of grace, 1933: During the first nine months of this year the arrest records, the fingerprint records of 241,000 persons were studied. Those arrested at nineteen years of age made up the largest of all the age groups. It numbered 12,418 individuals, charged with larceny, burglary, robbery, assault, rape and criminal homicide. Seventeen hundred were 15 years of age or younger; 20 per cent. were under 21, and three out of five were under 30. These figures cover the entire nation. In New York the percentage of youthful criminals was even greater. At Sing Sing, 50 per cent. were under 25 years, and 80 per cent. are under 30 years.

Irving W. Halpern: A recent survey completed by the Probation Department of the Court of General Sessions of the county of New York . . . reveals strikingly that the offenders twenty-five years of age and under represented 53.71 per cent. of the 12,744 criminal offenders whose histories were investigated . . . over a five-year period, . . . that those who were twenty-one years of age and under . . . numbered 33.87 per cent.

CHILDREN'S COURTS

Charles L. Chute: Hardly any well-informed person to-day will deny the importance of juvenile courts. They are the first line of defense set by society to deal with delinquency . . . when the home, the school, the church and other normal agencies fail.

Judge Cornelius F. Collins: Children's courts

have grown up throughout the whole country which have made marked progress and achieved important success, performing their functions with conspicuously successful results in the direction of prevention . . . and permanent reformation. The scope of these courts includes the whole of the domestic relations, husband and wife, parent and child, guardian and ward, and their interrelations and government.

Charles L. Chute: We now have juvenile court laws in every state but two. Sometimes they are called children's courts, as in New York State, and in recent years some of them have become domestic relations courts, with a broader jurisdiction, to deal not only with children but with parents. We have had a mass of legislation on this subject, but it is still quite inadequate and not uniform. Age limits vary, jurisdiction to deal effectively with parents is often lacking, and, worst of all, in many states the juvenile court has only a partial jurisdiction.

SCHOOL EXPERIENCE

Frank J. O'Brien: One of the greatest needs in schools to-day is for more . . . individualization. . . . If a person enters a hospital or puts himself under the care of his private physician, he is not treated en masse with others of the same age or profession, . . . and yet in . . . the education of our children—we continue, for the most part, to use those methods of mass education, which have been employed for decades. . . .

Individualization, based upon a knowledge of each child, . . . is . . . expensive as compared with the cost under our present methods. When we actually believe the fact that the misfits in school . . . make up in large measure our big army of juvenile delinquents and later form a very large percentage of the criminal group, the true significance of the so-called "different" child . . . becomes more evident. When we reason a step further and realize the cost to society of these social misfits as represented by the budgets for running our courts, probation departments and institutions, not to mention the costs as represented by the police department, district attorney's office, houses of detention, loss of life and property and human productivity, we can rightfully ask, "how can we continue to be satisfied with the results we are obtaining to-day?"

EDUCATIONAL RESEARCH AND STATISTICS

SPECIAL CLASSES FOR PHYSICALLY AND MENTALLY HANDICAPPED PUPILS

IN 1915 certain special classes for handicapped children in Minnesota public schools began to receive state aid. The statute of that year applied to the deaf, the blind, the mentally subnormal and the defective in speech. The last-mentioned group is not under consideration in this study. In 1921 similar aid was extended to classes for crippled children. The state aids studied herein are given to school districts upon a per pupil basis, according to amounts specified in the statutes. These amounts are now prorated according to a subsequent statute, due to large demands for state aids in other public school work. The tables submitted indicate, consequently, the prorated sums for special class aids. The first is designated as Table I.

FACTUAL TRENDS

Observation of the data in Table I reveals the fact that the peak of total expenditures for special classes having mentally subnormal children was reached during 1930–1931, while the greatest amount for state aid given such classes occurred in the previous year. It should be observed also that in the latter year the state aid sum was 59.2 per cent. of all expenditures for that year and that a year later, when total expenditures reached the peak, the ratio was 57.0 per cent. The latter percentage was but in excess of the last and the lowest percentage for the decade, which began with 79.6 per cent. and, with one exception, decreased with each succeeding year.

It should not be assumed, however, that local communities were carrying voluntarily a greater share of the cost burden as the years advanced. The truth may be that the state aid appropriations for this type of work were fairly constant from one biennium to the other. It is true, moreover, that prorating established by law for special classes as well as other types of public school endeavor is a factor which needs consideration here. This fact is illustrated in the succeeding tables by the increasing amounts for state aid in the other types of special classes for successive years, noticeably in the later years of the period.

The number of school systems apparently has

TABLE I

A Distribution Showing Total Expenditures, State Aid and Percentages, Together with Numbers of School Systems, Teachers and Pupils Enrolled in Special Classes for the Mentally Subnormal in Minnesota Public Schools during the Years 1923–1932

Year	Total expenditures (a)	State aid (a)	Per cent. of total expenditures	Number		
				School systems	Teachers	Pupils enrolled
1922–1923	$ 258,825	$ 206,086	79.6	42	148	2,460
1923–1924	288,051	213,089	73.9	44	156	2,609
1924–1925	321,317	217,309	67.6	47	171 (e)	2,825
1925–1926	342,007	231,616	67.7	48	183 (f)	2,982
1926–1927	369,874	240,257 (b)	64.9	50	197 (g)	3,307
1927–1928	377,096	238,191	63.1	49	202 (h)	3,278
1928–1929	387,252	243,330 (c)	62.8	47	207 (i)	3,334
1929–1930	410,535	243,405	59.2	46	218 (j)	3,419
1930–1931	415,621	237,119 (d)	57.0	45	213 (k)	3,400
1931–1932	410,929	226,119	55.0	43	209 (e)	3,322
Total	$3,581,507	$2,296,521	64.1			(av.) 3,093.6

(a) Amount to nearest dollar.
(b) Including $1,056 earned in 1925–1926.
(c) Including $90 earned in 1927–1928.
(d) Including $90 earned in 1929–1930.
(e) Including two part-time teachers.
(f) Including one assistant, one part-time teacher and one full-time teacher for less than one year.
(g) Including one assistant and one part-time teacher.
(h) Including one part-time teacher and one full-time teacher for less than one year.
(i) Including one part time teacher and three full-time teachers for less than one year.
(j) Including one part-time teacher and four full-time teachers for less than one year.
(k) Including one part-time teacher.

little or no relation to total expenditures or state aid for this type of work, since the peak was reached in the fifth year of the decade with receding numbers thereafter. The number of teachers and the pupil load, with one exception in the latter group, increased annually up to and including the year 1929–1930, decreasing somewhat in the two remaining years of the decennium.

Consideration of the data in Table II shows, with one exception, an increasing annual total expenditure for special education of the deaf

TABLE II

A Distribution Showing Total Expenditures, State Aid and Percentages, Together with Numbers of School Systems, Teachers and Pupils Enrolled in Special Classes for the Deaf in Minnesota Public Schools during the Years 1923–1932

Year	Total expenditures (a)	State aid (a)	Per cent. of total expenditures	Number		
				School systems	Teachers	Pupils enrolled
1922–1923	$ 21,650	$ 21,568	99.6	4	12	104
1923–1924	25,676	24,566	95.2	4	14	111
1924–1925	29,894	29,238	97.8	4	16	141
1925–1926	34,916	31,274	89.5	4	17	146
1926–1927	37,928	36,432	96.0	4	18	162
1927–1928	37,694	34,440	91.3	4	18	159
1928–1929	38,410	34,213	89.0	4	19	167
1929–1930	39,337	34,004	86.4	5	20	186
1930–1931	47,212	40,763	86.3	6	21	196
1931–1932	44,462	37,436	84.1	6	20	206
Total	$357,179	$323,934	90.6			(av.) 157.8

(a) Amount to nearest dollar.

TABLE III

A DISTRIBUTION SHOWING TOTAL EXPENDITURES, STATE AID AND PERCENTAGES, TOGETHER WITH NUMBERS OF SCHOOL SYSTEMS, TEACHERS AND PUPILS ENROLLED IN SPECIAL CLASSES FOR THE BLIND IN MINNESOTA PUBLIC SCHOOLS DURING THE YEARS 1923–1932

Year	Total expenditures(a)	State aid(a)	Per cent. of total expenditures	Number		
				School systems	Teachers	Pupils enrolled
1922–1923	$ 30,445	$ 30,115	98.9	5	16	138
1923–1924	36,495	36,126	98.9	5	19	154
1924–1925	44,317	40,999	92.5	5	23(b)	205
1925–1926	47,581	41,516	87.2	5	23(b)	213
1926–1927	48,928	44,957	91.8	5	23(b)	213
1927–1928	50,122	46,312	92.3	6	24(b)	225
1928–1929	50,200	45,864	91.3	6	23(b)	213
1929–1930	52,886	46,295	87.5	6	25(c)	224
1930–1931	53,160	48,019	90.3	6	24(d)	231
1931–1932	54,393	47,431	87.2	7	24	233
Total	**$468,527**	**$427,634**	**91.2**			**(av.) 204.9**

(a) Amount to nearest dollar.
(b) Including two part-time teachers.
(c) Including two part-time teachers and three teachers for less than one year.
(d) Including two part-time teachers and one teacher for less than one year.

in Minnesota public schools up to and including the year 1930–1931, the next to the last year of the period studied. State aid amounts show successive annual increases for the first five years, with fairly constant amounts for the next three years, and with the crest reached in the same year as that of total expenditures. The percentages which state aid sums annually bear to the other begin with 99.6 and close with 84.1, decrease being consistent for seven out of nine years. The number of school systems probably has significance after the eighth year. There is a consistent increase in the enrolment year by year and consequently in the number of teachers. This has definite bearing upon total expenditure.

The data presented in Table III are concerned with the progress of special classes for the blind in Minnesota public schools. Total expenditures for the period increased consistently for each year, showing that the sum for the last year was approximately 80 per cent. greater for that year than for the first. Substantial increases in state aid appeared annually for the first six years with slight decreases for the next two years, but with the peak of such aid reached in the ninth year. The percentages which state aids are of total expenditures vary, after the second year, from decrease to increase and back again until 87.2 is indicated for the final year. The slow growth in number of school systems may not be as important in relation to total expenditures as pupil enrolment, increase and size of the teaching personnel. Pupils enrolled had increased approximately 60 per cent. during the decennium.

The growth of special instruction and care of crippled children in Minnesota public schools during this period, while limited to no more than three large school systems, presents an interesting development in this field. The data are indicated in Table IV. Total expenditures were considerably more than trebled during the decade, while state aid was doubled generously. The increases were fairly consistent with the former, but less so for the latter. Pupils enrolled and numbers of teachers were more than doubled during the period.

SUMMARY AND CONCLUSIONS

(1) The grand total expenditures for the four types of state-aided special classes for defectives in Minnesota public schools reached the sum of $4,917,599 for the ten-year period.

The grand total state aid of $3,435,301 for such classes was 69.8 per cent. of the grand total expenditures.

The total expenditures of $3,581,507 for mentally subnormal children in this period was 72.8 per cent. of the grand total expenditures.

TABLE IV

A DISTRIBUTION SHOWING TOTAL EXPENDITURES, STATE AID AND PERCENTAGES, TOGETHER WITH NUMBERS OF SCHOOL SYSTEMS, TEACHERS AND PUPILS ENROLLED IN SPECIAL CLASSES FOR THE CRIPPLED IN MINNESOTA PUBLIC SCHOOLS DURING THE YEARS 1923–1932

Year	Total expenditures(a)	State aid(a)	Per cent. of total expenditures	Number		
				School systems	Teachers	Pupils enrolled
1922–1923	$ 26,509	$ 26,509	100.0	1	8	143
1923–1924	31,246	30,833	98.6	1	10	140
1924–1925	37,759	29,734	78.7	1	11(b)	156
1925–1926	31,347	28,839	91.9	1	12(b)	186
1926–1927	45,030	36,877	81.8	2	13(b)	217
1927–1928	58,291	41,005	70.3	2	14(b)	218
1928–1929	58,951	36,320	61.6	2	14(b)	241
1929–1930	69,712	47,872	68.6	2	15(c)	247
1930–1931	66,798	50,255	75.2	2	14(c)	266
1931–1932	84,743	58,968	69.5	3	19(c)	367
Total	**$510,386**	**$387,212**	**75.8**			(av.) **218.1**

(a) Amount to nearest dollar. (b) Including one part-time teacher. (c) Including two part-time teachers.

The total state aid of $2,296,521 for mentally subnormal children in special classes was 66.8 per cent. of the grand total state aid.

(2) With five exceptions in the four types of special classes for defectives throughout this period, the total expenditures increased for each succeeding year.

The increases in state aid for such classes in the same period appeared less often. There were twelve exceptions to the tendency to increase.

State support became noticeably less for mentally subnormal children and crippled children in these classes during the more recent years of the decade.

The number of school systems in itself probably was not significant, except as it might have affected total expenditures for crippled children.

The number of teachers increased with the enrolment, which in turn directly affected total expenditure. Owing to the prorating feature of the statute, however, the state aid did not increase in the same proportion as did the total expenditure.

IMPLICATIONS OF THIS STUDY

The data presented in this study and the conclusions regarding their significance lead one to a consideration of three problems for immediate and future study. These are indicated as follows:

(1) Questions of public educational policy involving administrative principles and the philosophy underlying public education are being asked as to (a) the relationship of special classes to the larger program of public education, (b) the effect upon special classes if administrative policies change and if a new philosophy of education is evolved.

(2) Retrenchment policies in public education as well as in other fields have become general, probably for an indefinite period. If retrenchment for special classes is imperative, to what types should it be applied?

(3) A study of the practical outcomes of special classes is as necessary as it is desirable. At no time has it been as essential as at present. Such inquiry is applicable to state-aided and non-state-aided classes alike. A recent study suggesting what may be attempted commends itself for consideration to the personnel of bureaus of research or others in position to undertake such endeavor.[1]

KENNETH NILSON

STATE DEPARTMENT OF EDUCATION
ST. PAUL, MINNESOTA

[1] Alice Channing, "Employment of Mentally Deficient Boys and Girls," U. S. Department of Labor, Children's Bureau. Publication No. 210.

NEW BOOKS IN EDUCATION

LAING, ALEXANDER. *Wine and Physic.* Pp. xii + 157. Farrar and Rinehart. $2.00.

RANDALL, OTIS E. *The Dean's Window.* Pp. viii + 323. Stratford. $2.50.

YOAKUM, GERALD A. and ROBERT G. SIMPSON. *An Introduction to Teaching and Learning.* Pp. x + 498. Macmillan. $2.50.

SCHOOL AND SOCIETY

WITH WHICH ARE COMBINED THE EDUCATIONAL REVIEW, ESTABLISHED IN 1891, THE TEACHERS MAGAZINE, ESTABLISHED IN 1878, AND THE SCHOOL JOURNAL, ESTABLISHED IN 1874.

Volume 39 SATURDAY, JUNE 30, 1934 Number 1018

WHERE IS AMERICAN RADIO HEADING?[1]

By LEVERING TYSON

DIRECTOR, NATIONAL ADVISORY COUNCIL ON RADIO IN EDUCATION, INC.

I

AMERICAN radio is heading in one of four directions.

First, the system might remain substantially the same as it is now with program practises changed to meet what the license-holders interpret as the wishes of the radio audience.

Second, the competitive element in the present system might be retained to some extent with the Federal Government doing one of two things—either regulating by law the types of programs that shall be given preferential consideration on the air, or providing facilities over which certain types of programs will be given preference, including programs for which the Federal Government itself, or some branch of it, might be entirely responsible.

Third, the Federal Government might take over the control of radio, delegating authority, including direction of programs, to a licensee or licensees, as has been done in Great Britain.

Fourth, the Federal Government might take over absolute control of all phases of radio, as has been done in Russia, Germany and Italy.

II

I am not sure that any one can assume the rôle of a prophet and indicate which of these directions will be followed. A fifth annual meeting such as this seems a fitting time to survey the whole situation, and I'll go no farther back than the conference called by the Secretary of the Interior, Ray Lyman Wilbur, in May, 1929.

III

Public broadcasting in America was then less than ten years old. It had had a glamorous history. Stations had sprung up like mushrooms in those early days. The underlying legislative control was then, as now, the Radio Act of 1927. The Davis amendment had been passed only a short time before. The confusion caused by practically uncontrolled operation of stations had been arrested by the passage of this act, and about 600 license holders were broadcasting regularly. Of these about eighty were classified as educational. The broadcasting industry had begun to feel a sense of security after earlier instability. We were at the height of the Harding-Coolidge-Hoover era. The great engineer who had sponsored the development of competitive commercial radio in this country had just taken office and was riding high. Rugged individualism was rampant. For two years the National Broadcasting Company had demonstrated the possibilities, commercial and other, of network broadcasting. The Columbia Broadcasting System had been organized and had

[1] An address delivered before the Ohio Radio Institute, May 2, 1934.

already proved that it was going to be an active competitor to the senior chain. The curve in broadcasting as a business was pointing upward. In the early days the novelty of radio had caught the public's imagination. In 1929 spectacular elements which to-day are commonplace were still unique enough to blanket most thinking on the subject of the ultimate rôle broadcasting might play in American life.

From the first educators echoed the sentiment extolling the wonders of radio. Stations owned and operated by schools, colleges and universities had not been able to keep up with the rapid development of commercial radio and were beginning to drop away. So-called educational programs had had quite a vogue on commercial stations all over the country. As the demands for time on the air increased, these programs became less prominent and many disappeared entirely. It has been said that the "power trust" or the "radio monopoly" forced educational stations off the air so as to grab favorable wavelengths. Another reason advanced has been that this type of station could not get enough money to operate. Another, that the type of programs produced is generally uninteresting and "too academic." Still another, that educators refused to adopt techniques in their programs that could compete successfully with the commercial programs' enormous audiences. This was the usual reason given by commercial stations for relegating "educational" programs to what educators regarded as poor time. But whatever the reason for these conditions, by 1929 it was evident that educators would have to give serious thought to radio if it was to be used either for broadcasting into the schools and colleges, or in adult education.

The meeting called by Secretary Wilbur in May, 1929, led to the appointment of one of the innumerable investigating groups which lived and died during the consulship of Herbert Hoover. The purpose of this committee was indicated by the secretary as follows:

> The possibilities of radio as an educational tool appeal to educators, broadcasters, manufacturers, and the public at large. This general interest led to a conference in my office at Washington on May 24. Those present by unanimous vote requested that I should appoint a committee to make a thorough fact-finding study of the situation.[2]

Please note that he included representatives of broadcasters, and manufacturers on his committee.

IV

Now let's see what has happened since 1929. The great engineer began to be unhappy before the year closed. The era which he typified ended in a roar that is ringing in our ears yet. The economic earthquake shook the foundations of the Republic. We are still operating our American system under the dear old Federal Radio Act of 1927, as amended. The underlying basis on which American broadcasting was commenced has not been materially modified, even though it is well known that the Act of 1927 was a compromise. The licensing authority has been concerned chiefly with relatively petty administrative problems. It has been engaged largely in the defense of its power to make and to modify assignments of frequencies. Contrary to early expectations, it has not substantially reduced the number of stations. Its policies have been so largely shaped by personal, sectional and political considerations that it has not initiated any comprehensive investigation or published any useful findings (comparable, for example, to the service and reports of the Interstate Commerce Commission on railroad consolidation) looking toward a more satisfactory disposition of facilities. As a result broadcasting is in practically the same hands to-day as it was in 1926. On the whole, broadcasting is a purely private

[2] From Report of the Wilbur Committee, page 7.

enterprise for private gain. The tendency of the licensing authority, whether or not as deliberate policy, has been to crystallize the *status quo,* and you all know the darkey's definition of the *status quo:* "Rastus, *status quo* am de Latin words fo' de mess we's in!" With the operation of prevailing economic forces this tendency has had the effect of vesting the control of the most desirable facilities in a relatively few private agencies. Broadcasting has become a profitable and powerful business. It has been and is a discouraging business to others to whom the less desirable facilities have been made available and to the public to whom certain of the commercialized aspects of broadcasting are offensive. To top it all off, radio has become and is little more now than a political football in Washington.

Early in the fall of 1933 President Roosevelt appointed an interdepartmental committee under the chairmanship of Secretary of Commerce Daniel C. Roper to make a study of the entire communication situation in this country. The final report was sent to the President early in 1934, who forwarded a special message to Congress on the subject. Bills were then introduced purporting to carry out the terms of the President's message.

It is not my purpose to criticize these bills, or the report of the Roper Committee which produced them, or the President's message which stimulated their introduction in Congress. He is a brave man indeed who to-day will venture criticism of the President's program, even though it would appear that the President is not responsible for lapses of his subordinates or perhaps of Congress. However, in proposing the new Communications Commission, at least from an analysis of the proposed legislation to create it, it would seem that the administration has no program or policy except to consolidate communications control. That is, broadcasting hasn't been given much, if any, consideration. So much for the legal phases of the subject.

V

From the engineering standpoint there has been a great deal of progress in the last five years. Transmission and reception today are as good as we want to make them. Our engineers have developed apparatus to a point where we can put on the air whatever we want to go into a microphone. Our radio manufacturers can build receivers capable of reproducing with wonderful fidelity whatever these transmitters put on the air. The development of the portable receiver has been popularly acclaimed. To-day, almost literally, we can listen to radio wherever we may be.

There have been amazing developments in the electrical recording process, and today there are indications that the uses to which transcriptions can be put will increase definitely and regularly with experience.

It is apparent that the process of television has been solved. Refinements are needed of course and will come. Its general use and adaptability is "still around the corner." That much abused corner now seems definitely to be not a technical but rather an economic one. The latest opinion of radio engineers is as follows:

> Television is reaching the stage where the mechanics of the problem will be forgotten and attention concentrated on the program itself. Its utility in education and in home entertainment is likely to grow as economic conditions change to permit the establishment of service (rather than experimental) transmitters and the marketing of reasonably priced receivers.[3]

In respect to television I believe the uncertainty of its ultimate development has been heightened by a sincere question as to how widely its use will be welcomed. Do

[3] Report, Engineering Committee, National Advisory Council on Radio in Education, 1934, chapter on television.

we really want television so very badly? Of course we could have asked some years ago why we would ever want broadcasting. As yet comparable advantages for television have not appeared, and in my opinion that is one reason why it has not been developed practically. The process is extremely expensive. Up to this time advantages in its operation have not warranted its enormous expense, particularly since no means have been provided for supporting it. Thus far advertising has provided the bulk of the revenue necessary to finance the broadcasting of sound. The experience we have had with some broadcasting raises a serious question whether advertising either could or should support television.

There is definite indication that facsimile broadcasting can be more generally applied. Its usefulness is apparent in a wide variety of ways. This process has been perfected for some years and its applications at present are being carefully studied. That it will soon be economically possible there seems to be no doubt whatsoever.

VI

What has happened in broadcasting since 1929? One of the last industries to feel the blighting effects of the depression, commercial success persisted for some time after the crash. But hard times in other fields, reflected in lowered advertising appropriations, knocked eventually at studio doors. In the last few years, in order to get revenue to operate stations, the ears of the American public have been literally flogged with selling talk for a variety of cathartic, cosmetic and pharmaceutical products. This has led to vocal and tacit protest, the force of which, if organized, could easily be translated into remedial legislation at any session of Congress. This feeling has grown up in spite of spectacular achievements in program production. But broadcasting has few friends. There is continuous guerilla warfare with the press. There has been a violent surge of criticism against certain types of so-called "children's programs." And so on. The broadcaster is belabored on one side by economic forces which no one could control; on another by an outraged public opinion against "disgusting" advertising; on still another by advertising agency statistics to prove that certain types of programs bring "results." And he is continually faced with the cold hard fact that the show must go on! He can't rest to take stock. The transmitter must operate every hour for which he is licensed. Aside from economic and other problems, visualize for a moment the stupendous task faced by the broadcasters in providing programs acceptable to the American audience practically every hour in the day. It is no wonder the combined intelligence that has been assembled has not solved it. It is no wonder that broadcasting seems like a tired and bewildered man and that it has lost much of the sprightliness which characterized it five years ago. There is little if any appearance of leadership. The industry sold out to the advertising agency when it lost its control over programs. It has not won and very likely has lost the first skirmish in its controversy with the press in which, by the laws of human progress, it is right. Because it is tired and bewildered it lacks courage to tackle an issue; it would rather temporize, and the pressure to keep out of the red, particularly in times of economic difficulty, seems to have sidetracked the fundamental concept that broadcasting is a public service.

VII

Now let us look at what happened in educational broadcasting circles after Secretary Wilbur appointed his committee in the spring of 1929. On that committee he named representatives of education, of the broadcasters, of the manufacturers, of the public at large and of the government. The American Association for Adult Education had previously undertaken a survey of broadcasting, as had the Payne Fund. All agencies interested in the subject, including the industry, which had been included definitely by the secretary, supported this attempt by the government to consider a complicated problem. I am frank to state I do not think that in the years since 1929 we have advanced the cause very much, if at all. Presumably those interested in educational broadcasting represent organized thinking. If educators will not adopt a scientific and objective attitude toward important questions of public concern where shall we look for such consideration? Yet what have we done since 1929? Let me give the principal events in chronological order.

December 31, 1929: Secretary Wilbur's committee ceased operations. Soon after this date Commissioner Cooper, as chairman of the committee, held a meeting in the New York offices of one of the commercial networks to decide what recommendations should be contained in the committee's report.

January, 1930: Meetings were held in New York at which recommendations were made to form the National Advisory Council on Radio in Education. These meetings were held with the full knowledge and sanction of Secretary Wilbur and Commissioner Cooper, who attended.

February 15, 1930: The Wilbur committee forwarded its report to the secretary.

Spring of 1930: The Council was formed. Operations were to begin as soon as organization could be effected and conferences held to formulate a program.

June, 1930: The first Ohio Radio Institute was held prior to the annual meeting of the National Education Association in Columbus.

October 13, 1930: Meeting held in Chicago called by Commissioner Cooper, presumably of same groups assembled by Secretary Wilbur, but actually in interest of institutionally owned and operated stations. At this conference, although no meeting of the Council had yet been called, no members elected or program adopted, the Council was repudiated as smoke screen of the broadcasting industry, the "power trust," the "radio monopoly"—or what have you. Mandate given at this meeting to form committee to recommend to Congress legislation to set aside 15 per cent. of channels for education. There were two effects of this meeting. It definitely threw down the gauntlet to the broadcasting industry. It also indicated conclusively that the educational forces were not going to agree in their consideration of the problems of educational broadcasting in the manner proposed by Secretary Wilbur. The forces have been scattered since that date.

October 14, 1930: The Council board met in Chicago. Decided not to abandon the cooperative idea back of the Wilbur committee, in spite of action of meeting of previous day. Schedule of constructive activities decided upon, emphasizing among others two main objectives—the accumulation of useful data concerning broadcasting and experimentation with programs.

January, 1931: Fess Bill introduced in Congress, carrying out mandate of October 13 meeting. Formation of National Committee on Education by Radio announced.

February, 1931: Campaign on behalf of Fess Bill begun. Controversy with industry started.

May, 1931: First annual assembly of Council held in New York, at which committees reported experimental programs ready for air.

But why continue this detail farther? The campaign for the Fess Bill was pushed vigorously; over several sessions of Congress hearings on it were never even held and it never got out of committee.

In spite of efforts to protect educational stations, their number decreased steadily until to-day there are only several dozen. Resolutions condemning the broadcasting industry actually or by innuendo were introduced and passed by various national organizations. Listeners' societies were formed to protest against broadcasting program practises. The adoption of the essential features of the British system of radio control and operation as a substitute for the American system was urged, and debates on this question were organized in schools and colleges all over the country. Bills to investigate broadcasting were introduced in Congress.

Program experimentation of the Council began in 1931 and has continued ever since. Annual assemblies have been held for presentation of reports of committees and consideration of the latest developments. The Ohio Radio Institute has held its meetings each year. But, in so far as uniting on conclusions that can solve the problem of educational broadcasting, we seem to be no farther advanced than in 1929. A concerted attack on the subject is no more clearly indicated now than it was then. The educators present a disappointing spectacle, and the broadcasters have laughed at us up their sleeves in the last three and a half years over our failure to make the most of our opportunities. We have a chance to take broadcasting by the neck and shake its teeth loose. They know it. Instead of that we have wasted time in fruitless and unwarranted disagreement, in a destructive attack upon the American broadcasting system and its supporters without proposing constructive measures to inspire confidence that we know what we are driving at.

VIII

I don't mean to imply that the period since 1929 has been entirely wasted. We have had five more years' experience in broadcasting and we have learned something, I hope. More people know about the complexities of radio now than they did in 1929, and many know more about the demands which the microphone makes upon the broadcaster. Yet because we have failed to set our own house in order we have not convinced any one, including ourselves, how radio can be used in education, nor have we solved basic problems in program production. These are fundamental questions. We might have been spending this time in arriving at some of these basic considerations. Educators, reasonable in everything else, have gone on the air with programs that actually invite the audience to turn them off at the end of sixty seconds. I include programs that have been put on the air under the auspices of my own organization in this category. We can not get far trying to perpetuate something that interests only a relatively few people, for we have yet to convince educators that radio is a generally useful instrument for formal classroom purposes. If we are going to push for its wider uses, we must compete on level ground for audiences that are accustomed to listen to a type of radio program which differs from that we have produced so far. We can only conduct this competition successfully by uniting every resource.

IX

To sum up the whole situation: The so-called American system of broadcasting has given the public good programs, variety and first-rate technical performance. It is better on the whole than systems in force elsewhere, but, as administered by the Federal Radio Commission under the Act of 1927, so many abuses and injustices have developed that on the whole radio broadcasting in this country has had a disappointing history. Many proposals for changes have been advanced. Broadcasting is peculiarly sensitive to political, sectional and class interests. It has produced a swarm of lobbyists, special pleaders and cranks, many of whom are engaged in advancing purely selfish interests. In consequence few, if any, of the plans for change are based on careful or comprehensive consideration of the public interest or of the limitations of the art. Piecemeal revision of the broadcasting structure is destined to be disappointing. Changes designed to promote the maximum beneficial use of available facilities are needed. This could not be planned without a careful objective investigation of the whole situation, conducted by a group of competent individuals who would be independent of Congress and who would begin and conduct their deliberations outside of the many existing controversies and irrespective of legislation existing or proposed. This is a job the educational world in America should and could get behind unitedly.

X

So where are we heading, on the basis of the last five years? We had our fill of rugged individualism and are tasting the bitter fruits. As Professor Orton, of Smith College, has said, "What individualism really means in matters of this sort is the practise of proceeding helter-skelter without any plan until an impossible situation has developed, and all sorts of vested interests have been created, and then trying to impose a plan retrospectively in face of innumerable technical and legal obstacles."[4] We are confronted by exactly that.

It is my personal belief that the present situation will not continue unchanged. The broadcasting industry has shown a disposition to temporize with its problems, and its attitude has been purely opportunistic. This indicates fundamental weakness. If it wakes up it has enormous power available to defend the *status quo*. If there is latent intelligence that intelligence long ago should have prompted it to take the lead in proposing changes which would make American radio what it ought to be, and is not—a public servant. If the American people continue to be satisfied with radio programs, present conditions may continue indefinitely. Broadcasting will then be relegated to the minor rôle of a mere entertainment enterprise.

I hardly think this will happen, however, because the government itself is now too much interested. I am inclined to think the radio industry will attempt to put its house in order, that broadcast advertising will continue, and that the government will gradually regulate the allocation of facilities so that at least a partial government parallel to the commercial system will provide opportunity for establishing certain public services in broadcasting.

Don't forget we are proceeding pretty rapidly already toward government control of many features of American life, a condition which was foreign to our national way of thinking less than a decade ago. This tendency might throw radio into the hopper with the rest. We might wake up some morning to discover that Congress or the administration in power at the time had decided to take over broadcasting. The profit motive, more insidious than the mere idea of competition, has been in the saddle. The supremacy of that motive, in radio as everywhere else, generally is inconsistent with public welfare. The government will be derelict in its duty if it does not provide opportunity to use broadcasting facilities for the public service motive at least on a fifty-fifty basis with the profit-making motive.

XI

I have stated in effect that intelligence has not been a prominent characteristic of the broadcasting industry, particularly in its recent history. In respect to broad-

[4] Professor William A. Orton, "America in Search of a Culture," Chapter XIII.

casting an identical charge can be made against educators. This is worse, for educators are supposed to be intelligent, whereas you can always give broadcasters the benefit of the doubt. Educators have in the radio an instrument the perfection of which was a significant event in social history. They have paid cursory attention to it, and a certain type of lip-service. In the last analysis it will go where the American public wants it to go. If the people continue to be satisfied with their radio fare, it won't be changed, either by broadcasters or government. If educators can succeed in producing and offering programs the people will want, they will be broadcast, either by broadcasters or by government. If the American people, in their comparative youth as a nation, have not risen to a level where they regard broadcasting as a cultural opportunity, the government of that people will not take control of radio for that purpose, either in modified form, as in Great Britain, or in complete form, as in Russia. It might seize it for purposes other than cultural, but you can't force intellectuality down democracy's throat unless it opens wide its mouth. So far its teeth have been tightly clinched.

So unless we have a political upheaval which will prompt seizure of radio by the government for its own purposes, and I don't believe that is imminent, I think we are faced with the two possibilities I mentioned: First, a continuation of the present system; second, a system in which ample opportunity will be provided by law for the broadcasting of public services, such as education.

Broadcasting is now a business in America. I believe that business will remain a business, but I believe American broadcasting will change. How it should change will be the subject of constantly increasing discussion from now on. The foremost educators of the country ought to lead in that discussion, and their contribution to it should be constructive suggestion. It will be worth any effort.

SUPERVISOR-TEACHER RELATIONSHIP AND MENTAL HYGIENE[1]

By ALEXANDER FICHANDLER
PRINCIPAL, PUBLIC SCHOOL 189, BROOKLYN, N. Y.

It is obvious that a teacher's value to her pupils and therefore to the community is directly related to her mental and emotional health. She may be ever so well trained for her occupation; she may be thoroughly familiar with the theory of teaching; she may command the technique of her profession; but if her personality is thwarted, distorted or disintegrated, if she is not happy, not only is she alone the victim, but her pupils also suffer.

The foregoing is self-evident and requires no further elaboration. The problem is: To what extent can the supervisor, in his relations with the teacher, improve her mental and emotional health, and therefore, improve the quality of her teaching?

I

A person can not do his best unless he is happy in his work. But it is undoubtedly true that in the present social order, a vast majority of human beings are but square pegs placed in round holes, and therefore can not do their very best.

This applies with particular force to teachers, who are not completely happy, because they are not doing the sort of thing

[1] Address delivered at the conference of the New York Principals' Association.

for which they are fitted or which they like to do. The experienced supervisor knows of numerous cases where teachers who were extremely inefficient and ineffective with a class of twelve-year-olds became the opposite with a class of seven- or eight-year-olds. He also knows of many teachers who were complete failures in teaching academic subjects, but proved very successful in teaching art, literature, music, etc.

It is clear, therefore, that one of the most important services which a supervisor can perform is the proper assignment of teachers. This requires a study of a teacher's personality, an inquiry into her preferences as to subject or grade, and a knowledge of her cultural and professional background. With such material in hand, the supervisor can assign a teacher to such activities as will increase her satisfaction and happiness, and will therefore improve her general attitude towards her work and her children.

II

A study of mental hygiene reveals that a fundamental factor in happiness is the sense of security. In order to be happy, a person must feel that he "belongs." The stoker in Eugene O'Neill's "Hairy Ape" is a tragic illustration of this principle. We do not feel happy in a strange group or isolated or in an unfriendly atmosphere. In such situations, we are frequently almost paralyzed and, no matter how we try, our efforts lack the vitality and enthusiasm which usually characterize our activities when we feel secure.

In the school, it is therefore necessary to make the teacher feel that she "belongs." The new teacher must be made to feel comfortable from the first moment that she arrives. She should be introduced to as many others as possible. She should be made acquainted with only a few, the most important general rules, with the assurance that she is not expected to become thoroughly familiar at once with all routine regulations, and that she will probably become familiar with them in time.

During her first few days or weeks, there will be no destructive criticism. She will receive sympathetic, encouraging and friendly visits from her supervisor, who will repeat again and again, "Is all well? Can I do anything for you? Can I help you?" She will be praised for anything worth praising, no matter how slight. She will be made to feel at home. Her requests and appeals will be received cordially and, if possible, will be acted upon favorably. She will be made to feel confident that she is welcome, that she can solve her own problems and that, if necessary, the supervisor will help her.

Inevitably, there will be created in the teacher a feeling of security which is essential to happiness and successful effort. Then she will probably go on cheerfully to solve her problems and to achieve her aims.

III

A frequent cause of unhappiness is a sense of inferiority. In all probability, there is not a person alive who is not a victim of this malady to a greater or lesser degree. Teachers are not exceptions. Like the rest of the human race, many, if not all, feel a real or imaginary inferiority, and therefore are less capable of living happily and functioning successfully.

The remedy is well known. Sympathy, encouragement, achievement and praise are the most potent remedies for this affliction. The supervisor is of strategic importance in this connection. His criticisms must be friendly and sympathetic; his suggestions must be constructive; his visits must not be merely tolerated, but rather wanted and welcomed. He must not let a visit pass without finding evidence of the teacher's effort, initiative and originality. And finally he must praise, praise, praise—provided, of course, there is something worth praising.

At teachers' meetings, the supervisor may describe notable achievements of individual teachers, both to the advantage of the entire school and the greater glory of these teachers.

Altogether, from the mental hygiene point of view, a supervisor can do nothing more important than to create in teachers a sense of worthiness and confidence, to encourage and stimulate originality and initiative and, in other ways, seek to overcome their sense of inferiority.

IV

One of the prerequisites for a healthy mental state is a healthy attitude towards one's occupation. The person who performs mechanical and routinized tasks, who feels that he is but a cog in a wheel, can not feel particularly enthusiastic about his job. On the contrary, he generally dislikes it.

A similar situation obtains among teachers. The teacher who is told specifically what to do and does exactly what he is told, who must follow directions, who is not consulted on the various matters affecting his work—in short, one who merely holds on to a job—is clearly not in the best of mental states. A proper mental state can be secured only if the opposite prevails. A good, healthy attitude exists where teachers participate in the administration of the school, where they are consulted on school policies, where they express their opinions freely, where they feel responsible for the success of the organization, where, in short, they feel that the school is theirs and not the supervisor's. It is such an environment that brings forth activity, enthusiasm and happiness.

In addition, teachers should be made to realize that their job is not merely to teach the three R's, but rather to help create a better social order. They will then become aware of the dignity of their profession and of its tremendous social significance. They should know that a teacher who develops in her children the capacity for questioning, challenging and discussing is helping to create an intelligent democracy, and is increasing the possibility of a better life for humanity.

Doubtlessly, participation in the administration of the school and the realization of the social importance of her job will produce in the teacher an attitude which will go a long way towards making her a completely happy human being.

V

It may be thought that a teacher's personality is too delicate a matter for the supervisor to be concerned with. But, after all, is it not the most important? For we know full well that the introvert, shut-in, unsocial, morbid, frustrated teacher certainly can not function as well as one with an integrated personality.

It is true that in some such cases the supervisor is helpless. There may be home, family and personal situations which he can not control and which produce undesirable personality traits. But there are many cases where he can and should be of use. Tactfully, he may suggest to a teacher that she ought to have more recreation, should go to theaters, dances and parties, should indulge in sports, should take up a hobby, should wear more becoming clothes, etc. He may encourage the shy teacher to mix with the others of her group, to study for advancement, to take up social activities and otherwise lead a richer and fuller life.

It is quite true that not all supervisors will be willing or should be permitted to undertake this task. There are some whose own personalities make it difficult for them to attempt it. But there is no doubt that this kind of work will probably benefit the school as much as some of the other activities of the supervisor.

VI

And, finally, it is important to emphasize that the methods employed by a supervisor in establishing such relationships with the teachers as will promote their mental health and happiness must, in the long run, percolate downward. Teachers who receive helpful, sympathetic, encouraging, friendly, democratic, understanding treatment from their supervisors will inevitably extend similar treatment to their children. Sooner or later, the entire school will be permeated with an atmosphere that is conducive to mental health and happiness for all—supervisors, teachers and children.

EDUCATIONAL EVENTS

VISIT OF TEACHERS OF THE BRITISH EMPIRE TO OBERAMMERGAU

Two thousand educationists, teachers and students of the British Empire, according to the London *Times,* have been invited by the Municipality of Oberammergau to attend a special performance of the Passion Play on August 10 and to be the guests of the villagers in their homes. A letter to the press, signed by Lord Moynihan, Lord Baden-Powell, the Bishop of Chichester, is in part as follows:

The presentation of the Passion Play at Oberammergau in 1930 made so deep an impression on the Executive Secretary of the National Council of Education of Canada that he was moved by a great desire that when next it was presented the greatest possible number of teachers and students from Canada might share his experience. This desire has gradually taken a wider range. Now, through the National Council of Education of Canada (and the Foreign Students' Bureau of Berlin) the Municipality of Oberammergau has invited 2,000 educationists, teachers and students (including senior boys and girls of the secondary schools and teachers in training) of the British Empire to attend a special performance of the Passion Play on August 10, and, moreover, to be guests of the villagers in their homes. The original invitation was for 5,000, the capacity of the new auditorium, but at the suggestion of the National Council of Education it is now limited to the number mentioned. . . . Those who desire to avail themselves of it are asked to apply at once through their respective organizations or schools. The number of places reserved for students is limited.

It may be added that the German railways have offered to each registered member of the company exceptional facilities, together with greatly reduced rates. The French authorities have agreed to collaborate in the arrangements in so far as the French part of the journey to and from Oberammergau is concerned and have accorded the most generous of concessions. It is hoped that the British railways will cooperate in similar manner. Mr. E. W. Beatty, chancellor of McGill University and president of the Canadian Pacific Railway, will play the part of host to a large number of Oberammergau's guests for the crossing from Southampton to Cherbourg in the *Empress of Britain* on July 28, while the Norddeutscher Lloyd has agreed to the chartering of the s. s. *Stuttgart* for a special crossing from Dover to Bremen on August 5, upon most reasonable conditions. The National Council of Education of Canada, which, in conjunction with a special London committee, is undertaking the arrangements for this pilgrimage, proposes to organize a short conference on "The Teaching of Christ and International Good Will." The conference will be preceded by a simple service in the great auditorium, in which the Passion Play orchestra and choir will take part. The hope is that the urgent need of peace and good will throughout the world may be realized afresh in the wonderful atmosphere of Oberammergau and in the light of the great memories of Calvary and Easter.

THE EMERGENCY IN EDUCATION

THE Committee on Education of the House of Representatives, to whom was referred the bill to provide for the cooperation by the Federal Government with the several states and territories and the District of Columbia in meeting the crisis in education, reported favorably with the recommendation that it pass without amendment.

It is the opinion of the committee that it was established beyond all doubt that an emergency situation does exist in education and that Federal aid is necessary for the coming fiscal year if the schools of this country are to remain open and if the children are to be given the instruction to which they are entitled.

Dr. George F. Zook, the Commissioner of Education, some time ago called together representatives of thirty-two national organizations and formed a committee, called the "Federal Advisory Committee on Emergency Aid in Education," to consider the problems of education from an emergency-need standpoint. On January 6, 1934, this committee reported to the commissioner its recommendations; and out of this committee there was formed the National Committee for Federal Emergency Aid for Education, under the chairmanship of James H. Richmond, superintendent of public instruction for the State of Kentucky. This committee, in consultation with the heads of education in the various states relative to educational needs for 1934–35, made an estimate of the amount of federal aid required. It is stated, however, that it by no means follows that these states will receive what they have requested. The need will be determined by the Federal Emergency Relief Administration acting with the Commissioner of Education.

Commissioner Zook estimates on the basis of present rates of compensation and normal school terms that $75,000,000 will take care of the school needs for 1934–35 and the committee is in agreement with his estimate. The report closes with the following statement by the committee:

> This committee believes that the conditions in many states can be alleviated by loans where there is adequate security available and that large sums of money in the form of gifts should not be awarded in these cases. This committee, however, has no jurisdiction over the matter of loans, but it is merely suggesting as an aid to the entire problem that many of the wealthy states which are in need of large sums of money should properly be cared for by loans.
>
> This committee believes that privately supported, free-tuition schools in need should be eligible for aid upon application. These schools are doing a splendid work and in many instances, where public schools have closed, through lack of funds, these schools have taken in pupils who would otherwise be without benefit of any education. It is not expected that many will apply for aid but it is believed that they should have the right to the assistance if desired.
>
> This committee is unalterably opposed to any policy of Federal control of education, believing that education is essentially a state and local matter. Thus in carrying out the provisions of this act the committee insists that no Federal officer shall control the instruction or administration in education in any state.
>
> This committee is also opposed to any permanent policy of the Federal Government to assist the states in education but is in favor of this act as an emergency measure only and for one year, namely, the fiscal year ending June 30, 1935.
>
> There is no doubt that there is an emergency in education to-day, brought on in part by the economic depression but also caused in no small measure through the fault of many of the states themselves; by their management without foresight; by the unwise use of the taxing power; by failure to reorganize antiquated taxing systems and to make proper allocations for education, and by the great failure to consolidate rural schools wherever possible, which failure is causing many states to make large unnecessary expenditures of money each year. The committee believes in granting this aid for next year because the states can not entirely correct these evils before the year 1934–35, but they can and should make a start in order to eliminate the necessity of coming back to Congress for relief after 1934–35.

THE TWENTY-FIFTH ANNIVERSARY OF THE JUNIOR HIGH SCHOOL AT BERKELEY

THE twenty-fifth anniversary of the founding of the junior high school in Berkeley, Calif., will be celebrated by junior high schools of the city during the school year 1934–35, according to plans formulated recently by a committee appointed by Dr. Lewis W. Smith, superintendent of schools, to have general charge of the observance.

Plans for the observance include a special meeting of the Berkeley board of education to commemorate the action of the Berkeley board on December 21, 1909, establishing the junior high school in Berkeley, publication of a booklet describing the history and development of the junior high schools during the past 25 years, and special activities in the junior high schools commemorating the opening of the first schools.

Authorized by the Berkeley board of education upon recommendation of F. F. Bunker, former superintendent of schools, "lower high school" units were first established in January,

1910, at the McKinley and Washington Schools with C. L. Biedenbach, now principal of Berkeley High School, as principal of the McKinley School and G. W. Monroe as principal of the Washington School. Because of the fact that the seventh, eighth and ninth grades at the McKinley School were segregated in one building and administered as a unit from the opening of the school, the McKinley Junior High School claims the distinction of being the first junior high school in the United States. In 1916 the junior high school grades from the McKinley School were transferred to the Willard Junior High School, while the Washington Junior High School pupils were transferred to the Edison building to form the Edison Junior High School. The Franklin and Whittier Schools were organized as "intermediate" schools in the fall of 1911, retaining the ninth grade pupils and organizing the seventh, eighth and ninth grades on the departmental plan. These schools became the Burbank Junior High School and the Garfield Junior High School, respectively, when the pupils were transferred to the new buildings in 1916.

The membership of the committee includes C. L. Biedenbach, now principal of Berkeley Senior High School, who was principal of the McKinley School when it was organized as a junior high school; Morris C. James, deputy superintendent of schools, who was superintendent during the early years of the junior high school in Berkeley; and the present principals of the Berkeley junior high schools, H. H. Glessner, D. L. Hennessey and L. L. Standley.

MOVING PICTURES AND SCHOOL CHILDREN

AT the instance of Dr. Harold G. Campbell, superintendent of the New York City schools, Dr. John S. Roberts, associate superintendent in charge of visual instruction, will make an immediate study of the industry with the view of determining how the schools might exert pressure for more wholesome films.

Dr. Campbell's letter to Dr. Roberts follows:

In view of the nation-wide movement by churchmen of all faiths, educators, civic leaders and public-spirited citizens generally to compel the production and exhibition of better motion pictures, may I ask you, as associate in charge of visual instruction in our schools, to make a special study to determine how the public schools may help to bring about the desired end. There is little doubt in my mind that much of the good that the schools are doing, especially in the field of character training and the development of right social attitudes, is being undermined and thwarted by substandard motion pictures.

Professor Ben Wood, of Columbia University, has pointed out that when a questionnaire was sent by Roger W. Babson to the school principals in New England asking which had the greatest influence in molding the character of our young children—the school, the church or the home—70 per cent. of the principals scratched out all three and answered "the movies."

Dr. Bernard Sachs, president of the New York Academy of Medicine and an authority on child psychology, has called attention to the adverse effect that certain films have upon the minds and behavior of children. I inclose a recent paper by Dr. Sachs on the subject of the motion picture and the prevention of crime in youth.

May I suggest that you contact Professor Wood, Dr. Sachs, the Motion Picture Research Council, of which Mrs. August Belmont is the head, and other individuals and agencies who have concerned themselves with the problem.

If, on the basis of your study, you think it would be helpful, you have my authorization to inform Mr. Will Hays that the largest school system in the world is determined that the character of its children shall not be undermined by inferior motion pictures. I have long been amazed at the blindness of the motion picture industry and its failures to take full advantage of the educational possibilities of the movies. While we in the schools are struggling along with inadequate appropriations for visual instruction, millions of dollars are being spent to produce and exhibit in theaters attended by children films of the very worst description.

We have long since abandoned the idea that education consists simply of instruction given and received in school. We know that children are being "educated" during every hour of the day, as much perhaps, while they are out of school as while they are in school. The movies are playing a large part in this "out of school education" and we, who are charged with the development of their character, attitudes and habits, are vitally concerned that the part played and the influence exerted by the movies shall be helpful rather than destructive.

I am in accord with you that more use should be made of the motion picture as an auxiliary to teaching in the schools, but we are hampered by the lack of appropriations to purchase or rent equipment and films. Meanwhile we should not permit children to be "uneducated" or misguided by the visual instruction they receive from inferior movies outside of school.

Please go into the entire matter and be assured that you will have my cooperation and that of the entire school staff.

THE NEWLY ELECTED PRESIDENT OF REED COLLEGE

DR. DEXTER MERRIAM KEEZER, who has been elected president of Reed College, Portland, Oregon, will take up his new work in September. A correspondent writes from Portland:

"The appointment of Dr. Keezer culminates a two-year search for some one qualified by sympathy and experience for the ideals of progressive education for which Reed has pioneered since the founding of the college in 1911. Dr. Keezer will become the fourth president of Reed College. He will succeed President Norman F. Coleman, who two years ago asked to be relieved of administrative responsibilities in order to devote more of his energies to teaching. Dr. Coleman will remain on the Reed staff.

"Dr. Keezer brings to the position sound academic training, broad teaching experience, rich journalistic experience and, through his present activities in the NRA, important contacts with the administration in its reconstruction efforts.

"Dr. Keezer after an undergraduate career interrupted by over-seas duty during the war completed his A.B. degree at Amherst in 1920. His M.A. degree was received from Cornell and his Ph.D. was conferred in 1925 by the Brookings Graduate School of Economics and Government, in Washington, D. C.

"He has taught at Cornell University as an instructor in economics, as associate professor in economics at the University of Colorado, and likewise at the University of North Carolina, and as visiting lecturer in citizenship at Dartmouth College.

"In publications Dr. Keezer collaborated on 'Problem Economics' with Addison Thayer Cutler and Frank Garfield, and on 'Public Control of Business' with Stacy May, of the Rockefeller Foundation. He contributed three articles for the Encyclopedia of the Social Sciences: 'Business,' 'The Press' and 'The Federal Trade Commission.'

"His newspaper experience began as a reporter on the Denver *Times* and as correspondent in the Washington bureau of the Scripps-Howard newspapers. From 1929 to 1933 he served as associate editor of the *Baltimore Sun*.

"In August, 1933, Dr. Keezer was appointed executive director of the Consumers' Advisory Board of the National Recovery Administration and recently he was made chief of the newly created Consumers' Division of the National Emergency Council.

"At present in association with Dr. Keezer in the Consumers' Division is Dr. William T. Foster, who as a young man became the first president of Reed College when it was established as an endowed, non-sectarian co-educational institution in 1911. Dr. Foster was succeeded in 1921 by Dr. Richard F. Scholz, who served as president of Reed College until his death in 1924.

"Since its beginning Reed College has gained a reputation as one of the outstanding progressive colleges of the country for its devotion to intellectual achievement, its avoidance of intercollegiate athletics, its integrated curriculum and oral examinations, and its daring policies of academic freedom."

TRIBUTE TO THE LATE DR. WILLIAM OXLEY THOMPSON

IN honor of the late Dr. William Oxley Thompson, president of the Ohio State University, memorial services were held at the university on June 9. Dr. David Kinley, president emeritus of the University of Illinois, who was intimately associated with Dr. Thompson in the work of the National Association of State Universities and the Association of Land-Grant Colleges, was the principal speaker.

Dr. Kinley said in part: "Dr. Thompson's contention that the trustees who represent the people of the state were better able to judge wisely of the needs and expenditures of their institution than was any political officer or any bureaucrat who viewed the university from the point of view of financial organization and control was sound. And I agree with him.

"In my opinion it is unreasonable to assume that temporary officers like governors and directors of finance, appointees of the governor, should be able to criticize or reduce budgets or supervise expenditures with anything like an approach to the intelligence, gained through intimate daily contact with the problem, found in university authorities. His remedy was to go back to the people. President Thompson was opposed to bureaucratic control by state as well as by federal offices. He stood for the integrity and independence of the colleges and universities.

"In somewhat recent conversations I found him solicitous about these new dangers that in his opinion, and I think correctly, are threatening our publicly supported educational institutions. He remarked that 'we shall have to fight the battle for public education over again.' The new challenge comes from those advocating curtailment of free public education, especially of the higher grades, because of increasing cost. He held rightly that in a democracy an educated 'followership' is as necessary as an educated leadership, unless that democracy is to merge into an aristocracy, a monarchy or a tyranny.

"Commenting on one phase of this situation, however, I may quote him to the effect that discontent due to excessive cost has led to 'an increased activity of supervising financial officers. . . . Under the plea of meeting the emergency, the reduction in appropriations has been made quite as much upon the judgment of such financial officers as upon the judgment of educational authorities.'"

Turning to a discussion of the state university idea, Dr. Kinley quoted Dr. Thompson as saying: "'The state's right to maintain education in all fields of study is unquestioned.' These state universities have enlarged the field of education, especially by stimulating the study of the sciences and their applications; have broken down the tradition of a conflict between the practical and the cultural; and have given a new and broader idea of true culture and a deeper insight into and appreciation of civilization and response to its claims.

"To quote Dr. Thompson again, 'We should recognize the demand for people educated and trained in all the agencies and arts that contribute to our civilization.' This argument does not rest on the basis of personal or individual needs. The state has in view social and public efficiency and service rather than individual advantage. It is sufficient now to be able to justify a public expenditure for education on the ground of public use and service."

HONORARY DEGREES CONFERRED AT HARVARD UNIVERSITY

NINE honorary degrees were conferred by Harvard University at its commencement on June 21. These were: the doctorate of laws on Charles C. Burlingham, '79, lawyer, former president of the New York Board of Education, of the Welfare Council, and of the Association of the Bar of the City of New York; Dr. Tyler Dennett, professor of international relations at Princeton University and president-elect of Williams College; Dr. Harold Willis Dodds, president of Princeton University; Dr. Abbott Lawrence Lowell, president-emeritus of Harvard University; Dr. Charles Ferdinand Martin, dean of the Medical Faculty and professor of medicine at McGill University, past president of the American College of Physicians; Dr. Edward Lee Thorndike, '96, professor of educational psychology at Teachers College, Columbia University. The degree of doctor of science was conferred on Dr. Thomas Hunt Morgan, director of the William G. Kerckhoff Laboratories of the California Institute of Technology, and the degree of master of arts was conferred on John Douglas Merrill, '89, editor of the *Harvard Alumni Bulletin*, and on Herbert Haseltine, sculptor, of New York and Paris.

The citations by President James Bryant Conant follow:

DOCTOR OF LAWS

CHARLES C. BURLINGHAM—A disinterested champion of good government, who, for more than fifty years, has used his talents for the benefit of his fellow-citizens.

TYLER DENNETT—Notable biographer and historian, learned adviser of our Department of State, the president-elect of Williams College, we welcome him to New England.

HAROLD WILLIS DODDS—Distinguished for his services in the realm of public affairs, the new president of a sister university, whose past we admire and whose future is assured by his leadership.

PRESIDENT-EMERITUS LOWELL—For twenty-four years our resolute captain, who enlarged and deepened the life of this university and preserved untainted the vitalizing spirit of liberty.

CHARLES FERDINAND MARTIN—A leader of Canadian medicine and administrator who has developed brilliantly a distinguished medical school.

EDWARD LEE THORNDIKE—Educational psychologist, the foremost American pioneer in developing those new types of measurement which supplement our oldest forms of examination.

DOCTOR OF SCIENCE

THOMAS HUNT MORGAN—A renowned zoologist whose experimental skill and penetrating insight have laid bare the mechanism of heredity.

MASTER OF ARTS

JOHN DOUGLAS MERRILL—During the many years of selfless labor, a patient and devoted interpreter of this university to the alumni.

HERBERT HASELTINE—A son of Harvard, a master of the art of sculpture, who has given the world a unique record of the beauty of domestic animals.

EDUCATIONAL NOTES AND NEWS

WILLIAMS COLLEGE conferred on June 18 the degree of doctor of laws on its retiring president, Dr. Harry A. Garfield, and the degree of doctor of humane letters on Dr. Tyler Dennett, president-elect. Following the presentation of the degree by Williams College, Dr. Garfield, acting for President James L. McConaughy, conferred on Dr. Dennett the doctorate of laws of Wesleyan University.

IN accordance with a special vote of the board of trustees the degree of doctor of laws was conferred on June 21 by Bowdoin College on Dr. Kenneth C. M. Sills, president of the college for fifteen years.

THE University of Pittsburgh conferred at commencement the doctorate of laws on Dr. Lee P. Sieg, dean of the College and Graduate School and acting dean of the School of Education, president-elect of the University of Washington.

DARTMOUTH COLLEGE at commencement conferred the degree of doctor of laws on Edward D. Duffield, chairman of the Board of Trustees of Princeton University; on Harlan Fiske Stone, associate justice of the United States Supreme Court, formerly dean of the school of law at Columbia University, and on Dr. Craven Laycock, who retires this year as dean of the college. The degree of doctor of letters was conferred on Perley Oakland Place, professor of Latin, Syracuse University, and the degree of doctor of pedagogy on José Padin, Commissioner of Education, Puerto Rico.

AT Colby College six honorary degrees were conferred on June 18, including the doctorate of laws on Professor Shailer Mathews, dean emeritus of the University of Chicago Divinity School, and on Dr. Frederick M. Padelford, dean of the University of Washington Graduate School. The degree of doctor of education was conferred on Patrick T. Campbell, superintendent of schools, Boston. The commencement address was given by Dr. Padelford.

TRINITY COLLEGE conferred the honorary degree of master of arts on Clarence Willard Gleason, teacher of Greek and Latin at the Roxbury Latin School since 1889, last year acting head master of the school. The degree of doctor of divinity was conferred on William Greenough Thayer, Ipswich, Massachusetts, formerly head master of St. Mark's School, Amherst, 1885.

THE degree of doctor of science was conferred at commencement on June 4 by Middlebury College on Dr. Herbert Eugene Walter, professor of biology at Brown University and assistant director of the Cold Spring Harbor Biological Laboratory, and the degree of doctor of letters on Philip A. Knowlton, of the Macmillan Company.

THE honorary degree of LL.D. was conferred on President Mary E. Woolley, of Mount Holyoke College, at the ninety-ninth commencement of Wheaton College, Massachusetts.

AMONG degrees conferred by Brown University on June 18 was the doctorate of laws on Dr. Ada Louise Comstock, president of Radcliffe College; the doctorate of letters on Charles Evans, of Chicago, librarian and bibliographer, and the doctorate of humane letters on Dr.

George Sarton, of the Widener Library, Harvard University.

THE Connecticut State College at Storrs conferred the honorary degree of master of letters at its fifty-first commencement exercises on Miss Edwina Whitney, librarian of the college, who retires on July 1 after serving for thirty-four years.

DR. FREDERICK WINGATE RAYMOND, of Chicago, has been elected president of Defiance College, Ohio.

JAMES B. WELLES, superintendent of schools at Roslyn, L. I., has been appointed principal of the State Normal School at Geneseo, N. Y.

THE REV. DR. P. E. MONROE, of Concord, North Carolina, has been elected president of Lenoir-Rhyne College, Hickory, North Carolina, a Lutheran institution. He succeeds Dr. H. Brent Schaeffer, whose resignation becomes effective on July 1.

J. W. RALEY has been elected president of the Oklahoma Baptist University at Shawnee.

DR. WALTER D. AGNEW has been reelected president of the Woman's College of Alabama at Montgomery for a third five-year term.

THE Alumnae Association of Simmons College, Boston, presented recently to the college a portrait of President Emeritus Henry Lefavour, painted by Edmund C. Tarbell. President Lefavour served the college for more than thirty-one years.

DEAN BERNICE BROWN CRONKHITE, of Radcliffe College, since 1923 dean of the college, has been elected dean of the Graduate School and chairman of the committee on admissions. She is succeeded as dean of the college by Mrs. Frances Ruml Jordan. Mrs. Jordan has been acting dean of the college during the recent absence on leave of Dean Cronkhite.

DR. JOHN W. BOWLER, as senior member of the department of physical education of Dartmouth College, has presented his resignation, effective at the end of the next academic year, availing himself of a year's leave of absence. At that time he will be seventy years of age and will have been connected with the department of physical education since 1901.

PROFESSOR JAMES B. MUNN will become chairman of the Department of English in Harvard College next year. He will succeed Professor John Tucker Murray, who will be on leave of absence during a part of the year.

DR. WILLIAM WELCH FLEXNER, of Bryn Mawr College, son of Dr. Simon Flexner, of the Rockefeller Institute for Medical Research, has been appointed assistant professor of mathematics at Cornell University.

REGINALD COGGESHALL, who was for five years on the staff of the *New York Herald* in Paris and has been for the past two years an assistant professor in the Department of Journalism at the University of Minnesota, has been appointed to a similar post in the School of Journalism of Columbia University. He will organize there a course in foreign correspondence. Mr. Coggeshall will represent Columbia as a member of the group which will make a six weeks' tour of Germany under the auspices of the Carl Schurz Foundation.

DR. GUIDO BECK, professor of physics in the German University at Prague, formerly of the University of Vienna and the University of Leipzig, will be a resident professor of physics in the University of Kansas during the year 1934–35, under the auspices of the Emergency Committee in Aid of Displaced German Scholars and of the Rockefeller Foundation. Professor Beck will conduct a seminar on problems of atomic nuclei and a course on the Dirac theory of electrons.

FOUR new department chairmen have been named at the University of Nebraska in accordance with the regulation that chairmanships be released when their incumbents become seventy years old. New chairmen are: Dr. D. A. Worcester, department of educational psychology and measurements, to succeed Dr. Charles Fordyce; Dr. W. C. Brenke, mathematics, to succeed Dr. A. L. Candy; Professor E. F. Schramm, geology, to succeed Dr. E. H. Barbour; and Dr. J. E. Kirshman, economics, to succeed Dr. G. O. Virtue. In Teachers College, other changes are: The transfer of Dr. A. R. Congdon from the department of educational psychology and measurements, to the department of secondary education with title of professor; Dr. S. M. Corey, promoted to the rank of professor, transferred from the department of history and principles of education, to the department of educational psychology and measurements; Dr. P. G. Johnson, now supervisor and instructor of physical and biological sciences in Teachers College High School, advanced to rank of assistant professor of secondary education and supervisor of physical and biological sciences. Professor C. K. Morse, now assistant professor, has been named assistant director of the university extension division, with rank of professor.

Archie M. Palmer, who has been associate secretary of the Association of American Colleges for the past five years, has been made executive secretary of The Cornellian Council of Cornell University, to fill the vacancy caused by the death of Harold Flack.

Dr. Robert P. Lane, of the department of industrial science of Dartmouth College, has been appointed executive director of the Welfare Council of New York City.

Dr. Willis R. Whitney, vice-president of the General Electric Company, has been appointed chairman of the education committee of the Board of Trustees of Union College.

Dr. Henry Noble MacCracken, president of Vassar College, left on June 23 with Mrs. MacCracken for Mexico, where they will spend July. Dr. MacCracken has been invited by the rector Abagado Manuel Gomez Morin to deliver several lectures at the National University of Mexico, in Mexico City.

Dr. William C. Bagley, of Teachers College, Columbia University, spoke at the commencement exercises on June 19 of the Bridgewater Teachers College. His address was on "The Teaching Profession in the Years that Lie Ahead."

President Raymond Walters, of the University of Cincinnati, gave the commencement addresses in June at Wilmington College and the Ohio Mechanics Institute.

President Frank L. McVey, of the University of Kentucky, delivered an address on "Philosophy for To-day" at the commencement exercises of the University of Cincinnati on June 15.

Dr. Cornelius Weygandt, professor of English literature at the University of Pennsylvania, delivered the commencement address at the university on June 20.

Dr. Louis I. Dublin was the principal speaker at the general session of the twenty-sixth annual conference of the Special Libraries Association, which opened in New York City on June 20. Mayor Fiorello La Guardia spoke at the dinner in the evening.

Denis W. Brogan, a member of the staff of the London School of Economics and Political Science, will be one of the speakers in a series of lectures and courses on current problems in labor and industry, in population trends, in agriculture, in government, in currency and on the Far East, to be given as a part of the program of the coming summer session at Western Reserve University.

An International University Conference has been arranged by the Association of University Teachers to be held at Oxford from June 29 to July 2. This conference will be the first attempt to form an organ of direct cooperation between universities of all countries. Among the subjects to be discussed are: university organization, vocational instruction, interchange of teachers, opportunities for research by foreign students, academic freedom.

An International Conference on Education is to be held in South Africa in July of this year. The conference, which will be conducted under the auspices of the New Education Fellowship of England, has received the support of South African Government Departments as well as of a large number of educational and social organizations. Two sessions will be held, one in Cape Town from the 2nd to the 13th of July, the other in Johannesburg from the 16th to the 27th of July. The list of speakers invited to address the conference includes Professor Pierre Bovet (Switzerland), Dr. William Boyd, Dr. F. M. Earle (Scotland), Professor Mabel Carney, Miss Helen Parkhurst, Professor John Dewey (United States), Professor Fred. Clarke (Canada), Lord Eustace Percy, Miss Beatrice Ensor (England), Dr. William Stern (Germany), Professor Giovanni Gentile (Italy), Professor Andre Siegfried (France). The Chief Executive Officer of the Australian Council for Educational Research, Dr. K. S. Cunningham, has been asked to speak on "Rural Education in Australia," and to give an account of the work of the council.

THE Fifth International Conference on Family Education will be held in Brussels in August, 1935. This conference will be concerned with a number of aspects of the home life of children, the development of character and the relationship between school and home. It is proposed to hold an exhibition in connection with the conference.

IN connection with the study of library instruction in teacher-training agencies to be made this year by a joint committee of the American Association of Teachers Colleges and the American Library Association, there will be organized in the School of Library Service at Columbia University a graduate seminar under the direction of Lucile F. Fargo, research associate and director of the joint-committee study. The seminar will extend over two semesters, beginning with the winter session, 1934, and will carry 2–4 credits per semester. It will be open to a limited number of students eligible for matriculation for an advanced degree who have had teaching, administrative or library experience in the field of library instruction for teachers. Each member of the seminar will be expected to make an individual contribution to the solution of problems such as the following which will form the agenda for general discussion: Studies and experiments under way, Methods of testing and evaluating library use by teachers-in-training and teachers-in-service, Library science curricula for teachers: Analysis and evaluation of current curricula in terms of usefulness to teachers, Integration with the instructional program of the teacher-training institution, Objective determination of content and faculty, laboratory facilities, opportunities for practice work.

TWENTY-FIVE members of the Riverdale Country School Glee Club, Riverdale-on-Hudson, New York, will sail on the S. S. *Leviathan* June 30 for a two months' bicycle tour of England. The boys will be entertained at various English schools where they will give concerts. They will also visit other places of historic and general educational interest. The trip, which is being undertaken as a good-will tour, has the endorsement of the English Speaking Union and the American University Union of London. Not only will the boys sing their way through England, but they will meet the English boys in athletic sports and exchange lessons in baseball for cricket. In addition they have received invitations to sing before Rotary Clubs and other organizations during the summer. Included in the itinerary are Exeter, Bath, Oxford, Stratford, London, Warwick, Rugby, Oundle, Bedford, Boston, Lincoln, York, Edinburgh, Carlisle, Ambleside, Liverpool, and many other famous English towns. Almost the entire trip will be made on bicycles, which will be obtained upon landing at Plymouth. The Riverdale Glee Club has won recognition during the past season in concerts given in and about New York. Last March the club sang at the final Young People's Concert of the Philharmonic Symphony Society of New York at Carnegie Hall; in May they gave a concert at the National Broadcasting Company studios over a national hookup, and later in the month they appeared in concert at Town Hall. The trip to England, which was arranged by Frank S. Hackett, head master of the Riverdale group of schools, will be under the leadership of Mr. D. Earl Gardner, assistant head master, James A. Giddings, director of the Glee Club, and Jack Stoll, pianist accompanist.

THE twelfth annual English Scandinavian Summer School, of which Miss Gladys Wright is the founder and principal, will be held at Milner Court, Sturry, Kent, from August 1 to 18, inclusive. The school is open to women educationists and provides facilities for studying the modern methods of physical education in the English language. Special attention is given to the modern development in gymnastic teaching known as the Björksten Modern Method.

THE Colby College Board of Trustees on April 14 adopted a reorganization of the physical education and athletic branches of the college. Beginning next autumn, there is to be a new department entitled: "The Department of Health and Physical Education." Within this will be three divisions as follows: (1) Medical and nursing services; (2) Intramural games; (3) Intercollegiate athletics. The purpose of the change was stated by President Franklin W. Johnson as follows: To subordinate athletics to a position on a par with the intramural program, to emphasize the close relation between the medical and recreational aspects of health, and to end the confusion and overlapping of functions that existed when the college administration and Athletic Association were jointly responsible for the conduct of intercollegiate sports.

PLANS for the organization of the first permanent professional children's theater resulted in the issuing of a certificate of incorporation for the project on May 9. It will be known as the American Children's Theater. The new theater is a non-profit institution and will be devoted to the special needs and interests of New York's million and a half children of school age. It will be modelled on the plan of the state-endowed children's theaters of Europe. Among the incorporators are Dr. John Dewey and Dr. George S. Counts, of Columbia University; Dr. Henry Hadley, former conductor of the Philharmonic Symphony; Mrs. Thomas K. Schmuck; Mrs. Peter Grimm; Wendell Phillips Dodge, an associate of the late David Belasco; and Lasas Galpern, for many years associated with the children's theater movement in Europe. A long list of noted educators, musicians, artists, dramatists, public officials and leaders in New York's theatrical and social life will serve as sponsors and patrons. The first performance is scheduled for some time in the fall.

DISCUSSION

SCHOOL SUBJECTS OR ACTIVITIES

Two books[1] have recently appeared which should cause the teaching profession to ponder seriously upon the place our familiar school subjects are likely to have or should have in the future school curriculum. Should school consist of only so-called pupil "activities" which exist on their own account or should "activities" have a place in school only in so far as they further the fundamentals of education which are generally conceived in terms of school subjects? The two books under consideration leave the reader in a confused state of mind.

Considerable disagreement on this issue is to be noted in the writings of the many contributors to the part of the Yearbook which deals with the activity movement. In Chapter IV are presented six types of teaching activities so arranged on a subjects-activities scale that the first type has a maximum emphasis on school subjects and the last a maximum emphasis on activities. One has the feeling after reading this chapter that the authors favor a swinging of educational practises toward the sixth or "activities" type.

Mead and Orth appear to lean in a similar direction. The very title of the book, "The Transitional Public School," suggests that the type of institution portrayed is merely a go-between, a make-shift, a temporary adjustment away from the traditional school toward a more ideal type. That this ideal school is also to be characterized by a maximum of "activities" may be inferred from a footnote in the book on page 64 which states, "The reader should hold in mind that the purpose throughout this book is to describe the work of the *transitional school;* to make it easier for the everyday teacher to make the shift further and further into the activity-unit form of organization."

First, a word concerning the meaning of "activities." Most writers in referring to this term apparently have in mind one or the other of two types. One is a rather brief, more or less isolated kind of activity, such as a visit to the local post-office, keeping daily temperature readings, making an Indian tepee, etc. The other is a fairly large or comprehensive unit of experience such as an "Indian" unit, a unit on "Transportation," and so on. As contrasted with the customary artificial activities of the traditional school, which were chiefly mental in character—memorization, reading *about* experiences—the more recent use of the term is confined in the main to overt types of activities, concrete rather than abstract, real and life-like. The Yearbook, however, presents no clear-cut definition of the term.

The writer of the present discussion can distinguish at least four types of teaching which are characterized by varying emphases on activities:[2]

[1] National Society for the Study of Education, Thirty-third Yearbook, Part II, *The Activity Movement,* Bloomington, Illinois: Public School Publishing Company, 1934.

C. D. Mead and F. W. Orth, "The Transitional Public School," New York: The Macmillan Company, 1934.

[2] These might be compared with other similar lists, such as six types suggested by a committee

(1) Emphasis merely on school subjects, including drill, memorization, etc.

(2) Emphasis on school subjects, including practical application or attempts at concreteness. An illustration of such an activity might be ''Making a shelter such as the Tree Dwellers first used for a house'' or ''Have children make a movie of some story very much enjoyed.''

(3) Emphasis on school subjects, but the latter so skilfully ''clothed'' in activities that the child is conscious only of the activities. Skills, facts or subject objectives are tested for at the end of the school term or at the end of a unit. Special drill or remedial work on school subjects is given when and where necessary.

(4) Emphasis entirely on activities. Both teacher and pupils are conscious only of the activities. School subjects are included merely when or where needed in the progression of the unit of activity. There is absent any checking or special drill on school subjects.[3]

It is the opinion of the writer that the teaching profession should face squarely the issue as to what is the place of school subjects in the education of the youth who pass through our institutions of learning. One question relating to this problem, concerning which apparently no agreement exists, is: Shall activities be injected into school subjects or shall school subjects be injected into activities? Both points of view seem to have adherents. Mead and Orth (p. 64), in describing the type of school they recommend, state: "It will be seen that such common branches of learning as arithmetic, spelling, geography, etc., form an integral part of the program and into them are injected dynamic units of work which eventuates into an activity program organized partly in subjects and partly in units of work." These authors, on the other hand (p. 14), quote Kilpatrick as championing a different point of view. The latter states: "This new curriculum consists of experiences. It uses subject matter, but it does not consist of subject matter." Mead and Orth then interpret Kilpatrick's philosophy by saying "Instead of 'subjects' into which we inject experiences, we are to have 'experiences' (enterprises, activities) into which we inject subject matter."

The answer to the question stated in the paragraph above lies, it seems to the present writer, in the answer to still another question: Are activities a means or an end in education? A few statements in the society's Yearbook do imply that activities might be considered as the ends and not the means. For example, in an elaboration of the fifth of the six types of teaching activities, comments such as the following appear (p. 74): "There is no attempt to utilize these enterprises in the school program merely as vehicles of learning. . . . The curriculum is, rather, emergent." However, most writers appear to conceive of activities as the *method* phase of education rather than the aims or ends. The following are typical of some of the opinions expressed in the Yearbook. Kilpatrick (p. 64) writes: "The activity movement, considered simply from the theory side, is restricted to the 'method' aspect of education . . . the activity conception by itself does not and can not suffice for a complete curriculum theory.[4] Heyl (p. 116) cites as one of the problems in connection with the activity movement that of the "Danger of the activity becoming an end, not a means toward fundamental learnings." Dewey (pp. 82 and 83) states, "there is nothing in the bare concept of activity that gives helpful direction to the educational program. . . . The settled point is that activity as doing is a means rather than an end." Oberholtzer (p. 136) referring to the activity curriculum in the schools of Houston, Texas, remarks, "the activities were chosen as the chief medium of the learnings of the classroom." Lane (p. 120) prefers the term "informal program" to "activity program" "because the activities are seen as means to an end, the end being the building up of a happy and successful group

in the Yearbook on pages 69 to 75 or five types presented by Brueckner in the Yearbook on pages 212 to 214.

[3] This last type appears to exist largely in theory. Courses of study, even though based on activities, generally do not reach this extreme practise. A good case in point is the Training School Course of Study for the kindergarten through the third grade by the State Teachers College, Farmville, Virginia. This course is one of the better, more recent ones organized on an activity basis. It is interesting to note, however, that the second half of the course consists of a list of objectives arranged according to school subjects which represent the expected outcomes of the activities.

[4] Are the two quotations from Kilpatrick, cited in the present and the preceding paragraph, inconsistent? They are not necessarily so. The *child* may be engaging in an activity for its own sake, whereas the *teacher* may be concerned with the ends the activities are designed to serve.

life." Furthermore, one of the statements by the committee of the society that prepared the Yearbook, with respect to which there was a measure of agreement among the members, reads as follows (p. 184): "The activity movement, under whatever name pursued, represents the psychological aspect of the educative process, and needs for its completion and direction a correlative social theory." It is thus apparent that there is fair agreement that activities should be considered as means and not as ends.

What, then, should be the ends toward the attainment of which school instruction is given? An examination of the contentions of the many contributors to the Yearbook reveals that these may be classified, in the main, into two types: first, those fundamental knowledges and skills which are customarily conceived in terms of school subjects and, secondly, certain traits, most of which could be subsumed under the term "character." The latter include such attitudes or abilities as, a tendency on the part of the child to cooperate with his fellows, ability to plan his work, tolerance toward opinions which conflict with his own, a habit of evaluating the results of his efforts, etc.

The necessity for the inculcating of character traits such as those mentioned above does not seem to be disputed by the teaching profession. However, much verbal warfare seems to be waging over the place of the so-called "fundamentals" in the school program. The writer, however, has difficulty in understanding why there should be contention over the need for the teaching of subject-matter. That there should be debate over the method of teaching these fundamentals, on the other hand, can by him be easily appreciated. To learn to perform a unique activity—the number of possible different activities is legion—does not appear to the writer to be of great significance. However, when one has acquired control over the elements which are common to experiences—call them generalizations, principles, subject-matter, or what we will—a person has indeed then the means by which he should be in a position to meet effectively the many challenging problems of life. Again, we are born into an environment or society in which a rather fixed language or means of communication, for example, is in vogue, an environment in which an inflexible number system is in use; we are more or less doomed to live a life under conditions where rather fixed customs prevail and institutions of one kind or another are to be found. If educators should train children without the former having their eyes steadily fixed upon the elements which are common to people's experiences and if these educators should train the children without carefully instructing them in the peculiar character of the natural and social world in which they are living and probably will continue to live, the "education" given could scarcely be worthy of the name.

If these, then, are the ends of education, are so-called "activities" the best means or method for their accomplishment? Traditional education has emphasized memorizing and lesson learning—activities exceedingly limited in scope. Newer conceptions of education stress a greater variety of activities so that the student gets practise in the multifarious tasks that constitute efficient current living. To form a trait of cooperation, children should be placed in situations where cooperation is necessary; to form an ability to initiate, pupils perforce need to be given practise in initiating. To insure the carry-over of verbal learnings, generalizations, principles or subject-matter from school to actual situations in life, some practise in engaging in natural situations seems necessary. Because activities, as conceived by present-day educators, are varied in nature and, secondly, because activities on account of their likeness to life-like situations should transfer readily to life as it is lived outside of school, they may be the best means of arriving at the goals sought through public-school instruction.

If the ends of school work may be considered to be both subject-matter and worthwhile character traits and the best means of their achievement to be pupil "activities," which one (ends or means) shall be made the core or center of attention? Probably in the initial stages of learning children may be so taught that they conceive of activity as something which exists on its own account—the teacher, on the other hand, constantly keeping in mind the ends. However, increasingly with time, it seems, pupils may share with their teacher a knowledge of the goals toward which their efforts are being focussed.

HERBERT T. OLANDER
UNIVERSITY OF PITTSBURGH

THE RIGHTS OF THE TEACHER

SCHOOL DISTRICT No. 72, Coffey County, Kansas, held their school board meeting out of the geographical limits of their district at the county superintendent's office. At this meeting the board hired one Dunfield for eight months, commencing September 5, 1932, and ending with the school year 1933, at $72.50 a month. When Dunfield presented himself for work on September 5, he was told his contract was not recognized. Dunfield appealed to the courts, and it was held that when a school board meets outside the school district and hires a teacher at such a meeting, that contract, although signed by the proper officers, is not binding on the school district.[1]

Corpus Juris recites:

> Boards possess such powers, and such only, as have been expressly conferred upon them by statute or are necessarily implied from those so conferred or from the duties imposed upon them, and "a fortiori" such an officer or board can have no authority which the state in its sovereign capacity could not delegate or confer. All persons who deal with school boards and officers are presumed to have knowledge of the extent of their powers, and the manner in which such powers may or must be exercised.[2]

> In the absence of a statute permitting it, a meeting can not validly be held outside the geographical limits of the district for which the board acts.[3]

> Where place at which meeting of board shall be held is prescribed by statute, a meeting held elsewhere is without authority, and proceedings held thereat are void.[4]

Where the question involved has arisen, the decision in the immediate case is law, and there seems to be no contrary opinion.

From the teacher's view-point, I desire to discuss this case. Apparently, the courts presume the last action of a school board is the desire of the community. They work out rules of law which they believe will set up that desire, regardless of the rights of the teacher who has depended on the contract.

Some one should be responsible, if a contract, proper on its face, is sent to a teacher, and that teacher is made to believe he has a position for the coming year.

It is my contention that a teacher is entitled to some consideration, and if the interpretation of the laws are not such, they should be made to cover just such cases as this Kansas one. What school teacher knows whether all the "red tape" that is necessary to make a valid contract has been complied with? What teacher knows whether the school board met within the geographical limits of the school district, or in a house just outside the district, or, in fact, whether the school board met at all to consider his contract? What difference should it make?

In another case, a contract was held void because one member of the school board had not been notified that a board meeting was called for the purpose of electing a teacher. A contract was sent to the teacher, who did not know of any irregularity of the board meeting. The contract was signed by the proper officers, and yet the contract was held void because one member of the board was not notified of the meeting.[5]

If the courts continue to require that all details set up in the statute be complied with, then teacher organizations should have state laws passed requiring that teacher contracts recite that all these details have been complied with. Board members who sign such a contract should be responsible and under bond to pay any teacher whose contract is found null and void because of conditions beyond teacher control. Teachers as well as communities must be protected. If an outgoing school board should hire a teacher not desired by the incoming board, that teacher should not lose his position because of a technicality. If he does, those board members who signed the contract or their bondsmen should be held responsible.

Much difficulty would be prevented if statutes provided that the school board be required to hire all their teachers for a period of one or more school years within a definite time after

[1] *Dunfield* v. *School District No. 72, Coffey County*, 28P (2d) 987: (1934).
[2] 56 *Corpus Juris* 331, 332.
[3] 56 *Corpus Juris* 336.
[4] 56 *Corpus Juris* 336.

[5] *Martin* v. *School District No. 3, Ramsey County (Minn.)* 204 N.W. 320; Paul G. H. Jarvis, "Recent Supreme Court Decisions on Teacher Contracts," where this *Martin* v. *School District No. 3* case is more fully discussed, SCHOOL AND SOCIETY, 24: 153–156, 1926.

their election, and thus prevent school boards which no longer have the confidence of the community to hire teachers, except for the purpose of filling unexpected vacancies. It may be that in some states the date of the election of the school board will have to be changed, but the results would be worth it.

PAUL G. H. JARVIS
HUMBOLDT SENIOR HIGH SCHOOL
ST. PAUL, MINNESOTA

SPECIAL CORRESPONDENCE

MEXICO'S PROGRAM OF RURAL EDUCATION

"A FEW wise men in the midst of millions of illiterates" was the fruit of the old school system in Mexico, but the revolution brought a radical change in policy and education has gone rural, has been put in the path of the poor. Why not? From the illiterate mass came the bulk of the soldiers who followed Madero, Carranza, Villa, Zapata, Obregon and Calles. They won the right not only to lands and political dominance but also to a schooling, and necessity demanded that they exercise this right if they were to continue in their newly acquired ascendency. Hence the education of the peasants became the chief concern of Mexican statesmen and the founding of schools in rural districts the predilection of the educators, at least after the Federal Ministry of Education was organized in 1921.

Rural schools demand rural teachers. What can a city-bred teacher do far off from all the conveniences of civilization where oftentimes even the language is different from his own, being Indian rather than Spanish? Rural normal schools had to be established in rural communities, where young "campesinos" could be gathered and without separating them from their native environment be trained and inspired with a zeal for the betterment of their fellows. Eighteen such schools have been opened at strategic points over Mexico, very, very few for such a large country, in fact, just a drop in the bucket but a tremendously important one.

Hecelchakan is the fortunate town chosen as the site for the normal school which is to supply the Peninsula of Yucatan with rural teachers. I met some of its first graduates teaching in Valladolid and they showed me how they are carrying out the methods which they had learned at their alma mater. With great enthusiasm they took me through their school and related to me how different it had been when they took it over a year before. No benches, no chairs, no desks then. Indeed, there were not many pupils to begin with, either. They had started from scratch except for a large building in ill repair. The young principal and his male assistant had set up a carpenter shop in one room and with the larger boys as apprentices had gone to work making school furniture. By the time I arrived they had equipped the school quite well, even to an interesting museum of natural history. The young ladies of the staff had gone about visiting in the homes after school hours, endeavoring to make friends with the habitual truants and their parents. They had made a census of the entire settlement and a chart showing the location of each home and other useful information.

The laws of Mexico provide for compulsory education for children where schools are available, but these young teachers of Valladolid had not wanted to resort to the civil authorities to force the children to come to school and since the parents would not send them nor oblige them to study when they did come they had to set about winning the cooperation of parents and children in other ways. Equipment for playing basketball and other games was secured, and the students who were regular in attendance were allowed to use it. Later on the teachers pooled their savings and bought a dynamo to provide electric lighting for the school and playground as well as to run a moving picture show. Parents who send their children to school faithfully are given a free ticket to the movies each week, and children who live up to the requirements are also given complimentary tickets. Parties are held from time to time and other attractions offered. In short, the drab is being taken out of the lives of the peasants, and as a result the school is winning their affections.

In the early stages of a school everything depends upon the teachers, and Hecelchakan Normal and kindred centers are turning out the kind who make good. One of them was sent to Quintana Roo, the backwoods of Maya Land. The citizens of the village to which he had been assigned did not want such an innovation as a school and they frankly told him so, but nevertheless he took possession of a large communal hut and invited the children to come and learn how paper talks. Being very small of stature, however, he did not inspire the respect of the Indians and they came one night and burned down the hut, thinking that in this way they could get rid of him. He refused to be defeated and would sleep out under the trees of the forest at night and come back to town during the day to show love and helpfulness. Within a month he had so won the primitive folk over to his program that they put up a new and better hut expressly for the school.

It is remarkable that only two years in normal after a scant four or five years' course in the grade schools can prepare such teachers. I learned the secret at Hecelchakan. The spirit of crusaders there imbibed gives the graduates a David-like determination and daring in the face of gigantic difficulties. Students and directors live together as one large family consecrated to the sole aim of redeeming the "campesinos."

Classroom work is supplemented by week-end practise trips, when the students mingle with peasants to demonstrate and develop their ability to impart what they have learned. Zeal and endurance is put to the test by long trips on foot into unhealthy, backward sections where for days they get along on poor food and no comforts. Those who can not stand it or do not like the life of itinerant apostles of learning quit and go home. The rule now is to pick all prospects from the ranks of the "campesinos" themselves, so that new recruits are not foreign to the hardships of rural life.

Products of the rural normal schools are in great demand. The entire class which graduated last year from Cerro Hueco, Chiapas, was given immediate employment, and the director of education for the state is anxiously waiting for more. The educators of Mexico will rejoice when the output of normal-trained rural teachers catches up with the ever-quickening pace at which villages and hamlets on mountain slopes or in jungle fastnesses and over desert sands are receiving schools. The number of federal rural schools has increased from 309 in 1922 to 7,504 in 1933, but approximately two million children in fifty thousand communities are still unreached. Governmental plans call for the founding of twelve thousand new schools during the next six years, so that it will be quite a while before the eighteen normal schools can supply sufficient rural teachers.

In the meantime the poorly trained emergency teachers are being improved by means of teachers' institutes, by the tutelage of visiting inspectors, by pedagogical journals and circulating libraries, and by a novel and extremely interesting institution called "the cultural missions." A cultural mission is composed of thirteen specialists as follows—a trained educator as leader, an ethnologist, an economist, a social worker, a doctor, a nurse, an agronomist, two manual arts teachers and a teacher each for popular arts, rural industries, physical education and music. There are fourteen of these cultural missions and their ministry has been itinerant until last year. Each mission would go in a group from town to town endeavoring to cover as much territory as possible, holding campaigns of several weeks' duration, fanning into a flame the ardor of the villagers for progress and giving practical demonstrations to the local teachers of the methods enjoined by the ministry of education. The thrilling experiences of these pilgrim educators would fill volumes. They accomplished much, but only fourteen such teams for such a large country with transportation facilities so poor in rural districts was spreading the butter very, very thin. It has been decided that their work will be more abiding and in the end will accomplish more if they are localized in regions contiguous to sections served by normal schools, and so in the future they will be permanent missions concentrating their efforts within a limited radius.

The whole educational program is vast in its scope. It does not seek the uplift of the individual as such but rather the transformation of entire communities. Its objective is to bring the primitive three fourths of the population of Mexico en masse up to the standard of living both economically and socially of the remaining one fourth and indeed to excel this by avoiding some of the undesirable features of the superior minority. What is expected of the rural teachers is almost incredible and would be absolutely impossible of attainment were it not for the spirit which animates them. The only way to give an accurate idea of their duties is to rehearse a list of them as taken from a circular of instructions.

For each teacher there should be an enrolment of fifty children in daytime classes and twenty-five adults in night classes. The children should be taught reading, writing, arithmetic, natural science, geography, history, manual training, drawing, rules of health, including sex knowledge, agriculture and some trade. They should also be organized into scouting clubs, Junior Red Cross societies, cooperative organizations and into committees for self-government, cleanliness, sports, festivals, savings, upkeep of buildings, temperance campaigns and for the protection of wild life.

When you realize that in the majority of cases there is only one or at most two teachers to attend to all this, you decide that Mussolini with his many portfolios doesn't have much over the rural teachers of Mexico. However, that is only a partial list of their responsibilities. At least twenty-five adults as well must be convinced that they should enrol in the evening classes, and they must be taught in such an interesting fashion that the average attendance will keep up to twenty.

Furthermore, the teacher should so organize and influence the whole community that the fruit of his efforts will be manifested sooner or later in the following ways. The highways leading into town will be kept clean and in good repair. New roads will be built when needed. Signs will be put up to direct the traveler. Trees will be built along the highways and over the hills by way of adornment and reforestation. The streets in town will be kept free from weeds, grass and roaming animals. The names of the streets will be painted clearly at each corner. The houses will be painted or whitewashed and each one will be swept and sprinkled daily. Every kitchen will have a chimney (the custom for centuries having been to let the smoke find its way out through the tile or thatch as best it might). People will no longer sleep on the floor in the kitchen but will secure beds and erect separate rooms for sleeping. Each home will secure a hygienic water tank, an outhouse, chicken roosts, corrals for pigs, rabbits and sheep away from the family living quarters, and a fenced yard with flower and vegetable gardens. These as well as beehives will be so managed according to the example and instructions given at the school that they will provide a real source of income and thus raise the standard of living as regards food and clothing.

Apart from the influence of the teacher being evidenced by these transformations in the individual homes his efforts in the community should further result in the establishment of a public library, a central market, a park, an open-air theater, a playground, a public cemetery, street lights, a slaughter house, an athletic field with benches for the spectators, a system of keeping vital records, a central emergency clinic, and a clean, municipal water supply (although he should teach the people to boil and filter their drinking water). Besides all this, the teacher should put forth every effort to get the people to erect a telegraph or telephone line to connect the town with the outside world, and he should make arrangements for the periodic carrying of mail where these facilities are lacking. He should vaccinate all the inhabitants against smallpox each year. He should organize temperance campaigns so effectively that they will result in a radical reduction in the number of the village saloons and ultimately in their complete extinction. Each week community gatherings of a social nature are to be held under the auspices of the school and contests in matters of health and cleanliness should be conducted in connection with them. All fanatical ideas both as regards ecclesiasticism and Indian religions are to be uprooted through the instruction and example given by the teacher and he should make the "campesinos" independent of all capitalistic interests by introducing new industries and organizing cooperative associations.

The opposition of the rural schools to capitalism makes them rather unpopular with the average plantation owner. According to law every plantation which is situated over three kilometers from any town and has over twenty children living on its premises is obliged to maintain a school at its own expense. This rule has been frequently disregarded because of the negligence or connivance of local authorities, but its enforcement has now been intrusted to the federal ministry of education instead of to the individual states and steps are being taken to compel the interests affected to finance schools for their employees. It has been estimated that this will result in the opening up of at least fifteen hundred new schools at no added expense to the government.

One young director of education, though delighted over the new arrangement, almost winced when he showed me the order to enforce it. "That means more enemies for me," he said. "The worst is that in this state, the revolution was not a complete upturn for the lower classes as in the rest of the country. Certain elements of the upper strata merely turned revolutionary in name and took control without vitally changing the outlook of society. That makes it necessary for us to develop our program without the proper backing of popular sentiment, whereas in other states the federal schools quite generally enjoy the support of a public opinion moulded by the revolution."

Yes, this mass movement toward an all-inclusive education, this startling crusade of a whole nation toward a new world was not only born of the revolution but also depends upon it for strength to succeed. They are mutually dependent, in fact, the one upon the other as mother and child. When the child grows up the mother will be assured of ample and permanent support. "No outcome of the Mexican Revolution," as Dr. Frank Tannenbaum has well said in his very illuminating book on Mexico, "Peace by Revolution," "is more significant than the rural educational movement that has grown from it. . . . It is the most modern, yet most delicate and sensitive, large scale movement of cultural stimulus and social awakening that can be recorded in America, and perhaps in the world."

W. CAMERON TOWNSEND

QUOTATIONS

MISS ABBOTT AND THE CHILDREN'S BUREAU

MISS GRACE ABBOTT, who retires this week as head of the Children's Bureau of the United States Department of Labor, has been one of the indispensable figures in the creation of the American conscience in regard to child welfare. If to-day it is comparatively easy to persuade any American community that its children must be safeguarded against disease and malnutrition, that for their youthful shortcomings must be meted out a different punishment from what is given to hardened criminals, and that young folks are better off in school than in factories, a large part of the credit must be assigned to the Children's Bureau.

Steadily, constructively, with unswerving fidelity to the truth and no deference to political expediency or flashy popularity, its two chiefs, Julia Lathrop and Grace Abbott, have for twenty-two years directed its activities in the unromantic field of collecting statistics, issuing pamphlets containing advice to mothers and aiding all sound measures for improving the general well-being of 43,000,000 American children. That their work is far from completed, and that the depression has complicated the problem a thousandfold, the Children's Bureau workers would be the first to admit. Theirs, however, is the kind of faith that plods steadily ahead. They work hardest when most needs to be done.

Miss Abbott has served under five Presidents, going to Washington first in 1917 in the administration of Woodrow Wilson as director of the child labor division of the bureau. When the first Federal child labor law was declared unconstitutional she served as adviser on the War Labor Policies Board, and in other positions of responsibility in child welfare fields, until her appointment in 1921 to succeed Miss Lathrop. The integrity and wisdom of her conduct of the bureau led to her being widely supported in 1930 as a candidate for Secretary of Labor to succeed James J. Davis. This opportunity she is generally believed to have sacrificed when she differed with President Hoover in his desire to transfer the activities of the Children's Bureau from the Department of Labor to the Public Health Service of the Department of the Treasury. The bureau remained where it was. So did Miss Abbott.

When, two years later, Miss Frances Perkins became Secretary of Labor, one of her first official utterances was a promise that the Children's Bureau would not be molested. The somewhat harassed secretary, confronted with tremendous seething throughout the labor world, and with internal problems in other nooks of her department, expressed profound thanks that the Children's Bureau was one thing she need not worry about.

In her new post as professor of public welfare in the School of Social Service of the University of Chicago Miss Abbott will have the good wishes of all citizens who have applauded her Washington service, and for generations to come millions who know nothing about her will benefit from that service.—*New York Herald-Tribune.*

AN ELECTIVE STATE BOARD OF EDUCATION

CALIFORNIA TEACHERS ASSOCIATION is putting before the voters of California at the November election as amendment to the Constitution which makes the State Board of Education elective rather than appointive, by the Governor, as it is at the present time.

The Attorney General's Office, at the request of our Association, has given us a circulation title for our proposed initiative measure. The circulation title for our initiative petitions, which we are anxious to have every teacher in the state help circulate, reads as follows:

Making State Board of Education Elective; Abolishing Superintendent of Public Instruction; Providing for Director of Education. Initiative. Repeals Section 2, amends Section 7, Article IX of Constitution. Abolishes office of Superintendent of Public Instruction. Declares State Board of Education shall consist of ten members, each elected from a district for ten-year term, each district comprising two congressional districts. Prescribes rotation in office. Empowers board to fill membership vacancies, appointee holding until next general election. Requires board appoint Director of Education, removable at pleasure, and fix his salary; Superintendent of Public Instruction continuing in office until appointed director qualifies.

California has an unsatisfactory state organization for its educational system. We have a Superintendent of Public Instruction elected by the people of the state at the same election at which a Governor of the state is elected. The Governor under our present organization appoints the State Board of Education, with which the Superintendent of Public Instruction must work. This poor organization has been responsible for some very difficult situations in the past, handicapping the welfare of public education.

This amendment calls for a new organization in the State Department of Education whereby the people of the state select their Board of Education. This Board in turn selects the Director of education who serves at the will of the Board and at a salary determined by the Board. Our present Superintendent of Public Instruction and his immediate predecessors have served the schools of this state at unreasonable personal financial sacrifices. If California expects to maintain indefinitely a public school system that is worthy of the best interests of childhood, she must not continue the present organization and must not expect able State Superintendents to continue indefinitely to render educational leadership for a financial return that is entirely out of keeping with the importance of the office.

The reorganization of the State Department of Education is a matter of outstanding importance and significance to the future welfare of the public school program of our state. The children of California deserve the best possible type of educational organization, insuring a Board of Education elected by the people for only one purpose, that of determining the educational policies of the state and administered by a Director of Education whose entire time can be given to his professional obligations.—*Willard E. Givens, president of the California Teachers Association, in the Sierra Educational News.*

REPORTS

FOUNDATION FOR THE ADVANCEMENT OF SOCIAL SCIENCES OF THE UNIVERSITY OF DENVER

THE Foundation for the Advancement of Social Sciences of the University of Denver has now completed ten years of service under the guidance of Dr. Ben M. Cherrington, executive secretary. In 1924 Mr. James H. Causey presented to the university $1,250,000 with the stipulation that the income be used to "advance understanding and good will in social, industrial and international relationships." Mr. Causey, Chancellor Frederick M. Hunter, of the University of Denver; Dr. Heber R. Harper, of Columbia University and formerly chancellor of the University of Denver, and Dr. Ernest Wilkins, president of Oberlin University, were appointed trustees to organize the foundation. They called upon Dr. Cherrington, then of the University of California, to act as executive secretary and to inaugurate the work of the foundation.

Dr. Cherrington's first step was to submit his problem to 150 prominent men and women all over the world. Compiling their answers, he found that most of them emphasized the need for an American awakening to the post-war position of the United States in international life, to an understanding based on a knowledge of world affairs and a view-point that would effectively serve as an active agency for peace.

After two years of study, research and observation of the methods of somewhat similar organizations, Dr. Cherrington resolved a four-point policy to serve as the basis for the Denver foundation. This four-point program has for its first step the dramatization of world affairs for large numbers of persons, and this has been promoted by the inauguration of a series of fortnightly luncheon meetings at which prominent lecturers are presented. At the first meetings, about 200 persons attended, but now nearly 1,000 guests come to each luncheon.

The function of the second step of the program is to reach the various community and professional groups. For example, Dr. Cherrington frequently invites a group of lawyers who have expressed their interest in the work of the foundation to join him in a series of evening meetings. This group may discuss codification of international laws, prevention of crime or the World Court. Several educators recently approached the foundation with the idea of organizing a discussion group on citizen training in Germany and Russia. This phase of the work proceeds through the service, social and business clubs of the city. Miss Elizabeth M. Fackt, assistant to the executive secretary, is responsible for reaching the women's organizations.

The intensive study groups constitute the third step. The first group of this sort was formed seven years ago and is still meeting one night a week for detailed study of world affairs. Five other groups are now extant and each group is limited to 40 or 50 persons. The efforts of Dr. Cherrington and his assistants are incorporated into the fourth step of the program. Study materials are sent to each individual who requests them. Since each person wishing to attend the meetings must ask for reservations himself, the directors are able to get into communication with every individual who has signified an interest. The foundation is now housed in a wing of the new Reed Library on the campus of the University of Denver.

EDUCATIONAL RESEARCH AND STATISTICS

RECENT TRENDS IN ENROLMENT AT THE UNIVERSITY OF ILLINOIS

FOR a great many years SCHOOL AND SOCIETY has published annually its article on "Statistics of Registration in American Universities and Colleges," presenting data collected from the institutions, exclusive of junior colleges, approved by the various regional associations. The following facts taken from recent articles by President Raymond Walters are interesting because of their bearing upon the trends during the years of the depression. The data presented for November, 1930, represented an increase of 3½ per cent. in the number of full-time students attending the institutions concerned over the preceding year.[1] The next year, 1931–32, showed a further increase of six tenths of 1 per cent. over 1930–31,[2] but the figures for November, 1932, were lower by 4½ per cent. than those for the preceding year.[3] The following year, 1933–34, showed a further drop of 5 per cent. over 1932–33.[4] Thus the first two years of the period of the depression showed small gains, while the last two years brought slightly larger losses.

1 SCHOOL AND SOCIETY, 32: page 787, 1930.
2 *Ibid.*, 34: page 782, 1931.
3 *Ibid.*, 36: page 737, 1932.
4 *Ibid.*, 38: page 781, 1933.

The facts just presented are based upon total enrolments in several hundred colleges and universities, and, therefore, do not necessarily reflect the exact trends in any single one of them. Many institutions have undoubtedly experienced much greater variations and even different types of variation than the average trends already cited represent. In view of this fact it is interesting to note what has happened to the enrolment during recent years in a single large institution. The study which is here reported is based upon the number of full-time classified undergraduates who were enrolled in the University of Illinois during the first semester of each year since 1924–25. Table 1 shows the number of students enrolled in the university for these years and the increase or decrease from each year to the next. It should be noted that, although the total enrolment increased gradually during the first three years shown, it decreased every year between 1926–27 and 1933–34, except for 1929–30 and 1930–31. The period of the depression did not show any decline in the total enrolments until 1931–32 and it exhibited its greatest effects in the following year. The reduction was smallest for the last year shown. The total decline from the peak reached in 1930–31 represents a loss of 2,083, or 21.4 per cent. of the enrolment for that year. The loss for 1933–34 represents only 2.4 per cent. of the enrolment for the peak year.

The enrolment for men and women, however, did not follow exactly similar trends. They exhibited tendencies of opposite character to a minor degree in the years 1927–28 and 1928–29, but the greatest differences between the sexes occurred in 1930–31 and 1933–34. In 1930–31 there was a considerable increase for the men but a loss for the women, whose enrolment, then, as the table shows, was affected a year earlier by the depression than was that of the men. This difference is probably due to the fact that college attendance is much more closely and directly dependent upon the economic conditions of the family in the case of the women than of the men. Thus, at the University of Illinois at least, a much larger proportion of men than of women engage in remunerative occupation while in residence. During the year 1933–34 the enrolment of women increased slightly,

TABLE 1

ENROLMENTS OF CLASSIFIED UNDERGRADUATES IN THE UNIVERSITY OF ILLINOIS FOR THE FIRST SEMESTER OF EACH YEAR FROM 1924–25 TO 1933–34

Year	Men		Women		Total	
	Number	Change over preceding year	Number	Change over preceding year	Number	Change over preceding year
1924–25	5678	+397	2372	+236	8050	+633
1925–26	6249	+571	2710	+338	8959	+909
1926–27	6566	+317	2831	+121	9397	+438
1927–28	6587	+ 21	2763	− 68	9350	− 47
1928–29	6454	−133	2774	+ 11	9228	−122
1929–30	6704	+250	2846	+ 72	9550	+322
1930–31	6972	+268	2748	− 98	9720	+170
1931–32	6547	−425	2494	−254	9041	−679
1932–33	5710	−837	2158	−336	7868	−1173
1933–34	5435	−275	2202	+ 44	7637	−231

while that of men continued to diminish. The decline which came with the depression, therefore, seems either to have run its course or to have reached a temporary halt for the women, but is still in process for the men.

The recent declines just referred to may be analyzed in somewhat greater detail as follows. According to Table 1 the year 1929–30 marked a peak in the enrolment of women, and the reduction which followed reached a low point in 1932–33. During this period the enrolment decreased from 2,846 to 2,158, a loss of 688, or 24.2 per cent. of the former figure. The peak in the enrolment of men came in 1930–31, and the decline has continued since that time up to the present. The reduction so far has been from 6,972 to 5,435, a loss of 1,537, or 22.1 per cent. It might be reasoned that each of these two declines constitutes a cycle, which may be regarded as complete for the women because of the small increase in their numbers for the present year (1933–34) and which, at the worst, will result in only a small further reduction for the men next year—sufficient to bring the percentage of reduction up to approximately the same point as that already reached by the women. If such an equalization does occur, we may expect a decrease of about 150 in the total number of men to be enrolled in the university in 1934–35. This loss would be very small in comparison with the losses of the last three years and might, especially if it is assumed to represent the highest decline probable, be regarded as an encouraging sign. On the other hand, it is quite possible, of course, that any one or more of various factors may operate to upset any expectations which the recent trends seem at present to justify.

The results of a study of enrolments by individual classes during the last eight years are presented in Tables 2 and 3, the former being introduced simply because it serves as the basis for deriving the latter. The first and second rows of Table 3 show a decline in the freshman enrolments for each year over the preceding year except for 1929–30 and 1933–34, and with the additional exception of 1930–31 for the men only. The increase in the freshman enrolment for 1933–34, particularly the gain of 21.3 per cent. for the women, is very encouraging, not only because of the increase itself but also because it may presage a favorable freshman enrolment for the following year. The third and fourth rows of Table 3, which represent the losses in a class from its freshman to its sophomore year, are characterized by very large decreases for all years, losses which are in fact so large that they might well be regarded as cause for concern over the problem of student mortality at this point. The reductions shown in these two rows for the year 1933–34, however, are distinctly low in comparison not only with those for the recent years of diminishing enrolments but also with those for all preceding years. In other words, the sophomore class of this year has exhibited very unusual holding powers.

TABLE 2

CLASSIFIED UNDERGRADUATE ENROLMENTS IN THE UNIVERSITY OF ILLINOIS SHOWN SEPARATELY FOR EACH CLASS BY MEN AND WOMEN, FOR THE FIRST SEMESTER OF EACH YEAR FROM 1926–27 TO 1933–34

Sex and class	Enrolment for: 1926–27	1927–28	1928–29	1929–30	1930–31	1931–32	1932–33	1933–34
Men								
Freshmen	2931	2818	2682	2810	2988	2475	1886	1982
Sophomores	1620	1580	1500	1533	1634	1516	1296	1222
Juniors	1218	1322	1284	1368	1345	1531	1393	1214
Seniors	797	867	988	993	1005	1025	1135	1017
Total	6566	6587	6454	6704	6972	6547	5710	5435
Women								
Freshmen	1016	994	933	1005	921	815	649	787
Sophomores	660	613	637	673	618	551	469	454
Juniors	656	672	652	691	647	616	528	529
Seniors	499	484	552	477	562	512	512	432
Total	2831	2763	2774	2846	2748	2494	2158	2202

TABLE 3

PERCENTAGES OF INCREASE OR DECREASE IN CLASSIFIED UNDERGRADUATE ENROLMENTS FROM THE FIRST SEMESTER OF ONE YEAR TO THAT OF THE NEXT SHOWN SEPARATELY FROM EACH CLASS BY MEN (M) AND WOMEN (W.) THESE DATA ARE FOR THE UNIVERSITY OF ILLINOIS FROM 1926–27 TO 1933–34

Increase or decrease from:		Percentages for: 1926–27	1927–28	1928–29	1929–30	1930–31	1931–32	1932–33	1933–34
Preceding freshman class to present freshman class	M	− 7.3	− 3.9	− 4.8	+ 4.8	+ 6.3	− 17.2	− 23.8	+ 5.1
	W	− 15.1	− 2.2	− 6.1	+ 7.7	− 8.4	− 11.5	− 20.4	+ 21.3
Preceding freshman class to present sophomore class	M	− 48.8	− 46.1	− 46.8	− 42.8	− 41.9	− 49.3	− 47.6	− 35.2
	W	− 44.8	− 39.7	− 35.9	− 27.9	− 38.5	− 40.2	− 42.5	− 30.1
Preceding sophomore class to present junior class	M	− 8.1	− 18.4	− 18.7	− 8.8	− 12.3	− 6.3	− 8.1	− 6.3
	W	+ 28.1	+ 1.2	+ 6.4	+ 8.5	− 3.7	− 0.3	− 4.2	+ 12.8
Preceding junior class to present senior class	M	− 17.0	− 28.8	− 25.3	− 22.7	− 26.5	− 23.8	− 25.9	− 27.0
	W	− 13.2	− 26.2	− 17.9	− 26.8	− 18.7	− 20.9	− 16.9	− 18.2

The interesting feature about the fifth and sixth rows of Table 3 is the fact that for each of the first four years shown the junior men suffered a loss, while the women in this class experienced a gain, due probably to large numbers of women transferring to the university with two years of work from normal schools and teachers colleges. Beginning with 1930–31 both groups showed a loss for each year, except that for the last year the women again gained. This gain of 12.8 per cent., then, represents a return to the earlier trend and, furthermore, compares very favorably with most of the previous gains. The loss for the junior men of 1933–34 has never been smaller and has been equaled only once. This junior class, therefore, has also shown a high survival rate for the present year. The seventh and eighth rows of Table 3 show a loss for both sexes every year, with the losses for 1933–34 being roughly comparable to those of preceding years. Before leaving the discussion of this table it should be pointed out that the recent reductions in enrolment which were referred to in connection with Table 1 may now be explained, in case of the men, chiefly in terms of large decreases in the freshman and sophomore classes and, in case of the women, by heavy losses in the first three classes. These losses were accompanied by merely normal mortality rates among junior and senior men and among senior women. In view of this fact it seems reasonable to expect that survival rates will not be unusually low in the upper classes next year.

The facts presented in the preceding paragraphs, then, offer several very encouraging signs as to enrolment trends in the immediate future, some of the facts indicating a marked slowing down of the processes of decline of the last few years and others showing an actual cessation. These facts, together with the absence of any adverse indications, justify a feeling of considerable satisfaction as to the prospective enrolment for the year 1934–35. Although this study is not concerned with predictions, it seems sound to assume that if any reduction in enrolment occurs next year, it is likely to be relatively small, and that at least a slight gain should occasion no surprise. Such statements of prospects should always be qualified, of course, to the effect that they are based only upon a knowledge of recent trends and that they may be nullified or even completely reversed by the operation of unforeseen or unexpected factors of many kinds.

On the other hand, however, the importance of attempts at anticipating future enrolments at this time must not be underestimated. During the past few years instructional provisions at many institutions of higher learning have been adjusted downward in response to the curtailment of financial resources as well as to the reduction of enrolments. That is, the number of courses and sections of courses, and the size of the instructional staff, have been reduced. With a return of larger numbers of students these provisions must again be expanded, but such expansion will in turn demand increased financial resources. Such demands can frequently not be met at a moment's notice but must be anticipated considerably in advance so that the plans and preparations necessary to satisfy them can be made. Thus it becomes necessary to anticipate future increase in enrolment, an event, which, according to the present study, may not be far away for the particular institution concerned.

EDWARD F. POTTHOFF
UNIVERSITY OF ILLINOIS

NEW BOOKS IN EDUCATION

BACON, SAMUEL F. *An Evaluation of the Philosophy and Pedagogy of Ethical Culture.* Pp. viii + 182. Catholic University of America.

BREEN, MARY J. *Partners in Play.* Pp. 130. National Recreation Association. $0.75.

COLLMANN, R. D. and others. *Comparative Intelligence of English, American and Australian Children.* Pp. 70. Melbourne University Press. 3s.

COX, SIDNEY and EDMUND FREEMAN. *Prose Preferences.* Second series. Pp. vii + 499. Harper's. $2.00.

CUNNINGHAM, K. S. and W. T. PRICE. *The Standardization of an Australian Arithmetic Test.* Pp. 116. Melbourne University Press. 4s, 6d.

HOGAN, JOHN G. *Heralds of the King.* Pp. 190. Stratford. $1.50.

HOY, ALICE. *The Teaching of History and Civics in Victorian Secondary Schools.* Pp. 78. Melbourne University Press. 2s, 6d.

Manual of Nursery School Practice. Pp. 215. 38 figures. Iowa Child Welfare Research Station, University of Iowa.

Our Public Schools. Pp. ix + 208. Illustrated. National Congress of Parents and Teachers, Washington, D. C.

PHELAN, ANETTE M. *A Study of School Health Standards.* Pp. 249. American Public Health Association. $2.50.